THE NEW BLACKWELL COMPANION TO
THE SOCIOLOGY OF RELIGION

BLACKWELL COMPANIONS TO SOCIOLOGY

The *Blackwell Companions to Sociology* provide introductions to emerging topics and theoretical orientations in sociology as well as presenting the scope and quality of the discipline as it is currently configured. Essays in the Companions tackle broad themes or central puzzles within the field and are authored by key scholars who have spent considerable time in research and reflection on the questions and controversies that have activated interest in their area. This authoritative series will interest those studying sociology at advanced undergraduate or graduate level as well as scholars in the social sciences and informed readers in applied disciplines.

The Blackwell Companion to Major Classical Social Theorists
Edited by George Ritzer

The Blackwell Companion to Major Contemporary Social Theorists
Edited by George Ritzer

The Blackwell Companion to Political Sociology
Edited by Kate Nash and Alan Scott

The Blackwell Companion to Sociology
Edited by Judith R. Blau

The Blackwell Companion to Criminology
Edited by Colin Sumner

The Blackwell Companion to Social Movements
Edited by David A. Snow, Sarah A. Soule, and Hanspeter Kriesi

The Blackwell Companion to the Sociology of Families
Edited by Jacqueline Scott, Judith Treas, and Martin Richards

The Blackwell Companion to Law and Society
Edited by Austin Sarat

The Blackwell Companion to the Sociology of Culture
Edited by Mark Jacobs and Nancy Hanrahan

The Blackwell Companion to Social Inequalities
Edited by Mary Romero and Eric Margolis

The New Blackwell Companion to Social Theory
Edited by Bryan S. Turner

The New Blackwell Companion to Medical Sociology
Edited by William C. Cockerham

The New Blackwell Companion to the Sociology of Religion
Edited by Bryan S. Turner

Also available:

The Blackwell Companion to Globalization
Edited by George Ritzer

THE NEW BLACKWELL COMPANION TO

The
Sociology Of
Religion

EDITED BY
BRYAN S. TURNER

A John Wiley & Sons, Ltd., Publication

This edition first published 2010
© 2010 Blackwell Publishing Ltd

Blackwell Publishing was acquired by John Wiley & Sons in February 2007. Blackwell's publishing program has been merged with Wiley's global Scientific, Technical, and Medical business to form Wiley-Blackwell.

Registered Office
John Wiley & Sons Ltd, The Atrium, Southern Gate, Chichester, West Sussex, PO19 8SQ, United Kingdom

Editorial Offices
350 Main Street, Malden, MA 02148-5020, USA
9600 Garsington Road, Oxford, OX4 2DQ, UK
The Atrium, Southern Gate, Chichester, West Sussex, PO19 8SQ, UK

For details of our global editorial offices, for customer services, and for information about how to apply for permission to reuse the copyright material in this book please see our website at www.wiley.com/wiley-blackwell.

The right of Bryan S. Turner to be identified as the author of the editorial material in this work has been asserted in accordance with the UK Copyright, Designs and Patents Act 1988.

Library of Congress Cataloging-in-Publication Data

The new Blackwell companion to the sociology of religion / edited by Bryan S. Turner.
     p. cm. – (Blackwell companions to sociology)
  Includes bibliographical references and index.
  ISBN 978-1-4051-8852-4 (hardcover : alk. paper)   1. Religion and sociology.   I. Turner, Bryan S.
  BL60.B53 2010
  306.6–dc22

                                    2009041472

A catalogue record for this book is available from the British Library.

Set in 10/12.5pt Sabon by Toppan Best-set Premedia Limited
Printed and bound in Singapore by Fabulous Printers Pte Ltd

1   2010

Contents

Notes on Contributors

Afe Adogame holds a PhD in History of Religions from Bayreuth University, Germany. He now teaches Religious Studies/World Christianity at the University of Edinburgh, UK. His special fields of teaching/research include: Religion and the African Diaspora, African Religions, Sociology of Religion, and Method and Theory in the Study of Religion. Dr Adogame has ethnographical expertise in African Christian communities in continental Europe (especially in Germany and the UK) and in the USA. He is the author of *Celestial Church of Christ: The Politics of Cultural identity in a West African Prophetic-charismatic Movement* (1999); (co-edited) *European Traditions in the Study of Religion in Africa* (2004); *Religion in the Context of African Migration* (2005); *Christianity in Africa and the African Diaspora: The Appropriation of a Scattered Heritage* (2008); and *Unpacking the New: Critical Perspectives on Cultural Syncretization in African and Beyond* (2008). He is on the Editorial Board of several scientific journals including the *Journal of Religion in Africa*; *African Diaspora: A Journal of Transnational Africa in a Global World*; *International Studies in Religion and Society*; and is Associate Editor of the *Studies in World Christianity*.

Richard T. Antoun is Professor Emeritus of Anthropology at the State University of New York in Binghamton. A Fulbright Scholar and past president of the Middle East Studies Association, he has taught at Indiana University; Manchester University, England; and as visiting professor at the American University if Beirut, Cairo University, and the University of Chicago. On the basis of extensive fieldwork in Jordan and Iran, he has written four books: *Arab Village: A Social Structural Study of a Transjordanian Peasant Community* (1972); *Low-Key Politics: Local-level Leadership and Change in the Middle East* (1979); *Muslim Preacher in the Modern World: A Jordanian Case Study in Comparative Perspective* (1989); and *Documenting Transnational Migration: Jordanian Men Working and Studying in Europe, Asia and North America* (2005). A fifth book is comparative and cross-cultural: *Understanding Fundamentalism: Christian, Islamic and Jewish Movements* (2001). This book has just been reprinted in a second edition, which features a new chapter on the transnational aspects of fundamentalism since 9/11, including the connections/misconnections between religion and violence and featuring a segment on Afghanistan and Osama bin Laden.

Steve Bruce was born in Edinburgh in 1954 and educated at the Queen Victoria School, Dunblane. He studied sociology and religious studies at the University of Stirling. He taught at Queen's University, Belfast, from 1978 to 1991 when he became Professor of Sociology at the University of Aberdeen. From 2002 to 2007 he was additionally the Head of the School of Social Science. In 2003 he was elected a Fellow of the British Academy and in 2005 he was elected a Fellow of the Royal Society of Edinburgh. His published work in the sociology of religion includes: *God Save Ulster: The Religion and Politics of Paisleyism* (1986); *Religion in the Modern World: From Cathedrals to Cults* (1996); *Conservative Protestant Politics* (1998); *Choice and Religion: A Critique of Rational Choice Theory* (2000); *Fundamentalism* (2001); *God Is Dead: Secularization in the West* (2002); *Politics and Religion* (2003); and *Paisley* (2007).

Joseph M. Bryant is Professor of Sociology at the University of Toronto, where he holds a cross-appointment in the Department for the Study of Religion and the Department of Sociology. He is the author of *Moral Codes and Social Structure in Ancient Greece: A Sociology of Greek Ethics from Homer to the Epicureans and Stoics* (1996), and co-editor, with John Hall, of *Historical Methods in the Social Sciences: Vol. I. Historical Social Science: Presuppositions and Prescriptions; Vol. II. Foundations of Historical-Sociological Inquiry; Vol. III. The Logic of Historical-Sociological Inquiry; Vol. IV. Social Worlds in Flux: Legacies and Transformations* (2005). His work has appeared in a variety of journals, including the *British Journal of Sociology, History of Political Thought, Archives européennes de sociologie, Method & Theory in the Study of Religion, Philosophy of the Social Sciences*, and the *Canadian Journal of Sociology*. He is currently engaged with two monograph projects: the first tentatively titled, *Was Early Christianity a Rational Choice? A Case Study in Applied Philosophy of Science*; to be followed by *The West and the Rest Revisited: Global Histories, Revisionist Narratives, and the Logic of Historical Explanation*.

Simon Coleman is Professor and Head of Department at the University of Sussex, and Editor of the *Journal of the Royal Anthropological Institute*. Previously, he has been Reader in Anthropology and Associate Dean of Social Sciences and Medicine at the University of Durham. His research interests cover Sweden, the UK, and Nigeria, and he has worked on charismatic Christianity, pilgrimage and hospital chaplaincy, as well as retaining more general interests in both anthropological pedagogy and fieldwork methodologies. Publications include *Pilgrimage Past and Present in the World Religions* (1995, with John Elsner) *The Globalisation of Charismatic Christianity* (2000), *Reframing Pilgrimage: Cultures in Motion* (2004, ed. with John Eade), *The Cultures of Creationism: Anti-evolutionism in English-speaking Countries* (2004, ed. with Leslie Carlin), *Locating the Field: Space, Place and Context in Anthropology* (2006, ed. with Peter Collins), and *The Discipline of Leisure: Embodying Cultures of "Recreation"* (2007, ed. with Tamara Kohn).

Current interests involve tracing the links between charismatic Christianity and migration between West Africa and Europe.

Grace Davie has a personal Chair in the Sociology of Religion in the University of Exeter. She is a past-president of the American Association for the Sociology of Religion (2003) and of the Research Committee 22 (Sociology of Religion) of the International Sociological Association (2002–6). In 2000–1 she was the Kerstin-Hesselgren Professor in the University of Uppsala, where she returned for the 2006–7 academic session. In January 2008, she received an honorary degree from Uppsala. In addition to numerous chapters and articles, she is the author of *Religion in Britain since 1945* (1994), *Religion in Modern Europe* (2000), *Europe: The Exceptional Case* (2002), and *The Sociology of Religion* (2007); she is co-editor of *Predicting Religion* (2003) and co-author of *Religious America, Secular Europe* (2008).

Stephen Ellingson studies religion, social movements, and culture. He is the author of *The Megachurch and the Mainline* (2007), which won the 2007 Distinguished Book Award from the Society for the Scientific Study of Religion, and he is co-author of *The Sexual Organization of the City* (2005). He is currently investigating the emergence and impact of religious environmentalism in the United States. He is an associate professor of sociology at Hamilton College. Before coming to Hamilton, Ellingson taught and directed a Lilly Endowment grant at Pacific Lutheran Theological Seminary. He received his PhD in sociology from the University of Chicago.

John H. Evans is Associate Professor of Sociology at the University of California, San Diego. He has been a visiting member of the School of Social Sciences at the Institute for Advanced Study in Princeton, NJ, a post-doctoral fellow at the Robert Wood Johnson Scholars in Health Policy Research Program at Yale University and has held a Visiting Professorial Fellowship at the University of Edinburgh. He is the author of *Playing God? Human Genetic Engineering and the Rationalization of Public Bioethical Debate* (2002) and co-editor (with Robert Wuthnow) of *The Quiet Hand of God: Faith-based Activism and the Public Role of Mainline Protestantism* (2002). He has also published many articles on opinion polarization in the USA over abortion, homosexuality, and related issues; science and religion; the sociology of religion; and the structure of public bioethical debates. His research focuses on the sociology of religion, culture, knowledge, science, and, in particular, bioethics. He is completing a book tentatively titled *The Religious Citizen and Reproductive Genetics: Avoiding the Abortion Debate and the Culture Wars?*

Michael S. Evans is a PhD candidate in Sociology and Science Studies at the University of California, San Diego. His interdisciplinary research interests include religion, science, politics, and culture. Some of his recent work on religion and science has been published in the *Annual Review of Sociology* (with John H. Evans) and *Public Understanding of Science*. He also recently published an article on values and monetary systems in *Environment and Planning A*. He is currently writing a dissertation that examines American public debates about religion and science in terms of representation, democracy, and morality.

Dennis F. Kelley holds a doctorate from the University of California, Santa Barbara, and is an Assistant Professor in Religious Studies and American Indian Studies at Iowa State University. With Suzanne Crawford, he edited *American Indian Religious Traditions: An Encyclopedia* (2005). He has published in Suzanne Crawford (ed.), *Religion and Healing in Native America*, and M. E. Sharpe (ed.) (2005) *Death and Religion in a Changing World*. He is a member of the American Academy of Religion, the California Indian Studies Association, the American Sociological Association, and the Society for the Social Scientific Study of Religion.

Pattana Kitiarsa is Assistant Professor in the Southeast Asian Studies Programme, National University of Singapore. He holds his doctoral degree in Sociocultural Anthropology from the University of Washington, Seattle. Considering himself as an ethnographer of human religious experience, he has combined the discipline of anthropology of religion and the area-based Southeast Asian Studies. Pattana's research interests are centered on two main areas: Buddhism and transnational labor migration. He has published both in Thai and English in the fields of religious commodification, Thai popular Buddhism, and transnational Buddhism. He has also developed a keen interest in understanding the religious aspects and implications of topics like transnational labor migration, Thai-style boxing, popular music, and films. He edited the volume, entitled, *Religious Commodifications in Asia: Marketing Gods* (2008).

David Lehmann is Reader in Social Science at the University of Cambridge. He has been a Visiting Professor in Ecuador, Brazil, and France and a Visiting Fellow at the Institute of Advanced Study of the Hebrew University. He is the author of *Democracy and Development in Latin America: Economics, Politics and Religion in the Postwar Period* (Polity, 1990); *Struggle for the Spirit: Religious Transformation and Popular Culture in Brazil and Latin America* (1996) and, with Batia Siebzehner, *Remaking Israeli Judaism: The Challenge of Shas* (2006). He has written numerous articles on fundamentalism and on globalization in relation to religion, and is currently working on the spread of multiculturalist ideas and policies in Latin America.

Victor Lidz is Associate Professor in the Department of Psychiatry and Director of its Division of Substance Abuse Treatment & Research at the Drexel University College of Medicine. He has been on the faculty of that medical school and its predecessor institutions since joining Hahnemann University of the Health Sciences in 1991. He previously taught in departments of sociology at the University of Chicago, the University of Pennsylvania, Saint Joseph's University, and Haverford College. He received his AB degree in Government from Harvard College in 1962 and his PhD in Sociology in 1976. As a graduate student in the former interdisciplinary Department of Social Relations, he studied with Talcott Parsons, Robert N. Bellah, Erik Erikson, David Maybury-Lewis, and Ezra Vogel, specializing in the sociology of religion and political sociology, and served as Parsons' research assistant from 1963 to 1968. Lidz has been contributor to and co-editor of *Readings on Pre-Modern Societies* (with Talcott Parsons), *Explorations in General Theory in the Social Sciences: Essays in Honor of Talcott Parsons* (with Jan J. Loubser, Andrew Effrat, and Rainer C. Baum), *The Nationalization of the Social Sciences* (with Samuel Z. Klausner), and *After Parsons: A Theory of Social Action for the 21st Century* (with Renee C. Fox and Harold J. Bershady). He is currently co-editor of the Lit Verlag series, Studies in the Theory of Social Action, with Helmut Staubmann.

Gabriele Marranci is an anthropologist by training, working on religion with a specialization in Muslim societies. His main research interests concern identity, Muslim migration/immigration, urban sociology, globalization, fundamentalism, political Islam, secularization processes, criminology, and anthropology of music. He has published widely in these subjects. He is Visiting Senior Research Fellow at the Asia Research Institute, National University of Singapore. He is the founding editor of the journal *Contemporary Islam: Dynamics of Muslim Life*, and also, with Bryan S. Turner, the book series *Muslims in Global Societies*. He is the author of four monographs, among which *The Anthropology of Islam, Understanding Muslim Identity: Rethinking Fundamentalis*, and *Faith, Ideology and Fear: Muslim Identities within and Beyond Prisons*.

Andrew McKinnon (PhD Toronto) is Lecturer in Sociology at the University of Aberdeen. Previously, he was Assistant Professor at the University of Toronto and subsequently a Visiting Lecturer in the Czech Republic (Anglo-American University of Prague). He is an Associate Editor of the *Canadian Journal of Sociology*, a member of the Associate Board for *Sociology* and a member of the Editorial Board for the book series Studies in Critical Research on Religion. Among his publications are articles in *Critical Sociology, Method and Theory in the Study of Religion, Journal for the Scientific Study of Religion*, and *Sociological Theory*. His theoretical interests include the classical tradition, critical theory, and the role of metaphor in sociological thinking; current empirical projects include a study of the conflict over sexuality in the global Anglican Communion and the historical sociology of energy systems.

Philip A. Mellor is Professor of Religion and Social Theory and Head of the School of Humanities at the University of Leeds. His publications include *Religion, Realism and Social Theory: Making Sense of Society* (2004), and, with Chris Shilling, *The Sociological Ambition: Elementary Forms of Social and Moral Life* (2001) and *Re-forming the Body: Religion, Community and Modernity* (1997).

Alan Mittleman is Professor of Modern Jewish Thought and head of the Department of Jewish Thought at the Jewish Theological Seminary. He serves as Director of the Seminary's Louis Finkelstein Institute for Religious and Social Studies. Prior to that, he was Professor of Religion at Muhlenberg College from 1988 to 2004. He is a member of several learned societies and is a Fellow of the Jerusalem Center for

Public Affairs. He is the author of three books: *Between Kant and Kabbalah* (1990), *The Politics of Torah* (1996), and *The Scepter Shall Not Depart from Judah* (2000). He is also the editor of four books: *Jewish Polity and American Civil Society* (2002), *Jews and the American Public Square* (2002), *Religion as a Public Good* (2003) and *Uneasy Allies: Jewish and Evangelical Relations* (2007). His many scholarly and popular articles, essays, and reviews have appeared in such journals as *Harvard Theological Review*, *Modern Judaism*, *Heythrop Journal*, *Jewish Political Studies Review*, *Journal of Religion*, and *First Things*. He is a contributor to *The Cambridge Companion to American Judaism*. His study of the role of hope in political theory, *Hope in a Democratic Age*, was published in 2009. His current book project is *A Short History of Jewish Ethics*. Professor Mittleman holds a BA (Magna cum Laude) from Brandeis University and an MA and PhD (with distinction) from Temple University. He is the recipient of an Alexander von Humboldt Foundation Research Fellowship and served as Guest Research Professor at the University of Cologne (1994 and 1996). From 2000 to 2004, Professor Mittleman served as director of a major research project initiated by The Pew Charitable Trusts, "Jews and the American Public Square." As an active participant in interfaith dialogue, he was part of a leadership delegation that met with Pope John Paul II.

Catherine Newell obtained her PhD in Religious Studies from The School of Oriental and African Studies (SOAS), University of London. She also holds BA and MA degrees from SOAS in Thai and Religious Studies. Her work focuses upon the history of Buddhist traditions in South and Southeast Asia, with particular reference to Thailand. Her PhD thesis explored the apparently "unorthodox" meditation practices at the heart of the Dhammakaya Temples of contemporary Thailand. Her current research examines the interrelated histories of Thai meditation traditions, Forest Monks, and state reform of Buddhism in Thailand from 1767 to the present, tracing back into the pre-modern period the "unorthodox" meditation lineages identified in her PhD.

Lionel Obadia is currently Professor in Social and Cultural Anthropology at the University of Lyon 2, in the Department of Anthropology. He is the Director of the CREA (Centre for Research and Studies in Anthropology). He received his PhD in anthropology in 1997, from the University of Lille 1 (France), and became Assistant Professor in the University of Lille 3 (from 1998 to 2004). He gave courses in the Institute of Oriental Languages and Civilizations in Paris (1996–7), the Ecole Pratique des Hautes Etudes (Paris, 2002–4), and was professor invited at the chair, Baron Satsuma in Buddhist Studies in Louvain (Belgium, 2000). Specializing in religion, he worked in the 1990s on the Westward and global diffusion of Buddhism, doing fieldwork in France, Europe, and Israel. Since the early 2000s, he has embarked upon new fieldwork in Himalayan shamanism among the Sherpas of Nepal. He has published several books in French on *Religion* (2005, tr. in Korean, 2006), *Witchcraft* (2004), *Buddhism in the West* (1999 and 2007, Italian edn. 2009), the *Anthropology of Religion* (2007, Greek edn. 2009), and *Buddhism and Modernity* (forthcoming, Wiley-Blackwell).

Pratap Kumar Penumala is a full Professor at the University of KwaZulu Natal, South Africa and currently is a Visitng Professor at Colorado College, Colorado. His publications include *The Goddess Lakshmi* (1997) and *Hindus in South Africa* (2000). His edited volumes include *South Asians in the Diaspora* (with Knut Jacobsen, 2004) and *Religious Pluralism in the Diaspora* (2006). He has also been a Series Editor for the Numen Book Series. He has published over fifty papers and articles in various journals.

William Ramp is an Associate Professor in the Department of Sociology at the University of Lethbridge, in Alberta. His writing on topics related to those treated here has appeared in the *Journal of Classical Sociology*, the *Canadian Journal of Sociology*, *Economy and Society*, and several edited collections. His interests include social and anthropological theory, implicit religion, historical sociology, and cultural and material history. His research focuses on religious and political interpretations of Durkheim, Foucault, and Bataille, the "moral geography" of early twentieth-century agrarian progressive movements in North America, the cultural history of modern selfhood and moral agency, and the aesthetic, religious, and political discourses involved in European middle-class and aristocratic constructions of personality, society, and the material world in the late nineteenth and early twentieth centuries. Recent publications include "Blood money: Gambling and the formation of civic morality," in Cosgrave and Klassen (eds.), *Casino State: Legalized Gambling in Canada* (2009); "Le Malin Génie: Durkheim, Bataille and the prospect of a sociology of evil," in Pickering and Rosati (eds.), *Suffering and Evil: The Durkheimian Legacy* (2008); "Transcendence, liminality, excess: Durkheim and Bataille on the margins of sociologie religieuse," *Journal of Classical Sociology* (2008), and "Religion and the dualism of the social condition in Durkheim and Bataille," *Economy and Society* (2003).

Rachel Rinaldo is an Assistant Professor of Sociology at the University of Virginia. She received her PhD in Sociology from the University of Chicago in 2007. Her research examines how transnational shifts such as modernity and religious revival affect women and possibilities for social change. Her dissertation explored these questions about gender, religion, and globalization through ethnographic fieldwork on Muslim and secular women activists in Jakarta. Her article, "Envisioning the nation: women activists, religion, and the public sphere in Indonesia," *Social Forces* (2008) examines how Muslim women activists are increasingly legitimate participants in the ongoing re-imagination of the Indonesian nation-state. Another article, "Muslim women, middle class habitus, and modernity in Indonesia," *Contemporary Islam* (2008) investigates the ways pious practices are linked to the production of new forms of middle-class subjectivity. Rachel is currently working on a book about women, Islam, and the public sphere in Indonesia.

Fang-Long Shih is a Research Fellow at the Asia Research Centre at the London School of Economics (LSE), where she convenes the Taiwan Research Programme and co-edits the eJournal *Taiwan in Comparative Perspective*. She is also a Visiting Lecturer on Chinese society and religions at the School of Oriental and African Studies. Dr Shih is a specialist on family, gender, death ritual, modernity, globalization, politics, and feminism within the context of Chinese religious culture. She regards religion as being always embodied in political, economic, and social processes. She is co-author of a historical survey and analysis of local religion in I-Lan County, Taiwan (2003), and a contributing author and co-editor of the book *Re-Writing Culture in Taiwan*. She argues that scholars write religion from within situated positions, and she considers questions of translation, context, and location in the (re-)writing of religion in Taiwan (2009). Dr Shih is particularly concerned with the double issue of "women and religion," focusing on "maiden-death" practices, which she reads as texts reflecting and negotiating both traditional gender relations and wider processes of economic and political change that have occurred during modernization and globalization (PhD thesis, University of London 2004).

Chris Shilling is Professor of Sociology at the University of Kent at Canterbury, having lectured previously at the Universities of Portsmouth and Southampton. His publications include *Re-forming the Body: Religion, Community and Modernity* (with Philip Mellor, 1997). *The Body and Social Theory* (2nd edn., 2003), *The Body in Culture, Technology and Society* (2005), and (as editor) *Embodying Sociology: Retrospect, Progress and Prospects* (2007). His latest book is *Changing Bodies: Habit, Crisis and Creativity* (2008), and he is also editor of the Sociological Review Monograph Series.

Jeremy Stolow teaches media history in the Department of Communication Studies, Concordia University, Montreal. He is also a member of the Centre de recherche sur l'intermédialité (Université de Montréal), and sits on the International Advisory Board of the Center for Religion and Media (New York University). A social theorist by training, Jeremy's principal area of research is religion and media. His publications include *Orthodox By Design* (forthcoming), a book-length study of the cultural politics surrounding ArtScroll, a major Jewish Orthodox publishing house, *Deus in Machina* (forthcoming), an edited book on religion and technology in historical and cross-cultural perspective, and articles appearing in various edited books and journals, including *Theory, Culture and Society*, *Material Religion*, and *Postscripts*. His current research investigates religious frameworks of reception of electrically mediated communications technologies in the latter half of the nineteenth century, focusing on elective affinities between the development of transatlantic telegraphic networks and the spread of modern Spiritualism across and around the Atlantic world.

John Torpey is Professor of Sociology at the Graduate Center, City University of New York. He is the author or editor of six books: *Intellectuals, Socialism, and Dissent: The East German Opposition and Its Legacy* (1995); *The Invention of the Passport: Surveillance, Citizenship, and the State* (2000; French, Portuguese, and Japanese translations); *Documenting Individual Identity: The Development of State Practices in the Modern World* (ed. with Jane Caplan, 2001); *Politics and the Past: On Repairing Historical Injustices* (2004); *Old Europe, New Europe, Core Europe: Transatlantic Relations after the Iraq War* (ed. with Daniel Levy and Max Pensky 2005; with Japanese, Chinese, and Turkish translations forthcoming), and *Making Whole What Has Been Smashed: On Reparations Politics* (2006). His articles have appeared in *Theory and Society, Sociological Theory, Sociological Forum, Journal of Modern History, Political Power and Social Theory, Journal of Classical Sociology, Contemporary Sociology, Genèses: Sciences sociales et histoire, Journal of Human Rights, Dissent, Contexts, openDemocracy, Frankfurter Rundschau, The Nation,* and *The San Francisco Chronicle.* During 1995–6, he was a Jean Monnet Fellow at the European University Institute in Florence.

Bryan S. Turner was Professor of Sociology at Cambridge University (1998–2005) and Professor of Sociology in the Asia Research Institute at the National University of Singapore (2005–9), where he was the research leader on globalization and religion. He is concurrently the Alona Evans Distinguished Professor of Sociology at Wellesley College USA (2009–12) and the Director of the Centre for the Study of Contemporary Muslim Societies at the University of Western Sydney Australia (2009–). He has published *Weber and Islam* (1974) and *Religion and Social Theory* (1991). He edited *Islam: Critical Concepts* (2003), the *Cambridge Dictionary of Sociology* (2006), and the *New Blackwell Companion to Social Theory* (2009). Professor Turner is a Research Associate of the Groupe d'Etude des Methodes de l'Analyse Sociologique, Centre National de la Recherche Scientifique, Maison des Sciences de l'Homme, France. He is a member of the American Sociological Research Association (2009–) and a Fellow of the Australian Academy of the Social Sciences.

Andrew Wernick, a social theorist, intellectual historian, sociologist of culture, and jazz musician, is Professor of Cultural Studies and Sociology at Trent University in Canada where he has chaired several departments and was the founding director of the Center and MA Program for Theory Culture and Politics. He is also a Visiting Professor and member of the Cultural Studies PhD degree committee at Ivan Franko National University in Lviv, Ukraine, and is Life Member in Residence at Clare Hall, Cambridge. His writings on social theory and contemporary culture have appeared in *C-Theory, Theory Culture & Society*, and *Angelaki* and in many anthologies. He is the author of *Promotional Culture* (1991), a seminal text in the study of advertising, and *Auguste Comte and the Religion of Humanity* (2001), the first major study of Comte's later work. He co-edited the collections *Shadow of Spirit: Religion and Postmodernism* (1993) and *Images of Aging: Cultural Representations of Later Life* (1994), and is on the Editorial Boards of C-Theory, *revista de la Publicidad* and *TOPIA: Canadian Journal of Cultural Studies*.

Matthew Wood is Lecturer in Sociology at Queen's University Belfast, where he teaches on social theory and is the Programme Director for the MA in Sociology. He previously taught sociology at the University of Cambridge and Richmond, the American International University in London. His doctoral research in the University of Nottingham comprised ethnographic study of a religious network of groups and practices involving spirit possession, meditation, healing, and divination. *Possession, Power and the New Age: Ambiguities of Authority in Neoliberal Societies* (2007) questions the view that we are witnessing the rise of spirituality based on self-authority. Following that research, at Roehampton University he began investigating the effects of social and cultural globalization in London Methodism. Through ethnography and surveys, this research explores how processes of globalization interweave with racialization and religious revitalization as Methodism experiences shifts in its internal balance of power between professional ministers and lay leaders. Publications arising from this include "Breaching bleaching: integrating studies of 'race' and ethnicity with the sociology of religion," in Beckford and Walliss (eds.), *Theorising Religion: Classical and Contemporary Debates* (2006) and "Carrying religion into a secularising Europe: Montserratian migrants' experiences of global processes in British Methodism," *Anthropological Journal of European Cultures* (2009). With Véronique Altglas, he has recently translated a paper by Pierre Bourdieu on reflexivity in the sociology of religion: "Sociologists of belief and beliefs of sociologists" is forthcoming in *Nordic Journal of Religion and Society*.

Fenggang Yang is Associate Professor of Sociology and Director of the Center on Religion and Chinese Society (CRCS) at Purdue University. He received his BA from Hebei Normal University (Shijiazhuang, China) in 1982, MA from Nankai University (Tianjin, China) in 1987, and PhD from the Catholic University of America (Washington, DC) in 1997. His sociological research has focused on religious change in China and immigrant religions in the USA. He is the author of *Chinese Christians in America: Conversion, Assimilation, and Adhesive Identities* (1999), the co-editor (with Tony Carnes) of *Asian American Religions: The Making and Remaking of Borders and Boundaries* (2004), and the co-editor (with Joseph B. Tamney) of *State, Market, and Religions in Chinese Societies* (2005) and *Conversion to Christianity among the Chinese* (a special issue of the *Sociology of Religion: A Quarterly Review*, 2006). His articles have been published in the *American Sociological Review, Journal for the Scientific Study of Religion, Sociology of Religion, Amerasia Journal, Journal of Asian American Studies, the Sociological Quarterly,* and *Asia Policy*, including one that won the "2002 Distinguished Article Award" of the Society for the Scientific Study of Religion ("Transformations in new immigrant religions and their global implications") and one that won "2006 Distinguished Article Award" of the American Sociological Association's Section of the Sociology of Religion ("The red, black, and gray markets of religion in China"). His current research focuses on the political economy of religion in China, Christian ethics and market transition in China, faith and trust among business people in China, and Chinese Christian churches in the USA.

Geneviève Zubrzycki is Associate Professor of Sociology at the University of Michigan. She received her PhD from the University of Chicago in 2001 and was a postdoctoral fellow at the University of Virginia's Center on Religion and Democracy in 2002. Her research focuses on the linkages between national identity and religion at moments of significant political transformation, collective memory, and the politics of commemorations, and the role of symbols in national mythology. Through an investigation of memory wars between Poles and Jews at Auschwitz, her book *The Crosses of Auschwitz: Nationalism and Religion in Post-Communist Poland* (2006) examines the historical constitution of the relationship between Polish national identity and Catholicism and its reconfiguration after the fall of communism. It received the American Sociological Association's Distinguished Book Award from the Sociology of Religion section, the American Association for the Advancement of Slavic Studies' Orbis Best Book Prize, and the Polish Studies Association's Best Book Award.

Introduction

Mapping the Sociology of Religion

BRYAN S. TURNER

INTRODUCTION: DEFINING THE FIELD AND THE ROLE OF THE *COMPANION*

In the modern world, religion, contrary to the conventional understanding of modernization as secularization, continues to play a major role in politics, society and culture. Indeed that role appears if anything to be increasing rather than decreasing and hence in recent years that has been a flurry of academic activity around such ideas as "political religion," "religious nationalism," and "post-secular society." In broad terms, religion appears to be increasingly an important component of public culture rather than a matter of private belief and practice (Casanova 1994). Of course the salience of religion in modern culture depends a great deal on which society we are looking at. Religion – in the form of Pentecostalism, fundamentalism, charismatic movements, and revivalism – appears to be flourishing in much of South America, Africa, and Southeast Asia. Religions are also reviving under the somewhat more liberal government policies of contemporary China and Vietnam. However in Europe and North America the growth of diasporic communities with large religious minorities is also changing the cultural map of what were thought to be predominantly secular societies. There is naturally the temptation to think that after 9/11 and the terrorist bombings in London, Madrid, and elsewhere that the revival of interest in religion is in fact a function of the political importance of understanding Islam as the *Terror in the Mind of God* (Juergensmeyer, 2003). There has indeed been a growth of scholarly interest in Islam, including the study of "radical Islam," "political Islam," and so forth, but one ought to avoid such narrow, popular and often prejudicial labels when considering Islamic revivalism. In most Muslim societies, there is very little evidence of political radicalism and on the contrary Islamic revivalism is not necessarily connected with youth alienation or anti-modern attitudes (Pew Research Center 2007). It is important for academics to avoid such popular, prejudicial, and political attitudes. The *New Blackwell Companion to the Sociology of Religion* attempts to understand and describe the prominence of religion in modernity and therefore takes a comprehensive and (in the neutral meaning of the term) catholic approach to the study of religion in society. In response to narrow views of religion, handbooks and companions can play an important role in both defining and defending the field of the study of religion and religions.

In the modern publishing market, handbooks, and companions have played a significant role in shaping the field of the study of religion. The *New Companion* takes its place alongside such publications as *A Reader in the Anthropology of Religion* (Lambeck 2002),*The Oxford Handbook of Global Religions* (Juergensmeyer 2006), the *Sage Handbook of Sociology of Religion* (Beckford and Demerath 2007), and the *Oxford Handbook of the Sociology of Religion* (Clarke 2009). The original *Blackwell Companion to Sociology of Religion* (2001), which was edited by Professor Richard K. Fenn, was divided into three sections – Classical and Contemporary Theory, Contemporary Trends in the Relation of Religion to Society, and the Sociology of Religion and Related Areas. The *New Blackwell Companion* is divided into a section on the foundations which examines basic theoretical traditions and their later development in the sociology of religion. This section is accompanied by chapters that follow the contemporary development of the field looking at new theoretical frameworks such as the idea of religious markets. One major issue in modern sociology is the debate around secularization. The *New Companion* looks at processes of secularization and re-sacralization, and at new institutional developments beyond the classical church–sect typology such as the growth of the urban megachurch. In classical sociology, Max Weber was a major figure in establishing the importance of the comparative and historical study of religion. The *New Companion* follows this Weberian tradition in examining contemporary issues around the comparative study of the world religions as well as the revival of traditional or indigenous religious practice in modern China. One major aspect of the contemporary debate about religion is the question of religion in the public sphere and the question about the "post-secular" features of the modern world. (See chapters 28 and 29.) There is a growing interest in issues about public religions, nationalism and politics. (See chapter 27.) The *New Companion* concludes with an examination of the debate about public religions and politics in multi-faith and multicultural societies. The globalization of religion including various forms of religious revivalism has transformed politics and public life and therefore many of the conventional liberal solutions such as the separation of church and state no longer appear relevant.

This comparison of the original Blackwell *Companion* and the *New Companion* demonstrates just how radically the world has changed in such a short period of time. One can therefore safely predict that a reviewer examining this *New Companion* within the next decade will also be forcefully struck by the intensity of social change in which our current preoccupations may appear less urgent and pressing. In chapters 28 and 29, there are two attempts to consider how current developments might throw some light on the future of religion. Perhaps our only safeguard against intellectual arrogance is to recognize the limitations of our current concerns in the light of anticipated future developments including the rise of radically new forms of religiosity with deepening globalization. For example, the original Blackwell *Companion* contained relatively little comparative sociology and did not, for rather obvious and intelligible reasons, deal with re-sacralization, globalization, postmodernity or violence which have become the topics that have most influenced recent developments in both the sociology and philosophy of religion. The distinctive and laudable intellectual preoccupation of the original *Companion* was on interdisciplinarity including perhaps somewhat unusually the interdisciplinary relations between sociology and theology. I have also tried to follow that preoccupation by including anthropological, historical, and philosophical perspectives in this current work. In contemporary sociology, perhaps the vitality of religion in the modern world is demonstrated by the large number of recent publications on the sociology of religion.

The special characteristics of the *New Companion* are examined in the following discussion. At this stage I may note that this new volume seeks to strike a balance between covering traditional topics and exploring such new and emerging areas in the field as the body and religion (chapter 9), feminist theory and religion (chapter 10) and women and piety movements (chapter 26). It also considers contemporary developments in religion such as "spirituality" (chapter 12), globalization (chapter 21), popular religion (chapter 24) and commodification (chapter 25). In the late nineteenth century, Charles Darwin's evolutionary theories began to create difficult questions for the biblical account of creation. In the modern world, issues around stem-cell research and cloning have intensified these issues. Many challenges to modern religion have come from scientific and philosophical analysis of religion and some of these debates are considered in chapters13, 28, and 29. This volume is dominated by two major themes: secularization and globalization. The issue of secularization was a dominant assumption of much sociology in the 1960s when secularization was seen to be a necessary component of modernization. This connection has in modern sociology been vigorously challenged and contrasted views of secular society are considered in the *New Companion* by Steve Bruce (chapter 5) and by Grace Davie (chapter 7). One aspect of this debate has been the contrast between the continuous strength of religion in the United States (see chapter 6) and the relative weakness of traditional Christianity in Europe. To explore this issue more systematically, there are various chapters (from 14 to 19) on comparative religion dealing with Christianity, Judaism, Islam, Buddhism, and Hinduism. The other major issue is the globalization of religion which is considered specifically in chapter 21, but also in chapters 22 through to 27. Although anthropological studies of religion have paid close attention to the transformation of aboriginal religion under the impact of both colonialism and globalization, the sociology of religion often neglects this issue. In the *New Companion* Dennis Kelly explores American Indian sacred traditions, providing an important insight into an aspect of religion in the United States that is often overlooked in the mainstream literature.

Within an academic field that is changing rapidly, what then is the intellectual role of the handbook or companion in more general terms? Firstly, a companion should provide a distillation of the principal achievements of the field, striking a delicate balance between the pursuit of established topics and the inclusion of issues that may in the long run turn out to be merely fashionable and ephemeral. Secondly, it must find a compromise between the dominant tradition of American sociology which can often be parochial and the rest of the world where many of the important social changes in religion are in fact taking place. Thirdly, it needs to establish openness to different disciplinary approaches, since many of the innovative theoretical developments in the study of religion are taking place in adjacent disciplines such as philosophy, history and anthropology. For example, the contemporary discussion of post-secularism and of the differences between the sacred and the religious is often dominated by philosophy rather than sociology. Finally, a companion needs to be sensitive to the very diverse methodologies – ethnographic, historical, archival, quantitative, and so forth – that compete for a presence in the study of religion and religions. While recognizing the value of interdisciplinarity, these four tasks or objectives should in principle establish why the *sociology* of religion has a distinctive contribution to make over and against other disciplines in the humanities and social sciences.

If we look at the history of such handbooks or companions, we can detect both the decline of the subfield of the study of religion from its heyday in the 1960s and 1970s and its contemporary but often problematic revival in the late twentieth and twenty-first centuries as sociologists have come to reject the secularization thesis, paying more attention to different forms of religion and spirituality. There is also a greater awareness of the importance of the comparative study of religion if we are to avoid ethnocentric interpretations. Within this more complete and comparative research agenda, unsurprisingly Islam, fundamentalism, political religion, public religions and religious nationalism have become dominant topics of this modern revival. Indeed one major factor in the current interest in religion is the association – real or otherwise – between radical religions and terrorism. Handbooks and companions of sociology typically appear to assume that there is a distinctive, sharp and unambiguous division between anthropology and sociology, but such a division appears often to be especially inappropriate in the study of religion. Where would Émile Durkheim's sociology of religion have been without access to anthropological research into aboriginal religion in Australia? Where would the sociology of religion be without Clifford Geertz, Ernest Gellner, and Mary Douglas? To take a contemporary example, one of the most influential commentaries on modern Christianity has been undertaken from a decisively anthropological perspective to understand Christian belief as the belief of the Other namely Talal Asad's *Genealogies of Religion* (1991). An evaluation of the status of sociology, at least in the field of the study of religion, has to consider this strange separation – indeed isolation – of disciplines in the modern university. While most handbooks of the sociology of religion tend to be rich in the treatment of Weber, Durkheim and Simmel, I seriously doubt that one can grasp the nature of religion as a generic topic of intellectual inquiry without taking seriously the legacy of Bronislaw Malinowski, Victor Turner, Clifford Geertz, or Melford Spiro. While modern companions tend to separate sociology and anthropology, the early classical textbooks had a very different approach. For example, Roland Robertson in his Penguin readings in the *Sociology of Religion* (1969) managed successfully to incorporate the work of Mary Douglas, E. E. Evans-Pritchard, Ernest Gellner, Clifford Geertz, Peter Worsley, J. W. Fernandez, and G. Lienhardt into an account of the sociological study of religion. In order to address this problem, important developments in the anthropology of religion are explored in this *New Companion* in chapters 2 and 4.

Although some degree of interdisciplinarity has been a characteristic feature of religious studies from the very beginning, it is very doubtful that in the modern period one could study the sociology of religion without some engagement with both theology and philosophy (see chapters 28 and 29 in this volume). To take some prominent examples, the study of secularization is seriously impoverished when separated from recent philosophical debates about the intellectual authority of religious belief systems in for example Jacques Derrida and Gianni Vattimo's *Religion* (1998). The recent work of philosophers and theologians should also play an important part in the development of sociological theories of religion (Milbank et al. 1999). Some of the more interesting criticisms of the sociological treatment of religion have come from philosophy and theology – for example John Milbank's *Theology and Social Theory* (1990). In modern philosophy, works such as Richard Rorty and Gianni Vattimo in *The Future of Religion* (Zabala 2005) and Hent de Vries's work on *Religion and Violence* (2002) have been influential. Over a longer period, Harvey Cox's theological interpretation of *The Secular City* (1965) remained an influential interdisciplinary statement. The contributions of women's studies and feminist theories of religion have also become more prominent in recent years. Feminist critiques of religion as represented by Julia Kristeva, Luce Irigaray or Carol P. Christ have begun to make their way into mainstream debates in sociology (Anderson and Clack 2004; Hawthorne 2009). These are of course especially potent in the case of modern Islam (Mernissi 2003). In this volume, feminist approaches to religion and gender are explored by Fang-Long Shih in chapter 10. These initial comments offer a broad-brush overview of some issues in the field and now I shall turn to consider some specific themes in more detail.

KEY THEMES

Key themes in the contemporary sociology of religion include re-sacralization, fundamentalism, and religious revivalism as illustrated not only by Islam but by Pentecostalism and charismatic movements. As a result the study of religion, like the study of society more generally, has abandoned the idea of a unitary process of modernization by accepting the idea of "multiple modernities" and by stressing the survival of local cultures against the juggernaut of globalization (Eisenstadt 2000). The idea that secularization is an inevitable outcome of modernization has been widely challenged by contemporary research and historical analysis (Smith 2008). We might argue that a unitary theory of modernization has been replaced by a macro-theory of globalization which, in the concept of "glocalization" at least, recognizes the diverse and divergent interactions between the global and the local (Niezen 2004). However, one major weakness of much modern sociology of religion, including the usual range of textbooks, is in fact the strange neglect of globalization. An obvious exception is the work of Mark Juergensmeyer in his *Global Religions* (2003) and *The Oxford Handbook of Global Religions* (2006). While Juergensmeyer's *Handbook* is in many ways comprehensive, it failed to deal adequately with the history of Christian missions from the late eighteenth century onwards and the collection did not engage with political religions, nationalism and the clash of civilizations. In this regard, James Beckford's *Social Theory & Religion* (2003) made an important conceptual contribution to the field, providing an entire chapter on "Globalisation and Religion" and in the introduction to the Sage

Handbook he correctly observes that, since the mid-1980s, religion "presents major challenges and opportunities to social scientific explorations of globalisation" (Beckford and Demerath 2007: 7). These developments have forced sociologists to think about social processes in a transnational or global framework, thereby bringing into question much of the national framework of traditional research.

In the 1960s and 1970s, the sociology of religion was, in addition to its Western focus, without question narrowly pre-occupied with the application of the church–sect typology to religious organizations. Bryan Wilson (1967 and 1970) was the outstanding figure in this institutional analysis of religion. More recent developments in the sociology of religion have involved a movement away from concentrating on institutions such as the church–sect typology to a focus on so-called de-institutionalized or post-institutional forms of popular religion. These forms of religion have in the past been variously described in terms of "invisible religion" (Luckmann 1967) "implicit religion" (Bailey, 1990 and 2009) or "new age religion" (Heelas 1996). There has also been some concentration of research on modern cults rather than mainstream organizations for example in Lorne L. Dawson (2003) *Cults and New Religious Movements*. However, the preferred term that has more recently pre-occupied sociologists of religion is "spirituality" in which individuals "pick and mix" their religious beliefs and practices in a manner that is perfectly consistent with the fluid subjectivities of modern society. These developments are considered by Matthew Wood in chapter 12. Claims both for and against the importance of spirituality in modern societies are both plentiful and contested (Heelas 2009). There is said for example to be a divorce, especially in contemporary America, between religion and spirituality (Cimino and Lattin 1998; Fuller 2001). The result is that there is increasing attention given to these new developments in relation to youth cultures (Bender 2003) rather than to religious organizations. Modern spirituality also illustrates an argument about the de-institutionalized character of contemporary religion put forward originally by Grace Davie (1994 and chapter 7 in this volume) that religiosity involves "believing without belonging."

There is therefore a general trend away from the study of organizational forms of the mainstream churches (Hamberg 2009). In addition, because the church–sect typology from Ernst Troeltsch onwards reflected the history of Christianity, it was not particularly useful in the analysis of non-Western religions and hence the departure from organizational analysis has also been associated with a greater emphasis on the comparative study of religious forms. This trend has been reinforced by the contemporary focus on Islam – a religion in which there has been historically greater emphasis on local consensus and devolved authority rather than on a centralized system of religious power. The crisis of authority in modern Islam is therefore all the more critical (Reid and Gilsenan 2007; Volpi and Turner 2007). Furthermore, the distinction between church and state or the Augustinian separation of the two cities was not characteristic of early Islam in which the caliphate combined the religious and the secular as a defense against communal feuding. The *New Companion* follows the work of Max Weber in placing a significant emphasis on comparative religion including a chapter on Islam by Gabriele Marranci.

A perennial problem for handbooks of the sociology of religion has been how to incorporate a comprehensive analysis of religion in the United States without ignoring the rest of the world. American religiosity has been a persistent focus of the sociology of religion for various reasons. Firstly, as a matter of fact contemporary sociology of religion has been dominated for decades by American sociologists such as William Bainbridge, Robert Bellah, Peter L. Berger, Charles Glock, Will Herberg, Gerhard Lenski, Talcott Parsons, W. C. Roof, Rodney Stark, Guy E. Swanson, and J. Milton Yinger. Secondly, American society has provided an important contrast to northern Europe since the time of Thomas Jefferson's Virginia Statute on Religious Freedom. With the separation of church and state, American religious denominations flourished and hence there is a continuing issue around "American exceptionalism." (See John Torpey in chapter 6 in this volume). Thirdly, a number of influential theories of modern religion have emerged from this specifically American experience of religion and religious organizations such as the civil religion debate which is closely associated with Robert Bellah (Bellah and Tipton 2006), the idea of spiritual market places (Berger and Roof), the economic models of religious behavior (Bainbridge and Stark) and finally the idea of new spiritualities (Roof and others). The recent publication of Parsons's *American Society* (2007) has also served once more to remind us of the centrality of religion to the sociological understanding of American society. Many of these issues are explored by Victor Lidz in chapter 3.

The sociology of religion has been in the postwar period largely dominated by American sociology and hence in editing a *New Companion* it is often difficult to achieve a successful balance between North America and Europe. Many early textbooks of the sociology of religion such as Louis Schneider's *Religion Culture & Society* (1964) left little space for understanding religion outside the American context. By contrast Norman Birnbaum and Gertrud Lenzer in editing *Sociology and Religion* (1969) drew overwhelmingly from a European tradition of social philosophy including selections from Nietzsche, Troeltsch, Mannheim, Goldmann, Adorno, and Schelsky. With too much emphasis on American sociology, there is an inevitable marginalization of the work of European sociologists such as the tradition associated with George Bataille (1992) or the more recent work of Daniele Hervieu-Leger in *Religion as a Chain of Memory* (2000) or Steve Bruce in *Politics & Religion* (2003) or David Martin in *Pentecostalism* (2002). There is also in general a problematic neglect of the work of Niklas Luhmann whose *Religious Dogmatics and the Evolution of Society* (1984) offered a unique theoretical understanding of religious communication. In this respect the *New Companion* attempts to reflect both North American and European traditions, by including both European and American sociologists.

Globalization studies have been a major development in the social sciences over the last three or four decades but most textbooks on globalization have ignored religion – for example Saskia Sassen's *A Sociology of Globalization* (2007), David Held's Held et al. (1999) *Global Transformations* (1999) or David Harvey's *The Spaces of Hope* (2000). Most existing texts that do examine religion and globalization tend implicitly to conflate the study of global religion and the comparative sociology of religion. For example, the Sage *Handbook* has a concluding section on "Case Studies from around the World" but the result is somewhat ad hoc and incomplete – official religions in China, central and eastern Europe after Communism, Judaism, and Israel, state Shinto in postwar Japan, and Mexico. A more satisfactory approach can be illustrated by Stephen Sharot's *A Comparative*

Sociology of World Religions (2001) which, employing Max Weber's notions of elites and virtuoso religion, managed to provide a more coherent, comprehensive, and systematic approach. Other valuable contributions have appeared in Manuel Vasquez and Marie Marquardt's *Globalizing the Sacred* (2003) and Peter Clarke's *New Religions in Global Perspective* (2006) but perhaps the most consistent theoretical account of religion and globalization has come from Peter Beyer in *Religion and Globalization* (1994). Jeremy Stolow's chapter 24 on popular religion and the global media explores an important aspect of this process of cultural globalization.

The globalization issue can also be seen as an element in the discussion about public religion, politics of identity and diasporic communities. Jose Casanova's *Public Religions in the Modern World* (1994) was the pioneering contribution to this discussion. Underpinning the debates about "political theology," "religious nationalism," "political Islam," and "religion and violence" is a deeper question about the nature of secularism and secularization. This development raises a fundamental question, not only about what counts as religion, but also what counts as the secular? There appears to be, especially in political theory, a widespread assumption that the liberal model of secularism dating from the Treaty of Westphalia in 1648 is in crisis, because assumptions about the privatization of conscience and the clear separation of religion and politics no longer hold. A modern handbook of the sociology of religion needs to look fairly determinedly at the range of concepts that grew up around liberal tolerance – secular, secularism, secularity, secularization and laicity. The notion of the secular has a complex history from St Augustine's idea of the two cities to Richard Hooker's defense of Anglicanism as a national religion, through John Locke's vision of religious tolerance to the Enlightenment and the French Revolution. It has of course also exercised the minds of modern thinkers such as Cox in his *The Secular City* (1965), but the most compelling examination of these issues has been undertaken by Charles Taylor in two significant works – *Varieties of Religion Today* (2002) and *A Secular Age* (2007).

In the process of exploring secularization, Taylor has also shown how important William James was to the early development of the sociology of religion for example in the work of Durkheim. James's pragmatism is – with the exception of Jack Barbalet (1997) – largely ignored in the study of the development of the sociology of religion. More generally one might say that accounts of the evolution of the sociology of religion neglect the importance of pragmatism not only in America but for European social thought as well (Baert and Turner 2007; Croce 1995). The analysis of secularism is therefore an important prior step to any understanding of the contemporary relation between religion and politics, and in any exploration of the secular it is unwise for sociology to stray too far from philosophy. To do so is to ignore at our own cost the work not only of Taylor but also of Alasdair MacIntyre, Jean-Luc Nancy and Hent de Vries. One could argue that the best illustrations of British sociology in general and of the sociology of religion in particular have always combined philosophy and sociology such as MacIntyre's *Secularization and Moral Change* (1967) and with Paul Ricoeur *The Religious Significance of Atheism* (1969). Even Ludwig Wittengenstein appears to fall out of the frame of reference of much sociology of religion, despite his pivotal position in the debate about practice in relation to belief (Arrington and Addis 2001). In *On Certainty*

(1969) and in his *Remarks on Frazer's Golden Bough* (1979), Wittgenstein rejected or at least brought into question assertions about the absolute truth or falsity of religious beliefs, insisting that they had to be set within a "language game," but more importantly that we should look more determinedly at religious practices not beliefs.

THE "NEW PARADIGM" IN THE SOCIOLOGY OF RELIGION

In the last couple of decades, a new theoretical paradigm has been heavily promoted in American sociology of religion, which has been variously called the "new paradigm," the religious markets approach, or the economic interpretation of religion. (See David Lehman in chapter 8 in this volume.) These approaches, which have been influenced in various ways by rational choice theories, are associated with figures such as Rodney Stark, Roger Finke, Laurence Iannaccone, and R. Stephen Warner (Hamilton, 2009). This "new" approach is often contrasted disparagingly with "old" European theories of religion. European sociology, it is alleged, has been too much focused on the meaning which social actors require to make sense of life, and by contrast the new paradigm is concerned with the economic dimensions of religious behavior, including both demand for and supply of religious beliefs, practices and objects. On the whole, the religious markets approach favors supply side explanations, taking particular note of how state responses to religious pluralism may or may not encourage religious competition. This approach to religion and politics has often produced valuable insights into how states manage religious diversity (Gill, 2008). The economic approach to religion has also generated important insights into how with the decline of communism for example has given rise to flourishing religious markets in for example post-communist China. (See Fenggang Yang in chapter 19 in this volume.)

The rational choice model has also been used to explain the vibrant nature of religion in America since the colonial period when compared to Europe. Before engaging in this description of the new paradigm, we should note that Alexis de Tocqueville, who was as an "old" European struck forcibly by the extraordinary religiosity of Americans during his famous journeys around the "new" society, continues to throw light on the issue of "American exceptionalism" in religious matters. In his *Democracy in America* (2000 [1835–40]), Tocqueville dwelt on the reconciliation of popular religiosity and democracy. While in Catholic France the relation between church and state had produced endless conflict, in America the moral force of popular religion was important in creating social harmony. Tocqueville as an "old" European was not interested in "true" religion, but in the social and political benefits of American religiosity as an aspect of civil society. Later European visitors such as Max Weber and Ernst Troeltsch were equally struck by this contrast between secular Europe and the religiosity of America. Weber arrived in 1904 for the World Congress of Arts and Science in St Louis and published an article in 1906 on the "churches and sects of North America" (Loader and Alexander 1985). The legacy of Tocqueville's analysis has of course been somewhat transformed by subsequent interpretation to emphasize the role of religious pluralism, self-realization, individualism, and voluntary association membership as manifestations of the democratic revolution, as essentially the democratization of religion (Wolin 2001). The democratic assumption that everybody has religious opinions and that all opinions are equally valid and important has contributed to the American religious marketplace, where priestly authority and ecclesiastical hierarchy do not find comfortable locations. In this sense, writers like David Martin (2002) are correct to see Methodism with its commitment to the priesthood of all believers, Arminian theology of salvation, lay participation, emotional subjectivity and congregational autonomy as the harbinger of religious modernization, the logical outcome of which is the proposition that everybody has his or her own personal religion. In this sense the evangelical religions of the eighteenth and nineteenth centuries paved the way to the eventual rise of modern post-institutional spirituality. (See Matthew Wood in chapter 12 in this volume.)

What are the principal components of the new paradigm? First, whereas traditional European social theory had emphasized the centrality of secularization to modernization alongside urbanization, increasing literacy and democratic politics, the new paradigm takes note of the resilience of religion, not only in the United States but globally. In European sociology in the 1960s, Bryan Wilson (1966) in *Religion in Secular Society* claimed that the churches were in rapid decline as a result of a general process of secularization and in *Contemporary Transformations of Religion* (1976) he argued that religion (that is Christianity) had survived in America at the cost of its orthodox theological content. Wilson sought to explain the prominence of Christian belief and practice in America by saying that it had simply accommodated belief and practice to the predominant values and life styles of a consumer society. In short the form of Christianity survived but only at the costs of its contents. While David Martin's work on secularization provided a more complex picture, he too was struck by the contrast between America and Europe in his *A General Theory of Secularization* (1978). Authentic, that is orthodox, religious belief and practice could only adjust to modern society by ejecting any demanding beliefs and practices, and embracing popular culture, that is through a process of cultural compromise. American religion had in fact abandoned much of its tensions with the world – a factor which Weber thought in his analysis of Protestantism was essential to religion as a lever of social change. Another version of these arguments appeared in Bellah's account of the growth of a civil religion in America in his "Civil Religion in America" (1967) and through a subsequent series influential publications (Bellah and Tipton 2006). (See Victor Lidz, chapter 3, in this volume.) Bellah argued that alongside Christianity there was a vibrant national religion composed of American values which treated American history as an unfolding of salvation. Christianity remained influential in public life when refracted through the lens of a civil religion. This development was an essential element in the historical exceptionalism of America. (See John Torpey in chapter 6 in this volume.)

Wilson was well known in British society for his conservative views on education, youth culture and the universities. This cultural conservatism was also evident in his critical views of American popular religion as a corruption of authentic religion. By contrast, American sociologists, such as Talcott Parsons, were impressed by the strength of religion in the United States (Turner 2005). Bellah, a former student of Parsons, while taking a more critical view of American civil religion, nevertheless recognized its importance with respect to American democracy. Perhaps because of their democratic presuppositions, American sociologists have been less inclined to question the authenticity of either mainstream Christianity or civil religion in American history. The apparent revival of fundamentalism globally has reinforced that viewpoint, and the "old" European theory of inevitable secularization has continued to be somewhat on the defensive with respect to the American tradition. (See Steve Bruce, chapter 5, in this volume.)

Second, the new model directs research attention towards the function of religious or spiritual markets in which there is a competition for "brand loyalty" from consumers of religious meaning, practices and objects. The notion of spiritual markets has been explored empirically and systematically by Wade Roof in *Spiritual Marketplace* (1999). It is impossible to understand religion in contemporary America without taking into account the impact of the "baby boomers" on religious practice and consciousness. Roof made an important contribution to the study of religion and generational change in his *A Generation of Seekers* (Roof 1993), in which the postwar generations were religious seekers, but also eclectic in their religious "tastes." The "culture wars" of the postwar period re-organized the map of mainstream religion in North America just as it challenged establishment culture generally. Employing life histories and a panel study, Roof argued that the boundaries of popular religion had been constantly redrawn under the impact of large postwar generations, facilitated by an expanding religious marketplace. American denominational pluralism as a spiritual marketplace in the absence of an established church continues to encourage organizational innovation and cultural entrepreneurship. The market for religious innovations can be seen as a response to massive social change in contemporary America in which an expanding consumer culture has produced the reflexive self as the principal conduit of and companion to expanded consumerism. In the market place of seekers, Roof identified five major subcultures: dogmatists (for example fundamentalists and neo-traditionalists) mainstream believers, born-again Christians (including evangelicals, Pentecostalists, and Charismatics), metaphysical believers and seekers, and secularists. While Americans may invest less time in voluntary associations and are less certain about traditional Christian values than in previous generations, they are significantly involved in spiritual searching that has produced a deeper emphasis on self-understanding, self-awareness and self-reflexivity. As the baby boomers came to maturity, they moved out of the narcissistic culture of the 1960s into a deeper, more serious "quest culture." If traditional religious cultures depended heavily on the continuity of the family as an agency of socialization, the transformation of family life and the entry of women into the formal labor market have radically destabilized religious identities and cultures. Despite these important contributions to research by Roof and others, it could be legitimately claimed that the sociology of religion has paid insufficient attention to generation as a variable by comparison with gender, class and ethnicity.

Despite the emphasis on individualism, choice and religious emotionality in consumer life style, religious conservatism continues to thrive, and more liberal forms of Christianity often appear to be in retreat. While Roof has explored American spirituality beyond the boundaries of institutionalized religion, sociologists continue to be concerned to understand the appeal of the conservative churches.

The explanation of the success of conservative Christian churches is in common-sense terms perhaps somewhat obvious. Conservative Protestants have more children, and discourage contact with people who are secular, childless or divorced. Christian families tend to stick together and people in conservative churches retain their membership, because they want their children to be raised through a traditional religious education. We can understand why people stay in conservative churches, but why proportionately do more liberals join conservative churches than vice versa? Why are the mainline churches such as the Unitarians, Presbyterians and Methodist denominations either stationary or in decline, while the more conservative denominations such as Southern Baptist Convention and the Assemblies of God are flourishing?

One classic explanation for organizational success was provided by Dean Kelley (1977) in terms of a theory of the costs of commitment. Kelley's thesis was that the specific contents of a religious message are less important for success than the demands for commitment that it places on its members. Ultimately the costliness of commitment is measured by control over members' lifestyles, the development of a strong church, and the seriousness of religious involvement. Churches tend to be successful when they develop a totalitarian and hierarchical form of authority and when they can create and sustain homogeneous communities. These successful congregations are unlike liberal religious groups that impose few sanctions and modest demands on their members. We might say in terms of markets that the importance of membership of any association is a function of the demands on entry and exit. Kelley's thesis has been widely influential. However, Joe Tamney's research in *The Resilience of Conservative Religion* (2002) provides only partial support for the strong church thesis. Tamney argued that conservative congregations support a traditional gender division of labor and conventional gender identities; in a society, which is deeply divided over gender issues, such ideological reassurance can be psychologically attractive. Furthermore, given the general uncertainties of everyday life in modernity, the certainties of religious teaching on morality can also be psychologically supportive. Clearly traditional religious orientations may serve to articulate political commitments around major issues relating to abortion, gay and lesbian sexuality, education, and the family. Tamney concluded by accepting Roof's notion of American society as a spiritual marketplace in which the loyalty of congregations cannot be taken for granted, because religion has to be sold, alongside other cultural products. In middle America, the religious market is volatile and people moving in and out of congregations in search of an appropriate niche just as customers move in and out of different areas of the secular marketplace.

Thirdly, these sociological ideas about religious markets, demand for religious services, and consumption of religious phenomena are primarily influenced by rational choice theory as an approach to modern spirituality. The paradigm has several interesting substantive claims such as the notion that the religious demand for meaning is more or less constant across time – that is the demand for meaning will remain more or less static (Finke and Stark 1992; Stark and Finke 2000). Hence variations in religious behavior are influenced by supply rather than by demand. Religious pluralism in America, by offering innumerable outlets for religious taste, promotes greater involvement. The theory in making a useful distinction between demand for and supply of religious products, effectively explains the proliferation of religious groups in the United States, switching between denominations by customers, the inflationary character of the market, and the resulting hybridization and experimentation that is characteristic of modern religiosity. Of course these markets are also global, because religious commodities and beliefs can travel rapidly. (See chapter 25 on religious commodification in this volume.) These emerging markets cannot be easily controlled by traditional religious authorities. While sociologists have become excessively concerned to understand religious fundamentalism, hybrid popular religion has also flourished alongside and in competition with more orthodox forms of fundamentalist faith and practice. Unlike popular forms of spirituality, fundamentalist churches succeed because of their strictness that is by the exacting demands they make on their members. Laurence Iannaccone's argument (1994) is that religions of high-demand such as Jehovah's Witnesses aim to avoid the free-rider problem – joining without paying – by monopolizing the commitment of their followers. Paradoxically the new spirituality is also flourishing but makes few systematic demands on its followers who adopt a flexible attitude towards both belief and practice. I shall turn to this issue of the fragmentation of both society and religion in my conclusion.

Finally, the new model raises important questions about the elitist assumptions in such dichotomies as official and popular religion, the great and little tradition, or virtuoso and mass religion that have been common in "old" European theories. These elitist features can be traced back to Kant's reflections on religion in *Religion within the Limits of Pure Reason* (1960). It is valuable to consider Kant through the framework of Jacques Derrida's "Faith and Knowledge" (1998). In his reflections on the Kantian legacy, Derrida followed Emile Benveniste's *Indo-European Language and Society* (1973) in which the word "religion" (*religio*) has two distinctive but related roots. First, *relegere* means to bring together, to harvest or to gather in, and secondly, *religare* from means to tie or to bind together. The first meaning recognizes the importance of religious foundations in creating the social bonds of human groups, and the second meaning points to the disciplinary functions of morality that are necessary for creating and controlling human beings. While the first meaning acknowledges the role of the cult in forming human associations, the second recognizes the regulatory practices of religion in the discipline of the self. According to Kant's framework, in cultic religions individuals seek favors from the gods through prayer and offerings, including ritual sacrifice Such cultic practices promise to bring healing and wealth to its followers, but by contrast religion as a system of moral precepts commands human beings to change their earthly behavior in order through enlightenment and freedom from unreflecting tradition to lead a better moral life.

The clear implication of Kant's distinction was that (Protestant) Christianity was the only true "reflecting faith," and in a sense therefore it provided the model for all authentic religious intentions. It ultimately defined what was to count as "religion." Kant's distinction was fundamentally about those religious injunctions that call human beings to (moral) action and hence demand that humans assert their autonomy and responsibility. In order to have autonomy, human beings need to act independently of God. In a paradoxical fashion, Christianity implies or indeed requires the "death of God" because it calls people to freedom and hence the Christian faith is ultimately self-defeating.

These Kantian distinctions were found their sociological parallel in the sociology of Max Weber. In the *Sociology of Religion* (1966), Weber made a distinction between the religion of the masses and the religion of the virtuosi. While the masses seek comfort from the gods and lesser spiritual beings, the virtuosi or the spiritual elite fulfil the ethical demands of a religious way of life in search of personal enlightenment. The religion of the masses requires saints and holy men to satisfy the needs of ordinary men and women, and hence charisma is inevitably corrupted by the demand for miracles and spectacles. More importantly, Weber distinguished between those religions that reject the world (such as inner-worldly asceticism) by challenging its secular conventions and those religions (such as other-worldly mysticism) that seek to escape from the world through mystical flight. The former religions (primarily the Calvinistic radical sects) have had revolutionary consequences for human societies in the formation of rationalism as the real basis of modernity. These traditions in the Abrahamic faiths provided a sharp contrast to the "Asian religions" where the legacy of Confucianism had no connection with notions about personal salvation (Turner 2009a). The implication of this Kantian legacy is paradoxical, because Christianity gives rise to a process of secularization that spells out its own self-overcoming. This distinction was particularly important in Weber's analysis of Buddhism in his *The Religion of India* (1958: 206), where he described "ancient Buddhism" as "a specifically unpolitical and anti-political status religion, more precisely a religious 'technology' of wandering and of intellectually schooled mendicant monks." (See chapter 17 in this volume.)

The new paradigm has important, and testable, features (Beckford 2003; Warner 2004), but is it a new model? The concept of a spiritual supermarket was originally developed by Peter Berger in his analysis of the crisis of religious plausibility. Secularization and the crisis of plausibility were produced by individuals "shopping around" to satisfy their spiritual needs. Berger (1969: 137) wrote that "the religious tradition which previously could be authoritatively imposed, now has to be *marketed*. It must be "sold" to a clientele that is no longer constrained to "buy." The pluralistic situation is, above all, a *market*." While it is not entirely obvious that the new paradigm is in fact "new," it has the intellectual merit of forcing us to think about how religion is marketed, and how it has become a commodity alongside other consumer objects. It also provides creative ways of understanding the relationship between the state and religion, because the supply side of religion is often dependent on state policies towards religious competition in civil society. Although the new paradigm has produced interesting insights into many aspects of religious markets, the paradigm has also been criticized precisely because of its emphasis on free markets, individual choice and subjectivity (Bastian 2006; Robertson 1992). For some critics, Bourdieu's notions of habitus and field avoids some of the problems that critics believe are connected with the idea of the autonomy of consumer choice.

FUNDAMENTALISM

Much of the discussion about the revival of religion in modern history has focused on the growth of fundamentalism. In the twentieth century, the growth of Pentecostalism and its charismatic manifestations were dramatic, and as a result approximately one quarter of a billion people are now adherents, or one in twenty-five of the global population (Martin 2002). There are different forms of Pentecostal revivalism that are shaped by its social audience. In Latin America and Africa, Pentecostalism finds an audience among the "respectable poor" whose ambition is successfully to enter the modern world; in West Africa and Southeast Asia, it is most prevalent among the new middle classes, including members of the Chinese diaspora. (See Afe Adobe in chapter 22 in this volume.) There are important social minorities who are also attracted to Pentecostalism in Nepal, the Andes, and inland China. In Latin America Pentecostalism functions as a religion of the oppressed, offering them hope, social membership and some basic welfare services, but in North America and Europe, where liberal Christianity is obviously still dominant, Pentecostalism spreads through charismatic movements inside the existing churches and denominations.

Following Martin, we can best understand Pentecostalism sociologically through a reflection on the social history of Methodism, which in the first instance spread in the eighteenth and nineteenth centuries through the working and lower middle classes with an Arminian theology that is a universal doctrine of salvation and an emphasis on emotional responses to Jesus as a personal savior. However, through education, discipline, teetotalism and literacy, the Methodist laity moved up the social ladder and eventually abandoned their Methodist chapels for a variety of destinations such as the Anglican Church, the Labour Party or merely indifference. Contemporary Pentecostalism has similar characteristics. The "Pentecostal virtues" include personal betterment through educational achievement, self control, social aspiration, and hard work. These technologies of the self produce socially mobile people, but Pentecostalism also offers psychological liberation. Martin argues that there is an elective affinity between Pentecostalism and the spread of global liberal capitalism and what Talcott Parsons called "the expressive revolution" (Parsons, 1963). Pentecostalism is a social movement that is devolved, voluntary, local and fissiparous; it works within a competitive religious market that offers spiritual uplift, social success and emotional gratification. While Methodism supplied the work ethic of early capitalism, Pentecostalism is relevant to the work skills and personal attributes of the post-industrial service economy, especially the attributes of self-monitoring and a refusal to accept failure.

Martin's *Pentecostalism: The World Their Parish* is important sociologically because it raises important questions about the assumption that "fundamentalist movements" like Pentecostalism are traditional, or indeed anti-modern. By contrast, Pentecostalism is highly congruent with the flexible, plural world of liberal capitalism, and appears to promote rather than reject the emotional individualism of late modernity. In the popular press, "fundamentalism" is normally but mistakenly equated with "radical Islam," and radical Islam is understood to be hostile to modernity. Part of the problem is of course how to define fundamentalism (Antoun 2001 and chapter 23 in this volume). The definition of fundamentalism revolves around a number of themes. According to Richard Antoun, "Scripturalism" requires a literal belief in the inerrant and unchanging nature of the fundamental scriptures, and the quest for legitimacy and authority by reference to those scriptures. In addition, there is the search for purity and piety in world that is seen to be impure; there is a willingness to see the relevance of traditional scriptures to contemporary issues;

"totalism" is the rejection of the divorce between the sacred and the profane, and by contrast the assertion of the relevance of religion to all spheres of life; "activism" involves confrontation with the secular world, by violent means if necessary; and a world view that understands the modern world in terms of an endless struggle between good and evil.

On the basis of information from existing sociological research, who are the fundamentalists? In terms of their core membership and leadership, fundamentalists in Islam are typically recruited from the educated but often alienated urban social classes. They are often highly educated but alienated by their lack of social mobility and limited economic success in developing societies. In short, fundamentalists are recruited from social groups that have typically failed to benefit significantly from secular nationalist governments and their aborted modernisation projects. In *Understanding Fundamentalism*, Antoun (2001) suggested that fundamentalism is not necessarily a traditional protest against modernity, but rather a selective protest against aspects of the modernization process. This approach suggests that fundamentalism refers to the selective process whereby certain technological and organizational innovations of modern society are accepted and others are rejected. Antoun also directs our attention to the process whereby an individual accepts a practice or belief from another culture (the secular world) and integrates it into their value system (the religious world). One illustration of the process of selective modernization is the use of television and radio by fundamentalist Christian groups in the United States. For example, Pat Robertson's CBN is now the third largest cable network in America, and funds the CBN University offering courses on media production techniques. Another example is James Dobson's radio programme *Focus on the Family* that offers psychological advice and counselling services. This programme has evolved into the equivalent of a Christian call center that receives over one thousand daily calls on a toll-free number. Similarly among Islamic radical groups, modern technology is also avidly embraced. The militant Hezbollah group has an information network in Beirut with mobile phones, computers and multiple-version web site. Antoun also considered various forms of controlled acculturation for Jewish and Muslim fundamentalists involving various strategies of physical separation. In Israel, Jewish fundamentalists who have to take university courses in academic settings that are secular and liberal have negotiated special arrangements for example to be taught by men. In Saudi Arabia, fundamentalists have used distance learning techniques to ensure that men can avoid contact with women who may be "immodestly dressed." We can conclude that fundamentalist groups are not wholly opposed to modernity, and have adapted various modern technologies to improve their organizational and communications effectiveness. We could take this argument further claiming that fundamentalists are specifically hostile to traditional religion which in their view has compromised the fundamental tenets of faith, and that by embracing modern technology and organizational structures fundamentalist movements are, often as an unintended consequence, ushering in radical modernity. This view is of course perfectly compatible with the Weber thesis in which the Protestant sects were the reluctant midwives of rational capitalism. Reformed Islam with its emphasis on discipline, asceticism, hard work and literacy, and its hostility to traditional Islam in the shape of the Sufi lodges, may have similar cultural consequences.

The Media and the Future of Religion

The major changes that have taken place in religion can give us some insight into broader changes in the social fabric. We can summarize both existing trends and suggest some possible developments in the future. Globalization and the spread of Internet use are significant aspects of social change that have also transformed religion in important ways. (See Jeremy Stolow, chapter 24 in this volume.) By employing the notions of communication and complexity from the sociology of Luhmann, we can argue that whereas religious communication in an age of revelation was hierarchical, unitary and authoritative, communicative acts in a new media environment tend to be horizontal rather than vertical. They are also diverse and fragmented ther than unitary and integrated, and the authority of any message – religious or otherwise – is constantly negotiable. The modern growth of diverse foci of interpretation in a global communication system has produced a general crisis of authority at least in the formal system of religious belief and practice. While some authors (Clarke 2006) argue that disputes over authority have been a persistent part of Islamic history, one can argue that in modern Islam there has been an inflation of sources of (lay) authority since almost any local teacher or *mullah* can issue a *fetwa* to guide a local community by setting himself up with his own blog.

In addition new media provide multiple channels of access and promote discursive interaction through such blogs. The result is that the new media bring about a certain level of the democratization of information. Although there is obviously a digital divide, more and more people have access to interactive religious sites, and the result is a democratization of religion. Many young Muslims bypass their local *ulama* and *imams* in order to learn about Islam in English from pamphlets and sources such as *The Muslim News* and *Q-News*. The majority of these Muslim users of the Internet are resident in Europe and North America and they are typically university students undertaking technical degrees in engineering and computing. Because Internet access is often too expensive to be available in many communities in Asia and Africa, it is again the student population of Western universities who are accessing the Internet for religious and political purposes. While there is evidence that the Internet is used by radical activists against the West, the Internet can also promote reasoned argument in a context where everybody can in principle check the sources for themselves. The majority of sites are not developed by official Muslim organisations such as the Muslim World League and these alternative Muslim sites provide opportunities for discussion outside the official culture. It is for this reason that the Internet is a means of bypassing many of the traditional gatekeepers of Muslim orthodoxy. These Internet sites also serve to reinforce the individualism which many observers have associated with neo-fundamentalism because the global virtual *ummah* is the perfect site for individuals to express themselves while still claiming to be members of a community on whose behalf they are speaking (Mandaville 2001). These developments are not of course confined to Islam and one general feature of the globalization of religion is the spread of Internet sites for worship, study and discussion. Buddhist meditation techniques originating in Tibet are now widely available in the form of short-cut *vispassana* sessions on video-cassettes and on the Internet, thereby creating large Buddhist networks between Asia and California (Obeyesekere 2003: 74). (See chapter 17 in this volume.)

Modern media contribute to a growing individualism that is very different in content from the ascetic individualism of early Protestantism. This religious subjectivity in the media is a facet of the "expressive revolution" to which I have already alluded and which had its roots in the student revolts of the 1960s. In the new individualism, people invent their own religious ideas giving rise to the new forms of spirituality. The result has been a social revolution flowing from both consumerism and individualism. Religious life styles are modeled on consumerism in which individuals can try out religions rather like they try out new fashions as in any leisure activity. New industries have emerged offering everything from spiritual advice, to pilgrimage packages, to religious holidays and to dating agencies. Globalization thus involves the spread of personal spirituality which typically provides not only practical guidance in the everyday world, but also subjective, personalized meaning. Such religious phenomena are often combined with therapeutic or healing services, or the promise of personal enhancement through meditation. Spirituality appears to be closely associated with middle-class singles who are thoroughly engaged with Western consumer values, and who experience no contradiction between personal piety and consumer capitalism.

Because the modern structure of authority tends to be devolved, there is a trend towards the hybridization of religious traditions. This hybridity is reinforced through globalization and through the processes of borrowing from different religious traditions in a global religious market. Courtney Bender in *Heaven's Kitchen* (2003) provides a description of "Anita" – an informant from the kitchen which is known as "God's Love We Deliver." Anita "attended the Sunday morning services at the Episcopalian and Catholic churches on her block. She spirit channeled, took astrology courses, read Deepak Chopra, and dabbled in Catholic mysticism. She grew up in a Jewish family, but since childhood she had been attracted to the "mysterious" black habits that Catholic nuns wore. She recently learned that she had been "a nun in a past life." Anita emphatically told me that her inner spirit guided here to ideas that would be "helpful" (Bender 2003: 72). This lifestyle and mixture of beliefs give a clear picture of the hybridity of modern spirituality. From an orthodox perspective, such hybridity also appears to be iconoclastic. We live increasingly in a communication environment where images and symbols play a more important role in public life than the written word. This visual world is therefore iconic rather than one based on a written system, and this iconic world requires new skills and institutions that no longer duplicate the hierarchies and institutions of the written word. It is also a new experimental context in which the iconic can also be the iconoclastic as Madonna in her Catholic period switched to Rachel and for a while explored the Kabbalah (Hulsether 2000).

Although some sociologists have argued that the Internet creates new communities, the growth of privatized spirituality points to the decline of the social and the erosion of community. In the past, Protestant individualism was combined with a deep involvement in church life and community activity. The social life of the New Age does not build communities and is entirely compatible with the individualism of consumer society. In short, the new forms of religiosity do not appear to build new publics. Contemporary interpretations of such developments tend therefore to be pessimistic (Rieff 2006). The principal characteristics of religion in modern society are its individualism, the decline in the authority of traditional institutions (church and priesthood) and awareness that religious symbols are constructs. Bellah's predictions about modernity in his article on "religious evolution" have been clearly fulfilled in the growth of popular, de-institutionalized, commercialized, and largely post-Christian religions (Bellah 1964).

In a differentiated global religious market, these segments of the religious market compete with each other and overlap; the new spirituality is genuinely a consumerist religion and while fundamentalism appears to challenge consumer (Western) values, it is in fact also selling a life style based on special diets, alternative education, health regimes and mentalities. All three aspects of modern religion share a degree of consumerism, but they are also distinctively different; and gender is a crucial feature of the new consumerist religiosity where women increasingly dominate the new spiritualities; women will be and to some extent already are the "taste leaders" in the emergent global spiritual market place. While globalization theory tends to emphasize the triumph of modern fundamentalism (as a critique of traditional and popular religiosity), perhaps the real effect of globalization is the emergence of heterodox, commercial, hybrid, popular religion over orthodox, authoritative, professional versions of the spiritual life. Their ideological effects cannot be controlled by religious authorities, and they have a greater impact than official messages. However, whereas Protestant individualism contributed to building social groups and communities, modern spirituality with its stress on subjectivity is unlikely to become socially constructive in the same manner.

CONCLUSION: WHAT IS AT STAKE IN THE SOCIOLOGY OF RELIGION?

Religion as an institution was a major topic of classical sociology. From Karl Marx to Max Weber, to Émile Durkheim and Georg Simmel, and to Talcott Parsons and Niklas Luhmann, the analysis of religion played a central role in the study of modernization, urbanization and the industrial transformation of society. In twentieth-century sociology, Parsons's essays on religion and his notion of "the expressive revolution" have been deservedly influential (Robertson and Turner 1991). Niklas Luhmann's controversial theory of the nature of religion as a system of communication provided new insights into the place of religion in differentiated social systems. Although one can cite these influential figures, it is remarkable that the study of religion played almost no role in the work of many postwar sociologists. In this respect, one can think of Norbert Elias, Alvin Gouldner, Luc Boltanski, Anthony Giddens, and Pierre Bourdieu. In recent years, there have been various attempts to suggest that Bourdieu's notions of habitus, practice and field are helpful in the study of religion (Furseth 2009; Rey 2007). Bourdieu's work on habitus has inspired some aspects of recent interest in the body and religion for example in the work of Chris Shilling and Philip Mellor in this volume. Nevertheless, religion played only a minor role in Bourdieu's work as a whole. Against the background of this intellectual history, I want to suggest that the approach of Durkheim to the sacred remains valid to the central tasks of sociology not because his approach to the elementary forms of religion are beyond criticism but because Durkheim, through the study of religion, raised issues that remain central to sociology as such. I conclude this account of the contemporary map of the sociology of religion by a retrospective evaluation of the legacy of Durkheimian sociology.

He was centrally concerned with the analysis of the sacred in society. However, in the modern debate about public religions, it has become fairly commonplace to make a distinction between the sacred (the fundamental collective experience of sacredness as a distinctive force) and the religious (the institutions and beliefs that give expression to religions). We can conceptualize the religious and the sacred as two spheres of social reality that overlap but are yet separate and distinct. I turn to these issues in the final chapter of this volume and hence in this opening discussion I am more concerned to explain and defend Durkheim's account of the sacred rather than concentrating on the division between the sacred and the religious. Much of this *New Companion* is concerned to criticize the secularization thesis and its association with a monotone view of modernization. This critique has either directly or indirectly resulted in a revival of interest in Durkheim's sociology in general and his views about the sacred in particular.

The current renaissance in the fortunes of the sociology religion – arising from the globalization of religion, the security crisis and the apparent failure of secularism as a strategy for managing religions – cannot tell us as such why the sociology of religion would matter from the point of view of sociology as a whole. One still wants to ask : what is at stake here? What appears to me to be at stake is the very nature of the social itself. Sociologists have been interested in religion because it is assumed to contain the seeds of social life as such. This insight was the real point of Durkheim's critique of rationalist theories of religious belief – as it was also an important insight in Wittgenstein's approach to language and meaning. Religion will not crumble before the flames of rationalist critique or fall apart as a consequence of scientific experiment, because religion is deeply embedded in the actual social structures that make social life possible. Durkheim claimed that rational objections to Christian belief simply missed the point that religious commitment is bound up with a particular way of life and with membership of a particular community. Religious beliefs rather like the rules of cricket are neither rational nor irrational, but relevant or not relevant to the ongoing existence of a community. The question that faces modern sociology is whether the social is being dismantled by such processes as globalization, and if so whether religion can still successfully express the form of life of a community. Is the death of institutionalized religion and the rise of the new spirituality a sign of the erosion of the social? What is the social in a global world of mobility, flows and networks?

During the period in which the secularization paradigm was dominant in sociological theory, Durkheim's fortunes in professional sociology were relatively low. However, the contemporary revival of religion globally, especially in the political sphere, has also seen a revival of the idea that religion is somehow critical to the actual constitution of the social world. The current crises around politics and religion which is encapsulated in the notion of a "post-secular society" have made Durkheim's sociology of religion once more a dominant concern of social and political theory. As a result, contemporary philosophers such as Charles Taylor (2007) when seeking to analyze nationalism, multiculturalism and pluralism constantly invoke Durkheim as a source of inspiration and as a paradigm for understanding the public role of religion. What then is the deep theoretical structure of *The Elementary Forms of the Religious Life* (1995) that remains so compelling?

Classical sociology can be understood as the quest to define "the social," and hence Durkheim's attempt to understand "social facts" in *The Rules of Sociological Method* (1958) remains central to sociology as a whole. In more precise terms, the focus of this sociological tradition was initially presented in *Primitive Classification* (Durkheim and Mauss 1963) where Durkheim and Mauss attempted to understand the general schema of logical classification as manifestations of social structure. Classical sociological explanations are sociological in the strong sense of the term, because they do not refer to individual dispositions as causes of action, but give some primacy to collective arrangements or social structures. Of course, not all sociological explanations assume or adhere to Durkheim's *Rules*. Insofar as sociological explanations do not employ references to social structure or social facts in Durkheim's sense, they may be regarded as residing outside this strong program (Turner 2009b), but they may nevertheless contain explanations that one can regard as sociologically important and convincing. If one wants to grasp "the social" as a topic of social science and if one wants to understand sociology, as opposed to psychology or history, one has to read Durkheim. By extension, anybody who wants to understand the sacred and the public sphere in modern societies would be well advised to take Durkheim seriously. Much of Durkheim's sociology as a whole is discussed at length by William Ramp in chapter 2 of the volume, but in this final section I need to revisit Durkheim in order to give an account of the specific importance of the sociology of religion. That is, I need to return to Durkheim in order to answer the question – what is at stake in the study of the sacred?

There is a double meaning to Durkheim's notion of the "elementary." At one level "elementary" does mean "primitive" and hence Durkheim's sociology was a reflection on the early field work that had been carried out in Australia by Baldwin Spencer and F. J. Gillen (1997) an anthropologist and a colonial magistrate and published as *The Northern Tribes of Central Australia* in 1904 . But Durkheim's intention was also to give a sociological account of the fundamental forms of the collective structures of consciousness. The subtitle of the earlier work on primitive classification perhaps makes their intellectual intentions more transparent namely "a study of collective representations." These primitive forms of collective representation are the elementary principles of cultural classification. We cannot understand forms of consciousness by a study of the consciousness of separate individuals. More specifically, we cannot grasp the structure of thought through a psychological study of the contents of human minds. The social comes before the individual, and thus to understand – or to classify – consciousness, we need to study its social forms. The explicit thesis of Durkheim's study was that it is society itself that presents the mind with these "primitive forms," namely the elementary forms of classification.

What was the originality of Durheim's study of religion? Durkheim was of course in many respects a rationalist and positivist in his approach to sociology. Despite Durkheim's rationalism, he came to see the religious as the wellspring of social life. According to Talcott Parsons's famous observation in *The Structure of Social Action* (1937), Durkheim at the conclusion of his career came to recognize that it was religion that produced society, not society that produced religion. Durkheim's sociology of religion broke decisively with the intellectual context of nineteenth-century individualism, evolutionary thought and cognitive rationalism. Much of his intellectual effort went into attacking Herbert Spencer who in combining both individualism and evolutionary thought had become profoundly influential not only in Europe but in China and Japan in their quest to comprehend modernization. Before Durkheim and modern anthropology, rationalist theories of religion treated the religious beliefs of primitive society as irrational or at least as mistaken views of reality. Primitive religion was defined as animist, because it proposed that natural phenomena were governed or animated by spirits. Natural science would eventually show that primitive magic and mythology were based false beliefs, and hence the spread of science would lead eventually to the demise of religion. Durkheim was especially critical of such rationalist views, emphasizing the continuing sociological importance of religion to social cohesion.

In the context of the anthropological research that became available in the nineteenth century, Christian intellectuals felt it was necessary to explain the differences between primitive rituals such as a communal meal and Christian practice such as the Eucharist. One solution was to appeal to evolutionary theory itself in order to argue that Protestantism was the most highly evolved religion, and that its rituals and beliefs were essentially abstract propositions that could be justified by rational argument. Protestant theology attempted to express religious truths through metaphors that have replaced ideas about actual relationships. In Protestant Christianity, the idea of divine fatherhood had become completely dissociated from the physical notion of natural fatherhood and the Eucharist had become a ritual of remembrance rather than the presence of the living God. Alasdair MacIntyre (1969) in *The Religious Significance of Atheism* made much use of Mrs Humphrey Ward's novel *Robert Elsmere* (1914) as an account of the intellectual climate of the late Victorian world in which there was a drift of nineteenth-century Protestantism from an evangelical faith to a secular justification of religious practice and eventually to humanism and socialism. *Robert Elsmere* which was published in 1888 became an instant success in charting the rise of an ethical interpretation of the Christian message in which the Bible was seen to be a moral treatise rather than a sacred text.

It was against this background of individualistic, rationalist and psychological theories of religion that Durkheim's generic definition of religion was intellectually interesting and influential. According to his famous definition, religion is not a belief in a high god or gods, but rather a unified system of beliefs and practices based upon a classification of social reality into sacred and profane things, and furthermore these beliefs and practices unite its adherents into a single moral community. Durkheim re-directed attention away from individuals to social groups or what he called a moral community. Religion as a classificatory system that is grounded in the dichotomy between the sacred and profane is thus set apart from magic which was seen by Durkheim to be an individual and instrumental activity. For Durkheim, there is no church of magic and religion survives because it satisfies a basic social function, not a psychological one. Thus Durkheim argued there is no society that can exist that does not need at regular intervals to sustain and reaffirm its collective life – its historical narrative, shared emotions and dominant ideas.

In this sense there are no false or irrational religions, because religion is the self-representation of society that is its collective representation. In these arguments

Durkheim was influenced by pragmatism, specifically James's *The Varieties of Religious Experience* (1963). From a pragmatist position, it does not make sense to ask about the veracity of religious classificatory practices; rather classificatory systems are only more or less useful in helping us to cope with reality rather than true or false in explaining reality. Religion is primarily a collective activity based on a classification of things into the sacred (set apart and forbidden) and profane (part of the everyday world). Because religion is collective, it is experienced as obligatory in the life of the individual. In this sense, it is what Durkheim called a "social fact" – a phenomenon outside the individual, existing independently and exercising moral force over society. Finally it makes little sense to have a strong evolutionary view of religion. In modern society, while the collective sense of the sacred may be less vivid, the same or similar functions can still be detected. Therefore when Durkheim employed words like "elementary" and "primitive" he was not adopting an evolutionary scheme, because for him the primary meaning of "elementary" is "basic" or "foundational."

We might re-state Durkheim's thesis to argue that political and social beliefs receive their authoritative force from classificatory systems that are collective and public, and which are sustained by a shared emotional life. We can assume that the argument is based on the following sequential structure in which collective rituals produce shared emotions giving rise to a social effervescence. Through this process collective classifications are given some political authority. This argument raises an obvious question about modern society, namely what happens to the authority of classificatory systems where the force of collective emotions are diminished by the secularization of religious systems? Durkheim anticipated this question when he wrote that the history of scientific classification is, in the last analysis, the history of the steps by which the element of social affectivity has been progressively weakened, diluted and ultimately undermined, thereby leaving more space for the reflective thought of individuals. However, Durkheim believed that this element of shared affectivity could never be entirely absent from a viable functioning society.

The implication of Durkheim's argument is that the collective and emotional character of classificatory practices in modern societies has broken down, and that with modernity there is an inevitable erosion of the authority of religious belief and a greater indeterminacy about religious practice, as individuals become more reflective about underlying classificatory principles. They are no longer taken for granted belief systems and social relations are subject to processes of individualization. However, under certain circumstances such as a revolutionary moment or a collective threat to a society in wartime collective symbolism once more becomes crucial. The lasting value of Durkheim's work is therefore the insight it gives us into traumatic events, collective emotions and symbols in modern politics.

Why has there been a revival of religion in the public sphere? Why have forms of religious nationalism become so prevalent? One answer is that religious cosmologies and collective symbolization have a collective force that was not fully available to the ideological systems of communism and nationalism. By contrast, religion allows a national community to express its history in deep-rooted myths or sacred time as if that national history had a universal significance, namely to express the mythical history of a nation in terms of a story of suffering and survival about humanity as a whole. The classical illustrations would be Poland, Mexico, and the

Philippines or more recently East Timor. Poland above all conceptualized itself as the Crucified Nation of Europe. We might note the obvious point that these are Catholic societies in which Roman Catholic symbolism, especially the figures of the Crucified Christ and the lamenting Virgin Mary, as Geneviève Zubrzycki (2006) demonstrated in *The Crosses of Auschwitz*, is crucial to their historical self-understanding as imagined communities. (See Zubrzycki's account of nationalism and religion in chapter 27.) The Protestant Churches have been more readily the vehicles for expressive individualism and subjectivism and perhaps less able to function as national vehicles of collective action. The exceptions might be Protestant nationalism in Scotland and Northern Ireland. Reading Durkheim's classic study of religion thus continues to offer us a creative sociological insight into these on-going tensions between nationalism religious revival and individual subjectivity in modern cultures, proving a stimulus to the constant renewal of sociological theory.

In the final chapter on post-secular society, I argue that we should conceptualize secularization at two levels: the political and the social. At the level of the state, in societies that are increasingly complex and diverse, there is a growing trend that we may broadly designate as "the management of religion." In this sense the old liberal paradigm is being replaced by a new alliance between states and religion to regulate public space. We can argue that both Émile Durkheim and Max Weber remain critically relevant to these debates. The idea of a post-secular society means basically that secular authorities can no longer simply ignore religion and that a liberal framework demands mutual recognition of competing religions. The specific issue in recent history has been the inclusion of diasporic Muslim communities into Western societies. These political developments are in some ways rather separate from the ebb and flow of religion in terms of the everyday social world. In this respect, Durkheim's perspective on the sacred and the profane remains the dominant paradigm of sociological inquiry. The sociology of religion remains important because the intersections of these two fields – the public religions of the civil sphere and the religious practices of everyday social sphere – constitute the central dimensions of the problem of "the social" in the modern world.

Note

Some aspects of this introduction first appeared as "Reshaping the sociology of religion: globalization, spirituality and the erosion of the social," *Sociological Review* (2009), 57 (1): 186–200.

Bibliography

Anderson, P. S. and Clack, B. (eds.) (2004) *Feminist Philosophy of Religion: Critical Readings*, London: Routledge.

Antoun, Richard T. (2001) *Understanding Fundamentalism: Christian, Islamic, Jewish Movements*, New York: Rowman and Littlefield.

Arrington, R. L. and Addis, M. (ed.) (2001) *Wittgenstein and Philosophy of Religion*, London: Routledge.

Asad, Talal (1991) *Genealogies of Religion: Discipline and Reasons of Power in Christianity and Islam*, Baltimore and London: Johns Hopkins University Press.

Baert, P. and Turner, B. S. (eds.) (2007) *Pragmatism and European Social Theory*, Oxford: Bardwell Press.

Bailey, Edward I. (1990) The implicit religion of contemporary society: some studies and reflections, *Social Compass* 37 (4): 483–97.

Baily, Edward I. (2009) Implicit religion, in Peter B. Clarke (ed.), *The Oxford Handbook of the Sociology of Religion*, Oxford: Oxford University Press, 801–16.

Barbalet, Jack (1997) The Jamesian theory of action, *Sociological Review*, 45 (1): 102–21.

Bastian, Jean-Pierre (2006) La nouvelle economie religieuse de l'Amerique latine, *Social Compass* 53 (1): 65–80.

Bataille, Georges (1992) *Theory of Religion*, New York: Zone Books.

Beckford, James (2003) *Social Theory and Religion*, Cambridge: Cambridge University Press.

Beckford, James and Demerath III, N. J. (2007) *The Sage Handbook of Sociology of Religion*, London: Sage.

Bellah, Robert N. (1964) Religious evolution, *American Sociological Review* 29: 358–74.

Bellah, Robert N. (1967) Civil religion in America, *Daedalus* 96 (winter): 1–27.

Bellah, Robert N. and Tipton, S. M. (eds) (2006) *The Robert Bellah Reader*, Durham, NC, and London: Duke University Press.

Bender, Courtney (2003) *Heaven's Kitchen: Living Religion at God's Love We Deliver*, Chicago and London: University of Chicago Press.

Benveniste, Emile (1973) *Indo-European Language and Society*, London: Faber and Faber.

Berger, Peter L. (1969) *The Social Reality of Religion*, London: Faber and Faber.

Beyer, Peter (1994) *Religion and Globalization*. London: Sage.

Birnbaum, N. and Lenzer, G. (eds.) (1969) *Sociology and Religion: A Book of Readings*, Inglewood Cliffs: Prentice Hall.

Bock, D. (2004) *Breaking the da Vinci Code*, Nasville: Nelson Books.

Bruce, Steve (2003) *Politics & Religion*, Cambridge: Polity.

Casanova, José (1994) *Public Religions in the Modern World*, Chicago: University of Chicago Press.

Christ, Carol (1998) *Rebirth of the Goddess*, London: Routledge.

Christ, Carol (2003) *She Who Changes*, Houndsmill: Palgrave.

Cimino, R. and Lattin, D. (1998) *Shopping for Faith: American Religion in the New Millennium*, San Francisco: Jossey-Bass.

Clarke, Peter B. (2006) *New Religions in Global Perspective*, London: Routledge.

Clarke, Peter B. (ed.) (2009) *The Oxford Handbook of the Sociology of Religion*, Oxford: Oxford University Press.

Cox, Harvey (1965) *The Secular City: Secularization and Urbanization in Theological Perspective*, London: SCM.

Croce, P. J. (1995) *Science and Religion in the Era of William James: Eclipse of Certainty 1820–1880*, Chapel Hill and London: University of North Carolina Press.

Davie, Grace (1994) *Religion in Britain 1945: Believing without Belonging*, Oxford: Blackwell.

Dawson, L. L. (2003) *Cults and New Religious Movements: A Reader*, New York: Oxford University Press.

Derrida, Jacques (1998) Faith and knowledge, in Jacques Derrida and Gianni Vattimo (eds.), *Religion*, Cambridge: Polity, 1–78.

Derrida, Jacques and Vattimo, Gianni (eds.) (1998) *Religion*, Cambridge: Polity.

Durkheim, Émile (1958) *The Rules of Sociological Method*, New York: Free Press.

Durkheim, Émile (1995) *The Elementary Forms of the Religious Life*, New York: Free Press.

Durkheim, Émile and Mauss, Marcel (1963) *Primitive Classification*, Chicago: University of Chicago Press.

Eisenstadt, S. N. (2000) The reconstruction of religious arenas in the framework of "Multiple Modernities," *Millennium. Journal of International Studies* 29 (3): 591–611.

Fenn, R. K. (ed.) (2001) *The Blackwell Companion to Sociology of Religion*, Oxford: Blackwell.

Finke, R. and Stark, R. (1992) *The Churching of America 1776–1990*, New Brunswick: Rutgers University Press.

Fuller, R. C. (2001) *Spiritual but Not Religious: Understanding Unchurched Americans*, New York: Oxford University Press.

Furseth, Inger (2009) Religion in the works of Habermas, Bourdieu and Foucault, in Peter B. Clarke (ed.) *The Oxford Handbook of the Sociology of Religion*. Oxford: Oxford University Press. pp. 89–115.

Glock, Charles Y. and Stark, Rodney (1965) *Religion and Society in Tension*, Chicago: University of Chicago Press.

Hamberg, Eva M. (2009) Unchurched spirituality, in Peter B. Clarke (ed.), *The Oxford Companion to the Sociology of Religion*, Oxford: Oxford University Press, 742–57.

Hamilton, Malcolm (2009) Rational choice theory: a critique, in Peter B. Clarke (ed.), *The Oxford Companion to the Sociology of Religion*, Oxford: Oxford University Press, 116–33.

Harvey, David (2000) *The Spaces of Hope*, Berkeley: University of California Press.

Hawthorne, Sian (2009) Religion and gender, in Peter B. Clarke (ed.), *The Oxford Handbook to the Sociology of Religion*, Oxford: Oxford University Press, 134–51.

Heelas, Paul (1996) *The New Age Movement*, Cambridge: Blackwell.

Heelas, Paul (2009) Spiritualities of life, in Peter B. Clarke (ed.), *The Oxford Handbook of the Sociology of Religion*, Oxford: Oxford University Press, 758–82.

Held, D., McGrew, A., Goldblatt, D., and Perraton, J. (1999) *Global Transformations: Politics, Economics and Culture*, Cambridge: Polity Press.

Hervieu-Leger, D. (2000) *Religion as a Chain of Memory*, Cambridge: Polity.

Hulsether, M. D. (2000) Like a sermon: popular religion in Madonna videos, in B. D. Forbes and J. H. Mahan (eds.), *Religion and Popular Culture*, Berkeley: University of California Press, 77–100.

Iannaccone, L. R. (1994) Why strict churches are strong, *American Journal of Sociology* 99 (5): 1180–1211.

James, William (1963) *The Varieties of Religious Experience: A Study of Human Nature*, New York: University Books.

Juergensmeyer, Mark (2003) *Terror in the Mind of God: The Global Rise of Religious Violence*, Berkeley: University of California Press.

Juergensmeyer, Mark (2006) *The Oxford Handbook of Global Religion*, New York: Oxford University Press.

Juergensmeyer, Mark (ed.) (2003) *Global Religions: An Introduction*, Oxford: Oxford University Press.

Kant, Immanuel (1960) *Religion within the Limits of Pure Reason*, New York: Harper and Row.

Kelley, D. (1977) *Why Conservative Churches Are Growing*, New York: Harper and Row.

Kitzinger, E. and Senior, E. (1940) *Portraits of Christ*, Harmondsworth: Penguin.

Lambeck, M. (ed.) (2002) *A Reader in the Anthropology of Religion*, Malden: Blackwell.

Loader, C. and Alexander, J. C. (1985) Max Weber on churches and sects in North America: an alternative path toward rationalization, *Sociological Theory* 3 (1): 1–13.

Luckmann, Thomas (1967) *Invisible Religion: The Problem of Religion in Modern Society*, London: Macmillan.

Luhmann, N. (1984) *Religious Dogmatics and the Evolution of Societies*, New York and Toronto: Edwin Mellen Press.

MacIntyre, Alasdair (1967) *Secularization and Moral Change*, Oxford: Oxford University Press.

MacIntyre, Alasdair and Ricoeur, Paul (1969) *The Religious Significance of Atheism*, New York: Columbia University Press.

Mandaville, Peter (2001) *Transnational Muslim Politics: Reimagining the Umma*, London and New York: Routledge.

Maresco, P. A. (2004) Mel Gibson's *The Passion of the Christ*: market segmentation, mass marketing and promotion, and the Internet, *Journal of Religion and Popular Culture* 8 (3): 1–10.

Martin, David (1978) *A General Theory of Secularization*, Oxford: Blackwell.

Martin, David (2002) *Pentecostalism: The World Their Parish*, Oxford: Blackwell.

Mernissi, Fatima (2003) *Beyond the Veil: Male–Female Dynamics in Muslim Society*, London: Saqi Press.

Milbank, John (1990) *Theology and Social Theory: Beyond Secular Reason*, Oxford: Blackwell.

Milbank, J., Pickstock, C., and Ward, G. (eds.) (1999) *Radical Orthodoxy: A New Theology*, London and New York: Routledge.

Niezen, R. (2004) *A World beyond Difference: Cultural Identity in an Age of Globalization*, Oxford : Blackwell.

Obeyesekere, G. (2003) Buddhism, in Mark Juergensmeyer (ed.), *Global Religions: An Introduction*, Oxford: Oxford University Press, 63–77.

Parsons, Talcott (1937) *The Structure of Social Action*, New York: McGraw-Hill.

Parsons, Talcott (1963) Christianity and modern industrial society, in E. A. Tiryakian (ed.), *Sociological Theory, Values and Sociocultural Change: Essays in Honor of Pitrim A. Sorokin*, New York: Free Press, 33–70.

Parsons, Talcott (2007) *American Society: A Theory of the Societal Community*, Boulder: Paradigm

Pew Research Center (2007) *Muslim Americans: Middle Class and Mostly Mainstream*, Washington, DC.

Reid, Anthony and Gilsenan, Michael (ed.) (2007) *Islamic Legitimacy in a Plural Asia*, London and New York: Routledge.

Rey, Terry (2004) Marketing the goods of salvation: Bourdieu on religion, *Religion* 34: 331–43.

Rey, Terry (2007) *Bourdieu on Religion: Imposing Faith and Legitimacy*, London: Equinox Publishing.

Rieff, Paul (2006) *My Life among the Deathworks*, Charlottesville and London: University of Virginia Press.

Robertson, Roland (1992) The economization of religion? Reflections on the promise and limitations of the economic approach, *Social Compass* 39 (1): 147–57.

Robertson, Roland (ed.) (1969) *Sociology of Religion: Selected Readings*, Harmondsworth: Penguin.

Robertson, Roland and Turner, Bryan S. (eds.) (1991) *Talcott Parsons: Theorist of Modernity*, London: Sage.

Roof, Wade C. (1993) *A Generation of Seekers: The Spiritual Journeys of the Baby Boom Generation*, San Francisco: Harper.

Roof, Wade C. (1999) *Spiritual Marketplace: Baby Boomers and the Remaking of American Religion*, Princeton and Oxford: Princeton University Press.

Sassen, Saskia (2007) *A Sociology of Globalization*, New York: W. W. Norton.

Schneider, Louis (ed.) (1964) *Religion Culture and Society: A Reader in the Sociology of Religion*, New York: John Wiley & Sons.

Sharot, S. (2001) *A Comparative Sociology of World Religions: Virtuosos, Priest and Popular Religion*, New York and London: New York University Press.

Smith, G. (2008) *A Short History of Secularism*, London: I. B.Tauris.

Spencer, B. and Gillen, F. J. (1997) [1904] *The Northern Tribes of Central Australia*, London: Routledge/Thoemmes Press.

Stark, Rodney and Finke, R. (2000) *Acts of Faith: Explaining the Human Side of Religion*, Berkeley: University of California Press.

Tamney, Joseph B. (2002) *The Resilience of Conservative Religion: The Case of Popular, Conservative Protestant Congregations*, Cambridge: Cambridge University Press.

Taylor, Charles (2002) *Varieties of Religion Today*, Cambridge, MA: Harvard University Press.

Taylor, Charles (2007) *A Secular Age*, Cambridge, MA: Belknap Press.

Tocqueville, Alexis de (2000) [1835–40] *Democracy in America*, Chicago: University of Chicago Press.

Turner, Bryan S. (2005) Talcott Parsons's sociology of religion and the expressive revolution: the problem of Western individualism, *Journal of Classical Sociology* 5 (3): 303–18.

Turner, Bryan S. (ed.) (2008) *Religious Diversity and Civil Society: A Comparative Analysis*, Oxford: Bardwell Press.

Turner, Bryan S. (2009a) Max Weber on Islam and Confucianism: the Kantian theory of secularisation, in Peter B. Clarke (ed.), *The Oxford Handbook of the Sociology of Religion*, Oxford: Oxford University Press, 79–97.

Turner, Bryan S. (ed.) (2009b) *The New Companion to Social Theory*, Oxford: Wiley-Blackwell.

Vasquez, Manuel A. and Marquardt, Marie Friedmann (2003) *Globalizing the Sacred. Religion across the Americas*, New Brunswick: Rutgers University Press.

Volpi, Frederic and Turner, Bryan S. (2007) Introduction: making Islamic authority matter, *Theory Culture & Society* 24 (2): 1–19.

Vries, Henk de (2002) *Religion and Violence: Philosophical Perspectives from Kant to Derrida*, Baltimore and London: Johns Hopkins University Press.

Ward, Humphry (1914) *Robert Elsmere*, London: John Murray.

Warner, R. S. (2004) Enlisting Smelser's theory of ambivalence to maintaining progress in sociology of religion's new paradigm, in J. C. Alexander, G. T. Marx, and C. L. Williams (eds.), *Self, Social Structure and Beliefs: Explorations in Sociology*, Berkeley: University of California Press, 103–21.

Weber, Max (1958) *The Religion of India*, New York: Free Press.

Weber, Max (1966) *Sociology of Religion*, London: Methuen.

Wilson, Bryan (1966) *Religion in Secular Society*, London: Watts.

Wilson, Bryan (1967) *Patterns of Sectarianism: Organization and Ideology in Social and Religious Movements*, London: Heinemann Educational Books.

Wilson, Bryan (1970) *Religious Sects: A Sociological Study*, London: Weidenfeld & Nicolson.

Wilson, Bryan (1976) *Contemporary Transformations of Religion*, London: Oxford University Press.

Wittgenstein, Ludwig (1969) *On Certainty*, Oxford: Basil Blackwell.

Wittgenstein, Ludwig (1979) *Remarks on Frazer's Golden Bough*, Retford: Brynmill.

Woodhead, Linda and Heelas, Paul (eds.) (2000) *Religion in Modern Times: An Interpretive Anthology*, Oxford: Blackwell.

Zabala, S. (ed.) (2005) *The Future of Religion*, New York: Columbia University Press.

Zubrzycki, Geneviève (2006) *The Crosses of Auschwitz: Nationalism and Religion in Post-Communist Poland*, Chicago and London: University of Chicago Press.

Part I

The Foundations

1

The Sociology of Religion
The Foundations

Andrew McKinnon

The classics have long played an important role in sociological theory and research, perhaps particularly about religion. While there are some who have deplored the ongoing conversation with classical sociological writers like Durkheim, Weber, Marx, and Simmel, as mere "ancestor worship" (Stark 2004), most other sociologists of religion have seen this heritage as an invaluable resource. What texts and which authors have counted as "classics" has admittedly changed – before the 1980s, few sociologists of religion would have included Marx, for example. In fact, one of the ways in which theory in the sociology of religion appears to change is when classic texts get reinterpreted, when some end up relegated to the dustbin, or when new classics are added to the established pantheon. So, even if Rodney Stark doesn't approve of the established classics, he still wants to make Adam Smith a classic sociologist of religion (Stark 2006), and most critics of the predominance of the classics have still found themselves having to position their arguments in debates with reference to these same classics (O'Toole 2001).

It is perhaps regrettable that more attention is not given to contemporary theory and debates in sociology of religion, but it is probably also understandable given the centrality of the "religion question" in the classics and its comparative marginality in contemporary theory. The classics are important in sociology of religion, in their own right, however, for two reasons. First, because a discipline's classic texts form the context of all subsequent sociological conversations (Alexander 1987); they provide a great deal of our most important vocabulary, the inspiration for many of our methods, and the starting point for most of our conversations about the social world – even if their world is occasionally very different from ours. An understanding of their texts is a cost of admission into the field of sociological research on religion (Bourdieu 1990: 30).

Second, classics are works that contemporary communities continue to find important and useful, and – somewhat paradoxically – sources of innovation. Classic texts are not simply collections of sociological rules to be mastered, nor compilations of hypotheses to be tested. Rather they "inspire imitation, invite elaboration and provoke discussion ... [A] surplus of sociological signification ... is the most indelible mark of a genuine disciplinary or sub-disciplinary classic. From this point of view, classics are not terminal destinations but rather points of embarkation for departure on future intellectual journeys" (O'Toole 2001: 140–1). For this reason, every generation will read and interpret the classics in new ways – posing its own questions and challenges to the ancestors. The classics have important challenges for us, as well. Marx and Weber set the bar for scholarship very high with their innovative ways of understanding religion, but also with the breadth and depth of their historical, comparative, and philosophical knowledge – not to mention the scope of their research questions.

This chapter will introduce the work of Marx and of Weber on religion; in this volume, Durkheim is grouped with the anthropological foundations, and thus will be discussed at length in the following chapter. My aim is to introduce Weber and Marx as classic thinkers in the sociology of religion, and thus it does not touch on the many other topics with which Marx and Weber concerned themselves. While I make every effort to provide a good place to start for readers new to these classics, this is my own interpretation of Marx and Weber, and it will inevitably differ from that of other readers. I am particularly interested in the historical and literary dimensions of their work, and my interpretations reflect that concern. Since all elucidation is necessarily partial, there is no substitute for reading and re-reading these classic works for oneself. I hope I will have provided both a solid starting point for doing so, and some sense of the rewards of engaging with the work of both Marx and Weber firsthand.

MARX

Although Marx is now usually (and quite appropriately) included as one of the key "classic" writers for sociologists of religion, his work has a more problematic status within the sub-discipline compared with the work of Durkheim and Weber, whose positions are much more secure. There are, I suggest, two reasons for this. The first is that Marx never devoted much of his formidable intellect to the study of religion: he simply left us a small number of works dealing with religion (and even there religion is a secondary concern), and these are mostly from his early writings. Second, it is easy to construe Marx as fundamentally antagonistic towards (or dismissive of) religion. Often Marx is introduced in sociological texts on religion, only to be dismissed again as an example of economic reductionism. That is to say, many writers unsympathetic to Marx will argue that for Marx religion and religious change are entirely derived from changes in the economy (construed as a reflection of class interests or the mode of production itself) – a view which has never found very many supporters. A related problem stems from the fact that Marx is well known to have described religion as the "opium of the people," though few have stopped to take a second thought about what that phrase could have meant in the 1840s when Marx wrote it (McKinnon 2005). Unlike Weber and Durkheim, Marx has never really had a significant following within sociology of religion – partly for intellectual, but also for political reasons. This does not mean that Marx has been wholly without influence, nor does it mean that his work does not provide important points of departure, some of which remain only partially explored to this day.

Marx was born in the city of Trier in 1818, three years after it had become part of the Kingdom of Prussia (later part of Germany). He came from a long line of rabbis on both sides of his family, but his family was Protestant, his father having converted for a career in the civil service. He studied law at the University of Bonn before moving to the University of Berlin where he encountered the philosophy of G. W. F. Hegel, who had taught at Berlin and died only a few years before Marx arrived. In 1841 he submitted his doctoral dissertation (on Greek Philosophy) at the University of Jena, where Hegel had written his early (and arguably his greatest) work, *The Phenomenology of Spirit* ([1807] 1994).

Marx's radical politics made an academic career (where the state had enormous power over academic appointments) unlikely, and he managed to quickly get himself into trouble in journalism as well. In 1843 the newspaper Marx edited, *Die Rheinische Zeitung*, was closed by the Prussian authorities and Marx, fearing jail (not unreasonably) fled to Paris, Brussels then to Cologne. Each of these moves brought with it further political problems before Marx and his family settled in London (ironically the capital of the most powerful empire in the world), which in those days had a large community of political refugees, in 1849. It is in the period after leaving Germany, but before arriving in London, that Marx begins to identify his radical democratic politics as *Communist*, an emerging political tradition which Marx (and his collaborator Friedrich Engels) would try to shape with their famous *Communist Manifesto* ([1848] 1967). While living in London, Marx continued to write for newspapers and to be involved in radical politics; it was here that he began his major research, still unfinished at the time of his death in 1883, entitled *Capital: A Critique of Political Economy* (1967). In this period Marx's writing becomes more focused on what we would now call "economics": it is an attempt to understand the basic dynamics of a capitalist society.

Some writers, following the French Marxist theorist Louis Althusser (1965), have seen a strict separation between the "early" and the "late" Marx (the latter being understood as more "scientific"). While most scholars would not accept this as a rigid divide, it is clear that while certain themes carry through the whole of Marx's writing life, his vocabulary does undergo some significant change, and his work becomes much more clearly focused on "economic" issues, as opposed to the more "philosophical" debates in which he was engaged with Hegel's descendents known as the "Young Hegelians." Although Marx had sharp differences with this group of philosophers, at an early stage in his work Marx is very much one of them.

When Marx began his studies, Hegel was the dominant philosophical figure, and although he had died before Marx arrived in Berlin, his work continued to be the starting point for all German philosophical debates. For Hegel, history was the progress of consciousness about human freedom, but what this meant continued to be a hotly contested question. The "Old" (or more accurately the "Right") Hegelians took this philosophy as a means of justifying the Prussian State and its constitutional monarchy as the highest instantiation of the idea of human freedom. This was further supplemented by a defense of orthodox (Lutheran) Christianity, which was the official state religion, and which Hegel had seen as the highest point in religious evolution. This view was challenged by those Hegelians who were united primarily by their shared opposition to these two positions, the radical supporters of enlightenment and democracy who are referred to as the "Young" or "Left" Hegelians. There is a good case to be made that the two groups in fact correspond roughly to the work of the Young and Old Hegel – as a young man Hegel had been an enthusiast of the French Revolution, even seeing Napoleon's invasion of Prussia as rational progress (Hegel 1807; Hyppolite 1969); he later became the official philosopher of the Prussian state, and it is not difficult to read his late masterpiece, *The Philosophy of Right* (1821), in support of a Right Hegelian position, though many contemporary Hegel scholars would dispute this view (for an overview see Houlgate 2005: 181ff.).

The Left Hegelians, among whom Bruno Bauer and Ludwig Feuerbach exercised the greatest influence on the young Marx, were primarily interested in questions of religion – or at least, that was what they wrote most about. This may be in part due to the fact that there was greater freedom to write controversially on questions of religion than would have been permitted to write about politics in like manner – religion became politics by other means. Nonetheless, their published views on religion (both were avowed atheists) were sufficient to block Feuerbach from an academic appointment, and for Bauer to lose his. In both cases, the state recognized that (in a situation where there is a state religion) there were political implications to their critiques. While Marx later turned critical of his erstwhile colleagues, both were very influential in the development of his thought. Bauer, from whom Marx took a course on the prophet Isaiah in 1839 (McLellan 1973: 34), argued that religion was part of the process of developing self-consciousness, but that the final stage of human self-consciousness must entail the exit from religion: if we recognize that God is a human creation we will come to the point of being able to see ourselves clearly (without needing the mediating idea of God). Feuerbach mostly sang from the same hymn book as Bauer did, but he differed from Bauer on two points. First, while Bauer was primarily preoccupied with Biblical studies and theology, Feuerbach was more interested in religion as a "secret anthropology" that – properly interpreted – would disclose the human *essence*. Second, while Bauer focused on religion as distorted cognition, Feuerbach was much more concerned with the emotional aspects of religious projection onto God or the gods (God as love, as jealous, as compassionate, and so forth) and with the way such attributions to God take *away from* humankind in equal measure – for Feuerbach, this is how humans alienate themselves from their own essence (Harvey 1995).

This is where Marx enters the debate, with his "Towards a critique of Hegel's philosophy of right: introduction," his most substantial engagement with the question of religion ([1844] 1977), and also the locus of his famous metaphor of religion as the "opium of the people." Marx had been exiled from Prussia and taken up residence in Paris, where he had come into contact with working-class socialism. In Paris he had begun to develop a dialectical understanding of social change in which the property-less classes are the ones who have the capacity to bring about a society without property (and hence classes). The proletariat begins to assume a much greater role in his thinking about social change, and his social criticism begins to develop a sociological analysis accordingly, but the logic of his thinking is still largely consonant with his Left Hegelian colleagues.

Despite its title, *Towards a Critique* actually has very little to say about Hegel's *Philosophy of Right*; rather, it is an "*Aufhebung*" of Feuerbach's critique of religion. This Hegelian keyword is notoriously hard to translate, and can mean quite opposite things: taken-up or kept, canceled, or abolished. In Hegelian and post-Hegelian philosophy it means both – it points to a contradiction between two countervailing tendencies or forces that must be resolved by a synthesis of the two. Marx never defined this term, but we get a good definition of it from Engels, who did. Engels writes that "*Aufhebung*" means "'Overcome and Preserved'; overcome as regards form, and preserved as real content" (Engels 1969: 166).

There are three senses in which the form of Feuerbach's work needed to be overcome in order to preserve the real content. First, Marx observes that Feuerbach's religious anthropology is essentially asocial: "Feuerbach resolves the religious essence into the human essence. But the human essence is no abstraction inherent in each single individual. In its reality it is the ensemble of the social relations" (Marx 1977: 157). Second, the form of Feuerbach's inquiries is essentially theological, even if his conclusions are atheistic. The question of the existence of God is essentially theological, and Marx thinks that the political questions themselves are far more important than the question of whether God exists or not (though he clearly thought not). What matters are not religious questions, but social and political examinations. Finally, Marx argues that Feuerbach's work is speculative, and in the end, fundamentally idealist (even though Feuerbach claimed to be materialist): if people come to the right intellectual conclusions about God – that he is a projection of our own human powers – we will inevitably re-appropriate those powers for ourselves. Marx may not be right in his understanding of Feuerbach, but it is clear that Marx is convinced that thought is not sufficient to change the world: it will take a revolution.

For Marx, the criticism of religion, although "essentially finished" (Marx 1977: 64) is not an end in itself; it is rather simply a means for addressing other questions. Marx takes the latest developments of post-Hegelian philosophy, and he turns them into an action-oriented critique of the social world. If the conclusion of the Young Hegelians is that "man is the highest being for man" (p. 69), then "categorical imperative" as far as Marx is concerned, is "to overthrow all relations in which man is a debased, enslaved, forsaken, despicable being" (p. 69). The point of Marx's essay is not that "Man makes religion, religion does not make man" (this was Feuerbach's thesis and claim to infamy) but rather the point is to overcome the situation in which human beings are "debased, enslaved and forsaken." Feuerbach's philosophical point is here but a premise or an "assumption" (*Voraussetzung*) from which Marx proceeds. It does not, however, make atheism in and of itself the more progressive position, since Marx wants to move beyond these theological questions altogether; by the end of his life Bauer was still an avowed atheist, but he had abandoned his radical democratic politics altogether and become an influential advisor to the Kaiser.

For stylistic reasons, it is sometimes difficult to distinguish quotations, summary and ironic responses to another author from Marx's own analysis, a problem which has often led readers of *On the Jewish Question* to conclude that Marx was an anti-Semite. As David McLellan (1969: 75–7) has shown, this conclusion is only tenable if we read Marx's essay in isolation from Bauer's argument to which Marx is responding – and Bauer was an anti-Semite. Readers have often come up against similar problems separating Marx's social and political analysis of religion from Feuerbach's psychological and theological argument to which Marx is responding critically.

Marx's summary of Feuerbach takes up the first three paragraphs of the essay and Marx's own analysis of religion begins in the fourth. There Marx writes:

> Religious suffering is at the same time an *expression* of real suffering and a *protest* against real suffering. Religion is the sigh of the oppressed creature, the heart of a heartless world, and the spirit of a spiritless situation. It is the *opium* of the people.
>
> The [Aufhebung] of religion as the illusory happiness of the people is the demand for their real happiness. The demand to give up the illusions of their condition is a demand to give up a condition that requires illusion. The criticism of religion is there-fore the germ of the criticism of the valley of tears whose halo is religion.
>
> Criticism has plucked the imaginary flowers from the chains not so that man may throw away the chains without any imagination or comfort, but so that he may throw away the chains and pluck living flowers. The criticism of religion disillusions man so that he may think, act, and fashion his own reality as a disillusioned man comes to his sense; so that he may revolve around himself as his real sun. Religion is only the illusory sun which revolves around man as long as he does not revolve around himself. (1977: 64, translation amended, emphasis original)

These passages begin with an essentially dialectical logic. Religious suffering, is both "expression of" and "protest against" real suffering, both of which Marx highlights by underlining. Sergio Rojo writes,

> The characteristic of the definition which Marx gives to the two terms "expression of real suffering and protest and against real suffering" constitutes a dialectical relation, an unstable equilibrium, which mutually influence each other, even if, historically, one aspect has prevailed over the other. (1988: 210, my translation)

Unlike in Feuerbach's analysis, religion is not an "abstract" expression of the human essence. Rather, expanding on the "expression," he highlights the social dimension by writing that religion is the spirit and heart of a spiritless, heartless social situa-tion; religion is a sigh that bears witness to oppression. While religion was an "expression" of suffering for Feuerbach (though not social and political suffering, poverty and oppression), it is by no means a "protest" against that suffering (espe-cially in its socio-political forms).

Marx underlines *expression*, *protest*, and *opium*, suggesting that "opium" embodies the contradiction between expression and protest. Opium, then, is the moment of *Aufheben* "in which negation and preservation (affirmation) are brought together" (Marx 2002: 87). The "traditional" readings of religion as "opium of the people" neglect both this context and dialectical movement, in which opium, as a condensed signifier, brings together both expression and protest in one moment. Marx's use of this metaphor forces us to look at it dialectically: opium/religion as expression and protest.

Readers seldom stop to think about what Marx means when he writes that reli-gion is "opium of the people" because it seems quite obvious: religion is an addictive pain-killer that distorts our perception of reality. Such an understanding would have been quite foreign in Marx's context. Opium was an important medicine (one Marx used himself (Regnault 1933; McLellan 1973: 337)), but it was also used as a means of infant-doping. It was the source of wild visions of another world (Coleridge's *Kubla Khan* [1813] and De Quincey's *Confessions of an English Opium Eater* [1821]), but also a major commodity and an important source of tax revenue for the British Empire. It was sometimes used for inducing sleep, but it was the cause of two international conflicts referred to as the "Opium wars," the first of which had just ended (in 1842). The irony was not lost on Marx when he wrote that "the occasion of [the second] outbreak has unquestionably been afforded by the English canon forcing upon China that soporific drug called opium." (Marx and Engels 1975: vol. 12, 93). Far from being a simple metaphor about the role of religion in society, it embodies the contradictions that Marx sees at the heart of religion, as *expression of*, and *protest against* real misery.

Marx wrote very little about religion after this essay, and these are generally occasional comments or even asides and footnotes in other works. It is therefore questionable whether it is even possible (or desirable) to reconstruct a systematic sociology of religion from these fragments. Alternately, one could argue that religion is best treated under the general umbrella of "ideology" or "alienation," concepts which derive from his thinking about religion and about which he did write considerably more. This would mean treating religion as if it were not a specific phenomenon with its own analytic demands, as if it were any other element of culture. Regardless of how one were to develop Marx's sociology of religion into a more systematic program, it is clear that it needs to be treated as a contradictory phenomenon, and not simply as an "expression" of class suffering (or interests) but as both an expression and a protest.

The Marxian tradition as it developed later has tended to emphasize rather one-sidedly the role of religion as the expression of interests rather than of suffering, but also its role in social control as an extension of that "expression." While this is a helpful corrective to the Durkheimian notions where religion appears as an expression of the group (without any reference to power), it tends to minimize the role of religion in social protest. Thus, Marx's collaborator, Friedrich Engels (1966) and Karl Kautsky both tended to see religion as a direct expression of class interests and as a form of social control. On the whole Kautsky tended to be much more simplistic than Engels in reducing religion to class interests.

Unlike Marx, Engels did engage in the empirical study of religion and society; *The Peasant War in Germany* (1966) is his study of sixteenth century "religious" conflict. Engels argues that while the war between the radical, communist peasants and the nobility was framed in terms of religious language, religion was the "clothing" that covered class interests. In the late Middle Ages, religion provided the language by which power was justified, but it was also (and partly because it was the hegemonic language) the only medium in which dissatisfactions could be expressed (see Turner 1991: 71–80). Ernst Bloch, another Marxist thinker, takes Engels work as a starting point, but Bloch argues that Engels overstates the primacy of economic forces. In Bloch's historical study of Thomas Münzer, the leading figure of the rebellion ([1921] 1964), Bloch contends that Münzer is both a theologian *and* a revolutionary, and not simply a revolutionary dressed up as a theologian. In like vain, he argues that religion does not simply hide the "real" (political, class) interests, but that (particularly in the sixteenth century) neither religion nor economics can be readily reduced to the other – rather, they exist as a complicated whole. How we are to understand the relation between the two remains somewhat unclear, though Bloch's study provides a seriously under utilized resource for Marxian sociology of religion. This book is the most sociological of all of Bloch's books, and bears the marks of Bloch's engagement with the thought of his teacher, Max Weber, whom I will discuss below.

In many respects, Bloch exemplifies the challenge for all Marxian sociology of religion: to critically analyze the relationship between religion and the relations of production, domination, and exploitation without ending up with Kautsky's economic reductionism. How to accomplish this without becoming a Weberian has long been the challenge, and it has been taken up with greater or lesser success not only by Ernst Bloch (Dianteill and Löwy 2005), but also by Antonio Gramsci (Gramsci 1971; Billings 1990), several members of the Frankfurt School (Mendieta 2005; Brittain 2005) and Lucien Goldman ([1956] 1964).

MAX WEBER

Max Weber was a generation younger than Karl Marx, born in Erfurt, Thuringia, then part of the Kingdom of Prussia in 1864. Weber's father, with whom he had personal difficulties, was a lawyer in the Prussian Civil service, and it was his career trajectory that Weber seemed to be following when he left home to study law and history at the universities in Heidelberg, Göttingen, and Berlin. Weber's early studies were marked more by drinking and dueling (a passion he inherited from his father, and from which he bore a scar on his cheek for the rest of his life) than by great studiousness. Weber's father was a hard working bureaucrat, but not particularly pious; it was on his mother's side of the family that Weber could see the confluence of the Protestant Ethic with the Spirit of Capitalism. His mother came from a long line of Huguenot (originally French) Calvinists, including both academics and industrialists (Marianne Weber 1975).

Weber earned his doctoral degree in 1889 with a dissertation on medieval firms, and his *Habilitationschrift* (a second dissertation that gave him the license to teach in a German university) two years later on the topic of Roman agricultural history and its implications for Western law. After teaching for a short period of time at the universities of Berlin, Freiburg and Heidelberg, Weber had a nervous breakdown. It is often suggested that this breakdown resulted from the guilt he suffered when he threw his father out of the house shortly before he died. Whatever the cause of the illness, it left Weber incapacitated and unable to teach, or, initially, to write. Revived by a trip to the St Louis World's Fair in 1904, on his return Weber wrote two essays which together would comprise his most famous work *The Protestant Ethic and the Spirit of Capitalism* ([1905–6] 2002). While Weber worked prodigiously in the following years, he only went back to teaching at the end of the First World War (in Vienna and Munich). He died of complications from influenza in 1920.

If sociologists the world over were asked to elect a single-most important classic text in the discipline, the odds are very good that *The Protestant Ethic and Spirit of Capitalism* would come out on top. Although it is common to speak of Weber's "thesis," the meaning of the book and the truth of its claims (which depend on how one interprets the "thesis" of the book) continue to be debated. There is considerable ambiguity about Weber's essays, and it is not unfair to say that this is one of the reasons it has remained a classic text (Baehr and Wells 2002): it is open to interpretation and re-interpretation as each new generation of sociologists encounters the text bringing its own questions and concerns to the reading of it.

Weber begins with the observation that the most economically developed areas in turn of the century Europe tended to be Protestant, rather than Catholic, and that the histories of the Protestant Reformation (particularly in its Calvinist form) and modern capitalism seem to have been intertwined in particularly intense ways. Some of the data Weber used to make his claims about the contemporary predominance of Protestants in industry have subsequently been questioned (cf. Samuelsson, 1957) but he is by no means the first to have noticed the "elective affinity" of the capitalists for Protestantism.

Weber's essays are often seen as a riposte to Marx (or at least to the Marxism of Karl Kautsky who was at the time the intellectual spokesman of the Social Democrats), because Weber emphasizes the role of "ideal factors" in the historical shaping of social formations. The degree to which this is the case is easily exaggerated – to the gross distortion of Weber's text. In fact, while Weber was partially responding to the crudities of orthodox Marxism, his narrative is arguably influenced more by the work of Nietzsche (Kent 1983; Hennis 1988; Kemple 2001) and of Goethe (Albrow 1990; McKinnon forthcoming).

A key, but often inadequately understood, term in Weber's essays of 1905–6 on the Protestant Ethic is the notion of "elective affinity," an idea that serves (sometimes only implicitly) to connect the various forces and elements in Weber's argument. Weber took the term from a novel by J. W. von Goethe entitled *Elective Affinities* ([1807] 1994). This minor masterpiece is the story of a couple, Eduard and Charlotte, and the changes that follow when two new people are added to their household. The first to arrive is Eduard's best friend, Captain, and a little while later Charlotte's niece Ottilie. Eduard soon falls in love with Ottilie, and Charlotte develops an intense attraction for Captain. Goethe foreshadows these events with an extended conversation between Charlotte, Eduard, and the Captain about "elective affinity" (*Wahlverwandtschaften*). Substances with an elective affinity have a very strong attraction to one another, and in their interaction "modify one another and form...a new substance altogether." Through this conversation, Goethe develops a "chemistry" of social relations that applies both to intimate relations and to interactions between groups, including different "vocations" (*Berufbestimmingen*), classes, and status groups (*Stände*). "Imagine," Captain explains,

> an A closely bound to a B and by a variety of means and even by force not able to be separated from it; imagine a C with a similar relationship to a D; now bring the pairs into contact; A will go over to D, C to B without our being able to say who first left the other, who first with another was united again. (p. 35)

When Ottilie arrives, we will soon sense the attraction between her and Eduard, and the subsequent growing mutual affection of Charlotte and the Captain; the arrival of D (Ottilie) sparks a chain of reactions. The old (marriage) bond between A and B is broken, and a new configuration of relations emerges: A "goes over to" D and B joins with C. As in a chemical equation, the bonds created between two elements create a substance that may be very different from either of the elements so united. But such merging of the two people (the "two joined as one" of a marriage bond) creates a whole that is greater than the sum of its parts: an alkali and acid join together to form a salt. Some elements sue for divorce to marry another.

In the *Protestant Ethic* essays, Weber contends that religious beliefs and practices made an important contribution to the breakdown of economic traditionalism, and the emergence of modern rational capitalism. Several Protestant beliefs and practices came together to form what would become the "Spirit of Capitalism," a spirit with a particular elective affinity with the capitalist practices of small-scale business-people. From Luther came the notion of the calling ("Beruf") – faithful Christians should serve God devotedly in their occupations, rather than fleeing the world to serve God behind the monastery walls. The Calvinists added an important ingredient. God, they believed, predestined souls to salvation or damnation; in the words of the Westminster confession: "By the decree of God, for the manifestation of His glory, some men and angels are predestinated unto everlasting life; and others fore-ordained to everlasting death" (Westminster Confession III: 3). This created an insatiable need for reassurance which they achieved through a disciplined life-conduct (*Lebensführung*): they worked hard and since they did not spend on luxuries, but reinvested their money in the work to which they were called, their enterprises flourished. The elect "may, from the certainty of their effectual vocation, be assured of their eternal election" (Westminster Confession III: 8).

In abbreviated or simplistic textbook versions of the tale, it often sounds as if Weber's "thesis" is that the Protestant Reformation "caused" capitalism. Although Weber does believe that Protestant beliefs and practices were important for the rise of *modern* capitalism, his argument is severely distorted by such cause and effect tales that are typically premised on metaphors from physics or statistics – Talcott Parsons accidentally promoted this by translating "elective affinity" as "correlation." Weber, however, is clear that this is not what he is arguing, and introduces the notion of "elective affinity" here to clarify what he does mean. Weber writes:

we have no intention of defending any such foolishly doctrinaire thesis as that the "capitalist spirit"... let alone capitalism itself, *could only* arise as the result of certain influences of the Reformation. The very fact that certain important *forms* of capitalist business are considerably older than the Reformation would invalidate such a thesis. We intend ... to establish to what extent religious influences *have in fact* been partially responsible for the qualitative shaping and the quantitative expansion of that "spirit" across the world, and that concrete aspects of capitalist culture originate from them.

In view of the tremendous confusion of reciprocal influences emanating from the material base, the social and political forms of organization and the spiritual content of the cultural epochs of the Reformation, the only possible way to proceed is to first investigate whether and in what points particular "*elective affinities*" between certain forms of religious belief and the ethic of the calling can be identified. At the same time, the manner and general direction in which, as a result of such *elective affinities* the religious movement influenced the development of the material culture will be clarified as far as possible. Only <u>then</u> can the attempt be made to estimate the degree to which the historical origins of elements of modern culture should be attributed to those religious motives and to what extent to others. (2002: 36, emphases in original)

With these words, Weber concludes his first essay. He uses the notion of elective affinity both to sum up his first essay, and to introduce the themes with which he will be preoccupied in the second essay. Neither Luther nor Calvin's teachings fit very well with, let alone seek to promote, capitalist practices (on the after-image of Luther's theology of labor in Marx and Habermas, see Glenna 2008). In the first essay, however, Weber argues that certain forms of Protestant belief and the vocational ethic interacted, and together they formed a new whole which will become the "spirit of capitalism."

While Weber does not describe the relation of the spirit and form of capitalism as an elective affinity, when he goes to clarify the argument of his essays in response to Felix Rachfahl, one of his earliest critics, he does so precisely in these terms. If the elective affinities of certain religious beliefs and the vocational ethic contributed to the growth and development of the capitalist spirit, it remains to be seen how the capitalist "spirit" and the capitalist "form" are related. This, Weber clarifies with the notion of elective affinity. "What are we to understand by the "spirit" of capitalism in relation to "capitalism" itself?" Weber asks:

> As far as "capitalism" itself is concerned, we can only understand by this a particular "economic system," that is, a form of economic behavior toward people and goods that can be described as "utilization" of "capital"... A historically given form of "capitalism" can be filled with very different types of "spirit"; this form can, however, and usually will, have different levels of *"elective affinities"* to certain historical types of spirit: the "spirit" may be more or less adequate to the "form" (or not at all). There can be no doubt that *the degree of this adequacy* is not without influence on the course of historical development, that "form" and "spirit" (as I said previously) tend to adapt to each other, and finally, that where a system and a "spirit" of a particularly high "degree of adequacy" come up against each other, there ensues a development of (even inwardly) unbroken unity similar to that which I had begun to analyze. (2002: 263)

As Frank Parkin suggests, Weber presumes that the "spirit" and "form"[1] (1983: 42) exist independently historically – in some times and locations we will find neither a capitalist form nor capitalist spirit. In other periods and places we will find the capitalist form without the capitalist spirit (the "pariah capitalism" of Jewish merchants in medieval Europe); elsewhere we can find the capitalist spirit even though the capitalist form has not been fully developed (Benjamin Franklin). Where both were present (in particular Protestant centers of production) the result was of world-historical consequence: this was the unique situation which led to the development of Modern Capitalism.

Rather than looking for the presence or absence of both the capitalist spirit and form, we need to keep in mind Weber's contention that there are *numerous* economic forms and *numerous* economic spirits, all of which have varying degrees of adequacy to one another. Some of these have a "particularly high degree of adequacy" and will be drawn together by very strong mutual attraction. What those, with such an elective affinity, produce is a phenomenon of "unbroken unity," like an acid and an alkali that together form a bond to produce a salt.

Goethe's elective affinity metaphor helps us to clarify Weber's argument in the *Protestant Ethic*. Weber describes two elective affinities: the first produces the spirit of capitalism, and the second produces modern capitalism. First, Weber argues that there is an elective affinity between the ethic of the calling and the asceticism of certain Protestant groups. This "chemical reaction" of these two elements produced something quite different from either of them: the spirit of modern capitalism, as it appears in Weber's example of Benjamin Franklin, whose ethic is different from either of the two elements, though it emerges from it. The second elective affinity Weber describes is the attraction of the "spirit" of capitalism (described above) and the "form" of capitalism that had long been found in small pockets of Bourgeois merchants. It is the "chemical reaction" of this spirit and this form that joined together to give us modern capitalism.

Elective affinities (as chemical reactions) cannot really be understood in the same terms of cause and effect drawn from physics or statistics. Rather, pursuing the chemical metaphor, the elements form bonds and together produce a new substance because of the characteristics of each element, and this is better understood as a kind of "emergence." As the noted Italian chemist Pier Luigi Luisi describes it, "emergence describes the onset of novel properties that arise when a certain level of structural complexity is formed from components of lower complexity" (2002: 183). The properties of water "are not present in hydrogen and oxygen, so that [water's] properties... can be considered as emergent ones" (p. 189). Water is formed from hydrogen and oxygen, but we would not normally say that it is "caused" by either of these elements. In other words, the debate about whether Weber's argument is best understood as a "strong" or a "weak" causal claim is largely irrelevant. Weber presupposes a metaphor that is not best understood in these terms. Modern capitalism is a phenomenon with emergent properties formed by the elective affinity of the form and spirit of capitalism, but not reducible to its component parts.

While *The Protestant Ethic* is undoubtedly Weber's best known and most carefully read book, it was by no means his last word about religion, nor, some would say, is it necessarily his most important (O'Toole 1984). In the period following the publication of the *Protestant Ethic* essays in 1905–6, Weber worked on a massive project on the comparative economic ethics of the world religions, completing volumes on the religions of China ([1915] 1951), India ([1916–17] 1958) and Ancient Judaism ([1917–20] 1952) before his death, leaving undone intended volumes on Medieval Christianity and Islam. He did nonetheless bring this project to a provisional close, publishing these volumes together with an introduction (*The Social Psychology of the World Religions*, [1915] 1946a, and *Intermediate Reflections (The Religious Rejections of the World and Their Directions*, [1915] 1946b). Also important is the section on religion in Weber's posthumously published *Economy and Society* (1978: 399–634), though some (cf. Tenbruck 1980) have challenged the claim that this volume should be seen as what Roth claimed was "the sum of Max Weber's scholarly vision of society" (Weber 1978: xxxiii). Nonetheless, for anyone interested in Weber's incisive analysis into the sociological study of society, both of these sources will be important.

Weber's interest in, and thoughts about, the comparative ethics of the world-religions were certainly stimulated by his ongoing conversations with his neighbor, friend and colleague, the liberal theologian Ernst Troeltsch (1865–1923). One can trace in the respective writings of Troeltsch and Weber the development of their ongoing discussions on the nature of religious ethics in history, particularly as these relate to the typology of different kinds of religious forms: the church, the sect and mysticism (Nelson 1975). In his magnum opus, *The Social Teaching of the Christian Churches* ([1911] 1976), Troeltsch is particularly concerned with understanding the relationship between the social teaching of different Christian groups (from the beginning to 1800) and the social form of that group. Religious ideas, Troetsch argues, are only comprehensible within the context of the different religious forms that have prevailed historically. The church is a broad organization, which is able to receive the masses from the time of their birth. As an organization it adjusts itself to the world by ignoring the "need for subjective holiness" (at least of the masses) and it dispenses salvation by means of the sacraments. The sect, by contrast, will be a narrower group because it is a voluntary society into which you must choose to belong. Here the emphasis is on subjective holiness and adherence to moral laws. Mysticism is the least coherent of the social forms, emphasizing inward personal experience which tends to undo all forms of social organization (Troeltsch [1911] 1976: 993–1013). One can clearly see Weber's influence in this book, especially in Troeltsch's discussion of sects, but Troeltsch's project seems to have been one of Weber's inspirations for embarking on the comparative ethics of the world religions, which broadens the study of the relationship between ethics and social organization far beyond the Christian world.

Troeltsch, dealing exclusively with the Christian tradition, never has the problem of having to define religion in general. Weber has sometimes been criticized for having failed to do so, despite the breadth of his project, insisting instead that it is preferable to conclude one's studies with a definition (1978: 399), rather than beginning with one (as Durkheim did, for example). Unfortunately, since Weber did not live to see the conclusion of his research project, we can only guess as to what his conclusion might have entailed. There is good reason to infer that Weber presumed a modern, denotative and commonsense understanding of what counted as religion (O'Toole 1984: 135–7; McKinnon 2002): Christianity, Judaism, Islam, Hinduism, Buddhism, as well as other phenomena that look like one of these, is a religion, and that these usually have a god or gods (Confucianism being a notable exception).

Whereas for Émile Durkheim religion and magic were completely different phenomena, Weber drew no sharp distinction; rather magic forms the core of his analysis of primitive religion, and an ongoing, important component of popular religion. Whereas in prayer, people beg the gods for something that they need, in magic, they compel the gods to act on their behalf (1978: 422ff.). In practice, the distinction between asking and compelling is a thin one, especially when set rituals for supplication or sacrifice are involved. For Durkheim, it was this practical purpose of magic, "the technical, utilitarian ends" he called it (2005: 58), as much as its purported non-collective nature, that made magic so different from religion. On the other hand, for Weber the most elementary religion is thoroughly practical, oriented not to the "hereafter," but to this world.

Formulating what he sees as the implicit definition of religion in Weber, Theodore Steeman argues:

> Religion is man's continuous effort to deal rationally with the irrationalities of life. Religion arises out of the *Not* [poverty, hardship] of existence, its ambiguities and conflicts, and gives the necessary *Begeisterung* [spirit, enthusiasm] to live. It makes life's precariousness acceptable, gives life preciousness and prescribes a way of life that makes living worthwhile. (1964: 56)

Whether this really amounts to a definition of religion may be questionable, but it does provide a good description of both the this-worldly nature of religious impulses, and the connection between these and the problem theodicy all of which are crucial in Weber's sociology of religion. Religion comes from the need to give meaning in the face of the difficulties of life, and the ubiquitous experience of hardship, suffering and death. Religion starts, for Weber, not with the experience of collective effervescence, but rather with the problems of embodied existence (Turner 1991).

Religion is thus "heavily concerned with the basic needs and routines of mundane existence while offering the opportunity of transcending them in the search for meaning and the good life" (O'Toole 1984: 140). Just as in Marx where we find a dialectical tension at the heart of religion, for Weber religion may "be the means by which human beings adjust to their natural, social, economic, political, and intellectual environments, it may also, *a fortiori*, be the means by which these are transcended or changed" (pp. 140–1). Some religions tend strongly towards adjustment to the world, like Confucianism which "reduced tension with the world to an absolute minimum ... The world was the best of all possible worlds" (1951: 227). This was the phrase Leibniz used in his *Theodicy* ([1709] 1985), which both invented the term Weber uses to discuss the problem of evil, and provided a classic defense of the status quo (the book was devoted to Queen Sophie Charlotte of Prussia). Confucianism promoted an ethic for living a good life, on learning to adjust to the natural and social world, and this made Confucianism popular with many rulers in East Asia (including in Japan where state-Shinto is a form of neo-Confucianism), who promoted it for its contributions to social harmony and integration.

In similar fashion, Weber argues that Hinduism also adjusts people to the social world, harmonizing the religious beliefs and the experience of the social and natural world. Hinduism is first and foremost a series of prescribed ritual practices, and for historical reasons it is an amazingly broad canopy for diverse beliefs (Haan 2005). Significantly, for Weber, the belief in reincarnation provides a *theodicy* which justifies the existence of the caste system and an individual's place within it. In the *karma* theodicy, people's place in the social hierarchy is the result of their good or bad behavior during a previous lifetime. According to this view, promoted by the Brahmins (the highest caste), only by behaving appropriately to one's station can one hope to improve ones lot in the next life. For the lower orders, who do experience the need for salvation (conceived as being reborn higher in the eternal order of things) this is accomplished by proper ritual conduct appropriate for their station, and worldly needs met by means of magic (which is not far removed from such ritualism).

For Weber not all religion is concerned with salvation. Confucianism is a religion that is not, nor is the Hinduism of the Brahmins (the priestly elites), although the lower classes are concerned with their salvation. Salvation in Weber's sense is for those who feel the need to be saved – from economic deprivation, poor health, or psychological states such as guilt, shame, or fear of death. Generally speaking, Weber argues (following Nietzsche rather than Marx) that elite classes are much less likely to feel these needs (and hence recognize their need for salvation) than the lower orders (1946a: 274–6).

The "salvation religions" (*Erlösungsreligionen*), exist in (and promote) tension with "the world." In Weber's view, Christianity, Islam, Judaism, Buddhism and Jainism are all religions of salvation, although within these traditions there are different ways of responding to this tension. Mystics, who exist in all of the major salvation religions, attempt to merge their soul with the divine reality, escaping all "worldly" distractions in order to do so (early Buddhism is the clearest type for Weber).

In contrast to mysticism, "other-worldly asceticism" involves self-mastery in the interests of devotion, but does not involve the mystical flight from the world, but a physical flight from the world into religious communities. Here Weber seems to have the medieval European monasticism foremost in his mind – monks could devote themselves to saying the mass and living in exclusive service to the divine, unencumbered by the demands of daily living outside the monastery. What Weber calls "inner-worldly asceticism" (*innerweltlich askese*) has been less common historically, but it plays a vital role in the development of Western rationalism. (Although it would have been better if the first generation of translators had opted for the less literal rendition "this-worldly" asceticism, "inner-worldly" has become the standard technical term). The Puritans, who are the heroes of Weber's *Protestant Ethic* are the archetype of inner-worldly ascetics. They have eschewed the mystic's union with God, and the other-worldly ascetic's escape from the world to the monastery. The remaining route for dealing with the tensions between the world of sin and the demands of God is to change the world in accordance with God's precepts. If the mystic tries to be the vessel of God, the ascetic, especially the ascetic of the inner-worldly type, tries to be God's tool for transforming the world. It is for this reason that he devotes himself to his calling in the world with such devotion. He is called upon to be God's tool in that occupation, doing God's work in the world.

Like Marx, Weber recognizes that some religious beliefs and practices will appeal to some groups and not to others. Weber has often been seen as responding to Marx in a more positive manner in these later writings, although the passages in question show more critical dialogue with Nietzsche, who (for reasons quite different from those of Marx) argued that traditional elites (especially the warrior nobles) have been quite indifferent to salvation religions ([1887] 1994). In both his comparative ethics on the world religions and in the posthumously edited sections on religion in *Economy and Society* (1978) Weber argues that certain classes and status groups (*Stände*) have tended to act as "carriers" of particular kinds of religion, and this is as important for the religious ideas and practices as for the groups that embody them. Thus, the "masses" (including working classes and peasants) will tend to be drawn to salvation religion, if one is available and successfully promoted, but will otherwise opt for more pragmatic religious practices such as magic.

Weber's claims were often more specific, as well, as a few examples will suffice. The non-salvation religious ethics for living a good life (such as Confucianism) have tended to have an elective affinity with literate elites, early Islam was carried by a conquering warrior class, Judaism by a "pariah people" and Christianity by itinerant and later urban artisans (1946a: 268–9). These religious beliefs were carried by these groups, but they were also shaped by them in the context of their religious and everyday needs. As Werner Stark puts it, the social world

> is no place for disembodied spirits; even ideas must have bodies if they are to last, and so they are on the lookout for appropriate social groupings who can take them in and carry them along. But human groupings, of whatever kind, will, for their part, always be on the lookout for appropriate ideas to give expression to their essence and their strivings, for, material as this life is, it nevertheless has a spiritual side to it. (1958: 257)

For Gerth and Mills (Weber 1946: 61–5) and those who have followed them, elective affinities involve the mutual attraction of ideas and interests, but this is not all that the elective affinities join, nor does an elective affinity join two forces which remain separate (ideas on the one hand, and interests on the other). In Weber's texts, we find examples of ideas having an elective affinity with other ideas, and structures with other structures (McKinnon forthcoming). Further, the relationship between carriers and the religious beliefs and practices are (at least in potential) mutually constitutive. The "practical rationalism" of urban commercial groups whose "whole existence has been based upon technological or economic calculations and upon the mastery of nature and of man…" made the teachings of the Protestant Reformation appealing to these groups, but such "practical rationalism" of the carrier group also profoundly shaped Protestant beliefs and practices. Weber's controversial notion of pariah peoples (Abraham 1992; Bodemann 1993), which he applied to both Jews in Europe and to lower Hindu castes, is another example whereby the *Stand* is the synthesis of particular sets of beliefs that articulate with a particular social location, here social marginality, to form something distinctive that cannot be reduced to one or other element. Thus, in Weber's later work as well, elective affinity is more than simply a connection, but rather a synthesis of the two forces in which the product is more than the sum of its parts.

CONCLUSION

Along with Émile Durkheim, who will be discussed in the next chapter, Marx and Weber have not only bequeathed to us many of sociology's most important conceptual tools for the sociological study of religion, but they are writers that also continue to challenge us. Their work provides ongoing interpretive challenges, but their arguments constantly push us to ask bigger questions, to think more carefully, broadly and more imaginatively. Whereas contemporary sociology of religion, not uncommonly, seems preoccupied with angels on the head of the proverbial pin, Marx and Weber both guide us (and goad us) towards less parochial concerns. The legacies of Marx and Weber demand that we think about the relationships between religion and other aspects and forces of social life (capitalism, domination and subordination, the state, the needs and suffering of the body), and to explore those relationships without becoming mere "specialists without spirit."

Note

1   For reasons I have never understood, Parkin substitutes "substance" for Weber's "form"; I have replaced it here with Weber's original term.

Bibliography

Abraham, G. (1992) *Max Weber and the Jewish Question: A Study of the Social Outlook of his Sociology*, Urbana: University of Illinois Press.

Albrow, M. (1990) *Max Weber's Construction of Social Theory*, London: Macmillan.

Alexander, J. (1987) The centrality of the classics, in A. Giddens and J. Turner (eds.), *Social Theory Today*, Stanford: Stanford University Press, 11–57.

Baehr, P. and Wells, G. C. (2002) Editors' ntroduction, in Max Weber, *The Protestant Ethic and the "Spirit" of Capitalism and Other Writings*, London: Penguin.

Billings, D. (1990) Religion as opposition: a Gramscian analysis, *American Journal of Sociology* 96 (1): 1–31.

Bloch, E. (1999) [1921] *Thomas Münzer: Théologien de la Revolution*, tr. Maurice de Gandillac, Paris: Union Générale.

Bodemann, M. (1993) Priests, prophets, Jews and Germans: the political basis of Max Weber's ethno-national solidarities, *Archives Europeenes de Sociologie* 34: 224–47.

Bourdieu, P. (1990) *In Other Words: Essays Towards a Reflexive Sociology*, Stanford: Stanford University Press.

Brittain, C. C. (2005) Social theory and the premise of all criticism: Max Horkheimer on religion, *Critical Sociology* 31 (1–2): 153–68.

Dianteill, E. and Löwy, M. (2005) *Sociologies et Religion: Approches Dissidentes*, Paris: Presses Universitaires de France.

Durkheim, E. (2005) [1911] *Les Formes Élémentaires de la Vie Religieuse*, Paris: Quadrige and Presses Universitaires de France.

Engels, F. (1966) *The Peasant War in Germany*, New York: International Publishers.

Engels, F. (1969) *Anti-Dühring*, London: Lawrence and Wishart.

Glenna, L. L. (2008) Redeeming labor: making explicit the virtue theory in Habermas's discourse ethics, *Critical Sociology* 34 (6): 767–86.

Goethe, J. W. (1994) *Elective Affinities*, Oxford: Oxford University Press.

Goldmann, L. [1956] (1964) *The Hidden God*, London: Routledge and Kegan Paul.

Gramscin, A. (1971) *Selections from the Prison Notebooks*, New York: Progress.

Haan, M. (2005) Numbers in nirvana: how the 1872–1921 Indian censuses helped operationalize Hinduism, *Religion* 35: 15–31.

Harvey, V. A. (1995) *Feuerbach and the Interpretation of Religion*, Cambridge: Cambridge University Press.

Hegel, G. W. F. (1994) [1807] *Hegel's Phenomenology of Spirit*, tr. Howard P. Kainz, University Park: Penn State Press.

Houlgate, S. (2005) *An Introduction to Hegel: Freedom, Truth and History*, Oxford: Blackwell.

Hyppolite, J. (1969) *Studies on Marx and Hegel*, tr. John O'Neill, New York: Harper and Row.

Kemple, T. M. (2001) The trials of homo clausus: Elias, Weber, and Goethe on the socio-genesis of the modern self, in T. Salumets (ed.), *Norbert Elias and Human Interdependencies*, Montreal and Kingston: McGill-Queen's University Press, 137–48.

Kent, S. (1983) 'Weber, Goethe, and the Nietzschean allusion: capturing the source of the 'iron cage' metaphor, *Sociological Analysis* 44 (4): 297–319.

Leibniz, G. (1985) [1709] *Essays on the Goodness of God, the Freedom of Man and the Origins of Evil*, tr. E. M. Huggard, Lassalle Illinois: Open Court.

Luisi, P. L. (2002) Emergence in chemistry: chemistry as the embodiment of emergence, *Foundations of Chemistry* 4: 183–202.

Marx, K. (1967) *Capital: A Critique of Political Economy*, New York: International.

Marx, K. (1977) [1844] Towards a critique of Hegel's philosophy of right: introduction, in D. McLellan (ed.), *Karl Marx: Selected Writings*, Oxford: Oxford University Press, 63–74.

Marx, K. (2002) Critique of Hegel's dialectic and general philosophy, in J. Raines (ed.), *Marx on Religion*, Philadelphia: Temple University Press, 75–93.

Marx, K. and Engels, F. (1967) [1848] *The Communist Manifesto*, London: Penguin.

Marx, K. and Engels, F. (1975) *Marx-Engels Collected Works*, New York: International Publishers.

Mendietta, E. (2005) *The Frankfurt School on Religion: Key Writings by the Major Thinkers*, New York: Routledge.

McKinnon, A. M. (2002) Sociological definitions, language games and the "essence" of religion, *Method and Theory in the Study of Religion* 14: 61–83.

McKinnon, A. M . (2005) Reading "opium of the people": expression, protest and the dialectics of religion, *Critical Sociology* 31 (1–2): 15–38.

McKinnon, A. M. (forthcoming) The chemistry of capitalism: Weber's protestant ethic and the attractions of elective affinity, *Sociological Theory*.

McLellan, D. (1969) *The Young Hegelians and Karl Marx*, London: Macmillan.

McLellan, D. (1973) *Karl Marx: His Life and Thought*, New York: Harper.

Nelson, B. (1975) Max Weber, Ernst Troeltsch and Georg Jellinek as comparative historical sociologists, *Sociological Analysis* 36 (3): 229–40.

Nietzsche, F. (1994) [1887] *On The Genealogy of Morality*, tr. Carol Diethe, Cambridge: Cambridge University Press.

O'Toole, R. (1984) *Religion: Classical Sociological Approaches*, Toronto: McGraw-Hill.

O'Toole, R. (2001) Classics in the sociology of religion: an ambiguous legacy, Richard K. Fenn (ed.), *The Blackwell Companion to Sociology of Religion*, Oxford: Blackwell, 133–60.

Parkin, F. (1983) *Max Weber*, London: Routledge.

Regnault, F. (1933) Les maladies de Karl Marx, *Revue Anthropologique* 43: 293–317.

Rojo, S. V. (1988) La religion, opium du peuple et protestation contre la misère réele: les positions de Marx et de Lénine, *Social Compass* 35 (2–3): 197–230.

Samuelsson, K. (1957) *Religion and Economic Action: A Critique of Max Weber*, New York: Harper and Row.

Stark, R. (2004) Putting an end to ancestor worship, *Journal for the Scientific Study of Religion* 43 (4): 465–75.

Stark, R. (2006) Economics of religion, in Robert Segal (ed.), *The Blackwell Companion to the Study of Religion*, Oxford: Blackwell, 47–67.

Stark, W. (1958) *The Sociology of Knowledge*, London: Routledge and Kegan Paul.

Steeman, T. M. (1964) Max Weber's sociology of religion, *Sociological Analysis* 25 (1): 50–8.

Tenbruck, F. (1980) The problem of thematic unity in Max Weber's sociology of religion, *British Journal of Sociology* 31: 316–51.

Troeltsch, E. (1976) [1911] *The Social Teaching of the Christian Churches*, tr. Olive Wyon, Chicago: University of Chicago Press.

Turner, B. S. (1991) *Religion and Social Theory* (2nd edn.), London: Sage.

Weber, Marianne (1975) *Max Weber: A Biography*, tr. Harry Zohn, New York: Wiley.

Weber, M. (1946a) The social psychology of world religions, in H. Gerth and C. W. Mills (eds.), *From Max Weber: Essays in Sociology*, New York: Oxford University Press, 267–301.

Weber, M. (1946b) Religious rejections of the world and their directions, in H. Gerth and C. W. Mills (eds.), *From Max Weber: Essays in Sociology*, New York: Oxford University Press, 323–59.

Weber, M. (1951) *The Religion of China*, New York: Free Press.

Weber, M. (1952) *Ancient Judaism*, tr. H. H. Gerth and D. Martindale, New York: Free Press.

Weber, M. (1958) *The Religion of India*, tr. H. H. Gerth and D. Martindale, New York: Free Press.

Weber, M. (1978) *Economy and Society*, ed. G. Ross and C. Wittich, Berkley: University of California Press.

Weber, M. (2002) *The Protestant Ethic and the "Spirit" of Capitalism and Other Writings*, New York: Penguin.

2

Durkheim and After
Religion, Culture, and Politics[1]

WILLIAM RAMP

Émile Durkheim's contributions to the study of religion are widely acknowledged, but are also sometimes viewed as imposing ruins whose rubble might at best serve as building material in quite different edifices. In this chapter, I propose that if reconstruction of the sociology of religion is in order, Durkheimian concepts and theories are potential cornerstones that builders reject at their peril. A neo-Durkheimian renaissance may yet transform the architecture of social inquiry (Strenski 2006; Pickering 2002, Shilling and Mellor 2001), and the terrain of its theoretical debates. Of course, this new scholarship is not univocal. It is marked by an emerging divergence of culturalist, realist and other interpretations (Smith and Alexander 2007; Frauley and Pearce 2007; Pearce 2006; Mellor 2004), and by debate over the postmodern recruitment of Durkheim (Rosati 2004; O'Neill 1990). It also struggles with interpretive legacies which have led some to downplay or deny Durkheimian affinities (Alexander 1988a: 6–7). In North America, for example, the creativity of neo-Durkheimian cultural analysis contrasts with a conservative and functionalist Durkheim still retailed in some undergraduate texts. While this chapter emphasizes the diversity and potential of Durkheimian approaches to the study of religion, it also locates these in a historical context and indicates some of their old and new challenges.

Renewed interest in Durkheim may owe opportunity to a particular impasse in the sociology of religion. In the 1980s, rational-choice theory re-energized the field, demonstrating the surprising vitality of contemporary religious phenomena – surprising, at least, in light of its projected demise in some versions of secularization theory. But subsequently, rational-choice models of religious action and motivation were themselves alleged to be overly economistic and conceptually narrow. Advocates and detractors of rational choice launched and counter-launched increasingly sophisticated studies as intellectual weapons against each other. If this battle had no clear victors, there was, perhaps, a victim: Christian Smith (2008) noted that "larger intellectual concerns or theoretical frameworks" came to seem "amorphous and wearied" in relation to it. Nonetheless, he sensed possibility beyond the stalemate for more nuanced approaches to the study of belief, embodiment, and emotions in religious life, and for a *rapprochement* between cultural and genetic explanations of religious phenomena. One might also hope that a critical revisitation of conceptual resources, and work in new fields like that of implicit religion, might encourage better conceptualization of religious motivation, both in sociology and in evolutionary psychology, than reductionistic models drawn selectively from modern theism or modern individualism.

Smith's own survey of these opportunities is framed within an uncannily Durkheimian ontology. The real, he says, exists "whether we know or understand it," becoming "actual" when its powers and capacities are activated as "events in the world." Our experience of this actuality, in turn, constitutes the empirical. Smith's critical realism posits a non-reductive understanding of realities "existing on multiple, though connected, levels," operating "according to [their] own characteristic dynamics and processes." The real includes more than material objects: "emergent phenomena, such as social structures and human cognition, are also real, insofar as they possess emergent, durable, causal power"; thus, "meaningful cultural reasons ... possess causal powers for humans." This "anti-foundationalist" approach differs from "empirical" or "scientific" realism because of its "reasoned resistance to modernity's absolute separation of fact from value, and readiness to engage in normative critical theory without (because of its ontological realism) collapsing into ideology and crass academic political activism" (Smith 2008: 1576–7). Similarly, Durkheim claimed that religion constitutes a set of social facts; that it is real even if (partially) non-material; that it has an actual presence in the world of events and actions, and that it can be studied empirically – but that such study must grant its *sui generis* character and not reduce it to the effects of individual self-interest or psychology. Over the past thirty years, Durkheimian ideas have been redeployed in cross-cultural and historical studies of the social and symbolic aspects of embodiment and emotional life, of politics, revolution and war. This work raises pointed and anti-foundationalist questions about the conceptual apparatus of the sociology of religion, and about the boundaries and relations which constitute and divide the spheres of religion, science and politics, of social inquiry and social engagement, of the immanent and the transcendent, the natural and supernatural.

RELIGION AS DURKHEIM UNDERSTOOD IT

The Elementary Forms of Religious Life[2] was the culmination of Durkheim's work on religion, but another text, *The Rules of Sociological Method*, haunts its pages. The *Rules* represents itself as a sort of Cartesian summative direction for social inquiry, but is, as Gane (1988) shows, better read as a threefold strategy: an attempt to further a "radical Enlightenment project" aborted in the revolutions of 1789, 1848, and 1871; a set of provocative methodological suggestions for understanding a perceived contemporary social crisis; and an audacious sociology of sociology. Alexander suggests that the *Rules* also seems to anticipate the future direction of Durkheim's thinking (which he represents as idealist) rather than to sum up a position arrived at. But the *Rules* advances a realist rather than an idealist conception of the social: social facts are real and are known as such by resistance to the imagination; they have an external, even coercive aspect. This realist element still marks the definitional strategy of *The Elementary Forms*, which emphasizes the resistance of actual religious phenomena to presuppositions about them, and attributes to the sacred the character of an interdict with real force. Durkheim does discuss subjective aspects of religious experience (as he had earlier explored subjective states associated with types of suicide), and he does stress the communal, performative and attractive aspects of religion. But he also asserts that one can only understand the subjective side of religion – including the subjective experience of its coercive force – by acknowledging that this experience is bound up with a *collective* power, existing in its own right as something *real*, and experienced as something that *actually* sweeps participants out of particularized subjectivity. Religion lives through our participation, but the plural signifies an order of reality with its own rules of operation.

Durkheim rejected any reductive grounding of the "causes" of religion in psychological motivation or material substrate, and in emphasizing the theoretical centrality of the concept of representations, he also rejected empiricism (Durkheim 1995: 370–1; Stedman Jones 2000). Society is both a disposition of persons and things, and a structure of representations. Neither is reducible to the other; both are actualized through actions and their material consequences; both also organize and structure action. Any *theory* of religion, like religion itself, exists inescapably only as a particular articulation of representations (Pickering 2000). Religion *is* a materialized performance; as the embodied action of sacrifice is necessary to the life of the gods, so the contingency of human life is made sense of and allayed both cognitively *and* practically (Paoletti 2000). But Durkheim grounds such performance resolutely in *social* life and in the life of *collective* representations: if his use of causality is creatively ambiguous, he does not stray far from the admonition of the *Rules* to relate social effects to social causes. Just as he had "de-constructed" the heterogeneous complexity of suicidal actions (Gane 2000), here he de-centers religious agency while emphasizing its subjective, affective, embodied and grounded aspects (Shilling 2005; Mellor and Shilling 1997). This is only an apparent paradox: members of the collective find themselves and their meaningful lives in that collective, and are shaped by active participation in it. The modern individual agent, likewise, is represented by Durkheim not as an analytical starting-point but as the end result of a long and complex historical formation in which Christianity played a significant part.

One of Durkheim's most controversial propositions, contested by Gaston Richard, among others, was that religious veneration of deities or totems honors society itself (Durkheim 1973a, 1974), a proposition seen by some as reducing God to a sort of social organon, and by others as illegitimately deifying the social (for recent assessments, see Pickering 1984; Steiner 1994; Watts Miller 2002). Alexander's more nuanced interpretation (1988b: 189) is that sacralizing elements of the social order rhetorically articulates and concretizes that order as meaningful, voluntarily building and rebuilding (in response to cultural crises) a palpable sense of collective significance. Another way to decipher what Durkheim meant by associating deity and the social is to suggest that he was describing a *process*, one actualized in observable and collective form but also experienced and enacted subjectively, which "makes sense" but not as a rational or propositional procedure. No one suggested that a god be invented to guarantee a social order; rather, gods, spirits, totems and other sacred entities came to be as symbolic and shared expressions of deeply felt social forces carrying people out of quotidian particularity and into cosmic participation; expressive entities which in turn defined them but which they had to propitiate, preserve, love. As the gods were fed, so were we fulfilled. The symbolic expressions shaping and resulting from such movements were not mere mental imagery, but originated in concrete gestural actions by which elements of the material world were set apart or given up; a "visible solemnity, the very strangeness whereof and differences from that which is common doth cause popular eyes to observe and mark the same" (Hooker 1888: 232–3). But in being made "strange," they are also *made central* (Watts Miller 1996: 142). The discrete specificity of mundane life is bestowed with renewed significance when particular elements of the social and natural world are taken up to embody a totality located at once beyond and at the center of ordinary life. Here, the objectivity of the sacred meets the actuality of sacrifice, and generates something new. For Durkheim, this process of objectification was key to what makes the social a society. If society is a structure of representations – and *représentation* encompasses both an act and the symbolic object which is its product – it is only through *réprésentations* that its members are able to imagine themselves *as* members or participants in the social realm, or to imagine social entities as something they are part of. Religion, in this sense, is perennial, and central to the emblematic constitution of social life. Society itself is an "immense writing machine," and all social surfaces "are imprinted with its text" (Gane 1992: 82; Durkheim 1995: 233).

Durkheim (1995: 33–44) identified four definitive features of religion: (1) it is collective, (2) it is composed of both beliefs and practices, (3) it articulates a fundamental distinction between sacred and profane, and (4) it is conceptually distinct from magic, which is instrumental, not obligatory, and not essentially collective). The core definition of the sacred (which resonates with a tradition of anthropological studies of liminality and of rites of passage from van Gennep to Victor Turner and Maurice Bloch) is that it is set apart from everyday life and use, placed under an interdict. The profane, by contrast, is available to ordinary touch, sight, use or consumption. To Durkheim, sacredness does not inhere in any essence of things, but is a consequence of repeated actions which *make things so* in participants' representations of them and relations to them in specific ritual contexts. The sacred does not always involve awe and veneration; some things are negatively sacred; set apart by repugnance, disgust and fear. But all sacred things, whether positively or negatively, represent elements of the collective. Durkheim and Mauss (1967) argued that religious representations, including sacred/profane designations, provided primal forms of classification in terms of which societies mapped out, defined, and inscribed themselves and the cosmos. Representations of space, time, number, or cause do not reflect universal, abstract categories in the Kantian sense; rather, such categories, and modern systems of logic, are but the end development of a process of abstraction and universalization that began with *concrete* representations of the world of things in terms of the symbolically encoded relations characteristic of a given *human* order. In its cognitive aspect, Durkheim says, religion lies at the origin of scientific forms of classification. But it is not any given *content* of classificatory schemas that makes a system religious; even the categories of natural and super-natural are not universally definitive of religion.

Durkheim asserts that the sacred serves a "totemic" function in social life, trans-lating the collective into a set of concrete signifiers. The notion of "society" is an abstraction only from the standpoint of the sociologist. Further, the sacred is not simply perceived but acted toward, organizing the differential – and deferential – disposition of people and things.[3] This emphasis on embodied rites (actions, often with an affective substance, which reinforce and negotiate distinctions between sacred and profane, and negative and positive sacred) accompanies an emphasis on collective effervescence and the demarcation of sacred times and spaces in which collective energies are generated and released; in which everyday life is temporarily set aside, and in which members are swept away, taken out of themselves into another reality. But if society is constituted as a structure of limits and differences, collective effervescence threatens it, and must be contained within temporal, spatial and ritual boundaries. When the containment does not work, revolution or destruc-tion ensues. Collective effervescence joins profound, embodied and emotional responses to an experience of de-differentiation (Ramp 1998) which, for all its danger, can also invigorate social forms, connecting and unifying differentiated members of a collective, providing an energized sense of totality in terms of which they may define and orient themselves within a meaningful and sensibly causal cosmos (Durkheim 1995: 211–16, 369–71). When effervescence spills out of or sweeps away established boundaries, it may destroy, but it can also allow the cre-ative assembly of a new disposition of things and people (Datta 2008).

These dynamics of differentiation and de-differentiation have an analogue in Durkheim's discussion of the soul. Ensoulment is not a central preoccupation of contemporary sociology, but it was clearly important to Durkheim's argument (2005) that modern individuals have a dual nature, differentiated from each other, yet bearing within themselves something universal. In a society which values the individual, each stands for all; each bears the image of humanity, thereby undertak-ing responsibilities and possessing rights. Each is subject to expectations of auton-omy and conscience. Each brings a common sense of meaningful human personhood to bear on the particular, limiting and often solitary circumstances of individuation. The ancestor of this consciousness of self, this conscientious individuality, is the soul, which develops in the process by which members of a society come to be dif-ferentiated (and by which societies are also particularized and emplaced in the cosmos) and come to sense, and make sense of that state. This soul lives on while we die in the sense that it is the principle of society within us; the collective living in and through each of us, giving our differentiated particularity a transcendent meaning.

For Durkheim, religion is thus immortal. Though its particular manifestations come and go, its action is fundamental. It is, if you will, the representational and emotional essence of sociality. Even modern science does not escape it entirely. Scientific forms of classification descend from religious ones (Durkheim and Mauss 1967); the culture of scientific naturalism generates the idea of the supernatural as its expelled binary opposite; science as a collective institution holds sacred the idea of truth (Durkheim 1995: 24–5, 36n45, 429, 433–47). Yet science transcends reli-gion, conscious of its workings in a way that religion itself cannot be.[4] It sees the face of the social behind the mask of religion, but this is different from the religious perception of forces at work behind the mask of nature. Science faces the sublime indifference of the universe which religion peoples with forces, spirits, or purposes. There is no more to the social than what it is. Such a view lends pathos to Durkheim's final years. *The Elementary Forms of Religious Life* was a veiled meditation on the retreat of transcendence in European societies in the face of calculation, analysis, utility and routine, but such traditional religious forms as were still available to him were of no comfort in mourning the death of his son (Pickering 2008a). War work on behalf of the nation manifestly did not fill the void he felt as a parent and even perhaps as a citizen. Perhaps he worked for the future, his fierce dedication to duty in service of a receding dawn.

As a systematic body of fieldwork developed in the twentieth century, Durkheim's concept of totemism was criticized as arbitrary, neither as fundamental nor as universal as he had thought. His definition of religion was faulted as so broad it made the social indistinguishable from the religious; his definition of the sacred as "unusable" in fieldwork. While he demonstrates the weakness of common assumptions about religion, his own process of definitional elimination was anchored in a loosely collective and perhaps arbitrary sense of what may be called religious (Lukes 1973). For all that, the very looseness and audacity of Durkheim's theoretical formulations, like his methodological ones, gives his discussion of religion a creative flexibility of application (Gane 1988, 2000; Fields 1995: xliii–xlix) that serves it well in comparison to models based on, say, "belief in a supernatural entity," or a motivating fear of death, or a cost-benefit model of individual action. Holbraad (2006) argues, against claims that Durkheimian conceptions of *mana* and "force" are ethnographically unsound and lack rigor, that Durkheim and Mauss used these terms to test the categorical boundaries of Western thinking in ways that (especially) today might provide for new, post-scientistic ways of thinking about alterity, about the agency of things, and about the *ontological* status of both concepts and realities (see also Wexler 2007: 215–16; Henare et al. 2006). If so, Durkheim and Mauss *themselves* may yet transform the very terms of the realist/culturalist debates presently waged in their names.

Durkheim's identification of "religious" elements at work in modern individualism, nationalism and socialism indicates other possibilities for future study. The historical development of a collective veneration of the individual, a central element of modernity, occurred not only as a philosophical process but also in new forms of education (1977), law, and punishment (1986)5, and sexual morality (Durkheim et al. 1979). The collective value placed upon the individual is codified in legal and penal codes but also acted out visibly, as in the institution of property, which Durkheim insisted was religious in two senses. First, forms of property in Continental European law codes descend from religious rites: for example, the ancient Roman *familia* enacted itself as a distinct social unit by re-enacting the gift of its ground from the gods, who retreated to liminal zones marked by *termini*, the loci of offerings returned for this gift. Second, property is *sacred* – set apart, or untouchable – to all but its proprietors; something also true of modern individual property which, Durkheim argues, descends from communal forms and still depends on collective assent (Durkheim 1992). The transfer of property is a liminal act, requiring ritual elements such as signing ceremonies, handshakes or the like. Due regard for the sacredness of personal property becomes a sign of regard for the sacredness of individual *persons*; theft or other forms of property violation commonly are experienced as personal desecrations.

The sacredness of individual persons is also enacted through sexual morality. In a civilization in which the sanctity of the individual is paramount and the individualization of persons is mapped on to the individualization of bodies, the sexual act threatens the boundaries of personhood, and renders participants vulnerable (something also diversely noted by St. Paul and Georges Bataille). A de-mystifying reduction of sex to biology or technique, or a stripping away of modesty codes would, in such a context, be a mistake (Durkheim et al. 1979). Instead, one must recognize the proper basis of modern sexual morality; its relation to individual rights. Modesty codes, of course, have much to do with the history of patriarchy, but the logic of Durkheim's argument seems to anticipate their possible democratization, and a questioning of sexual double standards as women gain status as individual persons with property rights and legal autonomy. Similarly, the historical development of manners and courtesy codes can be said to involve an embodied sacralization of personhood, and Goffman's exemplary discussion of deference (1956) gives a concrete demonstration of the cult of the individual enacted in everyday interaction rituals.

THE GENESIS OF *SOCIOLOGIE RELIGIEUSE*

While historical discussions of Durkheim's intellectual trajectory often reflect present-day interpretive agendas, the development and reception of Durkheimian sociology are actualities which merit understanding in their own right, along with their consequences. Durkheim's engagement with others and with the concerns of his place and time gave his sociology of religion a characteristic shape (Besnard 1983). Three elements in its formation stand out: the religious features which shaped French civic nationalism; the intellectual context in which Durkheim developed and defended his ideas; and the colleagues who, with Durkheim, formed a collective *équipe* for the scientific study of the social.[6] Of particular importance are the intellectual and political issues which engaged Durkheim as an inheritor and supporter of a secular, rationalist vision of French civic life who was nonetheless soberly apprised of the limits of rationalist individualism.

Religion and politics were closely but peculiarly entwined in nineteenth-century France. Roman Catholic ascendancy had never been fully assured nor monocratic. Historically, monarchs had vied with popes and cardinals for hegemony, and following the Reformation, France suffered protracted instability amounting at times to civil war, as a strong Protestant minority fought for supremacy or survival, depending on dynastic vagaries and the monarchy's struggle against the centrifugal tendencies of nobles and regions. This instability was only resolved, partially, with the murder or expulsion of the majority of the Huguenot population, and the consolidation, under Louis XIV, of the absolute monarchy. The splendor of the Sun King's rule was contingent on a constant theatrical and ritual performance of legitimacy with a distinctly religious aura (Muir 2005: 281–2), both allied to and in tension with the forms and policies of the Church. The Revolution – in particular, the execution of "*citoyen Capet*" – was thus a double blow, against the Church and also, profoundly, against a quasi-religious veneration of the person of the King as the embodiment of France.[7] But the Revolution itself was not utterly antireligious. Its task was less to erase Christendom or Sovereignty than to give their decapitated forms new content, immanentized in the sovereignty of the People and worship at the throne of Reason, installed in Notre Dame.

The ambiguous legacy of the Revolution incited a febrile instability in post-revolutionary politics. Durkheim noted (1973b: 60), a century later, that "the critical period begun with the fall of the *ancien régime* [had] not yet ended." A thoroughgoing anticlericalism vied with a Catholic counter-revival which sought to dedicate the entire nation to the Sacred Heart (Jonas 2000). But even secular rationalism provided soil for quasi-religious offshoots such as Comte's short-lived church of humanity, a serious if failed attempt to make sense of the interplay of religion, politics and science (Wernick 2001). Durkheim's own politics were aligned with secular republicanism, and thus anticlericalism and rationalism; never more explicitly than in his support of the Dreyfusards (Goldberg 2008). This was a natural position for a someone of Jewish descent to take, as it was for the small but intellectually influential Protestant community. But Durkheim's advocacy of secularism and rationalism was systematic and considered. His entire sociology could be seen as an extension of an effort by educators and public figures under the banner of *morale laïque* (Pickering 2006, 2008b; Stock-Morton 1988) to found an intellectually defensible secular morality, countering Christian claims that non-theistic moral systems were unsustainable. Durkheim, further, sought to link *morale* – and also politics – to *une culture spécialement sociologique* which would transform both. But this involved consideration of communal, emotional and symbolic aspects of religion (Rosati 2008: 243–7), and by extension, of similar features in civic and economic life, which sat uneasily with a faith in individualistic, secular rationalism. In re-acquainting his readers with the religious and emotional dimensions of sociality, with the religious origins of science, and with the collective and embodied dimensions of individualism, Durkheim aroused suspicion among those who might otherwise have been natural allies; not only secular anticlericals of rational-utilitarian bent, but also liberal Jews and Protestants who sought more intellectualized, ethicalized and de-ritualized versions of their inherited traditions. This led to a wounding rift in 1907 with Gaston Richard, a Protestant convert and collaborator on the *Année Sociologique*, over Durkheim's characterizations of Protestantism, over the role of the individual in religious life, and over what Richard saw as Durkheim's conflation of deity and sociality (Pickering 1979, 1984: 435–9, 2008b: 70–4).[8] Durkheim characteristically defined the obligatory aspect of religion as the inculcation of *social* imperatives, arguing that even the remnants of communalism and superstition so embarrassing to liberal modernists had their reasons, albeit ones unrecognized in any rational sense by participants. In making such claims, however, Durkheim drew upon resources available to him from French political history: his study of religion, even when it involved an ethnography of societies situated at a vast remove from contemporary France, had a European edge. *The Elementary Forms of Religious Life* was not only an attempt at a theory of religion but a perspective, "from far away" (Rosati 2008), on a society in which the collective, ecstatic and affective dimensions of religion had become attenuated, and in which the aura of sacredness had been corroded by the humdrum of modern economic and bureaucratic life.

While Durkheim's anthropological approach to religion is usually traced through his reading of Frazer, Robertson-Smith, and Australian ethnographic literature, its specific development is still debated. Parsons (1937) proposed that Durkheim's latter-day, "idealist" turn to the study of religion provided him a sociological solution to the Hobbesian problem of order, derived from the insight that cultural systems, manifest in the form of a values consensus, defined and bound together social actors in identifiable and coherent systems of action. While differing with some features of Parsons' argument, Jeffrey Alexander (1986a, 1986b) concurred that a fundamental, if complex shift in Durkheim's thinking between 1893 and 1900, allowed resolution of the "theoretical problem" of how to understand society as more than the consequence of economic or material factors; as at once "determinate, organized and voluntary." Durkheim himself claimed – in a passing remark – that his discovery of the work of William Robertson Smith had freed him to rethink his entire sociology (Pickering 1984: 62–70). Alexander (1986b), however, argues that this encounter was invoked retrospectively to rationalize a transition already underway toward a more subjectivist, non-materialist and voluntaristic understanding of the collective sacralization of society and the formation of "crystallized emotions." This "spiritualization" of his understanding of order gave Durkheim an answer both to "instrumentalist materialism" and to theories which linked social order too readily to coercion. Alexander sees this as Durkheim's great contribution to sociology, though continually endangered by the Scylla and Charybdis of theoretical individualism or materialist determinism. He suggests that Durkheim's own tendency to "idealism" needs correction by re-emphasizing the performative aspects of social life (if you will, performance as "actualization" in Christian Smith's sense). However, such claims are entangled in present-day disputation. Pearce suggests that they disengage a voluntarist and subjectivist Durkheim from the material realities of social life (Pearce 2006; Smith and Alexander 2007). Mestrovic (1985, 1988) detects a lingering Parsonianism in the notion that Durkheim's sociology of religion provides a theoretical solution to a problem of order, proposing instead that it was driven by a Schopenhauerian agenda to understand human will sociologically. Like Alexander, Massimo Rosati identifies a shift in Durkheim's later writing about religion, but one in which emphasis on communal and embodied emotional life, exemplified in the concept of collective effervescence, displaced an earlier focus on duty and obligation.

THE DURKHEIMIANS AND RELIGION

Durkheim sought to establish sociology as a collective project, an ambition appropriate both to the nature of its object, and to the enterprise of science, which he characterized as set apart from and transcending the personal concerns of its practitioners and contributors. Nonetheless, his personality dominated the *Année Sociologique* collective, as his own theoretical project dominated (with a few signal exceptions) its approach to religion, and that project did in some sense die with him. Among his students and successors, distinctively Durkeimian themes and approaches to the sociology of religion persisted, but did not add up to the same enterprise.

In *The Elementary Forms*, Marcel Mauss is present alongside Durkheim: the concept of collective effervescence comes from Mauss and Beuchat's study of Inuit culture (1979).[9] Mauss contributed much to the developing anthropological discourse about religion, identifying ritual and religious elements at work in reciprocity and gift exchange (Mauss 2002), in the development of the concept of the person and of the soul (Mauss 1985), in sacrifice (Hubert and Mauss, 1964), and especially in magic (Mauss 1972). Unlike Durkheim, Mauss argued that religion and magic had once formed a primordial unity and that both exhibited collective features. The "activation of society" was both cause and effect of magic; further, while magic (in the eyes of the anthropological beholder) involved a variety of incompatible ideas joined together, it formed, for participants, a whole more real than each of its parts (Nielsen 1998: 161). Like Henri Hubert (1999), Mauss emphasized the alternation of whole and part, totality and particularity in time and space as central features of social life and religious cosmology. Mauss also privileged the idea of a "force" embodied in *mana* over the concept of the totem, though such nuances indicate a reworking or extension of Durkheim's approach rather than a break with it, as Durkheim's own references (1995: 192, 324–5) to the force of the sacred demonstrate. It has been suggested that despite Mauss's emphasis on what he called the "total social fact" (a distinctive social phenomenon with ramifications in many areas of social life), his anthropology took a more individualist turn, foregrounding the particular interests or obligations of participants in gift giving and sacrifice. Further, Durkheim's penchant for systematic forms of social analysis and explanation was foreign to Mauss's personal predilections. However, Mauss never repudiated the place of reciprocity and sacrifice, as social phenomena, within a social totality, and his study of the gift is as much about recognition as about reciprocity; as much about the extension of a universe of shared meaning as about obligations and interests. Further, the essay on the gift is driven by a political intent similar to Durkheim's, to identify, from a viewpoint "far away," something profoundly out of joint in European modernity. In that sense, the idea that Mauss intended mainly to *distinguish* "commodity societies" from "gift societies" is mistaken.

Robert Hertz's untimely death left only hints of his potential as a theorist of religion, but he was nonetheless an important figure in the Durkheimian legacy. His reputation rests on a few short works, none translated into English before 1960: a study of the cult of St Besse (1985) incorporating – unusually for the first generation of Durkheimians – personal observation; two studies of death and the right hand, respectively (1985), and fragments of an unfinished thesis on sin and expiation (1994). Hertz linked the sacred to concerns about pollution, arguing that social rituals attempt not only to distinguish sacred from profane, or right from left sacred, but also to deal with the intrusion of disorder into the categorical structure of social life. This anticipated Mary Douglas's association of "dirt" with disorder, and his preoccupation with binary categories prefigured the work of Lévi-Strauss.

POST-DURKHEIMIAN EXTENSIONS: PARSONS AND AFTER

The oft-repeated identification of Durkheim's sociology of religion with functionalism has a complex history that can only be outlined here. Alfred R. Radcliffe-Brown, who coined the term "structural-functionalism," corresponded with Durkheim, emulated his tendency to ambitious theoretical schemata, and adapted elements of his approach into a sophisticated theory of the functional integration of society. However, he neglected the profoundly historical aspect of Durkheim's thought and distanced himself from the implicit evolutionism of Durkheim's contrast between simple and complex social forms. His real aversion was to the broad-brush evolutionary theory of an earlier generation of philosophical anthropologists; by contrast, he emphasized the synchronic interrelation of social institutions, the ways in which ritual reinforced social structure and function, and the connections of people to roles. Radcliffe-Brown was attracted to the analogy between social and biological "organisms" in *The Division of Labour*, and he also employed a basic principle from *Primitive Classification*; that systems of symbols could be linked to the structural features of social organization. Ultimately, his theoretical enterprise did not survive him: a growing emphasis on detailed fieldwork (Evans-Pritchard, Malinowski, Bateson) instead of global speculation undermined some of his theoretical propositions (Bell 1997: 34), and redirected anthropological emphasis toward the meaning of ritual, belief and symbol systems in their own right and for participants. Nonetheless, Radcliffe-Brown's preoccupations left a mark, during his peripatetic academic career, on the Chicago school of anthropology and, perhaps surprisingly (given the way in which sociological "paradigms" are diced-up in North America), on Erving Goffman.

The American recuperation of Durkheim by Talcott Parsons, Robert Merton, and Harry Alpert, followed a long hiatus during which American social psychologists who regarded individual behavior as a starting-point of social analysis had identified Durkheimian sociology with a "group mind fallacy" (see Gehlke 1915; Tiryakian 1962; Morrison 2001). But Parsons saw in Durkheim a solution to the problem of theorizing the relation of voluntaristic individual action to social order. For Merton, *Suicide* modeled a systematic scientific approach to the social free of the moralizing reformism that supposedly clung to midwestern community sociology. These recuperations occurred in part through a reading of Radcliffe-Brown, and in part from Parsons' exposure to systems theory *via* L. J. Henderson and W. B. Cannon. However, Parsons' sociology of religion should not be reduced simply to a functionalist account of its role in social integration or as a solution to the individual action/social order dilemma. What also fascinated him was a Kantian dichotomy between religion as moral duty and as a vehicle to express interests in salvation or healing (Turner 2005), expressed culturally in American individualism as a dichotomy between self-control and self-expression. Parsons saw in Durkheim's discussions of the development of modern individualism a way to theorize the functional recuperation of the Judaeo-Christian tradition in modernity, and latterly dedicated himself to this recuperation through a systems-theoretical contextualization of the human condition in terms of highly developed forms of autonomous individualism (Joas 2001). An analogous concern to understand the fundamentals of the human condition in the cultural context of the contemporary quest for authenticity lies at the heart of Jeffrey Alexander's contemporary rethinking of Parsons.

Another student of Parsons, Robert Bellah, similarly concerned to understand the consequences of individualism in American life, did so uniquely by developing

Durkheim's comments about religious aspects of political or national symbolism and ritual into a systematic analysis of "civil religion" in America (Bellah 1967).[10] Bellah later doubted that any one identifiable "civil religion can be said to operate on the American civic and political scenes," and became more interested in the individualization of religious expression. However, the concepts of the sacred and of collective effervescence, of the nation as an imagined moral community, and of civic nationalism as a phenomenon involving both beliefs and rites collectively held, still have purchase in the analysis of political events (Hunt 1988; Tiryakian 1988; Alexander 1988b). Bellah also sought to intervene in public civic discourse, conceiving of the "central tradition of the American civil religion not as a form of national self-worship but as the subordination of the nation to ethical principles that transcend it in terms of which it should be judged." Convinced that "every nation and every people come to some form of religious self-understanding," Bellah argued that it seems "responsible to seek within the civil religious tradition for those critical principles which undercut the everpresent danger of national self-idolization" (Bellah 1991: 168). In a sense, like Durkheim, Bellah moved from a "sociology of religion" toward a "religious sociology," applying fundamental religious insights to a sociological analysis of the secular present.

A Durkheimian emphasis on the centrality of symbolic classification marked the work of British anthropologist, Mary Douglas, who had a large North American following.[11] Her discussions of pollution and taboo, and of the classificatory transgressions of "dirt" are clearly related to the concepts of sacred and profane, though Douglas distanced herself from a Durkheimianism she associated with Radcliffe-Brown (Alexander 1988a: 9). A Durkheimian sensitivity to the manner in which rites incorporate participants into a totality whose compass both escapes their grasp and founds their existence, marks Victor Turner's studies of civic ritual and *communitas*, as does the idea of collective effervescence. A similar affinity marks Durkheim's attention to the negotiation of spatial and temporal boundaries around the sacred and Turner's concept of the liminal as a transitional phase between structures (Turner 1969, 1974). Clifford Geertz defines the study of religion in a characteristically Durkheimian manner (though without invoking Durkheim), as the recognition of meaning as "autonomous" (that is, public and social) and "materially embodied," and as involving some "conception of 'limit,' or 'ultimate,' or 'existential' problems," inciting a continual need to stave off chaos by reasserting collective morale and recognizing its cosmic conditions. Religion thus "tunes human actions to an envisaged cosmic order and projects images of cosmic order onto the plane of human experience" (Geertz 2005: 7; see also Ramp 2008). Today, however, religions have been "disentangled" from the traditional geographical and social sites of their formation, and "jumbled" together as their individualized carriers migrate to different areas of the globe. In the process, religion becomes "a portable *persona*, a movable subject position." Concurrently, relations between religious convictions and the "the workings of everyday life" have become "less simple, less immediate, and less direct – more in need of explicit, conscious, organized support" (Geertz 2005: 9). These changes, particularly the individualization of religious experience and observance, are – as Durkheim claimed with respect to the "cult of the individual" – outcomes of and responses to specific historical and cultural developments, not evidence of the ultimate basis of religion in individual psychology or agency.

Durkheim's observation that, in sacrifice, humans actively provide for the needs of their gods, ensuring the survival of the fabric of meaning they lend to the cosmos, and his vivid descriptions of piacular rites by which wounded communities restore themselves and resolve the ambiguous status of the recently dead, both resonate with a latter-day "performative" turn in anthropology, to which Turner, inspired by Goffman, contributed (see also Giesen 2006), as did Geertz's studies of symbolic performance (Geertz 1973; Alexander, 1988a: 7). Alexander (2006) and others employ Goffman's theatrical analogy (while eschewing his tendency to represent action as individualized self-presentation strategies) to examine a "de-fusing" of the elements of social performance in complex modern societies, and the conditions under which actors, audiences and scripts may be "re-fused" in a successful verisi-militude. Over such performances today – in traditional religious settings, in politics, in media productions, in everyday life, in the context of the expected and predict-able, and in moments of crisis – there hovers the spectre of inauthenticity. This condition, Alexander suggests, results from a separation of elites who carried out central symbolic actions from their mass audiences, an estrangement of "means of symbolic production" from the mass of social actors, and a disconnection of written foreground texts from background collective representations (2006: 45). In axial-age civilizations and their modern descendants, social experience is marked by de-contextualization and the institution of distinctions between, for example, meta-physics and ritual, the local and the general, the particular and the universal (Alex-ander 2005). Consequently, social performances, always to some degree particularized but calling on ideological universals, bear a formidable burden of "achievement" in attempting to knit together disparity and achieve authenticity – a situation remi-niscent of Geertz's observation of strained relations between religious convictions and everyday life. While Alexander criticizes Durkheim's attempt to find "elementary" forms of *all* religious life in Australian aboriginal societies, like Durkheim, he characterizes differences between pre- and post-axial age societies in terms of social and cultural complexity. These and other Ango-American re-appropriations of Durkheim rework a range of ideas and tropes into uniquely synthetic accounts of the religious constitution of self and civic life, person and polity; an enterprise which Jeffrey Alexander and others involved in the Yale-centered "strong program" in cultural sociology have attempted to realize with formidable ambition.

Religious aspects of modern individualism, both historical and contemporary, are also central to Hans Joas's (2008a) discussion of self-transcendence as an actual-ity (not merely a "need") which religion interprets, opening up "ways" of experi-ence. Joas also stresses the social and religious dimensions of human dignity in a critique of Foucault's history of punishment (2008b). Modern forms of punishment reflect ambivalence over the status of convicted criminals, who partake in the sacred-ness accorded the individual person even though convicted of violating that sacred-ness in assaults on others. This ambivalence appears in tensions between support for rehabilitation or prisoner rights, and calls to avenge criminal desecrations of personhood. Demands for vengeance cannot be dismissed as mere backward-looking survivals; they are responses to violations of *contemporary* forms of sacred-ness related to human dignity as a "religion of modernity" (2008a), and constitute powerful collective forces.

SOCIOLOGIE SACRÉE: FRENCH DURKHEIMIANISM

The influence of Durkheimian sociology in France weakened between the world wars for several reasons: the academic fate of "official Durkheimianism," the eroding legitimacy of the Third Republic, and political divisions which fed that erosion. In postwar France, as elsewhere, some who pursued Durkheimian topics or ideas, even using Durkheimian language, distanced themselves from his perceived legacy. Nonetheless, a conduit between Durkheim and postwar French thought persisted in the effect of Saussurian semiotics on a generation of anthropologists and comparative mythologists, including Emile Benveniste, Georges Dumézil and also Claude Lévi-Strauss, who brought a Durkheimian and Hertzian emphasis to the study of symbolic classification. While Levi-Strauss identified more with Mauss than Durkheim, distancing himself from the idea that such classifications reflected a synchronicity between social organization and symbolic structure, Dumézil (1988), in a manner reminiscent of Durkheim and Mauss, identified a mythical structure common to various Indo-European cultures – the four cardinal directions and their center – with an organizing principle in five-part divisions of peoples (see also Allen, 2000). Similarly, Dumézil's studies of the fragmentation of a primordial totality represented in stories of origin recall Durkheimian tropes of origin, differentation and ecstatic reunion. Michel Foucault mentioned Durkheim only occasionally and somewhat dismissively, but their methodological approaches bear comparison, as do their respective treatments of the concepts of the soul (Hecht 2003: 316), of discipline, and of governance (Ramp 1999, 2000). Datta (2008) contends that Foucault and Durkheim may be brought into dialogue by interpreting the concept of collective effervescence as a moment at which the dissolution of one way of ordering the relation of people and things makes possible the constitution of a new and revolutionary *dispositif* – an interpretive strategy equally applicable to political revolutions and to religious revivals.

René Girard continued a Gallic penchant for philosophical anthropology with a uniquely Christian treatment of scapegoating (Girard 1987; Graham 2007) as something central to the human social condition, which Christ's self-sacrifice disarms and annuls. Girard employed a non-Durkheimian theory of mimesis, but his identification of the sacrificial victim as an ambiguously sacred figure symbolizing what the collective expels has acknowledged Durkheimian roots. Independently of Girard, American sociologist Kai Erikson (1966) penned a luminous account of the Salem witch trials as outcomes and objectifications of anxieties over collective self-definition in the Massachusetts Bay Colony at crucial points in its history. Mike Gane (1994: 57–8) identified an incipient Durkheimian analysis of "normal violence" exercised against vulnerable social inferiors in times of transition, and Dan Stone (2004), in a manner reminiscent of both Durkheim and Caillois, evoked the concept of collective effervescence to mark the genocidal potential of ecstatic de-differentiation accompanied by the identification of collective enemies. Durkheim-influenced approaches to the sociology of suffering and evil (Pickering 2008a; Alexander et al. 2004; Alexander 2001) and of collective responsibility (Rosati, 2008) also contribute significantly to this literature.

The postmodern Durkheim renaissance beginning in the 1980s featured renewed attention to the sacred and to affective states associated with it, and derived from readings of Georges Bataille, Maurice Blanchot (Hart 2004), and Bataille's *Collège de Sociologie* colleagues, Roger Caillois and Michel Leiris. Caillois noted a duality in games and play, which involve moments of individual or collective frenzy but also of circumscription, often involving rules about touching. Games in particular exhibit both an escalating exuberance of improvisation (*paidia*) and petty and seemingly overdone rules and conventions governing difficulty (*ludus*) (Caillois 2001a: 12). Here is an emphasis, characteristic of Durkheim and Mauss, on a symbolic structuring of persons, actions, bodies and things, accompanied by moments of excitement, governed by collective rules whose purpose is not utilitarian but *the establishment of meaning itself*. But a Durkheimian (and Hertzian and Maussian) legacy is most explicit in Caillois's linking of the sacred to social occasions of cleansing and purification, or remission of sin, and in his weaving of collective effervescence into a disturbing comparison of festival and war (Caillois 2001b: esp. ch. 4)

The Durkheimian aspects of Georges Bataille's *oeuvre* are widely acknowledged but much debated (Richman 1997, 2002; Gane 2003; Riley 2005, 2006). Bataille related elements of Durkheimian sociology to Nietzchean assertions about consciousness in which the legacies of Hegel, Kant, Freud, and especially Marx, also persist (Bataille 1988d, 1989); for example, assertions about individual sovereignty "beyond good and evil" in the face of death and dissolution, about the foreignness of "base matter" to human ideals, and about profound contact with others as necessarily wounding and violating, paradoxically bound up with both ecstasy and failure. These concerns are grounded in a central assertion that biological life, consciousness and the social, though they take form as "organisms," are all defined by excess (Bataille 1988a, 1988b, 1988c, 1991): Bataille thereby located a Maussian emphasis on effervescence and the force of the sacred, and Durkheim's notion that transgression inevitably accompanies order, in a materialist matrix. Structure and limit are necessary to rational consciousness and social life (a Durkheimian trope), but are accompanied by an energy which promotes (on one hand) ecstatic transgression and (on the other) an *overproduction* of meaning which laughter, comically, debases and dissolves.

Bataille's anthropology is Durkheimian in its treatment of the sacred as symbolic, set apart and removed from use, and Maussian in its emphasis on the real force and power of the sacred. Bataille characterized the sacred as the site of heterogeneous forces repulsive to order and rationality; hence his Hertzian emphasis on its negative aspects. But like Durkheim and Mauss, he also claimed that the sacred and heterogeneity had been displaced or suppressed in modern life – except for the protean excesses of capitalist overproduction, and war. This made modern Europe ripe for fascistic seduction, diverting the energy of heterogeneity into an excessive and paradoxical devotion to order, aggression, and a spectacular aesthetic of violence (Bataille 1985). His creative use of Durkheim, Freud and Marx in this analysis still, perhaps especially now, merits attention. His attention to transgression and heterogeneity; to the sacred sites at which these are both indicated and reserved, and to the heterogeneous force expressed in collective movements and spectacular events, was widely emulated, in the work of Baudrillard (Baldwin 2008; Mellor and Shilling 1997, 1998; Maffesoli 1993, 1996; Mellor 2000; Richman 2002).

CONCLUSION: DURKHEIM AND THE CO-IMPLICATION OF SOCIOLOGY AND RELIGION

One may legitimately question the extent to which these various elements of a Durkheimian approach to the study of religion are *uniquely* Durkheimian, and whether they offer a coherent alternative to other approaches. Many of them reside in the work of others, often modified, unattributed, or in service of other theoretical schemes (just as elements of Durkheim's own thinking derived from Mauss, Hubert, and others outside the *Année* circle, such as Sylvain Lévi). Conversely, some find Durkheim's formulations restrictively monistic or arbitrary. Despite the explosion of recent neo-Durkheimian scholarship, no unified "Durkheim school" in the sociology of religion has emerged. It can at least be said that Durkheim was at the center of a way of conceiving and researching social life distinctive in its time and place, conveyed in a discourse which employed distinctive terms, tropes, metaphors and ways of arguing, which articulated particular elements of concern and emphasis, both scientific and, to borrow Durkheim's term, "moral." After his death, and the dissolution of the first *Année* group, this discourse became fragmented and variable as elements of it were incorporated into different languages, disciplines and theoretical enterprises, sometimes recombining and sometimes diverging.

If there is no continuing school, it is still possible to talk of a cluster of distinctive concepts, approaches and concerns marking a unique approach to religion as a social phenomenon. Those who propagate Durkheimian ideas and concerns tend to be critical of approaches to religion which focus on status and economic motivations, cost-benefit calculations, or individual psychology (Neubert 2008; Joas 2008a; Mellor 2004; Richman 2003), just as Durkheim criticized utilitarian or individualistic explanations of social phenomena. They emphasize emotional and collective aspects of religious life, but also structured and structuring networks of symbols, boundaries and prohibitions. Central to most of this work is attention to the sacred, and a sense of the profound co-implication of the religious and the political, whether in the civic deployment and celebration of sacred symbols, in ecstatic redispositions of persons and things in new and revolutionary configurations, or in darker manifestations of violence and authoritarianism. Also still present is Durkheim's attention, strikingly analogous to Freud's,[12] to dualisms defining the modern condition, and to the signs and sites of ecstatic de-differentiation and totality marked off from, or within, everyday particularity. Today, the emblems of a previous century's ecstatic mobilization, visions of utopia, sacred tradition or mythic origin, suffer fatal crises of authenticity. But the sacred and collective effervescence stubbornly resist death by the thousand cuts of individual interest, recurring anew in so-called fundamentalist movements, and in corporate gatherings from charismatic churches to Burning Man festivals. Less evident today, but present in much of the work examined above, is Durkheim's own emphasis on the historical development of religious and social forms, or his stillborn incorporation of religious sociology into a larger project on *la morale*, though Joas and Alexander address issues similar in emphasis and scope. More evident than in Durkheim's day is a Bataillian emphasis (sometimes lacking Bataille's ambivalence) on transgression, an emphasis which might incite future questions about its status in and consequences for the conceptual schema or ethico-political orientation of the study of religion.

What also remains active is a fundamental ambiguity which triggered several early criticisms of Durkheim: his insistence that religion is "real," central to social life, and in some sense perennial, and contrarily, that religion is also structurally "unconscious" of its true nature; that it, and its claims to ultimate validity, can be explained by a science which treats it as a "fact." Durkheimian sociology is sympathetic to religion, refusing rationalist dismissals of its ritualistic and emotional aspects, as well as of its more baffling modes of classification and belief. It counters the reductive definitions of religion in much of the so-called "new atheism" today. Nonetheless, it is profoundly agnostic in its refusal of the terms on which religion offers itself. Durkheim argued that science, including social science, descends from religious modes of logic and cognition, still betrays religious elements in its institutional organization, and, like religion, makes meaning in the face of the cosmos. But science does so differently, he claimed, and not as an equal *magisterium* (Lacroix 1979). This makes a Durkheimian approach to religion at once attractive and unsettling to religiously committed scholars. Yet, apart from early critics like Richard, and later ones like Hecht, sustained re-examination of Durkheim's sociological atheism has been somewhat rare.

The Durkheimian emphasis on religion as "real" recalls us, finally, to our opening discussion about the status of the social, and of religion, as objects of study. The position that Durkheim was a realist, not a positivist, has stout defenders, but debate continues about what kind of realist he was, and whether he did or did not latterly abandon a schema in which symbolic classifications were conceived of as rooted in "real" dispositions of persons and things. One can argue that he asserted a sort of culturalist realism; that religious manifestations, as social facts, are real in a derivatively Cartesian sense, as emergent properties with their own causal configurations. Alternatively, the *actuality* of religion may be located in its performative status; not as a "thing" or set of things existing as such but as a set of active performances, at once ordered and contingent, responsive to and generative of collective universals but also localized and contextualized. As Durkheim would have noted, such discussion about the epistemological and ontological status of religion (about its existence, and about how it is known sociologically as something in relation to, but also other to the knower), has "religious" dimensions. The debate relies on a collective framework of meaning, and is performed by scholars organized in professional bodies who hold certain presuppositions about truth sacred. But the encounter of religion and sociology raises another order of questions about transcendence, and about encounter, which Bataille in his tortured way faced most clearly. Religion, in at least some of its forms, purports to be about an encounter, whether with a personal presence, an impersonal force, or a universe of being to which we are insensitive and blind. Some representations of science superimpose epistemological questions on ontological ones, so that, for example, questions about God become debates over whether there is "a" being whose "existence" is empirically verifiable. A Durkheimian might reassert the importance of ontology, but also ask if epistemological and ontological issues in the philosophy of science are not variants of questions of otherness and encounter, differentiation and totality, faced existentially, historically and socially, in discourse and embodied performance, in other spheres of life and in other times.

Notes

1 I thank W. S. F. Pickering and Paul Datta for critical comments on an early draft of this chapter while taking full responsibility for my interpretation of their comments.
2 The convention for the English translation of this title is now established by Fields' (1995) translation. Watts Miller and Pickering suggest that "elemental" is a better choice than "elementary."
3 I am indebted to Paul Datta for this formulation.
4 Durkheim (1958) made a similar point about the relation of social science to socialism, yet his attraction to Saint-Simon as a founder of both modern socialism and of social science reflects a shared ambiguity: both saw religion as, in a sense, an inescapable "practical" expression of a given state of knowledge (see also Durkheim 1995: 432). A similar ambiguity haunts Althusser's latter recognition of the practical unavoidability of "ideology."
5 Foucault's study of the reformation of punishment, though articulated differently, was arguably anticipated by Durkheim (Ramp 1999).
6 On the vexed question whether Durkheim's Jewishness affected his theory of religion, I would reiterate Strenski's (1997) caution about speculation.
7 The disturbing religious implications of the decapitation of Louis XVI reappeared, a century and a half later, in the writings of both Georges Bataille and Georges Dumézil.
8 A similar dynamic motivated Durkheim's criticism of Guyau's proposal that a secular ethical individualism would ultimately replace god-projections (Watts Miller 1996).
9 It is arguable that van Gennep independently came up with a similar idea.
10 Smelser latterly developed similar interests.
11 Alexander (2006b: 60–2) applies a Douglasian concept of pollution to a discussion of "civil narratives of good and evil."
12 Lacan's engagement of Durkheim and Freud is central to the cultural theory of Zizek.

Bibliography

Alexander, J. (1986a) Rethinking Durkheim's intellectual development I: on "Marxism" and the anxiety of being misunderstood, *International Sociology* 1 (1): 91–107.
Alexander, J. (1986b) Rethinking Durkheim's intellectual development II: working out a religious sociology, *International Sociology* 1 (2): 189–201.
Alexander, J. (1988a) Introduction: Durkheimian sociology and cultural studies today, in J. C. Alexander (ed.), *Durkheimian Sociology: Cultural Studies*, Cambridge: Cambridge University Press, 1–21.
Alexander, J. (1988b) Culture and political crisis: "Watergate" and Durkheimian sociology, in J. C. Alexander (ed.), *Durkheimian Sociology: Cultural Studies*, Cambridge: Cambridge University Press, 187–224.
Alexander, J. (2001) Toward a sociology of evil: getting beyond modernist common sense about the alternative to "the good," in M. P. Lara (ed.), *Rethinking Evil*, Berkeley: University of California Press, 153–72.

Alexander, J. (2005) The dark side of modernity: tension relief, splitting, and grace, in E. Ben-Rafael and Y. Sternberg (eds.), *Comparing Modernities: Pluralism versus Homogeneity. Essays in Homage to Shmuel M. Eisenstadt*, Leiden: Brill, 171–82.

Alexander, J. (2006a) Cultural pragmatics: social performance between ritual and strategy, in J. C. Alexander, B. Giesen, and J. L. Mast (eds.), *Social Performance: Symbolic Action, Cultural Pragmatics, and Ritual*, Cambridge: Cambridge University Press, 29–90.

Alexander, J. (2006b) *The Civil Sphere*, New York: Oxford University Press.

Alexander, J., Eyerman, R., Giesen, B., Smelser, N., and Sztompka, P. (eds.) (2004) *Cultural Trauma and Collective Identity*, Berkeley: University of California Press.

Allen, N. J. (2000) *Categories and Classifications: Maussian Reflections on the Social*, London and New York: Berghahn Books.

Baldwin, J. (2008) Lessons from witchetty grubs and Eskimos: the French anthropological context of Jean Baudrillard, *French Cultural Studies* 19: 333–46.

Bataille, G. (1985) The psychological structure of fascism, in Bataille, *Visions of Excess: Selected Writings, 1927–1939*, ed. and tr. A. Stoekl with C. R. Lovitt and D. Leslie, Jr, Minneapolis: University of Minnesota Press, 137–60.

Bataille, G. (1988a) Sacred sociology and the relationships between "society," "organism," and "being," in D. Hollier (ed.), tr. E. Wing, *The College of Sociology (1937–39)*, Minneapolis: University of Minnesota Press, 73–102.

Bataille, G. (1988b) Attraction and repulsion I: tropisms, sexuality, laughter and tears' in D. Hollier (ed.), tr. E. Wing, *The College of Sociology (1937–39)* trans E. Wing, Minneapolis: University of Minnesota Press, 103–12.

Bataille, G. (1988c) Attraction and repulsion II: social structure, in D. Hollier (ed.), tr. E. Wing, *The College of Sociology (1937–39)*, Minneapolis: University of Minnesota Press, 113–24.

Bataille, G. (1988d) *Inner Experience*, tr. L. A. Boldt, Albany: SUNY Press.

Bataille, G. (1989) *Theory of Religion*, tr. R. Hurle, New York: Zone Books.

Bataille, G. (1991) *The Accursed Share 1: Consumption*, tr. R. Hurley, New York: Zone Books.

Bell, C. (1997) *Ritual: Perspectives and Dimensions*, New York: Oxford University Press.

Bellah, R. (1967) Civil religion in America, *Dædalus: Journal of the American Academy of Arts and Sciences* 96 (1): 1–21.

Bellah, R. (1991) *Beyond Belief: Essays on Religion in a Post-Traditionalist World*, Berkeley: University of California Press.

Besnard, P. (ed.) (1983) *The Sociological Domain: The Durkheimians and the Founding of French Sociology*, Cambridge: Cambridge University Press.

Caillois, R. (2001a) *Man, Play and Games*, tr. M. Barash, Urbana and Chicago: University of Illinois Press.

Caillois, R. (2001b) *Man and the Sacred*, tr. M. Barash, Urbana and Chicago: University of Illinois Press.

Datta, R. P. (2008) Politics and existence: totems, *dispositifs* and some striking parallels between Durkheim and Foucault, *Journal of Classical Sociology* 8 (2): 283–305.

Douglas, M. (2002) *Purity and Danger: An Analysis of Concepts of Pollution and Taboo*, London: Routledge.

Dumézil, G. (1988) *The Destiny of a King*, tr. A. Hiltebeitel, Chicago: University of Chicago Press.

Durkheim, É. (1958) *Socialism and Saint-Simon*, Yellow Springs: Antioch Press.

Durkheim, É. (1973a) *Moral Education: A Study in the Theory and Application of the Sociology of Education*, New York: Free Press.

Durkheim, É. (1973b) The intellectual elite and democracy, in R. N. Bellah (ed.), *Emile Durkheim on Morality and Society*, Chicago: University of Chicago Press, 58–60.

Durkheim, É. (2005) The dualism of human nature and its social conditions, *Durkheimian Studies* 11 (1): 35–45.

Durkheim, É. (1974) *Sociology and Philosophy*, tr. E. Pocock, New York: Free Press.

Durkheim, É. (1977) *The Evolution of Educational Thought: Lectures on the Formation and Development of Secondary Education in France*, tr. P. Collins, London: Routledge & Kegan Paul.

Durkheim, É. (1986) Two laws of penal evolution, in S. Lukes and A. Scull (eds.), *Durkheim and the Law*, Oxford: Blackwell.

Durkheim, É. (1992) *Professional Ethics and Civic Morals*, tr. C. Brookfield, intro. B. S. Turner, London: Routledge.

Durkheim, É. (1995) *The Elementary Forms of Religious Life*, tr. K. Fields, New York: Free Press.

Durkheim, É. and Mauss, M. (1967) *Primitive Classification*, tr. R. Needham, Chicago: University of Chicago Press.

Durkheim, É., Jacques-Amédée, Doléris, and Bureau, Paul (1979) A discussion on sex education, in Durkheim (ed. W. S. F. Pickering, tr. H. L. Sutcliffe), *Essays on Morals and Education*, London: Routledge and Kegan Paul, 140–8.

Erikson. K. T. (1966) *Wayward Puritans: A Study in the Sociology of Deviance*, New York: John Wiley.

Fields, K. (1995) Translator's introduction: religion as an eminently social thing, in Durkheim (tr. K. Fields), *The Elementary Forms of Religious Life*, New York: Free Press, xvii–lxxiii.

Frauley, J. and Pearce, F. (eds.) (2007) *Critical Realism and the Social Sciences: Heterodox Elaborations*, Toronto: University of Toronto Press.

Gane, M. (1988) *On Durkheim's Rules of Sociological Method*, London: Routledge.

Gane, M. (1992) *The Radical Sociology of Durkheim and Mauss*, London: Routledge.

Gane, M. (1994) *Harmless Lovers? Gender, Theory and Personal Relationships*, London: Routledge.

Gane, M. (2000) The deconstruction of social action: the "reversal" of Durkheimian methodology from the *Rules* to *Suicide*, in W. S. F. Pickering and G. Walford (eds.), *Durkheim's Suicide: A Century of Research and Debate*, London: Routledge, 22–35.

Gane, M. (2003) Review: Michèle Richman, *Sacred Revolutions, Durkheim and the College de Sociologie*, *Durkheimian Studies* 9: 100–2.

Geertz, C. (1973) Deep play: notes on a Balinese cockfight, in Geertz, *The Interpretation of Cultures*, New York: Basic Books, 412–53.

Geertz, C. (2005) Shifting aims, moving targets: on the anthropology of religion, *Journal of the Royal Anthropological Institute* (new series) 11: 1–15.

Gehlke, C. E. (1915) *Emile Durkheim's Contributions to Sociological Theory*, New York: Columbia University Press.

Giesen, B. (2006) Performing the sacred: a Durkheimian perspective on the performative turn in the social sciences, in J. C. Alexander, B. Giesen, and J. L. Mast (eds.), *Social Performance: Symbolic Action, Cultural Pragmatics, and Ritual*, Cambridge: Cambridge University Press, 325–67.

Girard, R. (1987) *Things Hidden Since the Foundation of the World*, tr. S. Bann and M. Metteer, Stanford: Stanford University Press.

Goffman, E. (1956) The nature of deference and demeanor, *American Anthropologist* 58 (3): 475–99.

Goldberg, C. A. (2008) Introduction to Emile Durkheim's "Anti-Semitism and social crisis," *Sociological Theory* 26 (4): 299–323.

Graham, E. T. (2007) The danger of Durkheim: ambiguity in the theory of social effervescence, *Religion* 37 (1): 26–38.

Hart, Kevin (2004) *The Dark Gaze: Maurice Blanchot and the Sacred* (Chicago: University of Chicago Press).

Hecht, J. M. (2003) *The End of the Soul: Scientific Modernity, Atheism, and Anthropology in France*, New York: Columbia University Press.

Henare, A., Holbraad, M., and Wastell, S. (2006) Introduction: thinking through things, in A. Henare, M. Holbraad and S. Wastell (eds.), *Thinking through Things: Theorising Artefacts Ethnographically*, London: Routledge, 1–31.

Hertz, R. (1960) *Death and the Right Hand*, ed. R. and C. Needham, New York: Free Press.

Hertz, R. (1985) St. Besse: a study of an Alpine cult, in S. Wilson (ed. and tr.), *Saints and Their Cults: Studies in Religious Sociology, Folklore and History*, Cambridge: Cambridge University Press Archiv.

Hertz, R. (1994) *Sin and Expiation*, tr. R. Parkin, preface W. S. F. Pickering, Oxford: British Center for Durkheimian Studies, Occasional Paper 2.

Holbraad, M. (2006) The power of powder: multiplicity and motion in the divinatory cosmology of Cuban Ifá (or mana, again), in A. Henare (ed.), *Thinking Through Things: Theorising Artefacts Ethnographically*, London: Routledge, 189–225.

Hooker, R. (1888) *The Laws of Ecclesiastical Polity: Books I–IV*, London: Routledge.

Hubert, H. (1999) *Essay on Time: A Brief Study of the Representation of Time in Religion and Magic*, ed. R. Parkin, intro. F.-A. Isambert, Oxford and New York: Berghahn Books.

Hubert, H. and Mauss, M. (1964) *Sacrifice: Its Nature and Function*, Chicago: University of Chicago Press.

Hunt, L. (1988) The sacred and the French Revolution, in J. C. Alexander (ed.), *Durkheimian Sociology: Cultural Studies*, Cambridge: Cambridge University Press, 25–43.

Joas, H. (2001) The gift of life: the sociology of religion in Talcott Parsons' late work, *Journal of Classical Sociology* 1 (1): 127–41.

Joas, H. (2008a) *Do We Need Religion? On the Experience of Self-Transcendence*, Boulder: Paradigm Publishers, Yale Cultural Sociology Series.

Joas, H. (2008b) Punishment and respect: the sacralization of the person and its endangerment, tr. S. Susen, *Journal of Classical Sociology* 8 (2): 159–77.

Jonas, R. (2000) *France and the Cult of the Sacred Heart: An Epic Tale for Modern Times*, Berkeley: University of California Press.

Lacroix, B. (1979) *The Elementary Forms of Religious Life* as a reflection on power (objet pouvoir), *Critique of Anthropology* 4: 87–103.

Lukes, Steven (1973) *Émile Durkheim: His Life and Work. A Historical and Critical Study*, Harmondsworth: Penguin.

Maffesoli, M. (1993) *The Shadow of Dionysus: A Contribution to the Sociology of the Orgy*, Albany: State University of New York Press.

Maffesoli, M. (1996) *The Time of the Tribes: The Decline of Individualism in Mass Society*, London: Sage.

Mauss, M. (1972) *A General Theory of Magic*, London: Routledge and Kegan Paul.

Mauss, M. (1985) A category of the human mind: the notion of person; the notion of self, tr. W. D. Halls, in M. Carrithers, S. Collins, and S. Lukes (eds.), *The Category of the Person: Anthropology, Philosophy, History*, Cambridge: Cambridge University Press, 1–25.

Mauss, M. (2002) *The Gift: The Form and Reason for Exchange in Archaic Societies*, tr. W. D. Halls, intro. M. Douglas. London: Routledge.

Mauss, M. and Beuchat, H. (1979) *Seasonal Variations of the Eskimo: A Study in Social Morphology*, London: Routledge & Kegan Paul.

Mellor, P. A. (2000) Rational choice or sacred contagion? "Rationality," "non-rationality" and Religion, *Social Compass* 47 (2): 273–92.

Mellor, P. A. (2004) *Religion, Realism and Social Theory: Making Sense of Society*, Thousand Oaks: Sage.

Mellor, P. A. and C. Shilling (1997) *Re-forming the Body: Religion, Community and Modernity*, London: Sage.

Mellor, P.A. and Shilling, C. (1998) Lorsque l'on jette de l'huile sur le feu ardent: secularisation, homo duplex et retour du sacré, *Social Compass* 45 (2): 297–320.

Mestrovic, S. (1985) Anomia and sin in Durkheim's thought, *Journal for the Scientific Study of Religion* 24: 119–36.

Mestrovic, S. (1988) Durkheim, Schopenhauer and the relationship between goals and means: reversing the assumptions in the Parsonian theory of rational action, *Sociological Inquiry* 58 (2): 163–79.

Morrison, K. (2001) The disavowal of the social in the American reception of Durkheim, *Journal of Classical Sociology* 1 (1): 95–125.

Muir, E. (2005) *Ritual in Early Modern Europe* (2nd edn.), Cambridge: Cambridge University Press.

Neubert, F. (2008) Indicating commitment: the notion of *dépense* in the study of religion and ritual, *Journal of Classical Sociology* 8 (2): 306–20.

Nielsen, D. A. (1998) *Three Faces of God: Society, Religion, and the Categories of Totality in the Philosophy of Emile Durkheim*, Albany: SUNY.

O'Neill, John (1990) Religion and postmodernism: the Durkheimian bond in Bell and Jameson, in G. Shapiro (ed.), *After the Future: Postmodern Times and Places*, Albany: State University of New York Press, 285–99.

Paoletti, G. (2000) Representation and belief: Durkheim's rationalism and the Kantian tradition, in W. S. F. Pickering (ed.), *Durkheim and Representations*, London: Routledge, 118–35.

Parkin, R. (1996) *The Dark Side of Humanity: The Work of Robert Hertz and Its Legacy*, Amsterdam: Harwood Academic Publishers.

Parsons, T. (1937) *The Structure of Social Action: A Study in Social Theory with Special Reference to a Group of Recent European Writers*, New York: McGraw-Hill.

Pearce, F. (2006) A modest companion to Durkheim, *Durkheimian Studies* (new series) 12: 149–60.

Pickering, W. S. F. (1979) Gaston Richard: collaborateur et adversaire, *Revue française de sociologie* 20: 163–82.

Pickering, W. S. F. (1984) *Durkheim's Sociology of Religion: Themes and Theories*, London: Routledge.

Pickering, W. S. F. (2000) Representations as understood by Durkheim: an introductory sketch, in W. S. F. Pickering (ed.), *Durkheim and Representation*, London: Routledge.

Pickering, W. S. F. (ed.) (2002) *Durkheim Today*, intro. K. Thompson, Oxford: Durkheim Press, Oxford and New York: Beghahn Books.

Pickering, W. S. F. (2006) Introduction: Durkheim's contribution to the debate on the separation of church and state in 1905, *Durkheimian Studies* (new series) 12: 8–10.

Pickering, W. S. F. (2008a) Looking backwards and to the future, in W. S. F. Pickering and M. Rosati (eds.) *Suffering and Evil: The Durkheimian Legacy*, Oxford and New York: Berghahn Books, 163–77.

Pickering, W. S. F. (2008b) Reflections on the death of Emile Durkheim, in W. S. F. Pickering and M. Rosati (eds.), *Suffering and Evil: The Durkheimian Legacy*, Oxford and New York, Berghahn Books, 11–27.

Pickering, W. S. F. (2008c) The response of Catholic and Protestant thinkers to the work of Emile Durkheim: with special reference to les formes elementaires, *Durkheimian Studies* (new series) 14: 59–93.

Ramp, W. (1998) Effervescence, differentiation and representation in *The Elementary Forms*, in N. J. Allen, W. S. F. Pickering, and W. Watts Miller (eds.), *On Durkheim's Elementary Forms of Religious Life*, London: Routledge, 136–48.

Ramp, W. (1999) Durkheim and Foucault on the genesis of the disciplinary society, in M. S. Cladis (ed.), *Durkheim and Foucault on Education and Punishment*, Oxford and New York: Durkheim Press and Berghahn Books, 71–103.

Ramp, W. (2000) The moral discourse of Durkheim's *Suicide*, in W. S. F. Pickering and G. Walford (eds.), *Durkheim's Suicide: A Century of Research and Debate*, London: Routledge, 81–96.

Ramp, W. (2008) *Le malin génie*: Durkheim, Bataille and the prospect of a sociology of evil, in W. S. F. Pickering and M. Rosati (eds.), *Suffering and Evil: The Durkheimian Legacy*, Oxford and New York: Berghahn Books, 118–35.

Richman, M. (1997) Rejection and renewal: Durkheim in the 20th century, *Modern & Contemporary France* 5 (4), 409–19.

Richman, M. (2002) *Sacred Revolutions: Durkheim and the Collège de Sociologie*, Minneapolis: University of Minnesota Press.

Richman, M. (2003) Myth, power and the sacred: anti-utilitarianism in the *Collège de sociologie* 1937–9, *Economy and Society* 32 (1): 29–47.

Riley, A. T. (2005) "Renegade Durkheimians" and the transgressive left sacred, in J. C. Alexander and P. Smith (eds.), *The Cambridge Companion to Durkheim*, Cambridge: Cambridge University Press, 274–301.

Riley, A. T. (2006) The institutional "missing links" in the genealogical tree connecting Durkheim to Foucault: a micro-sociology of the journals and personal relationships that made poststructuralism Durkheimian, paper presented at the annual meeting of the American Sociological Association, Montreal, Canada, Aug. 10, www.allacademic.com/meta/p105555_index.html, accessed March 16, 2009.

Rosati, M. (2004) Book review: *Sacred Revolutions: Durkheim and the College de Sociologie*, *European Journal of Social Theory* 7 (4): 552–5.

Rosati, M. (2008) Inhabiting no-man's land: Durkheim and modernity, *Journal of Classical Sociology* 8 (2): 233–61.

Shilling, C. (2005) Embodiment, emotions and the foundations of social order: Durkheim's enduring contribution, in J. C. Alexander and P. D. Smith (eds.), *The Cambridge Companion to Durkheim*, Cambridge: Cambridge University Press, 211–38.

Shilling, C. and Mellor, P. (2001) *The Sociological Ambition: Elementary Forms of Social and Moral Life*, Thousand Oaks: Sage.

Smith, C. (2008) Future directions in the sociology of religion, *Social Forces* 86 (4): 1561–89.

Smith, P. and Alexander, J. C. (2007) Imagining Durkheim: The Cambridge Companion and two recent review essays, *Durkheimian Studies* (new series) 13: 125–9.

Stedman Jones, S. (2000) Representation in Durkheim's masters: Kant and Renouvier I. Representation, reality and the question of science, in W. S. F. Pickering (ed.), *Durkheim and Representation*, London: Routledge, 37–58.

Steiner, P. (1994) *La Sociologie de Durkheim*, Paris: La Découverte.

Stock-Morton, P. (1988) *Moral Education for a Secular Society: The Development of Morale Laïque in Nineteenth-Century France*, Albany: SUNY.

Stone, D. (2004) Genocide as transgression, *European Journal of Social Theory* 7 (1): 45–65.

Strenski, I. (1997) *Durkheim and the Jews of France*, Chicago: University of Chicago Press.

Strenski, I. (2006) *The New Durkheim*, Piscataway: Rutgers University Press.

Tiryakian, E. A. (1962) *Sociologism and Existentialism: Two Perspectives on the Individual and Society*, Englewood Cliffs: Prentice-Hall.

Tiryakian, E. A. (1988) From Durkheim to Managua: revolutions as religious revivals, in J. C. Alexander (ed.), *Durkheimian Sociology: Cultural Studies*, Cambridge: Cambridge University Press, 44–65.

Turner, B. (2005) Talcott Parsons's sociology of religion and the expressive revolution, *Journal of Classical Sociology* 5 (3): 303–18.

Turner, V. (1969) *The Ritual Process; Structure and Anti-structure*, Chicago: Aldine.

Turner, V. (1974) *Dramas, Fields and Metaphors: Symbolic action in human society*, Ithaca: Cornell University Press.

Watts Miller, W. (1996) *Durkheim, Morals and Modernity*, London: Routledge.

Watts Miller, W. (2002) Alla ricerca di solidarietà e sacro, in M. Rosati and A. Santambrogia, (eds.), *Durkheim: Contributi per una rilettura Critica*, Rome: Meltemi, 141–68.

Wernick, A. (2001) *Auguste Comte and the Religion of Humanity: The Post-theistic Program of French Social Theory*, Cambridge: Cambridge University Press.

Wexler, P. (2007) Mystical Jewish sociology, *Journal for the Study of Religions and Ideologies* 6 (18): 206–17.

3

The Functional Theory of Religion

VICTOR LIDZ

The functional theory of religion focuses on relationships between religion and other social institutions, in both synchronic and diachronic perspectives. Its guiding notion has been that religions shape the values that ground the major institutions of societies and that, reciprocally, many practical circumstances in a society condition its religious life. Functional theory has particularly emphasized long term effects of religion on other institutions, including strata formation and legal, political, economic, educational, and cultural institutions. In the cases of the world religions, such as, Christianity or Buddhism, functional theory has focused on religion's part in shaping trends of development for entire civilizations.

This chapter examines the writings of three major contributors to the functional theory of religion, Talcott Parsons, Niklas Luhmann, and Robert N. Bellah.

TALCOTT PARSONS

Parsons' early masterwork, *The Structure of Social Action* (Parsons, 1937), established the basic framework for the functional theory of religion. It found this framework in a theoretical convergence among four early twentieth-century social scientists, Alfred Marshall, Vilfredo Pareto, Émile Durkheim, and Max Weber. Parsons argued that all four figures had treated norms as well as ends, means, and conditions as categories essential to *all* social scientific analysis, making the concept of norms a universal category for sociology. Every sociological analysis must attend to normative regulation of actors' choices of ends and of means toward their ends. At the macrosocial level, attention to normative orders is essential for understanding social institutions and the functioning of society. Durkheim and Weber played the major roles in Parsons' convergence argument, and both identified religious beliefs and institutions as central to normative orders.

Durkheim's *The Elementary Forms of Religious Life*, Parsons argued (1937: ch. 11), focuses on "ultimate values" as the core of normative orders maintained by members of society. A normative order's capacity to bind the conduct of members of society depends on what Durkheim called "moral authority." He sought to understand the source of moral authority in terms that apply to all societies. Durkheim started with a distinction between the sacred, or things "set apart" for special respect, and the profane or everyday. All cultures imbue sacred things with powers that make them dangerous if not given due respect. Religion is a system of beliefs and practices relating to sacred entities. Beliefs about the sacred are "existential references," not norms, as they do not relate to practical action (Parsons 1937: 422). Their concern is not with the empirical world, but with "non-empirical reality," as in the idea of Zeus. Yet, as symbols, they "concretize" religious experience and attract special attitudes of respect. Societies are moral communities that share ideals, and sacred beliefs provide the special respect that elevates ideas into ideals. It is by common possession of sacred ideals that a society becomes in its essence "a religious phenomenon."

Parsons relates religion to social control, noting with Durkheim that members of society impose religious beliefs on one another. The attitude of respect for sacred things is obligatory; a person who fails to show respect is sanctioned. Religious rites engage the members of society in displaying respect for the sacred. In performing rites, an individual goes through special procedures to exit the profane world, engage the sacred, and manipulate sacred symbols. Religious ritual expresses ultimate-value attitudes collectively and what Durkheim called its "effervescence" strengthens "sentiments of respect" for them (Parsons 1937: 433–7). Feelings of respect give moral authority to ultimate values and the broader sets of norms, integrated with the values, that regulate the details of everyday relationships.

While Durkheim probed elementary and universal aspects of the relation between religion and society, Weber gave little attention to the "gardens of magic" in religions of simpler societies. He concentrated on world religions based on transcendental conceptions of the sacred and capable of transforming traditional normative orders.

Parsons' (1937: ch. 14) discussion of Weber started with his analysis of the Protestant ethic and its transformation of the economy, politics, law, and social stratification. Weber's understanding of rationalistic bourgeois capitalism encompassed the continuously profit-oriented enterprise, its bureaucratic organization independent of the state, use of formally free labor, methodical exploitation of technology, reliance on rationalistic law regulating property and contract, and the price mechanism (Parsons 1937: 508ff.). Although capitalism has existed in many historical forms, this combination of elements never existed before modern times.

Weber argued that the distinctive characteristics of modern capitalism emerged only under the sway of a *spirit* of modern capitalism, an economic ethic legitimated by a set of ultimate values. Against materialist explanations, he maintained that a spirit of modern capitalism arose first, embracing the earning of money as a duty, not a tolerated evil; the rational pursuit of profit by whatever ethical means, including innovation; and the highly disciplined expenditure of human effort (Parsons 1937: 513ff.). Weber illustrated this economic ethic with Benjamin Franklin, who, raised in a Puritan family, became an entrepreneur before modern capitalist institutions existed.

Weber turned to the evolution of Calvinist ethics toward endorsing disciplined labor in worldly callings and ascetic saving of capital, both factors favoring the growth of capitalism (Parsons 1937: 515). Calvinist theology promoted this evolution with its idea of an absolutely transcendental Creator God, the doctrine of predestined damnation or salvation, and the belief that humankind's mission is to create the kingdom of God on earth. Yet, Weber emphasized not Calvinism's theology but its shaping of the religious interests of believers (Parsons 1937: 521ff.). Not knowing whether one was saved or damned created intolerable stress, so committed Puritans presumed that apparent contribution to building the kingdom of God on earth signified one's status as saved. Presumptive saints experienced justification in working hard, saving capital, investing methodically, and exercising discipline over workers, who might be damned.

Having demonstrated a connection between Calvinism and modern capitalism, Parsons observed, Weber sought further proof not in more detailed historical studies, but in comparative research on civilizations with sophisticated cultures and great wealth that did not develop modern capitalism. Parsons discussed his analyses of Confucian China (Parsons 1937: 542–52) and Hindu India (pp. 552–63).

In traditional China, an ethic of parental authority, filial piety, and duty to superiors culminating in the emperor pervaded the entire society. Regarded as the Son of Heaven, the emperor mediated between the cosmic order of Heaven and the human realm. Mandarins, educated in traditional Confucian culture emphasizing ceremonial proprieties, nearly monopolized political administration. They provided justice through their courts, collected taxes, and maintained local status orders, but their effectiveness was limited by lack of administrative staffs. Merchant groups, when they accumulated wealth, sought prestige by buying land, adopting "idle" gentry lifestyles, and raising sons to become mandarins. Continuous capitalism was disvalued and the status order prevented the emergence of a true bourgeoisie.

The Chinese ethic was worldly, valuing wealth, comfort, and harmony. It supported education in ceremonial propriety and the life of "self-controlled, dignified, polite" gentleman living harmoniously within the accepted Confucian order. The ethic stressed rational adjustment to the given world, not, as in Puritanism, mastery of the world in the service of God.

Weber's analysis of India focused on the caste system. The caste system had not been present in India from time immemorial, but was created by Brahmans and their religious ethic. The castes were endogamous, largely local, and hereditary, and the system of castes was "extraordinarily heterogeneous," yet hierarchically ordered in terms of castes' degrees of ritual purity. The status of a caste in terms of relative ritual purity set the etiquettes for its members interaction with members of other castes. Traditional lines of work figured importantly in the castes' statuses. At the top of hierarchy were Brahmans, priestly groups whose ethic of ritual purity grounded the entire order. They often served princes as advisors and administrators, but did not hold public authority in their own right. Some castes included merchants, but the caste system prevented them from becoming bourgeois and traditionalistic work practices blocked rational capitalism.

The caste order was supported by the doctrines of dharma and karma. Dharma stipulated that people must live by the traditional duties, including ritual duties, of their castes. Breaking from these duties led to expulsion from the caste and loss of social status. Conduct with respect to caste dharma affected one's karma or "permanent indestructible effects" (Parsons 1937: 558) of one's actions upon one's soul, and, given belief in transmigration of souls, one's fate in future incarnations. Caste-appropriate conduct enhanced one's karma, leading to future incarnations in higher castes, whereas violating dharma could result in demotion in caste. Hindu beliefs thus reinforced the traditionalism of the entire caste system.

From Weber's studies, Parsons appropriated two themes for his own theory. First was the tension between traditionalism and rationalism, including the ways rationalism can overcome traditionalism and create new social orders or render traditional institutions sacred and resistant to change. Second was the idea of directions of rationalization. Ethical prophecy, as in the Old Testament prophets, involves a prophet who presents himself as "the instrument of a divine will" (Parsons 1937: 568) conveying commands and norms to followers. If God is conceived as transcendent, the ethical prophet can initiate breaks with tradition and promote a new normative order, action in the world having great meaning. This is inner-worldly asceticism, held with intensity by Puritanism. By contrast, exemplary prophets model the way to salvation. Religious orientation becomes mystical, worldly affairs are radically devalued, and escape from worldly entanglements results, as in monasticism.

Integrating Weber with Durkheim, Parsons derived a framework for analyzing relationships between religion and normative structures of societies. Societies must be moral communities in order to sustain their solidarity. Religious beliefs provide principles for moral communities, while religious rituals promote commitment to the principles. In long-term perspective, religious ethics establish moral impetus and direction for rationalizing societal institutions. In adopting these general propositions, Parsons was influenced by their empirical validity as well as their importance in integrating a theoretical system.

The four-function paradigm

In the 1950s and 1960s, Parsons developed the "four-function paradigm," a radically different conception from previous lists of functional requisites of social systems based on empirical generalization. Derived by analyzing the concept of *action system*, the functions define four general dimensions or aspects of all empirical action systems. This analytic approach permits compilation of knowledge about how each of the functions is served across empirical settings and about general relationships among the functions. The four functions are pattern maintenance, integration, goal attainment, and adaptation. Their best known application defines four functionally specialized subsystems of society (cf. Parsons 1961, 1966):

- The economy (adaptation) involves production and allocation of basic resources for use by individuals and collectivities. Its institutions include markets for labor and capital, entrepreneurial roles, the legal complexes of property, contract, credit, and employment, and the organizational structures of business firms.
- The polity (goal attainment) coordinates the pursuit of society's collective ends. Government agencies at all levels, including the administrative, executive, legislative, and judicial institutions, are primary components. Various

non-public organizations and the participation of citizens are also central to modern polities.

- The societal community (integration) encompasses social classes, status and 'life style' groups, ethnic and other 'primordial' groups dynamically interrelated under law and informal norms to shape a society's form of solidarity. Phenomena of cleavage and conflict are important as well as solidarity.
- The fiduciary system (pattern maintenance) promotes the development, continuation, and transmission (or reproduction) of a society's values and shared culture. Institutions of religion, family and kinship, socialization, and education make up the fiduciary system. Change in fiduciary systems, especially in religious ethics, has been the greatest force of long term institutional change.

The fiduciary system was conceived as a set of latent structures that establish a society's identity in all of its components, analogous to a genome's effect on all of an organism's tissues and cells. The core of a society's fiduciary system consists of its value system, which derives a normative consistency from highly generalized premises, such as, Confucian "inner-worldly mysticism" mandating adjustment to worldly conditions as they are. The general premises are complemented, in a tree-like structure, by multiple levels of differentiated values that specify their implications for specific institutional settings. The tree-like structure penetrates from the pattern maintenance subsystem of a society through the pattern maintenance sectors of the other subsystems (economy, polity, and societal community) to their functionally defined subsystems. One implication is that the values of different subsystems, while sharing a common pattern, emphasize different contents, and there may be conflict between values of different subsystems, as between ideologies common among business executives and among university faculty.

Parsons held that Norbert Wiener's cybernetics clarified the special role of value systems in the regulation of action systems. Wiener demonstrated that in mechanical systems elements high in information can control or guide elements high in energy, as when a helmsman keeps a steamship on course or a thermostat controls a furnace's output. Parsons observed that Freud had discerned a human cybernetic relationship when he compared the ego's relation to the id to a rider guiding a horse. Freud also noted that riders can lose control and horses become runaways. Similarly, ids can break free of the civilizing controls of egos. Control relationships are inherently problematic, because energic mechanisms can break free of informational guidance.

The tree-structure of a society's value system, Parsons argued, provides society's informational controls. Core values, articulated in religious ethics, establish a pattern of evaluative preferences by which subordinate values and norms shape social institutions throughout the society's economic, political, integrative, and lower-level pattern maintenance subsystems. Parsons also emphasized that cybernetic relationships involve two-way dynamics: control, but, equally important, conditioning relationships, set by the limits of energic elements. A ship with a weak engine may not stay on course in a storm, regardless of how capably steered. The institutionalization of a religious ethic may break down when conditioning factors are disrupted, as in times of economic, political, or stratificational stress, such as, the French, Russian, or Chinese Revolutions. Parsons suggested that cybernetics resolves the division in sociology between theories emphasizing "ideal" factors, including religion, and theories emphasizing "material" factors, portraying both as essential and complementary, and with many grades between the purely ideal and purely material.

American society

In the late 1950s, Parsons planned a volume using the four-function paradigm to develop a comprehensive analysis of American society. Several draft chapters were completed before his collaborator, Winston White, left academic life, ending the project. Three chapters on American values are Parsons' only attempt fully to explicate his idea of a societal value system (Parsons and White, unpublished).

The analysis of American values has three key aspects. First, the American value-pattern is placed in a series of cultural variants in Western civilization, starting with ancient Hebrew and Greek elements integrated into early Christian thought. The analysis emphasizes continuities, such as, the conception of God as a transcendent Creator, the valuation of historical change, and theology incorporating logic. It also underscores emergent changes, including ascetic monasticism in medieval Europe, the Reformation turn to inner-worldliness, and the ascetic Protestantism of the Puritans. Parsons (1968) later wrote a similar but more detailed account of the development of Christianity.

Second, Parsons argued that a value-pattern of "instrumental activism" has generally been stable in America since colonial times. Stress on *pattern* stability is complemented by analysis of change in the *content* of specific value complexes related to such changes as industrialization in the nineteenth century and the growth of governmental activism in the 1930s.

Third, several levels in the value system are distinguished, from cultural premises about the nature of humankind and its purposes on earth, to general moral principles of social relationships, to the ideal characteristics of society, to ideals pertaining to specific societal subsystems and institutions. The analysis also explored the functional differentiation of the value system, attending to tensions between values of different institutional settings.

The characterization of a unifying pattern of American values started with the ascetic Protestant heritage of most seventeenth- and eighteenth-century colonists. The Protestant doctrine of each individual's direct responsibility to God, without mediation by any human institution, even churches, for implementing His commandments grounded a profound individualism. Over the centuries, this individualism has led to many Constitutional, legal, and customary protections for individual autonomy. It also grounded a profound activism, as individuals, defined themselves as instruments of God, responsible for bringing society into closer relationship to His ideals. Parsons term for this value-pattern, "instrumental activism," highlights the commitment to mastering everything in the human condition to the extent possible. Instrumental activism stresses the development and perfection of *means* for social action. At the macro-social level, it gives development of the economy priority over other societal subsystems. More than in other societies, economic institutions gain the lion's share of resources. Success in economic roles becomes the primary basis of status-recognition and social stratification. Instrumental activism has religious dimensions, yet many secular strivings derive their meaning from congruent expectations of mastery, whether athletes in their training, scholars in their research, entrepreneurs in expanding businesses, or homeowners purchasing appliances to make housework efficient.

Parsons (1960) also described what he called the denominational pattern of American religious organization. Impressed by Will Herberg's argument that American society, formerly Protestant in its religious identity, had after World War II integrated Catholics and Jews to a new degree, Parsons interpreted his conclusions by reference to Ernst Troeltsch's (1960) distinction between churches and sects. Churches coincide in membership with politically organized societies, generally taking part in legitimating state institutions. Sects stand ethically outside politically organized society, viewed as corrupt, and withdraw from or commit to changing the societal order. Parsons understood American religions to be neither churches nor sects, but a third form, denominations. American religions do not expect to coincide with the society in membership, as all are minorities. Few stand in sectarian opposition to the social order. Most broadly accept American institutions – their democratic aspects, economic activism, and relative openness to social mobility – while remaining critical of particular policies and institutions. They also expect recognition and acceptance for themselves and their members on a basis of formal equality.

Religion and social evolution

In the 1960s, Parsons proclaimed a revival of the theory of social evolution and began to write about social change over the sweep of human history and in comparative perspective. The evolutionary project resulted in two small books (Parsons 1966, 1971; see also Lidz and Parsons 1972), which together outline a six stage theory of societal development:

1   small non-literate societies without hierarchical structures;
2   larger non-literate tribes with central chiefdoms, simple class divisions, local cults, and small produce markets;
3   "archaic" societies with literate priestly groups, religious belief systems of cosmic scope, institutions of kingship and social classes, continuous agriculture, craft workshops, and extensive trade and markets;
4   "historic" empires legitimated in terms of world religions, with multi-ethnic populations, extensive systems of political authority, partially rationalized legal systems, upper classes with great wealth, and economies that concentrate great wealth and support large populations;
5   the "early modern" nation-states of Europe, legitimated in terms of Reformation or Counter-Reformation cultures, with monarchies and landed aristocracies, urban populations and an emerging bourgeoisie, nascent science and technology, and more active economic production;
6   "late modern" societies with inner-worldly religious and moral orientations, industrial production, various degrees of democratic institutions, expanding middle classes, systems of higher education, and advanced science and technology.

Parsons recognized two forms of society that fell between his other types and profoundly shaped human history. He used the term "seed-bed societies" for classical Greece and ancient Israel (Parsons 1966: ch. 6). Their institutions were archaic, yet they became centers of "historic" cultural innovation. Western and more recently world civilization have been affected by the Hebraic idea of a universal Creator God and ethical prophecy and by Greek conceptions of citizenship in the *polis* and *logos* as a standard of validity for cultural beliefs. Parsons also acknowledged the special status of Medieval society in Europe. Its political organization, fragmented by feudal hierarchies based on vassalage, was archaic. But its Christian religion, monastic asceticism, Roman legal tradition, commercial and eventually bourgeois-dominated cities, and nascent universities led to Renaissance and Reformation Europe (Parsons 1971: ch. 3).

The analysis of modern civilization highlighted the emergence since the Reformation of a system of societies with similar institutions, yet distinctive differences among them (Parsons 1971: chs. 4–7). Growth of the system has been due to the outward press of factors originally centered in Northwestern Europe, the United Kingdom, and North America, but by the late twentieth-century extended to most of the world. These factors include: inner-worldly values of Christian origin, but often in secular ideologies deriving from the Enlightenment; the appeal of democratic political forms to expanding middle classes; and the dynamic effects of economic markets and enterprises mobilizing raw materials, labor, and capital on a global basis. Parsons emphasized that societies around the world are developing variants of modern institutional orders adjusted to their particular value systems, often ones created by reordering heritages based in world religions. Analysis of religiously and ideologically rooted value systems is essential to understanding how particular societies establish niches in the evolving international system. Parsons attended particularly to variation among European societies, to institutional differences between the United States and the then Soviet Union, and to Japan as a model non-Western modern society.

For each evolutionary type of society, Parsons included comparative materials to suggest ranges of variation. In discussing archaic societies, he compared the ancient Egyptian and Mesopotamian kingdoms. His analysis of historic empires compared Chinese, Indian, Islamic, and Roman civilizations. His comparisons examined institutional differences in all four subsystems of the various societies. While emphasizing the independent importance of structures in each subsystem of society, Parsons argued that focus on long-term courses of societal development leads causal analysis to focus on cybernetically controlling factors. Thus, his analyses of archaic Egypt and Mesopotamia concentrate on their religious cosmologies and contrasting beliefs about kings' mediating roles between the sacred and profane orders. His analyses of historic empires emphasized religious beliefs and ethics as well as status groups that were the chief "carriers" of religious values, following Weber's treatments of the Chinese mandarins, Indian Brahmans, and Roman senatorial class.

The general action system

Parsons' conception of the social system is *analytic* in that it abstracts the system of interaction, social relationships, and institutions from the concrete social action of individuals. A logical implication is that social systems must be complemented by other systems that also shape social action. In the 1960s, he developed a four function analysis of what he called the general action system (Parsons 1977: ch. 10), the system of components based on meaning that directly contribute to social action. In a late formulation:

- Culture is pattern maintaining, as core beliefs and values establish principles for the entire action system.
- The social system is integrative, with its institutional components stabilizing relationships among actors over time.
- Personalities are goal attaining, their motivational structures enabling individuals to exercise *agency* in implementing action.
- The mind, differentiated from personality as G. H. Mead (1934) distinguished it from self, is adaptive. Mind mobilizes the intelligent capabilities and knowledge of individuals as resources for action.

Concrete social action draws upon elements of all four systems. Parsons explored ways in which certain general types of action draw on specific components of culture, social systems, personalities, and minds. He analyzed in detail the "cognitive complex" (Parsons and Platt 1973) involved in creating intellectually disciplined knowledge. There is also a "religious complex" that includes cultural, social, personality, and mental components of religious action. Several essays (in Parsons 1978) attempted cultural analysis of religious beliefs and "cultural codes" as sources of social values and implied a religious complex, but did not specifically formulate it (Lidz 1982 proposed a formulation).

The human condition paradigm

In the 1970s, Parsons developed the "human condition paradigm" for analyzing the general action system's location within extra-action environments and their effects on human social life. The paradigm treats the general action system as integrative for a system that includes the physico-chemical environment as adaptive, the biosphere or environment of all living things, including human organisms, as goal attaining, and the "telic system" as pattern maintaining (Parsons 1978: ch. 15). The telic system is a reformulation of "ultimate reality" that had long figured in Parsons' interpretations of Weber (Parsons 1937, 1963).

Parsons made two new points in formulating the telic system. First, openness to problems of meaning – to concerns over the nature of ultimate reality, the significance of one's existence in the cosmos, one's fate as saved or damned, or ultimate justice in the world (theodicy) – may affect any social relationship or institution. Where normative orders fail to secure the meaningfulness of social action, problems of meaning may arise, erode personal or collective commitments, and stimulate processes of change. Parsons held that problems of ultimate meaning are especially salient to religious belief and action, but hardly limited to them. They may arise with frustration in economic or political action, in relation to social status, in scientific work, or with illness, disability, or impending death.

Second, Weber's concepts of inner-worldly and other-worldly, asceticism and mysticism can be treated as defining transcendental limits of possible orientations to the human condition. As categories of the telic, they fall beyond direct human experience and empirical knowledge, but can be known through indirect evidence of limits to the orientations of actual socio-cultural systems, especially religious systems. Parsons ventured that there can be no human orientation to action that is not simultaneously in some degrees inner-worldly or other-worldly and ascetic or mystical. Transcendentally grounded religions establish specific orientations among myriad possibilities within these parameters. Such religious orientations fatefully shape the institutional orders that may rationally be legitimated as well as the problems of meaning that may be experienced by individuals living within them.

Niklas Luhmann

For Luhmann, articulating a systems theory was the necessary starting point for all sociological analysis. His conception of systems derived from engineering, second order cybernetics, evolutionary biology, physiology, and macro-economics (Luhmann 1995). Especially important was the biologist, Humberto Maturana's conception of *autopoesis* or self-reproduction of a system (Luhmann 1998, 2002a). Parsons' theory was also a key reference, but Luhmann rejected his four function theory and understanding of cybernetic hierarchy, thus his attempt to understand religion in terms of a general societal function and high-in-information controls over societal development (Luhmann 1982a, 1995). While criticizing Weber's analysis of ascetic Protestantism's part in the development of modern institutions, Luhmann sustained the interest in the rationalization of institutions and its religious sources.

Luhmann viewed the evolution of systems as a fundamental reality. Following Maturana, he treated evolution as a result of three independent but interrelated processes: variation in the operations of a system, selection among variants, and stabilization of selected variants over time (Luhmann 1995, 1998). By reference to these three general processes, he claimed that social evolution is continuous with biological evolution. Like biological systems, societies must manage their relations with their environments, including other societies, the personal systems of members, and physical, chemical, and biological environments. A society with internally differentiated systems, for example, political and economic systems, must also manage their relations with one. Processes of variation and selection result in differentiated and autonomous systems, and stabilization of an autonomous system requires continuation of its *autopoesis* in relation to multiple internal and external environments.

As a newly differentiated system gains autonomy from its environment, it reduces the complexity of that environment. Its *autopoesis* achieves a simpler, more efficient manner of operating, based on a new functionally specific rationality, for example, efficiency in economic transactions or methodical demonstration in science (Luhmann 1995). In modern societies, many functional systems maintain *autopoeses* and rationalities or principles of coordination independent of other systems. There is no longer one rationality, as economy, polity, law, religion, science, and so forth, maintain separate rationalities (Luhmann 1995, 2002a).

Luhmann adapted Parsons' idea that, besides money mediating economic relationships, there are other symbolic media, such as, political power and influence, that operate in other societal subsystems. In Luhmann's theory, every differentiated system requires its own "communications medium" to represent its internal conditions to environing systems (Luhmann 1995: ch. 4). The various media are integral to the *autopoeses* of their respective systems, to their salient forms of rationality, and to communication among systems (Luhmann 2002a: part 3).

For Luhmann, a religious system gains differentiation through the same general processes as other systems – variation, selection, and stabilization – but its rationality and communications medium are specific to its functions. Tracing a religious system's development requires understanding its characteristic rationality and form of medium as well as the consequences of its autonomy for other systems, especially in modern society with its many autonomous systems (Luhmann 2002b).

Luhmann's evolutionary analysis of religious systems did not emphasize a clear sequence of stages, but did concentrate on transitions from archaic religions to religions with rationalized dogmas to contemporary "secularized" religions emphasizing private belief (Luhmann 1982b, 2002b). He related these transitions to effects on economies, polities, law, science, and the arts, emphasizing rationalization in all systems. His examples came mainly from European Christianity, mostly Catholicism, with some discussion of the Reformation. His empirical base is narrow, and one may ask how far his insights extend to non-Western religions.

Citing studies of African and New World tribes as well as ancient Egypt and Mesopotamia, Luhmann characterizes archaic religions as having loosely integrated cycles of myths and rituals that sustain intense religious involvement. They also provide ideological grounding for political, economic, and legal systems that are so closely integrated that they scarcely operate autonomously (Luhmann 1984). Religious systems began to develop autonomy from other institutional systems by criticizing ancient kings, their courts, and the social justice they provided. Luhmann mentions the Buddha's criticisms of the Hindu caste order and Old Testament prophets' criticisms of kings and their courts. The prophets' criticisms led to a conception of God as universal, omnipotent Creator later incorporated in Christianity, a process of dogmatization that stabilized autonomous rationality for the religious system, differentiating it from other systems (Luhmann 1984).

For Luhmann, dogmatization transforms an open world of indeterminate possibilities into a determinable world. It selects among possibilities to establish a restricted but stable framework of sacredly validated grounds for religious experience and commitments (Luhmann 1982b: ch. 2, 1984). Dogmatization responds to functional pressure for greater coherence and consistency in religious belief, a pressure strengthened when writing facilitated more continuous, focused, and critical reflection. This pressure is apparent in the "God-concept," which, in Christian dogma, became a complexity-reducing principle, embracing the "world-universal" and guiding all aspects of life. Philosophically disciplined dogmatics, theology, emerged to defend core religious beliefs through a long series of controversies. The resulting conception of God absorbed "all of the contingency of an increasingly complex world, including evil and chance" (Luhmann 1984: 52) As God became a "perfect person" outside of time and nature, it "guaranteed" all the selections that make the world determinable (Luhmann 1984: 54). It provided ultimate comfort for facing life's disappointments, frustrations, and anxieties. The rituals of life transitions were supported by a soteriology that determines personal status as saved or damned at the end of life.

Christian dogma, including its soteriology, transformed a prophetic conception of history centering on the fate of a people, Israel, into a universal concept of time extending from the Fall of Man to the Last Judgment (Luhmann 1984: 81ff.). With this expanded idea of the meaning of human experience, dogma accommodated principles legitimating economic activity, political and social hierarchies, and scholastic law, while also restricting them ethically. Medieval society thus had a religious coherence despite its political and economic segmentation.

Dogmatization established a religious code enabling "faith" to serve as a communications medium (Luhmann 1984: 57). Faith had been important to Christian religiosity from Roman times, but as dependence on ritual, the sacraments, and priestly guidance waned, religious communication centered ever more on personal expressions of faith. Reformation doctrines of "justification by faith alone" replaced ritual as the efficacious modality of religious experience with a more unified medium of faith (Luhmann 1984: 59ff.).

As it developed, Christian dogma de-socialized the world, defining the human order, subject to God's commandments, as a sphere separate from nature and the transcendental sacred (Luhmann 1984: 50ff.). The Enlightenment transformed this understanding of the human sphere into modern notions of epochs defined by secular historical events. The "temporal horizon" also changed, such that action is planned "with an eye no longer to past but future selections" (Luhmann 1982a: 321–2). The changed understanding of time and history was part of a broad secularizing transition that differentiated system principles of economy, polity, law, science, and the arts from religion. The Enlightenment brought subsystems of society autonomous rationalities that had previously been blocked by religious orientation to the world as a unity under God's implicit relation to all action and experience (Luhmann 1995: 461). The late eighteenth century thus launched a new era in which greater autonomy from religion facilitated cumulative development in all societal systems.

The present situation of religious dogma and faith has been conditioned by the vast social changes of two centuries of increasingly secularized, globalized, and complex economic, political, legal, scientific, and other systems. Given secularization of system principles, religion no longer has direct legitimating relations to them and is no longer directly implicated in societal structure (Luhmann 1982b: ch. 4, 2002b: ch. 8). Religious dogmas have also been subject to radically rationalistic criticism since the Enlightenment. A result has been to privatize faith, which now circulates as expressions of highly personal experience not as dogma shared by members of society. Faith has been liberated from dogmatics, and religious experience has been individualized, radically removed from the broader social order (Luhmann 1982b: 232ff., 2002b: ch. 9). The eventual fate of a religious system based on privatized faith is unclear.

ROBERT N. BELLAH

Bellah commands a vast fund of knowledge in the history, sociology, and anthropology of religion. Early in his career, committed to comparative research, he developed expertise in Japanese, Chinese, and Islamic civilizations. His writing on American

religion has a broad background in the history of Christianity and Western civilization. He has said that his unifying task is to understand contemporary civilization
in the broadest comparative perspective. After well over fifty years of publication,
he is now writing his *magnum opus* to address the evolutionary meaning of human
experience against a background of the frames of meaning provided by the several
world religions.

Bellah's early writings used Parsons' four function paradigm and cybernetic
theory, helping to shape Parsons' own later understanding of religion. His later
works refrain from the formal functional paradigm, but continue to draw analytic
distinctions following its logic. He has affirmed (Bellah and Tipton 2006, introduction; epilogue in Madsen et al. 2002) that all of his writings draw on Parsons' early
integration of Durkheim's and Weber's frameworks. Some of his essays reexamine
their frameworks to probe that integration more deeply.

Early essays (Bellah 1970: ch. 1 and appendix) addressing the cultural, social,
and personality aspects of religion indicate the breadth of Bellah's engagement with
religion In discussing the theologically elaborated beliefs of world religions, Bellah
(1970: appendix) distinguishes four modalities of religious symbol systems, characterized as the God of justice, who upholds a moral order; the God of love, as in
"the Christ who died for me;" Divine power sustaining "objective universalistic
laws," as in Natural Law deriving from Stoicism; and the ground of Being, as in
Buddhist nirvana. Complex religious cultures develop beliefs relating to all four
aspects, which are identified, respectively, with the adaptive, goal attainment, integrative, and pattern maintenance dimensions of religious belief systems.

The essay identifies religious social action with the pattern maintenance sector
of society's pattern maintenance subsystem. Within that sector, it distinguishes four
subsystems of religious action: religious ethical action (adaptive), worship (goal
attainment), religious therapy or practices addressing the balance between gratification and deprivation, frustration, and anxiety (integrative), and faith or commitment
to a belief system (pattern maintaining). This paradigm is an abstract functional
grid, leaving open how particular empirical religions in their historical settings fulfill
the several functions, perhaps stressing certain functions over others. Bellah proposed that Weber's "problems of meaning" can be classified as challenges to the
four components of religious systems: guilt and shame as senses of personal inadequacy in religious ethical action; loneliness, including fear of death and isolation,
as a failure of the worship system; existential suffering as inadequacy of religious
therapy; and meaninglessness as failure to find grounds of faith in the belief system.

Bellah notes that religion contributes essentially to socialization. Religious rituals
are often parts of transitions between life stages, as in confirmations that signal
entry into adulthood. Moreover, the meaning of socialization is often reflected in
religious beliefs, as when sacred figures are symbolic fathers, mothers, sons, or
daughters. As psychoanalysts have underscored, many religions project Oedipal
emotions into myths and other beliefs. In a later essay, Bellah (1970: ch. 5) compared the Oedipal themes prominent in Western religion to themes in Confucian
culture that emphasize the Freudian latency stage. Chinese culture has accentuated
latency-like submission to parental authority and controlled expression of affect as
having special ethical meaning. A similar ethical emphasis is reflected in ideals of
interpersonal harmony, even suppression of independent initiative. In teaching,

Bellah has proposed that Hindu religion, with its elaborate milk symbolism, emphasizes early childhood dependence on a mother's caring as an ethical model for relationships.

Japan and modernization

In the 1950s, Japan's experience as the first "modern" nation outside the Western cultural sphere commanded special interest. Bellah sought to understand Japan's modernization following the model of Weber's emphasis on Puritan ethics as a source of modern capitalism. Bellah's *Tokugawa Religion* (Bellah 1957) argued, contrary to conventional analyses, that religious movements of the Tokugawa Period provided a certain functional equivalent of the Protestant ethic as sources of Japan's rapid industrialization after the Meiji Restoration.

Bellah identified not only worldly asceticism in Tokugawa religious ethics, but also differences between Japanese and Western values and social structure. Japanese values emphasized not the independent conscience and activity of the individual, but commitment to collectivities – families, villages, cities, merchant shops, feudal domains, or the national polity – and loyalty to their heads (Bellah 1957: ch. 2). Heads of collectivities, including feudal lords, did not hold autonomous authority, but were obligated to superior collectivities. Even the emperor owed loyalty to his ancestors and the sun god. Beyond loyalty, commitment to a collectivity involved stringent duties of performance. If the requirements of one's role were not fulfilled, expulsion might result, whether from family, village, or lord's domain. The emphasis on effective service to collectivities at all levels of organization, culminating in duty to emperor and nation gave primacy to political values over values of other societal subsystems.

Tokugawa religious movements emerged in a context of ancient religious heritages. The oldest heritage involved widespread local cults, seasonal ceremonies, and Shinto cults maintaining myths of the sun goddess, emperor's lineage, and emperor (Bellah 1957: ch. 3). Shinto's focus on the emperorship sacralized the nation and duties to heads of collectivities. Insofar as Shinto remained the central religion, it closed off belief in transcendent sources of value. It portrayed the sun goddess, royal lineage, emperor, and nation as merged into one sacred source of value and obligation, while also shading into all superiors. Sacralized authorities were viewed as giving "blessings" that dependents had to reciprocate with commitments to service.

Confucian and Buddhist borrowings from China complemented Shinto, providing metaphysical significance to religious commitments. Neo-Confucian metaphysics emphasized the harmony of heaven and its political meaning, instilling political loyalties with the ethics of filial piety. Buddhist movements, based in cults across the country, taught moral cultivation of the self and overcoming selfishness in fulfilling duties to superiors. As Confucian, Buddhist, and Shinto themes merged, understandings of devotion to superiors, especially the emperor, grew more spiritualized.

In the Tokugawa period, ascetic versions of these ethical doctrines arose and gained popularity. Bellah (1957: chs. 5 and 6) traced the outlooks of several religious movements. The Kokugaku school centered on myths of the emperor's harmony with the sun goddess, rejecting Confucian ethics and Buddhist metaphysics to underscore loyalty to superiors. The Mito school viewed "God, emperor, lord, and father" as identified with one another in a national family ordered by ideals of filial piety. Its ethics paired a "great filial piety" due emperor and nation with a "small filial piety" due parents. The Jodo Shinsu Buddhist sect stressed an asceticism of hard, honest work in one's occupation, in return for Amida's blessings, as a path to salvation. The Hotoku peasant movement promised worldwide well-being and salvation if earned by hard work in return for metaphysical blessings. The Shingaku movement (Bellah 1957: ch. 6) was initiated by the curious Ishida Baigan, a clerk for Kyoto merchants, who after years of studying Confucian and Buddhist classics taught whomever would listen to him. Shingaku eventually established teaching centers for students throughout Japan. It valued overcoming personal desires with asceticism to achieve mystical union with heaven and nature. It held that people of all stations in life could emulate the samurai ideals of service and sacrifice. Honesty, austerity, and devotion to service carried to extreme forms in conducting business yielded new respect for merchants and their contributions to the nation, countering earlier prejudice. Under the Meiji, Shingaku was suppressed, but its ethics entered schoolbooks and thus contributed to the discipline of merchants and workers who staffed the new multi-industry zaibatsu corporations and the thousands of small workshops that supplied them.

Japanese modernization, Bellah demonstrated, was guided by values that emphasized activism on the part of political organization. It was led not by bourgeois entrepreneurs, but by samurai whose positions the Meiji validated anew. The doctrine of bushido, the spiritualized status ethic of samurai, shaped the leadership of large-scale Japanese enterprise, complemented by Shingaku-influenced ethics of honesty and austerity among the staff of the zaibatsu, workshop owners, and merchants. Japan's political values and the samurai status ethic enabled it to concentrate the capital and sustain the organization to embark on modernization. Bellah stressed that the religious culture that shaped Japan's modernization differed radically from the values underlying Western modernity (Bellah 1957: conclusion).

Although a model for studies of religion and modernization, *Tokugawa Religion* proved controversial in Japan. The distinguished scholar, Maruyama Masao, argued that greater emphasis should be given to aspects of Japanese culture that had promoted the 1930s militarism and involvement in World War II. Bellah (2003a: ch. 4) acknowledged that the extraordinary adaptability in the *contents* of goals pursued through Japan's characteristic emphasis on performance left the society open to unfortunate policies, including militarism. He also suggested that a deeper issue was Maruyama's unease about the application of general social scientific analysis to Japan's unique culture.

Religious evolution

Bellah's most important contribution has been his schema of religious evolution (Bellah 1970: ch. 2), which provided an essential source for Parsons' schema, discussed above. The crux of Bellah's evolutionary analysis derives from Weber's comparative studies, portraying the emergence of world religions based on transcendental conceptions of the sacred and the resulting critiques of traditional social orders as the central watershed of human experience. Bellah characterizes this watershed, following Karl Jaspers (1966), as the "axial age," the millennium that encompasses the Old Testament prophets, the classical Greek philosophers, Jesus, the early Church Fathers who received Greek "logos" into theology, Confucius and his followers, the Brahman priests who developed Hindu religious ethics and *dharma*, the Buddha, and Mohammed. Each of these charismatic movements envisioned a sacred domain that transcends the experiential world and confronts traditional social order with new ethical ideals. Each of the religious movements also developed a soteriology offering a form of salvation after life and motivating ethical conduct through hope of ultimate participation in the sacred.

All of the world religions expanded beyond their archaic societies of origin, embracing diverse peoples and legitimating larger-scale civilizations. With larger civilizations came new institutions of social stratification, education, law, authority, and economic production as well as new ritual systems and types of educated religious specialists. Each of the world religions established its own modes and directions of rationalization, including distinct religious ethics and patterns of legitimating social institutions. A consequence was that the evolutionary paths of the axial societies diverged from one another, each becoming increasingly different from the others over time, and each creating particular barriers toward later modernization.

Among religions not based on an axial transformation, Bellah distinguished the non-literate or primitive from the archaic. For non-literate religions, he underscored the close relationship between the sacred and human realms. The sacred places, objects, and beings of their symbol systems have special powers, but pertain to things familiar in the environment. At the level of ritual, participants believe they can become mythical beings and participate directly in the sacred. This enables times of ritual activity, such as, the Australian corroborees, to become occasions of institutional creativity. Enacting sacred beings, tribal members can impart sacred legitimacy to new patterns of conduct. More recently, Bellah (2003b) has suggested that emotionally intense "primitive" rituals, with song, dance, and mimetic symbolization, likely facilitated the primordial evolution of culture among early human societies.

Archaic religions have the resource of ritual specialists attached to cult centers, who, with literacy, can extend reflection on religious beliefs over years, even generations. Over time, literate priests can integrate belief systems encompassing the ideas and symbols of multiple ritual centers. Archaic belief systems become cosmic in scope, locating the meaning of times and places within cycles of eras and large territories. Symbolism becomes monumental, as in Egyptian temples and pyramids. Political authorities are portrayed as larger than life. Class distinctions become prominent and privileged kinship groups gain legitimacy for lifestyles of luxury. Bellah (Bellah and Tipton 2006: ch. 17) has recently portrayed the exceptional legitimacy accorded kings as a core development of archaic religions. Archaic kings are mediators between sacred sources of harmony and the human realm, whose mediation is believed essential to rightly ordered society. Bellah suggests that, through the axial age and down to modern times, political figures have continued to embody some of the awe archaic peoples ascribed to royalty. Modern political leaders still derive aspects of their authority from traditions dating back millennia.

Modern religion originated in the Reformation with a "collapse," as Bellah (1970: 36) put it, of the hierarchical dualism between the transcendental and worldly realms, thereby realigning the relation of God to individual consciences. The Church's monopoly in mediating God's salvation to its members gave way to the idea of an unmediated relationship between God and human consciences. The sacraments became commemorations of historical events, not conveyors of salvation. Each individual conscience thus confronted God's omnipotence directly, responsible to Him immediately. Service to God came to involve, in Bellah's phrase, "the whole of life." The Church hierarchy also collapsed. Protestant churches became associations of faithful members, who were viewed as potentially equal in God's eyes. With Calvinism, the asceticism of medieval monasticism turned to worldly callings and individuals became instruments of the Lord commanded to build the "kingdom of God on earth."

Worldly activity, in science, economics, politics, and other domains, gained a new ethical dignity, legitimating new modes of rationality. The ensuing centuries brought worldly doctrines of economic enterprise, political order, jurisprudence, science, and the arts, establishing them as autonomous institutional domains. Belief in the ultimate equality of human consciences gradually undermined the legitimacy of aristocracies, creating legitimacy for democratic orders and confidence that ordinary citizens can conduct civil affairs. These developments originated in Calvinist societies, but have spread to other Protestant and Catholic nations.

Tentatively, Bellah identified a next phase of religious evolution, starting with Kant's critique "of the traditional metaphysical basis of all the religions" (Bellah 1970: 40), which undermined the dualism between transcendental sacred and profane worlds. Instead, the world becomes "infinitely multiplex," "an infinite possibility thing" (Bellah 1970: 40). Religious action loses metaphysical grounding, instead gaining anchorage in the ethical structures of society. Bellah identified Schleiermacher as the key theologian addressing the significance of Kant's critique of metaphysics, but also Bonhoeffer, Bultmann, and Tillich, who sustained the theological tradition in the twentieth century when religious thought no longer monopolized understanding of ultimate grounds of human existence. Bellah was formerly optimistic that popular religion would adapt creatively to liberal intellectual trends, but recent writings (Bellah and Tipton 2006: chs. 12–15) on contemporary American religion conclude with a pessimistic call for a new Great Awakening. He has suggested that the modern phase of religious evolution needs rethinking (epilogue in Madsen et al. 2002; Bellah and Tipton 2006, introduction and section II).

In an essay on religion and modernization in Asia, Bellah (1965) addressed the situation of societies with venerable axial religious traditions that are now confronted with modern cultural and institutional forces. The confrontation has come in various forms, including Christian missionaries in China, Western colonial rule in India, Indonesia, or Indo-China, and Turkey's wars with European powers. In all cases, the Asian societies encountered the productivity of the West, its political and military efficacy, and its cultural resources, including science, technology, and secular ideologies. Asian societies have been caught between commitment to indigenous religious tradition and efforts to remake their institutions to capture the wealth and efficacy of modernity.

Bellah discerned four modalities of religious response to this situation: adopting Christianity; maintaining tradition relatively unchanged; "reformism," advocating direct adoption of Western models; and neotraditionalism, revitalizing traditional cultural frameworks as a basis for adopting modern technique. He also identified three types of secular belief systems, liberalism, nationalism, and socialism, that may be adopted in pure form, combined with one another, or combined with a religious orientation. They may also be transformed into secular religions, as socialism has been in China.

Christian, reformist, and liberal orientations have in pure forms been advocated primarily by Western educated elites. In several countries, they have provided stimuli to early modernizing movements, but have rarely appealed to the masses. Only the Philippines have undergone widespread conversion to Christianity, and that occurred during Spanish colonization. In China and Japan, Christians have at times played key modernizing roles, criticizing traditional customs, but their ability to provide broad leadership has been limited. Reformism and liberalism confront the difficulty that mobilizing popular participation is necessary for modernizing economies, polities, and class structures, but religious and secular orientations linked to Western culture rarely appeal to people who have not had Western forms of higher education. Reformism's principal success has come in India where the penetration of British-sponsored educational ideals was the greatest and the post-colonial transition involved parliamentary politics. Yet, "Sanskritization," the mobilization of popular caste groups through neotraditional appeals, figures prominently in Indian politics.

Strict traditionalism has rarely proved viable, given the radically changed life-situations of communities engaging modern economic, political, and cultural forces. However, neotraditionalist orientations have combined mass appeal in terms of special values embodied in local axial traditions with capacity to accommodate elements of modernity, especially technology, formal organization in economic production, political bureaucracy, mass media of communication, and greater flexibility in class and status orders. Bellah cited Japan's modernization as a prototype of the transformative potential of neotraditionalism, although acknowledging the debacle of 1930s militarism and the limited development of citizenship and democratic institutions until the postwar institutional changes. Bellah also noted the "stagnation" that neotraditionalism produced in Nationalist China and some Muslim and Buddhist societies (1965: 215).

In a number of societies, including Japan, China, and Vietnam, nationalism has played a prominent role in mobilizing masses for modernization, but in combination with neotraditionalism or socialism. Nationalism seems an effective component of modernizing orientations, but insufficient by itself where ethical discourse is sufficiently transcendent to limit particularistic appeals. Bellah notes that secular nationalism has had its greatest appeal in religiously or ethnically divided societies where neotraditionalism would be divisive.

Communist China has been the one Asian nation to adhere exclusively to a socialist orientation, although for decades in sacralized form, given the status accorded to Mao Tse-tung and the intense activism demanded of party cadre. Socialism has had broader appeal as an element of more complex modernizing orientations. In India, a socialist element has combined with modernizing liberalism and nationalism. In Vietnam, it has combined with nationalism. Indonesia and several Arab countries include socialist elements with neotraditionalism.

Threaded through Bellah's essay are a few notable themes. First is the salience of religion in the setting of contemporary modernization. Religion plays a fateful role in nations suspended between traditional, religiously anchored cultures and the impending world of modernity. Second is the adaptability, within limits, of historic religious traditions as they confront modern institutions. The established religious tradition of a people does not by itself dictate their fate, as it may adapt its ethics and combine with other orientations. Third, understanding the modernizing potential of historic Asian civilizations requires analysis of how the masses can be mobilized with appeals for social change. Without popular mobilization, often through neotraditional appeals, modernization remains limited to the experience of elites.

American society

Bellah has had a long-standing interest in the relations between religion and the American republic, extending to the characteristics of many institutions, including community, education, and family life. From the Cold War to the war in Vietnam to the Iraq War, Bellah has also attended to the shaping of foreign policy by religiously grounded premises about the mission of the American nation. A major theme has been that the nation must recognize that its policies, formulated by individuals subject to original sin and often affected by *hubris*, are subject to profound error. Bellah calls for awareness of the fallibility of the nation and for greater respect for the cultures of other nations.

His publications on American society began with "Civil Religion in America" (Bellah 1967). Although the term civil religion was adopted from Rousseau, the essay's argument is Durkheimian: the nation's solidarity requires that citizens have a religious foundation for their commitments to it. Given the many denominations active in American society, the civil religion must be independent of particular denominations, so that the commitments it generates can be honored by all citizens. Bellah examines the religious language used on such public occasions as presidents' inaugural addresses and ceremonies on national holidays. He documents that God is uniformly invoked, but in terms acceptable across the spectrum of Judaeo-Christian beliefs. God is invoked as the transcendent Creator who sets missions for the nation and as Judge of the nation's conduct. The God of the civil religion is not concerned with individual salvation, but with law and proper social order.

Bellah proposed that American civil religion has responded to three times of crisis. The first extended from the start of the Revolution through ratification of the Constitution, with civil religion validating the nation's independence in terms of a universally significant redemptive mission, a theme that had surfaced earlier during the evangelical Great Awakening. The second great crisis was the Civil War, during which Abraham Lincoln, speaking of the transcendent trial the nation was suffering and the recompense it was paying for the abomination of slavery, emerged as the civil religion's foremost prophet. After his assassination, "with the Christian archetype in the background (Bellah 1970: 178)," he became the civil religion's central figure, symbolizing sacrifice for continuation of the union. The third crisis began after World War II with upheavals in the international arena – the Cold War and many independence movements. Bellah argued that awareness of "higher judgment" (Bellah 1970: 185) is essential for the nation to avoid the jingoism of the Mexican-American War and the Manichean logic that justified the War in Vietnam supporting a military dictatorship as part of the "free world" because of its war with a communist state. He noted that the religious civil disobedience of the civil rights and anti-war movements invoked the prospect of higher judgment of the nation's policies and laws.

The conception of civil religion was extended in *The Broken Covenant; American Civil Religion in Time of Trial* (Bellah 1975). Bellah's critical stance toward American society in this work led to a strong reaction by Parsons and tension in their intellectual relationship. In the preface, Bellah states his personal conflict between "affirmation and rejection" of a "cruel and bitter" American society. Acknowledging the millennial hopes of American society, he denounces their "distortions and perversions." America has seen corrosion of its morality with "a decline in all forms of obligation: to one's occupation, one's family, and one's country" (Bellah 1975: x). Commitment to freedom has devolved into simple liberty to pursue one's self-interest. While there has been liberation from the discipline of Puritanism, "virtue and conscience" have been replaced by utilitarian individualism and a utopian view that technical expertise can manage policy without religious guidance.

The book lays out in fresh detail the biblical archetypes, figurations, and myths in terms of which American society, from its colonial origins, has defined its identity and mission. Bellah outlines the Edenic view of an unspoiled New World, the Mosaic "errand into the wilderness" of Puritan settlers, Americans as a Chosen People occupying a Promised Land, the society as a City on a Hill or New Jerusalem, and the tradition of Jeremiad sermons. All of these figurations have in one context or another provided meaning to the purposes of life in America. For a people whose literacy, until the twentieth century, centered on reading the Bible, the use of archetypes provided a depth of orientation that no other cultural resource could supply. Bellah's mastery of the "logic" of figurational use of biblical myths and his adept identification of instances of it in various historical settings is unique in the sociology of religion. His analysis connects the civil religion to the Protestant heritage of American society while also maintaining the distinction between civil religion and religion in a generic sense.

The church polity and political organization of the New England colonies were based on a doctrine of internal covenants of the heart among the presumptive elect and external covenants binding all members of the community to church and government. The two covenant types were complementary in that internal covenants could not bind all of society and external covenants lacked the committed spirit of moral direction. Bellah (1975: ch. 1) writes that covenant doctrine long gave legitimation to the republic, including understanding of the Constitution as external covenant. He acknowledges that Montesquieu's conception of republics as based on the virtue of citizens also provided legitimation, supplementing the covenantal source by affirming that citizens might have the virtue to respond to inner spiritual guidance. However, Bellah claims that the main enduring source of legitimation for the Constitutional order has been utilitarian, Lockean if not Hobbesian. The utilitarian perspective interprets the Constitution as a morally neutral framework to mediate among conflicting interests, undermining any idea that the republic needs citizens to be committed to substantive moral principles. The republic is now increasingly subject to the kind of corruption that the Founding Fathers most feared, dependence of the common citizens on large interests. Bellah reaches these conclusion without considering in any detail the philosophic, moral, and legal design of the Constitution, as in the Federalist Papers, or the cumulating legal heritage of Constitutional interpretation.

The republic's decline, Bellah emphasizes, has been complemented by loss of the meaning once embedded in a biblical heritage. The religious symbolism of biblical Protestantism has been "pruned," its meaning weakened as broader pan-Judaeo-Christian themes have been emphasized (Bellah 1975: ch. 6). Bellah reminds us that in former times biblical figuration provided effective stimulus to redress wrongs, as in the anti-slavery movement. While again acknowledging the religious impetus to the civil rights and anti-war movements, he fears that the tepid mainline religions can no longer provide guidance. While the early evangelical movements gave moral direction to the nation, empowering common citizens, twentieth century evangelical preaching is Arminian and carries no moral weight. Preachers can no longer use biblical figuration, because their congregations lack the biblical literacy to follow its meaning. New religious movements of the 1970s drew on Asian as well as European traditions, experimented with communal forms, and attracted committed adherents, but as small sects had minimal macro-social impact (Bellah 1975: ch. 6; also Bellah and Tipton 2006: ch. 11). Religious commitment in the general citizenry is thin, as evidenced by the frequent changes in denominations, often in response to the marketing efforts of particular churches.

Bellah (1975: ch. 6) also notes that biblical traditions have long been invoked to purposes entangled with the worst of American experience. The Edenic conception of the American wilderness legitimated the treatment of Native Americans. The saint versus sinner dichotomy in Protestant theology legitimated the enslavement and later discrimination against African Americans. Discriminations against Catholics and Jews also had roots in Protestant ethics, starting for Catholics with principles of church polity. Thus, the civil religion's ways of defining American identity have created outcastes and classes of individuals subject to immoral social control.

The crux of Bellah's critique of American society in an era of weakened civil religion concerns growing reliance on utilitarian individualism, which devalues community institutions. Americans live basically as isolates and as utterly dependent on the dominant corporations. They live for careers and "success" with little concern for larger meanings of life. Capitalism has become "the great expropriator" of private property, as citizens own less and less of the productive property and depend increasingly on serving corporations as bureaucrats (Bellah 1975: 131). Concern for corporate profits outweighs interest in the public good. The cities are domains of "ugliness, chaos, and despair" (Bellah 1975: 132). Poverty, powerlessness, and political vulnerability are growing. Bellah declares that the nation's punishment is to be the most modern society on earth, with all the human costs that entails.

A later volume (Bellah and Hammond 1980) placed civil religion in comparative perspective. Bellah wrote on the Italian civil religion, emphasizing its diverse and conflicting sources and the resulting challenges for Italian national solidarity. In another chapter, he compared the Japanese and American civil religions, discussing the non-axial nature of the Japanese civil religion along with its collectivist values. In the introduction, Bellah addressed controversies that his original essay on the civil religion had engendered. He acknowledged that, dating back to the Roman Empire, Christianity had been in conflict with civil religions. In Rousseau's usage, civil religion is contrasted to Christianity. In American traditions, the so-called separation of church and state, though not part of the First Amendment, generates suspicion about any relationship of religion to public authority. Yet, going back to Savanarola and Calvin, there have been Christian republics and to a degree the New England colonists saw themselves in that heritage.

Bellah cites Tocqueville's discussion of religion's contribution to citizens' efficacy in the political processes of the republic. He adds that revivalism promoted a sense of national community through much of the nineteenth century. In the early decades of after independence, both a revolutionary "civil millennialism" and rationalistic Deism amounted to public theologies. With the decline of biblical religion and rise of liberal individualism, civil religion and republican moral frameworks have become ever more attenuated. Bellah contrasts the spirit and philosophic quality of the Lincoln-Douglas debates with the listless debates of recent presidential elections. He concludes that the republic has indeed become "corroded beyond repair" (Bellah, 1980: 18), and that only a new Great Awakening may revive it.

For *Habits of the Heart* (Bellah et al. 1985), a collaborative updating of Tocqueville's assessment of American democratic society, Bellah drafted chapter 9 on religion. A small sample of subjects drawn from various communities across the country, occupations, and ethnic, religious, and educational backgrounds was interviewed. Their religious lives show diversity, as they were from various Protestant denominations, Catholic, and Jewish. They were active in religious organizations to markedly different degrees, their beliefs ranged from conventional to quite unique, with one subject believing in her own religion, and they differed in the degree to which religious action was personally meaningful. Bellah placed the interview materials against the historical background of American religion and suggested that contemporary religious life has changed radically from its antecedents. He commented on the decreased intensity in personal involvement in church activities and the churches' remove from responsibility for the lives of their communities.

Bellah identified a continuum on which the subjects' religious lives fell, between an inner, vaguely mystical individualism concerned with self-realization and external religion oriented to a God who mandates an objective order for right living. The subjects found their personal orientations on this continuum and associated with people whose orientations somewhat matched their own. Yet, their religious lives focused on personal morality and meaning largely divorced from involvement with non-religious institutions and relationships. A vacuity of meaning was thus unavoidable as compared with the historical efforts of mainline churches to relate religious teachings to the whole of life. Bellah seems more optimistic that the Catholic Church is relating Christian ethics to the larger problems of the society, but his hope apparently derives more from pastoral letters of the Bishops than experiences of Church members.

From interviews with clergy, Bellah suggests that American churches are struggling to determine in what degree they should be church-like or sect-like. The various denominations try to resolve this matter in particular ways, but generally take positions that are church-like in some ways and sect-like in others. Bellah perceives a new tendency for Protestant, Catholic, and Jewish denominations to form a broad central alliance or "communion of communions" (Bellah, et al, 1985: 239) for exchanging views and coordinating action on public matters while also respecting denominational differences.

In *The Good Society* (Bellah et al. 1991), Bellah was the primary author of chapter 6 entitled "The Public Church." Bellah had ceased using the term civil religion, given the confusions it aroused (Bortolini 2008). However, the public church was not a direct substitute, as it refers to beliefs and symbols by which religions in the generic sense give moral framing to public life. By public, Bellah did not mean governmental but the institutional life of the citizenry independent of government, similar to Parsons' conception of societal community. As Bellah emphasizes, religion has from the start of American history been engaged in public life.

The chapter centers on the United Methodist Church, as representative of mainline Protestantism, and its efforts to be a public church. It is based on interviews with Methodist clergy and with the denomination's representatives in its Washington offices, where it pursues its interests in national policy, often with other denominations through the National Council of Churches. Bellah finds a structural but also a cultural gap between the national organization of Methodists and local congregations. National officials are concerned directly with issues of the public church and are troubled by the erosion of energy for addressing them in local Methodist churches. But local clergy see their primary duty as helping members with spiritual and practical needs. They are pleased with the energy and warmth of their congregations. They find that members respond to "prophetic" biblical preaching while also being open to elements of modern theology. Where they feel called to go beyond attending to members' needs, they are oriented first to local charitable works and occasionally local public issues that affect the churches and their members. Issues of the public church in the national arena generally fall outside their circles of concern.

The church's national representatives are aware of the declining influence of mainline churches and rising influence of evangelical churches. Methodist leaders acknowledge that their loss of influence is due to a lack of social vision among the mainline churches. They also know that religious pluralism has created many churches too small and decentralized to exercise national influence. No strong leadership has arisen among the many churches and there is a concern that "the churches have lost their social mission" (Bellah et al. 1991: 192).

Bellah perceives a division in public church advocacy between the conservative-evangelical and liberal churches. Conservatives advocate hard work in economic roles, respect for governmental authority, and personal moral conduct. The liberals favor civil rights, world peace, overcoming poverty, and preserving the environment. Bellah hopes for reconciliation, noting that excessive concentration on single issues narrows moral vision, restricting the potential of the public church. He emphasizes that religious commitment should transcend national loyalty. All major denominations in America accept the legitimacy of the Constitutional republic, but they should retain a transcending loyalty to God and capacity to critique national institutions and policies.

In the years since *The Good Society*, Bellah has continued to essay the relationships of religion to American public institutions (Bellah and Tipton 2006: chs. 13–17). With increasingly powerful rhetoric, he has elaborated his understanding that Lockean utilitarian individualism, atheistic and deterministic, and Constitutional liberalism have undermined the religious and moral foundations of the republic. The result is Hobbesian conflict and corrupting concentration of power in the large corporations. Government is driven to abandon the poor, the disabled, the disinherited while the narrow expertise of policy specialists lead the country into debacle after debacle in foreign as well as domestic matters.

The new understanding that Bellah brings to his later discussions is an insight that American individualism has roots not only in Lockean utilitarianism, but even more radically in the ascetic Protestant conception of the individual conscience in immediate relationship to God and His commandments. The result has been to deepen Bellah's perception of the morally ambiguous quality of American Protestantism from its earliest foundations. His story is no longer about declension, but of "flaws" in the basic religious ethics of ascetic Protestantism (Bellah and Tipton 2006: ch. 15). This account returns to Parsons' analysis of the origins of the American value system, but with a radically changed judgment.

CONCLUSION

This chapter has considered three paradigm-shaping contributors to the functional theory of religion, but other scholars have also worked within that framework, many of them students of Parsons or Bellah. Their topics have included religious movements, the religious foundations of particular societies or civilizations, and the religious legitimation of specific institutional spheres, economic, political, legal, medical, or familial. The body of scholarship in the functional theory of religion is substantial, but lacking younger researchers with the scope of Bellah's comparative knowledge. Luhmann's variant of functional theory has attracted widespread interest, but the resulting scholarship has rarely focused on religion.

The basic importance of functional theory is threefold. First, it has articulated the functional relations of religion to other institutions in society with greater specificity than other theories. A core concept concerns the cultivation of the values that ground the commitments of individuals, families, status groups, and other collectivities. In aggregation, the commitments shape legitimation for political, economic, stratificational, educational, and cultural institutions. Second, functional theory provides an analytic for understanding the distinctive qualities of particular civilizations and hence differences among civilizations. Although most comparative research is conducted under the headings of economic and political analysis, the ability to capture the characteristics of particular societies remains shallow unless religio-ethical patterns of legitimation are examined. Third, Bellah's variant of functional theory has provided sociology's sharpest questioning of the legitimacy of modern civilization. His critiques, often prophetic in tone, have been directed mainly but not exclusively at American society. He finds the unbounded individualism, weakness of community and lifeworld institutions, economic inequality, ever-expanding material production, distrust of ethical regulation of economic and political transactions, lack of understanding of other civilizations, often brutal foreign policy, and threat to the environment calling into question the religious and moral direction, or lack thereof, of American civilization.

Since Parsons synthesized Durkheimian and Weberian principles into a foundation for the functional theory of religion, there have been two major theoretical advances. The first is the four function paradigm, which facilitates more differentiated and yet generalized conceptualization of legitimating relationships between religion and other social institutions. The second is the evolutionary typology of religions, developed by Bellah and integrated into a broader societal schema of developmental stages by Parsons. Lidz (2005) has argued that the Bellah-Parsons typology of stages, while having profound implications for comparative analysis, follows a logic basically different from evolutionary biology. A challenge for future work is to resolve the conceptual differences between true evolutionary theory and the developmental and historical understanding of human civilizations.

A second challenge for future work is to analyze processes of legitimation, in the setting of modern civilization, while conceptualizing the differentiation of cultural as well as social systems. Bellah's reference to Kant's critiques as the key source of modern religious thought passes over another of their implications, emphasized by Ernst Cassirer (1955). Kant's critiques provide transcendental grounding for secular moral and ethical thought independent of religious thought. The tradition of the Enlightenment stands for the importance of differentiated cultural frameworks as elements of the modern human condition. What we mean by "modernity" is largely the independence of ethical, artistic-expressive, and scientific cultures from religion. This does not mean that religious culture lacks salience to the contemporary human condition or that the myths, archetypes, and figurations of public religion no longer contribute to legitimation processes. However, understanding contemporary issues of the legitimation of institutions and socio-political policies requires analysis of secular moral-ethical culture, the artistic-expressive mobilization of motivation, and scientific-technical assessments of consequences as well as religious ethics. Integrating attention to the differentiation of modern culture with the sociology of religion is a next large task for functional theorists.

Bibliography

Bellah, Robert N. (1957) *Tokugawa Religion: The Values of Pre-Industrial Japan*, New York: Free Press.

Bellah, Robert N. (1965) Epilogue: religion and progress in modern Asia, in Bellah (ed.), *Religion and Progress in Modern Asia*, New York: Free Press, 168–229.

Bellah, Robert N. (1967) Civil religion in America, *Daedalus* 96 (1): 1–21.

Bellah, Robert N. (1970) *Beyond Belief: Essays on Religion in a Post-Traditional Society*, New York: Harper and Row.

Bellah, Robert N. (1975) *The Broken Covenant: American Civil Religion in Time of Trial*, New York: Seabury.

Bellah, Robert N. (2002) Epilogue. Meaning and modernity: America and the world, in Richard Madsen, William M. Sullivan, Ann Swidler, and Steven M. Tipton (eds.), *Meaning and Modernity: Religion, Polity, and Self*, Berkeley: University of California Press, 255–76.

Bellah, Robert N. (2003a) *Imagining Japan: The Japanese Tradition and Its Modern Inter-pretation*, Berkeley: University of California Press.

Bellah, Robert N (2003b) The ritual roots of society and culture, in M. Dillon (ed.), *Hand-book of the Sociology of Religion*, Cambridge: Cambridge University Press, 31–44.

Bellah, Robert N. and Hammond, Phillip E. (1980) *Varieties of Civil Religion*, San Francisco: Harper and Row.

Bellah, Robert N., Madsen, Richard, Sullivan, William M., Swidler, Ann, and Tipton, Steven M. (1985) *Habits of the Heart: Individualism and Commitment in American Life*, Berkeley: University of California Press.

Bellah, Robert N., Madsen, Richard, Sullivan, William M., Swidler, Ann, and Tipton, Steven M. (1991) *The Good Society*, New York: Knopf.

Bellah, Robert N. and Tipton, Steven M. (eds.) (2006) *The Robert Bellah Reader*, Durham, NC: Duke University Press.

Bortolini, Matteo (2008) Nothing fails like success: Robert N. Bellah and the civil religion debate, paper presented at the International Institute of Sociology, Prague, Czech Repub-lic, June.

Cassirer, Ernst (1955) *The Philosophy of the Enlightenment*, Boston: Beacon.

Jaspers, Karl (1966) *The Great Philosophers: The Foundations, the Paradigmatic Individuals: Socrates, Budda, Confucius, Jesus; The Seminal Founders of Philosophic Thought: Plato, Augustine, Kant*, New York: Harcourt, Brace, Jovanovich.

Lidz, Victor M. (1982) Religion and cybernetic concepts in the theory of action, *Sociological Analysis* 43 (4): 287–306.

Lidz, Victor M. (2005) Social evolution in the light of the human condition paradigm, in R. C. Fox, V. M. Lidz, and H. J. Bershady (eds.), *After Parsons; A Theory of Social Action for the Twenty-First Century*, New York: Russell Sage, 308–33.

Lidz, Victor M. and Parsons, Talcott (eds.) (1972) *Readings on Premodern Societies*, Engle-wood Cliffs: Prentice-Hall, 308–33.

Luhmann, Niklas (1982a) *The Differentiation of Society*, New York: Columbia University Press.

Luhmann, Niklas (1982b) *Funktion der Religion*, Frankfurt am Main: Suhrkamp Verlag.

Luhmann, Niklas (1984) *Religious Dogmatics and the Evolution of Societies*, Lewiston: Edwin Mellen Press.

Luhmann, Niklas (1995) *Social Systems*, Stanford: Stanford University Press.

Luhmann, Niklas (1998) *Observations on Modernity*, Stanford: Stanford University Press.

Luhmann, Niklas (2002a) *Theories of Distinction: Redescribing the Descriptions of Moder-nity*, Stanford: Stanford University Press.

Luhmann, Niklas (2002b) *Die Religion der Gesellschaft*, Frankfurt am Main: Suhrkamp.

Madsen, Richard, Sullivan, William M., Swidler, Ann, and Tipton, Seven M. (eds.) (2002) *Meaning and Modernity; Religion, Polity, and Self*, Berkeley: University of California Press.

Mead, George Herbert (1934) *Mind, Self, and Society*, Chicago: University of Chicago Press.

Parsons, Talcott (1937) *The Structure of Social Action*, New York: McGraw-Hill.

Parsons, Talcott (1960) The pattern of religious organization in the United States, *Structure and Process in Modern Society*, New York: Free Press, 295–321.

Parsons, Talcott (1961) An outline of the social system, in T. Parsons, E. A. Shils, K. D. Naegele, and J. R. Pitts (eds.), *Theories of Society 1, 2 vols.*, New York: Free Press, 30–79.

Parsons, Talcott (1963) Introduction to Max Weber, *The Sociology of Religion*, tr. Ephraim Fischoff, Boston: Beacon Press, xix–lxvii.

Parsons, Talcott (1966) *Societies: Evolutionary and Comparative Perspectives*, Englewood Cliffs: Prentice-Hall.

Parsons, Talcott (1968) Christianity, in David L. sills (ed.), *International Encyclopaedia of the Social Sciences*, vol. 2, New York: Crowell, Collier and Macmillan, 425–47.

Parsons, Talcott (1971) *The System of Modern Societies*, Englewood Cliffs: Prentice-Hall.

Parsons, Talcott (1977) *Social Systems and the Evolution of Action Theory*, New York: Free Press.

Parsons, Talcott (1978) *Action Theory and the Human Condition*, New York: Free Press.

Parsons, Talcott and Platt, Gerald M. (1973) *The American University*, Cambridge, MA: Harvard University Press.

Parsons, Talcott and White, Winston (2001–2) (Unpublished) Manuscripts on American Society, Talcott Parsons Papers at the Harvard University Archives at HUG (FP) 42.45.2 Box 8.

Troeltsch, Ernst (1960) *The Social Teachings of the Christian Churches*, 2 vols., New York: Harper Torchbooks.

4

Recent Developments in the Anthropology of Religion

Simon Coleman

In 1963, the scholar Clifford Geertz (1926–2006) famously remarked that the anthropology of religion had "made no theoretical advances of major importance" since the end of World War ll (1973: 1).[1] Geertz's apparent dismissal of his sub-discipline mirrored debates over the role of religion itself in many parts of the world at the time, as commentators predicted that secular modernity was becoming a global phenomenon (cf. Cox 1965). Decades earlier, the study of religion had played a key part in the formation of the discipline – through the work of such figures as Tylor, Marett, Malinowski, Boas, Fortune, and Evans-Pritchard – but now seemed to have little future.

Looking back from the perspective of the present, we see that both religion and its anthropological study have gained a much higher profile in recent years than was expected by scholars in the 1960s. Geertz himself initiated some of the richest debates from the 1960s and beyond. The Society for the Anthropology of Religion is now one of the newest and most dynamic groupings of the American Anthropological Association, and shows no sign of running out of subject matter, while the ethnographic study of religion has contributed to numerous mainstream analytical and theoretical concerns, ranging from understanding processes of transnationalism and migration to redefining what is meant by "the field," or by cultural change and continuity. Yet, Geertz's remark – both a description and a provocation – is one that still raises important questions for contemporary anthropologists of religion. What is the purpose of the "anthropology of religion" as a sub-field, and what are its connections with the discipline as a whole – politically, epistemologically, analytically? Or, engaging with Geertz's own attempts to characterize religion, should we see our "theorizations" of religion as inextricably bound up with – and therefore limited – by how we define it in the first place? More radically, there is the question of whether the very idea of the "anthropology of religion" hinders understanding in the sense that it encourages us artificially to mark off an area of study that should not be separated from other areas of life.

In the following, I propose to give an inevitably highly partial picture of the contemporary state – and the recent past – of the anthropology of religion. Rather than trying to include every possible author, I have chosen to highlight some of the main themes that I consider relevant to understanding debates in the anthropology of religion over the past forty years or so. I have also chosen to include attitudes to the study of Christianity as a kind of linking thread between sub-sections, partly because of the remarkable transformations it has undergone as an ethnographic field of study, and partly because I think it acts as a useful index for assessing changing attitudes in the sub-discipline. However, one of my points is going to be that we need be wary of constructing rigid distinctions between "past," "modern," and even "postmodern" constructions of the subject. Contemporary anthropologists – and certainly Geertz himself – have been haunted (or one might say inspired) by the ghosts of past writers. Contrary to the implications of Geertz's remark, we might say that to draw on the past is not simply to echo or be trapped by it, much as contemporary biological research draws on Darwin but is hardly constrained by nineteenth-century paradigms. Lambek (2002: 4) sees the contemporary anthropology of religion as drawing on a significant number of such sources, including Boas's tracing of intimate connections between religion, language and poetics, Durkheim's understanding of religious phenomena as social, Marx's attention to power, alienation, fetishism, mystification, and Weber's attention to the place of religion in transitions to modernity. But he still feels able to talk of how it has "made great strides in its inquiries" (p. 13), for instance in its appreciation of the intellectual complexity and aesthetic richness of other people's religious expressions, or in its posing of fundamental questions relating to human difference.

Despite being partial, this chapter should also be seen as a provocation in its own right –not only to delve more deeply into the anthropological study of religion but also to consider the political and analytical challenges inherent in locating – constructing – religion as an object of study. This is an issue that runs through all of the sub-sections of the chapter, and it takes us into some of the most basic questions that permeate the discipline of anthropology as a whole, relating to the opportunities as well as the limitations of cross-cultural comparison, but also to the links between the cultural expressions and the physical make-up of humans. Overall, it seems to me that our attitude towards the sub-discipline should be a kind of benevolent skepticism. We must remember that we are always complicit in deciding what it is that constitutes "religion" as a discrete object of study. Indeed, one of the defining features of a contemporary anthropology of religion might be the heightened realization of the very slipperiness of the task that we have set ourselves. But that does not mean that we should abandon the project.

"DEFINING" RELIGION: HUMAN ESSENCE OR HISTORICAL PRODUCT?

In discussing how contemporary anthropologists should define religion, Morton Klass (1995: 17) begins by taking the reader to a distant (and fictional) time and place. He quotes Parson Thwakum from *The History of Tom Jones*, a comic novel by the English writer Henry Fielding that was originally published in 1749. Thwakum displays a commendable attempt to avoid ambiguity in his own definition: "When I mention religion I mean the Christian religion; and not only the Christian religion, but the Protestant religion; and not only the Protestant religion, but the Church of England." It seems safe to say that this declaration is meant to move us from the general to the particular, while illustrating all too clearly the power of definitions to make politically loaded claims on the world even as they purport simply to describe reality. In its very triumphalism, Thwakum's definition throws into high relief anthropology's challenge in attempting to move, at least some of the time, from the particular to the general. And while this problem plagues all areas of anthropology, I mention it here because definitional issues have been a highly significant dimension of recent debates in the anthropology of religion.

One of the chief *agents provocateurs* in such debates has been Geertz himself. Indeed, Geertz's attempt to give the study of religion a more general theoretical significance was expressed in a definition that has proved both influential and controversial. For him, religion was "(1) a system of symbols which acts to (2) establish powerful, pervasive, and long-lasting moods and motivations in men [*sic*] by (3) formulating conceptions of a general order of existence and (4) clothing these conceptions with such an aura of factuality that (5) the moods and motivations seem uniquely realistic" (Geertz 1973: 4). Note that, unlike Parson Thwakum, Geertz does not move us in a form of definitional involution towards a particular church or institution. The attempt to seek a general theoretical significance for the study of religion clearly depends on creating an object of study that is of relevance to the human condition as a whole – what Geertz here calls "a general order of existence." Such order depends on symbols organized into a system, and moreover a system that does things, acting on the social and cultural world and helping to give form to "the extreme generality, diffuseness, and variability of man's innate (that is, genetically programmed) response capacities" (p. 68).

Whereas Thwakum makes his own religious allegiance abundantly clear, Geertz's self-presentation is more circumspect, but importantly provides a hint of the ideological distancing common to scholarship by referring to how moods and motivations "seem" uniquely realistic. Of course Geertz's definition does not emerge out of an intellectual vacuum. As Fiona Bowie points out (2006: 5) his conception brings together Durkheim's symbolic functionalism – the sense of religion as a collective social act – with Weber's concern for meaning – the presentation of religion as a system for ordering the world. The assumption is that comprehension of the world rather than chronic confusion is indeed possible, and that such comprehension (of the gods, of suffering, of life's purposes) depends crucially on meanings that are public – intersubjective and shared (Geertz 1973: 64). For them to be religious requires a sense of reaching beyond the everyday since (p. 68): "A man can indeed be said to be "religious" about golf, but not merely if he pursues it with passion and plays it on Sundays: he must also see it as symbolic of some transcendent truths."

While symbols are given utmost significance in Geertz's presentation of religion, his theory also depends on a particular theory of ritual practice, since the persuasive authority formulated by symbols – contained in models "of" and models "for" reality – is attained through its performance and portrayal. Thus: (p. 76) "In a ritual, the world as lived and the world as imagined, fused under the agency of a single set of symbolic forms, turn out to be the same world." The attempt to understand the world as both experienced and imagined also helped to signal Geertz's distance from such figures as Lévi-Strauss, whose French "structuralism" focused on cultural meanings divorced from the actions and interpretations of living, identifiable people.

Geertz's work on religion is part of a wider anthropological worldview, and moreover a theory of how to understand and study culture as a whole. Indeed, Geertz came to be known as the major exponent of a form of "interpretive anthropology" that explored religion as a source of meaning and understanding alongside other such tools available to humans, including commonsense, science and aesthetics. Anthropology could not therefore be seen as a "hard science," and such a standpoint drew not only on classical social theorists but also on Geertz's original training in English and philosophy. In his work we see echoes, for instance, of Wittgenstein's emphasis on language as carrier of specifically social meaning.[2]

Geertz's discussion of religion involves a search for generality that is part of his desire to develop a theoretical stance of broad utility. And yet it is precisely this search for the generic that has attracted some of the sharpest criticism of his presentation of religion. Probably the best-known critique has come from Talal Asad, an anthropologist whose background contrasts fascinatingly with that of Geertz, even though both have produced ethnographic studies of Islam. Brought up in Pakistan, Asad's training took place in the United Kingdom, and he spent some time working with Evans-Pritchard at Oxford before eventually moving to the United States. In contrast to some of the intellectual forebears mentioned for Geertz, in Asad's work we see sophisticated echoes of Nietzsche, Foucault and Said. The result is an anthropology that is acutely aware of the politics of representing religion (not least in relation to understandings of the "Western" and the "non-Western"), and focuses on the need to construct "genealogies" of both religious and secular ways of viewing the world (cf. Asad 2003). For Asad, therefore, Geertz's definition runs into immediate problems in its attempt ultimately to capture a transcultural, panhuman phenomenon divorced from particular cultural, social and political contexts (see Bowie 2006: 5). It is the very attempt to grasp religion's "essence" (and to claim that such an essence exists) that helps to divorce religion from the domain of power. In this view, not only is a universal definition of religion an impossibility, but that definition itself must be seen as the historical product of ideologically charged, discursive processes (1993: 29).

Asad's famous essay "The Construction of Religion as an Anthropological Category," which forms part of his book *Genealogies of Religion* (1993), shows how conceptions of religion as a phenomenon ideally kept separate from politics, law, science have emerged from a unique, Western, post-Reformation history, and one that fits all too well with the interests of both secular liberals to confine the influence of religion, and liberal Christians to defend its continued existence. In studying religion as a discursive formation, we need therefore to concentrate less on symbols that allegedly implant "dispositions" and to focus more on how religion forms part of wider authorizing and disciplinary practices. For instance, in the European Middle Age the Church and other authorities regulated pagan practices, authenticated particular miracles and relics, authorized shrines, compiled saints' lives, required regular telling of sinful thoughts, controlled popular movements, and so on, and sought "the subjection of all practice to a unified authority, to a single authentic source that could tell truth from falsehood" (p. 121). It was only in the centuries after the Reformation that more contemporary notions of "belief," "conscience" and "sensibility" began to emerge, while in the seventeenth century, following the fragmentation of the Roman church, the earliest systematic attempts at producing a universal definition of religion were made. Such attempts at universalism were the product of a new social and intellectual context, in which different systems of belief could be compared with each other as well as with the propositions of natural science. By 1795, according to Asad, Kant was able to produce a "fully essentialized" idea of religion, counterposing a general notion of "religion" with different and specific historical confessions (p. 122).

We should begin to see the implications of Asad's argument for Geertz's characterization – and definition – of religion. The very notion that religion can be seen as involving "symbolic meanings" linked to ideas of "general order" expresses a specific Christian history, and one that has pushed towards the abstraction and universalization of religion. Geertz runs the risk of referring to meaning without looking at the social processes through which "meaning" is constructed (p. 123). Furthermore, the argument has implications for Geertz's view of the significance of ritual, since to understand how religious faith is constructed we need to examine not only sacred performances that are explicitly marked as such, but also the range of disciplinary practices that are evident in any given context.

If Geertz sees "meaning" everywhere, alongside the search for some kind of "order," Asad's basic assumption seems to be that "power" is a fundamental dimension of all cultural and social phenomena. The critique of religion and of Geertz is therefore in itself a rather generic one, and raises the question of whether the observer can ever escape from (or recognize fully) the discursive formations in which they find themselves. However, Asad's genealogical method surely shows how an appreciation of historical change can test notions of the "universal"; in doing so, it indicates some of the ways in which Geertz's definition is not quite as far from that of Pastor Thwakum as we might have expected, not least as both converge around broadly Christian sensibilities. At the same time, Asad's standpoint does indicate one key parallel with that of Thwakum: the sense that expressions of religion might be about "identity" as much as they are about "Truth."

The dispute between Geertzian and Asadian views of religion also resonates with a parallel debate that has occurred in recent decades over the notion of "belief." Issues of private versus public expressions of religiosity as well as the importance of historical context have again come to the fore (Lindquist and Coleman 2008). The discussion started with Rodney Needham's (1972) exploration of the wide range of possible uses of the concept: as a common word in the English language, as a psychological term designating an inner state, as an identifying peg, and as a basic concept in Western philosophical tradition. To vagueness was added the charge of parochiality, as outlined by Malcolm Ruel's examination of (1997: 100) "the monumental peculiarity of Christian 'belief.'" Ruel notes (1997: 101ff.) that the original Greek word (*pistis*) expressed the idea of trust, denoting conduct that honored an agreement or bond. Only in the apostolic writings of the New Testament was there added a sense of conversion and a common conviction that distinguished and united Christians as a community. Over time, the sense and definition of belief not only marked out Christian from non-Christian, but also true believers from the heretics. Thus, over the course of Christian history: "Trust in a personified God becomes conviction about a certain event, the Christ-event of history, becomes an initiatory declaration, becomes a corporately declared orthodoxy, becomes an inwardly organizing experience, becomes values common to all men" (p. 109). All these connotations are implied when we label orthodoxies, received ideas, collective representations, or the ontological foundations of other people's worlds as "beliefs" – a potentially far-reaching claim if we think of the language of many ethnographies, whether the focus is on religion or not. Ruel argues that the deployment of the term belief implies misleadingly that people's ideas are necessarily formulated as coherent orthodoxies; that people are committed to them and hold them unquestioningly; that these ideas are experienced as inner states; that they can be cited as simple explanations of personal and group behavior.

As with the juxtaposition of the views of Geertz and Asad, we see here worries about the hidden assumptions in the "universalizing" language used to describe others. Ethnographic description sometimes seems to be guilty of translating other "faiths" into Western categories. Religion as "essence" and religion as discursive formation are once again in conflict. However, the problem is arguably even more insidious than that evident in relation to definitions, since at least a definition lays itself open to explicit critique, whereas the simple deployment of the word "believe" in an ethnography risks going unnoticed. On the one hand, when trying to describe Kuria religion, Ruel (1997: 5) found that it simply did not fit with Western, Christian notions of supernaturalist speculation, so that it was not appropriate to say "the Kuria believe x or y." On the other hand, we might add that the discourse of belief can itself create a particular form of distance in ethnographic accounts, implying that "their" beliefs are mere delusions in comparison with "our" (usually secular) knowledge of how the world functions.

This last point, concerning the organization of ideas relating to religion and the world at large, indicates how questions over belief resonate with much larger debates in anthropology over "rationality." The question of whether non-Western others thought like those in the West was foundational in the work of a figure such as Frazer, as his *Golden Bough* (1922) traced the apparent shift in human thought from magic, to religion, to science, while Evans-Pritchard's *Witchcraft, Oracles and Magic among the Azande* (1937) was an ethnographic response to the claim by Lévi-Bruhl that "primitive" societies thought in pre-logical and mystical ways. A more contemporary ethnography by Luhrmann (1989) on witchcraft in London explores notions of "belief" and "rationality" that indicates the relative fuzziness of both, even among so-called sophisticated urbanites. Various elements work together in process she calls "interpretive drift" – the gradual transformation in interpreting events, making sense of experiences. Her informants do not deliberately change the way they think about the world: rather, they pick up intellectual habits over time, and learn new ways of drawing connections between events. Commitment to what one does as a witch is not a simple assertion that one possesses objective truth about the world. Rather, theories of magical practice both assertions about the real world, and "let's pretend" fantasies. One way in which witches and magicians gain this "seriously playful" involvement with their practice is through the language they deploy to describe their experience. Thus, they may learn to use a literal language to describe events which have not occurred "in reality" but have been imagined, while using a metaphorical language to describe actual events, feelings and impressions. When a magician says "Loki is loose tonight" she may take this reference to the Nordic god as a mystical manner of describing observable, unruly behavior: the god cannot be seen (presumably), but the behavior can. On the other hand, a magician may say after a ritual that "I could taste the salt spray" when he has been standing inside a Gloucestershire house for the whole time, far from the sea, thus deploying a physical, tactile language to describe experience.

Such work, indicating the sometimes playful, exploratory nature of "religious" commitment, not only complicates further our understanding of belief, but can also challenge some of the assumptions anthropologists have had about the existence of ordered religious and cultural "systems." Luhrmann's informants often inhabit and are successful within other contexts that invoke the tenets of rationality and science, such as their work lives. Witchcraft may almost become a kind of part-time cosmology, or one that competes with others during one's everyday life.

RITUAL, SOCIAL ORDER, AND CHANGE

Geertz's interpretative anthropology was meant in part to be a reaction against older forms of British functionalist anthropology, which had emphasized static social structures as opposed to more dynamic and evolving cultural systems. A broadly similar concern is evident in the work of another significant figure in the realm of symbolic anthropology, Victor Turner (1920–1983). Like Geertz, Turner produced an analysis of the working of religious symbols in ritual, although one more Durkheimian in its emphasis on social structures, in contrast to Geertz's more Weberian search for meaning. Turner shared with Asad the experience of moving between British and north American institutions in his career. However, in other respects his intellectual trajectory traced a path opposite to that of Asad, as his theoretical and personal stances moved him away from an original interest in Marxism and towards an insider's as well as an ethnographic exploration of religious faith.

Turner's doctoral work in the 1950s on the Ndembu of (then) northern Rhodesia was heavily influenced by Max Gluckman, whose experience of living and carrying out fieldwork in South Africa formed the basis of a politically engaged, anti-colonialist stance to anthropology. A founder of the so-called Manchester School, Gluckman's work combined Marxism with structural-functionalism, as well as developing a methodological focus on examining the rules of social interaction through the use of case-studies. It was Gluckman who urged Turner initially to study the principles of Ndembu social organization with the words: "Until you've mastered that, you're in no position to analyze ritual."[3] However, while Turner retained an interest in the case-study method as well as in tracing the management of conflict within social situations, he moved away from some of the other emphases of the Manchester School. In 1957 he resigned from the British Communist Party and renounced Marxism, and in subsequent years wrote extensively on Ndembu ritual, as well as becoming a Catholic.

Turner (1967: 19) defined ritual as "prescribed formal behavior for occasions not given over to technological routine, having reference to beliefs in mystical beings and powers." Ritual in turn is seen as a kind of storehouse of supernaturally charged, authoritative symbols (Turner 1968: 2) – the smallest units of ritual that retain the specific properties of ritual behavior, which can take the form of objects, activities, words, relationships, events, gestures, or spatial units (Turner 1967: 19). The Turnerian symbol acts less as a Geertzian vehicle of "culture" and more as a catalyst, within observable social processes, able to instigate social action, reinforce social norms, resolve conflicts. Rituals may even compensate for the lack of other forms of effective societal control such as political authority or bonds of kinship, acting within charged, often conflictual processes of "social drama" to remind participants of central values. In the process a symbol can bring together natural necessities and social desires; it "represents both the obligatory and the desirable ... an intimate union of the material and the moral" (Turner 1967: 54).

How can symbols work in such a way? Turner (1967: 28–9, 50–5, 1968: 18–19) argues that symbols are effective because they condense many different associations in a single object, bringing together apparently different meanings that are interconnected through analogous qualities, or by associations in fact or thought. At the same time, the symbol combines two distinct poles of significance: at the "ideological" or "normative" pole, a cluster of meanings refers to the moral and social order, to broad principles of social organization; at the "sensory" or "orectic" pole, natural or physiological phenomena and processes are represented, arousing desires and feelings at a more basic level. Thus, in the Ndembu ritual *Nkula*, a "ritual of affliction" that deals with female patients' reproductive or menstrual troubles, portions of the mukula tree are used (Turner 1968: 52–88). This tree exudes a red gum, referred to by the Ndembu as the "blood of mukula." In the ritual context, this "blood" refers at the same both to the orectic pole of childbirth and to the normative pole of matriliny.

We see how Turner's work emphasizes ritual performances and action rather than "belief." Symbols "work" not because their meanings are one-dimensional, or can be spelled out precisely, but because of their "multivocality," a quality that through richness of associations demonstrates the virtues of ambiguity in ritual contexts, especially where social order is ultimately to be emphasized in contexts of potential schism. Turner further developed his interests in the mediation of both change and ambiguity by taking up older work on rites of passage, by Arnold van Gennep (1873–1957), which had presented such rites as being made up of a tripartite structure of forms of separation from the everyday, then a liminal or transitional/"threshold" phase, and a final phase of incorporation back into society (1909). Turner was particularly interested in liminality as a ritual expression of creativity, a point at which social order and structure could be temporarily reversed or marginalized. It could be seen as providing the ritual space for a kind of "anti-structure," which Turner located in Western as well as non-Western contexts. According to this view, if in so-called tribal societies initiands usually have to engage with liminality out of social necessity, for instance in order to undergo rites of passage that turn them from children into adults, in Western contexts the liminal is replaced by a more "liminoid," voluntary embrace of the anti-structural that may be experienced through such activities as theater, poetry, art, and religion. Thus in his essay "Liminal to Liminoid in Play, Flow and Ritual" (1974) Turner sees leisure time in "industrial" societies as involving both "freedom from" the institutional obligations prescribed by bureaucratic organization and "freedom to" enter or create new symbolic worlds of entertainment, sports, games, and so on.

Through exploring such themes of anti-structure and "in-betweenness," Turner became one of the first theorists to see the parallels between an apparently "secular" activity such as tourism and a "sacred" one such as pilgrimage. Such intellectual interests combined with more personal concerns in the book *Image and Pilgrimage in Christian Culture* (1978), co-written with Edith Turner. Based on chapter-length case-studies of individual pilgrimage complexes, such as Lourdes, the Virgin of Guadalupe, Walsingham, and so on, part of the originality of this book (for the time) is its bringing together of studies of history and ethnography, materiality and myth, in defining the "field" of pilgrimage as extending beyond any single place or time. However, it also develops an important concept within Turner's work, and one that clearly builds on his interests in anti-structure and transition. Pilgrimage is seen as a prime context for the development of *communitas*, a state of temporary separation from mundane structures, hierarchies and identities, and incorporation into a broad commonality of feeling with fellow pilgrims. One influence behind this idea was his experience of being in the trenches during wartime – a context where the extremity of the situation renders participants decidedly equal.

In considering Turner's work we must acknowledge the tremendous utility of many of the concepts that he developed. The "multivocality" of symbols, the creative dimensions of "liminality," the experience of "communitas" – all have proved influential. At the same time, the juxtaposition of structure and anti-structure has proved a rather crude way of thinking about social change. Furthermore, the notion of communitas often seems to emphasize a theological ideal rather than a sociological reality, not least as pilgrimage sites reveal themselves to be sites of contestation and competition over symbolic and material resources (Eade and Sallnow 1991). We might think again of Asad's critique of Geertz's lack of appreciation of the significance of struggles over power and identity, and ask in Turner's case how his work might be re-interpreted through the framework of the very Marxism that he came to reject in his early career.

An important recent redeployment of the notion of the rite of passage is provided by Maurice Bloch in his book *Prey into Hunter* (1992), a text that indeed brings power, coercion and conflict back into the analysis of ritual. As part of such reanalysis, the emphasis of the book rests less on the liminal, other-worldly aspect of ritual and more on the everyday world, the brute realities of the here and now. Bloch therefore presents his text as an attempt to provide a general understanding of the "politics" of religious experience, and in doing so he argues for the existence of a basic grammar underlying a number of different types of ritual across cultures, ranging from initiation to sacrifice, possession, fertility rituals and funerals.

Bloch's thesis is that (pp. 5–6) an "irreducible core" of the ritual process involves a symbolically or physically violent conquest of the present world by the transcendental. Drawing on the rite of passage model, he sees the first part of the ritual as moving participants away from the here and now towards a powerful transcendent realm. In the return, that realm continues to be associated with those who made the initial move in its direction, so that the return to the ordinary world becomes a kind of conquest of that world. So the ritual expresses a form of "rebounding violence": willing cooperation by the initiate with a transcendental attack on his or her vitality is followed by a violent recovery of that vitality from an external source. Ritual initiands do not just experience the sacred; they bring it back into the world in order to conquer it. The person moves from from being "prey" into being a "hunter," embracing a state where the powerful transcendent element dominates the frail human element.

Thus Bloch's analysis of the Orokaiva rite of passage in Papua New Guinea, taken from Andre Iteanu's work (1983), traces the movement of children through the ritual process. Initially, children are driven out of the village (the everyday world) into the bush, where spirits live, by people who come from the bush dressed in birds' feathers and pigs' tusks, shouting "bite, bite, bite." Children are "turned into" pigs, taking on new life. They are then rounded up on a platform reminiscent of the ones on which dead bodies are placed, blindfolded and taken to a hut where they are not allowed to eat normal food, wash, speak or look outside. They are told they are dead, and have become spirits. Children are then taught to play sacred flutes and bullroarers that represent the voices of the spirits and are taught spirit dances. They gain the right to wear spirit masks, a privilege they maintain after the ritual. In this sense they are given permanent elements of the transcendental that they will take back with them to the everyday world. After a time of seclusion, children return to the village, wearing feathers themselves and themselves shouting "bite, bite, bite." They climb onto a similar platform to the one they had been on, and distribute pig meat. They are now part-spirit, having been turned from prey into hunter.

If Turner's work is based on a dichotomization of sacred and profane realms, mediated by ritual, Bloch's analysis provides more of an exploration of the relationship between the two. In common with Turner, however, his schema is intended to provide a much more general model of human behavior. He is attempting to explain the often-noted fact that religion furnishes an idiom of expansionist violence to people in a whole range of societies, a ritual idiom which under certain circumstances becomes a legitimation for actual, outwardly directed violence. We note for instance that (p. 17) Orokaiva initiation ends with an open-ended menace to outsiders which can become the beginning of serious hostility. More generally, "rebounding violence" requires the presence of particular circumstances for it to legitimize military expansionism, including both the presence of outsiders and the resources to act in such a manner. One example is provided by Japan in Bloch's argument: in that country's history Buddhism has provided the path of the exit of vitality while Shintoism has contained the path of its triumphal and forward-looking return (p. 63): "Renunciation on the part of the subjects and of the Buddhist monks could then lead to the rebounding vitality of the Emperor in much the way the renunciation of the Hindu Brahman could lead to the conquering sacrificial strength of the king."

Bloch does occasionally refer to the Judaeo-Christian heritage of much of the West. He talks, for instance (p. 32) of how the lives of Christian saints illustrate the process of the person turning against the mortal, bodily aspects of themselves in favor of supernatural invasion. Or he argues (p. 96) that "the aggressive ideology of rebounding conquest has…been very evident in Christianity … This element was particularly evident during the crusades or when religious fervor could be backed by military might, as in the periods of European colonial expansion." Arguably, in reflecting on more recent history, we might seek parallels with Jewett and

Lawrence's (2003) analysis of the role of violence associated with zealous nationalism in the United States. They trace the ways in which (p. 5): "The ideas of holy
war have been combined with a distinctively American sense of mission in language
that fuses secular and religious images. In major developments of American life – the
Civil War, the settling of the western frontier, the World Wars, the Cold War, the
Vietnam War, the Gulf War, and the so-called war on terrorism – these ideas have
continued to surface." Even where physical force has not been deployed, the symbolic violence of transformation has been deployed – either "killing" or "converting" the other in Jewett and Lawrence's terms.

From the work we have seen so far, it seems that ritual contexts can orient participants in authoritative ways, even if analysts disagree over such questions as to
the degree of freedom or coercion inherent in these types of performance. Ritual is
generally perceived to contain particular "framing" qualities, heightening social
experience, even if the distinction between the sacred and the secular is clearly a
problematic one. A major contribution to work that examines the "orienting"
properties of ritual itself is provided by Roy Rappaport in his final work, *Ritual
and Religion in the Making of Humanity* (1999). Part of Rappaport's point is that
whereas simple messages leave the responses of receivers to their own devices, rituals
often specify their responses very precisely. For instance ritual is full of conventional
utterances and acts – "I name this ship," "I swear to tell the truth" – which achieve
conventional effects.[4] The formal characteristics of ritual, the gravity and solemnity
characteristic of many performance, also aid its effects. Acceptance of performance
does not imply "belief," however: it is a public act, not a private state, visible both
to witnesses and to performers, even as the performer may transcend personal doubt
through carrying out the performance.

In common with most of the other analysts we have dealt with so far, Rappaport
is fundamentally concerned with the articulation of public meanings and commitments to ritual and social orders. His emphasis on the conventionality of such action
may be over-drawn, however – not least in the pilgrimage contexts I have encountered in Anglican Walsingham, for instance, where some pilgrims enact a distinct
ambiguity over their commitment to pilgrimage institutions precisely through their
"camping up" and exaggerating ritual performances in public (Coleman and Elsner
1998). We might also ask for more of an analysis of the audience for ritual: if the
public nature of ritual is significant, what kinds of publics gather round ritual forms?

Rappaport, Bloch, Geertz, and Turner tend to focus on set-apart, marked, major
ritual forms in the making or reinforcing of society. In this discussion, Asad takes
a slightly different approach in his desire to locate overtly religious action within a
range of disciplinary practices that permeate all of life. Other influential work on
ritual has moved more in this direction, such as Catherine Bell's (1992) emphasis
on "ritualization" rather than ritual. Her argument that ritual is neither a distinct,
autonomous activity nor necessarily a property of all action. However, it prompts
the observer to look for circumstances where action is "set aside" in some way, and
where culturally specific expressions of fixity, formality and repetition may contribute to the production of ritualized action. Thus such discussion of ritual partially
echoes that of defining religion, where initial assertions of the marked off quality
of the phenomenon are challenged by scholars who are skeptical of the assertion of
such boundaries, by either informants or fellow theorists.

Conversions to "Modernity"? Studying Religion in
the Post-colonial World

Whether or not they have focused explicitly on questions of power in their work, most of the scholars we have looked at so far have had to deal – both personally and intellectually – with issues relating to post-colonialism. We saw for instance how Turner's fieldwork began in the politically charged framework of the Manchester School, or how Asad's work has been prompted in part by attempting to deconstruct anthropologists' constructions of the Other. More generally, concerns over the political uses of knowledge have combined with worries over the objective status of knowledge itself. As Lambek (2002: 471) notes (and as we have seen in the work of Asad and Ruel), such self-consciousness can prompt the analyst not only to look at the historical roots of particular structures of inequality, but also to recognize the historicity of all social formations, religion included.

Some of the most effective work in this area has looked at past processes of colonization, where religion has formed part of the tangled encounter between colonizers and colonized, for instance as the former have attempted to move the latter towards an engagement with "the modern." Peter Van der Veer (1996: 3) notes that the nineteenth-century colony was an ideal arena for heated debates among the British about the location of religion in modernity. Conversion of others became gradually marginalized in Europe and transported to the non-Christian, colonized world. We see again here an example of the close intersection between religious action and wider disciplinary practices, a theme that has been powerfully explored in the work of Jean and John Comaroff in their analyses of Christian missionary activity on southern Africans. More particularly, their use of historical analysis as well as contemporary ethnography helps to put into temporal as well as political context the dialectic between "traditional" pre-colonial Tshidi values and the post-colonial world of modern South Africa in which the Tshidi are a marginalized group, part agricultural peasants and part urbanized proletariat (Bowie 2000; Comaroff 1985). Mission in the nineteenth century, while ostensibly about "religious" matters, helped to reshape Tshidi sociality, personhood and everyday practices, preparing Africans to be docile laborers at the bottom end of an emerging capitalist economy (Lambek 2002). At the same time, the Comaroffs show some of the nuances involved in such relationships. For instance, in the nineteenth century representations of the heathen "other" of the "dark continent" provided cultural means through which to reflect on threatening working classes at home. Furthermore, Tshidi have been able to appropriate aspects of Christian culture, combining them with other cultural resources in order to create spaces for resistance against their marginalization. For instance, the rich symbolism of Zionist dress codes contrasts with the uniforms of mission churches and with everyday work clothes (Bowie 2000: 81). Zionist men wear white skirts, blurring stark Western contrasts between male severity and female opulence (Comaroff 1985: 270) and personifying a distant, biblical world of Victorian mission, away from the problems of the present.

Such work illustrates the sometimes jagged juxtapositions involved in colonial and post-colonial encounters, but also the complexities of the dialogues and interactions that may occur – through articulations of language, the body, space, personhood, and so on. The notion of "modernity" is itself given a Christian genealogy, but one where the very nature of what constitutes the modern may be unclear, contested. Thus a central concern of Webb Keane's recent work *Christian Moderns* (2007) is with the idea of fetishism, a product of the missionary encounter that involves the imputation to non-Christian others of a false, dangerous, but sometimes seductive lack of distinction between humans and non-humans, subjects and objects, and therefore of a misunderstanding of the grounds of human agency. In such work we have the "Christian" placed alongside the "modern," but also see a wish to disrupt conventional "West versus the rest" divisions. For Keane, the interesting encounters are not inherently between sharply defined peoples or cultures, but between what he calls "representational economies." The very bringing together of "representation" and "economy" in one phrase, like the words Christian and modern, encourages a very close examination of articulations among language ideology, speaking (and reading and writing) practices, concepts of the person, moral values, and political institutions in any given "representational economy," including those of Calvinist missionaries or indeed Western anthropologists.

Both the Comaroffs and Keane use analyses of the colonial and post-colonial encounter to reflect not only on the colonized, but also on the culture of the colonizers. They also bring the study of Christianity itself to the fore (cf. Robbins 2007). Cannell notes (2006: 3) that Christianity "has seemed at once the most tediously familiar and the most threatening of the religious traditions for a social science that has developed within contexts in which the heritage of European philosophy, and therefore of Christianity, tends to predominate." To some degree, a "genealogy" of Christianity reveals it to have been, in Cannell's terms (p. 4), the "repressed" of anthropology over the period of the formation of the discipline. At the same time, the focus on such a religious formation brings familiar questions with it: how do we characterize the "logic" of a whole religion without engaging in universalizing claims about its transcultural, transtemporal "essence"? What is often striking here, as Cannell points out, is not only what anthropologists have chosen to emphasize about Christianity, but also what has been largely ignored. Thus (p. 7) while most writing on Christianity in the social sciences has focused on its ascetic aspects, on the ways in which Christian teaching tends to elevate the spirit above the flesh, Christian doctrine has always had another dimension, in which flesh is an essential part of redemption. More generally, Christianity can all too easily become a trope for the examination of "modernity." Cannell argues (p. 11), for instance, that the Comaroffs, despite their valuable accounts of the reception of missionization in South Africa, tend to subordinate the exploration of Christianity to the narrative of modernization itself, as well as to resistance to orthodox Christian practice.

Certainly, one of the most notable aspects of the burgeoning contemporary "anthropology of Christianity" is that it contains so many examples of Pentecostalism and charismatic Christianity, two areas that were largely ignored by many anthropologists a few decades ago, even when such Christians were missionizing in their "fields." The reversal of such an ethnographic taboo appears to reflect a change in anthropology itself, as it turns its gaze on to the cultural relativities of "the modern" and to its own genealogies, as well as engaging deeply with religious processes that are explicitly and self-consciously transnational in scope. At the same time, and ironically, such depictions of Christianity can limit our understandings of its range and significance if they prompt a focus on Christianity that is almost exclusive an anthropology of the birth and diffusion of "modernity."

GLOBALIZING RELIGION

As work on colonialism and post-colonialism indicates, anthropologists have not confined themselves to small-scale, synchronic studies in recent years. Increasingly, religion is seen as a medium of global activity, both through travel and through the creation of transnational imaginaries. Thus Steven Vertovec's (2000: 1–2) tracing of the "comparative patterns" of the Hindu diaspora indicate not only that "Hinduism" is an ever-malleable phenomenon, but also that the great challenge for analysts is to stop looking to India as the ideal culture, the yardstick against which other forms of Hinduism are to be measured. In such orientations towards India we perhaps see hints again of an anthropological essentialism, an assumption that "proper" Hinduism emerges from a particular territory. At the same time, contemporary anthropological emphases on heterogeneity may be in interesting tension with the views of some adherents in India and beyond who increasingly choose to present a nationalist and "fundamentalist" image of Hinduism, and India as a key site of religious orientation for such a viewpoint. Scholars must also take into account some of the effects of novel articulations of Hinduism in diasporic space. As Vertovec notes (pp. 34–5), a certain sharpening of self-awareness is a trend common in diasporas, fostered by self-reflection stimulated among minorities in new contexts of religious and ethnic pluralism. He discusses the ways in which the condition of diaspora may stimulate members of a faith to formulate "universal" accounts of the particular religion and its teaching. Such confrontation with religious otherness can be seen to engender processes of reification, removing modes of understanding from embeddedness in the flow of daily life, in a curious parallel to the Geertzean general formulations of religion that we saw towards the beginning of this chapter.

Transnational forms of religion are also increasingly mediated through novel forms of electronic technology. Vertovec (p. 155) draws on Gillespie's well-known work on *Television, Ethnicity and Cultural Change* (1995), which looks at the transformational ties television and film create between India and the diaspora in the form of Bombay movies, or concrete links between relatives and friends made through video letters and home movies of rites of passage. Thus, he notes that, when watching episodes of the Hindu epics the Ramayana or Mahabharata made for TV in India, Hindus in Britain may light incense or conduct puja before or after viewing.

Similarly, Dale Eickelman and Jon Anderson (1999) refer to the role of new media in the "Muslim world." Such media help to redefine Muslim publics, creating emergent forms of space and interaction beyond face-to-face communication, but also beyond the immediate control of the state. Thus, for Eickelman and Anderson a new sense of a public is emerging throughout both Muslim-majority states and Muslim communities elsewhere, shaped by increasingly open contests over the authoritative use of the symbolic language of Islam. One potential effect of such interaction, as we also see with diasporic Hinduism, may be the development of both "narrowcasting" among small interest groups and attempts to homogenize certain aspects of devotion for broad consumption. For these authors (p. 10): "The publics that emerge around these forms of communication create a globalization from below that complements and draws on techniques of globalization known in finance and mass marketing," while the professional who are often those who deploy the media most effectively "are both producers and consumers, forming communities on their own scale: interstitial, fluid, and resting on shared communications, a minimal definition of what constitutes public space."

The globalization of religious forms, and in particular their connections with patterns of migration, also has implications for a post-colonial anthropology. Old "sending" missionary contexts have become new missionary fields, as Europe and North America become targets for religious as well as economic migration. Thus Ukah (2005) refers to the process of "reverse mission" in relation to African Christian churches in Europe, an expansion which he sees as coinciding with processes of globalization. Church founders combine rhetorics of remissionizing the West with roles as immigration or visa consultants. Strikingly, such churches may also present contemporary transformations of older capitalist logics. Churches not only produce religious goods and services, but have also evolved an entrepreneurial and market logic which guides and informs involvement in the production, distribution and marketing of economic goods such as video-films, books, music cassettes, DVDs and CDs. Following Cannell, we should not view the significance of these churches only in terms of their articulation of Christian forms of modernity; and yet nor should we ignore their role in creating novel forms of citizenship and economic action in a landscape of agency that transcends – or perhaps it is more accurate to say renegotiates – national and political borders.

COMMON THEMES AND EMERGENT TRENDS

In my final remarks I shall resist mentioning the numerous themes and significant writers that I have failed to mention. Instead, I wish briefly to revisit just a few of the common substantive and analytical threads that have emerged since the 1960s, as well as suggesting a (very) few of the directions that the anthropology of religion is beginning to take in the twenty-first century.

One theme has been present, implicitly, in every section: that of the body, and associated processes of embodiment. We saw for instance how Geertz referred to human beings' "innate response capacities"; Asad, meanwhile, was concerned with a more Foucauldian and Marxist notion of the disciplining of the body, which had some parallels with the work of the Comaroffs on missionary encounters and even that of Bloch on ritual as coercive practice. Bell's concept of ritualization builds in part on Bourdieu's (1977) development of the notion of the habitus, the assertion that humans take on embodied dispositions and institutionalized bodily habits that mediate between custom and innovation. In a sense, habitus provides another way in which to think of the regularization of social order occurring in contexts that include, but also go far beyond, explicitly ritual frames. In its emphasis on experience, much of such work on the body takes us beyond Mary Douglas's (1966) useful (but curiously disembodied) depiction of the body as bounded symbolic system, and this is a trend has continued in contemporary anthropology through important work looking at the inscription of moral order on the experience of the "gendered" body (Boddy 1989; Austen-Broos 1997), or the construction of self-processes in the constitution of the sacred self (see e.g. Csordas 1994).

A very different approach that invokes other aspects of the physical body is provided by the newer forms of cognitive anthropology that have focused on religion. Thus Pascal Boyer's work, in such books as *The Naturalness of Religious Ideas* (1994) and *Religion Explained: The Evolutionary Origins of Religious Thought* (2001), finds the explanation for religious beliefs and behaviors in the way all human minds are said to work (there are echoes here of both Chomsky and Lévi-Srauss). In effect, religious concepts and norms can be "explained" as by-products of our cognitive architecture. The recurrent properties of religious concepts and norms that are detected in different cultures have emerged from standard cognitive systems that have evolved outside of religion, such as agency-detection, moral intuition, and contagion-avoidance. It is hard to imagine an approach more different to that of Asad, as universal properties of the body are said to lead to universally detectable trends.

Boyer's work largely by-passes another trend that has developed since Geertz was writing in the 1960s, and which has permeated anthropology as a whole: an increased awareness of the politics of carrying out fieldwork as well as of representing the religious systems of others. Asad's work is an example of such heightened political awareness, as is the work of the Comaroffs, but we see it also more implicitly in Tanya Luhrmann's decision to focus the ethnographic gaze (and moreover one concerned with rationality) back on to white, middle-class informants – people rather close in background to herself. Thus a recent book edited by James Spickard, Shawn Landres and Meredith McGuire (2002) talks in its sub-title of "Reshaping the Ethnography of Religion" through a focus on such issues as insider/outsider problems in understanding religions, questions of negotiating researcher identity, and issues of the relative power of researcher and researched.

These forms of heightened self-consciousness are illustrated well by the treatment of Christianity in the anthropology of religion. Once largely implicit in the discipline, perhaps ignored by researchers more interested in "exotic," non-textual religions, it is beginning to take a much more prominent place within a discipline keen to anatomize its own origins and assumptions. And yet, as we have seen, old problems have arisen even in contemporary analyses of this religion. How do we avoid essentialism – or at least a crude theologizing – in defining the central themes of such an internally heterogeneous religious formation? And how do we avoid looking at some aspects of Christianity (those that give us access to our concerns with transnationalism and modernity) but not others?

Much of the anthropology of religion of the present is marked by its hybrid quality, in the sense that scholars who study religion do not necessarily see themselves as cutting themselves off from studies of the economy, political formations, medical systems, and so on. The heterogeneity of the sub-discipline provides challenges to its identity but is also perhaps one of its greatest achievements. It may be that in the future we will not wish to talk of "the anthropology of religion" making few theoretical advances – not only because of the quality of the work being produced, but also because the anthropology of religion will primarily be seen as "anthropology" rather than a parochial sub-field.

Notes

1   Also quoted in Morris (1987: 313); Klass (1995: 2); Lambek (2002: 6).
2   Lambek (2002:6) also refers here to the influence of the philosophers Langer and Ryle on Geertz. See also Ortner (1999).
3   Gluckman as quoted in Turner (1985: 4); in Deflem (1991).
4   Austin (1962) calls these "performative utterances" and "illocutionary acts." Searle (1969) sees them as "speech acts."

Bibliography

Austen-Broos, Diane (1997) *Jamaica Genesis: Religion and the Politics of Moral Orders*, Chicago: University of Chicago Press.
Austin, John (1962) *How to Do Things With Words*, Oxford University Press: Oxford, England.
Asad, Talal (1993) *Genealogies of Religion: Discipline and Reasons of Power in Christianity and Islam*, Baltimore and London: Johns Hopkins University Press.
Asad, Talal (2003) *Formations of the Secular: Christianity, Islam, Modernity*, Stanford: Stanford University Press.
Bell, Catherine (1992) *Ritual Theory, Ritual Practice*, Oxford: Oxford University Press.
Boddy, Janice (1989) *Wombs and Alien Spirits*, Toronto: University of Toronto Press.
Bloch, Maurice (1992) *Prey into Hunter: The Politics of Religious Experience*, Cambridge: Cambridge University Press.
Bourdieu, Pierre (1977) *Outline of the Theory of Practice*, Cambridge: Cambridge University Press.
Bowie, Fiona (2000) *The Anthropology of Religion*, Oxford: Blackwell.
Bowie, Fiona (2006) Anthropology of religion, in Robert Segal (ed.), *The Blackwell Companion to the Study of Religion*, Oxford: Blackwell, 3–24.
Boyer, Pascal (1994) *The Naturalness of Religious Ideas*, Berkeley: University of California Press.
Boyer, Pascal (2001) *Religion Explained: The Evolutionary Origins of Religious Thought*, New York: Basic Books.
Cannell, Fenella (2006) The anthropology of Christianity, in Fenella Cannell (ed.), *The Anthropology of Christianity*, Durham, NC: Duke University Press, 1–50.
Coleman, Simon and Elsner, John (1998) Performing pilgrimage: Walsingham and the ritual construction of irony, in Felicia Hughes-Freeland (ed.), *Ritual, Performance, Media*, London: Routledge, 46–65.
Comaroff, Jean (1985) *Body of Power, Spirit of Resistance: The Culture and History of a South African People*, Chicago: Chicago University Press.
Cox, Harvey (1965) *The Secular City: Urbanization and Secularization in Theological Perspective*, New York: Macmillan.
Csordas, Thomas (1994) *The Sacred Self: A Cultural Phenomenology of Charismatic Healing*, Berkeley: University of California Press.
Deflem, Mathieu (1991) Ritual, anti-structure, and religion: a discussion of Victor Turner's processual symbolic analysis, *Journal for the Scientific Study of Religion* 30 (1): 1–25.
Douglas, Mary (1966) *Purity and Danger: An Analysis of the Concepts of Pollution and Taboo*, London: Routledge and Kegan Paul.

Eade, John and Sallnow, Michael (eds.) (1991) *Contesting the Sacred: The Anthropology of Christian Pilgrimage*, London: Routledge.

Eickelman, Dale F. and Anderson, Jon W. (1999) Redefining Muslim publics, in Dale Eickelman and Jon W. Anderson (eds.), *New Media in the Muslim World: The Emerging Public Sphere*, Bloomington and Indianapolis: Indian University Press, 1–18.

Evans-Pritchard, Edward (1937) *Witchcraft, Oracles and Magic among the Azande*, Oxford: Clarendon Press.

Frazer, James (1922) *The Golden Bough*, London: Macmillan.

Geertz, Clifford (1973) [1966] Religion as a cultural system, in *The Interpretation of Cultures*, New York: Basic Books, 87–125.

Gillespie, Marie (1995) *Television, Ethnicity, and Cultural Change*, New York: Routledge.

Iteanu, Andre (1983) *La ronde des échanges. De La Circulation aux Valeurs Chez Les Orokaiva*, Cambridge: Cambridge University Press.

Jewett, Robert and Lawrence, John (2003) *Captain America and the Crusade against Evil: The Dilemma of Zealous Nationalism*, Grand Rapids: Eerdmans.

Keane, Webb (2007) *Christian Moderns*, Berkeley: University of California Press.

Klass, Morton (1995) *Ordered Universes: Approaches to the Anthropology of Religion*, Boulder: Westview Press.

Lambek, Michael (ed.) (2002) *A Reader in the Anthropology of Religion*, Oxford: Blackwell.

Lindquist, Galina and Coleman, Simon (2008) Against belief? *Social Analysis* 52 (12): 1–18.

Luhrmann, Tanya (1989) *Persuasions of the Witch's Craft: Ritual Magic and Witchcraft in Present-Day England*, Oxford: Blackwell.

Morris, Brian (1987) *Anthropological Studies of Religion: An Introductory Text*, Cambridge: Cambridge University Press.

Needham, Rodney (1972) *Belief, Language, and Experience*, Oxford: Blackwell.

Ortner, Sherry (ed.) (1999) *The Fate of "Culture": Geertz and Beyond*, Berkeley: University of California Press.

Rappaport, Roy (1999) Enactments of meaning, in *Ritual and Religion in the Making of Humanity*, Cambridge: Cambridge University Press, 104–38.

Robbins, Joel (2007) Continuity thinking and the problem of Christian culture: belief, time and the anthropology of Christianity, *Current Anthropology* 48 (1): 5–17.

Ruel, Malcolm (1997) [1982] *Belief, Ritual and the Securing of Life: Reflexive Essays on a Bantu Religion*, Leiden: Brill. Originally: Ruel, Malcolm, Christians as believers, in J. Davis (ed.), *Religious Organization and Religious Experience*, London: Academic Press, 1982.

Searle, John (1969) *Speech Acts: An Essay in the Philosophy of Language*, Cambridge: Cambridge University Press.

Spickard, James V. and Landres, J. Shawn (2002) Whither ethnography? Transforming the social-scientific study of religion, in James V. Spickard, J. Shawn Landres, and Meredith B. McGuire (eds.), *Personal Knowledge and Beyond: Reshaping the Ethnography of Religion*, New York: New York University Press.

Turner, Edith (1985) Prologue: from the Ndembu to Broadway, in Edith Turner (ed.), *On the Edge of the Bush: Anthropology as Experience*, Tucson: University of Arizona Press, 1–15.

Turner, Victor (1967) *The Forest of Symbols: Aspects of Ndembu Ritual*, Ithaca: Cornell University Press.

Turner, Victor (1968) *The Drums of Affliction: A Study of Religious Process among the Ndembu of Zambia*, Oxford: Clarendon Press.

Turner, Victor (1974) Liminal to liminoid in play, flow and ritual: an essay in comparative symbology, *Rice University Studies* 60 (3): 1–14.

Turner, Victor W. and Turner, Edith (1978) *Image and Pilgrimage in Christian Culture: Anthropological Perspectives*, New York: Columbia University Press.

Ukah, Asonzeh (2005) Reverse mission or asylum Christianity? African Christian churches in Europe, unpublished paper, presented at a workshop on "Afrikanische Pfingstkirchen in Deutschland und Afrika," held at the Free University of Berlin, Germany, July 21–2.

Van Gennep, Arnold (1909) *Les Rites de Passage*, Paris: E. Nourry.

Van der Veer, Peter (1996) Introduction, in P. van der Veer (ed.) *Conversion to Modernities: The Globalization of Christianity*, London: Routledge, 1–21.

Vertovec, Steven (2000) *The Hindu Diaspora: Comparative Patterns*, London: Routledge.

Part II
From Secularization to Resacralization

5

Secularization

STEVE BRUCE

INTRODUCTION

The peoples of pre-industrial Europe were deeply religious. The extent to which they were orthodox Christians varied but most understood the world through basically Christian lenses. They knew the Lord's Prayer and the Hail Mary and could make the sign of the Cross. They knew the ten commandments, the four cardinal virtues, the seven deadly sins, and the seven works of mercy. They paid their taxes to the church. They were baptized, christened, married and buried by the church. They believed sufficiently in hell and in the status of Holy Writ for swearing oaths on the Bible to be an effective means of control. They avoided blaspheming. Even the most humble left something in their wills for the church and the wealthy willed large sums for priests to say masses post-mortem on their behalf. Most knew they had to make reparation to God for their sins, in this life or in the next. When the clergy of the Middle Ages complained of irreligion, their target was not secularity but the persistence of pre-Christian superstitions or the use of the church's rituals in an instrumental magical manner (Bruce 2002: 45–59).

As societies industrialized, their people divided. Some became well-informed "true believers"; others fell away. The once-pervasive religious worldview gave way to an increasingly secular public culture. By the middle of the nineteenth century, religion had become so separated from everyday life that we could count its supporters (Crockett 1998: 131) and declining support in turn reduced the social and political power of religious institutions. The introduction of social surveys in the twentieth century allowed us to assess religious belief (Gill et al. 1998; Field 2001). Whether we count membership, church attendance, religious ceremonies to mark rights of passage, or indices of belief, we find that across the industrial world there has been a major decline in all religious indices (Bruce 2002).

It is vital to appreciate that the decline of the churches in Europe has been general and nearly universal. In the less developed countries of the former communist bloc, there has been a small increase in church adherence since 1990 but given that even there, young people are marked less religious than their parents, this seems highly likely to be a brief blip. Leaving aside the above-average religiosity of migrants from Africa, Asia and the Middle East, almost every section of British Christianity has experienced unremitting decline since at least the middle of the nineteenth century: typical weekly church attendance has fallen from around 50 percent of the population to 7 pecent. Using the very large data set of the European Social Survey 2002–3, David Voas (2009) has demonstrated that, despite their very different political histories, countries as diverse as Holland, Portugal, Slovenia and the Netherlands East show very similar trajectories of decline in religiosity. The date at which decline begins varies but, once begun, the trajectories are remarkably similar. This is important because it tells us that the causes of decline are not to be found in particular local deficiencies. Because it gives them hope of being able to remedy the problem, it is tempting for church people to suppose that some particular feature of their belief-system, ritual, or structure is at fault. That secularization is widespread is the sociologist's justification for supposing that the cause lies above and beyond the defects of any particular religious expression.

Understanding Secularization

Explaining the decline in the power, prestige and popularity of religion has exercised such a large number of scholars that we can represent their work as a "secularization paradigm." Figure 5.1 represents a synthesis from a variety of sources. Some of the scholars cited would dissent from other elements of the general synthesis but brevity prevents me elaborating such disagreements.

Monotheism (R1)

Following Weber, Berger (1969) in sketching the deep background to secularization begins by noting how the monotheism of Judaism and Christianity contributed to the rationality of the West. The Egyptian, Roman, and Greek worlds were embedded in a cosmic order which embraced the entire universe with no sharp distinction between the human and the non-human. In contrast, the single Jewish God was remote. He would end the world he created but in-between it could be seen as having its own structure and logic. He made consistent ethical demands and he was beyond magical manipulation. We could learn his laws and obey them but we could not bribe, cajole or trick him. As the Christian Church evolved, the cosmos was re-mythologized with angels and semi-divine saints. The idea that God could be manipulated through ritual, confession, and penance undermined the tendency to regulate behavior with a standardized ethical code. However, this trend was reversed as the Protestant Reformation again demythologized the world, eliminated the ritual and sacramental manipulation of God, and restored the process of ethical rationalization.

Making formal what pleased God made it possible for ethics to become detached from beliefs about the supernatural. Codes could be followed for their own sake and could even attract alternative justifications. In that sense, the rationalizing tendency of Christianity created space for secular alternatives.

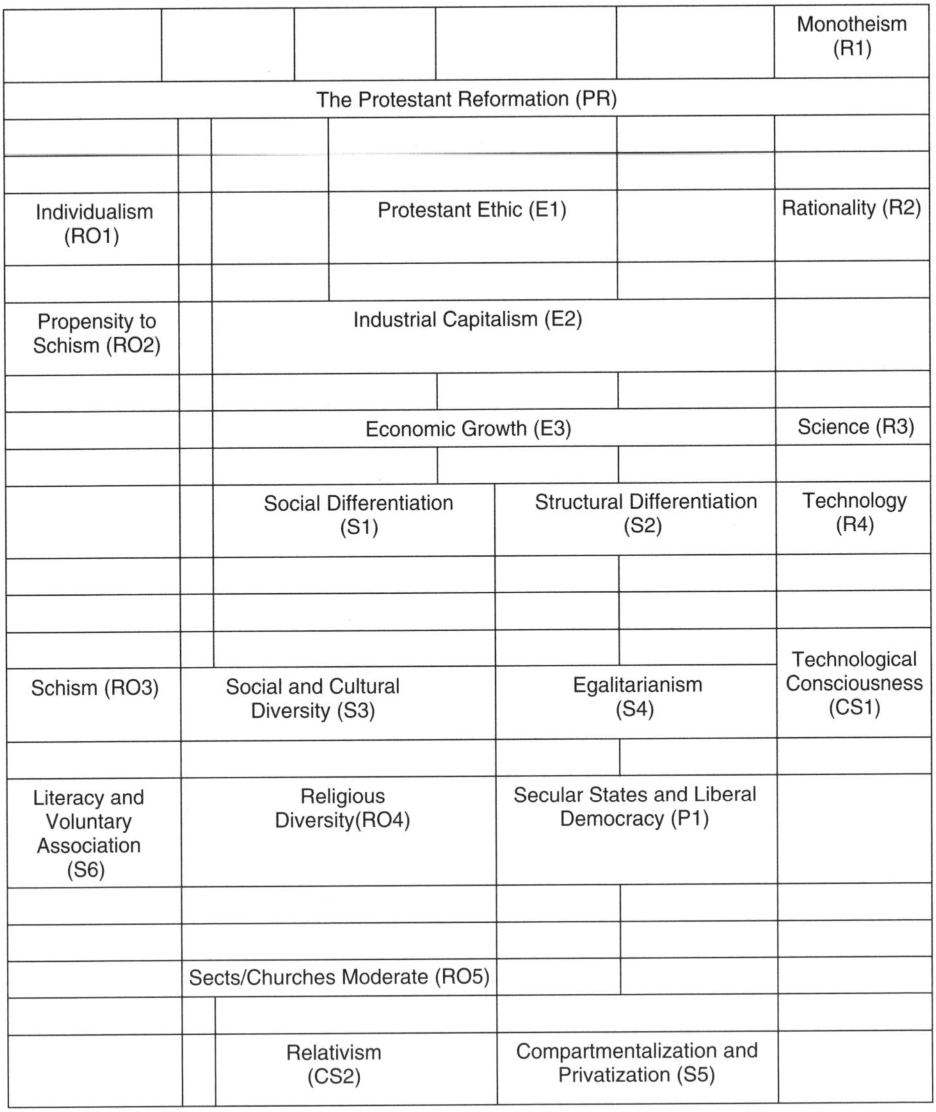

						Monotheism (R1)
The Protestant Reformation (PR)						
Individualism (RO1)		Protestant Ethic (E1)				Rationality (R2)
Propensity to Schism (RO2)		Industrial Capitalism (E2)				
		Economic Growth (E3)				Science (R3)
		Social Differentiation (S1)	Structural Differentiation (S2)			Technology (R4)
Schism (RO3)		Social and Cultural Diversity (S3)	Egalitarianism (S4)			Technological Consciousness (CS1)
Literacy and Voluntary Association (S6)		Religious Diversity(RO4)	Secular States and Liberal Democracy (P1)			
		Sects/Churches Moderate (RO5)				
		Relativism (CS2)	Compartmentalization and Privatization (S5)			

Figure 5.1 The secularization paradigm
Key: R = Rationalization; RO = Religious organization; E = Economy; S = Society; P = Polity; CS = Cognitive style.

The Protestant ethic (E1)

Weber argues that the Reformation inadvertently created new attitudes to work and capital accumulation (Weber 1976; Marshall 1980). Pre-reformation, especially pious people displayed "other-worldly asceticism": cultivating the purity of their souls by cutting themselves off from the world in monasteries and in hermitages. Luther argued that any legitimate occupation, performed diligently, glorified God. By arguing against confession, penance and absolution, the Reformers deprived people of a way of periodically wiping away their sins. They thus increased the strain of trying to live a Christian life and made it all the more important to avoid temptation; hence the additional premium on work. With other changes, the result was Weber's "this-worldly asceticism"; an attitude of disciplined self-control well-suited to the rise of rational capitalism. The link E2 to E3 represents the fact that those countries that first adopted industrial capitalism prospered ahead of their rivals and, as we will see, prosperity itself weakens religious commitments.

Structural differentiation (S2)

Modernization entails structural (or functional) differentiation: social life fragments as specialized roles and institutions are created to handle specific features or functions previously embodied in one role or institution (Parsons 1964). The family was once a unit of production as well as the institution through which society was reproduced. With industrialization, economic activity became divorced from the home. It also became increasingly informed by its own values (that is, there is a link from R2 to S2). At work we are supposed to be rational, instrumental and pragmatic. We are also supposed to be universalistic: to treat customers alike, paying attention only to the matter in hand. The private sphere, by contrast, is taken to be expressive, indulgent and emotional.

Increased specialization directly secularized many social functions which were once dominated by the church: education, healthcare, welfare, and social control. Either the state directly provided such services or, if churches remained the conduit, the work became increasingly governed by secular standards and values.

Social differentiation (S1)

As society fragments, so does the people. Economic growth created an ever-greater range of occupation and life-situation, which because it was accompanied by growing egalitarianism, led to class avoidance. In feudal societies, masters and servants lived cheek-by-jowl. Such proximity was possible because the gentry had no fear that the lower orders would get ideas "above their station." As the social structure became more fluid and the defense of hereditary inequality more difficult, those who could afford to do so replaced the previously effective social distance with literal space.

The plausibility of a single moral universe in which all people have a place depends on the social structure being stable. With new social roles and increasing social mobility, communal conceptions of the moral and supernatural order fragmented. As classes became more distinctive they created salvational systems better suited to their interests. The great pyramid of pope, bishops, priests, and laity reflected the social pyramid of king, nobles, gentry and peasants. Independent small farmers or the rising business class preferred a more democratic religion; hence their attraction to such Protestant sects as the Presbyterians, Baptists and Quakers.

Modernization was not simply a matter of religion responding to social, economic and political changes. Religion itself had a considerable effect on social and cultural diversity (S3). To explain this I must go back a stage to the link between the Reformation, the rise of individualism and schism.

Individualism (RO1)

Martin noted a major effect of the Reformation when he wrote that "The logic of Protestantism is clearly in favor of the voluntary principle, to a degree that eventually makes it sociologically unrealistic" (1978: 9). Belief systems differ greatly in their propensity to fragment. To simplify, some religions claim a unique truth while others allow that there are many ways to salvation. The Catholic Church claims that Christ's authority was passed to Peter and then fixed in the office of the Pope. It claims control of access to salvation and the right to decide disputes about God's will. If those claims are accepted, the Church is relatively immune to fission. As to depart from Rome goes to the heart of what you believed as a Catholic, such departures are difficult and are associated with extreme upheavals, such as the French Revolution. Thus as Catholic countries modernized they split into the religious and the secular: so in the twentieth century Italy, Spain and France had conservative Catholic traditions and powerful Communist parties.

Protestantism was vulnerable to schism because it rejected institutional mechanisms to settle disputes. Asserting that everyone can equally well discern God's will invites schism. Tradition, habit, respect for learning, or admiration for piety might restrain but could not prevent division. The Reformation produced not one church purified and strengthened but competing perspectives and organizations.

We might add a secular version of RO1. Individualism gradually developed an autonomous dynamic as the egalitarianism located in the diagram as S4. It is placed there to stress that individualism and the closely associated social reality of diversity (S3) could only develop in propitious circumstances and those where provided by structural differentiation (S2) and economic growth (E3).

The link between modernization and inequality is paradoxical. Industrialization produced both greater social distance and a basic egalitarianism (S4). The Reformers were not democrats but they inadvertently caused a major change in the relative importance of community and individual. By removing the special status of the priesthood and the possibility that religious merit could be transferred (by, for example, saying masses for the souls of the dead), they re-asserted what was implicit in early Christianity: that we are all severally rather than jointly equal in the eyes of God. That equality initially lay in our sinfulness and our responsibilities but the idea could not indefinitely be confined to duty. Equal obligations eventually became equal rights.

That was made possible by changes in the economy (Gellner 1983, 1991). Economic development brought change and the expectation of further change. And it brought occupational mobility. As it became more common for people to better themselves, it also become more common for them to think better of themselves. However badly paid, the industrial worker did not see himself as a serf. The serf occupied just one role in an all-embracing hierarchy and that role shaped his entire life. A tin-miner in Cornwall in 1800 might be oppressed at work but in the late evening and on Sunday he could change clothes and persona to become a Baptist preacher: a man of prestige. Such alternation marks a crucial change. As social status became more task-specific, it became possible for people to occupy different positions in different hierarchies. That made it possible to distinguish between the role and the person who played it. Roles could still be ranked and accorded very different degrees of power or status but the people behind the roles could be seen as in some sense equal.

Societalization

Societalization is the term Wilson gives to the way in which "life is increasingly enmeshed and organized, not locally but societally (that society being most evidently, but not uniquely, the nation state)" (1982: 154). If social differentiation (S1) and individualism (RO1) are blows to small-scale communities from below, societalization is the attack from above. Close-knit, integrated, communities gradually lost power and presence to large-scale industrial and commercial enterprises, to modern states coordinated through massive, impersonal bureaucracies, and to cities. This is the classic community-to-society transition delineated by Tönnies (1955).

Following Durkheim, Wilson argues that religion draws its strength from the community. As the society rather than the community becomes the locus of the individual's life, so religion is denuded. The church of the Middle Ages baptized, christened, married and buried. Its calendar of services mapped on to the seasons. It celebrated and legitimated local life. In turn it drew strength from being frequently re-affirmed by the local people. In 1898 almost everyone in my village celebrated the harvest by bringing tokens of their produce to the church. In 1998, a very small number of people in my village (only one of them a farmer) celebrated by bringing to the church vegetables and tinned goods (many of foreign provenance) bought in a supermarket that is itself part of a multi-national combine. Instead of celebrating the harvest, the service thanked God for all his creation. Broadening the symbolism of the celebration solved the problem of relevance but it lost direct contact with the lives of those involved. When the all-embracing community of like-situated people working and playing together gives way to the dormitory town or suburb, there is little left in common to celebrate.

Differentiation and societalization reduced the plausibility of any single overarching moral and religious system and thus allowed competing religions. While they may have had much to say to private experience, they could have little connection to the performance of social roles or the operation of social systems because they were not society-wide. Religion retained subjective plausibility for some, but lost its objective taken-for-grantedness. It was now a preference, not a necessity.

Again it is worth stressing the interaction of social and cultural forces. The Reformation's fragmentation of the religious tradition (RO3) hastened the development of the religiously neutral state (P1). A successful economy required a high degree of integration: effective communication, a shared legal code to enforce contracts, a climate of trust, and so on (Gellner 1991). This required an integrated national culture. Where there was consensus, a national "high culture" could be provided through the dominant religious tradition. The clergy could continue to be the school teachers, historians, propagandists, public administrators, and military strategists. Where there was little consensus, the growth of the state was secular.

Schism and sect formation (RO3)

The Reformation stimulated literacy (S5). With everyone required to answer to God individually, lay people needed the resources to meet that new responsibility. Hence the translation of the Bible into vernacular languages; the rapid advance in printing;

the spread of literacy and the start of mass education. Competition between sects was a further spur. And as Gellner and others argue, the spread of education was both essential to, and a consequence of, economic growth. The sectarian competitive spirit of the RO line interacted with the requirements of the E and S line to produce a literate and educated laity, which in turn encouraged the general emphasis on the importance and rights of the individual and the growth of egalitarianism (S4) and liberal democracy (P1).

Protestant sects also had a direct influence on P1 by providing a new model for social organization. Reformed religion was individualistic but it encouraged individuals to band together for encouragement, edification, evangelism and social control. As an alternative to the organic community in which position was inherited and ascribed, the sectarians established the voluntary association of like-minded individuals coming together to pursue common goals.

Social and cultural diversity (S3)

Diversity created the secular state. Modernization brought with it increased cultural diversity in three ways. Peoples moved and brought their language, religion and social mores into a new setting. Second, the expansive nation-state encompassed new peoples. Third, especially common in Protestant settings, economic modernization created classes which created competing sects. Hence the paradox: at the same time as the nation-state was trying to create a unified national culture out of thousands of small communities, it was having to come to terms with increasing religious diversity. The solution was an increasingly neutral state. The idea of having one legally established state church to which all subjects or citizens should belong was abandoned altogether (the United States) or was neutered (the British case). While freedom from entanglements with secular power allowed churches to become more clearly spiritual – to concentrate on their core task – their removal from the center of public life reduced their contact with, and relevance for, the general population (P2 and P3).

Separation of church and state was one consequence of diversity. Another was the break between community and religious worldview. In sixteenth century England, every significant event in the life cycle of the individual and the community was celebrated in church and given a religious gloss. The church's techniques were used to bless the sick, sweeten the soil, and increase animal productivity. Testimonies, contracts and promises were reinforced by oaths sworn on the Bible and before God. But beyond the special events that saw the vast majority of parishioners troop into the church, a huge amount of credibility was given to the religious worldview simply through everyday interaction and conversation. People commented on the weather by saying God be praised and on parting wished each other "God Speed" or "Goodbye" (an abbreviation for "God be with you").

Diversity also called into question the certainty that believers could accord their religion (Berger 1980). Ideas are most convincing when they are universally shared. The elaboration of alternatives provides a profound challenge. Believers need not fall on their swords when they find that others disagree with them. Where clashes of ideologies occur in the context of social conflict or when alternatives are promoted by people who need not be seriously entertained, the cognitive challenge can be dismissed (Berger and Luckmann 1966: 133). Nonetheless proliferating alternatives removes the sense of inevitability. When the oracle speaks with a single clear voice, it is easy to believe it is the voice of God. When it speaks with twenty different voices, it is tempting to look behind the screen.

Compartmentalization and privatization (S5)

Believers may respond to the fact of variety by supposing that all religions are, in some sense, the same (RO5). Another possibility (and they are not incompatible) is to confine one's faith to a particular compartment of social life (S5). With compartmentalization comes privatization: the sense that the reach of religion is shortened to just those who accept the teachings of this of that faith, As Luckmann puts it:

> This development reflects the dissolution of *one* hierarchy of significance in the world view. Based on the complex institutional structure and social stratification of industrial societies different "versions" of the world view emerge ... With the pervasiveness of the consumer orientation and the sense of autonomy, the individual is more likely to confront the culture and the sacred cosmos as a "buyer." Once religion is defined as a "private affair," the individual may choose from the assortment of "ultimate" meanings as he sees fit. (1970: 98–9)

Casanova (1994) argues that differentiation need not cause privatization. The major churches, having now accepted the rules of liberal democracy, can regain a public role. They achieve this not by the old model of a compact between a dominant church and the state, but by acting as pressure groups in civil society. This is true but it misses the point that religious interest groups are now forced to present their case in secular terms. For example, abortion is not opposed as unbiblical but because it infringes the universal human right to life.

The secular state and liberal democracy (P1)

Social innovations, once established, can have an appeal that goes far beyond the initial motive to innovate. Secular liberal democracy evolved as a necessary response to the egalitarianism (S4) made possible by structural differentiation (S2), and to the social and cultural diversity (S3) created by a combination of the fissiparousness of Protestantism (RO2) and social differentiation (S1). But it became attractive in its own right and in the late nineteenth century societies that had no great need for them introduced the same principles as part of wider political reforms. Despite dissent being largely contained within the Lutheran tradition, the introduction of representative democracy and the weakening of the monarchy (or Grand Duchy) in the Nordic countries was accompanied by a weakening of the Church (which largely retained its diverse social functions by presenting them universally as secular social services).

The moderation of sects and churches (RO5)

Niebuhr elaborates a small but important element of the paradigm in his extension of Troeltsch's comments on the evolution of sects (1962). Niebuhr notes that time and again radical sects (for example, the Quakers or the Methodists) became comfortable denominations, on easy terms with the world they once despised as unGodly. The commitment of those born into the sect is invariably weaker than that of those who made sacrifices through an act of choice. And the environment of the second, third and fourth generations was almost always more seductive. Most sectarians prospered ahead of the average, partly for the "Protestant Ethic" reasons elaborated by Weber (E1) and partly because their asceticism made them widely trusted. It is no accident that most of the British banking system developed from family firms run by Quakers: the Barclays, Backhouses, Trittons and Gurneys. Increasing wealth (and the possibilities of social status and public acceptance that came with it) increased the costs of asceticism. Not surprisingly, most sectarians moderated.

Michels (1962) identifies a further source of moderation in his study of oligarchy in left-wing trade unions and political parties. Most sects began as primitive democracies, with little formal organization, but gradually acquired a professional leadership. Especially after the founder died, there was a need to educate and train the preachers and teachers who would sustain the movement. If successful, there was a growing organization to be coordinated and managed. There were assets to be safe-guarded and books to be published and distributed. With organization came paid officials who had a vested interest in reducing tension between the sect and the wider society. They could also compare themselves to the clergy of the established church and (initially for the status of their faith rather than their own reward) desire the same levels of training, remuneration and social status.

If the sect can isolate itself from the wider society so that its culture forms the "taken-for-granted" backcloth to life then it can sustain itself. The Amish, Hutterites and Doukobhors, who created isolated agricultural communes, provide examples. But in most cases the sect is only slightly insulated and cannot avoid the social-psychological effects of diversity described above. Having failed to win over the bulk of the people to its radical message and having to come to terms with being only a "saved remnant," the sect finds good reasons to moderate its claims and comes to see itself, not as the sole embodiment of God's will, but simply as one expression among others of what is pleasing to God.

The moderation of sects is mirrored in the moderation of the national churches. Faced with widespread defection and the loss of authority, most churches reduced their claims and came to view themselves as just one among others. The change was rarely made quickly or willingly but by the start of the twentieth century most state churches were cooperating with other Christian organizations. By the end of it, most were presenting themselves as the senior spokesman for all religions against a largely secular climate.

Economic growth (E3)

The effect of prosperity on Protestants sects can be generalized. Increasing affluence often reduces religious fervor and traditionalism (Inglehart 1990, 1997).The poor and dis-possessed can find solace in a belief system that promises that those who have little in this life will have everything in the next. As they prosper, the no-longer-poor re-write their faith so that its loses much of its power. US Pentecostalists such as Oral Roberts (Harrell 1985) and Tammy Faye Bakker (Barnhart 1988) grew up in impoverished conditions which made it easy and satisfying to denounce flashy clothes, make-up, Hollywood movies, social dancing and television. When they could afford what had been the work of the Devil, they compromised their principles. Morals were slower to change but attitudes to sexuality were also relaxed. For example, divorce, though still regretted, is widely accepted. This does not of itself mean that US Pentecostalists are becoming less religious but that the erosion of distinctive ways of life makes the maintenance of distinctive beliefs harder because it increases positive interaction with people of more liberal religious views or none (Shibley 1996).

Science (R3) and technology (R4)

Critics of the secularization paradigm mis-represent it by elevating science to a central position: "it is science that has the most deadly implications for religion" (Stark and Finke 2000: 61). A zero-sum notion of knowledge, with rational thought and science conquering territory from superstition was carried into sociology by Comte and Marx among others but it is not part of the modern secularization paradigm. We recognize that modern people are quite capable of believing untruths and hence that the decreasing plausibility of any one body of ideas cannot be explained simply by the presence of some (to us) more plausible ones. The crucial connections are more subtle and complex than those implied in a science v. religion battle and rest on nebulous consequences of assumptions about the orderliness of the world and our mastery over it.

One line was drawn by Merton in his work on Puritan scientists (1970). He argues that many seventeenth-century Protestant scientists were inspired to natural science by a desire to demonstrate the glory of God's creation, by the rationalizing attitude of the Protestant ethic and by an interest in controlling the corrupt world. The result was the same irony that followed from the rationalization of ethics. By demonstrating the fundamentally rule-governed nature of the material world, the Puritan scientists allowed their heirs to do science without framing their work within the assertion that "This shows God's glory."

More important than science was the development of effective technologies. Religion is often practical. Holy water cures ailments and prayers improve crop quality. Wilson argues that technology secularizes by reducing the occasions on which people have recourse to religion. Farmers need not stop praying to save their sheep from maggots because an effective sheep dip becomes available but as the accumulation of scientific knowledge gave people insight into, and mastery over, areas that had once been mysterious, the need and opportunity for recourse to the religious gradually declined. A perfect example can be seen in the contrast response of the Church of England to the Black Death of 1348–49 and the HIV/AIDs so-called "gay plague" of the 1980s. In the first, the Church called for weeks of fasting and prayer. In the second, it called for more government investment in medical-scientific research.

More generally, as Martin puts it, with the growth of science and technology "the general sense of human power is increased, the play of contingency is restricted, and the overwhelming sense of divine limits which afflicted previous generations is much diminished" (1969: 116). If people are to be religious in the modern world they are more likely to be drawn to self-constructed individualistic "New Age" spiritualities (where they decide what they will believe) than to traditional authoritarian faiths.

Technology and consciousness (CS1)

In exploring the psychology of modern work, Berger et al. (1974) argue that, even if we are unaware of it, modern technology brings with a "technological consciousness" that is difficult to reconcile with a sense of the sacred. An example is "componentiality." Modern work assumes that the most complex entities can be broken down into parts that are infinitely replaceable. Likewise actions can be reduced to elements that can be indefinitely repeated. This attitude is carried over from industrial work to workers (a management style known after its heroic promoter as "Fordism") and then to bureaucracy generally. While there is no obvious clash between these assumptions and the teachings of most religions, there are serious incompatibilities of approach. There is little space for the eruption of the divine.

To summarize the R line, the effects of science and technology on the plausibility of religious belief are often misunderstood. Direct clash is less significant than the subtle impact of naturalistic ways of thinking. Science and technology have not made us atheists but the underlying rationality and the subtle encouragement to self-aggrandizement make us less likely than our forebears to entertain the notion of a divine force external to our selves.

Relativism (CS2)

Finally we come to the bottom line. The Christian Church of the Middle Ages was firmly authoritarian and exclusive in its attitude to knowledge. There was a single truth and it knew what it was. Increasingly social and cultural diversity combines with egalitarianism to undermine all claims to authoritative knowledge. While compartmentalization (the idea that my God rules my private life but need not rule the lives of others or my engagement in the public sphere) can serve as a holding operation, it is difficult to live in a world which treats as equally valid a large number of incompatible beliefs, and which shies away from authoritative assertions, without coming to suppose that there is no one truth. We may continue to prefer our world view but we find it hard to insist that what is true for us must also be true for everyone else. The tolerance which is necessary for harmony in diverse egalitarian societies weakens religion by forcing us to live as if we could not be sure of God's will. A remarkable example of the problem is inadvertently given by the Bolton Interfaith Council which, in a pamphlet encouraging people to walk around various worship sites in the city, has pages on "What Christians believe," "What Muslims Believe" and "What Hindus Believe" which present all three faiths as if they were equally correct. It is difficult to imagine how a young resident of Bolton, looking for a home for her incipient spiritual interests, could be recruited to any version of any of the three traditions by such relativism.

The consequence, visible over the twentieth century in liberal democracies, was a decline in the commitment of, and then in the number of, church adherents. Relativism debilitates faith by removing the best reason to ensure one's children are socialized in the faith. If all faiths (and none) offer a road to God, if there is no hell to which heretics get sent, then there is no need to ensure the transmission of orthodoxy.

RETARDING TENDENCIES

The secularization paradigm suggests that social and structural differentiation, societalization, rationalization, individualism, egalitarianism, and increasing social and cultural diversity undermine religion. However, most proponents would add an important qualification: except where religion finds or retains work to do other than relating individuals to the supernatural. The many and varied instances of that work can be summarized under the headings of cultural transition and cultural defense.

Cultural transition

Where social identity is threatened in the course of major social transitions, religion may help negotiate such changes or assert a new claim to a sense of worth. Religio-ethnic groups can ease the move between homeland and new world. The church offers a supportive group which speaks your language and shares your values but also has contacts with the new social milieu.

There is another manifestation of the tendency for religion to retain significance, even temporarily to grow in significance, and that is in the course of modernization itself. Modernization disrupted communities, traditional employment patterns, and status hierarchies. By extending the range of communication, it made the social peripheries and hinterlands more aware of the manners and mores of the center and vice versa. Those at the center of the society were motivated to missionize the rest, seeking to assimilate them by socializing them in "respectable" beliefs and practices. Sectors of the social periphery in turn were motivated to embrace the models of respectable performance offered to them, especially when they were already in the process of upward mobility and self-improvement (Brown 1987). Industrialization and urbanization gave rise to revival and reform movements.

Cultural defense

Religion often acts as guarantor of group identity. Where culture, identity, and sense of worth are challenged by a source promoting either an alien religion or rampant secularism and that source is negatively valued, secularization will be inhibited. Religion can provide resources for the defense of a national, local, ethnic, or status group culture. The role of Catholicism in Polish national resistance to Soviet communism is a good example (Szajkowski 1983).

In the process of functional differentiation, the first sphere to become freed of cultural encumbrances is the economy but religio-ethnic identity can constrain economic rationality. Employers often hire "their own" and even in consumption religion may over-ride rationality. Northern Ireland's small towns often have a Protestant butcher and a Catholic butcher where the market can profitably sustain only one. At times of heightened tension, Protestants and Catholics boycott each others' businesses and travel considerable distances to engage in commerce with their own sort.

Cultural defense also inhibits "societalization." A beleaguered minority may try to prevent the erosion of the community. Those who order their lives in the societal rather than the community mode may be regarded as treacherous and punished accordingly. In ethnic conflicts (Bosnia or Northern Ireland, for example) those who marry across the divide are frequent targets for vigilantes.

Finally, religio-ethnic conflict mutes the cognitive consequences of pluralism because the prevalence of invidious stereotypes allows a much more thorough stigmatizing of alternative cultures. The shift to relativism as a way of accommodating those with whom we differ depends on us taking those people seriously. Where religious differences are strongly embedded in ethnic identities, the cognitive threat of the others is relatively weak. Scottish Protestants in the nineteenth century deployed caricatures of the social vices of the immigrant Irish Catholics as a way of avoiding having to consider them as Christian.

THE RATIONAL CHOICE ALTERNATIVE

There is a radically different reading of the consequences of diversity. Stark argues that the religious vitality of the USA is explained by it having a free market in religious goods and considerable competition between the providers of such goods. Diversity allows all to find a religion that suits their interests, it keeps down costs and thus makes the creation of new religions easier, and it provides the clergy with incentives to recruit a following (Young 1997).

Small parts of the rational choice or "supply side" model are supported by evidence but only studies produced by Stark and his associates support the general approach. Attempts to replicate that work, either by comparing religious vitality and diversity for different areas within one society or by cross-cultural comparison, fail to find positive effects of diversity. Across Europe church adherence is far higher in countries dominated by one religion (Poland and Ireland, for example) than in diverse cultures such as Britain's. In the Baltic states of Lithuania, Latvia and Estonia, overwhelmingly Catholic Lithuania has far higher rates of church adherence than has the more mixed Latvia and Estonia.

A detailed critique of the supply side approach must be found elsewhere (Bruce 1999; Jelen 2002). I will make just two points. Whatever support the supply side model finds by comparing diversity and religious vitality in different places at the same time is overwhelmed by the conclusions drawn from looking at any one place over time. Whether we take Canada, Australia, Norway, Scotland, or Holland we find that religion was far more popular and powerful in 1850, 1900, or 1950 than it is at the end of the twentieth century. As these societies became more diverse so they became more secular.

Second, the rational choice model of human behavior works best for fields where general demand is high but brand loyalty is low. We are not socialized into a culture that bans us from buying a certain car: we are free to maximize. For most of the world, religion is not a preference; it is an inherited social identity, closely tied to other shared identities. It can only be changed at considerable personal cost. Hence this paradox. Only in largely secular societies, were there is little religious behavior left to explain, will people have the attitude to religion supposed by the rational choice model.

The Irreversibility of Secularization

It is always possible that the secularization of the West is merely temporary and that there will be a resurgence of religious interest. Many commentators believe the human condition is such that people will always need religion: that the desire for the supernatural and what it can offer is somehow "hard-wired" into our constitution. Hence long-term and widespread secularization is impossible. When one religious tradition declines another will fill the gap. The obvious evidential problem is that Christianity has now endured at least 150 years of decline and each wave of contenders for replacement (the Pentecostal movements of the 1920s, the charismatic movements of the 1960s, the new religious movements of the 1970s and the New Age spirituality of the 1990s) has failed to make even a small dent in the growing numbers of people free from any organized religious interest.

But there is also a logical problem. The idea that some innate or intrinsic spiritual need will provoke a religious revival neglects the role of culture in shaping human behavior. It supposes that individual needs translate into action outcomes in an unmediated fashion. It misses the point that biological and psychological drives are shaped by and articulated in a particular culture. Even if there are basic questions that most people will ask themselves (such as "what is the meaning of life?"), we cannot assume that large numbers will frame the question in the same terms, let alone embrace the same answer. On the contrary, the authority of the autonomous individual prevents such consensus. While it is common to ascribe to individualism every manner of social vice and to yearn for a more communal way of life, there is no sign that the people of the West are willing to give up their autonomy. The communalist always want everyone else to "get back" to his or her basics.

Brevity requires me to state this bluntly: shared belief systems require coercion. The survival of religion requires that individuals be subordinated to the community. In some settings (religio-ethnic conflicts, for example) individual autonomy is constrained by shared identities. In the stable affluent democracies of the West the individual asserts the rights of the sovereign autonomous consumer. We choose our electrical goods; we choose our gods. Unless we can imagine some social forces that will lead us to give up that freedom, we cannot imagine the creation of detailed ideological consensus. It is not enough to suggest that some calamity may disrupt our complacency. Without a pre-existing common culture, large numbers will not interpret a disaster in the same way and hence will not respond collectively. When the common culture of a society consists of operating principles that allow the individual to choose, no amount of vague spiritual yearning will generate a shared belief-system.

To conclude, the secularization paradigm argues that the decline of religion in the West is not an accident but is an unintended consequence of a variety of complex social changes that for brevity we call modernization. It is not inevitable. But unless we can imagine a reversal of the increasing cultural autonomy of the individual, secularization must be seen as irreversible.

Key Texts

Berger, P. L. (1969) *The Social Reality of Religion*, London: Faber and Faber.
Bruce, S. (2002) *God is Dead: Secularization in the West*, Oxford: Blackwell.
Martin, D. (1978) *A General Theory of Secularization*, Oxford: Basil Blackwell.
Stark, R. and Finke, R. (2000) *Acts of Faith: Explaining the Human Side of Religion*, Berkeley: University of California Press.
Wilson, B. R. (1982) *Religion in Sociological Perspective*, Oxford: Oxford University Press.

Bibliography

Barnhart, J. E. (1988) *Jim and Tammy: Charismatic Intrigue Inside PTL*. Buffalo: Prometheus Books.
Berger, P. L. (1969) *The Social Reality of Religion*, London: Faber and Faber.
Berger, P. L. (1980) *The Heretical Imperative: Contemporary Possibilities of Religious Affirmation*, London: Collins.
Berger, P. L. and Luckmann, T. (1966) Secularization and pluralism, *International Yearbook for the Sociology of Religion* 2: 73–84.
Berger, P. L., Berger B., and Kellner, H. (1974) *The Homeless Mind*. Harmondsworth: Penguin.
Brown, C. (1987) *The Social History of Religion in Scotland since 1730*, London: Methuen.
Bruce, S. (1996) *Religion in the Modern World: From Cathedrals to Cults*, Oxford: Oxford University Press.
Bruce, S. (1999) *Choice and Religion: A Critique of Rational Choice Theory*, Oxford: Oxford University Press.
Bruce, S. (2002) *God Is Dead: Secularization in the West*, Oxford: Blackwell.
Casanova, J. (1994) *Public Religions in the Modern World*, Chicago: University of Chicago Press.
Crockett, A. (1998) A secularizing geography? Patterns and processes of religious Change in England and Wales, 1676–1851, unpublished PhD thesis, University of Leicester.
Field, C. D. (2001) The haemorrhage of faith? Opinion polls as sources for religious practices, beliefs and attitudes in Scotland since the 1970s, *Journal of Contemporary Religion* 16: 157–76.
Gellner, E. (1983) *Nations and Nationalism*, Oxford: Blackwell.
Gellner, E. (1991) *Plough, Sword and Book: The Structure of Human History*, London: Paladin.
Gellner, E. (1994) From kinship to ethnicity, in E. Gellner (ed.), *Encounters with Nationalism*, Oxford: Blackwell, 34–46.
Gill, R., Hadaway, C. K., and Marler, P. L. (1998) Is religious belief declining in Britain? *Journal for the Scientific Study of Religion* 37: 507–16.
Hadaway, C. K., Marler, P. L. and Chaves, M. (1993) What the polls don't show: a closer look at church attendance, *American Sociological Review* 58: 741–52.
Harrell, D. E. (1985) *Oral Roberts: An American Life*, Bloomington: Indiana University Press.

Inglehart, R. (1990) *Culture Shift in Advanced Industrial Societies*, Princeton: Princeton University Press.

Inglehart, R. (1997) *Modernization and Postmodernization: Cultural, Political and Economic Change in 43 Societies*, Princeton: Princeton University Press.

Jelen, T. (ed.) (2002) *Sacred Markets, Sacred Canopies: Essays on Religious Markets and Religious Pluralism*, New York: Rowan Littlefield.

Luckmann, T. (1970) *The Invisible Religion: The Problem of Religion in Modern Society*, New York: Macmillan.

Marshall, G. (1980) *Presbyteries and Profits: Calvinism and the Development of Capitalism in Scotland, 1560–1707*, Oxford: Clarendon Press.

Martin, D. (1969) *The Religious and the Secular*, London: Routledge and Kegan Paul.

Martin, D. (1978) *The Dilemmas of Contemporary Religion*, Oxford: Blackwell.

Merton, R. K. (1970) *Science, Technology and Society in the 17th Century*, New York: Fetting.

Michels, R. (1962) *Political Parties: A Sociological Study of the Oligarchic Tendencies of Modern Democracy*, New York: Free Press.

Niebuhr, H. R. (1962) *The Social Sources of Denominationalism*, New York: Meridian.

Parsons, T. (1964) Evolutionary universals in society, *American Journal of Sociology* 29: 339–57.

Shibley, Mark (1996) *Resurgent Evangelicalism in the United State: Mapping Cultural Change since 1970*, Columbia, SC: University of South Carolina Press.

Stark, R. and Finke, R. (2000) *Acts of Faith: Explaining the Human Side of Religion*, Berkeley: University of California Press.

Szajkowski, B. (1983) *Next to God … Poland: Politics and Religion in Contemporary Poland*, New York: St Martin's Press.

Tönnies, F. (1955) *Community and Association*, London: Routledge and Kegan Paul.

Voas, D. (2009) The rise and fall of fuzzy fidelity in Europe, *European Sociological Review* 25: 155–68.

Weber, M. (1976) *The Protestant Ethic and the Spirit of Capitalism*, London: George Allen and Unwin.

Wilson, B. R. (1982) *Religion in Sociological Perspective*, Oxford: Oxford University Press.

Young, L. A. (1997) *Rational Choice Theory and Religion: Summary and Assessment*, London: Routledge.

6

American Exceptionalism?

JOHN TORPEY

THE IDEA OF AMERICAN EXCEPTIONALISM

During the recent US presidential election campaign, one heard fairly often the notion that the United States was unique among the states of the world – that, indeed, its peculiarities justified its characterization in terms of something called "American exceptionalism." Typically, this notion was invoked as a shorthand way of ascribing to the United States the status of what former Secretary of State Madeleine Albright has described as the "indispensable nation." This version of American exceptionalism relates to the image of the USA as the bearer of a divine mission, a light unto the nations, John Winthrop's shining "city on a hill." This variant of the idea (which I shall call AE 1) reflects a conception of the country as providential in character, singular in the annals of the ages, and destined to bring democracy and freedom to far-off lands. Needless to say, this is the version of American exceptionalism that led Woodrow Wilson to suggest that the United States had a mission to "make the world safe for democracy," and it in part underlies the Bush administration's grandiose vision of bringing democracy to the Middle East, starting in the beachhead of Iraq. It is this version of American exceptionalism that the international affairs scholar Andrew Bacevich (2008) has recently insisted has come to an end in the wake of a failed, overreaching bid for empire by a country that expects no more of its citizens than that they continue to shop in the face of disaster.

To a sociologist, however, it is somewhat odd to hear the term "American exceptionalism" applied to these features of American life. For many social scientists, the notion of American exceptionalism tends to be more strongly associated with a *negative* judgment about the USA. That assessment derives in considerable measure from the century-old study by the German sociologist Werner Sombart (1905), which asked, *Why Is There No Socialism in the United States?* and from kindred assessments of the relatively harsher socioeconomic characteristics of American life as compared to those obtaining in modern Europe. Sombart's question was often answered with Tocquevillean arguments to the effect that ordinary Americans, having a little bit of property rather than being condemned to proletarian penury as they had been in Europe, were ill-disposed towards schemes purporting to offer heaven on earth. (This is the understanding of "American exceptionalism" that led John McCain to attack Barack Obama during the 2008 presidential election campaign for his plans to "spread the wealth," a prospect that would seem to have an intrinsic appeal to most people, especially lower down the social order.) Tocqueville (2000) also famously addressed the Americans' propensity to conduct their affairs in civil society, through voluntary associations, rather than relying on the state to do things for them, and this has fed into a view of American political culture as anti-statist. Finally, the great French historian saw individualism as an ever-present danger in American life, but also as a quality allowing the individual to achieve and advance irrespective of family lineage. The prominent American sociologist Talcott Parsons (1977, 2007) viewed the United States as the quintessential modern society, one committed in unparalleled fashion to an egalitarianism based on individual achievement, especially of an educational sort – that is, to a meritocracy. The political sociologist Seymour Martin Lipset (1996) would eventually see the combination of economic laissez-faire, meritocratic individualism, anti-statism, and populism – which we might call AE 2 – as a veritable "American creed."

It is no coincidence that Lipset here resorts to a quasi-religious terminology. While Louis Hartz (1955) rested his mid-twentieth-century case for American exceptionalism on a supposedly primordial *Liberal Tradition in America*, others such as Lipset and Robert Bellah tend to understand American exceptionalism as rooted above all in the religious peculiarities of American experience. They, too, are following Tocqueville in the latter's view that – the non-establishment clause of the Constitution notwithstanding – religion is the first of American *political* institutions. The 2008 election campaign, from which Barack Obama emerged as the victor, delivered frequent reminders of the centrality of religion to Americans' thinking about who can – and can't – be president, as some of his opponents cast aspersions on his supposed Muslim faith (he is a Christian, though his father was a Kenyan Muslim). Similarly, the sociologist Penny Edgell and her colleagues (2006) have found survey evidence that Americans regard atheists as less likely to share their values than any other major cultural group, including gays and Muslims. Then of course there's the argument, by such authors as G. K. Chesterton and Richard Hofstadter, that the United States doesn't so much *live by* a creed as *constitute* one. Only thus can one understand the curious notion of "Americanism" as a political ideology, a matter distinct from purely cultural notions such as *Deutschtum* or *italianitá*.

But what sense is there in speaking of "exceptionalism" at all? In one of his many writings on the topic, Lipset – perhaps the chief exponent of the notion since it was originated by Alexis de Tocqueville himself – argued that the concept was "double-edged." Far from suggesting the "superiority" of the United States vis-à-vis other societies, as many critics of the notion of exceptionalism have held, the idea merely pointed to the distinctiveness of American society compared to others. Indeed, Lipset (1996: 18) wrote, "we are the worst as well as the best, depending on which quality is being addressed." To be sure, Lipset's protestations of even-handedness sometimes seem belied by the comparatively congratulatory tone of his writings about the United States. He claimed to "believe that [he was drawing] scholarly conclusions" when he wrote, "[T]here can be little question that the hand of providence has been on a nation which finds a Washington, a Lincoln, or a Roosevelt when it needs him" (Lipset 1996: 14). (Were Lipset alive today, my guess is that he would have added Obama to that list.) It is more than a little odd for a social scientist to claim to explain historical outcomes by invoking divine intervention. Nonetheless, having sought to mollify potential dissenters with an initial avowal of impartiality, Lipset proceeds to argue that the United States is "exceptional" in a variety of ways – political, religious, racial – that can be traced above all to its origins as "the first new nation," the first modern colony to break away from its imperial overlord and begin the political world anew. Lipset assures us that the notion of "exceptionalism" is simply a value-free, scientific usage that helps us make sense of the peculiar features of American life when compared to the folkways of other nations.

If it is merely a neutral characterization for "uniqueness" or "distinctiveness," however, the question then arises why the notion of "exceptionalism" needs emphasizing at all. After all, it is a commonplace among historians, at least, that all processes and developments are in some sense "unique"; they have their own rhythms and particularities that can't simply be shoe-horned into larger models. Lipset's stress on the notion thus in part reflects disciplinary considerations; as a social scientist, he was more interested in patterns, and variations therefrom, than in "unique," unrepeatable events or experiences. But then one might argue simply, as Aristide Zolberg (1986) has done, that there are "as many exceptionalisms as there are cases under consideration," and that we should discard the notion of "exceptionalism" entirely in favor of comparative historical macroanalysis.

In all events, not all exceptionalisms are the same, as we have seen; AE1 is a "good" exceptionalism, whereas AE2 is a "bad" one. Rather than characterizing the notion of exceptionalism as "double-edged," it might therefore be more useful to say that there are (at least) two "exceptionalist" theses: a "good" one that views the United States as singularly virtuous – democratic, egalitarian, anti-authoritarian, etc. – and a "bad" one that regards the United States as distinctively harsh and ungenerous – lacking the public policies that more "civilized" countries have adopted to protect their populations from the vagaries of fate, and inclined toward penal policies and practices that have uniquely uncivilized consequences, especially for the poor and non-white (see, e.g., Whitman 2003). There are also more narrowly tailored versions of the notion of "American exceptionalism," such as Michael Ignatieff's (2005: 1–2) invocation of the term to characterize the United States' contradictory support for and tendency to ignore human rights treaties and conventions.

Despite their traditional commitment to chronicling the "unique," historians have in recent years become increasingly uncomfortable with claims about the "uniqueness" of American life identified by comparative sociologists (and socialists) ever since Tocqueville. A good example of this discomfiture can be found in Thomas Bender's tellingly titled, *A Nation Among Nations: America's Place in World History* (2006). Bender insists that American history has traditionally been taught as a story of the rise of an upstart isolate, a sort of hegemon-in-training that had little need of the rest of the world and got the history it needed to rationalize that stance, so to speak. Bender is concerned that this sort of autistic historiography ill prepares Americans for the "globalized" world in which they now find themselves.

He therefore thinks it urgent that the study of American history be placed firmly in a "global context." The putatively self-aggrandizing idea of "exceptionalism" is inconsistent, in this view, with any understanding of history that takes seriously the unavoidable fact that any and all individual nations are also but one among all the other nations. Thus, Bender (2006: 296–7) concludes, "On the spectrum of difference the United States is one of many, and there is no single norm from which it deviates – or that it establishes."

Valuable though Bender's critique of "exceptionalism" may be with regard to our understanding of the place of the United States in world history, it tends to elide the reality that there are, in fact, peculiarities of American life relative to the West European countries from which the United States largely went forth that cannot be gainsaid. For example, it is a fact that the United States, alone among the countries with which it is normally compared (mainly in Western Europe, but perhaps also Japan), has (as of 2008) no national health insurance system. Its practice of the death penalty – including, in some cases, against minors – puts it in the company of some of the world's most egregious violators of human rights. The United States has exceptionally high rates of interpersonal violence compared to those reference group societies, and has long done so (see Mennell 2007: 133ff.). Perhaps the notion of American exceptionalism makes some sense after all?

Yet this sort of comparison can be extremely misleading; the notion of "exceptionalism" suggests that these kinds of differences are both substantial and enduring, and it is by no means obvious that such claims can be sustained across an array of relevant indicators. In a recent study of the death penalty, for example, Carol Steiker (2005) has noted that until approximately 35 years ago, any notion of "exceptionalism" would have gone in the other direction, so to speak, for at that time it was the United States, not Europe, which was in the vanguard of the movement to abolish capital punishment. Indeed, such punishment was briefly invalidated by the Supreme Court's decision in *Furman v. Georgia* (1972). While the American position on this issue now appears to stand in stark and unflattering contrast to the European (the European Union officially opposes capital punishment), Steiker contends that this outcome was contingent, depending more on the myriad pressures facing the Supreme Court at a particular historical moment than on any timeless American commitment to capital punishment. Moreover, the elimination of the death penalty in Europe had little to do with popular opinion on the matter, for majorities of the populations of Britain, France, and Germany supported the death penalty at the time of its abolition in each country. Rather, Steiker argues, this outcome was predicated upon the greater power of government bureaucrats to realize their preferences than would be possible in the United States. David Garland (2005) has argued even more forcefully that American practice with regard to the death penalty has been out of line with that of its usual reference group societies since only the 1970s, and that any effort to attribute its current anomalous stance to some deeply American cultural traits is therefore misguided. Indeed, the situation today (at least outside of Texas) is much as Tocqueville described it (2000: 38) 175 years ago: "One never saw the death penalty laid down more profusely in the laws, or applied to fewer of the guilty." Nonetheless, Tocqueville (2000: 39) noted that this "puritanical" penal legislation was "strongly imprinted with the narrow spirit of sect," a legacy of the biblical character of the religion of the first settlers. He had no doubt that religion, laws, and politics marched hand in hand in America as a result of the peculiar "point of departure" of the Americans.

THE RELIGIOUS ROOTS OF AMERICAN EXCEPTIONALISM:
CLASSICAL VIEWS

If the heart of American exceptionalism is to be found in its religious experience, what is it about that experience that is "exceptional"? The answer here tends to revolve around the formative role of sectarian Protestantism and the peculiar relationship between church and state that it shaped in the United States after the American Revolution. While Puritan theocrats played a major role on the New England scene in the colonial period, they were also confronted with considerable religious pluralism. There were Puritans elsewhere, of course, but they generally had to compete with an established (Catholic or Episcopal) Church, not with other Protestant sects. The eventual constitutional result of the religious diversity of the colonies was that no religion was to be officially established at the federal level (there were established religions at the state level until well into the nineteenth century), and everyone was free to practice any belief they wished. This posture was a considerable novelty from the perspective of early modern European caesaropapist systems in which it went without saying that the state had some sort of divine sanction with a particular theological coloration. Tocqueville (1998) would later argue that the church's place in the *ancien regime* explained the anti-clerical character of the French Revolution (a pattern subsequently repeated in many Latin American countries that inherited the tradition of divine legitimation). As a result of these earlier experiences, separation of church and state on the European continent would typically come to serve the protection of the state from religion; in the United States, in contrast, it was primarily religion that was to be protected from the state (Offe 2005: 36–7). Notwithstanding the concern to protect religion from state interference, the close historical relationship between religious dissent and political freedom led to a situation in which "god talk" in the public sphere came to be regarded as much more acceptable in the United States, as compared to most of Europe since World War II, at least.

Tocqueville claimed that the "point of departure" was of fundamental importance for understanding the way of life of any people, that one could see in the infant what one would see in the adult. But societies are not persons; why should the "point of departure" be so important? Supposedly its significance derived, according to Tocqueville, from the fact that "peoples always feel [the effects of] their origins. The circumstances that accompanied their birth and served to develop them influence the entire course of the rest of their lives." These axioms, nominally about societies in general, Tocqueville regarded as particularly pertinent to the American case. "[T]here is not one opinion, one habit, one law, I could say one event, that the point of departure [of the Americans] does not explain without difficulty." Yet part of the reason that Tocqueville laid such stress on this factor in his analysis of *Democracy in America* seems to have been simply because there *appeared to him to have been* such a point of departure in Tocqueville's reading of the American trajectory; no such point could be so easily identified in the case of the European countries with which he was always implicitly comparing America. The latter is "the only country where ... it has been possible to specify the influence exerted by the point of departure on the future of states" (Tocqueville 2000: 28–9). This hardly makes a compelling case for the enduring subsequent importance of the "point of departure."

There is an intriguing parallel here with Weber's "Protestant ethic thesis" and the critiques thereof. As Frank Parkin (1982: 65–70) has pointed out, the explanatory weight placed on Protestant doctrine in accounting for the rise of "rational capitalism" is at odds with the discussion in Weber's "Prefatory Remarks" to the *Collected Essays in the Sociology of Religion* (see Weber 2002a: 356–72), of which the *Protestant Ethic and the Spirit of Capitalism* was only the first installment. In those remarks, Weber notes that there are a variety of ways in which the West diverged from the East – in architecture, mathematics, science, art, law, and much else beside. It is therefore difficult to ascribe special significance to the religious factor, which on Weber's own account is not the only relevant variable. Tocqueville's emphasis on the point of departure seems similarly problematic, given that it was the only "point of departure" he could clearly identify and hence not necessarily as significant as he suggested. There were also a number of other factors that made America different from Europe, such as the (timing of the) frontier experience or the relative laxity of English control over their colonies as compared to the absolutist experience, but to some degree these were all bundled together into Tocqueville's notion of the "point of departure."

Be that as it may, Tocqueville (2000: 267) famously argued that he could see "the whole destiny of America contained in the first Puritan who landed on its shores," and many have followed his lead in this regard. Tocqueville speaks here to the oft-remarked influence of the Puritans on American character and life and their supposed dominance in determining its values (see, e.g., Bercovitch 1975). Critics such as Thomas Bender (2006: 44) insist that, contrary to "the usual narrative of American history, which conventionally sees American development as a continuous process of westering from the northeastern colonies ... [p]eople and influences arrived in [America] from all points of the compass and in every region." This one might characterize as the multiculturalist theory of the origins of the United States; it is a view that harmonizes suspiciously with contemporary ideological fashions, though that doesn't necessarily mean that it is wrong.

One might also object that there are enduring and important regional peculiarities that cast doubt on any claim that the New England experience should predominate. Tocqueville (2000) dealt with the thorny problem of the South by insisting that it was "American, but not democratic"; the fact that the lengthy chapter on "The Three Races" in America (which takes up one-quarter of Volume I) is a separate discussion suggests that Tocqueville was not entirely sure where it fit into the overall picture and how it could be squared with the notion of New England Puritanism's dominance. Here the work of David Hackett Fischer (1989) is exemplary; Fischer shows in copious and convincing detail how the "folkways" established in different parts of the (later) United States by four different British settler groups have persistently shaped regional and national politics since their arrival. Fischer's perspective, which emphasizes the durability since the seventeenth and eighteenth centuries of these regional cultures, is a sort of halfway house between Tocqueville's stress on the point of departure and his general insistence on the national level of analysis. In this connection, Bender (2006: 297) makes the important point that "exceptionalist claims about America tend to obscure … internal differentiation," because they privilege the national over the regional level of analysis. It would indeed be a mistake to think that there are no significant regional differences in the United States, a fact to which Tocqueville himself called attention in his treatment of the differences between North(east), South, and West. One might add that to say "Europe" is also always to say too much; there is of course considerable variety across European countries, such that it becomes very difficult indeed to speak of any specifically "European" patterns.

And yet it may still be the case that the Puritans of New England imparted a decisive influence to the country's long-term trajectory. Tocqueville argues (2000: 32) that the reason it was the Puritans rather than other groups who ultimately set the tone for American life had to do with the "rigor of their principles," which led them in search of a place sufficiently abandoned by others of their kind that they could "live there in their manner and pray to God in freedom"; they went to New England, he said, "to make *an idea* triumph." The other colonies had been founded by "adventurers without family." By contrast, "the emigrants of New England brought with them admirable elements of order and morality; they went to the wilderness accompanied by their wives and children." The contrast that Tocqueville draws between swash-buckling adventurers and God-fearing, sober-minded family men neatly parallels Max Weber's distinction between "booty" capitalism, which was based on the prospects for profit deriving from opportunities to loot and pillage, and modern "rational" capitalism, which was based on the ascetic devotion to labor in a calling. The predominance of the Puritans in subsequent American experience is reflected in the fact that the United States would eventually become the country most unwaveringly committed (rhetorically, if by no means necessarily in practice) to free-market capitalism, as well as a country with a tradition of religiously motivated social reform and moralistic foreign policies. To be sure, as the country developed, its religious life also tended to divide along class and racial lines (see Niebuhr 1929); Martin Luther King's observation remains true that the most segregated hour in American life takes place at eleven o'clock on Sunday morning. And yet, as Lincoln observed of religion during the Civil War, "Both [sides] read the same Bible, and pray to the same God"; evangelical religion is as alive among blacks as among whites today, but the political positions it supports tend to differ considerably.

One important feature of the Puritans' influence on American character and life flowed from their special devotion to a Jewish-style "covenant" between themselves and God (see Weber 2002a: 112). Such covenants implied the believers' obedience to God and the expectation that He would punish them for transgressions, at the same time that they could expect His favor as a reward for compliance with the terms of the covenant. It was in terms of such a mutually binding promise that the idea of America as a "City on a Hill," a "New Jerusalem," was adumbrated in John Winthrop's 1630 sermon aboard the *Arbella*. The idea of the covenant remained predominant in the thinking of New England Puritans until the mid-eighteenth century (Noll 2002: 39).

That the covenant has been broken time and again, and indeed from the very beginning (among other reasons because the "City on a Hill" was on "*somebody else's hill!"* [Bellah 1998: 618]), does not necessarily nullify the importance of the Puritan idea of an agreement with God that undergirds much American thinking about the world. It is notable in this regard that much of the criticism of Islam in America has come from the Christian right wing, which tends to see the American destiny as strongly bound up with the sense of the United States as the earthly instrument of a specifically Christian God. These affinities between conservative Christian church and state came to the fore in the contretemps between Virginia Republican congressman Virgil Goode and Minnesota representative Keith Ellison, the first Muslim elected to Congress, in the aftermath of the 2006 mid-term congressional vote. In a letter to a constituent, Goode inveighed that Americans needed to limit immigration in order to reduce the numbers of Muslims entering the country and thus to "preserve the values and beliefs traditional to the United States of America."[1] However broadly they are actually held, these "values and beliefs" are typically said to be those of the Puritans – obedience to God, devotion to family, commitment to the community.

The predominance of the Puritans in early colonial America was of special significance because of the distinctive nature of their spiritual outlook. As Tocqueville (2000: 35) described it, "One must not believe that the piety of the Puritans was only speculative or that it showed itself foreign to the course of human things. Puritanism … was almost as much a political theory as a religious doctrine." Tocqueville concurs here with Weber's later argument that Puritanism was not "world-rejecting," except in the sense of "this-worldly (*innerweltliche*) asceticism" and its tendency to view the world as an arena in which to carry out God's divine plan for the world. And, according to Tocqueville (2000: 32), the political theory of which Puritanism partook "blended at several points with the most absolute democratic and republican theories." Among other things, this posture entailed a deep commitment to education, though generally of a more vocational and unphilosophical kind, so that the believer could nurture a direct, unmediated relationship with God through knowledge of the Bible. The result of this sympathetic attitude toward useful knowledge was the founding of numerous schools and institutions of higher learning, of which the most symbolically important remains Harvard. While those in the interior west of the United States may not genuflect before the cultural power of that august institution, the aura of the college at Cambridge continues to radiate brightly across the country and, indeed, across the oceans. Regional differences notwithstanding, no university in the American South can begin to rival Harvard in symbolic authority; not for nothing is Vanderbilt's nickname "the Harvard of the South." Even Stanford and Chicago, despite their great prestige within the academic world, lack the charisma of Cambridge in the eyes of the ordinary mortal.

As the example of Harvard may suggest, while the Puritans' political ideas may have been democratic in certain respects, they were deeply exclusionary in others. Here Weber's more searching analysis of the consequences of Protestantism supersedes Tocqueville's insights into American habits. Weber (1946b: 332–3; see also Morgan 1966: 185–6) described the doctrinal situation as follows:

> As a religion of virtuosos, Puritanism renounced the universalism of love, and rationally routinized all work in this world into serving God's will and testing one's state of grace. … In this respect, Puritanism accepted the routinization of the economic cosmos,

which, with the whole world, it devalued as creatural and depraved. This state of affairs appeared as God-willed, and as material given for fulfilling one's duty. In the last resort, this meant in principle to renounce salvation as a goal attainable by ... everybody. It meant to renounce salvation in favor of the groundless and always only particularized grace. In truth, this standpoint of unbrotherliness was no longer a genuine "religion of salvation."

In Weber's view, in other words, the Puritans had abandoned to their fate those who failed the test of religious qualification, particularly as this is demonstrated by success in one's calling. If one regards wealth as a sign of merit, then poverty can only be seen as a sign of failure and hence of the lack of grace and of desert. Calvinist Protestantism thus made of poverty a *moral failing*, and it has been largely treated as such in the United States ever since – with the significant exception of the response to the Great Depression of the 1930s, when so many were thrown out of work that the notion of individual responsibility for this fate was at least somewhat undercut.

In a comment on the above passage from Weber, Robert Bellah (1999: 298) has written: "In thinking about the meaning of these words of Weber's in contemporary America, it would be well to remember that American Protestantism, and to some degree American religion generally, is the lineal descendant of that Puritanism that Weber describes as having so abandoned the ethic of brotherliness that it is no longer a religion of salvation. Only in this way can religion and the capitalist economy be reconciled." Bellah thus suggests that Americans' willingness to countenance comparatively large disparities between rich and poor have roots in American religious traditions as much as in a story one might tell about class and class struggles that might be more familiar to Europeans. His remark presupposes that there is a tension between religion and capitalism in American life that others have not necessarily seen. For example, José Casanova (2006: 22) has argued pointedly that "there is little historical evidence of tension between American Protestantism and capitalism." It seems true that most of the religiously generated reform in American history has targeted what one might characterize as moral turpitude – slavery, drink, segregation, war. Critiques of the capitalist economy are more likely to have come from avowed Catholics, who may be seen as defending populations that typically entered the American labor market at the bottom. Be that as it may, Gorski (2003: 163–4) has argued that the stingy "liberal welfare states emerged only in areas heavily influenced by Reformed Protestantism," whereas the welfare state in historically Lutheran or Catholic milieux has been comparatively more generous and less punitive in character (see also Kahl 2007).

Despite their avowedly democratic commitments, Americans are prepared to accept sharply exclusionary tendencies as well, especially where these can be framed in terms of just deserts. Weber had commented on the exclusivism of American life in remarks on America penned after his return to Germany from a trip to the USA in 1904: "Anyone who ... imagines 'democracy' to be a mass of humanity ground down to atoms, is profoundly mistaken, at least as far as American democracy is concerned. It is bureaucratic rationalism, not democracy, which leads to this thoroughgoing 'atomization'... The genuine American society – and we are talking here about the 'middle' and 'lower' strata of the population – has never simply been such a heap of sand. Neither has it ever been an edifice where anyone who comes along could expect to find open doors. It always was, and remains, riddled with all kinds of 'exclusiveness'" (Weber 2002b: 213). In Weber's view, the exclusivism of the Protestant sects – not the inclusiveness of a "church" – permeated the structures of American society as a whole. What made American society truly distinctive was its teeming religious pluralism, but these religious "conventicles" played midwife to a society characterized by intense in-group inclusivism combined with strongly exclusivistic elements. At the same time, Weber thought the country was being increasingly Europeanized and secularized, and that this exclusivism was being carried forward in his time by the many clubs he observed during his stay in the country (see Ringer 2004: 136–7). While there may indeed have been some Europeanization, the trend has widely been seen to go in the other direction – toward Europe's Americanization – in the twentieth century.

And yet, despite their exclusionary tendencies, Weber (2002b: 212) noted, "it is only the sects that have succeeded in combining positive religiosity and political radicalism." This was especially true with regard to the deepest violation of Christian egalitarianism in American life, namely racial slavery. Thus, according to the historian Winthrop Jordan (1967: 300), "It was men deriving from a specifically *Puritan* religious tradition who advanced the equation of slavery and sin," and thus cast it beyond the pale of any truly righteous person. More broadly, Weber detected in the country's Puritan roots a deep "hostility to authority" that contrasted sharply with prevailing attitudes in Germany, but with a novel, communitarian twist as well. "The traditional American aversion against performing personal services is probably linked," Weber wrote, "to the … [Puritan emphasis upon] the 'public' welfare or 'the good of the many' as against the 'personal' or 'private' benefit of individuals, as well as to other weighty reasons that follow from 'democratic' sentiments. … [This is also true of] the relatively greater immunity of formerly Puritan peoples against Caesarism" (quoted in Ringer 2004: 139–40). Clearly, the religiosity of the Puritans was, especially from our current perspective, quite complex, nurturing tendencies toward both individualism and community-mindedness at the same time (see also Bercovitch 1975). The cultivation of the individual conscience is a key mechanism underlying these elements of sectarian faith.

This is the secret underlying much American progressive and radical thought and activism; it flows out of the churches, rather than being opposed to them, as has been more common in the case of Western European countries (see McLeod 1997: ch. 7; Young 2006). This is the aspect of American life that feeds its most successful reformist impulses; Martin Luther King, Jr. is undoubtedly its chief modern exemplar, but abolitionism, which was originally advanced most vigorously by the Quakers, was an important case of religiously inspired reform as well. The story of opposition to the Vietnam War would similarly be unthinkable without the contribution of the Berrigan brothers, William Sloane Coffin, and a host of other Christian and Jewish clerics.

The many sects (and other religions) that abounded in American life from almost the beginning were free to develop without a state church overshadowing them. In this institutional context, and as a result of the importance of religious liberty from the early days of the colonies, American political culture came to be suffused with religiosity, but of a non-denominational (though strongly Protestant) sort. In his well-known discussion of the quasi-religious characteristics of American presidents' inaugural addresses, Bellah thus wrote of the (small-u) "unitarian" God of the American civil religion, who was meant to be inclusive of all believers in God without preferring any faith in particular. Bellah (1970: 175) also noted, however, that the God invoked as the ultimate source of sovereignty in American life was "also on the austere side, much more related to order, law, and right than to salvation and love." Such a judgment strongly echoes Weber's characterization of Puritanism as having "objectified everything and transformed it into rational enterprise, dissolved everything into the pure business relation, and substituted rational law and agreement for tradition" (Weber 1951: 241).

Here it is necessary to delve more deeply into the "Protestant ethic," and especially that of the Calvinists, in order to make sense of their distinctive and enduring impact on American society. In attempting to establish the role played by religious ideas in the rise of rational capitalism, Weber was struck above all by the historically novel and peculiar nature of the idea of predestination. With this theological innovation, Calvin and his followers had devised a system of religious salvation that left the individual completely bereft and without assistance in his aim to insure the fate of his eternal soul. As a result, the follower of Calvinism – a doctrine of "pitiful inhumanity," in Weber's view – experienced "a feeling of unprecedented inner *loneliness*" (Weber 2002a: 73, tr. slightly revised). The effect of this "inner loneliness" was to produce a highly disciplined seeker after salvation, precisely because salvation could never be assured. Yet it also encouraged a joylessness and disdain for sensual pleasure, which was deemed irrelevant to the goal of salvation. The result was the "sober and pessimistically colored individualism" that persists in the "national character" of countries with a Puritan past (Weber 2002a: 74; translation slightly revised). This quality endures, as Weber suggests, in contexts other than the American – such as in the UK, (northern) Germany, and the Netherlands.

The sober religious background to the American experience is also one of the reasons why, as Hannah Arendt (1965: 56) once claimed, the American Revolution remained "an event of little more than local importance" as compared to the world-historical significance of the French Revolution. In her comparative analysis of modern revolutions, Arendt was much influenced (though not necessarily always convinced) by Tocqueville. The basic difference between the two revolutions, Tocqueville (1998) argued, was that the Englishmen who first settled in North America had gone there in quest of a place to practice their religion in peace; in short, their religious and political aspirations overlapped. In France and elsewhere on the Continent, in contrast, the church had become a prop of the state, which was ruled by "divine right of kings." The entanglement of the church in an earthly power grown oppressive made it an appealing target of reformers and revolutionaries. Yet this was not, according to Tocqueville, a product of the revolutionaries' anti-religious views, but rather a by-product of the church's deviation from its proper vocation as saver of souls. The result of this transgression was that, "among us [in France] … the spirit of religion and the spirit of freedom almost always move in contrary directions. Here [in the United States] I found them united intimately with one another: they reigned together on the same soil" (Tocqueville 2000: 282).

The synergies between religion and liberty in the origins of "America" led to sharp differences between American self-understanding and that of Continental

Europe. The British writer G. K. Chesterton put the matter succinctly, asserting that America was "the only nation in the world founded on a creed," as a result of which the United States became a "nation with the soul of a church." The comparative piety of Americans is a fact that is in certain respects unintelligible to Europeans, especially of the left, because they tend to have inherited the anti-clericalism of the Enlightenment and of Continental radical traditions. Even Max Weber, whose deep sensitivity to the cultural importance of religious ideas was a hallmark of his sociology and indeed of his understanding of American society, could comment in response to his early twentieth-century travels in the United States that Americans' powerful religiosity was "an element which affects their life in a way that must seem to us grotesque and frequently repellent" (Weber 2002b: 204). In a striking continuity, this distaste for religion on the secular European left was reflected in the 2003 manifesto against the Iraq war penned by Jürgen Habermas and Jacques Derrida (2005: 10), in which it was claimed that "a president who opens his daily business with public prayer, and associates his significant political decisions with a divine mission, is hard to imagine" – despite the fact each day's proceedings in the British houses of parliament begin with such a prayer.

Much was written during the Bush years about a "widening Atlantic" and a "divided West" (see e.g. Habermas 2004; Kopstein and Steinmo 2008), yet this is hardly a long-enduring matter. So pronounced a sense of antagonism between the two would have been unthinkable during the Cold War era, and the chill seems likely to thaw again with a new enemy shared on both sides of the Atlantic: ill-regulated market capitalism and deep economic malaise. One might suggest that the European-American relationship is somewhat like a river that flows together for a time, then divides into parallel channels, then re-unites again further downstream. The character of the relationship varies over time as a function of a variety of factors, not least those of foreign affairs and international relations.

THE PLACE OF AMERICA IN THE RECENT COMPARATIVE SOCIOLOGY OF RELIGION

In the United States, the free exercise of religion has been much associated in recent scholarly analysis with religious pluralism and a vibrant religious "marketplace," whereas more intimate connections between church and state are said to have led to religious disinterest among the population (see Stark and Finke 2000; Pfaff 2008). The "religious economies" or "supply-side" school proceeds from the quasi-economic assumption that there exists a constant demand for religious adherence, as a result of which – assuming a free market with little state support or regulation – religious entrepreneurs compete in the market of souls to offer a more appealing product. That market thinking and language are a pervasive part of American religiosity today cannot be doubted, as the burgeoning profession of "church growth consultants" demonstrates. Indeed, in a comment on the move of several American Episcopal parishes to secede from the Anglican Communion due to its liberal stances on gays and lesbians, one observer noted, "I think this organization does not have much of a future because there are already a lot of churches in the United States for people who don't want to worship with gays and lesbians. That's not a market niche that is underserved" (quoted in Goodstein 2008). It is by no means clear that the competition for souls between various churches is an even one, however, as mainline Christian denominations have been forced to go head-to-head with a more promiscuous "seeker" spirituality. One study has found extensive concessions to the bland theology of the megachurches in the efforts of a Lutheran denomination to ward off decline (Ellingson 2007). In any event, the emergence of the supply-side perspective is striking from the point of view of a sociology of religion that once held that religious pluralism would march hand-in-hand with *secularization*, on the basis of the notion that if there are many fundamental truths, none of them can be correct (Berger 1967).

Yet the claims of the supply-siders are much contested. Indeed, an authoritative meta-analysis of research addressing the relationship between religious pluralism and religious participation (aka religious "vitality") found the putative association between the two "not supported" by the data (Chaves and Gorski 2001). The empirical shortcomings of the supply-side theory have been stressed by defenders of secularization theory such as Ronald Inglehart and Pippa Norris (2004), who insist that the American case has come to be overused by critics seeking to make their point about the inadequacy of traditional modernization-cum-secularization theory. In Inglehart and Norris's view, secularization remains a satisfactory characterization of the main trends in the world today. They argue that it is the vulnerable who are most inclined toward religion, and that the wealthy countries of the world have successfully mitigated some of the more severe risks to which people are exposed, reducing their interest in religious interpretations of their situation. The United States is an outlier among its peers in terms of religious attachment, however, a finding they ascribe to the higher levels of inequality in American life, the relative weakness of the welfare state, the stress on personal responsibility for one's fate, etc.[2] If one accepts that the vagaries of existence are greater and that the American social safety net is much less finely meshed than those in European societies, the argument appears plausible. If, however, one is persuaded by the analysis of Peter Baldwin (2009) that the US welfare regime is broadly comparable to those of the (many) European societies, this argument seems less compelling. More generally, one wonders about the persuasiveness of an approach that ascribes religiosity to feelings of vulnerability when millions of European workers in the nineteenth century abandoned the churches, despite their nominal concern for the poor, as bastions of the status quo. Of course, many of them were defecting for another "church," one more attuned to the realities of their situation (McLeod 1997: ch. 7).

The "religious economies" thesis better characterizes predominantly Protestant than Catholic contexts. Religious observance remains stronger in the latter than in the former, despite the fact that there is little competition for souls among different faiths in Italy, Ireland, Poland, Austria, and Spain (see Inglehart and Norris 2004). Still, the case of Sweden, where the Lutheran Church was only recently disestablished and the population is among the most secular in the world, drives home the point that state sponsorship can be very bad for religious vitality. It was such contexts that gave rise to the phrase "belonging without believing," because often church membership was essentially a requirement of citizenship in Scandinavia though not a good guide to actual faith commitments.

These observations remind us that another discourse of "exceptionalism" has arisen in recent years, this time with regard to Europe (see Davie 2002). The context here is that of a worldwide resurgence of religion: the explosion of Christianity, particularly in its evangelical and Pentecostalist forms, in parts of the world in which it had previously been unfamiliar, as well as of Islam, especially in its more exacting variants. Against this background, the extensively secularized faith-scape of contemporary Western Europe appears as a striking anomaly. Of course, the universe of comparison is different than the one that produced the notion of "American exceptionalism," which is based on a comparison with the wealthy countries of the OECD; the "European exceptionalism" with regard to religion, however, derives from a comparison with the world as a whole. Still, the invocation of the term throws into high relief one of the most distinctive characteristics of European societies when viewed from the perspective of a global upsurge of faith. Consistent with this trend, secularized European intellectuals often seem baffled by the presence of religiosity in their midst, or in other parts of a putative "West" that has come to be divided by faith (among other things, to be sure). "But maybe Europe does not provide the universal model," writes Martin (1990: 4), "and maybe Europe only illustrates what happens when social change occurs in states where religion has been tied to governments and to old elites." Presumably Martin is referring only to Western contexts, as ties between religion and old elites have been more the global norm than the exception.

Yet the widely presumed gap in religious belief and practice between the United States and Europe, though real enough in certain respects, tends to shrink somewhat on closer inspection. The religiosity of Americans, insofar as it is measured by church attendance, tends to be over-stated, whereas that of Europeans is to some extent under-appreciated. Thus it has been found that, whereas roughly two in five Americans *tell* researchers that they went to church last week, a study of their *actual* attendance revealed a figure closer to only one in five (Hadaway et al. 1993). These findings are generally interpreted to indicate that people are telling researchers what they think they should say. From the European side, meanwhile, despite the marked decline of church attendance especially since the 1960s, the religious scene can be understood to some degree in terms of a penchant for "believing without belonging" (Davie 1994; see also Greeley 2003). Some insist that the differences in religiosity between the United States and Europe are more a matter of kind than of degree, and that we need to focus simply on our specific differences, not on some self-congratulatory notion of American exceptionalism (Demerath 1998).

These scholarly efforts remind us that we must be careful about how we define religion and hence how we "count" it. Some scholars have tended to give more sway in their analyses of religious activity to "individualized" as opposed to "churched" religion (see Heelas 2006; Hervieu-Léger 2006), but others reject individualized religion as "impotent" in terms of their impact on society (Bruce 2006). Some religions making an appearance on the Western scene lack churches, congregations, and the related institutional trappings, which makes their practice difficult to assess in terms of traditional notions of "participation." Meanwhile, the influx of substantial Muslim populations has both intensified religious pluralism and recalled Europe to its Christian roots, while relatively unfamiliar Protestant denominations (Pentecostalists) are making new headway and the Pope is embarked on a major effort to revivify Catholic faith on the continent. It appears to be an uphill slog, though religious enthusiasm appears to have grown considerably in other parts of the world.

Notwithstanding the possibility of a "European exceptionalism," is there really a bad "exceptionalism" (AE2) that Americans are fated to play out over and over again, as the social scientists' version of the thesis implies? Any observer of the partial nationalization of the US financial system and the broad return to government pump-priming in response to the financial crisis of 2008 might well doubt that Americans are somehow congenitally averse to state intervention in social and economic life. Yet it is also true that the Secretary of the Treasury, former Goldman Sachs chairman Henry Paulson, resisted coming to the conclusion that the Federal government should assume the role of lender of last resort until British Prime Minister Gordon Brown insisted that that was the only way to handle the mess. Similarly, while Americans have indicated an increasing desire to create a system of universal healthcare coverage, including a stated willingness among many to pay higher taxes in order to do so, they also tend not to support the creation of a government-sponsored "single-payer" system (despite the fact that they already have one in the Medicare and Veterans Affairs systems, respectively). There does seem to be a kind of "default setting" of anti-statism in the United States, even if it often remains at the level of the rhetorical rather than the real, and this is clearly connected to the voluntary character of American religiosity from earliest times and the peculiarities of Reformed Protestant theology.

To be sure, historians have come to detest the very idea of American exceptionalism, rejecting the notion that the USA deviates from some broader, normative pattern in a fashion reminiscent of once-dominant but now outdated views of a German *Sonderweg*. From this perspective, the United States is simply one case among others, with no peculiarities that place it outside a range of possibilities familiar to observers of the European scene. Insistence on some special particularity of the United States, embellished with the moniker of "American exceptionalism," thus appears to be a cover for claiming that the USA is in some way either especially virtuous or especially egregious – and in a fashion that one would not tolerate if the label were applied to any other country. Assertions about American "indispensability" in world affairs, or about the supposed American enthusiasm for capital punishment, are good examples of this sort of tendentiousness.

Yet still, there remains a sense in which the United States constitutes a modern society that is different in fundamental ways from its usual reference group of comparison countries, overwhelmingly those in Western Europe. The relative obliviousness of the sociological classics – Marx and Durkheim, though less so Weber – to the fact that the United States was a legitimate sibling in the family of modern societies has helped obscure this fact. The decline of secularization theory – crudely put, of the equation of "modernization" with "secularization" – has resulted in considerable part from coming to terms with the fact that the United States has been more given to religious observance than its Western European cousins. Growing numbers of scholars have found it necessary to grapple with Tocqueville's claim (2000: 284) that "disbelief is an accident; faith alone is the permanent state of humanity," moving the United States to a more central place in thinking about modernity. One cannot *assume* some timeless, quasi-primordial "American exceptionalism," but its religious trajectory did impart to the country a different cultural dynamic than that of the European societies from which it predominantly went forth. Intriguingly, the United States also has a new "exceptionalism" to add to its list: the first country in the Euro-Atlantic "North" to place a black person in the top position of political leadership. This development has done remarkable things to restore AE 1 to its formerly exalted place in the eyes of the world. Although Parsons's conception of the United States as the most progressive and egalitarian society on earth came to grief on the shoals of Vietnam and a subsequent period of sharpened economic inequality, he was not altogether wrong to hold that much of the world would look to the United States for its own bearings – a fact attributable to a considerable degree to the USA's conception of itself as having a providential place in the annals of history.

Notes

1   Available at: www.wonkette.com/politics/virgil-goode/congressman-assures-constituent-i-will-deport-keith-ellison-223197.php
2   It should perhaps be added that, ultimately, they profess (p. 240) not really to understand *why* the United States is so unusually religious.

Bibliography

Arendt, Hannah (1965) *On Revolution*, New York: Penguin.
Bacevich, Andrew (2008) *The Limits of Power: The End of American Exceptionalism*, New York: Metropolitan Books.
Baldwin, Peter (2009) *The Narcissism of Minor Differences: How America Resembles Europe – An Essay in Numbers*, New York: Oxford University Press.
Bellah, Robert (1970) Civil religion in America, in Robert Bellah, *Beyond Belief: Religion in a Post-Traditional World*, New York: Harper and Row, 168–89.
Bellah, Robert (1975) *The Broken Covenant: American Civil Religion in Time of Trial*, New York: Seabury Press.
Bellah, Robert (1992) Afterword: religion and the legitimation of the American republic, in Robert Bellah, *The Broken Covenant: American Civil Religion in Time of Trial* (2nd edn.), Chicago: University of Chicago Press, 164–88.
Bellah, Robert (1998) Is there a common American culture? *Journal of the American Academy of Religion* 66 (3), 613–25.
Bellah, Robert (1999) Max Weber and world-denying love: a look at the historical sociology of religion, *Journal of the American Academy of Religion* 67 (2), 277–304.
Bender, Thomas (2006) *A Nation Among Nations: America's Place in World History*, New York: Hill and Wang.
Bercovitch, Sacvan (1975) *The Puritan Origins of the American Self*, New Haven: Yale University Press.
Berger, Peter (1967) *The Sacred Canopy*, New York: Anchor Doubleday.
Bruce, Steve (2006) Secularization and the impotence of individualized religion, *Hedgehog Review*, 8 (1–2): 35–45.

Casanova, José (2006) Secularization revisited: a reply to Talal Asad, in D. Scott and C. Hirschkind (eds.), *Powers of the Secular Modern: Talal Asad and his Interlocutors*, Stanford: Stanford University Press, 12–30.

Chaves, Mark and Gorski, Philip S. (2001) Religious pluralism and religious participation, *Annual Review of Sociology* (27): 261–81.

Davie, Grace (1994) *Religion in Britain since 1945: Believing without Belonging*, Cambridge, MA, and Oxford: Wiley-Blackwell.

Davie, Grace (2002) *Europe: The Exceptional Case: Parameters of Faith in the Modern World*, London: Darton, Longman and Todd.

Demerath, N. J. (1998) Excepting exceptionalism: American religion in comparative relief, *Annals of the American Academy of Political and Social Science* 558: 28–39.

Edgell, Penny, Joseph Gerteis, and Douglas Hartmann (2006) Atheists as "other": moral boundaries and cultural membership in American society, *American Sociological Review* 71(2): 211–34.

Ellingson, Stephen (2007) *The Megachurch and the Mainline: Remaking Religious Tradition in the Twenty-First Century*, Chicago: University of Chicago Press.

Fischer, David Hackett (1989) *Albion's Seed: Four British Folkways in America*, New York: Oxford University Press.

Garland, David (2005) Capital punishment and American culture, *Punishment & Society* 7 (4): 347–76.

Goodstein, Laurie (2008) Episcopal split as conservatives form new group, *New York Times* December 4, pp. A1, A32.

Gorski, Philip S. (2003) *The Disciplinary Revolution: Calvinism and the Rise of the State in Early Modern Europe*, Chicago: University of Chicago Press.

Greeley, Andrew M. (2003) *Religion in Europe at the End of the Second Millennium: A Sociological Profile*, New Brunswick: Transaction.

Habermas, Jürgen (2004) *Der gespaltene Westen: Kleine politische Schriften X*, Frankfurt am Main: Suhrkamp.

Habermas, Jürgen and Jacques Derrida (2005) February 15, or, what binds Europeans together: plea for a common foreign policy beginning in core Europe, in Daniel Levy, M. Pensky, and J. Torpey (eds.), *Old Europe, New Europe, Core Europe: Transatlantic Relations After the Iraq War*, New York and London: Verso, 3–13.

Hadaway, C. Kirk, Marler, Penny Long, and Chaves, Mark (1993) What the polls don't show: a closer look at U.S. church attendance, *American Sociological Review* (58): 741–52.

Hartz, Louis (1955) *The Liberal Tradition in America*, New York: Harcourt Brace Jovanovich.

Heelas, Paul (2006) Challenging secularization theory: the growth of "New Age" spiritualities of life, *Hedgehog Review* 8 (1–2): 46–58.

Hervieu-Léger, Danièle (2006) In search of certainties: the paradoxes of religiosity in societies of high modernity, *Hedgehog Review* 8 (1–2): 59–68.

Ignatieff, Michael (2005) Introduction: American exceptionalism and human rights, in M. Ignatieff (ed.), *American Exceptionalism and Human Rights*, Princeton: Princeton University Press, 1–26.

Inglehart, Ronald and Norris, Pippa (2004) *Sacred and Secular: Religion and Politics Worldwide*, New York: Cambridge University Press.

Jordan, Winthrop (1967) *White Over Black: American Attitudes Toward the Negro, 1550–1812*, New York: Norton.

Kahl, Sigrun (2007) Religious ethics and the spirit of welfare: how the Reformation shapes Welfare-to-Work policy in Europe and the United States, paper delivered at the Annual Meeting of the American Sociological Association, New York.

Kopstein, Jeffrey and Steinmo, Sven (eds.) (2008) *Growing Apart? America and Europe in the 21st Century*, New York: Cambridge University Press.

Lipset, S. M. (1996) *American Exceptionalism: A Double-Edged Sword*, New York: Norton.

Martin, David (1990) *Tongues on Fire: The Explosion of Protestantism in Latin America*, Oxford and Cambridge, MA: Blackwell.

Martin, David (2005) *On Secularization: Toward a Revised General Theory*, Burlington: Ashgate.

McLeod, Hugh (1997) *Religion and the People of Western Europe, 1789–1989* (2nd edn.), Oxford and New York: Oxford University Press.

Mennell, Stephen (2007) *The American Civilizing Process*, Malden, MA: Polity.

Morgan, Edmund S. (1966) *The Puritan Family: Religion and Domestic Relations in Seventeenth-Century New England* (new edn.), New York: Harper and Row.

Niebuhr, H. Richard (1929) *Social Sources of Denominationalism*, New York: H. Holt & Co.

Noll, Mark A. (2002) *America's God: From Jonathan Edwards to Abraham Lincoln*, New York: Oxford University Press.

Norris, Pippa, and Inglehart, Ronald (2004) *Sacred and Secular: Religion and Politics Worldwide*, New York: Cambridge University Press.

Offe, Claus (2005) *Reflections on America: Tocqueville, Weber, and Adorno in the United States*, Malden, MA: Polity.

Parkin, Frank (1982) *Max Weber*, London and New York: Tavistock.

Parsons, Talcott (1977) *The Evolution of Societies*, ed. Jackson Toby, Englewood Cliffs: Prentice-Hall.

Parsons, Talcott (2007) *American Society: A Theory of the Societal Community*, ed. Giuseppe Sciortino, Boulder: Paradigm.

Pfaff, Steven (2008) The religious divide: why religion seems to be thriving in the United States and waning in Europe, in J. Kopstein and S. Steinmo (eds.), *Growing Apart? America and Europe in the Twenty-First Century*, New York: Cambridge University Press, 24–52.

Ringer, Fritz (2004) *Max Weber: An Intellectual Biography*, Chicago: University of Chicago Press.

Sombart, Werner (1979) [1905] *Why Is There No Socialism in the United States?* tr. Patricia M. Hocking and C. T. Husbands, New York: M. E. Sharpe.

Stark, Rodney, and Roger Finke (2000) *Acts of Faith: Explaining the Human Side of Religion*, Berkeley and Los Angeles: University of California Press.

Steiker, Carol (2005) Capital punishment and American exceptionalism, in M. Ignatieff (ed.), *American Exceptionalism and Human Rights*, Princeton: Princeton University Press, 57–89.

de Tocqueville, Alexis (1998) [1856] *The Old Regime and the Revolution*, tr. Alan S. Kahan, 1998, Chicago: University of Chicago Press.

de Tocqueville, Alexis (2000) [1835–40] *Democracy in America*, tr. Harvey Mansfield and Delba Winthrop, Chicago: University of Chicago Press.

Weber, Max (1946a) Class, status, party, in Hans Gerth and C. Wright Mills (eds.), *From Max Weber: Essays in Sociology*, New York: Oxford University Press, 180–95.

Weber, Max (1946b) Religious rejections of the world and their directions, in Hans Gerth and C. Wright Mills (eds.), *From Max Weber: Essays in Sociology*, New York: Oxford University Press, 323–59.

Weber, Max (1951) *The Religion of China: Confucianism and Taoism*, tr. Hans H. Gerth, Glencoe, IL: Free Press.

Weber, Max (2002a) *The Protestant Ethic and the "Spirit" of Capitalism and Other Writings*, ed. Peter Baehr and Gordon Wells, New York: Penguin.

Weber, Max (2002b) "Churches" and "sects" in North America, in Peter Baehr and Gordon Wells (eds.), *The Protestant Ethic and the "Spirit" of Capitalism and Other Writings*, New York: Penguin, 203–21.

Whitman, James (2003) *Harsh Justice: Criminal Punishment and the Widening Divide between America and Europe*, Oxford: Oxford University Press.

Young, Michael (2006) *Bearing Witness against Sin: The Evangelical Birth of the American Social Movement*, Chicago: University of Chicago Press.

Zolberg, Aristide (1986) How many exceptionalisms? in I. Katznelson and A. Zolberg (eds.), *Working-Class Formation: Nineteenth-Century Patterns in Western Europe and the United States*, Princeton: Princeton University Press, 397–455.

7

Resacralization

GRACE DAVIE

INTRODUCTION

The notion of resacralization – a bit like its alter-ego secularization – can mean all things to all people. Indeed the two ideas very largely depend on each other. Those scholars, for example, who are of the opinion that secularization is a necessary concomitant of modernization are unlikely to be persuaded by the idea of resacralization on any long-term or significant basis. Those, conversely, who are less persuaded by the inevitability of secularization, will take a different view: resacralization is not only possible in the modern world, but likely. Its presence, moreover, must be determined empirically – it should not be ruled either in or out on an a priori basis. This chapter starts from the latter position, recognizing not only that there is considerable evidence for resacralization in the modern world, but that this evidence is subtle, complex and constantly changing. These are not simple black and white issues, but ongoing relationships that change and adapt over time for a wide variety of empirically verifiable reasons.

The discussion, however, must start by probing a parallel question. Is it the case that a process identified as resacralization is taking place in parts of the late modern world, or is a different explanation rather more accurate: namely that social scientists (among them sociologists of religion) are now more ready to acknowledge the continuing significance of religion? In other words, the shift is as much in the perspective as it is in the reality being observed. Religion is indeed resurgent in many parts of the world (that is clear), but it is also more readily *recognized* as a continuing and powerful force in both individual and social lives. And if the latter is the case, the logic leads us in a rather different direction: it is the absence not the presence of religion that requires an explanation, even in late modernity.

Exactly the same point can be made even more sharply by considering three pivotal events in the late twentieth and early twenty-first century. These are the Iranian revolution of 1979, the fall of the Berlin wall in 1989 and the attack on the Twin Towers in 2001. The striking thing about all of these episodes is that Western social science failed completely to see what was coming. Why was this so? It would be naïve in the extreme to say that each of these events was simply, or even primarily, a religious event. All of them were both motivated by and depended on a wide variety of economic, political, social, and cultural factors. It would be equally foolish, however, to exclude religion from the analysis – indeed it was the visible presence of religion and religious motivation in all three episodes that shocked the world, not least the Western pundits.

Why was it, for example, that a pro-Western, relatively secularized Shah was obliged to flee before an Iranian Ayatollah clearly motivated by conservative readings of Islam? Such a scenario had not been anticipated. And why was it that an aggressively secular ideology, not a religious one, collapsed so comprehensively throughout the Soviet bloc – a part of the world that has seen subsequently a marked, if uneven, renaissance of both Christianity and Islam? And why, finally, did the terrifying events of 9/11 come as such a bolt from the blue? Quite simply the unimaginable had happened, requiring – amongst many other things – a radical rethink of the paradigms that are supposed to explain, and indeed to predict the events of the modern world. Hence an inevitable, if somewhat disturbing, question: could it be that a more careful grasp of the continuing place of religion in the late modern world – that is of its capacities to resist Western influence in the Muslim world, to withstand harassment and persecution in the Soviet bloc, and to motivate terrorism across the globe – might have led to more accurate predictions of these events?

There are no easy answers to this question. One point, however, is clear: the realization that such factors might be important, together with the growing visibility of both religion and religious movements right across the globe, have led to some hard questions in almost all of the economic and social sciences. Two areas of thinking in particular illustrate the need for reappraisal: secularization and secular feminism. The first in its more extreme forms ruled out the possibility that being religious was compatible with being modern – a claim that is increasingly called into question. The second blinded Western scholars from seeing the importance of religion (frequently as a liberator) for women in many parts of the developing world – an ever more evident fact.

Bearing all these points in mind, this chapter will be structured as follows. It will look first at the reasons why classical sociology, including the sociology of religion, has had such difficulty coming to terms with the continuing significance of religion. A strong emphasis will be placed on the Eurocentric nature of this thinking. It will then consider the empirical challenges to the "classical" point of view, paying attention to those parts of the world where this challenge is sharpest – notably the global south. The third section deals with the sociological response to these changes, outlining the views of those scholars who are attempting to come to terms with these changes, recognizing that some of them, at least, had misgivings from the outset about the dominant paradigm. The fourth section returns to the European case, using this to illustrate the complexities of the present situation within which many different trends are taking place simultaneously. Not only is Europe an "exceptional case," in the sense that it is markedly more secular than almost all other global regions, it is itself changing. Some of these changes are accounted for by the arrival of the "rest of the world" in Europe; others, however, are generated from within

Europe itself – and include resacralization. A short conclusion gathers the threads together, noting both the complexity of the present situation and the need for imaginative responses to this. The religious factor must be taken into account, that much is clear, but not is isolation. It must moreover be carefully embedded into the core of the new paradigms that emerge to deal with this new situation – not simply tagged on as an optional or fashionable extra.

ACCOUNTING FOR THE CLASSICAL PARADIGM

Sociology, and within this the sociology of religion, has developed from a particular historical context – a set of circumstances which has colored not only the subject matter of the discipline but the tools and concepts which emerged in order to understand that context better. Central to this endeavor was a pre-occupation with the upheavals taking place in Europe at the time of the industrial revolution and, as part and parcel of this, a sensitivity to the impact that these were having on the nature and forms of religious life in this particular global region. Out of this situation emerged a pervasive, but ultimately false assumption: namely that the process of modernization was *necessarily* damaging to religion. Exactly what form the damage might take and its possible consequences for individual and social life were major topics of debate, but its inevitability was increasingly taken for granted – unsurprisingly given the evidence surrounding the early sociologists. The traditional structures of religious life, deeply embedded in the economic and political order of pre-modern Europe, were crumbling visibly under the mutually reinforcing pressures of industrialization and urbanization.

The process itself is significant for the development of sociology. Even more far-reaching, however, were the conceptual implications that came with it, as sociology looked for ways not only to describe but to explain the "damage" being done. An overwhelming preoccupation with secularization as the dominant paradigm in the sociology of religion should be seen in this light; it emerged from the specificities of the European case in which it worked relatively well – an understanding of secularization was clearly important to late nineteenth and early twentieth century Europeans. The next stage in the argument is, however, more difficult. The empirical connections present in Europe gradually – but inexorably – turned into theoretical assumptions, with the strong implication that secularization would necessarily accompany modernization whenever and wherever the latter occurred. More than this: Europe became the case against which all other cases were measured and, it is often implied, found wanting. The connections between modern and secular became normative. With this in mind, it becomes easier to understand why European sociologists, just as much as European journalists, have considerable difficulty accepting the fact that religion is, and remains, a profoundly normal part of the lives of the huge majority of people in the late modern world.

Exactly what is meant by the secularization thesis, however, is far from straightforward. Its various ramifications are explored elsewhere in this volume. But the essence is clear enough: the sociology of religion has been dominated by a frame of reference which has its roots in a global region with a *particular*, as opposed to typical, experience of religion and religious change. A crucial part of the evolution of the sub-discipline lies (and will continue to lie), therefore, in its capacity to discern the implications of these beginnings for the formation of sociological thinking and to escape from them where necessary.

The last phrase is important. Not everything in or about the secularization thesis needs to be discarded. Important insights have emerged not only from the thesis itself, but also from the European context which need to be carried forward into the twenty-first century. One of these, paradoxically, is the aspect of secularization which the Europeans resisted for longest – the gradual separating out of different and more and more specialized institutions (political or educational for example) as part of the modernizing process. Societal functions that were previously dominated by the church (education, healthcare etc.) become increasingly autonomous. It is equally important to grasp, however, that institutional separation – a normal and "healthy" part of modernization – need not bring with it either the marginalization of religion to the private sphere, or the decline in religious activity (Casanova 1994). Neither have occurred in most parts of the modern or modernizing world; nor are they likely to in the foreseeable future.

Before turning to these cases in more detail, it is helpful to place the argument set out above in an epistemological framework. Here the emphasis lies on the contrasting natures of the European and American enlightenments. If the former, especially in its French forms, took on a markedly anti-clerical (if not strictly speaking anti-religious) turn, the latter was very different: it is not an exaggeration to say that the American enlightenment was built by means of religion rather than against this. The contrast can be summarized as follows: in Europe,[1] enlightenment thinking can be seen as a "freedom from belief" (epitomized in a hegemonic Catholic Church); in America, conversely, the enlightenment becomes essentially a "freedom to believe," a statement with entirely different implications for the relationship between religion and modernity (Himmelfarb 2004).

The next step in the process is equally significant: that is to appreciate that the social sciences – in all their diversity – emerge from the European enlightenment. As a result, they have built into them a markedly secular bias. Auguste Comte, for example, understood "modern" as leaving both God and the supernatural behind. These unworldly attributes are replaced by the natural and the scientific, which become the primary – indeed the definitive – modes of explanation for the modern person. A distinctive epistemology emerged, which embodied above everything else a notion of the future that was realizable through human agency. Epistemologies, however, very frequently turn into ideologies: a mutation in which religion is seen as not only irrelevant (something to be left behind), but damaging both to modern societies themselves and to the scientific study of them.

The process should not be oversimplified. Each one of the founding fathers of sociology, for example, paid close attention to religion. They did this in very different ways, but all four – Karl Marx, Max Weber, Émile Durkheim, and Georg Simmel – recognized the significance of religion as an integral factor in the upheavals taking place in Europe in the nineteenth and twentieth centuries. Integral yes, but unlikely to endure, at least in its existing forms. The twin processes of industrialization and urbanization would, sooner or later, erode the power of religion – a process welcomed by Marx, rather less so by the others, who wondered what might emerge to replace this. There was no doubt, however, about the outcome: modern societies

were envisaged, for good or ill, as secular societies. This assumption sinks deeply
into the consciousness of European intellectuals, among them social scientists. Its
consequences are both direct and indirect: among the former can be found a marked
reluctance to take religion seriously (it is not worth bothering about); among the
latter (when the former policy fails) a pervasive tendency to construct it as a problem
– something, in other words, to be overcome. Neither is helpful in the modern
world.

CHALLENGING THE CLASSICAL PARADIGM

Difficulties emerge, in fact, as soon as this way of thinking is applied outside Europe.
The first challenge comes from the America case – which is hardly surprising, given
the very different beginnings of American society already alluded to. Here is a situation in which the dominant forms of post-enlightenment thinking (secular as well
as religious) are carried by the myriad Protestant denominations that constituted
the bedrock of American society, rather than by the secular parties that arose in
opposition to the Catholic Church in much of modern Europe.

What emerges in the United States is in fact a "spiral up," in which nation building (the federal state), economic development (the coming of industrial society),
urbanization (the building of new cities such as Chicago, Detroit, or Pittsburgh),
and a developing religious market all encourage each other (Finke and Stark 1992).
These factors are not in tension with each other and never were – instead they were
mutually supportive as wave after wave of immigrants moved into America's
growing cities bringing their particular form of (mostly) Christianity with them.
This is a far cry from the situation on the other side of the Atlantic where the twin
processes of industrialization and urbanization were necessarily inimical to the
static, territorially bound state churches that still dominated much of European
society. Unable to move easily into the growing cities of industrial Europe – indeed
unable to move anywhere, given their parochial base – these churches (already
demoralized by an anti-religious enlightenment) were disadvantaged from the outset.
Hence, in Europe, a "spiral down" – as economic, social, political, and philosophical factors came together to undermine the confidence of an already weakened
institution.

How then did social science react? The first step was to create, or rather to build
on to, the notion of American exceptionalism. America, in other words, became an
exceptional case – an indisputably modern society but one in which socialism and
socialist parties were conspicuous by their absence and vibrant religion by its presence (Lipset 1997). The exception was "explained" by the particular history of the
United States, but the assumed connections between modernization and secularization remained intact. Bit by bit, however the argument as a whole begins to shift.
Instead of arguing that there are particular reasons for the religious vitality of
modern America which require close and careful analysis – a subject that preoccupied scholars for much of the postwar period – Europe begins to emerge as the
exceptional case. The parameters of the debate alter accordingly. European forms
of religion are no longer seen as the global prototype; they become instead one
strand among many which make up what it means to be European. Or to put the

same point in a different way the relative secularity of Europe is not a model for export – it is something distinct, peculiar to the European corner of the world. What then has been the nature of this strand in the latter part of the twentieth century and what will it be like in subsequent decades? We will return to this question in the final section of this chapter.

In the meantime, it is important to place both Europe and America in a global context – that is, in a world which – in Peter Berger's inimitable phrase – is "as furiously religious as ever" (Berger 1999). The facts are undeniable; they cover the world's press on a daily basis and form the subject matter of increasing numbers of scholarly publications. One such became very rapidly a best-seller. Philip Jenkins in *The Next Christendom* (2002) drew attention to the exponential growth of Christianity in the global South, recognizing that the future of religion lay neither in Europe, nor in the United States but in Latin America and sub-Saharan Africa – amongst younger rather than older generations and in vibrant rather than "respectable" forms of religion. The shift in religious demography is the key to understanding this process. Indeed in Jenkins' opinion, the growth in Christianity is set to eclipse even the development of Islam, recognizing nonetheless that that the latter – so far at least – has caught the attention of far more people in the modern world.

The potential for violence in this respect has not gone unnoticed. Amongst other things, it reflects a shift in the understanding of global politics, from one based on ideology (the essence of the Cold War), to one rather more centered on identity (or identities) within which religion finds a natural place. Samuel Huntington's celebrated "clash of civilizations" (Huntington 1993, 1997) articulates this metamorphosis, offering ample space for religion in the ensuing debate. The controversial nature of this work lies in Huntington's conceptualization of civilizational (and within this religious) relationships as a "clash" rather than a dialogue. The potential for conflict – especially that between Islam and its neighbors – follows from this. Rightly or wrongly, it has become a pervasive frame of reference, for public as well as professional commentators. It is rooted in a growing awareness that religions of all kinds are increasing rather than declining in their political significance; it is essential that social science pays close attention to the implications of these changes.

These transformations, moreover, are happening in all world faiths and in almost all global regions with the possible exceptions of Western Europe and Japan.[2] Take, as a start, the global regions dominated by Christianity. We have already mentioned the United States, Latin America, and sub-Saharan Africa. Add to these the countries of the Pacific Rim – the Philippines, South Korea, and China – and the picture becomes ever more convincing. In South Korea, the European trajectory is largely turned on its head: a nation that industrialized extraordinarily fast between the 1960s and 2000 became increasingly religious in the same period, noting that Buddhism was growing as fast as Christianity. Any assumed connection between modernization and secularization becomes increasingly hard to sustain.

It now looks as though something similar might be happening in China, bearing in mind that the systematic study of religion in this part of the world is still in its infancy and – given the stance of the current regime – is not always easy to effect. One statistic, however, illustrates the significance of what seems to be taking place. According to a 2006 survey by the Pew Global Attitudes Project, 31% of the Chinese public considers religion to be very or somewhat important in their lives,

compared with only 11% who say religion is not at all important.[3] A third of any
population normally denotes an element worth taking into account. A third of the
Chinese population, however, is an enormous number of people – more or less the
equivalent of the entire population of Europe. Even more important is the fact that
in China, as in much of the developing world, it is the middle classes (urban, educated and critically engaged in the economic development of their countries) who
are attracted to religion, including Christianity. They are emerging moreover from
a context devastated by an aggressively secular cultural revolution. This is resacralization on an almost unimaginable scale.

India offers a rather different case. Here extraordinarily rapid advances in technology develop alongside a distinctive spirituality which has always been there – but
in no way does the former displace the latter. The point is nicely illustrated by the
software engineers in Bangalore who place garlands round their computers on
Hindu festivals (Berger 2002: 10–11). Rather more disturbingly the political divisions of the subcontinent remain inextricably linked to religion in ways that are not
always conducive to peaceful co-existence. That in turn leads to an awareness of
the Muslim world in all its manifest diversity: moderately secular Turkey is quite
different from Shi'ite Iran and neither has much in common with the Sunni dominated parts of the Middle East and/or the Gulf. Generalizing about Islam is as
dangerous as generalizing about Christianity. That does not mean however that it
is wise – or indeed safe – to ignore the religious factor in our efforts to understand
the global regions dominated by this world faith, or indeed any other. In the Middle
East, for example, an endemic and long-standing conflict is *increasingly* expressed
in terms of religion: Hamas is markedly more religious that the Yasser Arafat's PLO,
and the influence of Orthodox Judaism is without doubt more developed in Israel
than in was in the mid-postwar decades. Indeed a 1990s book on diplomacy that
fails to mention religion in either its contents list or its index now looks increasingly
– even absurdly – anachronistic (Kissinger 1994).

One final point completes this section. It moves away from the world of international politics and into the world of the everyday – a realm in which gender
becomes a highly significant factor. Take, for example, the significance of women
in Pentecostalism in Latin America, remembering that Pentecostalism is the fastest
growing form of Christianity in the modern world. In this context, Brusco's classic
work amongst Pentecostals in Colombia offers much food for thought. Her data
are striking and concern the marked changes in behavior that can be observed
among newly converted *men*. No longer, following Brusco, is 20 to 40 percent of
the household budget consumed by the husband in the form of alcohol. Nor are
"many of the extra-household forms of consumption that characterize masculine
behavior in Colombia, such as smoking, gambling and visiting prostitutes" allowed
to continue (Brusco 1993:147). More positively, the men withdraw from the (public)
street and, alongside their wives, begin gradually to assume responsibilities in both
the church and the home (the private sphere). What emerges is a rather more secure
economic existence for the family and, crucially, an education for the children –
itself a decisive factor in inter-generational mobility. The household becomes an
effective corporate group.

Few would dispute that Latin American women are advantaged by such changes.
This, however, is not the whole story; nor is it "liberation" in the Western sense of

the term. The men in question may indeed withdraw from the street but they maintain with vigor the traditional headship role, both in the family and in the churches. In an article entitled very aptly "The Pentecostal gender paradox," Bernice Martin (2000) explores this tension further. Her conclusions are not only provocative, but central to the argument of this chapter. In relation to the Pentecostal experience, Western feminist perspectives (just like the traditional versions of secularization) are not only inappropriate, they are themselves part of the problem in so far as they have blinded many Western academics to much that was happening in the developing world. Interestingly, the observers *sur place* (anthropologists, missiologists and development workers), were quicker to appreciate the changes taking place – not least their very positive effects for the women in question.

RETHINKING SOCIAL SCIENCE IN THE LIGHT OF A RENEWED AWARENESS OF RELIGION

The interrelated streams within this chapter can be clearly seen. On the one hand, are the unexpected changes in the ordering of the modern world, in which religion plays a major role; and on the other, are the attempts by the various branches of social science to come to terms with what is happening – bearing in mind that the latter involves perception as much as reality. That said, even those already interested in religion and aware of its continuing importance to human living have been taken by surprise. It is hardly an exaggeration to say that religion now dominates the agenda in many parts of the world. What is to be done?

The first task is to gather as much information as possible and to ensure both its accuracy and its freedom from bias. The second is to adjust social scientific perspectives in light of the data, rather than allowing a particular theoretical view to drive the agenda. That the latter can occur is well-illustrated by the case of Pentecostalism in the global south. As David Martin explains in a semi-autobiographical essay (Martin 2000), it was not easy to persuade the social scientific establishment that they should take Pentecostalism seriously – the more so given the nature of this particular phenomenon (its emotional, seemingly irrational, dimensions flew in the face of "scientific" explanation). "It was incorrect even to report what theory forbade" (2000: 27). The fact that this was an indigenous movement of some power for certain kinds of communities in (initially) Latin America, rather than an imposition of American imperialists was equally difficult to convey.

Martin, in fact, is a crucial player in this debate, in that right from the start he has been less convinced than others about the inevitability of secularization. As early as the 1960s, for example, he expressed serious misgivings about the concept itself. These were voiced in a much quoted article, published in the *Penguin Survey of the Social Sciences*, under a provocative, title "Towards eliminating the concept of secularisation" (Martin 1965). Such were the confusions surrounding the concept that it might be better to abandon it altogether. It is, however, Martin's classic text, *A General Theory of Secularization* (1978), that offers the key to his thinking in this area. The initial chapter takes the form of a five finger exercise in which Martin sets outs the different trajectories that the secularization process takes in different parts of the world and the key reasons for these contrasts. Not only does he underline the marked difference between Europe and America, he also points out the different patterns in different parts of Europe. The analyses that follow, many of which have become classics in the literature, work through the detail of the different cases.

Just over a decade later, Martin published a further article, with an equally significant title. The initial pages of "The secularization issue: prospect and retrospect" recall Martin's earlier analysis – i.e. that theories of secularization were essentially one-directional in so far as they embodied "covert philosophical assumptions, selective epiphenomenalism, conceptual incoherence, and indifference to historical complexity" (1991: abstract). The second section articulates a by now familiar theme: the connections between stronger versions of the secularization thesis and the European context from which they emerged. In other words, there are particular circumstances or conditions in West Europe that account for the relatively strong indicators of secularization that can be discerned in this part of the world (and even here, more in some places than in others). But outside Europe (and even in the parts of Europe than experienced communism at first hand), very different outcomes have occurred. The active religiosity of the United States, the massive shift to the south of global Christianity, and the emergence of Islam as a major factor in the modern world order are some of these – all of which are ill-served by theories that emerge from a European context. The question moreover is urgent: it becomes abundantly clear that we need new and different concepts if we are to understand properly the nature of religion in the modern world.

Martin himself has worked in two areas in particular: on the post-communist situation in Central and East Europe and on the exponential rise of Pentecostalism in the Southern hemisphere (see above). It is these empirically driven cases that have led him to articulate even more forcefully than before his initial misgivings about the secularization thesis. The penultimate paragraph of the 1991 article contains a final sting in the tail. The very factors that across Europe accounted for the erosion in the historical forms of religion (the negative associations with power and the rationalist alternative associated above all with the French Republic) are themselves in decline, liberating spaces hitherto occupied by opponents of certain forms of religion. At precisely the same time, new forms of religion (both Christian and non-Christian) are flooding into Europe, not least a significant Muslim population. The outcome of this entirely new combination will provide the theme of the following section.

It is important first to consider Peter Berger's contribution to the debate – recognizing in this case a volte-face in sociological thinking. Berger has moved full circle, from an advocacy of secularization as a central feature of modern, necessarily plural societies, to a trenchant critique of this position. Here is a clear case of a scholar who has altered his theoretical position in light of the data that are emerging all over the world. Specifically, the continuing religious activity of many Americans and the increasing salience of religion in almost all parts of the developing world fly in the face of his earlier ideas. It is worth quoting from Berger himself to appreciate this change of heart:

My point is that the assumption that we live in a secularized world is false. The world today, with some exceptions, to which I will come presently, is as furiously religious as ever. This means that a whole body of literature by historians and social scientists loosely labeled "secularization theory" is essentially mistaken. In my early work I contributed to this literature. I was in good company – most sociologists of religion had similar views, and we had good reasons for upholding them. Some of the writings we produced still stand up …

Although the term "secularization theory" refers to works from the 1950s and 1960s, the key idea of the theory can indeed be traced to the Enlightenment. The idea is simple: Modernization necessarily leads to a decline of religion, both in society and in the minds of individuals. And it is precisely this key idea that turned out to be wrong. (1999: 2–3)

Following this line of argument, secularization should no longer be the assumed position for theorists in the sociology of religion. The task of the sociologist shifts accordingly: he or she is required to explain the absence rather than the presence of religion in the modern world. This amounts to nothing less than a paradigm shift in the discipline. And if this is the case, the implications for policy as well as for sociological theory are immense. It is crucially important, therefore, that we – academics, journalists, politicians, policy makers and practitioners – get it "right."

By no means everyone is in favor of the new perspective. Bruce, for example, describes Berger's change in view as an "unnecessary recantation" (Bruce 2001). In a chapter devoted to precisely this aspect of Berger's work, Bruce argues that "his original contributions to the secularization approach remain valid, that he is confessing to sins that he did not commit, and that his arguments against his own case are unpersuasive" (2001: 87). Bruce takes each of Berger's arguments – the growth of conservative and evangelical churches in the United States, the decline of liberal churches, the persistence of religion (if not church-going) in other Western societies, and the vitality of religion in other parts of the world – offering in each case an alternative view in line with his own perceptions of secularization. In so doing he raises a crucial question: will the societies of the second and third worlds follow the model that Bruce claims to be irrefutable in modern liberal democracies? Is there, in other words, a necessary connection between increasing prosperity and a decline in commitment to religious orthodoxies? The answer can only lie in painstaking empirical inquiry.

Empirical inquiry, moreover, calls for accurate data concerning religion in every part of the modern world. An important resource in this respect is the World Values Study (itself an extension of the older European Values Study) – an investigation of ambitious proportions, currently reaching more than 80 societies in six continents and almost 80 percent of the world's population. It is a study of socio-cultural and political change, in which questions about religion (indeed many different aspects of religion) form a central part. Huge data sets have emerged from these inquiries which have led to an extensive list of publications.[4]

Significant here is the work of Ronald Inglehart (the instigator of the WVS) and his various associates. Working with Pippa Norris, for example, Ingelhart has identified an increasingly observable paradox, pointing out that *both* the following statements are true (Norris and Inglehart 2004). On the one hand it is clear that the populations of virtually all advanced industrial societies have been moving toward more secular orientations in the past 50 years, but on the other the world as a whole now has more people with traditional religious views that ever before – these people constitute a growing proportion of the world's population. The first statement is, in fact, an affirmation of the secularization thesis, in so far as it argues that the demand for religion varies systematically with levels of societal modernization, human development, and economic inequality. But the process is necessarily self-limiting in so far as exactly the same combination of factors – i.e. modernization associated with secularization – will lead to a decline in fertility. Hence, proportionally speaking, the growth (not decline) of the proportion of the global population that continues to affirm their faith in more rather than less traditional forms of religion.

Inglehart and his associates (1997, 2000) also introduce a second and even more important dimension to their argument, namely the diversity between nations, or groups of nations as they engage in the modernization process. It becomes increasingly clear, for example, that different societies follow different trajectories even when they are subject to the *same* forces of economic development. This is a "both/and" situation. On the one hand the rise of industrial society and its subsequent mutation into post-industrial forms are associated with coherent and empirically discernible cultural shifts. On the other, the systems which emerge at each stage in this evolution are path dependent: more precisely they reflect Protestant, Catholic, Islamic or Confucian backgrounds each of which display distinctive value systems. The associated differences, shaped very largely by the cultural (and more specifically religious) heritage in question, persist even after controlling for the effects of economic development.

Such an approach is both similar to and different from Shmuel Eisenstadt's work on *multiple* modernities – the final approach to be considered in this section. The notion that modernities might be plural rather than singular is even more radical in the sense that it rejects a great deal of the corpus of social scientific writing from the time of the founding father onwards. The following paragraph sets out this agenda; it is unequivocal in its critique:

> The notion of "multiple modernities" denotes a certain view of the contemporary world – indeed of the history and characteristics of the modern era – that goes against the views long prevalent in scholarly and general discourse. It goes against the view of the "classical" theories of modernization and of the convergence of industrial societies prevalent in the 1950s, and indeed against the classical sociological analyses of Marx, Durkheim, and (to a large extent) even of Weber, at least in one reading of his work. They all assumed, even only implicitly, that the cultural program of modernity as it developed in modern Europe and the basic institutional constellations that emerged there would ultimately take over in all modernizing and modern societies; with the expansion of modernity, they would prevail throughout the world. (Eisenstadt 2000: 1)

Right from the start, therefore, Eisenstadt challenges both the assumption that modernizing societies are convergent, and the notion of Europe (or indeed anywhere else) as the lead society in the modernizing process.

It is important, however, to grasp the positive as well as the negative aspect of Eisenstadt's idea. In the introductory essay to an interesting set of comparative cases, Eisenstadt suggests that the best way to understand the modern world (in other words to grasp the history and nature of modernity) is to see this as "a story of continual constitution and reconstitution of a multiplicity of cultural programs" (2000: 2). A second point follows from this. These on-going reconstitutions do not drop from the sky; they emerge as the result of endless encounters on the part of human agents, individuals, and groups, all of whom engage in the creation (and recreation) of both cultural and institutional formations, but within *different* economic and cultural contexts. The crucial point to emerge from Eisenstadt's work is the continued, and in some cases renewed space for religion and for religious movements within these unfolding interpretations. The forms of religion, moreover, may be as diverse as the forms of modernity. Indeed the examples that follow in the special issue of *Daedalus* offer Christian, Muslim, Hindu, and Confucian illustrations. In the volume as a whole, religion is more noticeable by its presence than by its absence.

Are these, however, examples of re-secralization – strictly speaking – or is it simply the case that religion has always been present in most parts of the modern world, but has not always been perceived as such, particularly by Europeans? The final section of this chapter returns to Europe with this recurring question in mind. Here, if anywhere, is a secular modernity, but one that cannot remain in isolation from what is happening elsewhere. What emerges is a complex case.

ACCOUNTING FOR COMPLEXITY: THE EUROPEAN CASE

One way of understanding the place of religion in modern Europe is to consider six very different factors, which push and pull in different directions – hence the complexity.[5] The six factors are: the role of the historic churches in shaping European culture; an awareness that these churches still have a place at particular moments in the lives of the great majority of the population; an observable change in the churchgoing constituencies of the continent, which operate increasingly on a model of choice, rather than a model of obligation or duty; the arrival in Europe of groups of people from many different parts of the world, with very different religious aspirations from those discovered in the host societies; the reactions of Europe's secular elites to the increasing salience of religion in public as well as private life; and – finally – a growing realization that the patterns of religious life in modern Europe are somewhat different from those in the rest of the world.

The starting point concerns the undisputed role of the historic churches in shaping European culture, bearing in mind that other factors (notably Greek rationalism and Roman organization) must also be kept in mind. One example will suffice: the Christian tradition has had an irreversible effect on the shaping of time and space in this part of the world. Both week and year follow the Christian cycle, even if the major festivals are beginning to lose their resonance for large sections of the population. The same is true of space. Wherever you look in Europe, there is a predominance of Christian churches, some of which retain huge symbolic value. This is not to deny that in some parts of Europe (notably the larger cities) the skyline is becoming an indicator of growing religious diversity. Europe is evolving, but the legacies of the past remain deeply embedded in both the physical and cultural environment.

Physical and cultural presence is one thing: a "hands-on" role in the everyday lives of European people quite another. Commentators of all kinds agree that, with very few exceptions, the latter is no longer a realistic aspiration for the historic churches of Europe. That does not mean, however, that these institutions have entirely lost their significance as markers of religious identity. In my own work, I have explored these continuing ambiguities in two ways: first through the notion of "believing without belonging" and, second, through the concept of "vicarious religion" (Davie 1994, 2000, 2007). The latter is particularly important.

By vicarious, I mean *the notion of religion performed by an active minority but on behalf of a much larger number, who (implicitly at least) not only understand, but, quite clearly, approve of what the minority is doing.* The first half of the definition is relatively straightforward and reflects the everyday meaning of the term – that is, to do something on behalf of someone else (hence the word "vicar"). The second half is more controversial and is best explored by means of examples. Religion, it seems, can operate vicariously in a wide variety of ways: churches and church leaders perform ritual on behalf of others (notably the occasional offices) – if these services are denied, this causes offence; church leaders and churchgoers believe on behalf of others and incur criticism if they do not do this properly; church leaders and churchgoers embody moral codes on behalf of others, even when those codes have been abandoned by large sections of the populations that they serve; churches, finally, can offer space for the vicarious debate of unresolved issues in modern societies. The last of these is particularly significant – it explains, for example why the populations of many European countries continue to pay attention to both the appointments and the pronouncements of religious professionals in societies which, on other indicators, are markedly secular.

Rather different are Europe's diminishing, but still significant churchgoers – those, in other words, who maintain the tradition on behalf of the people described in the previous section. Here an observable change is clearly taking place, best summarized as a shift from a culture of obligation or duty to a culture of consumption or choice. What was once simply imposed (with all the negative connotations of this word), or inherited (a rather more positive spin), becomes instead a matter of personal choice: "I go to church (or to another religious organization) because I want to, maybe for a short period or maybe for longer, to fulfil a particular rather than a general need in my life and where I will continue my attachment so long as it provides what I want, but I have no *obligation* either to attend in the first place or to continue if I don't want to."

As such, this pattern is entirely compatible with vicariousness: "the churches need to be there in order that I may attend them if I so choose." The "chemistry," however, gradually alters, a shift that is discernible in both practice and belief, not to mention the connections between them. There is, for example, an easily documentable change in the patterns of confirmation in the Church of England. The overall number of confirmations has dropped dramatically in the postwar period, evidence once again of institutional decline. In England, though not yet in the Nordic countries, confirmation is no longer a teenage rite of passage, but a relatively rare event undertaken as a matter of personal choice by people of all ages. As a result, there is a very marked rise in the proportion of adult confirmations among the candidates overall – by no means enough, however, to offset the fall among teenagers. In short, even in Europe, voluntarism (a market) is beginning to establish itself *de facto*, regardless of the constitutional position of the churches.

The fourth factor concerns the growing number of incomers in almost all European societies. There have been two stages in this process. The first was closely linked to the urgent need for labor in the expanding economies of postwar Europe – notably in Britain, France, Germany, and the Netherlands. The second wave of immigration occurred in the 1990s and included, in addition to the places listed above, both the Nordic countries and the countries of Mediterranean Europe (Greece, Italy, Spain, and Portugal) – bearing in mind that the latter, until very recently, have been countries of emigration rather than immigration. There are economic reasons for these shifts – the implications for religion are, however, crucial, but they vary from place to place. Britain and France offer an instructive comparison. In Britain immigration has been much more varied than in France, both in terms of provenance and in terms of faith communities. Britain is also a country where ethnicity and religion criss-cross each other in a bewildering variety of ways (only Sikhs and Jews claim ethno-religious identities). The situation in France is different: here immigration has been largely from the Maghreb, as a result of which France has by far the largest Muslim community in Europe (between 5 and 6 million) – an almost entirely Arab population. Rightly or wrongly, Arab and Muslim have become interchangeable terms in popular parlance in France.

Beneath these differences lies however a common factor: the growing presence of other faith communities in general, and of the Muslim population in particular, is challenging some deeply held European assumptions. The notion that faith is a private matter and should, therefore, be excluded from public life – notably from the state and from the education system – has been widespread in Europe. Conversely, many of those who are currently arriving in this part of the world have markedly different convictions, and offer – simply by their presence – a challenge to the European way of doing things. European societies have been obliged to re-open debates about the place of religion in public as well as private life – hence the heated controversies about the wearing of the veil or other religious insignia, about the rights or wrongs of publishing material that one faith community in particular finds offensive, and about the location of "non-European" religious buildings. There have been moments, moreover, when a lack of mutual comprehension, together with an unwillingness to compromise on many of these issues, have led alarmingly fast to dangerous confrontations, both in Europe and beyond. All of these factors are evidence of deprivatization, as much in Europe as elsewhere (Casanova 1994).

Such episodes raise a further point: that is the extent to which the secular elites of Europe "use" these events in order to articulate alternatives – ideological, constitutional, and institutional – to religion. It is important to remember, however, that such elites, just like their religious counterparts, vary markedly from place to place. Key in this respect is David Martin's underlying point: namely that the *process* of secularization has taken place differently in the two countries. What in Britain, and indeed in most of Northern Europe, occurred gradually (starting with a de-clericalization of the churches from within at the time of Reformation), became in France a delayed and much more ideological clash between a hegemonic, heavily clerical church and a much more militant secular state. As a result, what is known as "la guerre de deux Frances" dominated French political life well into the twentieth century. The legacies still remain in the form of a self-consciously secular elite, and a lingering suspicion concerning religion of all kinds – the more so when this threatens the public sphere. The fact that these threats are no longer Catholic but Muslim does not alter the underlying reaction. In Britain, something rather different occurs: *overlapping* elites (both religious and secular) work together to encourage mutual respect between different world faiths, a policy admirably illustrated following the (attempted) bombings in London in the summers of 2005 and 2006.

That said, Britain now plays host to some aggressively secular voices: resurgent religion brings with it resurgent atheism. The latter, however, is as much evidence of resacralization as the former. Both have taken not only Britain but Europe by surprise, and both require very careful scrutiny. The crucial point can be put as follows: a global region that had become markedly secular for all the reasons outlined above is now obliged to address complex issues regarding the place of religion in the public sphere on a regular basis. And precisely because European societies have become secular they have lost the instincts, concepts and vocabulary that would enable this debate to take place in an informed and constructive manner. It is for this reason that these exchanges very often become not only destructive but futile – reduced to sterile arguments in which advocates of religion of all kinds are derided by those who see religion per se as a delusion, and a harmful one at that (Dawkins 2006). Such conversations, or rather the lack of them, take place at every level of society: very few of them are helpful.[6]

The same point can be considered as follows. Until recently, it has been customary to argue that religion had been sidelined from the mainstream of Europe, but continued to exist in the private sphere. One way of capturing this shift was to talk about "believing without belonging" (see above), an approach that is similar to Thomas Luckmann's "invisible religion" or "little transcendences" (Luckmann 1967, 1990). All of these ideas acknowledged the continuation of the sacred, but in private, often understated forms, requiring innovative and sensitive research tools in order to be properly understood. Important questions had to be asked, moreover, about the capacity of these non-institutional forms of religion to sustain themselves over the long term. Could this be done in any meaningful way? Before that question could be answered, however, the re-emergence of religion at the very center of public debate began increasingly to demand attention, and of a very different kind. And it is this shift, paradoxically, that reveals the extent of the erosion that has undoubtedly taken place: the narratives of religion (in the sense of a coherent and usable knowledge of any world faith, including Christianity) can no longer be assumed. Hence the impossibility of intelligent debate.

One final step is important: that is to see Europe from the outside. *Europe: The Exceptional Case* (Davie 2002) does this by reversing the "normal" question: instead of asking what Europe *is* in term of its religious existence, it asks what Europe *is not*. It is *not* (yet) a vibrant religious market such as that found in the United States; it is *not* a part of the world where Christianity is growing exponentially, very often in Pentecostal forms, as in the case in the Southern hemisphere (Latin America, Sub-Saharan Africa and the Pacific Rim); it is *not* a part of the world dominated by faiths other than Christian, but is increasingly penetrated by these; and it is *not* for the most part subject to the violence often associated with religion and religious difference in other parts of the globe – the more so if religion becomes entangled in political conflict. It is, however, a global region that is itself changing and to which the adjective post-secular is increasingly applied.[7] Paradoxically the term resonates rather better in Europe's religiously plural cities than it does in the rural areas which – until recently – were considered the bastions of traditional religion.

CONCLUDING REMARKS

These considerations go straight to the heart of an urgent and as yet unresolved question which summarizes the essence of this chapter: *is secularization intrinsic or extrinsic to the modernization process?* The answer requires our close and interdisciplinary attention. Taken to its logical conclusion, it demands in fact a fundamental rethinking not only of the paradigms of the sociology of religion, but of social science *as a whole*, in order to take on board the abiding significance of religion in the modern world. Religion continues to influence almost every aspect human society – economic, political, social and cultural. No longer can it be relegated to the past or to the edge of social scientific analysis. Hence the challenge for the economic and social sciences: to rediscover the place of religion in *both* the empirical realities of the twenty-first century *and* the paradigms that are deployed to understand this. In short, social science itself, just as much as its subject matter, must respond to the demands of re-sacralization.

Notes

1   It is important to remember that the enlightenment in Europe took on different forms in different places. Only in France was this aggressively anti-religious. Elsewhere – in Italy, Germany, Scandinavia, and Britain – the possibilities for accommodation were greater.

2   The Japanese case is contentious. Some commentators argue that Japan is an example of secular modernity; others are less sure – maintaining that Japan remains a highly religious place, but one in which the evidence is not easily grasped using Western tools of analysis.

3   See http://pewforum.org/docs/?DocID=301. Clearly both the questions asked in this poll and the statistics which emerge must be treated with caution given the specificities of the Chinese case. That said, the growth of religion in general and of Christianity in particular merits very careful attention.

4   For the European Values Study, see www.europeanvalues.nl/index2/htm; for the World Values Study see http://wvs.isr.umich.edu.

5   A longer version of this section and its implications for social science can be found in Davie (2006).

6   Examples of these exchanges can be found in almost every form of media. The use of blogs and of public posts following published articles is increasingly common and reveals very directly a lamentable standard of discussion.

7   Precisely this point lies at the heart of Jürgen Habermas' recent work on the place of religion in the public sphere. Habermas' reformulations of his political philosophy are a direct response to the renewed presence of religion in public debate (Habermas 2006).

Bibliography

Berger, P. (1999) *The Desecularization of the World: Resurgent Religion and World Politics*, Grand Rapids: Erdmans Publishing.

Berger, P. (2002) The cultural dynamics of globalization, in P. Berger and S. Huntington (eds.), *Many Globalizations*, New York: Oxford University Press, 1–16.

Bruce, S. (2001) The curious case of the unnecessary recantation: Berger and secularisation, in L. Woodhead, P. Heelas, and D. Martin (eds.), *Peter Berger and the Study of Religion*, London: Routledge, 87–100.

Brusco, E. (1993) The reformation of machismo: asceticism and masculinity among Colombian evangelicals, in D. Stoll and V. Garrard-Burnett (eds.), *Rethinking Protestantism in Latin America*, Philadelphia: Temple University Press, 143–58.

Casanova, J. (1994) *Public Religions in the Modern World*, Chicago: University of Chicago Press, Chicago.

Davie, G. (1994) *Religion in Britain since 1945: Believing without Belonging*, Oxford: Blackwell.

Davie, G. (2000) *Religion in Modern Europe: A Memory Mutates*, Oxford: Oxford University Press.

Davie, G. (2002) *Europe: The Exceptional Case. Parameters of Faith in the Modern World*, London: Darton, Longman and Todd.

Davie, G. (2006) Religion in Europe in the 21st century: the factors to take into account, *Archives européennes de sociologie/European Journal of Sociology/Europaeisches Archiv für Soziologie* 47 (2): 271–96.

Davie, G. (2007) Vicarious religion: a methodological challenge, in N. Ammerman (ed.), *Everyday Religion: Observing Modern Religious Lives*, Oxford University Press, New York, 21–36.

Dawkins, R. (2006) *The God Delusion*, London: Bantam Press.

Eisenstadt, S. (2000) Multiple modernities, *Daedalus* 129: 1–30.

Finke, R. and Stark, R. (1992) *The Churching of America, 1776–1990: Winners and Losers in Our Religious Economy*, New Brunswick: Rutgers University Press.

Habermas, J. (2006) Religion in the public sphere, *European Journal of Philosophy* 14 (1): 1–25.

Himmelfarb, G. (2004) *The Roads to Modernity: The British, French and American Enlightenments*, New York: Alfred A. Knopf.

Huntington, S. (1993) The clash of civilizations, *Foreign Affairs* 72: 22–50.

Huntington, S. (1997) *The Clash of Civilizations and the Remaking of the World Order*, New York: Simon and Schuster.

Inglehart, R. (1997) *Modernization and Postmodernization: Cultural, Economic and Political Change in 43 Societies*, Princeton: Princeton University Press.

Inglehart, R. and Baker, W. (2000) Modernization, cultural change and the persistence of traditional values, *American Sociological Review* 65: 19–51.

Jenkins, P. (2002) *The Next Christendom: The Coming of Global Christianity*, New York: Oxford University Press.

Kissinger, H. (1994) *Diplomacy: The History of Diplomacy and the Balance of Power*, New York: Simon and Schuster.

Lipset, S. (1997) *American Exceptionalism: A Double-Edged Sword*, New York: Norton.

Luckmann, T. (1967) *The Invisible Religion: The Problem of Religion in Modern Society*, New York: Macmillan.

Luckmann, T. (1990) Shrinking transcendence, expanding religion? *Sociological Analysis* 5: 127–38.

Martin, B. (2000) The Pentecostal gender paradox: a cautionary tale for the sociology of religion, in R. Fenn (ed.), *The Blackwell Companion to Sociology of Religion*, Oxford: Blackwell, 52–66.

Martin, D. (1965) Towards eliminating the concept of secularisation, in J. Gould (ed.), *Penguin Survey of the Social Sciences*, Penguin, Harmondsworth, 169–82.

Martin, D. (1978) *A General Theory of Secularization*, Oxford: Blackwell.

Martin, D. (1991) The secularization issue: prospect and retrospect, *British Journal of Sociology* 42: 465–74.

Martin, D. (2000) Personal reflections in the mirror of Halévy and Weber, in R. Fenn (ed.), *The Blackwell Companion to Sociology of Religion*, Oxford: Blackwell, 23–38.

Norris, P. and Inglehart, R. (2004) *Sacred and Secular: Religion and Politics Worldwide*, Cambridge: Cambridge University Press.

Part III
New Developments

8

Rational Choice and the Sociology of Religion

David Lehmann

A Tribe and Its Leader

The case of rational choice is one of a tribe within the broader tribe of sociologists of religion, identified by a distinctive sense of embattlement and by a particular jargon. The writing of the highly prolific founding scholar, Rodney Stark, is interspersed with dismissive, even offensive, remarks and often sarcastic attacks on the secularization thesis and its defenders (Stark and Finke 2000: 60–1), on those who would despise deductive theory or simply do not know what real theory is (Stark 1997), on historians who accept the secularization thesis or versions thereof or who write approvingly of a long-term trend towards liberalization – notably Martin Marty (Finke and Stark 2005: 7–8 and 244–7) – on Émile Durkheim (Stark and Finke 2000: 7), on intellectuals and theologians in general, placed sarcastically in quotes as "learned professors" (Finke and Stark 2005: 87,133) on journal editors who would not publish his papers (Stark 1997: 9–11), and on structural functionalism ("more like astrology than astronomy" (Stark 1997: 5; Lehmann 2001) The list is very long.

The school can be said to have announced its birth in Stark and Bainbridge's *A Theory of Religion* (1987), and to have its existence confirmed by Stephen Warner in a 1993 paper whose title referred to "a new paradigm" (Warner 1993) and highlighted the use of concepts drawn from economics as its hallmark. It is variously referred to as "rational choice," "supply side," "market theory of religion" and "economics of religion" and its main claims have been summarized with admirable clarity by Alejandro Frigerio (Frigerio 2007):

1   Pluralism is the natural situation of religious economies.
2   Pluralism strengthens the religious economy.
3   Monopoly religions are inefficient.
4   There are no effectively monopolistic religions, but rather regulated [religious] markets.

5 Variations in religious behavior are best explained by variations in supply than by variations in individual religious needs.
6 Secularization is a misnomer: the phenomena it refers to are better described as a desacralization of society.
7 Desacralization does not necessarily bring a diminution of the importance of religion in the lives of individuals. (translation/paraphrase by D. L.)

Stark's writing –that is, the books and articles he has written himself and those written with his colleagues, principally William Sims Bainbridge and Roger Finke – is also sprinkled with *obiter dicta*, containing overarching and sometimes over-bearing verdicts on human nature and on history in general: "What is history but the record of the choices that humans have made and the actions they have taken on the basis of their choices?" (Finke and Stark 2005: 282); or "Most people desire immortality" (Stark 1997: 7). These statements are not really truth claims at all, but affirmations of self-sufficiency, intrusions or excursions into and away from the arguments of a text. They are particular striking because they appear not only in the retrospective texts published since the mid-1990s, but also in the austere *Theory of Religion* (1987) which is rooted in the more considered type of axiomatic theo-rizing which Stark has thought out very carefully: this is the procedure which meets his exacting criteria of what is a "big theory" ("make social systems emerge from micro-axioms," as George Homans, the prominent exchange theorist and precursor of rational choice, had called for in his 1964 address to the American Sociological Association (Stark 1997: 5).

The approach to the subject is indeed unique and self-sufficient: that is to say, it draws on almost no other contributions to the sociology of religion, or indeed to sociology generally, builds its own theory of human motivation from scratch – with only passing mentions of Freud, Darwin, or Wilson – and exhibits only a schematic notion of social structure, or stratification. Indeed, even the economists who pre-sumably hover behind the basic maxim of their framework merit little mention beyond a deferential nod (Stark and Finke 2000: 45). (Iannacone has corrected this absence as we shall see.) But a more elaborate understanding of economics would have helped: for example a distinction between maximization and optimization would offer a basis for a more sensitive account of motivation.

In explaining this unadorned way of presenting his ideas, shorn of ancestral invocation or legitimation, Stark complains that much of what goes by the name of sociological theory is little more than "ancestor worship" (Stark 1997: 21): for him, the merits of a founder of a school have little to do with those of applying its insights many generations later (biology students do not study Darwin, he notes, in Young 1997: 21), so he takes little trouble to place himself in a tradition or intel-lectual lineage. This adds further to the distinctiveness of his writings, setting them apart from the mainstream in which it is customary to use footnotes and potted histories of a concept as markers of allegiance to one or another school of thought. It does, however, leave his version open to the criticism that it is an over-simplifi-cation and conceivably inspired by a mission: at the very start (p. 2) of *The Future of Religion* (jointly authored with Bainbridge) it is stated, baldly, that "social sci-entists have misread the future of religion [and] not only because they so fervently desire religion to disappear."

The separation is to some extent mutual. The endorsements on the covers of Stark's books are written by people who are not known for their contributions to the study of religion – like the grand theory specialist Randall Collins (see the 1996 edition of *A Theory of Religion*) – or by others – like Andrew Greeley and Christian Smith (see *Acts of Faith*) – whose research is admittedly and perfectly respectably driven by a concern for the survival of one or other religious institution or tradition. Leading figures like David Martin, Robert Wuthnow, or José Casanova ignore Stark, Iannacone, and their circle, albeit mistakenly. David Martin has never mentioned Stark or Rational Choice and Wuthnow does not mention them even in a 2005 book entitled *America and the Challenges of Religious Diversity* (Wuthnow 2005), in which one chapter title includes the words "shopping in the spiritual marketplace." It is hard to believe that a scholar of Wuthnow's erudition had not considered whether to include a discussion of rational choice approaches to this subject.

Religious Commitment

Mention of the discrete religious commitment of Greeley and Smith leads us to the thorny question of that of Stark himself and his circle. This is complicated. Stark's work, as has been mentioned, is littered with expressions of contempt, even hostility, directed at theologians, erudite clergy and intellectuals. In *A Theory of Religion* Stark and Bainbridge describe themselves as "personally incapable of religious faith" (p. 23). Stark's contribution to the Laurence Young volume (Young 1997) recounts his academic career, and in a 2007 interview quoted on Wikipedia he slips in a swipe at the intelligentsia: "I have trouble with faith. I'm not proud of this. I don't think it makes me an intellectual" as if to set himself apart from the standard atheistic stance of intellectuals as he sees them. The same entry also quotes an interview given to the American Enterprise Institute and reproduced in the Mormon magazine *Meridian* www.meridianmagazine.com/ideas/050210darwin.html in which he describes himself as neither a Darwinist nor a creationist, but denounces anti-creationism at length as an atheist campaign against religion.

Stark's (Finke and Stark 2005) disparagement of an out-of-touch or elitist intelligentsia goes hand in hand with much more positive language used in connection with the religion or religiosity of the people. *The Churching of America* can be thought of as an extended homage to popular religion – a term which the authors do not use but which fits their purpose.

Yet their reverence for the popular is not unlimited. The book gains much of its credence from a rich vein of data from the Bureau of the Census which had previously, according to Finke and Stark, been dismissed by demographers on the grounds that, being the result of responses from Church officials, the data they contained would be wildly inflated. The authors' response is disarming: it is only when individuals, not churchmen, are asked their religious affiliation that the statistics are inflated: "Ever since the start of public opinion polling in the late 1930s surveys have found that approximately 85–95% of the population claims a religious affiliation." In contrast Church officials' Census returns are more modest and quite stable over time (2005: 13–14). So although they clearly believe – and their data clearly show – that at least in the United States Christian religion survives and grows thanks to popular religion, theirs is not a naïve enthusiasm for popular spontaneity: indeed, they live up to their supply-side moniker by expressing greatest enthusiasm for the entrepreneurial preachers who would stir up the presumed latent religiosity among the people. Their theory of religious motivation is, as we shall see, not a very populist one at all.

Stark and colleagues have no compunction in describing popular religion's openness to mobilization and to what some might describe as manipulation. Uncharitable or snobbish commentators might say that the methods they describe in the marketing of religion are no different from those used in promoting mundane consumer items. They emphasize entrepreneurship and the supply side, and the importance of preachers' ability and willingness to engage with the daily lives and needs of their actual and potential followings: these themes in turn reflect a powerful assumption about humans' disposition to religious affiliation, namely that it is present in human existence and ready to be tapped. This is no longer as controversial an assumption as it might have been a generation ago: cognitive anthropology and psychology have given us reason to believe that the functioning of our brains does indeed predispose us to religion – though it is a predisposition, not an inevitability, and it predisposes us to give credence to supernatural agency generally, not to the institutionalization of religion. Interestingly, when Pascal Boyer, one of the most prominent exponents of the cognitive approach to religion, comes to explain institutionalized religion, he takes a straightforward rational choice approach – though he does not use the term itself, preferring "coalition-building" (Boyer 2001, 2004; Atran 2003; Lehmann 2005).

The rational choice school takes its name not from cognitive science, but from a basic quasi-economic axiom, namely that "humans seek what they perceive to be rewards and avoid what they perceive to be costs" (Stark and Bainbridge 1987: 27). The challenge is then to show how not only immediate and material offerings but also soulful longing or yearnings for salvation, or discourses on the transubstantiation or on Rabbinic law, can be seen to flow from this axiom. We will come to this, but the approach also calls itself supply side because the rational choice theorists are also deeply interested in the organization and entrepreneurship required to respond to this basic feature of human behavior by providing rewards and cost-reducing resources.

The supply side explains how preachers reach their audience: the dedication of circuit preachers riding thousands of miles on horseback in eighteenth and nineteenth century United States enabled them to hone their skills, endlessly rehearse their exhortations, and accumulate a wealth of quasi-ethnographic experience. The camp meetings organized by Methodists and Baptists required meticulous organization and fund-raising, just as modern-day evangelicals use a battery of media and marketing resources, and immigrant leaders set up community halls. All this does not in itself detract from the supernatural or spiritual appeal of the outcome – it is merely a necessary condition for any successful event from the Christmas pantomime to a collective spiritual experience. And indeed the camp meetings were characterized by all sorts of trances and ecstasies, much to the distaste of the establishment clerics whom Finke and Stark love to mock (2005: 95).

If the truly thriving religion is the religion of the people, and if the most enthusiastic or committed forms of religious life (sects especially) tend to be overrepresented among the disempowered, is this not a version of Marx's "opium of the people"? Are Stark and his circle trying to promote the religion of untutored spontaneity or of the manipulated masses? Are they secret elitists, contemptuous of the intellectual and theological elite but resigned to the admission that the masses are a disposable mass ready to follow the best that the science of marketing can offer?

COMPENSATORS

That is indeed a question which arises in respect of Stark's concept of a "compensator," which was central to the books he wrote with Bainbridge. Although it was set aside in *Acts of Faith*, written with Finke, this was for presentational rather than substantive reasons. The concept of "compensator" emerged out of a formally structured sequence of axioms, definitions and propositions which start on p. 27 of *A Theory of Religion* (Stark and Bainbridge 1987) by defining the complementary words "reward" and "cost" and by page 36 have reached proposition 15: "Compensators are treated by humans as if they were rewards." Rewards are "anything which humans will incur costs to maintain" and costs are "whatever humans attempt to avoid." (By its end the book has accumulated 7 axioms, 104 Definitions and 344 Propositions.) The argument is that when the rewards sought by individuals are not achievable they may accept intangible substitutes which are also called "explanations" (*A Theory of Religion*, p. 36), though some might call them consolations or even sublimations. The generality of the rewards and the explanations is crucial: since no answer to "fundamental questions of meaning" can be unambiguously evaluated some people accept "untestable and extremely general explanations" as compensators. Note that the word "general" is important: even though it is a very vague word, it is used repeatedly in these texts to emphasize the ultimate or fundamental nature of the questions the compensators are supposed to answer. And the authors affirm that "many humans do often desire answers" to "questions of ultimate meaning" – though the only evidence offered is that the "Neanderthal performed burial rites" (p. 39). Religion is a term to describe systems of generalized compensation based on supernatural assumptions (p. 39). Cognitive scientists (like Boyer and Atran) take it almost for granted that if religion is "hard-wired" in our brains, it is, as already mentioned, the religion of what might be called naive supernatural belief and definitely not the religion of the afterlife or of eternal damnation or salvation. Given Stark and his colleagues' aversion to theology, it might have been expected that they would relegate eternal truths to a lower level of explanatory force than that accorded to it through the compensator concept. But while naive supernatural belief is counted as magic by them and does not qualify as religion, the importance they attach to a universal human search for ultimate meaning sits uncomfortably with their persistent denigration of theology.

The appeal of the compensator idea lies in one crucial implication, namely the uncertainty and inherent untestability of these very generalized expectations, for later in the theory we find (1) that the poor and the powerless tend to be those most drawn to them, since the more fortunate and more powerful can gain real rewards and are not drawn to compensators, and (2) that the power to convince people, or the power that comes to those in whom others place their trust, is quite significant (pp. 43, 140). In other words, high-status members of a religious organization are less dependent psychologically on the truth value of eschatological futures, or on the supernatural guarantors of future benefits. They have less to gain from believing in those prospects than their followers. Indeed, a rather chilling pair of propositions claims that those who gain real rewards have little vested interest in recognizing the limitations of those intangible rewards while those with few real rewards, taking refuge in compensators, will have a vested interest in denying the worth of real rewards: that is, the model has a built-in polarization between the skepticism or realism of the elite and the naïveté of the relatively deprived (p. 141). Stark and Bainbridge and later Finke are keen to clarify that nothing they write has any implication for the truth or falsehood of religious explanations – but this apparently rather cynical account does little to enhance religion's attractiveness. Stark and Bainbridge are not worried about cynicism, but they do go out of their way to pre-empt an accusation of Marxism. Theirs, they say, is not a Marxist claim that "the powerful will profit while the poor pray" (p. 44) because even the rich and powerful believe in some general compensators. The issue of Marxism is surely peripheral: a more significant question is that of power and uncertainty, which Stark and colleagues do address.

The uncertainty of outcomes in the religious marketplace is very important. Uncertainty links in to power, especially in sects where the followers are drawn from among the poor and disempowered (for reasons which Stark and colleagues explain) and compensators are more general, or vague and almost unspecifiable, than in what they call "mainline" religion – i.e. Christian denominations. Religious specialists can define, interpret and manipulate the meaning of their promises. "Since it has proven impossible to determine what the gods promise and desire, the terms of exchanges with the gods are freely defined by the specialists" (1987: 98). The reasoning behind this is largely that it is also in the interest of specialists to provide some benefits for their followers even as they impose strict demands on them (notably in respect of sexual activity, for example, or dress, or contributions in time and money), but the argument could go further, by invoking the substantial investment which followers make in the most sectarian movements and the consequent resistance to any evidence of failure. This is brought out by the argument that individuals who invest most in the positive self-image conferred by adherence to the cause and its cosmology (general compensators) tend to be the most powerless, and therefore are unlikely to take on the risks of revolt (1987: 140).

Eventually, as already noted, it was decided to set aside the idea of a compensator. In *Acts of Faith*, Stark and Finke (2000: 88) use the expression "otherworldly rewards," and in a footnote explain that that the term compensator "implies unmeant negative connotations about the validity of religious promises" (p. 289) – in other words its use led some readers to think that compensators were compensating for the impossibility, even dishonesty, of those promises. It now sufficed, they said, "to analyze aspects of the religious means of fulfilment of such explanations and the issues of risk and plausibility entailed therein" (p. 289) In other words, they looked to use a term which left room for a range of plausibility and did not even hint at the notion of zero plausibility. No commentator seems to have asked whether their usage of the word compensator might not have a Freudian origin on account of its resemblance to sublimation or displacement.

Secularization and Waves of Renewal

Stark and colleagues have a strong claim to be precursors of the reversal of consensus which has questioned the concept and the reality of secularization and its measurement. In *A Theory of Religion* (Starke and Bainbridge 1987) an argument is developed to the effect that secularization is self-limiting, and that, taking place in a "cosmopolitan society," it tends to encourage more sectarianism than in a society with a single dominant religious culture. This is for several reasons: religious institutions of a lax or liberal kind, which exist in low tension with society as a whole, which "modernize their values" and "embrace temporal values" (Finke and Starke 2005), are led by salaried religious specialists and comfortable lay members, and pay little attention to the provision of the sort of general compensators which are of benefit to their less advantaged followers. Their learned theological disquisitions often dismiss as superstition cherished ideas about the supernatural, confer little value on proselytization, and care little for the religiosity of everyday life. They – the elite – have plenty of rewards in this life, and have little need for the consolations ("compensations") of life after death, salvation and eternal happiness. They also may have many other satisfactions outside the life of their coreligionaries, whereas the less powerful have more restricted sources of reward.

Even if not many of these more humble people disaffiliate, for reasons principally of inertia, those who do leave will, in a "cosmopolitan" society where the religious arena is tolerant and competitive, be able to choose from a variety of alternatives. Disaffiliating from the low-tension denominations, they will gravitate to the "high-tension" sectarian alternatives rich in those ill-specified and unattainable consolations (the "general compensators" or general "otherworldly rewards"). They may not be many, but they will be an increasing proportion of the overall religious or observant population. In addition, the claim is that people from a religiously disaffected or unaffiliated background, if they do seek religion, are more likely to join high-tension religious groups – i.e. sects or even cults (Starke and Bainbridge 1987: 303). The interpretation is again somewhat chilling: the elite can do without religion, or at least with a religious affiliation which is undemanding and even flattering to their status, and have little if anything to gain from making their institutions more welcoming or even of benefit to the mass of the disempowered. The wording seems to suggest that the disempowered include not only the lower reaches of society but even the middle ranges of empowerment and income: all these are left to console themselves with promises which will be realized only when it is too late.

The notion of high-tension is evidently central to this argument. It means "broad sub-cultural deviance" (Starke and Bainbridge 1987: 121) or, quite simply, sects and cults and hostility to a notional liberal mainstream: denunciation of abortion, of sexual permissiveness, and same-sex marriage, for example (Finke and Stark 2005: 278). It is sub-culturally, not morally, deviant. Membership in sects is costly, and so the leaders must maintain a high level of tension to preserve the idea that their followers' objectives – to attain impossible compensations – are far superior to the illusory rewards of more comfortable members of society. But if a sect survives – and many do not – its leaders seem, in this model, to develop a life of power and high income and manage their followers by giving them positions of responsibility, or simply minor tasks, while keeping them in a state of deprivation, poverty, and powerlessness. This interpretation is puzzling because the tone of so much of this rational choice writing is, if not sympathetic to sects, then certainly hostile to hierarchies and institutionalized churches. Maybe we should welcome the frankness of the following (p. 248): "In contemporary America... members of high-tension sects will be heavily recruited from among low-income, low-IQ, uneducated, female, older, non-white, handicapped, neurotic and otherwise less powerful persons." Chapter 8 of Stark and Bainbridge (1987) is mostly devoted to showing that most sects disappear before they can grow to a significant size, while those which do grow must gradually reduce tension with their environment, a model which feeds back into the waves of secularization and desecularization.

This version of the secularization thesis does not deny a contemporary falling away in church attendance, but it regards this as part of secular fluctuations which will never end, and it also offers a theory to predict the increasing power of the leaders of sects, evangelical churches and what we might call conversion-led movements to set the agenda in public debates about religion. Yet it also foresees a constant ebb and flow between more and less institutionalized religious organization.

The fluctuations are well described in Finke and Stark (2005). The idea of a decline in religion just after the Revolution turns out to be a decline in attendance at established churches and neglects rapid growth of Methodists and Baptists. (pp. 59–60). This fits neatly with the Stark thesis – which is also that of Adam Smith – that maintained churches tend to lose their followings (pp. 53–4). The revivals, waves and great awakenings which have been the received wisdom of US history turn out, on this account, to be inventions, both in the sense that a closer examination shows they were not exceptional upsurges, and also in the sense that although they were particularly shocking and surprising to those who commanded the media at the time – namely the erudite clergy of the denominations – they were routine for their organizers. And Finke and Stark's main point is to emphasize the meticulous planning which lay behind these campaigns, downplaying the theme of spontaneity and thus of outbursts of innate religious fervor (pp. 87–92). These occasions may have appeared uncontrolled, but in fact they took place in well organized contexts.

When it comes to contrasting the USA with Europe the theme of a salaried clergy recurs with much rhetorical flourish. Not only have the established churches of Europe maintained an indolent clergy with little incentive to deliver – they have also never really been very religious nor above all very Christian at all. *Acts of Faith* (Stark and Finke 2000) assembles various sources to show that levels of church attendance even in medieval Europe were quite low. "The Christianity that prevailed in Europe was an elaborate patchwork of state churches that settled for the allegiance of the elite and for imposing official requirements of conformity, but made little effort to Christianize the peasant masses" (p. 69). So the assumptions made about Europe by standard secularization theory are wrong because the continent – a least in the West – was not very religious, or at least not very Christian, in the first place.

The treatment of Europe, marked as Bruce shows (see *infra*) by a very superficial historiography, is an illustration not only of Stark's focus on the USA, but also of a certain animosity towards Europe, depicted here as a more or less heathen space. There is disquieting ignorance, as when, in Finke and Stark (2005) it is said, with reference to the Catholic Church, that "in many parts of Europe the head of state holds veto over the appointment of bishops" (p. 131). This was still at least half true in Franco's Spain, but Franco had been dead for thirty years when the book was published. (Of course the state does have a role in non-Catholic episcopal appointments in England and several Scandinavian countries, but the process is too consensual to allow anything so strong as a veto.) Further on we shall come to Steve Bruce's exposure of many other errors.

Despite the aspiration to completeness, signified by the formal structure of *A Theory ...*, Stark and colleagues leave some threads untied. They describe the more or less inevitable process of sect institutionalization, and one can see how this fits into the idea of waves of revival followed by periods of calm, but does this mean that the contemporary upsurge has been a passing phase, or does it apply at a more micro – or maybe meso – level? If the model is local, then local churches and sects can evolve in waves, but at a national or global level the waves would not be visible.

In this connection too a recognition that the wave of conversion-led religious movements may have brought about deep changes in the last two or three generations in what it means to be religious would have been necessary to complement the model's formal and empirical merits. This change may have taken different forms and had differing impacts in different parts of the world, but given the school's enthusiasm for religious revival and participation, the fact that most Protestants worldwide are now Pentecostals should not have been overlooked – a trend whose implications will be examined further on.

THE "CLUB" MODEL

This section considers a second "wave" of rational choice theories, spearheaded by tighter economic reasoning and even modeling, and which is more applicable across cultural and geographical boundaries.

Iannacone and Stark speak of each other like two lonely warriors who met one day and saved each others' lives. This fits with their outsider status in their own disciplines. When Iannacone began to work on religion in the 1980s economists were liable to look with disdain on "real world" problems, let alone on problems which lay outside the traditional purview of their subject. That has changed and today economists have extended their reach to crime, healthcare and much besides.

Iannacone's contribution has been to bring some rigor to the formulation of the rational choice approach, drawing on Olson's short, but highly influential book *The Logic of Collective Action* (Olson 1965) and the institutional economics which it prefigured. Olson's original examples had been taxes, trade unions and voluntary organizations. We pay taxes because the penalty for not doing so is punishment by the state. The benefit to each individual tax-payer is hard if not impossible to relate to the taxpayer's own contribution. But why do we join a trade union if the wages negotiated by its officers will in any case be paid to all the employees of a firm? How can the trade union deal with this now-famous "free-rider" problem? Answer: under a closed shop agreement the firm has agreed only to employ members of the union. (Closed shops are much rarer now in North America and Western Europe than they were in the 1960s of course.) Why do we join a voluntary organization? Here the answer is not so obvious to those who adopt an economistic view of motivation, but Olson finds that voluntary organizations very often provides all sorts of "separate and selective incentives" of direct personal benefit to encourage members to contribute their dues: academic associations provide subscriptions to their journals at a fraction of the price to non-members; Touring Clubs and Automobile Associations provide insurance, manuals, maps, etc. Charitable donations are tax-deductible as is membership of professional associations, and participation in voluntary associations can bring social contacts and status. An important feature of Olson's model, though, is the theme of interest groups' involvement in regulating market access – as in the case of the closed shop – and this is highly relevant to the rational choice analysis of religion precisely because sect leaders build barriers around their following so as to restrict access to the benefits membership brings.

Turning now to religion, this model can be applied with particular force to the most demanding sects. It is a response to the question why people who are – or appear to be – under little compulsion would voluntarily join an organization which imposes a tight dress code, makes very heavy demands on their time, requires members to have very large families, and so on. The reference is not to weird cults, but to the thousands of evangelical and Pentecostal churches scattered around the globe, to ultra-Orthodox Judaism, and to North American Christian fundamentalism. Much "commonsense" sociology has explained the growth of Pentecostalism in poor countries with reference to migration, social disintegration and the consequent search for meaning or for a refuge from the loss of secure values. Norris and Inglehart confirm this intuition with data from a host of national surveys which show that "levels of societal and individual security … seem to provide the most persuasive and parsimonious explanation for variations in religiosity" (Norris and Inglehart 2007: 47). That is the demand side. No doubt gross numbers of religious participants are of interest, but more precise explanations are needed for the particular form of "strong" religiosity which has become so vociferous and influential in many countries despite its relatively small number of followers. That is where the supply side comes in.

Iannacone explains that religious movements provide benefits for their followers: not just – maybe not particularly – salvation, but "worship services, religious instruction, social activities, and other quasi-public 'club goods'" (Iannacone 1997: 1482). In tightly knit groups like the chapels of the Assemblies of God or the ultra-Orthodox Jewish neighborhoods of Stamford Hill (London), Crown Heights (Brooklyn, New York) and Ramat Shlomo (Jerusalem) one can count on quite a lot of social support and mutual aid, but, as in Olson's trade union case, how to discourage free riders, who would take advantage of these benefits without truly believing? The question is serious enough when the group itself provides the support – chapels which collect charitable gifts for their members for example – but it becomes even more serious when the group has access to some special external benefit. This can arise when the pastor of a chapel has preferential access to a politician to whom he has promised the votes of his congregation – though that is certainly a relationship involving multiple moral hazards. More concretely, among ultra-Orthodox Jews there is the question of access to charitable funds, to centers of religious learning (yeshivas), and in Israel exemption from military service and access to the small but regular government subsidy to married men engaged in full-time Torah study. This has been explored in depth by Eli Berman (Berman 2000) who seizes on the Israeli case to explain the self-imposed burdens borne by the ultra-Orthodox in terms of the free-rider problem: membership has to be burdensome to discourage those who would join or remain only for the sake of these exemptions and benefits. The issue is not a person's contribution in labor or time, but the sincerity of their moral or ideological commitment. The substantial material benefits available in Israel do, of course, make it a very suitable case study. No wonder Iannacone concludes: "many of the bizarre and apparently pathological practices of deviant groups can function as rational, utility-enhancing attempts to promote solidarity and limit free riding" (Iannacone 1997: 1489). In Jewish New York there are few such concrete benefits beyond the famed fund-raising talents of some leaders, and among Assemblies of God, who do not have access to a relatively wealthy international network, the benefits are even less concrete: but since the followers of the Assemblies are overwhelmingly drawn from low income groups, their calculus may be different and their needs more modest. The benefits of belonging to a chapel in a very low-income and low-security urban neighborhood are probably to do with social contacts and social recognition, which in a location where levels of trust and institutional presence are abysmally low can be very substantial indeed. More research on the economics of low-income Pentecostal churches would be welcome, but it is not easy, because it would be regarded as intrusive: secularization theorists and mainstream sociologists generally have said very little about the financial side of religion, as if they were slightly embarrassed by it, whereas Stark and Iannacone and Berman have engaged with that subject with perhaps excessive enthusiasm.

This is not entirely surprising: among secularization theorists – who show little overt enthusiasm for religious observance – religious motivation tends to be a matter of ethos, while rational choice advocates are both less apparently skeptical about religion and more down-to-earth in their interpretations of religious behavior. For them, if Pentecostals, say, are obliged to contribute regularly (tithing), then the proliferation of small churches illustrates their dream of graduating to the point where they too can make a respectable preacher's living from those selfsame tithes. David Martin's notion of the pastor as a model of upward social mobility and the church as a type of social escalator (Martin 1990: 283) though the task of collecting evidence to support this observation and related claims about the social origins and destinations of Pentecostal churchgoers and activists, is still pending, and may face almost insuperable difficulties as a research project. The data used by Iannacone for example are drawn not from inquiry into church finances, but from surveys which in a much less intrusive way ask individuals about their own religious contributions, such as US National Opinion Research Center's General Social Surveys (Iannacone 1997: 1472) – data of a type which Stark himself seems to regard with a degree of wariness.

Berman has pursued these themes into new territory by applying the model to violent political groups claiming a religious inspiration. In a working paper published on the National Bureau of Economic Research website in Washington DC he compared Taliban, Hamas and a short-lived Jewish underground which aimed to blow up the Temple Mount in Jerusalem (Berman 2003). Here the religious factor in the argument recedes into the background but still the model derived from Iannacone remains: only, because the surrounding society in Afghanistan and the Occupied Territories of Palestine possess no effective state, the sacrifices demanded of militants are even tougher. So the strategy of the Taliban pre-2001 was to drive a wedge between their personnel and the local population in order that the former's loyalties would not be divided; thus they retained a degree of power by providing the security which their enemies, warlords and Mujaheddin, had failed to provide (Berman 2003; Berman and Iannacone 2006). The argument is neither that the violence has a religious explanation nor that the religious rhetoric is just a mask for violent politics. Rather, it seems to be that religious organizations like others may adopt new aims, and this may involve using violence as a survival strategy or as a way of pursuing political power – in which case they are little different from other organizations, especially in an environment where the state is weak or scarcely existent. For its part the Jewish underground collapsed at an early stage because Israel has a functioning state and the population cannot be persuaded to pay for alternative protection from a dangerous environment. Paradoxically, using the club theory, he points out that rebels in Afghanistan and the Hezbollah and Hamas all accentuated the "required levels of sacrifice" precisely when they received substantial external funding which in the case of Hezbollah and Hamas enabled them to branch into social assistance on a very large scale and thus to become an attractive target for free riders (Berman and Iannacone, 2006). The draconian measures then came into their own.

RATIONAL CHOICE'S FIERCEST CRITIC

Like Stark and Iannacone, Berman makes a point of excising emotions and belief from his analysis, and this is one of the main aspects of rational choice theory attacked by Steve Bruce in an unusual book-length critique (Bruce 1999). Like Stark, Bruce feels victimized by journal editors, complaining in his Preface of biases in their procedures, and like Stark he can use some intemperate language, expressing the hope in the same Preface that this book will be "the stake through the vampire's chest." His brandishing of his adversaries' nationality – "a handful of US sociologists" (p. 2); "US economists may find it hard to believe but" (p. 141) – is in poor taste, as is his allusion to "the entrepreneurial world of US fundamentalism." But these lapses should not detract from the seriousness of Bruce's arguments and the detail of his critical analysis. Some of his criticisms take up points already raised in this contribution, albeit more sharply: his doubts about compensators, his complaints about Stark and Bainbridge's "atheistic premises" (p. 34). Bruce's most important contribution is his deployment of a far wider range of information across many more countries, cultures and periods and with much more scholarly care than is found in supply-side writing. He shows for example the fallacy of Stark's assumption that a country with a state church places that church in a monopoly position (pp. 44–54), and the superficiality of the assumption that monopoly is an imposition, by quoting in some detail the examples of England and Scotland from the Reformation onwards, and of twentieth-century Poland. He reminds us of the fundamental importance for a church of its identification with national or tribal identities as in Serbia and Russia (p. 116), Ireland and of course Poland again. In the process the role of competition in the religious field becomes more and more multifarious and context-dependent and one is led to agree with his quotation from the historian Hugh McLeod on the impossibility of sociological generalization about religion across a broad range of countries (p. 115). Certainly, Bruce leaves the empirical claims of rational choice theory, especially about the relationship between religious activity and competition or deregulation, severely weakened.

On the other hand, he himself recognizes that when applied to the United States those claims have much validity (p. 120). One reason for this is that behind the words "market" and "competition" there lies, in the United States case, a proliferation of ethnically homogeneous religious-cultural niches in which there is not really much competition at all. So that market, because of the country's size and because of the pattern of immigrant settlement and residence, looks more segmented than is allowed – something to which we shall return.

Bruce's other main objection is more theoretical and concerns religious motivation. He will not accept the refusal of the rational choice approach to consider altruism and idealism in religion (p. 141), and he does not think "that people believe in God because they get a good return on that belief" – an oversimplification even of the supply-siders' concept. Instead he says both that people perform spiritual exercises because they want to go to heaven, and that "most people believe because they are socialized into a culture of belief" (p. 157). But these are merely statements of opinion, and involve precisely the delicate issue of the relationship between belief and action which the rational choice advocates choose, prudently, to sidestep. He does not accept the idea, central to much social science, of a model which explains actions independently of motivations, and so in the end his argument with Iannacone is as much about metaphors (viz. the notion of a "return" on, or an investment in, religion) as about propositional claims (p. 56). He does, nonetheless, uncover many puzzles – not least that of how writers who do not conceal their enthusiasm for organized religion refuse to take seriously the question of belief as a motivator in religious participation, preferring to adduce more mundane, lateral costs and benefits.

REFINING AND THICKENING RATIONAL CHOICE

The rational choice approach can be improved, firstly by taking on a less provocative name: a term such as "the sociology of everyday life" would be preferable if only because the approach is not claiming that religious belief as such is rational.

It would also nuance an otherwise provocative emphasis on the use of economics. Rationality is about means towards ends, yet it is essential to take into account that the ends of religion are different from other ends in that their attainment is unknowable. Bruce's criticism could be reformulated as a complaint that Stark and colleagues, aside from their highly contestable concept of the compensator, barely recognize that religious organizations are different from any other. To improve the approach requires taking certain basic theoretical and empirical points into account.

The first empirical point which the theory needs to admit is the decline in religious participation and observance, however defined, almost throughout the world – another point on which Bruce insists repeatedly and correctly. The debate about the facts – the "secularization debate" – is no longer of intellectual interest. The serious challenge is to interpret the growing influence of evangelical and fundamentalist movements within this shrinking religious field and their disproportionate – and possibly growing – political and cultural influence beyond the religious field in certain geographical, cultural and ethnic contexts. Linked to this is the prominence of conversion in these movements. At a time when Pentecostalism is a vast global mass movement, it no longer makes sense to say people joining conservative sects with extremely heterogeneous followings are returning to traditions with which they already identify (as Bruce claims). Indeed, even the phenomenon of return – as is now common among a vocal and influential minority of Jews and Muslims – is itself a radical conversion in psychological and social terms.

These conversion phenomena are characterized by a higher degree of holism in the lives of individuals than is perhaps usual. Following Frigerio (Frigerio 2007), just as people live their identities in the personal, social and collective spheres and do not necessarily integrate them in the way we observe among fundamentalists, returnees and, to a lesser extent, evangelicals, so also the variety of ways in which religion itself is experienced must be allowed for. He is critical of simplistic assumptions that "once upon a time" there was complete Catholic domination in Argentina, and that this has now collapsed as beliefs diversify. He presents opinion poll data which seem to show that Argentinians expressed more Catholic beliefs, quantitatively and qualitatively, in 1999 than in 1984. The data lack a counterpart in religious observance and participation, but the point he insists on is that religious change can take many directions, for in that country although the market has opened up the religious landscape, which has become more varied with the growth of Pentecostal sects and possession cults like umbanda imported from Brazil, yet, to believe the response to surveys, the population seems to have become more Catholic than before. He concludes by evoking Pierre Sanchis' idea (Sanchis 1993) that Catholicism could be a *habitus*, a frame within which Argentines think their participation in all sorts of religious subcultures, just as in France even the most ferociously lay are described sometimes as "catholaïque." But the main message is that categories such as monopoly, belief and even Catholic have fuzzy edges.

If the economic model is to be maintained then the supply-siders should invoke another economic concept, moral hazard, to take account of the impossibility of knowing whether the benefits of religion have been attained. Stark and indeed Bruce recognize that one way for religious institutions to deal with failure to meet expectations is to branch out into social services of various kinds. Sects do not have this opportunity unless – as in the Islamist cases mentioned – they obtain external funding – or rather sects take up the opportunity when external funding is made available. For the issue is not one of tactical opportunity: rather it is the structural, pervasive moral hazard not just of unattainability, but of the awareness of not ever being able to know whether the proclaimed end has been attained by anyone. It is possible that the worldwide success of the Gospel of Health and Wealth is a consequence: that Gospel sets worldly success side-by-side with, maybe even ahead of, otherworldly salvation as a goal, but significantly the attainment of the dreams of wealth thus purveyed is made conditional on conversion and exorcism procedures which place great power in the hands of pastors and officiants. The pattern is noticeable particularly in highly centralized neo-Pentecostal churches, with their transnational reach, strong one-man leadership and enthusiasm for up-to-date methods of communication and marketing (Lehmann 1996, 2009). So long as the follower remains in the church the authority will be able to decide whether the exorcism has been done correctly and to offer explanations as to why the desired outcomes have not yet been attained: in this environment there is little practical difference in attainability between the promised prosperity and peace and eternal salvation itself.

Although Iannacone recognizes that "religions are risky business" and that "their fundamental assertions lie within a realm of "radical uncertainty" beyond the range of empirical verification," he is surely wrong to conclude that subscribing to a religion is a strategy "to hedge one's bets" (Iannaccone 2002: 210), trading finite losses in this life for the possibility of infinite rewards in the next, because whereas investors eventually find out whether an investment has gone sour or not, the overwhelming majority of religiously committed Christians and Muslims are perfectly aware that neither they nor anyone else will ever know the result of their "wager" on the afterlife.

Evangelical and Pentecostal churches nowadays have multiplied to such an extent, and their basic model has exhibited such a remarkable capacity to adapt and create without sacrificing its core recognizability, that wholesale generalization is barely possible any more. But because of the core elements of exorcism and healing and the accompanying moral hazards, the variable of power, already recognized by Stark, must be taken into account – power to determine what counts as salvation as healing and as exorcism – as must the fund-raising and tithing which are central to these organizations' survival.

The power factor is also important among ultra-Orthodox Jews who presented such a suitable case for Berman. Here the availability of subsidy from the state and from Jewish charities around the world place leaders in a clear position of power as well as presenting them with a strong imperative to issue ever more stringent rulings on the subject of dress, marriage, sex and whatever anyone brings before them. But the pressure for stringency may also come from below. Nowadays large families and the culture of permanent Torah study makes their followers' lives humdrum, even poor: when so many depend to some extent on the limited benefits of membership, it is not surprising that they look out for signs of insincerity among their co-religionaries. (cf. (Lehmann 2008) Unsurprisingly, researchers detect much anxiety about gossip and the evil eye.[1]

Conversion – the extreme case of exercising choice in matters religious – accentuates the power factor because converts – including the Jews and Muslims who renounce a secular lifestyle and become returnees to strict observance – tend to change their lifestyle, their social circle and their jobs, and become heavily dependent on their new community as well as anxious to conform and to serve.

Thus the phenomenon of conversion has changed the landscape underlying the theses of rational choice theorists and of their opponents: converts and returnees have become a major force in religious life worldwide, undermining the hold of the traditions which for Bruce are a strength – albeit a declining one – and for Stark and colleagues a weakness. This in turn goes together with an ever more open religious marketplace where entry is easy and consumer protection almost non-existent.

CONCEPTUALIZING AND MISCONCEIVING THE MARKET

At this point the rational choice advocates' concern with regulation becomes analytically interesting, but their faulty conceptualization is brought to light. Their simplistic assumptions about monopoly and state control have to be clarified and it has to be understood that the unattainability of convincing certification of the quality of the salvific and material goods offered by religion and so strongly emphasized by sects and conversion-led movements is a central feature, not just a detail. It relies, to be convincing, on an inward-looking culture whose followers are taught that the best they can do for society as a whole is to persuade ever more people to abandon "the world" and join them.

This "mainline" sector of religion may not enjoy much approval from Stark or Finke, but it is open to the world and by operating according to classic secular rules of bureaucratic impersonality, it usually avoids the opacity of the sects. In contrast, in large neo-Pentecostal churches a single leader exercises authority across all spheres but has little influence in the broader society.

Thus far we have concentrated on the core assumptions of rational choice, but it is necessary to return to the claims which have provoked most controversy and which were listed in the quote from Frigerio at the start of this article, concerning the relationship between religious monopoly, religious growth and secularization. One of the most single-minded applications of rational choice has been that of Andrew Chesnut (Chesnut 2003), who celebrates the collapse of the monopoly of the Catholic Church in the late twentieth century as a result of the erosion of state protection and the entrepreneurial culture or Pentecostalism (Chesnut 2003: 58–60). The result has been not only a proliferation of Pentecostal churches but also a response by the Catholic Church itself in the form of the Charismatic Renewal, which has many Pentecostal features while remaining under the wing of a member of the hierarchy, and of the adoption of modern methods of marketing and performance monitoring in dioceses and parishes (Guerra 2002, 2006). In Frigerio's view these changes are less drastic than authors might imagine, because the church in Latin America (as elsewhere) has itself a long history of internal diversity and weak central control, and he also criticizes those who assume the existence of an earlier period of total monopoly, as well as those, like the early Peter

Berger (of *The Sacred Canopy*) (Berger 1967) who idealize traditional religious observance and devotion in contrast to a contemporary period of fragmentation and of this-worldly, commercialized religiosity (Frigerio 2007, 2008). In this Frigerio reinforces Stark's critique of secularization theories – while offering a different reading from that of Chesnut, a true believing follower of Stark.

Frigerio also goes further in refining the concept of a market and of regulation. Rational choice, in the image of the US model of free exercise and no establishment, takes it for granted that less regulation brings more religious participation, because it enables religious entrepreneurs to explore and exploit all manner of market niches, or consumer preferences. Iannacone's statement that "government regulation of religion tends to reduce individual welfare, stifling religious innovation by restricting choice, and narrowing the range of religious commodities" (Iannacone 1997: 1489) needs qualification. But Frigerio points out that all markets are regulated in some way, that there is a continuum from monopoly to pluralism, and that regulation is not only a matter of state action: political and social pressures and the media also frame and condition the place of religion and religions and so the formal picture offers only an incomplete guide to the situation. Similarly Roberto Blancarte, in concluding an extensive essay on Mexico, emphasizes the relative character of the separation of spheres between between Church and State, or between religion and politics (Blancarte 2007). Indeed, after a period of intensive constitution-making and reform in Latin America since the Brazilian Constituent Assembly gathered in 1987, which has reduced, though not always eliminated, the prerogatives of the Catholic Church in the state, we have seen a resurgence of the Church's influence on politics, notably with regard to education and health.

Markets are also institutions and no theory or philosophy denies the need for public regulation to ensure, or try to ensure, fair dealing. Like the informal sector of the economy, the mass of Pentecostal sects operate in an unregulated institutional void where denominations and ancient churches are only sketchily present. In the informal economy regulations governing wages, health standards, contracts, and minimum standards are irrelevant, wages and productivity are very low, and so entry is easy. The similarity to Pentecostal churches is brought home forcefully by Omar McRoberts' study of religious districts in Boston (McRoberts 2005) in which "the glut of vacant commercial spaces… provided ample space for religious institutions looking for cheap rents" (p. 139). It is a market far more deregulated than anything the rational choice theorists – who do not claim to be extreme libertarians – might imagine in the way of free competition. The pattern whereby Christianity's most rapid expansion is carried forward by evangelical or charismatic churches which enjoy a dominant position in economically depressed areas, may simply reflect lack of competition rather than the merits of religion as a social good.

Supply-siders often write in tones of approval, sometimes enthusiasm, of the large numbers taking part in religious activity, yet they do not tell us why they adopt such a tone – especially since, as has been stated, some of their interpretations rest upon religion's social and psychological rewards, not on its truth value. Their underlying conception of what it means to be religious, and what society should expect from religion, is entirely implicit.

While it is true that the headlong growth of charismatic religion contradicts some versions of secularization theory, it must also be remembered that the Christianity which is growing is found in quite different social and geographical locations from the Christianity which has lost millions of adherents, participants and members in the secularization process. Similarly, while Judaism in general suffers a demographic crisis, the numbers and influence of the ultra-Orthodox are growing through the return movement. The minutiae of secularization debates, so well represented in the disputes between Bruce and Stark et al., sometimes make the sociology of religion itself look like an inward-looking sect, and they distract from the other story – namely the change brought about in the meaning of what it is to be religious by conversion-led and charismatic movements.

We may thus conclude by asking what is at issue? The rational choice question seems to be what are the conditions in which religious organization thrives, but the question whether its survival is good for the rest of society remains tantalizingly out of bounds: the authors' tone may convey a positive view of religious organization, but they do not engage with the issue at all. Perhaps this is because they do not want to raise issues of the truth of religious claims, and perhaps it is because they do not want to enter into the discussion of the benefits religion might, or might not, bring to society as a whole: that, after all, would detract from an implicit idea that religion is its own justification. Stark's open contempt for religious trends which seek to provide non-religious goods – i.e. liberal, non-exclusionary churches and synagogues– is a source of deep division separating him from Bruce and no doubt many others who see mission diversification as a path for sects out of their ghetto-like existence, towards eventual church or denominational status where, one might deduce, they fit into secularized societies. These differences are not purely academic, they are about belief and commitment.

Notes

I wish to thank the Institute of Advanced Studies at the Hebrew University for its hospitality and support during the writing of this piece.

1   Observation based on field research by the author with Batia Siebzehner in Israel 2005–7.

Bibliography

Atran, S. (2003) *In Gods We Trust: The Evolutionary Landscape of Religion*, New York: Oxford University Press.

Berger, P. L. (1967) *The Sacred Canopy: Elements of a Sociological Theory of Religion*, Garden City: Doubleday.

Berman, E. (2000) Sect, subsidy, and sacrifice: an economist's view of ultra-orthodox Jews, *Quarterly Journal of Economics* 115 (3): 905–53.

Berman, E. (2003) Hamas, Taliban and the Jewish underground: an economist's view of radical religious militias, *National Bureau of Economic Research Working Paper 10004*, www.nber.org/papers/w10004.

Berman, E. and Iannacone, L. (2006) Religious extremism: the good, the bad and the deadly, *Public Choice* 128 (1–2): 109–29.

Blancarte, R. J. (2007) Mexico: a mirror for the sociology of religion, in J. Beckford and N. J. Demerath (eds.), *The Sage Handbook of the Sociology of Religion*, London: Sage.

Boyer, P. (2001) *Religion Explained: The Human Instincts That Fashion Gods, Spirits and Ancestors*, London: Heinemann.

Boyer, P. (2004) Religion, evolution and cognition, *Current Anthropology* 45 (3): 430–3.

Bruce, S. (1999) *Choice and Religion: A Critique of Rational Choice Theory*, Oxford: Oxford University Press.

Chesnut, A. (2003) *Competitive Spirits: Latin America's New Religious Economy*, New York: Oxford University Press.

Finke, R. and Stark, R. (2005) *The Churching of America, 1776–2005*, New Brunswick: Rutgers University Press.

Frigerio, A. (2007) Repensando el monopolio religioso del catolicismo en la Argentina, in M. J. Carozzi and C. Ceriani (eds.), *Ciencias sociales y religión en América Latina: perspectivas en debate*, Buenos Aires: Biblos/ACRSM.

Frigerio, A. (2008) O paradigma da escolha racional: mercado regulado e pluralismo religioso, *Tempo Social* (São Paulo) 20 (2): 17–39.

Guerra, L. (2002) *Mercado religoso no Brasil: competição, demanda e a dinamica da esfera da religião*. Petropolis, Vozes: CATAVENTO.

Guerra, L. (2006) Mercado Religioso na Paraíba: a competição e o aumento da racionalização das atividades das organizações religiosas, *Religião e Sociedade* 26 (2): 155–86.

Iannacone, L. (1997) Introduction to the economics of religion, *Journal of Economic Literature* 36 (3): 1465–95.

Iannaccone, L. (2002) A marriage made in heaven? Economic theory and religious studies, in S. Grossbard-Schechtman and C. Clague (eds.), *The Expansion of Economics: Towards a More Inclusive Social Science*, Armonk: M.E. Sharpe.

Lehmann, D. (1996) *Struggle for the Spirit: Religious Transformation and Popular Culture in Brazil and Latin America*, Oxford: Polity Press.

Lehmann, D. (2001) Charisma and possession in Africa and Brazil, *Theory, Culture and Society* 18 (5): 45–74.

Lehmann, D. (2005) The cognitive approach to understanding religion, *Archives des Sciences Sociales des Religions* 131–2: 199–213.

Lehmann, D. (2008) The miraculous economics of religion: an essay on social capital, *Social Compass* 55 (4): 457–77 (French).

Lehmann, D. (2009) Religion and globalization: a comparative and historical perspective, in L. Woodhead, H. Kawanami, and C. Partridge (eds.), *Religions in the Modern World: Traditions and Transformations*, Abingdon: Routledge.

Martin, D. (1990) *Tongues of Fire: The Pentecostal Revolution in Latin America*, Oxford: Blackwell.

McRoberts, O. (2005) *Streets of Glory: Church and Community in a Black Urban Neighborhood*, Chicago: University of Chicago Press.

Norris, P. and Inglehart, R. (2007) Uneven secularization in the United States and Western Europe, in T. Banchoff (ed.), *Democracy and the New Religious Pluralism*, New York: Oxford University Press.

Olson, M. (1965) *The Logic of Collective Action*, Cambridge, MA: Harvard University Press.

Sanchis, P. (1993) Catolicismo: entre tradição e modernidades, *Comunicações do ISER* (Rio de Janeiro) 44: 9–17.

Stark, R. (1997) Bringing the theory back in, in L. Young (ed.), *Rational Choice Theory and Religion: Summary and Assessment*, London: Routledge.

Stark, R. and Bainbridge, W. S. (1987) *A Theory of Religion*, New York: P. Lang.

Stark, R. and Finke, R. (2000) *Acts of Faith: Explaining the Human Side of Religion*, Berkeley: University of California Press.

Warner, R. S. (1993) Work in progress towards a new paradigm for the sociological study of religion in the United States, *American Journal of Sociology* 98 (5): 1044–93.

Wuthnow, R. (2005) *America and the Challenges of Religious Diversity*, Princeton: Princeton University Press.

Young, L. (1997) *Rational Choice Theory and Religion: Summary and Assessment*, London: Routledge.

9

The Religious Habitus
Embodiment, Religion, and Sociological Theory

PHILIP A. MELLOR AND CHRIS SHILLING

INTRODUCTION

The origins of sociology are commonly associated with post-Enlightenment rational-ism, positivism and the instrumentalization of modern societies. What is frequently neglected in accounts of the emergence of the discipline, however, is that many of its founding figures also analyzed the *ontological foundations* of human beings. These foundations informed those emotions, passions and collective bonds that not only underpinned and coexisted with the rational dimensions of society, but pos-sessed the capacity to challenge these parameters. It was this concern, in fact, that contributed significantly to the general attention classical sociology devoted to the phenomenon of religion (Nisbet 1993; Levine 1993), and to its specific interest in the centrality of religion to two key sociological problems. First, the study of religion was understood to be core to the challenge of identifying and comprehending those social processes through which embodied subjects become incorporated into social groups. This was because religion both structured people's conscience and con-sciousness, and sought to harness their *bodily affects* and *practices* in line with collective norms. Second, the analysis of religion also highlighted the importance of examining how social phenomena not only shaped embodied subjects, but could *themselves* be structured and limited by the physical qualities, capacities and poten-tialities of these subjects. Sociologists generally acknowledged that religion responded to certain human needs and/or experiences (associated, for example, with human frailty, suffering, and finitude) and also recognized that it appeared to be patterned, at least in part, on the basis of these phenomena. Religion, in short, provided an exemplar of the dynamic interrelationship that existed between social phenomena in a rapidly modernizing Western world, and the ontological properties of embodied humans as they acted in and on this milieu.

The founding figures differed considerably in their conclusions about religion in the light of these problems, of course, and about the nature and development of social and cultural phenomena. Nonetheless, they all saw questions about religion, the embodied potentialities and limits of humans, and the creation and evolution of different patterns of human community, as intimately related and central to the sociological enterprise. Furthermore, their growing awareness that modern societies were developing a distinctively technological culture, characterized by processes of instrumentalism that rendered religion increasingly marginal to social life, only intensified this interest. Such developments raised questions about whether the rationalized demands of this culture could continue to bind people into social groups, and whether these demands could be seen as in some way "out of joint" with the embodied ontological needs of humans (Turner 1991); needs that had traditionally been addressed through religious meanings and practices.

This chapter focuses on the most influential classical sociological conceptions of this relationship between religion, the embodied ontology of humans and modernity, before switching attention to more recent sociological accounts built upon them. We begin with Weber, who analyzed Protestantism as promoting a divergence between the need of individuals for religious meaning and the rationalization of modern life, and contrast this with Durkheim's account of religion. Durkheim's focus on the "contagious" circulation of emotional energies, and their expression through symbols and regulation through rituals, presupposed the *enduring* significance of the link between religion, embodiment and society, even in highly rationalized modern societies.

In many respects the accounts of Weber and Durkheim are diametrically opposed, reflecting broader oppositions between the methodological individualism of much German social thought and the methodological holism characteristic of the French philosophical tradition, yet both identify embodiment as a vital mediator of the relationship between religion and modernity. This is the context in which we suggest in the second part of this chapter that the notion of a *religious habitus* can be used to build a bridge between these different classical perspectives, and illuminate key themes in the subsequent development of sociology's engagement with religion, embodiment, and society.

In general terms, the habitus refers to a socially structured bodily disposition that promotes particular orientations to the world. As a concept, it enables us to view the body-society relationship from the starting point of either the collectivity (the approach usually ascribed to Durkheim) or the embodied individual (the methodological position with which Weber is ordinarily associated). The idea of a *religious* habitus, moreover, allows us to explore what is distinct about how religion is connected to the embodied potentialities and frailties of humans, and how it seeks to harness those qualities to the re/creation of specific social and cultural orders. In analyzing this issue further, we examine some of the preconditions of, the distinctive stages involved in, and the issues raised by, the foundation and construction of a religious habitus. These involve the biological openness of our species being, links between the accumulation and expenditure of energy and the constitution of collectivities, the role and costs of sacrifice and sacrificial rites in this process, and the importance of bodily techniques and body pedagogics for the perpetuation of particular forms of religion. These themes have featured prominently in contemporary accounts of religion and embodiment and enable us to suggest that, despite its apparent marginalization within technological culture, religion remains integrally involved in the development of human society in the current global era.

CHARISMA, RATIONALIZATION, AND
TECHNOLOGICAL CULTURE

Weber's concepts of "charisma" and "rationalization" are central to his account of those processes through which embodied subjects are incorporated into, and subsequently dislocated from, social groups. Charisma originates from the inability of mundane bodily experience to answer problems of suffering and fortune, and provides a "supernatural" sense of power over the inexplicable (Gerth and Mills 1948). Weber (1968: 216) took the notion of charisma from Christianity, where it referred to the gift of divine grace, but used it to signal a powerful form of authority projected onto, and recognized as embodied within, particular individuals. It is the recognition, or "revelation," of this authority that is not only the inter-corporeal basis of religion, but a fundamental source of social creativity. While the "other-worldly" experience of charisma possessed a human basis, it stands apart from, takes precedence over, and provides an incentive to reinterpet and reorder the mundane world of daily life (Weber 1968: 432–3).

The creative power of charisma does not endure in Weber's analysis, however, as revelation and change gives way to a routinization of religious life conducive to the establishment of tradition and, subsequently, its further systematization via a process of rationalization. In modern societies, this rationalization becomes widespread so that the potentially revolutionary power of charisma inevitably wanes, signalling the dominance of bureaucratic organization and "the diminishing importance of individual action" (Weber 1968: 1148–9).

Ironically, Weber (1968: 1146) identifies Protestantism as one of *the* motor forces implicated in the loss of the inter-corporeal basis of charisma and the progressive rationalization and secularization of the modern world. Weber's (1991) account of the "elective affinity" between Protestantism and capitalist culture is well known. Focusing on the ways in which Protestantism came to see worldly activity in general, and work in particular, as a divine calling, he argued that it promoted a highly ordered and ascetic pattern of religious individualism. The rationalization of labor for the glory of God stimulated a culture centered on capitalistic productivity and, more broadly, an instrumentalization of the world necessary for the emergence of a distinctively technological culture (Weber 1991: 160, 102–5, 36, 72, 1968: 65, 24–6). What is less well known, however, is that, for Weber, this elective affinity is tied to important changes in the human experience of embodiment.

In Weber's narrative (1991: 13), the "disenchantment" of the world promoted by Protestantism renders charisma redundant, in the sense that a world ruled by rational calculation has no room for experiencing the other-worldly, but this redundancy could only be achieved via a disciplined regulation of the body and its affects. Protestantism, indeed, did not simply reject the sensuality of some aspects of medieval Christian religiosity, but reordered the religious priority attached to the senses, so that sight, which could be trained to read the Word of God, dominated touch and smell. In its asceticism, furthermore, Protestant sought to police the body in relation to the temptations of pleasure and sensuality that might undercut the disciplined exercise of a worldly calling (Mellor and Shilling 1997: 112).

A key point of Weber's (1991) analysis is that in so far as "Protestant" aspects of embodiment endure, they do so implicitly, robbed of religious justifications and legitimations. As rationalization processes advance in the modern world, social and natural realities become differentiated into specific spheres, many of which are defined as "secular" and, therefore, deemed to be free of religious censorship and control. This is particularly important with regard to the technological aspects of modern culture. While the Aristotelian notion of *technē* reflected an assumption that human techniques for controlling nature and society operated in harmony with a universal natural order, for Weber the accumulating technological knowledge of modernity was increasingly free of any religious or moral frame of reference (Maley 2004: 71). Heidegger's (1993) later suggestion that the essence of technology involves an instrumental rationalism of total mastery over nature develops this argument. Instrumentalism involves "enframing" nature, calling upon the environment to be "immediately on hand" as a "standing reserve" forced to yield its properties and potential to any efficiency-based demand placed upon it. Consequently, the defining property of modern technology is the insistence on domination and control *irrespective* of the properties of the material it is involved with, something that reaches a point where knowledge, morals and information come to be judged purely in terms of their productive utility, and where people themselves are regarded as a standing-reserve.

In this context, and in so far as they endure, religious attempts to enframe nature, society and humanity in moral and metaphysical forms are challenged by the routines of everyday life, wherein the "psycho-physical apparatus of man is completely adjusted to the demands of ... the tools, the machines" (Weber 1948: 149, 1968: 1156; Maley 2004: 75, 79). This is why, for Weber, secularization is not simply about the critical scrutiny applied to religious doctrines, or even to empirical data about such issues as church attendance. Instead, what modern secularizing processes entail is the promotion of a *form of embodied existence* that renders religious commitment marginal to the core of social and cultural life.

There is a great deal of crossover between Weber's arguments and those of Simmel, another figure central to the German tradition of sociology. Like Weber, though without recourse to the notion of charisma, Simmel (1997: 43) sees the origins of religion *within* the embodied potentialities of individuals. Prior to the emergence or continued existence of specific *forms* of religion in social life, there exists a "religious" impulse embodied in individuals, an impulse which seeks to unify divergent experiences and sensations, overcome internal conflicts, and provide a sense of self and world as meaningful, interrelated phenomena. Similar to Weber, however, Simmel (1997: 9) is convinced that these individual religious impulses are made problematic by the rationalization and complexity of the modern world. Thus, for both theorists, there is a tension between social creativity (located in the embodied potentialities of [interacting] individuals), and social stagnation (located in what are perceived to be the inhuman structures of the modern world) and a tendency to dwell upon the potentially bleak resolution of this tension in favor of the latter (Mellor 2004). This is reflected in Weber's (1991) despairing comment that a "polar night of icy darkness and hardness" awaits humanity, a comment which exemplified his view of the violence visited by modernity on embodied subjects, yet which stands in stark contrast to the analysis of this relationship offered by Comte and, more especially, Durkheim.

EMOTIONS, SYMBOLS, AND RITUALS

Auguste Comte gave us the word "sociology," and first accounted for its systematic nature and scope as a discipline centered on the acquisition of "positive facts" about society through methods of observation, experiment, comparison, and history. While rigorously eschewing theological and metaphysical speculation, however, Comte came to see religion as a fundamental dimension of social life precisely because it flowed from, and engaged creatively with, aspects of human embodiment which he understood to be necessary for the development of social meaning and order. Increasingly conceiving of sociology itself as a religious project, a move leaving him vulnerable to accusations of eccentricity and even insanity, he sought to promote his vision of the "positive society" by attempting to balance what he saw as the Enlightenment's over-emphasis on rationalism and the intellect with the emotional solidarity and symbolic richness of religion (Aron 1964; Pickering 1993; Reedy 1994). Durkheim ridiculed Comte's attempt to create a "religion of humanity," and his confusion of this with the sociological project. Nonetheless, he accepted Comte's view that the religious generation and regulation of emotions, symbols and rituals captured something universal about the embodied basis of a society.

In line with the French philosophical tradition's focus on the collectivity, Durkheim's primary sociological interests were in the "supra-individual" elements in social life relating to social actions, feelings, beliefs, values, and ideals (Lukes 1973: 115). Durkheim did not ignore the embodied ontology of humans in his writings, though, and attributed great importance to the *homo duplex* nature of individuals for the establishment of collective phenomena. For Durkheim (1973) the egoistic pole of our *homo duplex* character has to be stimulated by "*sui generis* forces developed in association" with others if the social and moral side of our being is to be harnessed to the creation and reproduction of collective representations and groups (Durkheim 1974: 24–6, 1995: 213). This understanding of the relationship between humanity's *homo duplex* character and the emergent, embodied unity of social symbols, and also of social life more broadly, is developed most systematically with regard to his stress on the foundational role of religious phenomena for society and culture. This is evident in his last major work, *The Elementary Forms of Religious Life*, a study in which he propounded a theory of the constitution of religious society, that was also a theory of society in general, and that additionally contained within it a theory of the embodied ontology of humanity.

For Durkheim, the fundamental processes through which social life is constituted have a religious character: the emergence of society is marked by a contagious circulation of emotional energies that produce distinctive experiences and collective representations of what he calls the "sacred." Durkheim refers to these energies through the notion "collective effervescence," a term which refers to the emotionally stimulating effects of congregation during which "a sort of electricity is generated" from people's closeness which "quickly launches them to an extraordinary height of exaltation" (Durkheim 1995: 217). This is the primary means through which the sacred is unleashed, experienced by, and spread between people. Defining the sacred as "things set apart and forbidden" from the profane world of every day life, which not only represent a group to itself but bind individuals into a powerful sense of moral community, Durkheim argues that there can be no society without this physical and cognitive sense of this sacred, and that the sacred/profane polarity has been a central feature of human thought and culture throughout history (Durkheim 1995: 44, 34–6).

If collective effervescence is the raw emotional phenomenon out of which solidarity experienced as the sacred is able to emerge, *ritual* provides the means through which this emotional energy can be intensified, regulated and replenished. In this respect "cults," systems of rituals, can be distinguished into "positive" and "negative" types: the former are focused on the potentially sacrilegious encounter with the sacred, such as in the Christian Eucharist where God is eaten symbolically/sacramentally; the latter serve to maintain the separation between sacred and profane through, amongst other things, taboos. Consequently, at the heart of religious life is the tension between coming into contact/not coming into contact with the sacred, mediated through a ritual process where this tension is kept "charged" with a sort of emotional electricity. Furthermore, different types of rituals channel emotional energies in ways that are directly related to the cyclical pattern of social life, so that some deal with profusions of energy, such as we find at feasts, while others deal with depletions of social energy, such as "piacular" rites, where the aim is to "restore to the group the energy that the events [e.g. deaths] threatened to take away" (Durkheim 1995: 415–6).

Symbols constitute a potent outcome of this ritually mediated effervescence for two main reasons. First, they express the transfigured world of sensed realities brought about by emotional contagion, and express an experience of moral community. Second, they are not simply abstract representations of collective experiences and identifications, but retain the emotional charge that created them (Durkheim 1995: 239, 221). Thus, the flag of a country is often treated as sacred, and a soldier will struggle to defend it on the battlefield because the symbol carries the emotional charge that binds that soldier to the community he seeks to defend: "the soldier who dies for his flag dies for his country" (Durkheim, 1995: 222). The development of a symbolic order in a society is a product of those processes through which collective feeling becomes conscious of itself, but also a further means of ensuring that this consciousness, the conscience collective, retains its emotional power in the hearts and minds of individuals.

Durkheim's arguments concerning the social origins and power of these collective representations were central to a number of later, highly influential studies of symbolic and ritual orders (e.g. Douglas 1966; Turner 1969), and had a decisive influence upon well known studies of the symbolic dimensions of contemporary culture (e.g. Berger 1967; Bellah 1970). Furthermore, his suggestion that we should understand religion as an emotionally potent grouping of people around collective experiences and symbols of the sacred has been exploited by studies of a diverse range of contemporary social and cultural phenomena, including patriotic or nationalist ceremonies (Tiryakian 1995, 2004; Alexander 2004; Collins, 2004), everyday social interactions (Maffesoli 1996), consumerism (Featherstone 1991; Ritzer 1999), and communications media (Dayan and Katz 1988).

Studies such as these raise important questions about the embodied character of social life in the light of Weber's account of technological culture. In particular, how is it that the relationship between religion and embodiment continues to hold in a society that is increasingly rationalized? For Weber, as we have noted, modernity promotes a form of embodied existence that renders religious commitment marginal to the core dimensions of social and cultural life. For Durkheim (1995: 1), in contrast, the embodied character of religion expresses something "fundamental and permanent" about humanity, so, ultimately, it cannot be in contradiction to modern technological culture. The differences between these theorists, though, can be overemphasized.

First, the tension between the effervescent vitalism of the "primitive" cultures Durkheim studied in *The Elementary Forms of Religious Life*, and the diminution of emotional energies, and thus of the sacred, in modernity was already prominent in his *Suicide* and *The Division of Labor in Society*. This tension encouraged later, neo-Durkheimian, work to attend to how *specific forms* of religion engaged with human embodiment, thereby bringing it closer to some of the comparative religious concerns that mark Weber's work. Second, both Weber and Durkheim attend in their different ways to the dynamic interrelationship that exists between humanity's *embodied constitution* and its openness to distinctively *social forms* of construction, elaboration and development.

This is the context in which notion of a religious habitus can constitute a bridge between Weber's and Durkheim's work by enabling us to trace the relationship between society and embodiment from the starting point of either the collectivity or the individual. Thus, on the one hand, as the embodiment of the *social*, the habitus is concerned with those external forces that manage to shape the body. On the other hand, however, it is also necessarily concerned with how the body's *own* needs and potentialities make it unevenly receptive to different social forces and may themselves impact on societal factors. The notion of the religious habitus can also be used as a framework for contextualizing a range of key themes that have marked the sociological analysis of religion and the body.

RELIGION AS HABITUS

The sociological development of the notion of *habitus*, which dates back to Aristotle and St Thomas Aquinas, is associated initially with Mauss (1950) but found its fullest expression in Elias's (1987, 1991) analysis of the transformations in manners and etiquette in Western history, which emphasized how the embodied subject is highly permeable with regard to large-scale social processes. Its best known and most influential deployment, however, remains Bourdieu's (1977) account of the pre-cognitive, embodied predispositions which promote particular forms of orientation to the world, organize each generation's senses and bodily experiences into particular hierarchies, and predispose people towards particular ways of knowing and acting.

Within the sociology of religion there have been a number of empirically oriented studies that draw upon this notion of the habitus, with its view of the body as "the principle generating and unifying all practices" (Bourdieu 1977: 124), such as

Csordas's (1994) analysis of the embodied character of Catholic charismatic healing. The notion's importance for the sociology of religion goes beyond specific studies, however, and rests on its theoretical significance across a range of thematic areas. In mainstream sociology, the deployment of the term habitus has tended to focus on such issues as how long term shifts in monopolies of violence and the division of labor impact on people's embodied character (Elias), or on how an individual's location within various "social fields" shapes their tastes and preferences (Bourdieu). Analyses of religion, in contrast, allow us to focus on how the habitus is also grounded in fundamental features of human existence relating to the material, bio-logical constitution of being human, as well as to the specific social milieu inhabited by individuals. The first of these features concerns what Turner (1991: xxii) has referred to as the inherent openness, flexibility and vulnerability of humans.

Biological openness

Turner (1991) has identified the importance for the sociology of religion of the German tradition of philosophical anthropology, a tradition associated with Gehlen and Plessner but ultimately having Nietzschean sources. Its key argument suggests that the instinctual character of humans is, in relation to other animals, significantly under-determined. Humans are "world-open," so their relationships with social and natural environments are vulnerable and require investments of meaning, discipline and training. The most influential expressions of these ideas in the sociology of religion are associated with Berger (1967) and Luckmann (1967).

Working together, Berger and Luckmann (1966) developed a highly influential sociology of knowledge which emphasized the "biological unfinishedness" of humans. They argued that the ontological condition of human being left people vulnerable to anomic experiences of life's meaninglessness and futility, and that cultural constructions of meaning helped shield individuals from this potential terror. In their subsequent books, Berger and Luckmann applied these arguments specifically to religious phenomena.

For Berger (1967), the importance of religion across history reflects the fact that, though it is a socially constructed product, its symbolic contents locate human life and destiny within a sacred cosmos transcendent of day-to-day realities. This cosmos functions to reassure individuals of the meaningfulness and reality of their lives; providing them with an existential framework in which they can act, construct a role-based identity, and develop a structured habitus that, biologically, they lack. It is in this context that Berger (1967: 63–5) develops Weber's interests by analysing a range of theodicies (from the "irrational" desire for absorption in the Other evident in religious mysticism through to the highly rationalized account of the universal significance of every human action in the *karma-samsara* complex in Indian religion) as cultural constructions that do not aim to provide happiness or rewards but *meaning*, particularly with regard to the brute fact of death (Berger 1967: 80).

Berger's use of philosophical anthropology in his analysis of human embodiment allows him to draw together the work of Durkheim and Weber, both of whom recognized the importance of culture for people's ontological needs. Like Durkheim, he emphasizes the collective, *sui generis* nature of society and culture, the symbolic expression of this as "the sacred," in strict opposition to the profane, the importance of symbols and rituals for the development and maintenance of religious phenomena, and the central role of religion across history in terms of the integration of individuals into social orders (Berger 1967: 7, 27). It is Berger's view of humans as biologically "unfinished," and his understanding of the existential consequences of this, however, that informs his view of the sacred not simply as the symbolic expression of collective social dynamics, but as connected to meaningful orders of *variable solidity* in relation to the potentially terrifying consequences of our "world openness." This analytical move transforms the sacred/profane polarity into an order/chaos dichotomy whose social significance is measured primarily in terms of individuals' experiences of existential reassurance or anxiety. Consequently, the Durkheimian model of religion and society is reframed here in terms closer to Weber. Like Weber, the importance Berger is then able to attribute to the contents of particular religions allows him to analyze the relative efficacy of different belief systems, and to implicate Protestantism in rationalization and secularization and in his bleak assessment of modernity.

Not surprisingly, since they developed their sociology of knowledge collaboratively, Luckmann's (1967) approach to religion is similar to Berger's. He too offers a theoretical model centered on biological unfinishedness and the sacred as meaningful order. Where he differs and leans more toward a Durkheimian framework than Berger, is in his argument that the *functions* of religious systems of meaning can be assumed by a wide variety of social phenomena while their specific *contents* are of far less importance. This allows Luckman to suggest that major world religions can be replaced by "functional equivalents" found among a diverse range of, often apparently "secular," phenomena classed as "invisible religion." For Luckmann, the functional equivalents of religion endure, albeit in a reconfigured form. For Berger, at least until a more recent change of heart, the fate of religion is inextricably tied to the relative effectiveness of its theodicy.

The relationship between the threats posed by biological openness and existentially reassuring (religious) meaning systems have been discussed by more recent influential thinkers. While not acknowledging the influence of Berger, Giddens (1990, 1991) offers similar arguments about the importance and frailty of culture. Where Berger (1967: 23) talks of "marginal situations" such as death threatening individuals's ontological security, Giddens (1991: 112) refers to the same phenomena as "fateful moments." Giddens (1990: 109) also locates the significance of religion in the domain of existential concerns, though he strongly emphasizes the undermining of religious cosmology by the reflexively organized knowledge of modernity. This recalls Berger's (1967: 156) emphasis on the fundamental importance of "plausibility structures" in his philosophical anthropology and the "crisis of plausibility" for religion initiated by modern technological culture. A major difference between Berger and Giddens, however, is that while Berger continues to ground his concerns about within a consideration for the biological materiality and vulnerability, Giddens (1991) ultimately erases the significance of embodiment altogether by suggesting that it becomes absorbed within the self-referential systems of modernity.

Turner, in contrast, retains a strong hold on the importance of the embodied constitution of humans in his enduring concern with the *material* dimensions of meaning and its consequences for people's biological "incompleteness." The primary focus of Turner's (1991) sociological engagement with religion and the body is on religious discourses and practices involved in attempts to control and regulate our socially receptive bodies. This draws on Foucault, as well as on his own interest in the Hobbesian "problem of order." Here, Turner (1991: 2, 12–13) argues that "the question of meaning" should be seen as a material issue rather than a theoretical one, in the sense that religion is to do with the "experience of physical and physiological reality," and, as such, lies at the heart of the interchange of nature and culture in the construction of what it is to be human.

Turner's interest in the "biological unfinishedness" of humans is developed in his later work. In collaboration with Rojek, for example, his Hobbesian focus continues, but is supplemented by Feuerbach's interest in the sensuous embodiment of humans whose societies furnish them with cultural systems that "complete their unfinished ontological characteristics" (Turner and Rojek 2001: 215–16, 32). In this model, humanity's embodied "ontological frailty" is manifest not only in cultural and social forms (providing humans with the meanings, values and identities they inherently lack), but in biological (disease, ageing, death), and psychological (fear, anxiety) forms too. These are seen as the inevitable parameters in which people develop particular forms of habitus, and their enduring ontological significance helps explain the epistemological structures of religion and its continued appeal.

Turner has reached contrasting conclusions regarding Durkheimian and Weberian debates about the fate of religion in technological culture (Turner 1991: xvii–xviii; Turner 2002: 117). Nonetheless, the merit of his focus on biological openness, along with that of Berger and Luckmann, is that it locates questions about people's embodied mode of orientation to their habitus at the heart of the sociology of religion. More recently, his considerations have also been extended to such areas as the possible consequences for religion of new technologies (Turner 2006, 2007).

The focus on biological vulnerability in this section highlights not only the importance of and the fundamental organic need that humans have for a *habitus*, but suggests that religion has a vital role to play in enabling individuals to develop a *viable* orientation to their world. The significance of the body for religion is not confined to its openness or vulnerability, however, and others have drawn attention to the importance of a range of emotions, energies and impulses central to religion. Their emphasis on the *socially structuring* potential of embodiment, as opposed to its capacity and need to be *structured* as a defense against world openness, characterizes the sociological interest in religion as a form of *expenditure*.

The accumulation and expenditure of energy

A notable development in the Durkheimian tradition is the idea that the emergence and maintenance of religion and society is connected to the accumulation and discharge of physical and emotional energy, a process most clearly evidenced in "primitive" societies. Caillois's (1950) account of the effervescent vitalism of the "feast" is a notable expression of this trend. Feasts are occasions, he suggests, in which religious rites channel an excess of food and energy into an effervescent contact with the sacred which leads to the revitalization of society (Caillois 1950: 227).

This focus on "primitive" expenditures of energy also featured in Mauss's (1973) study of the emotional intensity of the communal months in Eskimo communities, an analysis which became key to his account of the economy of energy involved in gift exchange. Developed with reference to his analysis of the potlatch, Mauss (1969) emphasizes how the expenditure of wealth becomes part of an emotionally saturated pattern of obligations generating social solidarity. These obligatory reciprocal expenditures provide an inter-corporeal basis for the periodic revitalization of collective relationships in which people incorporate "the other" into themselves.

In a similar argument, Bataille (1967) used Durkheim's account of the embodied basis of the sacred to develop a theory of a "general" economy; an economy (based upon "excess" and "expenditure") which underpinned the "restricted" economy (based on scarcity and production) that was the subject of classical economics. For Bataille, the excess of this general economy arises from a surplus of emotional energy that necessarily accumulates because it arises from human embodiment. This excess cannot be conserved within the body, and therefore must be expended. In primitive societies, this expenditure was characteristically achieved through religious activity.

Having located their analyses in the context of primitive societies, each of these theorists questions whether the vitalism of traditional bodies, collectivities and religious process can be maintained in modernity. Caillois (1950) doubts whether the "stirring effervescence" of the past could reoccur in a modern era characterized by a profane devitalization. Mauss's (1969) argument about the emotional basis to gift economies was developed as part of a critique of the rationalism and utilitarianism of modern culture. Relatedly, Bataille's (1992: 93–100) view of modernity, like that of Weber, was that it depended on an exclusion of the sacred that was not, following Durkheim, ultimately viable, and that would eventuate in a return of virulent and highly destructive sacred energies (Bataille 1992).

The writings of Caillois, Bataille, and Mauss provide us with a different approach towards the foundations of a religious *habitus* than those whose concern is with the cultural "completion" of our biological unfinishedness. Rather than emphasizing ontological "deficiencies," they focus on the creative potential of people's emotional energies and the potential frailty of modern attempts to structure the *habitus* in relation to what it apparently excludes.

Such a focus on the accumulation and expenditure of energy provide an important but relatively undifferentiated account of the collective consequences of one dimension of the embodied potentialities of humans. Accounts of *sacrifice* provided by Mauss and others, however, analyze in more detail the benefits and costs of this "economy," for both individuals and collectivities. Specifically, they examine how expenditures of energy need to be *harnessed* for them to recreate collectivities, involve potentially violent *interpersonal dynamics*, and entail significant *individual costs*. In so doing, these theorists supplement a concern with the biological need humans have for a "world completing" habitus, and the overall social structuring potential of their embodied energies, with an interest in the specific social trajectory and (sometimes negative) consequences resulting from the ritual mediation of human energy.

Sacrifice

Building upon Sylvain Levi's account of the Brahmanical notions of sacrifice, Hubert and Mauss (1964) identify this ritual as key to the consolidation of social groups. It is the expenditure during sacrificial rituals of people's energies, of collective resources, and even of the lives of victims, that provides an especially potent means through which a habitus conducive to the reproduction of community is forged (Mauss 1900). Bataille (1988, 1967) even suggests that ritual sacrifice is *necessary* for the revitalization of the sacred and the "revirilization" of society. For Bataille, those occasions when a sacrificial victim is plucked from the "world of utility," and brutally removed from profane life, become the means through which individuals reinforce community via a violent experience of solidarity.

If sacrificial rituals can reinforce community, however, the notion of sacrifice also illuminates the costs borne by individuals engaging in social processes. These costs reach beyond those sacrificial victims discussed by Bataille and relate to energetic expenditures required of individuals engaging in *any* social processes. Durkheim (1973: 163) introduces us to what is involved here. Despite his focus on the religiously and socially *productive* consequences of emotional effervescence, Durkheim acknowledges that society demands "perpetual and costly sacrifices" from individuals by obliging them to surpass their personal interests for collective ideals. His adoption of the individual perspective on this occasion moves us closer to Simmel (1990: 82) who suggests that all social interaction involves sacrifice. Simmel defines this sacrifice in bodily terms as an expenditure of personal energy. This expenditure is not wholly negative – it enables humans to fulfil the social aspects of their *homo duplex* natures, stimulating social emotions that bind individuals into communities – but it "drains" the emotional reserves of individuals (p. 82). In contrast to Durkheim, however, Simmel argues that the costs of this sacrifice may sometimes be too great. While an individual's religious habitus necessarily requires a *form* in which it can be expressed, this form may at times prove too damaging for the religious *contents* of the individual personality. Bataille also acknowledges the sacrifices involved for individuals in becoming part of a religious collectivity. For Bataille, indeed, all contact with the sacred entails a violent rupture from the profane world humans normally inhabit. Prefigured in the temporary obliteration of differentiation during orgasm, encountering the sacred promotes an annihilation of the individual which reaches its end point in death but which also signals the human yearning for undifferentiated community that is the essence of the religious impulse.

Taken together, the analyses in this section reveal a particularly important strand within the modern study of religion: "primitive" forms of culture are held to reveal the fact that the vitality and cohesion of a society depends upon ritually enacted death and personal sacrifice. Girard's (1977) account of sacrifice as the embodied basis of religion and culture offers the most striking development of this tradition of sociological thought. Building upon Durkheim's (1995: 417) reference to the "ambiguity" of the sacred, Girard (1977) argues that the link between religion and violence is foundational. He argues that "sacrifice," literally making sacred, expresses the sacralization of acts of collective violence against innocent victims in that it involves the victimization of an external "scapegoat" as a way of defusing intra-communal tensions.

This has proved an influential and controversial position. Nevertheless, Girard provides an original account of how the embodied constitution of humans renders sacrifice a social necessity, and how religions must necessarily seek to structure the habitus of their followers in relation to this foundational sacrificial mechanism. For Girard, human nature is, instinctively, informed by desire. The objects of desire are not fixed, however, but are shaped interactively: humans have an embodied predisposition to desire what others desire (Girard 1987: 26, 2001: 15). This mimesis is the primary source of social integration, in that it unites individuals through the regulation of their desires, but is also a potential source of disintegration, in that the rivalries it stimulates can provoke violence within a community.

It is on this basis, according to Girard, that religion promotes social cohesion through the direction of violent energies to an external, scapegoat, sacrificed in the interests of social solidarity. This sacrificial substitution must be concealed if it is to have its intended effect of restoring harmony and order – it must be believed that the victim is "guilty" of provoking the violence that threatens a community – but, once this has been effected, the restoration of order which results from the expression of mimetic violence is attributed to the sacrifice of the victim. Having been "made sacred," the victim becomes incorporated into subsequent mythological features of the religion (Girard 1977: 4–5). Thus, culture is based on sacrifices, on the collective murders that unite individuals into a moral community, which are then concealed within religious mythologies.

Having arrived at this recognition, Girard does not glamorize "primitive" culture and its embodied dynamics. Rather than lamenting the progress of modernization, indeed, he celebrates it as separating the modern habitus from the world of violence and the lies that preceded it. In this context, and against those who view modernity as bleak and disenchanted, he identifies the legal apparatus of the modern system of justice as a bulwark against the contagious violence of religious culture (Girard 1977). Furthermore, and controversially, he identifies this system with the moral imperatives of Christianity, which he distinguishes firmly from "pagan" religiosity.

For Girard, Christianity is an exception to the general pattern of violence central to primitive religion because it engages with human embodiment in a highly distinctive way. He argues that although the New Testament presents Christ as the sacrificial victim, the text is written not by the perpetrators of collective violence, as in other mythologies, but from a position emphasizing his innocence, thereby deconstructing the ritual sacrificial mechanism foundational to other cultures. He also notes how the New Testament interprets Christian conversion as a *new birth*, with a *new body*, presenting Christ as the primary mimetic model for all humans to follow, and repeatedly emphasizes the dangerous consequences of "worldly" communities where the human predisposition towards mimesis takes on violent forms (Girard 2001: 13).

Girard's concern with the distinctive ways in which religions seek to structure human embodiment leads us away from highly general discussions about "energies" towards issues concerning the construction of *particular forms* of religious habitus. This is reinforced by Hertz's (1960) analysis of how religious forms as diverse as Maori religion and the iconography of Christian visions of the Last Judgement engage with, and build upon, the near-universal preponderance of the right hand in human culture. They do this in their use of left/right symbolic dichotomies and it is on the basis of this engagement with the body that they then advocate radically different religious practices and techniques intended to result in different forms of religious habitus (Hertz 1973: 100–1).

These analyses suggest that, irrespective of their embodied foundations – be they the world openness of our biological vulnerability or the accumulation and expenditure of energies – a process of *corporeal learning* is required for the formation of any specific religious habitus. Dramatic collective activities may promote an effervescence that binds people together, with the accumulation and discharge of energies facilitating the creation of, and contact with, the sacred, but religions take on specific forms as a result of the long-term deployment of distinctive techniques. This learning of technique is a vital element in the construction of a religious habitus.

Technique

Mauss (1950) makes the point that the most seemingly natural actions of the embodied subject, such as walking and squatting, are actually learnt through processes of apprenticeship in culturally specific contexts. Describing these as "techniques of the body," Mauss provides an early account of their centrality to religion when reporting on those Yogic mystics, Taoist priests, and others, who employ methods of breathing as a means of transforming their consciousness and achieving transcendence. For Mauss, techniques of the body provide the material substratum of a habitus, religious or other, and result in people developing particular orientations, identities and histories.

Mauss's study of prayer develops these thoughts in relation to Christianity (Mauss 2003). While prayer appears to constitute an "effusion of a soul, a cry which expresses a feeling," it is also the product of centuries of development which not only serves to structure the embodied experiences of individuals in particular ways, but also integrates them into the Church (Mauss 2003: 33–6). Norris (2005) offers a similar view of prayer as primarily "transmitted and learned through the body." Techniques of the body are the medium through which collectively sanctioned religious norms come to reshape individual consciousness, the senses and the emotions (Norris 2005: 182).

Archer's (2000: 185) argument that religion is primarily to do with practice, wherein the exercise of spiritual "know how" is more important than assent to dogmatic principles, is also of note here. She suggests that religion is "a codification of practice," that there is no such thing as a non-liturgical religion, and that the center of Christian life is in the bodily disciplines of prayer, pilgrimage and physical contemplation as well as in the corporeal reception of the Body of Christ in the Eucharist (Archer 2000: 184–6). What she does not do, however, is examine how these patterns of religious "know how" within Christianity develop over time. In this respect it is useful to turn to Asad's (1993) analysis of the changing bodily practices and experiences engendered by Christianity across Western history.

Asad's analysis of medieval Christianity focuses on the body as the active center of a form of life that embraced not only "religion," in the sense of private belief, but the entire social, cultural and experiential reality of "Christendom." Embodied practices, not beliefs or discourses, provided the precondition and medium for the constitution of Christian religiosity (Asad 1993: 76). In a similar vein to Bossy (1985: 170), however, Asad contrasts this embodied religion with the emergence of a different understanding in the Protestant Reformation. Here, there was a "subli-mation of blood into belief" that facilitated the deconstruction of existing patterns of Christian solidarity (and the development of the modern sense that religion is, primarily, a matter of individual understanding, faith and conviction), and also signalled a reconstruction of the embodied aspects of religiosity. This can be conceptualized as a shift from the "carnal knowing" of the medieval era to the "cognitive-apprehension" of belief-oriented Christianity in the Reformation; a re-formation of the embodied basis of religion and culture away from the sacred "eating community" of Catholicism and towards Protestantism's discursive symbol-ization of religion centered on the Bible (Mellor and Shilling 1997: 103).

Pedagogics

This interest in the techniques promoted by particular religions and the manner in which they engage with the body's openness and energies in seeking to stimulate specific types of experience, often in tension with other institutions, has been sys-tematized recently in the study of body pedagogics. The study of body pedagogics examines how, and to what degree, the orientations, dispositions, values, and tech-niques validated by cultural forms, including those of religion, are actually embod-ied in individuals. In so doing, it highlights how religious identities are part of, and are forged within, broader cultural approaches to the body, and depend for their deployment in daily life on whether they become embodied in people's experiences, dispositions and actions. Specifically, the study of body pedagogics involves the examination of three, analytically distinct, factors: first, the central religious, edu-cational, institutional and other means or activities through which people encounter the key values, techniques and dispositions validated by a culture; second, the expe-riences of those engaged in these activities as they acquire, or fail to acquire, these cultural attributes; and third, the actual embodied outcomes resulting from this attempted process of cultural transmission. It is these outcomes which provide the embodied basis on which a religion is subsequently reproduced or subject to change (Shilling and Mellor 2007).

The notion of body pedagogics has affinities with Mauss's notion of techniques of the body, as well as Foucault's (1988) conception of "technologies of the self," which has been a significant influence on the sociology of religion. Its theoretical focus is wider, however, in addressing the means of transmission and the issue of experience glossed by Mauss, and the phenomenological and ontological dimensions of embodiment neglected by Foucault. Another important difference separating the conception of body pedagogics from the writings of Mauss, Foucault, and, indeed, Bourdieu, is its realist underpinnings. These are designed to recognize and respect the distinctive ontological properties of what is involved in the attempted transmis-sion of religious culture, in people's experiences, and in the actual embodied out-comes of this process. Thus, the focus on cultural means or activities directs attention to the practical techniques and material affordances, as well as the belief systems, employed in the organization and delivery of religious culture. The concern with experience focuses on people's immediate emotional feelings and bodily sensations when participating in these activities, and the subsequent reflective internal conversations they have about their responses. The concern with embodied outcomes focuses on whether these means and experiences have actually resulted in changes to people's values, to their capacities and dispositions for different types of action, and in any other physiological aspect of their bodily selves.

This approach aims to analyze how cultural means, people's experiences and embodied changes interact and alter over time, but does so with a particular interest in the relationships between religious body pedagogics and those of modern technological culture. Drawing upon Heidegger's (1993) account of technological culture, as well as that of Weber (1991), Shilling and Mellor (2007) examine how, while the enhanced efficiency associated with the technological body in the modern age is associated with an unprecedented degree of control over the external environment, this has developed at the expense of those experiences of transcendence and immanence that are variously central to the embodied dynamics of religious traditions. It is the exclusion of these experiences that is signalled by Heidegger's (1993) focus on the absence of *technē* from technological culture, so that individuals are increasingly unable to relate to their natural and social environments in a manner free from rational instrumentalism. The exclusion of these experiences also underpins sociology's long held interest in the difficulties individuals confront in avoiding a sense of fracture, fragmentation and anomie in rationalized, industrialized societies.

It is in the light of these concerns that Shilling and Mellor (2007) compare the body pedagogics of technological culture with religious forms as diverse as Taoism and charismatic Christianity. In contrast to Taoism's emphasis on the "immanent" aspects of the transcendence/ immanence dynamic that is a key feature of religious culture, charismatic Christian body pedagogics are seen as having a more "transcendent" focus, even though God, through Christ and the Holy Spirit is also immanent in the world through the embodied experience of Christians. Analyzing this form of religion as one "integrated around the key notion of transformation" (Martin 1990: 163), and productive of "rituals of rupture" that seek to reconfigure an individual's relationship to society and culture (Robbins 2004: 128), it is argued that the pedagogic focus is on bringing about physical and spiritual rebirth. Here, the Protestant worldly asceticism Weber associated with the origins of modern instrumental rationalism has given way to a re-formed "Protestant Ethic," both newer and, in its recovery of biblical body symbolism, older than the model he envisaged.

A key conclusion of this approach is that, in contrast to totalizing analyses of technological culture, humans are not "hailed" to assume specific subject positions but are, at most, prepared and disciplined to construct their lives according to specific sets of practices, rituals, and priorities. Furthermore, while the transmission of a specific religious habitus may be rendered difficult in by the competing pedagogic processes associated with technological culture, this culture is by no means destined to grow in strength (Shilling 2008). On the one hand, it has been associated the spiralling incidences of phenomena such as suicide attempts, clinical depression, eating disorders, drug abuse and other "risk behaviors," which are read as symptoms of frail, mortal bodies struggling in the "cybernetic eternity" that is technological culture (Virilio 2000: 40–2). On the other hand, it may be that the failure of

the technological habitus to engage meaningfully with important aspects of embodiment facilitates the continued need for individuals to immerse themselves in religion
as a result of the ontological condition of their existence as humans. As Turner
(1991) has argued, issues of meaning and religion possess a material, bodily basis
which is not simply rendered obsolete by the onwards march of modernity.

CONCLUSION

The study of religion became central to sociology not only because of its apparent
opposition to the rationalization processes located at the very heart of modernity,
with their attendant promotion of a human centered view of the world, but because
religion was characterized by ritual mechanisms and belief systems that engaged
with longstanding human needs, dispositions and potentialities. As such, it threw
into sharp relief questions about the relationship between social groups and the
embodied constitution of their members. In exploring these issues we outlined how
Weber's and Durkheim's writings enagage with the embodied aspects of religious
life, and how these relate to other components of society and culture. Suggesting
that the notion of the religious habitus offers a theoretical bridge not only between
the apparently incommensurate views of Weber and Durkheim, but across a variety
of other engagements with religion and the body, we then examined the themes of
biological openness, expenditure, sacrifice, technique and pedagogics as distinctive
elements in the constitution of this habitus. Three main conclusions can be drawn
from the examination of these themes.

First, analysing the embodied dimensions of religions is central to understanding
their social and cultural significance: there has been considerable theoretical variation in the perspectives considered in this paper, but all of them emphasize that
religiosity is not just a matter of beliefs and values, but is to do with *lived experiences*, *practical orientations*, *sensory* forms of knowing and patterns of *physical*
accomplishment and technique that impact upon day-to-day lives in far-reaching
ways. Despite the diversity of the perspective we have considered, all of them suggest
that these bodily aspects of religion are central to its capacity to integrate individuals
into social and cultural unities, but also crucial in illuminating the limits of social
and cultural influences relative to human embodiment.

Second, the range of perspectives on religion and the body considered in this
chapter can be interpreted as converging around the notion of the habitus as the
key to understanding religion sociologically. In general terms, a habitus refers to
the embodied predispositions which promote particular forms of orientation to the
world, but in the course of our discussion we have addressed a number of features
of embodiment specific to religious life: these have included the the existential reassurances and anxieties reflective of human frailty, the stimulation and regulation of
emotions relative to the sacred, and the development of rituals, techniques and
pedagogics with the aim of stimulating particular forms of consciousness and experience, including those related to transcendence and immanence.

A third point to be made is that, in a globalized world characterized by the
increased interaction between technological culture and a variety of religious forms,
the importance of developing a satisfactory understanding of the religious habitus

is particularly acute. In an era marked, for some, by an emerging "clash of civiliza-tions" wherein religion takes an absolutely central role (Huntington 1996), a focus on the embodied commonalities and differences across different religious contexts must surely become key to the sociological engagement with the renewed impor-tance of religion to global affairs.

Living in a different social and cultural context to the globalized world of the present, sociology's classical figures made a point of emphasizing the particular importance of studying religion to the sociological project, and sought to clarify the embodied basis upon which its social and cultural significance had developed. In the light of further developments in the discipline, and in relation to changes in the contemporary world, their emphasis remains as important as ever. It is the capacity of religion to develop a particular, embodied habitus that accounts for its potent social and cultural influence; it is this capacity that also makes the body central to the sociology of religion, and the sociology of religion central to the sociological project in general.

Bibliography

Alexander, J. C. (2004) From the depths of despair: performance, counterperformance and "September 11," *Sociological Theory* 22 (1): 88–105.

Archer, M. (2000) *Being Human*, Cambridge: Cambridge University Press.

Aron, R. (1964) *Main Currents in Sociological Thought I*, London: Weidenfeld and Nicolson.

Asad, T. (1993) *Genealogies of Religion*, Baltimore: Johns Hopkins University Press.

Azari, N. et al. (2001) Short communication: neural correlates of religious experience, *Euro-pean Journal of Neuroscience* 13: 1649–52.

Bataille, G. (1967) *The Accursed Share I*, New York: Zone.

Bataille, G. (1988) The sorcerer's apprentice, in D. Hollier (ed.), *The College of Sociology 1937–39*, Minneapolis: University of Minnesota Press.

Bataille, G. (1992) *Theory of Religion*, New York: Zone.

Bellah, R. (1970) *Beyond Belief*, New York: Harper and Row.

Berger, P. (1967) *The Sacred Canopy*, New York: Doubleday.

Berger, P. L. and Luckmann, T. (1966) *The Social Construction of Reality*, Harmondsworth: Penguin.

Bossy, J. (1985) *Christianity in the West, 1400–1700*, Oxford: Oxford University Press.

Bourdieu, P. (1977) *Outline of a Theory of Practice*, Cambridge: Cambridge University Press.

Caillois, R. (1950) *L'homme et le Sacré*, Paris: Gallimard.

Collins, R. (2004) *Interaction Ritual Chains*, Princeton: Princeton University Press.

Csordas, T. (1994) *The Sacred Self*, Berkeley: University of California Press.

Dayan, D. and Katz, E. (1988) Articulating consensus: the ritual and rhetoric of media events, in. J. Alexander (ed.), *Durkheimian Sociology: Cultural Studies*, Cambridge: Cambridge University Press.

Douglas, M. (1966) *Purity and Danger*, London: Routledge and Kegan Paul.

Durkheim, É. (1973) The dualism of human nature and its social conditions, in R. Bellah (ed.), *Émile Durkheim on Morality and Society*, Chicago: University of Chicago Press.

Durkheim, É. (1974) Individual and collective representations, in *Sociology and Philosophy*. New York: Free Press.

Durkheim, É. (1995) *The Elementary Forms of Religious Life*, New York: Free Press.

Elias, N. (1987) The changing balance of power between the sexes – a process-sociological study: the example of the ancient Roman state, *Theory, Culture and Society* 4: 287–316.

Elias, N. (1991) *Symbol Emancipation*, London: Sage.

Featherstone, M. (1991) *Consumer Culture and Postmodernism*, London: Sage.

Foucault, M. (1977) *Language, Counter-Memory, Practice*, Oxford: Blackwell.

Foucault, M. (1988) The ethic of care for the self as a practice of freedom, in J. Bernauer and D. Rasmussen (eds.), *The Final Foucault*, Cambridge, MA: MIT Press.

Gerth, H. and Mills, C. W. (1948) *Introduction to From Max Weber: Essays in Sociology*. London: Routledge and Kegan Paul.

Giddens, A. (1990) *The Consequences of Modernity*, Cambridge: Polity.

Giddens, A. (1991) *Modernity and Self-Identity*, Cambridge: Polity.

Girard, R. (1977) *Violence and the Sacred*, Baltimore: Johns Hopkins University Press.

Girard, R. (1987) *Things Hidden Since the Foundation of the World*, London: Continuum.

Girard, R. (2001) *I See Satan Fall Like Lightning*, New York: Orbis.

Heidegger, M. (1993) The question concerning technology, in D. Krell (ed.), *Martin Heidegger: Basic Writings*, London: Routledge.

Hertz, R. (1973) The pre-eminence of the right hand: a study in religious polarity, in R. Needham (ed.), *Right and Left*, Chicago: University of Chicago Press.

Hubert, H. and Mauss, M. (1964) *Sacrifice: Its Nature and Function*, London: Cohen and West.

Huntington, S. (1996) *The Clash of Civilisations and the Remaking of World Order*, New York: Simon and Schuster.

Levine, D. (1993) *Visions of the Sociological Tradition*, Chicago: University of Chicago Press.

Luckmann. T. (1967) *The Invisible Religion*, New York: Macmillan.

Lukes, S. (1973) *Emile Durkheim*, Harmondsworth: Penguin.

Maffesoli, M. (1996) *The Time of the Tribes*, London: Sage.

Maley, T. (2004) Max Weber and the iron cage of technology, *Bulletin of Science, Technology and Society* 24: 69–86.

Martin, D. (1990) *Tongues of Fire*, Oxford: Blackwell.

Mauss, M. (1900) Sylvain Lévi, *La doctrine du sacrifice bans les Brâhmanas*, *L'Année sociologique* 3: 293–5.

Mauss, M. (1950) Les techniques du corps, *Sociologie et Anthropologie*, Paris: Presses Universitaires de France.

Mauss, M. (1969) *The Gift*, London: Routledge and Kegan Paul.

Mauss,M. (1973) *Sociologie et anthropologie*. Paris: Presses Universitaires de France.

Mauss, M. (2003) *On Prayer*, Oxford: Berghahn Books.

Mellor, P. A. (2004) *Religion, Realism and Social Theory*, London: Sage.

Mellor, P. A. and Shilling, C. (1997) *Re-forming the Body*, London: Sage.

Nisbet, R. (1993) *The Sociological Tradition*, New Brunswick: Transaction Books.

Norris, R. (2005) Examining the structure and role of emotion: contributions of neurobiology to the study of embodied religious experience, *Zygon* 40 (1): 181–99.

Pickering, M. (1993) *Auguste Comte: An Intellectual Biography I*, Cambridge: Cambridge University Press.

Reedy, W. (1994) The historical imaginary of social science in post-Revolutionary France: Bonald, Saint-Simon, Comte, *History of the Human Sciences* 7 (1): 1–26.

Ritzer, G. (1999) *Enchanting a Disenchanted World*, London: Pine Forge.

Robbins, J. (2004) The globalisation of Pentecostal and charismatic Christianity, *Annual Review of Anthropology* 33: 117–43.

Shilling, C. (2008) *Changing Bodies: Habit, Crisis and Creativity*, London: Sage.

Shilling, C. and Mellor, P. A. (2007) Cultures of Embodied Experience: Technology, Religion and Body pedagogics, *Sociological Review* 55 (3): 531–49.

Simmel, G. (1990) *The Philosophy of Money*, London: Routledge.

Simmel, G. (1997) *Essays in Religion*, ed. J. Helle, New Haven: Yale University Press.

Tiryakian, E. (1995) Collective effervescence, social change and charisma: Durkheim, Weber and 1989, *International Sociology* 10 (3): 269–81.

Tiryakian, E. (2004) Durkheim, solidarity and September 11, in J. Alexander and P. Smith (eds.), *The Cambridge Companion to Durkheim*, Cambridge: Cambridge University Press.

Turner, B. S. (1984) *The Body and Society*, London: Sage.

Turner, B. S. (1991) *Religion and Social Theory*, London: Sage.

Turner, B. S. (2002) Sovereignty and emergency: political theology, Islam and American conservatism, *Theory, Culture and Society* 19 (4): 103–19.

Turner, B. S. (2006) *Vulnerability and Human Rights*, University Park: University of Pennsylvania Press.

Turner, B. S. (2007) Culture, technologies and bodies: the technological utopia of living forever, in C. Shilling (ed.), *Embodying Sociology*, Oxford: Blackwell.

Turner, B. S. and Rojek, C. (2001) *Society and Culture*, London: Sage.

Turner, V. (1969) *The Ritual Process*, London: Routledge.

Virilio, P. (2000) *The Information Bomb*, London: Verso.

Weber, M. (1948) Science as a vocation, in H. H. Gerth and C. W. Mills (eds.), *From Max Weber: Essays in Sociology*, London: Routledge.

Weber, M. (1964) *The Religion of China*, New York: Free Press.

Weber, M. (1968) *Economy and Society*, London: University of California Press.

Weber, M. (1991) *The Protestant Ethic and the Spirit of Capitalism*, London: Harper Collins.

10

Women, Religions, and Feminisms

Fang-Long Shih

Introduction

"Are females inferior?" – Feminist critiques often begin with this question (Delphy 1987: 80), and it is especially pertinent to investigations of religions. The first major feminist engagement with religion, Elizabeth Stanton's *Woman's Bible* (1895–8), attributed Christian women's inferior status to the misrepresentations of women in the Bible and patriarchal readings of the text. However, the double issue of "women and world religions" did not become a major scholarly concern until the 1980s, when a series of collected essays appeared (Sharma 1987; Carmody 1988; Holm and Bowker 1994; Sharma 1994). These essays typically drew upon and extended the phenomenological approach to various religious traditions or areas, and they interpreted women's voices and lives from within both the framework of the particular religion and the authors' own feminine perspective. Some scholars argued that both religious texts and scholarship about religions were inherently androcentric, and that only a very distorted perspective on women's subjectivity could be found in either (Gross 1987: 38). Others who sought to recover and interpret female experience agreed that world religions share the "common feature of being patriarchal," but argued that "we cannot avoid the androcentric text which muffles our stethoscope and prevents us from hearing the heartbeats of real women" (Young 1987: 2–3).

Patriarchal patterns among different religions which have frequently been explored and critiqued include: male images of the divine and male leadership in the Abrahamic religions; the superiority of male *karma* in Buddhism; patrilineal ancestor worship in Chinese society; husbands as divine in Hinduism; and male master-hood in Daoism. Overall, females are considered inferior to males and therefore incapable of attaining the same level of religious achievement as men. Hence, women need to be protected and under the control of men; practices also examined include: Christian witch-hunting, which secures the dominance of the male priesthood over women's potentially rival religious power; Confucian footbinding, which promotes chastity by making it difficult for women to move about; Hindu *sati*, in which a widow is immolated on her husband's funeral pyre so that she will be reunited with him in the next life; and Muslim *purdah*, in which women should not expose themselves to public view and thus must be veiled when outside the home.

However, the claim that patriarchy is the structuring grammar of all religions is debatable, and there are interpretations and evidence both for and against the idea. For example, there are anthropological studies of Southeast Asian religions (and cultures) which suggest that the organizing principle of these religions/cultures is not so much gender hierarchy as gender complementarity (Meñez 1999). Further, the phenomenological approach to "women and religion" cannot be combined successfully with feminist approaches (but see Sharma and Young 1999: 8, 13). Feminism takes as its point of departure the links between religions and economic, political and social spheres, while the phenomenological approach regards religion as a *sui generis* phenomenon, with an underlying essence distinct from its sociological, economic or political contexts. Central to its method is *epoché*, or "value-neutrality" (for a critique of the phenomenology of religion see Tremlett 2007); this is completely at odds with feminism, which is, by definition, a "value-saturated" perspective or series of perspectives.

Twenty years on from the "women and world religions" volumes of the 1980s, it is time to re-examine and re-think the conjunction of feminism and religion from a sociological perspective, including asking whether there is such a thing as "a feminist critique of religion." This chapter argues that there is in fact no such thing, for good or ill. If it were otherwise, we would recognize a coherent set of ideas, propositions, practices and convictions across all religions that unite feminists in criticism. A feminist critique of religion – like any other kind of critique – needs to agree as to what religion is, and there is no agreed definition of religion either among feminists or indeed among any other group.

Moreover, the same problem of definition exists in relation to what exactly feminism is. What would be the key moments in a "herstory" (Nestle 1982, quoted in Schwarz 1984: x) of dissent and counter-narrative through which a series of feminisms might be discerned? What exactly is meant by "women" as a category is also unclear: Whenever someone claims "we women," I wonder what "women"? Does this "women" category include me? Does it refer to my mother in Taiwan? Does it apply to the Hasidic woman next door? Many other women have experienced the same uncertainty but, as Toril Moi has argued, "we do not have to believe that the word "woman" always carries heavy metaphysical baggage" (Moi 1999: 10), and I would like to stress the diversity of women's thoughts about what feminism is (or should be), the different practices through which women assert themselves as feminists, and the multiple subject positions from which feminisms have been and are articulated. The question of difference and diversity among women and feminisms is one with the question of their perspectives, which are articulated in various socio-religious, economical, political, and historical locations and situations. The absence of a conceptual monolith regarding "woman," "feminism," and "religion" may well be more of a blessing than a curse. The gaps and spaces leave plenty of room for new voices. Hence, the title of this chapter is phrased as "Women, Religions and Feminisms."

The pluralistic development of feminisms can be categorized into two loose but distinctive positions: "liberal feminism" and so-called "radical feminism." There have been substantial debates between liberal and radical feminisms in the domain of religions and among scholarship on religions. As I discuss below, one area of debate concerns feminist theology/thealogy. For example, in the West some liberal Christian feminists have promoted a "Women-Church" movement, while other radical feminists have rejected Christianity in favour of a "Goddess Religion"; there are comparable debates in other social and religious contexts. Further, among radical feminist theorists, writing in the context of post-structuralism or postmodernism, there are differences between what I call "ontological French feminism" and "epistemological feminism." I note below the significant features of feminist ontological and epistemological arguments and strategies that have been used to critique both certain aspects of particular religions and the ways religions have been studied. The final part of this chapter presents an empirical case study. To complement existing literature, I draw attention to a gendered analysis of and a feminist approach to women and Chinese religious culture. In particular, I demonstrate how both the incompleteness of socio-religious structure and the role of female agents allow for new discursive and physical spaces in which alternative practices and conceptions regarding women can emerge.

In the Context of Feminist Theology/Thealogy

Religious liberal feminism

Liberal feminism has its roots in the feminist appropriation of the liberal tradition of equal rights. The first full statement is perhaps *A Vindication of the Rights of Women* (1789) by Mary Wollstonecraft. Wollstonecraft argued that women are rational rather than biological agents, whose "inferiority" is due primarily to inferior education and which could be redressed by equality of opportunity. In the late nineteenth century, Hubertine Auclert became the first woman to describe herself as a "feminist," while campaigning for women's suffrage (Bock 2002: 163). The suffrage movement between the 1880s and 1920s is regarded as "first wave" feminism. Contemporary liberal feminism, also known as "second-wave" feminism (coined by Marsha Lear in 1968), continues to seek inclusion within the current social order and full equality for women before the law as citizens. They further campaign for women's labour, sexual and reproductive rights, such as equal access to all professions, equal pay for equal work, free access to contraception and abortion, and opposing domestic and sexual violence. Liberal feminism, with its emphasis on equality in education, law, labour, welfare, and sex, has also been called "egalitarian feminism."

Religious liberal feminists have what might be called an agenda of accommodation with the religious "system" as it stands. Over the last thirty years, attaining the right to ordination has become a primary focus for liberal feminists in Christianity, Buddhism and among other religions. Liberal feminist theologians have rallied around this issue, and a number of Christian organizations, such as the American Episcopal Church since 1976 and the Church of England since 1992, now accept the ordination of women to the priesthood (Pears 2004). Within Buddhism, the discontinuance of the female monastic order (the *bhikkhuni sangha*) for a thousand years in the Theravada tradition has gained the attention of Buddhist feminists worldwide. Despite resistance from the male Theravada hierarchies, the Mahayana *bhikkhuni* of East Asia have helped to restore this monastic tradition for their Theravada sisters in Southeast Asia, with international ordinations from 1996. By 2006 there were about five hundred *bhikkhunis* in Sri Lanka, which contrasted with the 1993 situation, when the term "*bhikkhuni*" was forbidden (King 2008).

However, recent studies of female priests' experiences reveal that "even if the proportion of women priests in the Church of England increases to make these numbers comparable with men, there is no guarantee, or indication, that their presence will radically reshape the ordained ministry in the Church of England" (Thorne 2000: 134–5, in Pears 2004: 76). It has become clear to many feminist theologians that gaining admission to all levels of the Church's hierarchy is not enough in itself, and that there is a need to transform fundamentally the very institution and its structures and to ask how women can transform the Church and Christianity.

In fact, various perspectives on different forms of "women and Christianity" have emerged since the 1970s, growing out of disagreement or dissatisfaction with the insufficiencies of the liberal feminist preoccupation with ordination. Some worked to develop a feminist critical hermeneutics by transforming the Bible as a resource for women's liberation (Fiorenza 1984), some attempted to establish an alternative community or "Women-Church" (see below), some intended to build a "Mother-Church" with a reconnection to values of care to justice (Cunneen 1991), while others turned away from Christianity to a more radical Goddess Religion (see below) (for general texts on goddesses see Starhawk 1979; Preston 1982; Olson 1990).

Women-Church

The division among religious feminists became particularly sharp in 1979; some claimed that male images of the divine cannot simply be rejected but must be displaced by an alternative religion of the Goddess (see Carol and Plaskow 1979), while others argued that the total rejection of Judaeo-Christianity by Goddess feminists amounted to "unresolved dependence on the patriarchal authority" (Ruether 1979: 309). As Fiorenza (1984) explained, Goddess feminists share the same view as patriarchal Christian apologists, in that they both assume that the Bible is a mythical archetype which cannot be critically evaluated, but must be either accepted or rejected. Feminist theologian Rosemary Ruether considered that the creation of feminist spirituality "needs synthesis and transformation, not separation and rejection" (Ruether 1980: 847). She therefore called on women to undertake an exodus from patriarchy, but not out of the church, in an attempt to establish an alternative Women-Church.

Among Women-Church feminists, Ruether advocated "claiming the prophetic-liberating tradition of biblical faith as a norm through which to criticize the Bible" (Ruether 1983: 23–4). According to Ruether,

The maleness of Jesus was read as re-enforcing the view that maleness was necessary for normative humanity ... Views of femaleness as lacking normative and full humanity, as more prone to sin ... skewed the message of equal redemption in Christ. By the second generation of the Christian movement ... women were being defined as those who had been created second and sinned first. They are to keep silent, accept their subordination to the male and bear children in order to be "saved. (Ruether 1998: 11)

Further, Ruether declared that "biblical religion" with its traditions of exodus from oppression toward liberation could be re-employed to express the feminist community's exodus from patriarchy (Ruether 1983: 62, 205–6). In *Sexism and God-Talk* (1983), Ruether looked to alternative resources within the Christian heritage, seeking to transform the sexist language associated with the male God into gender-neutral or androgynous language. In *Women-Church* (1985), Ruether called on women to withdraw from traditional male-dominated communities and gather together, developing "the critical culture that can give them an autonomous ground from which to critique patriarchy" (Ruether 1985: 59), inventing new words, new prayers, new symbols, and new praxis to bring about liberation from patriarchy. In "Women-Church" (1990), Diana Trebbi comes to re-define the Church as "the people of God" where there is no relation to a patriarchal structure. And the principal claim of Women-Church "is to represent a church based on a "discipleship of equals" that can incorporate the charisma of Christ more authentically than the present hierarchy and clergy" (Trebbi 1990: 350).

The Women-Church approach has prevailed especially in the so-called Third World. In *The Church of Women* (2005), Dorothy Hodgson explores how Maasai Catholic women in Tanzania operate their "church of women" in terms of struggles over gendered meanings of authority, morality and approaches to evangelization. The Maasai church of women "provided frequent opportunities on a regular basis for women to meet as a group, talk to one another, sing, and pray" and also "provided both formal and informal leadership opportunities for women" (Hodgson 2005: 183). A senior member told Hodgson, "When we meet we have a service. Often we take a collection to help sick people or the family of someone who has died, or we go to help work on the farm of someone who is sick or the family of someone who has died" (Hodgson 2005: 186). She concludes that the church of women

enabled [Maasai] women to reaffirm and reinforce their claims to spiritual and moral superiority in opposition to the increasingly material interests of men ... It was also a domain of their lives where they experienced and expressed significant power ... all this occurred in a historical context where they had lost substantial economic and political rights and autonomy ... to men. (Hodgson 2005: 256–8)

Feminist theology in a third world context, "expresses itself as a liberation theology in a much stronger sense, as it develops within situations where the oppression of women and the denial of their full humanity often occurs on a much larger scale and to a much greater degree than in the First World" (King 1994: 3–4). The theologies of third world women stress the importance of their own struggle, working to gain their liberation from patriarchy while simultaneously fighting for the

economic and political liberation of their own countries. These concerns are also
shared by minority groups in the West; for example, black American Christian
women have taken up the term "womanist theology" (Williams 1994: 77–88;
Crawford 2002), referring to a black feminist theology defined in their own historical and social contexts. Black women have struggled not only against the sexism
of black men but also against the racism of white men and women.

Ruether has long struggled to transcend the dilemma "between an androcentric
one-nature and a complementarian two-nature anthropology" (Ruether, 1998: 65)
of gender, which led her to develop the concept which she calls the "Human One";
namely, what "a holistic humanness in mutual relation would mean for transformed
women and men in a good society" (Ruether 1998: 65). However, her idea of the
"Human One" has been challenged by women in Asia, Africa, and Latin America
and by postmodernists. Encountering feminist postmodern critiques (referring to
Nicholson, 1990), Ruether is aware that "postmodernism has rejected the whole
idea of universals, not only of essential maleness and essential femaleness, but also
of essential humanness." This is because that "all ideas of an essential human self
and universal values are declared social constructions that veil the cultural imperialism of dominant groups of Western men and women" (Ruether 1998: 65).

Postmodern feminist theologies emphasize situatedness and particularity. Among
them, women's theologies of non-Western cultures put special emphasis on "*doing*
theology. It is a theology as an activity, as an ongoing process rooted in praxis,
interdependent with and compassionately committed to life, justice, and freedom
from oppression" (King 1994: 16).

Religious radical feminism

Some religious women realized that full equality cannot be achieved merely through
inclusion and accommodation in prevailing socio-religious structures and institutions, and have turned to more radical forms of feminism. They argue that the
suppression of women comes from the categorization of women as an inferior
"class" to men on the basis of gender, and that this categorization goes to the very
heart of notions of law, philosophy and theology. These radical feminists pursue a
deconstruction that "hold[s] open a space of radical indeterminacy within the way
it explores the category of women" (Elam 1994: 59). They all assert the necessity
of displacement by a different kind of gendered theology, philosophy and law: some
focus on consciousness and culture while others on the unconscious and the psyche.

Goddess Religion

For Goddess Religion feminists, neutralizing the sex of God is not enough, as this
transformation still does not include women. In *Beyond God the Father* (1973),
Mary Daly reveals that, if God in "his" heaven is a father ruling "his" people (Daly
1973: 13), then God-Father "functions to legitimate the existing social, economic,
and political status quo, in which women and other victimized groups are subordinate" (Daly 1973: 19). In "Why women need the Goddess" (1979), Carol Christ
states that although female power is not altogether denied in patriarchy, it is not
recognized as legitimate and autonomous. As long as the word "Goddess" remains

unspeakable, female power is not explicitly and fully expressed. Therefore, only through discovering the Goddess can the female self be affirmed and the traditional view of female inferiority be overcome. As claimed by Starhawk,

> The mystery, the paradox, is that the Goddess is not "she" or "he" – or she is both –but we call her "she" because to name is not to limit or describe but to invoke. We call her in and a power comes who is different from what comes when we say "he" or "it." Something happens, something that challenges the ways in which our minds have been shaped in images of male control. (Starhawk, 1987: 21)

In contrast to the term "theo-logy," Naomi Goldenberg has coined a gendered term "thea-logy" (Goldenberg 1979: 96). In order to understand the thealogy of the Goddess, Christ argues that one has to demolish the worldview and way of thinking rooted in biblical religion and Western culture. Goddess feminists seek to approach the Goddess non-empirically through dream and non-ordinary experiences. According to Christ, the prevailing scholarship is presented "as objective, rational, analytical, dispassionate, disinterested, and true," but is in fact "rooted in the passion to honor, legitimate, and preserve elite male power." Christ, by contrast, admits that Goddess feminist "scholarship is passionate, is interested, is aimed at transforming the world we have inherited" (Christ 1997: 33–4). Aspects of Christ's argument anticipate the claims of scholars such as Harding and Haraway, that I will examine below.

Since the 1980s Goddess-centered symbols, languages, and rituals have received renewed interest, and the Goddess has become increasingly popular, particularly in North America, Europe, Australia, and New Zealand. Many women have been searching for their own ideas of the Goddess in their own ways. In *Rebirth of the Goddess* (1997), Christ provides two examples: Christine Downing was led to the Goddess through dreams: "When I sleep there in the cave I dream that within the cave I find a narrow hole leading into an underground passage. I make my way through that channel deep, deep into another cave well beneath the earth's surface. I sit down on the rough uneven floor, knowing myself to be in her [the Goddess] presence" (Downing 1981: 3, in Christ 1997: 4–5). For Caz Love, the Goddess became an inspiration for her thoughts after a pilgrimage to Crete: "What I did not expect was how profoundly the pilgrimage would affect my perceptions of our culture … experiencing … the huge presence of the Goddess in the sites, the land, in all of us … I am sad and angry that I will never grow up in a society that reveres nature and the feminine, with a mother who grew up in beauty and love and equality" (Love 1996: 4, in Christ 1997: 6–7).

The rebirth of the Goddess helps to break the hold of male control so that women no longer look to males for the divine and the saviour. Also, one can re-connect oneself with all powers in the universe;

> Finding the Goddess has felt like coming home to a vision of life that we had always known deeply within ourselves: that we are part of nature and that our destiny is to participate fully in the cycles of birth, death, and renewal that characterize life on this earth. We find in the Goddess a compelling image of female power, a vision of the deep connection of all beings in the web of life, and a call to create peace on earth. (Christ 1997: xiii)

The revelation of the Goddess challenges dualism, demonstrating "that death be honored equally with life, darkness equally with light, woman equally with man." Rather than "a 'changeless' God who stands above the world," the Goddess connects "us to a divinity who is known within nature and who personifies change. Instead of portraying God primarily as the 'light shining in the darkness,' Goddess rituals value the darkness as a place of transformation" (Christ 1997: 30). As Goddess priestess Starhawk puts it,

> The ritual, the magic, spins the bond that can sustain us to continue the work over years, over lifetimes. Transforming culture is a long-term project ... If we cannot live to see the completion of that revolution, we can plant its seeds in our circles, we can dream its shape in our visions, and our rituals can feed its growing power. (Starhawk 1982: 180)

Obviously, there are certain problems inherent to an approach that appears to reject empirical research, and the claim that evidence-based research is gendered is highly debatable. I will return to this point below. But, there is no denying the significance of this scholarship to the study of religions in general.

In the Context of Post-structuralism/Postmodernism

Ontological French feminism

The term "French feminism" is a publishing trademark promoted by the *Mouvement de Libération des Femmes* (MLF), referring to a theoretical movement that uses French texts in Anglo-American academic contexts. Radical French feminism emerged in the 1970s as an "anti-feminist feminism" in contrast to American-originated liberal theoretical feminism (Joy et al. 2002: 1–12). It claims to re-think what was then called "women's experience," recognizing contradictions which inhere in the specific definitions of women's nature and social role in specific power relations. It argues that the psychosexual dynamic is central to women's oppression, and draws on "Psych et Po" (Psychanalyse et Politique), "to 'psychoanalyze' the 'political' and to make 'political' the 'psychoanalytic' distinction of the sexes" (Joy et al. 2002: 5). French feminists thus concern themselves with the psychology of women.

The label "French feminism" is in particular applied to the writings of Hélène Cixous, Luce Irigaray, and Julia Kristeva. These authors engage critically with the writings of Freud and Lacan as products of phallo-centristic thought and further appropriate Derrida's ideas about deconstruction. They adopt post-structuralist positions, assuming that meaning is not something fixed but is rather fluid and changing. Their writings offer speculations about the ground of "the feminine" in an attempt to radicalize feminists' imaginations via metaphorical transformations of language. I therefore characterize them as feminists concerned with ontological issues in the context of post-structuralism. Cixous, Irigaray, and Kristeva all agree that women's experience cannot be articulated in a language and cultural system that effaces or hierarchizes difference, and their explorations of women's relation to writing, sexuality, and language have led to tentative speculations about the feminine. In addition to the American-originated liberal feminist focus on equality, French feminism has added another dimension: "the feminism of sexual difference" (Joy et al. 2002: 4). For them, men and women are equal but different subjects.

Hereafter, I look mainly at Cixous's and Irigaray's work relating to religion, and Kristeva's book *About Chinese Women*. We can see important points of convergence between Goddess feminist Christ and French feminists Cixous and Irigaray. I also note the work of Gayatri Chakravorty Spivak, who, like the others, has been influenced by post-structuralist theory. However, she rejects ontology, and her engagements with post-colonial theory and criticisms of French feminism provide a bridge to the following issue of feminist epistemology.

In "The Laugh of the Medusa" (1976 [1975]), Cixous undertakes a search for an *écriture feminine* (a feminine writing) or voice through which to begin the dismantling of the "masculine order" as developed in Western Christian culture. As Cixous puts it, "Woman must write her self: must write about women and bring women to writing, from which they have been driven away as violently as from their bodies ... Woman must put herself into the text – as into the world and into history – by her own movement" (Cixous 1976 [1975]: 875). She emphasizes that there is "no general woman, no one typical woman" (Cixous 1976 [1975]: 876). Nevertheless, through such a writing, her body could be heard and her dark unconscious might be brought to light and serve as a resource to break the cultural codes that have mastered and negated her. Cixous urgently demands that women learn to speak: "We must kill the false woman who is preventing the live one from breathing. Inscribe the breath of the whole woman" (Cixous 1976 [1975]: 880).

In "Sorties" (1986 [1975]), Cixous further demonstrates how phallo-centrism and logo-centrism (primacy of the word as law) subject thought to a binary system that appropriates and destroys the Other. She advocates the practice of feminist writing to disrupt and transform the logic of the "Selfsame," arguing that in the masculine order "thought has always worked through opposition ... Superior/Inferior" (Cixous 1986 [1975]: 63–4). Moving beyond Carol Christ's dualism, Cixous shows that this binary thought is not merely a sign of duality but also of hierarchy, and that hierarchy carries the violence of the Law. "All these pairs of oppositions are *couples*," such as man/woman, culture/nature. These oppositions always involve a battle and the "'victory' always comes down to the same thing: things get hierarchical. Organization by hierarchy makes all conceptual organization subject to man" (Cixous 1986 [1975]: 64). Cixous asks: "What would happen to logocentrism, to the great philosophical systems, to the order of the world in general if the rock upon which they founded this church should crumble?" (Cixous 1986 [1975]: 65). Further, what would happen if there could be a "feminine practice of writing" through which the ruling binary system could be, at the very least, subverted? (Cixous 1986 [1975]: 92)

Cixous' feminine writing is a style that privileges transgression. Hollywood (2003) argues that for Cixous, God and monotheism are responses to doubt created by the arrival of the Law. Cixous' writing, which defies the conventions of philosophy and the academy, is supposed to transgress that Law and give voice to its Other, namely woman. According to Cixous, woman "is able not to return to herself ...

going everywhere to the other" and that woman "has never 'held still'; ... she takes pleasure in being boundless, outside self, outside same, far from a 'center'" (Cixous 1986 [1975]: 87, 91).

Berkowitz notes that Cixous is attracted by stories from the Judaeo-Christian tradition, where she finds "in the fluidity with which they treat time, place and character ... a narrative mode subversively near to dream, that is, to the unconscious which preserves the memory of time before the Law" (Cixous 1993: 67, in Berkowitz 2003: 177), or, a trace of a pre-patriarchal age. It is in and through this poetic language – reading it, writing it, experiencing it and being transformed by it – that Cixous envisions the dissolution of binary thought and the knowing subject (God-Man) that it has created and privileged ever since. For Cixous, a feminine writing can "never be theorized, enclosed, coded – which doesn't mean that it doesn't exist. But, it will always exceed the discourse governing the phallocentric system" (Cixous 1986 [1975]: 92, 1976 [1975]: 883). That is, "defining a feminine practice of writing is impossible with an impossibility that will continue" (Cixous 1986 [1975]: 92).

However, there is a theoretical problem regardless as to whether we sympathize with Cixous' project. The Law appears as an event without history and resistance to its essentialisms is posed in terms of "woman" and "the feminine" occupying, it seems, the very grounds of hysteria, strangeness and alterity that they were assigned by the masculinist order from the start. Moreover, Cixous, like Carol Christ, does not offer any historical specificity or empirical evidence to support her arguments; *écriture feminine*, in its eschewal of all conventions and norms of evidence-based argument, marks a turn to the aesthetic and the literary and the abandonment of the political.

Irigaray, like Cixous, privileges the irreducibility of the feminine and has tried to develop a kind of feminine writing that presupposes certain ontological claims. In "Equal or different?" (1991 [1986]), Irigaray asks: "Demanding to be equal presupposes a term of comparison ... What do women want to be equal to? Men? ... Why not to themselves?" (Irigaray 1991 [1986]: 32). She insists that "the exploitation of women is based upon sexual difference, and can only be resolved through sexual difference" (Irigaray 1991 [1986]: 32). In "Sexual difference" (1991 [1984]), Irigaray claims that "sexual difference is one of the important questions of our age, if not in fact the burning issue." Moreover,

> In politics, some openings have been presented to women, but these have resulted from partial and local concessions on the part of those in power, rather than from the establishment of new values ... For the work of sexual difference to take place, a revolution in thought and ethics is needed. (Irigaray 1991 [1984]: 166)

Rejecting, in common with Haraway and Harding (see below), any correspondence theory of truth, Irigaray argues that knowledge must account for difference, and that the body becomes an important site of critical reflection on the problem of difference. There are biological differences between bodies; however, the meaningfulness of these differences is not biologically given or self-evident, but constructed in relation to cultural values. Irigaray is also critical of the primacy given in knowledge to the eyes, and she equates the phallus with sight and the ideal of objective truth through facts and data. The vagina, for Irigaray, stands for touch, which in turn becomes a metaphor for a tactile and feminine mode of writing.

According to Irigaray, religion is fundamental to the discovery, affirmation and achievement of sexual difference. In "Divine women" (1993 [1985]), Irigaray accepts that we need a God, a mirror to model, to become, which signifies "fulfilling the wholeness of what we are capable of being" (1993 [1985]: 61). However, she questions the Christian representation of God as the projection of idealized "man" through which masculine subjectivity is defined. She argues that women have had their own access to the divine blocked, noting that the Virgin Mary was able to become divine only through having a son. Claiming, in the light of Goddess feminists, that the absence of a divine representation has limited women's ability to develop their identity, Irigaray urges women to explore ways of becoming divine, through which feminine subjectivity would be founded.

Irigaray further constructs a problematic history of origins whereby, "in the beginning," women and daughters had access to the divine and the divine was rooted in the earth and nature. However, patriarchy emerged as male gods replaced goddesses, and eventually a patriarchal genealogy was established that outlawed the recognition of maternity, along with a new, masculine linguisticality that denies women their own discourse. Much of this is premised upon essential differences between men and women: as Roy notes, for Irigaray "woman has a pronounced taste for the relational, for relationships with other subjects and nature" whereas man prefers "the object ... over the relationship between subjects, the constructed over the natural" (Roy 2003: 16).

In *Between East and West* (2002 [1999]), Irigaray continues to explore a new ethics of sexual difference but turns towards Eastern traditions, which, with their goddesses, for her appear more "feminine." Morny Joy notes that Irigaray's association of indigenous elements found in contemporary Hinduism with what she understands as "gynocratic culture" is based on "secondary sources [such] as J. J. Bachofen, in general, and Mircea Eliade, in particular" (Joy 2003: 54). She contends that "Irigaray's work would seem to be written without reference to issues in contemporary scholarship in Anglo-American feminism, to recent historical research of early India, or to post-colonialist discussions" (Joy 2003: 55). In particular, Irigaray has failed to consider why Hindu women are still subordinate to men if their goddesses are as powerful as male gods; Joy observes that "whatever realization of self is allowed to a woman comes to her only as a reflection of the spiritual stature of her husband" (Joy, 2003: 60). Thus we can see that Irigaray's project, while constituting "an important intervention in the phallocentrism of Western culture" (Poxon 2003: 48), is nevertheless beset with problems. Irigaray uncritically reproduces orientalist stereotypes about Eastern spiritualities; she essentializes woman which limits the possibility of her becoming and she makes no mention of issues such as race, class or ethnicity. As such, Irigaray's writing appears "more spiritual rather than theoretical in nature" (Joy 2003: 55).

Kristeva, like Cixous and Irigaray, accepts the premise that the structure of Western thought and philosophy consists of hierarchically arranged binary oppositions. But, in contrast with Cixous and Irigaray, she believes that these can be at least temporarily undone, overcome or transgressed by focusing on the moments at which apparently stable meanings collapse in on themselves. These breaks and ruptures in meaning are the moments at which binary distinctions between the masculine and the feminine are transgressed. For Kristeva, woman is "an eternal dissident in relation to social and political consensus, in exile from power, and therefore always singular, fragmentary, demonic, a witch." Further, "a woman's experience can only be negative, one that says 'not that' and 'not yet'" (Kristeva 1977: 529, in Kristeva 1987: 113). Kristeva is particularly interested in "negative" experiences/deconstruction, such as abjection, suffering and horror that, temporarily at least, destroy the subject's conventional anchor in the world and cause the subject to lose itself: "in that thing that no longer matches and therefore no longer signifies anything, I behold the breaking down of a world that has erased its borders: fainting away. The corpse, seen without God and outside of science, is the utmost of abjection" (Kristeva 1982 [1980]: 4).

Kristeva's *About Chinese Women* (1977 [1974]) provides a bridge between Western feminisms and my own case study on women and "Chinese religion" below. For Kristeva, Christianity was the key form of patriarchal symbolic repression in the West, while in China the key form of patriarchy was the family. During her visit to China in 1974, Kristeva glimpsed the possibility of a new kind of China which was undergoing a transition from the patriarchal Confucian system toward "a socialism without God or Man" (Kristeva 1977 [1974]: 201). As an atheist brought up in socialist Bulgaria, she believed that religion had "provided a clever way of dealing with female paranoia, bringing it to heel and reducing it to masochism, the only perverse solution allowed women" (Kristeva 1987, 1977: 116). She saw in the Cultural Revolution new values to replace religion, values that could "respond to the psycho-social characteristics of women, and so propose another ethics in which women could partake" (Kristeva 1987, 1977: 116). Her understanding of the Cultural Revolution in China as an attack on Confucian patriarchy was certainly naïve. It is an historical irony that today, "communist" China is in the process of rehabilitating and re-inventing "Confucianism" as the new ideological glue to hold China's atomized society together.

Spivak, quoting Clément, acknowledges French feminist writing/action as working "to change the imaginary in order to be able to act on the real, to change the very forms of language which by its structure and history has been subject to a law that is patrilinear, therefore masculine" (Clément translated in Spivak 1988: 145). Spivak adds to these issues of race and class in relation to gender, demonstrating how both colonialism and Western feminists have marginalized third world women through a form of what she calls "epistemic violence." She argues that the distinction of "French" from "Anglo-American" feminisms is superficial, as both are unaware of the "inbuilt colonialism of First World feminism toward the Third" (Spivak 1988: 153). In particular, Spivak notes that Kristeva's speculations about an ancient matriarchal China are based on an orientalist "primitivistic reverence" (Spivak 1988: 138) gleaned from evidence in "two books by Marcel Granet ... and Lévi-Strauss" (Spivak 1988: 137):

> Not only has Chinese writing maintained the memory of matrilinear pre-history (collective and individual) in its architectonic of image, gesture, and sound; it has been able as well to integrate it into a logico-symbolic code capable of ensuring the most direct, "reasonable," legislating – even the most bureaucratic – communication: all the

qualities that the West believes itself unique in honouring, and that it attributes to the Father. (Kristeva 1977 [1974]: 57, in Spivak 1988: 138)

According to Spivak, Kristeva's reading of China – and I might suggest these remarks are equally pertinent regarding Cixous and Irigaray – sees "speculation" transformed into "historical fact" (Spivak 1988: 137). The inconvenience of detailed research, whether archival or ethnographic, has never prevented them from articulating grand claims which, when subject to close analysis, have little basis in fact. Such criticisms echo thoughts from feminists who place a particular emphasis on epistemology.

Epistemological feminism

Feminisms between the late 1960s and the mid-1980s tended to reflect the viewpoints of white, middle-class women of North America and Western Europe. In the "Introduction" to *Feminism/Postmodernism* (1990), Linda Nicholson notes the irony that feminist scholars "falsely universalized on the basis of limited perspectives" (Nicholson 1990: 1). In other words, they reproduced the same mistakes that had formed the foundation of their own critique in the first instance.

However, since the late 1980s a series of feminist critiques of methodology and epistemology have arisen, foregrounding questions concerned with theory of knowledge and method over ontology: most notable in this group are Donna Haraway and Sandra Harding, and I have called them "epistemological feminists." Questions epistemological feminists ask include: Are conventional methods of science gendered? Can there be a feminist science? They thus pay particular attention to the actual modes of producing scientific knowledge. Their work interrogates the status of knowledge, challenges the structure of the academy, exposes the myth of objectivity, and reveals the gender biases they claim are built into the fabric of the sciences. This is part of their attempt to transform the research process and thus research outcomes, and the methodological questions they address are indeed central to any feminist critique of the study of religions broadly conceived.

This epistemological turn was anticipated in the 1970s by Mary Daly, who was one of the first to reflect seriously on questions of method in the feminist analysis of religion. As I noted in the above section on feminist theology, Daly argues that, "If God in "his" heaven is a father ruling "his" people, then it is in the "nature" of things and according to divine plan and the order of the universe that society be male-dominated" (Daly 1973: 13). Intertwined with this problem, she poses another question of method: "It would be a mistake to imagine that the new speech of women can be equated simply with women speaking men's words" (Daly 1973: 8). As such, Daly urges women not only to re-think philosophy and theology but also to re-consider "the god Method," which

prevents us from raising questions never asked before and from being illumined by ideas that do not fit into pre-established boxes and forms. The worshippers of Method have an effective way of handling data that does not fit into the Respectable Categories of Questions and Answers. They simply classify it as nondata. (Daly 1973: 11)

Daly thus powerfully connects the theology of God – Father–Legislators with the problem of what she calls "the tyranny of methodolatory" (Daly 1973: 11). This is her attempt to start to think of method in gendered terms.

Feminist scholars of the late 1980s noted that the sciences were structured to make appeals to laws and universals that, once understood, revealed the essence of the real. Some, following Daly, attributed this feature of the sciences "to an earlier, more religiously based belief that the purpose of scholarship was to make evident the word of God as revealed in his creations," and further noted that as "the relation of God to the basic ordering principles of the universe grew increasingly distant, Western scholarship remained committed to the discovery of such principles" (Nicholson 1990: 2). As such, "a [Western] vision of true scholarship" was one "that replicates 'a God's eye view' " (Nicholson 1990: 2), or, one that replicates a "god-trick of seeing everything from nowhere" (Haraway 1991: 189).

The paucity of inquiry into knowledge production is a cultural problem, especially when it seems that knowledge comes from nowhere, when in fact all knowledge comes from somewhere. All knowledge involves a close relationship to theory. It is always informed by theory even if this is not acknowledged (Skeggs 1995). The feminist critiques of the Cartesian Knowing subject to be found in the writings of Freud, Lacan and Derrida are at the same time critiques of "the disembodied pretensions of the masculine knower," and if *écriture feminine* was an attempt to embody a new kind of writing, "stand-point" feminism is an effort to authorize an alternative, scientific gaze (Butler 1990: 327).

Haraway, writing as a feminist scientist, advances what she calls "an argument for situated and embodied knowledges" against "various forms of unlocatable, and so irresponsible, knowledge claims" (Haraway 1991: 191). On the one hand, there are social constructivists, postmodernists and relativists for whom there are no facts, only rhetoric and power, and on the other, there are positivists and empiricists for whom facts are value-free and given directly to experience, waiting patiently to be discovered. Haraway seeks a middle way:

> I think my problem and "our" problem is how to have simultaneously an account of radical historical contingency for all knowledge claims and knowing subjects, a critical practice for recognizing our own "semiotic technologies" for making meanings, and a no-nonsense commitment to faithful accounts of a "real" world. (Haraway 1991: 187)

In this search for a viable model of objectivity, Haraway attends to the metaphor of vision in scientific discourse and seeks to locate it and thereby bestow on it an ethics of knowledge. As such, she argues for the "embodied nature of all vision" as a means of reclaiming the "sensory system that has been used to signify a leap out of the marked body and into a conquering gaze from nowhere" (Haraway 1991: 188). Thus, a feminist objectivity or a feminist empiricism would be what she calls "situated knowledges" (Haraway 1991: 188) through which "we might become answerable for what we learn how to see" (Haraway 1991: 190).

Harding, like Haraway, is interested in the possibility of a feminist empiricism against the conventional idea that legitimate or true knowledge comes from no particular standpoint and represents no specific social grouping. She asks whether there can be value-free knowledge in a society "deeply stratified by gender, race and class" (Harding 1991: 110). Feminist empiricism challenges the norms of conventional science because it undermines the basis upon which the sciences were constructed and implicitly demands recognition that all forms of knowledge have a social basis (Harding 1991: 117). She also argues that feminist standpoint theory shows "how research directed by social values and political agendas can nevertheless produce empirically and theoretically preferable results" (Harding 1991: 119) and that it can "direct the production of less partial and less distorted beliefs" (Harding 1991: 138). But this begs the question: can research engaged in from and on behalf of a particular point of view claim validity as a knowledge claim, or, is it just a species of postmodern relativism? Moreover, when Harding argues that feminist empiricism can correct distortions and eliminate prejudices, does she re-inscribe the twin-notions of pure observation and fact before theory? Is feminist empiricism, then, a kind of super-positivism?

Harding also writes against the crude opposition of objectivism to relativism as the only positions in the debate. For Harding feminist standpoint theory is a solution to the bind:

> A feminist standpoint epistemology requires strengthened standards of objectivity. The standpoint epistemologies call for recognition of a historical or sociological or cultural relativism – but not for a judgemental or epistemological relativism. They call for the acknowledgement that all human beliefs – including our best scientific beliefs – are socially situated, but they also require a critical evaluation to determine which social situations tend to generate the most objective knowledge claims. They require, as judgemental relativism does not, a scientific account of the relationships between historically located belief and maximally objective belief. So they demand what I call strong objectivity in contrast to the weak objectivity of objectivism and its mirror-linked twin, judgemental relativism. (Harding 1991: 142)

According to Harding, then, objectivism is unable to account for the social changes that made science possible and the political and economic contexts that facilitated research into particular questions and problems, because it clings to the naïve view that the story of science is a story of the steady accumulation of knowledge of the world. Relativism is objectionable because it refuses to evaluate that which it seeks to understand, and can as such easily become an excuse for irrationalism or even terror.

A CASE STUDY FROM CHINESE RELIGIOUS CULTURE

In this section, I will augment my theoretical and methodological discussions with a case study drawn from my own research on women and Chinese religion. I take as my starting point Henrietta Moore's *Feminism and Anthropology* (1988), which is not an attempt to overthrow or deconstruct anthropology but rather a means to further a more complex reading and analysis of what anthropology is about and how it might promote greater awareness of gender issues in different parts of the world. As she says, "the justification for doing feminist anthropology has very little to do with the fact that "women are women the world over," and everything to do with the fact that we need to be able to theorize gender relations in a way which ultimately makes a difference" (Moore 1988: 198). My own work – the writing of this chapter and my own research – is likewise from this perspective.

Chinese patriarchal patterns

Writing within the academic tradition of "women and religions," I will begin by identifying, like the "women and world religions" scholars of the 1980s, the patriarchal patterns of "Chinese religion." However, a phenomenological approach is inappropriate, as religion is not a separate or autonomous realm of belief and practice in traditional Chinese culture. "Chinese religion" (for discussion of the problem of writing about Chinese religion in the singular see Feuchtwang 2005) is tightly bound and deeply embedded within culture and society – the supernatural realm is intertwined with the social; the world of the living and the world of the dead interact, and to be considered a socially complete person in Chinese society it is necessary to achieve ancestor status in the world of the dead. As such, I refer generally to "Chinese religious culture" (Shih 2009) and I combine sociological and gendered perspectives to investigate how ancestor-hood is gendered and how the status of women has been constructed in the Chinese socio-religious order (for a more detailed discussion see Shih 2004: ch. 2).

The Chinese world of the dead has long been understood in structural-functionalist terms as a reflection of the social order of the living world, containing ancestors, ghosts and gods, with each spirit category corresponding to a certain group in society. The human counterparts of gods are the imperial bureaucracy, the human equivalents of ancestors are kin, and the human counterparts of ghosts are strangers (Wolf 1974). Therefore, I ask: Which women become ancestors? It is a "sacred" thing in Confucian ancestor-worship that humans have capacity to give life, and therefore, human life is passed down from generation to generation in an unbroken chain. The family, as the custodian of the chain of life, comes to be enshrined as a "sacred" institution (Kelleher 1987) which is patrilineal and composed of those who are related within a male line (their wives as dependents and their daughters as temporary members). For a female to be accorded ancestor status, according to the rules peculiar to the Chinese patrilineal system, she must marry and have sons. The Chinese word for ancestor 祖 was originally written as 且, representing a phallus. Ancestral status enhances the fertility of the family/patrilineal line and ensures its ability to reproduce itself. The practice of patrilineal ancestor worship has had a formative effect on Chinese women's self-perception: to be fully socially acceptable, they have to marry and bear sons.

Which women become ghosts? Those women who for some reason break the link with their kin groups and after death are unidentifiable and neglected. Women who die unmarried or commit suicide (particularly if due to divorce, infertility, or for failing to bear sons) are believed more likely to become ghosts whom nobody is obligated to take care of as ancestors. This inspires Chinese society to view unmarried women, divorced women, infertile women, and sonless widows as socially anomalous, and to keep them at a distance, in an attitude comparable to that held towards ghosts.

Which women are identified as goddesses? In popular Chinese belief, deities are typically depicted in anthropomorphic form and are usually identified as the spirits of former human beings who led unusually meritorious lives. The two most popular female deities are the goddess of Mercy, named Guanyin (also Kuan-yin), and the goddess of the Sea, named Mazu (also Ma-tsu). Both goddesses were once human: Guanyin is identified with the Princess Miaoshan (Dudbridge 1978) and Mazu with Moniang Lin; both successfully reconciled the requests for religious and for filial piety. They resisted marriage and thus retained their purity, but at the cost of angering their fathers. However, this was compensated for by their sacrifice of themselves to save their fathers: Miaoshan offered her arms and eyes to cure her father, while Moniang used her power to save her father from drowning. The worship of Guanyin and Mazu emphasizes a specific feature of Chinese goddesses, in that both have a paradoxical identity: devoid of sexuality they are fertility goddesses; childless they become divine mothers, granting children to their devoted followers. This combination of virginity and motherhood, seen in the iconography of the goddesses, has become the role model for Chinese women. Movements associated with Guanyin or Mazu include the *buluojia* 不落家, who, at the turn of the twentieth century, worked in the silk industry in Guangdong and arranged for their husbands to have sons by concubines so they themselves could retain the status of motherhood while remaining virginal (Topley 1975).

In *A Room of One's Own* (1998 [1929]), Virginia Woolf illustrates how women act in a way that mirrors socially constructed gender patterns rather than acting for themselves. I regard the above system as the mirror model for Chinese women: legitimate womanhood is married mothers of sons; marginal womanhood is women who are either unmarried, or divorced, or infertile, or sonless; and ideal womanhood is women who combine motherhood and virginity.

Of course, I am aware that, for the purpose of this analysis, I have uncritically used existing literature which is inherently androcentric, and have also viewed everything from nowhere, regarding traditional Chinese religious culture as a whole and assuming a relatively high degree of homogeneity and continuity. Moreover, this mirror model and the claim that patriarchy is the structuring grammar of Chinese religious culture are debatable. Historian Patricia Ebrey (2003) argues that critiques of Neo-Confucianism have over-estimated the power of ideas articulated by male philosophers and their influence on women's actual lives. She instead attests that female mentalities were not solely shaped by philosophers, and that social and economic structures could be shaped by female agents. There are also anthropological studies of Chinese culture which draw our attention to other ties than patrilineal bonds; Margery Wolf (1972) focuses on the uterine linkage between mother and children, and Charles Stafford (1995) similarly focuses on the cycle of nurturing between mother and children. Both works demonstrate how women manipulate their positions as mothers to advance their interests and desires. Furthermore, Steven Sangren argues through a close reading of the Miaoshan story, that through her sacrifice "Miaoshan is producing for herself the subject position of filial sacrificer – that is, she is producing for herself the role defined as a prerogative of the filial son" (Sangren 1997:142).

A feminist approach to Chinese religious culture

Anthropology of Chinese religion has tended to analyze ancestor-worship in terms of a structure which determines the characteristics of Chinese gender identity. However, I seek to shift the focus to study a category outside ancestor-worship – maiden-death – that provides a space in which other identities might emerge. I focus on the fact that some dead maidens have attained continuity in the living world through practices that constitute forms of correction to exclusion/pollution/home-lessness. I regard these as "corrective practices" which serve as "texts" that can be read as reflections of and negotiations with traditional gender relations and wider processes of economic and political change. My research is itself a "corrective prac-tice," and thus a "political" activity.

The corrective practice described below refers to a maiden temple in Sam-giap 三峽姑娘廟, Taipei County, Taiwan that involves the "adoption" of goddess worship and the "inversion" of ancestral orthopraxy. The goddess of the Sam-giap maiden temple is addressed as Siann-Ma 聖媽 "the Efficacious Grandmother," who is believed to be effective in responding to the needs of the worshippers. It is said that the goddess was a local unmarried woman from the Ng family named Bhan-niu 尾娘. She had been born in 1813 and died aged 17 in an accidental fire, and some years later, she returned to her family in a dream in which she "demanded to be a maiden." The Ng family granted her "a piece of land" as her "dowry" and built a small stone shrine on the land to house her spirit.

The majority of maiden-spirits who appear to their families demand a "husband" and are provided with a ghost marriage. As a result, they are re-integrated into the patrilineal system. However, the spirit of Bhan-niu wanted to keep her unmarried status. Her dowry was a piece of land upon which a shrine was built to house her. It is normally the case that when a family member falls ill and the illness cannot be cured by a doctor, the cause is attributed to haunting by a neglected family-spirit, in most cases a maiden-spirit. The family normally follows the advice of a Daoist master to open communication with the spirit by burning incense and conducting a calling-spirit-home ritual. It is believed that ash from incense offered to a deceased maiden represents her spirit, and this ash is brought home and placed in a red sachet with a sheet of paper bearing the identity of the deceased maiden.

A temporary altar is then set up to house the maiden-spirit at home. The family begins to offer their deceased maiden food, clothing, and money. It is always said that after the maiden-spirit has been worshipped an ill person soon recovers from his or her illness. When accommodation outside the home is found, the maiden-spirit (i.e., the red sachet) is sent to her new "home," which is usually, though not always, a Buddhist monastery. However, this is very expensive, and poor families can instead deposit their deceased maiden's red sachet "secretly" in a maiden temple, donating some money for incense and candles. At the Sam-giap temple, the maiden-spirits (i.e., the red sachets) are hung up on boards beside the statue of goddess Siann-Ma. Interestingly, the *gap-lo* 合爐 practice in ancestor-worship is re-employed in the Sam-giap maiden temple. Traditionally, the *gap-lo* practice is employed to integrate a newly dead family member into a family lineage. Accord-ingly, every year on the temple's rebuilding anniversary, a *gap-lo* practice is held to adopt newly dead and homeless maiden-spirits. This is done by opening each red sachet and then pouring the individual spirit's ash into the goddess Siann-Ma's incense-burner.

From this case study, we see a succession of cultural and gender transformations. The Sam-giap maiden temple was conceived in the language of ancestral orthopraxy, and yet, at the same time, this language articulates many contradictions. For example, there are the demands for perpetual maidenhood from the daughter and for the gift of dowry land from the father. To be a maiden means to remain single and to resist marriage, while a dowry is usually the gift given by a father to his daughter for her wedding. "Marriage" is, of course, the primary means by which a family excludes its daughters from their lineage, but here it operates to solve the problem of Bhan-niu's homelessness and the threat of pollution to her family.

Critically, this contradictory response not only generates a space for the dead Bhan-niu but later also provides room to accommodate other maiden-spirits where the damage done to them by their exclusion/pollution/homelessness is corrected or healed. Being a maiden, Bhan-niu's spirit lacked any identity and was situated in a socially marginal position. However, by naming her Siann-Ma, the villagers attempt to create a recognizable identity for Bhan-niu's spirit as a grandmother, granting her a legitimate position as a female ancestor. As such, the disordering tension between the polluting maiden-spirits and the living villagers is re-configured as a relationship between a "grandmother" and her "descendants." It is interesting to note that a public relationship with a female "ancestor" is authorized in the Sam-giap maiden temple. Here, we witness the inversion of the private relationship with a male ancestor in patrilineage, and its replacement by a public relationship with a female "ancestor" in a maiden temple.

Furthermore, through the re-employment of the *gap-lo* ritual, the maidens after death have nevertheless attained social continuity with the living world: the adopted maiden spirits are connected to Siann-Ma and the Sam-giap temple worshippers and villagers, not because of particular kinship ties but by virtue of their membership in the temple and community. Here we witness the dissolution of kinship ties, and their replacement with community bonds.

Again, through the re-employment of the *gap-lo* ritual, the maiden-spirits are provided with a "home," not on an ancestral altar of the family house but in the incense- burner of the Sam-giap maiden temple. The fact that the adopted maiden-spirits' ashes are mixed with the temple goddess's ashes implies that the adopted maiden-spirits have some share of the incense offered to the temple-goddess. Whenever the temple-goddess is worshipped the adopted maiden-spirits are worshipped as well. As such, a different sense of community emerges: unlike lineage community with its emphasis on vertical relations of hierarchy, the focus in the Sam-giap temple is on horizontal relations of sharing and equality. Here we witness the dissolution of the hierarchical community of the lineage, and its replacement with an equal community of maidens.

Moreover, the communal worship of maiden-spirits in the Sam-giap maiden temple takes place on the temple rebuilding anniversary, rather than on the day for visiting ancestors or on the day for feeding hungry ghosts. This suggests that the maiden-spirits adopted by the temple are identified neither as ghosts nor as ancestors, but as a new category – "the companions of the maiden goddess."

To conclude, in this case study we see how spirit-adoption in the Sam-giap maiden temple constitutes an attempt to correct the problem of maiden-death. We also witness that the maiden-spirit Bhan-niu, who escaped re-incorporation through ghost marriage, has come to stand outside ancestral orthopraxy, which therefore never manages to constitute itself as a fully complete structure. Its incompleteness allows for new discursive and physical spaces in which a new category that disrupts the opposition of ghosts and ancestors emerges.

CONCLUSION

This chapter departs from the succession of books on "women and world religions" which appeared in the 1980s, and it passes beyond the religious liberal feminist quest for inclusivity. Instead, I have turned to various forms of religious radical feminism which have challenged the very heart of notions of theology, philosophy and law. Women-Church feminists create a women's space within theology; Goddess Religion feminists reinvent a gendered theology/thealogy; ontological French feminists try to develop a new language for philosophy; and epistemological feminists criticize God's view/Law to fashion a new model for science. Interestingly, this journey is circular; despite the various positions adopted by these groups of feminists, their conclusions sooner or later are all directed to the epistemological feminist viewpoint: questions of difference and diversity among men and women, and among women and feminisms, are all articulated from particular socio-religious, economical, political, and historical locations and situations. This is also my position. My research – the case study – demonstrates a particular approach that is both evidence-based and empirical but also passionately concerned and value-saturated; its objective validity lies in the "conversation" of which it is a part. Furthermore, while the work of radical feminists has influenced subsequent research projects, critiques do not always entail a rejection of liberal feminism. Indeed, all these efforts have contributed significantly to an incremental growth in awareness in the academy of the centrality of issues of women, religions and feminisms, and to increased appointments of women to senior academic posts in the study of religions. We can only guess – or dream – as to what exciting new paradigms will emerge in the near future.

Note

I am grateful to Taylor and Francis for granting permission for me to use a portion of my paper "Generation of a new space: a maiden temple in the Chinese religious culture of Taiwan" in the case study of this chapter. The paper was published in 2007 in *Culture and Religion* 8 (1): 89–104, and is available at www.informaworld.com.

Bibliography

Berkowitz, C. A. (2003) Paradise reconsidered: Hélène Cixous and the Bible's other voice, in M. Joy, K. O'Grady, and J. L. Poxon (eds.), *Religion in French Feminist Thought: Critical Perspectives*, London: Routledge, 176–88.

Bock, G. (2002) *Women in European History*, tr. A. Brown, Oxford: Blackwell.

Butler, J. (1990) *Gender Trouble: Feminism and the Subversion of Identity*, New York: Routledge.

Carmody, D. (1988) *Women and World Religions*, Englewood Cliffs: Prentice-Hall.

Carol, C. and Plaskow, J. (eds.) (1979) *Womanspirit Rising*, San Francisco: Harper and Row.

Christ, C. (1979) Why women need the Goddess: phenomenological, psychological, and political reflection' in C. Christ and J. Plaskow (eds.), *Womanspirit Rising*, San Francisco: Harper and Row, 273–87.

Christ, C. (1997) *Rebirth of the Goddess: Finding Meaning in Feminist Spirituality*, New York: Routledge.

Cixous, H. (1976) [1975] The laugh of the Medusa, tr. K Cohen and P. Cohen, *Signs* 1 (4): 875–93.

Cixous, H. (1986) [1975] Sorties, in H. Cixous and C. Clément, tr. B. Wing, *The Newly Born Woman*, Minneapolis: University of Minnesota Press, 63–132.

Crawford, A. E. B. (2002) *Hope in the Holler: A Womanist Theology*, Louisville: Westminster John Knox Press.

Cunneen, S. (1991) *Mother Church: What the Experience of Women Is Teaching Her*, New York: Paulist Press.

Daly, M. (1973) *Beyond God the Father: Toward a Philosophy of Women's Liberation*, London: Women's Press.

Delphy, C. (1987) Protofeminism and antifeminism, in T. Moi (ed.), *French Feminist Thought: A Reader*, Oxford: Basil Blackwell, 80–109.

Dudbridge, G. (1978) *The Legend of Miao-shan*, London: Ithaca.

Ebrey, P. B. (2003) *Women and the Family in Chinese History*, London: Routledge.

Elam, D. (1994) *Feminism and Deconstruction*, London: Routledge.

Feuchtwang, S. (2005) Chinese religions, in L. Woodhead, P. Fletcher, H. Kawanami, and D. Smith (eds.), *Religions in Modern World*, London: Routledge, 86–107.

Fiorenza, S. (1984) *Bread not Stone: The Challenge of Feminist Biblical Interpretation*, Boston: Beacon.

Goldenberg, N. (1979) *Changing of the Gods: Feminism and the End of Traditional Religions*, Boston: Beacon.

Gross, R. M. (1987) Tribal religions: Aboriginal Australia, in A. Sharma (ed.), *Women in World Religions*, Albany: State University of New York Press, 37–58.

Haraway, D. (1991) *Simians, Cyborgs, and Women: The Reinvention of Nature*, London: Free Association Books.

Harding, S. (1991) *Whose Science? Whose Knowledge? Thinking from Women's Lives*, Ithaca: Cornell University Press.

Hodgson, D. L. (2005) *The Church of Women: Gendered Encounters between Maasai and Missionaries*, Bloomington: Indiana University Press.

Hollywood, A. (2003) Mysticism, death and desire in the work of Hélène Cixous and Catherine Clément, in M. Joy, K. O'Grady, and J. L. Poxon (eds.), *Religion in French Feminist Thought: Critical Perspectives*, London: Routledge, 145–61.

Holm, J. and Bowker, J. (eds.) (1994) *Women in Religion*, London: Pinter.

Irigaray, L. (1991) [1984] Sexual difference, in M. Whitford (ed.), tr. S. Hand, *The Irigaray Reader*, Oxford: Blackwell, 165–77.

Irigaray, L. (1991) [1986] Equal or different? in M. Whitford (ed.), tr. D. Macey, *The Irigaray Reader*, Oxford: Blackwell, 30–3.

Irigaray, L. (1993) [1985] Divine women, in *Sexes and Genealogies*, tr. G. C. Gill, New York: Columbia University Press, 57–72.

Irigaray, L. (2002) [1999] *Between East and West: From Singularity to Community*, tr. S. Pluhácek, New York: Columbia University Press.

Joy, M. (2003) Irigaray's eastern explorations, in M. Joy, K. O'Grady, and J. L. Poxon (eds.), *Religion in French Feminist Thought: Critical Perspectives*, London: Routledge, 51–67.

Joy, M., O'Grady, K., and Poxon, J. L. (2002) Introduction: French feminisms and religion, in M. Joy, K. O'Grady, and J. L. Poxon (eds.), *French Feminists on Religion: A Reader*, London: Routledge, 1–12.

Kelleher, T. (1987) Confucianism, in A. Sharma (ed.), *Women in World Religions*, Albany: State University of New York Press, 135–59.

King, U. (2008) *The Search for Spirituality: Our Global Quest for a Spiritual Life*, New York: Bluebridge, 71–84.

King, U. (ed.) (1994) *Feminist Theology from the Third World: A Reader*, New York: Orbis.

Kristeva, J. (1977) [1974] *About Chinese Women*, tr. A. Barrows, New York: Urizen Books.

Kristeva, J. (1982) [1980] *Powers of Horror: An Essay on Abjection*, tr. L. S. Roudiez, New York: Columbia University Press.

Kristeva, J. (1987) Talking about *polylogue*, in T. Moi (ed.), tr. S. Hand, *French Feminist Thought: A Reader,* Oxford: Blackwell, 110–17.

Love, C. (1966) From *Ariadne's Thread (Newsletter of the Ariadne Institute for the* Study *of Myth and Ritual)* 4 (4).

Meñez, H. (1999) *Explorations in Philippine Folklore*, Manila: Ateneo de Manila University Press.

Moi, T. (1999) What is a woman? Sex, gender and the body in feminist theory, in T. Moi, *What Is a Woman? And Other Essays*, New York: Oxford University Press, 3–120.

Moore, H. (1988) *Feminism and Anthropology*, Cambridge: Polity Press.

Nestle, J. (1982) Living with herstory, keynote address for Amazon Autumn's Sixth Annual Lesbian Festival.

Nicholson, L. (ed.) (1990) *Feminism/Postmodernism*, New York: Routledge.

Olson, C. (ed.) (1990) *The Book of the Goddess: Past and Present*, New York: Crossroad.

Pears, A. (2004) *Feminist Christian Encounters: The Methods and Strategies of Feminist Informed Christian Theologies*, Aldershot: Ashgate.

Poxon, J. L. (2003) Corporeality and divinity: Irigaray and the problem of the ideal, in M. Joy, K. O'Grady, and J. L. Poxon (eds.), *Religion in French Feminist Thought*, London: Routledge, 41–50.

Preston, J. (ed.) (1982) *Mother Worship: Theme and Variations*, Chapel Hill: University of North Carolina Press.

Roy, M.-A. (2003) Women and spirituality in the writings of Luce Irigaray, in M. Joy, K. O'Grady, and J. L. Poxon (eds.), tr. S. G. Helfer, *Religion in French Feminist Thought*, London: Routledge, 13–28.

Ruether, R. R. (1979) A religion for women: sources and strategies, *Christianity and Crisis* 39: 307–11.

Ruether, R. R. (1980) Goddess and witches: liberation and countercultural feminism, *The Christian Century* 94: 842–7.

Ruether, R. R. (1983) *Sexism and God-Talk: Towards a Feminist Theology*, London: SCM Press.

Ruether, R. R. (1985) *Women-Church: Theology and Practice of Feminist Liturgical Communities*, London: Harper and Row.

Ruether, R. R. (1998) *Introducing Redemption in Christian Feminism*, Sheffield: Sheffield Academic Press.

Sangren, P. S. (1997) *Myth, Gender, and Subjectivity*, Hsinchu City, Taiwan: National Tsing Hua University.

Schwarz, J. (1984) Foreword, in T. Darty and S. Potter (eds.), *Women-Identified Women*, Palo Alto: Mayfield, ix–x.

Sharma, A. (ed.) (1987) *Women in World Religions*, Albany: State University of New York Press.

Sharma, A. (ed.) (1994) *Today's Woman in World Religions*, New York: SUNY Press.

Sharma, A. and Young, K. (eds.) (1999) *Feminism and World Religions*, Albany: State University of New York Press.

Shih, F.-L. (2004) Dead maidens in Taiwan: breaking down Chinese religious tradition, PhD thesis, School of Oriental and African Studies, University of London.

Shih, F.-L. (2007) Generation of a new space: a maiden temple in the Chinese religious culture of Taiwan, *Culture and Religion* 8 (1): 89–104.

Shih, F.-L. (2009) Re-writing religion: questions of translation, context, and location in the writing of religion in Taiwan, in F.-L. Shih, S. Thompson, and P.-F. Tremlett (eds.), *Re-Writing Culture in Taiwan*, London: Routledge, 15–33.

Skeggs, B. (1995) Introduction, in B. Skeggs (ed.), *Feminist Cultural Theory: Process and Production*, Manchester: Manchester University Press, 1–29.

Spivak, G. C. (1988) *In Other Worlds: Essays in Cultural Politics*. London: Routledge.

Stafford, C. (1995) *The Roads of Chinese Childhood*, Cambridge: Cambridge University Press.

Starhawk (1979) *The Spiral Dance: A Rebirth of the Ancient Religion of the Great Goddess*, New York: Harper and Row.

Starhawk (1982) *Dreaming the Dark: Magic, Sex, and Politics*, Boston: Beacon.

Starhawk (1987) *Truth or Dare: Encounters with Power, Authority, and Mystery*, San Francisco: Harper and Row.

Thorne, H. (2000) *Journey to Priesthood: An In-depth Study of the First Women Priests in the Church of England*, Bristol: Centre for Comparative Studies in Religion and Gender.

Topley, M. (1975) Marriage resistance in rural Kwangtung, in M. Wolf and R. Witke (eds.), *Women in Chinese Society*, Stanford: Stanford University Press, 67–88.

Trebbi, D. (1990) Women-Church: Catholic women produce an alternative spirituality, in T. Robbins and D. Anthony (eds.), *In Gods We Trust: New Patterns of Religious Pluralism in America*, New Brunswick: Transaction, 347–51.

Tremlett, P.-F. (2007) The ethics of suspicion in the study of religions, *DISKUS*, 8, www.basr.ac.uk/diskus/diskus8/Tremlett.htm.

Williams, D. (1994) Womanist theology: black women's voices, in U. King (ed.), *Feminist Theology from the Third World: A Reader*, New York: Orbis, 77–86.

Wolf, A. (1974) Gods, ghosts, and ancestors, in A. Wolf (ed.), *Religion and Ritual in Chinese Society*, Stanford: Stanford University Press, 131–82.

Wolf, M. (1972) *Women and the Family in Rural Taiwan*, Stanford: Stanford University Press.

Woolf, V. (1998) [1929] *A Room of One's Own/Three Guineas*, Oxford and New York: Oxford University Press.

Young, K. (1987) Introduction, in A. Sharma (ed.), *Women in World Religions*, Albany: State University of New York Press, 1–36.

Part IV
Institutionalization: Old and New Forms

11

New Research on Megachurches
Non-denominationalism and Sectarianism

STEPHEN ELLINGSON

INTRODUCTION

The emergence and rapid growth of megachurches in North America and Asia represent one of the most significant changes to Christianity in the past twenty to thirty years. A megachurch is customarily defined as a Protestant church that has at least 2,000 weekly attendees. The majority self-identify as conservative and often combine orthodox evangelical theology with practical, therapeutic religious messages. Many employ the latest in audio-visual technology in their worship services, and offer attendees a wide range of services and religious events (from day care to fitness classes to bible studies). In addition, many megachurches draw heavily on the marketing strategies and entrepreneurialism of the contemporary marketplace to effectively sell Christianity in a mall-like setting (replete with food court) and sell megachurch products (for example, sermon series, music, Sunday school curricula, or church growth consulting services) to other churches or church bodies (see Twitchell 2004: 47–108; Sargeant 2000: 106–62; Thumma and Travis 2007: 118–34 offer a more positive interpretation of megachurch entrepreneurialism). In short, megachurches are not only very large churches that experiment with tradition, liturgy and doctrine, but also draw on popular culture and a consumerist logic in order to attract an audience more familiar with rock and roll, shopping malls, and self-help culture than with traditional church liturgies, hymns, or symbols.

Megachurches are springing up in the suburbs and exurbs of the Sunbelt and Pacific Coast states and in major urban areas in South Korea and Southeast Asia. Megachurches may occupy campuses that cover dozens of acres and average about 4,000 weekly attendance; in Asia megachurches occupy denser but smaller campuses and they tend to be far larger (Hong 2000). In the United States., the median size of the main sanctuary is just over 1,000, however, a small percentage (5 percent) can seat 3,000 or more. In the United States, the number of megachurches has grown from approximately 50 in 1970 to over 1,200 in 2005 and the median five-year growth rates range from 33 percent for churches founded before 1945 to 250 percent for churches founded between 1995 and 2005 (Thumma and Travis 2007: 25; Goh 1999 and Tong 2008 report similar growth rates for megachurches in Singapore).

Despite the rapid proliferation of megachurches and their high visibility in the press, research on this phenomenon is still in its infancy. Scott Thumma, at Hartford Seminary, conducted national surveys of megachurch leaders in 2000 and 2005. Two other national surveys, the 2000 and 2005 Faith Communities Today and the 2001 United States Congregational Life Survey, also contain information about megachurches. Several other scholars have written on megachurches in their work to describe and explain "seeker" and "new paradigm" churches (Sargeant 2000; Miller 1999). Although much of the existing sociological research is descriptive in nature, scholars are beginning to develop explanations for the emergence, growth, and success of megachurches.

In particular, megachurches offer sociologists of religion an opportunity to expand and refine the general thesis on the restructuring of American religion; assess the claims of competing theories of religious change and innovation; and revisit church–sect theory. Megachurches reflect the move towards non-denominationalism in American religion and their growing influence across American Protestantism may presage a more widespread shift in the locus of religious authority and identity away from historic denominational traditions towards a more evangelical and generic Christianity.

As noted above, an important issue for scholars of contemporary religion is to explain the emergence and growth of megachurches. Historically, church–sect theory has been a useful tool for sociologists of religion to develop such explanations. Church–sect theory hinges on the key idea that religions exist in greater or lesser degrees of tension with the secular world and that it is the institutional move to increase or decrease tension that brings about religious conflict, innovation, and change. Historically, scholars have emphasized how sects, which exist in a heightened degree of tension with the world, create new religious forms and organizations by breaking away from world-accommodating churches in an effort to purify religion and then how sects gradually become churches as they age and struggle to maintain their tension with or distance from the surrounding culture (for example, Wilson 1959; Johnson 1957, 1963, 1971). Recently, scholars have turned to church–sect theory to explain the emergence of revitalization movements in Roman Catholicism and Methodism and to explain the growth of several post- or non-denominational religious bodies (Finke and Wittberg 2000; Finke and Stark 2001; McKinney and Finke 2002; Miller 1999). Megachurches challenge the utility of church–sect theory insofar as they are growing not by distancing themselves from the secular world but by pragmatically embracing it and mimicking the infotainment, consumerist, MTV culture of the American middle class, and in doing so they demonstrate how Christianity is relevant to those who live in a post-denominational world.

HISTORY, DEMOGRAPHICS, AND CULTURE OF MEGACHURCHES

Contemporary megachurches emerged in the 1970s and while many are affiliated with evangelical, charismatic or conservative denominations, the majority are functionally non-denominational. In addition, over one-third are formally non-denominational (Thumma and Travis 2007, 27). Megachurches tend to combine orthodox theological orientations with the therapeutic personalism that marks Baby-Boomer religiosity (Roof 1999; Wuthnow 1998). Megachurches often are described as innovators in church architecture and worship practices. The prototypical mega-church – Willow Creek Community Church in Illinois – looks more like a corporate office park or community college than a church. It seats several thousand in its theater-style worship space, minimizes overt displays of Christian symbols (for example, there is no cross in the sanctuary), and offers a wide-range of services and activities (for example, occupational and age-graded small groups, bookstores, cafes).

Megachurches have their theological and organizational roots in the revivalistic movements and the auditorium churches of the late nineteenth and early twentieth centuries (Loveland and Wheeler 2003). However, today's megachurches differ from their historic predecessors in terms of growth rate, building size, range of programs, and marketing know-how. Several scholars (Thumma and Travis 2007; Loveland and Wheeler 2003; Chaves 2006) date the emergence of contemporary megachurches to the 1970s when the number of such churches tripled (from 50 in 1970 to 150 in 1980). The number of megachurches climbed to 600 by 2000 and 1,210 by 2005 (Thumma and Travis 2007: 7). Forty-Four percent of megachurches have been founded since 1975, and they show more rapid growth rates than older churches. Moreover, most of the megachurches started in earlier decades did not reach megachurch size until the 1970s (Thumma and Travis 2007: 24). Roughly three-quarters of megachurches have experienced at least a 20 percent growth rate since 2000 and the average growth rate between 2000 and 2005 is 57 percent. Nearly 54 percent of megachurches have a weekly attendance of between 2,000 and 2,999 persons, and the average median attendance in 2005 was 3,585. However, only 4 percent have 10,000 or more weekly attendees (Thumma and Travis 2007: 8). The majority of megachurches are located in the suburbs of the Sunbelt states. Karnes et al. (2007) report on the spatial distribution of megachurches in the nine states with largest number of megachurches. They find megachurches concentrated in metropolitan areas with highly educated, relatively wealthy, young (adults with young families) and professional populations which is not surprising since mega-churches need the population and infrastructure of metro areas and the financial and human resources of educated middle-class attendees to succeed.

About two-thirds of megachurches are formally affiliated with a denomination and the other third are explicitly non-denominational. Most are affiliated with evangelical and conservative Protestant denominations. Only 11 percent of mega-churches are affiliated with one of the mainline denominations and like most of the other megachurches, the ties to the denomination are attenuated and often inten-tionally minimized among self-indentified seeker churches to avoid negative con-notations a denominational label may carry among a church's targeted audience (Thumma and Petersen 2003: 107; Sargeant 2000: 59; Thumma and Travis 2007). This move towards functional and formal non-denominationalism reflects the long-standing decline in the salience of denominational identity and traditions for many churchgoers and churches.

In order to capitalize on the declining interest or commitment to particular denominational traditions and thus to effectively reach groups with different religious capital and interests, many megachurches engage in a practice of "structured diversity" (Thumma and Travis 2007: 141–2). This refers to the effort by churches to meet the interests and needs of different sub-populations by offering multiple worship services in different formats or styles, and by providing a wide variety of fellowship groups that appeal to different age groups, lifestyle and interest cohorts. Thus it is common for megachurches to hold several services in a given week – an early Sunday morning traditional service for older adults; a praise service mid-morning on Sundays; a mid-week or Sunday evening rock service for teens and young adults and a Saturday evening jazz service.

Over 80 percent of megachurches are predominantly Caucasian, but roughly 10 percent of megachurches are predominately African-American, 2 percent are primarily Hispanic and another 2 percent are Asian (Thumma and Travis 2007: 28) In a national study of black churches, Tamelyn Tucker-Worgs (2001) identified 66 African-American megachurches. Like their white counterparts, the majority of African-American megachurches are located in the Sunbelt states, and average fewer than 4,000 weekly attendees. However there are several notable differences. Most black megachurches are in urban areas rather than suburbs; most attained mega-church size slightly later (after the 1980s), and 46 percent are Baptist. In addition, 60 percent of African-American megachurches have established separate 501C3 community development corporations. Unlike the predominately white mega-churches that have substantial social ministries (for example, programs to help the homeless, at-risk youth) the community development corporations at black mega-churches may be home to a credit union, be engaged in building affordable and transitional housing, run health clinics or job training programs, and provide a wide array of other social services (Tucker-Worgs 2001: 191–5). In addition, many churches have an explicit Afro-centric orientation in which ministers teach and preach from the perspective of black theology and in which art and symbols express an African-centered worldview (for example, murals with a black Jesus or heroes within African-American history).

Thumma and Travis (2007) describe four types of megachurches that vary in terms of worship styles, use of mass media, architecture, denominational ties, and constituencies. Thirty percent of megachurches fall into their category of Old Line/ Program-based churches. Many of these churches are among the oldest of all mega-churches and often are located in downtown or first-ring suburbs. Most are officially tied to a denomination and their theology, worship practices, programs, and organizational structure reflect their denominational backgrounds. This type of mega-church tends to self-identify as traditional and it is more likely to use formal liturgies, organ and choirs in its worship.

Another 30 percent of megachurches are seeker churches. These churches are among the most innovative and unconventional among the entire population of megachurches. Seeker churches have a strong, explicit mission to evangelize or reach the "unchurched" and are willing to experiment with worship styles, architecture, and religious ideas in order to make Christianity appealing and authentic to a boomer and post-boomer population alienated or indifferent to organized religion. Sargeant, who has written a masterful study of seeker churches with Willow Creek Community Church at the center of his analysis, notes that Willow Creek's auditorium, rituals and theologies reflect the organization's concern with "creating and maintaining a safe environment for seekers, an environment that is not unlike other places in the secular world" (2000: 61). In practice this means the absence of Christian symbols, a campus that looks like a "carefully maintained and slightly antiseptic professional buildings of suburban, corporate American," with the "conveniences of a shopping mall such as an atrium dining area and food court, as well as 'state of the art' facilities of a hotel conference center" (Sargeant 2000: 61; Hoover, 2000). It also means that Willow Creek and other seeker churches tend to be publicly non-denominational (even if they are formally affiliated with a denomination), eschew tradition, and intentionally minimize the distance between the outside world and the church by showing how Christianity is relevant and applicable to the world of middle-class suburbanites (Sargeant 2000: 58–73; also Thumma and Travis 2007: 39–40). More specifically, many Seeker megachurches tend to emphasize the personalistic aspects of faith – a believer's personal relationship with Jesus and the ways in which faith can help individuals address numerous domestic or personal issues (Sargeant 2000: 67) in order to demonstrate that Christianity is relevant.

Twenty-five percent of megachurches are Charismatic and/or pastor-focused. While many of these megachurches fall within the Pentecostal or charismatic theological tradition, they also emphasize the personal charisma of its senior minister and are the most likely group of churches to sponsor television ministries. They are among the most ethnically and racially diverse of all megachurches.

Finally, the newest set of megachurches, many founded since 1990, are New Wave or Re-envisioned churches. Many of these churches have multiple sites and are led by teams of pastors. They tend to reject the seeker church model and have returned to traditional symbols, language, and practices. For example, megachurches from the Vineyard Fellowship and Calvary Chapel, also known as "new paradigm churches" practice "postmodern primitivism" which is a return to ancient Christian symbols, language, and rituals, the minimization of doctrine, and an attempt to rediscover and follow the original scriptural narratives that guided the early church (Miller 1999). While such churches may embrace orthodox theology they also rely on cutting-edge audio-visual technology in their worship services, and tend to attract younger (under age 35) constituency (Thumma and Travis 2007: 40–1).

Megachurches are also on the rise throughout Asia. Hong (2000) notes that as the number of Protestants has grown in South Korea so to have the number of megachurches. He reports that in 1995 there were fifteen megachurches in the country. They ranged in size from 12,000 to 230,000 weekly attendees with eight averaging at least 20,000 attendees per week. He argues that there are three types of Korean megachurches; each emerged in a particular time period and each serves a specific audience. "Traditional" megachurches appeared at the end of World War II. They are aligned with the Presbyterian Church and emphasize orthodox doctrine and a pietistic faith. "Middle-class" megachurches emerged during the late 1970s with the development of a larger Korean middle class. Attendees tend to have higher incomes and more education than attendees of the other types of megachurches and middle-class megachurches tend to offer worship services and programs that emphasize an intellectualized faith. "Charismatic" megachurches represent the newest and most numerous types. They emerged during the explosive period of urbanization in the late 1980s and 1990s, and cater to a less educated and less wealthy population. As the name suggests these megachurches emphasize an emotive and experiential religiosity and services that celebrate manifestations of the gifts of the Holy Spirit (such as healing and speaking in tongues). Charismatic megachurches tend have stronger evangelism programs and a corresponding higher percentage of new converts among attendees than the other two types of megachurches.

Charismatic megachurches also have emerged in Singapore among Chinese Christians. Goh (1999) examines three such megachurches and finds that such churches combine the emotive and experiential aspects of Pentacostalism with the teachings and language of fundamentalism. Thus some of Singapore's megachurches promulgate an apocalyptic worldview and the separation of believers from unbelievers. These churches also are very authoritarian insofar as they demand attendees and members adhere to purity codes, demonstrate allegiance to church teachings, and participate in cell groups. In her case study of City Harvest Church, Joy Kooi-Chin Tong shows how the church wields "technologies of the self" to train and discipline attendees in order to both help individuals overcome the loss of identity and sense of belonging created by modernization, but also to ensure that the strict and hierarchical nature of the church is maintained:

> For instances, the practice of note-taking, as if the attendees "were going to sit an exam on this sermon," has cultivated a "teachable and expectant spirit" toward preaching. The requirement for its members to commit themselves to the church's teachings, by attending equipping class systematically, has helped shape people's views on certain issues, such as constant emphasis on the reward of offering has compelled the members to give lavishly; and severe teachings on gossiping and slandering has prohibited members from conversations related to the negative aspects or feelings toward church leaders. Also, leaders' supervision and peer pressures lead to conformity. From the "proper" way of worship (when to pray or raise hand), "proper" timing of responding to the sermons (i.e. the unified "yeah" response after the preacher has said something interesting or challenging), "proper" individual commitments such as tithe or even their future plans (i.e. the church encourages the youth to join the Bible Training Center before starting their first job), multiple technologies have in fact helped to train a certain type of Christian. Besides, disciplinary actions, taken by leaders to punish uncooperative attitude, are another effective way of regulating its huge membership. According to several of my informants, one of them was censured for her disagreement with the church's miraculous healing; another over her unwillingness to participate in the church building project. (Tong 2008: 9)

Finally, Asian megachurches share many of the common architectural and cultural features of their American counterparts. Worship services are held in large theater-like spaces and rely on similar kinds of audio-visual technologies. Church buildings may include cafes, bookstores, and meeting spaces for small groups. And like Willow Creek or one of the Vineyard megachurches, many Asian megachurches try to present the gospel in ways that resonate with the lifeworld experiences and cultural tastes of their middle and lower middle-class attendees so that religion becomes a resource to construct a resilient self or identity in a rapidly changing social world (Tong 2008; Goh 1999).

EXPLAINING THE EMERGENCE, GROWTH, AND SUCCESS OF MEGACHURCHES

Why did megachurches emerge in the late twentieth century and how can we account for their remarkable growth and success? Although much of the published work on megachurches is descriptive, a nascent sociological answer is emerging in the literature. The most common explanation draws on cultural and market theories of religious change. This type of explanation claims that growth is based on the ability of megachurch leaders to provide religious products that articulate with the religious interests and tastes of religious consumers. A second and related explanation draws on church–sect theory and stresses that megachurch growth is fueled by the ways in which they create a religious culture that is in clear tension with secular society. A third line of explanation emphasizes organizational dynamics. These are complementary rather than competing explanations, and still being developed by megachurch scholars. Below I review each explanation and discuss how existing theories of religious change can help us understand the growth of the megachurch.

Cultural/market explanations start from the key findings of work examining the restructuring of American religion. Namely, they claim that the decline of mainline Protestantism and concomitant rise of evangelicalism stems in part from changes in the religious interests and tastes of baby boomers, and the ability of megachurches to offer new religious products that fit the religious sensibilities of boomers and succeeding generations. Among these changes are the enshrinement of religious choice as an important value; the decline of denominational brand loyalty; the development of a therapeutic religious ethos; and anti-institutionalism. The first change is important because it signals the rise of a consumerist orientation to religion and the weakening of denominational brand loyalty. As religion became an achieved rather than ascribed identity, baby boomers were free to shop for a church (or a religious experience) that met their particular interests. The second change led to a new inward focus as religious consumers came to expect religion to be a tool in the individual's quest to develop the self. Finally, the strong anti-institutional bias appeals to the baby boomers' suspicion of organized religion with its hierarchical authority and inherited traditions (Roof and McKinney 1987; Miller 1999; Roof 1999; Sargeant 2000).

Loveland and Wheeler note that as evangelicalism grew in numbers, financial resources, and legitimacy entrepreneurs began to create a new religious culture that tapped into the anti-institutionalism, consumerist and therapeutic values of baby-boomers (2003: 114–24). They show how church growth experts adopted a marketing perspective to realize their goals of converting the unchurched and unsaved. These leaders argued that boomers live in a world of corporations and shopping malls and in order to attract boomers, church growth experts contended that churches needed to mimic the everyday world of the unchurched. Loveland and Wheeler (2003) discuss how Bill Hybels, the innovative pastor who founded Willow Creek Community Church, tried to make his church resonate with the experiences of his middle-class audience so that attending church would be meaningful.

In his view, the unchurched were as alienated by the architecture of the "traditional church" as by its worship services. He insisted that the physical facilities of Willow Creek should be such as to first win the respect of "unchurched Harry," and then make him feel comfortable and relaxed and therefore receptive to the seeker servicer. As a tour guide at Willow Creek explained, Hybels believed that a church should fit people's "life experience" and that "you shouldn't go through cultural shock when you go to church." In developing his architectural philosophy, Hybels noted the kind of secular buildings "unchurched Harry" found attractive– hotels, amusement parks, and corporate headquarters– and tried to make Willow Creek look and operate like them. He asserted that the Willow Creek buildings were purposely designed to look like a corporate headquarters. "What we want him [unchurched Harry] to do is just say, 'I was just at corporate headquarters for IBM in Atlanta Wednesday, and now I come to church here and it's basically the same'" (Loveland and Wheeler 2003: 123).

Twitchell (2004) and Tong (2008) link the success of megachurches to their deliberate efforts to commodify and brand a particular type of religious experience and identity. Twitchell argues that the population of megachurches is rapidly expanding because their product – a mix of "edutainment," FM type music, the mall or village commons, and "the therapeutic sensation of redemption, of epiphany, the promise of a new start, forgiveness – closely mirrors the consumer culture of the American, suburban middle class" (2004: 76). The genius of the megachurch, he argues, is that is it able to match its practices and products with the entertainment system (in terms of megachurch music, use of video screens and other technology), the mall (food courts and large parking lots), and several other lifeworld arenas of its attendees (for example, child care, fitness clubs), so that attendees are able to navigate seamlessly between the worlds of work, family, leisure, and religion (2004: 85–8). In effect, he makes a strong argument that megachurch success is based on a form of cultural isomorphism. He also argues that growth itself and size, two important values of the capitalist system, help fuel the expansion of megachurches as church shoppers come to define size and growth as markers of "redemptive success." Hong makes a similar claim about Korean megachurches, noting that Korean culture equates bigness with success, beauty, or greatness (2000: 109).

Tong makes a similar argument about Harvest City Church in Singapore, but grounds her explanation in Ritzer's concept of McDonaldization. A megachurch's success is driven in part by the ability of its leaders to routinize and standardize the ritual, educational, and leadership processes, and in part by developing a unique religious identity for a young audience. Tong argues that the church is intentionally "building an 'ultra-modern, energetic, and upwardly mobile' image, one that emphasizes the visible signs of wealth and success in a capitalist world" (2008: 10–11). Echoing Weber's notion of "elective affinity" from his discussion of the religions of different class and status groups, Tong notes that the megachurch offers a "brand – a lifestyle, a set of values, tastes, and symbols" – that validate the values of most of its middle-class attendees (an elective affinity argument refers to the degree to which the religious interests, needs, or questions of some group are met by or articulate with the goods and services offered by a religion. (Weber 1968 [1946]: 62–3, 284–5; Tong 2008: 11). In particular she argues that City Harvest Church relies on the gospel of wealth in which worldly success is interpreted as a sign of God's blessing, and thus fits neatly with the worldview and experiences of a rising middle class in which material accumulation is highly valued (2008: 12). At the same time, the church emphasizes the value of freedom and encourages attendees that as Christians they are free from the limits imposed by traditions, customs, and legalisms. Christian freedom or being "true to yourself," in the idiom of the church, is commonly framed in terms of consumption, lifestyle and personal appearance as Tong summarizes:

> In a series of sermons and articles regarding the freedom that Christians, Kong [the senior pastor] said, "What music do you listen to? What clothes can you wear? What art may you appreciate, what kind of car or house can you have ... these are not issues of right or wrong, sin or righteousness. They are simply matters of personal preference!" This is undoubtedly a liberating and comforting message for people in a consumer society, in which – individuals are encouraged to choose and display goods where the furnishings, house, car, clothing, the body or leisure pursuits to make their personal statement (Lyon 2000: 82). Nevertheless, it does seems that through teachings like this, Kong has in fact unwittingly given the consumer culture is spiritual endorsement on the one hand and set the trend of "liberal and trendy" Christianity on the other. (Tong 2008: 13)

In short, the megachurch succeeds because it effectively creates a religious identity and lifestyle that is consonant with the emergent middle-class identity and lifestyle of Singapore's young and upwardly mobile population.

The goal of constructing new religious identities in response of rapid social change also is the cornerstone of Goh's (1999) explanation for megachurch emergence and growth in Singapore. He combines the classic modernization argument with a Weberian elective affinity argument. Urbanization and industrialization in Singapore have led to the loss of identity and belonging among the lower middle class, while their rising economic expectations from their gains in education are frustrated. As a result the lower middle class find themselves in a situation of existential doubt or angst, much like Weber's Calvinists. Singapore's megachurches that combine Pentecostal worship, fundamentalist theology, and the tight integration into small fellowship groups provide members with a new transcendent identity and recurring transient religious experiences that help individuals resolve their existential doubt and find their place in a rapidly changing social world. Moreover, Goh notes that the three megachurches he studied have many of the characteristics of strict churches and rely on authoritarianism to discipline and structure religious life for members.

Explanations based on the tight cultural articulation between megachurch programs and the interests, experiences, and values of their audiences also characterize much of the work on American megachurches. Thumma and Travis (2007: 14–17) note that megachurches are appealing and successful because they make religion take place in a familiar institutional form (the shopping mall or movie theater), with familiar music (contemporary pop rock), and organize church "in a way that allows [individuals] choice and yet asks them to become serious in their commitments" (2007: 15). Similarly Sargeant and Miller in their studies of seeker and new paradigm churches respectively identify the ways in which megachurch leaders craft rituals and programs to resonate with boomer religious sensibilities. Sargeant shows how seeker churches intentionally minimize denominational worship traditions because their audiences desire a more authentic experience of the sacred that are obstructed by the older formal liturgies and rituals of mainline Protestantism. He also shows how leaders of megachurches craft their theological messages that emphasize the subjective and pragmatic benefits of belief for seekers looking to develop the self, find help coping with family conflict, or deal with the pressures of corporate work (Sargeant 2000: 64–83). Miller (1999) also argues that new paradigm churches are successful because they eschew the kinds of church traditions (for example, Bach chorales) that their audiences consider irrelevant to contemporary life and inauthentic. Such churches also are successful because they are organized non-hierarchically and non-bureaucratically which appeals to baby-boomers' anti-institutionalism. In short, these researchers rely on a Weberian elective affinity argument. Megachurches offer people access to the sacred in ways that conform to their artistic, cultural, and religious tastes and provide better answers to their audiences pressing existential questions about the self, morality, family, and/or work.

The second type of explanation draws on church–sect theory, although only Miller uses this theory explicitly. Church–sect theory posits that congregations grow when they embody the characteristics of sectarian groups, especially by making members separate themselves from the moral corruption of the outside world, and by offering intense experiences and exclusive religious benefits to members. However, Miller argues that new paradigm churches (which include Vineyard and Calvary Chapel church bodies, both of which have significant numbers of megachurches) are not "cultural separatists" (that is, churches that embrace rather than reject popular culture) and use features of contemporary culture to their own purposes (1997: 154). He combines the cultural/market approach with ideas from church–sect theory to develop a complex explanation for change. He argues that new paradigm church are growing in part because they provide a superior religious product – namely a profound experience of the transcendent –and in part because they use but do not capitulate to dominant secular values like most sects. In summary he writes:

> New paradigm churches eliminated many of the inefficiencies of bureaucratized religion by an appeal to the first-century model of Christianity; this "purged" form of religion corresponded to the countercultural worldview of baby boomers, who rejected institutionalized religion; with their bureaucratically lean, lay-oriented organizational structure, new paradigm churches offered a style of worship that was attractive to people alienated from establishment religion because it was in their own idiom ... The key point is that new paradigm churches appropriated elements of contemporary culture without accommodating to all its values. (1997: 183–4)

Montgomery's (1996) formal theory about religious economies follows Miller's argument about a more lenient form of sectarianism. He suggests that megachurches may be growing due to changes in the class status of their members. He argues that as incomes rise and individuals rise into the middle class they prefer less "strict" churches and thus act to "secularize" their denomination or religious body. Megachurches tend to cater to a middle-class constituency, but their evangelical identity pushes them towards a significant degree of tension with the secular world (especially in regards to personal morality or purity issues), and thus it seems plausible to argue that megachurches represent a more secular form of sectarianism or what Miller calls "postmodern" sectarianism (Miller 1999: 154).

Stark and Iannaccone's (1997) work on the Jehovah's Witnesses offers some insightful propositions about the growth of sectarian movements that may be usefully applied to megachurches. One important factor that encourages growth is ensuring continuity with conventional faiths of a culture but maintaining a moderate degree of tension with society. Megachurches do this by crafting theological messages and worship rituals that dovetail with the interests and questions of their audiences while still demonstrating that participation in the megachurch marks one as fundamentally different from those outside the church. Conversely, the study by Goh (1999) suggests that more sectarian-like may thrive in Asia. The current research does not explain why more moderate sectarianism works in the United States and a stricter form works well in Asia, but future research could address this lacuna by identifying the social (especially class), cultural, and organizational factors that produce the different forms of sectarianism.

Second, Stark and Iannaccone note that sects "will grow to the extent that they can generate a highly motivated, volunteer religious labor force, including many willing to proselytize" (1997: 147). Thumma and Travis found that megachurches are far more adept than mainline churches at making evangelism by members a high priority, although they note that pastors' role in evangelism may be more important (2007: 156–62). Third, according to Stark and Iannaccone, sectarian movements grow because they maintain fertility levels that offset member mortality. Although there is little data on the fertility and mortality rates of megachurch members, the high proportion of young adults and young adults with families suggests that demographics may be important in megachurch growth, especially to the extent that megachurches are able to successfully socialize their young.

Finally, some scholars focus on the organizational structures and dynamics of megachurches and how they influence growth. Thumma and Travis (2007) claimed that megachurch success can be attributed, in part, to the intentional efforts of church leaders and a significant percentage of members to engage in recruitment, and to develop programs that effectively incorporate people into the life of a congregation. They also note that worship is an important factor in megachurch growth. The key here is not just to provide exciting, joyful, and informal worship in which attendees experience the sacred, but also the church's willingness to change worship in order to stay relevant and/or meet the interests of important subpopulations.

Chaves (2006) takes a different organizational approach and looks at the population of megachurches to explain why they emerged. In a creative and insightful article he begins by raising the question: why have the number of very large churches increased and why have the number of people who attend very large churches increased since 1970? He reviews and then dismisses many of the common explanations for megachurch emergence and growth. First, megachurches are not growing because they are tapping into a market of people who are unchurched as much as they attract people who are already members of small churches. Second, the idea that megachurches grow because they are located in new suburbs seems intuitively correct, yet Chaves points out that the trend lines for suburbanization and megachurch emergence and growth do not match up. There was no real increase in suburbanization in the 1970s just as megachurches emerged. Third, he briefly shows that the innovations associated with megachurches are not very novel as many of their worship, fellowship, and organizational practices were implemented in large churches of the late nineteenth and early twentieth centuries. Fourth, he notes that the cultural argument that megachurches are more responsive to the changed religiosity and values of baby boomers is plausible and perhaps correct but there is no strong evidence to show that boomers and post-boomers are systematically different than older generations (Dillon and Wink's (2007) make a strong case for this claim). In the end, Chaves offers a novel economistic explanation. He argues that churches, like symphonic orchestras or theaters, are organizations that cannot reduce their costs by becoming more efficient. He notes that since 1970 church donations and incomes have failed to keep pace with rising costs across denominations. As a result many small churches have been forced to reduce programs and the quality of programs which in turn makes them less appealing and viable. He speculates that as quality has decreased among small churches, members have left and joined larger churches.

Chaves' explanation is parsimonious and intriguing yet he smuggles in a cultural explanation insofar as the mechanism for the change is the apparent loss of meaning in worship, programs, or fellowship that accompanies congregational decline. Similarly, church–sect explanations assume that sectarian religion is successful because it is more meaningful than non-sectarian religions, even as such explanations emphasize other organizational processes. Cultural/market explanations are helpful because they force us to consider how religion's most important characteristic, its system of meaning, influences growth and success. However, cultural/market explanations need to combine demand and supply side perspectives in order to provide a more complete and compelling account of megachurch development.

As suggested by this review, the field currently lacks an integrated theory to explain the rise and development of megachurches. While it is beyond the scope of this essay to develop such a theory, Thumma and Travis (2007) and Chaves (2006) urge scholars to develop explanations that combine multiple variables (for example, culture, social context and history, organizational structures and processes such as isomorphism). In particular, I suggest that a multi-causal approach will allow us to account for the complexities of church growth and success. Such an explanation should examine the independent effects of endogenous (for example, management styles and congregational cultures) and exogenous factor, such as geographic shifts in populations and societal changes in religiosity, and then look at the relationship between internal megachurch dynamics and external religious trends and pressures. Such an approach, for example, might entail studying how internal processes such as the ways in which megachurch leaders contextualize theological messages and worship services are shaped by the models provided by other megachurches or congregations in local and religious networks; how megachurch leaders develop and market new products based on perceived shifts in religiosity (for example, the desire to return to ancient traditions among younger attendees); or how megachurches effectively tap into the interpersonal networks of attendees to expand their potential audiences and thus strive to explain how and why megachurches are able to control local religious markets.

MEGACHURCHES AND THE PULL TOWARD
NON-DENOMINATIONALISM AND SECTARIANISM

It appears that the emergence and institutionalization of the megachurch has initiated a new phase in the restructuring of American Protestantism. Thumma and
Peterson claim that "megachurches are defining what Protestant America looks like
for the foreseeable future" (2007: 18). Although this picture is still developing,
several features of the new religious reality are taking shape. First, megachurches
reflect the continued growth of evangelicalism in terms of numbers and market
share. Second, megachurches may be reshaping the denominational system in the
United States both by intensifying the push towards non-denominationalism and by
creating new, decentralized quasi-denominations that may take on some of the
functions of older denominations without the costs or negative image of the older,
hierarchical denominational bodies. Third, they may be redefining Protestant religious culture as increasing numbers of congregations, across denominations adopt
the worship practices, educational materials, and theological ideas employed by
successful megachurches.

Thumma and Peterson note that megachurches have become quasi-denominations as they have taken on many of the functions older denominations once held
(2007: 129–32). Some megachurches have established national or international
networks of congregations such as the Willow Creek Association which has grown
to roughly 12,000 congregations since 1992 (www.willowcreek.com/AboutUs/),
while others have a more local emphasis. At the hub of the network the megachurch
provides ministers and church leaders with a wide variety of resources such as bible
study/small group guides and Sunday school curricula, worship music, and seminars
or conferences about evangelism and leadership. Ellingson (2007) shows how
nationally-known megachurches provide resources, models for ministry, and inspiration for several of the Lutheran churches he studied. In addition, megachurches
increasingly are taking on the education of future leaders, a role once the exclusive
domain of national denominational bodies. Thumma and Peterson note that 30
percent of megachurches have their own training and education institutions and
more partner with established seminaries to offer classes or serve as teaching
churches for seminary students, thus extending megachurches' ideas about evangelism, church growth, theology and worship to a wider audience than in their pews
(2007: 131).

At the local level, megachurches also exercise significant power. By their very size
and the real or imagined threat of "stealing members" from their competitors,
megachurches compel other churches to respond in order to survive. In Eiseland's
(1997) ethnographic study of the religious ecology of an exurban area outside of
Atlanta she identified three typical responses to the local megachurch. One congregation succumbed to isomorphic pressures and tried to become a megachurch,
although it followed a different path by establishing a number of branch churches
rather than growing one church to megachurch size. A second response was to
develop a new niche identity, grounded in a particular denominational tradition and
the congregation's history in the local community that stood in contradistinction to
the identity and programs of the megachurch. The third response was one of inac-

tion in the face of limited and declining resources. And as expected, the failure to respond to a new organizational challenger at all led to congregational decline.

The influence of megachurches on the religious landscape of the United States also reflects three broader changes: the move towards official and functional non-denominationalism; the move to embrace evangelicalism within older mainline Protestant congregations; and the move to rediscover traditions and/or revitalize older mainline denominations. Chaves (2004: 149) suggests that the growth of independent or non-denominational congregations in recent decades is an important development in American religion. First, they represent a growing share of the religious market as 20 percent of all congregations and 10 percent of all attendees are affiliated with a non-denominational church (Chaves 2004: 24–5). Non-denominational congregations' structural independence allows them the freedom to experiment in terms of worship, leadership, and diversity and thus they are becoming leaders in religious innovations. Second, the vast majority of independent congregations are aligned theologically with some form of conservative Protestantism (evangelicalism, fundamentalism, Pentecostalism) and use a less ceremonial, more enthusiastic style of worship; both of which make liturgical forms of worship and liberal-moderate theological orientations less prevalent and visible in the American religious landscape. Finally, the majority of independent congregations are members of some type of religious organizational network that provides a host of resources that once were primarily provided by national denominations. In addition, this growing non-denominational parachurch sector increasingly is providing Sunday school and adult education curricula, worship materials, and leadership resources for old mainline congregations (Ammerman 2005: 80–92), which may undermine the authority and legitimacy of these denominations.

The second recent shift in American religion is the move by older mainline Protestant congregations to adopt elements from evangelicalism or to remake themselves into evangelicals. This is one of the main findings from Ellingson's (2007) work on Lutheran churches in California. He argues that by adopting the music and educational curricula from evangelical providers, they are also adopting evangelical theology and ultimately the types of congregational mission and identity of evangelical congregations. McKinney and Finke (2002) argue that evangelical renewal movements (ERMs) have sprung up in nearly all of the older mainline denominations with the goal of "return[ing] to previous traditions and teachings, such as emphasizing biblical authority, rekindling efforts of evangelism, and renewing the traditional doctrines of their founders" (2002: 771). They also note how the ERMS are adopting conservative positions on homosexuality that have polarized many denominations in recent years. The attempts to remake old mainline Protestantism or at least groups of congregations within them coupled with the rise and growing influence of parallel religious networks or quasi-denominational associations of like-minded congregations may be creating greater polarization within denominations and weakening the authority of national bodies.

Yet the claims of the decline and demise of denominations, especially older mainline Protestant denominations tends to be overstated. Several recent national studies of American congregations indicate that denominational identity is still strong within many congregations and for many churchgoers. Hartford Seminary's Faith Communities Today study found that 62 percent of the 14,301 participating congregations claimed to have a strong denominational identity. Denominational heritage and traditions were strongest among historically black and strongly sectarian groups and weakest among moderate and liberal Protestant congregations (except for Episcopal and Lutheran (Evangelical Lutheran Church in America) congregations (http://hirr.hartsem.edu/research/quick_question22.html, accessed July 17, 2008)). Ammerman documents how many congregations are intentionally working to preserve denominational traditions and make clear denominational identities salient for members. She summarizes her findings from the Organizing Religious Work study in the following way

> In many of these congregations [that is, congregations that report that they express their denominational heritage "quite well" or "very well"], the effort is simply to make sure that the denominational ethos permeates worship and teaching. But in many others, the efforts are specifically didactic. As new members from other traditions join they are intentionally taught the distinctive beliefs and traditions of their new fellowship ... What distinguishes these congregations where denominational traditions are valued and sustained from those that resign themselves to their "genetic" fate is the way they undertake three key practices of congregational life –worship, mission, and education. In the face of multiple curricular choices, they opt for their own denomination's educational materials. In the face of vast changes and blending of worship styles, they emphasize the distinctiveness of their own tradition. And even when working with many other partners, they highlight the good programs and mission work of their own denomination. (http://hirr.hartsem.edu/bookshelf/ammerman_article3.html; Ammerman 2005)

Roozen's and Nieman's (2005) recent edited volume on denominations, that also draws on data from the Organizing Religious Work study, makes a strong case against the decline of denominationalism that pervades much of the scholarly and popular literatures on American religion. While the authors acknowledge that denominational identity tends to be weaker in the Calvinist traditions than in the liturgical ones, denominations are still a vital part of Protestantism in the United States. In a series of richly detailed cases studies that explore the theological, sociological, and historical features of eight denominations (that range from Assembly of God and Vineyard Fellowship to United Church of Christ, United Methodist, and the National Baptist Convention) scholars repeatedly point out how denominations try to make their historic traditions, resources, and governing structures relevant to congregations. The editors note that identity is a central issue confronting denominations. For some congregations like the United Church of Christ, this means remaking organizational identity to heighten its commitment to diversity; for some, like the Lutheran Church Missouri Synod, the question of identity swirls around the debate to either remain theologically and communally exclusive (and thus pure) or to open up the denomination to make it more congruent with contemporary evangelicalism (essays by Barman and Chaves on the UCC and Carlson on the LCMS).

As discussed earlier, research on megachurches in the United States indicates that they share features of both sects and churches, while megachurches in Asia tend to more closely resemble the classic sect. Miller's discussion of postmodern sectarianism and the discrepancy in orientations between Asian and American megachurches suggest that scholars should revisit the church–sect dichotomy to assess its explanatory power and utility. The church–sect dichotomy has remained in use, largely by scholars working out of market or rational choice approaches to religion, but it remains relatively static. For example, Finke's work on evangelical renewal movements within old mainline Protestantism and organizational revival within Catholicism illustrates how churches move towards sectarianism rather than the more common movement from sect to church, yet the basic contours of church–sect theory remain intact (Finke and Stark 2001; McKinney and Finke 2002; Finke and Wittberg 2000; Liu and Leung 2002 and Lu and Lang 2006 apply this theory to churches in China).

However, the work on American megachurches and new paradigm churches, emergent African-American sects, and British Christianity challenge the fundamental criteria by which sects and churches are differentiated – namely the degree of tension with a religious organization's surrounding environment. Sherkat (2002) shows that African Americans who belong to sectarian or non-denominational congregations are equal in educational attainment and income to their Methodist and Baptist peers (that is, church members), thus intimating that the former may not be as world-rejecting as past sectarians.

Miller's (1999) claim that new paradigm churches represent a postmodern sectarianism raises new questions about the usefulness of the key criteria for distinguishing between churches and sects because many megachurches and more generally evangelical congregations exist in low tension with much of Western culture. Such church bodies seem to embrace the powerful ethos of consumerism within Western capitalist societies, are quite willing and adept at using the latest audio-visual technology, the forms and content of popular music, film, television, and the World Wide Web, and freely borrow ideas and images from corporate culture. The stated goals of some megachurches to make the church experience mimic the experience one has in the mall, Starbucks cafe, or movie complex are signs of a low degree of tension with their surrounding environment. I contend that we are seeing a form of selective sectarianism in which congregations select some issues or features of contemporary society to reject, embrace other issues or aspects that are useful to fuel organizational growth and legitimacy, and remain silent on issues or features of the secular world that could threaten membership or attendance. Conservative church bodies and conservative movements within old mainline congregations often select issues surrounding personal morality (such as sexuality) and lifestyle (such as parenting) as the means to distance themselves from secular society and allegedly less religious or more accommodating churches, and to foster a strong in-group identity, often as an embattled minority within secular society (Wellman 1999).

Bruce and Voas (2007) discussion of decline of sectarianism and rise of religious tolerance in Great Britain offers help in explaining the shift towards selective sectarianism within Western Christianity. They note that sacrifice, a critical practice that validates sectarian rejection of the world, and religious purity increasingly have lost their stigma as the kinds of practices that once marked sectarians (for example, dietary and dress restrictions) are now practiced by many in the secular world. In addition, they argue that sectarian deviance is no longer punished or criminalized, and thus conclude that, "the absence of a hostile response not only reduces the sectarian's opportunity to make sacrificial commitment (and thus inadvertently reduces group cohesion). It also makes socialization more difficult" (2007: 13). They also note that while many Westerners are nostalgic for the type of community and fellowship the sect offers, they do not like to have their individual freedom restricted. This makes strict forms of sectarianism less appealing.

Selective sectarianism may be an emergent organizational form among megachurches and new paradigm type churches in the United States because they do not require significant sacrifices (it is not difficult to give up homosexuality when one is heterosexual) nor does this type of sectarianism challenge the dominant consumerist ethos of the surrounding environment which rejects personal sacrifices. Furthermore, megachurches and more generally, evangelicalism, create parallel but separate lifeworlds that largely mimic the culture and meaning systems, leisure and family spheres of secular society but give them Christian content which allows megachurch attendees and evangelicals to retain the benefits of consumer capitalism but avoid their alleged polluting effects.

FUTURE RESEARCH

Leading experts agree that megachurches will continue to play a significant role in the American religious landscape for decades to come, especially if the trend toward growing numbers of large churches and the increasing concentration of attendees in those large churches continues (Chaves 2006; Thumma and Petersen 2007). One possible scenario is that megachurches will continue to strengthen the move towards non-denominationalism and a more homogenous form of Protestantism anchored in evangelicalism (this argument is suggested by Ellingson 2007 and Miller 1999). A second scenario is that while megachurches will continue to expand, congregations within mainline and other denominations will push back to recover their historic traditions and develop niche identities and thus revivify some of the mainline denominations in decline. A third scenario (and one that Thumma and Travis (2007: 182–7) believe is unlikely given megachurches the ability to adapt and respond to changes in the surrounding culture) is that individuals will reject the large churches as they seek religious experiences in smaller, more intimate venues.

Given the growing importance of megachurches for American religion and the relative inchoateness of research on megachurches, there is no shortage of work to be done. It is time for scholars to move beyond descriptive research and develop more systematic and robust explanations that bring the study of the megachurch into the animating debates within the sociology of religion and within organizational and cultural sociology. First, as megachurches mature and begin to wield greater power within national and local religious ecologies, we need to assess their impact on other congregations and denominations. While Ellingson's (2007) and Eiseland's (1997) work is suggestive we still know very little about how and why megachurches are influencing mainline Protestantism or congregations within a particular community. Second, much of the data on megachurches come from surveys of pastors or church leaders rather than rank and file members. While this provides solid supply-side information, we have very limited demand-side or audience data (however, Thumma's 1996 study incorporates both demand and supply side data). Thus we do not fully understand why people attend; why they join, stay, or leave; how they experience the worship, fellowship, or theology of megachurches. In addition, without data from attendees of megachurches we cannot fully assess the accuracy of cultural/market explanations because we cannot know with certainty if and how megachurch programs resonate with the interests of audiences or help individuals address their religious questions. Conducting representative surveys and/or in-depth case studies of megachurch attendees would help us strengthen and refine cultural/market explanations.

Finally, megachurches offer a new avenue to develop church–sect theory. Because megachurches draw on many of the ideas, practices, and technologies within secular culture, they are not in strong tension with the outer world, yet their theology and creation of alternative Christian world in which attendees can live (recall that megachurches are total institutions of a sort) create sect-like exclusivity and separation. Perhaps we need to rethink the fundamental notions of *tension* and *strictness* on which the theory rests and consider the ways in which megachurches are creating a form of selective sectarianism – one that creates meaningful subcultures with semi-permeable cultural and social boundaries. One important avenue for future research will be to compare Asian and North American megachurches with an eye to explaining why the strict form of sectarianism seems to thrive in Asia while the more lenient form is dominant in the United States.

In sum, megachurches are a worldwide phenomenon that remains understudied despite their growing prominence since the 1970s. They represent an opportunity to extend accounts of how religion is being reshaped or restructured in the twenty-first century and develop new explanations of religious innovation, change, and power.

Bibliography

Ammerman, Nancy (2000) New life for denominationalism, *The Christian Century* March 15, http://hirr.Hartsem.edu/bookshelf/ammerman_article3.html.

Ammerman, Nancy (2005) *Pillars of Faith*, Berkeley and Los Angeles: University of California Press.

Bruce, Steve and Voas, David (2007) Religious toleration and organizational typologies, *Journal of Contemporary Religion* 22: 1–17.

Chaves, Mark (2004) *Congregations in America*, Cambridge, MA: Harvard University Press.

Chaves, Mark (2006) "All creatures great and small": megachurch in context, *Review of Religious Research* 47: 329–46.

Dillon, Michele and Wink, Paul (2007) *In the Course of a Lifetime: Tracing Religious Belief, Practices, and Change*, Berkeley and Los Angeles: University of California Press.

Eiseland, Nancy (1997) Contending with a giant: the impact of a megachurch on exurban religious institutions, in Penny Edgel Becker and Nancy Eiseland (eds.), *Contemporary American Religion*, Walnut Creek: Alta Mira Press, 191–219.

Ellingson, Stephen (2007) *The Megachurch and the Mainline*, Chicago: University of Chicago Press.

Finke, Roger and Stark, Rodney (2001) The new holy clubs: testing church-to-sect propositions, *Sociology of Religion* 62: 175–89.

Finke, Roger and Wittberg, Patricia (2000) Organizational revival from within: explaining revivalism and reforms in the Roman Catholic Church, *Journal for the Scientific Study of Religion* 39: 154–70.

Goh, Daniel P. S. (1999) Rethinking resurgent Christianity in Singapore, *Southeast Asian Journal of Social Science* 1: 89–112.

Hong, Young-gi (2000) The background and characteristics of the charismatic megachurch in Korea, *Asian Journal of Pentecostal Studies* 3: 99–118.

Hoover, Stewart (2000) The cross at Willow Creek: seeker religion and the contemporary marketplace, in Bruce David Forbes and Jeffrey H. Mahan (eds.), *Religion and Popular Culture in America*, Berkeley and Los Angeles: University of California Press, 145–59.

Johnson, Benton (1957) A critical appraisal of the church–sect typology, *American Sociological Review* 22: 88–92.

Johnson, Benton (1963) On church and sect, *American Sociological Review* 28 (3): 539–49.

Johnson, Benton (1971) Church and sect revisited, *Journal for the Scientific Study of Religion* 10: 124–37.

Karnes, Kimberly, McIntosh, Wayne, Morris, Irwin L., and Pearson-Merkowitz, Shanna (2007) A might fortresses: explaining the spatial distribution of American megachurch, *Journal for the Scientific Study of Religion* 46: 261–8.

Liu, William T. and Leung, Beatrice (2002) Organizational revivalism: explaining metamorphosis of China's Catholic Church, *Journal for the Scientific Study of Religion* 41: 121–38.

Loveland, Anne C. and Wheeler, Otis B. (2003) *From Meeting House to Megachurch*, Columbia and London: University of Missouri Press.

Lu, Yunfeng and Lang, Graeme (2006) Impact of the state on the evolution of a sect, *Sociology of Religion* 67: 249–70.

McKinney, Jennifer and Finke, Roger (2002) Reviving the mainline: an overview of clergy support for evangelical renewal movements, *Journal for the Scientific Study of Religion* 41: 771–83.

Miller, Donald E. (1999) *Reinventing American Protestantism*, Berkeley and Los Angeles: University of California Press.

Montgomery, James D. (1996) Dynamics of the religious economy: exit, voice and denominational secularization, *Rationality and Society* 8: 81–110.

Roof, Wade Clark (1993) *A Generation of Seekers*, San Francisco: Harper Collins.

Roof, Wade Clark (1999) *Spiritual Marketplace*, Princeton: Princeton University Press.

Roof, Wade Clark and McKinney, William (1987) *American Mainline Religion*, New Brunswick: Rutgers University Press.

Roozen, David A. and Nieman, James R. (eds.) (2005) *Church, Identity, and Change: Theology and Denominational Structures in Unsettled Times*, Grand Rapids: Eerdmans.

Sargeant, Kimon Howland (2000) *Seeker Churches: Promoting Traditional Religion in a Non-Traditional Way*, New Brunswick: Rutgers University Press.

Sherkat, Darren E. (2002) Investigating the sect–church–sect cycle: cohort-specific attendance differences across African-American denominations, *Journal for the Scientific Study of Religion* 41: 485–93.

Stark, Rodney and Iannaccone, Laurence R. (1997) Why the Jehovah's Witnesses grow so rapidly: a theoretical application, *Journal of Contemporary Religion* 12: 133–57.

Thumma, Scott (1996) The kingdom, the power, and the glory: megachurch in modern American society, Doctoral Dissertation, Emory University.

Thumma, Scott and Petersen, Jim (2003) Goliaths in our midst: megachurch in the ELCA, in Richard Cimino (ed.), *Lutherans Today: American Lutheran Identity in the 21st Century*, Grand Rapids: Eerdmans, 102–24.

Thumma, Scott and Travis, Dave (2007) *Beyond the Megachurch Myths*, San Francisco: Jossey-Bass.

Tong, Joy Kooi Chin (2008) McDonaldization and the megachurch: a case study of City Harvest Church, Singapore, in Pattana Kitiarsa (ed.), *Religious Commodifications in Asia*, New York: Routledge, 186–204.

Tucker-Worgs, Tamelyn (2001) Get on board, little children, there's room for many more: the black megachurch phenomenon, *Journal of the Interdenominational Theological Center* 29: 177–203.

Twitchell, James B. (2004) *Branded Nation*, New York: Simon and Schuster.

Weber, Max (1968) [1946] *From Max Weber*, ed. H. H. Gerth and C. Wright Mills, New York: Oxford University Press.

Wellman, James K. Jr (1999) Introduction: the debate over homosexual ordination: subcultural identity theory in American religious organizations, *Review of Religious Research* 41: 184–206.

Wilson, Bryan (1959) An analysis of sect development, *American Sociological Review* 24: 3–15.

Wuthnow, Robert (1998) *After Heaven*, Berkeley and Los Angeles: University of California Press.

12

The Sociology of Spirituality
Reflections on a Problematic Endeavor

MATTHEW WOOD

INTRODUCTION

The period since the turn of the millenium has seen the concept of "spirituality" attain ever greater purchase within the sociology of religion. In reaction to what are seen to be the failings of the concept of "religion," increasing numbers of sociologists, as well as scholars in other disciplines, have employed "spirituality" to describe *and* interpret certain shifts that they deem to be occurring in contemporary, particularly Euro-American, societies. For these sociologists, whereas "religion" conceptually captures institutions, traditions, the public world and external authority, and does so in an objectivist manner, it ill-serves the attempt to understand situations in which these are waning. Stressing a subjectivist approach, however, "spirituality" is judged conceptually competent to deal with such situations. The purpose of this chapter is to assess this argument. Just what sociologists mean by "spirituality" will be examined – and it will be shown that underlying their various meanings, sociologists use this term to describe people as exercising their own authority. In response, this chapter proceeds to subject the sociology of spirituality to epistemological, theoretical and methodological critique. In sum, by positing the existence of self-authority, the sociology of spirituality abnegates a properly *sociological* interpretation of the phenomena it addresses. Through its conceptual distinction between "religion" and "spirituality," this sociology lifts people out of their social contexts, with the result that it fails adequately to address social practice, social interaction, and the wider contexts of people's lives and biographies. Eliding sustained investigation into people's practical experiences with one another, and within institutions and organizations (however formal or informal), the sociology of spirituality primarily focuses upon texts, discourses and surveyed beliefs that serve to represent these people merely as *individuals*, not as social actors. The purpose of this critique, however, is not simply to draw attention to the misleading nature of an increasingly widespread sociological approach. It is also to ask whether sociologists in general have too often been unduly narrow in their conceptualization of religious practice and interaction – and thus unwittingly invited this misplaced reaction. In this respect, sociology has much to learn from its twin discipline, social anthropology.

THE RESHAPING OF RELIGION: SECULARIZATION AND SPIRITUALITY

Since the 1960s, the sociology of religion has paid considerable attention to the changing nature of religion. One element of this attention has involved debates surrounding the measurement and explanation of the process of secularization, whereby religious institutions, personnel, practices and beliefs are seen as declining in public – if not in private – significance. In part overlapping with these debates, from the 1980s there has emerged another element: a focus upon the *reshaping* of religion rather than its *decline*. Sociologists pursuing this second line of enquiry have sought to investigate those aspects of human life that they consider to be neglected by debates about secularization: practices and organizations that are non-orthodox and informal; private experiences; consumption of religious products; and the significance of religious discourses. More importantly, these aspects of human life are held to require a quite different conceptualization than that provided by the notion of "religion" in secularization debates; it is precisely for this reason that the concept of "spirituality" has been promoted.

A sense of what this new conceptualization seeks to capture is expressed by McGuire (2008b: 228):

> By "spirituality," I wish to convey a sense of an individual condition-in-process, sug-gesting experience – unfinished, developing, and open. ... In contrast to "religiosity," "spirituality" might be used to refer to patterns of spiritual practices and experiences that comprise individual "religion-as-lived" ... "Religiosity" could still be useful for describing individual religion in terms of such characteristics as formal membership or identification, rates of participation in religious services, frequency of prayer and scrip-ture reading, assent to church-prescribed creeds and moral prescriptions, and so on. It is extremely difficult, however, to operationalize such a notion of religiosity to apply to all Christian church-defined beliefs and practices, much less to all religions.

This focus upon individuals and their experiences is central to the sociology of spirituality, but what constitutes relevant experiences is much less clear, as demonstrated by Flanagan's (2007: 1–2) adoption of an essentially theological viewpoint:

> Spirituality signifies an indispensable dimension of what it is to be human. In the spirit, the social actor finds ambition, animation and exultation that all move and mobilise the self to reach beyond itself ... As a phenomenon, spirituality is something subjective, experiential, non-rational, unverifiable and serendipitous in its eruptions, all properties an enlightened sociology finds difficult to transpose into the ordering argot of the discipline.

An equally ambiguous position is adopted by Wuthnow (2001: 307):

> For present purposes, spirituality can be defined as a state of being related to a divine, supernatural, or transcendent order of reality or, alternatively, as a sense or awareness of a suprareality that goes beyond life as ordinarily experienced. Interest in spirituality is commonly expressed in beliefs about God and other divine beings, such as angels, and in experiences of such beings. But spirituality is not limited to such beliefs. For instance, some people refer to the spiritual as that which lies beyond the filtered experiences available to us because of our cultural categories; others use the term spiritual to designate that which encompasses all of physical, emotional, and mental experience.

Despite its lack of clear analytical meaning, Wuthnow (1998) contends that American "spirituality" has recently undergone "reordering," from a "spirituality of sacred spaces" contained within structured congregations to a "spirituality of seeking" in which individuals themselves negotiate their "personal relationships" to the "sacred." Linked to a view of individuals as socially mobile and as exercising choice, the notion of seekership is a dominant trope in the sociology of spirituality's interpretation of individuals' experiences. The role of institutions in such seekership has become the focus for most debate amongst sociologists of religion. Whilst Wuthnow is perhaps the foremost proponent of the view that spirituality continues to commonly take place within institutional, and more broadly communal, contexts, Verter (2003: 157–8) represents the position that institutions are largely irrelevant to spirituality (although, as shown in the following quote, he mistakenly attributes this view to precisely those American sociologists of religion who reject it):

> Though "spirituality" is notoriously ill defined, when used in opposition to "religion" (as in the lamentably common locution, "I'm not religious, but I'm spiritual"), it generally connotes an extrainstitutional, resolutely individualistic, and often highly eclectic personal theology self-consciously resistant to dogma. (Bellah et al. 1985 [1996]; Roof 1993, 1999; Wuthnow 1998)

In general, the sociology of spirituality's focus upon individual experience forms part of a broader sociological reaction against structural-functionalism. In place of attention being directed towards publicly observable social contexts and institutions, with the aim of interpreting their significance in terms of the structuring and functioning of society, there has grown an interest in private, cultural matters in the lives of individuals whether or not they relate to institutional dimensions of social life. Furthermore, central to this analytic shift is the view that the dominance of religious institutions over people is increasingly replaced by the autonomy of the individual. This draws strength from Luckmann's (1967) influential study of "modern society," *The Invisible Religion*, encouraging the argument that secularization itself, as part of modernization, led to the growth of spirituality. Again, sociologists of spirituality disagree on whether or not this involves decline in the significance (public or private) of institutions: Hanegraaff (1999) goes so far as to argue that secularization has involved the splitting of spirituality from religious institutions (in a form which he labels "New Age spiritualities"), such that it can be characterized as "secular religion."

SELF-AUTHORITY

As well as responding to broader sociological trends, the rise of the sociology of spirituality has occurred in response to the concept of "spirituality" (and "spiritual") itself becoming widespread in Euro-American societies, as McGuire notes (2008b: 228):

> The concept has been taken over in recent years by the mass media and advertising campaigns, such that one can buy a huge range of goods and services to enhance one's spirituality. Thus, one use of rhetorics of spirituality is marketing commodities. Analyzing this commodification of spirituality is one worthwhile task for a sociology of spirituality, but the banality of the concept has made it extremely difficult to use analytically.

Whilst this corporate takeover may indeed have been recent, it is clear that sociologists' use of the concept *followed* this – and has itself influenced the spread of the concept into other scholarly fields, such as studies in education, healthcare and social work – as well as developing in response to the increasing use of the word by people they were studying. Perceiving what they saw to be a shift in quotidian discourse, sociologists adopted "spirituality" as a keyword that could function not only as a description or label of people's orientations and beliefs, but also as a sociological category to analyze them.

In principle, it is possible to defend this method: the inductive construction of analytical categories from the discourses, worldviews, or beliefs of those who are studied has a long tradition within sociology, being particularly associated with Weber and the interpretive sociologists. Barker (2008), for example, constructs an ideal-typical distinction between religiosity and spirituality on the basis of reviewing the results from various social surveys. Whereas the former involves belief in "a transcendent, personal God," Barker (2008: 189–90) claims that spirituality involves belief in "the god within" such that the source of authority is "[p]ersonal experience" related to "the 'true self'" and "[i]nternal responsibility." This characterization of spirituality on the basis of respondents' views mirrors that of many other studies, including Furseth (2005), Lambert (2004), and Heelas and Woodhead (2005: 160, n.5; emphasis added) who assert that analysis can only proceed on the basis of "what we know to be the case: namely, what participants *have to say*."

However, the perennial danger of the inductive method is that people's discourses become sociologists' descriptions of social reality – in other words, that they are taken as *only* what can be known. Such a position is, in fact, quite distinct from Weber's method which, as Woodiwiss (2005: 59–65) explains, is more accurately described as realist, akin to the methods of Marx and Durkheim. In the case of the sociology of spirituality, a *naive* inductivism has meant that people's views that they are exercising authority over their lives have been translated into sociologists' declamations that such is in fact the case. Put simply, sociologists have turned respondents' discourses about controlling their lives into the analytical pronouncement that these people are indeed exercising self-authority.

Thus, Barker (2008: 200) concludes that "the beliefs and practices of [spirituality] ... by their very nature eschew both dogma and boundaries but celebrate individual choices and emphases"; from her interviews with Norwegian women, Furseth (2005: 167) claims that an individual who "speak[s] of spirituality" "actively picks and chooses to construct a world-view as a bricolage that she feels fits her life"; and Lambert (2004: 43) argues on the basis of the European Values surveys that there has been an evolutionary shift in religiosity such that "religion is relativized, passed through the filter of individual subjectivity, confronted by indifference or the autonomous spiritual quest." In perhaps the most influential study to date, Heelas and Woodhead (2005) distinguish between "subjective-life spirituality" that exists in "holistic" milieux (involving such activities as meditation, yoga and alternative therapies) and "life-as religion" that is primarily located within Christian congregations. Unlike the latter, the former is characterized by the *actual* exercise of self-authority (Heelas and Woodhead 2005: 2–3):

> It *is* a turn away from life lived in terms of external or "objective" roles, duties and obligations, and a turn towards life lived by reference to one's subjective experiences ... if I decide to heed those subjective states, to listen to what they are telling me, and to act on their prompting ... then *I am* turning away from life lived according to external expectations, to life lived according to my own inner experience.

Such unacknowledged transmutations of those discourses under study into sociological descriptions of reality are to be found *throughout* the sociology of spirituality, to the extent that this view about self-authority now seems paradigmatic, particularly since it remains unquestioned. Thus, even those who argue that spirituality is also to be found in churches likewise retain a distinction between people who do or do not exercise their own authority, as in Guest's (2007: 189; emphasis added) view that "traditional groups and organisations are increasingly open to or at least available for re-appropriation and reinvention" – but only, it seems, "in accordance with the *subjective predilections* of individuals." Similarly, Besecke (2001: 368) asserts that whilst "[t]he language of reflexive spirituality recognizes the authority and integrity of religious traditions" nevertheless, "only in the proverbial "last instance" does individual authority carry the trump" – which is simply to say that "individual authority" will *always* prevail over external authorities, but that there may be situations in which they coincide. The paradigm is further reinforced by the fact that sociologists who re-assert the secularization thesis against the view that religion is being reshaped in Euro-America still hold to the position that spirituality, whilst an insignificant phenomenon, is indeed characterized by self-authority (for example, Voas and Bruce 2007).

Commonly, the locus of authority in spirituality is sociologically seen not merely in terms of the individual, but in terms of the "self." In what he names "reflexive spirituality," Roof (1999: 42) claims that "in a very real sense, the self is elevated to a higher level of making spiritual choices and negotiating frameworks of meaning drawing off institutional and more popular-based religious discourses." Similarly, in Wuthnow's (1998: 154–6) terms, "spirituality of seeking" "focuses less on submission to a higher power and more on cultivating trust in oneself" or in "one's inner self." These pronouncements are not underpinned, however, by a sociological account of the self – indeed, Heelas (1998: 379) rejects "a *theoretical* view of the self," since he sees this as denying its "essential properties ... most notably *agency*." Of course, Heelas' assumption about the self's intrinsic agency *is* theoretical, but represents a philosophico-theological account that draws inspiration from the work of Charles Taylor. The theological concept of "fullness" as the moral/spiritual dimension of humanness in Taylor's (2007) latest tome, for example, is enthusiastically translated into Heelas' (2008) notion of "wellbeing spirituality."

The inductive approach pursued by the sociologists of spirituality therefore leads inexorably away from a *sociological* consideration of people's discourses and how these are embedded in their social practices, interactions and contexts. Instead, we are left with a picture of individuals whose essential selves exercise authority in their lives. This reinstates conceptual dichotomies of agency and structure, the individual and society, free will (or choice) and determinism, interiority and exteriority, and subjectivity and objectivity, which have long been recognized as interfering with the sociological enterprise, and which theoretical approaches have convincingly undermined (for a detailed discussion, see Wood 2007: 41–77).

In addition to the naivety represented by the transmutation of the concept of "spirituality" from people's discourses into a sociological description of reality, it is also the case that this is based on simplifying the discourses encountered. Discourses of spirituality have certainly become widespread in contemporary Euro-American societies in recent years. However, following the lead from corporate advertising and marketing, as already indicated by McGuire, sociologists have lifted out references to "spirituality" or "spiritual" from people's discourses, and interpreted these *selected* elements to represent a unique transformation of religion. Furthermore, these keywords are often fore-grounded in surveys, such that they demand a reaction from respondents. However, such surveys themselves show that "spirituality" and "religion" are inextricably linked for the majority of those who express, or identify with, either or both (Barker 2008: 194; Marler and Hadaway 2002; Zinnbauer et al. 1997).

As regards the meanings of such terms, whilst quotidian discourses about "spirituality" may refer to rejection or skepticism regarding church dogma, authority, and tradition, and to personal responsibility and self-authority, these are very often interwoven with discourses about duty, obedience, and submittance, and are redolent with social norms and morals – as in the discourse of "Sheila," a figure in Bellah et al.'s (1996: 221) study who is frequently taken as an archetype of spirituality (see also the cases discussed in Wood 2007: 92–3, 2009: 238–9). This belies any simplistic construction of analytical ideal-types. Bender (2003: 70) provides a rare but highly welcome criticism of this approach:

> Narratives by "religious seekers" may obscure personal and institutional connections and ties (in fact, one suspects that the similarities in seekers' narratives point to their participation in social networks where such language is cultivated), but this does not mean such stories are the only ones seekers tell about themselves. Likewise, the measure of a narrative's force cannot be found through interviews alone but must be coupled

with observation of the various contexts where we might understand how such self-descriptions shape individuals' activities, approaches, and values.

As should be clear from this discussion, people's discourses constitute important data that must be taken into account, but only by being placed within their social contexts. In one respect, this means the wider context of those other discourses in which they feature – hence the requirement not to selectively lift certain discourses or keywords away from those with which they are inextricably bound. In another respect, it means that sociologists must attempt to understand the *social (re)production and contestation* of these discourses – which can only be done by refusing to perceive people as mere individuals exercising self-authority, but instead situating them within their practical interactions with others. Whilst ethnographic methods are particularly suitable for attempting this, surveys and interviews are not irrelevant so long as they seek information about these issues. Manifestly, this is rarely attempted by sociologists of spirituality – even when, as we will see, respondents themselves raise the significance of their interactions with others. Disturbingly, even when ethnographic methods have been employed, the conclusions drawn typically downplay the significance of social interactions despite evidence to the contrary. In order to understand how such lacunae have arisen, the academic contexts that have led to the emergence of the sociology of spirituality are now considered.

THE GENEALOGY AND DISCIPLINARY CONTEXT OF THE SOCIOLOGY OF SPIRITUALITY

The transmutation of people's discourses into descriptions of social reality is symptomatic of the lack of control that the sociology of spirituality exercises over its concepts. In this it betrays its underlying scholarly orientation, which is primarily that of Religious Studies (and cognate disciplines such as History of Religions and Theology), not Sociology. The development of the sociology of religion from the 1960s aimed at the assertion of control over concepts and methods by connecting with classical sociological approaches to religion, in opposition to the church-directed religious sociology that had prevailed until that time (Luckmann 1967: 20). Despite this, it remained marginal within wider sociology (Beckford 1989: 13–17; Turner 1991: 2–7), with the result that it was more open to encroachment from non-social-scientific disciplines with the encouragement of inter-disciplinarity from the 1980s, as a result of policy-led shifts in higher education. Whilst it would be instructive to research the porous boundaries between the sociology of religion and these other disciplines in terms of personnel, publications and organizations, the significant issue is how *discourses and methods* prevalent in Religious Studies gained ground in the sociology of religion. Chief among these is the reliance upon texts coupled with inductivism, which as we have seen is a key characteristic of the sociology of spirituality – it is therefore no surprise to find common agreement between sociologists of spirituality and scholars working in these other disciplines, who also conclude that self-authority is a defining feature of spirituality. For example, as a historian of religions, Hanegraaff's interpretation is based upon a content analysis of popular books (see Hanegraaff 1996), leading him to conclude that New Age or secular spiritualities "are based upon the individual manipulation of religious as well as non-religious symbolic systems," an *individual creation* that in fact starts from "point zero" (Hanegraaff 1999: 152).

In order to understand this situation better, it is useful to sketch a genealogy which locates the sociology of spirituality in relation to two intersecting currents of thought that themselves relate to the dominant twin themes of post-1950s sociology of religion, namely secularization and new religious movements. The first of these currents can be characterized as "counterculture and consciousness" studies, which arose in America in response to social changes in the 1960s and 1970s (for example, Glock and Bellah 1976; Tipton 1982; Wuthnow 1976). Typically, these related the reshaping of the religious field to the so-called "baby boom" generation born in the postwar period, seen as asserting individual autonomy and as focusing on an inward turn that prioritized shifts in consciousness, often within the context of new religious movements. A related British formulation was Campbell's (1972) application of Troeltsch's notion of "mystical religion" to a countercultural "cultic milieu" characterized by individualistic seekership.

The second current is New Age studies, which in part grew out of the "counterculture and consciousness" sociology, but (developing in the late 1980s and 1990s) was marked by the encroachment of Religious Studies into the sociology of religion, and consequently by a much *less* rigorous sociological approach – as typified by Heelas' (1996) *The New Age Movement*, whose primary source of empirical data, as for Hanegraaff, was printed texts. As we have seen, both Wuthnow and Heelas subsequently became key figures in the sociology of spirituality. Significantly, however, the concept of "spirituality" is lacking from these earlier currents of thought – where it appears, it is generally in relation to Eastern religions (Ellwood 1987) or healing (McGuire 1988).

In both these currents of thought, but particularly in the latter, the sociological paradigm of self-authority is evident. In a piece on religious evolution, for example, Bellah (1969: 288; emphasis added) stated that, "[t]he historic religions discovered the self; the early modern religion found a doctrinal basis on which to accept the self in all its empirical ambiguity; modern religion is beginning to understand the laws of the self's *own* existence and so to help man take responsibility for his *own* fate." Likewise, Heelas (1996: 35; emphasis added) proclaimed that, "if there *is* too much external authority ... one can conclude that one is no longer with the New Age." Indeed, sociologists of religion in general came to see what they called the "New Age Movement" as that mode of religiosity (or, later, of spirituality) in which self-authority was most detached from institutions – although they disagreed about whether it was typical of reshaped religion or not.

Underpinning this paradigm of self-authority has been a theoretical conception of the individual and society that is essentially Durkheimian in its reduction of the social world to a relationship between the individual and society (Wood 2009: 240). Luckmann's (1967) Durkheim-inspired argument about the growth of individual autonomy has been central here, as also in Hervieu-Léger's (2008) linkage between spirituality and modern individualization/subjectivization. Luckmann (1996: 75) later argued that in its accentuation of this feature, "[t]he New Age movement illustrates the social form of the invisible religion." Whilst Beckford (1983) accurately diagnosed the weakness in Luckmann's sociology as removing attention from issues of social power, this criticism has gone unheeded by the sociologists of New Age and spirituality. More recently, analytic buoyancy has been provided by Giddens' (1991) thesis of self-reflexivity and detraditionalization – itself subject to sustained criticism for relying upon conceptual dichotomies (Wood 2007: 63–5). Thompson's (1996: 90) description of detraditionalization as a theory that supposes "individuals are obliged increasingly to fall back on their own resources to construct a coherent identity for themselves" reveals its attractiveness for the sociology of spirituality. Indeed, a raft of meta-narratives has been drawn upon in order to offer a sociological gloss to an increasingly Religious Studies oriented field: subjectivization, individualization, privatization, postmodernization, and globalization (Wood 2007: 30–6).

Given the claim that religion is being reshaped into a form in which individuals' self-authorities are paramount, it logically follows that sociological attention would be directed primarily to individuals' views and experiences, and only secondarily to the contexts of social authorities, structures and functions in which these occur – even for those scholars who maintain the significance of institutional contexts. That this is precisely what has occurred is shown by the nature of social research pursued in the sociology of spirituality, which displays a marked lack of attention to social interactions, and to the wider contexts of people's lives and biographies. In addition, because this sociology constructs the analytical categories of "spirituality" and "self-authority" on the basis of people's beliefs and discourses, it has privileged these over social practices – investigations of practices have tended simply to list those engaged with by individuals, not to see them as *social* activities.

The second half of this chapter will discuss the importance of reinstating these three sociological principles when researching phenomena that have been labeled as "spirituality": namely, the need to address social practice, social interaction, and the broader social contexts of people's lives and biographies. By following these principles, it will be shown that a quite different understanding is gained, such that it is manifestly unhelpful to make use of "spirituality" as an *analytical* concept. Whilst it is important to address those aspects of human life that the sociology of religion has too often neglected, their conceptualization in terms of "spirituality" as distinct from, or in tension with, "religion" only serves to re-establish analytic dichotomies that have long hindered sociological understanding.

SOCIAL PRACTICE

Attention to people's practices was one of the most important steps made in the development of the sociological method, enabling it to emerge as distinct from the speculative orientation of theological and philosophical enquiry. The key figure here is Marx, whose assertion of the centrality of the *practical* dimension of human life was developed early in his work, being his principal objection to the Hegelian philosophy of mind or consciousness: "[w]here speculation ends – in real life – there real, positive science begins: the representation of the practical activity, of the practical process of development of men" (Marx and Engels 1949: 15). Quite simply, Marx's eighth thesis on Feuerbach states that "[a]ll social life is essentially *practical*" (Marx and Engels 1949: 199). This was perhaps Marx's main legacy to Weber: whilst commentators often contrast the two by highlighting the latter's consideration of a social actor's values or meanings (set within a worldview or *Weltanschauung*), in fact Weber always sought to locate these in social action – which is why his *magnum opus* opens with a discussion of meaningful *action* as a methodological foundation (Weber 1978: 4–22). Subsequent shifts of focus away from practice towards structure or belief have more recently been redressed by social theorists, such as Bourdieu (1990) and Foucault (1980), whose perspectives have arguably reinvigorated the discipline, in particular by re-orientating it towards issues of power.

The recent orientation of some American sociologists towards "lived religion" has begun to highlight social practice, leading to a more fruitful understanding of people who employ a discourse of "spirituality." McGuire (2008b: 216), for instance, emphasizes the "lived" nature of "the individual's religion … not just symbols and cognitive frameworks, but also individual emotions, embodiment and experience." Consequently, she criticizes the sociologists of spirituality for "uncritically accepting … [respondents'] self-identification[s] of spirituality and religiosity as the basis for … sociological interpretation," and for thus failing "to distinguish the rhetoric and ideological uses of the term "spirituality" from the empirical and analytic referents" (McGuire 2008b: 218). However, as in Wuthnow's work, McGuire's (2008a) detailed analyses of practices tend to remain at the level of the individual, rather than exploring those social interactions that influence and constitute even private practices. This leads her to lapse into uncritically accepting another aspect of respondents' views, namely that they are "free to choose components of their individual faith and practice," which she interprets through Giddens' view of self-reflexivity in late modernity (McGuire 2008b: 223, 229).

The significance of the neglect of social practices by sociologists of spirituality can be highlighted by their lack of attention to practices of spirit possession that are so prevalent in those social networks in Euro-America that they would typically classify in terms of "spirituality" or "New Age spirituality." For example, evidence from a typical network, in the English East Midlands, which included meditation, channelling and holistic healing groups, and which intersected with anthroposophical, pagan and spiritualist groups, shows that channelling was a central practice, as were other practices (such as Reiki) which could be described as involving possession in that practitioners established a bodily communion with spirits or supernatural energies (for detailed discussion of this "Nottinghamshire network," see Wood 2007). Although many studies have recognized the popularity of channelling in similar networks elsewhere, most have merely focused upon the *texts or discourses* produced in channelling (for example, Brown 1997). However, attention to channelling and other forms of possession as practices is essential for two reasons. Firstly, this draws attention to the way in which gods, spirits and their intermediaries are seen as legitimate *authorities* – although not necessarily as the only or prime authorities. Such relations with authorities take place even in relatively informal, weakly institutionalized contexts, which should not therefore be interpreted as dominated by self-authority and bereft of power relations. Secondly, *as a form of practice* possession in these networks points to the way in which people who (as we will see) have typically undergone a process of de-churching, are able to instil their current activities (such as meditation, divination, or healing) with a religious dimension, due to the explicit connection with the supernatural.

Social Interaction

Without attention to social practice, it is unlikely that attention will be paid to social interaction – and this is precisely the case in the sociology of spirituality, which is only interested in the individual *as an* individual. It is only by paying attention to people's social interactions, however, that a better understanding of the Nottinghamshire network (introduced in the last section) can be gained. Here, people interacted with diverse *multiple* authorities that relativized each other: instead of involving relatively exclusive commitment to a group, tradition or practice (or to a common set of these), leading to a specific religious socialization, interactions with any particular authority (such as a channeler, a meditation group leader or a crystal healer) formed merely one element in people's religious lives. As such, the network and those involved with it can be described as relatively *nonformative*: authorities were relatively unable, and were not expected, to *formatively* shape individuals' experiences and expectations (Wood 2007: 70–4, 156–63; Wood and Bunn 2009: 290–9).

This conceptualization of the Nottinghamshire network in terms of a multiplicity of relativizing authorities does not simply refer to the existence of different groups, leaders and practices, but also to the fact that these did not *act together* in order to inculcate or socialize people in a particular way (including into a particular discourse or worldview, such as "New Age": Wood 2009: 244). This is quite different from other religious networks in which multiple authorities exist, but where these authorities support, rather than relativize, each other. Such was the case in the pagan, spiritualist and Anthroposophical groups and networks that partly overlapped with the Nottinghamshire network: although each of these milieux involved various groups and sources of expertise, nevertheless amongst participants there existed relatively strong social identities, core beliefs, senses of boundaries, senses of how their practices and rituals should be conducted, and presence of gossip and rivalry (Wood 2007: 137–53).

From this perspective, it is instructive to explore sociological studies of spirituality in Christian contexts. McNamara's (1992: 34) study of students and graduates from an American Catholic high school, for example, draws upon Giddens to argue that increasingly "the individual considers himself or herself the final arbiter and judge of what is to be believed and practiced." What is interesting in this study, however, is the way in which it clearly shows the continuing influence of religious authorities in the school – especially in terms of inculcating in the students a discourse of individual conscience or personal responsibility. So, the school's theology teachers "were pushing the students as far as they could in a reflective direction," in line with the Second Vatican Council's assertion of "the right of the individual conscience to be free from outside coercion" (McNamara 1992: 33, 114). Indeed, a range of personnel and practices at the school were employed in what amounted to a *coordinated* process of religious socialization, involving chaplains, counsellors, and "thought-out and constructed liturgies, ranging from student body Masses to off-campus retreats," with the result that there was an "enormous formative power of classroom and liturgical *rituals*" (McNamara 1992: 115). That, as McNamara's data shows, there was considerable divergence between some official Catholic positions and students' views, in particular regarding sexual morality, does *not* lead to his conclusion that students were developing an ability to exercise self-authority. Rather, it is essential to give sufficient weight to their other interactions – McNamara (1992: 124) himself notes, for example, that "certain moral, especially sexual, attitudes are formed largely through peer interaction."

In line with the rejection of analytical dichotomies already discussed, McNamara's conclusion that individual conscience is increasingly dominant should not be replaced by an interpretation of these students as determined by external authorities, whether their peers or their theology teachers. It is not a question of deciding whether self-authority or external authority prevails, but of re-conceptualizing the relationship between people such that they are seen as mutually constituting, rather than being individual repositories of essential wills to power. Another study of Christians is even more revealing in this regard. Yip (2003: 136) follows Heelas in arguing "that the self (that is, agency) and traditions (that is, structures) coexist and intermingle inextricably ... [but] that in the late modern context, the self (agency) seems to have the upper hand" – in other words, despite the possibility of mixing, the self is always distinguishable from, and exists in opposition to, that which lies outside it. Yip (2002: 201) develops this argument by studying the discourses of non-heterosexual Christians in Britain, claiming to identify a shift from church authority to self-authority: "[t]he self appears to be the ultimate reference point for the respondents' religious faith and practice ... the self, rather than religious authority structures, serves as the primary component of the framework within which the respondents engage in the doctrinal and practical reinterpretation of issues affecting their lives."

By setting up the "self" in opposition to "tradition," which reifies Christian churches in terms of their "official stances" and "traditional teachings," attention is diverted from considering practical interactions, even though Yip's (2002: 202) respondents were accessed through groups that it would be *essential* to sociologically investigate in order to understand their views – namely, the Lesbian and Gay Christian Movement, the Center for Creation Spirituality, secular gay groups and the nonheterosexual "scene." The lack of such investigation denies any sociological recognition of interactions that may play significant roles in the formation of people's discourses, including those of "spirituality" and self-authority. Furthermore, whilst Yip builds his argument upon respondents' discourses about self-authority, other discourses are not taken into account – such as one respondent's view that "[s]pirituality is about people coming together and talking and exchanging and finding ways of looking at the teachings they subscribe to; and applying to their lives and various relationships with other groups of people" (Yip 2002: 205–6).

Given that, as Yip (2002: 204) writes, "respondents in general still considered the institutionalized churches relevant to their everyday lives and spiritual nurturing," such that around 80 per cent still attended regularly, it is sociologically peculiar not to investigate, or at least raise the issue of, the various social interactions of respondents in these congregations. He treats churches as homogeneous institutions that attempt to reproduce orthodoxy in opposition to some participants' personal positions, rather than as sites of social conflict invoking various orthodox and heterodox factions affected by religious conflicts in wider Christian culture. In fact, like McNamara's study, Yip's research provides evidence not for the presence of self-authority, but for the relative *formativeness* of churches: diverse social authorities exist, but they do so on relatively common ground that supports the importance of the church, Christian faith and Christian identity, despite disagreements and heterodoxies. This is also attested by Dillon's (1999) research into why marginalized Catholics stay Catholic, despite resolutely opposing official positions over such issues as sexuality, women's ordination and abortion.

In other words, even research asserting the rise of spirituality indicates an enduring (though not uncontested or invariable) Christian identity that involves *relatively common* valuations of ritual and liturgical practice, and associated doctrines. This is quite different from the situation in the Nottinghamshire network, where there was a marked lack of contestation or even gossip, precisely because participants had little in common in terms of sense of identity and ritual. Thus, significantly different social phenomena have been classified under the label of "spirituality" simply because sociologists have uncritically accepted a selection from people's discourses that they are exercising their own authority. Concentration on the balance between self-authority and external authority (or tradition) has meant that attention has been diverted away from the sociologically crucial issue regarding the way in which multiple authorities may or may not support each other in patterns of socialization (conceptualized in my terms as the degree of formativeness or nonformativeness).

THE BROADER SOCIAL CONTEXTS OF PEOPLE'S LIVES AND BIOGRAPHIES

To reiterate, I am not arguing that discourses and subjective experiences are sociologically irrelevant, but that they should not be separated from practices and interactions. Furthermore, all of these must be contextualized within people's broader experiences and biographies in the religious and other social fields. Only by doing this can the sociology of spirituality's blind spot regarding *social power*, and the way this relates to processes of socialization and to social positions such as class, be addressed. The neglect of these issues is especially noticeable in those studies which have focused on the consumption of goods in what scholars usually name the "spiritual marketplace" (for example, Bowman 1999; Carrette and King 2005; Hamilton 2000; Lyon 2000). In distinction to important developments within the sociology of consumption (discussed in Featherstone 1991), these studies pay little interest to *how* goods are consumed, or to the *structural* features of the marketplace, or to the *contextualization* of this consumption in consumers' wider lives and biographies (for an exception, see the discussion of interactions related to reading experiences in Llewellyn, 2008).

It is particularly surprising that even people's *religious* backgrounds have been neglected by sociologists of spirituality. For example, their argument against the secularization thesis is that whilst religion (or religious behavior, such as church attendance) is falling, spirituality (or spiritual behavior) is increasing – leading not to decline but to a spiritual "revolution" (Bouma 2006: 12; Heelas and Woodhead 2005). But this ignores the fact that the most significant factor linking those classified within the "spirituality" bracket, in Euro-American societies, is that they were *regular churchgoers* in the past – Heelas and Woodhead's own dataset, for example, shows this to be case for 74 per cent of people in their "holistic milieu," a statistic that is disregarded in their analysis (Wood 2009: 245). Similarly, a noticeable feature of the Nottinghamshire network was that the majority of participants had been brought up as regular churchgoers. In other words, the growth of practices outside Christian churches in Euro-America, classified by scholars as "spirituality," rests upon a process of *de-churching*, whereby religiously socialized individuals cease to participate in the religion of their upbringing. This diachronic dimension is obscured when it is simply assumed that non-churchgoers are *un-churched*, as in Barker (2008: 191), Hunt (2003: 160) and Fuller (2001: 2–4). As already discussed, people involved in contexts such as the Nottinghamshire network, marked by multiple *relativizing* authorities (in other words by nonformativeness), experience neither *socialization* into a new form of belief, practice or identity, nor *subjectivization* in the sense of exercising self-authority (or learning to do so). Given these factors, their involvement is instead best interpreted as a manifestation of *partial* individual secularization: these sorts of contexts are primarily an outcome of the widespread process of de-churching in Euro-American societies since the 1960s (especially amongst women), and therefore provide support for the secularization thesis (Wood 2009: 244–6; Wood and Bunn 2009: 293–5). Indeed, the growth of quotidian discourses of spirituality seems primarily due to the growth of de-churched populations that remain partially religious.

This argument explains why it is the case that when studies of spirituality have taken into consideration some factors relating to people's broader lives – such as gender, generation and occupation – their significance tends to be misinterpreted unless attention has already been paid to social practices and interactions. For example, the *nature* of people's relationships with authorities, being relatively more formative (as in Christian contexts) or nonformative (as in the Nottinghamshire network), must be taken into account in order for the *significance* of their religious backgrounds to be understood. The same is true for the significance of social class: the ambiguous nature of nonformative relationships with religious authorities in the Nottinghamshire network, for example, can be shown to relate also to status ambiguity associated with lower middle-class positions in which middle-class professionalization goes hand-in-hand with working-class insecurity and job dissatisfaction (Wood 2007: 163–72).

In general, the sociology of spirituality suffers from a naive form of analysis in which data are interpreted by sociological meta-narratives (particularly those of detraditionalization and subjectivization, associated with Giddens) rather than being interpreted through knowledge of its local social contextualization. Englund and Leach (2000: 226), identifying a similar problem in some anthropological writing, argue against the imposition of "certain specific abstractions in the current discourse on modernity [especially by Giddens] and, in particular, around the concept of the person that those abstractions involve." In place of this, they promote the importance of ethnography for *contextualizing* people's beliefs and practices. This is not to deny the value of meta-narratives but to criticize the way they are utilized, namely the unreflective manner in which they are parachuted into analysis with scant regard for what is actually taking place on the ground.

Perhaps not surprisingly, it is an ethnographic study that avoids such lapses. Bender's (2003) discussion of lived religion amongst participants in an American non-religious charitable organization attempts to contextualize discourses about "spirituality" and "religion" in everyday life, without assuming that (selections from) these discourses should stand as sociological analysis. As already shown, Bender (2003: 69–70) argues that discourses relate to the specific social contexts in which they are produced; she thus rejects interviews as a sufficient sociological method, especially as the redundant analytical distinctions they promote have led scholars to "slip easily into normative critiques." Whilst Bender notes how, at times, some participants in her field setting articulated a discourse relating to "spirituality" which emphasized personal freedom and the rejection of institutional religion, her analysis sensibly refuses to mobilize this as an analytical category. Thus, Bender's (2003: 72; emphases added) account of "Anita," who articulated such a discourse, refers to "Anita's *religious* practices [and] ... *religious* teachings," just as it does for "Nancy" who articulated a "religious" discourse. This analytical orientation directs Bender's (2003: 72–3) attention towards the role of other people and contexts in Anita's life, such as a Catholic friend and Episcopalian priest whose invitations to church services meant that she now "made mass and vespers part of her weekly schedule," as well as continuing to channel and to take astrology courses. Consequently, as Bender (2003: 170–1, n. 24) writes:

> While it is absolutely necessary to take those who call themselves spiritual (or religious) at their word, relying on a conceptual notion of "religious practice" gives us the tools to analyze how such terms also play a role in structuring those experiences. For instance, when Emily [a Protestant churchgoer] tells us she is spiritual, we nevertheless also see her connections to a bona fide, anchoring religious tradition. Anita's spiritual narrative is less easy to engage on these terms. Individuals who call themselves their own spiritual guides use narrative forms that actively distance them from institutional connections. Such connections, and attendant constraints, may nevertheless be apparent if we employ a notion of "religious practice" to ferret out connections, communities, and accrued religious habits and language.

This analytical orientation is important because it prevents the separation of discourses and practices that should be analyzed together, whereas the positing of a conceptual distinction between "religion" and "spirituality" leads to the discourses and practices associated with each to be interpreted as bearing no relation, or as being in opposition, to each other. Indeed, ethnographic evidence shows that people's discourses, practices and interactions in contexts considered (by themselves or sociologists) as "spirituality" in fact relate explicitly to contexts labeled as "religion." In the Nottinghamshire network, for example, people drew their discourses and practices from, and related them to, traditions and institutions that they deemed "religious," as well as sharing with these an assumption about the existence and efficacy of supernatural beings and powers (Wood 2009: 241). Furthermore, as already shown, the most significant factor linking these people was their previous regular churchgoing. In other words, whilst "religion" and "spirituality" may sometimes and in some contexts relate to distinct discourses and practices, the clear linkage between these necessitates a *single* analytical category.

It is here that a theory of social fields proves its value, since this conveys the notion of a unitary (though only semi-autonomous) arena of practice, involving power-relations in competitions over capital – as theoretically developed most fully in the work of Bourdieu (1990). Bourdieu (1991) himself referred to the *religious* field and capital, and whilst his conceptualization of religion has rightly been criticized for introducing unwarranted assumptions into analysis (Verter 2003: 157), a theory of fields points to the need to retain *some* analytical category in order to articulate the synchronic and diachronic relations between people's practices. Therefore, to introduce a distinction between "spiritual capital" and "religious capital," as does Verter, is to reinstate the analytical distinction between "religion" and "spirituality" precisely at the point where a common analysis is required, namely in the analysis of a unitary field of practice. The unhelpfulness of this approach is demonstrated by the fact that, as already shown in Verter's (2003: 157–8) case, this introduces a misleading analysis of "spirituality" as "extrainstitutional" and "resolutely individualistic," as opposed to "religion." The same may be said for Davies' (2000: 196–7) identification of spirituality with habitus: whilst his reference to the bodily, imaginative and emotional dimensions of human life is admittedly essential for any properly sociological understanding of practice, interaction and context, given that Davies himself refers to "religious experience" and "authority in religion" it seems misleading to refer to habitus in terms of "spirituality" rather than "religion." This unacceptability of an analytical distinction between "religion" and "spirituality" logically extends to proposals for a new category to subsume both as sub-fields or sub-categories, as in Heelas and Woodhead's (2005: 6) notion of the "sacred landscape" and Knoblauch's (2008: 142) notion of "transcendence" (which, without irony, he describes as "less biased" than the concept of "religion").

If the concept of "religion" seems tied to assumptions about rigid institutionalization, hierarchization and conformity, then what sociologists must do is alter their conceptualization – not reinstate the structure-agency dichotomy by opposing the concept of "spirituality" to that of "religion." In this regard, sociologists would benefit by paying attention to the conceptualization of religion in the twin sociological discipline of social anthropology. Often addressing contexts that are weakly institutionalized and formalized, social anthropologists have nevertheless been able to utilize "religion" as a concept that retains analytical sharpness in addressing a wide variety of human religious experiences, practices and interactions (a good overview of which is provided by Bowie 2006), thereby avoiding the problematic recourse to "spirituality" as a second concept. Undoubtedly, that the concept of "spirituality" has been so little taken up in social anthropology is due in no small part to the discipline's ethnographic method that insists upon social contextualization.

CONCLUSION

This chapter has sought to pass a critical eye over a growing body of sociological work that addresses "spirituality." The sociology of spirituality uses this concept to encompass individualistic, subjective experiences, although there are disagreements about whether these occur in institutional settings. However, it was shown that this approach unquestioningly adopts some views by some respondents – nearly always on the basis of surveys, interviews or published texts – that they individually choose their practices and beliefs by asserting self-authority. The transmutation of this discourse into an analytical category has led to the reinstatement of a number of conceptual dichotomies, principally of structure-agency, that recent developments in sociological thinking have successfully begun to overcome – and thus represents an interpretative regression. This is associated with the entrance, into the sociology of religion, of discourses and methods associated with Religious Studies. Its consequences are seen in the fact that the sociology of spirituality typically pays little attention to three key sociological principles: the need to investigate social practice, social interaction, and the broader social contexts of people's lives and biographies. In other words, issues of social power that lie at the heart of sociological enquiry are neglected. Certainly, it is important to address the way in which people may think and talk about themselves and their activities in terms of "spirituality." However, whilst this may necessitate using the concept of "religion" in a more nuanced way, akin to social anthropological studies, this chapter has shown how analysis is ill-served by the establishment of a category of "spirituality" as distinct from that of "religion." Whilst scholars in Religious Studies may decide that "spirituality" retains analytical value for them, it is high time that sociologists pursued their studies on their own *sociological* terms.

Bibliography

Barker, E. (2008) The church without and the God within: religiosity and/or spirituality? in Barker, E. (ed.), *The Centrality of Religion in Social Life*, Aldershot: Ashgate, 187–202.

Beckford, J. A. (1983) The restoration of "power" to the sociology of religion, *Sociological Analysis* 44 (1): 11–32.

Beckford, J. A. (1989) *Religion and Advanced Industrial Society*, London: Unwin Hyman.

Bellah, R. N. (1969) Religious evolution, in R. Robertson (ed.), *Sociology of Religion*, Harmondsworth: Penguin Education, 262–92.

Bellah, R. N. et al. (1996) [1985] *Habits of the Heart* (revd. edn.), Berkeley: University of California Press.

Bender, C. (2003) *Heaven's Kitchen*, Chicago: University of Chicago Press.

Besecke, K. (2001) Speaking of meaning in modernity: reflexive spirituality as a cultural resource, *Sociology of Religion* 62 (3): 365–81.

Bouma, G. (2006) *Australian Soul*, Cambridge: Cambridge University Press.

Bourdieu, P. (1990) *The Logic of Practice*, Cambridge: Polity.

Bourdieu, P. (1991) Genesis and structure of the religious field, *Comparative Social Research* 13: 1–44.

Bowie, F. (2006) *The Anthropology of Religion* (2nd edn.), Oxford: Blackwell.

Bowman, M. (1999) Healing in the spiritual marketplace: consumers, courses and credentialism, *Social Compass* 46 (2): 181–9.

Brown, M. F. (1997) *The Channeling Zone*, Cambridge: Harvard University Press.

Campbell, C. (1972) The cult, the cultic milieu and secularization, in M. Hill (ed.), *A Sociological Yearbook of Religion in Britain 5*, London: SCM Press, 119–36.

Carrette, J. and King, R. (2005) *Selling Spirituality*, London: Routledge.

Davies, D. J. (2000) *The Mormon Culture of Salvation*, Aldershot: Ashgate.

Dillon, M. (1999) *Catholic Identity*, Cambridge: Cambridge University Press.

Ellwood, R. S. (1987) Introduction, in R. S. Ellwood (ed.), *Eastern Spirituality in America*, New York: Paulist Press, 5–43.

Englund, H. and Leach, J. (2000) Ethnography and the meta-narratives of modernity, *Current Anthropology* 41 (2): 225–48.

Featherstone, M. (1991) *Consumer Culture and Postmodernism*, London: Sage.

Flanagan, K. (2007) Introduction, in K. Flanagan and P. C. Jupp (eds.), *A Sociology of Spirituality*, Aldershot: Ashgate, 1–21.

Foucault, M. (1980) *Power/Knowledge*, London: Harvester.

Fuller, R. C. (2001) *Spiritual But Not Religious*, Oxford: Oxford University Press.

Furseth, I. (2005) From "everything has a meaning" to "I want to believe in something": religious change between two generations of women in Norway, *Social Compass* 52 (2): 157–68.

Giddens, A. (1991) *Modernity and Self-Identity*, Cambridge: Polity.

Glock, C. Y. and Bellah, R. N. (eds.) (1976) *The New Religious Consciousness*, Berkeley: University of California Press.

Guest, M. (2007) In search of spiritual capital, in K. Flanagan and P. C. Jupp (eds.), *A Sociology of Spirituality*, Aldershot: Ashgate, 181–200.

Hamilton, M. (2000) An analysis of the Festival for Mind–Body–Spirit, London, in S. Sutcliffe and M. Bowman (eds.), *Beyond New Age*, Edinburgh: Edinburgh University Press, 188–200.

Hanegraaff, W. J. (1996) *New Age Religion and Western Culture*, Leiden: Brill.

Hanegraaff, W. J. (1999) New Age spiritualities as secular religion: a historian's perspective, *Social Compass* 46 (2): 145–60.

Heelas, P. (1996) *The New Age Movement*, Oxford: Blackwell.

Heelas, P. (1998) Review, *Journal of the Royal Anthropological Institute* 4 (2): 379–80.

Heelas, P. (2008) *Spiritualities of Life*, Oxford: Blackwell.

Heelas, P. and Woodhead, L. (2005) *The Spiritual Revolution*, Oxford: Blackwell.

Hervieu-Léger, D. (2008) Religious individualism, modern individualism and self-fulfilment, in E. Barker (ed.), *The Centrality of Religion in Social Life*, Aldershot: Ashgate, 29–40.

Hunt, K. (2003) Understanding the spirituality of people who do not go to church, in G. Davie, P. Heelas, and L. Woodhead (eds.), *Predicting Religion*, Aldershot: Ashgate, 159–69.

Knoblauch, H. (2008) Spirituality and popular religion in Europe, *Social Compass* 55 (2): 140–53.

Lambert, Y. (2004) A turning point in religious evolution in Europe, *Journal of Contemporary Religion* 19 (1): 29–45.

Llewellyn, D. (2008) Forming community in the third wave: literary texts and women's spiritualities, in D. Llewellyn and D. F. Sawyer (eds.), *Reading Spiritualities*, Aldershot: Ashgate, 153–69.

Luckmann, T. (1967) *The Invisible Religion*, New York: Macmillan.

Luckmann, T. (1996) The privatization of religion and morality, in P. Heelas, S. Lash, and P. Morris (eds.), *Detraditionalization*, Oxford: Blackwell, 72–86.

Lyon, D. (2000) *Jesus in Disneyland*, Cambridge: Polity.

Marler, P. L. and Hadaway, C. K. (2002) "Being religious" or "being spiritual" in America: a zero-sum proposition? *Journal for the Scientific Study of Religion* 41 (2): 289–300.

Marx, K. and Engels, F. (1949) *The German Ideology, Parts I and III*, London: Lawrence and Wishart.

McGuire, M. B. (1988) *Ritual Healing in Suburban America*, London: Rutgers University Press.

McGuire, M. B. (2008a) *Lived Religion*, Oxford: Oxford University Press.

McGuire, M. B. (2008b) Toward a sociology of spirituality: individual religion in social/historical context, in E. Barker (ed.), *The Centrality of Religion in Social Life*, Aldershot: Ashgate, 215–32.

McNamara, P. H. (1992) *Conscience First, Tradition Second*, New York: State University of New York Press.

Roof, W. C. (1993) *A Generation of Seekers*, New York: HarperSanFrancisco.

Roof, W. C. (1999) *Spiritual Marketplace*, Princeton: Princeton University Press.

Taylor, C. (2007) *A Secular Age*, Cambridge, MA: Harvard University Press.

Thompson, J. B. (1996) Tradition and self in a mediated world, in P. Heelas, S. Lash, and P. Morris (eds.), *Detraditionalization*, Oxford: Blackwell, 89–108.

Tipton, S. M. (1982) *Getting Saved from the Sixties*, Berkeley: University of California Press.

Turner, B. S. (1991) *Religion and Social Theory* (2nd edn.), London: Sage.

Verter, B. (2003) Spiritual capital: theorizing religion with Bourdieu against Bourdieu, *Sociological Theory* 21 (2): 150–74.

Voas, D. and Bruce, S. (2007) The spiritual revolution: another false dawn for the sacred, in K. Flanagan and P. C. Jupp (eds.), *A Sociology of Spirituality*, Aldershot: Ashgate, 43–61.

Weber, M. (1978) *Economy and Society*, Berkeley: University of California Press.

Wood, M. (2007) *Possession, Power and the New Age*, Aldershot: Ashgate.

Wood, M. (2009) The nonformative elements of religious life: questioning the sociology of spirituality paradigm, *Social Compass* 56 (2): 237–48.

Wood, M. and Bunn, C. (2009) Strategy in a religious network: a Bourdieuian critique of the sociology of spirituality, *Sociology* 43 (2): 286–303.

Woodiwiss, A. (2005) *Scoping the Social*, Maidenhead: Open University Press.

Wuthnow, R. (1976) *The Consciousness Reformation*, Berkeley: University of California Press.

Wuthnow, R. (1998) *After Heaven*, Berkeley: University of California Press.

Wuthnow, R. (2001) Spirituality and spiritual practice, in R. K. Fenn (ed.), *The Blackwell Companion to Sociology of Religion*, Oxford: Blackwell, 306–20.

Yip, A. K. T. (2002) The persistence of faith among nonheterosexual Christians, *Journal for the Scientific Study of Religion* 4 (2): 199–212.

Yip, A. K. T. (2003) The self as the basis of religious faith: spirituality of gay, lesbian and bisexual Christians, in G. Davie, P. Heelas, and L. Woodhead (eds.), *Predicting Religion*, Aldershot: Ashgate, 135–46.

Zinnbauer, Brian J. et al. (1997) Religion and spirituality: unfuzzying the fuzzy, *Journal for the Scientific Study of Religion* 36 (4): 549–64.

13

Arguing against Darwinism
Religion, Science, and Public Morality

MICHAEL S. EVANS AND JOHN H. EVANS

1   INTRODUCTION

The sociology of religion has different understandings of how religion ought to be defined for purposes of analysis. Perhaps the most persistent divide is that between epistemological approaches to religion, which see religion as a defined area of knowledge (e.g. about the supernatural, or about the "irrational"), and meaning or cultural approaches to religion, which see religion as a way of making sense of social relations (Geertz 1973; Buckser 1996). However, in practice the methods of social science often obscure this distinction, since it is not practical to distinguish between what is in the minds of people and what they actually say in a survey, or what we analyze as a variable in quantitative analysis. In this chapter we explore a case where this difference matters. We analyze a longstanding debate in American public life over the origins, meaning, and significance of human life. Creationist challenges to evolution demonstrate the implications of defining religion in terms of cultural systems rather than epistemological content or status.

In contrast to the dominant academic narrative about religion and science (see Evans and Evans 2008), we claim that epistemological arguments are, and have always been, less important in motivating ordinary people to mount challenges to Darwinism. Far more important are concerns about public morality, more specifically the place of humans in the world and proper behavior towards fellow humans. Such concerns have mobilized a wide variety of challenges to Darwinism. And while such varied positions as Young Earth Creationism, Old Earth Creationism, Day-Age Creationism, Gap Creationism, Progressive Creationism, Creation Science, and Intelligent Design can be more or less treated as epistemologically "creationist," it is their qualities as moral criticisms of Darwinism that most tightly bind them together, both historically and sociologically speaking. Creationist challenges of all kinds are, and have always been, driven by moral claims.

At the same time, we argue that Darwinism has often been the grounds for making moral claims by scientists. It is not that religious challenges erroneously mix morality and science because challengers don't understand science. Rather, challengers understand full well that scientists are also making moral claims, and are acting to counter these claims. This contrasts sharply with the idea of "value-free" science. But we are not making a claim about epistemological standpoint and what science "really is." Rather, we use empirical historical and sociological data to demonstrate that such claims, whatever their epistemological status, are mobilized regularly in public discourse.

By ignoring the centrality of moral claims in these debates, scholars and policymakers have managed to miss the motivating factors behind debates and conflict over Darwinism. It is not surprising, then, that policies intended to redress this conflict have consistently failed to achieve traction. Of course, claiming higher epistemological status is one way to end debate. Hence the only partly successful strategy is for scientists to appeal to state enforcement of such status.

But if this debate is largely about values, state enforcement of a particular position is hardly a democratic way to go about it, and ignores the driving moral concerns that will continue to mobilize challengers to Darwinism. So challenges will persist, and perhaps even intensify. The good news is that liberal democracy has some useful ways of handling debates over public morality (rather than epistemology). We argue that acknowledgment of creationist challenges to Darwinism as battles over public morality opens up a new space for liberal democratic approaches to resolving the conflict. And we offer specific suggestions on how to go about it.

Finally, we use the case of creationist challenges to make two key points: one about religion in public life, and another about how to conduct research in the sociology of religion. First, we follow aspects of the arguments of Wolterstorff, Stout, and the later Rorty in arguing for liberal democracy as an ongoing debate and, in particular, in arguing that the only way such debate can reasonably continue is to address the moral concerns at the heart of such debate rather than resorting to "conversation-stoppers" like religious or scientific epistemological claims. Second, using creationist challenges as our evidence, we reiterate that there is a practical difference between sociological approaches to religion that are primarily epistemological and approaches that are primarily cultural. Epistemological approaches are largely blind to moral concerns, and therefore are less appropriate for understanding religion in public life.

WHO ARE THE CREATIONISTS?

As a preliminary step, we need to determine the social location of those persons who claim to not believe in evolution. Because of space constraints, and because of the historical prominence of creationism in American public debate, we generally focus on the American context. Of course there are examples of creationist activists with resources currently operating in various forms throughout the world. In Turkey, for example, Adnan Oktar's Science Research Foundation produces and distributes books such as *The Evolution Deceit* (Yahya 1999) and *The Atlas of Creation* (Yahya 2006) to advocate an Islamic version of Old Earth Creationism. And recently in the United Kingdom, evangelical Christian activists have pushed to teach creationism alongside evolution in privately-funded colleges (for example,

Emmanuel College, see Allgaier 2008), while the activist group Truth in Science has distributed Intelligent Design materials to UK schools (Zimmerman, 2006). But our focus here primarily is on the American context.

The 2004 General Social Survey asked a question of a random sample of Americans about the "truth" of evolution. We coded the 55 percent of the respondents who claimed that evolution was "probably not true" or "definitely not true" as not believing in evolution. That 55 percent of Americans do not believe in evolution is of course fodder for advocates of science. This lack of belief is more evenly distributed in the population than one might think. To map out the social location of lack of belief, we created a number of demographic variables. Fitting with the general stereotypes of critics of evolution, the first column in table 13.1 shows that those who are older, female, with less education, and living in the South are less likely to believe in evolution. Furthermore, evangelicals and black Protestants are less likely to believe than are members of other religious traditions.

Of course, some of these demographic differences may appear to be significant because, for example, women are more likely to be religious than men. So, we conducted an ordered logistic regression model predicting lack of belief in evolution. The second column shows these coefficients, where the magnitude of the coefficients are directly comparable because all of the variables are dichotomous. (Dashes indicate the comparison group. For example, the effect being an evangelical is in relation to not having any religious affiliation.) This regression equation shows that while education, Southern residence and gender determine one's view of evolution, these demographic characteristics pale in comparison to the effect of being either an evangelical or black Protestant. The evangelical effect is nearly 4 times the size of the largest demographic effect – education. Catholics and mainline Protestants have the same level of skepticism about evolution as do the non-religious. These data show that claiming to not believe in evolution is, in the American context, solidly located within the conservative Protestant tradition.

Table 13.1 Percentage of selected social groups who do not believe in evolution

	% who do not believe in evolution	Logistic regression coefficient
High school education or less	64	0.540[a]
Some college education or more	50	–
Younger in age	53	–
Older in age	58	0.179
Lives in south	66	0.384[b]
Lives outside of south	49	–
Woman	61	0.473[a]
Man	49	–
Evangelical	83	1.93a
Mainline Protestant	46	0.150
Black Protestant	69	0.998[a]
Catholic	46	0.232
Other religious tradition	37	−0.114
Non-religious	31	–

[a] = $p < 0.001$; [b] = $p < 0.05$.

Based on this statistical analysis, one would probably come to the conclusion, as many have, that organized opposition to Darwinism is the result of these conservative Protestants using a biblical literalist epistemology and the scientists using a secular materialist epistemology. But a scientific epistemology would reject much of conservative Protestant belief, such as the virgin birth and the resurrection, so why the persistent protest against this one claim about nature? The answer, we propose, is that the debate persists because all attempts to address the debate have missed its motivating feature: a concern over the link between Darwinism and morality.

THE HISTORY OF CREATIONIST CHALLENGES TO DARWINISM

We follow the conventional periodization of this history in terms of apparent changes in creationist tactics, though one of the points of this chapter is to indicate that the moral concerns at the heart of opposition to Darwinism remain consistent. There are three overarching points to consider as we review specific historical and contemporary evidence. First, while there have always been epistemological claims involved in debates over Darwinism, these do not explain how many epistemologically distinct positions coalesce into coherent challenges to, and defenses of, Darwinism. Second, there have always been moral claims by all parties involved, and these are more consistent across time and space than epistemological claims. The persistent thread from the days of Darwin to today's Intelligent Design movement is not in the pro-creation argument, but the anti-evolution argument (Numbers 1992; Scott 1997). Third, it is moral claims, not epistemological conflicts, that drive people to mobilize challenges. The concern of creationists in each of their historic incarnations is that when you teach evolution, you are implicitly teaching a certain philosophy at the same time, and that this philosophy undermines some forms of morality. So while it has always been epistemology and values together, our point is that focusing on epistemology misses the most important component of creationism.

This is not the usual way of talking about creationist challenges to Darwinism. Attempts to reconcile religion and science (for example, Haught 2000) focus primarily on the problem of reconciling apparent epistemological conflict. Well-meaning defenses of ID's intellectual history (for example, Fuller 2007) provide epistemological arguments for the inclusion of creationism in scientific debate. And even those scholars who acknowledge the moral concerns at the heart of creationism (for example, Nelkin 1982) tend to pass these over in favor of epistemological arguments.

Scopes

Upon publication of *The Origin of Species* in 1859, both supporters and detractors immediately recognized that Darwinism had moral implications, a concern that rose to even greater prominence following the publication of the *Descent of Man* in 1871. While philosophers might question the transition from "is" to "ought" on Humean grounds, it is clear that for many contemporaries, Darwinism implied some social challenges, especially when articulated in Herbert Spencer's (1864: 444) terms as "survival of the fittest." For example, William Jay Youmans, editor of *Popular Science Monthly*, wrote about natural selection:

> There is perhaps no greater or more serious problem confronting society today than this: how to pay just heed to the above law without injury to our own moral sensibilities and particularly to our sense of the sacredness of life. (Youmans, 1893: 122)

Concerns over moral implications of Darwinism led to legal restrictions on the teaching of evolution in public schools, the site of education for a rapidly increasing number of young Americans (Nelkin 1982; Larson 1997). Biology textbooks of the time, such as the popular *A Civic Biology* by George William Hunter (1914), often contained only a limited amount of material on evolution. But even that limited amount discussed moral problems. *A Civic Biology*, for example, suggested that "if the stock of domesticated animals can be improved, it is not unfair to ask if the health and vigor of the future generations of men and women on the earth might not be improved by applying to them the law of selection" (Hunter 1914: 261).

In May 1925, in order to test the constitutionality of an anti-evolution law passed only two months earlier, the American Civil Liberties Union provoked the State of Tennessee into prosecuting high school science teacher John Scopes for teaching the evolution lessons from *A Civic Biology* in a public school classroom. Creationists saw an opportunity to demonstrate that Darwinism implied an unacceptable and dangerous moral position that should not be publicly considered at all, much less taught to schoolchildren (Larson 1997). The defender of the creationist view was populist former Democratic Party presidential candidate William Jennings Bryan. According to Ron Numbers' canonical analysis of creationism, for Bryan:

> World War I ... exposed the darkest side of human nature and shattered his illusions about the future of Christian society. Obviously something had gone awry, and Bryan soon traced the source of the trouble to the paralyzing influence of Darwinism on the conscience. By substituting the law of the jungle for the teachings of Christ, it threatened the principles he valued most: democracy and Christianity. Two books in particular confirmed his suspicion. The first ... recounted first hand conversations with German officers that revealed the role of Darwin's biology in the German decision to declare war. The Second ... purported to demonstrate the historical and philosophical links between Darwinism and German militarism. (Numbers 1992: 538)

As a celebrity trial, the Scopes case drew immense attention, but not for its constitutional implications. As Dorothy Nelkin (1982: 31) put it, "the constitutional question ... was buried as William Jennings Bryan and Clarence Darrow clashed over questions of religion and morality." Though technically Bryan won the case, creationists failed to win public support for their concerns over Darwin and morality. In the popular account, creationists emerged from *Scopes* as ignorant bumpkins, while evolution supporters triumphed as proponents of reason and science, an impression reinforced in popular media most notably through the 1955 play *Inherit the Wind*, made into an 1960 Academy Award-nominated film starring Spencer Tracy as the fictionalized Darrow.

But while it seemed that Darwinism had triumphed in the popular imagination, the empirical fact is that the teaching of evolution in public high schools, and the inclusion of Darwin in biology textbooks, actually declined after *Scopes* (Grabiner and Miller 1974). In this sense Bryan was successful, as textbook publishers voluntarily self-censored their materials in order to avoid offending dominant sentiments. Notably, this was not just production of "special expurgated southern editions" of textbooks, but widespread "self-censorship by the New York-based publishing industry," implying that this was not simply a regional expression of religious sentiment (Grabiner and Miller 1974: 835). For all of the flash of the *Scopes* trial, there was little interest in, and much public resistance to, expanding the teaching of evolution in public schools.

To be clear, we are not claiming that religious activists forced the systematic removal of evolution from biology textbooks, a claim that remains in dispute over the details of particular terms, motives, and intent by publishers and authors (Ladouceur 2008). What is not in dispute, however, is that Darwinism in public schools did not expand after Scopes, and in several cases, for whatever reason, actually declined, giving activists less reason to press their objections. Without Darwinism moving into the sphere of public morality through the education system, creationists kept to themselves and their own organizations after *Scopes*. Creationists still worried about the moral claims of Darwinism, but by and large kept their arguments within the creationist community rather than public debate, founding organizations such as the Religion and Science Association in 1935 and the American Scientific Affiliation in 1941 (Nelkin 1982; Numbers 1992; Lienesch 2007).

Creation science

With the launch of Sputnik in 1957, the American government turned to funding science education in a concerted and systematic way through the National Defense Education Act of 1958. The Biological Sciences Curriculum Study (BSCS) brought together, perhaps for the first time, practicing scientists and practicing teachers to create a biology curriculum to be used in the nation's public schools (Lienesch 2007). The BSCS program made Darwinism, and evolution more generally, the cornerstone of biology education in America (see, for example, BSCS 1963). BSCS curricula also promoted the relationship between science and progress, and thus appeared to make Darwinism central to America's future development, not just in training scientists, but in educating all citizens to participate in American public life (Nelkin 1982). As one participant in the process put it, "one hundred years without Darwin are enough" (Muller 1959).

In response to the increase in teaching of Darwinism in public schools through the BSCS program and its curriculum products, creationists mounted challenges to BSCS textbooks on many different grounds, including indecency of images depicting reproductive organs, violation of remaining state anti-evolution laws, and violation of the First Amendment (Nelkin 1982). The tactics varied in their approaches, but the common concern remained that Darwinism had dangerous moral implications and should not be taught in schools.

One of the strongest challenges came from "creation science," where creationists dismissed Darwinism based on scientific claims stemming from the Bible. Creation science proponents agreed that students should learn science, but not that they should learn Darwinism. In 1961, Whitcomb and Morris published *The Genesis*

Flood, an account of geology and human origins based on biblical explanations of the world-girdling Noachic flood, drawing heavily on previous "flood geology" theories offered by George McCready Price in his 1923 creationist textbook *The New Geology*.

For Whitcomb and Morris, the claim to scientificity was as much about the need to replace Darwinian morality with a God and human-centered morality as it was about floods and geology. In *The Genesis Flood*, they wrote:

> [T]he morality of evolution, which assumes that progress and achievement and "good" come about through such action as benefits the individual himself or the group of which he is a part, to the detriment of others, is most obviously anti-Christian. The very essence of Christianity is unselfish sacrifice on behalf of others, motivated by the great sacrifice of Christ himself, dying in atonement for the sins of the whole world! (Whitcomb and Morris 1961: 447)

These sentiments were echoed by R. G. Elmendorf and the Pittsburgh Creation Society, who distributed a flyer with a pictorial diagram of the "evolution tree" of "evil fruits" growing from the root of Darwinism. These "evil fruits" include (but are not limited to) communism, racism, terrorism, abortion, socialism, crime, and inflation. The accompanying text concludes:

> What is the best way to counteract the evil fruit of evolution? Opposing these things one-by-one is good, but it does not deal with the underlying cause. The tree will produce fruit faster than it can be spotted and removed. A more effective approach is to chop the tree off at its base by scientifically discrediting evolution. When the tree falls, the fruit will go down with it, and unbelieving man will be left "without excuse" (Romans 1:21). That is the real reason why scientific creationism represents such a serious threat to the evolutionary establishment! (reproduced in Toumey 1994: 96)

Whitcomb and Morris founded the Creation Research Society in 1963 to promote creation science through the publication of a creationist journal and the development of a creationist biology textbook. In 1968, however, the decision in *Epperson v. Arkansas*[1] rendered anti-evolution laws unconstitutional, making it difficult to promote a text solely on the basis of its anti-evolution position. The CRS shifted its emphasis to promoting creation science as a legitimate scientific alternative to Darwinian evolution. In 1974 Morris produced *Scientific Creationism*, a guide to teaching creation science without explicit reference to biblical authority or even religious language (Morris 1974). Without the advantage of anti-evolution laws, creationists promoted the idea of "equal time" and "balanced treatment" for creation science and Darwinian science, and even obtained legal protection for such treatment in Arkansas and Louisiana (Gilkey 1985; Numbers 1992).

In 1982, however, *McLean v. Arkansas*[2] marked the beginning of the end for creation science in science classes. The *McLean* decision, written by Judge William Overton, struck down the Arkansas Balanced Treatment for Creation-Science and Evolution-Science Act on the basis that creation science violated the American Constitution's First Amendment prohibition on the establishment of religion. Overton acknowledged that creation science was in part a reaction to the introduction of the BSCS curriculum, even citing the moral concerns driving the challenge in the official opinion:

> Creationists view evolution as a source of society's ills, and the writings of Morris and Clark are typical expressions of that view.
>
> "Evolution is thus not only anti-biblical and anti-Christian, but it is utterly unscientific and impossible as well. But it has served effectively as the pseudo-scientific basis of atheism, agnosticism, socialism, fascism, and numerous other false and dangerous philosophies over the past century." (Morris and Clark, cited in *McLean v. Arkansas*)

Yet Overton focused his legal decision on epistemological issues, itemizing the ways in which creation science did not accord with scientific method or practice, and emphasizing that creation science was not, in his opinion, science at all. While this was not strictly necessary for rendering an opinion on the religious grounds for creation science, it nonetheless set an important cultural precedent for evaluating creationist challenges as epistemological, not moral, in nature. From *McLean* forward, the success of creationist challenges would be measured based on whether or not creationist theories were included in "science" as defined by judges in landmark legal cases, rather than the extent to which moral concerns resonated with a broader public. In 1987, *Edwards v. Aguillard*[3] came before the US Supreme Court, and largely based on Overton's reasoning about religious establishment in *McLean*, the court rendered a decision to strike down Louisiana's Creationism Act, the last remaining "equal time" law in the nation.

For creationists, discrediting evolution on scientific grounds was the most effective strategy for eliminating a dangerous source of moral justification for many of the ills of society. Many scholars studying creationists generally dismiss creation science as an instrumental strategy for navigating legal restrictions (for example, Spuhler 1985; Scott 1997). The *McLean* decision certainly seems to support this analysis. But it is clear that in the period following *Scopes*, the motivations for creationist challenges came from concerns over the increasing influence of Darwinism in public education, a point that even Judge Overton acknowledged in striking them down.

Intelligent design

McLean and *Edwards* instituted a legal regime where any hint of religious motivations could invalidate an attempt to promote an alternative to Darwinism. In response, the Foundation for Thought and Ethics reworked an existing creation science text to remove all references to creationism and replace them with the term "intelligent design." They published the resulting text in 1989 as *Of Pandas and People* (Davis and Kenyon 1989; Biever 2005). The term "intelligent design" (hereafter ID) refers to the idea that the world as we observe it could not have happened without intelligent guidance, an idea that traces back to such luminaries as Newton and Paley (Fuller 2007). Notably, however, ID does not necessarily require specific claims about God or a particular religious belief system (Discovery Institute 2007).

The most visible and active proponents of ID are fellows of the Discovery Institute, a "nonpartisan public policy think tank conducting research on technology, science and culture, economics and foreign affairs" (Discovery Institute 2007). The Discovery Institute's strategy for promoting ID is called the "Wedge Document," and while it was originally intended for internal use, it has been copied and widely circulated by opponents seeking to discredit ID (for example, Forrest and Gross 2004). The Wedge Document cites as motivation the serious moral concerns implied by the materialist conception of reality promoted by Darwinism, which:

> eventually infected virtually every area of our culture, from politics and economics to literature and art ... materialists denied the existence of objective moral standards, claiming that environment dictates our behavior and beliefs. Such moral relativism was uncritically adopted by much of the social sciences ... Materialists also undermined personal responsibility by asserting that human thoughts and behaviors are dictated by our biology and environment ... In the materialist scheme of things, everyone is a victim and no one can be held accountable for his or her actions.

As with creation science, ID proponents seek equal time for their position in public school science classes. Unlike creation science, ID proponents take special care to minimize the possibility that ID will be seen as religious. So far this strategy has met with limited success. In 2004, a school board in Dover, Pennsylvania voted to require a statement about ID as part of the public school curriculum. Shortly thereafter, a group of parents filed suit against the district, and the resulting decision in *Kitzmiller v. Dover*[4] once again struck down a creationist challenge based on the First Amendment establishment clause.

Recently ID proponents have once again taken up the idea of "equal time" and "teaching the controversy," but in the public rather than the legal arena. Popular author and TV host Ben Stein helped produce and promote the documentary film *Expelled: No Intelligence Allowed. Expelled* claims that alternatives to Darwinism have been suppressed, and that Darwinism is of grave moral concern:

> In a Darwinian framework, human beings are no better than any other animal and ultimately may be treated as animals by those who consider themselves to be greater, more human, enlightened or evolved ... Hitler and the Nazis followed Darwinian eugenics to an extreme, carrying "survival of the fittest" to the radical conclusion of exterminating "unfit" and "inferior" races like the Jews and Gypsies, and "weak" members of society like the handicapped. (Motive 2008: 14)

Unsurprisingly, reaction to ID from "defenders of science" in popular and academic venues has focused on ID's religious origins, as this is now the most effective legal way to prevent ID from inclusion in public school curricula (Pennock 2001; Forrest and Gross 2004). The central claim at the heart of Intelligent Design remains consistent with Bryan, Whitcomb, Elmendorf, and many other creationists since Darwin. For creationist challengers past and present, Darwinism implies a morality that devalues human life, causes unneeded conflict and competition, and pushes society in an actively harmful direction.

Darwinism as a Moral Project

It is clear that many creationists claim that Darwinism provides moral grounds for all sorts of evil in the world. But creationist challenges to Darwinism based on issues of public morality do not necessarily emerge from ignorance, misunderstanding, or a confusion of science with morality, as many defenders of Darwinism have claimed. Rather, they can be seen as a reaction to some prominent scientists, past and present, who have also mobilized Darwinism to support moral positions on human life, personhood, and social organization. Of course, Darwinism is very flexible. As historian Robert Proctor (1988: 16) has put it, "People generally found in Darwin what they wanted to find," and in Loewenberg's (1941: 363) terms, "Charles Darwin was all things to all men." But the point is that this is as true for scientists as it is for creationists. It is a mistake to portray creationists as people who don't understand science and are confusing it with morality. Rather, creationists are contributing to a multi-sided debate about the moral implications of Darwinism in which scientists are often willing participants.

Darwinism and social order

From its inception, Darwinism introduced new justifications for old practices and prejudices. Francis Galton, a half-cousin of Darwin, drew heavily on Darwin's theories to promote eugenics, the systematic intervention into human reproduction for purposes of improving "racial hygiene" (Galton 1883). Of concern to many proponents of eugenics was the idea society could succumb to degeneration, making it less fit for survival and therefore doomed to extinction. Yet many were confident that Darwinism provided the answer. As John Haycraft said in his lectures to the Royal College of Physicians (collected as *Darwinism and Race Progress*):

> [W]e can improve our race by adopting the one and only adequate expedient, that of carrying on the race through our best and most worthy strains. We can be as certain of our result as the gardener who hoes away the weeds and plants good seed, and who knows that he can produce the plants he wants by his care in the selection of the seed. (Haycraft 1895: 155)

Early American eugenics drew on Spencer, Darwin, and Galton to justify programs of forced sterilization for "mental defectives," "moral degenerates," and other "undesirables" to prevent the inheritance of their bad traits to later generations. The Eugenics Record Office, founded in 1910 at the Cold Spring Harbor Laboratory, promoted forced sterilization as good public policy and created standardized questionnaires to help with evaluation (Eugenics Archive 2008). By 1930, half of the states in the USA had some sort of eugenic sterilization law on the books. In Arizona, inmates of the State Hospital for the Insane could be sterilized if they were the "probable potential parent of socially inadequate offspring," and in Kansas any inmate of the state, including prisoners, could be sterilized if "procreation by him would be likely to result in defective or feeble-minded children with criminal tendencies" (Brown 1930: 23, 25).

Often, however, "degenerate" meant non-white or immigrant. Even the Scopes text *A Civic Biology* included a ranking of races from "the Ethiopian or negro type, originating in Africa" to "the highest type of all, the Caucasians, represented by the civilized white inhabitants of Europe and America" (Hunter 1914: 196). By 1924, based largely on data presented by Harry Laughlin of the Eugenics Record Office, the US Congress passed the Immigration Reform Act, setting quotas for immigrants according to their seeming fitness and levels of "social inadequacy." Immigration levels did not recover until the late 1980s (Eugenics Archive 2008).

Of course the most severe example of eugenics application is the systematic sterilization and extermination of those deemed degenerate by the Nazi regime, particularly embodied by the 1933 Law for the Prevention of Genetically Diseased Offspring. The Nazis "regularly quoted American geneticists who expressed support for their sterilization policies ... [and] frequently invoked the large-scale California experience with sterilization" (Paul 1995: 86). It is clear that Nazi policies drew on ideas about racial hygiene and degeneracy (Proctor 1988), and it is clear that American scientists admired such firm policies. Of course, the use of Darwin's ideas to legitimate prejudices reached their apotheosis in the Holocaust where, in Kevles' words, "a river of blood would eventually run from the [German] sterilization law of 1933 to Auschwitz and Buchenwald" (Kevles 1985: 118). (Again, to be clear, unlike ID advocates who say Darwinism necessarily led to the Holocaust, we are simply claiming that Germans of this era used Darwinism to legitimate the Holocaust.)

By 1944, Hofstadter could speak of "Social Darwinism" as one of the most influential trends in American public life, in which Darwinism "impelled men to try to exploit its findings and methods for the understanding of society through schemes of evolutionary development and organic analogies" (Hofstadter 1944: 4). Of course the concept of Social Darwinism is flexible, and historically the term has been employed by both advocates and opponents of particular social policies. And it is arguable whether Darwinism per se acted as the conceptual source for these actions (Hofstadter 1944), as a catalyst for many existing tendencies in American intellectual life (Bannister 1979), or as a sort of guiding worldview partly disconnected from its scientific origins (Hawkins 1997). But to reiterate, we are not saying that Darwin really said these things, and we are not saying that Darwinism inevitably leads to genocide. We are saying that some scientists also use Darwinism to make moral claims about social order, and that religious opponents of Darwinism were aware of their uses. Historically, this awareness would have been due to the ubiquity of the eugenics movement in America, which claimed to be "scientifically" solving social problem (Kevles 1985; Rosen 2004). Contemporary evidence of this awareness is in the constant reference to the Holocaust by ID advocates (for example, Motive 2008).

The moral status of humans

Darwinism has also been used to justify many different kinds of claims about the place of humans in the world. Immediately after Darwin, John Fiske described humans as the pinnacle and purpose of evolution:

The creature thus evolved long since became dominant over the earth in a sense in which none of his predecessors ever became dominant; and henceforth the work of evolution, so far as our planet is concerned, is chiefly devoted to the perfecting of this last and most wonderful product of creative energy. (Fiske 1884)

Some of Darwinism's proponents have also sought to replace existing moral systems with a system based on evolution. Following the horrors of World War II, there was a broader community of scientists attempting to find the meaning and purpose of human existence in evolution and biology, to create a secular " 'scientific' foundation upon which to reestablish our system of ethics and to rest 'our most cherished hopes' " (Kaye 1997: 42). If we could no longer look outside nature for purpose and direction – as most theologies had done – the foundation for ethics was to be found in the "objective" facts of evolution such as "greater complexity, biological efficiency and adaptive flexibility" (Kaye 1997: 41).

For example, Sir Julian Huxley, a British born biologist, grandson of famous defender of Darwin T. H. Huxley and brother of novelist Aldous Huxley was, according to one of his biographers, seeking "to create a religion of evolutionary humanism based on biology, and to bring these efforts to fruition through popularization and liberal political action" (Waters 1992: 2). A large part of what he called "evolutionary humanism" was the rejection of traditional religion, and its replacement with science and rationalism. As he wrote in 1961:

Evolutionary man can no longer take refuge from this loneliness by creeping for shelter into the arms of a divinized father-figure whom he has himself created, nor escape from the responsibility of making decisions by sheltering under the umbrella of Divine Authority . . . More immediately important, thanks to Darwin, he now knows that he is not an isolated phenomenon, cut off from the rest of nature by his uniqueness . . . he is linked by genetic continuity with all the other living inhabitants on his planet. (Huxley 1961: 19)

More recently, best-selling author and ethologist Richard Dawkins has condemned distinctions that reinforce the "speciesist imperative" and which give special place to humans:

I have argued that the discontinuous gap between humans and "apes" that we erect in our minds is regrettable. I have also argued that, in any case, the present position of the hallowed gap is arbitrary, the result of evolutionary accident. If the contingencies of survival and extinction had been different, the gap would be in a different place. Ethical principles that are based upon accidental caprice should not be respected as if cast in stone. (Dawkins 2003: 26)

Such claims are inescapably moral, and the authors directly and unapologetically use Darwinist thought about the origins of humans and the descent of man to legitimate these claims.

Evolutionary psychology

A particularly active branch of science is evolutionary psychology, which attempts to explain the moral behavior of contemporary humans as the result of evolutionary pressures in the era of evolutionary adaptation millions of years ago. Most famously and tendentiously, these evolutionary psychologists are particularly concerned with gender differences (Angier 1999). For example, the incredibly influential *The Moral Animal* by Robert Wright uses neo-Darwinian theory to explain differential monogamy by men and women (Wright 1994). Or, to take one of the more controversial claims, Steven Pinker claimed in the New York Times Magazine that contemporary high-school aged women sometimes engage in infanticide because their genes lead them to this act, with this genetic design being adaptive during the era of evolutionary adaptation, if no longer (Pinker 1997).

Since the vast majority of women do not kill their babies, at best we are left with a very slight genetic tendency toward this action. What would be left is what is commonly called "morality." But, scientists take this tiny sliver of genetic effect and then portray it as an explanation of "morality." If our genes 100% determined our behavior, then perhaps we could say that scientists are justified in using Darwin to promote a "true" morality. But, if genes are responsible for a small fraction of our behavior, then it probably appears to ordinary people that scientists are using Darwinism to promote their own morality. Since there is no direct evidence for the scientific claims, this seems an area ripe for social influences. As scholars have pointed out, it is interesting how all of these theories tend to legitimate morally condemned male behaviors (McCaughey 2008).

In sum, creationists are not alone in connecting Darwinism to morality. Many scientists also draw on Darwinism to make moral claims about the status of humans, our place in the world, and what ought to be done. Because scientists also link Darwinism and morality, we cannot say that creationists are entirely mistaken, ignorant, or confused when they challenge Darwinism on moral grounds. Rather, they are engaging in the same practices as those scientists who use Darwin to make moral claims, and are reacting to those claims.

We also note that the morally offensive policies that have been legitimated by reference to Darwinian truth, such as forced sterilization and the Holocaust, have been rejected when their bases as moral rather than scientific projects are revealed. This is instructive for our understanding of creationist challenges to Darwinism. In the remainder of this chapter, we apply this insight to creationist challenges in American public life, first by explaining how and why this debate has persisted for over a century in approximately the same form, then by demonstrating how treating creationist challenges as debates over public morality can restore the liberal democratic process to this particular dispute.

WHY THIS DEBATE PERSISTS

In this section we explain why this debate has persisted for over a century in approximately the same form. We focus specifically on three major epistemological approaches to resolving creationist challenges: science education, definitional enforcement, and movement suppression. Each of these approaches has failed to stop creationist challenges, and in fact may have increased support for creationist perspectives.

Knowledge deficit

The first influential epistemological approach to creationist challenges is the "knowledge deficit" model of science education. The knowledge deficit model assumes that people should agree with science because it is true, and that therefore lower levels of agreement (sometimes called resistance or opposition) are due to a deficit of knowledge about science. In this model, if people are better educated about science, then they will agree with it. Applying the model to this case means that if creationists do not think evolution is a true description of human origins, then it is because they do not understand it (probably because their religious beliefs interfere) and they need to be better educated.

There are two implications of this approach for creationist challenges. First, schools should not permit the interfering beliefs into the science classroom. Second, science classes should focus on teaching evolution as clearly and completely as possible. The BSCS, starting in 1960 and continuing into the present, has focused on the second strategy. The first strategy has been pursued at the local level through school board meetings and curriculum review (Binder, 2002), and at higher levels through legal intervention, as in *McLean*, *Edwards*, and *Kitzmiller*.

The problem is that there is little evidence to suggest that the knowledge deficit model underlying these strategies is correct. One of the biggest shifts in the academic field of "public understanding of science" happened when several studies showed that disbelief, resistance, and opposition to science had very little to do with level of knowledge (Sturgis and Allum 2004; Bauer et al. 2007). In many cases, people who support creationism test as well as those who fully agree with evolution (for example, Woodrum and Hoban 1992). Given the empirical limitations of the knowledge deficit approach, the "public understanding of science" literature has shifted from discussion of knowledge deficits to discussion of public exclusion, suggesting that participation, deliberation, and inclusion are far more important in developing "scientific citizenship" (Irwin 2001).

Empirically, however, it is clear that opponents of creationism in schools often hold to the knowledge deficit model even when there is evidence to the contrary. A recent case in the UK case illustrates this point (Allgaier 2008). In 2002 a media furor arose over the involvement of the Vardy Foundation, a Christian organization, in supporting a creationist conference at Emmanuel College (Gateshead). This coverage included accusations of teaching creationism in science classes, a particular concern given Emmanuel's origins as a City Technology College. Yet several public figures lined up in support of Emmanuel, not based on agreement with creationism, but on the basis that Emmanuel continued to earn top marks from the Office for Standards in Education (OFSTED). When asked about the controversy, Prime Minister Tony Blair praised the school for its achievements and OFSTED assessment results. But another set of public figures, including not only scientists such as Richard Dawkins and Peter Atkins, but also Michael Turnbull, the Bishop of Durham, pressed for OFSTED to reevaluate the school, and in the end, even for OFSTED to be reevaluated, because it could not be working if it positively assessed a school that allowed creationism in the classroom (Allgaier 2008: 184–5).

The Emmanuel case is interesting because it demonstrates how the knowledge deficit model fails in practice. Student outcomes were not only acceptable, but outstanding. Yet opponents of teaching creationism continued to argue that creationism in the classroom was threatening and dangerous to scientific education, and attempted to remove creationism anyway. Such unconditional opposition to creationism, based on assumptions about knowledge deficit rather than evidence, leaves no room for discussion of creationists' motivating concerns.

Defining science

The second epistemological approach to creationist challenges is to engage in active boundary work in defining what counts, and what does not count, as science. This is a defensive strategy, but it is particularly suited for the legal arena, where decisions are often made with reference to standard definitions. So, for example, even though the issue at stake in *McLean* and *Kitzmiller* was whether or not creationist challenges violated the Establishment clause, both Judge Overton and Judge Jones expended significant time and resources in defining what science is, so that they could say that creationism is not science. Such use of the courts is somewhat risky for science, as science is not particularly protected under law, and allowing courts to define science arguably devalues scientific expertise by conceding authority to law (Evans, M. S.: 2008). But it has been largely successful in American courts thus far.

The tactic of opposing creationism by defining it as "not science" is also very common in academia. Some of the most significant works on creationism and Intelligent Design (for example, Scott 1997; Forrest and Gross 2004) are basically extensive justifications of why creationism is not science. More recently, scholars have defended the exclusion of creationism by drawing out an intellectual history of scientific thought, and demonstrating that this intellectual history necessarily eliminates claims such as Intelligent Design from inclusion in the boundaries of science (for example, Clark et al. 2007).

There are many problems with this approach. The most significant philosophical problem is that, as science and technology studies scholars have thoroughly established, the boundaries of science are fluid, contingent, and negotiable. There is no essential or universal set of rules for demarcating "science" from "not science." So while the epistemological exclusion of creationism may be supported today, it is because of the boundary work being done to maintain it as such, not because it is essentially "not science" (Gieryn et al. 1985). Based on historical evidence, it is entirely possible (though uncommon) to construct a justification for Intelligent Design, for example, as the legitimate claimant to the label "science" (for example, Fuller 2008).

The most practical problem with this approach, however, is that it does not address the concerns that motivate creationist challenges. Challenges from creationists, while often shaped to the institutional context in which they operate (Binder 2002), are motivated by concerns over the link between Darwinism and morality, however construed. Those who spend their efforts defining science are fundamentally missing the point. We argue that this is a primary reason why creationist challenges persist. The epistemological approach of defining science is blind to the moral concerns at the heart of creationist challenges, and it is at best a temporary institutional remedy for a deeper cultural problem.

Suppressing challenges

The third epistemological approach is to suppress challenges using all available resources at every possible instance. This is an epistemological approach because it does not work without the conviction that what one is suppressing is false, and that what one is defending is true. Sometimes this takes the form of humiliation and name-calling. For example, coverage of the Scopes trial included cartoon images of William Jennings Bryan as Don Quixote charging a windmill labeled "evolution," while other cartoons portrayed a jury composed of talking monkeys. And more recently, Richard Dawkins (1989) has written "It is absolutely safe to say that if you meet somebody who claims not to believe in evolution, that person is ignorant, stupid or insane (or wicked, but I'd rather not consider that)."

More common, however, is to leverage all existing arguments to suppress challenges in court, in school boards, and in public debate. Examples of such "countermovement frames" include the claims that challengers are "not science" and should be dismissed from the classroom, that creationist challenges are political and therefore should be disallowed from participation in educational institutions, and that creationism as a religious movement has no place in secular civic life (Binder,2007: 558–9). There are significant organizational and financial resources behind these efforts as well, including the National Center for Science Education (NSCE), whose stated goal is to defend science education from creationist and other challenges. Drawing on extensive resources, this total approach to suppressing creationism on multiple fronts, for multiple reasons, using any available resources, has been largely successful in eliminating creationism from science classes in public schools.

However, there are two practical problems with this approach. The first is that suppressing movements actually strengthens challengers. As Binder (2007) points out, creationists simply retool for the new institutional context. Historically this is certainly the case, with Scopes, creation science, and Intelligent Design mounting very different kinds of institutional challenges and tactics. Consistent with our argument, however, these suppressed movements often return in greater force and with stronger resolve. We suggest that this is because these movements are not merely seeking proximate success in getting a book into classrooms, or a friendly face on a school board, but because they seek to challenge what they see as the moral implications of Darwinism for society.

The second practical problem with this approach is that it is profoundly anti-democratic. From an epistemological distinction, this criticism seems misplaced. If something is true, such as evolution, then it should not be subject to democratic debate. So when creationists call for "equal time," an epistemological approach would reject it out of hand as incompatible with a notion of science as truth, and stop the conversation based on an appeal to the epistemological status of scientific knowledge. But democracy is, among many other things, a process for debating what ought to be done. Creationists are motivated by their concerns over moral implications of Darwinism for society. So it is not misguided to suggest that suppression of creationist challenges is anti-democratic in that it suppresses discussion of what ought to be done. We recognize, however, that from an epistemological standpoint, such claims do not make sense, or are invisible.

The policy consequences of epistemological approaches play out in ways that perpetuate challenges. Continuing to argue and act as though epistemology is the main concern aggravates challengers, who are actually mounting a challenge based on morality, escalates the challenges and makes all sides feel aggrieved. It is a recipe for continued dispute, but not for democratic debate.

RELIGION IN PUBLIC LIFE

Epistemological approaches to creationist challenges seem not to work. While defenders of science continue to engage in tactics based on epistemological approaches, creationists continue to mount challenges that are seemingly about epistemology. But what really seems to drive them is what they see as the moral implications of Darwinism. We argue that the only way to address this conflict over public morality is to also treat it as a problem of public morality. That is, while debate about the epistemological issues can continue, the moral debate can only be resolved through liberal democratic debate, not through appeals to (or state enforcement of) special epistemological status for what are essentially moral issues.

Treating debates about Darwinism as debates about public morality implicates broader philosophical concerns about the place of religion and moral language in American public life. Historically, much of the debate about religion in public life is about whether religious reasons are sufficient on their own in a liberal democracy, or whether debate must occur with reasons that are accessible to everyone (Audi and Wolterstorff 1997). More recently, Wolterstorff (2003), Rorty (2003), and Stout (2004) have explored the idea that there are no such reasons accessible to everyone. Science can be as much of a "conversation-stopper" as religion, so we must focus on the validity of reasons and claims on their own terms. Despite their diverse philosophical commitments, these scholars agree that it is the reason-giving that is important to the process, not necessarily the epistemological status of these reasons.

So how do we keep the conversation about morality going? Here are some possibilities for how to take a liberal democratic approach to resolving these concerns, and what they might mean for our understanding of religion in public life.

Allow creationism in schools

The first possibility is to allow creationism into public schools, either as ID or in some other form (Binder 2007). The objection would be that this may damage the scientific knowledge of youths, but studies show that not believing in evolution does not lead to a lack of faith in other areas of science (Woodrum and Hoban 1992; Evans, J. H.: 2008). While an argument can be made that scientific education overall is lacking in effectiveness, it is difficult to claim creationism as the culprit (see also Binder 2007: 569–70).

Studies of creationism in the classroom indicate that introducing creationism into a classroom does not significantly interfere with the learning of evolution

(Lawson and Worsnop 1992; Verhey 2005). There is some evidence that allowing creationism in the classroom may increase acceptance of evolution, as creationist students are more likely to accept evolution if they think their views have been discussed with respect in the classroom (Dagher and BouJaoude 1997; Verhey 2005). Recently a prominent educational leader in the UK suggested that "when teaching evolution, there is much to be said for allowing students to raise any doubts they have (hardly a revolutionary idea in science teaching) and doing one's best to have a genuine discussion" (Reiss 2008). Discussion of creationism would then possibly lead to a discussion of the moral concerns of children with religiously-inspired creationist views, without excluding these discussions with conversation-stopping appeals to the epistemic authority of science or the epistemic authority of religion. The moral conversation could continue. As long as there is no teaching of creationism as true or authoritative, this should not violate constitutional restrictions (Greenawalt 2005). People would have to decide which is more important, the potential damage to the scientific literacy of the country or potentially resolving a moral conflict.

Moral disclaimer

The second possibility is to take a Humean approach and explicitly decouple Darwinism-the-"is" from Darwinism-the-"ought," which would allow the moral conversation to continue without conversation-stoppers. Teachers would have a discussion with students about the moral implications of Darwinism, hopefully engaging in the inevitable moral education that schools provide for students. They could say, for example, that the survival of the fittest organism should not be taken as a model for how humans should treat each other – which was a concern of William Jennings Bryan. They could note that even if mutations in organisms are random, it does not follow that human morality is random. The supposed moral lessons of Darwinism can all be explicitly counteracted in the classroom without any concern about the separation of church and state.

Some scientists already do this in their public lectures and commentaries. For example, in his response to the movie *Expelled*, Richard Dawkins wrote:

> [N]atural selection is a good object lesson in how NOT to organize a society. As I have often said before, as a scientist I am a passionate Darwinian. But as a citizen and a human being, I want to construct a society which is about as un-Darwinian as we can make it. I approve of looking after the poor (very un-Darwinian). I approve of universal medical care (very un-Darwinian). It is one of the classic philosophical fallacies to derive an "ought" from an "is." (Dawkins 2008).

But as demonstrated in the previous suggestion, it is not enough simply to say "don't derive an ought from an is." Students learn moral positions through participation in cultural systems, not through knowledge acquisition. So if the is/ought fallacy is where the moral concerns of creationists are detached from knowledge of evolution, this fallacy must be identified and explicitly engaged in the classroom throughout the process of learning.

CONCLUSION

Religiously inspired creationists have been making epistemological claims and conflicting with scientists for many decades. Institutional pressures, such as the legal system in the United States, have further pushed these debates in an epistemological direction, with debates coming to concern what is "religious" and what is "scientific." This has made many analysts miss the point that while there is an epistemological component to religiously inspired conflicts about Darwinism, the primary engine of grievance seems to be moral. These moral concerns on the part of the primarily conservative Protestants who oppose evolution are not due to an error on their part in thinking that Darwin has moral implications. Rather, Darwin has been used to promote the moral visions of many scientists. Therefore, the proper way to describe debates about Darwinism is that they are primarily moral, with one particularly effective weapon being the epistemology claim, typically used by scientists, to shut down discussion of creationism.

If we want to resolve this dispute about Darwinism, we must do so through discussion and deliberation. If through "conversation-stoppers" like explicit religious and scientific claims we declare conversation to be over, then this debate will continue on in mutated forms for many more decades. We discuss a few possibilities for allowing a conversation about Darwinism to proceed in the public schools (the only place where the topic would ever arise for ordinary citizens.) While opponents of creationism have the clear advantage legally, politically and socially, they should consider whether annihilation of their opponents is the wisest course. Not resolving these moral issues results in conservative Protestants feeling aggrieved at the hands of a "cultural elite" (for example, H. L. Mencken) for no particular reason. It is these grievances that contributed to the formation of the religious right in the USA in the late 1970s, and these grievances were still on display in the Republican Party during the 2008 American Presidential elections. Liberals should consider why they are feeding their opponents for arguably no good reason.

Notes

1   393 U.S. 97 (1968).
2   529 F. Supp. 1255, 1258-1264 (ED Ark. 1982).
3   482 U.S. 578 (1987).
4   400 F. Supp. 2d 707 (M.D. Pa. 2005).

Bibliography

Allgaier, J. (2008) Representing science education in UK newspapers: a case study on the controversy surrounding teaching the theory of evolution and creationism in science classes, PhD thesis, Centre for Research in Education and Educational Technology, The Open University, Milton Keynes.
Angier, N. (1999) *Woman: An Intimate Biography*, Boston: Houghton Mifflin.

Audi, R. and Wolterstorff, N. (1997) *Religion in the Public Square: The Place of Religious Convictions in Political Debate*, Lanham: Rowman and Littlefield.

Bannister, R. C. (1979) *Social Darwinism: Science and Myth in Anglo-American Social Thought*, Philadelphia: Temple University Press.

Bauer, M. W., Allum, N., and Miller, S. (2007) What can we learn from 25 years of PUS survey research? Liberating and expanding the agenda, *Public Understanding of Science* 16: 79–95.

Biever, C. (2005) Book thrown at proponents of intelligent design, www.newscientist.com/article.ns?id=dn8061, accessed September 11, 2008.

Binder, A. J. (2002) *Contentious Curricula: Afrocentrism and Creationism in American Public Schools*, Princeton: Princeton University Press.

Binder, A. J. (2007) Gathering intelligence on intelligent design: where did it come from, where is it going, and how should progressives manage it? *American Journal of Education* 113: 549–76.

Brown, F. W. (1930) Eugenic sterilization in the United States: its present atatus, *Annals of the American Academy of Political and Social Science* 149: 22–35.

Bryan, W. J. (1922) *In His Image*, New York: Fleming H. Revell.

BSCS (Biological Sciences Curriculum Study) (1963) *Biology Teachers' Handbook*, New York: Wiley.

Buckser, A. (1996) Religion, science, and secularization theory on a Danish island, *Journal for the Scientific Study of Religion* 35: 432–41.

Clark, B., Foster, J. B., and York, R. (2007) The critique of intelligent design: epicurus, Marx, Darwin, and Freud and the materialist defense of science, *Theory and Society* 36: 515–46.

Dagher, Z. R. and BouJaoude, S. (1997) Scientific views and religious beliefs of college Students: the case of biological evolution, *Journal of Research in Science Teaching* 34: 429–45.

Darwin, C. (2004) *The Descent of Man*, Penguin: New York.

Davis, P. and Kenyon, D. H. (1989) *Of Pandas and People: The Central Question of Biological Origins*, Dallas: Haughton Publishing.

Dawkins, R. (1976) *The Selfish Gene*, Oxford: Oxford University Press.

Dawkins, R. (1989) In short: nonfiction, *New York Times* April 9, 34.

Dawkins, R. (2003) *A Devil's Chaplain: Reflections on Hope, Lies, Science, and Love*, Boston: Houghton Mifflin.

Dawkins, R. (2006) *The God Delusion*, New York: Houghton Mifflin.

Dawkins, R. (2008) Lying for Jesus, http://richarddawkins.net/article,2394,Lying-for-Jesus,Richard-Dawkins, accessed September 11, 2008.

Discovery Institute (2007) Questions about intelligent design, www.discovery.org/csc/topQuestions.php#questionsAboutIntelligent.Design, accessed October 17.

ERO (Eugenics Record Office) (1933) Eugenical sterilization in Germany, *Eugenical News* 18: 89–93.

Eugenics Archive (2008) Image archive on American eugenics movement, www.eugenicsarchive.org, accessed September 11, 2008.

Evans, J. H. (2008) Testing religion and science conflict narratives, UCSD Department of Sociology.

Evans, J. H. and Evans, M. S. (2008) Religion and science: beyond the epistemological conflict narrative, *Annual Review of Sociology* 34: 87–105.

Evans, M. S. (2008) Rethinking *Kitzmiller*: religion, science, and the cultural logic of definition in American public life, presented at the 2008 SSSR Meetings, Rochester.

Fiske, J. (1884) *The Destiny of Man Viewed in the Light of His Origin*, Boston: Houghton Mifflin.

Forrest, B. and Gross, P. R. (2004) *Creationism's Trojan Horse: The Wedge of Intelligent Design*, Oxford: Oxford University Press.

Fuller, S. (2007) *Science vs. Religion? Intelligent Design and the Problem of Evolution*, Malden: Polity Press.

Fuller, S. (2008) *Dissent over Descent: Evolutions 500 Year War on Intelligent Design*, London: Icon.

Galton, F. (1883) *Inquiries into Human Faculty and Its Development*, London: Macmillan.

Geertz, C. (1973) *Interpretation of Cultures*, New York: Basic Books.

Gieryn, T. F., Bevins, G. M., and Zehr, S. C. (1985) Professionalization of American Scientists: Public Science in the Creation/ Evolution Trials, *American Sociological Review* 50: 392–409.

Gilkey, L. (1985) *Creationism on Trial: Evolution and God at Little Rock*, Minneapolis: Winston Press.

Grabiner, J. V. and Miller, P. D. (1974) Effects of the Scopes trial, *Science* 185: 832–7.

Greenawalt, K. (2005) *Does God Belong in Public Schools?* Princeton: Princeton University Press.

Harris, S. (2004) *The End of Faith: Religion, Terror, and the Future of Reason*, New York: W. W. Norton.

Haught, J. F. (2000) *God after Darwin: A Theology of Evolution*, Boulder: Westview Press.

Hawkins, M. (1997) *Social Darwinism in European and American Thought, 1860–1945: Nature as Model and Nature as Threat*, Cambridge: Cambridge University Press.

Haycraft, J. B. (1895) *Darwinism and Race Progress*, New York: Charles Scribner's Sons.

Hitchens, C. (2007) *God Is Not Great: How Religion Poisons Everything*, New York: Twelve Books.

Hofstadter, R. (1944) *Social Darwinism in American Thought, 1860–1915*, Philadelphia: University of Pennsylvania Press.

Hunter, G. W. (1914) *A Civic Biology: Presented in Problems*, New York: American Book Company.

Huxley, J. (1961) The Humanist frame, in J. Huxley (ed.), *The Humanist Frame: The Modern Humanist Vision of Life*, London: George Allen & Unwin, 11–48.

Irwin, A. (2001) Constructing the scientific citizen; science and democracy in the biosciences, *Public Understanding of Science* 10: 1–18.

Kaye, H. L. (1997) *The Social Meaning of Modern Biology: From Social Darwinism to Sociobiology*, New Brunswick: Transaction Publishers.

Kevles, D. (1985) *In the Name of Eugenics: Genetics and the Uses of Human Heredity*, Berkeley: California Universtiy Press.

Ladouceur, R. L. (2008) Ella Thea Smith and the lost history of American high school biology textbooks, *Journal of the History of Biology* 41: 435–71.

Larson, E. J. (1997) *Summer for the Gods: The Scopes Trial and America's Continuing Debate over Science and Religion*, New York: Basic Books.

Lawson, A. E. and Worsnop, W. A. (1992) Learning about evolution and rejecting a belief in special creation: effects of reflective reasoning skill, prior knowledge, prior belief and religious commitment, *Journal of Research in Science Teaching* 29: 143–66.

Lienesch, M. (2007) *In the Beginning: Fundamentalism, the Scopes Trial, and the Making of the Antievolution Movement*, Chapel Hill: University of North Carolina Press.

Loewenberg, B. J. (1941) Darwinism comes to America, 1859–1900, *Mississippi Valley Historical Review* 28: 339–68.

McCaughey, M. (2008) *The Caveman Mystique: Pop-Darwinism and the Debates over Sex, Violence, and Science*, New York: Routledge.

Morris, H. M. (ed.) (1974) *Scientific Creationism*, San Diego: Creation-Life Publishers.

Motive Entertainment. (2008) *Expelled Leader's Guide*, Westlake Village: Motive Entertainment.

Muller, H. J. (1959) One hundred years without Darwinism are enough, *Humanist* 19: 139–49.

Nelkin, D. (1982) *The Creation Controversy: Science or Scripture in the Schools*, New York: W. W. Norton.

Numbers, R. L. (1992) *The Creationists*, New York: Alfred A. Knopf.

Paul, D. B. (1995) *Controlling Human Heredity: 1865 to the Present*, Atlantic Highlands: Humanties Press.

Pennock, R. T. (ed.) (2001) *Intelligent Design Creationism and its Critics*, Cambridge, MA: MIT Press.

Pinker, S. (1997) Why they kill their newborns, *New York Times Magazine* November 2, 52–4.

Proctor, R. (1988) *Racial Hygiene: Medicine Under the Nazis*, Cambridge, MA: Harvard.

Reiss, M. (2008) Science lessons should tackle creationism and intelligent design, www.guardian.co.uk/science/blog/2008/sep/11/michael.reiss.creationism, accessed September 11.

Rorty, R. (2003) Religion in the public square: a reconsideration, *Journal of Religious Ethics* 31: 141–9.

Rosen, C. (2004) *Preaching Eugenics: Religious Leaders and the American Eugenics Movement*, New York: Oxford University Press.

Scott, E. C. (1997) Antievolution and creationism in the United States, *Annual Review of Anthropology* 26: 263–89.

Spencer, H. (1864) *Principles of Biology*, vol. 1, D, New York: Appleton and Company.

Spuhler, J. N. (1985) Anthropology, Evolution, and "Scientific Creationism," *Annual Review of Anthropology* 14: 103–33.

Stout, J. (2004) *Democracy and Tradition*, Princeton: Princeton University Press.

Sturgis, P. and Allum, N. (2004) Science in society: re-evaluating the deficit model of public attitudes, *Public Understanding of Science* 13: 55–74.

Toumey, C. P. (1994) *God's Own Scientists: Creationists in a Secular World*, New Brunswick: Rutgers University Press.

Verhey, S. (2005) The effect of engaging prior learning on student attitudes toward creationism and evolution, *BioScience* 44: 996–1003.

Waters, C. K. (1992) Introduction: revising our picture of Julian Huxley, in C. K. Waters and A. Van Helden (eds.), *Julian Huxley: Biologist and Statesman of Science*, Houston: Houston: Rice University Press, 1–30.

Whitcomb, J. C. and Morris, H. M. (1961) *The Genesis Flood: The Biblical Record and its Scientific Implications*, Philipsburg: Presbyterian and Reformed Publishing Company.

Wolterstorff, N. (2003) An engagement with Rorty, *Journal of Religious Ethics* 31: 129–39.

Woodrum, E. and Hoban, T. (1992) Support for prayer in school and creationism, *Sociological Analysis* 53: 309–21.

Wright, R. (1994) *The Moral Animal: Why We Are the Way We Are: The New Science of Evolutionary Psychology*, New York: Vintage.

Yahya, H. (1999) *The Evolution Deceit: The Scientific Collapse of Darwinism and its Ideological Background*, London: Ta-Ha Publishers.

Yahya, H. (2006) *Atlas of Creation*, Istanbul: Global Publishing.

Youmans, W. J. (1893) The bearing of the doctrine of evolution on social problems, *Popular Science Monthly* 44: 121–3.

Zimmerman, M. (2006) Creationism creep, *New Scientist* 2580: 4.

Part V
Sociology of Comparative Religions

14

The Sociology of Early Christianity
From History to Theory, and Back Again

Joseph M. Bryant

The history and sociology of Early Christianity occupies a singular place in the academic study of religion, at once privileged and unsettling. This is so for several reasons. The modern social sciences took their formative shape in the aftermath of the eighteenth century European Enlightenment, and the subsequent emergence of the multi-disciplinary research university over the course of the nineteenth century. Both of these developments were complexly framed and informed by the fact that their locus was a Europe still predominantly Christian in its identity, as well as in many of its customs and beliefs. Indeed, to a decisive extent, the cultural and institutional history of Europe is largely coterminous with, and deeply implicated in, the cultural and institutional history of the Christian Church.

The preponderate "presence" of Christianity in the formation of Europe has accordingly been paralleled by longstanding intellectual interests – theological, philosophical, and historiographical – in the unfolding destiny of that faith, from the time of origins to its increasingly contested place under the changing conditions of modernity. These concerns would be taken up anew and transformed by the emerging social sciences – anthropology and sociology, most notably – which, even as they endeavoured to widen the scope of inquiry to encompass the religious beliefs and practices of other cultures, remained indebted to the interpretive schemes that had crystallized during what might be called the "domestically focussed" phase of Christian scholarship on the Christian tradition. It is this partial dependence on – and continuity with – earlier modes of thought that looms large in contemporary criticisms of so-called Eurocentric paradigms and Orientalist discourses, wherein a distinctively Christian lens or prism has been discerned, and faulted, for providing the filter and focus through which all other cultures and religions have been perceived and evaluated (Said 1979; cf. Turner 1994). That an instructive measure of merit resides in these charges is now widely acknowledged, even as the polemical overstatements they contain, or have inspired, are also coming clearer to view. The diverse and shifting ethnocentrisms and social biases that render objectivity a methodological aspiration – rather than a consistently secure achievement – do not automatically entail a comprehensive invalidation of the scholarship so influenced, and distinguishing the cogent from the careless or the concocted remains an enduring, and shared, epistemological responsibility.

CHRISTIANITY AND THE ACADEMIC STUDY OF RELIGION

Before one can assess the extent to which Christian-centered scholarship has served to skew our understanding of religious phenomena in general, or the religions of diverse "others" specifically, a historic fact of paramount historiographical importance must be registered. I refer, of course, to the massively transformative rupture within Western Christendom occasioned by the Protestant Reformation, a sixteenth century sectarian development that created the social possibilities for the counterbalancing consolidation of two competing "discourses" over the Christian legacy. The venerable Catholic tradition, its legitimacy resting upon a spiritual charter laying claim to salvific powers bequeathed directly by Christ to the Church he purportedly founded, was hereafter directly assailed by a Protestant grand narrative that spoke of accumulating priestly corruptions, imported magical ceremonials, and a fatal falling away from the pristine faith of the Gospels (Smith 1990). With their confessional dispute turning so decisively on antithetical interpretations of Christian history, both sides were ineluctably confronted with the challenge of providing warrant for their respective positions and claims. Scholarship, in the service of theology and apologetics, would thus acquire not only a new urgency, but a new and progressive rigour and critical awareness, as the Christian past became contested ground for intensive intra-faith disputation. Here the Protestant quest to recover the "authentic meaning" of holy writ – put forth by Luther and Calvin as the indispensable and sole basis for living a genuine Christian life – provided the crucial prod, the opportune opening.

Translation of the biblical texts into the European vernaculars accordingly assumed a primacy in the Reformist agenda, not only for purposes of breaking the Church's interpretive monopoly on the divine word, but to make possible a Christianity wherein each believer could develop their faith through direct reading and reflection on God's revealed communication. Linguistic mastery of the ancient languages – the Hebrew and Aramaic of the Old Testament, the Greek and Latin variants of the New – necessarily entailed a corresponding comprehension of the social worlds within which those languages originally functioned, and thus a deepening engagement with the challenges of history and sociology. Indeed, out of the pressing need to develop a defensible *Hermeneutica sacra*, philological and historiographical skills and techniques were raised to new standards of sophistication. A prodigious outpouring of lexicons and grammars, manuscript studies, handbooks of antiquities, digests, and historical geographies soon brought the records of the past into the discerning light of critical judgement, with accuracy and comprehensiveness increasingly prized as the governing principles of interpretive inquiry. Pioneering archaeological excavations would yield material treasures of increasing abundance and variety, both of the sensational sort, such as Christian funerary art in the catacombs, and the quotidian, of which the soon-to-be innumerable inscriptions and papyri offered the most fascinating glimpses into the lives of ancient

Mediterranean peoples. Professional schools and academic associations dedicated to the tasks of retrieval and restoration provided in situ opportunities to study the intricately interwoven Classical and Christian pasts, all to be abetted by Europe's tightening colonial sway over many of the core regions of Rome's fallen empire: North Africa, Asia Minor, the Levant and Syria (Frend 1998). Scholarly bulletins, journals, and monograph series would henceforth report on the latest discoveries and provide forums for the communication of developing lines of interpretation and explanatory synthesis. Though still beholden and attentive to theological interests, the field of Christian studies had effectively reconstituted itself as an academic enterprise over the course of the nineteenth century, its operations of research increasingly self-disciplined by norms of objectivity and empirically based argumentation.

The result of all this unprecedented and relentlessly accumulating intellectual effort – now running to treatises in the thousands, articles and chapters well beyond counting – is that considerably more is known about the early history of Christianity than is the case for any of the other Axial Age religious traditions that emerged in the civilizational cores of the ancient Near East, the Indian subcontinent, and imperial China. Efforts, long overdue, to correct this historic imbalance in academic attentiveness are presently gaining instructive momentum, as the privileged focus on Christianity justifiably gives way to a more diversified distribution of research pursuits. There are certain inequitable "circumstances of data," however, that all but guarantee a continuing Christian primacy, at least as regards inquiries centered on questions of developmental origins. Consider, first, that Christianity emerges in a setting and an epoch marked by a highly advanced level of historical awareness and literacy, as fostered by the Hellenistic-Roman civilization within which the fledgling faith would make its way. With records of the Roman imperial state and local civic administrations providing reliable grids for temporal and regional anchorage, many of the more important aspects of the Christian advance – in textual production, cultic and organizational elaboration, doctrinal developments, conversion trends, schismatic and heretical fissuring – are often locatable within reasonably secure place-time contextualizations. Comparable possibilities are exceedingly rare for investigations into the much older traditions of Hinduism, Zoroastrianism, Buddhism, and Judaism, each of which would pass through their respective germinal phases during centuries for which surviving contemporaneous documentation – textual and material – is too sparse and fragmentary to permit robust efforts at social-historical reconstruction. Nor does the later arrival of Islam – postdating the advent of Christianity by more than half a millennium – confer any evidentiary advantages, as its regional emergence in an orally based culture of nomadic tribalism and limited urbanism would pass, not surprisingly, without adequate recorded notice. The historical narratives, Qur'anic commentaries, and juristic compendia that serve as our primary sources for the time of the Prophet and his religiously based confederacy were all either composed or redacted in the second and third centuries of the faith's existence, and variously reflect the fact that Muslims had, in the interim, become masters of a vast, multi-ethnic territorial empire, forcibly acquired within the astonishingly short compass of two overlapping generations. Here the sociological contrast with Christianity could not be more consequential, for the earlier faith – its incipient growth occurring in the absence of a centralized authority and manifesting in far more diverse geographical and cultural settings – would need to traverse some three centuries of divisively contested internal transformation before being presented, quite unexpectedly, with the opportunity of its own "imperial moment," under the sponsoring aegis of Constantine, the first Christian emperor (Turner 1976).

Over the course of Christianity's extended run as an illegal cult that sought the conversion of a hostile and sometimes persecuting world around it, a remarkably rich and diverse range of textual materials would be produced, the extant corpus of which furnishes the primary data for reconstituting the formation of the Jesus movement and the complex Church order into which it evolved. The multi-authored New Testament writings, generally presented in simple, unpolished Greek, were composed in various regions of Rome's empire over a period extending from c.50 to 120 CE. As subsequently canonized, this assemblage of narrative and epistolary documents offers a dense tangle of historical fact, theological assertion, disciplinary injunctions, ritual specification, and eschatological promise. Conjoined with the Hebrew Old Testament, which the emerging faith appropriated as divine prophecy of Christ's coming, these *biblia* formed the scriptures of the Christian movement, the sacred source for core beliefs and modes of conduct. An immensely larger corpus of non-canonical writings survives as well, consisting not only of voluminous ecclesiastical productions – exegetical works, treatises, synodal rulings, epistles by clerics and theologians, etc. – but also a significant number of texts that give voice to various "alternative Christianities" that were either marginalized or vanished during the prolonged intra-faith struggle to establish ideological coherence and institutional coordination. Commonly classified as Pseudepigrapha and Apocrypha, these Jewish and Christian documents – Prophetic and Wisdom texts, Gospels, Acts of the Apostles, Teachings, Apocalypses – were variously credited with sacred status in select communities, thereby posing difficult challenges for the harmonization of the Christian proclamation. Though this early multiplicity would gradually give way to a unifying orthodoxy increasingly capable of invidious labeling and coercive exclusions, the textual survival of so many diverse and contending views from these formative centuries allows for a close and balanced tracking of the ongoing factionalism, as well as informed appraisals of the social interests and resources in play.

From this relative abundance of evidentiary sources – richly supplemented by all that is available for the study of Second Temple Judaism and the wider Hellenistic-Roman world – it has proved possible to reconstruct not only the broad lines of Christian developmental history, but to discern many of the key sociological factors that shaped its emergence, facilitated its survival, and contributed to its eventual worldly triumph. Little wonder, then, that the academic study of religion, as its focus shifted towards historical and anthropological concerns, would exhibit a marked dependence on the massively detailed and integrated scholarship that was being produced on Christian origins, and which had already yielded compelling insights on such central issues as doctrinal evolution, cultic practices, authority structures, and recruitment dynamics. The enduring status of early Christianity as a "foundational case" thus hinges on more than the faith commitments and experiences of many of those involved in the academic enterprise; it reflects as well the fortuitously compliant fact that the surviving "records and relics" are, in many instances, adequate to the historiographical task.

As the sociology and anthropology of comparative religion advances, one can anticipate that the study of Early Christianity will retain its prominence, while significantly modifying its function and purpose. That is to say, all ethnocentric elevations of Christianity – as either the most advanced form of religion, or as a master exemplar for comprehending and explicating religious phenomena in general – must be neutralized and replaced by a strictly historical-sociological utilization and engagement. Contemporary scholarship has already progressed considerably along that path, and there is now far greater epistemological awareness that the faith commitments and cultural affiliations of intellectuals have, in many instances, conveyed those partialities into the interpretive process. Definitions and terminology, classifying schemes, developmental taxonomies, and universalizing claims have all been shown to be susceptible to insinuations of the ideological, and noticeably so in the academic study of religion, where theological interests have long exercised preponderate sway. Indeed, even in the absence of overt confessional agendas, Christian-centered presuppositions and standards have left their telltale marks on scholarship of the highest order and importance.

Consider, as a first example, Ludwig Feuerbach's pioneering philosophical-existential reflections on the "essence" of religion, as inferentially derived from his provocatively insightful "Theology is Anthropology" formula (1841). While not unaware that the world's religious traditions present an astonishingly diverse array of beliefs and practices, Feuerbach's foundational generalizations – on prayer, faith, providence, immortality, heaven – are all decisively informed by illustrative content drawn from the Judaeo-Christian variant, and commonly appear to presuppose the highly individualized religious actor of Protestantism as their anthropological basis. To insist, moreover, that the essence of religion resides in the "personal predicates" that an alienated humanity projects onto an imaginary supreme deity – God as Person, Father, and Judge, God is Merciful, Just and Holy, God is Love – is to essentially conflate religion with the atypical monotheistic faiths, an inference strikingly inconsistent with the stated anthropological ambitions of his theory. And while many of Feuerbach's interpretations offer suggestive possibilities for comparative application, significant and even radical modifications would be required to sustain their extension to major traditions such as Hinduism or Buddhism, to name only the most obvious contrast cases.

An implicit Christianizing is likewise on intermittent display in William James's classic, *The Varieties of Religious Experience* (1902). For in the course of sketching out, often with deft brilliance, various psychological processes and tendencies operative in humanity's transactions with the numinous and the sacred, James unselfconsciously "naturalizes" several of the defining predilections of Protestantism. A declarative affirmation of the "primordial" primacy of the so-called "personal" factor in religious life – "the feelings, acts, and experiences of individual men in their solitude" – provides the limiting frame for much of his analysis, curiously justified on the assertion that the "institutional branch" of religion is a derivative or "secondary" growth upon the former. Ecclesiastical organizations, James insists, are preoccupied with the "external arts" of soliciting divine favour, largely through ritual and ceremony; the "inner dispositions" of believers, in contrast, flow along more spontaneously and freely, passing directly "between man and his maker" (pp. 28–31). A "great partition" between the institutionally external and the spiritually internal has thus long divided the religious field, and increasingly so in modern times, with the weakening hold of ecclesiastical power and the rising prominence of "inward piety" in the lives of the faithful. In support of this Protestant-tinted view of religious history, James alludes to our third illustration of ethno-cultural bias: the grand models of social evolution then being proposed – in the wake of Darwin – by several of the founding figures of the new discipline of anthropology.

For Edward Burnett Tylor and James Frazer, the human adventure discloses as a complex yet progressive trajectory, passing from primitive savagery, up through barbarism, and continuing on to modern civilization. The onward course of this development, the two scholars agree, is to be explicated in terms of successively immanent advances in human rationality and knowledge. Tylor would be the first to articulate these propositions in his immensely influential two-volume study, *Primitive Culture* (1871), which strives to comprehend the evolutionary stages of the human adventure in reference to "the general laws of intellectual movement" that inform and propel cultural advance. Two bilateral lines in the "mental history" of our species are famously identified: a long and arduous quest to master the powers of nature, as indexed by an extended passage from savage reliance upon the magical arts to the civilizing triumph of genuine science; and a corresponding trans-formation of Man's spiritual beliefs, developing out of a universal and primordial animism, and continuing on – among the "higher nations" – to the successively more advanced forms of polytheism and monotheism. While alertly recognizing that social change is accompanied by the selective persistence of customs and beliefs from earlier eras – as registered in his celebrated theory of "cultural survivals" – Tylor was in little doubt that the cumulative directionality of human affairs heralded a future of continuing betterment.

The multiple volumes and editions of Frazer's *The Golden Bough* (1890–1922), its treasure trove of captivating detail gathered from a prodigious reading of folk-lore, myth, and missionary reports, offered a similarly reassuring tale of supersti-tions abandoned and rationalities embraced. The cognitivist bias that tilts Tylor's intellectualist approach to all things cultural is unhelpfully pushed to extremes by Frazer, who insensibly reduces magical belief and practice to little more than a "false science," and an "abortive art" – a fatally restrictive view that passes over the emotive and expressive aspects of the phenomenon that subsequent field-based anthropology, starting with Malinowski, would do so much to highlight. No less problematic is the simplistic developmental scheme Frazer erected on his "magic as faulty physics" premise, which proceeds by speculatively crediting the "shrewder intelligences" of mankind with a belated recognition of the "inherent falsehood and barrenness of magic." Agitated by this empiric discovery and alarmed over their inability to manipulate the forces of their environment, these "primitive philoso-phers" set off in search of a "new system of faith" that would provide solace and security in a world of recognized human limitations and vulnerabilities. Out of this mental leap forward the great "Age of Religion" would be born, inaugurated by the transformation of nature spirits into anthropomorphic deities, the ascendancy of priests over magicians, and an emerging preference for prayers and piety over spells and ceremonial (1922: 56–69).

For all the vast learning that Tylor and Frazer enviably display, the two "arm-chair" ethnographers were too deeply invested and immersed in their own time and place to comprehend the full expanse of human cultural diversity and historical change in anything like the requisite objectivity or balance. Indeed, their partisan commitments would on occasion extend to their benighted co-religionists in the Christian tradition. Tylor's unguarded remark that Roman Catholicism presents a "scheme" of great ethnological interest, owing to "its maintenance of rites more naturally belonging to barbaric culture" (vol. 2: 450), is paralleled by Frazer's equally invidious assertion that the true "universal faith, this truly Catholic creed, is a belief in the efficacy of magic" (1822: 64). But these were, after all, prejudices easily embraced during the heyday of Victorian optimism; and it might be expected that at the stirrings of a new academic discipline, efforts towards establishing or specifying the phenomena being proposed for study will race somewhat ahead of any cautious scrutinizing of epistemological points of departure. From the privileged vista of hindsight, it is perhaps not too surprising that an English Quaker and a Scottish Presbyterian would put forth allied evolutionary narratives of world history, premised on a shared claim that the magical and the superstitious had given way – among the superior races and classes – to modern science and the refined pieties of Protestantism (Tambiah 1990).

A reflexive attentiveness to these and similar socially based biases should thus permit a constructive reconfiguration of the academic study of religion, with Christianity assuming its proper role – not as standard or measure, not as *telos* – but as an integral case that carries both world-historical significance and remarkably rich informational content. Indeed, it is this relative advantage in the abundance and diversity of its available source materials that largely accounts for the fact that Christianity has served as the principal quarry from which the social sciences have hewn and fashioned many of their analytical categories and models for the study of religious phenomena. Nowhere is that dependence more obvious than in our continuing efforts to comprehend what is usually the most factually obscure and mythically shrouded period in the histories of religions: their origins and early development.

EARLY CHRISTIANITY IN SOCIOLOGICAL PERSPECTIVE

As a consequence of the fact that Protestants and Catholics would wage their theological battles on the terrain of history, with each side contesting the other's fidelity to a founding moment – i.e., the words and deeds of Jesus and his Apostles, as conveyed in the holy scriptures – a turn towards sociological comprehension was all but inevitable. Any cogent recovery of the original meaning and purpose of the sacred writings, their intended significations oft enshrouded in archaic ambiguities and allusiveness, could proceed only by deciphering the symbolic resources employed and by reconstituting the settings in which they functioned. The variegated customs, beliefs, rituals, and institutions of the diverse peoples comprising Rome's expansive empire were thus carefully researched and inventoried, with the aim of establishing those wider contexts of meaning and action within which the ministry of Jesus and the mission of the primitive Church unfolded. This broad effort at contextualization – generally pursued through a weaving together of meticulous social history with exacting philological mastery of the ancient languages – would bring about a gradual intellectual revolution in the allied fields of biblical studies and Church History, as traditional theological concerns were increasingly set within frames of analysis marked by growing sociological awareness. Sensational publications by prominent nineteenth-century practitioners of this "historical-critical" approach, such as F. C. Baur, David Friedrich Strauss, Bruno Bauer, and Ernest Renan, did much to both stimulate this current and widen its public recognition. Adolf von Harnack and Gustav Deissmann (founder of a famed study group on comparative religions that included Max Weber and Ernst Troeltsch) would deepen these lines of inquiry in the decades to follow, a development creatively paralleled across the Atlantic in the pioneering socio-historical scholarship of the Chicago School of Theology, led prominently by Shailer Mathews, the celebrated Social Gospel advocate and former student of Albion Small, one of the founders of American sociology. Central to the Chicago perspective, as carried forward by Shirley Jackson Case and Donald Riddle, was an insistence that Christianity could only be comprehended as a continuously and contentiously produced outcome, of successive generations working through the practical challenges of their own time, under the borrowed light of their accumulating traditions.

Establishing the "life situation" or *Sitz im Leben* of ancient authors and actors thus became a methodological norm in the study of early Christianity, with the result that the interjacent Jewish, Hellenistic, and Roman milieux – their respective political orders, economic arrangements, religious practices, rural–urban relations, class and status hierarchies, kinship patterns, and belief systems – were all assiduously examined for their possible mediating influences on the genesis and development of the new faith. This sociologically relevant scholarship would in turn provide much of the informational content that sociologists and anthropologists of religion would reflect and build upon – from the likes of Weber, Simmel, and Durkheim, to Malinowski, van Gennep, and Evans-Pritchard – as they aspired to greater theoretical comprehension and comparative range. A great many of the key orienting assumptions, typologies, and models in the study of religion were thus worked up from illustrative material drawn from the Christian case, extending to such phenomena as prophecy and millenarianism, ritual practices and group solidarity, mysticism and asceticism, soteriology, conversion dynamics, possession and exorcism, and sect formation.

Given the formidable language skills that are required for working with primary source materials in this field, it is altogether understandable that the pendulum of influence has generally swung in the other direction over recent decades, with biblical scholars and Church historians exploring new topical concerns and venturing fresh perspectives on old problems by turning, expressly and purposefully, to the social sciences for theoretical and comparative guidance (Holmberg 1990; Elliot 1993; Esler 1995; Horrell 1999; Theissen 1999). Virtually every prominent paradigm or theory in sociology, anthropology, psychology, and economics has been taken on and tested against the issues and data of the Christian case, typically in lagging lock-step with the passing popularity of these perspectives in their disciplines of origin. Where functionalist, phenomenological, and Marxist approaches were all the rage in the opening phases of this renewed engagement, preferences have more recently shifted towards Foucauldian, rational-choice, and postcolonial paradigms. Even a cursory perusal of the scholarship that is now routinely featured in the leading specialist periodicals – e.g., the *Journal of Biblical Literature, Jahrbuch für Antike und Christentum, Journal of Early Christian Studies, Church History*, or the *Journal of Ecclesiastical History* – will confirm that the embrace of social science perspectives has been sustained, encompassing, and of deepening analytical sophistication.

The sheer extent and diversity of this interdisciplinary research is such that a representative overview is no longer feasible in abridged compass, seeing as even partial bibliographic listings easily run to many hundreds of books and articles (Blasi et al. 2002). Several of the main lines of social scientific analysis can be linked, however, in the form of a selectively thematic historical sociology of early Christianity, explicating its beginnings as a reformist current within Judaism to its later ascendancy as the official religion of the Roman empire. Moreover, by charting the developmental course of the Christian movement – i.e., the series of internal and external challenges overcome, as registered in organizational adjustments and modifications in patterns of belief and practice – we gain a clearer sense of how the ongoing "social construction" of a major religious tradition unfolds. Other religious movements will, of course, be subject to the social structural and cultural specificities of their own locus of genesis; but the data-rich Christian case can nonetheless serve as a provisional heuristic to tease out causally significant analogues and variances across a spectrum of comparative possibilities. That is to say, whatever the differences in their formative historical contexts, new religious movements are typically constrained to negotiate a common set of problems and quandaries that pertain directly to continued viability, such as issues of leadership, group identity and personhood, recruitment, worldview coherence, membership loyalty and commitment, and disciplinary coordination. Those are precisely some of the concerns that have attracted the closest sociological scrutiny in the history of early Christianity.

Charisma and its routinization

One of the most influential of Max Weber's many contributions to comparative sociology is his ideal-type category of "charisma," which he utilized to examine situations where authority is exercised by individuals who are widely believed to possess extraordinary qualities and abilities. Owing to the perceived efficacy of their words and deeds, such individuals are able to establish personalized forms of command over those who, drawn to the charisma, come to comprise an inspired social following. Weber distinguishes this individualized mode of dominance from the more institutionalized forms of traditional and legal-rational authority, and insightfully identifies a broadly cyclical pattern wherein charismatic and institutionalized arrangements tend to give way to one another in successive fashion. The decisive historical-sociological importance of charisma thus resides in its great potential for initiating transformative change or revolutionary upheaval. Typically arising in response to crisis conditions that call into question the legitimacy or effectiveness of established authorities and practices, charisma is a galvanizing force and coordinating power that can usher in radical social changes through the mobilization of mass support. The charismatic figure, Weber notes, "seizes the moment" by summoning others to new demands and obligations, thereby proposing courses of action that variously challenge or subvert existing arrangements of custom or dominance (1978: 212–54).

Though Weber extends the application of the charisma concept across several domains of social action, including war, politics, and law, it is in the religious sphere that the phenomenon finds its greatest socio-cultural influence, in the enduring legacies of life regulation that flow from the careers of the historic founders and reformers of the world's diverse sacred traditions. Charisma here – as the perceived possession or attainment of an elevated holiness that is accompanied by extraordinary spiritual powers and insights – is thus both a catalyst for the transformation of traditional arrangements and an inspiration for the creation of new social forms and practices. How charisma manifests in any particular setting will be shaped by the norms and roles already existing (i.e., a Muhammad will not appear on the Ganges plain, nor will a Confucius offer his services in Mecca); and likewise with the culturally informed responses of those populations that will be judging the value of the charismatic claims and displays. Weber pointedly emphasizes the inherent fragility of charismatic authority, which not only diminishes upon failures to perform to the expectations of the follower group, but reaches a natural terminus with the leader's death. Charisma's historical efficacy is thus contingent upon its transfer into more stable or continuous media, through a process Weber calls the "Routinization of Charisma" (1978: 1121–48).

From the extended analyses and illustrative examples that are featured in his diverse writings, it is clear that Weber's thinking on the subject of charisma owed a great deal to the particular histories of Judaism and Christianity – traditions that are known to assign considerable import to the workings of the holy spirit and the bestowal of divine *charis* or "grace" in their authority structures and cultic operations. Conceptually as well, Weber acknowledged that the interpretive work of Church historians had provided suggestive leads for development. So close a connection between the theory and its case foundations has understandably raised questions about the applicability of the charisma-routinization model to other religious traditions, even in instances where highly personalized forms of authority are notably present (Freedman and McClymond 2001). It needs stating, however, that Weber's comparative sociology is not only premised on the fact that important distinctions are to be made among all the many prophets, sages, saints, and mystics who have entered into history's unfolding registry, his ideal-type methodology explicitly enjoins just such a procedure, in the form of a reciprocating movement between the empirical and the conceptual. That charisma is a relational phenomenon – rather than an autonomous or unalloyed personal force – is central to Weber's sociological understanding, and it is this awareness that ensures full analytical openness to the historically specific contexts within which charisma comes to operate. Indeed, this explanatory requirement for local particularization applies even in the case of his most celebrated exemplar.

The public execution of Jesus of Nazareth, c.30 CE, as an enemy of the Roman imperium and a blasphemer against the God of the Jews, is in itself a strong indicator that the crucified holy man had been the bearer of a charisma sufficiently potent to be deemed dangerous by the ruling authorities. Our evidence for this incident, as well as for all other aspects of the life of Jesus, is unfortunately neither contemporary nor neutral, and is limited in the main to what is contained in the texts that Christians themselves would begin composing over succeeding decades. The theological and ecclesiastical interests of later periods are thus perceptibly at work in the scriptural enterprise, the larger and express purpose of which is to present the career of Jesus as a divinely ordained "fulfilment" of prophecies contained in the Hebrew scriptures. The Jesus of sacred writ, in other words, has already been merged with the exalted and divinized *Christos* of the movement that arose in his name – a faith driven development that poses significant interpretive challenges for the sifting of historical fact from sacred mythologizing and legitimizing projection.

There is little reason to question, however, that Jesus presented himself initially as a teacher and prophet, seeing as these were recognized roles for those "filled with the spirit" in the Jewish tradition. The Gospel accounts also depict Jesus as a thaumaturge of unprecedented power, capable of mastering natural forces and crediting him with scores of exorcisms and miraculous healings. While theological interests are likely to have embellished these stories, similar accomplishments do find testimony across the length and breadth of the ancient Mediterranean, from literary texts reporting on the deeds of wonderworkers and sorcerers to *ex voto* inscriptions in the temples of numerous gods and goddesses, gratefully attesting to miraculous cures of divine favour. The portrait of Jesus as *didaskalos* or Rabbi, preaching and debating in the synagogues or before gathered crowds, is likewise persuasive as a historical depiction, its apparent realism enhanced by the fact that credible information is provided as to why the Nazarene's career would prove so polarizing. For as the Gospel summaries of his parables and public disputations make clear, Jesus displayed little hesitancy or caution in levelling scathing criticisms – at times damnatory – against representatives from two of the most influential religious affiliations of the day. The traditionalist Sadducees, upholders of the Torah as the sole binding authority for legal and ritual practice, were the leading party of the establishment, drawing their membership primarily from the higher ranks of the hereditary priesthood and the propertied aristocracy. Strict in their juridical enforcements and prudently disinclined to challenge Roman hegemony, the Sadducees were also noted for their opposition to the increasingly popular beliefs in immortality and bodily resurrection. Their principal rivals, the Pharisees, represented a broad-based reform movement, dedicated to achieving a more exacting application of purity norms and ritual compliance across all aspects of daily life. Exegetical extensions of the scriptures and supplemental requirements from the so-called "oral Torah," a cumulative body of observances handed down by learned sages, provided the commanding rationales for their pursuit of intensified holiness. Ardent believers in the resurrection, some of the more militant elements within the Pharisaic camp are known to have taken an active role in resistance efforts against Rome's client-king Herod (37-4 BCE), and also against subsequently imposed forms of direct Roman governance and control.

In his symbolic injunction to refrain from "taking bread" that contains "the leaven of the Pharisees and Sadducees" (Matthew 6:1–16), Jesus registers his committed opposition to both of these orientations. Though undoubtedly aware that important differences in belief and practice distinguished the two factions, Jesus finds them jointly culpable for giving priority to the outward and self-promoting forms of piety – a superficiality rendered damnable by their hypocritical disregard for divine intention and what he calls "the weightier concerns" of the Law, those being justice, mercy, and faith (Matthew 6:23; Mark 12). Rapacity and prideful arrogance are thus allowed to flourish, while the scribes and teachers insensibly agitate about external matters, such as the ritual purity of serving cups and plates, the technicalities of oath-taking, or straining to ensure a proper tithing for seasoning herbs! Genuine purity and holiness, Jesus insists, must entail an ethical intent and substance, as instructively indicated by his pronouncement that all things are made "clean" when what is served on the platters is shared with those in need (Luke 11:41). Privileged seating in the synagogues, honorific terms of address, the flaunting of costly apparel, making conspicuous show of fasting, prayer, and almsgiving: these are the vanities Jesus denounces, and against which he enjoins a deeper spirituality expressive of love of God and charity towards one's neighbour. Whether in debate over Sabbath observance, dietary rules, norms of table-fellowship, or the legitimacy of divorce, Jesus repeatedly overrules the formalism of existing practices by appealing to higher ethical considerations that will satisfy God's overriding call for righteousness. In so doing, Jesus not only echoes the demands for justice and purity of heart that had been voiced by Israel's earlier "men of God" – the great prophets Isaiah, Jeremiah, Amos – he is assuming the same mantle of inspired authority (Zeitlin 1988).

Did the Galilean holy man make yet greater claims to status and power? Seeing as the central figure in the Christian religion is, even to this day, referred to as Jesus *Christ*, the question might appear superfluous. For "Christ" is a transliteration of the New Testament *Christos*, which in turn is a direct translation into Greek of the Hebrew *mashiach*, "Messiah." Derived from the verb for "anointing," the term unambiguously points back to ceremonials that extended divine grace to kings and high priests upon their consecration. Lexical usage of the term in the Hebrew scriptures is thus largely restricted to conveying the theocratic notion that Israel's kings and priests were the "Lord's anointed," and thus chosen of God. In the wake of successive national disasters – the Assyrian conquest of northern Israel in 721 BCE, followed by Babylonian hegemony and the destructive sacking of Jerusalem and its Temple in 586 BCE – this political theology would require modification. In the prophetic literature that attended and followed these catastrophic events, eschatological concerns would rise to a new and urgent prominence, as efforts were made to brace Israel's faltering covenantal monotheism through repeated promises of a pending divine deliverance. The arrival of a warrior-king of the Davidic royal line, who is tasked with vanquishing the enemies of God's chosen people, is expected to initiate proceedings, which will entail an in-gathering of the dispersed tribes and a rebuilding of the Temple in a gloriously refounded Jerusalem – all this in prelude to the commencement of Yahweh's direct reign upon the earth. As further ethical reflection and emerging sectarian interests began to rework these eschatological dramas, the "settling of accounts" schemas were adjusted accordingly, with salvation being either exclusively reserved for Israel's "righteous remnant" (and encompassing, according to some verses, the resurrected dead), or extending more inclusively to include any and all nations that foreswear idolatry and "turn to the Lord." In later amended versions, this "end of days" scenario takes on the imagery of a perfected Eden – as in the "new heavens, new earth" pronouncement in *Isaiah* – wherein a redeemed humanity will live on in protracted bliss, amidst the docility of wild animals and the unlaboured fertility of the fields and trees.

These prophetic yearnings for deliverance, from the evils of social injustice and from foreign domination, would bequeath to later generations a fund of inspiring ideas and evocative images that both permitted and stimulated a deepening of Jewish eschatological reflection. In passing under the hegemony of one conquering empire after another – Persian, Macedonian, Roman – hopes for an effective and unified national resistance became increasingly difficult to sustain. As these geo-political disasters carried delegitimizing theological implications regarding Yahweh's power and fidelity to his people, circumstances pressed ever more insistently for the development of new lines of interpretation, to render history's calamitous turns comprehensible, and thus more endurable, while also offering reassurances that divine redemption was certain to occur. In the textual production that poured out in response to this ongoing crisis of a "captive" Israel, Torah scribes and sages would work their way towards a more expansive worldview, selectively adapting motifs, tropes, and symbols from the mytho-religious systems of the regionally dominant cultures – Babylonian, Persian, and Hellenistic – to creatively fortify their threatened covenantal belief system.

The resulting intellectual ferment yielded, as its principal expression, the volatile mixture known as Apocalypticism, a hybridized thought-pattern that characteristically proceeds along two axial lines of exposition. A dramatic disclosure of esoteric or concealed information commonly opens the communication, supplying both after-the-fact "prophecies" of significant historical events and a forecast of an ordained destiny that draws near. A graphic description of the violent overthrow of the present world and its supersession by a new transcendent order commonly follows, accompanied by an accounting of a Judgement Day that will bring eternal salvation to God's elect, and destruction or punishing damnation for his enemies. Great worthies of the past – Moses, Abraham, Ezra, the Twelve Patriarchs, etc. – are the usual conveyers of this revelatory knowledge of what lies "beyond and ahead," which they themselves obtained through visions, dreams, or otherworldly transport, often with the assistance of heavenly or supernatural intermediaries who explicate the mysteries and symbols presented. Fundamental to the apocalyptic paradigm is a strategic transpositioning of historical concerns onto the grander and deterministic cosmic plane of divine and demonic conflict, of light against darkness, good against evil. In keeping with earlier scriptural prophesies regarding the Lord's Anointed – "a Star out of Jacob, a Sceptre out of Israel" (Numbers 24:15–17), "a rod out of the stem of Jesse" (Isaiah 11:1) – Messianic agents are accorded a prominent role in the redemptive process, but within the surcharged atmosphere of apocalyptic eschatology they take on a greater supernatural aura or identity, even in instances where the traditional descriptor of Davidic king is retained (Collins 1998; Cohn 2001).

It is within the parameters of prophetic and apocalyptic eschatology that one must situate the charismatic intervention of Jesus of Nazareth, whose career trajectory will trace an arc that both begins and ends in questions of Messianic expectation and identity. Owing to the intrinsic bonding of the theological and the political that set the terms of Israel's compact with its sovereign God – land and divine favour in exchange for exclusive devotion – the issue of deliverance from the foreigner's might could never be fully confined to projective speculations of the literary imagination. Divinely assured prophecies of a future triumph must perforce occasionally spill forth from the markings on scrolls to the ground of immediate historical struggle, there to supply participants with interpretive frames for understanding and scripted programmes for action. From the closing years of Herod's reign up to the disastrous Jewish Revolt against Roman power (66–70 CE), the appeal of these eschatological hopes ran to a feverish pitch, as evidenced by the appearance of numerous would-be Messianic pretenders, armed claimants to the Davidic throne, and clandestine insurrectionary groups that braced their nationalist aspirations with theocratic ideals and uncompromising religious zealotry (Stegemann and Stegemann 1999; Horsley 1999). Jesus himself will appear in the midst of this roiling instability and violence, receiving his public authorization at the hands of John the Baptizer (c.6 BCE–30 CE), the fiery populist prophet and leader of an eschatological repentance movement that arose in anticipation of the imminent arrival of God's Kingdom. With egalitarian calls for justice and stern warnings that all sinners would be cast into the fire on the Day of Judgment, John drew immense crowds to the river Jordan for his baptismal cleansings (Luke 3:7–20). Viewed as a yet another dangerous rabble-rouser by Herod Antipas, Rome's sponsored ruler of the Galilee and Perea (4 BCE–39 CE), John was duly arrested and executed, but not before passing on his message – and apparent inspiration – to the man from Nazareth.

Though the Synoptic Gospels of Matthew, Mark, and Luke present their central figure in shades of ambiguity regarding his self-representation – partly through the trope of drawing attention to frequent bewilderment among his disciples at certain of his perplexing words and provocative acts – the dominant framing throughout is that Jesus is, in truth, the promised Messiah. That this was indeed the documentary intention is readily confirmable through Biblical Concordances, which conveniently list the aligned matches between Old Testament prophecies and their New Testament fulfillments or parallels. Every possible Messianic declaration, allusion, and symbol that can be found in the Hebrew scriptures thus finds – in Christian exegesis – a corresponding expression in the life of Jesus, beginning with his purported Davidic ancestry, the locus and timing of his birth, and continuing on through key events in his career, the meaning and purpose of his death and resurrection, and his predicted future reign in the everlasting kingdom to come. The extent to which these concordances represent subsequent literary "fittings" by the early Christian writers rather than historically authentic reportage is, of course, a question of longstanding dispute, and the pendulum of accreditation has swung with shifts in theological and scholarly fashion. Any case for outright skepticism, however, would appear to be fatally burdened by two rather formidable sociological considerations. First, the historical Jesus, like all acculturated actors, will have thought and acted in accordance with his religious tradition, taking normative guidance from the scriptures that decisively shaped and informed his beliefs, values, and daily practices. Having come forward as a prophet and redemptive agent, he is likely to have communicated his intentions by performing in those capacities in ways that will have been recognized and understood by his contemporaries. The Jesus of history, in other words, is all but certain to have attempted a realization of the sacred eschatological *mythos* that gave solace and hope to his subjugated people.

Secondly, had Jesus not ventured a selective compliance with certain Messianic expectations – such as stirring the Passover crowds by riding into Jerusalem "on a colt, the foal of an ass," as foretold in *Zechariah*; or provocatively "cleansing" the Temple precincts by expelling the money-changers, with overtones of *Isaiah*, *Jeremiah*, and *Malachi* – then the political and religious agitation that led to his public execution, wherein he was mockingly scourged, paraded and crucified as a would-be "King of the Jews," becomes incomprehensible.

An originating or founding "charisma" is of course always more likely to elude historical documentation than the institutional developments its sponsoring authority summons into being. We accordingly move onto firmer ground when we turn from questions of what Jesus might have said and done, to what his followers claimed he said and did, and to what they themselves would do in attempted compliance with his teachings and example. Approached from this angle, what stands out most clearly is that the belief in Jesus as the Messiah constituted the generative basis of the cult that would develop in his name, a datum indelibly inscribed not only in the appellative use of *Iesous Christos*, "Jesus the Messiah," to identify the movement's founder and inspiration for its faith, but also in the early and enduring designation of his devotees as *Christianoi*, "followers of the Messiah." Viewed sociologically, what this reinforcing pattern of identification points to is the decisive centrality of the figure of Jesus in the emergence of Christianity as a new religious movement. Indeed, there can be few cases in religious history where the "routinization of charisma" has been either more comprehensively accomplished, or more vitally sustaining over the long course of subsequent adaptation, than what followed upon the execution of the man Jesus.

In the Weberian model, the most direct response to the demise of a charismatic leader is the transfer of authority to blood relatives or to the departed's closest associates. Both of these forms of charisma preservation would manifest in the aftermath of the crucifixion, as the two preeminent disciples, Peter and John, were joined by one of the Lord's brothers, James the Just, to provide leadership for the fledgling faith association. These three "pillars" were assisted in preaching and missionary work by other apostles, including members from the original group of the Twelve who had been chosen by Jesus, and by yet others who were subsequently authorized to spread the "good news" and organize local groups of the converted. James the Just appears to have assumed *de facto* leadership of the entire movement, up to the time of his public stoning on the orders of High Priest Ananus, in 62 CE. Tradition further records that other brothers of Jesus were prominently active in evangelical work, and that the Lord's nephew, Simon bar Clopas, succeeded James as the head of the Jerusalem congregation. Paul of Tarsus, the principal missionary to the Gentiles, would assert his own apostolic status on the basis of a direct revelatory epiphany of the Risen Lord.

Apostolic authority thus supplied the crucial leadership functions for the earliest generations of believers, but other mediums for the preservation of the Saviour's charisma were also developed. The recollected words and deeds of Jesus provided sacrosanct guidance from the outset, in the form of oral traditions that were passed on through evangelical preaching and in hymns and prayer formulae. Greater stabilization would be achieved through textual production, which started with local recordings of anecdotal materials, such as action episodes or sayings, which were subsequently taken up and expanded upon in the literary narrations of the Gospel genre. Cultic practices offered a singularly potent instrumentality for charismatic mediation, seeing as the celebrants themselves would participate in and partake of the spiritual graces that faith in their Redeemer made possible. Two ceremonial re-enactments in particular would come to play an enduringly central role in the history of Christianity.

The ritual meal of the Lord's Supper, or Eucharist – so named for the prayers of thanksgiving, *eucharistia*, that followed the sharing of food and drink – appears to have started out as simple table fellowship among the brethren, before developing into a more symbolically surcharged sacrament. In addition to commemorating the Lord's last meal with his disciples, his sacrificial death, and his post-Easter resurrection appearances, this communal ritual also functioned in mystical fashion to bond each believer to Christ and his Church, through the ingestion of his "body and blood" in the consecrated bread and wine. Described in early second century Christian texts as "the spiritual food and drink of eternal life," "the medicine of immortality," the Eucharist came to be seen as a means for bringing believers into regular physical-pneumatic "holy communion" with their Savior. Consumption of the sacred meal was also believed to nourish and replenish the charismatic powers of the Holy Spirit that had been gifted in Baptism – the sanctifying cleansing that marked their full admission into the faith, and which was modelled after the baptism of Jesus by John as retold in the Gospels. Miraculously restored to purity through the "washing of rebirth," believers were thereupon infused with the Holy Spirit of God, an endowment that not only constituted a pledge of future "deliverance from death," but an instalment of grace that enabled Christians to "walk in a new life" of holiness prior to the pending arrival of the heavenly Kingdom. Through their combined operations, these two identity-defining sacraments thus issued in the creation and renewal of a "charismatic" community, i.e., an in-gathering of those who regarded themselves as spiritually transformed beings, redeemed by their faith in the Messiah and "chosen of God" for eternal salvation.

The modalities of charisma transfer and routinization surveyed above would in due course fall under the commanding sway of what Weber called "office charisma," the decisive and culminating step in the institutionalization of movements originating in virtuosic or heroic personal charisma. Here too the Christian evidence is confirmatory, for as first generation of disciples and apostles passed from the scene, and as the movement expanded outwards and numerically, it became increasingly necessary to establish differentiated roles and regular tasks to provide both leadership and functional coordination within the multiplying and dispersing cellular communities. Hence the gradual emergence of a clerical order responsible for liturgical ministrations and pastoral care, which began to form around local leaders – whether originally appointed by apostles or nominated by the congregation – who were identified and empowered not on the basis of their personal charisma, but by such assigned titles as overseers, elders, and assistants. An overlapping transition period extending over the first half of second century can be detected in the textual sources, but also a marked trend-line whereby the charismatic authority of missionary apostles and itinerant prophets begins to recede before the collegiate governance of bishops, presbyters, and deacons. In the decades immediately following, the so-called monarchical episcopate would rise to ascendancy, as bishops concentrated greater powers in their own office in response to the growing complexities of expanding congregations and to challenges posed by mounting doctrinal disputes and ensuing factionalism. One of the watchwords of the new order, "follow the bishop, as Jesus Christ follows the Father," offered a harbinger of things to come (Ignatius, *To the Smyrnaeans* 8.1).

Messianic millenarianism and salvation in the new covenant

Jesus attracted crowds and followers largely on the appeal of his eschatological preaching and the miracles he performed in declared confirmation of the onset of the Messianic age. He aroused suspicions among the Jewish and Roman authorities for those very same reasons, and was duly executed – publicly and degradingly – following the disturbances that attended his provocative entry into Jerusalem for the Passover festival. His death by crucifixion did not, however, mark the end of his influence, but elicited instead a response from his disciples that would exert world-historical significance over the millennia that followed, and which can be reasonably expected to do so for times yet to come. For rather than fade into oblivion, the movement Jesus had called into being waxed yet stronger, and would become more dynamic over time, as it refashioned and redirected its interests in the light of the revered leader's temporal passing.

By conventional understanding, Jesus had manifestly failed to achieve any sort of Messianic deliverance, and the imminent Kingdom of God he had promised showed no signs of supplanting the *imperium Romanum* any time soon. How, then, could his followers possibly account for so glaring an anomaly? The answer they provided came to form the central article of faith in the Christian tradition:

> He suffered under Pontius Pilate, was crucified, died, and was buried.
> On the third day he rose again.
> He ascended into heaven and is seated at the right hand of the Father.
> He will come again to judge the living and the dead.

These statements are from the *Apostles' Creed*, a composite formulary that gained prominence in the fourth century, but which incorporates a number of credal declarations dating back to the immediate post-Easter experience. One of our earliest surviving Christian texts, a letter from Paul to his Corinthian congregation, written c.54, already provides the essential affirmations: "Christ died for our sins … was buried … and raised to life three days later, as the scriptures foretold … he appeared to Peter, then to the Twelve together … (1 Corinthians 15:3–8). Paul not only reports that this teaching was "received" from those who instructed him after his own conversion (c.34), he immediately adds that the Lord had "appeared" to him as well, having called him to his apostleship at the very moment when he, as Saul, was on the road to Damascus to persecute his followers.

Mystical experiences, regardless of their specific psychological stimuli, must be interpreted in accordance with the linguistic means and cultural frames available for their description. The successes achieved by Jesus' disciples in preserving their fledgling movement thus depended less on the personal intensity or vividness of their "encounters" with the Risen Lord, than with the exegetical labours that yielded a preachable message of conviction and appeal. Having themselves participated in the eschatological drama that had been sparked by John and fanned by their own master, the followers of Jesus were already conditioned and disposed to interpret the eventful flows of the historical in theological-cosmic terms, for which the prophetic and apocalyptic texts provided authoritative guidance and possibility. The issuance of their midrashic deliberations would accordingly exhibit marked dependence upon inherited eschatological symbols and motifs – the books of Isaiah and Daniel, most crucially – even as creative modifications were introduced to accommodate the apparent incongruities implied by their leader's ignominious death. The doctrinal consensus attained took the form of a revamped *mythos*, centring on the notion of a Messiah crucified, resurrected, and ascended into heaven, whose pending return in power and glory will culminate in the bestowal of blissful immortality upon all those who enter into the New Covenant his atoning death inaugurated, and eternal damnation for all those whose "hardened hearts" refuse to accept this divine offer of redemption. That the core ideas of this refashioned Messianism were taught from early on is again confirmable from Paul's missionary correspondence, the first extant letter of which – pointedly composed to address rising concerns over the fate of believers who might die prior to Christ's promised return – offers the following capsulation: "What we are teaching you now is the word of the Lord, that we who are living at the time of the Lord's coming (*parousia*) will not precede those who have fallen asleep. For the Lord himself will descend from heaven with a cry of command, at the sound of the archangel and the trumpet of God. The dead in Christ will be raised first, then we who are living, who are left, will be caught up together with them in the clouds, to meet the Lord in the air ... For God did not appoint us to suffer his wrath, but to obtain salvation through our Lord Jesus Christ, who died on our behalf" (1 Thessalonians 4:13–5.10).

The eschatological teaching that Jesus was the heavenly Redeemer would provide the inspirational and ideological catalyst for the emergence of a new form of social organization: the Church of Christ. Through proselytizing efforts that spread astonishingly rapidly to include Gentile populations – not only in Palestine, but in Syria, Arabia, Egypt, Asia Minor, and beyond – the followers of Jesus succeeded in establishing small congregations of converts, generally termed *ekklesiai*, for their practice of "coming together" or "assembling" regularly for shared worship and in-group solidarity. By acknowledging Jesus as the Christ and by undergoing baptism in his Name, individuals were ritualistically enrolled in the eschatological New Covenant that Jesus is reported to have announced at the time of the Last Supper. The appearance and multiplication of these local Christ-confessing conventicles, their members enthusiastically animated by the workings of the Spirit, effectively marks the metamorphosis of Christianity into an apocalyptic sect. Though not the first such to appear in Jewish history – the separatist, communally organized Essenes, who prayed fervently for their own cosmic-scale Messianic deliverance (as the Dead Sea Scrolls confirm), can be traced back to c.150 BCE – the Christian sectarians would radically transform the apocalyptic impulse by channelling it in new directions.

Most decisively, and following growing contention within the movement, the Christian mission adopted a policy of universalistic, open recruitment, by dropping the initial requirement that Gentile converts to Christ undergo circumcision and commit to full *halakhic* compliance. One of the most forceful proponents of this policy, the indefatigable Paul, had actually embarked on this course prior to the formal settling of the dispute with the Apostolic Decree delivered by James, in c.49 (Acts 15:1–20). Paul's letters provide the clearest and most influential expressions of this Messianic "spiritual transcendence" of all socially established distinctions: "For by one Spirit we were baptized into one body, whether Jews or Greeks, slaves or free, and we were all made to drink of one Spirit" (1 Corinthians 12:13); "For in Jesus Christ you are all sons of God through faith ... There is no longer Jew or Greek, slave or free, male and female; for all of you are one in Christ Jesus" (Galatians 3:26–8). With a salvation offer pitched in that fashion, one can readily infer that those who will rise in status from the symbolic levelling are far more likely to find incentives to join than those who will fall. And that, not surprisingly, is the overall conversion pattern disclosed in the evidentiary sources, which indicate that the new faith drew its followers chiefly from the ranks of the marginalized, the disinherited, the oppressed, and the despairing.

For was it not to this broad and teeming constituency that the Kingdom had been specifically promised, in stirring words of timeless hope and consolation? The Sermon on the Mount, with its paired "blessings" and "woes," leaves little doubt as to the underlying social aspirations and resentments that inflamed the apocalyptic imagination: "Blessed are you poor, for yours is the Kingdom of God. Blessed are you who hunger now, for you shall be filled ... But woe unto you that are rich, for you have received your comfort. Woe unto you that are now filled, for you shall hunger" (Luke 6:20–5). Elsewhere in the Gospels it is foretold that "the meek shall inherit the earth" (Matthew 5:5); that the powerful are to be cast down, the lowly uplifted, the hungry fed, and the rich turned away (Luke 1:51–3); that "many who are now first shall be last, and the last shall be first" (Mark 10:31). Images of bountiful harvests and the feasting to come are prominent in the eschatological prophesies, and the Lord's Prayer itself conveys the urgency of subsistence anxieties with its pointed request for divine dispensations of "daily bread" (Matthew 6:9–13). The *Epistle of James*, an early circular letter comprised of sermons and sayings of the Lord's brother, is strikingly explicit on the centrality of social justice concerns in the early Church. Pointedly reaffirming that "God has chosen the poor in this world to be rich in faith and heirs of the Kingdom" (2:5), James preaches a sacred obligation to do charitable works, to ensure that "brothers and sisters who need clothes and who lack enough to eat" will be taken care of, and that "orphans and widows" will find comfort and support. Not only are the rich condemned for their oppression, and likened to flowers that will burn up in the heat of the scorching sun, James delivers an excoriating indictment of their greed and folly: "Come now, you rich, weep and wail for the miseries that shall come upon you. Your riches are corrupted, your garments moth-eaten. Your gold and silver is corroded, and the rust thereof shall bear witness against you, and consume your flesh like a fire. You have hoarded up treasure in these the last days!" (5:1–3).

The ideas, norms, and arrangements that would coalesce in these early Christ-confessing congregations are thus comprehensible as the defining elements of a distinctive sociological unity or syndrome, for which historians and social scientists variously employ the terms "apocalyptic" or "millenarian." Nor is it accidental that scholarly as well as popular understanding of this phenomenon is heavily reliant upon illustrative material drawn from the founding Christian experience, the salient features of which furnish a remarkably complete "archetypal" inventory: (1) an originating faith in the pending arrival of a supernatural deliverer; (2) expectations of a cosmic cataclysm that will yield a new heaven and a new earth; (3) belief in a compensatory and vengeful reversal of existing social hierarchies and injustices; (4) an upsurge and release of anticipatory joys and ecstasies that are collectively expressed in ritual gatherings to expedite the advent of the end-time; (5) a radical reconstitution of personal identities and communal bonds on the basis of divine election and attending spiritual transformation; (6) the subordination of established status distinctions to the higher claims of membership within the community of the saved; (7) the prominence of an egalitarian ethos of mutual sharing and support; and (8) a constituency recruited predominantly from the ranks of the variously disprivileged, the alienated, and the politically powerless.

A number of these themes will find their most famous, and influential, expression in the aptly named *Apocalypsis* of John, written shortly after Nero's murderous persecution of Christians following the great fire that devastated Rome in the year 64. With its graphic descriptions of the horrific plagues and scourges to be inflicted upon idolaters and all those who support the Great Whore, Babylon/Rome, John's revelatory text conveys the stark "saved or damned" polarity in imagery of striking power and vividness. Only those who abide in faith and resist the allures of the corrupt world will survive the avenging Christ's onslaught against Satan and his demonic and earthly minions. And it is here that the millennial idea receives its first textual codification, as Christ's *Parousia* – to "smite the nations" and "rule with an iron rod" – will inaugurate a glorious thousand-year reign of the resurrected Christian martyrs. There follows the release of Satan from the pit, the resurrection of all the dead, the final cosmic battle, the Day of Judgment, and – for the victors – the descent of the heavenly Jerusalem, wherein God's redeemed will live for eternity in perfected bliss.

The sociological inference to be made is clear: the emergence and consolidation of the Christ cult is the expression of millenarian dreams in action, a social imaginary that became deeply encoded in the cultic life of the Church and permanently inscribed in scriptures that were composed to give hope and direction to its converted followers. Instrumental, if not essential, in generating popular appeal, millenarian promises of imminent deliverance also carry the risk of diminishing support, should undue delays induce a crisis in confidence "when prophecy fails" (Festinger 1957). Already in the Gospels there are defensive statements warning that the Son of Man will return at a time known only to the Father, a position braced by parables alerting the faithful of the need for constant vigilance, as the Kingdom might arrive later than expected (Mark 13:32–7; Matthew 25:1–13; Luke 12:41–6). Much the same cautionary idea is found in Paul's catchphrase that the Lord will come "like a thief in the night" (1 Thessalonians 5:2). Particularly effective was a later decision to "loosen" or recalibrate the time horizon by alluding to a divine schema of temporality and purpose. Troublesome scoffers and doubters are to be reminded: "a day for the Lord is as a thousand years," and God "tarries" only because of his unsurpassed mercy, "that none should perish, and all should advance to repentance" (2 Peter 3:8–10, c.125?). Christian writings will confirm that doubt-induced defections were not uncommon, but by retaining a great many more than it lost, and by adding new converts through ongoing evangelization, it is clear that the problem of "prophecies delayed" had been successfully managed. The millenarian impulse, as securely sublimated into the eschatologically oriented rituals of the Church and the shared intensity of its congregational communalism, remained ever available for renewed summons in times of crises. Fresh outbursts of that fervor would manifest repeatedly in the centuries to come – and not only in the Christian world, but to wherever Christian ideas, texts, and missionaries would carry the visionary expectation (Cohn 1970; Thrupp 1970).

The sect–church dynamic

As a conversionist sect that aspired to universal recruitment, but only under restrictive terms of exclusive devotional commitment – the first such arrangement to appear in the ancient Mediterranean – the fortunes of Christianity in its post-apostolic phase of development would turn decisively on questions of membership. Though quantitative growth does not appear to have been distinctively rapid, it did sustain the multiplication of small Christ-confessing congregations across the empire, which typically arose in the major cities and lesser towns that served as the coordinating centers of governance, commerce, and culture. That a rurally based Jewish millenarian movement could expand beyond its indigenous socio-cultural locus – and not only attract, but integratively connect new constituencies in the wider Hellenistic-Roman world – was an astonishing achievement. How did it happen?

Christian writings candidly testify that the apostles generally encountered strong resistance from their fellow Judaeans to declarations that Jesus was the Christ resurrected. Nor was this opposition simply an expression of incredulity, or outrage, at the disturbing paradox of a crucified Messiah. A new scheme of redemption was being offered, in a "new" covenant that not only called into question the salvific adequacy of the "old," but included menacing threats that Jews who failed to acknowledge Jesus would lose their promised inheritance in God's Kingdom (Matthew 8:10–12). Matters became increasingly difficult with the growing openness towards Gentiles, and markedly so after their conversion was no longer conditional upon circumcision and *halakhic* adherence. This radically tolerant policy undoubtedly owed much to the foreshortened eschatological horizon that framed the thoughts and actions of Christ's apostles; but regardless of justification, the hazards for Jewish ethno-religious identity were unmistakeably dire. The arrests, whippings, and expulsions that were commonly meted out to Christian missionaries – whose confessional preaching is reported to have regularly sparked tumult in the synagogues, in Judaea and across the Diaspora – only confirms the intensity of feeling that was aroused by this perceived "usurpation" of an ancestral sacred legacy.

Jews did of course make up the founding constituency of the new sect, and for the first two generations, they also authored the majority of its texts and filled the leadership ranks of the earliest communities. Christian evangelizing during this period is also known to have gained adherents from among the Hellenized Jews of the Diaspora, who were possibly attracted by an opportunity to retain core beliefs and practices in the new faith, while letting go of the segregated marginality of ethnic identification (Stark 1996). All indications are, however, that most Christian congregations outside the Jewish homeland attained Gentile majorities rather quickly, a datum already implied by Paul's epistles, which regularly remind believers of their sinful pagan pasts as a way of calling them to stronger faith and service. Once the receptiveness of Gentiles had been confirmed by the early successes of Paul, Barnabas, and other missionaries, the demographic advantage was destined to result in a massive reconfiguration of the Christian support base.

As the Gentile mission gained momentum, the original Jewish-Christian congregations in Judaea were subjected to severe socio-political disruptions, none more consequential than the failed Jewish Revolt that resulted in the destruction of the Temple (66–70). Two subsequent uprisings against Rome, the Rebellion of the Exile that broke out in the eastern Diaspora (115–17), and the liberation war led by the Messianic figure Simon bar Kokhba (133–5), resulted in ruinous losses of life, economic devastation, and the expulsion of Jews from Jerusalem, which Hadrian refounded as *Aelia Capitolina*, a Roman colony dedicated to the god Jupiter. Christians, awaiting their own Messiah, had refrained from participating in these militaristic ventures, but the congregations in Judaea were nonetheless displaced amid the tumult, resettling in Transjordan and Syria, before spreading out to Egypt and Asia Minor. Two sectarian orders – the Ebionites and the Nazarenes – would preserve the original Jewish form of Christianity for centuries to come, remaining faithful to the Torah and to their own Gospels, and, most interestingly, resistant to developing Christological notions that Jesus was a divine rather than a human figure (Skarsaune and Hvalvik 2007).

In the intensified pursuit of Gentile converts, the early evangelists – themselves of humble or modest circumstances – continued to move in much the same social circles, drawing the majority of their recruits from the marginal, the disprivileged, and the working poor. Sociologically, this holds no surprises, for the Roman world was filled with such people, and featured a stratification system that rested upon a fundamental division between a ruling and cultured elite – comprising upwards of 5% of the empire's inhabitants – and a vast subject population. Merchants, urban artisans, and hired laborers, consisting of the freeborn, the servile, and the manumitted, constituted another 10%. The great remainder, estimated in the 85% range, toiled away in the agricultural sector, some as free peasants, but a greater number under terms of enslavement, indenture, or extortionate tenancy. Against this hierarchical distribution, the social catchment of the Church cannot be considered representative, for it was significantly underweighted at both ends of the spectrum, attracting precious few converts from the elite ranks and achieving only modest gains in the countryside. Most congregations were urban, and on the information available – textual and archaeological – their membership ranks were preponderantly filled with artisans, small traders, freedmen, slaves, and the indigent (Lampe 2003). Within these communities, however, there were also a few individuals of greater means – those successful in commerce, lower-ranking officials, the educated, women of property – who took on patronage and leadership roles, deploying their skills and resources for the benefit of their humbler co-believers. Through this within-group reproduction of the socially pervasive patron-client relationship, these otherwise limited and vulnerable communities were braced by the coordinating powers of literacy and the sustaining largess of charity. Considering that Christian ritual life would be conducted, over its first two centuries, in the cramped but secure spaces of so-called "house churches," which concurrently served as the private residences of wealthier members, the functional importance of the educated and prosperous few cannot be overstated (Meeks 1983).

The fact that pagan critics and Christian apologists would alike agree that the overwhelming majority of believers were drawn from the lower social ranks should not be taken to imply that the new cult was fundamentally a proletarian movement. The vengeful hostility and resentment against the rich and powerful that was bequeathed and carried in the apocalyptic tradition did retain its broad appeal, but Christian militancy was cosmologically rather than politically oriented. Nor can it be said that the urban masses and working poor rallied to the Church in numbers that approximated their demographic magnitude. Christianity would, in fact, long remain an affair of a distinctive minority, living interspersed among the roughly 60 million inhabitants of the Roman empire, which included some 3 to 4 million Jews:

c.100 CE	less than 40,000 Christians	= ~0.06% of total population
c.200 CE	perhaps 200,000	= ~0.33%
c.250 CE	perhaps 1 million	= ~2%
c.300 CE	upwards of 5 to 6 million	= ~8–10% range

As these demographic estimates indicate, the Christian growth-rate was not only modest, but the total number of believers, relative to the overall population, was strikingly limited (MacMullen 1984; Lane Fox 1987; Hopkins 1999). Why so?

The dilatory ascent of Christianity can be attributed to two interrelated sets of dissuasions, external and internal. Debuting as an end-of-the-world cult whose members prayed daily for divine deliverance from the present order, and whose teachings featured a sacrilegious charge that all the many gods and goddesses of ancestral belief were malevolent demons, suffices to explain why the Christian "good news" was generally greeted with outrage and hostility. Nor did the pedigree of this *nova superstitio* commend itself, seeing as its devotees offered hymns and worship to a deceased Galilean criminal, whose subversive promises of a "kingdom to come" had led to his crucifixion as an enemy of the Roman state. The illegality of the sect, a status dating from Nero's mass executions, rendered membership a capital offense, thus obliging the movement to cloak its practices in varying degrees of secrecy. Rumors accordingly abounded of transgressive rituals involving cannibalistic feasts (the consumption of Christ's "flesh and blood") and incestuous promiscuity ("brothers" loving "sisters"), depravities deemed credible given the notorious Christian disinclination to join their fellow citizens in everyday civic activities, common entertainments, and religious ceremonials. An obdurate refusal to participate in the imperial cult – a customary display of pious loyalty, normally entailing offerings to the gods and to the spirit of the emperor – provided yet further evidence of treasonous intent. Christian "atheism," moreover, was widely believed to alienate the favour of the protecting deities, as indicated by the floods, droughts, and plagues that now seemed to wrack the empire in unprecedented frequency.

Suspected of impiety, perversion, and disloyalty, the followers of Christ were duly subjected to sporadic persecutions, initiated in most instances by local officials acting in response to outbreaks of popular anger and agitation, but occasionally in conjunction with imperial directives (Ste Croix 2006). Arrests, tortures, incarcerations, and banishments were common, out of which would arise a significant body of honored Christians known as confessors. Martyrs – the conquering vanguard of the *militia Christi* – were also made, whether by summary executions, death under conditions of imprisonment or penal servitude, or through staged killings in public arenas. Their actual numbers lie hidden beneath the cultic veneration and pious exaggerations that celebrated their heroism, but plausible conjecture will not fall below several thousand, as a minimal counting (Frend 1967).

For those willing to incur the stigmas and potentially fatal hazards of participation in a despised and illegal cult, there awaited a series of arduous demands from within the movement. Entrance into the body of God's elect was screened and safeguarded by a requirement that converts renounce all attachments to the sinful world outside – styled the "pomp of the Devil" in the baptismal interrogation – and commit themselves fully and exclusively to the New Covenant in Christ. This commonly entailed a breach with kin and former associates, disengagement from civic responsibilities, and a rejection of all employments that were somehow tainted by idolatry. Following their baptismal cleansing and regeneration, Christians were expected to live "dead unto sin" thereafter, ever mindful of the need to remain "without spot and blameless" in anticipation of the imminent Second Coming (2 Peter 3:14). Exacting moral rectitude was thus required of those who had become living "temples of Christ," a charge made more urgent by repeated warnings that any return to "sin's dominion" risked the loss of the miraculous immortality that had been promised (1 Corinthians 3:16–17).

The phenomenon we are describing, sociologically considered, is a religious sect, a form of association that features intensified spiritual experiences for its members, strict demands on commitment and service to the movement, and promises of selective salvation for those who abide by the terms of admission. Expressly challenging the adequacy or legitimacy of existing religious arrangements or traditions, sects will invariably convey some degree of world-opposition, a circumstance that accounts for their preferential appeal to the unfulfilled and the alienated. To the extent that such movements attract notoriety – whether from scandalizing conduct or through recruitment successes – they will become the target of populist anger and repressive measures by the ruling authorities. So-called secessionist sects seek to avoid such confrontations through collective relocation, migrating to new or marginal lands to "wait out" the time of troubles that precedes the expected deliverance to come. Conversionist sects, in contrast, must venture forth, into the territory occupied by the Evil Power, to redeem all captives whose hearts remain open to the saving Truth.

Christianity followed the path of engagement, not only defying the Roman imperium – the murderous Great Whore of John's *Apocalypse* – but ultimately prevailing. It would do so, however, only through a fundamental reorganization of its forces – a military metaphor routinely invoked by Christian leaders themselves, who presented their campaign as the triumphant, conclusive phase in the cosmic confrontation between the "camp of God" and the "camp of Satan," the *castra Dei* against the *castra diaboli*.

No Christian in those early centuries will have entertained any hope or expectation of a triumph over Rome – the Dragon's sponsored beast – other than miraculous and eschatological. Under such a conception, perseverance until the end-time was the guiding strategy, living in the Spirit was the effective tactic. As for those netted by Satan's servants, their "baptism by blood" ensures their glory in the millennium that is imminent, and greater blessings still in the eternal paradise to follow. A courageous creed, undoubtedly, but one that would prove difficult to sustain, even for those empowered by graces bestowed by God. Already in the later texts of the New Testament, there is mention of doubters and scoffers who question the truth of what has been taught – an erosion of confidence that will only deepen as "waiting-time" to the promised redemption lengthens. An identifiable pastoral crisis would presently manifest in the guise of the *dipsychoi*, the "divided souls" or "double-minded" who are said to plague every congregation with their enervating doubts regarding God's salvific power: "We have heard these things even in the days of our fathers, and behold, we have grown old, yet none of these things has happened to us" (1 Clement 23:3 [c.96]). Waning eschatological trust will be accompanied by the yet greater problem of moral backsliding, as disconcerting numbers of believers begin to succumb to worldly temptations, returning once again to vanities and vices they had renounced at baptism (Bryant 1998).

The Christian movement – assailed from without by intensifying persecution, and convulsed from within by growing disconfirmation that its membership was fully capable of adhering to the purity requirements of the faith – could proceed no further on the basis of its founding sectarian zeal and enthusiasm. New arrangements were needed, to restore confidence in the attainability of salvation and to forestall desertions from those beset by doubt and burdened by sin. The terms of membership had to be – and were – progressively eased over time, chiefly through a series of renegotiations that centered on penitential practices. As a key boundary-maintenance mechanism, penitential discipline commonly serves to establish the determinant criteria for inclusion-exclusion, retention-expulsion. By shifting towards greater moderation in its understanding of the irrepressible reality of post-baptismal sin, the Christian leadership not only provided a brace to its faltering congregations, it opened the possibility for expanding its recruitment base beyond the limited circles of the religiously intense.

The first adjustment, announced in a sacred text of prophetic revelation (c.115), was cautiously minimalist and still animated by strong sectarian norms: owing to God's mercy, an emergency period of grace was offered, whereby sins accrued since baptism – but no future transgressions – could be wiped away by heartfelt repentance. By the end of the second century, an institutionalized sacrament of penance is in place, its function limited to a one-time remission of sins for those who failed to keep their baptismal "seal" intact. A more decisive break with sectarian principle came with an episcopal override of the traditional distinction between forgivable sins, such as dishonesty, greed, or drunkenness, and the unforgivable "mortal" sins, transgressions so heinous that the gifted Holy Spirit instantly vacated the soul of the perpetrator, rendering the offender "dead unto Christ." Reformist bishops of Carthage and Rome led the way (c.220), issuing rulings that the sins of fornication and adultery were henceforth remissible within the Church, conditional upon diligent penitence. The empire-wide persecution launched by the emperor Decius, in the year 250, would force an even greater "accommodation," as overwhelming numbers of Christians "lapsed from the faith" by offering the mandated sacrifices to the gods. Notwithstanding the firm scriptural injunction that those who deny Christ will lose their salvation, moderate and laxist bishops – increasingly prone to invoking the title Catholic or "universal" – pushed through a reform that extended absolution to the most grievous sins in the Christian moral economy: idolatry and apostasy. All that remained to complete this tempering of the sectarian spirit – i.e., its subordination to the higher virtue of merciful indulgence for the weak and wayward – was to lift the requirement of personal holiness from members of the clerical order. That, too, would be accomplished, following the final wave of imperial persecution (303–11), when it was ruled that the ministrations of fallen and sinful clerics carried full spiritual efficacy. As an eminent bishop summed up the now dominant Catholic persuasion: "the Church is one, and its sanctity is derived from the sacraments, not weighed on the basis of pride in personal qualities" (Optatus, *On the Donatist Schism* 2.1).

Christians who opposed these penitential innovations – the Montanists, Kathari, the Egyptian Church of the Martyrs, Donatists, and others – proceeded to form their own sectarian communities, insistent that the baptismal pledge to purity was obligatory, and that congregations filled with the polluting presence of apostates, fornicators, and adulterers constituted a mockery of Christ's redeeming sacrifice. They would be called heretics and schismatics, and they would be progressively marginalized as the Catholic mainstream continued along its reformist path of remaking a millenarian sect into a world-accommodating church. Now functioning as a universal instrument for the attainment of salvation, and armed with an expanded sacerdotal capacity to bestow grace and restore to sanctity those in compliance with clerical authority, this Catholic Christianity would soon navigate yet another determinant transition: from persecution to imperial patronage – a status it could never have attained under its original apocalyptic charter and charismatic orientation.

Church and world

Having weathered the storms of persecution and the strains of sectarian expectation, the Catholic Church had achieved sufficient stability to ensure a continuing presence in a world that was still overwhelmingly resistant to its message. Its authority structures had been tightened in the episcopate and ministerial order; restrictions had been imposed upon acceptable thought and conduct through the closure of its scriptural canon, hereafter limited to the approved texts of the Old and New Testaments; a disciplinary regime had been fashioned that judiciously combined an insistence upon saintly virtue with merciful provisions for the remission of sins committed. There were, in addition, other possible attractors. Given its centrality in Christian discourse, the promise of life eternal must have held intrinsic appeal, perhaps enhanced by the peculiar notion – alien to the Hellenic-Roman worldview – of bodily resurrection. To the uneducated and toiling majorities of the ancient world, philosophical speculations about the immortality of the soul or mind will have lacked the tangibility and force of the Christian pledge that their bodies would be perfected for the perpetual delights of a restored Eden. The cultic importance of Jesus Christ as a unique man-god Redeemer suggests a similar preoccupation with salvation possibilities. Nor were terrestrial interests neglected. Charitable supports and altruistic bonds of solidarity greeted each new convert, whose dignity and self-worth were elevated by privileged inclusion among the "chosen of God." For the alienated and oppressed, the indigent and troubled, the sheltering arms of *Mater Ecclesia* provided not only material benefits and existential security, but also an ideology that allowed for the transvaluation of all worldly sufferings into a schema of assured miraculous deliverance. Intensified in-group attachments based on a spiritualized kinship terminology and norms of egalitarianism permitted a new and vibrant experience of *communitas*, invitingly free from hierarchical relations of dominance and deference.

And yet, a full two centuries after its founding, the Christian *religio* had managed to embrace only 2% of the inhabitants of Rome's empire.

This singularly important fact confirms that any proper analysis of the eventual Christian ascendancy must be conjunctural, dialectical, and track the ways in which the rising fortunes of the Church were conditioned by the declining fortunes of empire. For as the demographic trend-line indicates, the first real surge in Christian membership – rising from an estimated 1 million in year 250 to some 6 million in the year 300 – occurs in the latter half of so-called "crisis century" of Roman history. Christian teachings and the benefits of membership undoubtedly took on greater appeal in circumstances of social disorder and personal insecurity. Borders continuously breached by plundering nomads; mutinies within the ranks of the legions; ensuing civil wars that issue in repeated armed usurpations of the imperial crown; military expenditures that strain the fiscal capacities of the state; intensified taxation and coinage debasements as coping measures that lead to runaway inflation and commercial contraction; agrarian distress and a corresponding rise in social banditry: these are the interconnected and compounding disasters of the age, and their demoralizing consequences are to be seen, in part, in an increasing willingness of some to abandon the hallowed traditions of their forefathers for a chance at salvation through faith in Christ.

The conversion to Christianity by the emperor Constantine in the year 312 would prove epoch-making in its consequences. Under his patronage, and that of his imperial successors, Christianity will become a full partner in the affairs of empire, a fateful compact that led inexorably to the creation of Christian armies, Christian law, Christian education, Christian art ... in a word, a Christianized world. Forcefully assisted by the coercive powers the Christian state – which proceeded to close temples, ban sacrifices, and prohibit worship of the pagan deities, upon sentence of death – the Christians will have become, by the year 400, a numerical majority in their newly won terrestrial empire.

As Christianity continued on, surviving the fall of Rome, and later that of Byzantium, spreading outwards into new and distant regions, passing through the Middle Ages and on into a globalized Modernity, it would carry within it a binary code of social expression, which variously permitted and encouraged the opposing stances of world-opposition and world-accommodation. Sectarian disengagement from the corrupted world, a churching ambition to convert and master it: these have been the alternating orientations that have imparted to the Christian faith such remarkable adaptability under changing and variable circumstances. To comprehend the complex histories this tradition has produced, genealogies must accordingly be traced, back to the formative period of socio-genesis.

Bibliography

Blasi, Anthony, Duhaime, Jean, and Turcotte, Paul-Andre Turcotte (eds.) (2002) *The Handbook of Early Christianity: Social Science Approaches*, Walnut Creek: AltaMira.

Bryant, Joseph M. (1998) Wavering saints, mass religiosity, and the crisis of post-baptismal sin in early Christianity, *Archives européennes de sociologie* 39 (1): 49–77.

Cohn, Norman (1970) *The Pursuit of the Millennium*, New York: Oxford University Press.

Cohn, Norman (2001) *Cosmos, Chaos, and the World to Come*, New Haven: Yale University Press.

Collins, John J. (1998) *The Apocalyptic Imagination*, Grand Rapids: Eerdmans.

Elliot, Jack (1993) *What Is Social-Scientific Criticism?*, Minneapolis: Fortress Press.

Esler, Philip (ed.) (1995) *Modelling Early Christianity*, London: Routledge.

Festinger, Leon (1957) *A Theory of Cognitive Dissonance*, Stanford: Stanford University Press.

Feuerbach, Ludwig (1989) [1841] *The Essence of Christianity*, Buffalo: Prometheus Books.

Frazer, Sir James (1822) [1890] *The Golden Bough*, New York: Collier Books.

Freedman, David N. and McClymond, Michael (eds.) (2001) *The Rivers of Paradise*, Grand Rapids: Eerdmans.

Frend, W. H. C. (1967) *Martyrdom and Persecution in the Early Church*, New York: Anchor Books.

Frend, W. H. C. (1998) *The Archaeology of Early Christianity: A History*, Minnapolis: Fortress Press.

Holmberg, Bengt (1990) *Sociology and the New Testament*, Minneapolis: Fortress Press.

Hopkins, Keith (1999) *A World Full of Gods*, London: Phoenix.

Horrell, D. G. (ed.) (1999) *Social-Scientific Approaches to New Testament Interpretation*, Edinburgh: T. and T. Clark.

Horsley, Richard (1999) *Bandits, Prophets, and Messiahs*, Harrisburg: Trinity Press.

James, William (1982) [1902] *The Varieties of Religious Experience*, New York: Penguin.

Lane Fox, Robin (1987) *Pagans and Christians*, New York: Knopf.

Lampe, Peter (2003) *From Paul to Valentinus*, Minneapolis: Fortress Press.

MacMullen, Ramsay (1984) *Christianizing the Roman Empire*, New Haven: Yale University Press.

Meeks, Wayne (1983) *The First Urban Christians*, New Haven: Yale University Press.

Said, Edward (1979) *Orientalism*, New York: Pantheon Books.

Skarsaune, Oskar and Hvalvik, Reidar (eds.) (2007) *Jewish Believers in Jesus*, Peabody: Hendrickson Publishers.

Smith, Jonathan Z. (1990) *Drudgery Divine*, Chicago: University of Chicago Press.

Stark, Rodney (1996), *The Rise of Christianity*, Princeton: Princeton University Press.

Ste Croix, G. E. M. de (2006) *Christian Persecution, Martyrdom and Orthodoxy*, Oxford: Oxford University Press.

Stegemann, Ekkehard and Stegemann, Wolfgang (1999) *The Jesus Movement*, Minneapolis: Fortress Press.

Tambiah, Stanley (1990) *Magic, Science, Religion, and the Scope of Rationality*, Cambridge: Cambridge University Press.

Theissen, Gerd (1999) *The Religion of the Earliest Churches*, Minneapolis: Fortress Press.

Thrupp, Sylvia (ed.) (1970) *Millennial Dreams in Action: Studies in Revolutionary Religious Movements*, New York: Schocken.

Turner, Bryan S. (1976) Origins and traditions in Islam and Christianity, *Religion* 6 (1): 13–30.

Turner, Bryan S. (1994) *Orientalism, Postmodernism, and Globalism*, London: Routledge.

Tylor, E. B. (1871) *Primitive Culture*, 2 vols., London: John Murray.

Weber, Max (1922/1978) *Economy and Society*, Berkeley: University of California Press.

Zeitlin, Irving M. (1988) *Jesus and the Judaism of His Time*, London: Basil Blackwell.

15

Judaism

Covenant, Pluralism, and Piety

ALAN MITTLEMAN

The medieval Jewish philosopher, Saadia Gaon (d. 942), wrote that Israel is only a nation by virtue of its Torah, its divine teaching (Saadia Gaon 1948: 158). This comment on the character of Jewish nationhood – although by no means uncontested – captures essential features of the phenomenon to be explored in this chapter. Saadia's view entails, first, that the Jews *are* a nation, not simply a religious community or even an ethnicity. That is, their proper form is as a people with a distinctive language and culture formed in historical time and extended, at least in their formative period, over a bounded territory, enjoying self-governance, and living in accordance with their own law (Grosby 2005a: 20). His view also entails, however, that Jewish nationality is uniquely bound up with what, for lack of a better term, we shall call Judaism. It is Torah and not simply the "normal" characteristics of nationhood that condition Jewish nationality. Of course, it is far from unique for nations to link their identity to the worship of territorial gods; this is a phenomenon attested by the Bible itself. Israel's nationhood, however, hinges on the worship of a god who is understood to be the God of the universe – the one and only God – not a territorial deity whose primary function is to cement a national identity. What is unusual then about the Jewish case is that the Jewish people, Israel, holds to both a strong and ancient sense of nationhood and a religious outlook that might well have dissolved or relativized that sense (Grosby 2005b: 12). Christianity and Islam, for example, problematize nationhood on account of their monotheism. Judaism, on the other hand, supports both a rigorous universalizing monotheism and a normative assumption of nationhood. Nationhood has sacred, virtually sacramental value.

In this chapter, I want to consider how the core religious ideas and practices of Judaism relate to historical expressions of Jewish nationhood. In Hebrew terms, how are *torah* (divine teaching) and *am yisrael* (the Jewish people) mutually implicated?

DEFINING TERMS

A word about terminology is in order. Terms such as "religion," "nation," and "Judaism," as they are currently used by speakers of English, do not map neatly over functionally equivalent terms in pre-modern Hebrew. The modern provenance of the term "religion," as the concept of a genus comprising species such as "Hinduism," "Christianity," etc., fails to capture the modes of symbolic self-reference common among ancient and medieval, or even some modern, Jews. Wilfred Cantwell Smith has argued that the concept of religion is an Enlightenment construct designed to set culturally embedded patterns of devotion apart from allegedly meta-cultural, universal expressions of reason such as are found (allegedly) in philosophy (Cantwell Smith 1991: 43). Just as the British Raj designated as "Hinduism" anything that wasn't Muslim in the sub-continent, so too the Enlightenment branded everything that constituted a traditional historical (non-philosophical) piety as religion. On this view, when Europeans settled upon "Judaism" or "Judentum" or "Judaïsme" etc. to distinguish the way of the Jews, they created an artifact comparable (but presumably inferior) to Christianity. The construction of this "ism" provided speakers of European languages with a category by which to frame Jewish life that distorted as much as it described. For to frame the traditional way of the Jews solely as a religion is to reduce or circumscribe it. Judaism qua religion engendered a set of enduring, and unfortunate, conceptual problems. (For example, since Judaism is a religion and a religion is different from a nation are the Jews still a nation? If religion is something higher and purer than nationhood, to the extent that the Jews continue to assert Jewish nationality, do they not have a defective religion? If Judaism is a religion, does that not disqualify the Jews from the status of a people with a right to its own state – a claim frequently made by contemporary detractors of the State of Israel.) The problems manufactured by a semantic transaction, although not quite the equivalent of Wittgenstein's judgment that philosophical problems arise when language goes on holiday, remain salient for modern Jews. Whole books have been written to attempt to define Judaism with greater adequacy – I have in mind here Leo Baeck's *The Essence of Judaism* (1905) or Mordecai Kaplan's *Judaism as a Civilization* (1935) – than the logical grammar of the "ism" initially conveys.

Another corollary of the modern concept of religion is that religion is typically distinct from politics. Christendom, of course, differentiated church from state in legal, institutional and theological ways long before modernity. Nonetheless, the logical grammar of "religion," as a product of the secularizing thought of the Enlightenment, implies differences unknown in pre-modern times. Religion implies the private, politics the public. Religion implies the voluntary, politics the obligatory or compulsory. These distinctions are more or less alien to medieval Christendom, let alone to traditions such as that of the Jews, which do not distinguish "religion" clearly from "politics." Paradoxically, the Jews, although an exiled and powerless people for much of their history, kept alive a more integral sense of the theo-political nexus than Western peoples influenced by the Enlightenment. When Count Clermont-Tonnerre told the French National Assembly, which was contemplating the emancipation of the Jews, "the Jews should be denied everything as a nation, but granted everything as individuals," he referenced the abiding phenomenon of Jewish national and political self-understanding in an age when it had already become conceptually anomalous (Mendes-Flohr and Reinharz 1980: 104). When Napoleon called a "Sanhedrin" and an "Assembly of Notables" to ratify the emancipation, he gestured toward the very political cast of Judaism that he intended, dramatically, to dissolve. Thus, the dimensions of nationhood and politics, however notional under conditions of exile and the loss of sovereignty, are integral to "Judaism" but inherently problematic for religion as a modern construct.

The problem of "Judaism" as a foreign term inadequately coordinate with Jewish self-representation is exacerbated by a still deeper problem. The term from which European languages draw in deriving their equivalents of "Judaism" is the Greek ιουδαϊσμος. The striking thing about this term is that it was coined, or at least first used, by a Greek speaking Jew, the author of II Maccabees. Referring to the Jews who rose up against Syrian-Greek oppression, he writes "of the manifest interventions from heaven in favor of those who vied with one another in fighting manfully for Judaism: few though they were, they took the spoils of the entire country and drove out the barbarian hordes" (2 Maccabees 2:21; see also 2 Maccabees 8:1, 14:38). It is not quite clear what this abstract noun was meant to denote – perhaps the temple, the polis, and the laws which the next verse, not cited here, mentions. At any rate, the author constructed a concept intelligible to outsiders, who spoke of Hellenism (Ἑλλήνισμος). Thus, the term is relational – it requires an Other – and confrontational. It is forged in the context of conflict and opposition. *Ioudaismos*, as a descriptive term for the comprehensive way of life of the Jews, originates in a polemic against other ways of life. Had the Jews not lived in a pluralistic world with outsiders making claims on their loyalties, they would not have had to coin *Ioudaismos* (Neusner 1995: 232). It might have sufficed for them to refer to themselves as "Israel," a term that was more elastic and inclusive than *Ioudaismos*. An indication of this elasticity is that the early Church laid claim to being a new Israel; it did not think of itself as a new Judaism.

How then did the Jews, when speaking internally, name what we call Judaism? The Hebrew term that signifies Judaism in modern Hebrew, *yahadut*, does not appear in biblical or classical Hebrew writing. Up through the Middle Ages, there were various ways by which the Jews referred to their own comprehensive way of life. The most common of these was *torah*, a term which generically means teaching and refers both to divine teaching (and the human explication of divine teaching) and to the classical documents, such as the Pentateuch, in which that teaching is found. Thus, the pagan who sought instruction from the first century sage, Hillel, so that he might join the Jewish people, asked to be taught the whole of the *torah* while standing on one foot (Shabbat 31a). Similarly, when the tenth-century Jewish philosopher, Saadia, cited above, asked what constituted Jewish nationhood (*umma*), he indicated that the laws cum teachings (*toroteha*; plural with feminine pronominal suffix of *torah*) were decisive. Another option is found in the Mishnah, the earliest stratum of the Talmud, which makes reference to *dat yehudit*, Jewish custom, as a criterion for proper behavior (Ketubot 7: 14). Similarly, the ancient formula for entering into a marriage commits one to act "according to the custom of Moses and Israel" (*k'dat Moshe v'yisrael*) (Kiddushin 5b). Terms such as *torah*, with its resonance of teaching and law, and *dat*, in the sense of national custom, mark a semantic range broader than the modern concept of religion. The terms remain rooted in the concrete life of a distinguishable national community.

The first appearances of the rather more abstract term *yahadut* are found in the medieval talmudic commentator, Rashi, and the supercommentary on Rashi's work, Tosaphot. One such reference describes, curiously enough, the significance of how one ties one's shoes (Sanhedrin 74b). The Talmudic discussion concerns the grave topic of how a Jew should behave during a time of persecution, that is, under what circumstances should a Jew become a martyr rather than transgress Jewish law. One view has it that even the transgression of a "light commandment" in public should be avoided at the cost of martyrdom. What constitutes a "light commandment"? – even a change in the way one ties one's shoes. Rashi comments that if the gentiles tie their shoes one way and Jews tie theirs in another, then there is "an aspect of Judaism to the matter" (*tzad yahadut b'davar*). Although we are not dealing with a true commandment (*mitzvah*) but only with a custom (*minhag b'almah*), nonetheless this also affords an opportunity to honor God by acting in a Jewish manner. According to Rashi, God is sanctified in public before his Jewish covenantal partners (*haverav*). *Yahadut* thus seems to indicate the sum of all relevant Jewish customs; it indicates as well loyalty or fidelity to those customs in the face of challenge. Thus, as in II Maccabees, the term is used in the context of cultural and social confrontation. Other citations (e.g. Tosaphot to Gittin 34b) suggest that the term functions to mark the boundary between Jews and non-Jews. Jews used the term in their own discourse to highlight their collective difference from non-Jews. Were there no outside threat against which to react, Jews would not need such a terminological simplification and abstraction of their life-world.

Under the conditions of modernity, the outside has become the inside. "Judaism" is no longer a distillation of the laws and customs, of the comprehensive life-world of the people Israel, deployed for polemical, confrontational purposes. It has been accepted by Jews as an adequate descriptor for their own tradition. Indeed, it has been internalized as a token of the type "religion," a convenient shorthand to distinguish what differentiates Jews from their fellow citizens. That difference can be thought to be minimal when religion is held to be a private, purely individual spiritual matter.

By calling to mind elements of the genealogy of "Judaism," I do not mean to reject the use of the term, only to gain clarity about its conceptual origins and consequences. I mean also to suggest that we are ill-advised to seek, in the manner of many nineteenth- and early twentieth-century Jews, an "essence" of Judaism. We ought, again with reference to Wittgenstein, to see an ensemble of purposes and relations bundled into the term. "Judaism" indicates a family resemblance rather than a determinant essence. "Judaism" ought to be unpacked as indicating a range of phenomena, across which may be found an ongoing project by groups of Jews to articulate a sacred nation through law, culture, politics, and, until the quite recent emergence of what Charles Taylor calls "exclusive humanism" (Taylor 2007: 26), interpretations of divine intent.

What ideas, practices, traditions, and texts and what social groups thereunto related are key for a sociology of Judaism? Passing reference has already been made to monotheism. This is a primordial feature of Judaism, of which any sociology must take account. Monotheism, in its eventual, fully developed form, is original to Judaism. It is not, however, a Judaic monopoly. It is shared by both classical philosophy, which gestured toward an intellectual monotheism, and Christianity and Islam, which achieved it. Accordingly, it would be mistaken to see monotheism as a uniquely distinguishing feature of Judaism. (Those Jewish groups, such as Reform Judaism in the nineteenth and twentieth centuries that made "ethical monotheism" the exclusive "essence of Judaism" were usually intent on seamless acculturation to gentile society (Auerbach 1993).) The core ideas and practices which arguably distinguish Judaism are to be found more in the consequences of monotheism, as lived by a distinctive social group, than in monotheism per se.

As mentioned above, the maintenance of an acute sense of particularistic nationhood in tandem with an expansive monotheistic universalism is one such tradition. Another is a complex, internally conflicted understanding of authority: the absolute authority of the One God relativizes the authority of all men. The relativization of authority in turn supports an ongoing practice of pluralism, that is, a variety of expressions of Jewish belonging each claiming normative status with no higher court of appeal among them than the eventual judgment of history (Sagi 2007: 69). These expressions do not necessarily affirm the acceptability or validity of one another, in the manner of modern democratic pluralism (Galston 2005: 16). Indeed, their contempt for one another can be quite sharp. (Among the harsh judgments groups of Jews have pronounced on one another, the most famous is undoubtedly Jesus' condemnation of the Pharisees in Matthew, chapter 23. This condemnation – "hypocrites," "brood of vipers," "white washed tombs" – is not different in kind from other ancient, medieval and modern expressions of disapproval, however.) Nonetheless, there is a recognition of the fact that moral and intellectual competition and lack of resolution are ineradicable features of human social life; that life *inter homines* is irrefragably agonistic rather than harmonistic (Kekes 1993: 54). The condition of the builders of Babel also characterizes, to some extent, the people Israel. The cosmos as such, at least in the end, may be harmonistic, but a metaphysics of ultimate eschatological harmony cannot underwrite a social order, a present politics, in which conflict has been superseded. Conflict and dissent – and therefore a culture of rights, limited government, constitutionalism, and divided authority – are necessary. This phenomenology grounds my claim that Judaism is an ongoing contest over the constitution of sacred nationhood. The religious-political idea that gives expression to this pluralism is the concept of covenant (*berit*). Much of our analysis will focus on this core idea and its implications for the lived experience over the millennia of the Jews.

COVENANT

Modern scholars are divided on the origins of Israel. The biblical account locates the origin of the people Israel in a single family line. After repeated disappointments with humankind, God chooses a single individual to be His servant. He calls Abraham to leave his native Mesopotamia and settle in the far west, in Canaan. Over several generations the line of Abraham grows (and splits). It becomes as numerous as the sands of the sea and the stars of the heavens, as God promised, during its 400-year ordeal in Egypt. After this a charismatic leader, Moses, liberated over 600,000 Israelites. These lineal descendants of Abraham, in league with others who joined them, collectively become God's servants, His chosen nation, after they enter into covenant with Him at Mt Sinai. After a forty year sojourn in the wilderness, a generation uncorrupted by slavery conquered the land of Canaan under Moses' (not quite as) charismatic successor, Joshua. The people secured existence on their territories by annihilating the indigenous Canaanites. They had no peace, however. Their national life developed under threat from a Mediterranean people, the Philistines, in response to which they reorganized their loosely federated political system as a kingship. The normative status of kingship was highly contested. The biblical texts preserve both fear that an aboriginal federalism under the direct rule of God would be lost, as well as a sacralization of the king along the lines common to the older societies of the ancient Near East. (Eventually kingship was accepted, even projected onto the future in the concept of the messiah as the utopian eschatological consummation of history.) The Israelite state splintered into two unequal parts, one characterized by dynastic stability, indicating the full acceptance of the normativity of kingship, the other by continual upheaval, indicating the lingering power of direct, charismatic rule. Both states maintained a cultus, devoted primarily to the ancestral God, YHWH, although with admixtures of syncretism imported by the normal give and take of politics and international relations. Priests administered the cult. Both states generated a culture of opposition, in the phenomenon of prophecy, to religious syncretism, political abuse, and social injustice. Both states ultimately met their end in conquest by a great power. Some of the Israelites disappeared from the stage of history. Others, henceforth known as *yehudim* (inhabitants of Judah; Jews) endure to the present day.

While pious Jews (and Christians) accept the historicity of the beginning phases of this story, scholars do not. The historical verisimilitude of the account grows as the chronology develops. David, Solomon, and subsequent kings, and some of the prophets who criticized them, for example, are acknowledged as historical figures although there is no consensus on how much of the texts that purport to describe their activities is accurate (Greenspahn 2008: 3–20). Nonetheless, most scholars do not see the texts of the "former prophets" (i.e. Judges, Samuel, Kings) as sheer fiction. That is not the case with the narratives of the Pentateuch. Some scholars believe that Genesis and Exodus, for example, preserve cultural elements which suggest that their authors knew whereof they wrote. Others believe that these writings fabricated eponymous ancestors in order to give an identity to a later group in search of a usable past. The upshot is that there is no definitive scholarly account of the origins of Israel. There is, however, an emerging scholarly consensus.

Scholarship can neither prove nor disprove the existence of Abraham, Isaac, and Jacob and the account of Israelite origins articulated by the biblical narrative. The idea of descent from common ancestors has supported the millennial Jewish sense of the Jews as an extended family. Pious Jews will never abandon it. However, the critical scholarly view of a composite, non-familial origin for Israel also has great explanatory potential for later features of Judaism. Although it is not endearing, it is heuristic. As mentioned, there is no consensus among scholars on Israelite origins but there is movement in the direction of a consensus. A generation ago, there were three dominant views of how the people that called itself Israel emerged. First was the "conquest model," in terms of which the Joshua account of rapid conquest by an outside people, Israel, of Canaanite city states was believed to be historically veracious. Archaeology no longer supports this model. More precise dating of destruction layers has complicated, if not quite falsified, what was, from the perspective of traditional faith, welcome scientific support. By the mid-twentieth century, scholars hypothesized a second model, that of peaceful infiltration by an outside group – an account supported somewhat by the less than successful story of "conquest" in the Book of Judges. A third view was that of an indigenous peasant revolt. The people who emerged as Israel began as dissident Canaanites.

The emerging scholarly consensus takes elements from these models. In the words of a leading archaeologist, William Dever:

> [T]he early Israelites were a motley lot – urban refugees, people from the countryside, what we might call "social bandits," brigands of various kinds, malcontents, dropouts from society. They may have been social revolutionaries, as some scholars hold, imbued with Yahwistic fervor … They may have had some notion of religious reforms of one sort or another. There does appear to be a kind of primitive democracy reflected in the settlements and the remains of their material culture. Perhaps this group of people included some pastoral nomads, even some from Transjordan. I'm even willing to grant that a small nucleus of people who became Israelites had originally been in Egypt … Thus, it is quite possible that there were some newcomers in this mixture of peoples, who were, however, mostly indigenous Canaanites. (Shanks et al. 1992: 54)

What ultimately distinguished this "motley" group of Canaanites and others, who emerged in the central hill country in the early Iron Age, from other Canaanites was the worship of YHWH. They drew a boundary around themselves as a people formed by fidelity to an ancestral god. Just as the Ammonites worshiped Milcom and the Moabites worshiped Chemosh, the Israelites were those whose identity was tied to YHWH (Shanks et al. 1992: 129).

This was essentially Max Weber's view. Although he gave far more credence to the conquest model than do contemporary scholars, seeing YHWH as a war god whose forte is might, not order, he saw Israel as a confederation of disparate groups (*Eidgenossenschaft*) not less than Dever does (Weber 1952: 77; Mittleman 2000: 59–66). For Weber, the original aim of the confederation is war, the conquest of the land. Nonetheless, once that was accomplished, confederation – or to put it in more biblical terms, covenant – continued to order Israelite polity and *mentalité*. Weber was the first to stress the socio-political reality of covenant and to retrieve its practical significance from the realm of theology. Prior to Weber, as in Wellhausen, covenant was thought to signify a purely "religious" relationship between a demanding ethical God and His people. For Wellhausen, the primordial natural-familial bond between the father god and the human children was transformed by the literary prophets into an abstract, ethical relationship. Covenant is a symbol for this gain in transcendence and loss in immediacy. (Note the telltale signs of German Romanticism.) For Weber, by contrast, covenant connotes a socio-political form of organization, the oath bound confederation, which in turn has an affinity to ethically contingent ways of conceptualizing the divine-human relationship. The twentieth-century discovery of Hittite suzerain-vassal treaties that use covenantal

formulae lend credence to Weber's early emphasis on the socio-political phenomenology of the *berit*.

The idea of covenant has profound implications for the subsequent development
of the Jews and Judaism. To list a few of its features: (1) Covenant takes both
history and agency seriously. It requires as a condition that human beings (and God)
make morally binding, consequential decisions to link their lives (as it were, in the
case of God) together for mutual benefit. Covenant endows history, the temporal
dimension in which decisions are made and played out, with significance. There is
neither fate nor an "unbearable lightness of being." Being has moral weight and
worth. (2) Covenant preserves the unique distinctiveness of the covenanting parties.
It resists mystical absorption into an allegedly higher, all encompassing reality (the
"Godhead") as the consummation or amplitude of being. The consummation of
being is the fulfillment of the terms of the covenant, which ultimately have to do
with the attainment of a just socio-political order. (3) Covenant relates disparate
beings or groups through subscription to a common moral framework. Thus,
Abraham, due to his covenant with God, is able to challenge God's intended actions
at Sodom and Gomorrah: Will the Judge of all the earth not do justly? Abraham
asks (Genesis 18:25). This common framework, despite radical ontological difference, will have vast consequences for subsequent Judaism. (4) Covenant-making
requires consent. The choice of moral agents – although perhaps not entirely free
– in favor of covenantal relationship in turn assumes the dignity, rights, and moral
worth of those agents. Liberty is necessary for consent – hence the Israelites must
be freed from Egypt in order to accept the covenant. Covenanting also preserves
and transforms liberty. Consent remains an ideal, although it is an ideal in tension
with the non-consensual claims that kinship, family, social solidarity, and so on
make on the members of a nation. The Jewish tradition, in its own idioms, has had
to wrestle with the conceptual problems engendered by social contract theory, viz.
how is consent reconcilable with membership in a socio-political order into which
one has been born and to which one has not, in any explicit sense, consented.

Although direct historical evidence for this claim is lacking, one could argue that
the composite origin of Israel as a covenantal union of disparate groups under the
moral aegis of God has echoes throughout subsequent Israelite and Jewish experience. Covenantal origins bear covenantal consequences. The "Eidgenossenschaft"
retains its character even after a more organic model of nationhood takes hold. Let
us consider first the implications of covenantalism for questions of authority and
politics. The biblical story is one of ongoing contestation over the authority to define
how the challenge of sacred nationhood is to be realized. Various regime forms
ranging from charismatic founders (Abraham, Isaac, Jacob) and prophets (Moses,
Joshua to a lesser extent), to charismatic military leaders (the *shoftim* or "judges"),
to kings, to post-exilic governors are presented as plausible claimants for the best
regime under the relevant contingent historical circumstances. Each of these forms
is founded on a covenantal agreement of some sort. Within the Bible, rebellions
against authority, such as that of Korah (Numbers 16), are launched as competing,
warranted claims to holiness made with reference to covenantal norms. (Korah, for
example, argues against Moses and Aaron: "You have gone too far! For all the
community are holy, all of them, and the LORD is in their midst. Why then do you
raise yourselves above the LORD's congregation?": Numbers 16:3.) When one

regime form, kingship, achieves dominance an institutionalized form of challenge and opposition, prophecy, is generated. Prophecy attempts to hold the kings to the covenantal norms that legitimate their rule. The competing claims of both king and prophet are moderated by a third center of authority, the priesthood. The biblical experience, at least as presented by the canonical text, is thus one of division of power. The nation as a whole is founded on a covenant between God and Israel, which has as a consequence that the constituent members of the nation relate to one another as covenantal equals (*bnei berit*). No one center can claim complete authority. Each propounds its own normative ideals, all of which suffuse the Bible. The Bible, as a literary work, speaks in these many voices, its composite nature reflecting the divergent worldviews, traditions and interests of its authorships (Knohl 2003). The separation of powers in the Bible informed the tradition of political federalism in the West where some thought it to be an exemplar of political genius and others, notably Spinoza, thought it to be a recipe for political weakness and instability (Elazar 1995).

As mentioned, the biblical regimes are presented by the text as founded on covenant. The legal-constitutional framework, offered by God to Israel at Mt Sinai through the mediation of Moses, has to be consented to by Israel (Exodus 19:8, 24:3). The Bible presents the Sinai covenant as a founding: Israel ascended from a familial group, the descendants of Jacob, with whom a disparate multitude of refugees from Egypt (Exodus 12:38) associated themselves, to a proper nation. The covenant makes an *'am* (a people) into a *goy* (a nation), governed by a divine sovereign under a code of divine law and ready to take control of a bounded territory (Speiser 1964: 86). It is characteristic of covenants that they require periodic renewal, that there be public demonstrations of fidelity that both reenact the original founding and consecrate, in Abraham Lincoln's words, a "new birth of freedom." Thus we find episodes of covenant-renewal in the Bible (Deuteronomy 29:9–28; Joshua 24:1–28; Nehemiah 9). This theme loses some salience in subsequent Jewish cultures at least insofar as periodic public demonstration is concerned. Nonetheless, elements of consent and voluntarism remain. One scholar sees in the daily liturgical declaration of divine unity (the *Shema*, from the first word of Deuteronomy 6:4: "*shema yisrael*: Hear, Israel, the LORD your God, the LORD is one!") a rabbinic version of a covenant renewal ceremony (Levenson 1985: 82).

Alongside the paradigm of the Sinai covenant, there is another founding. "[W]ithin the national covenant lies another, restricted to one family, the royal house of David" (Levenson 1985: 99). Texts such as 2 Samuel 7: 11ff. and Psalm 89:4–5 speak of the covenant that God grants to David and his descendants to be kings over Israel forever. God, in a sense, ratifies the choice of the people, who elected David as their king (2 Samuel 5:3): David and the "elders of Israel" entered into a mutual covenant. Prior to the divine grant of rule to David, the decision of the people to choose David as their ruler was similar to earlier decisions to choose *shoftim*, "judges," as provisional warrior chieftains. God's grant of rule, however, seems to lock the Jewish people into monarchy as the necessary form of national polity forever after. This is not the case, however. The Davidic monarchy, as an effective political institution, ceased with the Babylonian conquest (586 BCE). Subsequent forms of civil governance, such as the post-exilic "Great Assembly," its successor, the Sanhedrin, the Patriarchate of late Roman times, and the Exilarchate of Sassanian and then Muslim Mesopotamia were analogized by the Jews to the Davidic monarchy. Thus, the Talmud, glossing Genesis 49:10 ("The scepter shall not depart from Judah, nor the ruler's staff from between his feet.") comments that " 'The scepter ...' these are the exilarchs who rule over Israel with a scepter. 'Nor the ruler's staff ...' these are the sons of the sons of Hillel, who teach Torah in the public domain" (Sanhedrin 5a). Monarchy retains value as an ideal – the ideal monarch becomes a future scion of David, the messiah. However, the full acceptance and legitimation of other forms of civil order allowed the Jewish people a continuous political existence in the absence of their own state. Until the eighteenth century, Jews commonly thought of themselves as a political nation in exile from their homeland but clinging to features of their early political community; their ideal was a full national polity governed according to the law of their Torah-constitution. It was only with the possibility of emancipation from medieval ghetto conditions and citizenship in the modern European states that the old surrogate of an *imperium in imperio* was abandoned for a more purely religious understanding of what constituted Judaism. Thus, we can see from this brief sketch that covenant, both as concept and as instrument, has been critical to Jewish adaptation and survival to a variety of political and historical conditions.

PLURALISM

Covenant, as mentioned, underwrites pluralism. The post-biblical experience of the Jewish people shows rival groups each claiming to represent the "kingdom of priests and holy nation" (Exodus 19:6) that Israel was meant to be. By Roman times, the various alignments included the Temple-centered Sadducees, the Essenes, priestly dissenters who established a counter-society in the Judean wilderness, the proto-rabbinic Pharisees, and the hyper-nationalist Zealots, whose military confrontation with the Romans brought about the destruction of the Temple and Jewish Jerusalem in 70 CE A plethora of literature not included by the post-70 CE rabbis in the scriptural canon but having sacred status for non-rabbinic Jews such as the Alexandrine community that produced the Septuagint indicates further versions of Judaism. Groups that began within the Jewish social and cultural matrix, such as the followers of Jesus, gradually took on a distinct identity of their own. The reasons for the evolving split between Jewish Christians and other Jews remain a matter of scholarly exploration and controversy. At any rate, the estrangement between Jews and (increasingly) gentile Christians shows that the covenantal matrix is not entirely elastic. It is possible to push the claim to best represent God's covenant partner, Israel, past a limit where the claimant loses Jewish status. The limits of elasticity are discovered within the give and take of social experience; they are not postulated a priori. Unlike the Christian experience of heresy, splits within Jewish history have been more a matter of law and custom than belief or creed. On one influential scholar's view, the parting of the ways began in earnest when sufficient numbers of Jews stopped treating Jewish Christians as fellow Jews by declining to marry them (Schiffman 1985).

Even after the dominance of the Pharisaic-Rabbinic group owing to the destruction or discrediting of its rivals, acceptance of rabbinic authority remained largely voluntary, i.e. covenantal in character (Berger 1998: 105). Maimonides comments that the enactments and decrees of the rabbis had authority because "all Israel agreed to abide by them" (*hiskimu aleihem kol yisrael*) (Maimonides, Mishneh Torah). Of course, Maimonides also argues that rabbinic authority is grounded in divine law: the rabbis are authorized by God to interpret the Torah. Nonetheless, the dimension of voluntary consent, a key dimension of covenantalism, is present. From approximately the seventh century to the eighteenth century, the rabbinic culture that created the Babylonian Talmud dominated Jewish life. The people granted their constitutional text authority. They allowed themselves to be formed by the norms, ideals, and intellectual project of the Talmud. This constrained the contestation over authority, but it did not diminish it. Talmudic Judaism is a culture of criticism. Within the rabbinic world, competing claims to authority flourished in the centuries long rivalry between the political and scholarly leaders of the Land of Israel and those of Babylonia, in the form of regional vs. centralized governance and in rabbinic vs. lay control of communities. There was also dissent from the claim of rabbinic Judaism per se to represent the normative ideal of the Jewish People, as in the ninth-century movement of the anti-rabbinic Karaites, in periodic eruptions of messianic fervor in which rabbinic norms and leadership were subverted and, in modernity, in nineteenth-century Reform Judaism and in the varieties of late nineteenth- and twentieth-century secularism and nationalism.

The Jewish experience of late antiquity and of the Middle Ages, in terms of the covenantal framework elaborated upon here, was one of trying to sustain the consciousness of nationhood, as well as some of the requisite institutions of nationhood, under the inimical conditions of exile and of the loss of sovereignty. Jews exploited whatever political possibilities were open to them to create institutions and to extend their reach. After the disastrous Bar Kokhba rebellion against the Romans in 132–135 CE, Jews reorganized their political and religious institutions in the Land of Israel. The Palestinian Jewish community was organized under a Patriarch (*nasi*), descended from the famous Pharisee, Hillel, and an assembly of rabbis who resuscitated the term "Sanhedrin" for their body. This dual structure harked back to the Hasmonean kings and Sanhedrin, as well as to the king and prophet structure of biblical times. The patriarchate was the political face of the Jewish community; the Sanhedrin was the more purely religious and legal one. These two institutions, representing the polar but integrated nature of Jewish life as national and religious, cooperated but also rivaled one another. None of this would have been possible had the Romans not decided to co-opt the Jews and diminish the possibility of future rebellion. Christian Roman emperors, however, became increasingly hostile to the Jews. The patriarchate was terminated by the Romans in 425 CE. The Sanhedrin was deprived of the ability to tax communities of the Roman diaspora for its support and was weakened as well.

Babylonia gradually replaced Israel as the center of Jewish life, although not without rivalry and contestation between them. The Jews, once again with imperial patronage, set up a parallel structure in Mesopotamia, with an exilarch (*resh galuta*), who claimed descent from King David, fulfilling the civic functions of rule and rabbinic heads of academies (which eventually produced the Babylonian Talmud) acting as legal and religious authorities. Eventually, the academies (*yeshivot*) consolidated. The head of the academy of Sura became known as the Gaon ("illustrious one"). The Gaonate, as the ultimate religious-legal authority, paralleled the Exilarchate, as the ultimate political authority (Elazar and Cohen 1985: 148). The Exilarchate endured until the beginning of the fifteenth century, although its power was greatly diminished as regional centers such as Spain and North Africa grew in importance. It lasted as long as it did not only due to sufferance of Muslim rulers but due to the abiding traditional authority vested by the people in the line of David. The rule of a Davidide, however notional, kept alive not only memories of ancient glory but anticipations of messianic revival. The Exilarchate stood as a symbol of national unity, even as the various other geographic centers within the lands of Islam and Christendom eclipsed it.

In Spain, the Jewish community initially replicated the polar governance structure with a civic, prince-like leader, the *nagid*, trying to exercise kingdom-wide authority and rabbis both cooperating with and checking his claims. Local communities (*kehillot*), sometimes in federation with one another, also grew and asserted their rights. In the German and French speaking lands, and eventually in Eastern Europe, Jewish life was always organized on a local community basis. The local community was a comprehensive "state within a state." The elected leaders of the community collected taxes, provided welfare, a court system, funding for religious institutions such as schools, kosher slaughter, ritual baths, the dowering of indigent brides, the salaries of ritual employees, etc. as well as represented the community to the Christian overlord. When circumstances permitted, as was the case earlier in Spain, individual communities federated with other communities and held annual conclaves to set policy, adjudicate disputes, etc. Thus, although Jews often had to settle for communal life on a local scale, their impulse was to articulate national institutions whenever possible.

The medieval order, although often perilous for Jews under both Islam and Christendom, was nonetheless something of a golden age for Jewish self-governance. *Kehillot* fit into the social order as tolerated corporations, chartered by local rulers or kings with the right to manage their own affairs in exchange for annual tax revenues. Jews developed sophisticated political and legal institutions. In Spain, they even had the right to administer capital punishment. Rabbis addressed questions of politics and economics – of public law – in their legal essays and rulings. Different theories of the grounds of public authority circulated. The extent to which *kehillot* were purely consensual or partly compulsory, democratic or republican was debated, as was the relationship between traditional Torah law, presumably rooted in divine authority, and humanly promulgated legislation (*takkanot*). The effort to retrieve the political theory of medieval Jewry has become an important scholarly field. Although falling far short of the mythic ideal of a sovereign nation in its own land living under its own law, the medieval Jewish community nonetheless displayed the normative thrust of Judaism, that is, Torah qua communal theo-political praxis.

In the lands of Islam, in Provence, and in the Iberian peninsula, under both Muslims and Christians, Jews participated extensively in the general culture and created works of science, philosophy, poetry and grammar that paralleled those of gentiles. Thomas Aquinas referred frequently in the *Summa* to "Rabbi Moses," that is, Maimonides, the leading representative of medieval Jewish intellectual culture. The medieval legacy of the Jews remains a fertile field, not just for scholarly research, but for popular interpretation. When Christians, influenced by romanticism in the nineteenth century, yearned for the Christian Middle Ages and retrieved, for example, Gothic architecture, Jews looked to the "Golden Age of Spain" and created a "Moorish" style for their synagogues. Modernizing Jews also retrieved great works of Jewish rationalism, such as Maimonides' *Guide for the Perplexed* and created a tradition of "Jewish philosophy" with which to argue their fitness for admission to modern intellectual culture. On the other hand, the modern acculturating Jews of Western Europe buried the mystical elements of their tradition (*Kabbalah*) out of a certain embarrassment with its magical and superstitious elements. It was only with the upsurge of neo-Romanticism in the first two decades of the twentieth century that such traditions were reclaimed. Their popularity today speaks to the "rubber cage" or "disenchantment with disenchantment" aspect of late modernity, as noted by Ernest Gellner (Gellner 1987: 152).

With the breakdown of the medieval corporate order and the rise of nation states in Europe, the self-governing status of the Jewish communities became anomalous. Coordinate with the Enlightenment, rulers in Austria, France, and the German states began to emancipate their Jewries. Emancipation conferred legal equality (never perfectly achieved) on individual Jews in exchange for the dissolution of historic Jewish communal structures. In principle, Jews became citizens rather than tolerated aliens existing under their own vestigial law in ghettoized enclaves. The success of this project varied from nation to nation, the residue of traditional hatred of Jews continuing to exist alongside Enlightenment ideas of human equality. Indeed, with the coming of a more secular age, traditional religiously formed currents of Jew-hatred were transformed into modern "scientific" varieties described by the nineteenth-century neologism, anti-Semitism. In Eastern Europe, where the largest communities of Jews lived, mostly within the Russian empire, modern trends came more fitfully.

Jews encountered modernity in some ways well-prepared and in other ways ill-prepared. The Talmudic culture of traditional Judaism prepared Jews for modernity insofar as education and intellectual achievement – albeit within the framework of a traditional religious canon – were long valued by the Jewish community. Meritocratic criteria for rabbinic leadership were valorized. The character of learning was abstract, dialectical, logical and literary; traditional Jews prized a skill set that could easily be transferred to a secular, scientific or humanistic framework. Furthermore, the Talmudic culture educated Jews into the ways of the sophisticated economy of late antiquity. Whereas European peasants were familiar only with the agricultural economy of the feudal order, Jews, despite their often reduced economic circumstances, preserved cultural knowledge of more advanced economic practices. They were thus well-positioned to take part in a modern capitalist economy. Social and legal exclusions also contributed to this aptitude. Jews were for the most part not allowed to own land; thus they served as economic middlemen rather than farmers. They were basically an urban people, even though they had been expelled from cities (when they were not simply expelled from countries altogether) in several lands in the late Middle Ages. When given the chance, they returned to cities or smaller commercial centers. The late twentieth-century Jewish nostalgia for the "shtetl" or small market town of Eastern Europe was purely romantic. Jews flocked to the cities of Eastern Europe when they were allowed to do so; the shtetl would have died on its own had it not been destroyed in the Holocaust.

The authority of the "state within a state" in which Jews lived had been chiseled away in the German speaking countries in the seventeenth and eighteenth centuries. Modernizing elements within the Jewish communities cooperated with German rulers in reducing the power of Jewish courts, rabbinic enactments, and the *kehillah*'s tax collecting functions. When the Emancipation demanded the end of the *kehillah*, many Jews were quick to comply. Citizenship seemed a far more desirable status than traditional Jewish collective life in a world where medieval corporations had less and less plausibility. The consequence of the unmaking of the traditional *kehillah* was three-fold. First, the Torah could no longer be practiced in a self-governing political context. The political part of the "theo-political" nexus of traditional Judaism had been severed. As such, Judaism had to be reconfigured as a religion in the modern, Western sense. In Germany, where most of the Jews of Western Europe lived, the cost of admission was high. Jews had to reform their tradition in radical ways, basically reshaping Judaism to accord with Protestant norms of what a proper religion should be. Second, the national dimension of Jewish consciousness had to be suppressed. Jews needed to think of themselves as Germans, Frenchmen, and so on who differed from their fellow citizens only in religion. The question of how a German Jew was to think, for example, of a French Jew – as brother or as stranger – became perplexed and fraught with political consequences. Third, since Judaism however transformed cannot be simply a private or creedal religion – since its communal dimension resists being reduced to a "gathered community" of individuals who come together to worship – new forms of Jewish communal life had to be created to substitute for the compulsory *kehillah*. These challenges indicate the way in which traditional Judaism ill-prepared Jews for modernity. A scattered diasporic nation that would retain its national consciousness was ill suited to a brave new world of nation states, each demanding unequivocal loyalty.

Nonetheless, the modern history of the Jews and Judaism should not be presented as a "subtraction story" (Taylor 2007: 27) but as one of subtraction and addition, of challenge and creative response. Let us consider how Jews responded, and Judaism adapted, to the three challenges enumerated above. On the first point, which historians of modern Jewry sometimes call the "confessionalization of Judaism," a determined effort was made by modern Jews to repress the political elements of Judaism. The iconic model of this is Moses Mendelssohn's *Jerusalem* (1783). Mendelssohn, a Berlin Jewish philosopher who was an advocate for both Enlightenment and Emancipation and a harbinger of Jewish acculturation, argued for a Lockean understanding of religion and state. Religion was to be a private matter, irrelevant to citizenship. The state was to be unconcerned with religious opinion. Freedom of opinion was to be sacrosanct (Mendelssohn 1983: 70). Judaism was redescribed along Lockean, interiorized lines. Mendelssohn argued that the theo-political constitution of Judaism in antiquity, paradigmatically, in the Bible, was appropriate only to the unique circumstances of that age (Mendelssohn 1983: 131). Subsequent embodiments of Judaism as a compulsory community with the power to banish, imprison, punish and tax were deviant. The ideal typical form of Judaism was a kind of church of freely assenting, like-minded individuals who practiced ceremonial customs infused with moral lessons. Mendelssohn thus justified in theory what had been worked out in practice by the Prussian state: the erosion of the integrity of the *kehillah* in the interest of the modernization of the state was now given a Jewish religious justification.

Unlike France, where the emancipation of the Jewish community occurred definitively under Napoleon, the emancipation of German Jewry was episodic and subject to reversal. (German Jews were not fully equal citizens until the founding of Bismarck's Reich in 1871.) The progress and reversal of emancipation led German Jews to modify their tradition more drastically than did Jews elsewhere. Reform Judaism, a highly confessional, denationalized, de-ritualized religion, which drew inspiration from the Protestant Reformation, arose in Germany. The movement was motivated partly by purely political considerations, that is, it was meant to convince the Germans that Jews were sufficiently like them to merit equal status. But it also reflected the fact that many Jews themselves had become alienated from traditional Judaism insofar as the decline of the *kehillah* and partial acculturation to German language and Enlightenment culture deprived traditional Judaism of its plausibility structure. Out of frustration with the laggard pace of Emancipation, some Jews converted to Christianity. Reform was meant to offer an appealing Jewish alternative. Reform Judaism began as the moderate reform of liturgical practice in the second decade of the nineteenth century (Meyer 1997: 123). Its proponents even argued their case in traditional Hebrew language rabbinic responsa. By the 1840s, however, the movement became ideologically self-aware and argued for a deeper, more consequential transformation of Judaism as a whole. Reform Judaism was inhibited in Germany by political supervision of religious life – some governments wanted to keep the Jews traditional precisely so they would not assimilate to the broader society. It flourished however in the USA, to which it was brought by German-Jewish immigrants after 1848. In the religious free market of the USA, Reform Judaism could take its tendency to the extreme and abolish Jewish dietary laws, Saturday as the Sabbath, reject traditional messianism, gender specific practices, the Hebrew language and so on. That Reform Judaism initially met the modernist resurgence of Jewish national consciousness, Zionism, with unalloyed hostility is unsurprising, given its premise. "Washington is our Jerusalem," a nineteenth-century Reform leader declared. Although Reform has allowed, even encouraged, the return of Hebrew and Jewish ritual practices back into its temples – a word it chose to distance itself from the traditional synagogue and allude evocatively to the Temple in Jerusalem – it hews to an Enlightenment *weltanschauung* where autonomy and ethics constitute the heart of religion. The stress on autonomy raises the covenantal theme of consent to high visibility but also stretches it to its limit. Contemporary Reform wrestles with the tension between its Enlightenment funded emphasis on individual conscience and its traditional Jewish inheritance of solidarity with the historic Jewish community. Reform, as did most other Jews, increasingly came to identify with Zionism. One way it negotiates the tension between individuality and solidarity is to work to remake the State of Israel along purely liberal, Western lines.

As is often the case in modernity, unreflective tradition was forced to become self-reflective traditionalism. As Reform grew into a movement, enlightened traditionalists began to push back, defending Talmudic forms of Jewish piety and practice in modern idioms. There was a moderate wing to this movement, which eventually grew into the form known in the USA as Conservative Judaism, as well as a more defiant traditionalism which became known, ironically by a word on loan from Christianity, as Orthodoxy. The Conservative moderates affirmed the full normativeness of traditional Jewish law but felt compelled, for reasons of intellectual honesty, to consider texts critically and historically. They accepted the canon of hermeneutics of the German university. The uneasy juxtaposition of traditionalist practice and historicist criticism imbued this tendency with an intellectual instability. Traditional piety is hard to sustain without some certainties about revelation, prophecy, authority, etc. all of which are eroded by historicity and criticism. What sustained Conservative Judaism, which flourished in the mid-twentieth century in the USA, was a sufficiently large population of Jews who wanted both traditionalism and modernism and were willing to live with the tensions. Enshrining intellectual tension as the hallmark of a religious movement appears to its partisans as honest and brave. Others view it as confused or compromised. Orthodoxy, by contrast, was developed by traditionalists who wanted the prerogatives of modern citizenship without incurring any intellectual debts to modernity. The Orthodoxy that developed in Germany was keen on emancipation and acculturation to prevailing norms of dress, speech, and high culture, all the while rejecting intellectual accommodation with modernity. It tried to retain a maximalist view of revelation, rejecting the Spinozist assumptions of the Higher Criticism practiced in German universities, that would underwrite full observance of traditional Jewish law. While Reform Jews rejected the normative authority of Jewish law altogether in favor of the autonomous moral conscience, Conservative Jews modified the law to adapt to current conditions. (A classic American example is the Conservative decision in the 1950's to allow driving on the Sabbath in order to cope with distances denizens of the new suburbs would have to travel to attend synagogue.) Orthodox Jews, however, would not modify the law as freely. If it was too far to walk to synagogue, then one should move. As worthwhile as gender equality may be in civil life, it has no warrant in certain precincts of Jewish law and liturgical practice. A current issue – the status of homosexuals – is a clear case in point. While both Reform and Conservative laities and leaderships have made their peace with, even enthusiastically embraced, sexual orientation equality, Orthodoxy cannot on principle. The term "orthodoxy" although originating in the controversies over the transformation of Judaism in nineteenth-century Germany, has come to stand for all varieties of principled arch-traditionalism today. Thus, Jewish traditional movements from Eastern Europe, such as Hasidism, which remained aloof from the paroxysms of nineteenth-century German Jews unselfconsciously call themselves "Orthodox," as do traditional Jews from Arab lands whose ancestors were untouched (or, thanks to colonialism, lightly touched) by the European developments sketched above.

All of these movements – and new ones have emerged in the late twentieth century as well – have in common that they are voluntary constellations of like-minded individuals. They are based on consent. The high salience of individual consent renders both national consciousness and thickness of community problematic. Jews in liberal societies, especially where anti-Semitism is marginal, are in no sense externally compelled to identify as Jews. It is for them a purely voluntary, consensual identity. (A recent slogan celebrated this condition as that of a "choosing people" rather than, traditionally, a chosen people.) As such, they can construct it however they wish. The rising construction of Judaism in the USA is personalistic, spiritual, and aesthetic. Judaism is felt to be a path to personal meaning and spiritual growth, not an obligatory solidarity with other Jews, an obligatory practice of traditional duties enunciated within a historic legal system, etc. (Cohen and Eisen 2000). Jews thus emulate trends in other traditions increasingly noted by sociologists of religion in America (Roof 2001). Heinrich Heine's satirical observation, as Christians do, so do Jews (*wie es christelt sich, jüdelt sich*) remains pertinent.

It is difficult to sustain the forms of community that modern Jews developed in the wake of the *kehillah*. Those forms, now in a state of transformation and arguably in a state of decline, corresponded to the two poles of the classic theo-political constitution. On the one hand, Jews organized religious societies around synagogues or, as they came to be called by Reform minded Jews, temples. (The locution not only recalled a glorious, classical past but also subtly indicated a vision of the future: Jews would no longer await a supernatural messiah to restore the Temple. Emancipation and assimilation in a liberal society or *Rechtsstaat* was incipiently the messianic age.) In the USA, synagogues and temples, although local organizations, federated with others of compatible outlook and formed national bodies, similar to Protestant denominations. American Jewry divided itself into denominations, which competed and occasionally cooperated with one another throughout the twentieth century. Early attempts to transplant the European *kehillah* to colonial American soil – the nascent Jewish community of New York in the seventeenth century was modeled after the London community – quickly proved unsustainable. Voluntarism rather than compulsion came to characterize American Jewish religious life almost from the start (Kaplan 2005). Absent a *kehillah* with a state chartered authority to punish dissent from religious norms, the practice of Judaism was left to the discretion of individual Jews. Diffuse social pressure and individual conscience rather than rabbinic authority backed by public sanction maintained the relevant norms. A study of synagogue constitutions over three centuries of American Jewish life shows a steady decline in public normativeness. In the eighteenth century, a member of a synagogue could be fined or expelled for public desecration of the Sabbath, cursing, or being seen near a house of prostitution. In the twentieth century, the only thing that could get one removed from the membership rolls of a synagogue was failure to pay dues (Elazar et al. 1992).

On the other hand, the communal solidarity of Jews, however undercut by the individualist assumptions of a liberal society, required expression. Synagogues, however various their activities, were insufficient. Jews began to form, by the nineteenth century, civic organizations that corresponded to some of the public functions of the medieval *kehillah*. A host of extra-synagogal organizations came into being. These were originally fraternal and charitable (e.g. Bnai Brith, founded in 1843). However, with the growth of a virulent new anti-Semitism in the late nineteenth century, Jews in various Western countries created defense organizations, such as the Alliance Israelite Universelle (1860) in France, the Central Verein Deutsche Staatsbürger Jüdischen Glaubens (1893) in Germany and the American Jewish Committee (1906). These typically tried to appeal to the better angels of the citizenry's nature, the norms of legal justice, the values of the constitution, etc. Today, however, the increasing religious personalism and diffuse spirituality of contemporary Jews coupled, at least in the USA, with the decline of anti-Semitism challenges the continued existence of century old Jewish civic structures.

The rise of anti-Semitism revealed a bitter irony of history. Jews were previously despised in the West because they were fundamentally different from everyone else. They were not Christian. With their successful emancipation and embourgeoisment, they became despised because they were too much like everyone else or, at least, like everyone else was supposed to be. They had learned the lesson that the paternalistic teachers of emancipation and enlightenment thought to teach them and became prominent, sometimes wealthy, often engaged citizens. Modern anti-Semitism revealed the flaw in Clermont-Tonnerre's promise: Jews became individual, liberal citizens, tied to their "coreligionists" by nothing other than "Mosaic faith" and yet they were still thought to be a distinctive (and objectionable) group and discriminated against on that basis. As noted above, in the late nineteenth century, French, German and other Jews established countrywide organizations to articulate their civic interests and defend themselves. These organizations also worked on behalf of oppressed Jewries abroad, for example, in the Russian empire and the Middle East. For other Jews, although such measures acknowledged the truth of the matter – that Jews remained, when all was said and done, a people – they did not go far enough. They conceded too much ground to the premise of the liberal society, namely that the "Jewish problem" could be solved on a case by case basis of fighting discrimination, educating against prejudice, asserting civil rights, etc. Furthermore, a century of concessions and adaptations to the liberal bourgeois order had damaged the national consciousness of the Jews and warped their essential nature. The "Jewish problem" was, in their view, a national problem – the proud European nation states could not respect a stateless, Weber would say a "pariah," people in their midst. Beholding the awful mockery of assimilationist ideals in the spectacle of the Dreyfus affair (1894), a disillusioned Theodor Herzl concluded that the Jews needed a state of their own.

Herzl gave impetus and leadership to a secular, Western, nationalist conception of Zionism that sought to solve the *Judenproblem*, as it was called in his native Vienna, in purely political terms. Herzl's approach was unappealing to the vast majority of Western Jews, who still put their trust in the liberal state. The Jews of Eastern Europe were a more receptive audience. The promise of a liberal solution to the misery of the masses of Russian Jews was virtually nil. Some of those Jews were drawn to democratic socialism in both its Jewish and secular versions, some to outright revolution, others to fidelity to the timeless traditional ways of piety, and still others to a precursor of Herzlian Zionism. In response to the pogroms of the 1880s some Russian Jews began to advocate settlement in the historic land of Israel. This movement was coordinate with a Jewish version of the previous century's Enlightenment called *Haskalah*. The practitioners of *Haskalah* (*maskilim*) sought to renew the viability of Hebrew as a modern cultural language, created secular poetry and prose (often in competition with the cultivation of the Yiddish language for similar purposes), and tried to create a modern identity for the Jews, drawing upon but not bound to traditional religiosity. This movement differed profoundly from the assimilationist paradigm that had been regnant in the West. In the Russian empire, the Jews lived, under miserable conditions, in a compact western zone called the Pale of Settlement. The very density of Jewish population, with a common language and culture, as well as the absence of an enlightened, liberal regime encouraged Jewish national consciousness and solidarity. Herzl's

Zionism combined with its Eastern European predecessor to produce a practical movement that outlived its founder and, within a half century of his death, succeeded in establishing a state in the historic land of Israel.

The history of the Zionist movement is rife with ideological differences, struggles – some of which were bloody – and opposition. Some of these differences remain salient and are refracted by contemporary political parties in Israel today. Many traditional Jews opposed Zionism as an infringement of the prerogatives of the messiah – a Talmudic passage has the Jews promising not to throw off the yoke of gentile domination until the messiah returns (Luz 2003: 25). Zionism, on this view, is a violation of the oath. More to the point, however, was the modernism – the unvarnished secular nationalism – of Herzl and his followers. Nonetheless, many traditional Jews also opted to endorse Zionism insofar as they were able to bracket out its secularism and view it as a practical mechanism for regaining the land of Israel, within which alone the full practice of traditional Jewish life was possible. At the beginning of the Zionist movement, therefore, a religious party developed. Although originally a minority, the outlook of "religious Zionism" dominates Orthodox circles today, at least those Orthodox who have made their peace with the modern world. Reform Jews in the USA, like liberal assimilationist Jews elsewhere, initially opposed Zionism insofar as it undercut their claim to have achieved equal citizenship and security in the diaspora. With the founding of the State of Israel in 1948, the prime minister of Israel, David Ben Gurion, met with the leader of the American Jewish Committee in New York to assure him that Israel would not try to represent American Jews. A truce was called. Many of the circles that were hostile to the Zionist project before World War II, however, accepted, even embraced Zionism when the full extent of the Holocaust became clear. As the consciousness of the Holocaust grew among world Jewry in the late 1960s and 1970s close identification with Israel became a sine qua non of Jewish identity. Philanthropic and political work on behalf of Israel is a major preoccupation of American Jews. Nonetheless, by the 1990s – the Sabra and Shatilla massacre may be seen as a turning point – tensions developed once again between American Jews, the largest diaspora, and Israel (Rosenthal 2001: 66). The liberal values that have deeply shaped the American Jewish outlook are often confronted with illiberal Israeli realities. The rather different societies in which these two Jewish communities live amount to discrepant "Jewish worlds," with increasing alienation, indifference and disengagement between them (Liebman and Cohen 1990). Creating greater reciprocity, knowledge and empathy has become a concern of both Israeli and American Jewish leaders and educators.

This survey has tried to show how Jews have both struggled continuously to maintain public institutions that express their self-understanding as a sacred nation and have indulged a pluralistic contestation over how that nationhood should be represented. Finally, let us consider how these themes have played out in the realm of traditional Jewish piety (*emunah*).

PIETY

As Martin Buber pointed out, Jewish piety or faith is characterized by a posture of trust in God more than it is by conceptual affirmations about God (Buber 2003).

The Hebrew word for faith, *emunah*, conveys the notion of trustworthiness or reliability. (Buber held, by contrast, that the New Testament term, *pistis*, pointed the Christian toward matters of belief rather than toward a deep, existential orientation.) Although Buber might have scanted Christian faith, he captured something correct about the religious life of the Jews. Matters of belief are secondary; the attitude of trust, the life of loyalty to the covenant, is primary for pious Jews. Belief has never been irrelevant but neither has the precise formulation of belief, as in Christianity, been central. It did acquire some centrality in the Middle Ages, in the highly rationalist project of Maimonides, but immediately became controversial. Maimonides tried to specify a set of key affirmations that a loyal Jew must make. His philosophical successors accepted that positive affirmations have their place but disagreed about what they were, how many of them there were, whether belief can be commanded, and so on (Kellner 2004). Thus, the matter returned to the status quo ante: Jewish faith entails the love and awe of God such that the Jew is to walk in God's ways and live by God's law (Deuteronomy 10:12). That is to say, piety means fidelity to Israel's covenant partner; it means living as a member in good standing of a sacred nation living according to its law.

Judaism has thus been characterized by the New Testament scholar, E. P. Sanders, as a "covenantal nomism" (Sanders 1977). (The term is meant to emphasize the role of law without the pejorative connotation of "legalism.") Law is central but not as a set of heteronymous or arbitrary duties, imposed by divine fiat. Law is expressive of an existential relationship both to God and country, as it were. Israel consents to enter a covenant with God, which entails service on the part of Israel and regard for Israel on the part of God. God gives commandments (*mitzvot*) as a way of concretizing what Israel's service means. The law is not an end in itself, let alone a way of "earning" salvation: it is a vehicle by which to demonstrate the love and awe that Israel has for its divine covenant partner. The duties of the Torah are to be undertaken in joy (*simcha shel mitzvah*) and with a constant demonstration of covenantal loyalty (*hesed*) toward God. God, for his part, shows *hesed* toward Israel, even when (especially when, on the traditional view) he chastises them for disobedience. *Hasidut* (the virtue of being loyal to the covenant in all one's ways) is the praxis of *emunah*.

In Weberian terms, Jewish *emunah* is an inner-worldly asceticism. The utter transcendence of God removes ontological likeness between the human and the divine from the realm of possibility. Thus, mysticism in the sense of *unio mystica* is impossible. What remains is *imitatio dei*. The relation between God and humanity is based on will not on substance, on ethics not on metaphysics. Avenues open to Christianity on account of its trinitarianism are closed to Jews. (I hasten to note, however, that Judaism did develop mystical traditions, the dominant one known as Kabbalah, which complicate to an extent the ideal-typical pattern I am sketching here.) The ontological unlikeness between God and man and the covenantal relationship are mutually supportive. Covenant entails that the covenanting partners retain their distinct identities. The linkage of their lives, as it were, is intimate and transformative but they do not become one being. Their relationship proceeds within the order of time and on the plane of history. The sorts of assertion made in the Upanishads, for example, in which the ontological integrity of human beings is subsumed in Brahman are not possible within a Judaic, covenantal context.

The lived experience of Jewish faith both gives expression to a rigorous monotheism and reinforces consciousness of belonging to a covenanted people. The dominant form that piety took in biblical times, animal sacrifice conducted by a sacerdotal caste, took place in a Temple founded by the royal family. The first Jerusalem Temple, built by Solomon (reigned c.965–928 BCE) and destroyed by Nebuchadnezzar in 586 BCE, was as much a political institution as a religious one. King David's conquest of Jerusalem consolidated its status as the capital of the nation. His son Solomon's construction of the Temple lent the capital the aura of a holy city, a status which it has never lost in the Jewish imagination. Although the Temple rituals had their own religious logic flowing from the presumed reality of sacred space, the social and political dimension of the centralization of the cultus must not be lost. The God of Sinai entered into a covenant with Israel that could be enacted, in principle, everywhere. The God of Zion, by contrast, can only be served on his holy mountain. Israelite faith negotiates the tension between affirming that God is the God of the universe and that God is the God of Israel (in the dual sense of land and people).

The holy days of biblical Israel, which remain the holy days of the Jews, typically have a national referent. The three pilgrimage festivals, Passover, Tabernacles and the Feast of Weeks, fuse recollection of periods of the agricultural year of ancient Israel with significant historical events. Passover (*Pesach*) commemorates the liberation from Egypt, a founding event of Israelite nationhood. Tabernacles (*Sukkot*) commemorates the long march through the wilderness toward the promised land. The Feast of Weeks (*Shavuot*) recalls another founding event – the acceptance of the Torah as the constitution of the nation at Mount Sinai. In addition to these, the New Year (*Rosh Hashanah*) and the Day of Atonement (*Yom Kippur*) add apparently ahistorical, purely "spiritual" or ethicized elements. However, as these holidays are related to the purification of the ancient Temple, its priesthood, and ultimately of all Israel they embody national referents as well. Subsequent late or post-biblical holidays, such as Purim or Chanukah, commemorate events in the life of various Jewish communities that were elevated to national significance. As such, the Jewish liturgical year conveys collective memories, historical consciousness, and a yearning for the Land of Israel in which the agricultural component could be practiced.

As a "covenantal nomism" Judaism cultivated the application of faith to every conceivable action and department of life. The covenant is comprehensive. Jewish law treats eating, sexuality, commerce, interpersonal relations, personal status matters such as marriage, divorce, childhood, adoption, issues of public and social justice, legal procedure, public policy, criminal matters, property, torts, liability, as well as typically "religious" matters such as sacrifice, tithing, prayer, and so on. The profane is meant to receive the sacred through the conscientious action of the Jew. The great breakthrough in the history of Judaism, begun by the much maligned ancient sect of the Pharisees, was to extend the purity laws regulating priestly conduct to ordinary Israelites (Neusner, 1989: 25). They encouraged all Jews, wherever they lived, to live *als ob* they were priests fit for service in the Temple. (Although note, the democratization of holiness had begun already within the corpus of the priestly writings of Scripture (Milgrom 2004: 213).) This democratizing move reduced the centrality of priesthood and Temple, such that when the second Temple was destroyed by the Romans in 70 CE, the Jews were able to recover and adapt to new historical vicissitudes. The Temple and its sacrificial service entered the collective memory. The synagogue, through daily prayer services that mirrored those of the Temple, practiced mimesis. A religion of ethical-ritual sanctification enacted in the midst of the profane by everyone replaced a hierarchical, space-bound formal cultus.

Rabbinic Judaism was a post-70 CE fusion of two separate streams of Second Temple culture. The Pharisees, with their emphasis on purity and impurity laws – and on exporting them beyond the priesthood – have already been mentioned. The other tradition was that of the scribes, the learned bookmen (who might have begun as Persian governmental officials in the time of Ezra) whose work focused on what we might call constitutional interpretation. The Bible itself reveals a process of late reworking of already ancient materials (as, for example, in the historical books of Chronicles vis-à-vis Samuel and Kings). The literary culture of ancient Israel that composed the books which eventually become canonized as scripture was continued in prophetic and scribal circles down into Roman times and beyond. The scribal mentality, often meticulous and conservative, sometimes daring and original, shaped the project of rabbinic Judaism and endowed it with both the reverence for received tradition and the flexibility to adapt it that allowed the Jews to survive under new and difficult conditions. A piety based on books and learning replaced one based on cult and sacrifice. Socially, a meritocracy based on learning replaced a hierarchy based on genealogy, although, as we have seen, presumptive descent from the house of David continued to endow charisma on Jewish civil leaders for generations.

Judaism is comprised by the historic practices of the Jewish people under the normative impress of texts and leaders the people themselves, in the mists of antiquity, consented to follow. A people, then as now, creates a constitution which in turns recreates them. Israel is thus, like America, a "new nation" based on choice, consent, principle and text, as well as an old nation formed by organic processes of kinship, descent, shared history and sentiment. The tensions between these poles enliven and exacerbate the ongoing contest over what it means to be a Jew.

Note

This chapter is dedicated to the memory of Daniel J. Elazar (1934–1999), friend and teacher, whose work it carries on.

Bibliography

Auerbach, J. (1993) *Rabbis and Lawyers: The Journey from Torah to Constitution*, Bloomington: Indiana University Press.

Berger, M. (1998) *Rabbinic Authority*, New York: Oxford University Press.

Buber, M. (2003) *Two Types of Faith*, Syracuse: Syracuse University Press.

Cohen, S. and Eisen, A. (2000) *The Jew Within*, Bloomington: Indiana University Press.

Elazar, D. (1995) *Covenant and Polity in Biblical Israel*, New Brunswick: Transaction Publishers.

Elazar, D. and Cohen, S. (1985) *The Jewish Polity: Jewish Political Organization from Biblical Times to the Present*, Bloomington: Indiana University Press.

Elazar, D., Sarna, J. and Geffen, R. (eds.) (1992) *A Double Bond: The Constitutional Documents of American Jewry*, Lanham: University Press of America.

Galston, W. (2005) *The Practice of Liberal Pluralism*, Cambridge: Cambridge University Press.

Gellner, E. (1987) *Culture, Identity and Politics*, Cambridge: Cambridge University Press.

Greenspahn, F. (Ed.) (2008) *The Hebrew Bible: New Insights and Scholarship*, New York: New York University Press.

Grosby, S. (2005a) *Nationalism: A Very Short Introduction*, Oxford: Oxford University Press.

Grosby, S. (2005b) The biblical "nation" as a problem for philosophy, *Hebraic Political Studies* 1 (1): 7–23.

Kaplan, D. (ed.) (2005) *The Cambridge Companion to American Judaism*, New York: Cambridge University Press.

Kekes, J. (1993) *The Morality of Pluralism*, Princeton: Princeton University Press.

Kellner, M. (2004) *Dogma in Medieval Jewish Thought*, Oxford: Littman Library of Jewish Civilization.

Knohl, I. (2003) *The Divine Symphony: The Bible's Many Voices*, Philadelphia: Jewish Publication Society.

Levenson, J. (1985) *Sinai and Zion: An Entry in the Jewish Bible*, San Francisco: Harper and Row.

Liebman, C. and Cohen, S. (1990) *Two Worlds of Judaism: The Israeli and American Experiences*, New Haven: Yale University Press.

Luz. E. (2003) *Wrestling with an Angel: Power, Morality and Jewish Identity*, New Haven: Yale University Press.

Mendelssohn, M. (1983) *Jerusalem: Or on Religious Power and Judaism*, Lebanon: University Press of New England.

Mendes-Flohr, P. and Reinharz, J. (eds.) (1980) *The Jew in the Modern World*, New York: Oxford University Press.

Meyer, M. (ed.) (1997) *German-Jewish History in Modern Times II: Emancipation and Acculturation 1780–1871*, New York: Columbia University Press.

Milgrom, J. (2004) *Leviticus: A Book of Ritual and Ethics*, Minneapolis: Fortress Press.

Mittleman, A. (2000) *The Scepter Shall Not Depart From Judah: Perspectives on the Persistence of the Political in Judaism*, Lanham: Rowman and Littlefield.

Neusner, J. (1989) *Judaism and its Social Metaphors: Israel in the History of Jewish Thought*, Cambridge: Cambridge University Press.

Neusner, J. (ed.) (1995) *Judaism in Late Antiquity II: Historical Syntheses*, Leiden: Brill.

Roof, W. C. (2001) *Spiritual Marketplace: Baby Boomers and the Remaking of American Religion*, Princeton: Princeton University Press.

Rosenthal, S. (2001) *Irreconcilable Differences? The Waning of the American Jewish Love Affair with Israel*, Lebanon: University Press of New England.

Saadia Gaon. (1948) *The Book of Beliefs and Opinions*, New Haven: Yale University Press.

Sagi, A. (2007) *The Open Canon: On the Meaning of Halakhic Discourse*, London: Continuum.

Sanders, E. P. (1977) *Paul and Palestinian Judaism*, Philadelphia: Fortress Press.

Schiffman, L. (1985) *Who Was a Jew? Rabbinic and Halakhic Perspectives on the Jewish-Christian Schism*, Jersey City: Ktav Publishers.

Shanks, H., Dever, W., Halpern, B. and McCarter, Jr, P. (1992) *The Rise of Ancient Israel*, Washington, D.C.: Biblical Archaeology Society.

Smith, W. C. (1991) *The Meaning and End of Religion*, Minneapolis: Fortress Press.

Speiser, E. (1964) *Genesis: The Anchor Bible*, Garden City: Doubleday.

Taylor, C. (2007) *A Secular Age*, Cambridge: Harvard University Press.

Weber, M. (1952) *Ancient Judaism*, New York: Free Press.

16

Sociology and Anthropology of Islam

A Critical Debate

Gabriele Marranci

No scholar has provided a critical study tracing the development of the sociology, or the anthropology, of Islam. In this chapter, I have no intention to try the endeavor. Not only would the space allowed be hardly sufficient for even a short overview, but also, as Varisco has rightly observed, the extremely difficult task of writing an anthropology or sociology of any religion by just tracing the specific studies conducted, for instance in a Christian, or in this case Islamic, context, would appear absurd since "It is easy to create unity out of diversity but seldom does it serve an analytic purpose" (2005: 135–6). Rather, here I shall offer a critical debate on how the sociology and anthropology of Islam have been debated and conceived as well as highlight some of the challenges, risks and weakness of sociological approaches to Islam.

As we shall see below, there is no agreement, and even little debate, about what a sociology, or even an anthropology, of Islam might be or even should be, even though the number of sociological and anthropological[1] studies of Islam have increased, particularly in the aftermath of 9/11. Yet many of these studies, as we shall see, show a certain Wittgensteinian "family resemblance": the contention that Islam as religion, cultural system or social structure is the main factor in shaping the lives of Muslims.

I have discussed in depth elsewhere (2008) the problems that cultural determinism has brought to a proper investigation of the dynamics of Muslim lives; yet in this chapter I will try to provide a glimpse of the danger of essentialism and the counterproductive effects which it had, and has, on the social scientific attempt to make sense of Muslims and their communities. To do so, we need to start from where the majority of scholars normally do: Islam as religion. I will then show how the history and theology of Islam have been central to the first sociological and anthropological studies of Islam even when, after the 1970s, sociologists, and more rarely anthropologists, left the village to explore the global village in their efforts to understand Islam and Muslims as a social and cultural phenomenon. In more recent years sociological studies of Islam and Muslims have tried to explain the increase in Islamic fundamentalism. Many of the theories and frameworks which were developed to understand the "exotic" Islam are now used to explain "Islamic fundamentalism." Muslims, in these studies, are often represented as a product of their own religion, as is, as we shall see in the last section, the understanding of Muslim women, resulting in a lack of studies focusing properly on gender. Indeed, while studies of Muslim women in Islam are so common that they are difficult to keep track of, studies which focus on Muslim men or even non-heterosexual Muslims are still today the exception.

ISLAM: THE HISTORICAL FACTS

If we could line up, one after another, all the introductory books that have been written about Islam, we would be surprised at the miles we could cover.[2] However, I think that, before discussing our main topic, the sociological and anthropological studies of Muslims and Islam, the reader may benefit from a very brief summary of the main historical milestones and theological tenets of Islam.

Islam is a monotheistic religion and part of the so-called Abrahamic family: Jews, Christians and Muslims have faith in the same God, which the latter call "Allah," a combination of the definitive article al- with ilāhun (meaning "a god"); so Allah means "the God," the only one to whom no associations are allowed. In other words, the Arabic term for "God" embeds the main symbol of the strong monotheism that characterizes Islam. As in any other monotheistic religion, divine revelation is central to Islam and, like in Judaism and Christianity, it is embodied in a written text that, in the case of Islam, Allah revealed to Muhammad (c.570–632). It took the Archangel Gabriel a span of twenty-three years to reveal the Qur'an to Muhammad, who received the first verse at the age of forty (for more, see Waines 1995). The first followers of the new religion started to memorize the Qur'an, which, however, the most powerful tribe in Mecca, the Quraysh (of which Muhammad was a member), perceived as a threat to the existing tribal tradition. This led to years of persecution which forced the newly formed religious community migrate in 622 CE (thus performing the Hijra, which also marks the year zero of the Islamic calendar) and find refuge in Yathrib (today Medina) where Muhammad established a multi-cultural and multi-faith political system based on the "constitution of Medina" or dustur al-medinah (Watt 1956). After a series of battles with the Quraysh, Muhammad entered Mecca in 629 CE, practically without any resistance. By the time of his death (632 CE), the community had expanded and the "Muslims" controlled the Arabian Peninsula. This would be only the beginning of a surprising expansion of the Islamic empire, which was not just the result of victorious battles but also advancement in technology, medical sciences, arts and commerce. It was not until the nineteenth and twentieth centuries that the Islamic empire saw a rapid and disastrous decline.

Yet the new community, united under the charismatic leadership of Muhammad, faced a fissure after his death. The early divergence between the two parties, which was mainly of a political nature, became increasingly theological. Yet the central debate, if we wish to condense the long dispute, focuses on the political and spiritual role of Muhammad's family. Muhammad died without indicating his successor as leader of the growing Muslim ummah. Hence, Muslims had only two options to resolve the succession issue. The first solution, advocated by the supporters of Alī ibn Abī Ṭālib, the Prophet's cousin, argued that the role of leader of the Muslims, or *khalīfa*, had to pass from Muhammad to one of his descendants, in this case Alī ibn Abī Ṭālib himself. Alī was a member of the Hāshim family, which, as we have seen, was part of the Quraysh tribe. Alī became Muhammad's son-in-law by marrying Fātima, his daughter. Opposed to the "party of Alī" (which would later be referred to as the "Shi'a," whose name means only "party") remained the majority of Muhammad's companions, who rejected the direct succession as an act against the Sunna. They argued that Muhammad had rejected the laws of tribal kinship, and for this reason had not named his successor among his own family. Among the two solutions available to find a leader, the position of the Sunni prevailed, and only four *khalīfa* later, Alī succeeded in being elected.

Like other *khalīfa* before him, Alī was assassinated in 661 CE. While the new khalīfa convinced Hasan, Alī's eldest son, to renounce his claim to the *khalīfate*, Ḥusayn, Alī's second son, refused to recognize Yazid I as the legitimate successor. In 680 CE, Yazid's forces attacked Ḥusayn's small army in Karbalā', in Iraq, exterminated Ḥusayn's supporters, and beheaded Ḥusayn himself. Today we can still visit the marvellous shrine in which the body and decapitated head of Imam Ḥusayn is venerated by Shi'i Muslims. In fact, Alī and his sons are considered martyrs (*shahīd*) and martyrdom plays a fundamental role in Shi'ism. Revolts against the Sunni *khalīfas* continued, as did the killing of Shi'i imams. The line of the Shi'i imams eventually numbered eleven, with the twelfth and last imam considered to have concealed himself. However, Shi'i Muslims believe that he will come back on the Day of Judgement, when perfect divine justice will be implemented. Among the many differences, one of the most important is that Shi'i Islam has developed a distinct Islamic school of jurisprudence based on the teaching of Jafar al-Sadiq (d.748 CE), in which human reasoning holds a particularly strong position. Still, today, tensions mark the relationship between Shi'i and Sunni Muslims (for more on Shi'a Islam see, for instance, Syed 1981).

Although the Qur'an is the most sacred source of Islam, Muslims consider the Prophet Muhammad to be the perfect example of what it means to be Muslim. Islamic scholars have divided the Sunna (examples of the life and sayings of the Prophet) into two main sources: the *sīrahs* and the *hadiths*. The sīrahs are narratives concerning the life and actions of the Prophet Muhammad, which can be compared to Jewish and Christian chronicles. The hadiths are the narratives of what Muhammad said in certain particular circumstances and, after the Qur'an, Muslims consider them the most important source of Islam. Two generations after the death of Muhammad, the hadiths, which in the beginning were transmitted orally, started to proliferate uncontrollably (Burton 1994; Hallaq 1999). It is not difficult to imagine that some Muslims manipulated, or even created, *hadiths* to justify their own behavior or to ease the Qur'anic rules. Indeed, it was not long before Muslim scholars recognized this issue and classified the *hadiths* according to four main different categories based on the reliability of the chain of narrators, or *isnād*.

The first category includes the *hadiths* which are considered sound or trustworthy, the second the hadiths which, though the chain of narrators shows some weakness, are still considered fair or good, the third those which are considered weak and finally the *hadiths* which have been considered as "sick" or "infirm" (i.e. false). The two collections of *hadiths* that are considered to be the most authoritative are those of Muhammed ibn Ismāʿīl al-Bukhārī (810–870) and Muslim ibn al-Ḥajjāj (d.875). The science of *hadiths*, thus, can be particularly complicated and requires years of study.

The Qur'an and the *hadiths* are central in the formation of what Muslims called sharīʿa. For example, it is from both the Qur'an and the *hadiths* that the five pillars of Islam (*arkāna al-islam*), fundamental to the *sharīʿa*, are derived. The arkāna al-islam are the shahāda, or profession of faith (witnessing the oneness of God and the prophethood of Muhammad), ṣalāt, or the five daily prayers, zakāt, almsgiving, ṣawm, or fasting in the month of *ramaḍan*, and ḥajj, the pilgrimage to Mecca to be performed at least once in a lifetime. Yet both the Qur'an and the sunna were still insufficient to resolve all the circumstances in which a legal decision had to be taken. After the death of Muhammad, the *ummah* had lost its supreme judge and guide for deriving the divine law from the Qur'an. Muslims needed a mechanism to maintain their legal system within God's will. The solution was a process in which *ijtihād* (individual opinion of a scholar) was based on analogical reasoning starting from the Qur'an and then the *hadiths*. Yet individual opinions could lead to disagreement, *khilāf*. For this reason, a new law was considered valid only if consensus, *ijmāʿ*, was reached (Dien 2004). Indeed, this facilitated the formation of many schools of Islamic thought, or *madhāhib*, of which only four are left within the Sunni tradition (i.e *ḥanafīs, ḥanbalīs, mālikis, and shāfiʿīs*, all derived from the names of their founders).

As we shall see in the following paragraphs, starting from Weber, sociologists and later anthropologists, considered the history and theology of Islam as the blueprint on which Muslim society, seen as a monolithic entity, and the "Muslim mind," seen as a product of cultural and social structures and functions, were built upon. As Said has argued (1978) the concept of Orient and Orientalism as a discipline are European (i.e. Western) discourses that are far from being neutral; they are ideological and the result of a certain power relationship marked by political interests. In other words, academics, no less than politicians, are responsible for transforming the Arabs, and Muslims, into the archetype of the "Other." This "Other" embodies the anti-Western by definition. According to an "Orientalist" perspective, Muslims not only lack some historical events that have enhanced Europe, such as the Enlightenment, but they also lack the capacity for representing (leave aside understanding) themselves. They need to be guided by the Western power. His observations, as we shall see below, are relevant to how studies of Muslim societies, and Muslim lives, were, and unfortunately sometimes still are, conducted.

SOCIOLOGY AND ANTHROPOLOGY OF ISLAM DEBATED

During my childhood in Italy, images of Islam and Muslims provoked fantasies of minarets, the Thousand and One Nights, Crusaders and Saladins, as well as my colonialist – he fought in Libya – grandfather's stories (Marranci 2006). Indeed, not many Muslims lived in Florence during the end of the 1970s. One of these few was the Berber door-to-door salesman from whom my mother bought my colorful socks. Abd al-Kader became a familiar figure with his Moroccan-French accent and the stories he offered in exchange of my mother's hot coffee during the cold Florentine winters. I sometimes had the occasion to watch him pray in our living room, and I remember patiently awaiting the end of the prayer to ask him as many questions I could: he made Islam a flesh and bone presence. During my years of study, books and teachers explained that Islam is a religion based on theological precepts and a particular history. During my research, I learned that the Islam of books, theology, and history is nothing more than a ghost hunted for by both the believers and academics alike. Indeed Abd al-Kader's interpretations of what Islam is makes Islam an "object" of this world. However, this object is a polythetic one since Abd al-Kader's Islam differed, for instance, from others since, despite sharing theological frameworks and history, it would be absurd to affirm that all Muslims lived and embodied the same Islam. Different contexts, such as economic status, education, ethnic background, heritage, age, social and political environments as well as epistemology and emotions affect how the brain makes sense of reality and forms "cognitive maps" that become real and part of the material world only through communication (Sperber 1996). It is only through this process that an idea, ethos and ideology of Islam may form and spread. Hence, it is essential to recognize the epistemological and (in Sperberian terms) epidemiological fact that people learn about Islam from others who have learnt about Islam from others, in an endless circle of communication. Hence, since interpretations are multiple, the personal embodiments of Islam are likewise multiple. It is not Islam that shapes Muslims, but rather Muslims who, through discourses, practices, beliefs and actions, shape Islam in different times and spaces.

Max Weber would have certainly disagreed with the above statement. Although Weber never developed a systematic sociological study of Islam, his understanding of it shows a monolithic view reminiscent of Said's Orientalists (Turner 1978). Indeed, as Turner has discussed "in Weber's sociology of Islam, the Shari'a created an administrative and legal environment which was not conducive to the growth of rational economic activity" (Turner 1974: x). Furthermore, Islam represented for Weber the antithesis of European Puritanism, since the German sociologists unquestioningly accepted a Christian-apologetic, similar to the Voltairian (Voltaire 1736/1905), view of Islam as violent, hedonistic, libidinous and oppressive towards women. The main elements, however, of what Weber saw as the failure of Islam vis-a-vis the rampant success of European capitalism, is the alleged lack of social and economic rationality. Turner (see 1974 and 1992) has offered a valid criticism of the several weakness, and few strengths, of Weber's take on Islam. Weber, however, was a man of his own time. Nonetheless, we shall see below how Weber's sociology of Islam has influenced, directly or indirectly, other more contemporary scholars such as Gellner (1981) and some of his students (see for instance Shankland 2003). Yet the Weberian legacy has also inspired much of the discussion about Islam in the post 9/11 world in the attempt to answer the, often rhetorical rather than analytical, question of whether Islam is compatible with the modern (Western capitalist) values of human rights and democracy.

Gellner (1981) was certainly the most Weberian of the sociologists and anthropologists who devoted their studies to Muslim societies (or rather Islam). He, together with Geertz, affected, and largely still influences, sociological and anthropological studies of Islam. In his most famous work, *Muslim Society*, Gellner's central argument argues that Islam cannot change. Far from being the religion of living Muslims with opinions, ideas, feelings, identities, Gellnerian Islam is an essence that remains constant in its model as a result of being based on three pillars: first, a strong eschatological scripturalism which does not offer room for any change since Muhammad is the last prophet; second, Islam rejects a clergy and consequently religious differentiation; and third, Islam rejects the division between church and state, since, according to Gellner (but see also Weber for the same argument) "it began as a religion of rapidly successful conquerors who soon were the state" (1981: 100–1). Yet the most important aspect of all is a "trans-ethnic" and "trans-social" characteristic of Islam, since, Gellner has argued, it does not "equate faith with the beliefs of any community or society [...] But the trans-social truth which can sit in judgement on the social is a Book" (1981: 101) so that no political authority can claim it. It is in this centrality of the "Book" as the ultimate authority and in the division and tension between what Gellner has defined as high Islam (urbanized and based on scripturalism) and low Islam (based on kinship and the charismatic power of the saint) that the fight for puritanism has led to the development of a religion, Islam, resistant to secularization. Gellner, consistent with his model, has stated that Muslims "could have democracy, or secularism, but not both" (1981: 60). In other words, if Muslim societies have democracy they would inevitably see secularism eroded in favor of an increasingly Shari'a based state. Only a dictatorship can impose a secular model of society, since it can manipulate and control, and so limit, the role and influence of Islam within society.

Kamali, among others[3], has strongly criticized Gellner's reading of Muslim society. Kamali has correctly noticed, "[Gellner] mixes the religious notion of umma, which is the concept of a religious community in relation to its Messenger, namely the Prophet, with the peoples residing in different Muslim countries ... This use of the notion of umma as a homogeneous phenomenon referring to the entire 'Muslim world' neglects the reality of different cultural and institutional arrangements in the various 'Muslim' societies. He fails to take into account in his discussion the sociocultural and even economic diversity of different Muslim countries." (Kamali 2001: 464) Gellner has been neither the first social scientist to focus on Islam as an independent variable, instead of a dependent one, as many sociological studies of North African villages (Fernea and Malarkey 1975; Abu-Lughod 1986) had previously done, nor the first one to offer a reductionist and monolithic reading of Muslims as expressions of Islam as a cultural, historical and legalistic system. Known to Gellner, but just fleetingly mentioned in his work, was the work of the American anthropologist Clifford Geertz. Indeed, we can say that Geertz's *Islam Observed* (1968) delivered the kiss that awakened the sleeping beauty (Marranci 2008) of anthropological studies of Islam. For the first time, an influential social scientist wrote a work featuring the word "Islam" in its title. Geertz's book inspired new generations of anthropologists, who redirected their attention to Islam as religion rather than to kinship, marriages and village rural life.

I have not the necessary space to summarize Geertz's work here, nor shall I provide a new critique or defence of this seminal study[4], nonetheless I need to emphasise here how, despite an innovative and interesting attempt to explain Islam through a "comparative" (Indonesia and Morocco) approach, Geertz ended in suggesting that myths and sacred texts (such as the Qur'an and *hadiths*) fully explain Muslim behavior (i.e. human behavior) and their social expressions. As in much of Geertz's theory of culture (1973) the "system of symbols" controls humans, and in this case, since the system of symbols is called "Islam," Muslims,

> If they are religious men, those everyday terms will in some way be influenced by their religious convictions, for it is in the nature of faith, even the most unworldly and least ethical, to claim effective sovereignty over human behavior. The internal fusion of world view and ethos is, or so I am arguing, the heart of the religious perspective, and the job of the sacred symbol is to bring about that fusion. (1968: 110)

Gellner and Geertz are not interested in understanding Muslims; rather they believed to have provided – similar to Weber's incomplete macro-sociological attempt – the ultimate explanation of Islam as a cultural and social system. In other words, Geertz and Gellner seem to ignore Alfred Korzybski's simple, but cognitively significant, observation that "the map is not the territory" (1948: 58). Indeed, what we have discussed at the beginning of this chapter (i.e. the historical development of Islam and its rituals) is nothing other than a "map," or actually a series of maps, representing a vast territory. Scholars such as Geertz and Gellner thought that the map "Islam" was more similar to the map of a "cultural" genome: a reality that conditions – variations allowed – how all Muslims (or at least the "real" ones) will behave, form societies and interact. Thus, knowing (scriptural) Islam means knowing (real) Muslims.

Something in the sociological and anthropological study of Muslim societies start to change with Gilsenan's *Recognizing Islam* (1982). Gilsenan's seminal book succeeds in avoiding essentialism since, instead of telling us what Islam is and how it shapes Muslims and their societies, Gilsenan has provided readers with an inspiring study of the different embodiments of Islam. He has stated, "I did not consider Islam to be a monolithic 'it,' an entity which could be treated as a theological or civilizational historical bloc, unchanging and essentially 'other' in some primordial way [...] I was and am concerned with more sociological questions of social and cultural variation in very different societies" (1982: 5). The shift from studying Islam to studying Muslims who practice Islam in different contextual environments has certainly provided the first right step towards a "paradigm" for a sociology/anthropology of Muslims and their societies. Nonetheless, even with Gilsenan's work (as many others during the 1970s and 1980s) we do not have a full discussion of what a sociology/anthropology of Islam might be. In fact, sociological and anthropological research on Islam has developed through specific studies and ethnographies, but without real coherence or discussion among the scholars (Abu-Lughod 1989; Fernea and Malarkey 1975).

During the mid-1970s, when anthropological research on Islam was at its dawn, el-Zein in a challenging article (1977) attempted to reopen a debate about what sociologists and anthropologists of Islam were actually studying. In his article that compared five different anthropological approaches (Geertz 1968; Bujra 1971; Crapanzano 1973; Gilsenan 1973; and Eickelman 1976), el-Zein asked his readers whether "in the midst of this diversity of meaning, is there a single, real Islam?" (1977: 249). He argued that no single "true" Islam can be spoken of by a scholar studying Muslim societies, and instead sociologists and anthropologists can only provide a social scientific analysis of Muslim life exclusively through the observation of the diverse interpretations of Islam. El-Zein's viewpoint, in particular when expressed by a practising Muslim, sounds very controversial (Eickelman 1981) and while his contribution started a diatribe on one Islam versus many Islams, it did not succeeded in facilitating the much needed discussion among sociologists and anthropologists studying Muslim societies and communities.

Nine years after el-Zein's effort, another anthropologist Talal Asad (1986b) engaged in the debate about how sociologists and anthropologists should approach Islam. Asad, in his *The Idea of an Anthropology of Islam*, has rejected both el-Zein's argument as well as Gilsenan's paradigm since both "[do] not help identify Islam as an analytical object of study" (1986b: 2). Asad has argued that scholars cannot ignore theological teaching since the starting point for a student of Islam should be the same from which Muslims start. Hence the centrality of the founding texts, the Qur'an and the *hadith*, since, according to Asad, Islam is neither "a distinctive social structure nor a heterogeneous collection of beliefs, artefacts, customs, and morals. *It is a tradition*" (1986b: 14, italics added). A tradition, Asad has argued, is conceptually linked to a past (marking the formation of the tradition), a future (marking the strategy of survival of the tradition) and a present (marking the inter-connection of the tradition with the social strata). Therefore, studying Islam means, Asad has proposed, to observe and explain the tension (i.e. the relation of power) that exists between historical, political, economic and social dynamics, which through orthopraxy try to change tradition, and the tradition itself, which tries to resist through orthodoxy.

As we can see, one of the main issues that the social scientific study of Islam has to face is its relationship with the theological and historical elements of Islam. Although scholars have debated openly over it, none of the above mentioned sociologists and anthropologists, for instance, actually started from theology itself as a foundation of the discipline. By contrast some Muslim sociologists and anthropologists have tried to develop a new approach, so called Islamic sociology or Islamic anthropology, starting from the "universality" of the Qur'an and developing what they have called an "Islamic methodology," which is not limited to the study of Muslim societies or cultures. Hence, at the beginning of the 1980s, the project for an Islamic anthropology was not a novelty (Mahroof 1981) and several Muslim scholars have attempted to Islamicize the social sciences (see Ba-Yunus and Ahmad 1985; Wyn 1988), particularly as a response to the Western materialistic approach. If the Western sociological approach to the study of Islam lacked, and still lacks,[5] a blueprint, Islamic sociology and anthropology surely have one: Islam itself, or at least its ethos.

The most representative champion of an Islamic sociology and anthropology of Islam is Ahmed's *Toward Islamic Anthropology* (1986). In his work, he has defined the Islamic anthropology of Islam as,

The study of Muslim groups by scholars committed to the universalistic principles of Islam – humanity, knowledge, tolerance, – relating micro village tribal studies in particular to the larger historical and ideological frames of Islam. Islam is here understood not as theology but sociology, the definition thus does not preclude non-Muslims. (1986: 56)

Ahmed's *Toward Islamic Anthropology* has received much attention through extended reviews and discussions,[6] but the majority of anthropologists have shown an overall skepticism towards his argument, with some vehemently rejecting it (cf. Tapper 1988). Indeed, Eickelman has rightly observed, "Islamic anthropology ... sounds very much like other anthropologies, except for the efforts to justify it in terms of perceived Qur'anic principles and to encourage Muslim scholars to use anthropological approaches" (1990: 241). Furthermore, there is a clear tautological contradiction in studying Islam and Muslims through the lens of the religion itself. Finally, since Ahmed's Islam can only be one, it means that an Islamic sociology or anthropology is conducted through a very selective process by which some Muslims' behavior is bound to contradict the Islamic paradigm informing the Islamic methodology.

It seems that even today we can repeat what Asad noticed twenty-three years ago, "no coherent anthropology of Islam can be found on the notion of a determinate social blueprint" (1986: 16). However, I wonder whether we really need a blueprint. Is not an anthropology/sociology of Islam just plain anthropology or sociology? The issue, as we have observed above, is that essentialism, more than any other field, has affected both academic and popular discourse on Muslims (Modood 1998; Donnan 2002; Grillo 2003; Matin-Asgari 2004; Geaves 2005). I call this essentialism the fallacy of the "Muslim mind theory" (Marranci 2009). Muslims, according to the "Muslim mind theory" believe, behave, act, think, argue, and develop their identity as Muslims despite their disparate heritage, ethnicities, nationalities, experiences, gender, sexual orientations and, last but not least, brains. In other words, their believing in Islam makes them a sort of cloned computer CPU: different styles, different colors, same process. Sometimes this fallacy is the result of generalizations, some of which are difficult to avoid (Marranci 2008). At other times, however, it is more ideological and the by-product of an extreme culturalist position within the social sciences.[7] In all cases, the root of it is the, latent or manifest, unrecognized fact that a Muslim person is primarily a human being.

Surely, social scientists should start from Muslims rather than from Islam. This means to understand Islam as a map of discourses on how to "feel Muslim" (Marranci 2008). As I have argued above, the main thing that Muslims share among themselves and others is certainly not Islam, but rather the fact that they are human beings. Hence, they communicate, act, interact, change, exchange, with both other humans as well as the environment. These relationships are marked by emotions – which as Damasio has suggested (1999 and 2000) are a reaction to stimuli – that produce feelings. I have argued (Marranci 2008) people define themselves as Muslims because, in one way or another, "Muslim" has a particular value attached for them. The value can certainly be explained rationally, but it is not necessarily rationally driven. For many people professing their credo in Islam, "Muslim" has an emotional component attached to it. In other words, they *feel to be* Muslim.

It is then, and only then, that the "feeling to be" is rationalized, rhetoricized, and symbolized, exchanged, discussed, ritualized, orthodoxized or orthopraxized. This simple fact resolves essentialist approaches such as those offered by Geertz, Gellner and among many others, el-Zein's idea of (1977) many Islams as being culturally rooted, or Asad's position that Islam is something that exists in itself, as, for instance, a tradition. All these approaches to the study of Muslims (and their societies) end, though by various routes, in explicit or implicit theological determinism. To avoid this, I have suggested (Marranci 2008) that we need to understand Islam as a map of discourses on how people feel to be Muslim, how this representation becomes part of an epistemological and, in Sperber's terms, epidemiological (1996) process, and finally (at the social level) how a person "feels Muslim" in such a way that the relevant others within the environment recognizes them as such.

FROM THE VILLAGE TO GLOBAL VILLAGE

During the 1960s until the end of the 1980s, sociologists and anthropologists studying Muslim societies have mainly focused on the Middle East and North Africa, where the village remained, with few exceptions (Gilsenan 1982), the center of ethnographies and sociological analysis. Certainly studies until the 1980s overlooked Western Muslims and Muslims seen as actors within the "global village." Starting from the end of the 1980s, young anthropologists and sociologists increasingly paid attention to new fields of research, such as Muslim immigrants, second generation Muslims, Muslim transnational networks, virtual ummahs and the integration/assimilation of Western Muslims. Nonetheless, this research remained marginalized within mainstream sociology and anthropology and was forced to find refuge in other more interdisciplinary fields such as migration studies, gender studies, education studies and global studies.

Yet while the "exotic" ethnographies ended entangled in kinship, Sufi saints and segmentary theories, the Western-based ethnographies of Muslim lives ended in a cultural hermeneutic that presents Islam as the ultimate shaper of migrants' lives. At the end of the 1980s, Europe, the USA and Canada saw an increase in the number of second-generation Muslims. The culture of Muslim migrants began marking even the urban spaces of the main Western metropolizes through new mosques, Islamic centers and madrasas. Yet in Western societies, and in particular France, Great Britain and Germany, governments failed to address the growing challenges of an unplanned multiculturalism. On the one hand, marginalization, discrimination, isolation and ghettoization became an embedded feature of the daily experience of Muslim communities. On the other, autochthonous non-Muslim populations felt threatened and challenged by the unfamiliar Islamic culture, which was known primarily through stereotypes.

It is in this complex social, political and cultural context that sociological studies of Western Muslim communities started to be published. We can observe differences between the traditional studies of Muslim societies and this new field of research, but also similarities, such as a certain, and perhaps inevitable, colonial heritage. Indeed, the Western colonial experience explains the presence of the Muslim communities settling in Europe as well as the specific community focus of migration studies. For instance, in the UK the research has concentrated on South Asians, in France on Northern African Muslims and in Germany on the Turkish community. Another similarity with the first "exotic" anthropological studies of Muslim societies is the political agenda marking some of the studies. As in the case of ethnographies focusing on the Middle East, studies of Muslim immigrants show certain recurrent "zones of theorizing" (Abu-Lughod 1989). Among these "zones" themes such as integration, Westernization, gender, second generations, education, and Islamism remain, by far, the most prominent.

The anthropology and sociology of the Middle East (or other Muslim countries) originated in serving the colonial administrations by providing an understanding of the "native" cultures and facilitating their control; while the social scientific works on Western Muslim communities originated in the increasing need to framework the "other" among "us." During the 1970s, Western societies perceived these immigrants as Algerians, Turks, Pakistanis, or in broader categories such as Arabs, North Africans and South Asians, rather than Muslims. Consequently, sociological as well as anthropological studies focused on the immigrants' national and ethnic backgrounds, rather than their religious affiliation (see for instance Dahya 1972, 1973, and 1974). At the beginning of the 1980s, many studies were still referring to the ethnic-national identity of these immigrants and their socio-economic status[8]. Yet the 1979 Iranian revolution saw an increasing number of these immigrants start to define themselves as firstly "Muslims" rather than as members of a particular nation, and this consequently reinforced the centrality of Islam within sociological and anthropological studies.[9] Thus Islam became the cultural-sociological main keyword to make sense of the immigrants' otherness (Saifullah-Khan 1979). The increase in Muslim women, both migrants and of Western origin, facilitated a high number of studies, mainly from a feminist perspective, which paid attention to their condition and emancipation (e.g. Saifullah-Khan 1975, 1976; Abadan-Unat 1977).

Another priority of these studies was, of course, the new second-generation of Muslims and the inevitable, but often damaging (Marranci 2006 and 2008), politically driven question of both assimilation as well as loyalty towards the given Western nation. This time it was a faulty rationale, what we may describe as a mistake of logical types, that affected many of the sociological and in particular anthropological studies: Islam, as a religion, was reduced to the same category of national or ethnic identity. One of the enduring versions of this faulty reasoning reads that young Muslims live in a form of permanent "in-betweenness" (Anwar 1976; and see also Watson 1997). Anwar (1976) has discussed the relationships between Pakistani Muslims in Britain and their relatives in Pakistan. There is a tendency to see religion as the main element that could prevent Muslims from integrating within the "modern," "civilized," and "secular" Western democracies. Some events have reinforced this perception: the Honeyford affair in 1984 (Halstead 1988), the Rushdie affair in 1989 (Asad 1990; Modood 1990; Halliday 1995), and the 1989 *Affaire du Foulard* (Bowen 2007). Many of the studies, however, missed the connection between the local and the global in understanding specific community dynamics as well as, in reality, the marginality of those involved in these protests.

Indeed, we must recognize that a sociology of Islam or an anthropology of Islam, today, cannot be other than global. We cannot study, for example, Muslims in Indonesia, Malaysia, Pakistan, Bangladesh, Algeria, Morocco, or Libya, without taking into consideration the transnational and global networks they are part of. Similarly, we cannot study Muslim communities in the West without paying attention to their connections with other Muslims in Islamic countries and other communities, both Muslim and non-Muslim. The global village as well as the new sense of interconnection between localities, and also the new limitations introduced by an increasingly globalized world, need to be taken into consideration in the study of Muslim lives. This is even more relevant today, in the aftermath of 9/11 and the deriving new world order. Yet, again, as we shall see below, it is more the idea of Islam as a blueprint rather than Islam as a cognitive map which has led the analysis of, for instance, radicalism and fundamentalism.

9/11, ISLAM, AND FUNDAMENTALISM

After the events triggered by 9/11, more sociologists and anthropologists have tried to answer the question: why do we have an increase of Islamic radicalism, which also includes extreme forms of violence? Unfortunately much of the sociological/ anthropological discussion of fundamentalism and radicalism among Muslims has shown similar ontological problems to those we have discussed above concerning the "exotic" as well as "Western" studies of Muslim communities. There are some clear differences between the studies authored before and after September 11. In the pre-September 11 studies, particularly those published between the end of the 1980s and the mid 1990s, scholars have mainly discussed Islamic fundamentalism as one species, though the most pernicious among the Abrahamic religions. For this reason, the discussion of Islamic fundamentalism has been often framed within a wider comparative approach to fundamentalism seen as characterized by family resemblances.

Typical of these studies is the representation of Islamic fundamentalism as a historical process, started by charismatic Islamic ideologues (such as Mawdudi, Al-Banna and Qutb),[10] and culminating in the 1979 Iranian revolution. Islam as a cultural and sociological blueprint surely matters in these studies.[11] Indeed, the Qur'an as a holy scripture provides, according to these academic works, the basis for the formation of a scripturalist ideology, from which those ideologues derived their political inspiration and actions. Hence, Islamic fundamentalism, according to this perspective is, as any other fundamentalism, an anti-Enlightenment force that rejects modernism and its main value of secularism in favor of a strict adherence to the scripture and in defence of an anti-relativistic, unique and superior truth.

Many post-9/11 studies appear to be influenced by the same framework which affected Gellner's analysis. Gellner has suggested that Islam, being a markedly secularization-resistant religion, is also the most vigorously fundamentalist. According to Gellner, Islam, as religion, shows some ideological historical elements conducive toward fundamentalism. The idea that the history of Islam, or Islam as a religion, can explain Islamic fundamentalism is certainly not limited to Gellner. Other scholars have offered similar views. The sociologist Steve Bruce has sociologically described Islam as the most fundamentalist of all religions, so that while he affirms "Religion has always been a disruptive force" (Bruce 2000: 1), Islam is taken to be the most disruptive of all. Indeed, according to Bruce, religion is the cause of fundamentalism itself, and so fundamentalisms differ among themselves.

Bruce has suggested that Islam has a totalitarian view of culture and life, in which the domain of religion and the domain of the world cannot be divided without compromising one's beliefs. What Bruce is suggesting, in contrast for instance with Tibi (1998), is that Islamic fundamentalists are not political opportunists manipulating Islam as a religion, but coherent believers who are not ready to compromise with the modern contemporary liberal reality which seeks to relegate faith to the private sphere (cf. Bruce 2000: 95–123). For Bruce, Islamic radicalism is as old as Islam itself since, as Weber suggested, it is part of its history (Bruce 2000: 40–65).

Sociological and anthropological approaches to Islam and Muslims similar to those presented here by Gellner and Bruce have an inherent fallacy in their explanations of Islamic fundamentalism: they falsely link Muslims' personal faith to their theological knowledge by failing to observe that many worshipers have no theological knowledge beyond the practical aspects of their prayers and festivities. Certainly, some Muslims may start to develop strong emotional and identity-derived understandings of their own religion. However, it is too great of a leap to conclude that, because they are Muslims who take seriously their understanding of Islam, they reject modernity (see also Marranci 2006, 2007, and 2008). I have argued (Marranci 2009) that some of these analyses have suffered from what I have called *comparative reductionism* and *Eurocentric historical evolutionarism* in which denotative, rather than connotative, characteristics are described as essential paradigms of Islamic fundamentalism, in a linear genealogy of ideologues and ideologies that originated in different places, within different Islamic traditions and during different geopolitical contentions. In other words, although Islamists such as Mawdudi, Al-Banna and Qutb share some similarities, it would be extremely simplistic to advocate that environment, political realities and personal experiences had no impact on their views because they derived them from interpretations of the same text, the Qur'an.

Another extremely flawed aspect of certain explanations of Islamic fundamentalism derives from what I have called *Eurocentric historical evolutionarism*. The majority of scholars who have discussed Islamic fundamentalism have explained it in terms of a rejection of "rational" Enlightenment values in favor of an "irrational," and thus fanatic, scripturalism. Of course, part of the struggle is the resistance of Islamic fundamentalists to the correlated products of Enlightenment, modernism and secularism. Although this may appear at first to be a very clear and successful explanation, it has serious faults. Not only do these authors essentialize the European experience of Enlightenment, but also they present it as a universal, and universally acceptable, phenomenon. Enlightenment, even within the European context, has never been a single event or way of thinking. The history of Enlightenment in France was very different from the history of Enlightenment in, for example, England. Furthermore, some historians even doubt that we can present Enlightenment as a single, clear historical fact, but that rather we need to consider it as a process. I am concerned that interpretations of Islamic fundamentalism strongly based on Eurocentric historical evolutionarism can actually obscure, instead of disclose, the reasons behind the existence of Islamic fundamentalism as a "human" (Marranci 2006), rather than a "cultural," phenomenon.

To avoid this weakness, other scholars have tried to cast light on the hidden folds of the fundamentalist psyche. Indeed, if Bruce, together with a majority of sociologists and political scientists, has rejected the idea that fundamentalists are people affected by an abnormal way of thinking about the world, other scholars (particularly within the field of psychology and feminist tradition) have suggested that this is precisely the case. Often alienation, compulsory disorders, inferiority complexes leading to a sense of superiority, self-esteem issues and authoritarianism have been discussed as the inner reason for which people turn towards Islamic fundamentalism (cf. Dekmejian 1985; Hoffman 1985). For instance, Hoffman appears to suggest that the main reason for turning to Islamic fundamentalism can be found in a bipartite process consisting of first a failed conversion to Western atheism, or strong secularism, and then a reversion to a new form of Islamic cultural identity. She has concluded that Islamic fundamentalism in Islamic societies, reclaiming traditional moral, economic and political values, has a strong appeal because the introduction of Western modernization has been experienced through the political failure of Arab nationalism; thus young people have suffered alienation. Hoffman has also discussed, following an established feminist tradition (Mernissi 1975; Sabah 1984), the reason for which sexuality is so prominent within Islamic fundamentalist discourse. She has accepted Mernissi's view that Islamic fundamentalist misogyny is derived from the frustration provoked by the traditional Muslim society, which prevents the fundamentalist from accepting his own sexuality, despite the alleged "sex-positive" Islamic norms.

This frustration is, according to many feminists, expressed through the oppression of and aggression towards women, seen as the main culprit responsible for the impure sexual desire. It is certainly undeniable that we can recognize in many of the Western feminist understandings of Islamic fundamentalism a strong Freudian influence (cf. Mernissi 1975 and Sabah 1984). Although I agree that psychological factors play a role in the formation of strong religious views and radicalization, studies based on psychological profiling of Islamic fundamentalists and fundamentalist groups end up over-generalizing. They produce a stereotyped taxonomy of assumed collective, trans-cultural and trans-sectarian "pathologies." Hood, Hill and Williamson (2005) have attempted to provide a psychological understanding of fundamentalism, including Islamic fundamentalism, which avoids the above-mentioned issues. To do so, they have embraced, however, many of the traditional culturalist views on fundamentalism, including the relevance of, in Gellnerian terms, the "Book." The result is an inconclusive mix of psychological and hermeneutical "Geertzian-style" analysis which adds little to previous understandings of Islamic fundamentalism.

Rather I have suggested (Marranci 2006 and 2009) that identity and emotions play a fundamental role in the phenomenon that scholars have referred to as Islamic fundamentalism, each time implying that it was a unitary "thing" possessing within itself defined characteristics. By contrast, it is my contention that what has been called Islamic fundamentalism is not a "thing" in itself, but rather a cluster of particular processes linked to two essential human aspects, identity and identification affected by emotional communication, which, for the benefit of shorthand, I have called "Emotional Islam" (Marranci 2009).

GENDER AND ISLAM: NOT ONLY WOMEN

Muslim women have attracted the attention of the West for as long as Western scholars have encountered Islam. The mysterious and exotic image of the harem mixed with the fear of powerful Muslim armies reaching Vienna, the door of Europe. Today, we may think that the morbid curiosity about Muslim women, seen as different, mysterious and in particular, complacent victims of the disproportionately virile oppression of the "Muslim man" is confined to eroticized romantic novels and travel journals within aged and dusty books. Today, to satisfy our judgmental curiosity about Islam and its female believers, we do not have the Christian polemicist caricature of Islam that Voltaire offered in his *Mahomet* ([1736] 1905). Rather, we have a by-product of our imagined, yet still much romanticized, idea of a civilized superiority in which White Western men and women alienate themselves within the illusion of possessing secular-based rights of gender equality. The curiosity is alive still, centuries after Voltaire's *Mahomet* and thousands more books on Islam and women.

Since the middle of the 1970s, feminist sociologists of both Muslim and non-Muslim origin started to gender Islam. The studies mainly addressed gender and Islam in the Middle East and North African regions (see Beck and Keddie 1978; Keddie 1991; Ahmed 1992; Tucker 1993) and focused on two main aspects: the conditions and status of Muslim women in Islam. These studies, however, immediately became a battleground between those who accused Islam – as a religion – of fostering gender inequalities and being oppressive towards women, and those – particularly Muslim feminists – who blamed local cultural traditions for the disadvantages and discrimination and exalted "real" Islam as the solution. The latter focused on the economic rights that Muslim women enjoyed within Islam, while the former focused on dress codes, particularly the "veil," as strong evidence of the patriarchal oppression of Islam on women. One of the first Muslim scholars to write a successful study of gender in Islam was the Moroccan sociologist Mernissi.

In 1975, Mernissi's *Beyond the Veil* became the successful matrix for future feminist studies of gender in Islam. Despite the subtitle "Male–Female dynamics," Mernissi focused only on women, basing her analysis on ethnographic studies she conducted with Moroccan women. She has not discussed the dynamics between genders within Moroccan society, but rather the impact that the discourse of sexuality in Islam has on Muslim women. The central topic of her book is sophisticated, but extremely monolithic. Mernissi focused on "the traditional Muslim view of women and their place in the social order" (Mernissi 1975: 1). She suggested the latter depends upon the attitude of the "Muslim mind" towards sexuality and *sharī'a*, which she has presented as a means of moral control. Indeed, we can read, "the link in the Muslim mind between sexuality and the *sharī'a* has shaped the legal and ideological history of the Muslim family structure and consequentially of the relation between the sexes" (1975: xv). The main argument is that men use Islam to control women's dangerous sexuality and impose patriarchal structures, of which Muslim women are responsible for the propagation and transmission (Roald 2001). Mernissi's Feminist–Freudian approach to Islam and gender has certainly shown some attractive insights, but also evident weaknesses.

Her analyses suffer from, I would say, Freudian reductionism. Mernissi has reduced Islam, as a religious system, to an inverted chastity belt, protecting the men from the temptation of a dangerous and uncontrolled female sexuality. This idea has found some support among other feminist scholars such as Hussain (1984) and Sabah (1984). Nonetheless, the most flawed aspect of Mernissi's argument is the idea that "a Muslim mind," forged by the rules and ethos of Islam, can exist. This essentialist argument is certainly not new, as we can easily trace it back to Orientalistic viewpoints such as those expressed by Baring (1908).[12]

During the 1980s, a new generation of feminist Muslim scholars paid particular attention to the topic of gender, colonialism and Islam, as in the case of Bodman and Tohidi (1998) and, in particular, Ahmed (1992). Partially rejecting the previous Freudian sexual-centric analysis and criticism, these new studies employed a postmodern and, often Fanonian, anti-colonial approach. Ahmed, in her book *Women and Gender in Islam*, has offered an interesting social and historical discussion and analysis of women in the Middle East. Ahmed has shown a very different approach from that advocated by Mernissi. She has recognized that Islamic societies did oppress women and continue to do so, but at the same time has rejected colonialist and Orientalist views of Islam. Ahmed has argued, "the political uses of the idea that Islam oppressed women and noting that what patriarchal colonialists identified as the source and main forms of women's oppression in Islamic society was based on a vague and inaccurate understanding of Muslim societies" (1992: 160).

Her criticism did not stop at the Orientalist and colonial heritage, but strongly extended to Western feminist ideas of Islam, "critical of the practice and beliefs of the men of their societies with respect to themselves acquiesced in and indeed promoted the European male's representations of the Other men and the cultures of the Other men and joined, *in the name of feminism*, in the attack on the veil and the practices generally of Muslim societies" (1992: 243, italics added). Ahmed, indeed, has suggested that the Western view of gender in Islam and the Western paternalistic attitude towards women in Islam could in reality cover an attempt to strip Muslim women not just of their veils but rather of their culture and Muslim identity.

It seems safe to argue that to date "gender in Islam" has meant nothing else than "women in Islam." This constant omission of proper gender studies of Islam, has, in more recent times, brought some anthropologists to argue that the study of gender "must be central to an anthropology of Islam" (Tapper and Tapper 1987). Surely we cannot deny that a certain traditional androcentric bias has prevented male anthropologists, especially during the 1970s and 1980s, from observing the active role that Muslim women had, and have, in their societies and in interpreting Islam. However, it is also true that feminist sociologists and anthropologists, who ideologically have focused on Muslim women as the victims of Islam, have overlooked the fact that gender also includes masculinity. We can only agree with Okkenhaug and Flaskerud that "men and masculinity in the Middle East are still almost non-existing research areas" (2005: 2). In other words, studies on gender in Islam have suffered from a generalized, when not politicized, reductionist understanding of both gender and Islam. The tendency of sociology and anthropology is often to focus on "issues," facilitating a constant emphasis on the difficulties and problems of the population studied. This increases the risk that scholars may present individuals, or a particular category within the studied society, as passively under the control of undetermined sociocultural forces.

Yet research on gender including masculinity and studies of masculinity in the context of Muslim societies are surprisingly rare (for exceptions, see Ghoussoub and Sinclair-Web 2000 and Lahoucine 2006) despite the attention that gender studies have paid to masculinity in other societies and cultures. Even less has been written concerning Muslim gays and lesbians. One of the reasons for this lack of attention to masculinity and homosexuality in Islam could be found in the fact that gender has not been understood as dynamics between subjects. In a contemporary sociological and anthropological approach to Muslim lives, we cannot reduce gender to femininity since it is only through the observation and analysis of the relationships between the genders that we can achieve a full picture (Pels 2000). Homosexuality has been even more an overlooked topic in studies of Muslim societies (Schmiduke 1999). Indeed, the topic is highly controversial since the orthodox interpretations of Islam agree that the Qur'an (through the story of Lot) has condemned non-heterosexual relationships and the Sunna condemns it in even harsher terms. Confusion, however, surrounds the correct punishment. Some ḥadiths describe the Prophet as being almost tolerant to homoerotic desires; while in others he is described as being very harsh in his request for punishment, which in some cases involved stoning both the culprits to death (Pellat 1992). These differences have marked the divergence on the matter expressed by the different Islamic Schools. Hence, the legislation available in different Islamic countries varies in the degree of severity of the punishment (Sofer 1992).

Nonetheless today, particularly among anthropologists, we can find pioneering studies focusing on non-heterosexual Muslims. For example, since 1999, Boellstorff has conducted fieldwork in Indonesia on non-heterosexual Muslims and written interesting ethnographies (2005) discussing the relationships that his respondents had with their Muslim non-heterosexual identities. Even more recent is the anthropological study of non- heterosexual ethnic minorities in the West. One of the first scholars to address the subject among the British South Asian community is the anthropologist Kawale (2003). Although Kawale has discussed not only first and second generations of South Asian gays and lesbians, but also bisexuals (indeed a novelty), she has, however, focused only on ethnicity. The majority of Kawale's informants may have been Muslims, since they were of Pakistani or Middle Eastern origin, but the difficult relations between religion, ethnicity and non-heterosexual identities have not been explored.

Thus, the research of Yip (2004a, 2004b, 2004c) and Siraj (2006) are innovative in this respect. In observing Muslim non-heterosexual social interactions with family and peers, Islam, seen as part of the identity formation, becomes the central topic of Yip's and Siraj's analyses. Yip has also found that the majority of non-heterosexual Muslims still practice their religion, though they tend to compartmentalize their lives so as to avoid a possible crisis of identity. He has emphasized how the Muslim communities explain this "Western disease" as being the result of an intense exposure to Western values, such as individualism and secularism. By contrast, Yip has found that many non- heterosexual Muslims explain their sexual preference as inevitable, since God created them with such a sexual orientation. This has led some of them to reinterpret the Islamic texts in such a way that non-heterosexuality is, if not justified, at least tolerated or not punished. Yip (2004c) has also emphasized how families of non-heterosexual Muslims see marriage as the most effective "cure" for their children's sexual preferences. Some non-heterosexual Muslims have given in to pressure to get married. In her study, Siraj has presented an extreme example in which a non-heterosexual Muslim remained married for thirteen years to a woman whom he neither loved nor sexually desired (Siraj 2006: 210–11).

This short review of approaches to the study of gender and Muslims suggests that sociologists and anthropologists, as other social scientists interested in understanding the dynamics of Muslim lives, would benefit from focusing more on gender, as a complex category of relationships, rather than focusing on Muslim women alone. Indeed, there is an urgent need in the sociology and anthropology of Muslims to avoid those recurrent "zones of theorizing" (Abu-Lughod 1989) which have affected the studies since the 1960s.

CONCLUSION

As we have observed in this chapter, there is no agreement among scholars as to what a sociology, or anthropology, of Islam might be. Yet we have to recognize that in the aftermath of 9/11 an increasing number of sociological research is now available which focuses, in one way or another, on Muslims and Islam. Hence we may wish to ask ourselves whether we need a sociology or anthropology of Islam today. My personal take on this question is that we surely do not need a sociology, or anthropology, of Islam any more than we need a sociology of Christianity or any other religious phenomenon. The risk of speaking of a sociology of Islam is to end in cultural essentialism which inevitably leads to understanding Muslims as being a product of Islamic "theology" or even history. It is clear to me that what sociologists and anthropologists study is not Islam as a religion, but Muslims and their social interactions, representations, and structures.

This means that we need to refocus on Muslims as human beings and study not just how "Islam makes them," but rather how Muslims, in various environments, through their own processes of feelings and emotions (Marranci 2006 and 2008) form different epistemologies based on their experience of what Islam may be in such circumstances and contexts. Indeed Islam per-se cannot exist; we need at least a mind[13] since, as many other private and pubic representations, it can only be made sense of through mental processes forming what we can call "cognitive maps."

Notes

1 I have decided to discuss sociological as well as anthropological approaches together since today very few differences can be perceived between the two disciplines. This is because, at least in the case of studies focusing on Islam, both have increasingly relied upon fieldwork and observation and the traditional division of qualitative (for anthropological approaches) versus quantitative studies (for sociological ones) has practically disappeared.

2 To mention just a few recent examples: Esposito 1988; Ahmed 2002; Armstrong 2002; Naser 2002; Brown 2003; Riddell and Cotterell 2003; Sonn 2004; Ernst 2004.

3 See, for instance, Anderson 1984; Asad 1986a, 1986b; Munson 1993, 1995; Roberts 2002; Rosen 2002; and more recently Marranci 2006 and 2008.

4 For a critical debate, and just to mention a few, see Crapazano 1973; el-Zein 1977; Marranci 2006 and 2008, but in particular Varisco 2005.

5 But see Marranci 2008 for a full discussion on the anthropology of Islam and possible new approaches to it.

6 See for example, Boase 1989; Elkholy 1984; Hart 1988; Tahir 1987; Tapper 1988; Young 1988; Edwards 1991; Varisco 2005.

7 For a general critique of the culturalist position in social sciences you can read Cronk 1999 and Sperber 1996.

8 See for instance Aldrich 1981; Bhatti 1981; Werbner 1980 and 1981; as well as Wilson 1981.

9 To cite just some examples, see Nielsen 1981; Mildenberger 1982; Qureshi 1983; Anwar 1982 and 1984; Barton 1986; Andezian 1988.

10 See for instance Dekmejian 1985; Arjomand 1995; Hoffman 1985; Khatab 2006a and 2006b.

11 Tibi 1998; Bruce 2000; Antoun 2001; Choueri 2002.

12 For an in-depth criticism of Mernissi's work, see Varisco 2005.

13 For those whom believe this includes God's mind.

Bibliography

Abadan-Unat, N. (1977) Implications of migration on emancipation and pseudo-emancipation of Turkish women, *International Migration Review* 11 (1): 31–57.

Abu-Lughod, L. (1986) *Veiled Sentiments: Honor and Poetry in Bedouin Society*, Berkeley: University of California Press.

Abu-Lughod, L. (1989) Zones of theory in the anthropology of the Arab world, *Annual Review of Anthropology* 8: 267–306.

Ahmed, A. S. (1986) *Toward Islamic Anthropology: Definition, Dogma and Directions*, Herndon, VA: International Institute of Islamic Thought.

Ahmed, A. S. (2002) *Discovering Islam: Making Sense of Muslim History and Society*, New York: Routledge.

Ahmed, L. (1992) *Women and Gender in Islam*, New Haven and London: Yale University Press.

Aldrich, H. (1981) Business development and self-segregation: Asian enterprise in three British cities, in C. Peach, V. Robinson, and S. Smith (eds.), *Ethnic Segregation in Cities*, London: Croom Helm, 170–92.

Anderson, J. W. (1984) Conjuring with Ibn Khaldun: from an anthropological point of view, in B. B. Lawrence (ed.), *Ibn Khaldun and Islamic Ideology*, Leiden: Brill, 111–12.

Andezian, S. (1988) Migrant Muslim women in France, in T. Gerholm and Y. G. Lithman (eds.), *The New Islamic Presence in Western Europe*, London and New York: Mansell Publishing, 196–204.

Antoun, R. (2001) *Understanding Fundamentalism*, New York: Alta Mira Press.

Anwar, M. (1976) *Between Two Cultures: A Study of the Relationships between Generations in the Asian Community in Britain*, London: Community Council.

Anwar, M. (1982) *Young Muslims in a Multi-Cultural Society: Their Educational Needs and Policy Implications*, London: Islamic Foundation.

Anwar, M. (1984) Employment patterns of Muslims in Western Europe, *Journal: Institute of Muslim Minority Affairs* 5 (1): 99–122.

Arjomand, S. A. (1995) Unity and diversity in Islamic fundamentalism, in M. E. Marty and R. S. Appleby (eds.), *Fundamentalisms Comprehended*, Chicago: University of Chicago Press, 179–98.

Armstrong, K. (2002) Islam: A Short History (revd. edn.), New York: Modern Library.

Asad, T. (1986a) The concept of cultural translation in British social anthropology, in J. Clifford, and G. Marcus (eds.), Writing Culture: The Poetic and Politics of Ethnography, Berkeley: University of California Press, 141–64.

Asad, T. (1986b) The Idea of an Anthropology of Islam, Washington, DC: Center for Contemporary Arab Studies.

Asad, T. (1990) Ethnography, literature, and politics: some readings and uses of Salman Rushdie's The Satanic Verses, Cultural Anthropology 5 (3): 239–69.

Ba-Yunus, L. and Ahmad, F. (1985) Islamic Sociology: An Introduction, Cambridge: Islamic Academy.

Baring, E. (Earl of Cromer) (1908) Modern Egypt, New York: Macmillan.

Barton, S. (1986) The Bengali Muslims of Bradford, Leeds: University of Leeds.

Beck, L. and Keddie, N. (eds.) (1978) Women in the Muslim World, Cambridge, MA: Harvard University Press.

Bhatti, F. M. (1981) Turkish Cypriots in London, Research Papers: Muslims in Europe 11, Birmingham: Centre for the Study of Islam and Christian-Muslim Relations, 1–20.

Boase, A. M. (1989) Review of Ahmed 1986, Arabia: the Islamic World Review 6: 65.

Bodman, H. and Tohidi, N. (eds.) (1998) Women in Muslim Societies: Diversity within Unity, Colorado: Lynne Rienner Publishers.

Boellstorff, T. (2005) The Gay Archipelago: Sexuality and Nation in Indonesia, Princeton: Princeton University Press.

Bowen, J. R. (2007) Why French Do Not Like Headscarves, Princeton and Oxford: Princeton University Press.

Brown, D. W. (2003) A New Introduction to Islam, Malden: Blackwell.

Bruce, S. (2000) Fundamentalism, Cambridge: Polity.

Bujra, A. S. (1971) The Politics of Stratification: A Study of Political Change in a South Arabian Town, Oxford: Clarendon.

Burton, J. (1994) An Introduction to the Hadith, Edinburgh: Edinburgh University Press.

Choueri, Y. M. (2002) Islamic Fundamentalism, London and New York: Continuum Books.

Crapanzano, V. (1973) The Hamadsha: A Study in Moroccan Ethnopsychiatry, Berkeley: University of California Press.

Cronk, L. (1999) That Complex Whole, Texas: Westview Press.

Dahya, Z. (1972) Pakistanis in England, New Community 2 (3): 25–33.

Dahya, Z. (1973) Pakistanis in Britain: transients or settlers?, Race 14 (3): 241–77.

Dahya, Z. (1974) The nature of Pakistani ethnicity in industrial cities in Britain, in A. Cohen (ed.), Urban Ethnicity, London, Tavistock, 77–118.

Damasio, A. R. (1999) The Feeling of What Happens: Body and Emotion in the Making of Consciousness, New York: Harcourt Brace.

Damasio, A. R. (2000) The Feeling of What Happens: Body, Emotion and the Making of Consciousness, London: Vintage.

Dekmejian, H. R. (1985) Islam in Revolution: Fundamentalism in the Arab World, Syracuse: Syracuse University Press.

Dien, M. I. (2004) Islamic Law, Edinburgh: Edinburgh University Press.

Donnan, H. (2002) Interpreting Islam, London: Sage.

Edwards, D. B. (1991) Review of discovering Islam: making sense of Muslim history and society, International Journal of Middle East Studies 23 (2): 270–3.

Eickelman, D. F. (1976) Moroccan Islam, Austin: University of Texas Press.

Eickelman, D. F. (1981) A search for the anthropology of Islam: Abdul Hamid El-Zein, International Journal of Middle Eastern Studies 13: 361–5.

Eickelman, D. F. (1990) Knowing one another, shaping an Islamic anthropology (review), *American Anthropologist* 92 (1): 240–1.

el-Zein, A. H. (1977) Beyond ideology and theology: the search for the anthropology of Islam, *Annual Review of Anthropology* 6: 227–54.

Elkholy, A. (1984) Toward an Islamic anthropology, *Muslim Education Quarterly* 1: 2.

Ernst, C. W. (2004) *Rethinking Islam in the Contemporary World*, Edinburgh: Edinburgh University Press.

Esposito, J. L. (1988) *Islam, the Straight Path*, Oxford: Oxford University Press.

Fernea, R. and Malarkey, J. M. (1975) Anthropology of the Middle East and northern Africa: a critical assessment, *Annual Review of Anthropology* 4: 183–206.

Geaves, R. (2005) The dangers of essentialism: South Asian communities in Britain and the "world religions" approach to the study of religions, *Contemporary South Asia* 14 (1): 75–90.

Geertz, C. (1968) *Islam Observed*, New Haven and London: Yale University Press.

Geertz, C. (1973) Deep play: notes on the Balinese cockfight, in C. Geertz, *The Interpretation of Cultures*, New York: Basic Books, 412–54.

Gellner, E. (1981) *Muslim Society*, Cambridge: Cambridge University Press.

Ghoussoub, M. and Sinclair-Web, E. (eds.) (2000) *Imagined Masculinity: Male Identity and Culture in the Modern Middle East*, London: Saqi Books.

Gilsenan, M. (1973) *Saint and Sufi in Modern Egypt: An Essay in the Sociology of Religion*, Oxford: Clarendon.

Gilsenan, M. (1982) *Recognizing Islam: Religion and Society in the Modern Middle East*, London: I. B. Tauris.

Grillo, R. D. (2003) Cultural essentialism and cultural anxiety, *Anthropological Theory* 3 (2): 157–73.

Hallaq, W. B. (1999) The authenticity of prophetic hadith: a pseudo-problem, *Studia Islamica* 89: 75–90.

Halliday, F. (1995) Islam is in danger: authority, Rushdie and the struggle for the migrant soul, in J. Hippler and A. Lueg (eds.), *The Next Threat: Western Perceptions of Islam*, London: Pluto, 71–81.

Halstead, M. (1988) *Education, Justice and Cultural Diversity: An Examination of the Honeyford Affair 1984–85*, London: Falmer.

Hart, D. K (1988) Review of Ahmed 1986, *Middle East Studies Association Bulletin* 15: 1–2.

Hoffman, V. J. (1985) Muslim fundamentalists: psychosocial profiles, in M. E. Marty and R. S. Appleby (eds.), *Fundamentalisms Comprehended*, Chicago: University of Chicago Press, 198–229.

Hood, R. W., Jr, Hill P. C., and Williamson, W. P. (2005) *The Psychology of Religious Fundamentalism*, New York and London: Guilford Press.

Hussain, F. (ed.) (1984) *Muslim Women*, London: Croom Helm.

Kamali, M. (2001) Civil society and Islam: a sociological perspective, *Archive of European Sociology* 53 (3): 457–82.

Kawale, R. (2003) A kiss is just a kiss ... or is it? South Asian lesbian and bisexual women and the construction of space, in N. Puwar and P. Raghuram (eds.), *South Asian Women in the Diaspora*, Oxford: Berg, 179–98.

Keddie, N. (1991) Problems in the study of Middle Eastern women, *International Journal of Middle Eastern Studies* 10: 225–40.

Khatab, S. (2006a) *The Political Thought of Sayyid Qutb: The Theory of jahiliyyah*, London: Routledge.

Khatab, S. (2006b) *The Power of Sovereignty: The Political and Ideological Philosophy of Sayyid Qutb*, London: Routledge.

Korzybski, A. (1948) *Science and Sanity: An Introduction to Non-Aristotelian Systems and General Semantics*, Lakeville: International Non-Aristotelian Publishing Co.

Lahoucine, O. (ed.) (2006) *Islamic Masculinities*, London: Zed Books.

Mahroof, M. (1981) Elements for an Islamic anthropology, in *Social and Natural Sciences: The Islamic Perspective*, Jaddah: KAA University and Hodder and Stoughton, 15–23.

Marranci, G. (2006) *Jihad Beyond Islam*, Oxford: Berg.

Marranci, G. (2008) *The Anthropology of Islam*, London and New York: Berg.

Marranci, G. (2009) *Understanding Muslim Identity, Rethinking Fundamentalism*, London and New York: Palgrave Macmillan.

Matin-Asgari, A. (2004) Islamic studies and the spirit of Max Weber: a critique of cultural essentialism, *Critical Middle Eastern Studies* 13 (3): 293–312.

Mernissi, F. (1975) *Beyond the Veil: Male–Female Dynamics in a Modern Muslim Society*, New York: Schenkman Publishing Company.

Mildenberger, M. (1982) *What Place for Europe's Muslims? Integration or Segregation?*, Research Papers: Muslims in Europe 13, Birmingham: Centre for the Study of Islam and Christian–Muslim Relations.

Modood, T. (1990) The British Asian Muslims and the Rushdie affair, *Political Quarterly* 62 (2): 143–60.

Modood, T. (1998) Anti-essentialism, multiculturalism and the "recognition" of religious groups, *Journal of Political Philosophy* 6: 378–99.

Munson, H. (1993) *Religion and Power in Morocco*, New Haven: Yale University Press.

Munson, H. (1995) Segmentation: reality or myth? *Journal of the Royal Anthropological Institute* 1 (4): 821–9.

Naser, S. H. (2002) *Islam: Religion, History, and Civilization*, San Francisco: Harper San Francisco.

Nielsen, J. S. (1981) *Muslims in Europe: An Overview*, Research Papers: Muslims in Europe 12, Birmingham: Centre for the Study of Islam and Christian-Muslim Relations.

Okkenhaug, M. and Flaskerud, I. (eds.) (2005) *Gender, Religion and Change in the Middle East*, Oxford: Berg.

Pellat, C. (1992) Liwāt, in A. Schmitt and J. Sofer (eds.), *Sexuality and Eroticism among Males in Moslem Societies*, Binghamton: Haworth Press, 152–67.

Pels, T. (2000) Muslim families from Morocco in the Netherlands: gender dynamics and father's roles in a context of change, *Current Sociology* 48 (4): 75–93.

Qureshi, R. B. (ed.) (1983) *The Muslim Community in North America*, Edmonton: University of Alberta Press.

Riddell, P. G. and Cotterell, P. (2003) *Islam in Context: Past, Present, and Future*, Grand Rapids: Baker Academic.

Roald, S. A. (2001) *Women in Islam: The Western Experience*, London and New York: Routledge.

Roberts, H. (2002) Perspective on Berber politics: on Gellner and Masqueray, or Durkheim's Mistake, *Journal of the Royal Anthropological Institute* 8: 107–26.

Rosen, L. (2002) *The Culture of Islam: Changing Aspects of Contemporary Muslim Life*, Chicago: University of Chicago Press.

Sabah, F. A. (1984) *Woman in the Muslim Unconscious*, New York: Pergamon Press.

Sageman, M. (2004) *Understanding Terror Networks*, Philadelphia: University of Pennsylvania Press.

Said, E. (1978) *Orientalism*, New York: Pantheon Books.

Saifullah-Khan, V. S. (1975) Asian women in Britain: strategies of adjustment of Indian and Pakistani migrants, A. Desouza (ed.), *Women in Contemporary India*, New Delhi: Manohar, 16–88.

Saifullah-Khan, V. S. (1976) Pakistani women in Britain, *New Community* 5 (1–2): 99–108

Saifullah-Khan, V. S. (1979) Pakistanis and social stress: Mirpuris in Bradford, in V. S. Saifullah-Khan (ed.), *Minority Families in Britain: Support and Stress*, London: Macmillan, 37–58.

Schmiduke, S. (1999) Homoeroticism and homosexuality in Islam: a review article, *Bulletin of the School of Oriental and African Studies*, University of London 62 (2): 260–6.

Shankland, D. (2003) *The Alevis in Turkey*, London and New York: Routledge Curzon.

Siraj, A. (2006) On being homosexual and Muslim: conflicts and challenges, in O. Lahoucine (ed.), *Islamic Masculinities*, London: Zed Books, 202–16.

Sofer, J. (1992) Sodomy in the law of Muslim states, in A. Schmitt and J. Sofer (eds.), *Sexuality and eroticism among Males in Moslem Societies*, Binghamton: Haworth Press, 131–49.

Sonn, T. (2004) *A Brief History of Islam*, London: Polity Press.

Sperber, D. (1996) *Explaining Culture: A Naturalistic Approach*, Oxford: Blackwell.

Syed, J. (1981) *The Origins and Early Development of Shi'a Islam*, London: Longman.

Tahir, M. A. (1987) Review of Ahmed 1986, *Muslim World Book Review* 8 (1): 8–10.

Tapper, N. and Tapper, R. (1987) The birth of the prophet: ritual and gender in Turkish Islam, *Man* (new series) 22: 69–92.

Tapper, R. (1988) Review of Ahmed 1986, *Man* 23 (3): 567–8.

Tibi, B. (1998) *The Challenge of Fundamentalism: Political Islam and the New World Disorder*, Santa Barbara: University of California Press.

Tucker, J. (ed.) (1993) *Arab Women, Old Boundaries*, New Frontiers, Bloomington: Indiana University Press.

Turner, B. S. (1974) *Weber and Islam*, London: Routledge.

Turner, B. S. (1978) *Marx and the End of Orientalism*, London: Allen and Unwin.

Turner, B. S. (1992) Islam, capitalism, and the Weber theses, in S. B. Turner, *Max Weber: From History to Modernity*, London: Routledge, 41–55.

Varisco, M. D. (2005) *Islam Obscured: The Rhetoric of Anthropological Representation*, Basingstoke and New York: Palgrave Macmillan.

Voltaire, F. A. M. (1905) [1736], Mahomet, in F. A. M. Voltaire, *The Works of Voltaire*, vol. 27, Akron: Werner.

Waines, D. (1995) *An Introduction to Islam*, Cambridge: Cambridge University Press.

Watson, J. L. (ed.) (1997) *Between Two Cultures: Migrants and Minorities in Britain*, Oxford: Blackwell.

Watt, M. (1956) *Muhammad at Medina*, Oxford: Oxford University Press.

Werbner, P. (1980) Rich man, poor man, or a community of suffering: heroic motifs in Manchester Pakistanis' life histories, *Oral History* 8: 43–8.

Werbner, P. (1981) From rags to riches: Manchester Pakistanis in the textile trade, *New Community* 9: 216–29.

Wilson, A. (1981) *Finding a Voice: Asian Women in Britain*, London: Virago.

Wyn, M. D. (1988) *Knowing One Another: Shaping Islamic Anthropology*, London and New York: Mansell.

Yip, A. K. T. (2004a) Embracing Allah and sexuality?: South Asian non-heterosexual Muslims in Britain, in P. Kumar and K. Jacobsen (eds.), *South Asians in the Diaspora*, Leiden: Brill, 294–312.

Yip, A. K. T. (2004b) Minderheit in der Minderheit: nicht Heterosexuelle Britische Muslime, in *Muslime unter dem Regenbogen: Homosexualitat, Migration und Islam*, Berlin-Brandenburg e.v. (Hg.), Berlin: Queverlag GmbH, 128–42.

Yip, A. K. T. (2004c) Negotiating space with family and kin in identity construction: the narratives of British non-heterosexual Muslims, *Sociological Review* 52 (3): 336–49.

Young, W. (1988) Review of Ahmed 1986, *American Journal of Islamic Social Science* 5: 2.

17

Approaches to the Study of Buddhism

Catherine Newell

Introduction

The mass migrations of Buddhist peoples and the spread of Buddhist traditions into Europe and North America particularly in recent decades mean that Buddhism now thrives well beyond its traditional Asian heartland. The Western academic study of Buddhism and Buddhist societies (as distinct from the rich history of scholarship within Buddhist traditions) is as long as the history of encounters between Western scholars and Buddhist countries. It crystallized in the mid-1800s and now encompasses a wide range of academic disciplines including Religious Studies, History, Sociology and Anthropology. In this chapter I explore this history of scholarly approaches to the study of Buddhist societies. The chapter falls into two sections of roughly equal length. In the first section I take a chronological overview of the early study of Buddhism and Buddhists, with particular reference to the experience of Buddhism under colonialism. In the second section I take a more thematic approach, exploring the different approaches taken by a selection of important scholars associated with important analyses of Buddhism in Burma, Sri Lanka, and Thailand. In conclusion I will assess how such academic approaches have shaped our understanding of Buddhists and Buddhist practice. The chapter will also introduce some of the key facts and terminology used in Buddhist Studies. By the end of the chapter the reader will have oriented him/herself in the contemporary Buddhist Studies landscape and should be well equipped to understand current debates.

About Buddhism

The Buddhist religion originated with the teachings of Siddhartha Gautama, the Buddha, who was born in Northern India over 2,500 years ago. Scholars of Buddhism refer to Gautama as "the historical Buddha" to distinguish him from other

Buddhas recognized by some or all Buddhist traditions. "Early Buddhism" is a rather contested label used to denote the period before the gradual emergence (over a period of many centuries) of Mahayana *sutras*, which were texts which explored new doctrinal interpretations of Buddhism, the earliest of which can be dated to around second century CE (Gethin 1998: 225).[1] What little we know about Early Buddhism has to be reconstructed from Buddhist literature and limited epigraphic and archaeological evidence. Early Buddhism featured a number of schools, conventionally counted as eighteen, though there is no clear historical evidence for this number other than within some traditional accounts. Fragments of the teachings and monastic rules of some of the eighteen schools have survived to the present day, often in translation, but the only complete canon we have is from the Theravada School. The most important of the eighteen schools, for our purposes, was the Sthaviravada, which due to disagreements with another, the Mahasanghikas, is associated with the first major schism of Early Buddhism, probably during the reign of Mahapadma Nanda around 362–332 BCE (Skilton 1994: 49). "Sthavira" is the Sanskrit word for "elder" (referring to senior monks), which in Pali is "Thera"; thus the historical Sthaviravada School, which did not survive to the present day, has come to be associated with the "Theravada" School. There is no firm evidence for a direct association between the two schools, and their exact if any relationship remains a moot point among scholars (Skilton 1994: 67). Nevertheless this identification with ancient Buddhist history and the association between Theravada and Sthavirada remains a key part of Theravada self-identity, and there is no reason to suggest that the two schools did not share similar doctrines and practices. Moreover, this association of Early Buddhism with Theravada has persisted in the minds of scholars, as we shall see below.

Beyond the Theravada Buddhists of contemporary South and Southeast Asia, there are Buddhists in North and East Asia who follow traditions based on the innovations of Mahayana thought. While Theravada is a school with its own closed canon and *vinaya*, Mahayana is an overarching term used to denote the philosophical basis for an array of diverse and geographically dispersed forms of Buddhism. Another important influential body of texts, the Buddhist Tantras, appeared from around the second century CE. Tantra was a pan-Indian movement which also had a major influence upon Brahmanism and other Indian religions. It incorporated texts, beliefs, and practices which aimed to transform the elements and mundane physical body into the means for spiritual attainment and transformation. Tantric rituals and techniques are particularly associated with the traditions of Tibet and Nepal, but have also been recorded in elements of practice in countries as diverse at Japan and Thailand. Tantric Buddhism is sometimes referred to as *Tantra-yana* or *Vajra-yana* Buddhism. Early Buddhist thought emphasized the path to personal salvation, and is sometimes called "*sravaka – yana*," that is, the vehicle of the individual *sravaka* or "listener." "Mahayana" means great vehicle, and some Mahayana sutras used the pejorative label "Hinayana" ("small" or "lesser" vehicle) to describe non-Mahayana Buddhists; unfortunately this label was taken up and used inaccurately by generations of Western scholars to refer to all Early Buddhism. Sometimes this confusion extends to include modern Theravada, due to confusion about the relationship between Early Buddhism and Theravada. Properly, "Hinayana" has only a very specific meaning in Indian history; there was no such single historical entity as "Hinayana Buddhism"(Cohen 1995: 20–2). These facts have not prevented a simplistic model of a linear development of Buddhism:

"Early" / Hinayana Buddhism → Mahayana → Tantrayana / Vajrayana

being used so widely as to have become the standard framework for describing Buddhist history, despite its fundamental inaccuracies.

In the main, this chapter operates in the context of Theravada Buddhist Studies. There are a number of reasons for this, primary amongst them the fact that there is a longer history of contact between Theravada countries and European academia as a consequence of colonial administrations in such Theravada countries as Sri Lankan and Myanmar (Ceylon and Burma under British rule), Laos, and Cambodia (French Indochina), alongside Thailand, which although not colonized still had considerable interaction with its neighbors' colonial rulers.

OVERVIEW OF EARLY BUDDHIST STUDIES

Buddhist Studies ... began as a latecomer to Romantic Orientalism, an off-shoot of Indology at a time when India was no longer in vogue. (Donald S. Lopez 1995: 2)

Serious Western scholarship of Buddhist traditions began to take shape in the 1850s, when Buddhism had been absent from India for centuries, having disappeared in circumstances still unclear but apparently at least partly prompted by the Muslim invasions of twelfth and thirteenth centuries (Skilton 1994: 143–5). Though Buddhism did flourish throughout the colonized East, in British Ceylon and Burma and French Indochina, the practice of Buddhism on the ground in those societies was not the appealing object of Victorian scholarship, which almost from its inception favored classical Buddhist texts as a means to understand and represent Buddhism (Hallisey 1995: 34–8; Almond 1988: 24–8). The reasons for this preference for a long-dead, absent Buddhism over the living traditions of South and Southeast Asia are complex, and in order to understand the development of Indological preferences and priorities in the early study of Buddhism we need to consider a number of factors.

The outlook and expectations of Western residents in India and Buddhist nations were shaped by discourse about the nature and location of religion which dated back to the Reformation. Protestantism downplayed the importance and efficacy of religious ritual and the soteriological mediation of a professional clerisy, and asserted the centrality of individual access to texts in understanding a religion. It emphasized the personal rather than the social focus of religion. This rational, ritual-free, "true" Christianity, based in scripture rather than tradition, was presented in contrast to Catholicism, which was seen to have moved far away from the original teachings of the Early Church, and to have allowed itself to be sullied by clerical hierarchy, devotionalism and excessive ritual. The superiority of Protestantism over the perceived idolatry and ritual of the Catholic Church was well established in the minds of many of the early European scholars of Buddhist Asia, particularly within the Anglo-German strand of scholarship. These factors and expectations of the nature and location of religion had a number of consequences for the study of Buddhism. "Buddhism" was effectively separated into two disparate poles, thus:

1 A rather idealized Buddhism of distant antiquity, reconstructed by scholars from texts in Pali and Sanskrit, with preference given to older texts.
2 The Buddhists of contemporary Asia, whose practices and preferences were perceived in specific contrast to this ideal.

Through this polarization, as Lopez explains, "Buddhism could be construed as a transhistorical and self-identical essence that had benevolently descended on various cultures over the course of history" (1995: 7). Moreover, in European scholars' appropriation of Buddhist scholarship we can perceive the "invention of an authentic Buddhism in Europe ... [against which] all of the Buddhisms of the modern Orient were to be judged and found lacking" (Lopez 1995:7) In this way, the living traditions of Buddhism were contrasted with an ideal of "Early Buddhism" which had itself been extracted from particular textual evidence by European scholars. Those traditions which most closely resembled this idealized Buddhism were esteemed over those with which it apparently had little in common.

Thus, the expectations of scholars about what religion is and where it is located also dictated assessments of the various Buddhist traditions which they encountered. A scholarly preference for Theravada Buddhism was established at this time, in part because Theravada's closed canon reflected unconscious Protestant expectations of a religion's proper textual basis, but it was also due to Theravada's perceived antiquity, and the belief that it was the living tradition closest to Early Buddhism, the absent, unknowable, yet most highly prized Buddhism of all. This was in marked contrast to the treatment of Tibetan Buddhism, which was seen to be characterized by a wealth of ritual and a vast pantheon of gods and goddesses.[2] Tibetan Buddhism was not even deemed to be Buddhism, and for some time was labeled instead "Lamaism," after the formal Tibetan title *bla ma* given to teachers (Lopez 1998: 15–45). "Lamaism" was explicitly equated with Catholicism during in this period, a comparison which persists (Lopez 1998: 16, 33, 1995: 261). Wedemeyer argues that scholarly accounts of Buddhist history are underpinned by an unacknowledged "model of decline," which perceives the development of Buddhist traditions as moving increasingly far away from the ideal of the Buddha (2001: 223–59).[3] Wedemeyer is specifically examining the way in which Mayahana and Tantric Buddhism have been represented as degenerations, even distortions of the historical Buddha's original message, but his observations are relevant for students of all traditions. The equation of Theravada with "Early Buddhism" persists in modern scholarship. It is still common for scholars to use the terms Theravada, "Early Buddhism" and Hinayana almost interchangeably, even though extensive research (for example, Cohen 1995: 1–25; Crosby 2003: 836–41) has now established that these are very different entities.

As we have seen, scholars of Buddhism had a stated preference for antiquity and canonicity, and prioritized languages and texts in Pali and Sanskrit, languages which were now deemed "Classical." Contemporary and historical vernacular sources, of which there was a rich, ongoing, iterative tradition, were perceived to be of less importance, relegated to a lower status early on and remain to this day less studied.

The kind of scholarship required by this approach to Buddhist Studies was essentially philological, that is concerned with understanding ancient cultures through the medium of classical languages and texts. The expertise of these early scholars of Buddhism whose names are still familiar to students today – T. W. Rhys Davids, Max Müller, Monier Williams – were primarily in the realm of classical Asian languages. The ability to use vernacular languages such as Burmese, Sinhala, Shan or Siamese was not as highly prized as proficiency in classical Buddhist languages of Sanskrit and Pali. But how reasonable was this emphasis on the canon?

We have already seen that Theravada Buddhism was elevated to the role of sole contemporary representative of Early Buddhism, in part because of its textual heritage, which in the reckoning of scholars meant the Pali Canon. Theravada Buddhist history asserts that the canon was fixed (that is, agreed upon and recited) at the first Buddhist council immediately after the death of the Buddha, and handed down as an oral tradition until the first century BCE in Sri Lanka when it was first written down. This account of the canon's provenance was accepted by early scholars of Buddhism, who regarded it as an apolitical, neutral record of Buddhism at the time of and just after the life of the Buddha. The behaviors and practices it described, particularly with regard to monastic conduct, were taken to be an accurate historical portrayal of the daily reality of Early Buddhist Society. Contemporary scholarship challenges this interpretation of the Pali canon on a number of grounds. It is not possible to accept that the traditional dating is valid for the canon as a whole, since many of the events it describes clearly postdate its ostensible compilation. In addition, the Pali canon is now understood to be only one of many redactions of early Buddhist texts, albeit the only one which has survived in full. Moreover, Schopen, whose work will be considered in more detail below, suggests of the Pali canon that "this material records what a small, atypical part of the Buddhist community wanted that community to believe or practice" (1997: 1). In line with Schopen, Collins deconstructs "the very idea of the Pali canon" (1990: 89–126), arguing that further research is necessary "on the actual possession and use of texts, in monastery libraries and elsewhere, and on the content of sermons and festival presentations to laity" (1990: 104). The work of both Schopen and Collins gives us pause to think about the meaning and purpose of the Pali canon in Buddhist history beyond the simplistic model of an impartial account of Early Buddhists which can be used as a benchmark against which to judge contemporary Buddhist practice.

If the presuppositions concerning religion and society of early scholars of Buddhism influenced how they went about their studies, they also had a profound impact upon the depiction they gave of "Early" Buddhism. Various ideas about Buddhism became popular at this time, many of which have persisted in scholarship and the popular mind. Great emphasis was placed on the personality and life story of the historical Buddha, and in particular on the task of constructing a coherent life story for the Buddha which corresponded with Western expectations of the genre of biography (Hallisey 1995: 34–8; Reynolds 1976: 37–61). This preoccupation mirrored the contemporary concern with the "historical Jesus," a Victorian theological and cultural project that developed a historical biography of Christ that unintentionally made him look like a benign and rational Victorian gentleman. In classical and vernacular Buddhist literature biographical information about the

Buddha did not appear in a single narrative; rather, descriptions of key events tend to be recounted independent of an overarching narrative framework. In Southeast Asia, the most important biographical narrative story is the *Vessantara Jataka*, which recounts Gautama's previous life before he was born into the life in which he would gain enlightenment. In Thailand and Laos, retelling this story is a highlight of the festival year, and lay and monastic devotees anticipate great merit from hearing it (Swearer 1995: 32–5). In contrast, Western scholars have tended to place less emphasis on such *jatakas* (stories of the Buddha's previous lives), and to focus instead on the narrative of Gautama's personal religious quest. Collating source material to build a biography was a key undertaking of Early Buddhist Studies and the popularity of viewing the Buddha's biography as a way into the religion can be seen to persist today, for example in the sustained popularity of Hermann Hesse's *Siddhartha*.

An offshoot of this preoccupation was that certain ideas and emphases about the Buddha's personality and motivations also gained currency, many of which are still held to be true. The Buddha was often portrayed by earlier Victorian popular and scholarly writing as a religious reformer equivalent to Protestant reformer Martin Luther (Almond 1988: 73–4); his Buddhism was perceived not as a new or separate religion but as a kind of reformed Hinduism, a hermeneutic strategy that sought legitimacy in medieval Hindu polemics that cast Buddha as an avatar or incarnation of Vishnu. Furthermore, as Almond notes, this "analogy between the Buddha and Luther, between Buddhism and Protestantism served not only to illuminate Buddhism, but also for anti-Catholic polemic" (1988: 73). A great stress was placed on the Buddha's pronouncements on the caste system, despite his comments on this being restricted to its relevance to soteriology. Perceiving the Buddha as radical, rational social reformer also reflected the Protestant perceptions of Christ that were in currency at the time, and fitted into a view of Buddhism as a rational religion which did not conflict with modern scientific thought.

While the earliest stratum of Buddhist scholarship portrayed the Buddha as a social reformer, towards the end of the nineteenth century scholars, influenced particularly by the work of Oldenberg, increasingly rejected this idea and moved instead towards a picture of the Buddha as aloof from society, and solely concerned with questions of personal salvation (Almond 1988: 75). This view of Buddhism, as a purely soteriologically orientated religion, is particularly associated with Weber (1864–1920), whose legacy looms over the study of all religions, especially Buddhism. Weber portrays Early Buddhism as an "other-worldly mysticism," as a religious path for world-renouncing monastics who focus single-mindedly on salvation (*nirvana* in Sanskrit, *nibbana* in Pali) and take no interest in mundane matters. There are a number of implications for this view of Buddhism. It denigrates lay religiosity, which Weber perceived as being concerned with ritual and merit making entirely unconnected to the goal of nirvana, and sets it in opposition to the "true" Buddhism of the renouncing monk. As contemporary Sri Lankan scholar H. L Seneviratne notes:

> The distinction was absolute: Buddhism represented a duality that consisted, on the one hand, of the monkhood on which was concentrated all rationality, morality, ethical stature and perfect goal-orientation, and, on the other, of an irrational amoral laity

immersed in a world of magic and mundaneity all living a life of loose or diffuse goal
orientations. (1999: 344)

This model denied monks any role other than that of the perfectly goal-orientated
nirvana-seeker, and limited their social interaction to dependence upon lay people
for alms. Thus any involvement of monks in ritual practices, life cycle ceremonies,
social service, temple construction or other mundane pursuits was incompatible
with this uncomfortably idealistic theoretical construction. Nor, for Weber, could
Buddhist monks or Buddhist institutions have any involvement with politics. For
Weber, Buddhism was "a specifically unpolitical and anti-political status religion,
more precisely, a religious "technology" of wandering and of intellectually schooled
mendicant monks" (Weber 1958: 206) A second layer of Weberian analysis con-
sisted of examining contemporary Buddhist societies and cataloguing the ways in
which they failed to implement or be consistent with their proper role, as
constructed by Weber. Seneviratne argues that Weberian typology employed
"Buddhism" to fill the role of "other worldly mysticism," and that his interpretation
thereof can only be understood as an "ideal type [which] expresses itself as an
empirical reality" (1999: 1); it was not meant to be taken as a portrait of
Buddhism.

Although Weberian analysis of Buddhism remains influential, some recent scholarship has begun to challenge some of its fundamental assumptions. This work has
been textual, historical and anthropological. The work of Schopen offers a new
interpretation of the scholarship concerning Early Buddhist history. Schopen's
oeuvre is concerned with Indian Buddhist monasticism and historical approaches
to it, and his research encourages us to review some of our fundamental expectations in attempting to assess and analyze Buddhism. He argues, very persuasively,
that in the attempt to establish a history of Early Buddhist monasticism certain types
of evidence and history have been prioritized over others. In particularly he points
out that material culture, that is, archaeological and epigraphic evidence of what
the monks, nuns and lay people of early Buddhism actually did, is devalued in place
of textual culture. For example, he presents the case of donative inscriptions found
at some of the earliest extant Buddhist monuments from second and first centuries
BCE, at Sanci and Bharhut (1997: 3–5). A succession of scholars had noted that
many of the inscriptions on the monuments showed that donations had been made
by Buddhist monks and nuns. It is natural to assume that in order to make such
donations, these named monks and nuns must have had money. However, the
monastic code by which they lived forbade the owning of personal property and
the handling of money. Given this apparent anomaly – the extensive evidence that
early Buddhist monks and nuns owned property which they could donate in apparent contravention of monastic code – the scholars all reached the same conclusion:
that the monks and nuns in question had "obtained ... by begging the money
required for making the rails and pillars" (1997: 3). The other possibility, that they
had possessed the means to make donations on their own behalf, despite this going
against monastic code, was discounted on the grounds that it conflicted with the
picture of monastic morality as painted in texts; that is, the archaeological and
epigraphic evidence of what Buddhists did was interpreted in a curiously round-
about way, indeed dismissed, in order to fit with what Buddhist texts stated was

Buddhist practice at that time. As Schopen puts it, "textuality overrides actuality" (1997: 7); for so long as a Buddhism could be comfortably reconstructed from ancient texts "what Indian Buddhists actually did was of no consequence" (1997: 9). When material history does not correspond with the expectations of Buddhist texts, it is explained in terms of those texts or simply ignored (1997: 8).

Schopen argues that the reason for this particular preference can be understood as part of the broader scholarly trend which has its roots in and is a latter-day expression of European Protestantism: "apparently neutral archaeological and historical method might well be a decidedly non-neutral and narrowly limited Protestant assumption as to where religion is actually located" (1997: 13). Elsewhere, Schopen explores a significant number of examples which counter the perceptions of Early Buddhism as non-worldly, text-based, soteriology-focused and exclusively monastic. He has also made important contributions to the debate surrounding the nebulous origins of Mahayana Buddhism, as well as challenging entrenched ideas about the contrasting roles of the lay person and the monk / nun in Early Buddhism. His work has been a tonic as much as a challenge to Buddhist Studies.

Summary

The model of Buddhism and the modes of Buddhist scholarship passed down from the earliest generations of Buddhist scholars are characterized by a number of features. I have noted that scholarship was marked by over-reliance on certain textual sources – preferably canonical, and in the classical languages of Pali and Sanskrit – despite the fact that this did not reflect the way in which texts were used in Buddhist societies. This approach, validated through its construction as an explicit hermeneutic by Weber, meant that a particular picture emerged about the nature of Early Buddhism, which was considered to be "true" or "pure" Buddhism, and from which contemporary Buddhist traditions were perceived as deviations. The appeal of a distant, dead religion over a living, present one had many dimensions, one of the most important being that it could be understood as an ancient civilization, now lost. In the colonial mindset it was the job of the European academic, whose more sophisticated learning was an advance on any "Eastern" indigenous scholarship, both to recover the original message and deliver it back to the Buddhists in whose charge it had become so distorted. As a consequence, Buddhist scholars effectively appropriated "Buddhism" as a category, meaning that

> Buddhism developed as something primarily said in the West … [while] Buddhism as it manifested itself in the East could only there be seen through the medium of what was definitively said about it elsewhere. (Almond 1988: 33)

In the assessment of these early European scholars, aspects of Theravada were equated with Early Buddhism, and projected as "authentic," while Tibetan and other tantric traditions of Northern Buddhism were dismissed as degenerations from this ideal and denigrated with the label "Lamaism." Early Buddhist scholarship created a focus on the personality and life of the Buddha, which was interpreted in a manner fitting the Victorian outlook, quite differently from its role within Buddhist traditions themselves.

From Text to Context[4]

Introduction

Many anthropologists have oversimplified … [the] relationship between text and context. Adopting the somewhat simplistic model of context (anthropologist's concern) vs. text (Indologist's concern), the text-context debate has been unnecessarily constrained to the level of what happens in the "field" (people's beliefs and practice) as against the "doctrinal" Buddhism (historical-doctrinal) as some unitary entity already understood in the west. (Gustaaf Houtman 1991: 235)

In the preceding section I introduced some of the approaches taken to the study of Buddhist traditions, and explored their ongoing consequences for the interpretations of Buddhist societies. One of these was the devaluation of the broader social setting of Buddhism, its function within the community and in particular the role of lay devotees and their interaction with monks and nuns. Moreover, a text-centered approach illuminated what happened in the field to only a certain, limited extent, and a new generation of scholars was frustrated by the limitations of this approach. From the 1970s onwards, some of the most important and exciting studies concerning Buddhists and Buddhist societies have emerged from the sphere of social sciences (see Houtmann 1991: 242–54 for a useful overview of this trend). The focus of their studies was not the textual history of Buddhism but how it was lived on the ground, its context rather than its text. As the spotlight moved onto Buddhists and Buddhist societies the ethnographies produced focused not so much on what Buddhists did as to why they did it. In this section I offer a short survey of some of the best known of these ethnographies.

Frank Reynolds has offered a "map" of those contemporary ethnographies which have addressed Theravada countries, which comprises four modes of scholarship, each with varying degrees of emphasis. The first category, his Mode I, emphasizes the use of "text/historical data and methods," that is, philology. Mode II denotes a typically ethnographic approach. The second two categories are characterized by a combination of these two emphases, what Reynolds describes as the "holistic" approach, informed by both text-historical and ethnographic scholarship and analyses, but with differing emphases. Mode III emphasizes the former, while Mode IV emphasizes the latter (Reynolds 1987: 114).

Spiro in Burma

One of the most important early anthropological studies of Buddhism was Spiro's 1970 *Buddhism and Society*. Spiro's study of Buddhism in the context of Burmese society was groundbreaking in a number of respects. His analysis was based on fieldwork in Burma, and his attempt to account for differences in lay and monastic religiosity, to understand Buddhism on the ground, was largely unprecedented.[5] Recalling Reynolds' taxonomy, *Buddhism and Society* would appear to fall into Mode IV, representing a holistic approach synthesizing textual and anthropological

methodologies with particularly sympathy for the latter. Reynolds, however, explicitly states that Spiro's *Buddhism and Society* is "the least ambiguous and most
influential expression of what I have called Mode II in Theravada scholarship"
(Reynolds 1987: 114), an assessment which is presumably based upon the scarcity
of anthropological studies at the time of Reynolds' writing.

Spiro is aware that his project is somewhat innovative, and prefaces his study
with the assertion that, as an anthropologist, he hopes to build upon the philological
and Indological basis, and advance upon it:

> so far as Buddhist scholarship is concerned, one might say that the anthropologist takes
> off where the textual and historical scholar ends, for the anthropologist is not con-
> cerned with religious texts per se, but with the interaction between the doctrines found
> in these texts and conceptions found in the heads of religious devotees, and conse-
> quently, with the relation between these religious conceptions and the general ordering
> of social and cultural life. (1971: 3)

It is clear, then, that Spiro feels that the anthropologist can improve upon
the Indological or philological scholars who have preceded him/her, using them as
the basis on which to build, by informing the doctrinal and literary framework
already established, and enriching it with proper, scientific analysis which needs to
come from a scholar trained in the social sciences. It is also clear, from this
quotation as well as from the study itself, that Spiro is confident where "Buddhist
doctrine" is located: in the texts, in contrast with their expression on the
ground, where they are translated into "the conceptions in the heads of religious
devotees."

The overarching analysis of Spiro's study argues that the practice and orientation
of the Burmese Buddhists he encountered can be understood as falling into three
broad categories:

1 nibbanic;
2 kammatic;
3 apotropaic.[6]

The first two, "nibbanic" and "kammatic," are understood to be operating within
a soteriological system, while the third, "apotropaic" is non-soteriological (Spiro
1971: 468); the three "mesh" together into a single overarching pattern, despite
apparent internal inconsistencies. Nibbanic Buddhism is "a religion of radical salvation," and applies only to monks (fully ordained nuns are not a feature of Burmese
Buddhism) (Spiro 1971: 64). Kammatic Buddhism can be understood as those
activities which centre upon the generation of merit with the intention of a better
future life. Spiro's third category, apotropaic Buddhism, features the use of magical
formulae, amulets and rituals to appease spirits, ward off dangers and maintain
good health and personal prosperity. Nibbanic Buddhism is associated exclusively
with monks, while kammatic and apotropaic orientations are seen as the sometimes
overlapping categories in which lay Buddhist activities operate. Spiro asserts that
the division between monastic and lay Buddhists he perceives is a reflection of
"primitive," that is, Early Buddhism, which featured

two classes of Buddhists: *upāsakas* or lay devotees, who remained in the world, and *bhikkhus*, the wandering mendicants who rejected the world. The former, however, are still far from the Path; their primary religious value consists in the support they render to those who have the spiritual attainments necessary to renounce the world. (1971: 64)

It is clear that Spiro still assesses Burmese Buddhists through an Indological lens, though he colored in the picture painted by Indologists with ethnographic local detail. In his account of the differences between lay and monastic Buddhists we can observe perpetuation of the tropes of early Buddhist scholarship, which denigrated lay religiosity and reduced it to the accumulation of merit gained by supporting the "true" Buddhist, the world-renouncing monk (Spiro 1971: 64). Spiro's scheme clearly favours the monastic ideal of the literate monk over the practice of the unlettered lay person. Spiro's model of the world-renouncing monk mirrors exactly the Weberian ideal type discussed above. However, while he elevates the monastic ideal he suggests that it is seldom found in the contemporary Burmese sangha. He argues that contemporary Burmese monks are not focused on the nibbanic path, and as such do not live up to this ideal (Spiro 1971: 358). Summaries of Spiro's interviews with monks in which he explores monastic motivation and dispositions appear under such subheadings as "need for dependence," "narcissism" and "emotional timidity" (pp. 338, 343, 348) and are notably unsympathetic.

Nevertheless Spiro's analysis and categories have remained influential. Samuel's 1991 study of Tibetans living in India and Nepal in the early 1970s, *Civilized Shamans*, proposes a similar threefold typology of motivations amongst Buddhists. He labels these as *bodhi* orientation (*bodhi* is the Sanskrit word for enlightenment), karma orientation and pragmatic orientation. These categories correspond with Spiro's *nibbanic, kammatic,* and *apotropaic* (summarized in Samuel 1991: 5–7; in more detail 199–243, 258–69). In *Civilized Shamans* they form the basis for his careful analysis of Tibetan society. Samuel identifies his study as anthropological, that is Mode II (1991: 5) and the technical vocabulary and analytical categories of the social sciences pervade his investigation to a far greater extent than in Spiro's book.

A large part of Spiro's study consists of explaining Buddhist doctrine, but this does not come from, in the main, Burmese informants or even Burmese-language sources, but rather from translations of Pali canonical material and European scholarship. It is clear that in spite of Spiro's pioneering use of anthropological methodology as his analytical framework, in many respects *Buddhism and Society* perpetuated many elements of early Buddhist Studies rather than holding them up to examination. Although it purports to be Mode II, in its reliance upon a limited textual basis of Pali canonical texts and translations thereof, it could be argued that in fact it fits better into Mode IV, "a more holistic approach ... [which] takes ethnography as its primary focus" (Reynolds 1987: 114)

Gombrich in Sri Lanka

Gombrich's work focuses on Buddhism in Sri Lanka. His training and expertise lie in classical Indology, but his work is often based upon and informed by fieldwork. His is a holistic approach which Reynolds would identify as Mode III. Gombrich has described himself as "an Indologist sympathetic to anthropology" (Gombrich and Obeyesekere 1990: ix). Gombrich's first book, *Precept and Practice*, appeared almost simultaneously with Spiro's *Buddhism and Society*, and like Spiro's, examines the practice of Buddhism in a rural, village setting, this time in Sri Lanka. In contrasting the "precept" and "practice" of his title, Gombrich examines Sri Lankan Buddhist practice in terms of the degree to which it reflects the textual norms of the Pali canon. In undertaking this task Gombrich perceives a distinction between what Buddhists "say they believe and say they do" and "what they really believe and really do" (Gombrich 1971: 5). Gombrich labels these two categories respectively as "cognitive" and "affective," and employs them to explore particular issues. An example of his use of these terms comes in his examination of the villagers' attitude towards the Buddha image. Gombrich's informants all assert that they know the Buddha to be dead, and thus beyond reach or influence, yet nevertheless they persist in treating a Buddha image as if it "contained or embodied the living presence of the Buddha" (1971: 166). Gombrich argues that this inconsistency can be understood in terms of what the villagers know to be doctrinal fact versus what they feel; "cognitively" they know that the Buddha is dead, but "affectively the Buddha is felt still to be potent, even when an image is not present" (1971: 167). The cognitive/affective division has been criticized, notably by Stanley Tambiah who described it as "simpleminded" (Tambiah 1984: 375). More recent scholarship concerning Buddha images in Theravada societies, notably Bizot (1994), Crosby (2005a), and Swearer (2004) suggest other, more sophisticated readings of the complex and multi-layered relationships between Buddhist texts, Buddha images and Buddhist practice.

Gombrich's approach – contrasting ethnographic data with ancient canonical norms – is similar to Spiro's, and indeed he makes similar distinctions between the types of Buddhist activity observed. However, while Spiro regards contemporary Burmese Buddhism as a kind of corruption of Early Buddhism, Gombrich's interpretation allows room for doctrinal orthodoxy, in that his Sri Lankan villagers and monks are aware of what they "should" believe even when they do not act in accordance with this. Thus his cognitive/affective distinction allows for a more nuanced understanding of the practice of rural Buddhists.

While *Precept and Practice* focuses on rural Sri Lankan Buddhism, much of Gombrich's subsequent work is associated with analysis of the disputed label of "Protestant Buddhism." This term was coined by Gananath Obeyesekere in 1970, and is used by some scholars to refer to the "new" Buddhism of the urbanized middle-class Sinhalese who emerged during British rule from the end of the nineteenth century. In a co-authored work, Obeyesekere and Gombrich outline its key features thus:

> the hallmark of Protestant Buddhism … is its view that the layman should permeate his life with his religion; that he should strive to make Buddhism permeate his whole society; and that he can and should try to reach nirvāna. (Gombrich and Obeyesekere 1990: 216)

Protestant Buddhism is a complex and multi-faceted phenomenon, but its main innovation is the idea that the path to nibbana is open to all, both lay and monastic. This brings with it the idea that carrying out such an undertaking without fully renouncing the world is possible, leading to the emergence of a "this-worldly asceticism." Gombrich, following Weber, would consider such "this-worldly" asceticism to be quite at odds with the ideals of Early Buddhism. Extending nibbanic Buddhism to the realm of the lay person would also challenge Spiro's model of Burmese Buddhism, in which even monks did not aspire to nibbana.

Another key element of Protestant Buddhism is the personal access to texts to enable independent study; this in particular reflects European Protestant values and this aspect of Protestant Buddhism could be understood in part as a response to missionary activity of the colonial period. Gombrich suggests that the urban middle classes who embraced Protestant Buddhism drew their understanding of Buddhism from scholarly English language translations of Pali sources, rather than the vernacular Sinhalese tradition (Gombrich and Obeyesekere 1990: 223). In this way contemporary Sinhalese Buddhists and scholars of Buddhism came to agree upon where "true" Buddhism was located (in the Pali canon) and the format by which to access it (via Pali Text Society editions and translations). The reasons for labeling this Buddhism "Protestant," then, are two-fold. First, its historical emergence coincided with Sri Lankan dialogue with Christian Protestant missionaries and disputes against British rulers, but secondly this interpretation of Buddhism came to incorporate a number of features of Protestantism itself, particularly the emphasis on the personal, individual focus of religion (Gombrich and Obeyesekere 1990: 7). Gombrich regards Protestant Buddhism as radically different from early Buddhism, and describes its emergence as "one of the great transformations in the history of Buddhism" (Gombrich and Obeyesekere 1990: 241).

Protestant Buddhism was initially associated with Sri Lanka and its unique experience under colonialism, but as a category it is broadly synonymous with "Buddhist Modernism." This was a label used first by Heinz Bechert (in German as "Buddhistischer Modernismus") (Bechert 1966). Bechert emphasizes the complex nature of the forces which shaped Buddhist Modernism, noting that

> there was a close interrelation between Buddhist resurgence in the East and the early phases of the spread of Buddhism in the West. This interrelation was not only organizational; essentially it concerned trends towards reinterpretation of Buddhism *as a system of thought*. (Bechert 1984: 275, my emphasis)

This "Buddhist Modernism" extends to incorporate the many thriving traditions of Buddhism in the West as evidenced by Lopez's 2002 *Modern Buddhism* which assesses contemporary Buddhism as a global phenomenon. The term "Protestant Buddhism" is highly problematic and remains contested by scholars, many of whom argue that as a concept it is neither valid nor helpful.

Tambiah in Thailand

Tambiah is associated with a series of ambitious studies that have Thai Buddhism as their touchstone. The first in his trilogy, *Buddhism and the Spirit Cults in Northeast Thailand* (1970) focused on Buddhist cosmology and the function and meaning of ritual in the Thai village context. The second, *World Conqueror and World*

Renouncer, was published in 1976 and explored the tension between Weberian perceptions of Buddhism as aloof from social engagement and politics and Buddhism's historical associations with and legitimating functions of "polity" in Thai history. The final volume in the trilogy appeared in 1984: *The Buddhist Saints of the Forest and the Cult of Amulets*. Like all of Tambiah's work this embraced a number of themes, here exploring contemporary Thai forest monks, Buddhist amulet usage and Buddhist hagiography.

Tambiah's work is too multi-faceted to appraise as a whole, and instead I will focus solely upon some salient aspects of his approach to the study of Thai Buddhism. Tambiah identifies himself as a social anthropologist (1984: 3) and his methodology has been classified by Reynolds as Mode IV, the holistic approach which combines ethnographic and text-historical methods, with a particular emphasis on the former. Reynolds comments that

> [Tambiah] argues for the ethnographic focus of his Mode IV method but maintaining that, in contrast to textual/historical study which can never give a fully holistic picture of Theravada Buddhism in a particular time and place, his ethnographic approach is able to generate a much more complete and encompassing synchronic description. (1987: 115)

Tambiah grounds his understanding of Buddhist doctrine in translated canonical and secondary material. Despite this, he is well known for his lampooning of what he labeled "Pali Text Society mentality," that is, the

> Linear view of the development of Buddhist from a pure, pristine, philosophical, salvation-search-oriented beginning, unstained and unsullied by the character and concerns of the social milieu in which it arose, to the later stages of ever-widening popularization and vulgarization and deviation from the initial purity, in which are at play all the human passions and this-worldly concerns of the masses. (1984: 7)

Tambiah here associates one thread of Buddhist Studies with the organization of the Pali Text Society, an organization on whose publications Tambiah appears to depend, at least in part, for his knowledge of Buddhism. For this reason he has been criticized by Houtmann, who comments

> even Tambiah, who is among the fiercest critics of the textual-historical Indological approach ... has blatantly reintroduced the Indological texts through the backdoor when he uses them as key points of departure ... How methodologically sound is it to claim at the outset that ethnography is contextual, yet to anchor such ethnography in the ancient text [as edited and translated] by Western Buddhologists? (Houtman 1991: 250)

In his *Buddhist Saints*, Tambiah explains that he was in part drawn to his subject by his observation of the proliferation of "popular Thai literature of magazines, books, and newspapers" concerning amulets and forest monks; despite this, he utilizes none of these Thai-language sources in his study (1984: 3). Moreover, in his study of Buddhist hagiography, Tambiah has been criticized for basing his analysis of the biography of Thai monk Ajarn Mun Bhuridatta (1870–1949) on the single biography which has been translated into English, which has been shown to be atypical of the genre by Thai scholar Tiyavanich (1997: 11).

Tambiah remains influential and his focus upon Buddhist Thailand served to open up a huge area of debate, and to move beyond scholarship which downplayed the importance and appeal of regional variation in Theravada Studies. Furthermore, he was part of a larger trend which saw local expressions of religion as valid and worthy of scholarship and which regarded them as more than a modern shadow of an idealized distant ideal. In spite of Tambiah's pioneering approach, there remain a number of fundamental problematics with his analysis, which regarded most Buddhist concepts as fixed in ancient canonical texts, and depended upon a text-historical approach as the baseline for his ethnography. His reluctance to embrace Thai-language material, whether popular or academic, is also unfortunate.

CONCLUSION

In the earlier section I explored the way in which the suppositions and emphases of the first generations of Buddhist Studies scholars shaped early Buddhist scholarship, and how this in turn impacted upon subsequent scholarship. Protestant notions about the nature and location of religion led to a particular stress on the importance of translating and editing certain texts, favoring the ancient over the contemporary and the "classical" (Pali and Sanskrit) over the vernacular (Thai, Sinhala, Shan, Lao, etc.). "Buddhist Studies" was largely a philological discipline. The model of Buddhism which emerged from such scholarship is a version of "Early Buddhism" which is created from the texts. This emphasized the personality and motivation of the Buddha in a way which did not reflect Buddhist traditions, it de-emphasized ritual, and its assessment of Buddhism as a properly soteriological tradition of a world-renouncing monk devalued both the role of the laity and Buddhism's social presence and functions. Moreover, the simplistic model of linear development of Buddhism promoted during this period fed into a rhetoric of decline which saw contemporary Buddhism as a modern, popular vulgarization of a once noble monastic tradition. Theravada Buddhism was judged to be the closest to "Early" Buddhism, while Tibetan Buddhism was largely neglected as an area of study, so distant did it seem to be from the ideals and teachings of the Buddha. Many of these fundamental tenets of Early Buddhist Studies have been challenged by the groundbreaking scholarship of such contemporary Buddhologists as Collins and Schopen.

The early 1970s witnessed the emergence of a new approach to studying Buddhist Societies, an approach which synthesized traditional philological research and anthropological analysis, building upon a text-historical basis with fieldwork in Buddhist societies. Scholars associated with pioneering this new approach include Spiro, Gombrich and Tambiah. Spiro and Tambiah in particular both associate themselves with anthropological "advances" upon traditional Buddhist scholarship, yet as I have shown, their understanding of basic Buddhist doctrine and Buddhist history are fundamentally rooted in such scholarship. The "holistic" approaches favored by Spiro and Tambiah do not extend to the use of vernacular languages in anything other than interviews (often via translators); thus we may see in their "new" approaches unwitting perpetuation of many of the hierarchies and assumptions of earlier scholarship.

The study of Buddhism and Buddhist societies has continued to grow since these innovatory holistic approaches of the 1970s and 1980s. A new generation of scholars has emerged, many of them writing from the perspective of Buddhist traditions themselves, who continue simultaneously to challenge and build upon previous scholarship. In Thailand and Laos, McDaniel synthesizes vernacular and classical language skills to study Thai Buddhism, particularly Buddhist texts and monastic education (2006, 2008). Thai scholar Tiyavanich has utilized a wide range of Thai- and Lao-language sources, as well as interviews to produce some exciting new studies of Thai Buddhism (1997, 2003). Scholars associated with the École Francaise d'Extrême-Orient (EFEO) such as Bizot, de Bernon, Gabaude, Skilling, and Filliozat have expanded our knowledge of Buddhist traditions in Cambodia, Thailand, Laos and Vietnam by studying Buddhism through its texts, its rituals and its ordination lineages (see, for example, Bizot 1992, 1994; Skilling 2007). In Sri Lanka, Samuels (2008) and Blackburn (2001) combine text-historical analysis with fieldwork. Schober works on contemporary Theravada societies and particularly on Burma and Sri Lanka, and has written on such themes as sacred biography (1997), manuscript culture (2009) and relics in Burmese Buddhism (2001).

Many scholars whose focus remains textual have illuminated understanding of Buddhist traditions and history, in part by moving to examine such diverse and previously neglected materials as regional chronicles, meditation handbooks and *kammavacca* texts relating to local ordination lineages (see Crosby 2000, 2005b; Skilton 1994). Tibet, previously unfavored by scholarship, has come to acquire a new appeal, shaped by the very Orientalist discourse which had earlier dismissed it. Tibet's geographical isolation is now viewed positively, as Tibetan Buddhism is perceived as somehow untarnished by the cultural and social decline which marked the twentieth century elsewhere. It also enjoys the image as the repository of a rich and largely unexplored textual tradition, and Tibetan Buddhist traditions are now regarded as amongst the most popular and visible forms of Buddhism, particularly in the West.

The present and emerging generations of scholars can be seen to have moved away in many respects from the rigid view of Buddhism and Buddhist Studies set in place when the discipline itself was in its infancy; indeed the very subject has now come to be understood as ideally interdisciplinary, embracing a range of linguistic and analytical skills in order to permit a more sophisticated and profound understanding of Buddhist traditions. Buddhist scholars will continue to embrace a range of approaches and to be informed by Buddhists themselves in order to explore this rich, diverse and ultimately rewarding area of inquiry.

Notes

The author would like to express her gratitude to David Azzopardi and Andrew Skilton for reading early drafts of this chapter and making a number of helpful comments and suggestions.

1 For ease of understanding, here I am using the term "Early Buddhism" differently from
   Bechert and Collins, who used it to apply to the shorter period of Buddhism before the
   rule of Asoka, (268–239 BCE) (see Collins 1990: n.4, 105).
2 In fact, a range of ritual practices, local "cults" and elaborate cosmologies were also
   features of Theravada Buddhism; however, scholars tended to de-emphasize or simply
   ignore these.
3 This academic model of decline should not be confused with the inherent expectation
   within the Buddhist tradition that the Buddha's teaching goes through subsequent cumulative decline whereby human life and behavior deteriorate until there is no attainment
   of higher spiritual states or access to the Dhamma possible until the arrival of a new
   Buddha.
4 This phrase in based on Houtmann's analysis of the development of Buddhist Studies
   (Houtmann 1991: 241), itself drawn from Tambiah (1984: 7).
5 Houtman notes that Winston L. King had attempted a similar project in his 1964 *A
   Thousand Lives Away*, to which Spiro owes some of his classifications (1991: 244).
6 Spiro also identified a number of further categories, adding millennial, eschatological,
   esoteric and normative, on which see Houtman (1991: 247).

Bibliography

Almond, Philip (1988) *The British Discovery of Buddhism*, Cambridge: Cambridge University Press.
Bechert, Heinz (1966) *Buddhismus, Staat und Gesellschaft in den Ländern des Theravāda Buddhismus* (vo. 1, Frankfurt and Berlin: Alfred Metzner; vols. 2 and 3, Wiesbaden, 1967 and 1973).
Bechert, Heinz (1984) Buddhist revival in east and west, in Heinz Bechert and Richard Gombrich (eds.), *The World of Buddhism*, London: Thames and Hudson, 273–85.
Bizot, François (1992) *Le Chemin de Lanka*, Paris: EFEO.
Bizot, François (1994) La consecration des statues et le culte des morts, in François Bizot (ed.), *Recherches Nouvelles sur le Cambodge*, Paris: EFEO, 101–39.
Blackburn, Anne (2001) *Buddhist Learning and Textual Practice in Eighteenth-century Lankan Monastic Culture*, Princeton: Princeton University Press.
Cohen, Richard S. (1995) Discontented categories: Hinayana and Mahayana in Indian Buddhist history, *Journal of the American Academy of Religion* 63 (1): 1–25.
Collins, Steven (1990) On the very idea of the Pali Canon, *Journal of the Pali Text Society* 15: 89–126.
Crosby, Kate (2000) Tantric Theravāda: a bibliographic essay on the writings of François Bizot and others on the Yogāvacara tradition, *Contemporary Buddhism* 1 (2): 141–98.
Crosby, Kate (2003) Theravāda, in Robert E. Buswell Jr (ed.), *Encyclopedia of Buddhism 2*, New York: Macmillan Reference USA: 836–41.
Crosby, Kate (2005a) Devotion to the Buddha in Theravada and its role in meditation, in A. S. King and J. Brockington (eds.), *The Intimate Other: Love Divine in Indic Religions*, Orient Longman, 244–77.
Crosby, Kate (2005b) Only if you let go of that tree: ordination without parental consent in the Theravada vinaya, *Buddhist Studies Review* 22 (2).
Gellner, David N. (2001) *The Anthropology of Buddhism and Hinduism: Weberian Themes*, New Delhi and New York: Oxford University Press.

Gethin, Rupert (1998) *The Foundations of Buddhism*, Oxford: Oxford University Press.

Gombrich, Richard F. (1971) *Precept and Practice: Traditional Buddhism in the Highlands of Ceylon*, Oxford: Clarendon.

Gombrich, Richard F. (1988) *Theravada Buddhism: A Social History from Ancient Benares to Modern Colombo*, London: Routledge and Kegan Paul.

Gombrich, Richard and Obeyesekere, Gananath (1990) *Buddhism Transformed: Religious Change in Sri Lanka*, Delhi: Motilal Banardsidass.

Hallisey, Charles (1995) Roads taken and not taken in the study of Theravāda Buddhism, in Donald S. Lopez, Jr (ed.), *Curators of the Buddha: The Study of Buddhism under Colonialism*, Chicago and London: University of Chicago Press, 31–61.

Hesse, Hermann (1998) *Siddhartha*, London: Picador.

Houtmann, Gustaaf (1991) The tradition of practice amongst Burmese Buddhists, PhD thesis, University of London.

Jong, J. W. de (1987) *A Brief History of Buddhist Studies in Europe and America* (2nd revd. edn.), Delhi, India: Sri Satguru Publications.

King, Winston L. (1964) *A Thousand Lives Away: Buddhism in Contemporary Burma*. Cambridge, MA: Harvard University Press.

Lopez, Donald S. (1998) *Prisoners of Shangri-La: Tibetan Buddhism and the West*. Chicago, London: University of Chicago Press.

Lopez, Donald S. (2002) *Modern Buddhism: Readings for the Unenlightened*, London: Penguin.

Lopez, Donald S. (ed. and intro.) (1995) *Curators of the Buddha: The Study of Buddhism under Colonialism*, Chicago, London: University of Chicago Press.

McDaniel, Justin (2006) Buddhism in Thailand, in Stephen C. Berkwitz (ed.), *Buddhism in World Cultures: Comparative Perspectives*, Santa Barbara and Oxford: ABC-CLIO, 101–28.

McDaniel, Justin (2008) *Gathering Leaves and Lifting Words: Histories of Monastic Education in Laos and Thailand*, Seattle: University of Washington Press, in association with Silkworm Books, Thailand.

Obeyesekere, Gananath (1970) Religious symbolism and political change in Ceylon, *Modern Ceylon Studies* 1; repr. in Bardwell Smith (ed.), *Two Wheels of Dhamma*, AAR Monograph 3, Chambersburg, 1972.

Reynolds, Frank E. (1976) The many lives of Buddha: a study of sacred biography and Theravāda tradition, in Frank E. Reynolds and Donald Capps (eds.), *The Biographical Process: Studies in the History and Psychology of Religion*, The Hague: Mouton, 37–61.

Reynolds, Frank E. (1987) Trajectories in Theravāda studies with special reference to the work of Stanley Tambiah, *Contributions to Indian Sociology* (new series) 21 (1): 113–21.

Samuel, Geoffrey (1993) *Civilized Shamans: Buddhism in Tibetan Society*, Washington; London: Smithsonian Institution Press.

Samuels, Jeffrey (2008) Is there merit in the milk powder? Pursuing punna in contemporary Sri Lanka, *Contemporary Buddhism* 9 (1): 123–47.

Schober, Julianne (2001) Venerating the Buddha's remains in Burma: from Solitary practice to the cultural hegemony of communities, *Journal of Burma Studies* 6: 111–40.

Schober, Julianne (2009) *Buddhist Manuscript Cultures: Knowledge, Ritual and Art*, ed. with Stephen C. Berkwitz and Claudia Brown, Abingdon and New York: Routledge.

Schober, Julianne (ed.) (1997) *Sacred Biography in the Buddhist Traditions of South and Southeast Asia*, Honolulu: University of Hawaii Press.

Schopen, Gregory (1997) *Bones, Stones and Buddhist Monks: Collected Papers on the Archaeology, Epigraphy and Texts of Monastic Buddhism in India*, Honolulu: University of Hawaii Press.

Seneviratne, H. L. (1999) *The Work of Kings: The New Buddhism in Sri Lanka*, Chicago: New University of Chicago Press.

Skilling, Peter (2007) Kings, sangha, and brahmans: ideology, ritual, and power in premodern Siam, in Ian Harris (ed.), *Buddhism, Power and Political Order*, Abingdon and New York: Routledge, 182–215.

Skilton, Andrew (1994) *A Concise History of Buddhism*, Birmingham: Windhorse.

Spiro, Melford E. (1971) *Buddhism and Society: A Great Tradition and Its Burmese Vicissitudes*, London: Allen and Unwin; orig. pub. Harper & Row, New York, 1970.

Swearer, Donald K. (1995) *The Buddhist World of Southeast Asia*, Albany: SUNY Press.

Swearer, Donald K. (2004) *Becoming the Buddha: The Ritual of Image Consecration in Thailand*, Princeton: Princeton University Press.

Tambiah, Stanley J. (1970) *Buddhism and the Spirit Cults in North-east Thailand*. Cambridge: Cambridge University Press.

Tambiah, Stanley J. (1976) *World Conqueror and World Renouncer: A Study of Buddhism and Polity in Thailand against a Historical Background*, Cambridge: Cambridge University Press.

Tambiah, Stanley J. (1977) The galactic polity: the structure of traditional kingdoms in Southeast Asia, *Annals of the New York Academy of Sciences* 293 (1): 69–97.

Tambiah, Stanley J. (1984) *The Buddhist Saints of the Forest and the Cult of Amulets*, Cambridge: Cambridge University Press.

Tiyavanich, Kamala (1997) *Forest Recollections: Wandering Monks in Twentieth-Century Thailand*, Honolulu: University of Hawaii Press.

Tiyavanich, Kamala (2003) *The Buddha in the Jungle*, Thailand: Chiang Mai; Seattle: Silkworm Books; Washington: University of Washington Press.

Weber, Max (1958) *The Religion of India: The Sociology of Hinduism and Buddhism* Glencoe, IL: Free Press; tr. Hans H. Gerth and Don Martindale of *Hinduismus und Buddhismus*, pub. as vol. 2 of the author's *Gesammelte Aufsätze zur Religionssoziologie*.

Wedemeyer, Christian K. (2001) Tropes, typologies and turnarounds: a brief genealogy of the historiography of tantric Buddhism, *History of Religions* 40 (3): 223–59.

Williams, Paul (1989) *Mahayana Buddhism: The Doctrinal Foundations*, New York: Routledge.

18

Sociology of Hinduism

Pratap Kumar Penumala

Introduction

Hinduism, unlike many other religions such as Judaeo-Christian and Islamic traditions, may be considered more a way of life because of its greater reliance on family traditions as opposed to a single unified doctrine, theology, institution and so on. The social reality does not always reflect what appears in the texts. However, Religionist scholars and Indologists generally relied far too heavily on the classical materials that are transmitted through Brahmanical texts. In discussing Hindu society, therefore, they tended to pay greater attention to notions of *Varna* and the fourfold division of Hindu society as mentioned in the *Rig Veda Samhita* and the *Manusmriti* (Laws of Manu). *Varna* literally means color, and as Brian K. Smith (1994) has shown, *Varna* as a hierarchical notion was a system that is also based on the notion that gods and the entire universe are classified in a hierarchical way. However, as he also identifies, in the early stages of Vedic society, the *Varna* system accounted only the twice born castes identified as Brahmanas (Priests), Kshatriyas (Warriors), and the Vaishyas (Commoners) very much like the Indo-European tripartite ideology as shown by Dumézil (1958a). In describing the Sociology of Hinduism, the *Varna* system was also taken far more seriously by many early social scientists dealing with Hindu society.

In this chapter on the Sociology of Hinduism, I shall first include some classicists who discussed Hindu society primarily through traditional categories of *Varna*, *Jati* (literally means birth group, and *Kula* (clan/family group) and the general Western notion of caste that was applied to Hindu society. Generally in most discussions, although *Varna* refers to a different type of classification, these terms are not clearly distinguished, and usually conflated with the term "caste." In this chapter, I shall also discuss the prospect of an Indian Sociology of Hinduism by pointing out the inadequacy of depending on the ideology of Brahmanism to understand Hindu caste as it is practiced in contemporary society. I shall then pay attention to the idea of a "dominant caste" and its role in contemporary Hindu society, especially in its political life. I shall then discuss the Hindu value of *Sannyasa* (asceticism) and *Bhakti* (devotion) and their role in shaping Hindu society. I shall then deal with what I refer to as "organized Hinduism" and its role in modern times. I finally deal with Hindus in their global context and discuss how the globalization of Hinduism has in some fundamental ways changed our understanding of modern Hindu society not only in India, but also in the Hindu diaspora. In all my discussion, my concern is to discuss Hindu society from a contemporary point of view and identify continuities and changes.

CLASSICISTS OF SOCIOLOGY OF HINDUISM

In this section, we shall note that most of the classical sociologists have turned their attention to the village and its basic social unit, caste (*Varna, Jati and Kula*). As Dumont recognizes, the emergence of a Sociology of India (I shall adapt it here as a Sociology of Hinduism as a default) certainly owes itself to the earlier work of Marcel Mauss (his analysis of Brahmana sacrifice – *Essay on Sacrifice*), Célestin Bouglé's essay on Indian castes (*Le Régime des Castes*), Mauss's work on *Borobudur*, Dumézil's work on Hindu *Varna* system, and Hocart's work on caste (Dumont 1970: 3). It is needless to labor the point that Indian Sociology owes significantly to Indology, or to use Dumont's own words "rests in part on the existence of Indology" (Dumont 1970: 1). But here, in identifying the influential figures for the emergence of a Sociology of Hinduism, I shall limit myself to a select few.

Not only M. N. Srinivas but many (David G. Mandelbaum, F. G. Bailey, McKim Marriot, Alan R. Beals, Marian W. Smith, and S. C. Dube, just to mention some) who contributed to his volume (Srinivas 1966a) paid a great deal of attention to the village not because there is any homogeneity among Indian villages, but on the contrary, as they differ so widely (Srinivas 1966a: 1–2). And it is in the village that these early anthropologists and sociologists found the institution of caste reflecting the microcosm of Hindu society. It is clear that by this time, perhaps thanks to the British census system in India, caste has been accepted as the most singularly important value of Hindu society, or as Srinivas put it, "an institution of prodigious strength" (Srinivas 1966a: 6). The work of M. N. Srinivas, however, introduces the notion of "dominant caste" – "A caste is dominant when it is numerically the strongest in the village or local area, and economically and politically exercises a preponderating influence. It need not be the highest caste in terms of traditional and conventional ranking of castes" (Srinivas 1966a: 7). He emphasizes the functional aspects of caste and demonstrates how they are linked through a system of shared economy and ritual (Srinivas 1966a: 27).

The notion of "dominant caste" not only underlines the many changes that have occurred in the practice of caste in recent years and it also problematizes the *Varna* system of classification. Srinivas noted that in the *Varna* model, although hierarchy and caste status is fixed, in practice caste groups constantly doubted each others claims of superiority. He gives the example of how Harijans (the name Gandhi gave to the Dalits/Untouchable castes in India) will not accept the cooked food of some Brahmin groups. He suggests, "[i]t is clear that vagueness or doubt regarding mutual position is not accidental or unimportant, but is an essential feature of caste as an ongoing system." Such doubt among castes about each others' sense of superiority, he says, "should not be regarded as exceptional in their behavior but as the typical product of a dynamic system in which there is some pushing and jostling in the attempt to go ahead" (Srinivas 1966b: 4). It is to nuance these changes that he deploys the notion of "Sanskritization" as an analytical concept to unpack the manner in which caste groups could move higher in the social hierarchy. He defines "Sanskritization" as "the process by which a "low" Hindu caste, or tribal or other group, changes its customs, ritual, ideology, and way of life in the direction of a high, and frequently, "twice-born" caste. Generally such changes are followed by a claim to a higher position in the caste hierarchy than that traditionally conceded to the claimant caste by the local community" (Srinivas 1966b: 6). But this process, he avers, is a complex one in which the dominant caste determines its social and political power through its landowning status.

This is a significant modern change from caste's fundamental affiliation to Hindu ritual. In other words, the modern transformation of caste seems to be defined more by its association with landownership than ritual hierarchy. A landowning Jat or Thakur in the Punjab might recognize the ritual superiority of the Brahmin but have claimed a higher secular status. Srinivas also emphasizes that "Sanskritization" did not always mean emulation of the Brahmanical model – "Thus if the locally dominant caste is Brahmin or Lingayat it will tend to transmit a Brahmanical model of Sanskritization, whereas if it is Rajput or Bania it will transmit Kshatriya or Vaishya models" (Srinivas 1966b: 14). But generally it is, in his thinking, from lower to higher order. To complete his analysis of caste changes and mobility, he deployed a supporting category, viz., "Westernization." He says, "[t]o catch up with the high castes, mere Sanskritization was not enough." For this reason the lower castes "became more determined to obtain Western education" (Srinivas 1966b: 91). He notes that in recent years many castes through higher education and economic power tended to claim higher caste status (e.g., Vellalas and Padyachis in Tamilnadu) (Srinivas 1966b: 94). He, however, did not entirely ignore the notions of purity and pollution that come to dominate in Dumont's work. He remarks that there is a greater pragmatism regarding the values of purity and pollution (Srinivas 1980: 195).

Despite the significant contributions made by M. N. Srinivas, Max Weber, and Louis Dumont in a sense set the stage for the Hindu sociological views that later scholars have come to either accept or reject. But there is little doubt that Srinivas' key notions of "dominant caste," "castes with landownership," "caste mobility" through "Westernization" and "Sanskritization" are embedded in both Dumont's work as well as in the work of many others, such as André Béteille. Weber's view on India and Hinduism received a good deal of criticism as well as appreciation. But one must concede to Weber for having created the idea of a "Sociology of Hinduism" which is part of his book title which dealt with Hinduism and Buddhism (Weber 1958b). In his typology of "world-rejection," viz., innerworldly *vs.* other worldly, mysticism *vs.* asceticism, mystical poet *vs.* ascetic poet, Robert Bellah (1980: 287) thinks that Weber locates the Hindu renunciation in the *bhakti* tradition of India. What Bellah is referring to is the idea that he deals with in the specific context of *bhakti* as a "personal inner relation of trust" (Weber 1958b: 307). It is here in the context of *bhakti* that he uses the expression "passionate inward devotion to the redeemer and his grace" (Weber 1958b: 307).

As a sociologist, Weber approaches Hinduism through caste, which he considers central to Hinduism. But the rigidity of caste lies in its inherent relationship to what he calls, "clan charisma." He says, "[t]he Hindu social order, to a large extent than anywhere else in the world, is organized in terms of the principle of *clan charisma*. "Charisma" means that an extraordinary, at least not generally available, quality adheres to a person." … And this "extraordinary quality adheres to sib members per se and not, as originally, to a single person" (Weber 1958b: 49). It is in this sense that Weber seems to think of caste as fundamentally a status group within which the leadership is passed down. Although he recognizes changes in the practice of caste, his organization of castes into the conventional four groups, viz., the Brahmins (priests), Kshatriyas (warriors), Vaishyas (traders/commoners) and Shudras (servants) betrays his dependency on the textual understanding of caste rather than actual field work. But what is more, he seems to take the *Varna* system, which betrays color, more seriously than other social scientists. He compares caste with race. He says, "[a]t best we can say that race or, better, the juxtaposition of racial differences and – this is sociologically decisive – of externally striking different racial types has been quite important for the development of the caste order in India" (Weber 1958b: 124). He goes on to say, "[t]he most striking contrasts in external appearance simply happens to be different skin color. Although the conquerors replenished their insufficient supply of women by taking women from among the conquered, color differences still prevented a fusion in the manner of the Normans and Anglo-Saxons" (Weber 1958b: 125). But the main point of Weber is that the intellectual soteriologies profiled in the Asian religions in general and in Hinduism in particular led to an otherworldly attitude conditioned by notions of *samsara* (transmigration) and *karma*[1] (Weber 1958b: 332). In other words, "[g]iven its world indifference, it could now assume the form of a flight from the world or, indeed, in an innerworldly manner, with, however, world-indifferent behavior: a protection against the world and one's own acts, not in and through both" (Weber 1958b: 332–3). Thus, for Weber caste remained a rigid institution.

Rejecting Weberian notion of individualism that is based on Western ideology, Dumont pays greater attention to the ideology of caste. In his characterization of (Hindu) India as *"hierarchicus"* and the West as *"equalis"* Dumont reinforced a structuralist view on India. For him, it is not so much caste itself, but the ideology of caste that seems more important. For this reason, he observes that in the notion of "dominant caste" in various parts of India, it follows the same pattern as the Brahmana–Kshatriya relationship (Dumont 1980). In order to understand Dumont, one has to not only read his most seminal work – *Homo Hierarchicus*, but also the essays that he himself collected in *Religion/Politics and History of India* (1980) as well as his volume on *German Ideology* (1994). In his work, Dumont makes two important assumptions – first, India is one. This unity is found, he says, "above all in ideas and values, it is therefore, deeper and less easily defined: on one hand it is social in the strictest sense, and this justifies our sociological perspective, it makes *Indian society as a whole* the true object of our study. On the other hand, this unity consists more in relations than isolated elements" (Dumont 1994: 5). Elsewhere, he refers to it as "holism" (Dumont 1986: 25). It is not the unity but diversity which is illusory for him. Second, as reflected in his later work on *Aequalis*, and in particular on the basis of his analysis of Karl Philip Moritz's work on aesthetics, he maintains his unequivocal stand on the idea of the "whole." For him it is a "self-sufficient whole" and in the chain of hierarchical levels each level finds its finality in the level above it (Dumont 1994: 79). Once we understand this, his rejection of Weberian individualism makes sense. It is all the more important for him to reject this individualism in Germany itself. For him a German, unlike his French counterpart, is one who thinks, "I am essentially a German, and I am a man through my being a German." "[T]he German speaks of something essential" (Dumont 1994: 3).

Perhaps, Dumont must be credited for having located Indian caste squarely in (Hindu) religion unlike De Nobili, Max Müller, and more importantly Max Weber – all of whom treated caste as a social institution or as an extreme form of Western idea of class. He also rejects the comparison of caste with race as it happens in South Africa (Dumont 1980: 24–7). For him the counter-category for equality is not necessarily inequality, but hierarchy which underlines "a certain consensus of values, a certain hierarchy of ideas, things and people" and this is "independent of natural inequalities or the distribution of power" (Dumont 1980: 20).

Central to the notion of hierarchy is the distinction, first, of purity and pollution which is not based on hygiene, but on religious grounds (Dumont 1980: 47). Secondly, he separated status and power which are often confused in the caste hierarchy, as Srinivas himself separated before him. Even though Dumont agrees that caste might have been influenced by the *Varna* system, it is more correct to say that it is the pure and impure "relationship established in the varnas between priesthood and royalty" that is at the core of caste hierarchy (Dumont 1980: 74). He is, therefore, dubious about the program of "Sanskritization" that the Arya Samaj[2] introduced. The untouchables in reality found out that their status did not change even after giving up degrading occupations, nor did the castes which made exorbitant claims about their status in the census reports obtained any "recognition in their environment" (Dumont 1980: 230). The central idea that Dumont pushed in his work on India is to suggest that caste status based on ritual or religious purity does not necessarily imply economic and political power. In his thinking, therefore, status and power must be separated.

Although André Bétteile in later years comes to critique Dumont for such structural reinforcement of India as "*hierachicus*" and the West as "*equalis*," in his earlier work (Béteille 1965) (which was published a year before Dumont's *Homo Hierarchicus* appeared in 1966) he demonstrated not only the increasing isolation of the Brahmin community in Tamilnadu from political and even economic power but equally importantly the increasingly violent and turbulent relationships between the land-owning castes and the Adi-Dravidas (Dalits/Untouchables) seem to reinforce a similar hierarchical pattern that existed between the Brahmin and their non-Brahmin tenants (who have since independence come to own land). In other words, the very ideology of purity and pollution that determined the relations between the Brahmin and his non-Brahmin tenant also determined the relationship between the new land-owning castes and their Dalit laborers. Nevertheless, Béteille's work on Sripuram in Tamilnadu departs both from Weber and Dumont in significant ways. With regard to Weber, he disagrees with the Weberian idea that castes are "status groups" and constitute homogenous communities (Weber 1958b). But Béteille argues "[i]t should be pointed out that castes constitute communities only at the local or narrow regional level. Thus, the Shri Vaishnavas of Sripuram, or even all the Brahmins of that village, can be spoken of as a community. It would be inexact, however, to speak of all Brahmins, or even all Shri Vaishnavas, as constituting a community" (Béteille 1965: 188).

The key contribution of Béteille is in defining caste in terms of what he calls "styles of life." He says, "[p]roperty and occupation enter as important elements in the style of life of a status group or community" (Béteille 1965: 188). But these elements do not necessarily unite the status groups. He, therefore, points out that "[t]oo much diversity of occupation or economic position may, however, disrupt the unity of a status group" (Béteille 1965: 188). It is here, he also moves away from Dumont's fundamental assumptions of purity and pollution as key operational categories embedded in caste. In this regard it is instructive to note a review comment made by Schwartzberg (a Geography specialist) – "One of the difficulties in venturing a judgment on *Homo Hierarchicus* is that it deals essentially with the ideological, and therefore nonmeasurable, foundations of a traditional, but fast-changing, society" (Schwartzberg 1973: 255).

Now, looking at both Dumont's position that separated status and power on the one hand, and Béteille's position that added economic concern as an important element in caste changes on the other, one needs to concede a grain of truth in Dumont's emphasis on status in relation to caste hierarchy. In his work on Bisipara village and witch-hunt, Bailey underlines the point that a witch-hunt is often a way to bring the person of Washermen caste back to his caste status despite his personal wealth (Bailey 1994). However, what it also underlines is that it is not enough for a low caste person to become wealthy in his personal life. When a caste as a whole becomes economically and politically powerful, then they claim to higher status, as it happened in the case of Nadars of Tamilnadu in the nineteenth century. Béteille's emphasis on economic factors, therefore, needs to be understood in relation to caste as a whole and not as individuals.

It is clear from these early accounts that caste has been the preoccupation of most Hindu sociological theories. Notwithstanding its presence in other religious communities (e.g., Sikh, Muslim, and Christian) it is seen as an inherent notion of Hinduism. On the extreme side, in the Weberian sense, "without caste there is no Hindu" (Weber 1958b: 29). Perhaps, it is better to say – "without caste there is no Indian," if one wants to include all other religions that exist in India. Notions of caste, *Jati*, and *Varna* have been linked in fundamentally religious ways. These early studies, especially those by Western sociologists and anthropologists, of course, tended to locate the caste discourse in the larger Western discourse of individualism, capitalism and socialism. However, can we isolate from these discussions what might be peculiarly Indian concerns in the Sociology of Hinduism?

PROSPECT OF AN INDIAN SOCIOLOGY OF HINDUISM

If Dumont was gracious enough to grant India a Sociology of India for which the first and foremost condition was to establish "a proper relation between it and classical Indology" (Dumont 1970: 2), what might be the relations that the Indian scholars would be concerned about in developing an Indian Sociology of Hinduism? Of course, it is ingenuous to think that one could separate the discourse of Indian

Sociology of Hinduism entirely from its Western roots. After all, both Sociology and Indology were products of a Western intellectual engagement with the other, that is, the non-European other. Nevertheless, we might endeavor to find some unique Indian concerns that may separate the Indian Sociology of Hinduism from its Western discourse.

In an effort to find specific Indian concerns, we cannot continue to rely on *Varna* based or predominantly Brahmanical ideas as our basis. For this reason, I find Brian K. Smith's recent work on *Classifying the Universe* (1994) as well as the work of Lawrence Babb (*Divine Hierarchy*, 1975) less helpful as they both in their respective ways reinforce the view that Brahman continues to be the best analytical tool to interpret caste hierarchy. Notwithstanding the numerous field-work based studies on Indian society that have demonstrated the alienation that exists between the *Varna* system and the caste system practiced in Hindu society, scholarship in some Indological and religionist writings seem to continue to assume the caste origins in the *Varna* system. While Babb's work argues for the pre-eminent place of Brahman priest in society when he says, "[h]is (Brahman) presence constitutes a two fold affirmation. His use of fully elaborated textual styles lends prestige to the family and confirms the nominal identity of the deity being worshipped; his presence also suggests the imagery of kingly sacrificial sponsorship. Also, by merely entering such a household the Brahman is stating, in effect, that the pollution of the household is sufficiently low to be innocuous to him. This is a direct validation of the high status of the family" (Babb 1975: 196). Smith's point that the *Varna* system that the Brahman's devised not only explicitly articulates "the social aspects" but it "projected itself into cosmological, supernatural, natural, and ritual contexts; the structure of society was mirrored in the structure of reality in all its dimensions" (Smith 1994: 49) is in the same vein. Smith's final comment further reinforces it – "[t]he Veda is the Brahmin's account of the world; it was written in part to establish and promote Brahmin interests; and while it certainly represents the ideals and hopes of the Brahmin community, it very probably distorts the historical, political, and social realities of Vedic India "as it was" in order to do so" (Smith 1994: 325).

Both Babb and Smith underline the ideological and social pre-eminence of the Brahman. But underlining the ideological pre-eminence, both of them fail to take into account the limitations of the category *Varna*, and also the internal divisions of the Brahmans. Veena Das's analysis of both *Varna* and *Jati* based on the *Dharmaranya Purana* is illuminating. She finds the binary oppositions posited by both Dumézil (1958a) and Dumont (1980) in the *Varna* scheme – the opposition between the Brahman and others – are not meaningful in society. For instance, she points out, "[t]he myths clearly say that the relation between the king and the Brahman does not alter, regardless of whether the king is a Kshatriya or Shudra. Therefore, it is clear that the four *varna* categories are not homologous entities" (Das 1982: 86).

But as André Béteille pointed out in his study, we need to take account of the notion of "dominant caste" more seriously to understand not only the increasing isolation of the Brahmin as a social and political force, but also the point made by Dumont that ritual or religious purity does not imply social, economic and political power. And McKim Marriot's (1955) important study on Indian villages also demonstrates that even when the illiterate villagers appropriated the Brahman gods, they

are "most attached, I would estimate, to the worship of four local godlings of no
refinement whatsoever." He also points out how they totally reverse the Sanskritic
"Gobardhan" (Go + Vardhan = Cow Nourisher) worship as "Gobar + dhan"
(Cowdung Wealth). This is what he calls Parochialization. It is worth noting here
that McKim Marriot proposed the notion of "Parochialization" to explain the
"downward devolution of great-traditional elements and their integration
with little-traditional elements." Instead of Srinivas' "Westernization" and "Sanskritization" notions, Marriot deploys notions of "Universalization" and "Parochialization." "Parochialization is a process of localization, of limitation upon the
scope of intelligibility, of deprivation of form, or reduction to less systematic and
less reflective dimensions" (Marriot 1955: 200).[3] The points made by Béteille,
Dumont and Marriot need to be taken seriously in our search for a sociology of
Hinduism.

Unless we accept the fundamental social changes that have gone on both in the
pre-European as well as in the post-European period of India, we cannot meaningfully write the Sociology of Hinduism that is relevant for today. Central to these
fundamental social changes is the control of land and based on that control the
emergence of the social elites in India. Bloomfield argued, "[w]e must recognize that
in many areas and certainly in the peripheral areas with which I am primarily concerned, there was considerable social mobility in pre-European times. Certainly the
British presence affected the direction and possibly the speed of movement, most
directly by providing new opportunities for economic gain, but it is significant that
the groups which took advantage of these new opportunities did so very largely in
terms of their old methods of action" (Bloomfield 1971: 61). The emergence of
"bhadralok" (social elite) in Bengal with their acquired social status on a par with
Brahmin, Baidya and Kayastha is only one such example. The sweeping social
changes during the nineteenth and the early twentieth centuries need also to be
understood in the competition between the so called "old elites" – the *bhadralok*
from Bengal, Brahmins in Maharashtra, and Brahmins in Tamilnadu, who were
initially the recipients of the benefits from their association with the colonial interests of the British – and the new elite emerging from Uttar Pradesh, Bihar and
Gujarat, who are non-Brahmanical counter elites. It is the new elite, with their
association with land control, who began to emerge as a political elite (Bloomfield
1971: 68ff.).

Therefore, in the search for the prospects for an Indian Sociology of Hinduism,
notions of dominant caste, social change, family and kinship relations will certainly
dominate the Indian scholarly attention. But in this search for an Indian Sociology
of Hinduism, one must first move beyond the cultural determinism that has for so
long reiterated the notion that Hindu society can be essentially understood through
the rigid categories of *Varna* and *Jati*, *Karma*, and *Samsara* albeit they are useful
backdrops of the past. Rather than being fixated by Weberian and Dumontian
models that have privileged classical cultural notions, one perhaps needs to take
note of the relations between land, politics and economics and the social changes
that they have been triggered in Hindu society. In this regard, it is equally important,
as Nathan Katz rightly pointed out in his study of caste in relation to Cochin Jews,
to "re-examine our presuppositions about the ideological framework of caste" (Katz
1989: 56).

It is even more important to recognize the economic interests of groups that created mobility in Hindu society not only socially, but more importantly in religious practice. The reshaping of Hinduism by modern Hindu gurus, movements and transnational movement of Hindus need to be accounted for, as well as the forces that organized Hinduism as a national social phenomenon, such as the Arya Samaj and the Rashtriya Svayamsevak Sang and the various Hindutva movements, need to be analyzed. For they move us beyond the cultural determinism, that is looking for explanations of Hindu society solely through its archaic cultural forms and enables us to see how Hindu society in modern times used its freedom to choose and become globally integrated. As T. N. Madan says, "[i]t is in the interplay between cultural tradition and individual life experience that choice making emerges as the condition and guarantor of human freedom and dignity" (Madan 1988: 140).

CASTE AND POLITICS

Crucial, therefore, to documenting the Sociology of Hinduism is the role Hinduism and its various social denominations have played and continue to play. For this, we need to understand the intrinsic relationship between caste and politics in Indian democracy. For it is here that Hinduism and India's political commitment for secularism come face to face. Dr B. R. Ambedkar, who, despite his low caste background, rose to the position of being the chairman of the committee that drafted India's constitution, located the most fundamental problem of Indian politics in the caste system and he located it squarely in the heart of Hinduism. He said, "Caste is a phenomenon peculiar to Hindu India"; "Caste has done enormous harm to the country"; "Caste is opposed to democratic concept" (Ambedkar 1970: 98). This system that is so peculiar to Hindu India has even infected the Muslim and Christian communities. And for this reason, he called for the annihilation of caste by means of legislating the institution of priesthood and Brahmanism. For in his view, "Brahmanism is the poison which has spoiled Hinduism." And he went on to say, "You will succeed in saving Hinduism if you will kill Brahmanism." He even invoked the support of Arya Samajists in this venture (Ambedkar 1970: 98).[4] Gandhi replied to Ambedkar's views by reiterating that "[c]aste has nothing to do with religion. It is a custom whose origin I do not know and do not need to know for the satisfaction of my spiritual hunger" (Gandhi's reply was also published in Ambedkar 1970: 107).

The enormous role of caste in modern Indian politics, therefore, necessitated Indian sociologists to clarify its relationship to politics. In describing the relationship between caste and politics, Kothari emphasizes three points – first, those who are arguing for the disappearance of caste from politics "lack any clear conception of either the nature of politics or the nature of the caste system." Second, those who view politics as an instrument of caste misunderstand "the developmental reality which consists not in any approximation to a pre-conceived framework of antecedent society, but in the changing interactions of the constituent elements in a dynamic situation." Third, those who want to emphasize the autonomous status of both caste and politics tend to explain "empirical phenomena in terms of a unified conceptual model that enables neat generalizations to be imposed on a complex reality"

(Kothari 1970: 4–6). For Kothari as a political sociologist, it is "not so much what happens to caste system as a whole as a result of its involvement in the political process but rather what structures and networks of relationships enter into the political process and how" (Kothari 1970: 7). Whether it is the Mahars of Maharashtra, Kshatriyas of Gujarat, Nadars of Tamilnadu, Reddis and Kammas of Andhra Pradesh, political sociologists generally dissociated caste from religion and pondered upon it as a key element in politics and economics. At the same time, Indian sociologists generally looked at caste as an institution that has undergone significant social changes – that this insight is largely due to the influence of Marxian approach to Indian society is not surprising. But as Khare remarks, generally Indian sociologists and anthropologists gave substantial focus to caste perhaps largely due to the influence of Dumont and as a reaction to his work. But later focus of Indian scholars shifted to the postcolonial discourses (Khare 2006: xiii).

ASCETICISM AND BHAKTI

If caste, Jati and family affinity as key values underscored Hindu sociology, two other key notions have, in a fundamental way, turned the tables around in Hindu society. These are – asceticism and *bhakti*. Here, I discuss them as two values in Hindu society and not merely as religious phenomena, not withstanding their religious significance. In a sense, they can be viewed as attitudes towards society and not just towards their transcendental goals. Both *bhakti* and ascetic attitudes not only reinforce the traditional religious practices, but they also radically transform them in ways that call into question the traditional social structures within which such religious practices are undertaken.

It is obvious to students of Hinduism that asceticism as a social institution has been accommodated as a fourth stage in the Brahmanical order of society. The significance of asceticism as a social value can be seen not so much because it is observed strictly in Hindu society in modern times as final stage in ones life, but because of its pervasiveness in the attitudes of Hindus. The many Hindu gurus, reformers and philosophers have not only emphasized it as an important value in society, but a number of them followed it. Shankara of the non-dual Vedanta philosophy of the eighth century and Ramanjua of the Srivaishnava tradition of the eleventh century are good examples of the earlier period. These are succeeded by a number of later examples, such as Kabir, Ramananda, and in more recent years many modern gurus, who have reinforced the value of ascetic attitudes. Many leaders of the Hindu reform movements, such as the Swami Dayananda Saraswati, Swami Ramakrishna Paramahamsa and Swami Vivekananda and in recent times Swami Prabhupada of the Hare Krishna movement and Satya Sai Baba and many others have set examples for such mode of life. Almost all of these reformers and gurus have placed materialism as a threat to the moral fiber of Hindu society. In other words, asceticism is understood as a counter value to materialism. Nirad C. Chaudhuri put it well when he said – "all the blindness that is to be found in respect of a life which will offer us a sense of fulfillment and happiness comes in the first instance from our incapacity to criticize life and next from a sordid materialism" (Chaudhuri 1970: 16).

Now and again, virtuosos like Gandhi, the man considered responsible for Indian independence from the British, and others could emerge as examples of such life style that reinforces an ascetic attitude. If the value of renunciation and the value of pragmatism are pitched against each other, what one might find is that renunciation remains an ideal in Hindu society, and one does not need to realize the ideal but sufficient to approximate to it. In other words, pragmatism embraces renunciation and domesticates it in society. As Milton Singer says, "[n]ot all householders live up to this theory, but one does meet engineers, lawyers, doctors who phrase their retirement in these terms, and younger men who walk out of their jobs in order to engage in more "spiritual" preoccupations" (Singer 1956: 83). In dealing with asceticism as a social value in modern Hindu society, one also needs to take account of the modern emergence of women who renounce family life and take up the roles of renunciants, and it is also here that one needs to see the changing status of Hindu women. Meena Khandelwal's account of Ananda Mata and Baiji in her work on *Women in Ochre Robes* (2004) provides an insight into how Hindu women are looking to other role models than epic characters of Sita and in particular looking for them in real society. Asceticism is one social value that Hindu women found an appropriate way to change social perceptions of women. Denton's field work in Benares on women ascetics explored not merely the religious and spiritual aspects, but rather more importantly the "social and personal roots of religiosity" (Denton 2004: 166).

So, for as long as we treat renunciation as a religious value, it defies its accountability in society. In the light of his research on Cochin Jews, Nathan Katz cautions – "Asceticism is such a familiar topic to scholars of religion. However, this research compels us to ask whether standard treatments of the subject have not been overly spiritualized. By exclusive concern with its spiritual orientation, do we perhaps fail to recognize asceticism's very down-to-earth meanings and rewards?" (Katz 1989: 56). He underlines the aspects of human motivation and behavior as important rather than spiritual motives. In particular, he identifies "status" as a motivation in asceticism as a practice (Katz 1989: 58). Here lies the fact that in Hindu society, while most Hindus may not be willing to renounce their family and possessions, they look up to others who are willing to do so, and confer up on them the status of being a virtuoso.

If asceticism thus confers on an individual a special status in society, *bhakti* as an attitude towards life equally reinforces this special status in Hindu society. From earlier times, *bhakti* provided an effective means to transcend social barriers both for Hindu men and women. Some of the medieval proponents of *bhakti*, such as Ramanjua (who was referred to earlier) engaged in social reform in his time by allowing lower caste converts to become priests in some of the Vaishnava temples. As *bhakti*, as an attitude, embraced ordinary folk it naturally went beyond caste boundaries. Even sacred places, pilgrimage centers, rivers, and temples became relatively important and not absolutely necessary. In other words, it relativized the normative social order. In doing so, it "neither tried to change the society nor alter the worldly pursuits" (Yocum 1973: 8). The *Bhagavad Gita* in two places urges the devotee to perform actions without concern (Gita 3:30, 18:66). The Srivaishnava commentator Ramanuja, in both places, reads it as not giving up actions but as follows – "[w]hile performing all *dharmas* – i.e., *karma-*, *jnana-* and *bhakti yoga*"

(Van Buitenen 1968: 174). In other words, it is an attitude that subsumes all actions without any attachment. A person who displays this sort of attitude is certainly seen as someone who is elevated to a special status in society, a virtuoso. That is why, the Gita's statement in 18:66 asking the devotee to give up all attachment, is preceded by an important caveat – "I shall tell it for your own good, for you are profoundly dear to me" (Gita 18:65). In other words, the devotee who displays this kind of *bhakti* as outlined in the Gita, is specially treated by God and this confers on him a special status in society.

In this sense, the Hindu view of a *sannyasin* and a *bhakta* elevate them to the position of virtuoso. They do not refrain from societal involvement, but by their involvement radically alter the social dynamics and relations. The Indian *gurus* and elevated teachers occupy this special position in Hindu society. By merely seeing them or being seen by them can confer merit on an ordinary person. This seeing (*darshan*) deepens the bond with the *guru*, says Kakar (1985: 850). In fact, the mutual viewing between the *guru* and the devotee is "a precondition for the devotee's salvation" (Kakar 1985: 846). He suggests, "[i]n practice, in the lives of a vast majority of the sect [Radha Saomi] members, the meditational regimen of the *yoga* takes secondary place to guru *bhakti* which is not a mere intellectual acceptance and respect for the guru as a teacher and guide. For one, the guru referred to is the *Satguru* ("True Master") who is the embodiment of the divine and is in fact the Supreme Being himself" (Kakar 1985: 844). The idea of the special place of the teacher/*guru* due to his special qualities as an interpreter of Hinduism and not just the techniques of interpretation is documented well (Lubin 2002). The role of the *gurus* and *sannyasins* in Hindu society, therefore, acquires an important significance for us to understand and document on Hindu sociology.

"ORGANIZED HINDUISM"[5] IN INDIA

So far I have tried to look at the larger milieu of the Hindu society through some of the issues of contemporary social significance. The issues that I dealt with so far only emphasized the complexity of the overall narrative of the Sociology of Hinduism. In the midst of these complexities in presenting the Sociology of Hinduism, we also need to pay attention to how Hinduism came to be organized in recent decades or even a century or more. The nineteenth century witnessed a range of such attempts to organize Hinduism and its society to present a more unified look about it. Brahmo Samaj, Arya Samaj and the Ramakrishna Mission certainly deserve mention in this regard. But to recount their stories at great length is certainly beyond the scope of this chapter. What is useful, however, is to identify what they have achieved toward "organizing Hinduism" in the new context. Did these early experiments achieve the goal of organizing Hinduism? Daniel Gold (1994) has provided useful account of the role of the Arya Samaj leading up to RSS (Rashtriya Svayamsevak Sangh) movement and their appropriation of Arya Samaj ideas in organizing Hinduism.

Although "Organized Hinduism" has its roots in the elite literati beginning from the Brahmo Samaj, under the Arya Samaj this phenomenon became "solidly established among the upper-middle classes." And with the RSS involvement, it became firmly established in the lower middle class and became less elite (Gold 1994: 537). Hinduism became organized by many different modern Hindu movements since those early attempts (hence Gold refers to them as "Organized Hinduisms"). However, under the leadership of the RSS organized Hinduism became more and more militant and radically politicized. Notwithstanding the disagreements between Sarvarkar of Hindu Mahasabha and the RSS leadership in the 1930s, the RSS came to align itself with political parties, first with the Bharatiya Jana Sangh Party (popularly known as Jana Sangh) and later with its successor, the Bharatiya Janata Party (Gold 1994: 572). However, their influence is perhaps more limited to the Hindi speaking North Indian belt (Gold 1994: 573). This increasing politicization of "organized Hinduism" in contemporary India sharply conflicted with the various minority groups in varied degrees. In different parts of India this polarization took different manifestations such as Hindu-Sikh conflict in Punjab, and Hindu–Muslim and Hindu–Christian tensions throughout India. For instance, in Kerala State Christians, with their higher social and economic status, presented socio-economic challenge to Hindus, whereas elsewhere the Christians, though presented a challenge in numerical terms, in socio-economic terms they remained subordinate to the political domination of the dominant Hindu castes. Nevertheless, as Gold points out, "even though the political situation of the eighties has highlighted organized Hindu response to Sikh separatism, the continuing presence of Muslims in India is likely to appear as a more genuine problem to Hindu Nationalists – and may indeed prove to be one that is more lasting" (Gold 1994: 579).

The attacks on Mumbai by unidentified Muslim group/s (which started on the night of Wednesday November 26, 2008) have highlighted Gold's point. It is worth underlining that as the body of the chief of Anti-Terrorism Squad of Mumbai was being carried away for its final cremation, thousands of Hindus who were in the procession shouted anti-Pakistan and anti-Muslim slogans and one of the Indian newspapers commented that this incident would certainly tilt the next national elections more in favor of the Hindutva led BJP. Notwithstanding the fact that mainstream Mulsim organizations led by All-India Muslim Majlis-e-Mushawarat, the umbrella body of Muslim organizations categorically condemned the incidents, the looming Hindutva response in the succeeding days and months cannot be underestimated. The call of the Muslim organizations to rise above politics to "unitedly face this threat and refrain from using it for petty political ends" (*The Hindu*, Nov. 28, 2008) will be tested in the complex Hindu–Muslim relations in India. In this context it is instructive to note what Sudhir Kakar says, "In both Hindus and Muslims, riot-time interactions deviated substantially from the code that governs their actions during normal times" (Kakar 1996: 132).

GLOBAL HINDUISM

What I am referring to as Global Hinduism is closely linked to what Daniel Gold (1994) has called "Organized Hinduism." Significant social changes can be seen among the Hindu diaspora in comparison with their counterparts in India. In an important sense, incorporation of the variety of accounts of Hinduism from the diaspora would no longer make caste as an *apriori* condition for the practice of

Hinduism. The rise of a new Hindu identity, transnational networks among Hindus across ethnic boundaries, would certainly change the face of Hinduism. Significant caste mobility, homogenization of linguistic groups across ritual and dietary practices have also occurred in the context of the diaspora which I have shown in my earlier work on the Hindus in South Africa (Kumar 2000: 1–13). Most of the accounts in the early diaspora communities indicate a greater collaboration between groups across caste and linguistic boundaries in establishing places of worship and a common Hindu identity. But Clothey points out that in places like Singapore, as individual caste numbers increased due to subsequent immigrations, there was a tendency to form caste or language based temples and shrines and associations (Clothey 2006). Due to difference in immigration patterns both in South Africa and other former European colonies in Africa, Asia and many Indian ocean islands, Hinduism is characterized by what might be described as popular or village forms such as worship of the village goddesses (e.g., Mariamman and Druapadiamman). The Sri Lankan form of Tamil Hinduism is dominant in Southeast Asia (Malaysia, Singapore). This has perhaps to do with the refugee policies of these countries in relation to Sri Lankan refugees.

The immigration patterns of the Hindus in the UK, Australia, continental Europe, and North America are very different from the early immigrations to various nineteenth century colonies. After the partition of India, a significant number of Hindus arrived in the UK, largely Punjabis and some Gujaratis who were later joined by the East African Gujarati merchants. Places like Southall and Leicester in the UK strong presence of Hindus is found. British Hinduism is generally dominated by the Gujarati and Punjabi Hindu practices with a minority of South Indian Hindu elements being present (Vertovec 2000). On the other hand, the Continental Europe is dominated by the Sri Lankan Hinduism, drawn mainly from its former Tamil roots. As such, while in Britain the Swaminarayan temples are very conspicuous, the Sri Lankan Saiva/Murukan and Mariamman worship practices are more common in the continental Europe. Sociologically speaking this would mean that those who represent Hinduism in the UK are of North Indian background whereas the Hindu views in the continental Europe are represented by the Sri Lankan Tamil Hindus. However, in the Netherlands, the Hindustanis from Surinam, who immigrated to the Netherlands after its independence, are more visible Hindus (Van Der Burg 2004). In terms of the social changes among Hindus in the UK, Eleanor Nesbit pointed out that while general association of vegetarianism with Hinduism is not common, conversion from non-vegetarianism to vegetarianism is not necessarily depended on religious values (Nesbit 1999: 397ff.). Such pragmatism in the observance of religious rituals in UK is also noted by Kim Knott (Knott 1986: 89).

The immigration to North America is relatively a recent phenomenon and consists mostly of the educated middle-class Hindus. Kurien points out that the percentage of Hindus among the total number of Indian Americans is between 45–65% (Kurien 2004: 368). A number of former East African Hindus did settle in the United States and Canada and the UK as well as Australia. The UK, Australia, and North America have, therefore, experienced Hindus who were twice immigrants, either from East Africa or in the last ten years increasingly from South Africa. Hindus in Australia, however, began to appear since the mid nineteenth century as part of the coolie labor system/indenture system (Hartney 2004: 437ff.). But, in Australia it is conspicuously dominated by Sri Lankan Tamil Hinduism.

The gradual increase in the appearance of Hindu temples in Australia, UK, continental Europe, and North America has had important consequences for both the Hindus in the daispora as well as for the host societies. It created both tensions and positive images of Hinduism in the West. The nature of Hinduism in these countries largely depended on the various Hindu communities that settled in these places.

In Australia, there was initially a strong objection to Hindu temples appearing. Objections ranged from more noise to intrusion into the White society. The "Scenic Protection Lands" Act was used to block the construction of the Hindu temple (Hartney 2004: 447). The public appearance of Hinduism in the form of temples in Germany (Luchesi 2004) and in Norway (Jacobsen 2006) seems less resisted. In fact, in both places incorporation of local public figures such as politicians and bureaucrats into the Hindu ritual practice is noteworthy. It is interesting to note that in the Murukan temple in Hamm, Germany a native German man was accepted as an assistant priest (Wilke (2006: 261). The resistance to the presence of Hindus in the UK has been captured by Richman (1999) and by Weller (2004). Weller's study in particular highlighted the fact that both Hindus and Sikhs experienced fairly high levels of discrimination in the UK. This is attributed to the fact that Hindus and Sikhs are "visible minorities" (Weller 2004: 486) and the continental European context perhaps still has not reached the stage of "visible minority" status. But in more recent years, Hindus seem to enjoy relatively better relations than their Muslim counterparts largely due to the impact of 9/11 and the subsequent attempts by the Hindu Council of UK to distance themselves from their South Asian Muslim counterparts and at the same time aligning themselves with the mainstream British society. In North America, there is not a great deal of reporting of negative sentiment toward the appearance of Hindus. It is perhaps due to the fact that they are more dispersed throughout North America, with the exception of Toronto and Vancouver in Canada and New Jersey in the United States.

Linked to the idea whether the Hindu presence has been effectively incorporated into the mainstream society or not, especially in Western societies, is the fact that most of the ritual places such as temples are located either in the relatively remote places and away from the mainstream society or in modified former industrial buildings. In relation to the idea of sacred space in Hinduism, some scholars have suggested that in the context of diasporic Hinduism, India is no longer exclusive in claiming Hindu sacred places. Many among the diaspora consider many local places, rivers and so on as sacred for them, e.g., a lake in the outskirt of Oslo city in Norway (Jacobsen 2004). But what is also important to take into account is the location of these sacred sites in the West – for example in Norway the "[t]he Sivasubramanyar Alayam is situated close to the edge of the city where the forest begins" (Jacobsen 2004: 144); in Germany a number of shrines were built inside the converted houses – "Outside there was normally no indication except may be an unobtrusive sign" (Luchesi 2004: 120); one of the largest Swaminarayan temples in New Jersey is built in the industrial area of Woodbridge by converting an existing industrial building. If we contrast this scenario to the classical locations of sacred places in Hinduism, temples are usually the centre of the towns and villages rather than outside the villages. Only the non-Brahmanical shrines and temples are built on the outskirt of the villages. The Hindu sacred spaces in the diaspora context certainly reverse the conventional Hindu orthodox views. For here, there are no conventional Hindu structures, such as caste, ritual leadership, to sustain a classical notion. Although, Hinduism is now placed on the global map as a world religion, ethnically speaking it has to content itself as one of the many minority religions in the West.

As a minority religion, nevertheless, it developed effective strategies to exert its influence in the West – by claiming moral and spiritual superiority, a claim that goes back to the early Hindu reformers such as Vivekananda. One of the important teachings of the Swaminarayans, especially to those who are living in the West is – "concentrate on leading a moral life whilst doing what you are going to do there. Never get involved in consuming liquor or flesh. Don't think we are inferior to the Americans; compared to them we are morally superior ... Don't forget your dharma. You should never forget your background wherever you are living" (Brear 1996: 222). Secondly, by ostentatiously decorating their temples and making them visibly attractive, the Hindus seem to enrich the rainbow colors in the West as it increasingly becomes multi-cultural and multi-religious. Whether or not these strategies have worked to their advantage varies from place to place.

While the issue of "Organized Hinduism" largely dealt within the context of sub-continental politics and religious tensions, in various degrees those issues do seem to affect the Global Hindus in the diaspora context. In particular, the Hindu–Muslim tensions are not limited to South Asia, as the terrorist crisis was unfolding in Mumbai (started on the night of Wednesday November 26, 2008) one of the Indian newspapers (*Indian Express*, Nov. 28, 2008) was already speculating that the terrorists in the Mumbai attack were probably British citizens of Pakistani origins. But the only gunman who was captured is reported to have disclosed that they were all Pakistani citizens and trained in Pakistan. While the Hindu–Muslim relations of South Asian context impact on the Hindu diaspora, the rise of Hindu nationalism needs also to be understood in the context of the ideology of multiculturalism also. In North America, Kurien has pointed that the ideology of multiculturalism has certainly exacerbated the Hindu militant nationalism (Kurien 2004). She points up that "[a]lthough often overlooked in the literature on immigrants and multiculturalism, within the sociology of religion, it is now well understood that religion and religious institutions often play a central role in the process of ethnic formation, particularly for immigrants to the United States" (Kurien 2004: 366).

It is for this reason, the various forms of Reform-Hindu groups and the modern *guru* based Hinduisms, coupled with the growing number of Hindu temples that have played a vital role in shaping Global Hinduism in the West need to be accounted for. Additionally and perhaps equally importantly, we need to take into account the earlier transportation of various forms of Hinduism to places in South East Asia. In particular the Hinduism presence today in Burma, Thailand, Laos, Sumatra, Java, and Cambodia and also Sri Lanka in South Asia needs to be accounted for. Linking Global Hinduism with the earlier Hindu presence will further help us understand the transnational dimension of Global Hinduism. Stanley Tambia had hinted on the prospects of transnational Hinduism. He suggested that transnational Hinduism need not be based on a symbolic link to homeland but there are "decentered" and "lateral connections" between global Hindus (Tambia 2002: 332). It is, however, the twice migrants for the most part who created the transnational networks among Hindus who led to the creation of "Global Organization of People of Indian Origin" (GOPIO). Although majority of this organization are Hindus, it is open to all Indians overseas.

In dealing with the Global Hinduism, we need to account for three more important factors. Babb has identified three distinct styles of modern Hinduism – the Radha Saomi, the Brahmakumaris and the Satya Sai Baba (Babb 1987). But here I wish to focus on two others coupled with the Satya Sai movement that Babb had already mentioned. They are – the Swaminarayan (Bochasanwasi Shri Akshar Purushottama Sanstha) movement and the Hare Krishna movement (International Society for Krishna Consciousness). The growing transnational nature of the Hindu society and the push towards freeing Hinduism from its ethnicity are reflected in these two important sociological phenomena that the modern Hindu Sociology has to take into account. While the Swaminarayans have created a transnational, but ethnically oriented Hindu movement in the West by emphasizing its unique identity as Gujarati, notwithstanding its efforts to give up caste restrictions (Brear 1996; Dwyer 2004; Williams 1998) the Hare Krishna (International Society for Krishna Consciousness) and the Satya Sai Baba movements have created transnational Hinduisms that have pushed the ethnic boundaries and made them global. While Brooks (1989) in his work tried to emphasize the success of the foreign devotees of the Hare Krishna movement in appropriating Indian meanings and in turn being accepted by the Indian devotees, Aghehananda Bharati points out that Brooks in his account of the Hare Krishnas "does not mention, for example, that Western devotees are not allowed into the sanctum of the older, more traditional pan-Indian Vaishnava shrines such as Jagannath-Puri in eastern India and Srirangam in southern India" (Bharati 1990: 585). However, the Hare Krishna followers consider themselves as traditional Vaishnava practitioners. In a sense it has combined in it the modes of Hindu life that is traditional and yet freed it from the conventional ethnic and caste restrictions. The Satya Sai movement, on the other hand, flourishes mostly as a lay organization being directly loyal to their God/Guru, Satya Sai Baba and at the same time goes beyond ethnicity in their following. Babb deals with the Satya Sai group not so much as a "religious movement" but as a "cult" because it is based on an individual's charisma through his miracles and does not have a definite worldview (Babb 1987). Nevertheless, others have criticized Babb's distinction between religious movement and cult as being not very distinct in the light of the data that he presents (Handoo 1989). The Sai Baba movement's focus is on Hindu spirituality rather than on its social tenets. It is, however, ethnically so diversified that the Chinese in Singapore could sing Indian *bhajans* in Chinese and in Japan they could do so in Japanese. These are fundamental changes in the Hindu sociology that distinguish the Satya Sais and the Hare Krishnas from the Swaminarayan's ethnic emphasis.

While the Hare Krishnas use a variety of strategies that include an aggressive vegetarianism campaign, adoption of modern techniques of music, food and popular Indian fashion couture and modern business strategies to attract the support of the wealthy Indian businessmen (Kumar 2008), the Satya Sai Baba followers too combine a variety of the same strategies. Of course, the attraction of Sai Baba's miracles is an additional factor in their success. The two modern Hindu viz., the

Hare Krishna and the Satya Sai groups have made Hinduism globally viable with their missionary zeal. The chief characteristics that are essential in the transnationalization of Hinduism – "[i]ncreased mobility and modern technological advances" "computers, modern printing and electronic transmission, audio-visual media, and the knowledge explosion" that Williams (1998: 858) identified in connection with the Swaminarayana Hinduism can also be applied to the others such transnational Hindu movements. Many scholars have studied the effective use of internet for religious propagation and religious practice by many Hindu organizations in the diaspora. For example, Manjeet Kripalani reported in 2001 (*Business Week*, 00077135, 02/26/2001, issue 3721) about the website (www.web-dunia.com) which offered Hindus the option to have virtual dip in the river Ganges instead of physically traveling to India.

Nevertheless, the transnational nature of Global Hinduism can both strengthen modern Hinduism and can also become a limiting condition in its effort to become more integrated into host societies where it finds itself. In the context of unclarified multiculturalism, as Kurien (2004) pointed out, it can isolate the Hindu community from the mainstream society and give rise to militant attitude toward their religious identity.

CONCLUDING REMARKS

In India, the Sociology of Hinduism included caste changes by means of economic mobility and new changes in the constitutional definitions of Economically Backward Classes. But in the context of Global Hinduism fundamental social changes occurred due to – (1) absence of the conventional structures to sustain caste; (2) opening up of Hindu practices to people of non-South Asian origin, and (3) increasing transnationalization of Hindu society. Most of the modes of religious practices, such as taking up priesthood and renunciation, are no longer limited to male members let alone to people of South Asian origin. The Arya Samaj has accepted female priesthood and established training centers for women priests; the Ramakrishna Mission globally has established women Ashrams where women of not only South Asian origin, but Western and East Asian women have also taken up the practice of Sannyasinis. The so-called popular Hinduisms are no longer limited to the South Asian villages, but they are found from South Africa to Germany and Canada. The rise of the middle-class Hindus and the simultaneous globalization of Hinduism and the growing terrorism concerns in South Asia are bound to bring even more fundamental changes that make not only Hindutva ideology more relevant but traditional and classical views of Hinduism vis à vis Brahmanical texts will become problematic. The question of Hindu representation in the West will continue to be a moot point, as seen in the context of the Californian State text book controversy, the book controversy around an American scholar's reference to Ganesha in psychoanalysis terms (Courtright 1985) both among lay Hindus as well as in academic circles. (See McDermott 2000, Smith 2000 – the entire *Journal of the American Academy of Religion* 68 (4) of 2000 was dedicated to the issue of "who speaks for Hinduism.") The diversity of Hindu practices in India as well as outside will move the debates around how Hinduism is represented outside India beyond the boundaries of "insiders" and the "outsiders." For, Hindu "insiders" would include not only the diverse Hindu practitioners from South Asia, but also the European, East Asian, and African Hindus. The "outsiders" are not only the non-practicing Hindus, the Orientalists and modern academics who study Hinduism, but also many Hindu academics and the many *laissez faire* Hindus.

Finally some issues need to be mentioned in relation to modern Hinduism in dealing with its sociology. And that is its relations to the other religions and the Dalits. It is clearly the "Organized Hinduism" that has consistently defined the Hindu identity in sharp distinction from the other communities – Muslims, Christians, Sikhs, and in more recent years increasingly the Dalits, all of whom have been perceived to have presented a serious threat to the political interests of the Hindutva and the political parties that have been supported by them (Bharatiya Janata Party). The issue of conversion on the other hand, is far more important in the relations between Hindus and Christians. Here the issues of Christians and Dalits vis à vis Hindus is conflated. That is, in so far as conversion to Christianity is mostly associated with the Dalit groups, attacks on Christianity and the Dalits is, at least on a social level, seem one and the same.

In recent years, by and large the Hindu–Muslim relations have been defined by the Ayodhya (Babri Mosque controversy) issue. But Hindu–Muslim relations have reached a more complex level with the Muslim terrorist attacks on Mumbai. The unconfirmed demands from the terrorists to claim back not only Kashmir, but also the former Muslim state in the south, viz., the Nizam of Hyderabad have certainly raised the levels of anxiety among not only Hindutva ideologues but also among the ordinary Hindus. In the light of these new concerns for Hindu society, it will be interesting to see how Hindu society will evolve in the coming decades.

Notes

1   The notions of transmigration (Samsara) and rebirth in Hindu society are generally determined by the idea that an individual accrues merits and demerits from their past actions (karmas). The soul of an individual, therefore, is understood to be caught in the round of births and deaths. The Hindu thinkers, such as Shankara of the eighth century, proposed knowledge as means to overcome this cycle of births and deaths and obtain ultimate liberation, while Ramanuja of the eleventh century suggested devotion combined by knowledge and ritual actions as means to liberation.

2   Arya Samaj was established in the nineteenth century by Swami Dayananda Saraswati with a view to turn Hinduism toward what he called Vedic Hinduism rejecting the image based temple rituals.

3   Glenn Yocum called it the "indigenization of Brahmanical traditions" in the context of Tamil bhakti (Yocum 1973: 17).

4   Ambedkar was not the only one who called for the elimination of caste in Hindu society. Radhakrishnan, in his *Religion and Society* (1947), called for the elimination of innumerable castes and outcastes. Nevertheless, he declined to give up his loyalty to Hindu spiritual values. But it is also noteworthy that he draws those spiritual values from the Upanishads and downplays the role of temples as "dull acquiescence and tedious routine"

(Radhakrishnan 1947). Surprisingly, Ambedkar's position on Hinduism is also quite similar in that he too emphasized the role of Upanishads and rejected the Vedas and what he called the old religion. Notwithstanding his many disagreements with Radhakrishnan, he seems to concede the role of Upanishads – "Liberty, Equality and Fraternity it may not be necessary for you to borrow from foreign sources and that you could draw for such principles on the Upanishadas" (Ambedkar 1970: 98).

5 I am adopting this phrase from Daniel Gold's essay "Organized Hinduism: from Vedic truth to Hindu nation" in Marty and Appleby (1994).

Bibliography

Ambedkar, B. R. (1970) [1936] *Annihilation of Caste*, Jalandhar: Bheem Patrika Publications.

Babb, Lawrence A. (1975) *Divine Hierarchy: Popular Hinduism in Central India*, New York: Columbia University Press.

Babb, Lawrence A. (1987) *Redemptive Encounters: Three Modern Styles in the Hindu Tradition*, Berkeley: University of California Press.

Bailey, Frederick George (1994) *The Witch-hunt, or the Triumph of Morality*, Ithaca: Cornell University Press.

Bellah, Robert N. (1980) Max Weber and world-denying love: a look at the historical sociology of religion, *JAAR* 67 (2): 277–304.

Béteille, André (1965) *Caste, Class and Power: Changing Patterns of Stratification in a Tanjore Village*, Berkeley: University of California Press.

Béteille, André (2007) *Marxism & Class Analysis*, New Delhi: Oxford University Press.

Béteille, André (ed.) (1969) *Social Inequality: Selected Readings*, Baltimore: Penguin.

Bharati, Aghehananda (1990) Review of *The Hare Krishnas in India*, by Charles Brooks, *American Ethnologist* 17 (3): 585–6.

Bloomfield, J. H. (1971) The regional elites: a theory of modern Indian history, Thomas R. Metcalf (ed.), *Modern India: An Interpretive Anthology*, London: Macmillan, 60–70.

Brear, Douglas (1996) Transmission of a Swaminarayan Hindu scripture in the British East Midlands, in Williams (1996), 209–27.

Brooks, Charles, R. (1989) *The Hare Krishnas in India*, Princeton: Princeton University Press.

Caughran, Neema (1998) Fasts, feasts, and the slovenly woman: strategies of resistance among North Indian potter women, *Asian Folklore Studies* 57 (2), 257–74.

Chaudhuri, Nirad C. (1970) *To Live or Not to Live: An Essay on Living Happily with Others*, New Delhi: Indian Book Co.

Clothey, F. W. (2006) *Ritualizing on the Boundaries: Continuity and Innovation in the Tamil Diaspora*, Columbia, SC: University of South Carolina Press.

Courtright, Paul B. (1985) *Ganesha: Lord of Obstacles, Lord Beginnings*, New York: Oxford University Press.

Das, Veena (1982) *Structure and Cognition: Aspects of Hindu Caste and Ritual*, Delhi: Oxford University Press.

Denton, Lynn Teskey (2004) *Female Ascetics in Hinduism*, Albany: State University of New York Press.

Dumézil, Georges (1958a) *L'Ideologie tripartie des Indo-Européens*, Brussels: Collection Latomus.

Dumézil, Georges (1958b) Métiers et Classes Fonctionnelles Chez Divers Peuples Indo-Européen," *Annales Economies, Sociétés, Civilisations* 13: 716–24.

Dumont, Louis (1970) *Religion/Politics and History of India: Collected Papers in Indian Sociology*, Paris and The Hague: Mouton.

Dumont, Louis (1977) *From Mandeville to Marx: The Genesis and Triumph of Economic Ideology*, Chicago: University of Chicago Press.

Dumont, Louis (1980) *Homo Hierarchicus: The Caste System and Its Implications*, tr. Mark Sainsbury, Louis Dumont, and Basia Gulati, Chicago: University of Chicago Press; first pub. in 1966 in French and 1970 in English.

Dumont, Louis (1983) *Affinity as a Value: Marriage Alliance in South India, with Comparative Essays on Australia*, Chicago and London: University of Chicago Press.

Dumont, Louis (1986) *Essays on Individualism: Modern Ideology in Anthropological Perspective*, Chicago: University of Chicago Press.

Dumont, Louis (1994) *German Ideology: From France to Germany and Back*, Chicago and London: University of Chicago Press; first pub. in 1991 under the title *Homo Aequalis II*.

Dumont, Louis (2006) [1971] *Introduction to Two Theories of Social Anthropology: Descent Groups and Marriage Alliance*, New York: Berghahn Books.

Dwyer, Rachel (2004) The Swaminarayan Movement, in Jacobsen and Kumar (2004): 180–203.

Gentes, M. J. (1992) Scandalizing the goddess at Kodungallur, *Asian Folklore Studies* 51 (2): 295–322.

Gold, Daniel (1994) Organized Hinduisms: from Vedic truth to Hindu nation, in Marty and Appleby (eds.): 531–93.

Gupta, Dipankar (ed.) *Anti-Utopia: Essential Writings of André Béteille*, New Delhi: Oxford University Press.

Gupta, Narmata and Arun K. Sharma (2002) Women academic scientists in India, *Social Studies of Science*, 32 (5/6): 901–15.

Halbfass, Wilhelm (1988) *India and Europe: An Essay in Understanding*, Albany: SUNY Press.

Handoo, Jawaharlal (1989) Review of *Redemptive Encounters: Three Modern Styles in the Hindu Tradition* by Lawrence A. Babb, *Asian Folklore Studies* 48 (2), 326–8.

Hartney, Christopher (2004) Performances of multiculturalism: South Asian communities in Sydney, in Knut A. Jacobsen and P. Pratap Kumar (eds.), *South Asians in the Diaspora: Histories and Religious Traditions*, Leiden: Brill, 435–53.

Hatcher, Brian A. (2007) Bourgeois Vedanta: the colonial roots of middle class Hinduism, *Journal of the American Academy of Religion*, 75 (2), 298–323.

Hess, Linda (1999) Rejecting sita: Indian responses to the ideal man's cruel treatment of his ideal wife, *Journal of the American Academy of Religion*, 67 (1): 1–32.

Jacobsen, Knut A. (2004) Establishing ritual space in the Hindu diaspora in Norway, in Jacobsen and Kumar (2006): 134–48.

Jacobsen, Knut A. (2006) Hindu processions, diaspora and religious pluralism," in Kumar (2006): 163–74.

Jacobsen, Knut A. and Kumar, P. Pratap (2004) *South Asians in the Diaspora: Histories and Religious Traditions*, Leiden: Brill.

Kakar, Sudhir (1985) Psychoanalysis and religious healing: siblings or strangers, *Journal of the American Academy of Religion* 53 (4): 841–53.

Kakar, Sudhir (1996) *The Colors of Violence: Cultural Identities, Religion and Conflict*, Chicago: University of Chicago Press.

Katz, Nathan (1989) Asceticism and caste in the passover observances of the Cochin Jews, *Journal of the American Academy of Religion* 57 (1): 53–82.

Khandelwal, Meena (2004) *Women in Ochre Robes: Gendering Hindu Renunciation*, Albany: SUNY Press.

Khare, R. S. (ed.) (2006) *Caste, Hierarchy, and Individualism: Indian Critiques of Louis Dumont's Contributions*, New Delhi: Oxford University Press.

King, Ursula (1989) Some reflections on sociological approaches to the study of modern Hinduism, *Numen* 36 (1): 72–97.

Knott, Kim (1986) *Hinduism in Leeds: A Study of Religious Practice in the Indian Hindu Community and in Hindu-Related Groups*, Monograph Series: Community Religious Project, Leeds: University of Leeds.

Kothari, Rajni (ed.) (1970) *Caste in Indian Politics*, New Delhi: Orient Longman Ltd.

Kumar, P. Pratap (2000) *Hindus in South Africa: Their Traditions and Beliefs*, Durban: University of Durban-Westville.

Kumar, P. Pratap (2004) Taxonomy of the Indian diaspora in South Africa: problems and issues in defining their identity, in Jacobsen and Kumar (2004): 375–92.

Kumar, P. Pratap (2008) Rathayatra of the Hare Krishnas in Durban: inventing strategies to transmit religious ideas in modern society, in Knut A. Jacobsen (ed.), *South Asian Religions on Display: Religious processions in South Asia and in the Diaspora*, London: Routledge, 205–16.

Kumar, P. Pratap (ed.) (2006) *Religious Pluralism in the Diaspora*, Leiden: Brill.

Kurien, Prema (2004) Multiculturalism, immigrant religion, and diasporic nationalism: the development of an American Hinduism, *Social Problems* 51 (3): 362–85.

Lawrence, Bruce B. (1976) *Shahrastani on the Indian Religions*, The Hague: Mouton.

Leslie, Julia (1991) Sri and Jyestha: ambivalent role models for women, in Julia Leslie and Madison Rutherford (eds.), *Roles and Rituals for Hindu Women*, Teaneck: Fairleigh Dickson University Press, 107–27.

Lubin, Timothy (2002) The virtuosic exegesis of the brahmavadin and the rabbi, *Numen*, 49 (4): 427–59.

Luchesi, Brigitte (2004) Tamil Hindu places of worship in Germany, in Jacobsen & Kumar (2004): 116–33.

Madan, T. N. (1988) The son as savior: a Hindu view of choice and morality, in George N. Appell and Triloki N. Madan (eds.), *Choice and Morality in Anthropological Perspective: Essays in Honor of Derek Freeman*, Albany: SUNY Press.

Madan, T. N. (1994) The double-edged sword: fundamentalism and the Sikh religious tradition, in Marty and Appleby (eds.): 594–627.

Marriot, McKim (1965) *Caste Ranking and Community Structure in Five Regions of India and Pakistan*, Poona: Deccan College Postgraduate and Research Institute.

Marriot, McKim (1966) Social structure and change in a U.P. village, in Srinivas (ed.) (1966a): 106–21.

Marriot, McKim (ed.) (1955) *Village India: Studies in the Little Community*, Chicago: University of Chicago Press.

Marty, Martine E. and Appleby, R. Scott (eds.) (1994) [1991] *Fundamentalisms Observed*, Chicago: University of Chicago Press.

McDermott, Rachel Fell (2000) New Age Hinduism, New Age Orientalism, and the second generation South Asian, *Journal of the American Academy of Religion* 68 (4): 721–31.

Mendelsohn, Oliver and Vicziany, Marika (1998) *The Untouchables: Subordination, Poverty and the State in Modern India*, Cambridge: Cambridge University Press.

Michaels, Axel (2004) *Hinduism: Past and Present*, Princeton: Princeton University Press.

Nesbit, Eleanor (1999) "Being religious shows in your food": young British Hindus and vegetarianism, in T. S. Rukmani (ed.), *Hindu Diaspora: Global Perspectives*, Montreal: Department of Religion, Concordia University, 397–426.

Olivelle, Patrick (Tr.) (1992) *Samnyasa Upanishads: Hindu Scriptures on Asceticism and Renunciation*. New York: Oxford University Press.

Olson, Carl (2007) *The Many Colors of Hinduism: A Thematic-Historical Introduction*. New Brunswick, NJ: Rutgers University Press.

Pennington, Brian K. (2005) *Was Hinduism Invented? Britons, Indians, and Colonial Construction of Religion*, Oxford: Oxford University Press.

Potter, Karl H. (1963) *Presuppositions of India's Philosophies*, Englewood Cliffs: Prentice-Hall.

Radhakrishnan, S. (1947) *Religion and Society*, New York: Macmillan.

Richman, Paula (1999) A diaspora Ramayana in Southall, Greater London, *Journal of the American Academy of Religion* 67 (1): 33–57.

Robinson, Catherine A. (1999) *Tradition and Liberation: The Hindu Tradition in the Indian Women's Movement*, New York: St Martin's Press.

Sagar, Sunder Lal (1975) *Hindu Culture and Caste System in India*, Delhi: Uppal Book Store.

Salmond, Noel A. (2004) *Hindu Iconoclasts: Rammohun Roy, Dayananda Sarasvati and Nineteenth Century Polemics Against Idolatry*, Waterloo, Ontario: Wilfred Laurier University Press.

Schwartzberg, Joseph E. (1973) A review essay on *Homo Hierarchicus*: an essay on the Caste System, *Annals of the Association of American Geographers* 63 (2): 253–5.

Singer, Milton (1956) Cultural values in India's economic development, *Annals of the American Academy of Political and Social Science* 305 (May): 81–91.

Smith, Brian K. (1994) *Classifying the Universe: The Ancient Indian Varna System and the Origins of Caste*, New York: Oxford University Press.

Smith, Brian K. (2000) Who does, can, and should speak for Hinduism? *Journal of the American Academy of Religion* 68 (4): 741–9.

Smith, Fred M. (1991) Indra's curse, Varuna's noose, and the suppression of the woman in the Vedic Srauta ritual, in Julia Leslie and Madison Rutherford (eds.), *Roles and Rituals for Hindu Women*, Teaneck: Fairleigh Dickson University Press, 17–45.

Srinivas, M. N. (1966a) [1955] *India's Villages*, New York: Asia Publishing House.

Srinivas, M. N. (1966b) *Social Change in Modern India*, Berkeley: University of California Press.

Srinivas, M. N. (1980) [1976] *The Remembered Village*, Berkeley: University of California Press.

Srinivas, M. N., Shaw, A. M., and Ramaswamy, E. A. (eds.) (2002) [1979] *The Fieldworker and the Field*, New Delhi: Oxford University Press.

Swatos, William H. & Lutz Kaelber (eds.) (2005) *The Protestant Ethic Turns 100: Essays on the Centenary of the Weber Thesis*, Boulder: Paradigm Publishers.

Tambia, Stanley (2002) Vignets of present day diaspora, in Eliezer Ben-Rafael with Yitzhak Sternberg (eds.), *Identity, Culture and Globalization*, Leiden: Brill, 327–36.

Van Buitenen, J. A. B. (1968) *Ramanuja on the Bhagavadgita: (Condensed Reading of His Gitabhashya with Copious Notes and an Introduction)*, Delhi: Motilal Banarsidass.

Vanaik, Achin (1997) *The Furies of Indian Communalism: Religion, Modernity and Secularization*, London: Verso.

Van Der Burg, Corstiaan J. G. (2004) The Hindu diaspora in the Netherlands: halfway between local structures and global ideologies, in Knut A. Jacobsen and Kumar, P. Pratap (eds.), *South Asians in the Diaspora: Histories and Religious Traditions*, Leiden: Brill, 97–115.

Vertovec, Steven (2000) *The Hindu Diaspora: Comparative Patterns*, London: Routledge.

Wadley, Susan S. (1977) Women and the Hindu tradition, *Signs* 3 (1), 113–25.

Wadley, Susan S. (1994) *Struggling with Destiny in Karimpur 1925–1984*, Berkeley: University of California Press.

Weber, Max (1958a) *Protestant Ethic and the Spirit of Capitalism*, tr. Talcott Parsons. With a foreword by R. H. Tawney, New York: Scribner.

Weber, Max (1958b) *The Religion of India: The Sociology of Hinduism and Buddhism*, tr. and ed. Hans H. Gerth and Don Martindale, Glencoe, IL: Free Press.

Weller, Paul (2004) Hindus and Sikhs: community development and religious discrimination in England and Wales, in Jacobsen and Kumar (2004), 44–97.

Wilke, Annette (2006) Tamil Hindu temple life in Germany: competing and complementary modes in reproducing cultural identity, globalized ethnicity and expansion of religious markets, in P. Pratap Kumar (ed.), *Religious Pluralism in the Diaspora*, Leiden: Brill, 235–68.

Williams, Raymond Brady (1998) Training religious specialists for a transnational Hinduism: a Swaminarayan Sadhu training center, *Journal of the American Academy of Religion* 66 (4): 841–62.

Williams, Raymond Brady (ed.) (1996) [1992]*A Sacred Thread: Modern Transmission of Hindu Traditions in India and Abroad*, New York: Columbia University Press.

Yocum, Glenn E. (1973) Shrines, shaminism, and love poetry: elements in the emergence of popular Tamil Bhakti, *Journal of the American Academy of Religion* 41 (1): 3–17.

Zaehner, R. C. (1969) *The Bhagavad Gita (with Commentary Based on Original Sources)*, Oxford: Oxford University Press.

Zelliot, Eleanor (1996) *From Untouchables to Dalit: Essays on the Ambedkar Movement*, New Delhi: Manohar Publishers.

19

Religious Awakening in China under Communist Rule

A Political Economy Approach

FENGGANG YANG

INTRODUCTION

In the existing literature of the economic approach to the study of religion, the supply-side theory (e.g., Finke and Iannaccone 1993; Stark and Iannaccone 1994; Finke 1997; Froese 2001) has been dominant, so much so that many people mistakenly equate the economic approach to the supply-side model.[1] This chapter develops a political economy approach and examines the demand-driven changes in the Chinese religious economy.

The supply-side theorists assume that religious demand in a society is relatively stable and religious change is largely driven by the supply-side shifts (Finke and Stark 1993; Stark and Finke 2000). However, the stability of religious demand is *assumed*, not proved. Some scholars employing the economic approach have pointed out the need to take "both demand and supply factors into account" to understand changes in religious market structures (Hamberg and Pettersson 2002: 99; also see Ellison and Sherkat 1995; Sherkat and Wilson 1995; Sherkat 1997).

The stable demand assumption becomes simply implausible when we examine religious change in China. After decades of atheist propaganda and religious repression, the Chinese express an exceptionally low level of religious beliefs and practices compared with people in other societies. On the other hand, there has been a gradual religious awakening in China in spite of the restrictive religious policy that aims at maintaining a reduced level of religious participation. The active demand for religion has been continuously increasing, rendering the religious regulations ineffective, resulting in the emergence of the black and gray markets in addition to the "red" market of religion (Yang 2006).

This chapter develops a political economy approach that takes power competition as an integral part of the religious market. First, the Communists regard the ideology of Communism as a competitive alternative to religious beliefs, and have deliberately tried to replace conventional religion with the atheist belief system of Communism. The political economy of religion must include atheism as a competitor in the religious market. Second, the faith-based organizations are perceived as one of the most serious threats to the Communist Party. This is why the Catholic Church has been treated as a serious threat, even though Catholics comprise less than one percent of the Chinese population. Third, the larger political economy of religion should also include alternatives to institutionalized religion. In addition to religious participation in formal religious organizations in the form of membership and attendance, other types of spiritual practices, such as "popular religion" or "folk religion," exist in all societies. Non-institutionalized spiritualities play important roles in the heavily regulated religious economies (Yang 2006). More importantly, these spiritual practices are also alternatives to the atheist orthodoxy. Applying the concepts of consumer behaviors in János Kornai's economics of shortage to the religious economy in China under Communist rule, we expect to see people *queuing up*, *searching*, *suppressing demand*, and *experimenting with substitutes* for religion.

RELIGIOUS REGULATION IN THE PEOPLE'S REPUBLIC OF CHINA

After the Chinese Communist Party (CCP) established the People's Republic of China (PRC) in 1949, it spent the first 17 years attempting to bring all religions under control, followed by 13 years of eradication measures before relenting to a policy of limited tolerance. The following brief account of this history is based on original sources from Chinese authorities (MacInnis 1989; RAB 1995; Ye 1997; CPS 1998; Gong 1999; RAB 2000; Luo 2001), as well as from Chinese observers in the West (Bush 1970; MacInnis 1989; Pas 1989; Potter 2003).

In the ideological lexicon of the CCP, atheism is a fundamental doctrine that manifests in two major forms: (1) scientific atheism and (2) militant atheism. Scientific atheism, as an offspring of the European Enlightenment movement, regards religion as illusory, nonscientific, and backward. Thus, the advancement of science and education will lead to the natural demise of religion. In contrast, militant atheism, as advocated by Lenin and the Russian Bolsheviks, treats religion as a dangerous narcotic and a troubling political ideology that serves the interests of antirevolutionary forces. As such, it should be suppressed or eliminated by the revolutionary force. On the basis of scientific atheism, religious toleration was inscribed in CCP policy since its early days. By reason of militant atheism, however, atheist propaganda became ferocious, and the power of "proletarian dictatorship" was invoked to eradicate the reactionary ideology (Dai 2001).

Examining CCP's religious policies through the lens of market analysis, we may distinguish different policies toward religious consumers (believers) and suppliers (leaders and organizations). Scientific atheism may contain sympathy for "deceived" consumers (believers), but it affords little tolerance for the "deceiving" suppliers (religious leaders and organizations). As soon as the PRC was established, militant atheism compelled the party to impose control and limitations on religious suppliers. Foreign missionaries, who were considered part of Western imperialism, were expelled, and cultic or heterodox sects that were regarded as reactionary organizations (*fandong hui dao men*), were banned. Further, major religions – Buddhism, Daoism, Islam, Catholicism, and Protestantism, which were difficult to eliminate and possessed diplomatic value for the isolated regime – were co-opted into national associations. Through tremendous government effort and a select few cooperative religious leaders, the China Protestant Three-Self (i.e., self-administration, self-support, and self-propagation) Patriotic Movement (TSPM) Committee was established in 1954. This was followed by the China Buddhist Association in 1955, the China Islamic Association in 1957, the China Daoist Association in 1957, and finally, the China Catholic Laity Patriotic Committee in 1957, which later became the China Catholic Patriotic Committee. In short order, previously existing denominational and sectarian systems within each religion were broken down and banned. Uniformity was imposed upon each of the five religions.

When the so-called Great Proletarian Cultural Revolution began in 1966, all religious sites were closed down. Many buildings were torn apart, statues of gods and religious artifacts were smashed, and religious scriptures were burned. Secretly keeping a religious scripture or an artifact was a crime, and some people took great risks to save scriptures, sculptures, and buildings in the name of preserving antiques or cultural heritages. The few remaining believers were forced to make public renunciations or were "wiped away like dust" into dark prison corners or reeducation-through-labor camps. The complete ban was imposed on both religious demand and supply.

Following the death of Chairman Mao Zedong in 1976, Deng Xiaoping gradually emerged as the paramount leader within the CCP. Under his leadership, the CCP set a new course for the country, focusing on modernization and economic reform. In order to rally people around the central task of economic development, the pragmatic CCP began to loosen control over various aspects of social life. Regarding religion, eradication was replaced with toleration. Beginning in 1979, a limited number of Protestant and Catholic churches, Buddhist and Daoist temples, and Islamic mosques have reopened for religious services.

China's economic reforms since 1978 have brought profound changes. In the past, under the ideology-driven central planning, the Chinese economy was a typical "shortage economy" of Communist-ruled countries (Kornai 1980, 1992), which was characterized by shortage in consumer goods, long queues in shops, long delays in services, and shortage throughout the production process. "The shortage phenomena under the classical socialist system are general, frequent, intensive, and chronic; the system is a shortage economy" (Kornai 1992: 233). The transition from central-planning to a market economy,[2] in spite of numerous challenges and missteps along the way, has been quite successful with remarkable, continual rapid growth of GDP. By the end of the 1990s, China's economy successfully entered the "post-shortage period" (Lü 2001). The Chinese Communist Party (CCP) itself has undergone far-reaching changes, including opening its door to welcome capitalists to join the party, even though the proletariat rhetoric remains. However, unlike the economic sector that has adjusted policies and upgraded regulations several times since 1978, many other social sectors lag behind in reforms, including the religious sector.

In 1982, the policy of limited tolerance was formally reinstated, inscribed in the edict "The Basic Viewpoint and Policy on the Religious Affairs during the Socialist Period of Our Country," now known as "Document No. 19" (Yang 2004). This central document has served as the basis for religious policy for over twenty years.

It grants legal existence to Buddhism, Daoism, Islam, Protestantism, and Catholicism under the government-sanctioned "patriotic" associations, but not to any group outside of the five religious associations, nor to other religions. Document No. 19 proscribes proselytizing outside of approved religious premises. In line with Document No. 19, the PRC Constitution of 1982 reaffirms freedom of religious belief, but clearly stipulates that only "normal" religious activities are protected.[4] Document No. 19 also insists that religion eventually will wither away, that religious organizations must be restricted and controlled, and that atheist education must be carried out unrelentingly (see MacInnis 1989 for an annotated English translation of Document No. 19). Compared with the violent eradication practices carried out during the radical Cultural Revolution[3] (1966–76), limited tolerance of religion was certainly a progress. Nonetheless, formulated at the very onset of the reforms focusing on economic modernization, Document No. 19 remains very much ideology-driven and reflects the Communist ideology to the dogmatist left. It merely acknowledged the impracticability of eradicating religion *in a short period of time*, and had to offer some justification for the limited tolerance policy while upholding atheist ideology.

China's religious policy has had no significant change since 1982. Of course, there have been some adjustments in the implementation of religious policy. For instance, since the mid-1990s the central and provincial governments have installed numerous administrative ordinances, climaxing in the latest Regulations on Religious Affairs decreed by the State Council that became effective on March 1, 2005 (see Chan and Carlson 2005 for an annotated translation). But there have been no substantial deviations from the basic policy established in Document No. 19. The CCP authorities have repeatedly emphasized the need to strengthen the religious control apparatus, to guard against foreign infiltration through religion, and to reinforce the propagation of atheism, all of which were inscribed in Document No. 19. The formal ordinances were enacted in the broad context of reforms that call for increasing rule by law (*fazhi*) instead of rule by personal will of officials. Rule by law may have legitimized greater freedom in some other social sectors, but religious regulations have become arguably more stringent. For example, in 1994, the State Council published two ordinances requiring all religious groups to register with the government and prohibiting foreigners from proselytizing in China. In 1996, the CCP and the State Council issued a joint decree to curb the building of temples and outdoor Buddha statues, and constricted authority to grant new building permits for religious venues to provincial-level governments. In 1999, the National People's Congress Standing Committee adopted a "Legislative Resolution on Banning Heretic Cults," which banned Falun Gong, other sectarian *qigong* groups, and some religious groups. In 2004, the CCP Propaganda Department, joint by the Organization Department, the Central Party School, the State Ministry of Education, and the Chinese Academy of Social Sciences, sent out a circular "Concerning Further Strengthening Marxist Atheist Research, Propaganda, and Education Work." About the fact that China's religious policy remains strict, there has been a broad consensus among China observers (e.g., Human Rights Watch/Asia 1993, 1997; Freedom House 2002, 2007) and scholars who have closely followed the development (Potter 2003; Kindopp and Hamrin 2004; Carlson 2005; Ying 2006). The strict regulations, however, have not achieved their goals of reducing religion and containing it to a low level. Instead, it has resulted in the triple markets, in which many religious activities operate in the underground or legally ambiguous areas (Yang 2006).

THE FAILURE OF ERADICATION

The ban of religion took effect in 1966 during the zenith of the Cultural Revolution, when all religious sites were closed down, many temples and churches torn down, religious scriptures burned, statues of gods and religious artifacts smashed, and believers forced to make public renunciations or sent to prisons or *laogai* (reeducation through labor) camps.

Having seen state eradication measures during the Cultural Revolution, many scholars once pronounced the death of religion in China (Welch 1961: 13; Treadgold 1973: 69; Pas 1989: 20; Lambert 1994: 9). However, religion disappeared only from the public scene. Not only did many people maintain their faith in secrecy, but persevering believers also gathered for worship at home or in the wilderness.

Ironically, the eradication measures created martyrs or living heroes who inspired other believers.[4] Some staunch believers survived in and out of prisons and labor camps. Some Christian groups managed to hold religious gatherings in secrecy at home or in the wilderness (Lambert 1999; Aikman 2003; Huang and Yang 2005; Yang 2006). At the Buddhist Shaolin Temple, over a dozen monks refused to return to their original villages during the Cultural Revolution. They stayed at the temple and became farmers in the "People's Commune" (*gongshe*) but secretly kept their practice. Eradication measures failed to eliminate religious believers and practitioners.

As it became apparent that religion could not be wiped out of people's minds and hearts in the near future, when the more pragmatic leadership under Deng Xiaoping took over the Chinese Communist Party (CCP) from the radicals in the late 1970s, they changed course. To rally the nation for economic reforms and development, the CCP authorities conceded to the religious demand, albeit withholding firm reservations, as seen in the Document No. 19. It was the persistent demand for religion that drove the policy change from eradication to limited tolerance. Moreover, once the total ban was lifted in 1979, a religious upsurge has outpaced regulatory expansion, in spite of accelerated efforts of control.

EFFECTIVE SUPPRESSION OF DEMAND FOR RELIGION

The failure of eradication is only in the sense that persevering believers survived the harshest eradication campaigns. However, the active demand for religion in China has been effectively reduced to an exceptionally low level in comparison with other societies. According to the World Values Surveys (WVS),[5] the overall level of religiousness in the People's Republic of China (PRC) is the lowest among all the countries included in the surveys (see table 19.1). In the year 2000 wave of the survey that included China for the first time, it shows that only 13.7 percent of the Chinese in the sample (N = 1000) claimed to be religious and only 6.0 percent

Table 19.1 Religiousness in the People's Republic of China, Taiwan, and other countries (%)

	P.R. China (N = 1,000)	Average of all 67 countries	Taiwan (N = 780)
Independent of whether you attend church/temple or not, would you say you are a religious person?			
A religious person	13.7	67.0	72.2
Not a religious person	55.3	19.9	22.1
A convinced atheist	24.0	4.2	1.7
No answer	0.2	0.8	
Don't know	6.8	4.0	4.1
Do you belong to a religious denomination?			
No	93.0	18.9	20.9
Yes	6.0	77.7	79.1
No answer		0.2	
Don't know	0.4	0.4	
Not asked in survey		2.6	
Missing	0.6	0.1	
Apart from weddings, funerals and christenings, about how often do you attend religious services?			
More than once a week	0.7	13.2	2.9
Once a week	1.5	18.5	4.0
Once month	0.9	10.7	7.3
Only on special holy days	5.4	18.5	20.9
Once a year	0.8	6.3	2.3
Less often	1.0	8.3	22.4
Never or practically never	88.9	22.7	38.6
No answer		0.4	0.1
Don't know	0.8	0.3	1.4
Not asked in survey		1.2	

Source: World Value Surveys, People's Republic of China and other 66 countries: 2000; Taiwan: 1995.

belonged to a religion, the lowest among the 67 countries in the survey. Of the 67 countries, the averages were 67.0 and 77.7, respectively. Meanwhile, 88.9 percent of the Chinese reported that they never or practically never attended religious services, whereas the average was 22.7 percent; and 24.0 percent of the Chinese claimed to be convinced atheists, while the average was 4.2 percent.

Some people might suggest that the Chinese have always been a nonreligious people, but such speculative claim is contrary to empirical observations. The received wisdom has been that the Chinese as a whole have never been religious. Hu Shih, one of the most influential Chinese intellectuals in the twentieth century, states, "China is a country without religion and the Chinese are a people who are not bound by religious superstitions" (quoted in Yang 1961: 5). Many Chinese scholars and Western Sinologists share this view (see Yang 1961; also see, e.g., Küng and

Ching 1989). However, this is a problem of armchair philosophers and theologians who read texts instead of observing people. For anthropologists and sociologists who have been there and done that, they report a totally different reality. "There was not one corner in the vast land of China [before 1949] where one did not find temples, shrines, altars, and other places of worship ... [which] were a visible indication of the strong and pervasive influence of religion in Chinese society" (Yang 1961: 6).

Furthermore, the 1995 wave of the World Values Surveys included Taiwan, a Chinese society that shares much the language and culture with mainland China. Using the same set of questions, people in Taiwan reported much higher religiosity, closer to the averages in the whole survey (see the right column in table 19.1). The huge difference between mainland China and Taiwan cannot be explained away merely by impugning methodological problems. The empirical findings of religiosity in Taiwan should also put the cultural difference argument to rest. The differences are not so much cultural, but political. Of course, it is possible that some PRC respondents were not willing to admit their real views of religion, especially when religion is politically suppressed and socially discouraged. If this is the case, it further indicates the importance of social and political factors in suppressing active demand for religion.

FORCED SUBSTITUTION OF COMMUNISM

In place of religion, the CCP has tried to indoctrinate people with Communist beliefs, a common practice in Marxist-Leninist states (Hollander 1982). "Within Marxist movements, and under Marxist-Leninist regimes, then, many devoted party activists and some average citizens accepted Marxian teachings *as if* they were a religious body of sacred precepts. Marxism, as a code of personal and group practices, satisfied emotional needs, provided transcendental guidance, and defined ethical ends" (Luke 1987: 114, emphasis in original). Some scholars have studied Communism as a sort of religion, such as a civil religion (Luke 1987) or a political religion (Zuo 1991; Burleigh 2000). However, labeling Communism as a religion is controversial at best (Shorten 2003). As staunch atheists, the Communists themselves insist on the irreligious or antireligious nature of the Communist ideology. As such, it is more appropriate to call Communism what it wants to be – a substitute for religion, or a pseudo-religion in the broad religious economy.

The CCP insistently propagates Communism as the "loftiest ideal and noblest belief" (*zui chonggao de lixiang he xinyang*). The Communist ideological system includes beliefs in an ideal future – the Communist Society, which is, in religious terms, like a paradise on earth, a society where no exploitation or inequality exists; the principle of production and distribution will be "from each according to his ability, to each according to his need." In order to advance into the Communist Society, revolutionary and progressive people need to offer unrelenting service to the people and the Communist Party and struggle against class enemies, counter-revolutionary and reactionary elements in society.

The organizational pillar upholding the Communist ideology lies in the organization of the Chinese Communist Party. In addition, the Chinese Communist Youth

League (CCYL) for young people ages 14 to 28 is a preparatory organization for the CCP. The Chinese Young Pioneers (*shao xian dui*, CYP) for elementary and middle school children is "to prepare the Communist successors (*jie ban ren*)." The CCP and CCYL are selective, open only to people who, in principle, have demonstrated their commitment to the Communist endeavor. CCP and CCYL constitutions require open denunciation of any belief in gods, spirits, or ghosts. The membership criteria of CYP are less stringent, so that a majority of students may join. Nonetheless, it is required to take a Communist vow to become a member.[6] The CCP and CCYL committees and branches are instituted in all grassroots work units, residential districts, villages, high schools, and universities, and the CYP in all elementary and middle schools. The grassroots Party and League branches are responsible for organizing periodical study meetings for all members. Members are required to pay monthly membership dues to the Party or League and participate in organized activities (*guo zuzhi shenghuo*). By the end of 2003, there were 68,232,000 CCP members and 3,341,000 grassroots branches, 71,070,000 CCYL members and 2,983,000 grassroots branches, and over 130,000,000 CYP members in 15,530,000 brigades.[7] Together, the CCP, CCYL and CYP members of 269,302,000 comprise about 20.7 percent of the total population, more than any organized religion in China today.

Are the atheistic communist campaigns effective? Many people express doubts about it, especially in light of the apparent disenchantment with Communist ideology during the reform era. However, in the World Values Surveys in 2000, one out of four Chinese respondents claimed to be "convinced atheists" (see table 19.1), the highest proportion among all the countries included in the survey. The level of effectiveness of the atheist propaganda may exceed many people's impression and take some sobriety to sink in. In sociology, socialization is one of the basic concepts, which denotes that what is taught in the formative years of youth often, consciously or unconsciously, remains over the rest of life for many people. Some evidences show that at least some Party and League members and aspirants appear to be genuinely inspired by the Communist idealism. In a 1994 survey of young people in Shanghai conducted by the CCYL Shanghai Committee, nearly half of the respondents claimed that the purpose of joining the political organization, i.e., the CCP or CCYL, was "for pursuing the ideal and the belief" (*wei le lixiang he xinyang*), that is, the Communist ideal and belief (Liu 1995).

At any rate, for those CCP and CCYL members and aspirants who are more or less sincere, Communism is the substitute for religion. Of course, it is probably a forced substitute for most of the people, as the alternatives were made inaccessible. According to János Kornai,

Forced substitution plays a major part in understanding the shortage syndrome. It should be distinguished from voluntary substitution. If a customer has hitherto chosen the first of two products, A and B, which are close substitutes for each other and both readily available on the supply side, and then changes to the other (substitutes B for A) because her tastes or the two products' relative prices have altered, the substitution can be considered voluntary. But if she buys B because A is unavailable, the substitution is forced. (Kornai 1992: 230–1)

In other words, "forced substitution" does not imply complete coercion. People always have choices, especially in the spiritual sphere. Communism is a forced substitute as religious alternatives are made unavailable.

Most Chinese people born in the PRC, especially those born before the 1980s, grew up without exposure to religion. Since 1979, although some religious groups have been allowed to exist, there have been too few of them for most people to encounter in daily life. During my field research in several cities in China, several times I asked for the direction to a nearby church or temple, but people simply had no clue that there was a church or temple in that neighborhood, even though the church or temple was only within a hundred meters away from where we were standing. Even if some people came into contact with religious believers, the accepted atheist ideology, antireligious discourses, and the lack of religious knowledge usually impeded their communication with the believers and hindered their understanding of religious symbols, beliefs, and practices. Many people habitually despise religious clergy. For the good intentioned ones, they may not know how to address a clerical person.

ALTERNATIVE SUBSTITUTES TO COMMUNISM AND INSTITIONAL RELIGION

Not all substitutes are the same. Instead of the forced substitute, individuals may seek alternative substitutes. According to Kornai,

> The customer abandons her original purchasing intention and instead buys something else that is more or less a substitute for it. It may be a close substitute, for instance, another kind of meat instead of beef, or a remoter substitute, some kind of deep frozen or canned meat, or it may be drawn from an even remoter sphere of substitutes: any kind of food stuff at all. (Kornai 1992: 230)

Moreover, besides settling for the forced substitute offered in the official market, some consumers may find unusual alternatives that are somewhat more proximate to the desired good. For instance, when beef and other types of standard meat are not available at the shops, instead of settling for the vegetarian diet, the woman shopper mentioned earlier might choose to hunt herself for game animals or exotic insects for food. This kind of substitution may involve some unusual acts beyond the market scope, but life sometimes drives people to hunt and gather instead of shopping at the market. Such alternative substitutes can be more satisfactory than total abstention.

This applies to the spiritual life. While some people have settled for Communism, other people find neither orthodox Communism nor irreligious materialism satisfy their spiritual needs. Many people thus have sought and experimented with spiritual alternatives that more closely proximate religion. Since the spiritual alternatives may be practiced without the religious label, form, or organization, it does incur the same costs as to practice institutionalized religion under restriction.

During the Cultural Revolution, the major form of alternative spirituality was the personality cult of Chairman Mao.

Communist Party Chairman Mao Zedong was glorified as "the great savior of the people" (*renmin de da jiuxing*) and "the Red Sun" (*hong taiyang*). People danced and sang to Mao's statue, and confessed sins and made vows before Mao's portrait (Zuo 1991). The "Little Red Book" of Mao's words was revered. Studying Mao's quotes was institutionalized into the daily schedule of government officials, school students, factory workers, and village farmers. Even mathematics and science lessons in all textbooks began with the words of Chairman Mao. (Yang 2006: 99)

The zest for Communism was surreptitiously replaced by the Mao personality cult. This may seem ironic, but is not difficult to explain in terms of economics of shortage. Noticeably, the personality cult is a common illness of the Communist regimes, Mao in China, Stalin in the Soviet Union, Tito in Yugoslavia, Castro in Cuba, Ho Chi Minh in Vietnam, and Kim Il-sung in North Korea. The forced substitute for religion – atheist Communism – gave way to an alternative substitute that deifies and worships the Communist leader. The individuals who practically worshipped Mao had experienced the feelings that were practically religious.

In reform-era China, there are two major forms of alternative spiritualities without being labeled religious. One is conducted in the name of carrying on traditional culture (e.g., folk religious practices). Another is carried out in the name of advancing science (e.g., healing cults of *qigong*). These comprise the main elements in the gray market of religion (Yang 2006).

In China, folk religion has been revived in the name of ancestral commemoration, community fairs, regional culture, or folklore preservation. In rural areas, many villages and towns have restored temples dedicated to historical heroes or immortals who have become accepted by the locals as tutelage gods, including Chairman Mao Zedong (Heibrunn 1997). They hold dedication ceremonies, temple fairs, or festival celebrations. The construction of such temples is often supported by the whole village. Most villagers and clansmen participate in the celebration of festivals and fairs related to the temples. As such, the celebrations are regarded as part of the local cultural tradition or folklore rather than a religion. Some of the temples and activities are better organized than others, such as the Three-in-One cult (*sanyi jiao*) in Fujian (Dean 1998), but most of them remain in a village without a permanent organizational structure. Similar "communal religion" has been observed by ethnographers in Southeast China (Dean 1993, 1998, 2003; Kuah 2000), Northwest China (Jing 1996), and North China (Fan 2003; Zhang 2001); in fact, it has spread throughout the country (Hou and Fan 2001). CCP policies toward folk religion are ambiguous. Different government agencies, different levels of the government, or different individual cadres often have contradictory attitudes and policies. Some of the folk-religious temples have been restored in the name of preserving cultural relic sites. Some new ones have been built in order to attract overseas investments and/ or tourists.

Besides the community-based folk religion, there are also popular practices performed by individuals, including fortune-telling (*suan gua*), physiognomy (*xiang mian*), glyphomancy (*ce zi*, analyzing the parts of written characters), *fengshui*, and the like. They have become widespread in the reform era. According to a report in *Religions in China*, the official magazine published by the State Religious Affairs Bureau, about five million people made a living through conducting fortune-telling in the mid 1990s (Zheng 1997). Many cities have a de facto "fortune-telling street" with dozens of fortune-tellers. A recent study by a researcher at the State Administration College has revealed that even a majority of Communist Party and government mid-level officials believe in some form of these superstitions (*Kexue Shibao* 2007). These superstitions (*mixin*) are more of magic than of religion. Nonetheless they include supernatural beliefs and to certain extent may meet people's need for the supernatural.

A more widespread form of alternate spiritual practice was *qigong*. The word *qigong* means, literally, the power of *qi* (air or breathing). Simply put, *qigong* is a form of physical exercise, meditation, and healing. But the *qigong* phenomenon in reform-era China was extremely complex, entangled with traditional Chinese medicine, modern scientism, body politics, and, now, international relations (Xu 1999; Chen 2003a, 2003b; Palmer 2007). What is evident, though, most of the *qigong* groups and practices are a form of quasi-religion, as this word is commonly understood (Greil and Robbins 1994). As briefly summarized in Yang (2006), first, almost all of the large *qigong* groups offer an explanatory system that employs Buddhist and/or Daoist concepts and theories. Only very few rudimentary *qigong* practices claim no supernatural element, thus are not much different from martial arts (*wu shu*) or general physical exercise (*ti cao*). Second, most of the *qigong* masters claim to be heirs of certain ancient Daoist or Buddhist lineages who have been sent by certain mystical masters to "go out of the mountains" (*chu shan*) and spread the *gong*. Third, the practices often involve meditating over religious images or cosmic principles, reciting mantras, and/or reading scriptures. Due to political and cultural reasons, *qigong* masters and practitioners insisted that they were not religious, and therefore not subject to religious regulations. However, they are comparable to New Age religions, occult, magic, or "client and audience cults" (Stark and Bainbridge 1985) in the West.

Compared with the forced substitute of Communist atheism that rejects the supernatural, quasi-religious or alternative spiritual practices can be considered more satisfactory because they include the belief in the supernatural. In the mean time, when the institutional religions become more accessible, the people who have practiced alternative spiritualities find it less difficult than the sincere atheists to turn to a conventional religion. Many testimonials of Buddhist converts appeared in Buddhist magazines have noted that practicing *qigong* led them to becoming interested in Buddhism. Venerable Master Jing Hui, the president of Hebei Buddhist Association, said that in China "many people begin to learn Chan (Buddhism) because they first practiced *qigong*."[8] Several people I have known for a long time have made a series of spiritual transitions, moving from professed Communist atheists to *qigong* practitioners, to Falun Gong followers, and then baptized into the Christian church. Evidently, practicing folk religion, popular religion, or *qigong* has eased the way toward joining some conventional religion.

SPIRITUAL AWAKENING IN THE REFORM ERA

However, substituting may not last long, and suppressing the active demand is not the same as wiping out the need, which could stay dormant or hidden in privacy.

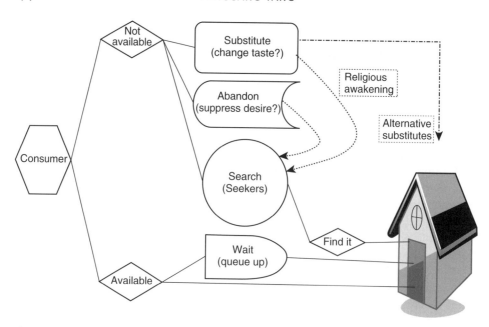

Figure 19.1 Consumer behaviors in a shortage economy of religion

Once religion becomes available again, the dormant may be awakened, and the hidden need for religion may be revealed. This is illustrated in the dotted lines and boxes in figure 19.1, about which Kornai had no discussion.

In reform-era China, the literature of creative writings first reflected this gradual spiritual awakening. The 1981 novella *When the Sunset Clouds Disappear* (*wanxia xiaoshi de shihou*) portrayed the protagonist, a Red Guard, as a man who had struggled with notions of science and Marxist dialectic materialism for many years. Fortuitously he ran into a Buddhist monk on the holy mountain of Taishan, and engaged in a long, enlightening conversation. This novella instantly became politically controversial but popular among the young people because of its departure from the ideological orthodoxy. It also stirred heated debates among readers about science and religion. Religious clergy, once ridiculed and driven out of the public sight, might hold some fascinating, enlightening truths to the questions with which many young people were struggling. This idea itself was subversive, but stimulated truth-seekers searching in religion as well as in other realms. Ten years later, the celebrated novelist Zhang Chengzhi, once a Red Guard himself, published the book *The History of A Soul* (*xinling shi*), which features his embrace of his rediscovered Islamic identity. Gao Xingjian, the best known Chinese writer in the West and winner of the 2000 Nobel Prize in Literature, has also written novels exploring spiritual themes with titles like *The Soul Mountain* and *One Man's Bible*. His characters were obviously spiritual seekers, but they commonly ended up hopelessly wandering without finding a spiritual home. Indeed, many Chinese intellectuals have explored spiritual issues and sought religious answers, including novelists (Li 1996), poets (Yeh 1996), artists (Cai 2002), and academic scholars (Yang 2004). Their publications both reflect upon and contribute to the growing popular interest in religion in the reform-era.

A case of the once suppressed need for religion reviving under new circumstances is Mr Niu Shuguang. I first met the amiable old man in Tianjin in 1984. At that time, he was a retired factory worker who volunteered to teach ancient Greek to graduate students at Nankai University. As we became close, he brought to me stacks of handwritten carbon-copied articles he had accumulated over many years, in which he made self-criticisms for his past beliefs in Christianity, clearly articulated the dialectic materialism of Marxism-Leninism-Maoism, and rebuked all religious beliefs as false consciousness and superstition. Through many conversations I learned that he was once a well-known Protestant minister in the 1940s and 1950s, was imprisoned in the late 1950s for his faith, and later was released and assigned to do manual labor at a factory. In prison and at the factory, he earnestly and scrupulously studied the *Complete Collections of Marx, Engels, Lenin, and Stalin,* and the *Selected Works of Mao Zedong.* He then declared and demonstrated repeatedly in writing that he had become a socialist new man, an atheist. The 1980s was a period of fast change. When some Protestant churches were reopened in Tianjin, Mr Niu made some strong remarks criticizing their superstitious ritual practices. His criticism sounded genuine to me. But things changed very fast in those days. Merely two or three years later, he accepted a faculty position at the Yanjing Christian Seminary in Beijing. He also reclaimed a book of the New Testament exposition he authored in the 1940s and early 1950s, which, unbeknownst to him, had been published in Hong Kong without the author's name. When I visited him at the seminary in Beijing a few years later, he spoke unapologetically about his recovered Christian faith. Mr Niu is but one of many believers who once suppressed their religion under the repressive regime. Both his atheism and recovered faith in Christ appear in sincerity.

SEEKERS QUEUING UP AT CHURCHES AND TEMPLES

The ideology-driven regulators want to reduce religion, and have repeatedly, alarmingly exclaimed about the "religious fevers" since the early 1980s. As predicted in the economics of shortage, the phenomenon of excessive demand for religion will persist. Visiting religious sites, it is indeed common to witness what appears to be excessive demand for religion. Religious seekers abound, and many queuing up for the scarcely available religious goods and services.

Overcrowded churches and temples are common scenes in today's China. During my fieldwork research since 2000 I visited many Christian churches in coastal cities and inland provinces. In most of these places I observed churches filled beyond capacity. In Beijing, for example, each of the churches offered multiple Sunday services to accommodate attendances. Folding stools were added in the aisles of the sanctuary. Some churches had overflow rooms with closed-circuit TV sets transmitting the service from the main sanctuary. In the southern city of Guangzhou, a youth service was held on Sunday afternoons. The attendance in summer 2000 always spilled outside, with dozens of people standing in the sun even when the temperature hovered around 37 degree Celsius (100 degrees Fahrenheit). In the southwestern mountainous city of Nanchong, Sichuan, a wooden building designed to hold 400 people was packed with some 600 worshippers three times every Sunday. In the northeastern coastal city of Dalian, the church held multiple services throughout the week. Each service was packed, with wooden pews designed for four people seating as many as six congregants, and the space between rows was smaller than that of economy-class seats in commercial airplanes. Many people had to arrive one or two hours before the scheduled start of service in order to get a seat in the sanctuary. For those who arrived on time, it would be too late for either the sanctuary or the overflow rooms. They had to sit on small plastic stools in the yard and listen to the choir and sermon on loud speakers. Tony Lambert (1999: 24–5), who visited many Protestant churches in various parts of China, reports the same – people arriving at church two hours before the service started in order to find a seat, and at times many left standing in torrential rain while attending the service.

Over-crowded conditions are not unique to Christian churches. Some Buddhist and Daoist temples have been similarly crammed beyond the physical capacity during holidays and festivals. According to news releases from the China Tourism Bureau and the official Xinhua News Agency, on the Chinese New Year's Day of 2004, Huayan Buddhist Temple in Chongqing City received over 40,000 "incense visitors" (*xiang ke*, i.e., pilgrims), and Lingyin Buddhist Temple near Hangzhou City received 45,100 visitors. In Shanghai, about 151,000 people visited Buddhist and Daoist temples on New Year's Eve alone. On the first six days of the Chinese New Year, the Beijing White Cloud Daoist Temple sold about 600,000 tickets to visitors. Holiday visitors to temples are not necessarily religious. However, when better measures of religiousness are not available, temple visits may be used as a proxy measure. [9] Choosing to visit a temple on New Year's Day or New Year's Eve can be considered an indicator of the visitor's priorities, who could instead, for example, visit family or friends for a dinner party. Even if the visitor was dragged to the temple by a friend or family member just for the "red-hot" fun (*re nao, hong huo*) (Chau 2006), the exposure to religious scenes, rituals, and the atmosphere might serve to stimulate the person's interest in religion, or awaken the religious need that had been dormant. Meanwhile, many people visited the temple with clearly religious beliefs and practices. For example, some people squeezed hard into the temple in order to burn the "first incense sticks" (*tou xiang*) or touch the zodiac symbols for blessings, which clearly indicates supernatural beliefs.

I observed the enthusiasm of religious seekers in Shenzhen, a coastal city near Hong Kong. Accompanied by a friend, I visited a church's weekly youth gathering, which was held on the third floor of an abandoned factory building. It was a humid and hot Friday in summer 2000. Later in the afternoon, rain began pouring. Given the location of the church on this rainy evening, I expected a small turn-out. However, when I entered the large, bare-bricked hall, I was surprised to find over 200 young people in attendance. At the church office, a woman pastor was chatting with a few first time visitors, including me. Fifteen minutes before the start of the night's gathering, as I remained in the small office, the pastor received three phone calls. All were from strangers who were asking for directions to the church and related information. And they all came. At the end of the gathering, some newcomers came to the office with questions. But the pastor was too busy to conduct a focused conversation with any of them. Though most of the visitors did not get their questions answered, they bought some books and left. Before leaving, some told the pastor that they would return.

Ironically, the overcrowding of churches and temples itself may serve to stimulate onlookers' interest in religion. In Dalian, I observed that some passersby became attracted by the attendance that spilled out onto the church yard. Some walked over to the sanctuary entrance for a closer look, taking a moment to listen attentively to the singing and preaching through the loudspeakers. Some attendants made friendly gestures to such onlookers by offering a stool or sharing the hymnal book or the Bible. Such friendly gestures might generate curiosity for the onlooker: why do these people do this? What do they believe? And why does believing religion make them behave in such ways? Such curiosities may ignite a spiritual awakening and search. I interviewed a woman from Anhui, who used to be a library clerk at a factory. When visiting Hefei, the capital of Anhui Province, she happened to see a church worship service gathering. She went in with curiosity about the devoted crowd. Followed by a series of incidents "led by God," as she described them, she converted to Christianity. Later, she became the founder of the first church at the county seat of her residence, and eventually fired up and led to develop over seventy churches throughout the county.

Besides stumbling upon temples and churches, seekers seek out religious believers as well. In Guangzhou, a Christian told me about an informal book club, whose participants were young, college-educated intellectuals. They chose some books of Western culture to read and discuss and eventually they decided to read the Bible because it was considered one of the most important books in Western culture. However, they encountered much frustration in their discussions of this book. Eventually they agreed to find "a true and educated Christian" to explain the true meaning of the Bible and Christian beliefs. This group of seekers was ready to be evangelized. Tony Lambert also reports, "In south China, soon after the events in Beijing [the student-led democracy movement and the Tiananmen massacre in June 1989], over 200 students came literally knocking on the door of the local TSPM church seeking answers to their anguished questions" (Lambert 1999: 156).

I even observed people queuing up for baptisms at a Christian church in Guangzhou. Inquirers were required to take a series of classes for two months, fill out an application form, and pass a long written exam before their application was even considered. A pastoral staff member would then interview the applicant to decide whether he or she was ready to be baptized. A waiting list for baptism is common in most churches that I have visited. My interviewees told me that sometimes these waiting lists occurred due to the lack of clergymen authorized to perform baptisms. More often it was due to quotas implicitly or explicitly imposed by the local Religious Affairs Bureau (RAB) and/or the Chinese Communist Party's United Front Department (UFD). Because of the atheist ideology and the desire to reduce religion, in a given city or county, if a religion, especially Christianity, grows too rapidly, the local RAB and UFD cadres may face reprimands, or a diminished chance for promotion. Consequently, local RAB/UFD cadres would press local religious organizations to slow down the admission of new converts.

Ironically, the hurdles for becoming a church member may serve as a mechanism to select the most knowledgeable and most committed believers, and disparage free-riders, resulting in, on average, a higher level of commitment among church members (Iannaccone 1994). In turn, these church members manifest a high level of enthusiasm for evangelism and for serving as role models inspiring to seekers and prospective converts. As a result, more and more people become active in their demand for religion.

THE CHRONIC SHORTAGE OF SUPPLY

All the demand-side dynamics described above are in response to the shortage of supply. Under the dominance of atheist ideology, the shortage of religious supply will persist. János Kornai (1980, 1992) argues that in a shortage economy the growth of firms is resource-constrained instead of demand-constrained. Basic resources for production include the physical space, input materials, and labor. In the religious economy, the resource-constraints are not so much due to the lack of resources, but regulatory restrictions. In China's religious sector, all of these resources, namely, religious venues, religious materials, and religious labor (clergy), are under tight control and restriction by the authorities, resulting in the chronic shortage.

First, the party and the state restrict the number of sites open for religious activities. All religious buildings were closed down during the Cultural Revolution. Since 1979, a limited number of temples, mosques, and churches have been reopened for religious activities. However, the number and the process of reopening have been tightly controlled. Following Document No. 19, the State Council decreed a document in 1983 stating that the reopening of temples, in principle, should limited to those that were used for religious activities immediately before the Cultural Revolution (Luo 2001: 317). The rest, if not occupied for other purposes, would remain to be treated as historical and cultural relics or tourist sites under the administration of other government agencies rather than the Religious Affairs Bureau. The implied rationale for the limited reopening of temples was that the extant religious believers were those people who had religion before the Communist liberation in 1949 and were incapable or refused to become socialist new persons. The new generations who grew up under the red flag in new China would need no religion.

The central-planning of religious sites continued in the 1990s. In 1991, a regulation specified that opening a religious site needs to be approved by county- or higher-level government (Luo 2001: 436). In 1996, stricter restriction was imposed, "it must be approved by the provincial-level government" (Luo 2001: 540). Interestingly, the central-planners at the time appeared to believe that the existing number of religious sites had been sufficient to meet the demand for religion in the population, as the 1996 document stated, "given that the existing Buddhist temples have basically met the need of believing masses for normal religious activities, in general no new temples should be constructed from now on" (see Luo 2001: 540).

In reality, however, the existing religious sites have been insufficient to meet the demand that, unexpected to the regulators, has been growing. A comparison with the United States in actual supply may be indicative. On average there are 6.5 government-approved religious sites for every 100,000 Chinese (85,000/1.3 billion), whereas there are about 117 religious congregations for every 100,000 Americans (350,000/0. 3 billion).[10] Put it another way, there is one church or temple for every 15,294 people in China, whereas one church for every 857 Americans. The contrast is stark to their extremes. Even if one insists that the Chinese have never been a very religious people whereas religious oversupply is a problem in the United States, the 18 times difference between these ratios is at least indicative of a certain level of shortage of religious supply in China.

We may also look at some comparisons within China itself. In Beijing, for example, in 1948 there were over 400 Buddhist temples, 72 Protestant churches, 65 Catholic churches, 46 Islamic mosques, and 65 Daoist temples. In 2002, a total of 107 temples, mosques and churches were open for religious services, including 5 Buddhist temples, 5 Protestant churches, and 5 Catholic churches in the urban districts. In Shanghai, the 280 Protestant churches present in 1949 were reduced to 23 in 1990, the 1950 Buddhist temples dropped to 19, the 392 Catholic churches to 43, the 236 Daoist temples to 6, and the 19 Islamic mosques to 6 (Qi 1991; Luo 1992). According to an oral briefing of a government official at a meeting in 2006 that I was present, there were 375 religious sites in Shanghai in 2005, including 85 Buddhist temples, 15 Daoist temples, 7 Muslim mosques, 104 Catholic churches, and 164 Protestant churches. It is true that there has been rapid increase in the reform era. However, the overall number has remained far less than that in the pre-PRC era. Moreover, the Chinese population has about tripled since 1949, from about 450 million to nearly 1.3 billion, and increased even more in Beijing and Shanghai metropolises. Besides, the shortage of supply is evident on the ground. Almost all of the government-approved temples and churches in China have been overcrowded, as described earlier.

Second, the party and the state restrict clergy and clergy formation. Since 1979, some religious schools or seminaries have been officially opened to train young clergy. By 1995, there were 32 Buddhist seminaries, 2 Daoist seminaries, 9 Islamic seminaries, 31 Catholic seminaries, and 17 Protestant seminaries. Most of the seminaries have had small enrollments in the dozens or hundreds. The CCP United Front Department (UFD) and government Religious Affairs Bureau (RAB) decide which schools to open and how many seminarian students to admit. Without government approval, no organization or individual is allowed to run a seminar or train clergy (Luo 2001: 392).

Due to the tight control, the number of clergy remains extremely low. According to the government-released numbers, Catholic priests and nuns increased from 3,400 in 1982 to 4,300 in 1995, Protestant ministers from 5,900 to 18,000, Muslim imams from 20,000 to 40,000, Buddhist monks and nuns from 27,000 to 200,000, and Daoist monks and nuns from 2,600 to 25,700. These are impressive increases. However, we have to keep in mind that the numbers of lay believers have increased even faster, and the laity/clergy ratios remain very imbalanced. In 1995 there were 930 Catholics to every priest or nun, 556 Protestants to every minister, and 450 Muslims to every imam (see table 19.2). In reality, the problem is even more acute, as the actual numbers of believers are definitely higher than the officially published estimates, and many older clergy suffered physical and psychological tortures and became too feeble to be active on duty.

Third, the party and the state restrict the publication and distribution of religious scriptures, books, and other printed materials. For example, a RAB and Police Bureau joint circular in 1988 insists: "Christian scriptures, books, and magazines must be approved by provincial-level government for printing and publishing. Only Christian organizations [approved by the government] may apply for the permit

Table 19.2 Believers and clergy of five religions in China

	Catholic	Protestant	Islamic	Buddhist	Daoist
Believers (millions)					
1982[a]	3.0	3.0	10.0	?	?
1995[b]	4.0	10.0	18.0	?	?
Clergy					
1982	3,400	5,900	20,000	27,000	2,600
1995	4,300	18,000	40,000	200,000	25,700
Clergy/believer ratio					
1982	1/882	1/508	1/500		
1995	1/930	1/556	1/450		

1 Li (1999) is an official in the CCP United Front Department.

2 The number of Muslims is the total population of ten ethnic minorities that consider Islam their ethnic religion, although many do not practice Islam.

3 Buddhist and Daoist believers are difficult to define and estimate because of the lack of formal membership in Buddhism and Daoism.

4 The professional ecclesiastics of different religions are not totally comparable because Buddhist and Daoist monks and nuns may not interact with lay believers, whereas Catholic priests, Protestant pastors, and Islamic Imams minister to the laity.

Sources: [a]Document no. 19; [b]Li 1999.

and do so according to state regulations of press. No other organizations or individuals are allowed to edit, print, or distribute Christian scriptures, books, magazines, and tracts" (Luo 2001: 392). The Amity Printing Company in Nanjing has printed tens of millions of copies of the Christian Bible, but this company holds a monopoly in the market. No other presses are allowed to print Bibles. And the distribution channel is also monopolized by the network of the government-approved Three-Self Patriotic Movement Committees. Document No. 19 also stipulates that religious scriptures, booklets, or pamphlets may not be distributed outside religious premises, even if that is by clergy or believers of the officially approved temples, mosques, and churches.

In sum, the regulation on religious supply has been restrictive. However, restrictive measures are not always enforceable. While religious activities, scriptures, and clergy formation are not allowed openly, some religious activities simply go underground. Foreigners have smuggled Bibles and religious publications to China. The control apparatus has been rounding up "self-designated evangelists" or ministers without government recognition (*zi feng chuan dao ren*), but such evangelists continue to rise and proselytize. Some sects, such as the Christianity-inspired Shouters, have experienced crackdowns since the early 1980s, but they still persist, spread, and mutate in organizational form. The black and gray markets of religion (Yang 2006) exist because of the shortage of supply under regulation.

Conclusion

This chapter describes the major religious changes in China under Communist rule. The China case amplifies the importance of political factors in the religious economy. The Chinese religious economy has been a "socialist economy" based on the atheist Communist ideology. The "socialist" economy is by nature a "shortage economy" (Kornai 1980, 1992). In a shortage economy, religious demand is far from stable. Religious demand has been substantially reduced, although never eliminated, and has been increasing in the reform era.

The reality of the religious situation in reform-era China shows that the restrictive regulations have failed to maintain religion in a lower level. While the regulations remain strict, religious revivals have been spreading throughout the country. The regulators have tried hard to spell out procedures and specifics, carry out periodical crackdowns on various religious activities, ban various religious or spiritual movements and organizations and severely punish their leaders. However, religious demand has kept growing. As the suppressing and substituting efforts fail to an ever growing degree, the restrictive measures imposed on the supply side ironically help stimulate even more interest in religion, or help awaken the dormant need for religion, thus increasing active demand for religion.

Changes in the shortage economy of religion under the Communists have been driven mostly by the demand-side dynamics, including queuing up, searching, substituting, and suppressing the demand for religion. The continuously rising demand for religion has forced the authorities to accommodate. The black and gray market religious groups and activities (Yang 2006) have become so large that the control apparatus is simply out of manpower to put them down without substantially draining resources or adversely affect the overall endeavor of economic reforms and social stability. The dramatic changes in the Communist-ruled societies in the last two decades show that moving away from the ideology-based central-planning economy toward a market economy is the only alternative to a total bankruptcy of the system. This is probably so as well in the religious economy.

The functional substitutes for conventional religion especially deserve more careful examination. They are not mere ideas or beliefs, but also have corresponding organizational bases. Near the end of *Suicide* (1951), Durkheim pondered about social institutions that could serve as functional substitutes for religious organizations to sustain the needed moral cohesion or social integration. He considered the schools, the political society or nationalism, the family, and the occupational group or corporation. Interestingly, the Chinese Communist Party has put all of these into practice – the systematic Communist education from kindergarten to college, the political organizations that nourish patriotism/nationalism, and the work unit (*danwei*) as the basic organ of society. Closer examination of such social experiments will be of great interest in both theory and practice. This will also lead the sociology of religion to the sociologies of education, politics, economy, family, culture, and indeed the general sociology of the whole society. After all, religion does not exist in isolation from other social institutions, and no society, including the most secular China under Communist rule, has existed without religion.

Notes

A version of this chapter was originally published in the fall of 2009 in the *Journal of Church and State* 51 (4).

1 Worse, some people even equate the supply-side theory as synonymous to the "new paradigm" of the sociology of religion, even though R. Stephen Warner, who first delineated the emerging new paradigm (1993), and several other scholars have insisted that the new paradigm has a broader scope, including various approaches and theories (see Jelen 2002).

2 Although the CCP-ruled Chinese authorities have insisted on calling it a "*socialist* market economy," while the meaning of "socialist" is debatable, since 2004 the Chinese government has repeatedly appealed to American and European countries in the World Trade Organization to recognize China's economy as a *full market economy*.

3 The Constitution of the People's Republic of China, including the version during the Cultural Revolution, has always included the article of protecting the freedom of religious belief. In practice, however, all temples, churches, and mosques were closed down when the Cultural Revolution broke out in 1966. Not until 1979 were temples, churches, and mosques allowed open for religious activities again.

4 Among the tens of thousands of intractable believers, the most well-known include the Catholic Bishop Gong Pinmei (Kung Pingmei; 1901–2000) in Shanghai, who was jailed between 1955 and 1985 before being exiled to the United States; Protestant minister Wang Mingdao (1900–1991) in Beijing, who was jailed between 1955 and 1979; Watchman Nee (1903–1972), the founder of the Little Flock Christian sect, who was jailed in 1952 and died in prison in 1972; Yuan Xiangchen (1914–2005) in Beijing, who was jailed between 1957 and 1979; Lin Xian'gao (Samuel Lamb; 1924–) in Guangzhou, who was jailed between 1955 and 1978. Lamb and Yuan have become the most renowned Protestant house-church leaders (Aikman 2003).

5 European Values Study Group and World Values Survey Association. European and World Values Surveys Integrated Data File, 1999–2002, Release I [Computer file], 2nd ICPSR version. 2004.

6 The formal vow for becoming a CYP member is: "I am determined to follow the teachings of the Chinese Communist Party, study hard, work hard, labor hard, and be prepared to sacrifice all for the Communist endeavor!" See CYP HomePage: http://cyc6.cycnet.com:8090/ccylmis/cypo/index.jsp.

7 Xinhua News Agency reports on May 3, 2004, and May 31, 2004, June 30, 2004.

8 See *Chan* magazine, no. 3 of 1991: www.chancn.com/magazine/index.asp.

9 "A tourist is half a pilgrim, if a pilgrim is half a tourist." This mantra-like saying, attributed to Victor and Edith Turner, is quoted in the preface of the latest collection of studies in pilgrimage and tourism (Swatos 2006: vii). This proximate measure of religiousness has been used by other scholars inside and outside China as well.

10 According to the Chinese government's *White Paper: Freedom of Religious Belief in China* in 1997, there were more than 85,000 sites for religious activities in the whole country. Some estimates put roughly 350,000 religious congregations in the United States (see Hadaway and Marler 2005). The US population is about 300 million, while the population in China is about 1.3 billion.

Bibliography

Aikman, David (2003) *Jesus in Beijing: How Christianity Is Transforming China and Changing the Global Balance of Power*, Washington, DC: Regnery Publishing.

Burleigh, Michael (2000) National Socialism as a political religion, *Totalitarian Movements and Political Religions* 1 (2): 1–26.

Bush, Richard C., Jr (1970) *Religion in Communist China*, Nashville and New York: Abingdon Press.

Cai, Rongan (2002) *Zongjiao re: linghun de tong chu – dui jinnian lai meishu chuangzuo liu xiang de yi zhong kao lü* (Religious fever: pains of souls – a thought about a trend of art creation in recent years), *Jiangxi Normal University Journal* 2: 74–7.

Carlson, Eric R (2005) China's new regulations on religion: a small step, not a great leap, forward, *Brigham Young University Law Review* 3: 747–97.

Central Party School (CPS) (1998) *Xin Shiqi Minzu Zongjiao Gongzuo Xuanchuan Shouce (Propaganda Manual on Ethnic and Religious Affairs in the New Era)*, Beijing, China: Religious Culture Press.

Chan, Kim-Kwong and Carlson, Eric R (2005) *Religious Freedom in China: Policy, Administration, and Regulation. A Research Handbook*, Santa Barbara: Institute for the Study of American Religion, and Hong Kong: Hong Kong Institute for Culture, Commerce, and Religion.

Chau, Adam (2006) *Miraculous Response: Doing Popular Religion in Contemporary China*, Stanford: Stanford University Press.

Chen, Nancy N (2003a) *Breathing Spaces: Qigong, Psychiatry, and Healing in China*, New York: Columbia University Press.

Chen, Nancy N (2003b) Healing sects and anti-cult campaigns, *China Quarterly* 174 (2): 505–20.

Dean, Kenneth (1993) *Taoist Ritual and Popular Cults of Southeast China*, Princeton: Princeton University Press.

Dean, Kenneth (1998) *Lord of the Three in One*, Princeton: Princeton University Press.

Dean, Kenneth (2003) Local communal religion in contemporary south-east China, *China Quarterly* 174 (2): 338–58.

Durkheim, Émile (1951) *Suicide: A Study in Sociology*, Glencoe, IL: Free Press.

Ellison, Christopher G. and Sherkat, Darren E. (1995) The "semi-involuntary institution" revisited: religional variations in church participation among black Americans, *Social Forces* 73 (4): 1415–37.

Fan, Lizhu (2003) The cult of the silkworm mother as a core of local community religion in a north China village, *China Quarterly* 174 (2): 359–72.

Finke, Roger (1997) The consequences of religious competition: supply-side explanations for religious change, in Lawrence A. Young (ed.), *Rational Choice Theory and Religion: Summary and Assessment*, New York: Routledge, 45–64.

Finke, Roger and Iannaccone, Laurence R. (1993) Supply-side explanations for religious change, *Annals of the American Association for Political and Social Science* 527: 27–39.

Finke, Roger and Rodney Stark (1993) *The Churching of America, 1776–1990: Winners and Losers in Our Religious Economy*, New Brunswick: Rutgers University Press.

Freedom House (2002) *Report Analyzing Seven Secret Chinese Government Documents on Religious Freedom*, Washington, DC: Hudson Institute.

Freedom House (2007) Freedom in the world: China (2007), www.freedomhouse.org/ template.cfm?page=22&country=7155&year=2007.

Froese, Paul (2001) Hungary for religion: a supply-side onterpretation of the Hungarian religious revival, *Journal for the Scientific Study of Religion* 40 (2): 251–68.

Gong, Xuezeng (ed.) (1999) *Minzu, Zongjiao Jiben Wenti Duben (Basic Questions Regarding Ethnicity and Religion: A Reader)*, Chengdu, China: Sichuan People's Press.

Greil, Authur L. and Thomas Robbins (1994) *Between Sacred and Secular: Research and Theory on Quasi-Religion*, Greenwich, CT: JAI Press.

Hadaway, C. Kirk and Penny Long Marler (2005) How many Americans attend worship each week? An alternative approach to measurement, *Journal for the Scientific Study of Religion* 44 (3): 307–22.

Hamberg, Eva M. and Pettersson, Thorlief (2002) Religious markets: supply, demand, and rational choices, in Ted G. Jelen (ed.), *Sacred Markets, Sacred Canopies: Essays on Religious Markets and Religious Pluralism*. Lanham: Rowman and Littlefield, 91–114.

Heibrunn, Jacob (1997) Mao more than ever, *New Republic* 216 (April): 20–4.

Hollander, Paul (1982) Research on Marxist societies: the relationship between theory and practice, *Annual Review of Sociology* 8: 319–51.

Hou, Jie and Fan Lizhu (2001) *Shisu yu shensheng: zhongguo minzhong zongjiao yishi (The Secular and the Sacred: The Religious Consciousness of Chinese People)*, Tianjin: Tianjin People's Press.

Huang, Jianbo and Yang, Fenggang (2005) The cross faces the loudspeakers: a village church perseveres under state power, in Fenggang Yang and Joseph Tamney (eds.), *State, Market, and Religions in Chinese Societies*, Leiden and Boston: Brill.

Human Rights Watch/Asia (1993) *Continuing Religious Repression in China*, New York: Human Rights Watch.

Human Rights Watch/Asia (1997) *China: State Control of Religion*, New York: Human Rights Watch.

Iannaccone, Laurence R. (1994) Why strict churches are strong, *American Journal of Sociology* 99: 1180–1211.

Iannaccone, Laurence R. (1995) Risk, rationality, and religious portfolios, *Economic Inquiry* 33: 285–95.

Information Office of the PRC State Council (1991) *White Paper on the Status of Human Rights in China*.

Jelen, Ted G. (ed.) (2002) *Sacred Markets, Sacred Canopies: Essays on Religious Markets and Religious Pluralism*, Lanham: Rowman and Littlefield.

Jing, Jun (1996) *The Temple of Memories: History, Power, and Morality in a Chinese Village*, Stanford: Stanford University Press.

Kexue Shibao (Science Times) (2007) Yiban yishang xianchuji gongwuyuan nan ju "mixin" (More than half of public service officials at the county or above levels have difficulty in resisting "superstitions"), May 11, 2007, www.sciencetimes.com.cn/htmlnews/ 2007511193241656179151.html.

Kindopp, Jason and Hamrin, Carol Lee (2004) *God and Caesar in China: Policy Implications of Church-State Tensions*, Washington, DC: Brookings Institution Press.

Kornai, János (1979) Resource-constrained versus demand-constrained systems, *Econometrica* 47 (4): 801–20.

Kornai, János (1980) *Economics of Shortage*, Amsterdam; New York; Oxford: North-Holland Publishing Company.

Kornai, János (1992) *The Socialist System: The Political Economy of Communism*, Princeton: Princeton University Press.

Kuah, Khun Eng (2000) *Rebuilding the Ancestral Village: Singaporeans in China*, Aldershot: Ashgate.

Küng, Hans and Ching, Julia (1989) *Christianity and Chinese Religions*, New York: Doubleday.

Lambert, Tony (1999) *China's Christian Millions*, London and Grand Rapids: Monarch Books.

Li, Pingye (1999) 90 niandai zhongguo zongjiao fazhan zhuangkuang baogao (A report of the status of religious development in China in the 1990s), *Journal of Christian Culture* (Beijing) 2: 201–22.

Li, Qiaomei (1996) Lun zhongguo dangdai zuojia de "zongjiao re" (On the "religious fever" among contemporary writers of China), *Guangdong Social Sciences* (Guangzhou) 4: 106–11.

Liu, Ping (1995) Duo Yuan Qu Xiang, Chong Shang Ge Xing, Zi Xin Zi Xing (Pluralist tendency, individualistic outlook, confidence and reflectivity), *Research of Modern Young People (Dangdai Qingnian Yanjiu* (Shanghai) 2: 1–5.

Luke, Timothy W. (1987) Civil religion and secularization: ideological revitalization in post-revolutionary communist systems, *Sociological Forum* 2 (1): 108–34.

Luo, Guangwu (2001) *1949–1999 xin zhongguo zongjiao gongzuo dashi gailan (A Brief Overview of Major Events of Religious Affairs in New China 1949–1999)*, Beijing: Huawen Press.

Luo, Weihong (1992) Shanghai zongjiao shinian fazhan chuyi (A preliminary discussion of the development of Shanghai religion in the past ten years), *Contemporary Religious Research* (Shanghai) 1: 23–9.

Lü, Wei (2001) Jin ru "hou duan quan shiq" ' de zhongguo jingji (Chinese economy entered the "post-shortage period") *Cai jing wenti yanjiu (Research on Financial and Economic Issues)* (Beijing) 3.

MacInnis, Donald E. (1989) *Religion in China Today: Policy and Practice*, Maryknoll: Orbis Books.

MacInnis, Donald E. (1973) The secular vision of a new humanity in People's China, *Christian Century March* 12, 1974: 249–53.

Palmer, David A. (2007) *Qigong Fever: Body, Charisma, and Utopia in China*, New York: Columbia University Press.

Pas, Julian F. (ed.) (1989) *The Turning of the Tide: Religion in China Today*, Hong Kong; Oxford; New York: Oxford University Press.

Potter, Pitman B. (2003) Belief in control: regulation of religion in China, *China Quarterly* 174 (2): 317–37.

Qi, Wen (1991) Shou ci zhongguo dangdai zongjiao xianzhuang yantaohui zai jing juxing (The first symposium on the present religious situation in contemporary China was held in Beijing), *Research on World Religions* (Beijing) 1: 145–8.

Religious Affairs Bureau (RAB) (1995) *Xin Shiqi Zongjiao Gongzuo Wenxian Xuanbian (Selection of Religious Affairs Documents in the New Era)*, Beijing, China: Religious Culture Press.

Religious Affairs Bureau (RAB) (2000) *Quanguo Zongiao Xingzheng Fagui Guizhang Huibian (Collection of Administrative Ordinances on Religion)*, Beijing, China: Religious Culture Press.

Sharot, Stephen (2002) Beyond Christianity: a critique of the rational choice theory of religion from a Weberian and comparative religions perspective, *Sociology of Religion* 63 (4): 427–54.

Sherkat, Darren E. (1997) Embedding religious choices: integrating preferences and social constraints into rational choice theories of religious behavior, in Laurence A. Young (ed.), *Rational Choice Theory and Religion: Summary and Assessment*, New York and London: Routledge, 65–85.

Sherkat, Darren E. and Ellison, Christopher G. (1999) Recent developments and current controversies in the sociology of religion, *Annual Review of Sociology* 25: 363–94.

Sherkat, Darren E. and Wilson, John (1995) Preferences, constraints, and choices in religious markets: an examination of religious switching and apostasy, *Social Forces* 73 (3): 993–1029.

Shorten, Richard (2003) The enlightenment, communism, and political religion: reflections on a misleading trajectory, *Journal of Political Ideologies* 8 (1): 13–37.

Stark, Rodney and Bainbridge, William Simms (1985) *The Future of Religion: Secularization, Revival, and Cult Formation*, Berkeley and Los Angeles: University of California Press.

Stark, Rodney and Finke, Roger (2000) *Acts of Faith: Explaining the Human Side of Religion*, Berkeley and Los Angeles: University of California Press.

Stark, Rodney and Iannaccone, Laurence R. (1994) A supply-side reinterpretation of the "secularization" of Europe, *Journal for the Scientific Study of Religion* 33 (3): 230–52.

Swatos, William H., Jr (ed.) (2006) *On the Road to Being There: Studies in Pilgrimage and Tourism in Late Modernity*, Leiden and Boston: Brill.

Treadgold, Donald W. (1973) *The West in Russia and China 2: China 1582–1949*, Cambridge: Cambridge University Press.

Warner, R. Stephen (1993) Work in progress toward a new paradigm for the sociological study of religion in the United States, *American Journal of Sociology* 98: 1044–93.

Warner, R. Stephen (2002) More progress on the new paradigm, in Ted G. Jelen (ed.), *Sacred Markets, Sacred Canopies: Essays on Religious Markets and Religious Pluralism*, Lanham: Rowman and Littlefield, 1–32.

Welch, H. (1961) Buddhism under the Communists, *China Quarterly* 6 (April–June): 1–14.

Xu, Jian (1999) Body, discourse, and the cultural politics of contemporary Chinese Qigong, *Journal of Asian Studies* 58 (4): 961–92.

Yang, C. K. (1961) *Religion in Chinese Society*, Berkeley and Los Angeles: University of California Press.

Yang, Fenggang (2004) Between secularist ideology and desecularizing reality: the birth and growth of religious research in communist China, *The Sociology of Religion: A Quarterly Review* 65 (2): 101–19.

Yang, Fenggang (2006) The red, black, and gray markets of religion in China, *Sociological Quarterly* 47: 93–122.

Ye, Xiaowen (2000) [1997]. Dangqian woguo de zongjiao wenti: guanyu zongjiao wu xing de zai tantao (Current issues of religion in our country: a reexamination of the five characteristics of religion), in Cao (ed.), *Annual of Religious Research in China, 1997–1998*, Beijing: Religious Culture Press.

Yeh, Michelle (1996) The "cult of poetry" in contemporary China, *Journal of Asian Studies* 55 (1): 51–31.

Ying, Fuk-Tsang (2006) New wine in old wineskins: an appraisal of religious legislation in China and the regulations on religious affairs of 2005, *Religion, State & Society* 34 (4): 347–73.

Zhang, Zhentao (2001) *The Cult of Houtu and the Music Associations in Hebei Province*. Hong Kong: Chinese University of Hong Kong CSRCS Occasional Paper 7.

Zheng, Wen (1997) Dui kanxiang, suanming deng mixin huodong bu ke deng xian shi zhi (Our concerns about physiognomy, fortune-telling and other superstitious activities), *Religions in China* (Beijing): 46–8.

Zuo, Jiping (1991) Political religion: the case of the cultural revolution in China, *Sociological Analysis* 52 (1): 99–110.

20

Native American Religious Traditions
A Sociological Approach

Dennis F. Kelley

Few academic topics produce as much contention and difference than the topic "religion." In addition, the academic study of Indigenous cultures has, at its very heart, the colonialist history of Euroamerica as its impetus. Nonetheless, there have been a great many insights into traditional cultures when these cultures are approached via the portal of sociology. Often, the role of religious scholarship on traditional societies provides insights helpful to the study of religion generally – what Native experts articulate about the practices of their various communities resonates with those in other traditions, such as the varieties of Hindu, Jewish, Muslim, or Christian practices. Therefore, the study of the multitude of distinct American Indian sacred practices must be juxtaposed against the very common articulation of lived worldview that accompanies the great majority of human communities. Of course, the nature of the historic interaction between the modern West and the aboriginal nations of the north American continent has provided a tangle of issues with which contemporary academic and non-academic understandings of Native culture must contend. This chapter is intended to be an overview of the scholarly issues within the sociological study of American Indian religious traditions. In order to accomplish this monumental task in a relatively brief essay, the focus here will be on a theoretical paradigm for understanding the general themes and tendencies in aboriginal North American religious traditions, with some specific examples provided for illustrative purposes, rather than an encyclopedic treatment of the various and unique traditions that make up the religions of aboriginal north America. We will therefore begin with a brief introduction to the history of the study of American Indian religious traditions, which will hopefully illuminate the current discourse. This introduction will be followed by the suggestion of a model for the study of Native American religions that incorporates three key features: the role of sacred places, the understanding of sacred power, and the utility of ritual protocols. These will be contextualized using examples from within the various tribal traditions that make up religious activity in Native north America.

BEGINNINGS

The way in which the academic community has approached American Indian traditions has changed drastically over time, not only reflecting new information gathered in the academic process, but changes in the wider political, religious, cultural, and economic spheres of American society, as well. Early in the process, the study of American Indian religions were often conducted by missionaries who needed a basic knowledge of Native traditions, so as to better manipulate and undermine them (Tinker 1993: 4). The earliest academic scholarship not motivated by Christian bias took shape in the late nineteenth and early to mid-twentieth centuries, a time when Native nations had either been forced on to reservations, or were relegated to the very bottom of social hierarchies. During this time, American Indians were suffering the demographic and cultural decline that resulted from the violent policies of conquest and assimilation. Scholarship responded to this crisis with what has become known as "salvage anthropology" (Hester 1968: 132), designed to rescue cultural data from what were seen as vanishing populations. With the political resurgence of Native communities in the 1960s and 1970s it became very clear to the wider public that Native nations and cultures were not vanishing at all, but are indeed flourishing. During this time, and owing much of their genesis to a course in American Indian History and culture taught at the University of California, Berkeley, more and more Native scholars took on the task of recording and reflecting upon their cultural traditions in an academic setting, and their presence provided the space for truly emic, or *insider*, perspectives on the material. This newfound political presence gave rise to collectives such as the American Indian Movement (AIM), and Native American interests and concerns became known to a much wider audience. This emic presence demanded that scholarship of Native communities recognize the political realities of contemporary Native nations, and the impact that scholarship can potentially have upon those politics. In contemporary scholarship, Native nations exert considerable control over access to cultural resources, and demand that academic studies reflect the concerns, interests, and values of the Native communities themselves, establishing whole new protocols and ethical approaches to these materials within academia. Many scholars, both Native and non-native, see themselves as working *for* rather than working *on* Native communities and cultures, and do so with a greater sense of humility and obligation to these Native communities, thus fitting directly into the ethos of applied sociologists and the models generated by them.

As mentioned previously, missionaries and traders, all of whom had a vested interest in learning about and understanding the Native communities with whom they hoped to work, wrote some of the earliest documents about Native religious traditions. Traders needed to know enough about Indian languages and cultures to successfully negotiate for goods. Missionaries, on the other hand, needed to know enough about the Native communities they encountered to successfully convert them to Christianity. However, much of the data derived from these sources has analytical value, and some of the most informative and most carefully researched documents of this era came from missionaries, such as the Jesuits who arrived in New France in the sixteenth century. To be certain, missionaries and traders all approached Native traditions with an inherent assumption of their inferiority. In their very vocation missionaries were assuming the superiority of Christianity over Native religious and cultural practices. Indeed, for most missionaries, conversion to Christianity simultaneously required a complete conversion to European culture, language, economy, and lifestyle. The texts that these individuals left behind reflect this assumption of cultural superiority. They rarely supplied the perspective of Native people themselves, but described these traditions as they were perceived by outsiders who did not fully understand the philosophies, cultures, or histories that put such religious practices into play.

By the nineteenth century, Native populations were decimated by diseases carried by European colonists; their traditional food resources were devastated by Euroamerican settlers; and their traditional hunting and gathering locations were stripped and leveled for farming or settlement. Following a series of bloody conflicts between the US Army and various Native nations around the continent, most tribes were interred on reservations by the American government where they faced starvation due to lack of resources and the federal government's failure to honor its treaty obligations to provide food, medical care, and other necessities. Restricted to reservations or left to fend for themselves in a country now openly hostile to their very presence, American Indian cultures seemed at the threshold of collapse. Observing the rapid rates at which Native communities were changing, many scholars feared that these cultures would be lost forever.

Unfortunately, in an era dominated by anthropological views guided by the (relatively) new Darwinian philosophy, it was assumed that this loss was inevitable. According to this evolutionary doctrine, all of human culture exists within a linear progression from savagery to civilization. According to this very ethnocentric view, European civilization was, of course, the most advanced and most evolved of all civilizations. As such, it was argued, it was the most fit to survive. Lesser-evolved cultures and societies must, of necessity, pass away so that Western Civilization could proceed. Indigenous cultures throughout the world were seen as less-evolved, having stagnated in their aboriginal cultures.

In addition, according to this view, a European had only to look at indigenous cultures to understand his or her own origins in ancient history. Fascinated with the idea of exploring their own origins, many scholars turned to Native American traditions for a glimpse into the primordial depths of the European, and larger human, psyche. Clearly, such perspectives were intensely problematic. First, they assumed the superiority of one culture over another. Second, they assumed that human civilization exists on an upward linear march toward a final end goal: that societies are necessarily evolving toward purer and better forms. It also assumes that other non-Western cultures had somehow stagnated, have not evolved as they should have, and, that indigenous cultures have remained unchanged for thousands of years. And finally, this social philosophy was entirely informed by the political and economic climate in which it took place. With Manifest Destiny (the belief that the United States was meant to dominate and take over the entire continent from Atlantic to Pacific), and a colonialist agenda that demanded absolute power over what was to become the United States, Euroamericans needed a philosophy that justified their expansion, their theft of land from Native nations, and the incredible devastation that this expansion wreaked upon Native populations. It justified and placated a nation struggling with a guilty conscience.

At the turn of the nineteenth and into the twentieth centuries, ethnographic scholarship struggled with this philosophical legacy. Some ethnographers, such as Franz Boas, challenged the idea of cultural evolution, and insisted that indigenous cultures be understood on their own, not as exemplars of humanity's evolutionary past. But most scholars were still driven by a sense that Native cultures were rapidly disappearing. From the 1880s to the 1950s, these scholars engaged in what has since been termed "salvage ethnography": to collect as much data and material about indigenous cultures and language as possible, before it was crushed underneath the onward march of civilization (Gruber 1970: 1,291).

Though these scholars made enormous contributions to the academic study of American Indian religious traditions, gathering huge amounts of data, and working to create a mode of study that was scientific in its methodology and critical of universalized laws of cultural evolution, aspects of their work remain problematic. While the work of early anthropologists and ethnographers contributed much to the contemporary approach to the academic study of American Indian religious traditions, they nonetheless shared a misperception common among many people of the time: the belief that Native people and cultures were fast disappearing. The urgency behind their work was driven by this belief, and their work reflects both the sense of urgency associated with it, and the assumption of the inevitable disappearance of American Indian cultures. While perhaps undertaken with the best of intentions, salvage ethnographers during this era demonstrated less caution and respect toward Native privacy and sacrality than perhaps should have been the case, and sacred objects, human remains, and details of rituals, ceremonies and songs were removed from the reservations to be housed in museums and anthropological journals. Many of these objects and examples of cultural knowledge were taken without the permission of their proper owners, and many human remains were taken in direct violation of Native communities' protests. Scientists often worked carelessly and aggressively, because, they reasoned, these cultures were about to disappear anyway.

It is true that Native cultures and languages were at risk, and the work of these early scholars was essential in preserving some of these data for future generations. However, the notion of the "vanishing Indian" implies the existence of a "true" Native culture, untarnished by cultural contact, and that culture change inherently meant culture loss. In their emphasis on classical traditions, many of these studies failed to see the means and methods of adaptation, accommodation, and resistance that many Native communities were undertaking. While Native cultures changed dramatically in the twentieth century, they were also successful at survival: as they navigated the changing political, social and economic climates, their religious practices reflected that navigation. Such traditions remained inherently "Indian," as expressions of Native communities, and, while many changes occurred, they maintained a strong connection with the ethical, philosophical and spiritual traditions that informed their earlier traditions.

It might also be noted that scholarship of the late nineteenth and early twentieth century was informed by their perspectives as outsiders; they were never able to fully embody the insiders' perspective on these cultures. As such, their work was directed by the questions and concerns of a non-Native academic community. Their methods, approach, and conclusions were likewise the result of a non-Native academic world. Their publications were written for non-Native audiences, and their collections of artifacts were set aside for the benefit and viewing pleasure of non-Native audiences. In the process, traditions were misinterpreted, sacred objects were mistreated and removed from their proper ritual context, the skeletal remains of Native ancestors were at times removed from Native burials, and the very real ethical and political concerns of the Native communities themselves were not always respected. Certainly this was not always the case, many of these scholars sought to respect the communities with whom they worked, and some testified in court cases on behalf of Native tribes. However, their position as outsiders, and the lack of Native voices to complement their own, meant that a one-sided perspective of Native traditions was presented to the public.

The ability of Native communities to survive the drastic changes of the eighteenth, nineteenth, and twentieth centuries is illustrated in the changing face of Native scholarship of the 1960s and 1970s. With the rise of the American Indian Movement, Native scholars entered the academic scene in greater force, insisting that Native traditions be understood and valued as they were perceived by the people themselves. Further, they insisted that academic scholarship be viewed within its political context, and that the political implications of scholarship be overtly recognized.

As has been noted, the political awareness of Native people was highly influential on the academic study of American Indian religious traditions. With a resurgence of a distinctly Indigenous identity emerging out of the reservation period and culminating with political acts such as the occupations of Alcatraz Island in California and Wounded Knee in South Dakota, a wider audience was available to those who had informed scholarship to share with regard to Native culture. This shift from ethnographic inquiry to that of cultural studies, mirrored in the development of Women's Studies, Black Studies, and Chicana(o) Studies at the level of the university, was at least punctuated, and perhaps indelibly influenced by, the publication of Vine DeLoria Jr's *God Is Red*. Matching the awareness of political and social concerns brought about by political mobilization, this philosophical treatise of the context within which American Indian people understand themselves in terms of worldview, juxtaposed against the totalizing force of Western intellectual support of the subjugation of Native people, not only opened the door for understanding American Indian religiosity as a valid area of philosophical, even theological inquiry, it kicked it wide open. Natives and non-Natives alike were challenged to view the traditional wisdom of this continent's indigenous peoples along side that of all human history. It is within the context of entering the discourse on religious belief, practice, and behavior, that began to produce scholarship in other areas, such as law and literature, dedicated solely to the American Indian experience. Seen as parts of a whole, then, much of the scholarship surrounding Native culture was a collaborative project involving sociologists, anthropologists, literary critics, art critics, linguists, lawyers, theologians, archeologists, and especially, Native American communities themselves, that highlighted the emerging holism which punctuates the discourse today. Emphasis is placed on the communal historic context of the information, with the current social and political aspects of Indian Country as a guide.

THE SIGNIFICANCE OF SOCIOLOGY

Once this discourse was established, it then became itself fodder for the kind of systemic analysis informed by Parsonian Sociology. The approach of Talcott Parsons was instrumental in bringing systems theory and cybernetics to a new generation of sociologists concerned with ethnicity, political power structures, and religious movements. Though contrasting somewhat from Parsons, thinkers such as Walter Buckley and Niklas Luhmann have applied systems theory in ways that frame my thinking with regard to ethnicity, and especially religions of discreet ethnic communities. In addition, the influential book *The Ecology of Freedom: The Emergence and Dissolution of Hierarchy* by Murray Bookchin gives contemporary sociologists of religion grounding in activist paradigms inherent in the discourse on Native American cultures. It is in this vein that I provide a theoretical model for the analysis of Native religious culture generally, and specific issues with regard to the ongoing interaction with these models of social organization and their impact on social and environmental issues relevant to the entire planet.

An important element in this process is the re-visioning of the idea of "religion." Again, it is here that the scholarship on Native cultures provides a direction that analysis of cultural groups in general can borrow from. "Religion" as a unique and separate category of experience does not reflect most Native cultures' experiences, where, in pre-Columbian realities, traditional spirituality encompassed nearly all areas of life, and operated in an integrated mode with the rest of cultural experience. Contemporary scholarship reflects this recognition, exploring religious and spiritual practices as they inform and are impacted by land rights, land use, politics, gaming, social networks, health and wellness, recreation, prisons, political reform, and language preservation (among other things). It is here, of course, that the work of Émile Durkheim has been most influential in the understanding of the role that religion plays in the development and maintenance of American Indian religious identity. The establishment of an contemporary "moral community" within modern Native populations, one that not only responds to individual spiritual needs but also unites the collective in a politically relevant system, is a key feature of what has been called the Native American "resurgence" (Nagle 1997), "revitalization" (Wallace 1956), and "reprise." The understanding of American Indian religious traditions through the lens of sociology, in other words, is to understand the ongoing utility of sacred traditions for Native communities navigating the complexities of their political realities.

This is the key to an application of this theoretical paradigm, that of the primacy of religious action and materiality to the process of utilizing active, physical, material expressions of communal identity that cement the individual to that community. What thinkers like Pierre Bourdieu, Talcott Parsons, and of course, Émile Durkheim have shown is that the collectivity supersedes the individual on a deep level in the human consciousness, and in particular, Bourdieu's notion of the *habitus* as "society written into the body" speaks to the inexorable link between the requirements of group membership and individual action. Using *habitus* and Bourdieu's connected use of "field," along with "cultural capital" assigned by both Natives and non-Natives to the idea of "Indianness" contributes to the larger social paradigms associated with power relationships in modernity. The very presence of Native communities in modernity can be seen as a living critique of the American project, thus, the expression of Indian identity is not confined to an individual desire for a more evocative spiritual life, as it is among many New Age adherents who attempt to employ some of the same material and active elements of Native culture, but rather an attempt to bind oneself to an autochthonous community, an ancestral tradition, that transcends many of the paradigmatic forms that the study of religion relies upon. In addition, the emphasis on issues of belief not only favors some of the world's religious traditions, but also can obscure important aspects of them. What I suggest here is that, if the cultural products and processes that have come to be called "religious" function in some way to form a collective identity as well as an individual one capable of conforming to the collective, then overt expression and externalized action are the markers for those individual and collective expressions. Exemplars for identity, then, are numerous in the discourse on religion, and the comparative project is furthered by the analysis of these actions in terms of collective systems much more so that becoming mired in the individuated beliefs that are used to rationalize them.

In addition, pan-Indian uses of cultural practices have served as examples of what I have elsewhere termed "employed exemplars," elements of performed and tangible culture that, in their use and display, allow for a collective representation of a communal ethos. Often, these elements of traditional culture provide urban Indian communities and reservations that have experienced some lapse with culturally specific elements around which to form identities, and the connected collective spirituality, as Indian people. Ceremonial practices, such as "sweating" – fairly ubiquitous in Indian Country and one of the most commonly retained religious practices – has taken a more central place in many Indian communities due to its availability in the contemporary world. The adoption of a pan-tribal standard, one that borrows heavily from the Lakota *inipi*, transcends specific tribally located ontologies that a view informed by the likes of Rodney Stark would require for the validation of the identity formed and maintained through it use. Practically, however, *behaving one's religion* is the more productive paradigm, not only for explaining the persistence of the sweat, but its distribution through various contexts in Indian Country. Therefore, an integration of the key concepts associated with Bourdieu's concept *habitus*, and the associated issues of social power, with the autopoietic foundations of socialcybernetics provides a rationale for establishing a Parsonian perspective that unites the basic motives and characters of these disparate traditions.

My sincere hope is that I have provided evidence for the consideration of the sociological approach to Native American sacred traditions to contexts within the academic study of religion generally. I aver that there are "blind spots" resulting from an over-emphasis on issues of belief and internally reflective paradigms that need to be addressed in Religious Studies, which I believe can be mediated by a more practice-centered approach. Looking at how religious action informs communal identities can provide a nuanced perspective to issues of religious conflict, religious nationalism, and globalization. Native Americans have *both* conformed to the Euroamerican category "Indian" by developing pan-tribal identities and networks, *and* maintained discreet tribal-specific traditions. The development of "pan-Indian" structures goes as far back as the first European contact, as the tribal groups most effected by initial colonial efforts found benefit in uniting in regional networks that belied many of the traditional divisions and even hostilities of pre-Columbian times. Of course many of those divisions were also maintained and even intensified as a result of the European encounter, as well. However, clearly Native communities quickly became aware that the European interlopers viewed them as "Indians" first, distinct regional communities second, and this tendency became an important organizational factor when the colonial projects of England, Spain, and France became clear. Today, there are many examples of this "pan-Indian" identity: the aforementioned sweating styles, common expressions of aboriginal spirituality in prayer and ceremony, and pan-tribal standards in ceremonial regalia and music. The important thing to note here is that the presence of these commonalities have been among the most important strategies for the maintenance of specific tribal traditions. Though this may seem somewhat counterintuitive, when viewed within the historical reality of what David Stannard has called the "American holocaust," it becomes clear that maintenance of a broad "indigenous" identity allowed communities to remain intact, both on reservations and in urban centers, so that the re-emergence of specific traditions could occur when the greatest opposition to the presence of American Indian communities had dissipated.

This is my justification, then, for using the tools of sociology and cultural studies to establish a set of three key principles that are both common to the various tribal traditions that make up Native American sacred culture, but also provide mobile categories for a reevaluation of the scholarship regarding religious identity generally. These categories are Locale, Sacred Power, and Protocol.

LOCALE

The reasons for choosing the term "locale" rather than "place" or "space" is significant and requires some discussion here. The concept "place" connotes a location in geographic terms. While it is true that land-based orientation is one of the key issues with regard to American Indian spirituality and that that set of issues will play prominently in the entirety of this work, geographic location is only one facet of the embedded quality of indigenous cultures. Much has been written on the topic of the importance of place to American Indian religious traditions and this central theme will be unpacked later in my argument. Suffice it to say here that my understanding of the category "locale" follows closely on that of historian of religion Jonathan Z. Smith's use of "place" in his seminal texts *To Take Place: Toward Theory in Ritual* (1992) and *Map is Not Territory: Studies in the History of Religions* (1993), illuminates the relationship between human activity and the construction of places.

"Taking place" is, of course, a dual-use phrase that alludes both to events occurring, and the actual apprehension of a territory – the implication in the phrase is that there is an active presence transforming "area," or space in a geographical sense, into "place." In *Map is not Territory*, Smith identifies what he calls "locative" cultures, as contrasting with "utopian" ones (Smith 1993: 309). This distinction is significant to this project in that it brings a religious discussion to bear on the economic factors leading to Anthony Giddens' term "disembededness." For Giddens, modernity is both "disembedded" and "post-traditional," key features in the development of an ideology associated with the historic, political, and economic reality of a post-Renaissance worldview. Modernity, then, has produced utopian and disembedded cultures. Smith places the religions of these cultures in juxtaposition to "locative" cultures – cultures that can be then referred to as "embedded" ones (Giddens 1991: 80).

For Smith, utopian religious systems are religions of " 'nowhere,' of transcendence" and correspond to the quality of the immigrant (Smith 1992: 310). The religious activity of the immigrant, then, centers on developing systems for accessing the transcendent, usually in the form of an omnipresent deity, through visions and/ or epiphanies, which renders a religious system capable of bringing a sense of the sacred *along with* the disembedded cultures, or perhaps more precisely, allowing for the assumption that the sacred is *everywhere*, and therefore, *nowhere in particular*. Religious disembeddedness and portable gods allow for the assumption of any new region entered into as potential "space," taken on authority of the immigrant's utopian sacred system.

In contrast, an imminent sense of the sacred, a sacredness that *resides* with the people, as in "embedded" spiritual systems, assumes the role of the territory in adhering to that sacredness. In fact it may be, for some indigenous religious systems, that it is the *place* that authors the proper sacred behaviors. In other words, the logic of these "locative" systems assumes the land itself is an actor, and perhaps the *key* actor in the development of the sacred behaviors appropriate to that land. If "sacred behaviors" can stand in for the academic term "religion," then the ultimate defining quality of indigenous religious systems may be the derivation of those systems from the landscape itself. Thus, the category "locale" used here begins with a sense of the deep connection between the sacred aspects of the universe and the physical reality of territory.

An example of this from within Indian Country has been shown in the brilliant work of Keith Basso, especially in his book *Wisdom Sits in Places*. Basso uses the storytelling tradition of the Western Apache as a model for how sacred knowledge is connected to specific aspects of the landscape. For the Western Apaches, the names of places within their territory are imbued with a sacredness that results from the original naming of these places by the ancestors. Each place has a name that places it in relationship to the sacred narrative of the Western Apache, and the associated stories provide wisdom in the form of socially relevant themes and cautionary tales that help contemporary Apaches live a life informed by the knowledge of their sacred tradition. What Basso shows is that even to say the names of the places becomes a sort of meditation, "quoting the ancestors," and that walking on the land is to place oneself in physical and temporal proximity to the very nature of the sacred universe.

In addition to the sacred nature of place in indigenous religious systems, there is also an assumption of human activity within that sphere which actualizes the religious system. Therefore, "locale" also refers to appropriate activities that occur in a place. While this aspect of the argument will be covered in the section on "protocol," it is important to stress that my sense of the category locale includes *both* the inherent sacredness of the landscape in indigenous religious systems, *and* the relevance of that sacredness to human activity in that landscape. While it is important to note that most, if not all, indigenous systems assume a sacredness that resides in the land itself, there is also the quality of appropriate community activity relative to that sacred landscape: indigenous communities see themselves as both occupying and being occupied by the land.

This is the key quality to the locale concept utilized herein: the landscapes live *in* the people as certainly as they live in the landscape. The inexorable link between the place and the religious system does not necessarily mean that the removal of the people from the place deflates the system, but that the system itself comes to be carried with the land held in the collective memory. Specific landscapes teach their people how to live anywhere, and it is the adaptability of the locative cultures to new settings in both cultural and geographic space that is the underlying assumption of the "locale" concept. There is an obvious theoretical turn here that connotes social construction – that it is the people themselves that produce the sacred landscape in a way that can be engendered and communicated by and to the people within the religious sphere. In this way, the sacralization and continued re-imagining of that sacred landscape can be understood through the work of Henri Lefebvre and his notion of the production of space/place.

In his book *The Production of Space* (1991), Lefebvre continued the intellectual work of the *Situationiste International* and their critique of urbanism by employing the Marxist concepts "alienation" and "appropriation" in discussing French gentrification projects in Paris. Essentially a critical analysis wherein the gentrification process is an act of displacing the community associated with certain areas of the city and replacing them with new groups who can pretend a locative identification, Lefebvre unpacks the sociocultural act of appropriation from within a Marxist paradigm, highlighting the power differentials associated with the gentrification process. For Lefebvre, appropriation is a "diversion" (*"detournement"*), a re-utilization of abandoned places, thereby infusing them with new meaning and identity, in part as a method for divesting local interest in social spaces such as markets and neighborhoods in order to open them to new investment by giving the spaces new identities. My entrance into this discussion is to expand on Lefebvre's idea by suggesting that it is possible to participate in a kind of re-appropriation through the employment of culturally specific objects and practices, as well as geographic space. The exemplary objects and actions with regard to the religious revitalization of American Indian communities (such as imagery and materials which connote "Indianess") then become contested *space*, politically charged items and acts of culture that vie for meaning in the equally contested territory of the imaginations of Native people *vis á vis* that of American society at large by providing iconic elements of Native American culture which can be employed in a kind of "counter-gentrification." These "exemplars" which vary greatly between the diverse tribal cultures, provide the stance from which space, and therefore identity, can be liberated from the control of the dominant culture and returned to the people of origin. Further, these exemplars gain in cultural *cachet* if they are available to physicality in a "religious" realm – in short, sacred items in use during sacred practices – and become what I have termed elsewhere "employed exemplars" (p. 23), items of cultural value that are *used in specific contexts*, becoming markers for cultural adherence.

For example, two tribal traditions, the Chumash of the central California coastal region, and the Makah of Neah Bay, Washington, have returned to their canoe traditions as an important element of their cultural revitalization. Thus, the canoe (a sacred object) is employed through paddling (a sacred practice), as a way to revitalize religio-cultural identity associated with a particular geographic region (a locale). As canoes are available to anyone, both native and non-native wishing to employ them in these particular places, it is the process of distinguishing *a certain kind* of paddling as "sacred" and thus unique to the native peoples of the region, that provides the framework for the cultural and concomitant religious revitalization.

Since the renaissance sparked by the Makah's participation in the excavation of an important site known as Ozette Village, the importance of the large, ocean-going cedar canoes to the social, spiritual, and economic turnaround currently underway cannot be overstated. A reservation that lies at the very outskirts of the continental USA, very little in the way of economic self-determination was open to the Makahs, rendering a tattered social fabric with the accompanying social ills of gangs, drug and alcohol abuse, and domestic violence. However, with the re-introduction (along with many canoe-oriented tribes throughout the Pacific Northwest) of traditional maritime cultural values, the community has experienced a virtual turnaround. Now teenagers proudly belong to canoe clubs, membership in which requires strict adherence to drug and alcohol-free lifestyles, respect for elders and others, and probably the most unique aspect for tribal communities burdened with the fallout of the reservation system, respect for themselves. The building, maintenance, and employment of these canoes in modern waters is an important aspect of the ongoing cultural reprise that the Makah associate with living a better life and passing that life on to future generations.

Similarly, in the process of learning the behaviors and skills required for the rowing of the Chumash canoe, or *tomol*, the Chumash have also begun to fashion a rhetorical system within which the *tomol* protocol and the actual requirements for paddling are transmitted to others, especially the young people. This rhetoric is consistemtly connected to issues of valuing the specific natural world seen as the homeland of the Chumash people. In fact, the canoe revival in Chumash communities has engendered a concomitant increase in environmental activism in the Santa Barbara and Ventura region of central California. The Chumash see themselves as stewards of these particular locales, and the *tomol* as the tool for managing that relationship. Thus, in the reprise of canoe culture for both the Chumash and the Makah, the canoe provides an opportunity to express what it is that comprises the traditional ethos, which is inherently associated with the homeland.

As Lefebvre has shown, much of the modern project is an appropriation of space; the abstracting of space in order to control meaning, much like the process described as "disembedding" by Giddens. It is the resulting abstract space that attempts to produce and impose social homogeneity. Seeing places as empty space to be traded as commodities allows for the dissolution of the lived social systems dedicated to those places, and it is partly in response to this social distanciation that indigenous attempts to exert traditional control in the reappropriation of places, objects, and practices operates. The traditional authority over the locale exists as a localized power to which the people are responsible for the ongoing maintenance of the homeland, a lived social space, that can be termed "sacred power."

SACRED POWER

It is beyond the scope of this chapter to fully interrogate the category "sacred power" as it is employed in the study of religion. However, it is imperative that my use of this term achieves clarity sufficient to the understanding of my overall argument. My use of this term conforms closely to Mircea Eliade's sense of something set apart from the "profane" or mundane (Eliade 1968: 10). The larger issues involve *how* and *why* things are "set apart." While there is much variety in the discussion of religious sacrality, there is also consensus as to the culturally located act of categorizing the "sacred," as well as the placing of items in that category (places, songs, objects, people, times, etc).

In the modern context, American Indian religious revitalization consists primarily of locating the community within the parameters of a (tribally defined) sacred universe, which constitutes, like defining terms and appropriating space, a political act. In other words, the processes associated with cultural and religious revitalization in American Indian communities assumes a certain level of lapse, which necessitates the revitalization in the first place. This context requires extensive discussion. It will have to suffice here to state that it is apparent that the histories of the aboriginal inhabitants of this continent have included pressures from the colonial efforts of Euroamericans. This pressure has led to the cultural and religious displacement that revitalization addresses. Revitalization and renewal of religio-cultural identity, then, occurs within the contested realm of signification (Long 1986: 61).

Defining the sacred, and acting in response to that defined quality, remains at the center of the revitalization process. It is often this act that precludes the individual impetus for indigenous renewal. Therefore, sacred power is both culturally located and contextual, following the definition of religion laid out above. Sacredness, then, can be seen as the manifestation of the principal organizing power in the universe. This follows closely Gregory Bateson and his approach using systemic theories in that the act of setting something, someone, sometime, or someplace apart as "sacred" is done to create markers for the assumptions that underpin a society, markers that protect these basic building blocks in the "schismogenic" nature of human culture (Bateson 1987: 112).

One key feature of American Indian cultures that highlight this process of marking can be seen is the particular creation narratives associated with the various tribal traditions. To be sure, this fact is also true for other of the world's religious traditions. But it is in the ongoing significance of the themes associated with Native American creation stories that also implies an assertion of specificity, one that is, again, an aspect of embeddedness that creates distance from the universality of the Christian paradigm used to counter aboriginal north American connections to the land and its traditions. A particularly cogent example of this lies in the Diné (Navajo) connection to the creatrix deity, Changing Woman.

For the Diné, their creation story is one of emergence, from underworlds into this one. However, the Diné people themselves were actually created in this world by a sacred being, Changing Woman, who used dead skin from her body along with minerals associated with the Diné landscape and ground corn in the colors of the four directions to share their actual bodies. The spiritual essence of the people travelled with the other sacred being in this journey through the successive underworlds into this one, but Changing Woman gave them their particular physical bodies once here. In addition, as her name implies, Changing Woman has a particular role in that She came into this world as an infant, but matured to menarche in twelve days. Her first menstrual period is marked with a ceremony, the *kinaldáa*, by the sacred beings, and it is this ceremony that is performed for all young women who come of age in Diné communities to this day. Thus, the concepts associated with this earth-based deity – fertility, productivity, and the feminine – represent the key concept associated with the sacred power of the universe. The woman's body is a microcosm of the universe, and menses are seen as connected to the natural rhythms of the land.

This example shows the totalizing concept "sacred power" as it emerges in the various discourses associated with the study of religion, but also the particularity with regard to American Indian sacred connections to locales. Unlike an anthropological conceptualization of the concept "sacred power" associated with the work of E. B. Tylor and James Frazer, a sociological approach renders a view that is more utilitarian, engaging the social systems associated with these concepts. In the Diné example, one isn't surprised to se the association of sacred power with the feminine rendering a matriarchal, and matrilocal society. In addition, the *kinaldáa* continues as one of the most important ceremonial complexes in Diné society, giving contemporary Diné an opportunity to empower their young women in ways that are complementary to modern feminist ideologies.

My attempt here is to orient the reader to my particular direction concerning the broad term "sacred" and the particular function that the term obtains in both religious circumstances and the study of those circumstances. In terms of concrete circumstances regarding this ineffable quality, the actions taken in a communal setting that adhere to the overall sacred quality assigned to that setting follow a general proprietary patina I will here term "protocol."

PROTOCOL

As emphasized in the section on "locale," the power that resides in and works with the people is linked inexorably to the landscape itself. This connection between locale and power is what constitutes the special relationship the people living in that locale have to the power of that locale. This relationship, following the logic of Durkheim, connotes the relationship the people experience with each other. The social structure is therefore reflected in the relationship between the people and the sacred power within the context of the locale. This relationship requires a system for enacting both the social responsibilities given the sacred locale, and the sacred responsibilities to the source and manifestation of that power. I use here the term "protocol" to refer to this system.

While the term "protocol" has a fairly broad usage, with etymological connections to issues of etiquette, agreement, and propriety, all of the connotations are nonetheless both communal and active. One utilizes or refers to a protocol, and does so in order to arrive at an agreed-upon standard. I take the key features of this operational category to conform to the category "ritual." However, my sense of sacred practice is at the center of this discussion, therefore the category protocol requires a much more extensive treatment. "Ritual," as a feature of protocol, requires its own clarification here.

Again taking my lead from J. Z. Smith, ritual connotes a "gnostic" quality within religion (Smith 1980: 125), which reflects what Smith calls "an exercise in the strategy of choice" (p. 116). This distinction, that ritual is a thoughtful and purposeful exercise, defies the term's vernacular use, which engenders issues of mindlessness and empty repetition. Ritual provides a systematized method for encountering and interacting with the sacred, and is therefore often repetitive with regard to actual practice, and can be rote in the sense of second-nature. However, Smith shows that repetition and unconsciousness can impart, or result from, focused attempts at generating meaning. Rituals are, at their base, communally meaningful prescribed actions which communicate and enact the proper ethos given the shared understanding of the structure of the sacred universe. The conscious incorporation of traditional activities associated with American Indian tribal cultures by Indians engaged in cultural and religious renewal, are examples of Smith's notion of strategy and choice, bringing Indian people to a larger sense of their cultural identity as well as communicating that identity to others, both Indian and non-Indian.

The Sacred Pipe Ceremonies of the Lakota provide an excellent window into this use of the concept. The Lakota, a tribal tradition associate with the Great Plains, employ a complex system of ritualized activities aimed specifically to maintain a moral community. Derived from an encounter with a sacred being called White Buffalo Calf Woman, the ceremonial complex associated with the Pipe were given to the Lakota at a time when the people were experiencing economic and social problems. Thus, these ceremonies, and in particular the meaning of the Pipe, are particularly focused on the maintenance of a tradition associated with a particular socio-historic community.

The Sacred Pipe (*cannupa wakan*) has become somewhat iconic in the imaginations of non-Indians with regard to Native rituals generally, but it is, rather, a Plains-specific tradition employing the act of smoking tobacco and non-intoxicating herbs in a ceremonial marking of unity – between people and between the people and the Earth – that can be directly compared with the Christian ritual known as *Eucharist*. The Pipe itself exemplifies the blending of the key aspects of the Lakota sacred universe and one assumes that the act of smoking with others binds that group in an obliged relationship to that universe.

In terms of protocol, then, rituals such as the Pipe Ceremony provide important opportunities to engage the sacred system for the purposes of learning and displaying the knowledge of one's proper role in that system. For indigenous communities, the embedded nature of that system warrants ritualized approaches to daily life, as well. Thus, protocol can be seen as ritualized interpersonal interactions, with the assumption that the other-than-human world obtains personhood, as well as the human. Sacred beings and the natural world warrant diplomatic status, as do the members of the human community. It is this quality, that of proper behavior given the sacred nature of the lived universe, that underpins the use of the term "protocol" herein, and protocol provides opportunities to engage in the strategies of identity formation and negotiation through the employment of ritual acts and paraphernalia.

Indigenousness, the autochthonous and lived experience of locale, sacred power, and protocol, provides the contextual backdrop for this discussion of sacred practices and their importance to the production and maintenance of religious identity. Indigenous identity is a growing movement worldwide, as people who trace their traditions to their lived locales attempt to reestablish control over their own cultural and religious destinies. My argument here is that culturally significant *practices* provide the key to the understanding of traditional religious identity, with the more individuated and internal issues associated with *belief* providing the supportive rationale for this identity. Further, I believe that this quality – that of the primacy of practice over a secondary role of religious belief – provides a helpful paradigm from which the sociological study of religions generally can proceed.

Pierre Bourdieu responds to Émile Durkheim and what Bourdieu calls the "gnoseological problems" Durkheim raised with regard to traditional society as revealing their political nature when raised in response to contemporary social structures (Bourdieu 1990: 24). Specifically, Bourdieu states that "forms of classification are forms of domination" and that a sociology of knowledge rests upon "symbolic domination" (p. 25). American sociology of the 1950s and 1960s, Bourdieu claims, took on the character of an orthodoxy, a *communis doctorum opinio* that is inappropriate for the sciences and served the demands of those in power that any discourse on the social world should be "kept at arm's length and neutralized" (p. 38). On a perusal of sociological reviews of the period, Bourdieu found "empty academic rambling about the social world, with very little empirical material ... [using] ... concepts that are only understandable if you have some idea of the concrete referent in the mind of the people using these concepts" (p. 39). It is my view that a post-Boasian American anthropology responded to the call for "salvage ethnography" rising out of the same social and cultural milieu which informed the sociology of the time, one that places the industrial West, in particular American-style free market industry, at the apex of human culture. The scientific exploration, classification, and archival of the non-industrial, "primitive" cultures, therefore, needed to be done before their inevitable disappearance "like the snow before the noontide sun," to quote one early archeologist of Chumash sites (Benson 1997: 28). Thus, the social sciences of the 1950s and 1960s were being informed by the same cultural stimulus described by Bourdieu. Led by Claude Lévi-Strauss, the structuralism loosely based upon Saussure's linguistic theories becomes a set of reified categories for social behavior above which the analyst can hover and observe, aware of their implications in a way that eclipses the minds of the subject. In addition, the so-called "primitive mind," is seen in this view as a window into our human past, setting up some of the most difficult barriers to the free expression of contemporary American Indian religiosity via the biases inherent in this ethnocentric position.

One example of these continuing biases is the ongoing, uncritical use of terms such as "conversion"when discussing missionization. This term is so misused as to be virtually worthless when attributed to the American Indian experience. The implication is missionaries completely transformed all the "converts" in their control into Christians in the fullest sense of that (also problematic) term. I am of the opinion that it is sociological inquiry, a generalized analysis of social and cultural movements associated with the structures that constitute and influence societies, which can address many of the problematic biases that exist with regard to the study of Native American religions.

CONCLUSION

American Indians are among those discreet ethnic groups that possess both a broad collective identity and localized and specific communal traditions. Therefore, like the discourse on the religious communities of the Indian subcontinent, religious diversity in Japan, or the religions of Africa, much effort must be made to avoid the perpetuation of stereotypes while trying to speak in the broadest terms possible. Like indigenous traditions around the world, Native American religions are inexorably connected to specific landscapes and are therefore oriented to small-scale societies associated with subsistence-level management of resources. This is not to say, of course, that they are in any way "simple." What I have attempted to show, through a few diverse examples, is that these cultures are indeed religiously complex in terms of philosophical concepts and social organization alike. This complexity contributes to the sociological interest of the study of these tribal traditions in that there is often a disconnect between the reality within the tradition and the perceptions held by outsiders. In addition, the politically motivated nature of the perceptual gap is itself an actor in the development of both individual tribal communities and their pan-Indian collectives, as well as the adaptation of these to modernity. The Chumash and Makah canoes are purposefully anachronistic so to better claim an aboriginal status which runs counter to the perceived shortcomings of modern society. The Diné kinaldáa provides an ongoing critique of marginalization, both gender and ethnic, for both Diné people and the non-Indian communities with whom they communicate. And the Sacred Pipe Religion gives contemporary Lakotas a spiritual foundation from which to forge an intact and relevant traditional community that has resisted some of the most virulent anti-Indian actions our government unleashed on Native America.

Max Weber's non-positivistic use of the concept *verstehen* calls us to view religious concepts in the sociohistoric context associated with the communities who employ these concepts. For Native Americans, this context has to include the American colonial project, a project that in many ways is still ongoing, and one that can rightly be viewed as genocidal. In his epilogue to *American Holocaust*, Stannard makes a comparison between the cognitive vicissitudes of white American views of Native peoples to the difference between pre and post WWII views of the Japanese. Prior to the war in the Pacific, many "experts" (including the curator of the Smithsonian Institution's Anthropology Division) held that the Japanese were inherently inferior to European-based peoples (the anthropology curator informed the president that the Japanese skull was 2,000 years behind ours in development), and that they were hopelessly incapable warriors who lacked the ability to pilot planes effectively or even shoot straight (due to their "slanted eyes."). After the attacks at Pearl Harbor and the US entry into the war on the

Pacific front, the view of Japanese people changed dramatically. They were then seen as "super-competent warriors" but "morally subhuman." This distinction allowed for the rationalization of the killing of civilians, shooting surrendering soldiers, and tossing the dying into pits with the already dead. Stannard makes this comparison at the end of his treatise in part to show the method for the moral justification of genocidal practices toward aboriginal north Americans. But it also highlights a concept more germane to the current work: the depiction of the minoritized community by the dominant culture directs very real consequences to those marginalized communities. It is in the spirit of Louis Wirth, then and applied sociology that this piece has been produced: one must fully understand three key aspects of American Indian cultures in order to place the religions of those cultures into a proper analytical perspective. First, the tribal traditions associated with Native America are varied and diverse, and it is with specific and important caveats that one approaches American Indian religions as a broad category. The second aspect speaks directly to this fact in that the political, economic and social reality of colonialism cannot be separated from the analysis. The search for a "pure" tradition unsullied by contact has done more to obfuscate the reality of Native America than to clarify it. And third, a theoretical model wherein the concepts locale, sacred power, and ritual protocols guide the evaluation of data from within Native religious contexts can render a set of principles from which both analytical and predictive models can aid in the sociological conceptualization of American Indian religious traditions.

Bibliography

Bateson, Gregory (1987) *Angels Fear: Towards an Epistemology of the Sacred*, New York: Macmillan.

Benson, Arlene (1997) *The Noontide Sun: The Field Notes of the Reverend Stephen Bowers, Pioneer California Archeologist*, California: Ballena Press.

Bourdieu, Pierre (1990) *In Other Words: Essays towards a Reflexive Sociology*, Stanford: Stanford University Press.

Eliade, Mircea (1968) [1957] *The Sacred and the Profane: The Nature of Religion*, Orlando: Harcourt.

Giddens, Anthony (1991) *The Consequences of Modernity*, Stanford: Stanford University Press.

Gruber, Jacob W. (1970) Ethnographic salvage and the shaping of anthropology, *American Anthropologist* 72 (6): 1289–99.

Hester, James J. (1968) Pioneer methods in salvage anthropology, *Anthropological Quarterly* (Dam Anthropology: River Basin Research, special issue) 41 (3): 132–146.

Long, Charles (1986) *Significations: Signs, Symbols and Images in the Interpretation of Religion*, Minnesota: Fortress.

Nagle, Joane (1997) *American Indian Ethnic Renewal: Red Power and the Resurgence of Identity and Culture*, New York: Oxford.

Smith, Jonathon Z. (1980) The bare facts of ritual, *History of Religions* 20 (1–2).

Smith, Jonathon Z. (1992) *To Take Place: Toward Theory in Ritual*, Chicago: University of Chicago Press.

Smith, Jonathon Z. (1993) *Map Is Not Territory: Studies in the Histories of Religions*, Chicago: University of Chicago Press.

Tinker, George (1993) *Missionary Conquest: The Gospel and Native American Cultural Genocide*, Minnesota: Fortress.

Wallace, Anthony F. C. (1956) *American Anthropologist* (new series) 58 (2): 264–81.

Part VI
Globalization

21

Globalization and the Sociology of Religion

Lionel Obadia

Introduction: Globalization and Religious Studies

Religion has often been, and still is, considered as a discreet – not to say evanescent – chapter of Globalization Studies (Robertson 1992; Waters 2001; Beckford 2003; Csordas 2007a). The recent increase in the number of publications on this theme, however, seems to demonstrate that such studies are not characterized by their scarcity, but rather by their proliferation, and it is already becoming difficult to outline the entire body of works devoted to religion and globalization. In consequence, this chapter only acquaints us with a small share of them, yet it aims to delineate a significant part. Indeed, Religious Studies have recently embraced this new theme, and its potential for updating their theoretical models, in a context in which religion inexorably and more ostensibly progresses toward new "modern" individual configurations of existence, social and territorial organization, new cultural and symbolic frames, and economic exchanges, worldwide communication and technological transfers, in the very heart of a globalization from which observers and theorists religion did not play any crucial role (Kale 2004). All things considered, the term "globalization" is still challenging since it assumes no unity in use and meaning. Under the aspect of diversity, theories of globalization nevertheless seem to come together in a few main models ("World"- systems – culture, – society or – capitalism – see Sklair 1999) or perspectives. To put it briefly, and risk extreme simplification, they subdivide among systemic theories of "world-something," inspired by structuralist-functionalist models, established on the idea that there exists an increasing connectivity and integration between societies, and theories of "flows," strongly influenced by diffusion models, underscoring human and cultural mobility. The first model relates to the "convergence" theory, that is structural homogenization, but the second is associated with fragmentation" theory, i.e. global differentiation.

Ulrich Beck attempted to map out the contours of the semantic field, and suggested differentiation between *globality* (the condition of the present-day world), *globalization* (worldwide processes) and *globalism* (ideologies of globalization)

LIONEL OBADIA

(Beck 1999). Martha Van Der Bly, however, called attention to ambiguities as inherent in the three main versions of globalization, when the term is promoted to a sociological concept (2005): "globalization-as-a-Condition" opposing "globalization-as-a-Process," "globalization-as-Reality" dissimilar to "globalization-as-Futurology," and "One-Dimensional-globalization" contradicting "Multidimensional globalization." Van Der Bly has cleverly pointed out that all these models introduce specific biases, whether they underestimate or overvalue temporal, human or conjectural parameters (Van Der Bly 2005). Yet, and in spite of the obvious problems the reference to "the global" induce, James Beckford suggests that globalization is a concept which is "good to think with" in relation to religion: the latter (religion) indeed challenges any theoretical attempt to simplify a phenomenon (globalization) so eminently diversified and complex (Beckford 2003). The relationships religions assume with globalization actually provide the intellectual basis of (or are shaped by) *globalisms*, which vary significantly from one another by national and local context.

New approaches to the study of religions in the globalist scope subsequently offer a wide-opened panorama of global perspectives (as in Robertson 1992; Beyer 1994, 2006; Beckford 2003), local ones (based on regional case-studies, as in Garrard-Burnett 2004; Beyer and Beaman 2007; Geertz and Warburg 2008) or comparative ones, either for New Religious Movements (Rothstein 2001; Clarke 2006) or world religions (Kurtz 2007; Esposito et al. 2008). Several authors have recently attempted to better circumscribe the relationships between religion and globalization. Thomas Csordas outlines three relationships, corresponding, respectively, to a correlative, a causal, and an identity link: "globalization *and* religion "distinguished from" globalization *of* religion" and "globalization *as* religion" (2007a: 265).

The analysis of the role of religion in the path of globalization is not consensual, but religion is regularly mentioned as a *parameter* or as one of the main historical forces in the accomplishment of globalization. In Martin Albrow's views, globalization is indeed considered as a "New Age" (1996). Albrow's stance espouses dominant models of history, cut up into substitutive sequences: in this model, the era of modernity is followed by either an era of postmodernity or an era of globalization. Since Karl Jaspers' theory of "Axial Age" (one of Albrow's influences), great religions of the world are frequently assumed to play a key role in "civilizational" transformations, whether they occur prior to or alongside globalization, although this is not always explicitly explained (for instance, see Tehranian 2007). Some authors have attempted to identify this role, at least historically. Göran Therborn, for example, introduced a model encompassing six "waves" of globalization, one of the first being characterized by the rise and the spread of world religions (c. fourth century), and the impetus they conferred to the geographic extension of cultures and societies, by virtue of their missionary expansionism (Therborn 2000). Are religions therefore subjugated to globalization or did they generate it? Scholars' views on this question are rather mixed, and the exact nature of the relationships between religion and globalization in ancient history remains unclear. Campbell (2007) has recently attempted to construct a more complex model, probing the *roles* of *religions* in each sequence of globalization. Still, in every case, religions (in particular, world religions) have always flowed over the boundaries of political units (Beyer 1994), and for that reason, long been deeply involved in what is nowadays called "globalization" (Juergensmeyer 2003b: 5).

Theories of Globalization, Theories of Religion: From Modernization to Globalization

Yet, fitting religion into a new conceptual frame such as globalization presupposes proving its relevance, especially with regards to pre-existing, prevalent theoretical models – such as "modernization" theories. To what extent was the modernity thesis *not* adequate in accounting for the contemporary mutations of religions, and why did it need to be replaced or supplemented by the globalization thesis? Experts in Globalization Studies do not agree about the relationships between *modernity* and *globalization*. Some of them, like Anthony Giddens (1990) consider both of them as two dimensions of the same contemporaneous condition – globalization should only be the extension of the process of modernity. Others, like Stuart Hall (1991) conversely disconnect the two on a double scale of their historical succession and their outcomes: modernity is supposed to have dissolving effects on (cultural, ethnic and religious) identities, whereas globalization, on the contrary, partakes of their reinvention. The first version of modernization theory that is secularization and disenchantment (Gauchet 1997), and the hypothetical "vanishing" of religion from the public sphere, failed to account for the "renewal" and the "de-secularization" of modern societies (Berger 2000). According to the second model of modernization, religion hence changes, and takes pluralistic, individualized, reflexive and hybrid forms, and globalization should facilitate these transformations, and accelerate them. But in many perspectives claiming to be "global," religions are nevertheless still reviewed under the conceptual umbrella of their "path to modernity," "globalization" simply providing an outlook on general environmental conditions for these differentiated (Esposito et al. 2008) or convergent (Beyer 2006) processes of modernization, or on a world reconfigured after the Cold War (Kurtz 2007). But the usually accepted parameters of globalization (worldwide economy, international diplomacy, transnational communications and informational transfers, intercontinental migrations and cultural pluralism ... among others) denote the relevance of an unambiguous distinction between globalization and Modernity (Simpson 1991; Lehmann 2002).

And in the context of globality, or in a modern world-system, religion has not only failed to vanish from public and political scenes, it even takes over them, to play a major (but sometimes subtle) role in the social and political organization of modern societies, and, above all, in the reconfiguration of international relationships (Beyer 1994). Accordingly, the theory of globalization bypasses the theory of modernization (at least in its first version) and offers a theoretical refutation to an interpretation of religious global history in terms of secularization (Beyer 1999; Robertson 2007). Globalization and modernization are thus unconnected in their forms and their processes, but not necessarily in their effects. And basically, modernization should rather be considered as a historical process while globalization should instead be seen as a geographic process – the evolution of beliefs and practices first, and their diffusion next. As such, modernization was associated with an inclusive series of intrinsic metamorphoses within religions (individualism, laicization, pluralism, relativization, privatization, hybridization and so forth) attributable to changes in their extrinsic conditions of living. But while the central issue of modernity was the secularization process and its alleged effects, the focal subject-matter of globalization is the worldwide religious take-over (Juergensmeyer 2005), and for that reason, in the "global village," "Never has the study of religion be more important or an understanding of the various traditions more crucial" (Kurtz 2007: 1). One of the promises to reconcile globalization and modernization theories has been made by Csordas, for whom religion in global settings partakes on a "re-enchantment on a planetary scale" (2007a: 259), a view that echoes the image of a globalization pictured as a global extension of modernity (Featherstone et al. 1995).

Globalization consequently (as modernization did in its time) helps define a prominent theoretical frame, which helps make transformations of religion (or religions) more intelligible. Then again, global approaches to religion neither stand for a theoretical unity, nor they have been designed *from* and *for* the study of religions. And many authors – whether or not their research falls under "religious studies" – prudently explore the complex relationships between religion and globalization. Malcolm Waters for instance deplores the lack of *sacriscapes* in the theory of global scapes coined by Arjun Appadurai (1990) (Waters 2001: 187) even though the term later succeeded in being defined (as "religioscapes") and is now widespread.

Roland Robertson is undoubtedly the first sociologist – at least officially – to be credited with initiating the examination of "religion and globalization" issues, in the mid-1980s. Robertson's emphasis was both cultural and political. His analysis of the adaptations of Japanese polytheism to modern and international conditions (1987) has rooted the reflection in a frame, which he had the chance to develop and expose later, allowing for both the proprieties of religious systems and those of their surrounding (local and global) conditions of existence (1992). While the project (or "civilizational program" – in Eisenstadt's words, 2001) of modernity included secularism – which remains one of its core values (Friedman 1994), globalization has similarly been considered as the worldwide expansion of modern secularism, rationalism, and scientism. But the previous spread of Christianity and the conversion of non-Western populations were also a matter of "conversion to modernities" (Van der Veer 1996), and "global rationalism." After much tension with religious ideologies, globalization finally found its own religious dimension, and ironically looked like "an immanent salvation religion" (Thomas 2007: 46). To a certain extent, and under certain conditions, globalization then resembles an (almost) religious doctrine (Csordas 2007a: 265). Beckford already alluded to the symbolic propinquity between globalist theories and religious cosmologies, both of them "totalizing" (a feature facilitating overlap between the two), and the appropriation of secular globalisms by religious voices, whether they praise the utopia of a global harmony or blame the excesses of globalization (Beckford 2003: 108ff.). Yet, some "grand narratives" of globalization, fashioned in the academic milieu, and succeeding the narratives of modernity, contain eschatological phraseologies, as for Constantin Van Barloewen who portrays the path to globalization as the shift from a modern civilization of *logos* (next to an antique civilization of *mythos*) towards a worldwide civilization of *holos* (that is "global"). A world where men and societies are connected and interdependent (2003: 18), asserts the German essayist, "needs" a "mystical" ideology balancing the realm of "scientism" (2003: 25).

Contrasted Images of Global Conditions

Moreover, Globalization Studies do not supply a unified image of contemporary global conditions, and nor do they agree on their impact on religions. At the opposite poles of the narratives of a world engaged in a "global" path stand two contrasted portrayals of "globalization." On the one hand, globality is pictured as a "multiverse of cultures" living in a "genuine interculturality" (Van Barloewen 2003: 28), and globalization offers a "chance" for spiritual traditions of humankind to live in concord (Küng 1991). On the other hand, globality is saturated with violence, and especially terrorism, which marks its bloody signature in every region of the world, in North America (the destruction of the World Trade Center towers), Japan (the assault of the Aum Shirikyo sect in the subway with sarin gas), Russia (the persecution of Chechen secessionism for religious and ethnic reasons), India (conflicts between Hindus and Muslims, Sikh secessionism), China (the oppression of Tibetan monasticism, the repression of the Falun-Gong sect), North Africa (Muslim fundamentalism) or Europe (the political control on cults and the self-destruction of so-called sects) ... among other examples.

Besides, globality exemplifies as well the contrary image of an "open" world, crossed by cultural flows and human mobility, where social and political boundaries have dissolved, and where religious beliefs and practices are subjected to a generalized circulation (Meintel and Leblanc 2003), a context supposed to be propitious to multiple borrowings, the fabric of genuine and hybrid cultural and religious forms (Luca and Burrell 1999). This immaculate image of globality sharply contrasts with the image of a world in tension, crossed over by conflicts, communal refuges, violence perpetrated in the name of religion (Kurtz 2007), and even a "globalization of intolerance" (Frunza 2002). These two pictures, somewhat simplistic if considered separately, are not mutually exclusive. The essays edited and presented by Mark Juergensmeyer in the volume *Religion in Global Civil Society* (2005) accurately demonstrate that, from anti-globalism to alter-globalism, from the takeover of public spheres by transnational networks to the attempts to reshape the norms of citizenship in the very heart of nation-states, religions assume ambivalent relationships with globalization, and they *always* acclimatize partially with, according to specific, and often local, issues.

So far, the tension between religion and globalization, which is a tension between *particularism* and *universalism* (Robertson 1992), is not embodied solely in the prosaic forms of negotiated frontiers between globalization and religions. It also floods in more spectacular forms (much more publicized, then) of conflict and violence, that have crystallized, after the 9/11 World Trade Center's destruction, Muslim fundamentalism all around the globe, and hence questioned the two faces of contemporaneous violence, and the exact role religions play in it, whether as an aggravating factor, or, quite the reverse, as an actor of prevention or resolution of political and ethnic conflicts. This modern propensity for conflict would be, in the first place, the responsibility of large socio-political units, such as "civilizations" outlined by Samuel Huntington (1996), or, in the second place, accountable of smaller entities, as Wilma Dunaway suggested, since the ethnic contemporary conflict-proneness is dependent on the tension between, on the one side, the forces of "cultural hegemony" (those that press certain compartments of globalized societies towards homogenization), and, on the other side, the defiance of "ethnic heterogeneity." In other words there exists a tension between the processes of integration of groups and societies into a world-system (mainly capitalistic), and the resistances of these groups and societies against the civilizational project that goes along with the extension of the global system (Dunaway 2003: 7).

For Waters (2001: 187), the globalized forms of fundamentalism are nothing else than the reactions against the alignment of (mainly non-Western) religions on the model of Protestant individualism, and globalized responses against the modern social hyper-differentiation: when modernity generates processes of (social, political, or cultural) fragmentation, fundamentalisms propose ideologically unifying responses – an idea aligned with the views of Jonathan Friedman, who maintains that "the globalization of fundamentalisms and of powerful nationalisms is part of the same [disjunctive] process, the violent eruption of cultural identities in the wake of declining modernist identity" (1994: 211). But the interpretation of the emergence and spread of a global Muslim fundamentalism allows the expression of divergent theories. According to Peter Beyer (2006), fundamentalism, whatever can be its confessional orientation (albeit mainly monotheistic), is indeed a consequence of a process of religion acclimatizing to globalization. If Muslim fundamentalism is opposed to the "imperialism" of nations that take advantage of a political and economic leadership in the context of globalization, it is nevertheless itself a exemplary form of global religions insofar as Muslim fundamentalists have been prompt to appropriate modern and wide-scale communication techniques and modes, in order to control the diffusion and the reception of religious messages (as illustrated the *fatwa* against Salman Rushdie, see Beyer 1994). But for others, these views are somewhat unified and stereotypical of both Islam *and* globalization (Arjomand 2004), and all the more when globalization paradoxically engenders these fundamentalisms against those indigenous democratic forces disposed to engage in and support globalization (Pasha 2002).

The problem of nationalist violence, which fundamentalism is supposed to embody, is that it has first been theorized as the expression of a secularized political trend, as "modern" (Gellner 1983; Juergensmeyer 1993), and afterwards acknowledged as "modern" *but* religious. As per Juergensmeyer (2003a), globalization did *not* generate religious violence but has merely intensified it, and spread it on a wide geographic scale, whilst marginalizing certain religious groups. Terrorism, when perpetrated in the name of religion, subverts spiritual symbolism in "narratives of struggle" and in a heroic valorization of violence, assumes different forms because it emerges from "cultures of violence" that surfaced in local contexts, with specific issues. Globalization accordingly offers religious violence a "global theatre" where it can be performed.

Further, the analysis of religious violence questions the relationship between globalization and social conflict. In Huntington's views (1996), this "conflictuality" is primarily "civilizational," relating to a kind of plate tectonics of civilizations that ignite at their points of friction. This thesis, which subsumes, in Huntington's standpoint, religion to civilization, is not however systematically confirmed, once the analysis improves its conceptual tools, and distinguishes, in the theoretical context, *religious* and *civilizational* conflicts (Fox 2001). One underlying and undisclosed topic in the debates upon the globalization of fundamentalism, in particular for

Islam (Roy 2004), is the conflict of cultural imaginations, pertaining to the Orientalist figuration of the Otherness, which blurs the classical modes of understanding of Muslim societies after colonialism (since Edward Said's *Orientalism*, 1978), those societies that have laid claim to their own version of globalism and intend to sidestep the (Western) modernist project (Turner 1997). These figures of a cultural and religious Other, far from dissolving in global settings, are on the contrary intensified and amplified by the current propinquity of societies (Turner 2001).

Religion *in* Global Society

To a certain extent, the issues regarding religion are more or less the same as those that have been questioned vis-à-vis culture, society or economy in the context of globalization, or global settings. The basic premise of the prominent theoretical frame of Globalization Studies, namely the "world-system theory," is the structural "unity" of the world, henceforth ordered as a "single society" (Beyer 1994, 1998, 1999). To a degree, it verges on the thesis of a standardization of societies, cultures and religions, one of the core tenets of modernization theory, but it comes to a different end in the globalist perspective.

Firmly embedded in a sociological perspective inspired by Émile Durkheim, which concedes that "society" is the conceptual matrix for understanding religion, and after Niklas Luhman, from whom he borrows the assertion that society is characterized by modes and forms of communication, Peter Beyer has, repeatedly, supported the idea that the study of a "global religion" must beforehand be grounded in a theory of "global society" (Beyer 1994, 1999, 2006). The "global religious system" of which he is a pioneering designer, is not, in Beyer's term, a religious tradition that has turned "global" that is whose doctrines and practices would have spread worldwide. This "global religion" assumes a diversity of forms and expressions, and epitomizes one of the subsystems of a global society, "not a mere agglomeration of religious 'things', but rather the social differentiation and social construction of a recognizably religious category of action or way of communicating which manifests itself primarily through numerous social institutions" (Beyer 1998: 8–9). In Beyer's view it is a religious and social differentiated system, such as those observed in the monotheistic and Western context, but with a global extension, which transcends the distinctiveness of specialized traditions. But if Beyer then opts for a structural and systemic image of an ordered world, the hypothetical new religious world "order" also and inversely corresponds to a chaotic *clash of civilizations*, following Huntington (1996), for whom, and in the perspective of the civilizational paradigm, the world "order" (of political units, and religious entities in the international context) is a dynamic and ever-changing continuous adjustment – and consequently a disorder.

Global Flows: A World of "Migrations" and "Missions"?

Ajrun Appadurai favors a different point of view on globalization. Without denying the existence of global structural forms (Appadurai 2001), he envisages the contemporary world as an enduring movement of men and women, ideas and practices, goods and money ... in a series of "flows" (Appadurai 1990). Albeit the minor attention Appadurai paid to religious flows, the Indian-born American anthropologist's views are, surprisingly, not distant from classical German social and historical sciences, which in the past formulated models of religious diffusion. And to some extent, present-day sociology is still inclined to carry on with the standard distinction traced by Max Weber between the expansionist dynamics of "World Religions," and an insular logic, inherent to "ethnic religions." But in the model of Beyer, the expansion of religions relates to two distinct processes, respectively missions and migrations (Beyer 1998: 18), or in the words of Juergensmeyer, transnationalism and diasporas (Juergensmeyer 2003b: 5). Csordas recently made the issue more complex by recognizing the *missionnization* versus *migrations* dichotomy in adding up two other processes, *mobility* (non-migratory diffusion) and *mediatization* (broadcasted diffusion) (Csordas 2007a: 262). Consequently akin to the *cosmopolitans* described by Ulf Hannerz (1996), global religious "virtuosi" travel the (real or virtual) world and spread their messages, whether in the direction of potential converts or followers, or of their own community members. In installing "evangelism" at the forefront of "the four faces of global culture," Peter L. Berger inflects his views on globalization towards an image of a world reticulated by missionary processes – in parallel to diplomatic networks and economic supranational elites (Berger 1997: 27). Of course, Berger confines his analysis to the example of the transnational expansion of North American evangelical Protestantism, which, while disseminating worldwide, should be considered in the universalization of Western modernism. The issue of religious missions in modern and/or global settings is nevertheless problematic. Robert L. Montgomery, for instance, explains the historical *Diffusion of religions* (Montgomery, 1996) in exclusive missionary terms. The worldwide diffusion of Tibetan Buddhism can also be justified in similar terms (Obadia 2001), but the modernity of the Buddhist, and more generally religious, missions is controversial (Learman 2005), and, as for religious violence, the contemporary *missionarization* processes can paradoxically be both rooted in ancient or recent times, and take advantage of global settings to intensify and grow.

Which religions? The empirical and theoretical field of sociology of religions in globalization is generally polarized between two categories of objects: world religions and new religious movements.

WORLD RELIGIONS AND GLOBALIZATION

Indeed, if there is any "globalization of religion," the problem is to identify which religion this process is all about. Indeed, on the one hand, Globalization Studies refer to "religion" in global conditions, just like an archetypal model above historically and socially embedded traditions, and on the other hand, sociologists and anthropologists observe locally and on a transnational level, expansive processes, missionary or migration strategies, sects or churches connected networks, and living traditions embarked on processes of change.

The French philosopher Jacques Derrida adheres to the idea of the global expansion of a "Latin" (that is Western and Christian) model, in his own words, a "*mondialatinisation*" (a contraction between *mondialisation* – globalization, in French – and *latinisation*, Derrida 1998: 48). But more recent research has improved this one-sided perspective, and injected into the analysis the complexity of the forms of religious traditions in globalization. In the systemic paradigm of Beyer, however, the Western monotheisms, and especially Christianity, have moulded, much more on a structural than on a cultural level, the shape of a "global religious system." According to Peter Beyer, indeed, "the global religious system bears the marks of its origins and early developments in Christian society" and "the contemporary global religious system therefore looks somewhat Christian, not in a religious sense, but only in a sense parallel to the way that globalization looks like Westernization" (1998: 4). The religious traditions of the contemporary world have therefore undertaken a process of patterning, on the structural and functional yardstick of Christianity, a tradition that has disjointed the sacred and the profane, that has brought about the distinctive autonomy of the religious "sphere" from other "spheres of human life, and that has lastly redefined its social and cultural spatiality consecutively from its recent confrontation with secularist ideologies. Consequently, the global religious system is socially differentiated, owing to the alignment of non-Christian and non-Western traditions on the standard model of Christianity: a corroborated hypothesis in the case of Islam and Hinduism (Beyer 2006), but also for the *African Indigenous Churches* (Venter 1999).

Religious reactions that are critical of globalization are, according to William H. Mott, as diversified as those against modernization (see Hefner 1998), and vary in line with their unique trajectory in (modern and) global settings. Judaism first accompanies it (since ancient times and as a diasporic religion), but turns into ethnicity and finally into nationality (with the rise of Zionism). Christianity first "politicizes" under a territorial entity (kingdoms and empires of the Middle East, and of Southern and Northern Europe), afterwards universalizes, and finally "humanizes" (after the era of Enlightenment). Islam initially assumes a universal and supra-cultural shape, before being marginalized by Euro-centered globalization, and finally becomes hostile to the "Westernization" of the world (Mott 2004: 184–7). According to the political scientist, the options of religious traditions are limited to a communitarian defence or alliance with fundamentalism (Spohn 2003), on the one side, or ecumenical coalitions or "social secularization," on the other (Mott 2004: 188–93). But as for theologians, the consequences of globalization are also conceivable as bringing about a "global and diversified ecumenicist community" (Küng 1991). Actually, the religious responses to globalization processes are much more complex and locally determined than these broad-spectrum theorizations. They can even unite in a similar anti-global charge in the opposed figures of the leader of Muslim fundamentalism (as Osama bin Laden) and of the Christian liberal movement (such as Dwight Hopkins) (Stahl 2007).

NEW RELIGIOUS MOVEMENTS AND GLOBALIZATION

Much more than world religions, which however colonize a wide lexical surface in the works on "Religion and globalization," the "new religions" have primarily exemplified the most genuine and typical religious forms of modernity, initially, and globalization more recently. Their increase in number and their worldwide diffusion are supposed to have captured scholars's attention much more than world religions (Rothstein 1996: 195). But some authors maintain, on the contrary, that scientific literature on this topic remains relatively small (Arweck 2007: 276). Yet, sociology's emphasis on "New Religious Movements" (NRM) builds on a particular perspective which is not exclusive of a broader approach on "religion" as a whole. But the rise and the expansion of the NRM offered sociology a new locus to confront its theoretical models with religious changes. Some religious movements are globalizing, others are adjusting themselves to global settings, and the New Age movement, torn between unity and diversity, nonetheless embodies a new "global religiosity" (Rothstein 2001). On account of their doctrinal and practical genuineness, but also owing to their expanding dynamics, the NRM should indeed typify the "exemplary" or "paradigmatic" cases of religious globalization (Clarke 2006), such as Protestant evangelism (Berger 1997), or the Catholic Charismatic Renewal (Csordas 2007b). Karel Dobbelaere (1998) maintains that, contrasting with world religions which remain anchored in their national contexts, the NRM tend to be supra-national, and therefore favor their connection with globalization – but this distinction is not so obvious, on the basis of the works of Elisabeth Arweck who demonstrated that the NRM can also intentionally limit their own expansion (Arweck 2007).

NON-INSTITUTIONALIZED, POPULAR, AND INDIGENOUS RELIGIONS

The scope of globalized religions is anything but confined to institutionalized religious systems. Within globality, other phenomena, much less tied up to a codified doctrine and a normative praxis, are also observable. For instance, Marian apparitions are multiplying in highly modern urban contexts (large cities throughout the planet, notably in North America), where spontaneous forms of pilgrimages are arranged, and, for some of them only, authenticated by Christian organizations (Vásquez and Marquardt 2000). Far from being overcome by modernity, the forms of popular religiosity have resisted and adapted, and have sprung up again in the very heart of contemporary societies, but for significantly diverse reasons, from a regional context to another. Akin to modernity, globalization seems to accelerate this process of revivification of popular religious traditions, which surface in Eastern Europe and the Balkans, notably, after the profound political transformations subsequent to the collapse of the Soviet bloc (in Bulgaria, see Valtchinova 2005).

Popular traditions, yet, not only "resist" or "revitalize," they also globalize. Following David Chidester's daring hypothesis (Chidester 2005), popular (North) American culture, which features analogically a true "religion" ("of fakes") globalizes alongside the *Cocacolonization, McDonaldization,* or *Disneyization* of the world. "If for a moment we take Coca-Cola, McDonald's, and Disney seriously as transnational religions, we can see the missions they represent as the religious challenges of globalization" alleges the American anthropologist (2005: 148). Of course, such a perspective, as a matter of fact heuristic, presupposes to acknowledge the initial axiom of an ontological identity (even suggested in an analogical perspective) between popular culture and popular religion. It entails, moreover, that the spreading processes of popular forms of religion align with the modes of diffusion of world religions, as well as with the networks and processes of globalization as a whole. Many other religions, whose theologies or ideologies are unfamiliar with the ideas of "universalism" or "mission," benefit from the global extension of human fluxes, communicational networks, of the dissemination of religious ideas, and the rebirth of the appeal to "spirituality": as we can see in the reinvention and/or diffusion of "ancient" pagan traditions, "ethnic" (that is "exotic") religions (such as the transatlantic Cuban *Santéria* (Brandon 1993), "primordial" traditions such as shamanism (partially disseminated by scholars who have studied it in an ethnographic perspective, and popularized its ideas and practices in their own countries – Michael Harner or Larry Peeters) but also neo-shamanism (Wallis 2003), transnational and modern-styled "antique" witchcraft (the *Wicca*), or, lastly, the worldwide manifestations of a "neo-magic" in the shadow of declining monotheisms (Parker Gumucio 2002). All these partake in a process the French sociologist Nathalie Luca calls "the revenge of oral traditions" (Luca and Burrell 1999). But here again, one can observe cases in which "ethnic" religions mould onto a universal model to globalize (as it is the case for the exportation of the cults of Orisha in the Yoruba tradition, see Olupona and Rey 2008), and many "magical" and "popular" revivals in the non-Western world are responses to the changes, roughly impelled by exported models of economic planning, or the local adoption of the norms of global capitalism (Hoogvelt 1978; Comaroff and Comaroff 1993). In these cases, the analysis remains, time and again, confined to the study of religious *systems* or *traditions*, insofar as they are engaged in (or target for) global processes. But another globalization process, that has yet received little attention is the diffusion of ideas, beliefs and practices disconnected from their institutions. These religious "flows" swarm on a worldwide scale, more or less independent from their symbolic and practical original matrixes (Csordas 2007a).

IMPACTS AND TRANSFORMATIONS

The breadth of the new configurations of religions and of religious landscapes, implies, for sociology, an adjustment of the pre-existing theoretical models of religious change, overlooked by the paradigms of the discipline founders (Marx, Durkheim, and Weber) who were all theorists of modernity, but none (except Marx to a certain extent) of globalization. Indeed, a major issue not only lies in the attempt to highlight the dynamic of religious change, but also in explaining *to what* and *how* religions adapt in globality.

RELIGIONS BEYOND TRADITIONS, CULTURES, AND NATIONS?

In a first and widespread theory, religions, like cultures and societies, are allegedly undergoung a process of *detraditionalization* – in relation to a broader process of modernization – otherwise labeled *deculturation* or *denationalization*, consisting in the dissociation between the religious system and its traditional socio-cultural context (see for instance, Giddens, 1990), and corresponding to a similar process, that is *deterritorialization,* or empirical *transnationalization* and ideological *universalization.*

For Robertson, Japanese polytheism has been propitious in the engagement of Japan in globalization, explaining the economic take-off of the country and the expansion of national NRM worldwide. In this process, the Japanese new religions were primarily "ethnic" (for national expatriates abroad) before becoming "universal" (and conversionist, see Robertson 1992: 84ff.). The Soka Gakkai movement, while initially "Japanese," gradually alleviated its national roots and identity – a case of *desethnicization* in favor of a *universalization* of its contents, and *transnationalization* of its organization (Liogier 2004). In contrast, the "cultural" (that is "exotic") features of Tibetan Buddhism, one of the key aspects of its successful expansion, have been preserved *in spite of* or even *because of* globalization (Obadia 2008).

The deterritorialization of cultures and societies is purportedly ineluctable in a world "without border and spatial boundaries" (Waters 2001: 5) and twice achieved by their movement and connectivity (Tomlinson, 1999). Cultures and societies nowadays belong to a brand new networked world, both technologically and sociologically speaking (Castells 2000). Following Derrida's formulation, religion currently aligns on "tele-techno-media-scientist, capitalistic, political and economic" facets of global society (1998: 65). A similar mode of organization configures transnational networks in which denominations and ethnicities superimpose and merge, and can assume original forms, and the unmistakable Western (Christian), African (Muslim) or Asian (Hindu or Buddhist) networks, overlap with multicultural international cults (such as Scientology) or Asian *Christian* networks (Goh 2004).

All the same, the consequences of this side of religious globalization are complex and sometimes antithetical. Against the diagnosis of fragmentation of socio-political entities and national religious systems, globalization produces new communities (imagined or not) and locally redesigns the (ideological) sense of national or regional unity. Globalization hence contributes to a re-territorialization of political and religious identities, at the broad level of whole "civilizations" (Huntington 1996) or the narrow regional scale (Casanova 2001). Processes of spatial and symbolic re-investment of territories, new geographies of pilgrimages, and the foundation of temples and the celebration of sacred places (McAra 2007; Kim 2008; Rothstein 2008) are occurring everywhere. Even spiritual practices among people only loosely connected to institutionalized socio-religious systems, adopted throughout the planet, such as Indian Yoga or Chinese Qi Cong, are still "connected to national identities" and, thus linked to a "spiritual nationalism" as demonstrated by Peter Van der Veer (2007). Territoriality still plays a crucial role in the realm of social imagination, in creating or rebuilding symbolic territories (Appadurai 2001), in re-establishing ideological topologies of religious Otherness (the West versus Orient), and it also assumes much more physical forms, while reconciling ritual performance, the embodiment of religious experience, and the sacralization of social spaces (McGuire 2007).

RELIGION: FROM FIELD TO MARKET?

One of the most critical changes in religions in global settings is perhaps the shift from a "religious field" – ruled, according to Weber and Bourdieu, by the social norms of monopoly relating to symbolic goods, and by the legitimate authority of religious institutions (see Rey 2007) – to a "spiritual market" (also labeled religious "supermarket" or "marketplace"), in which the predominant norm is not adherence but consumption. The "market" approaches to religion borrow the models and terminology of economics, and divides into two distinct but complementary models. The first one, namely "pluralism," aims at highlighting the adjustments of religious organizations to the contemporary logics of "supply-and-demand" (Stark and Bainbridge, 1985, or Finke and Stark, 1992, among others, quoted in Kurtz 2007: 15–16). The second one is based upon the sociology of religious individuals, regarded as "religious consumerism," the relevance but also the limits of which have been discussed by Gordon Mathews, who recognizes that people "pick" selected religious elements in a spiritual supermarket for their "personal use," but he otherwise insists upon the difference between *spiritual* and *material* supermarkets (Mathews 2000). According to French sociology, the "market" is a substitutive form of the previously dominant "field" (Hervieu-Léger 2000), but Bourdieu's theory of fields, when applied to a large scale (as does Robertson a propos a "global field": 1992), matches well in a global religious perspective, even subjugated to explicitly "economic" references and strategies (Khüle 2008). In a rather different perspective, James Spickard (2008) has shown that the economic metaphor also applied to structural transformations of religious organizations, which resemble "transnational corporations." The debates surrounding the issue of religion in globalization have prolonged the modernist and challenging question of the coexistence of religious traditions, be it a denominational multiculturalism, in which religions coexist in the same sociopolitical spaces, but maintain cultural and social frontiers between them, or be it a syncretic landscape, in which religions intermingle, by means of proselytizing or durable contacts. The comparison of national contexts, and the extreme cases with which their administrations have been confronted such as Rushdie's *fatwa* in Great-Britain (Beyer 1994) or the caricatures of the prophet Mahomet in Denmark (Riis, in Beyer and Beaman 2007) uncover the extensive variety of the *forms* and of the societal *responses* to religious diversity in the context of globalization.

ACCULTURATION AND SOCIAL CHANGE

As a result, religions, be they traditional or new, are subjected to the dialectics of "universalization" and "particularization" (Dobbelaere 1998), following the model framed by Robertson for societies and cultures in global settings (1992). The contemporary tension between religion and globalization is taking place in the mismatch between, on the one side, religious differentiations and antagonisms at the national or local scales, and, on the other side, the homogenizing convergences of traditions in the previously mentioned structural standardization – a tension that

Friedman depicts as a "cannibalizing dialectic between tendencies to homogeneity and tendencies to heterogeneity" (Friedman 1994: 210). But religions are also dependant on transformation processes which are neither *necessarily* associated with modernity, nor globalization. And besides, one question remains: what are the religious traditions acculturated to global settings, from the moment that their contemporary metamorphoses are labeled in terms of "adjustments" or "adaptations" to globalization?

A first but disputed response assumes that cultures – and thus religions – are acculturated to each other such that the globalizing world is the theatre of an extensive *creolization* (Hannerz 1996), in which religious identities (of systems and of social actors) become hybrid. Friedman, however, is opposed to these views, claiming that *creolization* is not in fact a "hybridization" but an *essentialization* of structurally homogeneous identities (Friedman 1994). For Robertson, religions can acculturate locally (or "glocalize" in his own terms, Robertson 1992) in new settings and cultural frames, or for Clarke, be locally "domesticated" (Clarke 2006). The works of Mikael Rothstein (1996) and of Margit Warburg (2001) offer rather different approaches to these questions. Warburg sees, in what Rosabeth Moss Kanter (1995, quoted by Warburg, 2001) identifies as the four main tendencies of globalization (mobility, simultaneity, pluralism, and bypass), the underlying processes of three different NRMs with quite different proprieties: ISKCON (or Hare Krishna, Hindu-oriented), Livets Ord (a Christian Swedish evangelical group)and Baha'i (an original syncretism), whilst Rothstein's analysis encompasses a wider variety of NRM (the family, Sai Baba, transcendental meditation, scientology, the Unification Church of Sun Myung Moon, the Soka Gakkai movement, and others). The two authors have demonstrated that globalization serves the expansionist purposes of these NRMs, in providing propitious techniques and channels for their diffusion (communication networks, missionary zeal, transnational flow, and so forth) but hold opposing views in their conclusions. Warburg maintains that there exists a dialectic relationship between the conservation of distinctive features of the groups and the adoption of global features – ending up not in a *local* but in a *global* acculturation. Rothstein is more circumspect. For him, the local populations who adhere to the transnational NRMs and adopt their religious standards, are more acculturated to the NRMs than the NRMs are acculturated locally. But in spite their specific features, these NRMs share similar properties in their models of diffusion, that is international distribution and network structuring (Rothstein 1996).

On the political level, Peter Beyer's dichotomy described differences between *conservative* and *liberal* options (Beyer 1994), respectively correlated to world religions and NRMs, and raised a theoretical controversy with regard to the Baha'i. The movement indeed exhibits liberal tendencies (syncretic, noteworthy), but aims at another conservative project of political global unification (Warburg 1999), and therefore is conferred an ambivalent conceptual status regarding Beyer's dichotomy, which hence provides evidence of theoretical limits (McGlinn 2003). On an ideological level, the global values – or values of global times or global societies – are also ambivalent. The same values (like global awareness, reflexivity, cosmopolitanism) can be *secular* and *humanistic*, on the one hand (Spickard 1999), and religious on the other. All things considered, globalization permanently presents the ambiguous face of a Janus.

Finally, a few recent models have attempted to unite, in a single frame of analysis, the diverse matrixes of religious reconfiguration in globalization. For Neil J. Smelser, four main tendencies delineate the morphology and dynamic of the religious global landscape: sectarian conflict, mutual tolerance, new cleavages in the boundaries of religion, and the emergence of a religion of globality. These seem to epitomize the parallel processes of fragmentation and "conflictuality," on the one hand, and adaptations and convergence, on the other, but in an encompassing global movement (Smelser 2003: 110–11). As for Thomas Csordas, he considers that globalization is the theatre where religious imaginations embed in the global economy and technology, where new pan-indigenous spiritual movements emerge, and where global flows now turn back Westward, and where global culture is becoming sanctified (Csordas 2007a: 262–5).

Sociology and the Global Religions: Between Caution and Expectations

In the same way that "culture matters for globalization" (Tomlinson 1999: 12), one can endorse another slogan: "religion matters for globalization." But as for culture, religion epitomizes an "ideological battleground of the modern world-system" (Wallerstein 1990). According to Thomas Csordas "the time has most certainly arrived for serious theorization of religion and globalization, and the globalization of religion" (2007a: 266). The globalization of religions compels the sociological analytical scope to "de-Westernize" and sociology itself, to become more comparative and transnational (Parker Gumucio 2002).

Whereas the global perspective requires a profound, but by no means integral, regeneration of the trends and scope of sociology of religions, it however does not seem to partake in a radical transformation within all the fields of knowledge of sociology. And the time of early conquests, which has delineated the first grand models ("world society," "world-systems," and "flows," among others) has almost concluded. Nowadays, critical voices and circumspect attitudes are expressed against the quick developments of the "think global" paradigm. The reference to globalization in a sociological analysis does not entail ineluctably establishing the concept on empirical grounds as demonstrated by Mauro Guillén (2002). A large section of sociologists even doubt its historical specificity. Obviously, however, sociological interest in the term derives from its theoretical and descriptive heuristic potentiality, and globalization refers accordingly to a set of conditions and processes, whose originality lies much more in their configuration and intensity than in the nature or form. Furthermore, assigning to "the global" the very *raison d'être* of the transformation of religions is as inaccurate as modernity, when the latter was the first and foremost "cause" of morphologic metamorphosis observed in the religious field of Western societies.

Several studies currently demonstrate that the dynamics of social or religious transformation and resistance to economic changes, for instance of a political and ethnic nature, are preceding globalization but identical to those usually attributed to it (in the case of South America, see Yashar 2007). Observing that religions globalize, or are affected by global processes, or when they are themselves vectors of globalization is nothing new, and globalization does not generate *only* new religious forms. The global changes in religions might be well considered as adaptations of ancient religious forms, rather than the production of original ones (Smelser 2003: 102), or, as Csordas puts it: "Perhaps we are simply beginning to recognize the same age-old waters of religion fill the newly constructed channels that flow between the local and the global" (Csordas 2007a: 265). Furthermore, the very historical and ontological identity of a *religious globalization* is in question; is it parallel with globalization as a whole, both of them then would have gone "hand in hand" as Kale (2004: 96), suggests, or is it *a part of* it or, lastly, *apart from* it – as I have suggested in the case of the globalization of Buddhism (Obadia 2004)?

What is new and proper to global contemporaneous forms is the extent to which religions globalize, the ideological adjustment they concede to global conditions, or the new morphologies (networked) that they adopt. The global does not however only epitomize a series of social, political, economic or technological conditions. It symbolizes also a theoretical paradigm compelling a change of focus, and urges the sociology of religion to think beyond national contexts, and in a comparative manner (Beyer 1999: Clarke 2006). Consequently, in adopting a global viewpoint, the sociological take on religion has changed somewhat and sociology nowadays thinks from "global rather than country or regional standpoint" and as Clarke emphasizes: "the impact of the phenomenon, to be fully appreciated, needs also to be seen for what it is, a religious reformation *on a worldwide scale*, and as such can only be fully understood in the context of *global society*" (Clarke 2006: xiii, emphases are mine).

Bibliography

Albrow, Martin (1996) *The Global Age*, Stanford: Stanford University Press.
Appadurai, Arjun (1990) Disjuncture and difference in the global cultural economy, re-ed. in: Mike Featherstone (ed.), *Global Culture. Nationalism, globalization and Modernity* (8th edn.), London, Thousands Oaks, and New Delhi: Sage, 295–310.
Appadurai, Arjun (2001) Grassroots globalization and the Research Imagination, in Arjun Appadurai, Arjun (ed.), *Globalization*, Durham, NC, and London: Duke University Press, 1–21.
Arjomand, Saïd Amir (2004) Islam, political change, and globalization, *Thesis Eleven* 76: 9–28.
Arweck, Elisabeth (2007) Globalization and new religious movements, in Peter Beyer and Lori Beaman (eds.), *Religion, Globalization, and Culture*, Leiden and Boston: Brill, 253–308.
Beck, Ulrich (1999) *What Is Globalization?*, Cambridge: Polity Press.
Beckford, James A. (2003) Globalization and religion, in *Social Theory and Religion*, Cambridge: Cambridge University Press, 103–49.
Berger, Peter L. (1997) Four faces of global culture, *The National Interest*, 49 (fall): 23–9.
Berger, Peter L. (ed.) (2000) *The Desecularization of the World: Resurgent Religion and World Politics*, Grand Rapids: Eerdmans.
Beyer, Peter (1994) *Religion and Globalization*, London: Sage.
Beyer, Peter (1998) The religious system of global society: a sociological look at contemporary religion and religions, *Numen* 45: 1–29.

Beyer, Peter (1999) Secularization from the perspective of globalization: a response to Dobbelaere, *Sociology of Religion* 60 (3): 289–301.

Beyer, Peter (2006) *Religions in Global Society*, London and New York: Routledge.

Beyer, Peter and Beaman, Lori (eds.) (2007) *Religion, Globalization, and Culture*, Boston: Brill.

Brandon, George (1993) *Santería from Africa to the New World: The Dead Sell Memories*, Bloomington: Indiana University Press.

Campbell, George Van Pelt (2007) Religion and phases of globalization, in Peter Beyer and Lori Beaman (eds.), *Religion, Globalization, and Culture*, Leiden and Boston: Brill, 281–302.

Casanova, Jose (2001) Religion, the new millennium, and globalization, *Sociology of Religion* 62 (4): 415–41.

Castells, Manuel (2000) [1966] *The Rise of the Network Society. The Information Age: Economy, Society and Culture I* (2nd edn.), Oxford: Blackwell.

Chidester, David (2005) *Authentic Fakes: Religion and American Popular Culture*, Berkeley: University of California Press.

Clarke, Peter B. (2006) *New Religions in Global Perspective: A Study of Religious Change in the Modern World*, London and New York: Routledge.

Comaroff, Jean and Comaroff, John (eds.) (1993) *Modernity and its Malcontents: Ritual and Power in Postcolonial Africa*, Chicago: University of Chicago Press.

Csordas, Thomas J. (2007a) Introduction: modalities of transnational transcendence, *Anthropological Theory* 7 (3): 259–72.

Csordas, Thomas J. (2007b) Global religion and the re-enchantment of the world: the case of the Catholic Charismatic Renewal, *Anthropological Theory* 7 (3): 295–314.

Derrida, Jacques (1998) Faith and knowledge, in Jacques Derrida and Gianni Vattimo (eds.), *Religion*, Stanford: Stanford University Press, 1–78.

Dobbelaere, Karel (1998) Relations ambiguës des religions à la société globale, *Social Compass* 45 (1): 81–98.

Dunaway, Wilma A. (2003) Ethnic conflict in the modern word-system: the dialectics of counter-hegemonic resistance in an age of transition, *Journal of World-Systems Research* 9 (1): 3–34.

Eisenstadt, Shmuel N. (2001) The civilizational dimension of modernity: modernity as a distinct civilization, *International Sociology* 16 (3): 320–40.

Esposito, John L., Fasching, Darrel, and Lewis, Tood (2008) *Religion and Globalization: World Religions in Historical Perspective*, Oxford and New York: Oxford University Press.

Featherstone Mike, Lash, Scott M., and Robertson, Roland (eds.) (1995) *Global Modernities*, London: Sage.

Finke, Roger and Stark, Rodney (1992) *The Churching of America, 1776–1990: Winners and Losers in Our Religious Economy*, New Brunswick: Rutgers University Press.

Fox, Jonathan (2001) Clash of civilizations or clash of religions: which is a more important determinant of ethnic conflict?, *Ethnicities* 1 (3): 295–320.

Friedman, Jonathan (1994) *Cultural Identity & global Processes*, London; Thousand Oaks; New Delhi: Sage.

Frunza, Randu (2002) Religious fundamentalism and the globalization of intolerance, *Journal for the Study of Religion and Ideology* 3: 5–15, www.jsri.ro/old/html%20version/index/no_3/sandu_frunza-articol.htm, accessed on the May 15, 2008.

Garrard-Burnett (2004) The third church in Latin America: religion and globalization in contemporary Latin America, *Latin America Research Review* 39 (3): 256–69.

Gauchet, Marcel (1997) *The Disenchantment of the World: A Political History of Religion*, tr. Oscar Burge, Princeton: Princeton University Press.

Geertz, Armin W. and Warburg, Margit (eds.) (2008) *New Religions and Globalization: Empirical, Theoretical and Methodological Perspectives*. Aarhus: Aarhus University Press.

Gellner, Ernst (1983) *Nation and Nationalism*, Ithaca: Cornell University Press.

Giddens, Anthony (1990) *The Consequences of Modernity*, Cambridge: Polity Press.

Goh, Robbie B. H. (2004) Asian Christian networks: transnational structures and geopolitical mappings, *Journal of Religion and Societies* 6: 1–13.

Guillén, Mauro F. (2002) Is globalization civilizing, destructive or feeble? A critique of five key debates in the social science literature, *Annual Review of Sociology* 27: 235–60.

Hall, Stuart (1991) Old and new identities, old and new ethnicities, in Anthony King (ed.), *Culture, Globalization, and the World-System*, London: Macmillan, 41–68.

Hannerz, Ulf (1996) *Transnational Connections: Culture, People, Places*, London: Routledge.

Hannerz, Ulf (1999) Cosmopolitans and locals in world culture, in Mike Featherstone (ed.), *Global Culture. Nationalism, Globalization and Modernity* (8th edn.), London, Thousands Oaks, and New Delhi: Sage, 237–51.

Hefner, Robert W. (1998) Multiple modernities: Christianity, Islam, and Hinduism in a globalizing age, *Annual Review of Anthropology* 27: 83–104.

Hervieu-Léger, Danièle (2000) *Religion as a Chain of Memory*, New Brunswick: Rutgers University Press.

Hoogvelt, Ankie M. (1978) *The Sociology of Developing Societies* (2nd edn.), London and Basingstoke: Macmillan.

Huntington, Samuel (1996) *The Clash of Civilizations and the Remaking of World Order*, New York: Simon and Schuster.

Juergensmeyer, Mark (1993) *The New Cold War? Religious Nationalism Confronts the Secular State*, Berkeley: University of California Press.

Juergensmeyer, Mark (2003a) *Terror in the Mind of God: The Global Rise of Religious Violence* (3rd edn.), Berkeley; Los Angeles; London: University of California Press.

Juergensmeyer, Mark (ed.) (2003b) *Global Religions: An Introduction*, Oxford: Oxford University Press.

Juergensmeyer, Mark (ed.) (2005) *Religion in Global Civil Society*, Oxford: Oxford University Press.

Kale, Sudhir H. (2004) Spirituality, religion, and globalization, *Journal of Macromarketing* 24 (2): 92–107.

Khüle, Lene van Der Aa (2008) Globalization, Bourdieu, and New religions, in Armin W. Geertz and Margit Warburg (eds), *New Religions and Globalization: Empirical, Theoretical and Methodological Perspectives*, Aarhus: Aarhus University Press, 95–108.

Kim, Hanna H. (2008) Mapping deterritoralization, sustaining belief: the Bochasanwas Shree Aksar Purushottan Swaminarayan Sanshta as ethnographic case study and theoretical foil, in Armin W. Geertz and Margit Warburg (eds.), *New Religions and Globalization. Empirical, Theoretical and Methodological Perspectives*, Aarhus: Aarhus University Press, 225–42.

Küng, Hans (1991) *Das Judentum*, Munich: Piper.

Kurtz, Lester R. (2007) *Gods in the Global Village: The World's Religions in Sociological Perspective* (2nd edn.), Thousand Oaks: Pine Forge Press.

Learman, Linda (ed.) (2005) *Buddhist Missionaries in the Era of Globalization*, Honolulu: Hawaii Press.

Lehmann, David (2002) Religion and globalization, in Linda Woodhead, Paul Fletcher, Hiroko Kawanami, and David Smith (eds.), *Religions in the Modern World*, London and New York: Routledge, 299–316.

Liogier, Raphaël (2004) *Le bouddhisme mondialisé*, Paris: Ellipse.

Luca, Nathalie, and Burrell, Jean (1999) Borrowings go round and round: transcending borders and religious flexibility, *Diogenes* 47: 3–10.

Mathews, Gordon (2000) *Global Culture/individual Identity: Searching for Home in the Cultural Supermarket*, London: Routledge.

McAra, Sally (2007) *Land of Beautiful Vision: Making a Buddhist Sacred Place in New Zealand*, Honolulu: University of Hawaii Press.

McGlinn, Sen (2003) A difficult case: Beyer's categories and the Baháí Faith, *Social Compass* 50 (2): 247–55.

McGuire, Meredith (2007) Sacred place and sacred power: conceptual boundaries and the marginalization of religious practices, in Peter Beyer, Lori Beaman (eds.), *Religion, Globalization, and Culture*, Leiden and Boston: Brill, 57–77.

Meintel, Deirde, and Leblanc, Marie-Nathalie (2003) La mobilité du religieux à l'ère de la globalisation, *Anthropologie et sociétés* 27 (1): 5–11.

Montgomery, Robert L. (1996) *The Diffusion of Religions: A Sociological Perspective*, Lanham and New York: University Press of America.

Mott, William H. (2004) *Globalization: People, Perspectives, and Progress*, Westport: Praeger.

Obadia, Lionel (2001) Tibetan Buddhism in France: a missionary religion?, *Journal of global Buddhism* 2: 92–105, www.globalbuddhism.org/.

Obadia, Lionel (2004) Le bouddhisme et la globalisation culturelle: modèles analytiques, controverses, et enjeux théoriques, in Jacques Scheuer and Paul Servais (eds.), *Passeurs de religions. Entre Orient et Occident*, Louvain la neuve (Belgium): Academia-Bruylant, 71–97.

Obadia, Lionel (2008) Esprit(s) du Tibet. Le bouddhisme tibétain en France: topographies paradoxales, territorialisation et économie de l'imaginaire tibétophile, in Monica Esposito (ed.), *Images of Tibet in the 19th and 20th Centuries*, Paris: EFEO, 119–53.

Olupona, Jacob K. and Rey, Terry (eds.) (2008) *Òrìsà Devotion as World Religion: The Globalization of Yorùbá Religious Culture*, Wisconsin: University of Wisconsin Press.

Parker Gumucio, Cristian (2002) Les nouvelles formes de la religion dans la société globalisée: un défi à l'interprétation sociologique, *Social Compass* 49 (2): 167–86.

Pasha, Mustapha Kamal (2002) Predatory globalization and democracy in the Islamic World, *ANNALS AAPSS* 581 (May): 121–32.

Rey, Terry (2007) *Bourdieu On Religion: Imposing Faith and Legitimacy*, London: Equinox.

Robertson, Roland (1987) Globalization and societal modernization: a note of Japan and Japanese Religion, *Sociological Analysis* 47: 35–42.

Robertson, Roland (1992) *Social Theory and Global Culture*, London, Thousand Oaks, and New Delhi: Sage.

Robertson, Roland (2007) Global millennialism: a postmortem on secularization, in Peter Beyer and Lori Beaman (eds.), *Religion, Globalization, and Culture*. Leiden and Boston: Brill, 9–34.

Rothstein, Mikael (1996) Patterns of diffusion and religious globalization: an empirical survey of new religious movements, *Temenos* 32: 195–220.

Rothstein, Mikael (2008) Religions globalization: a materialist perspective – assessing the Mormon temple in terms of globalization, in Armin W. Geertz and Margit Warburg (eds.), *New Religions and Globalization. Empirical, Theoretical and Methodological Perspectives*, Aarhus: Aarhus University Press, 243–60.

Rothstein, Mikael (ed.) (2001) *New Age Religion and Globalization*, Aarhus: Aarhus University Press.

Roy, Olivier (2004) *Globalised Islam: The Search for a New Ummah*, London: Hurst.

Said, Edward (1978) *Orientalism*, New York: Pantheon; London: Routledge and Keegan Paul; Toronto: Random House.

Simpson, John H. (1991) Globalization and religion, in Roland Robertson and William R. Garrett (eds.), *Religion and Global Order IV*, New York: Paragon, 1–18.

Sklair, Leslie (1999) Competing conceptions of globalization, *Journal of World-Systems Research* 2, http://jwsr.ucr.edu: 143–63.

Smelser, Neil J. (2003) Pressure for continuity in the context of globalization, *Current Sociology* 51 (2): 101–12.

Spickard, James V. (1999) Human rights, religious conflict, and globalization, *MOST: Journal on Multicultural Societies* 1 (1), www.unesco.org/most/vl1n1spi.htm, accessed on May 21st 2001.

Spickard, James V. (2008) Organisational transformations in global religions: rethinking the relationships between organisation, culture and market, in Armin W. Geertz and Margit Warburg (eds.), *New Religions and Globalization. Empirical, Theoretical and Methodological Perspectives*. Aarhus: Aarhus University Press, 109–27.

Spohn, Wilfried (2003) Multiple modernity, nationalism and religion: a global perspective, *Current Sociology* 51 (May): 265–93.

Stahl, William A. (2007) Religious opposition to globalization, in Peter Beyer and Lori Beaman (eds.), *Religion, Globalization, and Culture*, Leiden and Boston: Brill, 335–53.

Stark, Rodney and Bainbridge, William S. (1985) *The Future of Religion*, Berkeley: University of California Press.

Tehranian, Majid (2007) Globalization and religious resurgence: an historical perspective, *The Muslim World* 97 (July): 385–94.

Therborn, Göran (2000) Globalizations: dimensions, historical waves, regional effects, normative governance, *International Sociology* 15 (2): 151–79.

Thomas, George M. (2007) The cultural and religious character of world society, in Peter Beyer and Lori Beaman (eds.), *Religion, globalization, and Culture*. Leiden and Boston: Brill, 36–56.

Tomlinson, John (1999) *Globalization and Culture*, Chicago: University of Chicago Press and Polity Press.

Turner, Bryan S. (1997) [1994] *Orientalism, Postmodernism & Globalism*, London and New York: Routledge.

Turner, Bryan (2001) Cosmopolitan virtue: on religion in a global age, *European Journal of Social Theory* 4 (May): 131–52.

Turner, Bryan S. (2007) Globalization, religion and empire in Asia, in Peter Beyer and Lori Beaman (eds.), *Religion, Globalization, and Culture*. Leiden and Boston: Brill, 145–65.

Valtchinova, Galia (2005) Aspects of religious globalization in the Balkans: examples from postsocialist Bulgaria, *MESS (Mediterranean Ethnological Summer School*, vol. 6, Ljubljana (Slovenia): 167–182.

Van Barloewen, Benjamin (2003) *Anthropologie de la mondialisation*, Paris: Ed. des Syrtes.

Van Der Bly, Martha (2005) Globalization: a triumph of ambiguity, *Current Sociology* 53 (6): 875–93.

Van der Veer, Peter (1996) *Conversion to Modernities: The Globalization of Modernities*, New York and London: Routledge.

Van der Veer, Peter (2007) Global breathing: religious utopias in India and China, *Anthropological Theory* 7 (3): 315–28.

Vásquez, Manuel A. and Marquardt, Marie F. (2000) Globalizing the rainbow Madonna: old time religion in the present age, *Theory, Culture & Society* 17 (4): 119–43.

Venter, Dawid (1999) Globalization and the cultural effects of the world-economy in a semiperiphery: the emergence of African indigenous churches in South Africa, *Journal of World-Systems Research*, http://jwsr.ucr.edu/ 5: 104–26.

Wallerstein, Immanuel (1990) Culture as the ideological battleground of the modern world-system, *Theory, Culture and Society* 7: 31–55.

Wallis, Robert J. (2003) *Shamans/Neo-Shamans: Ecstasy, Alternative Archaeologies and Contemporary Pagans*, London: Routledge.

Warburg, Margit (1999) Baha'i: a religious approach to globalization, *Social Compass* 46: 47–56.

Warburg, Margit (2001) Religious organizations in a global world: a comparative perspective, *Global Dimensions*, www.cesnur.org/2001/london2001/warburg.htm, accessed Jujne 9, 2001.

Waters, Malcolm (2001) *Globalization* (2nd edn.), New York: Routledge.

Yashar, Deborah J. (2007) Resistance and identity politics in an age of globalization, *ANNALS, AAPSS* 610 (March): 160–81.

22

Pentecostal and Charismatic Movements in a Global Perspective

Afe Adogame

Introduction

The Pentecostal and charismatic movements represent some of the most popular and fastest growing religious movements within contemporary world Christianity. Pentecostals and charismatics have been estimated at over five hundred million adherents worldwide (Barrett and Johnson 2003: 24–5). Recent demographic statistics such as by the Pew Forum survey on Pentecostalism (2006), Philip Jenkin's *Next Christendom* (2002), and David Barrett's et al. *World Christian Encyclopaedia* (2001) are lucid indicators of the shifting contour of Christianity's center of gravity from the North to the South. It is estimated that two thirds of Pentecostal and charismatic movement's 523 million adherents live outside the West in areas such as Africa, Latin America, Asia, and Oceania, as do most of the nine million who convert to it each year (Barrett and Johnson 2002: 284).

Pentecostal and charismatic Christianity has emerged as one of the most prevalent segments of world Christianity in ways that result in phrases such as 'Pentecostal power' (Pew Forum Survey 2006), to illustrate this trend and the dynamic nature of the phenomenon. As the survey indicates, "By all accounts, Pentecostalism and related charismatic movements represent one of the fastest-growing segments of global Christianity. At least a quarter of the world's 2 billion Christians are thought to be members of these lively, highly personal faiths, which emphasize such spiritually renewing 'gifts of the Holy Spirit' as speaking in tongues, divine healing and prophesying" (2006: 1). This survey which provides analyses of the religious demography of 10 countries including Nigeria, Kenya and South Africa demonstrates how Africa along with Asia and Latin America are assuming significant global players in the dramatization and appropriation of world Christianity.

Statistics on Pentecostals and charismatic movements, as with other religious movements in the world, are often fraught with controversy and imprecision. The projected demographic figures indicated in many existing works may be largely contested on the one hand. So also is the criterion for categorizing these movements as Pentecostal or charismatic which, in itself, may be confusing as it varies from context to context. It actually depends on what definition of Pentecostalism and charismatic movements we adopt. Nevertheless, the value of any statistics is that it suggests that these movements have gradually carved out a niche for themselves within religious maps of the modern world, but also in terms of their demographic composition and geographical spread. It is even suggested that this brand of Christianity is now second in size to the Roman Catholic Church globally.

Pentecostal and charismatic movements are indeed dynamic phenomena that have captured the scholarly attention of social scientists, historians of religion, theologians, policy makers, the media and other wide-ranging publics. What constitutes Pentecostal and charismatic movements remains elusive just as explanations of their provenance are ever more contested in the face of newly emerging discourses and a revisiting of Pentecostal historiography. Their public visibility, mobility, and social relevance in local–global contexts have attracted further interpretive and analytic approaches. There is a common tendency to talk about the globalization of Pentecostalism and charismatic Christianity or Global Christianity (van der Veer 1996; Dempster et al. 1999; Coleman 2000; Jenkins 2002) and to give Pentecostalism the description "a religion made to travel" (Dempster et al. 1999).

These diverse academic scholarship, intellectual orientation and varied interpretations evident in a burgeoning literature have helped to reposition Pentecostal and charismatic movements from obscurity to center-stage of the global religious map. The various approaches to these religious movements are in themselves not mutually exclusive but have influenced and shaped each other in a dynamic way. This chapter concentrates on the sociological definitions, interpretation and analyses of Pentecostal and charismatic movements in the context of an evolving Pentecostal historiography. While our emphasis is largely sociological, it is important to point out that the social scientific interpretations and analyses are not exceptionally unique. They are sometimes born out of, or at least shaped by, a certain mutual cognition in which historical, religious studies and theological standpoints are complementary approaches – even if in a remote sense.

THE HISTORICAL ORIGINS

The emergence of modern Pentecostalism had earlier been located within religious events at the beginning of the twentieth century. Two interrelated events, one in Topeka, Kansas on 1 January 1901 under Charles Parham, and the other, the Asuza Street revival in Los Angeles in April 1906 under a black Holiness preacher, William Seymour were traditionally recognized as the historical origins of these movements (Synan 2001; Burgess and Van der Maas 2002). However, recent scholarship has demonstrated that Pentecostal outbursts occurred in other parts of the world, notably in Africa, Europe, Asia and Latin America contemporaneously and to some extent even well before the twentieth century. In global terms, Pentecostal origins are multifaceted, so are their opportunities, contexts and challenges. Thus, Pentecostalism as a global culture is to be understood in terms of parallel tracks and not simply as unilateral diffusion. Interpretations of Azusa Street as a birthplace of modern Pentecostalism have been relativized by growing awareness of other geographical foci. There are several developments independent of the Azusa Street narrative, although they may not have had the same resources and networks to globalize. Historically, the Azusa Street event was very significant in its capacity to launch into global networks, such as the pre-existing networks of immigrant and missionary networks. Thus, the human carriers of the Azusa street event were not only Americans, but immigrants from Europe, Latin America, Africa and Asia. From Los Angeles, news of the "outpouring of the Holy Spirit" spread across the United States and around the world through social networks involving both word of mouth and printed literature (Burgess and Van der Maas 2002).

Pentecostal identity is obviously central to any definition of Pentecostalism and the description of its growth globally. Pentecostals and charismatic movements have been defined from a variety of sociological, historical, phenomenological, and theological perspectives. The collective identity of Pentecostals and charismatics also emerged from each group's self-identity. We can suggest that a common feature of these varied definitions is that they are not mutually exclusive. In the broadest sense, the term "Pentecostalism" embraces what has been variously described as classical Pentecostals, neopentecostals, charismatics, neocharismatics, denominational Pentecostals (such as Charismatic Renewal groups), but also Christian and para-church organizations with Pentecostal-like experiences that have no specific traditional Pentecostal and charismatic denominational connections (see Burgess and Van der Maas 2002). In fact, the terms "pentecostal" and "charismatic" are often used loosely and interchangeably by churches in various contexts, thus complicating scientific attempts to achieve a precise definition. This complexity has therefore led some scholars to use both terms as a "compound-phrase" namely Pentecostal-charismatics or Charismatic-pentecostals. In fact, there is ample evidence of churches that describe themselves as both Pentecostal and charismatic in outlook, content and orientation. These varied definitions, meanings and contexts render a simple taxonomy of Pentecostal and charismatic movements almost impossible.

CHARACTERISTICS OF PENTECOSTAL CHURCHES

However, Pentecostal and charismatic movements are identified by their central emphasis on spiritual rebirth (baptism of the Holy Spirit) – evidenced by glossolalia, charismatic (spiritual) gifts, healing, deliverance, prophecy, exuberant worship, and a distinctive language of experiential spirituality. In spite of these common features, they differ on the meaning, symbolism, and level of emphasis of each characteristic. Irrespective of differences in the composition of these groups, their appeal and function are similar. In spite of the extraordinary degree of affinity of liturgy, organization, ideology and ethic in various cultural contexts, Pentecostal and charismatic churches should be viewed as diffuse global movements and not as centralized, international organizations. One feature of Pentecostal movements is their relative religious autonomy permitting them to develop independently within each local, cultural setting as opposed to becoming a centralized bureaucratic organization. The unprecedented growth of Pentecostal and charismatic movements in their various forms also occasioned a remarkable growth of ritual patterns, cultural attitudes, ecclesiastical structures, and complex strategies of expansion.

The lack of definitional specificity and standardization in such social scientific terms as Pentecostal and charismatic partly results from an "elastic" and broad understanding of the phenomena. These terms can become so general and broadly used as to be meaningless (Corten and Marshall-Fratani 2001: 4; Droogers 2001: 46; Kamsteeg 1998: 10–11). Sociologists of religion can sometimes take for granted the character of Pentecostalism without regard to its historical, phenomenological and theological dimensions. Rather sociological approaches of Pentecostalism investigate how Pentecostal and charismatic movements respond to changes within a variety of local and global contexts. The dynamics of religious change in different cultural contexts enables a more exact insight into the nature and impact of Pentecostal and charismatic movements. In short, this terminological confusion among social scientists is partly a consequence of their lack of attention to the actual history of Pentecostal and charismatic churches. As Robbins argued, although a basic historical framework cannot solve all definitional problems, it can establish more adequate terminological parameters (2004: 119). Social scientists who employ a variety of terms such as Protestantism, fundamentalism, evangelicalism, charismatic Christianity and so forth as analytic categories, sometimes mistakenly assume that local meanings can be applied universally and will therefore be widely comprehended in different contexts. Such juxtaposition of terms in different contexts often obscures a clearer definition of Pentecostalism.

To have a clear grasp of the sociology of Pentecostal and charismatic movements, it is important to examine some theoretical developments in sociology, particularly in the sociology of religion, that form the bedrock for understanding current debates about and analysis of Pentecostal and charismatic movements. We shall briefly sketch these developments here.

The secularization theory has a long history in the social sciences and played considerable role in the development of the sociology of religion (Berger 1967, 1999; Martin 1978; Hadden 1987). The resilience, renewed impact and relevance of religion in Western societies in the late twentieth century have challenged, more than ever before, secularization theories that predicted the declining significance – indeed the obituary of religion in social life- in the form of the diminished strength of religious organizations, the waning commitment of individuals and the transformation of their values, attitudes and consciousness. As Hadden argued, "secularization had never amounted to a testable theory but had simply been a taken-for-granted ideological reflex of antagonism towards religion and rationalist assumptions about modernity (Beckford 2003: 32). It was allegedly a 'doctrine' and an 'ideological bias' that was 'deeply internalized in the minds of our European and American founding fathers" and "is still firmly entrenched in the minds of contemporary sociologists" (Hadden 1987: 595). With three basic patterns of secularization, David Martin (1978) was successful in interpreting the multiple factors shaping the public and private significance of religion in Europe and North America since the sixteenth century.

Although a few sociologists (Wilson 1985, 1992; Bruce 1996, 2002) continue to defend versions of the secularization thesis, most scholars no longer adhere to the equation of modernity and secularization in dealing with religion. Even erstwhile ardent secularization theorists such as Peter Berger (1999) have now rejected the idea of secularization as a useful orientation. This outcome does not suggest that processes of secularization are not in fact noticeable in the Western world, particularly in Europe, but rather that the process is not necessarily a direct consequence of modernity. Where the fall in church attendance, dwindling membership, and the separation of church and state are canvassed as indices of secularization, it becomes problematic as to how we can universalize such tendencies in social contexts where there is ample evidence to suggest that the opposite is the case.

As Berger (1967: 109) pointed out, "while secularization may be viewed as a global phenomenon of modern societies, it is not uniformly distributed within them. Different groups of the population have been affected by it differently." Grace Davie's (1994, 2000) thesis of "believing without belonging" (especially in the European situation) has allowed us to reconsider "the inherited model" (Wilson 1985) of secularization and has been instrumental in promoting a more subtle interpretation of empirical indicators of religious belief and participation in religious organizations (Beckford 2003: 54). To further complete this picture, Hervieu-Léger (1999) even offers a reverse characterization of the European situation as "belonging without believing."

In response to this erosion of the secularization argument, sociologists of religion took on the significant task of re-drawing the global map of religion in the contemporary world. As a consequence scholars shifted attention from a consideration of the decline of religion to an examination of the new forms which religion, including Pentecostal and charismatic movements, have assumed at the individual, group and societal levels (Casanova 1994). Research interests began to focus on both the resurgence of old forms of religion and an unprecedented upsurge in new religious movements, including their socio-political impact on Latin America, North America, Europe, Africa, and Asia (Martin 1990, 2002; Stoll 1990; Lehmann 1996; Cox 1995; Davie 2000, 2001; Clarke 2006; Gifford 1998, 2004; Kalu 2000, 2008; Corten and Marshall Fratani 2001; Juergensmeyer 1993, 2005; Mullins 1994). Such works produced remarkable empirical evidence of religious vitality at the grassroots level of these respective societies.

CHANGING CONTOURS OF THE RELIGIOUS SITUATION

Martin (1990, 2002) best describes the explosion of the Pentecostal version of Evangelical Protestantism in Latin America. His works are distinctive in their historic focus, global reach, and analytic breath. They offer case studies which detail and compare the growth of Protestant churches throughout Latin America and the Caribbean, but also in Africa and Asia. Martin's *Tongues of Fire* (1990) approaches the phenomenon of Protestant growth from a historical perspective, providing an exciting macroanalysis of the spread of Pentecostalism in Latin America. His *Pentecostalism: The World Their Parish* (2002) complements *Tongues of Fire*, lending his treatment of Protestantism a global flavor by exploring the roots of the Pentecostal movement. His work demonstrates how Pentecostalism crosses cultural boundaries, appealing to diverse sectors of society in Latin America, Africa and South East Asia. While Martin's primary interest was in the social and religious appeal of religion, he has not ignored the fact that religion has significant political consequences. These developments raise a question about the current status of

Roman Catholicism in the continent. Thus David Stoll's *Is Latin America Turning Protestant?* (1990) seeks to explain the dynamics of competition between Protestantism and Catholicism, as well as the linkages between US churches, American foreign policy and Protestant evangelization in Latin America. Stoll characterizes Protestant growth in Latin America as a form of "awakening," describing it as "a period of religious ferment, in which masses of people arrive at a new sense of themselves and their society" (1990: 23).

Martin and Stoll perceive late twentieth century Pentecostalism in Latin America as comparable to the religious revival in North America, although they do not explain away Protestant growth in Latin America entirely on the basis of American mission initiatives and linkages. While Latin American Pentecostal movements were generally considered to be products of North American religious proselytism, studies from the 1990s (Stoll 1990; Martin 1990, 2002; Cox 1995) have clearly identified these movements as growing out of local religious impulses and experiences. They demonstrated that religion has been a potent factor in Latin American social life, demonstrating how social and political crisis have helped to fuel the resurgence of religious vitality. Thus, since 1990 there has been a perceived shift of focus in the analysis of the emergence of Latin American Protestantism from a preoccupation with the expansion of Anglo-American ideologies and religions toward a greater sensitivity to the role of poor, indigenous Latin American communities in creating cultural and political options for themselves. This shift of research attention has been partly informed by the literature on new social movements in a time of rapid social change. The exploration of Pentecostalism as a form of religious organization that is well suited to the needs of the marginal poor – a religion for the "dispossessed" and "disinherited" – has continued to shape the study of Pentecostalism in Latin America (Mariz 1994; Chesnut 1997, 2003). In actual fact, this change of focus has generated a transformation of the study of Pentecostalism elsewhere (cf. Corten and Marshall-Fratani 2001).

Peter van der Veer's (1996) *Conversion to Modernities* explores religious conversion to various forms of Christianity (including Pentecostal and charismatic churches as types of Protestantism) in the modern era as not only a conversion to modern forms of these religions, but also to religious forms of modernity. Conversion is understood as an innovative practice that is largely linked to the transformation of the social sphere. Van der Veer examined (religious) conversion to modernity as an effect of the interplay between Europe and the colonized world. This thesis was intended to provide a critique of the "simplicities" of conventional theories of modernization and secularization in which modern Europe was seen unilaterally to modernize its Others, whose role was thereby limited merely to a psychological reaction, both in the sense of being a weak response and also a retrograde action (Veer, 1996:7).

Since the 1970s the ascendancy to worldwide prominence of what was often described simply as "religious fundamentalism" stimulated further sociological research into Pentecostal and charismatic movements. Debates about the rise of so-called fundamentalist religions in the United States and about new religions in a global perspective (Beckford 1985; Barker 1989; Bruce 2001; Clarke 2006) were significant in serving as the basis for reconfiguring our understanding of the significant place of religion in society. In a strict sense, fundamentalism refers in fact to a specific development in the history of American Protestantism. Social scientists have been eager to learn who the religious fundamentalists are and what fundamentalism is. Why is a resurgence taking place and what are the distinctive characteristics, the global spread, and the possible connections to political violence?. *Exporting the American Gospel* (Brouwer et al. 1996) demonstrates, though controversially, how new Christian fundamentalism has taken hold in many nations in Africa, Latin America, and Asia. This new kind of Christian fundamentalism – described as a transnational religious culture – was epitomized by "a fresh hybrid of Pentecostal fervor, mainstream evangelicalism, and bible-believing millenialism distributed by modern means: innovative megachurches and parachurches, televangelism, and computerized churches" (Brouwer et al 1996). Unfortunately the interpretation of Pentecostalism and the charismatic movements has suffered from academic biases, because these religious movements do not measure up to secular scholars' notions about "intellectual progress," "progressive refinement," and religious ideas (Finke and Stark 1992: 4–5).

Although a survey of these and other related works over the past three decades reveals some progress in sociological research on such movements, there are evidently ongoing pitfalls in conceptualizing and understanding religious fundamentalism. Pentecostalism and fundamentalism may share certain affinities in that they both emerged in the early twentieth century and exhibit elements of the broader evangelical movement. The treatment of Pentecostalism as a branch of fundamentalism (Stoll 1990), its association with various brands of conservative Christianity (Woodberry and Smith 1998) and the assumption that they are in fact the same can hardly suffice historically and analytically (Cox 1995, 1997; Martin 1990, 2002; Spittler 1994).

Globalization and Religious Vitality

In exploring global Christian fundamentalism, Brouwer, Gifford and Rose (1996) went too far in privileging a new and unique kind of American fundamentalism that is spreading across the globe. Such narratives of "extraversion" and "ecclesiastical externality" prevalent in earlier accounts on Protestantism in Latin America (Martin 1990) and of "modern" or "new" fundamentalist Christianity in Africa (Gifford 1998, 2004); van Dijk 1995), mask indigenous innovation and creativity. They also hide local experiences and expressions that shaped these contexts. Recent works are uncovering the local impulses and vitality of indigenous Pentecostal movements and how they are responding to rapid social change, modernity and globalization (Martin 2002; Kalu 2008).

Some notable attempts at building a link between religion and globalization or globality are evident in the works by Roland Robertson (1985, 1987, 1992, 1994) and Peter Beyer (1994, 2001). Robertson is undoubtedly the pioneer in this academic endeavor. Since the mid-1980s, he has written extensively on the theory and processes of globalization. He talks about "the crystallisation of the entire world as a single place," "the emergence of the global-human condition," "the consciousness of the globe as such." On religion, Robertson based his analysis on how tensions in relations between state and religion across the globe arise from the politicization of religion, and the "religionization of politics" resulting from the process of globalization. Beyer (1994) attempted a theoretical and applied examination of globalization and its application to religion by combining four world-system theorists in order to show how globalization can be understood as a global economy (Wallerstein), a global culture (Robertson), a global society (Luhmann), and a global polity (Meyer). Beyer observes that both Christian and Islamic fundamentalist forms are flourishing in the new global environment. The expansion of Christianity, prior to the point at which the term "globalization" gained wide academic currency, has always been viewed as a transnational phenomenon with globalizing tendencies. For Beyer, globalization has been a vital resource for understanding the place of religion in a modern global culture.

Globalization as a concept has been employed by social scientists as an appropriate category for describing and interpreting the emergence of Pentecostalism as a cultural movement. In fact, Jenkins (2002: 7–8) defined it as "perhaps the most successful social movement of the past century." Religious traditions have the capacity for self-reflexive critical thinking about globalization (Beckford 2003: 105). The nascence and rapid expansion of the Pentecostal movement in the twentieth century lead to a recognition of Pentecostalism as an integral part of the globalization process but also as a product or consequence of it. The application of globalization to Pentecostalism therefore refers to its geographical expansion, demographic spread, and its cultural influence.

Globalization has stimulated a postmodern interest in fragmentation, not so much in relation to the global, but much more in relation to the local translations of the global.

Joel Robbins (2004) demonstrates how scholars "use Pentecostals and charismatics to support theories that construe globalization as a process of Westernizing homogenization and those that understand it as a process of indigenizing differentiation." Robertson's (1992: 73) innovative concept of "glocalization" is quite apt in exploring the interconnectedness between local and global contexts at the level of religious movements such as the Pentecostal and charismatic movements. Although the popular adagium has been "think globally, act locally," much of the thinking also takes place at the local level (Droogers 2001: 51). Thus, the globalization of Pentecostal and charismatic movements makes sense mainly in terms of its localization.

As André Droogers aptly points out, "this then is the somewhat gloomy globalizing world within which Pentecostal expansion occurs. In it, space and non-space intermingle, just as the global and the local – or even the fragmented ... Religion is part of the globalizing forces, as well as of the local translations. It is part both of the global impact and the local reaction" (Droogers 2001: 51). In other words, the rich, local varieties, manifestations, expressions and experiences of Pentecostal and charismatic Christianity shed significant light on considering them as a global phenomenon or as a "global culture" (Poewe 1994). Pentecostalism facilitates the translation from the global to the local and vice versa (Droogers 2001: 57).

It is within this context of globalization that questions about the "why" and "how" of Pentecostal expansion and success have become pressing and intriguing. The origin, *raison d étre* and explanations for the rapid proliferation and success of Pentecostalism have attracted varied interpretations depending largely on the academic persuasion and "paradigmatic preference" of the author. To account for the success of Pentecostal and charismatic churches in terms of attracting converts in large numbers and of its phenomenal spread globally, sociological theories concentrate on the role of deprivation and anomie as causes of growth (d'Epinay 1969; Anderson 1979; Chesnut 1997; Corten 1999). Pentecostalism was largely described as the religion of the poor, the masses, the disinherited, and displaced persons. It was also categorized as an urban phenomenon. Such interpretations undercut and undervalue significant dimensions of Pentecostal and charismatic cultures. The narrow emphasis on the *why* of conversion undermines *how* Pentecostal and charismatic movements negotiate or transform the cultures into which they are introduced. Droogers aptly posits internal religious characteristics of Pentecostalism and their articulation within the external circumstances of globalization as causes of growth (2001: 41). He aptly remarks, "In any case, now as before, whatever the theoretical framework, most attention is given to factors that are external to Pentecostalism itself. Only rarely are specific characteristics of Pentecostalism taken into account and a more idiosyncratic explanation sought" (Droogers 2001:41). Thus, while not underestimating the influence of external conditions, Droogers underscores the fact that, a far-reaching account of this expansion, must necessarily commence from "the particularities of a specific religion" and proceed from there to the impact of, and articulation with, external social processes, and not the other way round.

PENTECOSTALISM WITHIN THE AFRICAN CONTEXT

The most recent development within African Christianity is the emergence and increasing proliferation of Pentecostal and charismatic Churches, especially from the 1950s and 1960s onwards. There have been two waves of these Pentecostal movements. On the one hand there are the indigenous Pentecostal groups such as the Redeemed Christian Church of God, the Deeper Life Bible Church, Zimbabwe Assemblies of God Africa, International Central Gospel Church, Church of Pentecost, Church of God Mission International, Winners Chapel, Rhema Bible Church, Mountain of Fire and Miracles Ministries, Latter Rain Assembly, and the Household of God Fellowship and on the other hand there are those developments such as the Four Square Gospel Church, the Full Gospel Businessmen Fellowship International, Campus Crusade for Christ, Youth with a Mission, and Christ for all Nations, which exist as branches or missions of Pentecostal churches and organizations outside Africa. The former are largely independent and rely on hardly any external assistance, while some of the latter depend to a large extent on funds, literature, and sometimes personnel from their mission headquarters. The former have also embarked on transnational mission activities by planting branches in the United States, Canada, Europe, and other parts of the world.

The Pentecostal and charismatic churches have shaped African Christianity through their increasing involvement on the wider global stage. They have increasingly taken to proselytizing in North America and Europe, viewing the regions as "new abodes" and promising "mission fields" (Adogame 2005: 504, 2007). There are also groups existing as branches of mother churches with headquarters in Africa;

and others founded by African migrants in the diaspora. Examples include the Redeemed Christian Church of God, with headquarters in Nigeria and the Kingsway International Christian Center in East London. Both have a huge African membership with few non-Africans. The Embassy of the Blessed Kingdom of God for All Nations in Kiev in the Ukraine is a typical example of an African-led church with a majority non-African membership (Adogame 2008). Such African religions are significant within the framework of globalization, owing to the unique expression of African Christianity which they exhibit – a feature that could be described as their self-assertion and as the global preservation of their religious identity (Adogame 2003). They constitute international ministries that have implications on a global scale. As part of an increasing phenomenon of what they term "mission reversed" or "remissionization of Christianity to a secularized West," these African churches have systematically set out to evangelize the world. Notions of globalization and globality are appropriated as theological and ideological constructs, and thus feature prominently in their mission statements and strategies, as well as sermon rhetoric – although these notions are used and understood differently. It is common to find churches defining themselves as "global churches" and their mission as "global tasks."

The sociological analysis of African Pentecostal and charismatic movements has followed similar trajectories in recent debates within sociology of religion as a whole.

The literature on African Pentecostalism and charismatic movements has grown steadily in the past two decades. Until recently, research on the phenomenon in Africa has been dominated by social scientists from Western countries. African scholars have now joined them to fill in this academic vacuum. It is interesting to explore to what extent their methods and interpretations have opened up new vistas in research on the phenomena, but also contributed more broadly to knowledge of the field. At least three categories of scholarship can be discerned. Some scholars have taken as their starting point both theoretical premises about modernization and neo-Marxist perspectives in order to arrive at conclusions about the unprecedented expansion of Pentecostal and charismatic movements. Pentecostalism is portrayed as born, packaged, transmitted and delivered from the West, particularly from the United States through Azusa Street connections to other parts of the world, and shaped by North American religious proselytism and political hegemony (Gifford 1991, 1992, 1998).

A second school of thought differs significantly from this earlier one in that it emphasizes local, spontaneous and contemporaneous developments and manifestations of what could be identified as Pentecostalism. This view recognizes the Azusa street and other related events in the United States as only one instance of the spiritual event that occurred spontaneously and independently in different parts of the world (Kalu 2000, 2008; Anderson 1999, 2004, 2007; Ruth Marshall-Fratani 1998, 2001).

The third explanation, although somewhat related to the second, appears to occupy the middle position in that it places emphasis on what may be called an interactive or dialectical development of the phenomenon within and between cultural boundaries. This explanation does not necessarily recognize the root of the spectacular spiritual event in Azusa but looks at several local, indigenous and spontaneous spiritual events that have been transmitted to other contexts through many channels. Of course, it must be pointed out here that these categories are far from being exclusive. However, they are helpful in showing in an admittedly sketchy form, the conceptual and theoretical frameworks that are used in explaining this phenomenon.

The paradigmatic preferences of scholars have also influenced their analysis of these religious developments. The phenomenon has attracted the gaze of social scientists much more than historians of religion, secular historians and theologians. This is clearly evident from the volume and focus of the literature that is available on the subject. Apart from a few cases, most social scientists appear to prioritize causal factors that are external to Pentecostalism itself in contradistinction to its internal religious characteristics, in explaining the *raison d étre*, rapid expansion and relative success of these forms of Christianity (cf. Droogers 2001). More recent studies are gradually filling these lacunae by attempting to provide a wider, more ingrained and integrated explanation of the expansion and mobility of these movements. Scholars are now beginning to concentrate on the peculiarities of specific religious situations and the internal religious dynamics of Pentecostal and charismatic churches, and proceeding from these analyses to examine the influence of, and articulation with, external social processes (Kalu 2002, 2008; Maxwell 2000, 2006; Asamoah-Gyadu 2005; Marshall-Fratani 1998; Englund 2003). We should see these diverse approaches as complementary perspectives in understanding Pentecostal and charismatic growth and expansion in Africa and beyond.

Paul Gifford is one of the few scholars who had researched extensively on African Christianity, particularly on the phenomenon of Pentecostalism (Gifford 1998, 2004). In his writings, Gifford embraces conspiracy theories which point to the role of the Central Intelligence Agency (CIA) in serving US capitalist expansion through the support given to North American missionary organizations. By examining contemporary developments in Africa Christianity with regard to their public role, Gifford (1998) sought to locate Africa's churches in a wider context by employing socio-political concepts and tools in his data analysis. Using case studies of developments in Ghana, Uganda, Zambia and Cameroon, Gifford provides material that is both rich and extensive on the dramatization of Christianity on the African religious landscape. We might add however that he failed to recognize the colossal diversity and complexity of African Christianity. This failure sometimes resulted in wide generalizations and insensitivity to the historical and cultural complexity of African religion. Pentecostalism exhibits a complex diversity that must be taken into account in any attempt at assessing the nature, vitality and impact of Pentecostalism in Africa and beyond. Gifford provides an elaborate description of the growth of what he calls the "born again movement," its public character, as well as an appraisal of its appeal.

Gifford explored the American origins of the born-again upsurge, particularly its emphasis on the faith gospel or what has come to be known as the "gospel of prosperity." He argued that although the US evangelistic thrust (the agenda of the American New Religious Right) is undertaken on purely religious grounds (Gifford 1998: 316), it is nevertheless part of a wider American cultural project. Gifford glosses over indigenous religious creativity and innovation in his remarks that

"Creativity should not be so emphasized that it glosses over the West's cultural significance." According to him, "For all the talk within African church circles of localization, inculturation, Africanization, or indigenization, external links have become more important than ever. Through these links the churches have become a major, if not the greatest single, source of development assistance, money, employment and opportunity in Africa" (Gifford 1998: 308). This standpoint largely concurs with traditional explanations locating the origins of modern Pentecostalism in the United States. It is also similar to earlier explanations of the origin of Latin American Pentecostalism as products of North American religious proselytism and hegemony. The preponderance of "ecclesiastical externality" in explaining all dimensions of African Christianity, particularly Pentecostal and charismatic movements, has been thoroughly criticized on the grounds that it provided a one-sided, simplistic picture of a rather complex phenomenon (see Hexham and Poewe 1997; Maxwell 1998, 2000; Kalu 2008). David Maxwell (1998) has given specific attention on a particular version of the prosperity gospel as manifest in the Zimbabwe Assemblies of God Africa (ZAOGA). He argues that the movement's leadership draws upon various American versions of the prosperity gospel to legitimate their excessive accumulation but its own dominant prosperity teachings have arisen from Southern African sources and are shaped by Zimbabwean concerns. In explaining the development of the prosperity gospel, Maxwell draws upon both external and internal roots with the latter playing the dominant role.

Ogbu Kalu's *African Pentecostalism* (2008) remains the most comprehensive account of the role and social impact of African Pentecostal and charismatic Christianity, focusing on a broad range of issues such as identity, agency, gender and authority, media and popular culture, political discourses, and Pentecostal immigrant religiosity. Kalu critically engaged current scholarship, and was successful in balancing global processes with local identities. He combined the discourse on African Pentecostal and charismatic movements with a wider global, Western historiography by revisiting the debate on genealogy, emerging themes, development and mobility of Pentecostalism. Elsewhere, Kalu describes this religious development in Africa as "the third response," "an implosion of the Spirit" (2000: 106). Kalu appraised the social face and force of African Christianity in the last three decades of the twentieth century, while also arguing for the uniqueness and peculiarity of African Pentecostalism, contrasting its links to the Azusa street event and other external influences (2000: 104).

Other interesting treatments of African Pentecostalism have taken up a historical, phenomenological and theological focus, exploring issues of provenance, terminology, development and global impact within specific African contexts, particularly South Africa (Anderson 1999, 2004, 2007). Allan Anderson, like Kalu, adduces both internal and external roots in explaining the origin of African Pentecostalism. The external roots he explains are also "predominantly African cultural features, evident in the leadership of William Seymour, whose spirituality lay in the past" (Anderson 1999: 221). He contends that "one of the outstanding features of Pentecostals in the Third World (Africa) is their religious creativity and spontaneously indigenous character, a characteristic held as an ideal by Western missions for over a century." His combination of African Instituted Churches (AICs) and Pentecostal and Charismatic churches, both new and older varieties, as different expressions of

Pentecostalism in Africa underscores Anderson's theological as opposed to a socio-logical definition of Pentecostalism.

Karla Poewe's *Charismatic Christianity as a Global Culture* (1994) provided a global treatment of the history, spread and characteristics of Pentecostal and char-ismatic Christianity from an interdisciplinary perspective. This conceptualization of charismatic Christianity as a global religious culture is based on four main features: experiential, idealistic, biblical and oppositional. The work provides a comprehen-sive overview of a charismatic tapestry that transcends national, ethnic, racial and class boundaries. The homogenization of charismatic thought patterns and religious traditions in this work underplays the inherent diversity of the phenomenon as well as the heterogeneity of the Pentecostal tradition. Irving Hexham and Karla Poewe (1997) further highlighted the intercultural dynamics of these movements in inter-preting cults and new religions as "global cultures." They argued that, "new reli-gions such as charismatic Christianity are part of African life and must be interpreted as genuine expressions of African spirituality, not simply as a negative reaction to Europeans" (1997: 53). In support of the multi-directional process of globalization, Hexham and Poewe aptly remarked that "Just as American religion is exported throughout the world, so large religious organizations abroad export their products to North America" (1997: 45).

Some scholars of African Pentecostalism and charismatic movements adopted the concept of fundamentalism in describing the phenomenon in Africa (See Gifford, 1991, 1992; Van Dijk 1995, 2000; Maxwell 2001; Ter Haar 2003). In that way, they contributed to the wider discourse on fundamentalism, although they are largely unsuccessful in clarifying how the concept may fit within the wider discourse of global fundamentalism. Rijk van Dijk places particular attention on the "social meaning" of what he variously calls "Christian fundamentalism," "charismatic Pentecostalism," or "a religion of modernity" in sub-Saharan Africa. He examines the developmental history of charismatic Pentecostal churches as a fundamentalist turn in Africa Christianity, describes its basic ingredients and analyzes some of its "essential ideological parameters," and shows how "it draws its appeal from the ways in which it mediates, negotiates and mitigates modernity" (2000: 2). Van Dijk was critical of Gifford's explanation of Pentecostal resurgence as inspired by right-wing, highly conservative, bourgeois ideals and argued that "the public face of these new fundamentalist or Pentecostal movements should not deceive us as to their meaning and significance at a deeper level of social life in African societies" (2000: 25). Nevertheless, Gifford and van Dijk appropriated "Christian Fundamentalism" in reference to Pentecostalism and other "new dimensions of African Christianity," albeit in an imprecise, undefined manner.

The concepts "modernity," "modernization," "democratization," "urbaniza-tion," "transnationalism," and "appropriation of media" occupy special focus in the works of Gifford 1991, 1998; 2004; van Dijk 1995, 2000; Hackett 1998; Marshall-Fratani 1998, 2001; Meyer 1998, 1999, 2004; Maxwell 1998, 2001, 2006. Van Dijk shares a common view with other scholars in describing "charis-matic Pentecostals" as "primarily urban-based, with a focus on the influential middle classes of bourgeois, these churches are able to exert an unparalleled socio-political and moral influence on society" (2000: 14). The modernization discourse is usually located within the context of the city, and urbanization is seen as an

influential manifestation of the modernization process. There is always some reference to personal uprooting, alienation and the loss of a social and cultural framework in sociological accounts of these developments. It is problematic to generalize
about the claim which explains away Pentecostalism simply as an urban religion.
For instance, Gunilla Oskarsson's findings prove to the contrary through the case
study of Pentecostals in Burundi where it is a rural movement. He argued that the
biggest congregation is still to be found on the countryside, in the southern part,
where in many villages the Pentecostals constitute the majority of the population
(Oskarsson 1999: 414). Research on Pentecostalism and charismatic churches in
Africa often concentrate on urban areas because that is where change is most dramatic and obvious. But rural environments have their own dynamism that yearns
for attention as well. The urban religions, including Pentecostalism, provide a new
home and even a new family of "brothers and sisters," albeit based on artificial
kinship. As Droogers argues, although it may be an important element in explaining
Pentecostal expansion, this reasoning offers no help either in explaining its growth
in rural areas, or its growth among long established and successful urbanities. It
also does not contribute to our understanding of why some people choose one
particular urban religion rather than another (Droogers 2001: 49).

In her contribution to the study of Ghanaian Pentecostal religiosity, Birgit Meyer
(1998) discusses inter alia the connecting nexus between religion, memory and
modernity in a globalizing world. Meyer defined "charismatic" churches as "a
newer type of Pentecostalism recently emerged, especially in urban areas" (1998:
320). She examines "how Pentecostalism seeks to distinguish the present from the
past, at the same time being engaged in a dialectics of remembering and forgetting,
which has helped to construct the past." Meyer was apt in her emphasis that "the
proponents of Pentecostalization regarded the local gods and spirits as authentic
agents of Satan. They strove to exclude them, thereby placing themselves in a tradition of Africanization "from below" (1998: 320ff.)

Ruth Marshall-Fratani locates Nigerian Pentecostalism within the purview of
"transnationalism," the nation-state and the media, and discusses the new situation
in the world created during the last decades. One of her main objectives was to
show how and to what extent the current wave of Pentecostalism in urban Nigeria
evinces an instance of the creation of subjects "whose individual and collective
identities seem to have been formed in terms of a new type of negotiation between
local and global, one in which the media has a privileged role" (1998: 281). Her
second contention was with the relationship between Pentecostalism and the Nigerian nation-state. Marshall-Fratani concludes that even though Pentecostalism
hardly faces the real issues behind the workings of power, it nevertheless entails a
fairly bold attack on the Nigerian State.

Rosalind Hackett (1998) also directed her focus on religion and media, where
she demonstrates how what she characterizes as charismatic and Pentecostal movements in Ghana and Nigeria "are increasingly favoring electronic media as suitable
sites for transmission of their teachings and erecting of their empires." She attributes
the transformation of the religious landscape as a consequence of these developments. Hackett's recognition of the internal and external explanations for their
growth is underscored with her assertion that the majority of the charismatic movements are locally instituted, while some of their leaders were educated in the United

States and maintain some links and affiliations with leading American evangelists. She argues further that, with the extensive growth of viewing audiences and the enhancement of the electronic medium, evangelists with a powerful message and "a good dose of charisma" can attract a much larger following, which might in part explain the development of mega-churches in both Ghana and Nigeria in recent years. Although she tries to make a distinction between charismatics and Pentecostals, she never provides a definition for the nomenclature "Pentecostal." Moreover, the characteristics she adduced for them make her comparison somewhat confusing. What she describes as charismatic in Ghana is more suitably understood as Pentecostal in Nigeria and vice versa.

The gradual burgeoning of literature on Pentecostalism by African scholars has served to complement extant literature on the phenomenon, in a way that challenges the dominance of the field by largely European social scientists. The works by Matthew Ojo (1988a, 1988b, 2006), Kingsley Larbi (2001), Cephas Omenyo (2002) and Kwabena Asamoah-Gyadu (2005) are remarkable instances of how African scholars are contributing to the historiography of African Pentecostal and charismatic movements. These works place an emphasis on the complex internal dynamics and indigenous creativities that characterize the contemporary forms and structure of the charismatic and Pentecostal phenomena. Ojo (1988a, 1988b, 2006) is undoubtedly a pioneering figure in the study of charismatic movements and early Pentecostalism in Nigeria. Ojo's (2006) *The End Time Army* is an in-depth study of Charismatic movements in modern Nigeria, a religious phenomenon that emerged in Western Nigeria in the 1970s. He explored the significant impact of charismatic movements on the contextualization of Christianity in Africa. As he aptly enthused, new Charismatic movements have attained social prominence in Nigeria because of their appropriation of the media, by the attention given to them by the secular media, and because of their large, mostly educated youth membership.

From an insiders' perspective, Larbi (2001) dealt extensively on the origins, forms and development of Pentecostalism in Ghana, and explores the continuity and discontinuity between Ghanaian Pentecostalism and the indigenous religious imagination, as well as their peculiarities. Omenyo (2002) explores the Charismatic/Pentecostal phenomenon in Ghanaian mainline churches as one of the most challenging issues of Christianity in Ghana. Asamoah-Gyadu's (2005) *African Charismatics* represent a fascinating attempt at reconstructing the complexity of indigenous Pentecostalism in Ghana. By employing historical, phenomenological and theological approaches, the book provides sufficient insight into how far a polymethodic perspective can enrich our grasp of the dynamism of contemporary Ghanaian Christianity. Asamoah-Gyadu (2005) aptly demonstrates how some "imported" concepts employed in describing and analyzing new dimensions of African Christianity could be less-informing and more-concealing. The vulnerability of indigenous African Christianities to a certain hybridization of concepts sometimes obscures more than it reveals its dynamism and complexity. He drives home this point clearly, using the expression "charismatic" in Pentecostal vocabulary to show the peculiarity of its meaning and appropriation within local Ghanaian public and religious discourse and context. By explicating how terms and designations associated with Pentecostalism have come to mean different things in different contexts (2005: 1), he demonstrates how Ghanaian Pentecostalism(s) is both "like" and "unlike" Pentecostalism(s) elsewhere. In spite of their theological perspectives, these works have dealt extensively with the origins, forms and development of Pentecostalism in Ghana; while also exploring charismatic and Pentecostal phenomena in mainline churches.

CONCLUSION

The spontaneous, multifaceted provenance and phenomenal expansion of Pentecostal and charismatic movements since over a century, and their one billion mark projection by 2025 or 2050 (Barrett et al. 2001) is a vivid indication that the movement has and will probably continue to reshape and reconfigure the global religious landscape of the twenty-first century and beyond. Owing to the movement's mobility, public role and strategies of expansion, the increasing globalization of Pentecostal and charismatic movements but also the pentecostalization and charismatization of world Christianity will be commonplace. This fluid, elastic nature of the phenomena, particularly its influence on mainline Christianity will render a consideration of a distinctively Pentecostal identity more and more enigmatic. In fact, as new Pentecostal and charismatic movements continue to emerge, they will undergo, in the long run, institutionalization and bureaucratization processes likely to transform and change their nature, identity, texture, public (civic) role and modus operandi. Thus, the "why" and "how" of Pentecostal expansion and relative success globally will continue to pose a critical issue to sociologists and historians of religion as well as other social scientists, secular historians, theologians, policy makers and various publics in an era of increasing global insecurity and uncertainty. The movement's visibility, mobility and continued growth throws up future challenges to both Pentecostal/charismatic and non-pentecostals alike; world Christianity and its interaction with other religions; the local and global public spheres.

The perceived shifting contours and center of gravity of Christianity from the North (Western countries) to the South (Africa, Asia, Latin America) is now well evidenced by the rapid proliferation of Pentecostal and charismatic movements. Their demographic spread and impact cannot be understood only through presence and activities within the geographical confines of Africa, Asia, and Latin America. Rather, the sustained transnational ties, links and exchanges with Pentecostal and charismatic movements globally, has resulted in mutual enrichment, revitalization, transformation and change in each local religious context. African, Asian, and Latin American Pentecostals and Charismatics now form a visible part of global Pentecostalism and contribute to wider, global religious discourses. These "non-Western" Pentecostal and Charismatic movements are now expanding to Western countries, with a renewed effort towards "reverse-mission" (Adogame 2008). Migration also becomes a significant impetus for religious expansion and mobilization in that African, Asian, and Latin American immigrants have established Pentecostal and charismatic churches in new host, Western countries of Europe, North America, and elsewhere. Such a religious development has overarching implications. As most mainstream churches in Western societies continue to experience dwindling membership and decline in missionary significance by the late twentieth century, the impact of non-Western missions, particularly by Pentecostal and Charismatic movements to Europe and North America became strategically significant. The expansion of immigrant Pentecostal and charismatic Christianity opens new vistas, challenges for scholarly exploration of religious diversification and transformation in the context of growing pluralistic societies, a feature often undermined by the secularization debate. Pentecostal and Charismatic Christianity's expansion from the Southern hemisphere to the former "heartlands" of Christianity has helped to revivify Christianity in Europe and North America. The "reverse mission" trend has resulted in a major shift from the traditional understanding of "mission," and provided better sensibilities to, and appreciation of the multi-cultural nature of Christianity in the twenty-first century. Religious expansion or "missions" have now moved strategy from cultural transplantation to contextualization. The capacity of local Pentecostal and charismatic movements to encounter and oscillate within indigenous religious worldviews and cultures has further enriched the movement in terms of their remarkable religious, cultural and theological identity and pluriformity.

Bibliography

Adogame, A. (2003) Betwixt identity and security: African new religious movements and the politics of religious networking in Europe, *Nova Religio: The Journal of Alternative and Emergent Religions* 7 (2): 24–41.

Adogame, A. (2005) African Christian communities in diaspora, in Ogbu U. Kalu (ed.), *African Christianity: An African Story*, Pretoria: Department of Church History, University of Pretoria, 494–514.

Adogame, A. (2007) Raising champions, taking territories: African churches and the mapping of new religious landscapes in diaspora, in T. L. Trost (ed.), *The African Diaspora and the Study of Religion*, New York: Palgrave Macmillan, 17–34.

Adogame, A. (2008) Up, up Jesus! Down, down Satan! African religiosity in the former Soviet bloc: the embassy of the blessed kingdom of God for all nations, *Exchange: Journal of Missiological and Ecumenical Research* 37 (3): 310–36.

Anderson, A. (1999) World Pentecostalism at a crossroad?, in A. Anderson and W. J. Hollenweger (eds.), *Pentecostals after a Century: Global Perspectives on a Movement in Transition*, Sheffield: Sheffield Academic Press, 19–31.

Anderson, A. (2001) *African Reformation: African Initiated Christianity in the Twentieth Century*, Trenton: Africa World Press.

Anderson, A. (2004) *An Introduction to Pentecostalism: Global Charismatic Christianity*, Cambridge: Cambridge University Press.

Anderson, A. (2007) *Spreading Fires: The Missionary Nature of Early Pentecostalism*, London: SCM Press.

Anderson, A. and Hollenweger, W. J. (eds.) (1999) *Pentecostals after a Century: Global Perspectives on a Movement in Transition*, Sheffield: Sheffield Academic Press.

Anderson, R. M. (1979) *Vision of the Disinherited: The Making of American Pentecostalism*, Peabody: Hendrickson.

Asamoah-Gyadu, J. K. (2005) *African Charismatics: Current Developments within Independent Indigenous Pentecostalism in Ghana*, Leiden: Brill.

Barker, E. (1989) *New Religious Movements: A Practical Introduction*, London: Her Majesty's Stationery Office.

Barker, E. (ed.) (1982) *New Religious Movements: A Perspective for Understanding Society*, New York and Toronto: Edwin Mellen Press.

Barrett, D. B. and Johnson, T. M. (2002) Global statistics?, in S. M. Burgess and E. M. van der Maas (eds.), *New International Dictionary of Pentecostal and Charismatic Movements*, Grand Rapids: Zondervan.

Barrett, D. B. and Johnson, T. M. (2003) Annual statistical table of global mission: 2003, *International Bulletin of Missionary Research* 27 (1): 24–5.

Barrett, D. B., George T. K., and Johnson, Todd M. (eds.) (2001) *World Christian Encyclopedia*, 2 vols. (2nd edn.), Oxford and New York: Oxford University Press.

Beckford, J. A. (1985) *Cult Controversies: The Societal Response to New Religious Movements*, London: Tavistock.

Beckford, J. A. (2003) *Social Theory and Religion*, Cambridge: Cambridge University Press.

Berger, P. (1967) *The Sacred Canopy: Elements of a Sociological Theory of Religion*, New York, Anchor Books.

Berger, P. (ed.) (1999) *The Desecularization of the World*, Grand Rapids: Eerdmans.

Beyer, P. (1994) *Religion and Globalization*, London: Sage.

Beyer, P. (ed.) (2001) *Religion im Prozeß der Globalisierung*, Würzburg: Erzon Verlag.

Beyer, P. and Beaman L. (eds.) (2007) *Religion, Globalization and Culture*, Leiden and Boston: Brill.

Burgess, S. M., and Van der Maas, E. M. (eds.) (2002) *The New International Dictionary of Pentecostal and Charismatic Movements*, Grand Rapids: Zondervan.

Brouwer, S., Gifford, P., and Rose, S. D. (1996) *Exporting the American Gospel: Global Christian Fundamentalism*, London: Routledge.

Bruce, S. (1996) *Religion in the Modern World: From Cathedrals to Cults*, Oxford and New York: Oxford University Press.

Bruce, S. (2001) *Fundamentalism*, Oxford: Polity Press.

Bruce, S. (2002) *God Is Dead: Secularization in the West*, Oxford: Blackwell.

Casanova, J. (1994) *Public Religions in the Modern World*, Chicago: University of Chicago Press.

Chesnut, A. (1997) *Born Again in Brazil: The Pentecostal Boom and the Pathogens of Poverty*, New Brunswick: Rutgers University Press.

Chesnut, A. (2003) *Competitive Spirits: Latin America's New Religious Economy*, Oxford: Oxford University Press.

Clarke, P. (2006) *New Religions in Global Perspective: A Study of Religious Change in the Modern World*, London and New York: Routledge.

Coleman, S. (2000) *The Globalization of Charismatic Christianity: Spreading the Gospel of Prosperity*, Cambridge: Cambridge University Press.

Corten, A. (1999) *Pentecostalism in Brazil: Emotion of the Poor and Theological Romanticism*, New York: St Martin's.

Corten, A. and Marshall-Fratani, R. (eds.) (2001) *Between Babel and Pentecost: Transnational Pentecostalism in Africa and Latin America*, Bloomington: Indiana University Press.

Cox, H. (1995) *Fire from Heaven: The Rise of Pentecostal Spirituality and the Reshaping of Religion in the Twenty-First Century*, Cambridge, MA: Da Capo Press.

Cox, H. (1997) Into the age of miracles: culture, religion and the market revolution, *World Policy Journal* 14: 87–95.

Davie, G. (1994) *Religion in Britain since 1945: Believing without Belonging*, Oxford: Blackwell.

Davie, G. (2000) *Religion in Modern Europe: A Memory Mutates*, Oxford: Oxford University Press.

Davie, G. (2001) Patterns of religion in western Europe: an exceptional case, in R. K. Fenn (ed.), *The Blackwell Companion to Sociology of Religion*, Oxford: Blackwell, 264–78.

D'Epinay, C. L. (1969) *Haven of the Masses: A Study of the Pentecostal Movement in Chile*, London: Lutterworth.

Dempster, M., Klaus, B., and Petersen, D. (eds.) (1999) *The Globalisation of Pentecostalism: A Religion Made to Travel*, Oxford and Irvine: Regnum.

Droogers, A. (2001) Globalisation and Pentecostal success, in A. Corten and R. Marshall-Fratani (eds.), *Between Babel and Pentecost: Transnational Pentecostalism in Africa and Latin America*, London: Hurst and Co., 41–61.

Englund, H. (2003) Christian independency and global membership: Pentecostal extraversions in Malawi, *Journal of Religion in Africa* 33: 83–111.

Finke, R. and Stark, R. (1992) *The Churching of America: Winners and Losers in our Religious Economy*, New Brunswick: Rutgers University Press.

Gifford, P. (1991) Christian fundamentalism and development, *Review of African Political Economy* 52: 9–20.

Gifford, P. (1998) *African Christianity: Its Public Role*, London: Hurst and Co.

Gifford, P. (2004) *Ghana's New Christianity: Pentecostalism in a Globalising African Economy*, London: Hurst.

Gifford, P. (ed.) (1992) *New Dimensions in African Christianity*, Nairobi: All Africa Conference of Churches.

Hackett, R. I. J. (1998) Charismatic Pentecostal appropriation of media technologies in Nigeria and Ghana, *Journal of Religion in Africa* 28 (3): 258–77.

Hadden, J. K. (1987) Towards desacralizing secularization theory, *Social Forces* 65 (3): 587–611.

Hervieu-Léger, D. (1999) *Le Pilerin et le Converti. La religion en mouvement*, Paris: Flammarion.

Hexham, I. and Poewe, K. (1997) *New Religions as Global Cultures: Making the Human Sacred*, Boulder: Westview Press.

Hollenweger, W. (1988) [1972] *The Pentecostals*, London: SCM, 1972; repr. Peabody: Hendrickson, 1988.

Jenkins, P. (2002) *The Next Christendom: The Coming of Global Christianity*, New York: Oxford University Press.

Juergensmeyer, M. (1993) *The New Cold War? Religious Nationalism Confronts the Secular State*, Berkeley: University of California Press.

Juergensmeyer, M. (2005) *Religions in Global Civil Society*, Oxford: Oxford University Press.

Kalu, O. U. (2000) *Power, Poverty and Prayer: The Challenges of Poverty and Pluralism in African Christianity, 1960–1996*, Frankfurt am Main: Peter Lang.

Kalu, O. U. (2002) Preserving a world view: Pentecostalism in the African maps of the universe, *Pneuma* 24 (2): 110–37.

Kalu, O. U. (2008) *African Pentecostalism: An Introduction*, Cambridge: Cambridge University Press.

Kamsteeg, F. H. (1998) *Prophetic Pentecostalism in Chile: A Case Study on Religion and Development Policy*, Lanham: Scarecrow.

Larbi, K. (2001) *Pentecostalism: The Eddies of Ghanaian Christianity*, Accra: Center for Pentecostal and Charismatic Studies.

Lehmann, D. (1996) *Struggle for the Spirit: Religious Transformation and Popular Culture in Brazil and Latin America*, Oxford: Blackwell.

Lehmann, D. (2002) Religion and globalization, in L. Woodhead, P. Fletcher, H. Kawanami, and D. Smith (ed.), *Religions in the Modern World*, London and New York: Routledge, 299–315.

Mariz, C. L. (1994) *Coping with Poverty: Pentecostals and Base Communities in Brazil*, Philadephia: Temple University Press.

Marshall, R. (1991) Power in the name of Jesus, *Review of African Political Economy* 52: 21–37.

Marshall-Fratani, R. (1998) Mediating the global and local in Nigeria Pentecostalism, *Journal of Religion in Africa* 28: 278–315.

Marshall-Fratani, R. (2001) Mediating the global and local in Nigerian Pentecostalism', in A. Corten and R. Marshall-Fratani (eds.), *Between Babel and Pentecost. Transnational Pentecostalism in Africa and Latin America*, Bloomington: Indiana University Press, 80–105.

Martin, D. (1978) *A General Theory of Secularization*, Oxford: Blackwell.

Martin, D. (1990) *Tongues of Fire*, Oxford: Blackwell.

Martin, D. (2002) *Pentecostalism: The World Their Parish*, Oxford and Massachusetts: Blackwell.

Maxwell, D. (1998) "Delivered from the spirit of poverty?" Pentecostalism, prosperity and modernity in Zimbabwe, *Journal of Religion in Africa* 28 (3): 350–73.

Maxwell, D. (2000) Review article: *In Defence of African Creativity*, *Journal of Religion in Africa* 30 (4): 468–81.

Maxwell, D. (2001) African gifts of the spirit: fundamentalism and the rise of the born again movement, in P. Martyn (ed.), *Fundamentalism, Church and Society*, London: SPCK, 160–82.

Maxwell, D. (2006) *African Gifts of the Spirit: Pentecostalism and the Rise of a Zimbabwean Transnational Religious Movement*, Oxford: James Currey.

Meyer, B. (1998) Make a complete break with the past: memory and post-colonial modernity in Ghanaian Pentecostal discourse, *Journal of Religion in Africa* 28 (3): 316–49.

Meyer, B. (1999) *Translating the Devil: Religion and Modernity among the Ewe in Ghana*, Edinburgh: Edinburgh University Press.

Meyer, B. (2004) Christianity in Africa: from African independent to Pentecostal-charismatic churches, *Annual Review of Anthropology* 33: 447–74.

Mullins, M. R. (1994) The empire strikes back: Korean Pentecostal mission in Japan, in K. Poewe (ed.), *Charismatic Christianity as a Global Culture*, Columbia: University of South Carolina Press, 87–102.

Ojo, M. (1988a) The contextual significance of the charismatic movements in independent Nigeria, *Africa* 58 (2): 175–92.

Ojo, M. (1988b) Deeper Christian life ministry: a case study of the charismatic movements in independent Nigeria, *Journal of Religion in Africa* 18 (2): 141–62.

Ojo, M. (2006) *The End Time Army: Charismatic Movements in Modern Nigeria*, Religion in Contemporary Africa Series, Trenton: Africa World Press.

Omenyo, C. (2002) *Pentecost Outside Pentecostalism: A Study of the Development of Charismatic Renewal in the Mainline churches in Ghana*, Zoetermeer: Uitgeverig Boekencentrum.

Oskarsson, G. N. (1999) African Pentecostalism, *Swedish Missiological Themes* 87 (3): 405–18.

Pentecostal Power (2006) Pew Research Center Publications, October 5, 2006, http://pewresearch.org/pubs/254/pentecostal-power, accessed July 13, 2007.

Poewe, K. (ed.) (1994) *Charismatic Christianity as a Global Culture*, Columbia, SC: University of South Carolina Press.

Robertson, R. (1985) The sacred and the world system, in P. E. Hammond (ed.), *The Sacred in a Secular Age: Toward Revision in the Scientific Study of Religion*, Berkeley: University of California Press, 347–58.

Robertson, R. (1987) Church–state relations and the world-system, in R. Robertson and T. Robbins (eds.), *Church–State Relations: Tensions and Transitions*, New Brunswick: Transaction Books, 39–52.

Robertson, R. (1992) *Globalization, Social Theory and Global Culture*, London: Sage.

Robertson, R. (1994) Religion and the global field, *Social Compass* 41 (1): 121–35.

Robbins, J. (2004) The globalization of Pentecostal and charismatic Christianity, *Annual Review of Anthropology* 33 (2004): 117–43.

Spirit and Power (2007) Report of a 10-country survey of Pentecostals, Pew Forum on Religion and Public Life, October 2006, http://pewforum.org/publications/surveys/pentecostals-06.pdf, accessed July 13, 2007.

Spittler, R. P. (1994) Are Pentecostals and charismatics fundamentalists? A review of American uses of these categories, in K. Poewe (ed.), *Charismatic Christianity as a Global Culture*, Columbia: University of South Carolina Press, 103–16.

Stoll, D. (1990) *Is Latin America Turning Protestant?*, Berkeley: University of California Press.

Synan, V. (1997) *The Holiness-Pentecostal Tradition: Charismatic Movements in the Twentieth Century*, Grand Rapids and Cambridge: Eerdmans.

Synan, V. (2001) *Century of the Holy Spirit: 100 years of Pentecostal and Charismatic Renewal*, Nashville: Thomas Nelson.

Ter Haar, G. (2003) Religious fundamentalism and social change: a comparative inquiry, in G. Ter Haar and J. J. Busuttil (eds.), *The Freedom to Do God's Will*, London and New York: Routledge, 1–24.

Van der Veer, P. (ed.) (1996) *Conversion to Modernities: The Globalization of Christianity*, New York and London: Routledge.

Van Dijk, R. (1995) Fundamentalism and its moral geography in Malawi: the representation of the diasporic and the diabolical, *Critical Anthropology* 15: 171–191.

Van Dijk, R. (1997) From camp to encompassment: discourses of transsubjectivity in the Ghanaian Pentecostal diaspora, *Journal of Religion in Africa* 27 (2): 135–9.

Van Dijk, R. (2000) *Christian Fundamentalism in Sub-Saharan Africa: The Case of Pentecostalism*, Occasional Paper, University of Copenhagen, Copenhagen: Center of African Studies.

Wilson, B. (1985) Secularization: the inherited model, in P. E. Hammond (ed.), *The Sacred in a Secular Age*, Berkeley: University of California Press, 9–20.

Wilson, B. (1992) Reflections on a many sided controversy, in S. Bruce (ed.), *Religion and Modernization*, Oxford: Oxford University Press, 195–210.

Woodberry, R. D. and Smith, C. S. (1998) Fundamentalism et al.: conservative protestants in America, *Annual Review of Sociology* 24: 25–56.

23

Fundamentalism

RICHARD T. ANTOUN

INTRODUCTION

The preponderance of scholarly opinion in the West suggests that fundamentalism is a set of dogmatic beliefs, a creed, or a literal adherence to a sacred text considered infallible (scripturalism).[1] This chapter presents an alternative view: fundamentalism is an orientation to the world. The intellectual aspect of that orientation is termed "worldview," and the emotional/attitudinal aspect of that orientation is termed "ethos." This definition is far removed from other contrasting definitions of fundamentalism by authors writing from both within and without the varied fundamentalist traditions. Within the Christian tradition the "fundamentals" have been defined as belief in the Trinity, the divinity of Christ, and human nature's corruption by original sin.[2] From without the tradition as "movements that seek to return to orthodox, feudal value systems"; "repression of individuals and social groups" and "exertion of violence as an expression of power"; "a puritanical attitude...and the assertion of patriarchal authority"; and "a discernible pattern of religious militance by which self-styled 'true believers' attempt to arrest the erosion of religious identity, fortify borders of religious community, and create alternatives to secular institutions and behaviors."[3] This lack of intellectual agreement about what constitutes fundamentalism is both endearing and disturbing. The variety of definitions indicated is free-wheeling and provocative. But when anything and everything can stand for a concept, here fundamentalism, then the concept is no longer useful for purposes of description and analysis.

This is, then, an interpretive chapter. The definition and description of fundamentalism goes against the grain of much academic writing on the subject which is particularistic in scope, dichotomous in classification, and pejorative in evaluation. This account treats fundamentalism as a cross-cultural phenomenon as well as an ideal type and a genuine (though not incorruptible) form of religion. It contextualizes fundamentalism within the broad social, economic, and political currents that began at the end of the eighteenth century. The attitude taken toward fundamentalism is neither condemnatory nor praiseful, but rather empathetic (though not sympathetic which suggests support). That is, the aim is to understand the phenomenon rather than to boost or denigrate it. References to contrasting points of view appear in passing in the chapter, and in the list of works for further reading at the end.

This description of fundamentalism is confined to the monotheistic religions. The religious traditions of Islam, Christianity and Judaism are intimately related not only historically but also theologically. Muslims recognize the Hebrew prophets and even include Jesus as one of them! Moreover, all three religions accept Abraham as a significant seminal figure in their religious tradition and recognize that they share a common legacy. A review of Hindu, Sikh, or Buddhist fundamentalism would be valuable and make this study more widely cross-cultural, but such a review is beyond my expertise.[4] Fundamentalism, then, is an orientation to the modern world, both cognitive and emotional, that focuses on protest and change and on certain consuming themes: the quest for purity; the struggle between good and evil; the search for authenticity; totalism and activism; the necessity of certainty (scripturalism); selective modernization and controlled acculturation, millenialism, and the centering of the mythic past on the present (traditioning). Totalism is the orientation that views religion as relevant to all important domains of culture and society including politics, the family, the marketplace, education, and law. Activism is confronting the establishment, political or religious, by multiple forms of protest: legal, political, economic, and coercive. Scripturalism is the justification and reference of all important beliefs and actions to a sacred scripture and a proof-text claimed to be inerrant. That scripture, above all, has a powerful emotional appeal for the believer. Selective modernization is the process of selective acceptance of technological and social organizational innovations introduced by the modern world. Controlled acculturation is the process by which an individual accepts a practice or belief from another culture or the secular world on terms that integrate it into their value system. Traditioning is the process of making scriptural accounts, events, and images relevant to present-day activities. Millenialism is the Christian doctrine that the prophecy in the book of Revelation will be fulfilled with an earthly rule of a thousand years of universal peace and the triumph of righteousness. More generally for a number of religious traditions it is the belief that history will come to an apocalyptic end with the return of a divine redeemer, the reign of the righteous, and a judgment day for the Al Qaedaick and the dead.[5]

WHO ARE THE FUNDAMENTALISTS?

The social identity of fundamentalists has been a debatable question whose answer has often varied in terms of the fundamentalist movement discussed, the pertinent period in modern history, and the perspective taken. Five views are covered briefly below. Each view highlights certain aspects of fundamentalist recruitment that deserve attention.[6] Henry Munson, an anthropologist, has described fundamentalists in terms of a worldview that sees them choosing God's side in the ongoing and pervasive struggle of good against evil (Satan).[7] Fundamentalists differ among themselves in whether they regard this struggle as moral (with imperial rule as a punishment for an immoral people) and as necessitating a strict return to scripture (Qur'an) or whether the see the struggle political as well as moral and as necessitating not only moral reformation and a struggle against the oppressor but also the establishment of an Islamic state. In his application of this view to Morocco in the 1970s and 1980s, Munson distinguishes three fundamentalist types, ranging from most moral to most political. Implicit in these categorizations is the distinction between "religious" and "religious-minded" people.[8] These terms distinguish between people who spontaneously experience religion and those who are self-conscious in defense of their beliefs (and who feel most threatened by outsiders). Two of the three fundamentalist leaders of the movements Munson discusses were former inspectors in the Ministry of Education. And the supporters of the more political of the movements were students and members of the educated middle class with very few supporters from such categories as peasants, workers or rural migrants.

Bruce Lawrence, a historian of religion, has emphasized that in its leadership and core following, fundamentalism is a movement of secondary-level male elites.[9] These males are dominantly laymen, not clergy.[10] He notes that two prominent Muslim fundamentalist leaders in Pakistan, Abul-'Ala Mawdudi and Asrar Ahmed, were a journalist and a medical doctor, respectively, before turning their attention to religious reform; two other prominent Egyptian Muslim fundamentalists, Hassan al-Banna, and Sayyid Qutb were, respectively a teacher and a bureaucrat in the Ministry of Education. And Juhayman ibn Sayf al-'Utayba, who led the violent military takeover of the sacred mosque enclosure in Mecca in 1979, an audacious challenge to the Saudi state, was a soldier in the Saudi National Guard before he became a self-taught Muslim theologian. In the United States Pat Robertson is by training a lawyer, and James Dobson is a developmental psychologist, and although Jerry Falwell was trained in the ministry, he made his living as a talk-show host. Fundamentalists are very much men of the world in the world. In Egypt in the 1980s Lawrence records that that Muslim fundamentalists came from upwardly mobile educated middle class backgrounds and not from the dispossessed and downtrodden. In Saudi Arabia, Malaysia and Iran in the late 1970s they came from the petite bourgeoise, that is, from "marginalized out-of-power groups and estranged urban dwellers who continue to have rural roots and premodern values."[11] The male elite fundamentalist leaders in this period and the following decade were professionally and scientifically oriented. Quite often, they were unemployed or underemployed "frustrated engineers, disaffected doctors, or unpaid bureaucrats in meaningless public jobs.[12] Lawrence's description affirms the diversified social base of fundamentalist Muslim movements.

Martin Riesebrodt, a sociologist, compares the social composition of Protestant fundamentalists in the United States in the period from 1910 to 1928 with Shi'a Muslim fundamentalists in Iran from 1961 to 1979 and finds remarkable similarities. He argues that fundamentalists are neither a class nor a dislocated amorphous mass. Rather, they are segments of different classes sharing the same experience and reacting to it through the same set of religious symbols or, alternatively, segments of society having different experiences that are expressed through the same set of religious symbols.[13] A social movement whose members share a number of attributes such as religion, regional tradition, and economic position organize through a voluntary religious association to promote a certain worldview. They are brought together symbolically and socially by common images and ideas. Riesebrodt argues that fundamentalism is an urban protest movement recruited from all classes but featuring urban migrants, the traditional middle class, the clergy, and "border-crossers." Border-crossers include youth and white-collar bureaucrats of rural origins who come to the city, have received a secular education, are alienated from many aspects of rural culture, but are not modern in their worldview or ethos (e.g., they have conservative views of women and their dress, demeanor and participation in public life including education and work).[14] In Iran patron–client ties between particular local and regional religious leaders and their followers martialed economic support for schools, mosques, and hospitals, and for the revolution (of 1979).[15]

In the United States fundamentalism was also an urban phenomenon, arising and flourishing in the large northern cities of New York, Chicago, Philadelphia, Boston, Baltimore, and Minneapolis as well as in Los Angeles. The leaders of fundamentalist activity as well as the followership "came from confessions in which the conflict between modernism and orthodoxy was strongest, the Baptists and Presbyterians of the North."[16] Riesebrodt's demographic point is significant not only because it challenges the stereotype of American fundamentalism as a rural and small-town phenomenon, but also because it focuses on rapid urbanization, industrialization, and mass migration. These were the processes that were transforming the United States from a personalistic and patriarchal society to an impersonal and bureaucratic one, both in the communities and in the churches.[17] It is not accidental that the invective of the Protestant fundamentalists at the beginning of the twentieth century was xenophobic, citing "Rum and Romanism," and focusing on Roman Catholics and Jews. These were precisely the immigrant groups that were pouring into the northern cities where fundamentalism arose. It was they, the fundamentalists argued, that were eroding the moral values of the nation. The American south did not experience such mass migration, industrialization, and urbanization until much later.

Ian Lustick, a political scientist, has in one way broadend and in another way narrowed the application of the term fundamentalism by linking it with militant political activism. He defines fundamentalism as "a style of political participation characterized by unusually close and direct links between one's fundamental beliefs and political behavior designed to effect radical change."[18] Fundamentalists are identified by three attributes: uncompromisable injunctions, belief that their behavior is "guided by direct contact with the source of transcendental authority," and "political attempts to bring about rapid and comprehensive change."[19] By defining fundamentalism in this way Lustick was able to rule out other Jewish religious groups in Israel such as the *haredim* (ultra-orthodox Jews) as fitting the category. The latter regarded the Torah and other Jewish sacred scriptures as literally true and inerrant, and they were extremely pious as judged by their devotion to worship and their style-of-life (dress, diet, and demeanor). But the *haredim* "opted out of key political struggles over the course that Israeli society will take."[20] By definition, for Lustick, fundamentalists must not only be political activists, they must be militant political activists. Members of *Gush Emunim* (Bloc of the Faithful) are com-

mitted to claiming and settling the West Bank of the Jordan river – land already
settled by Palestinians – by force if necessary under the slogan, "The Land of Israel
for the People of Israel, according to the Torah of Israel."[21] On the other hand,
Lustick's definition of fundamentalists would include nonreligious political movements characterized by dogmatism, militancy, and justification by some ultimate
cause (e.g., the classless society). The core of *Gush Emunim* (around 20,000 in the
1980s) was supported by a much larger number of followers and sympathizers
(estimated at 150,000 in elections) connected in a social network with nodes in
religious schools, cooperative and collective settlements, parties, and political
lobbies in much the same way that Iranian fundamentalists are connected in a far-
flung social network whose nodes are mosques, prayer halls (*husayniyyahs*), and
bazaars where pious businessmen organize activities. Fundamentalists, then, are
not always, perhaps not usually, organized in formal corporate groups but rather
in informal networks within which, nevertheless, communication can be rapid and
efficient.

A fifth perspective is provided by Daniel Levine and David Stoll who discuss the
attraction of new Protestant religious movements among Roman Catholics in Latin
America. In explaining the attraction of such movements , Levine and Stoll have
emphasized five attributes: social change and mobility, the allure of modernity, the
small size of churches located on the urban periphery, the intense informal social
networks, and the evangelical component in the message.[22] The authors emphasize
the new clientele that have developed for Protestant missionary activity as a result
of urbanization, population shift, and expanded transport and communication,
beginning in the 1960s. The "new affiliations to Protestant churches are overwhelmingly drawn from men and women with an intense experience of change and mobility with hopes for improving personal and family life."[23] Fundamentalist churches
appeal to "the newly educated, including groups with technical training."[24] The
newly educated sense that the fundamentalist churches represent a "modern way of
living," with their emphasis on personal responsibility, literacy, the necessity to read
an "unmediated ... text," and a focus on intense spirituality and health and healing.[25]
Levine and Stoll also indicate that Protestant fundamentalist churches are better
able to adapt to changes occuring in Latin America because they are located on the
urban periphery where migrants land, and because they are small and unburdened
with the large bureaucracy the Roman Catholic Church must support. The authors
argue that there is a built-in dynamism of small, poor fundamentalist or evangelical
churches related to their "low thresholds."[26] These churches feature intense social
and religious life with small meetings, overlapping groups, and frequent home visits.
These low thresholds mean that "it is simple to organize a church and not very
difficult to gain recognition as a religious leader." The poorer the church, the more
it depends on expansion (in membership) to survive.[27] Finally, Levine and Stoll argue
that the essential component of the attraction of new Protestant movements in Latin
America is their evangelical character which they define in terms of three beliefs:
the reliability on the Bible as a final authority; the necessity of being "born again"
(i.e., of being "saved" as an adult through a personal relationship with Jesus Christ);
and "the importance of spreading this message of salvation to every nation and
person."[28]

THE GREAT WESTERN TRANSMUTATION AND
THE PROTEST AGAINST MODERNISM

Fundamentalist movements are defined, ideologically, by their opposition to and reaction against the ideology that suits the permissive secular society, the ideology of modernism.[29] Lawrence has characterized the ideology of modernism as one that values change over continuity, quantity over quality, and commercial efficiency (production and profit) over human sympathy for traditional values. The ethos of fundamentalism, its affective orientation, is one of protest and outrage at the secularization of society; that is, at the process by which religion and its spirit has been steadily removed from public life – from schools, offices, workshops, universities, courts, and markets, and even from religious institutions themselves – churches, mosques, and synagogues.

The elevation of change over continuity in our lives is evidenced by the constant upgrading of computer hardware and software, and, recently, by the energy crisis with its demand for constriction of budgets, consumer conservation, and producer proliferation of new sources of energy. The necessity of corporate businessmen to uproot themselves and their families and to adjust in the new suburbs where they relocated was described after World War Two by William H. Whyte in his best seller, *Organization Man* (1956). So common a part of life in corporate Europe and the United States is this phenomenon it has been termed *spiralism* by sociologists: one has to move spatially to climb hierarchically. Although human beings in peasant societies traveled occasionally to regional markets, they worked daily within walking distance of their homes, enabling cultivators to go out to their fields and return by nightfall. The urban revolution did not disrupt the unity of home and work; it was quite common for urban dwellers in the Chinese, Indian, and Middle Eastern civilizations to live in the same neighborhood where they worked; often, they lived and worked in the same building, working on the first floor, living on the second. The industrial revolution changed all that. The introduction of the factory required leaving one's home to go to work. During the last hundred years, particularly in the last twenty-five, the industrial revolution and the high-tech era have encouraged the rapid spread of transportation and communication networks, triggering mobility because of the proliferation of job opportunities provided by the complex, global capitalist system. Transnational migration has become a powerful force for change in Europe, Asia and North America.[30] In my own community, a small town in upstate New York, I am no longer able to get a newspaper, pick up prescription drugs, shop at a small supermarket, or repair my shoes at the nearby shopping plaza, as I was forty years ago when I moved to the community. All these small enterprises have been displaced by the proliferation of large shopping malls on the other side of town. The small city adjoining my town is now the locus of transnational migrants from Latin America, Asia, Africa, and Europe including Kurds, Somalis, Iraqi Arabs, Bosnians, Vietnamese, Laotians, Haitians, Puerto Ricans, Indians, Chinese, Russians, Brazilians, and Ukrainians. Only the latter were present in any numbers forty years ago.

Modernity's elevation of commercial efficiency over human sympathy is reflected in the increasing focus on the clock. Two political scientists, Lloyd and Susanne

Rudolph compared Gandhi's daily schedule to Benjamin Franklin's. In their diaries both men segmented the day's activities according to clock time, stipulating beginning and ending times for meals, bath, exercise, rest, study, sleep and worship. Gandhi was the more "modern" of the two, the more efficient and specialized in dividing activities by the clock, stipulating fourteen activities beginning at 4 a.m. and ending at 9 p.m., whereas Frankin stipulated eleven, beginning at 5 a.m. and ending at 10 p.m. Modern life is clock-conscious life and rules the day. However, the modern way of life submerges the important interpersonal ties that have bound societies together for thousands of years. Among these are ties of friendship. I recall many years ago being a visiting professor at the American University of Beirut, where a Lebanese colleague and I became good friends, eating meals together, visiting one another in off-work hours, and going on trips together in the Lebanese countryside. Late one morning he came to me as I was in the midst of preparing a class lecture I was to give in an hour's time, saying, "Let's go out for a cup of coffee and a smoke of the hubble-bubble pipe." I replied, "I'm sorry, I have to finish preparing my lecture." Although I noted he was disappointed, I thought little about the matter. A few weeks later he was busy preparing a lecture for a class he was to give in an hour's time, when his friend, a Lebanese professor, came in and said to him, "Come, let's go out for a cup of coffee and hubble-bubble smoke." He replied, "Okay, let's go." This incident demonstrated that I was tied to the clock and my obligation to produce a lecture. My friend and colleague was a good teacher and an excellent scholar, but he placed human sympathy and friendship first.

Also among these human ties are patron-client ties.[31] These ties are often discussed in a political or economic context, but such a discussion misses their human texture. During this same time (when I was a visiting professor in Beirut) I often had my shoes shined because of the dusty thoroughfares of a bustling entrepôt and because it was appropriate to my status in the university milieu. Outside the university gate there were six or seven men lined up next to one another who shined shoes. Fortuitiously, I chose one on the occasion of my first shoe shine; thereafter, the same man would always preempt the others and shine my shoes. Soon, he and I took it for granted that we were linked in a patron-client relationship. He always said he would give me a better shine than the others would, and I think he did because, over time, we developed a less instrumental and more personal relationship. Customarily, when I finished my shoe shine and went into the Lebanese restaurant opposite the gate, I experienced a similar relationship; the same waiter always came to serve me at the table, and every other patron at the restaurant had his or her own special waiter who offered superior service and jocular company. These interpersonal ties that informed the ethos of a premodern society are being diminished, even in the rural areas of Jordan. Before the 1970s the prevailing custom of the villages of the district where I did my research was that villagers who returned to the community after a long absence (six months or a year) always brought gifts to their close kinsmen. In this society this could mean a fairly large number of cousins, uncles and aunts as well as immediate family members. Close kinsmen reciprocated by inviting the returned villagers to their homes for a sumptuous meal, sometimes involving the slaughter of an animal. In the 1970s transnational migration from the village where I conducted my research to seventeen different countries for purposes of work, higher education, and military training became common.

Many villagers were coming and going with a frequency never before known. Now they could not afford to bring gifts every time they returned; they wished to save their money for their education, for the education of their children, or for commerical enterprises they might start in the village and its environs with their savings from working abroad. Yet these returned villagers still expected their close kinsmen to invite them for meals or at least invite them to their homes. On their side, kinsmen who remained in the village still expected their relatives to bring them gifts from abroad. Expectations were disappointed on both sides. A new ethos began to replace the old one, which was composed of hospitality, cordiality, and mutual affection. Villagers characterized the new ethos by the term *mujamala*, meaning politeness, but false politeness motivated by self-interest. That is, your kinsmen only visited you now because they wanted something from you, not because they had affection for you. What does this discussion have to do with fundamentalism? It is simply this: fundamentalism is a reaction, both ideological and affective, to the changes in basic social relationships that have occurred on a worldwide basis as a result of the social organizational, technological, and economic changes introduced by the modern world.

The changes in interpersonal relations described above are part of a historical shift in worldview and power relations that Bruce Lawrence, following Fernand Braudel, Marshall Hodgson, and Barrington Moore, has described as the "Great Western Transmutation" (GWT).[32] The GWT began at the end of the eighteenth century in Western Europe and changed the outlook of human beings toward the material world. As a result of the Enlightenment, the French Revolution, the commercialization and industrialization of life, and the scientific revolution, a worldview that had been preoccupied with moral and ultimate questions (such as the quest for salvation) now became involved with (commercial) puzzle solving in a world of expanding markets and opportunities. God's world was this new world and not the next world, and the work of the world was God's work, whereas before, the work of the world was to prepare for the hereafter. The GWT undermined the organic worldview that placed each class in its proper place and taught each man/woman to aspire only to their parent's role/status and led instead to the revolution of rising expectations. This new worldview also led eventually to the pluralization of private beliefs (in the United States regarding birth control, equal rights for women, prayer in the schools, affirmative action) and the relativization of public value (by which the government assumes dissent on issues of public interest and a "live and let live attitude" on the part of the populace). The GWT is tied to a shift in power relations in turn related to the bureaucratization and technicalization of violence. I remember as a high schooler going on the class trip to Washington DC and being taken into the Pentagon. I looked down one of the hallways and could not see the end of it! The Pentagon is the culmination of the bureaucratization and the technicalization of violence. Before the French Revolution (1789) there were ten world powers (measured by their ability to wage war successfully); after World War One (1919) there were six; after World War Two they had been reduced to two; and after the Gulf War (1991) by that standard only one, the United States. Over the course of two hundred years with respect to military, political and economic power there has been a reduction of winners and a proliferation of losers. This changing power ratio has had a direct impact on fundamentalism. Fundamentalism in its many manifestations worldwide is a movement of those who are or see themselves as losers in the struggle for power and recognition.

THE QUEST FOR PURITY

It remains to discuss some of the prominent attributes of fundamentalism.[33] Perhaps the most important is the quest for purity. Why so important? Because fundamentalists regard the world as impure and corrupt. Therefore, they must devise strategies to avoid that world, or alternatively, to confront and defeat it. Avoidance through flight is a fundamentalist reaction at one extreme; separation – physical, social or symbolic – is a second reaction to an impure world; and militant struggle to overcome and capture that world is a third reaction. The quite different reactions of fundamentalists to a common problem again illustrates that fundamentalists are not so much tied by a particular cultural content (Christian fundamentalists are driven by antipathy to evolution and positivist science, Muslim fundamentalists by outrage at Western colonialism, and Jewish fundamentalists by outrage at virulent anti-Semitism), but rather by their common orientation to the modern world: an orientation of outrage, protest and fear.

Flight has long been a strategy pursued by minoritarian religious groups who suffer oppression, discrimination or both. The Boers of South Africa (representing the Dutch Reform Church tradition) trekked 1,000 miles from Cape Province to the Transvaal in 1836 to escape the pervasive secular influence brought by English settlers and administrators representing the British Empire. The Egyptian fundamentalist group, "Excommunication and Flight" (*takfir wa hijra*), so named by the Egyptian press and public in the 1970s because they declared excommunicated the majority of Egyptian Muslims who, they argued, engaged in idolatrous behavior such as usury, fornication, prostitution, the mixing of sexes in public, and the drinking of alcohol (Stella, a national beer, was very popular in Cairo). Their own purified version of Islam followed the Prophet's tradition: they shaved their heads, cultivated trimmed beards, and wore black cloaks after his example. The movement split into two parts, one of which pursued the strategy of militant confrontation with the government, resorting to kidnapping government ministers and assassination. But the other branch abandoned their urban residences for caves in Upper Egypt near the desert to escape the reach of the government and the pressure for conformity.[34] Flight is a demonstration of protest and sometimes defiance. It allowed this group of Egyptian fundamentalists to avoid common national obligations such as military conscription and payment of taxes.

A second strategy is separation. One mode of separation is radical social and spatial separation (but not flight). Another branch of Excommunication and Flight remained within urban centers but formed their own "families" within these centers, living with like-minded fundamentalists of both sexes in crowded apartment buildings. They prayed separately in these buildings, refusing to attend mosques led by government-appointed (and therefore contaminated) preachers. They taught their children in their own homes rather than send them to public schools whose curriculum they regarded as corrupting; in their view all teachers in public schools were appointed by the corrupt central government. They refused intermarriage with those who were not members of their own religious movement. When they did marry they refused to be married by mainline religious officials; that is, the usual religious specialists who served the majority population. Another example of radical separation (but not flight) from an impure world is the case of the Reb Arelach *haredim* who live in the gated quarter of Mea Shearim in Jerusalem.[35] Israelis use this term to designate those Jews who defend the faith and keep the law without making the kind of compromises to the secular world common to the majority in Israel. The *haredim* designate themselves *erlicher Yidn*, virtuous Jews, not a sect of Judaism, but the true Jews. Like Excommunication and Flight they regard the central government of Israel with distrust and often hostility because they see that government as supporting a "permissive society" in which Judaism threatens to be overwhelmed by nightclubs, cinemas, television, immodesty of women (particularly their dress), hedonistic cross-sex relations, violations of kosher rules, and the secularization of education. To ward off the powerful flow of impure culture that emenates from the government, secular Jews, and foreign countries, the *haredim* have gathered in their own quarter of Jerusalem where they conduct their own way of life according to their own strict rules. They do not allow strangers to enter their quarter and strut their profane style-of-life with impunity. Immodestly dressed men and women who enter their quarter are heckled and sometimes stoned. Just before the Sabbath they close the gate to their quarter and permit no one in or out until the Sabbath ends twenty-four hours later. When they appear outside their quarter, the *haredim* are immediately set off by their dress and appearance. They are always in black and white, with men distinguished by beards and ear locks and women with hair covered.

A third mode of separative strategy is institutional and symbolic rather than physical and spatial, illustrated by the Bethany Baptist Academy (BBA), a Christian academy in a city of 50,000 in Illinois. The leader of the school told the anthropologist studying it, "The Bible says that we are in the world, but not to be of the world."[36] The academy urged students not to form close ties with non-Christians; not to date non-Christians; not to marry non-Christians; to prefer Christian candidates in the voting booth; and to carry back and apply their Christian ethics and Christian ethos in their homes. But there was no Christian yellow-page listing in the telephone book with names of preferred merchants and physicians, and BBA families had no restrictions placed on where they could live. Although certain occupations were preferred (minister, missionary) with a few exceptions (bartender, gambler, rock musician) occupations were open. It is important to note that "non-Christians" designated all those who were not "saved" (received Jesus in the form of the Holy spirit in adult life). Therefore, the world of the impure was far larger than might first appear. Because the BBA applied the principle of separation differently in different domains of culture, and because it did not constrain daily contact with nonbelievers in the workaday world, special devices were necessary to provide protection to core believers. These devices were symbolic and ethical. On the symbolic side, a dress code sets Bethany students apart from others: short hair for boys, nice dresses and stockings for girls, and the absence of blue jeans for both. More important on the symbolic side is a whole vocabulary of salvation that defines the quest for divine grace as well as the degree of its achievement: "being saved," "grown in the Lord," "testifying," "witnessing," "full-time Christian," "born-again,"the fallen faithful," "get in the word," "get right with the Lord," "the place the Lord wants you to be," and "we put the Lord first." Separation is defined in spiritual terms. All these symbolic statuses or processes have ethical correlates. In other words, one must be one's brother's as well as one's own keeper. Because the BBA did not segregate its students from the world at large, it had to develop other devices to ensure effective inculcation of its message. Besides its elaborate vocabulary of degrees of salvation and their ethical correlates, and along with constant monitoring, it developed "total teaching" and strived for a "total atmosphere." All classes including math and English were introduced by biblical lessons and religious messages. All school activities began with prayer, e.g., the bus driver or the coach prayed before the bus left on athletic trips. Parents were urged to support the teachings of BBA at home to produce the "total atmosphere" of a Christian home and "the full-time-Christian." Such were the dimensions of totalism.

Scripturalism and Traditioning

The focus on a divine scripture is a key attribute of fundamentalism, but not for the reasons usually given – the literal belief in an inerrant scripture as the world of God.[37] The scripture is so powerful, above all, for its numinous character, an unseen and majestic presence that inspires both dread and fascination. Every major mosque of every major Muslim city is adorned with the calligraphy of the Qur'an. This Qur'anic calligraphy is the closest presence of God on earth for the believing Muslim. The emotional impact of the scripture is manifested in Muslim daily prayers which are filled with Qur'anic verses. The emotional impact of the Protestant Bible was and still is reflected in the intimate notes written in the margins of verses that had/have particular meaning for the meditating Christian. Charles Hirschkind has provided new insights into how recitation of scripture impacts the believer. In his book, *The Ethical Soundscape* (2006) he has analyzed how Islamic sermon cassettes have communicated a powerful emotional but also ethical message that has driven the Islamic revival in Egypt in such a way as to overcome the power of the state to indoctrinate its own citizens with a basically nationalist ideology.[38] These cassette sermons are filled with verses of the Qur'an that are chanted by Muslim preachers and heard by taxi drivers and their passengers as they wend their way through the cacaphony of Cairo traffic. Hirschkind has argued that these Qur'anic verses register through the sensorium (the heart, the mind, the ears, the muscles, the entire body inside and outside) until the listener develops "an active belief" (to take action in the world rather than wait for the hereafter) and an "attitude of ... acceptance and responsibility infused with the emotions of fear, sadness and humility."[39] Moreover, he argues that the discussions triggered by these sermons lead to a process of collective rethinking involving argument, criticism and debate rather than simple indoctrination. In addition, scripture assuages that yearning for certainty felt by human beings in an increasingly uncertain world. This yearning was reflected in an early twentieth century public debate on the inerrancy of scripture before 10,000 people in New York City by a fundamentalist minister named Straton:

"Shall the highest interests of our natures be left to caprice and chance? Are we forever to grope in darkness and uncertainty? Are there no fixed standards? No

solid and enduring ground on which we can build our society and found our hopes
of Heaven? Is each one of us to be left to believe one thing one day – and that thing
perhaps different from everything our neighbors are believing – and another thing
tomorrow, and another thing the next day, and so on and on."[40]

Finally, the scripture is a guide to everyday behavior and an explanation of
repetitive and occasional events. When I was conducting anthropological field work
in a peasant village in Jordan during the winter months I would sometimes look up
at the partly cloudy sky in the morning and ask a villager if he thought it was going
to rain. He would often reply by reciting a verse from the Qur'an such as, "Hast
thou not seen that God knows whatsoever is in the heavens and whatsoever is in
the earth" (58: 7), i.e., Why are you asking me such a foolish question?

Traditioning is the process of collapsing the primordial, the ancient, the heritage
of the golden age with the present time, making them one and the same. By identifying with the good past and melding that past with the good present, a guide and an
explanation is provided for present situations and circumstances.[41] Samuel Heilman's
account of an ultra-orthodox (haredi) community in Jerusalem illustrates this
process.[42] He sat in on a sixth grade haredi class. He was interested in the class's
knowledge of modern geography, and the teacher asked the students to draw a map
of (modern) Israel and its neighbors. No one could list the names of the countries
surrounding Israel nor name the main bodies of water, the Dead Sea and the Sea of
Galilee. They had never heard of Saudi Arabia. But they did have a map of the world,
a globe hanging from the vestibule of the yeshiva (Jewish religious school). It was a
map of eastern Europe that spread-eagled the globe. However, it was a very particular eastern Europe, the eastern Europe of the rebbes (Jewish scholar-mystics) who
had founded the religious order in Russia and Poland more than a century before.
The central focus of the map was the town of Zvil (the rebbe of the Israeli order to
which the school was affiliated traced his descent to Zvil), and the surrounding cities
were all well-known centers of authentic Jewish life in eastern Europe a hundred
years previously. The past was made present in the geography taught as well as the
language (of the golden east European age), Yiddish. Of course, the students had an
excellent knowledge of scriptural geography, the geography of the Torah. For these
yeshiva students, the Israel of their imagination, biblical Israel – including all its
heroes and heroines – was far superior to modern (secularized) Israel.

The past was made present in many other aspects of haredi life. For instance,
Heilman attended the Friday night Sabbath religious observances at the Belz (another
east European town) yeshiva in Jerusalem, which culminated in a meal at the rebbe's
tish (the Yiddish world for table). He described it as a "classic east European meal"
that became ritualized. After each set of songs, all Belz tunes, the rebbe ate another
course, beginning with the breaking of the coiled challah bread and followed in turn
by gefilte fish, grape juice, chicken soup, farfel (little bits of noodles), honey-sweet-
ened carrots, chicken, and finally fruit compote. The haredi way of dealing with the
tragedy of the Holocaust was to intensify both worship and what they regarded as
the pure Jewish tradition (of eastern Europe) and to nurture a counterculture
through social separation. Traditioning in the Christian tradition was illustrated
above in the habit of avidly tracing and strictly applying biblical proof texts regarding various domains of culture and society (such as intermarriage and obedience to
parents).

The most interesting and politically problematic aspect of traditioning is its view of time and history. What is relevant is only today and the previous golden age(s). What happened in between (and the peoples involved) is/are irrelevant. Susan Harding has given the best explanation of the fundamentalist notion of time/history in *The Book of Jerry Falwell*.[43] She conducted field work in and around Lynchburg, Virginia, the center of Jerry Falwell's Moral Majority movement as well as Liberty University, founded by him in 1984. She listened carefully to the language that preachers and followers affiliated with his movement used. Three terms were continuously repeated relating to time/history and human destinies: prefiguring/fore-shadowing (used as synonyms) and fulfillment. The meaning of these concepts was illustrated by Falwell himself when discussing the mountain-top location of Liberty Baptist College (later Liberty University) in 1972. He gave a proliferation of scriptural references that prefigured the location of Liberty University: Noah's ark rested on a mountain; Abraham prepared to sacrifice Isaac on a mountain; Moses and Joshua viewed the Holy Land from a mountain; Jesus gave the Sermon on the Mount.[44] By implication Falwell became metaphorically Noah, Abraham, Jesus, Joshua, and Moses. Even bad events (in the present) are prefigured and lead to fulfillment unforseen by the individual. In 1973 when the Securities and Exchange Commission sued Falwell's Thomas Road Baptist Church for fraud and deceit in the sale of church bonds and declared it insolvent, it forced Falwell to modernize and expand his church: hire professional accountants, cut overhead costs, hire public relations experts, and an agency to coordinate fund-raising.[45] Fundamentalists constantly see their lives personally fulfilled in terms of prefigured events. This notion of time, history, and personal destiny is alien to the notion of the chain of cause and effect held by most historians and lay persons.

Selective Modernization and Controlled Acculturation

Because fundamentalism is often regarded by majoritarian, secularized groups as an ideology that resists change, most surprising are the attributes of selective modernization and controlled acculturation. Christian radio broadcasting and televangelism are dramatic examples of selective modernization.[46] The same year Jerry Falwell became an accredited preacher (1956) he became a televangelist and businessman (a primary function of televangelism is raising money for religious congregations). Pat Robertson founded his all-day Christian Broadcasting Network in 1961. The network evolved into 5,500 cable systems across the country. He developed the "700 club" while experimenting with the variety show, talk show, and country formats to find the most effective format for televangelism. James Dobson (with a PhD in child development and not religion) founded his radio program, "Focus on the Family," a weekday, half-hour program that combined religious wisdom with psychological discussion in the 1970s. By the 1980s his program received 200,000 letters a month and 1,200 telephone calls a day. For the 10,000 letters regarded as life-threatening, the program referred the writers to one of 19 family counselors, nationwide, who made therapist referrals. Every year Focus on the Family sent out 52 million pieces of mail and one million cassettes.[47] It's obvious that such massive communications involve the development of a complex social organization and bureaucracy as well as technological expertise and business acumen. The televangelists and Christian radio broadcasters martialed this sophisticated technological expertise, however, to communicate a specific and highly selective message: the immorality of the world, the cataclysm to come, the necessity for individual spiritual reform, and economic libertarianism and social traditionalism. Economic libertarianism assumes that economic interaction between rationally self-interested individuals in the market will lead to prosperity and social harmony; this policy has been labeled, *laisse-faire*. Social traditionalism is concerned with the breakdown of the family, community, religion, and traditional morality in American life due to the government's supporting abortion, affirmative action, busing, sexual permissiveness, the Equal Rights Amendment, and the prohibition of school prayer.[48]

Controlled acculturation is the process by which an individual of one culture accepts a practice or belief from another, but integrates that belief or practice within his/her own value system. When I initiated my research in Kufr al-Ma in rural Jordan in the 1960s I noted that women were restricted in their spatial and occupational mobility. Women never left the village unchaperoned by men and did not work outside the village. Both Islamic and tribal norms stipulated that the honor of women would be jeopardized by allowing them to mix socially with unrelated men.[49] When I returned to the village in the 1980s I discovered that substantial transnational migration for education and work had taken place, and that a number of village women were now working as teachers in villages up to twenty miles away; a few had gone to work on five-year contracts as teachers in Saudi Arabia. It was difficult for me to reconcile this development with both the practice and the norms I had observed in the 1960s. After further inquiry I discovered that there was a carefully elaborated pattern of controlled acculturation that allowed both spatial and occupational mobility. The key to this pattern was the kinship system and the bus driver! Teachers went to school and returned every day on the bus. The locations where they taught seemed haphazard with a number teaching in villages relatively far away, whereas few taught in villages relatively close. Tibne was the mother village from which the people of Kufr al-Ma (and many other villages) had originally come a hundred years before. The teachers only taught in villages that were the daughter villages of Tibne, i.e., where they had relations of kinship and former propinquity. Absent that opportunity, they only taught in villages in which the bus driver was of the "peoples of Tibne." Thus, the village could be quite far away. At the point where the bus driver of "the peoples of Tibne" was replaced by another (i.e., stranger), the people of Kufr al-Ma refused to allow their daughters/sisters to travel. The bus driver became the substitute chaperone. He was trusted to monitor and protect the teachers, and be sure they went and returned safely and unmolested by word or deed. The value of women's modesty and honor had been accommodated to occupational mobility. This is controlled acculturation.

FUNDAMENTALISM AND TRANSNATIONAL RELIGION AFTER 9/11

The terrorist attack on the World Trade Center in New York City on September 11, 2001 raises the question of the connections between terrorism and fundamentalism and more broadly between religion and violence. It also poses anew the question of the organization of terrorist movements and their relation to the organization of religious movements. Fundamentalism is one response to a broader religious process that Hervieu-Leger has described as the "cultural disqualification of all traditions bearing a unified code of meaning in a world committed to rapid change and extreme pluralization."[50] Global changes in communication, transportation, marketing systems, and social relations, along with the mass movement of peoples and information, have undermined the unified messages of all the world religions and their focus on a national and local hub of religious activity. One reaction is a shift away from the pursuit of salvation in local religious congregations and attendance to, "private religiosity oriented toward this-worldly realities and psychological fulfillment of the individual."[51] This can be termed a "do-it-yourself" approach to religion. Another reaction is the multiplication of transnational socioreligious networks. A debate has swirled around the composition and shape of such networks, in particular around the organization of the Taliban and Al Qaeda. The case of the Taliban in Afghanistan is interesting in this regard. The Taliban are a quite different fundamentalist movement than Al Qaeda in inspiration, organization, and composition. Shahrani has argued that the Taliban continue a long tradition of "internal colonialism" in Afghanistan by which the Pushtun-speaking tribes of the south and southeast have dominated the Uzbek and Tajik ethnic groups of the north.[52] An alternative view regards the Taliban as a transnational movement with a critical niche in a particular political economy: the trading of military arms for drugs (opium) through Afghanistan between Central Asia and Pakistan.[53] A third view regards the Taliban as an aberrant fundamentalist movement, drawing much of its power from the aura of purity and charisma of a holy man, Mullah Omar, who as its leader, because of his status, had the appearance of a neutral who could effectively mediate between the tribes, factions and ethnic groups.[54] A fourth view stresses the Taliban's application of the strategies of selective modernization and controlled acculturation to gain and maintain power through radio, mass street and brutal stadium spectacles, tanks corps, and machine guns mounted on Toyotas.[55] Canfield, Crews, and Tarzi have stressed the variegated composition of the Taliban. The movement has been embraced by different core and support elements affording different financial and material resources as well as different political perspectives: *madrasa* students and orphans from Pakistan; former anti-Soviet mujahidin commanders; defectors from the militias that fought the Russians and then one another in the civil war; former Pashtun officers working with the Communists; Pakistani military and technical advisors; dispersed Pashtuns from northern Afghanistan; the government of Saudi Arabia; and not least Osama bin Laden and Al Qaeda.

Whereas the Taliban is a religious movement spanning two countries, Afghanistan and Pakistan, Al Qaeda is a transnational movement spanning several continents and many countries, e.g., North Africa, Indonesia, the Philippines, Iraq, and the northwest territory of Pakistan. A debate has also swirled around its composition and the shape of its network with views oscillating between those who argue that it is centrally led and trained by a cadre focused on Pakistan and Afghanistan to those who argue that it is a loosely knit world-wide network that conducts its activities in different regions in an autonomous fashion, looking for inspiration only to its charismatic leader, Osama bin Laden.[56] Although Al Qaeda has undergone many transformations, if one accepts the first view stated above, there are generally three levels to its social structure: a trusted inner circle (many with blood ties to Bin Laden), the "soldiers" who carry out the missions; and a wide range of supporters/sympathizers who aid the movement financially, logistically by providing a room or recommending for a job or ideologically by transmitting its message through multimedia or word of mouth. Although bin Laden's vocabulary is political and anti-colonial, his struggle is religious against "global unbelief."[57] In his "Letter to the Americans," posted on the internet on October 14, 2002, Bin Laden raises and answers two questions, "Why are we fighting and opposing you?" and "What do we want from you?" and answers both. With respect to the latter question he demands that Americans accept Islam and stop both their oppression of other peoples and the debauchery within their own society.[58] Sayyid Qutb, perhaps the most influential fundamentalist writer of the twentieth century, enabled Al Qaeda as a militant movement justifying *takfir* (excommunication) and killing of "defeatist ulema" (Muslim scholars) and Sunni Muslims who cooperated with the government. Followers of Qutb in Iraq extended his militant message to Shi'a Muslims and Kurds because all were said to be unbelievers living a life of the *jahiliyya* (the time of ignorance before the prophecy of Muhammad) who repudiated their prayer and fasting by engaging in fornication, adultery, gambling, the drinking of alcohol, and the witnessing of pornography (in night-clubs).[59]

RELIGION AND VIOLENCE

What are the links between religion and violence and more specifically between fundamentalism and terrorism? By terrorism I mean public acts of destruction committed without a clear-cut military objective, usually against civilians, that arouse an overpowering sense of fear.[60] Although writers on the subject seldom do so, it is necessary to distinguish between different types of terrorism (state, criminal, religious, political, and pathological) if only because of their quite different motivations and implications.[61] Are fundamentalists violent people? I know of no reliable statistical study on this subject. My own judgment based on reading about various fundamentalist movements over a period of twenty-five years is that only a tiny minority of fundamentalists resort to violence, not to speak of terrorism. Fundamentalists pursue strategies of flight, radical separation, spatial separation, and institutional separation – none of which are violent – as well as confrontation. The great majority of confrontational acts are nonviolent: contesting elections, staging demonstrations, boycotting products, services and entertainments, propagandizing over radio and television, acting as pressure groups, and pursuing legal action in the courts. The great majority of fundamentalists are law-abiding people, like the general population of all nations.[62]

What is the justification for violence within the Islamic tradition, a tradition about which misinformation abounds.[63] To simplify a complex set of opinions over a long historical period, the justification for using violence by Muslim scholars has a minority and a majority tradition. For most Muslim scholars *jihad* is not holy war, but rather struggle, striving, perservering towards a fixed goal, fighting to defend ones's life or against an oppressive ruler, or against the evil in onself, e.g. miserliness and jealousy.

However, the minority scholarly tradition regards *jihad* as "the neglected duty." This is the title of an essay written by Abd al-Salam Faraj (doubtless inspired by Sayyid Qutb), the spokesman of Islamic Jihad, the movement responsible for assassinating Anwar Sadat, the president of Egypt, in 1981.[64] In this tradition the establishment of an Islamic state is necessary for the establishment of an Islamic society and the living of a Muslim life. Three criteria indicate the disappearance of an Islamic society: when Muslims become ruled by non-Muslim laws; when unbelief prevails in society; and when Muslims recite the profession of faith, pray and fast but undermine their worship by drinking alcohol, gambling, immodest dress, and indulging in fornication and adultery. According to this tradition, the Islamic state cannot be established by education and prosyletization because the evil state controls mass communication and because good people are usually a minority. These scholars justify holy war with Qur'anic proof-texts such as "Fight them (unbelievers) until there is no dissension and the religion is entirely God's" (Qur'an 7:39) and "Fighting is prescribed for you, though it is distasteful to you. Possibly you dislike a thing, though it is good for you and possibly you may love a thing though it is bad for you" (Qur'an 2: 216).

The majority scholarly interpretation of the religious justifiction for violence is quite different. Followers of this view cite the Qur'anic verse, "Let there be no compulsion in religion" (2:256). And they cite the practice of the Prophet, Muhammad, based on the biography of the Prophet written within one hundred years of his death by Ibn Ishaq.[65] During the first thirteen years of his prophecy Muhammad was neither a militant nor a political advisor. When his followers were oppressed he recommended flight, first to Ethiopia and later (622 CE) to the oasis of Medina, 200 miles to the north. He was called by the people of Medina to be neither a prophet nor a ruler, but rather an arbitrator (*hakam*) between competing tribes, a role for which he had been known in Mecca. Between 622 and 629 he waged a war of attrition against the Meccans involving raids with few casualties. In 629 Muhammad appeared before the gates of Mecca with a large army that could easily have taken the city.[66] The Meccans told him they would not allow him to enter the city, but if he came back the following year they would allow him peaceful entry. The Prophet led his army back to Medina, and the following year he returned, entering the city peacefully and performing the first Muslim pilgrimage at the Kaaba.

Several significant facts about these events should be noted for our discussion of the connection between religion and violence in the Islamic tradition. First, Muhammad did not destroy the Kaaba, the previous center of polytheistic tribal worship which he had denounced. Rather, he emptied it of its idols and made it the center of Muslim pilgrimage, the Hajj. Second, he did not allow his army to take revenge against the Meccan leaders who had derided his message, hounded him, and oppressed his followers. Rather, he declared a general amnesty for the Meccan population including those who led the opposition against him. And third, although Muhammad's entrance into Mecca in 629 was recorded as "the conquest of Mecca," it was achieved by negotiation and compromise and not force of arms. This culminating event of Muhammad's political career marks him as a man of peace, reconciliation, and compassion rather than a militant seeking revenge. The majority view, then, is that jihad is just war and striving to do good deeds in the familial (e.g., serving one's parents), political (e.g., opposing oppressive rulers), and religious spheres (e.g., performing pilgrimage) and not holy war against unbelievers.

What can we say, then, about the strength of fundamentalism as a socioreligious movement after 9/11? Fundamentalism remains a powerful transnational movement, though not the dominant force, demographically, in hardly any nation-state in the world today.[67] It remains a powerful force because change and uncertainty have become even more rapid and intense, and the secular state still holds powerful sway in most of the world.[68]

Notes

1   For a discussion of various views on the importance of scripturalism (and other attributes) to a definition of fundamentalism consult the following academic authors: Akenson 1992; Ammerman in Marty and Appleby 1991; Armstrong 2000; Beale 1986; Carpenter 1988; Euben 1999; Harding 2000; Heilman 1992; Lawrence 1989; Lustick 1988; Marty and Appleby 1991; Moussalli 1999; Shepard 1987; and Silberstein in Silberstein 1993. One should also consult what leaders of fundamentalist movements themselves have to say including the following fundamentalists: Dobson 1970; Falwell 1980; Jones 1985; Kahane 1972; Khomeini 1981; Mawdudi 1985; Mutahhari 1988; Qutb n.d.; Robertson and Slosser 1982; and Rowland on Begin 1985.
2   See Gardiner in Pesso-Miquel and Stierstorfer 2007.
3   These contrasting views/definitions of fundamentalism were gathered from within the covers of a single volume. See *Fundamentalism and Literature*, pp. 109, 125, 126, 147, and 169.
4   South Asians have pursued a wide variety of orientations and strategies to cope with change in the modern world including fundamentalism. In fact, India's Bharatiya Janata Party is the largest movement of religious nationalism in the world. Its victory in the Indian elections of 1999 allowed it to form the governing coalition at the national level. Sikh fundamentalism has been active for many years as a movement fighting both secular nationalism and Hindu nationalism. The selective bibliography at the end of the chapter includes a few titles on fundamentalism in South and Southeast Asia.
5   Millenialism will not be dealt with in this chapter. For those interested in this attribute of fundamentalism see the Left Behind series novels of Tim LaHaye and Jerry Jenkins, e.g., 1995, 1996, 1997, and 2007. See also Cook 2005.
6   The question of who fundamentalists are, socially, is different from the question of how fundamentalism is defined/described as a phenomenon in the modern world. The latter question is addressed in the following sections.
7   See Munson 1984: 20–1.
8   A distinction made by Clifford Geertz as quoted in Munson 1993.
9   See Lawrence 1989: 100.
10 Ayatollah Khomeini is the exception. Munson's ministry of education inspectors are more the rule.
11 Lawrence 1989: 196.
12 Lawrence 1989: 197.
13 See Riesebrodt 1990.

14 Riesebrodt 1990: 185–9.

15 For details of this kind of patron-client relationship in a revolutionary and prerevolutionary context see Fischer, 1980. For a more general view of clergy-state relations in Iran see Akhavi, 1980.

16 Riesebrodt 1990: 73.

17 See Riesebrodt 1990: ch. 2.

18 See Lustick 1988: 5.

19 Lustick 1988: 6.

20 Lustick 1988: 7.

21 Lustick 1988: 83.

22 See Levine and Stoll, in Rudolph and Piscastori 1997 for details of the argument.

23 Levine and Stoll 1997: 72.

24 Levine and Stoll 1997: 72.

25 Ibid.

26 Levine and Stoll 1997: 73.

27 Ibid.

28 "Fundamentalist" and "evangelical" are overlapping categories. However, Many Christians identify themselves as either one or the other. The split between evangelicals and fundamentalists in the United States took institutional form in the early 1940s, with the evangelicals seeking greater accommodation with the modern world by accepting cultural and structural pluralism and functional rationality. In this chapter fundamentalists are defined by the presence of certain attributes (e.g., protest against the modern world, concern for purity, activism and totalism, traditioning, etc.) whereas evangelicals are distinguished by their view that Christians must be "born again." Not all fundamentalists are evangelicals in this sense, and not all evangelicals share all the attributes of fundamentalism. For divergent views on this distinction see Ammerman 1987 and Harding 2000.

29 Ideology refers here to "an action-oriented system of beliefs capable of explaining the world … justifying decison(s), identifying alternatives, and … creating the most all-embracing and intensive social solidarity possible." This is Paul Sigmund's definition as quoted in Lawrence 1989: 76. In short, an ideology is an action-related system of ideas focused on this (and not the next) world.

30 For the structure and culture of the pre-industrial city see Sjoberg, 1960; for the recent impact of transnational migration on the migrants and on the home community in one Jordanian village see Antoun 2005.

31 For a discussion of how patron–client ties operate in the Mediterranean and the Middle East see Gellner and Waterbury 1977.

32 For details see Moore 1966 and 1972; Hodgson, 3 vols., 1974; Braudel, 3 vols., 1981–4 and 1980; and Lawrence 1989.

33 A full description and analysis of the attributes of fundamentalism is to be found in Antoun 2001 and 2008. For a discussion of how fundamentalism relates to the state and to bureaucracies, particularly when the bureaucrat is also a fundamentalist, see Antoun, August 2006.

34 See Kepel 1984 for a detailed description of this movement in the 1970s and 1980s.

35 See Heilman 1992 for details.

36 See Peshkin 1996 for details.

37 For various versions of the literalist scriptural interpretation see Ammerman 1987; Beale 1986; Bendroth 1993; Kepel 1994; Lustick 1988; Marty and Appleby 1991 and 1992; Munson 1984 and 1983; and Peshkin 1996.

38 See Hirschkind 2006.

39 Hirschkind 2006: 180.

40 As quoted in Carpenter 1988.

41 See Heilman 1992 for a definition and illustrations of this concept.

42 Heilman: 57ff.

43 See Harding 2000 for details.

44 Harding 2000: 113–14.

45 Harding 2000: 116–17.

46 See Bruce 1990 for details.

47 See the article by the *New York Times* religion correspondent, Steinfels, June 5, 1990, for details.

48 See Himmelstein, in Liebman and Wuthnow 1983 for details.

49 See Antoun, August, 1968 for details.

50 Hervieu-Leger in Rudolph and Piscatori 1997: 106.

51 Hervieu-Leger: 110.

52 See Shahrani in Crews and Tarzi 2008.

53 See Crews and Tarzi, "Introduction" and Canfield in Crews and Tarzi 2008 for details.

54 See Canfield, Crews and Tarzi, Sinno, and Cole, in Crews and Tarzi 2008. Cole's essay develops the Taliban's policy towards women.

55 See Cole for details.

56 For examples of opposing views of Al Qaeda see Gerges 2005; Burgat 2008; Sageman 2008; and Hoffman, May/June, 2008.

57 See Lawrence, *Messages to the World: The Statements of Osama Bin Laden*, 2005, for the best collection in English of Bin Laden's speeches and communications.

58 See Lawrence 2005 for a full statement of this and other letters sent out by Bin Laden over the years. Robert A. Pape, a political scientist, has an alternative view of Al Qaeda. He stresses that Al Qaeda pursues non-religious political goals, e.g., the withdrawal of Western combat forces from Saudi Arabia, Afghanistan, Iraq, and other Muslim countries. He views Al Qaeda as engaged in an anti-imperial struggle that can be dealt with by Western countries through dialogue that recognizes the legitimate interests of other countries. See Pape's (2005) book.

59 The most influential of Qutb's books is *Milestones* (n.d.). On his works and his influence see Haddad in Esposito 1983 and Shepard 1996.

60 For an insightful discussion of the anatomy of terrorism and its ramifications in five different terrorist movements see Juergensmeyer 2000. See also the articles of Ann Speckhard (2005 and 2006) on the case of Chechen terrorism, particularly on the part of women.

61 See Eqbal Ahmad's discussion of these differences recorded in a speech given in Boulder Colorado, October 12, 1998 entitled "Terrorism: Theirs and Ours" and included as a chapter in a book edited by Benbelsdorf, Cerullo, and Chandrani 2006.

62 For a more detailed discussion of the connections between religion and violence see Antoun in Gluck (in press); and Antoun, *Understanding Fundamentalism* 2nd edn., 2008, ch. 7.

63 For insightful discussions of how the Western tradition of maligning Islam developed historically see Daniel 1962 and 1966. The morbid focus on violence, martyrdom, and death attributed to Islam and its civilization by Western critics has been examined perceptively by Hirschkind 2006. He discovered in his study of Egyptian sermon cassettes that a very large number did indeed focus on death. But the theme developed is that death is the inevitable and proper end of life; and that the knowledge that one is destined to die should encourage positive and ethical behavior in life. See Hirschkind 2006: 178.

64 See Faraj in Jansen 1986 for the details of the argument.

65 Thus the saying common among knowledgable scholars of Islam that this religion was born "in the full light of history." See Gillaume, *The Life of Muhammad: A Translation of Ibn Ishaq's Sirat_Rasul Allah*, 1955.

66 All these events are recorded in Ibn Ishaq's biography.

67 I would argue that fundamentalism is demographically not even dominant in Iran where the fundamentalists rule. Remember, the Iranian revolution of 1979 was a grass-roots movement, fought by a coalition of forces: shopkeepers, peasants, intellectuals, industrial workers, students, and religious leaders. The latter took the leading role in the revolution because their mosques and prayer-halls were the only rallying places left open after the Shah's repression. After the revolution the religious leaders through their militias suppressed the other coalition members and seized power. I would also argue that Saudi Arabia is not a fundamentalist state. The fundamentalist (Wahhabi) clergy dominates a religiously conservative populace, but the Saudi elite rules by tribal norms and not religious norms, although it enforces slamic law on a selective basis.

68 An example of the continued power of the secular state, albeit with a strong fundamentalist challenge, in the United States was the controversy over a provision of a Pentagon bill that would allow military chaplains to offer sectarian prayers at non-denominational military events. "The long-standing custom has been to offer a non-sectarian prayer, for example citing God rather than Christ" (*The New York Times*, 9/19/06). Many ecumenical groups spoke against the provision, saying that sectarian prayers would create division among the military. Evangelical groups argued that "refusing (evangelical) chaplains the chance to pray in Jesus' name infringes on their religious liberty" (*The New York Times*, 9/19/06). The evangelicals were not able to prevail. The Republican Party's recent (August 2008) nomination of governor Sarah Palin of Alaska to be its candidate for vice-president of the United States dramatizes the continued relevance of a fundamentalist perspective at the highest political levels in the United States. Uncertainty and change mark her personal life (a Downs-syndrome infant and a pregnant, unmarried teenage daughter) as well as her political life (Alaska is undergoing a huge economic boom accompanied by gross governmental and corporate corruption). The ideology of fundamentalism provides governor Palin a moral compass to lead her through difficult times. Addressing the Assembly of God church in her home town of Wasilla, Alaska, "the governor encouraged a group of young church leaders to pray that 'God's will' be done in bringing about the construction of a big pipeline in the state'." She told them that "her work as governor would be hampered 'if the people of Alaska's heart isn't right with God'" (*The New York Times*, 9/6/08). Religion and politics are inextricably intertwined in her world-view. Note, however, that John McCain, the presidential candidate of the Republican Party has never been associated with fundamentalists or their ideology. Although in 2008 he mended his political fences with them, in the 2000 primary campaign in South Carolina he refused to associate himself with Bob Jones University or deliver an address there.

Bibliography

Ahmad, Eqbal (2006) Terrorism: theirs and ours. In Carollee Bengelsdorf, Margaret Cerullo, and Yogesh Chandrani (eds.), *The Selected Writings of Eqbal Ahmad*, New York: Oxford University Press.

Akenson, Donald H. (1992) *God's Peoples: Covenant and Land in South Africa, Israel and Ulster*, Ithaca: Cornell University Press.

Akhavi, Shahrough (1980) *Religion and Politics in Contemporary Iran: Clergy–State Relations in the Pahlavi Period*, Albany: SUNY Press.

Ammerman, Nancy (1987) *Bible Believers: Fundamentalism in the Modern World*, Piscataway: Rutgers University Press.

Ammerman, Nancy (1991) North American protestant fundamentalism, in Martin E. Marty and R. Scott Applesby (eds.), *Fundamentalisms Observed*, Chicago: University of Chicago Press.

Antoun, Richard T. (1968) On the modesty of women in Arab Muslim villages: a study in the accommodation of traditions, *American Anthropologist* 70: 671–97.

Antoun, Richard T. (2001) *Understanding Fundamentalism: Christian, Islamic Jewish Movements* (1st edn.), New York: Rowman and Littlefield.

Antoun, Richard T. (2005) *Documenting Transnational Migration: Jordanian Men Working and Studying in Europe, Asia and North America*, New York: Berghahn Books.

Antoun, Richard T. (2006) Fundamentalism, bureaucratization and the state's co-optation of religion: a jordanian case study, *International Journal of Middle East Studies* 38: 369–93.

Antoun, Richard T. (2008) *Understanding Fundamentalism: Christian, Islamic and Jewish Movements* (2nd edn.), New York: Rowman and Littlefield.

Antoun, Richard T. (in press) Religious fundamentalism and religious violence: connections and misconnections, in Andrew Gluck (ed.), *Religion, Fundamentalism and Violence: An Interdisciplinary Inquiry*, Scranton: Scranton University Press.

Armstrong, Karen (2000) *The Battle for God*, New York: Alfred A. Knopf.

Beale, David O. (1986) *In Pursuit of Purity: American Fundamentalism since 1850*, Greenville: Unusual Publications

Benbelsdorf, Carollee, Cerullo, Margaret, and Chandrani, Yogest (eds.) (2006) *The Selected Writings of Eqbal Ahmed*, New York: Oxford University Press.

Bendroth, Margaret (1993) *Fundamentalism and Gender: 1875 to the Present*, New Haven: Yale University Press.

Braudel, Fernand (1980) *On History*, Chicago: University of Chicago Press.

Braudel, Fernand (1981–4) *Civilization and Capitalism 15th–18th Century*, 3 vols., London: Collins.

Bruce, Steve (1990) *Pray TV: Televanglism in America*, London: Routledge.

Burgat, Francois (2008) *Islamism in the Shadow of al-Qaeda*, Austin: University of Texas Press.

Canfield, Robert (2008) Linkages between fraternity, power and time in central Asia, in Robert Crews and Amin Tarzi (eds.), *The Taliban and the Crisis of Afghanistan*, Cambridge, MA: Harvard University Press.

Carpenter, Joel A. (1988) *The Debates between John Roach Stanton and Charles Francis Potter*, New York: Garland Publishing Company.

Cole, Juan (2008) The Taliban, women and the Hegelian private sphere, in Robert Crews and Amin Tarzi, *The Taliban and the Crisis of Afghanistan*, Cambridge, MA: Harvard University Press.

Cook, David (2005) *Contemporary Muslim Apocalyptic Literature*, Syracuse: Syracuse University Press.

Crews, Robert and Tarzi, Amin (2008) *The Taliban and the Crisis of Afghanistan*, Cambridge, MA: Harvard University Press.

Daniel, Norman (1962) *Islam and the West: The Making of an Image*, Edinburgh: Edinburgh University Press.

Daniel, Norman (1966) *Islam, Europe and Empire*, Edinburgh: Edinburgh University Press.

Dobson, James (1970) *Dare to Discipline*, Wheaton: Tyndale.

Euben, Roxanne (1999) *Enemy in the Mirror: Fundamentalism and the Limits of Modern Rationalism*, Princeton: Princeton University Press.

Faraj, Abd al-Salam (1986) The creed of Sadat's assassins, in Johannes J. G. Jansen (ed.), *The Neglected Duty*, London: Macmillan.

Falwell, Jerry (1980) *Listen America!*, Garden City: Doubleday.

Fischer, Michael M. J. (1980) *Iran: From Religious Dispute to Revolution*, Cambridge, MA: Harvard University Press.

Gardiner, Anne B. (2007) Jonathan Swift and the idea of a fundamental Church. In Catherine Pesso-Miquel and Klaus Stierstorfer (eds.), *Fundamentalism and Literature*, New York: Palgrave Macmillan.

Gellner, Ernest and Waterbury, John (1977) *Patrons and Clients in Mediterranean Societies*, London: Duckworth.

Gerges, Fawaz (2005) *The Far Enemy: Why Jihad Went Global*, Cambridge: Cambridge University Press.

Gillaume, Alfred (1955) *The Life of Muhammad: A Translation of Ibn Ishaq's Sirat Rasul Allah*, Oxford: Oxford University Press.

Haddad, Yvonne (1983) Sayyid Qutb: ideologue of Islamic revival, in John L. Espositio (ed.), *Voices of Resurgent Islam*, Oxford: Oxford University Press.

Harding, Susan (2000) *The Book of Jerry Falwell: Fundamentalist Language and Politics*, Princeton: Princeton University Press.

Heilman, Samuel (1992) *Defenders of the Faith: Inside Ultra-Orthodox Jewry*, New York: Schocken Books.

Hervieu-Léger, Danièlle (1997) Four faces of Catholic transnationalism, in Susanne Rudolph and James Piscatori (eds.), *Transnational Religion and Fading States*, Boulder: Westview Press.

Himmelstein, Jerome (1983) The New Right, in Robert C. Liebman and Robert Wuthnow (eds.), *The New Christian Right: Mobilization and Legitimation*, New York: Aldine de Gruyter.

Hirschkind, Charles (2006) *The Ethical Soundscape: Cassette Sermons and Islamic Counterpublics*, New York: Columbia University Press.

Hodgson, Marshall (1974) *The Venture of Islam: Conscience and History in a World Civilization*, 3 vols., Chicago: University of Chicago Press.

Hoffman, Bruce (2008) The myth of grassroots terrorism: why Osama bin Laden still matters, *Foreign Affairs*, 87: 133–8.

Jones, Bob (1985) *Cornbread and Caviar*, Greenville: Bob Jones University Press.

Juergensmeyer, Mark (2000) *Terror in the Mind of God: The Global Rise of Religious Violence*, Berkeley: University of California Press.

Kahane, Meir (1972) *Never Again: A Program for Jewish Survival*, New York: Pyramid Books.

Kepel, Gilles (1984) *Muslim Extremism: Thew Prophet and the Pharaoh*, Berkeley: University of California Press.

Kepel, Gilles (1994) *The Revenge of God: The Resurgence of Islam, Christianity, and Judaism in the Modern World*, University Park: Pennsylvania State University Press.

Khomeini, Sayeed Ruhollah (1981) *Islamic Revolution: Writings and Declarations of Imam Khomeini*, Hamid Algar (tr. and annot.), Berkeley: Mizan Press.

Lawrence, Bruce (1989) *Defenders of God: The Fundamentalist Revolt against the Modern Age*, San Francisco: Harper and Row.

Lawrence, Bruce (ed.) (2005) *Messages to the World: The Statements of Osama Bin Laden*, New York: Verso.

Lahaye, Tim and Jenkins, Jerry (1995) *Left Behind: A Novel of the Earth's Last Days*, Wheaton: Tyndale.

Lahaye, Tim and Jenkins, Jerry (1996) *Tribulation Force: The Continuing Drama of Those Left Behind*, Wheaton: Tyndale.

Lahaye, Tim and Jenkins, Jerry (1997) *Nicolae: The Rise of Antichrist*, Wheaton: Tyndale.

Lahaye, Tim and Jenkins, Jerry (2007) *Kingdom Come: The Final Victory*, Carol Stream: Tyndale.

Larson, Gerald (1995) *India's Agony over Religion*, Albany: SUNY Press.

Levine, Daniel H. and Stoll, David (1997) Bridging the gap between empowerment and power in Latin America. In James Piscatori and Susanne H. Rudolph (eds.), *Transnational Religion and Fading States*, Boulder: Westview Press.

Lustick, Ian (1988) *For the Land and the Lord: Jewish Fundamentalism in Israel*, New York: Council on Foreign Relations.

Marty, Martin and Appleby, R. Scott (1992) The Glory and the Power: The Fundamentalist *Challenge to the Modern Age*, Boston: Beacon Press.

Marty, Martin and Appleby, R. Scott (eds.) (1991) *Fundamentalisms Observed*, Chicago: University of Chicago Press.

Mawdudi, Sayyid Abul-'Ala (1985) *Let Us Be Muslims*, ed. Khurram Murad, London: Islamic Foundation.

Moore, Barrington (1966) *Social Origins of Dictatorship and Democracy: Lord and Peasant in the Making of Modern War*, Boston: Beacon Press.

Moore, Barrington (1972) *Reflections on the Causes of Human Misery and upon Certain Proposals to Eliminate Them*, Boston: Beacon Press.

Moussalli, Ahmad S. (1999) *Historical Dictionary of Islamic Fundamentalist Movements in the Arab World, Iran, and Turkey*, Lanham: Scarecrow Press.

Munson, Henry (1984) *The House of Si Abd Allah: The Oral History of a Moroccan Family*, New Haven: Yale University Press.

Munson, Henry (1993) *Religion and Power in Morocco*, New Haven: Yale University Press.

Mutahhari, Murteza (1988) *Islamic Hijab: Modest Dress*, Chicago: Kazi Publications.

Oberoi, Harjat (1994) *The Construction of Religious Boundaries: Culture, Identity and Diversity in the Sikh Tradition*, New York: Oxford University Press.

Pape.Robert (2005) *Dying to Win: The Strategic Logic of Suicide Terrorism*, New York: Random House.

Peshkin, Alan (1996) *God's Choice: The Total World of a Christian Fundamentalist School*, Chicago: University of Chicago Press.

Pesso-Miquel, Catherine and Stiersorfer, Klaus (eds.) (2007) *Fundamentalism and Literature*, New York: Palgrave Macmillan.

Qutb, Sayed (n.d.) *Milestones*, Cedar Rapids: Unity Publishing Company.

Riesebrodt, Martin (1990) *Pious Passion: The Emergence of Modern Fundamentalism in the United States and Iran*, Berkeley: University of California Press.

Robertson, Pat and Slosser, Bob (1982) *The Secret Kingdom*, Nashville: T. Nelson.

Rowland, Robert (1985) *The Rhetoric of Menahem Begin: The Myth of Redemption through Return*, Lanham: University Press of America.

Sageman, Marc (2008) *Leaderless Jihad: Terror Networks in the Twenty First Century*, Philadelphia: University of Pennsylvania Press.

Shahrani, Nazih (2008) Taliban and Talibanism, in Robert D. Crews and Amin Tarzi (eds.), *The Taliban and the Crisis of Afghanistan*, Cambridge: Harvard University Press.

Shepard, William (1987) Fundamentalism: Christian and Islamic, *Religion* 17: 355–78.

Shepard, William (1996) *Sayyid Qutb and Islamic Activism: A Translation and Critical Analysis of Social Justice in Islam*, Leiden: Brill.

Silberstein, Laurence (1993) Religion, idelogy, modernity: theoretical issues in a study of Jewish fundamentalism, in Laurence Silberstein (ed.), *Jewish Fundamentalism in Comparative Perspective: Religion and the Crisis of Modernity*, New York: New York University Press.

Sinno, Abdulkader (2008) Explaining the Taliban's ability to mobilize Pushtuns, in Robert Crews and Amin Tarzi (eds.), *The Taliban and the Crisis of Afghanistan*, Cambridge, MA: Harvard University Press.

Sjoberg, Gideon (1960) *The Preindustrial City: Past and Present*, New York: Free Press.

Speckhard, Ann and Akhmedova, Khapta (2005) Black widows: Chechen female suicide terrorists, in Yoram Schweitzer (ed.), *Female Suicide Terrorists*, Tel Aviv: Jaffe Center Publlication.

Speckhard, Ann and Akhmedova, Khapta (2006) The making of a martyr: Chechen suicide terrorism, *Studies in Conflict and Terrorism* 29: 429–92.

Steinfels, Peter (1990) *The New York Times* June 5, 1990.

Van der Meer, Peter (1994) *Religious Nationalism: Hindus and Muslims in India*, Berkeley: University of California Press.

Whyte, William H. (1956) *Organization Man*, New York: Doubleday.

24

Religion, Media, and Globalization

Jeremy Stolow

Who today can ignore the dramatic ways religion has acquired new prominence in public life, and has done so on a global scale? Islamic outreach movements, *jihadi* websites, Pentecostal prayer rallies, international blockbuster movies like Mel Gibson's *The Passion of the Christ*, Roman Catholic World Youth Days, advertising campaigns on city buses promoting atheism, and New Age meditation retreats – these are only some examples of the religious dimensions of globalization, and global dimensions of religion, that seem to sweep millions of people into action, binding them together as petitioners and faithful followers, but also as audiences, target groups, clients, bystanders, or even enemies. Such globally resonant forces certainly have come to occupy greater attention among academics, journalists, and policy makers. It is far from clear, however, what we can and should safely assume about such phenomena, and more generally, about the place of religion in the contemporary world order. For one thing, diagnoses couched in the language of "religious revival," "the return to religion," or the "clash of civilizations" obscure more than they reveal since, as this chapter aims to show, they rarely take seriously enough the role of media. Simply put, the technologies, institutional arrangements, circulatory systems, and shifting modalities of reception that together make up "media" are indelibly present in any account of the growing visibility or the new political salience of religious symbols, practices, and identities on the contemporary world stage. More than just instruments used by religious, non-religious, or even anti-religious actors, media constitute an environment that makes it possible for religion to sustain a presence in both public and private life. It is within and through mediated environments that so-called religious folk increasingly carry out their business of seeking knowledge, performing rituals, proclaiming faith, proselytizing to others, embarking on moral campaigns, or engaging in holy wars. To the extent that these circuits mediated communication extend more than ever before across the entire world, reaching the most remote hinterlands and penetrating into the most intimate parts of everyday life, there is no way to talk about religion and globalization without at least implicitly invoking the "middle term" of media. In the following pages, I will try to make good on this claim, with reference to some illustrative examples, and on these terms to highlight an agenda for further research among sociologists of religion.

RELIGIOUS? GLOBAL? MEDIATED?
SOME PROBLEMS OF TERMINOLOGY

When talking about religion, media, and globalization, it is important to guard against the nominalist error of assuming that each of these three things can somehow be separated from, or combined with the others, as fully distinguishable variables used to measure possible patterns of growth, decline, concentration, dispersal, or other types of change. Let us start with the term "religion." It is admittedly difficult to avoid the methodological convenience of allowing this word to refer to a realm of action, power, and knowledge that is distinct from many other arenas and dimensions of social life, such as science, politics, or economic exchange, to name a few. But this is no license for sociologists of religion to reify the religious field, for instance, as something that "comes before" globalization, or that stands "outside" media. Such a danger is particularly acute in cases where the word "religion" is assumed to refer to matters of individual belief, or even to the institutional organization of groups of people united by shared beliefs, since the very notions "belief" and "faith" are embedded in a larger set of narratives that originate in a particular – not a universal – cultural, historical, and geopolitical context. As demonstrated by a growing body of scholarship, the academic study of comparative religions, framed by Orientalist scholarly canons of philology and archaeology, cannot be disentangled from its roots in the history of the Christian Inquisition and in the work of missionaries, and related legacies of competition and exchange between Christian and non-Christian representatives both within and beyond the borders of Europe, including the Church's encounter with witches, Jews, Muslims, Hindus, Buddhists, and the many varieties of so-called "primitive" religion, found throughout the world (see, e.g., Chidester 1996; Masuzawa 2005; van der Veer 1996). It was out of this dialogic arena that universal definitions of religion emerged: the idea that in every society there existed a phenomenon called "religion," the essential features of which could then be compared in terms of localized forms of belief, practice, and institutional organization. Such efforts at constructing equivalencies had as their consequence that things hitherto possessing no referent in their native idiom could now be understood within the classificatory system of comparative religions.

This is not the place to review the ways such comparisons have accorded privilege to Christianity as a normative principle, and in particular have advanced a definition of religion on the model of post-Reformation Protestant ideals of voluntary association and private belief. At their worst, such comparative gestures have done little more than confer legitimacy on what Jacques Derrida (2002), in a related context, provocatively named the power of *mondialatinisation* [globalatinization]: the metaphysical and political promotion of ostensibly universal (but in practice unavoidably particularist and territorializing) ways of seeing and knowing the world, inscribed by the discourses of Roman imperialism and Christian brotherhood. In this sense, the history of comparative religions can be tied to the historical constitution of the West as "father" of the family of nations, and self-appointed guardian of "the civilized world." For the purposes of this discussion, suffice it to say that it is not tenable (not even for the most well-intentioned comparativist) to render commensurable the disparate forms of knowledge, practice, performance, and discourse, ways of organizing space and time, structures of authority, and patterns of economic and symbolic exchange, as they are found in different places around the world, and to succeed in making all these things fit into a single framework called *religion*.

But even if we presuppose – just for heuristic purposes – the existence of communities, institutions, and movements that can safely be called "religious," we have further definitional problems associated with the pronounced *public visibility* of "religious things" on the contemporary world stage. Any attempt to divide the universe into religious and non-religious spheres brings one into contact with the highly charged language of "the secular," and students of the sociology of religion are well served to bear in mind the discipline's own history of confusing and unconvincing claims about "secularization," and the uses of that term as a master narrative, an interpretive lens, and a normative ideal against which one is supposedly able to measure forms of religious publicity, their visibility, and their political relevance in the modern world. Indeed, theories of secularization have – often silently – worked to organize the dominant historical narratives about the rise of modern nationalism, and its institutions, governmentalities, disciplinary techniques, political subjectivities and resources for imagining community. So, for instance, the Westphalian cartography of a world divided into autarchic nation-states depends upon an image of the public life of the nation marked by the retreat of "traditional" (read: religiously inscribed) forms of power and authority, and with this, a decline in belief, a slackening of faith, and a generalized devolution of the sacred into the private sphere of personal choice. Implicit assumptions about secularization can readily be found in national historiographies, as well as in the prescriptions of modernization theorists, and others who seek to align different societies along a single, teleological trajectory leading to a future, secular world. These are the terms on which social formations identified with "religious" modes of thought and practice continue to be located on the far side of modernity, not least so-called fundamentalist, or other putatively illiberal religious movements that have emerged in recent decades.[1]

The dominant narratives of nation-state formation continue to operate within this frame of secularization by focusing on the penetration of the modern state's instrumentalities and disciplinary powers into local spaces of everyday life, and the production of "national civil subjects" through such institutional mechanisms as schools, factories, prisons, hospitals, transportation systems and mass media. What is too often left unsaid, however, is that many of these disciplinary powers are themselves derivations of religious forms of communication and conduct, and that religion thereby provides a key condition of possibility of the nation-state. Readers of Max Weber's studies of the Protestant Ethic will find this argument familiar, since Weber famously proposed that modern subjectivity is rooted in the forms of asceticism associated with Puritan ideas of inner loneliness, predestination and rational labor (Weber 1958). One might expand this argument by suggesting that a "religious interior" colors the entire spectrum of discourse and practice through which modern institutions imagine and conduct themselves. Nationalist myths of birth and awakening, of destiny and sacrifice, the cult worship of the "glorious dead," or the specter of enemies or hard times, are all parasitic upon religious narratives of creation and salvation, and theodicies of the problem of evil. By the same token, the history of moral missions to organize the health, wealth and welfare of both citizens at home and colonial subjects abroad cannot be recounted without acknowledging how such efforts secured legitimacy through the mobilization of sacred vocabularies, such as in America's proclamation of its "manifest destiny," or the British Empire's "special burden," which was just as much the burden of the Christian as that of the white man (Hutchison and Lehmann 1994; Hastings 1997; van der Veer and Lehmann 1999; Smith 2000). Even more fundamentally, it has been argued, modern conditions of sovereignty, of biopolitical power, or the transcendental force of law – so central to the self-definition of modern political institutions – rest upon much older, mystical foundations of fate, and assumptions about the expiatory character of divine violence (Benjamin 1978; Agamben 1998).

In sum, it is at best specious, and at worst politically dangerous, to try to enforce a distinction between, on the one hand, things that are ostensibly "religious" in nature, and on the other, the range of "properly political" activities and concerns that are presumed to fall within the remit of territorial nation-states, and their putatively secular institutions of governance, in the realms of policing, education, diplomacy, or the provision of health and welfare. This division not only understates the sacred foundations of modern nationalism and state authority (as political theologians have long insisted), it also distorts our vision of the most recent period of global religious restructuring. By treating signs of religious activity as local evidence of a world-wide pattern of religious revival or the "return" to religion, one risks producing what, following Arjun Appadurai (1996: 141), we might call "germ theories" of social life, according to which illiberal, implacable, or even violence-prone populations, in this case marked by their religious commitments, are regarded as an invading force, sapping the life-blood of its national host, and upsetting the procedures and norms of the modern national imaginary, including the ideals of deliberative democracy, liberty of the person, or freedom of speech (an issue to which I shall return below). In all these ways, religion is confirmed as a return of the repressed, or to make use of Jürgen Habermas's famous term, as the sign of a "refeudalization" of modern public spheres (Habermas 1989: 142ff.).

Such descriptions are particularly unhelpful for any serious study of contemporary forms and modalities of religious discourse, conduct and imagined community in relation to globalizing forces and trends. For one thing, as even a casual observer can note, patterns of adherence to religious community have existed on a transnational scale for centuries. Religious communities might even be thought of as prototypical forms of what we often refer to today as "global society." Religious organizations have indeed provided the infrastructure for some of the oldest forms of association connecting distant local cultures, as suggested by the long histories of Christian missionary societies, Muslim Sufi brotherhoods, and Buddhist monastic orders, and their movements across vast territories, following along trade routes or in the footsteps of conquering armies, establishing footholds in new lands as providers of healthcare, welfare and education, and drawing new populations into their orbit through religious conversion. More generally stated, religious communities have seen world empires and kingdoms come and go; some of them have been around much longer than most nations; and there is no reason to assume that they will not outlive the current world order defined by the distribution of sovereign states and the family of nations. In this sense, the religious field constitutes a map of the world superimposed upon, but never reducible to the geography of nation-states, dividing the globe according to its own frontiers – such as the world of Christendom or the Islamic world – and with its own capital cities, such as Jerusalem, Vatican City, Wittenberg, Mecca, Najaf, Varanasi, Amritsar, Lhasa, or Ile-Ife.

All the same, it is undeniable that this religious field has undergone a dramatic restructuring over the course of the past one hundred and fifty years – a process that has gained considerable momentum since the late 1970s. However hesitant to define "religion," and however much it finds itself entangled in the prejudicial language of secularism, the sociology of religion nevertheless requires an analytical framework that can account for these recent changes. Throughout the world, scholars have noted significant patterns of reorganization of the institutional structures and cultural frameworks of religious life, transfigured by the global profusion of new techniques for self-cultivation increasingly being conducted outside the "customary" institutional sites of religious practice, and beyond the reach of "traditional" religious authorities. This has brought to the fore new questions about religion and the self, and the relation of religious subjectivity to matters of bodily health, security, pleasure, or mastery of the senses. We would be naïve to suppose that this expansion of the religious field has nothing to do with the proliferation of recent conflicts carried out "in the name of religion," from the intimate micropolitics of religious prescriptions for personal conduct (such as dress codes), to the globally resonant activities of crusading states, holy warriors, and other international agents.

Of signal importance, I suggest, is the growing, and increasingly globalized *public visibility* of religious actors, religious actions, and religious modes of discourse. This expanding visibility is centrally, deeply, and inextricably tied to the range of technological, symbolic and economic shifts that have given rise to the modern global media landscape. Over the course of the past century, and especially since the 1970s, new institutions and technologies of communication have radically altered the global mediascape, engendering new possibilities for both long-distance and evermore intimate forms of talk, travel, broadcast, narrowcast, surveillance, visualization, and archivization, in all these ways radically altering the spatio-temporal contexts of social life, of knowledge and practice, and of cultural identity and difference (see, e.g., Castells 2000–2004; Thompson 2005). It should therefore hardly surprise us that this geography of economic flows, symbolic exchanges and technological materialities has also radically altered the terms of *religious* identity, thought, and practice, and has been doing so on a world-wide scale.

Of course, links between religion and mediated communication are very old. In most religious traditions, the business of preaching, evangelizing, interpreting sacred meanings, pronouncing judgments, exorcizing malignant spirits, or expelling heretics has crucially depended on the historically available technologies and methods for fixing, reproducing and circulating words, images, and sounds. Religious institutions and communities have rarely if ever limited their activities to face-to-face modes of communication. In the Abrahamic faiths (Judaism, Christianity, and

Islam), for instance, it seems impossible to distinguish the origins of religious community from the evolving material conditions of production of written texts, including such things as techniques for inscribing on stone, clay, or leather, or the training of scribes, librarians, recitational experts, and other handlers of textual matter. In these and other traditions, we can also recall long histories of religious performance that have always depended upon a material culture of statues, masks, costumes, regalia, temple architecture, animal parts, and other "media" of religious communication. We might go so far as to suggest that, like a Kantian *noumenon*, one might be able to think of, but one can never perceive anything that could be called a "non-mediated" form of religious community, or a "pre-mediated" mode of fashioning religious selves, since it is only in and through its mediation that religion is made phenomenologically available.[2]

Nevertheless, we should not assume any simple continuities in the historical relations between media, religious institutions, communities of conviction, or modes of religious action. In our contemporary moment, perhaps more than ever before, it appears that mediated performances and media products precede, and thereby predetermine, all varieties of religious experience. Through a dizzying array of genres, aesthetic forms, technologies, and performative repertoires – such as instruction manuals, pop-psychology books, Internet blogs, comic books, rap music, bumper stickers, audio-cassettes, video games, or televized and cinematic versions of religious epics and mythologicals – media have extended the religious field beyond what Danièle Hervieux-Léger (2000: 132–7) calls "the civilization of the parish," that is to say, the geographical confines of routine institutional participation and face-to-face interaction, and the localized boundaries of ritual time. Ever-accelerating processes of mediatization have led to an ever-greater blurring of the distinctions between, say, pilgrimage and tourism, between religious ritual and news event, between religious festival and entertainment, or between the powers attributed to icons, artistic, and scientific images (and thereby, the organization of visualizing practices within the institutional spaces of temples, museums, and laboratories). In all these ways, the "place" of religion in contemporary life has undergone a significant shift. This shift is registered, not only at the level of practice among actually existing institutions and communities of faith, but also at the level of broader, cultural constructions infused by religious imagery and figures of discourse, including notions of transnational belonging and multicultural citizenship, tolerance and intolerance, hospitality and war, or faith and credit, to say nothing of the "religious" experiences associated with the finitude of the human body, and the uncanny, magical, and even sacred powers attributed to the advanced technologies and scientific projects that are reshaping our life-worlds, from nuclear energy to genetically modified foods, stem cell research, organ donation, or digital archives. In short, there is no way to make sense of current repositioning of the religious field without a detailed appreciation of the evolving media systems that underpin religious publicity, daily practice, and imagination, both historically and in the present.

The terms religion, media, and globalization thus point to an extraordinarily fecund field of research, at the very same time that they carry with them a deeply problematic and oftentimes confusing conceptual baggage. Given the impossibility of arriving at an Archimedean point from which to survey the range of objects, processes, and relationships that emanate from this conjunction, in the remainder of this chapter I shall offer a brief, synthetic account of some selected, but hopefully instructive, case studies, and thereby point toward future paths of inquiry for sociologists of religion.

The Case of Religious Print

One of the most familiar cases of religious mediation comes, not from our own times, but from the crucible of European modernity, the Protestant Reformation, and its felicitous relationship with the advent of print. There is insufficient space here to try recount the long and complex history (and considerable debate) surrounding Gutenberg's press and the legacy of the European print revolution of the fifteenth and sixteenth centuries, if indeed it is reasonable to invoke the term revolution in this context. But it is nonetheless impossible to ignore the pioneering efforts of early modern European religious intellectuals to avail themselves of the new medium, most famously in the case of Martin Luther, Bible translator, pamphleteer, and foremost architect of the Protestant Reformation.[3] Whether for good or ill, agents of religious mediation who followed in Luther's steps were decisively influenced by the relationships they began to forge with printer's shops, book markets, and with the very materiality of the print medium, absorbing its logics of standardization, circulation, and public address. Through the circulation of printed works, a distinct new arena of possibility was opened up for religious agents to debate opponents, win followers, or consecrate their own legitimacy and authority by claiming to speak in the name of the masses. Thanks to the printing press, Elizabeth Eisenstein has argued, "the social penetration of literacy, which was linked with Bible-reading, changed the character of group identity ... Religious affiliation thus entered into diverse forms of social agitation and mobility, political cleavage and cohesion" (1979: 422).[4]

The uptake of print as a communications medium thus had deep, dramatic, and seemingly irreversible repercussions for the social organization of peoples along "religious" lines. In the case of early modern Europe, print helped to link individuals together into new "commonwealths of learning," while at the same time facilitating a Balkanization of the established sodalities of religious community that made up Western Christendom. The spread of Bibles translated into vernacular languages, for instance, fragmented a cosmopolitan elite of religious literati, defined by its shared familiarity with sacred manuscripts written in Latin or Greek. In these and other ways, new forms of sociability emerged within and through the circulation of print commodities, mounting a significant challenge for the established hierocratic bureaucracies, and undermining their longstanding, monopolistic claims over the production, authorized interpretations, and the teaching of written texts. This is perhaps nowhere more poignantly exemplified than in the history of Roman Church's increasingly desperate attempts to control the spread of printed books. The *Index Librorum Prohibitorum*, initially promulgated in 1559, required incessant revision in the face of lax local authorities, dauntless underground publishers and smugglers, and a seemingly inexorable growth in the European appetite for new books (Febvre and Martin 1976: 244–7; Burke 2000: 141–5). But if, in the eyes of the sixteenth-century Roman Church, print seemed at best a risky medium on account of the unruly conduct of readers, Protestants tended to see instead a providential opportunity for expanded reach, to which they responded through the translation and dissemination of Bibles, code books, tracts, pamphlets, and other religious writings. Evangelist publishing campaigns were thus founded on an assumption that "the capacity of like-minded men to cite the same chapter and verse and to govern their daily lives accordingly, hinged on their access to identical copies of whole Bibles, and hence on the output of sizeable standard editions" (Eisenstein 1979: 364). The work of creating and distributing vernacular Bibles were was crucially tied to a broader effort to secure the assent of new communities of "solitary readers who [would receive] silent guidance from repeatedly re-reading the same book on their own" (Eisenstein 1979: 366).

However, efforts to place Bibles in the hands of "common" readers were fraught with problems of reliability and control. For the very technology that made it possible to spread God's word so widely also imposed new constraints and entailed new forms of anxiety about its transmission. Circulating outside the authority of any form of religious hierocracy, and liable to fall into the hands of any interested party, sacred works translated and printed in vernacular tongues enjoyed at best a precarious claim to their own authenticity. This can be inferred from the intense efforts on the part of Protestant authors and publishers to secure for their readers the "original" and "true" meaning of Christian scripture. "It is surely one of the ironies of Western civilization," Eisenstein summarizes, "that Bible studies aimed at penetrating the Gothic darkness in order to recover pure Christian truth – aimed, that is, at removing glosses and commentaries in order to lay bare the pure "plain" text – ended by interposing an impenetrable thicket of recondite annotation between Bible-reader and Holy Book" (1979: 700).

As suggested by this (admittedly rushed and certainly only partial) account, the printed word quickly came to constitute a strategically decisive arena in which religious community could be imagined and religious authority could be re-engineered. For Christians, Jews, Muslims, and other religious communities, the creation of print markets entailed new circulations of knowledge and power aligned with the emerging conditions and performative imperatives to "reach the people" through the technological reproduction of identical texts, and through the distribution of print matter within an impersonal public sphere. Print's apparent capacity to educate, reform, control, or liberate "the masses" resonated among religious intellectuals as well as their interlocutors, including lay readers, potential converts, and even heretics, whose increased access to texts provided them new opportunities to read against the grain of authorized interpretations. Thanks to rising literacy rates, a succession of technological revolutions, and the growing accessibility of dispersed populations, modern religious movements increasingly resembled one another in their common reliance upon the standards of popular success associated with the mass reproduction of printed texts, and with the print medium's attendant protocols for "effective communication."

The social logic underlying this expanding universe of print-mediated religious publicity can be further illustrated with reference to the work of Christian missionary societies, beginning in the late eighteenth century. British organizations such as the London Missionary Society (founded in 1795), the Religious Tract Society (1799) and the British and Foreign Bible Society (1804), and their US counterparts, the American Bible Society (1816) and the American Tract Society (1825), were among the most innovative and energetic agents for the global spread of print. They viewed the printed word as a (if not *the*) key instrument in their efforts to save souls and stamp out heathen customs, wherever the rapidly expanding networks of roads, ships, and railways could take them, both "at home" and in far-flung corners of the earth, as evident from their unprecedented capacities to produce and distribute inexpensive, portable, and reliable reproductions of Bibles, catechisms, tracts, pamphlets, and other works of a religious nature.[5] In so doing, missionary societies found themselves at the vanguard of larger economic and social pressures to transform the print industry, which up to that time was governed by an artisanal mode of production, organized around the labor of individual master printers, their trusted assistants, and their limited distribution networks of shopkeepers and colporteurs, who all tended to share an understanding of publishing as an activity of learned gentlemen engaged in the transference of symbolic property from authors to a select audience of readers.[6] Groups such as the American Bible Society have been credited for playing a key role in advancing the economic and institutional arrangements, and even the technological capacities for mass printing and mass distribution of the written word, through their pioneering experiments with new techniques to make inexpensive wood-pulp paper, steam power, cylinder presses, and eventually the development of cost-effective stereotypography, as well as their embrace of increasingly efficient and reliable systems of inventory, accounting, marketing, and transportation of print commodities (Nord 2004; Wosh 1994). Through such work, missionary societies not only extended printed copies of sacred literature to new classes of readers, but also, at the same time, helped to reposition the markers for "appropriate reading," as printed works increasingly moved beyond their "traditional" locations of schools or houses of prayer into the public spaces of factories, railway cars, ships, and town squares, and even onto the parlor bookshelf, as a centerpiece of bourgeois domestic life.[7] Through their material presence in these diverse social scenes, print commodities could now embody the ideals of religious edification as well as personal ownership and domestic display, reflective of the forces that were redefining print-mediated publicity along the axis of an expanding consumer culture. These rapidly evolving modes of circulation allowed for new possibilities of translation, contact, and exchange, and thereby a recalibration of the lines that both divided and connected the private and the public, the local and the distant, or for that matter, the imperial metropolis and its colonial periphery.

Even a casual survey of the unabated expansion of religious publishing up to the present makes it hard to deny that subsequent media revolutions – such as those based on the recording of sounds and images, the use of electricity for broadcasting, or more finely grained processes for spatializing and disseminating information in and through computer platforms – have not at all obviated the interactions that first began in the sixteenth century to forge imagined communities through the circulation of printed works, as Benedict Anderson has famously described in his account of "print capitalism" (Anderson 1991: 37–46). On the contrary, industries and markets for printed works have not only survived the impact of electronic media, but have intensified their productive capacities and expanded their reach. Nineteenth-century trends in the field of religious publishing thus continue to be felt in the present day, a period when the book market – and religious print in particular – has been experiencing a particularly dramatic growth.[8] Commensurate with the growing capacity of religious consumers to exercise demand for commodities that will meet their ideological and affective expectations and needs, the market for religious print has been injected with new vigor, as a growing number of presses – especially small-scale operations, and even desktop publishers – enter into the fray. These producers cater to increasing numbers of readers (as well as turning already established groups of readers into "return customers"), addressing evangelical Christians in the United States, Pentecostals in Brazil, Islamic pietists in Egypt, Pakistan, and Indonesia, Hindu nationalists in India, Jews living in the English-speaking diaspora, and many others who wish to deepen their understanding, reinforce their commitments, and ignite their imaginations through the consumption of religious print matter. Over the past half century, the United States alone has seen an exponential growth rate of Christian Bibles, recently estimated at over seven thousand different editions, the majority of which constitute an almost completely uncharted territory for the scholarly eye (Gutjahr 2001: 338). And beyond such canonical works, markets catering to different faith groups have experienced a veritable explosion of publication of legal codices, hymnals, manuals and catechisms, as well as a vast array of "substitute products," parasitic upon the genres of writing found in the mainstream market, including "religious" adventure novels, self-help literature, autobiographies, popular science, news reportage, or comic books.

Far from being a merely residual field of cultural production, of only marginal significance for sociological accounts of the contemporary world order, religious print evinces an ongoing and vital process of constituting and reconstituting religious publicity, illustrating new variations on longstanding themes that are proper to the *longue durée* of print, and its socioeconomic, symbolic and performative logics of "permanence through inscription" and "mass connectivity through circulation." But sad to say, studies of the history and contemporary situation of religious print remain in short supply. In part, this is because sociologists of religion, among others who might have things to say about the socio-economic conditions, the institutional organization, the action-networks, or the communicative environments of religious print culture, have largely ceded the study of this terrain to scholars concerned principally with the hermeneutics of textual exegesis, and only secondarily with the social contexts of production, circulation, and reception of print commodities.

THE DANISH CARTOON IMBROGLIO

If the contemporary religious publishing industry has remained, for the most part, an unfamiliar and ill-considered topic for many social scientists today, nothing could stand in sharper contrast than the intense interest that has been given to the global circulation of religious images, as well as the eruption of dramatic controversies about images. Whether it be the appearance of religious leaders such as the Pope or the Dalai Lama in the international news, the circulation of images of vast crowds at major religious events, or the depiction of shocking acts of desecration of religious images, such as the singer Madonna's *Confessions Tour* of 2006, or the Taliban's televized destruction of the Buddhist statues at Bamiyan, Afghanistan in 2001, it would seem impossible to account for the prominence of religious themes in the world today without trying to account for the specific ways this prominence is communicated in a visual register.

The example I want to focus on here will be familiar to many readers, since a great deal has already been written about the publication, and republication, of twelve cartoons containing satirical depictions of devout Muslims and of the Prophet Muhammad. These cartoons originally appeared on 30 September 2005, in the Danish newspaper, the *Jyllands-Posten*, which had commissioned them as part of an article entitled "The Face of Muhammad." The publication was intended as a commentary on what the editors of the paper perceived to be a dangerous trend toward self-censorship in the Danish press, based on a fear of including Muslims in the repertoire of objects of ridicule and mockery freely available to cartoonists and political satirists. The cartoons were subsequently reproduced either in part or in their entirety in at least 143 newspapers in 56 different countries,[9] and they also have appeared on dozens of websites, establishing the transnational, if not global, resonance of the imbroglio surrounding what have come to be known as the "Danish cartoons."[10] From their initial appearance to their international circulation, these images pitted champions of "free speech," enshrined in the genre of the political cartoon – and especially defenders of "freedom from religious authority" – against a range of audiences and actors for whom the images were insulting, injurious, and (for at least some) a violation of religious taboo. The conflict culminated in a series of dramatic conflagrations staged on city streets and within the circuits of global media – ranging from violent riots, to campaigns to ban Danish consumer goods, to the bombing of embassies – in waves of activity that began in late 2005 and that have shown no signs of abating at the time of writing this text, in early 2009.[11]

This globally resonant event has been explained in various ways, not least by noting how it builds upon a much longer history of interdependency, exchange, competition, conquest, and occupation that for centuries have linked a putatively Christian Europe with a putatively Muslim Middle East. Many have also noted how this case illustrates the ways patterns of migration, settlement, labor, inter-generational tension, racism, and social exclusion have defined the specific experiences of recent generations of Muslim-minority communities living in the West, and at the same time, how the local dynamics of intercultural relations between Danish Muslims and their neighbors get linked up with social movements located in far-away Muslim-majority countries, such as Pakistan, Iran, or Syria. So much was evident from the interventions of political and religious elites, who petitioned the Danish government to take "responsible action" against the *Jyllands-Posten*,[12] or the pronouncements of scholars, populist leaders, and local politicians urging their own governments to impose diplomatic sanctions, as well as calling upon Muslims around the world to organize boycotts of Danish goods, and even, in a few dramatic cases, calling for the assassination of the cartoonists. Beyond the elite level, it was striking how, once they entered the public realm, the Danish cartoons were so readily integrated within existing patterns of political protest that have long defined the position of Islamic movements within larger geopolitical dynamics of local state authoritarianism, American military hegemony, and the gross inequities of the international petrodollar economy. Violent marches outside Danish embassies in Damascus, Beirut, Tehran, Islamabad, and many other cities appeared to be directed, not only against offending parties in far-away Denmark, who were shielding the cartoonists from the punishment it was claimed they deserved, but also against the corrupt, undemocratic, and only nominally Islamic government authorities at home.

This is all familiar enough. I only wish to highlight two dimensions of this story which I consider to be particularly relevant for a broader study of religion, media, and globalization, and which, perhaps, have not received the attention they deserve. The first has to do with the accelerating pace of telecommunications technologies and the forms of visibility they enable. Indeed, as I have already suggested, the Danish cartoon affair is relevant before anything else as a public spectacle, produced not simply by its principal actors, but also through the global circulation of printed and electronic texts, the reporting of rumors, and the cascading flow of images (including the images of protestors against images). Taken together, these circuits of perception and visibility invite us to rethink the politics of so-called "religious revival" in our current global moment. Among other things, they offer a vantage point for situating the most recent phases of cultural and political revolution often referred to as "the Islamic Awakening." Through the lens of modern media, their capacity to construct detailed visual representations of the *umma* [the world community of Muslims], and to link distant local contexts through the circulation of such images, the Islamic Awakening cannot be reduced to simplistic accounts of reactionary, anti-modern reflex. On the contrary, within this global mediascape, it is impossible to separate the so-called Islamic radicals, protesting on city streets from the systems of circulation that render such protests visible, and that enable the participation of a diverse and refracted global audience. Protestors who seek to challenge what they perceive as the inequities of a world system that marginalizes Islam, and Western journalists and public intellectuals who claim to act in defence of a liberal civil order under threat from religious fundamentalism, are both of a piece with the mediatic construction of the global as a unitary field of visibility: a proscenium upon which political conflict is choreographed, performed, and made available for global consumption.

My second observation is that the Danish cartoon affair also touches on the very question of visibility and its status in the borderlands dividing "religious" and "secular" systems of legitimacy in the modern world. It has often been stated that Muslims around the world have taken offense at the publication of the cartoons because they violate a fundamental prohibition within Islam against the visual representation of the Prophet. There is much that could be said here about the specific religious texts upon which such claims have been founded, and the traditions of interpretation and accommodation with what in any event should be regarded as a much-exaggerated principle of Islamic aniconism [aversion of sacred images]. Traditional Islamic proscriptions against *shirk* [idolatry] were never automatically translated into prohibitions against pictorial art, as evident from the numerous instances, both historical and contemporary, of strategies to legitimate the representation of the Prophet in Islamic art (such as through the depiction of his face as a featureless void emanating light). By the same token, we should exercise caution here in assuming that Muslims find the Danish cartoons "blasphemous," since it is at best indiscriminate to try to substitute the term *blasphemy* for terms indigenous to Islamic discourse such as *kufr* [unbelief] or *ilhad* [heresy]. It would be more appropriate, perhaps, to note instead the ways that blasphemy continues to exist (however dimly recognized) as a legal norm within numerous Western societies. Indeed, despite their self-proclaimed secularism, several countries in Europe still retain blasphemy laws within their penal codes, including Denmark itself, as well as Germany, the UK, the Netherlands, Ireland, and Spain. Moreover, such laws – even if only rarely exercised – are organized around the normativity of Christian dogma, and it is notable that no Muslim group living in the West has ever succeeded in provoking their enactment.

But lastly, we might also note how the so-called secular world also depends on its own system of forbidden images. Consider, for instance, the complex taboos surrounding images of the bodies of dead soldiers, of naked children, or of tortured bodies, as consecrated in the ethos of professional journalistic practice, and also enshrined in national, and even international laws (such as in the case of the Geneva Code's proscription against the circulation of images of prisoners of war). In a similar vein, it might be useful to compare the moral outrage ascribed to Muslim opponents to the Danish cartoons to other instances of institutionalized violence with regard to offensive or forbidden images, as in the cases of the Netherlands, Spain, Switzerland, Poland, Thailand, and Brunei (to name a few) where laws of *lèse majesté* prohibit citizens from producing insulting images of their own heads of state.[13] A particularly apt case emerged in Spain in 2007, when two cartoonists were found guilty of *lèse majesté* for having depicted Crown Prince Felipe and his wife Letizia engaged in a sexual act, on the cover of their weekly satire magazine, *El Jueves* – although, tellingly, unlike the Danish case, there was no subsequent rush among periodical publishers either inside or outside Spain to reprint the offending image.[14]

As these and other cases might lead us to conclude, rather than assuming as self-evident that it is morally opprobrious to produce and display images such as those published by the *Jyllands-Posten* – and that, by contrast, no reasonable person should take offense at a mere cartoon – we would be better served to reflect on the power of images to excite, incite, inspire, or offend the sensibilities of both "religious" and "secular" constituencies, and thereby to inquire into the terms on which such divisions are enacted. One fruitful line of inquiry would be based on a study of the origins of the Western secular aversion of images of the humiliated and suffering body. In this respect, it is important to recall how, in contrast with certain secular visual regimes, for many religious actors – one thinks here of the many spectacles in both the Roman Catholic as well as *shia* Muslim world in which flagellants engage in dramatic acts of self-mortification – images of suffering bodies are not at all offensive, but on the contrary serve as legitimate objects of adoration and imitation. That kind of analysis suggests, perhaps, that the Danish cartoon imbroglio has not simply revolved around a contest between secular-liberal proponents of free speech and intolerant zealots determined to overturn such rights. Instead, we can begin to see this conflict in terms of two divergent, and colliding, economies of visibility, each organized by distinct notions about what constitutes a forbidden image, and each resting on distinct ideas about the relationship of pain, truth, and their commensurability.[15]

CONCLUSION

The history of religious print and the contemporary politics of globally circulating religious images offer but two points of departure for a more wholesale re-assessment of stock assumptions about the relationship between religion and media. Their study also bring questions about religion to bear on the theoretical assumptions of many media sociologists, communications historians, and others concerned with the impact of technologies, institutions, and practices of media on social life. It is hard to ignore, for instance, the obdurate and widespread persistence, both within and outside scholarly circles, of a characterization of communications technologies, beginning with the printing press and culminating in the twentieth and twenty-first century spread of film, television, and the World Wide Web, as key agents precipitating the shift from societies ruled by "the divine right of kings" to the modern situation of societies governed by the promise of "power by and for the people." Of course, scholars from diverse perspectives have long interrogated these mythologies about collective deliberation and popular self-determination, enshrined in such liberal ideals as "freedom of the press" or "consumer sovereignty." But as I hope I have managed to suggest in and through the examples discussed in this chapter, the sociology of religion has something distinctive and important to add to the conversation, to the extent that it is able to identify, in finely grained detail, the structural, dynamic, and lived tissues that connect religion, media, and globalization together as three dimensions of a single social field. There is much that awaits our attention.

Notes

1   For more on this topic, see the chapter on "Secularism" in this volume. Some of the most analytically productive strands of discussion about "the secular" have been taking place outside the sociology of religion, see, inter alia, Asad (2003), Jakobsen and Pelligrini (2008), Mahmood (2006), Taylor (2007). See also the ongoing debates in "The Immanent Frame," a blog developed by the Social Sciences Research Council (USA): www.ssrc.org/blogs/immanent_frame/

2   Elsewhere (Stolow 2005) I have elaborated this claim in greater detail. Leading texts in current discussions about religion and media include de Vries and Weber (2000), Meyer and Moors (2006), Morgan (2008).

3   For a useful overview of the role of print in the Protestant Reformation, see Dickens (1974), Edwards (1994), Gilmont (1998), Scribner (1981).

4   Eisenstein's account of the impact of the print on Early Modern Europe has been the subject of ongoing dispute, among other things for its putative technological determinism. See, for instance, the debate between Eisenstein and one of her most trenchant critics, Adrian Johns, in *The American Historical Review* 107 (1), 2002: 84–128.

5   On the global impact of nineteenth-century Christian missionary societies, see Comaroff and Comaroff (1991), van der Veer (1996), Ward (1992). On the global diffusion of Christian print, see Hofmeyer (2003), Howsam (1991), Sugirtharajah (2001), Wosh (1994). Some scholars have suggested that the diffusion of print technology and its social

logic of address not only facilitated the global spread of Christianity, but also led to the "Protestantization" of non-Christian religions. Gananath Obeyesekere (1970) has famously referred to the rise of a form of "Protestant Buddhism" in nineteenth-century Sri Lanka, in which Buddhist intellectuals responded to missionary work by indigenizing print technologies and their modes of knowledge-ordering and public-making.

6 For discussion of the economic organization of print publishing, and the relationships among authors, printers, and their publics in the English-speaking world, and in particular early (colonial) American history, see Amory and Hall (2007), Tebbel (1987). On the industrialization of print production in the nineteenth century, see Casper et al. (2007), Kaestle and Radway (2009).

7 See, inter alia, Altick (1998), Brown (2004), Gutjahr (1999), Ledger-Lomas (2009), Morgan (1999). More general treatments of the shifting locations of print matter and the practice of reading throughout this period include Casper et al. (2007), Kaestle and Radway (2009); Vincent (1993).

8 "Religious publishing" is of course a highly ambiguous and contested category, since no one can say with confidence what precisely constitutes a "religious" as opposed to a "non-religious" book. For discussion of the definition of "religious" publishing, see Tebbel (1987: 449–452). Cf. Garrett (1999), Gutjahr (2001), Riess (2000a, 2000b), Winston (1999, 2003). With this caveat in mind, it is instructive to review the data produced by organizations such as the Christian Booksellers Association, which suggest that by the mid-1990s the Christian book industry in the US had developed into an industry worth over $2.5 billion per year, accounting for somewhere between 5% and 10% of the total US book market, depending on what is being counted (Kress 2000; Milliot 2001). This output – enormous by any reasonable standard of measurement – is abetted by the existence of a broad network of publishing houses, outreach organizations, church and para-church groups, retail sellers, and, it would also appear, a large population of consumers with disposable incomes. Comparable evidence exists with respect to various religious print industries outside the Christian world. For instance, on the role of publishers in contemporary transnational Jewish public spheres, see Stolow (forthcoming); on the Islamic book market in Egypt, see Gonzalez-Quijano (1998).

9 As reported by Olesen (2007: 302).

10 The Danish cartoon affair has already been analyzed from a range of perspectives. See, inter alia, Berkowitz and Eko (2007), Goldstone (2007), Keane (2009), W. Keane (forthcoming), Olesen (2007), Saunders (2008).

11 For a time-line of protests around the world, up to June 2008 (the bombing of the Danish embassy in Pakistan), see: www.mapreport.com/countries/cartoon_protest.html.

12 See, for instance, the Open Letter signed by 11 ambassadors from Muslim-majority states, sent to the Danish Prime Minister in October 2005: http://gfx.tv2.dk/images/Nyhederne/Pdf/side1.pdf and http://gfx.tv2.dk/images/Nyhederne/Pdf/side2.pdf.

13 For its part, Denmark sets forth in §115 of its penal code a provision that allows a judge to double the punishment for acts of libel (usually, four months imprisonment) in cases where the state's regent is the target. Available at: www.retsinformation.dk/Forms/R0710.aspx?id=113401.

14 For details, see: http://news.bbc.co.uk/2/hi/europe/7092866.stm.

15 This proposal rests on insights that have already been developed in recent discussions about the power of religious images and the politics of iconoclasm in religion, art, science, and other domains. See, inter alia, Flood 2002, Latour and Weibel 2002, Meyer 2008, Morgan 1998, Pinney 2004, Rajagopal 2001, Spyer 1998.

Bibliography

Agamben, Giorgio (1998) *Homo Sacer: Sovereign Power and Bare Life*, Stanford: Stanford University Press.

Altick, Richard D. (1998) *The English Common Reader: A Social History of the Mass Reading Public, 1800–1900* (2nd edn.), Columbus: Ohio State University Press.

Amory, Hugh and David D. Hall (2007) *A History of the Book in America 1: The Colonial Book in the Atlantic World*, Chapel Hill: University of North Carolina Press.

Anderson, Benedict (1991) *Imagined Communities: Reflections on the Origin and Spread of Nationalism* (2nd revd. edn.), London: Verso Books.

Anderson, Benedict (1994) Exodus, *Critical Inquiry* 20 (2): 314–27.

Appadurai, Arjun (1996) *Modernity at Large: Cultural Dimensions of Globalization*, Minneapolis: University of Minnesota Press.

Asad, Talal (1993) *Genealogies of Religion: Discipline and Reasons of Power in Christianity and Islam*, Baltimore: Johns Hopkins University Press.

Asad, Talal (2003) *Formations of the Secular: Christianity, Islam, Modernity*, Stanford: Stanford University Press.

Benjamin, Walter (1978) Critiques of violence, in Peter Demetz (ed.), *Reflections: Essays, Aphorisms, Autobiographical Writings*, New York and London: Harcourt Brace Jovanovich, 277–300.

Berkowitz, Dan and Lyombe Eko (2007) Blasphemy as sacred rite/right: "the Mohammed cartoons affair" and maintenance of journalistic ideology, *Journalism Studies* 8 (5): 779–97.

Brown, Candy Gunther (2004) *The Word in the World: Evangelical Writing, Publishing, and Reading in America, 1789–1880*, Chapel Hill: University of North Carolina Press.

Burke, Peter (2000) *A Social History of Knowledge: From Gutenberg to Diderot*, Cambridge: Polity Press.

Casper, Scott, Jeffrey Groves, Stephen Nissenbaum, and Michael Winship (eds.) (2007) *A History of the Book in America 3: The Industrial Book, 1840–1880*, Chapel Hill: University of North Carolina Press.

Castells, Manuel (2000–4) *The Information Age: Economy, Society and Culture*, 3 vols. (2nd edn.), Oxford: Blackwell.

Chidester, David (1996) *Savage Systems: Colonialism and Comparative Religion in Southern Africa*, Charlottesville: University Press of Virginia.

Comaroff, Jean and Comaroff, John (1991) *Of Revelation and Revolution: Christianity, Colonialism and Consciousness in South Africa 1*, Chicago: University of Chicago Press.

Coser, Lewis, Charles Kadushin, and Powell, Walter (1982) *Books: The Culture and Commerce of Publishing*, Chicago: University of Chicago Press.

Derrida, Jacques (2002) *Acts of Religion*, ed. Gil Anidjar, New York and London: Routledge.

Dickens, A. G. (1974) *The German Nation and Martin Luther*, London: Edward Arnold Publishers.

Edwards, M. U., Jr (1994) *Printing, Propaganda, and Martin Luther*, Berkeley: University of California Press.

Eisenstein, Elizabeth (1979) *The Printing Press as an Agent of Change: Communications and Cultural Transformations in Early Modern Europe*, Cambridge: Cambridge University Press.

Febvre, Lucien and Martin, Henri-Jean (1976) *The Coming of the Book: The Impact of Printing, 1450–1800*, tr. David Gerard, London and New York: Verso.

Flood, Finbarr Barry (2002) Between cult and culture: Bamiyan, Islamic iconoclasm, and the museum, *Art Bulletin* 84 (4): 641–59.

Garrett, Lynn (1999) Bibles and sacred texts: betcha can't own just one, *Publishers Weekly* 246 (41): 33.

Gilmont, Jean-François (ed.) (1998) *The Reformation and the Book*, Aldershot: Ashgate.

Goldstone, Brian (2007) Violence and the profane: Islamism, liberal democracy, and the limits of secular discipline, *Anthropological Quarterly* 80 (1): 207–35.

Gonzalez-Quijano, Yves (1998) *Les gens du livre: Édition et champ intellectuel dans l'Égypte républicaine*, Paris, CNRS Éditions.

Griffiths, Paul J. (1999) *Religious Reading: The Place of Reading in the Practice of Religion*, New York: Oxford University Press.

Gutjahr, Paul C. (1999) *An American Bible: A History of the Good Book in the United States, 1777–1880*, Stanford: Stanford University Press.

Gutjahr, Paul C. (2001) The state of the discipline: sacred texts in the United States, *Book History* 4: 335–70.

Habermas, Jürgen (1989) *The Structural Transformation of the Public Sphere: An Inquiry into a Category of Bourgeois Society*, Cambridge, MA: MIT Press.

Hastings, Adrian (1997) *The Construction of Nationhood: Ethnicity, Religion and Nationalism*, Cambridge: Cambridge University Press.

Hervieu-Léger, Danièle (2000) *Religion as a Chain of Memory*, New Brunswick: Rutgers University Press.

Hofmeyer, Isabel (2003) *The Portable Bunyan: A Transnational History of the Piligrim's Progress*, Princeton: Princeton University Press.

Howsam, Leslie (1991) *Cheap Bibles: Nineteenth-Century Publishing and the British and Foreign Bible Society*, Cambridge: Cambridge University Press.

Hutchison, William and Hartmut Lehmann (eds.) (1994) *Many Are Chosen: Divine Election and Western Nationalism*, Minneapolis: Fortress Press.

Jakobsen, Janet and Ann Pelligrini (eds.) (2008) *Secularisms*, Durham, NC: Duke University Press.

Kaestle, Carl and Janice Radway, eds (2009) *A History of the Book in America 4: Print in Motion: The Expansion of Publishing and Reading in the United States, 1880–1940*, Chapel Hill: University of North Carolina Press.

Keane, David (2008) Cartoon violence and freedom of expression, *Human Rights Quarterly* 30 (4): 845–75.

Keane, Webb (2009) Freedom and blasphemy: on Indonesian press barons and Danish cartoons, *Public Culture* 21 (1): 47–76.

Kress, Michael (2000) Slicing the market pie (religion update), *Publishers Weekly* 247 (13): S16–S18.

Latour, Bruno and Weibel, Peter (eds.) (2002) *Iconoclash: Beyond the Image Wars in Science, Religion, and Art*, Cambridge, MA: MIT Press.

Ledger-Lomas, Michael (2009) Mass markets: religion, in David McKitterick (ed.), *The History of the Book in Britain, 1830–1914*, Cambridge: Cambridge University Press, 324–58.

Mahmood, Saba (2006) Secularism, hermeneutics, and empire: the politics of Islamic reformation, *Public Culture* 18 (2): 323–47.

Mandaville, Peter (2001) *Transnational Muslim Politics: Reimagining the Umma*, London and New York: Routledge.

Masuzawa, Tomoko (2005) *The Invention of World Religions or, How European Universalism Was Preserved in the Language of Pluralism*, Chicago: University of Chicago Press.

Meyer, Birgit (2008) Powerful pictures: popular Christian aesthetics in southern Ghana, *Journal for the American Academy of Religion* 76 (1): 82–110.

Meyer, Birgit and Moors, Annelies (eds.) (2006) *Religion, Media and the Public Sphere*, Bloomington: Indiana University Press.

Milliot, Jim (2001) Do religion sales add up?, *Publishers Weekly* 242 (15): 25.

Morgan, David (1998) *Visual Piety: A History and Theory of Popular Religious Images*, Berkeley: University of California Press.

Morgan, David (1999) *Protestants and Pictures: Religion, Visual Culture, and the Age of American Mass Reproduction*, New York and Oxford: Oxford University Press.

Morgan, David (ed.) (2008) *Key Words in Religion, Media, and Culture*, London and New York: Routledge.

Nord, David Paul (2004) *Faith in Reading: Religious Publishing and the Birth of Mass Media in America*, New York and Oxford: Oxford University Press.

Obeyesekere, Gananath (1970) Religious symbolism and political change in Ceylon, *Modern Ceylon Studies* 1 (1): 43–63.

Olesen, Thomas (2007) The porous public and the transnational dialectic: the Muhammed cartoons conflict, *Acta Sociologica* 50 (3): 295–308.

Pinney, Christopher (2004) *Photos of the Gods: The Printed Image and Political Struggle in India*, London: Reaktion Books.

Rajagopal, Arvind (2001) *Politics After Television: Hindu Nationalism and the Reshaping of the Public in India*, Cambridge and New York: University of Cambridge Press.

Riess, Jana (2000a) Tracking the mega-categories (religion update), *Publishers Weekly* 247 (22): S16–S18.

Riess, Jana (2000b) New genres, emerging audiences (religion update), *Publishers Weekly* 247 (34): S4–S8.

Saunders, Robert (2008) The ummah as nation: a reappraisal in the wake of the "Cartoons Affair," *Nations and Nationalism* 14 (2): 303–21.

Scribner, Robert W. (1981) *For the Sake of Simple Folk: Popular Propaganda and the German Reformation*, Cambridge: Cambridge University Press.

Smith, Anthony D. (2000) The "sacred" dimension of nationalism, *Millennium: Journal of International Politics* 29 (3): 791–814.

Spyer, Patricia (ed.) (1998) *Border Fetishisms: Material Objects in Unstable Places*, London and New York: Routledge.

Stolow, Jeremy (2005) Religion and/as media, *Theory, Culture and Society* 22 (4): 119–45.

Stolow, Jeremy (forthcoming) *Orthodox By Design*. University of California Press.

Sugirtharajah, Rasiah S. (2001) *The Bible and the Third World: Precolonial, Colonial and Postcolonial Encounters*, Cambridge: Cambridge University Press.

Taylor, Charles (2007) *A Secular Age*, Cambridge, MA: Harvard University Press.

Tebbel, John William (1987) *Between Covers: The Rise and Transformation of Book Publishing in America*, New York and Oxford: Oxford University Press.

Thompson, John B. (2005) The New Visibility, *Theory, Culture and Society* 22 (6): 31–51.

van der Veer, Peter (ed.) (1996) *Conversion to Modernities: The Globalization of Christianity*, London and New York: Routledge.

van der Veer, Peter and Harmut Lehmann (eds.) (1999) *Nation and Religion: Perspectives on Europe and Asia*, Princeton: Princeton University Press.

Vincent, David (1993) *Literacy and Popular Culture: England, 1750–1914*, Cambridge: Cambridge University Press.

Vries, Hent de and Weber, Samuel (eds.) (2000) *Religion and Media*, Stanford: Stanford University Press.

Ward, W. R. (1992) *The Protestant Evangelical Awakening*, Cambridge: Cambridge University Press.

Weber, Max (1958) *The Protestant Ethic and the Spirit of Capitalism*, tr. Talcott Parsons, New York: Charles Scribner's Sons.

Winston, Kimberly (1999) Bibles and sacred texts: of the making of many scriptures, *Publishers Weekly* 246 (41): 34–41.

Winston, Kimberly (2003) You can judge a (good) book by its cover, *Publishers Weekly* 250 (41): 32–8.

Wosh, Peter J. (1994) *Spreading the Word: The Bible Business in Nineteenth-Century America*, Ithaca: Cornell University Press.

25

Toward a Sociology of Religious Commodification

Pattana Kitiarsa

Introduction

The symbiotic interrelation between religious faiths/institutions and market economy has always loomed large in the sociology of human religious experience. In this chapter, I discuss the definition, scope, contents, and significance of religious commodification. My discussion deals particularly with how and why religious commodification has become invisible and noticeable across major religious traditions. I use an ethnographic case study of the mega amulet cult of Chatukham-Rammathep in Thailand to supplement my interpretation of how religious commodification has emerged as one of prominent aspects of private and public religious life. I propose that religious commodification as a key sociological concept and a form of complex religio-cultural phenomena must be understood through its contextualized backgrounds, processes, and implications. My stance is different from the view that modernization and commodification have either degraded or damaged religions. Rather, I suggest that religious commodification has produced some lively and open landscapes of interpretation across religious traditions and societies. To some extent, religious commodification exists everywhere as it forms a crucial part of complicated human religious ventures. Indeed, the rise and fall of a faith is inseparable from its marketable qualities and entrepreneur leadership. My argument is that religious commodification is a problematic, yet persistently growing field of sociological investigation particularly in the studies of post-9/11 public religion. The emergence of the sociology of religious commodification at the turn of the twenty-first century offers an alternative way and method for the sociology of religion to speak critically about complex tension and fragmentation of modern/postmodern social life. It also reflects how an academic discipline deals with the global explosion of religious faiths and movements at both conceptual and phenomenal levels.

TOWARD A SOCIOLOGY OF RELIGIOUS COMMODIFICATION

Religious commodification is a rising conceptual and methodological orientation with strong potentiality to help dissect what Grace Davie (2007: 1) calls "tension between global realities and sociological understanding." The highly dynamic market economy and religion convergence is created through market mechanism, technological advancement, and global flows of people, capitals, and information, including religious symbols and institutions. On the supply side, religions reinvent themselves in order to compete for attention and affiliation from "consumers" in the "spiritual marketplace" (Roof 1999; see also Einstein 2007). In addition, religious commodification entails multi-faceted processes involving an ever-increasing expansion of marketized religious faiths, pervasive fragmentation of social life, and proliferation of choices pertinent to "the modes of believing and the structure of sensibilities" (Ward 2006: 179). In short, religious commodification, while spurring production and consumption of marketized religious goods, has unveiled some widespread trends of refashioning pieties and inspiring prosperity. It strongly re-affirms the "continuing significance of religion in late modern society" (Dillon 2003: 4).

Religious commodification demands our attention and the sociology of religion significantly responds to them. In their discussion of American consumption of religious and spiritual material goods, Park and Baker (2007: 502) describe the considerable expansion of religious publications as "unnoticed by academics but not by mass audiences." This observation may correctly indicate some key aspects in the overall picture of the studies of religious commodification. However, with the presence of some major titles, like *God in Popular Culture* (Greeley 1988), *Selling God* (Moore 1994), *Spiritual Marketplace* (Roof 1999), *Jesus in Disneyland* (Lyon 2000), *Commodifying Everything* (Strasser 2003), *Branded Nation* (Twitchell 2004), *Investing in Miracles* (Wiegele 2005), *Brands of Faith* (Einstein 2007), *Shopping for God* (Twitchell 2007), and *Religious Commodifications in Asia* (Kitiarsa 2008a), it is difficult to ignore religious commodification as a field of sociological investigation. The commercial religious culture, religious consumption, marketized faith, and other forms of religious commodification are proliferating.

DEFINING RELIGIOUS COMMODIFICATION

Out of many areas of the current sociology of religious experience, the phenomena of religious commodification across major religious traditions have quietly but consistently attracted some scholarly attention. Mara Einstein (2007: 12, 14) reminds us about some crucial principles of religious commodification that market and religion are not at war against each other. Instead, religion adopts market logics. It has built its moral and spiritual empires based on market principle and model. Most modern evangelical religions always brand themselves as consuming packages with intent to conquest the world of religious marketplace. In other words, most religions aim at roaming and conquering the world. They take the world as their competing grounds.

What I mean by religious commodification is rather broad, inclusive, and complex historical and religio-cultural phenomena. The term itself implies sets of purposeful acts to convert religious symbols and institutions into marketable and consumable commodity despite the fact that profit and other forms of material gains are often carefully packaged and subtly placed underneath. By religious commodification, I mean an emerging multifaceted and multidimensional marketized process which turns a religious faith or tradition into consumable and marketable goods. It is an interactive and iterative relationship between religion and market, simultaneously involving both market force commodifying religion and religious institution taking part in marketplace and consuming culture. My definition concurs with Moore (1994: 5), who suggests that religious commodification in the USA Protestant context is embedded in "the ways in which churches have grown by participation in the market, or more specifically how religious influences established themselves in the form of commercial culture." Growing out of the historical juncture between market economy and a perennial ambition of mass expansion among leaders and communities of religious faiths, religious commodification gives birth to diverse forms of market and media channeled devotion and piety. It entails the process of how a religion takes the form of commodity and marks "a shift [in pieties at both individual and collective levels] from obligation to consumption" (Davie 2007: 144).

Elsewhere (Kitiarsa 2008b), I discuss some useful definitions of "religious commodification." According to *The Oxford Dictionary of English* (1989), it is defined as "the action of turning something into, or treating something as, a (mere) commodity; commercialization an activity, and so on, that is not by nature commercial" (OED 1989: 563). The English usage of "commodification" began only in the 1970s, even though the word "commodity" has existed since the fifteenth century. The most crucial idea deriving from this definition is perhaps centered on the phrase that "commercialization an activity, and so on, that is not commercial by nature." In *Commodifying Everything: Relationships of the Market,* Strasser (2003: 3) discusses this OED definition of commodification and goes on to suggest that "there is something ordinary or commonplace about commodities. Things and activities "not by nature commercial" are special, and commodifying them ... can get a culture into trouble." Religion appears to fit the bill. Commodification or commercialization has brought many religious traditions in trouble. It generates debates and creates tensions within religious communities and between religious authorities and the public. Indeed, the social life of any religion always encounters dilemma. By nature, religion stands and preaches against greed and vices rooted in desire, illusion and material madness. It perpetuates Durkheimian senses of moral community centered on the sacred binding and clothing people with "feeling, emotion, and compassion as foundations of moral action" (Turner 1991: xiii). Religious faiths and activities are not supposed to be involved in the business of making money, let alone being run by people with modern market strategies or being treated as commodities. In reality, most religions are unfortunately unable to resist the market force and culture. They are treated as consumer goods in the marketplace. Religion-market connection has been ever expanding and intensifying. In short, I suggest some growing possibility that "religious commodification helps redefine religions as market commodities as well as exchange in the spiritual marketplace. It further expanded the transnational connections of religious organizational and market networks" (Kitiarsa 2008b: 6).

CONTEXTUALIZING THE STUDIES OF RELIGIOUS COMMODIFICATION

An entry point to understand the academic merit of religious commodification is to take it as a complex historical and cultural process. In the words of Ward (2006: 184), "what we believe and the practices that produce, reinforce, and modify that believing are historically and culturally embedded." Religious commodification is by all means not an occurrence specifically meaningful to modern or postmodern religious conditions. As part of human religious experience, it has existed in both premodern and modern times. It has grown out of our socioeconomic life. It has become part of major events and ways of expressing our religiosity which have gradually structured and organized our religio-cultural world. Religious commodification is indeed a very old practice connoting the fact that religious leadership and community had to rely on socioeconomic power and other material support by engaging with or responding to religious demand of the mass. Religion cannot prosper without money and other strong material foundation. Although the birth and expansion of all faiths have involved certain forms and degrees of religious commodification from the very beginning, the "growing worldliness of religion" (Moore 1994: 3) has been more evident and produced socioeconomic and cultural impacts in the past two centuries, particularly in Protestant America and almost everywhere in the world beyond Northern and Western Europe where public religious affiliation has drastically decline (Berger 1999; Berger et al. 2008; Twitchell 2007).

Acts of turning religious elements into commodities, marketing them, and consuming them are rather perennial. Ward (2006: 185) suggests that religious commodication "is nothing new. Many of the great Medieval churches in Europe are built on the funds of the commodification of religion in terms of endowing chantries to sing masses for souls following death." He insists that "what is new is the technology that can facilitate a global systematization of this commodification. Now all and any specific religious tradition ... can be branded and sold worldview – Christian angels, Jewish kabbalah, the Hindu arts erotica, Confucian meditations, Haitian voodoo dolls, Islamic tiles, celtic blessings" (p. 185). It is not exactly the point that the advancement of science and technology would emancipate human beings from primitive belief and practice as the Enlightenment once promised. In contrary, the market logic involving in the commodification of religion and magic in our postmodern life reminds us that everything in the world is marketable with no exception to old or new religion or magic (Strasser 2003). "The belief in the operation of angels, demons, and the appearance of ghosts was a medieval commonplace, the object of enlightenment ridicule and is again finding support in certain contemporary sections of western society" (Ward 2006: 183). Putting aside a recent debate on *"Religious America, Secular Europe?"* (Berger et al. 2008), everywhere else on the globe, particularly in Asia and other Third World countries, Weber's classic statement that "the world remained a great enchanted garden"

(Weber 1963: 270) is still very much valid and highly significant. It is safe to say that propitiating and worshipping the sacred throughout the world are massively relevant to our contemporary social life. The explosion of large-scale religious commodification can only validate such popular religious practices. It complicates the process of growing worldliness of religions. It establishes religions more firmly within the realm of commodity relationship.

There is no doubt that religious commodification is part and parcel of modernization. Religion has always interacted and interwoven itself with modernizing forces, especially the state and the market. Commodification is the product of such a historical and cultural dialectical process. In her discussion of commodification as market-driven human enterprise, Strasser (2003: 3) argues that "there is no limits to the reach of the commodity relationship, and implicitly asking whether everything, indeed, can be commodified." When a religion is commodified through modern market institution, it shows the fact that religious community is ready to adjust itself to changes. Most religious traditions are capable of modernizing themselves. Bellah (1970: 72) reminds us more than three decades ago that "it has been impossible for religion to remain entirely indifferent to modernization." In Southeast Asian contexts, Alatas (1970: 270) reiterates a similar finding from the same era that "in the case of the great world religions such as Islam, Christianity, and Buddhism ... we may suggest that in some places they are neutral, in some places they encourage, but nowhere do they hinder modernization and economic development." This line of argument seems very much applicable to most religious traditions across the world at the turn of the twenty-first century.

Market and the emergence of consumerism are two widely cited factors, giving birth to, nurturing and shaping the rise of religious commodification. Market has become a major driving force in modern life and society. Weber (1947) reminds us long time ago that human beings were dominated by strong desires and efforts to make money. The market force, informed by certain religious ethos (i.e., the Protestant ethics), has produced some overwhelming effects on humans' life far beyond material acquisition and consumption. When Weber visited the USA in the early twentieth century, he described religious affiliation among European immigrants in America as "impressively strong church-mindedness" (Weber 1947: 303). Protestant ethics' influence was deep and pervasive on the American's life. He noted that "church affiliation in the USA brings with it incomparably higher financial burdens, especially for the poor, than anywhere in Germany" (p. 302) and "the question of religious affiliation was almost always posed in social life and in business life which depended on permanent and credit relations" (p. 303). For him, the Americans' economic success was a prime model of how the spirit of capitalism behind the powerful forces of Protestant ethics was developed and put to work. In other words, Protestant ethics' influence is one of fundamental aspects of the wide spread phenomena of religious commodification decades later.

Consumerism is another cornerstone of religious commodification. The late John Paul II once asserts that "consumerism more or less did to Western Europe what communism did to the East. Communism functioned by reducing people to mere servants of production. Consumerism does the same only in reverse; it makes them servants of consumption. In both cases the human person is reduced to an object of material things ... Thus they become enslaved in a lifestyle and a value system injurious to and diminishing their true vocation as human beings" (Conway 2006: 143). Following a similar line of thought, Loy (1997) describes how the churches particularly in the US contexts have participated in religious marketplace and general influence of market forces over modern life as "near complete commodification of the world." He argues that the post-Communist world has enthroned market as the supreme force with strong spiritual metaphors and connotations. "The collapse of communism makes it more apparent that the Market is becoming the first truly world religion, binding all corner of the globe into a worldview and set of values whose religious role we overlook only because we insist on seeing them as 'secular'" (Loy 1997: 1). Perhaps, the fiercest criticism of consumerism and global market influences over the church comes from the following statement delivered by Bishop Kenneth L. Carder of the United Methodist Church in Mississippi, USA, Carder (2001: 1). He argued that "the myths, rituals, and methods of the consumerist driven market have now invaded the church, been baptized by the church, ritualized by the church until the message of the gospel is so filtered through the consumerism of the global market that the Gospel of Jesus Christ itself has become another commodity to be exchanged for self-fulfillment, personal success, institutional advancement, and now even national security."

FUNDAMENTALISM, DE-SECULARISM, AND PIETISM

I further locate my discussion of religious commodification under three growing themes in the current sociological debates of human religious experiences, namely (1) global concerns over fundamentalism and militant religious movements, (2) some persisting criticisms over the secularization thesis, and (3) growing trends of privatizing piety and religiosity.

First, the study of religious commodification is often shadowed by the attention to religious fundamentalist and militant movements. As a global religio-cultural phenomenon, it seems to be uncharacteristically subsumed under the overwhelming public concerns of, and scholarly responses to, the emergence of global fundamental and militant religious movements. Dillon (2003: 3) observes that "the terrorist events of Tuesday morning, September 11, 2001, and their aftermath renewed our awareness that religion matters in contemporary times." The world since the 9/11 terrorist attack has paid more attention to radical religious fundamentalism and terrorism than the intensive interplay between religion and market. Commercializing or commodifying religion is a nightmare for orthodox religious gatekeepers, whether they are individuals or institutions. It is often viewed as a threat to religious orthodoxy and establishment. Its mundane outlook and money-involved activity are taken as signs to degrade the aura of canonical sacredness and orthodox religious sensitivity.

The sociology of religion has strongly revived at the turn of the twenty-first century. There is no greater stimulation to such a renewed scholarly interest than the global fundamentalist and terrorist threats and panic responses by policy makers and related authorities around the world. According to Jeff Haynes (1997: 719), "religious fundamentalists, feeling that their way of life under threat, aim to reform society in accordance with religious tenets: to change the laws, morality, social norms and, sometimes, the political configurations of the country." If generations of scholars had devoted their attention to the multiple impacts of modernization (secularization and civic religion in 1950s and 1960s and to new social movements and religious constructions of gender in 1970s and 1980s), fundamentalism and religions in the contexts of globalization and transnationalization have emerged major themes for the sociological investigation in 1990s and 2000s. The following are series of major works focusing on such themes, for example, *Fundamentalism* (Bruce 2000), *Global Fundamentalism* (Lechner 1993), *Holy War: The Rise of Christian, Jewish, and Islamic Fundamentalism* (New 2002), *Holy Wars: The Rise of Islamic Fundamentalism* (Hiro 1989), *Jihad vs. McWorld* (Barber 2003), *Religion and Globalization* (Beyer 1994), and *Religions in Global Society* (Beyer 2006), to name just a few. The sociology of religion as a site of knowledge production and a method of thinking about and understanding human religious experiences has become intellectually vibrant and politically relevant once again.

The post 9/11 world has produced some distinctive features of religio-political and economic landscapes. The sociology of religion furiously responds to such a global trend of change across international borders and over major religious traditions. Towards the end of the twentieth century and the beginning of the new millennium, the multiple subjects pertinent to religion have captured the interest and imagination of many anthropologists, political scientists, sociologists, and scholars across different disciplines. As a consequence of the waves of terrorist attacks by Islamic militants in places like New York, London, Madrid, Mumbai (India), Nairobi (Kenya), Karachi (Pakistan), Bali (Indonesia), etc., plus the US military campaigns in Afghanistan and Iraq, scholars studying the interfaces of religion and society have seriously turned their attention to investigate complex issues of ethno-religious fundamentalism and religion-inspired radical movements. The threat of fundamentalism and terrorism make religious and ethnocultural differences even more visible and critical in the multi-ethnocultural world.

Second, religious commodification subtly contests the secularization thesis. Market has become a major channel to gain access to, express, and spread popular religiosity. As a sociological concept, it is placed on the opposite side of the wall against the secularization stance. It demonstrates some paradoxical relationships to the preexisting thesis of secularization. The presence of religious goods and some enormous efforts to "sell" religious faiths via market and media channels have demonstrated the growing mundaneness of religious teaching and beliefs at the outset. Indeed, religious commodification has reiterated the weakness of secularization thesis and witnessed how the modern world is "as furiously religious as ever" (Berger 1992: 32), with perhaps an exceptional cases of Northern and Western Europe. In *Selling God: American Religion in the Marketplace of Culture*, Laurence Moore argues against the wrongfulness of the secularization thesis which assumes that "sectors of society and culture are removed from the domination of religious institutions and symbols" (Berger 1969: 107). Such modernist and secularist assumptions are "so dead wrong" (Moore 1994: 5). Nonetheless, the secularization thesis is not completely useless. He suggests that "much of what we usually mean by speaking of secularization has to do not with the disappearance of religion but its commodification" (Moore 1994: 5). With the market as an irresistible force of penetration, a religious faith has inevitably become worldlier and more secular.

Finally, religious commodification underscores the growing trend of the pietization of religion among modern/postmodern subjects. Taking religion as consumer goods has enabled individuals to personalize their piety and religious sensibility. Weber (1965: 44) reminds us that piety as a concept has its root in Christianity and Judaism, referring to "behavior acceptable to god." It "leads from the rational wish to insure personal external pleasures for oneself by performing acts pleasing to the god, to a view of sin as the unified power of the anti-divine ... into whose grasp man may fall" (p. 44). Belief and practice pertinent to religious piety connote the senses of reverence and obedience to God or gods. Privatized piety provides some greater freedom to the individual to choose a faith, make decisions on how to practice or express belief, perform religious duties and show a sense of belonging to a community of certain faith. Piety in this sense is a choice embedded and bounded by tradition and personal religious training. Piety allows an individual to make decisions to fulfill religious goals and to define selfhood by taking sides and rooting himself into a religious faith (Mahmood 2005). Berger (2008: 15) describes the pietization of spirituality in the consuming Western European world as follows: "I am religious, but I cannot identify with any existing church or religious tradition." Religious commodification offers one of the most accessible ways for individuals to consume as well as to actively engage in a certain religious faith rather than passively following or being born into a spiritual or religious community. Therefore, the privatization of religion has redefined the "given-ness qualities" (Geertz 1973) of religious traditions in the manners that fit desire and meet the demands of the late modern or postmodern social life.

THE MAKING OF MARKETABLE RELIGIOUS COMMODITIES

Three fundamental aspects of the sociology of religious commodification involve the following questions: what constitutes religious commodities? How a religion is transformed into sets of marketable goods? And why is religious commodification significant in understanding late modern or postmodern religiosity? The first question demands some detailed descriptions of actual religious goods available in everyday religious marketplaces. The second one asks for an elaboration of processes and forces in converting and transforming certain religious elements into commodities. The final inquiry seeks an explanation of the position of religious commodification in the contemporary world.

Religious goods come in various colors and shapes. Religious commodities can be categorized into many groups based on their physical, cultural/institutional, and symbolic properties. Most religious goods share common properties like other economic goods, such as scarcity, highly valued, or in demand such as, historical statues, images, and pieces of art work. Some are commodities embedded with both use and exchange values, such as publication, music, and clothes. Many are simply manufactured goods for mass markets like souvenirs, stickers and postcards. Others are fetishized products such as amulet and talisman, which are produced through special sacralized rituals and marketized procedures. However, these goods have possessed some distinctive features which set them apart from other general consumers' products.

First, religious commodities are closely associated to sacred biographies of the founders of the faith, major historical events, or marked localities. In this case, historic places, buildings, and events recorded in the cannons are major attractions to the followers. They can be easily turned into pilgrimage destinations and tourist attractions.

Second, many religious commodities are usually produced, controlled, and manipulated institutionally by certain organizations. Religious goods are the products of organized efforts. Institutionalization is one of the powerful machineries for religious branding, advertizing, and marketing. It guarantees historical authenticity and stimulates some genuine emotion and devotion. In reality, "churches, synagogues, temples, and mosques play an important role in the way every religion is shaped, even for people who are not in them" (Ammerman 2007: 8).

Third, religious commodities are filled with symbolic meanings, sacred quality, and charismatic reputations. Berger (1969: 26) defines "sacred" as "a quality of mysterious and awesome power, other than man and yet related to him, which is believed to reside in certain objects of experience." It is this sacred quality that makes a religious commodity out of a mundane object. Symbolism contains powerful religious messages and generates a sense of membership and identity. In this way, religious goods are made worship-able religious icons, especially in the cases of charismatic personalities. The owners of religious goods are often found themselves in powerful moods with special spiritual messages or supernatural sentiments.

Fourth, religious commodities are particularly promoted through public events like ritual, celebration, festival, and religious tourism. Producing, marketing, and consuming religious goods are fundamental aspects of popular religion. Publicly accessible religious events are important to display the effective use of religious goods. They have become occasional marketplaces, where buying, selling, and exchanging of religious commodities actually take place. Public events not only bring manufacturers, sellers, and consumers together, but also create mood and atmosphere which stimulate business exchange in the names of worshipping the sacred and expressing one's religious identity.

Finally, religious commodities are channeled to the public via mass media. In modern societies around the world, publicly accessible media, such as TV, radio, newspaper, or internet are employed as vehicles to advertise religious goods to mass society. With the power of mass media, religious goods are the most important part of what Ammerman (2007) calls "everyday religion."

The next question is concerned with methods or strategies in the making of certain religious commodities. Studies of current religious commodification across major religious traditions (Einstein 2007; Henn 2008; Iannaccone 1991; Jackson 1999a, 1999b; Roof 1999; Smith 2001; Twitchell 2004; Wiegele 2005; Wilson 2008) have revealed the following methods: (1) manufacturing and marketing religious goods with particular emphasis on charisma and extraordinary leadership, (2) publishing business for religious publications, (3) broadcasting religious messages and shows via mass media, including television, radio, newspapers, internet, and other online media, (4) commercial film, sport, and other forms of popular culture; (5) pilgrimage and religious tourism; (6) adopting business/market strategies of modern corporate firm, such as megachurches and other prosperity theology and cults. I do not mean to exhaust religious commodifying methods and strategies, but these methods adequately represent the major bulk of commodification methods in modern society.

Commodifying methods are widely found across religious traditions and societies. In the study of the commercialization of Thai Buddhism (*phuttha phanit*), I argue that such a process requires both venues and tactics, which are rooted in the history and religious culture of Thailand. Thai Buddhism is transformed into a commodity and widely marketized and consumed as a prosperity religion by the complex forces of capitalist economy and modern life style. Engined by the large-scale merit making industry, the prosperity cult of *phuttha phanit* represents a religio-cultural space where popular Buddhism has converged with the market economy, consumer practices, and the quest for personal and cultural identities (Kitiarsa 2008c: 120–1). In the study of the rise of El Shaddai and popular Catholicism in the Philippines, Wiegele (2005: 2) reports practices like seed-faith offerings, positive confession, and prayer requests for miracle and healing as methods to gain the movement's material success and popularity. In Japan, Reader and Tanabe (1998: 8) discover that "… the promise of this-worldly benefits is an intrinsic element within Japanese religion in general." Practical or worldly benefits are very important to attract the general public. "Buddhist temples have long been as active as the new religions in promoting the practical benefits that can be acquired through venerating their figures of worship and through prayers, petitions, and the purchase of talismans and amulets" (p. 8). In Islamic societies, such as in Indonesia, religious commodification is also increasingly visible. Muzakki (2008) reports the public sermon via broadcasting media such as TV and radio has become commercially involved. In the process, it has transformed Islam into symbolic commodity. Lukens-Bull (2008) also points out that young Indonesian Muslim use religious stickers to promote Islamic values and to express their everyday religious identities.

The widespread of marketized forms of religiosity gives us a firm idea that "religion is everywhere" and "religion in the marketplace of culture has become an ordinary commodity" (Moore 1994: 256). Religious commodification begs key questions: why does commodification rule the religious marketplace? What does religious commodification mean in the postmodern world? There are many possible ways to discuss some answers to these important questions. However, discussions about the issues pertinent to how and why religious commodification has become so imperative and prominent in the post or late modern world must start with the following premises.

First, the premise on specific characters of postmodern life and society. Religious commodification is product and process of postmodern conditions. Following Ward (2006), I use the term "postmodernity" as the sign of time and it is employed in studies of religious commodification as an index of changes in modes of believing and structure of sensibilities. Davie (2007: 144) suggests that there would be two forms of the sacred likely to emerge in postmodern times: one that affirms fragmentations and another creates islands of security. Her thoughtful words are worthy of quoting the full length:

What are the forms of the sacred most likely to flourish in late modernity and how can their relative success be explained ... Two possibilities emerged in this respects: on the one hand, the types of religion that followed or affirmed the fragmentations of late modern societies, including the many different manifestations of the new age; and on the other, the forms of religion that create islands of security with the uncertainties of rapid economic, social and cultural change, including a tendency towards fundamentalism. (Davie 2007: 144)

Postmodern life and society are characterized as highly uncertain and fragmented. It is implied from Davie's thesis that religious commodification is associated with fostering religious beliefs and practices which follow or affirm postmodern uncertainty and fragmentation. By the late twentieth century, the modernist theme on "tension between religious faith and modern western rationality" (Kurtz 1995: 7) seems to be less relevant. Religious commodification directs our attention to everyday practice and human experience of changing conditions which are often defined as turbulent, traumatic, and dislocating. It opens space of belief and redefines landscape of practice in which people embrace more relevant and consumable religious messages and goods with the assistance of technologies which fit their life style.

Second, the premise on consumers' identities and pleasure-seeking individuals. Religious commodification grows out of the fertile soil of consumerism. It is facilitated by market means of exchange and consumption. It is redesigned to fit the moral and spiritual needs of the postmodern social life, where people's religious piety and religiosity are drastically different from previous generations. Bauman (1995: 69) argues that "in the postmodern, consumer-oriented society, individuals are socially formed under the auspices of the pleasure-seeker or sensation-gatherer role instead of the producer/soldier role formative for the great majority of society member ... in the modern era." He further elaborates his point on new religiosity that "men and women haunted by uncertainty postmodern-style do not need preachers telling them about the weakness of man and the insufficiency of human resources. They need assurance that they can do it – and a brief as to how to do it" (Bauman 1998: 68–9).

Finally, the premise on market-religion convergence. I argue that religious commodification is a joint invention by religious institutions, market forces, and demand from consumer-cum-religious pleasure and identity seekers. Einstein (2007) asks the following sets of questions in her studies of branding faiths in American: why was religious shopping an expanding trend? Why were megachurches so popular? How did marketing play a part in this, and why was religious marketing proliferating now? Why religious marketing has proliferated? Her answers to these questions are: (1) religion is a product; (2) "religious products ... have become branded in much the same way that consumer products have been branded. Religious organizations have taken on names, logos or personalities, and slogans that allow them to be heard in a cluttered, increasingly competitive marketplace" (p. xi); (3) there is a high level of media saturation; and (4) people as religious consumers have more freedom to choose the religion of their choice (p. 7). Religious commodification grows out of the market-religion connection. They are more closely related than we could possibly imagine as illustrated in the case of a mega amulet cult in the following section.

RELIGIOUS COMMODIFICATION IN THAILAND: THE MEGA AMULET CRAZE OF CHATUKHAM-RAMMATHEP

The pluralistic situation is above all a market situation. In it religious institutions become consumer commodities. And ... a good deal of religious reality comes to be dominated by the logic of market economies. (Berger cited in Moore 1994: 7)

I draw an example of current religious commodification from the cases of prosperity cults in Thailand (Jackson 199a, 1999b). Investing in and consuming of series of religious goods is contagious in this mainland Southeast Asian country. Thailand is a flourishing Eden of popular religious cults and the Thai people are devout worshippers as much as consumers of marketized faiths. The popular cult of amulets in Thailand such as Chatukham-Rammathep has its deep roots in the traditional belief and practices concerning traditional magic and supernaturalism. Swearer (1987: 119) reminds us that between the tenth or eleventh century to the fifteenth century, the religious situation in mainland Southeast Asia "was fluid and informal, with Buddhism characterized more by miraculous relics and charismatic, magical monks than by organized sectarian traditions." According to Tambiah (1984: 5), "sacralized amulets in the form of small images of the Buddha or famous saints, or medallions struck with the faces and busts of the same, and amulets of other shapes and representation, are an old phenomenon." Soontravanich (2004: 4) suggests that worshipping of amulets, natural objects like *mai ruak* (species of small bamboo), cowry, jackfruit seed or *wan* (medicinal plant with or without roots), among the Thais must have begun "since prehistoric days and take a more sophisticated development with the advent of Hindu-Brahmanism and Buddhism." He further notes that "the pre-nineteenth century Thai amulets were non- or, at best, quasi-Buddhist." They were quasi-Buddhist amulets in the sense that they "were made or consecrated by Buddhist monks using Buddhist *mantra* and *yantra* mixed with indigenous and Hindu-Brahmanist sacred rituals, but none carried the image of Buddha or Buddhist saints" (p. 5). Indeed, beliefs in and practices of amulet and spirit worship, in principle, are immoral and against Buddha's teachings. Thai Buddhist scholars have often taken these cults as signifiers of crises involving the incompetence of the Buddhist Sangha, the penetration of consumerism and moral weakness of Thai society. (Phra Phaisan Visalo, 2003; Phra Dhammapitaka, 1995a, 1995b, 1996; Aeusrivongse 2002).

History and myth are chaotically intermingled in framing the stories behind most famous amulets. The plots in the stories behind the rise of amulet figures are concerned more with miracles than proven historical facts. They represent a "pluralistic, market situation" (Berger cited in Moore 1994: 7), which has proven a perfect ground for religious commodification. However, history and myth never completely or convincingly set themselves apart from one another because most mythical stories of most amulets need to be grounded in "known" ancient history or "sacred biographies" (Schober 1997) of Buddha or gods and goddesses from other religious traditions to validate their believability and creditability. This politics of modern historiography is important in understanding the influence of Protestantism on the cult of Chatukham-Rammathep.

The deities or devas (*thep*), whose names and legends have inspired the flourishing of this mega amulet cult, are usually of multiple origins. There are many versions of the stories of the origin of Chatukham and Rammathep. As the amulet's central logo, these two separate deities are often identified as the aliases to former rulers of the ancient Srivijaya Kingdom, a pan-Malay world ancient kingdom centered in Palembang, Sumatra (*The Nation*, April 17, 2007), which as many Thais claimed was located in contemporary Southern Thailand. Some authors link Chatukham and Rammathep legends to King Chantaraphanu and Phaya Srithamma Sokkarat, the founders of Nakhon Si Thammarat (Vallibhotama 2007; Sitthicharphutikun 2007; *The Nation*, April 17, 2007) and others relate them to the Brahmanistic devas or guardian spirits of the great Buddhist stupa at Wat Mahathat, whose names are "Khattukham" and "Rammathep" (Payangluang 2007; Kasetsiri 2007: 72). Many authors also present Maha Deva Chatukham and Rammathep as Avalokitesvara or a bodhisattva, who embodies the compassion of Buddha in the Mahayana Buddhist tradition (Payangluang, 2007). Chatchai Sukrakan and Pricha Noonsuk (cited in Rotphet, 2007) summarize the four possible sources of the origins of Chatukham-Rammathep as follows: (1) Avalokitesvara boddhisattava; (2) spirits of the kings who founded Nakhon Srithammarat, e.g., Chantharaphanu; (3) Brahma and Vishnu, the two guardians at the entrance of the great chedi; and (4) Khattukham and Rammathep, whose two statues are located besides the staircases of the chedi.

The flowering of the multiple versions of Chatukham-Rammathem stories shows that the production of this popular history has flourished outside and beyond the professional historian's authorization and monopolization. The histories of these two deities involve more legends and myths than history. Aeusrivongse (2007: 287) announces that "I do not trust the historical information behind the cult of Chatukham-Rammathep." As an authoritative figure in the modern Thai historiography, he believes that Thai-language research on the history and archeology of Srivijaya, ancient city of Ligor (Nakhon Si Thammarat's old name in Malay), or Hindu-Brahmanistic devas is far from adequate. The Thai public is fed with myths, legends or tales created by authors, spirit mediums, Buddhist monks or amulet specialists/traders associated with the commercialization of this mega amulet.

In the cult, it is often the case that "believing precedes rationality. Principle and logic are secondary to a devout belief" (Sitthicharphutikun 2007: 105). In contrast to the poverty of historical research on the cult, the production of Chatukham-Rammathep popular history is very intense and widespread. The cult of Chatukham-Rammathep owes its existence to a series of religious ceremonies associated with the establishment of Nakhon Si Thammarat's holy city pillar shrine (*lak muang*) and the search for its guardian in 1987. It is unusual that a historic city like Nakhon Si Thammarat was without a pillar shrine and the city leaders led by two prominent policemen, the late crime-buster Police Major General Phan Phantharak Ratchadet (Khun Phan) and the provincial police chief, Police Colonel Sanphet Thammathikun, took it as their joint responsibility for the city's spiritual stability and fertility to found the pillar shrin. Nakhon Si Thammarat in the mid-1980s was ranked among the top five cities with the highest crime rate in Thailand. Its leaders believed that the city had endured some bad omen since it had no formal holy pillar shrine, even though some took the grand chedi at Wat Mahathat as one. As many legends have it, Chatukham-Rammathep, the guardians of the grand chedi at Wat Phra

Mahathat, were identified through the mouthpiece of a spirit medium and chosen to serve at the new city pillar shrine (*Cho Chatukham-Khun Phan* 2007). The first batch of this mega amulet was consecrated and manufactured in order to provide funding support for the construction of the city pillar.

The consecration, manufacturing, and marketing of amulets to raise funds to support monastic and civic development projects is common in Thai Buddhist communities throughout the country. The 1987 Nakhon Si Thammarat's Lak Muang amulet was no exception. The master narrative of Chatukham-Rammathep's "amulet building" (*sang watthu mongkhon*) involved three key characters, who twenty years later would become legendary figures, namely, the late Khun Phan, Sanphet and Phong (also known as Ko Phong). The latter is the local Sino-Thai spirit medium. Khun Phan was a legendary crime-buster and a local hero who had built his life-long reputation as a man with genuine knowledge in magic, supernaturalism and traditional medicine. He was particularly famous for his magical invulnerability. Weapons can give him no harm due to his supernatural potency (*Cho Chatukham-Khun Phan* 2007). The first two men (Khun Phan and Sanphet) were the former leaders in the city's police force and attempted to restore stability and confidence of the public amidst of the spread of crimes in the areas. These three men served in the local committee, whose task was to set up the city's holy pillar shrine. The committee produced a batch of spectacular Chatukham Rammathep amulets, which were usually larger than regular Buddhist amulets with a size of "5 cm diameter and cost 39 Baht" (*Pattaya Daily News*, April 17, 2007). Soon, many local and Bangkok-based amulet collectors and specialists (*sian phra*) denounced the first-batch of Chatukham-Rammathep as "awkwardly big and not pretty" (*thoetha mai ngot ngam*) (*Cho Chatukham-Khun Phan* 2007: 10). The name of Chatukham-Rammathep was still unknown. The inquisitive response from the amulet-trade community was "who are the Chatukham and Rammathep?" Most amulet specialists, traders, and collectors often referred to the debut of Chatukham-Rammathep in late 1980s as an inconvenient free gift or souvenir from Nakhon Si Thammarat. Many people involved in the fund-raising tasks were forced to keep several boxes of the strange amulets (pp. 10–11). The old-style marketing of the first batch of Chatukham-Rammathep thus failed and it would take more creative and modern ways of promotion and advertisement to introduce this sacred product to the Thai religio-cultural marketplace.

FETISHIZING AND MARKETING A MEGA AMULET

An amulet is usually invented through delicate ritual as well as marketing means and the Chatukham-Rammathep is no exception. It was brought to life by a group of creators, sellers, and buyers or collectors. Its sacred reputation as a fetishized or an auspicious object with some extraordinary marketing values was largely spurred by a combination of some factors. First, this amulet is firmly associated with a very special place in the Thai Buddhist universe, Wat Mahathat Maha Worawihan, Nakhon Si Thammarat. The ancient chedi with its long history and deep-rooted legends renders itself as fertile soil for the amulet cult bearing the names of its guardian deities. Second, Chatukham-Rammathep has built up its fame and reputation on the shoulders of Khun Phan, a well respected, retired police and local magician. Khun Phan was as popular as Chatukham-Rammathep itself. Series of his images were reproduced and sold along with the amulets. His well-attended and widely publicized funeral in early 2007 demonstrated how well Chatukham-Rammathep had registered in the mind of the public (*Cho Chatukham-Khun Phan* 2007). Finally, Chatukham-Rammathep is perhaps the most intensively marketized and promoted religious commodity in the history of Thai amulets. Its marketing involves massive advertisement campaigns. According to Neilsen Media Research (Thailand), the period from January to March 2007 saw a boom in the Chatukham-Rammathep advertisements in major newspapers such as *Khao Sod Daily*, *Kom Chad Luek*, *Thai Rath*, *Daily News*, and *Matichon Daily*, with an estimated record revenue of more than 70 million Baht (around 2 million USD) (Janchitfah 2007).

As a mega business on the rise, Chatukham-Rammathep was peerless. As a commodity, the Chatukham-Rammathep amulets need to "satisfy their buyers" (Moore 1994: 10). It had grown like no other industry in 2006 and 2007, when the country's economic succession was in deep trouble due to the political instability. It was perhaps the only industry which showed some bright spot in the country with a reputation of inconsistent economic performance. Based on an estimation by Narong Bunsuaikhwan and Suwan Bandit, scholars from Walailak University in Nakhon Si Thammarat, in the past two decades, more than 80 million sets (*ong*) from a total of 400 batches (*run*) of this mega amulet were produced and circulated in the market (cited in Rotphet, 2007; Songsiri, 2007). This estimation is astounding: 80 million sets of Chatukham-Rammathep for a country of 65 million people. If the numbers hold true, this mega amulet has flooded the country by its sheer physical presence alone. A study carried out by the Research Centre of Thai Farmers' Bank estimates that there would be more than 300 batches and varieties of Chatukham-Rammathep in the amulet markets since its first presence in 1987. In 2007, the economic scale of this mega amulet industry was estimated at around 40 billion Baht (around $1.2 billion), creating jobs and incomes for people from different socioeconomic classes throughout the country. It also helped prolong the business lifeline for the mass media, printing (e.g., books, posters, and brochures), transportation, and local tourist industries (*Matichon Weekly*, 2007a: 76). *Matichon Weekly* (2007b: 9). The country's top news magazine described the "occult economy" created by Chatukham-Ramathep as "Chatukam-nomics" fueled by the "Theva[Deva] Marketing" strategies. Comaroff and Comaroff (2001: 19–23) remind us that the occult economy's common feature is "the allure of accruing wealth from nothing." Even though the nature of this undisclosed economy entails both material and ethical aspects, it often marks or sparks "the real or imagined production of value through … magical means." It is no surprise that people in the industry of Chatukham-Rammathep have carefully produced and packaged their amulet goods and turned to print (and internet) media to stimulate large-scale consumption. In these "print-as-commodities" (Anderson 1991: 37), miracle-filled stories and extraordinary images of deva amulets or talismans are very instrumental means to raise profits for people involving in the amulet and printing industries alike.

Thailand's amulet trade is an important example of what Marx (1992, ori. 1867) called "commodity fetishism." In Marxism, commodity is a key factor organizing the social life in the capitalist society. People's social relation is determined by market mechanism through dominant means of exchange such as money and commodities. However, the amulet, as an inanimate object worshipped for its supposed magical powers, assumes its fetish form through both religio-cultural processes and market economy institutions. Tambiah (1984: 5) suggests that there are two main processes turning sets of raw materials (*muan san*) into fetish objects of worship (*watthu mongkhon*): "the objectification and transmission of charisma." In the cult of Chatukham-Rammathep, these two processes are immensely intensified and elaborated through the advent of modern marketing promotion and massive advertisement campaigns through the country's top mass media channels.

A religious fetishized object is "animated with a will and mind of its own" (Taussig 1993: 218). The modern-day animation and fetishization of a religious object indeed requires very modern means of fetish-making and inventing. The fetishization of Chatukham-Rammathep is best illustrated by some tempting "ready-made" recipes. According to Inthep (2007: 14), the four strategic components essential to a successful marketing promotion of the Chatukham-Rammathep amulet include: (1) popular printing blocks (*phim di*); (2) raw materials that stand out (*muan san den*): (3) attractive and solid statement of intention of why and where the proceeds from selling Chatukham-Rammathep would go to (*chut prasong chatchen*); and (4) complete series of elaborated consecrated rituals (*phithi krop*) led by renowned masters of ceremony (mostly magic monks) (*chao phithi*). Indeed, these four components in the making of a Chutukham-Rammathep amulet are mechanical ritual processes of transforming simple sets of materials into animate objects of worship with expected magical power. Each component has previously existed in the Thai amulet tradition prior to the production of the first Chatukham-Rammathep in 1987. However, no amulet-making venture has ever reached the economic, political, and religious magnitude and scale of Chatukham-Rammathep.

CONCLUSION

In this chapter, I have discussed the emergence of the sociology of religious commodification, which I believe has become one of the key areas of investigation in the larger field of sociology of religion in recent decades. My argument on the increasing interest in the studies of religious commodification is accompanied by a detailed case study of the rise of the mega amulet industry in contemporary Thailand, particularly the cult of Chatukham-Rammathep. Religious commodification is driven by the postmodern condition. It responds to the uncertain and fragmented character of our contemporary social life. It deeply involves a process of turning religious faiths (e.g., material symbols, icons, institutions, historic places, etc.) into consumable goods, of marketing them through the use of a wide range of media, and of consuming such commodities by individuals or communities of certain faiths. People have diverse reasons to purchase and possess market-channeled religious goods, such as personal values, subjects of worship for supernatural beliefs, business investment, or identity markers.

However, religious commodification is a problematic concept. From the standpoints adopted by religious leaders and communities, religious commodification is generally viewed negatively. It ruins and is harmful since money and profit run against the foundation of the faiths. They argue that market participation by any faith shows the signs of its growing worldliness and of market domination. Therefore, religious commodification is counterproductive to religions, which have built around the aura of sacredness and timeless teachings. Market or commodity logics serve as an inconvenient truth, especially from the orthodox religious stance. From sociological perspectives, religious commodification has carried with it a sense of theoretical uneasiness. Commodification, marketization, or consumption of religious goods are evidence to counter modernist or secularist arguments. Market and media make religions more accessible to the public and convert religions into popular cultural practices in modern societies, but they are just fashionable trends, while other sectors of modern social life have increasingly rationalized and moved away from the influences of religious traditions or institutions. In addition, religious commodification is likely to subvert the theoretical authority of conventional approaches such as, charisma, fundamentalism, gender, piety, textual and symbolic analysis. Emphasizing on market logics and growing mundane aspects of religious life has invited some critical concern over an unnecessary focus on a rather superficial part of religious life.

My suggestion is that the problematization of the concept is debatable, but the sociology of religious commodification is on the rise. As a religio-cultural phenomenon, religious commodification is pervasive and imperative across religious traditions and societies throughout the world. As a sociological topic, religious commodification has the potential to fill intellectual gaps in the sociology of religion which is overwhelmed by studies of issues like fundamentalism, secularization or de-secularization, and the politics of piety.

Note

The author wishes to thank Bryan Turner for his academic guidance and encouragement. For the Romanized transcription of Thai-language terms, I follow the Royal Thai General System of Transcription (RTGS), sanctioned by the Royal Institute of Thailand (Ratchaban-dittayasathan), available at: www.royin.go.th/upload/246/FileUpload/416_2157.pdf, accessed May 23, 2009.

Bibliography

Aeusrivongse, N. (2002) Kon Yuk Phra Sri-an: Wa Duai Satsana Khwam Chuea Lae Sintham [Prior to the Era of Ariya Maitreya: On Religion, Belief, and Morality], Bangkok: Samnakphim Matichon.

Aeusrivongse, N. (2007) Chatukham Rammathep: Kho Sangket Chak Nidhi Aeusrivongse [Chatukham Rammathep: an observation from Nidhi Aeusrivongse], in Cho Chatukham-Khun Phan [Inside Chatukham-Khun Phan] (3rd printing), Bangkok: Samnakphim Matichon, 286–90.

Alatas. S. H. (1970) Religion and modernization in southeast Asia, Archives of European Sociology 11: 265–96.

Ammerman, N. T. (2007) Introduction, in N. T. Ammerman (ed.), Everyday Religion: Observing Modern Religious Lives, New York: Oxford University Press, 3–18.

Anderson, B. (1991) *Imagined Communities: Reflections on the Origin and Spread of Nationalism* (revd. edn.), London: Verso.

Appadurai, A. (ed.) (1986) *The Social Life of Things: Commodities in Cultural Perspective*, New York: Cambridge University Press.

Bangkok Post (2007) Jatukam fever reaches new heights, June 11.

Bauman, Z. (1995) *Life in Fragments*, Oxford: Blackwell.

Bauman, Z. (1998) Postmodern religion? in P. Heelas (ed.), *Religion, Modernity, and Postmodernit*, Oxford: Blackwell Publishers, 55–78.

Barber, B. R. (1995) *Jihad vs. McWorld*, New York: Times Books.

Barber, B. R. (2003) *Jihad vs. McWorld*, London: Corgi.

Bellah, R. N. (1970) *Beyond Belief: Essays on Religion in a Post-Traditional World*, New York: Harper and Row.

Berger, P. (1969) *The Social Reality of Religion*, London: Faber and Faber.

Berger, P. (1992) *A Far Glory: The Quest of Faith in an Age of Credulity*, New York: Doubleday.

Berger, P. (2008) Religious America, secular Europe?, in P. Berger, G. Davie, and E. Fokas (eds.), *Religious America, Secular Europe? A Theme and Variations*, Aldershot: Ashgate, 9–21.

Berger, P. (ed.) (1999) *The Desecularization of the World: Resurgent Religion and World Politics*, Grand Rapids: Eerdman.

Berger, P., Davie, G., and Fokas, E. (eds.) (2008) *Religious America, Secular Europe? A Theme and Variations*, Aldershot: Ashgate.

Beyer, P. (1994) *Religion and Globalization*, London: Sage.

Beyer, P. (2006) *Religions in Global Society*, London: Routledge.

Bruce, S. (2000) *Fundamentalism*, Malden: Polity Press.

Carder, K. L. (2001) Market and mission: competing visions for transforming ministry, *Hickman Lecture*, Duke Divinity School, www.pulpitandpew.duke.edu/kencarderlecture.pdf, accessed January 29, 2009.

Cho Chatukham-Khun Phan [Inside Chatukham-Khun Phan] (2007) Bangkok: Samnakphim Matichon (3rd printing).

Comaroff, J. and Comaroff, J. L. (2001) "Millennial capitalism: first thought on a second coming, in J. Comaroff and J.L. Comaroff (eds.), *Millennial Capitalism and the Culture of Neoliberalism*, Durham, NC: Duke University Press, 1–56.

Conway, E. (2006) The commodification of religion and the challenges for theology: reflections from the Irish experience, *Bulletin ET* 17 (1): 142–63.

Davie, G. (2007) *The Sociology of Religion*, London: Sage.

Dillon, M. (2003) The sociology of religion in late modernity, in M. Dillon (ed.), *Handbook of the Sociology of Religion*, Cambridge: Cambridge University Press, 3–15.

Einstein, M. (2007) *Brands of Faith: Marketing Religion in a Commercial Age*, London: Routledge.

Geertz, C. (1973) Religion as a cultural system, in *The Interpretation of Cultures: Selected Essays*, New York: Basic Books.

Greeley, A. M. (1988) *God in Popular Culture*, Chicago: Thomas More Press.

Haynes, J. (1997) Religion, secularization and politics: a postmodern conspectus, *Third World Quarterly* 18 (4): 709–28.

Henn, A. (2008) Crossroads of religions: shrines, mobility and urban space in Goa, *International Journal of Urban and Regional Research* 32 (3): 658–70.

Hiro, D. (1989) *Holy Wars: The Rise of Islamic Fundamentalism*, New York: Routledge.

Iannaccone, L. R. (1991) The consequences of religious market structure: Adam Smith and the economics of religion, *Rationality and Society* 3 (3): 156–77.

Inthep, P. (2007) Chatukham Lam Talat Khaeng Konlayut Sut Phitsadan [Chatukham roams the market with exotic competitive strategies], *Nation Sutsapda [The Nation Weekender]* 16, 790 (July 20): 14.

Jackson, P. A. (1999a) The enchanting spirit of Thai capitalism: the cult of Luang Phor Khoon and the post-modernization of Thai Buddhism, *South East Asia Research* 7 (1): 5–60.

Jackson, P. A. (1999b) Royal spirits, Chinese gods, and magic monks: Thailand's boom-time religions of prosperity, *South East Asia Research* 7 (1): 245–320.

Janchitfah, S. (2007) Marketing faith, *Bangkok Post* May 6.

Kasetsiri, C. (2007) Thao Khattukham Thao Rammathep [Khattukham and Rammathep Deities], *Matichon Sudsapda [Matichon Weekly]* 27, 1391 (June 1–7): 72.

Khomchadluek (2007) Chatukham Neu Manut [Human-flesh Chatukham Amulet], August 31.

Kitiarsa, P. (ed.) (2008a) *Religious Commodifications in Asia: Marketing Gods*, London: Routledge.

Kitiarsa, P. (2008b) Introduction: Asia's commodified sacred canopies, in P. Kitiarsa (ed.), *Religious Commodifications in Asia: Marketing Gods*, London: Routledge, 1–12.

Kitiarsa, P. (2008c) Buddha Phanit: Thailand's prosperity religion and its commodifying tactics, in P. Kitiarsa (ed.), *Religious Commodifications in Asia: Marketing Gods*, London: Routledge, 120–43.

Kurtz, L. (1995) *Gods in the Global Village: The World's Religions in Sociological Perspective*, Thousand Oaks: Pine Forge Press.

Lechner, F. J. (1993) *A Future for Religion? New Paradigms for Social Analysis*, Newbury Park: Sage.

Lechner, F. J. (2004) Global fundamentalism, in F. J. Lechner and J. Boli (eds.), *The Globalization Reader*, Malden: Blackwell, 326–9.

Loy, D. (1997) Religion and the market, www.religiousconsultation.org/loy.htm, accessed January 29, 2009.

Lukens-Bull, R. (2008) Commodification of religion and the religification of commodity: youth culture and religious identity, in P. Kitiarsa (ed.), *Religious Commodifications in Asia: Marketing Gods*, London: Routledge, 220–34.

Lyon, D. (2000) *Jesus in Disneyland: Religion in Postmodern Times*, Cambridge: Polity Press.

Mahmood, S. (2005) *Politics of Piety: The Islamic Revival and the Feminist Subject*, Princeton: Princeton University Press.

Marx, K. (1992) [1867] *Capital 1: A Critique of Political Economy*, New York: Penguin Classics.

Matichon Weekly (2007a) Patihan Chatukham-Rammathep [The miracles of Chatukham-Rammathep], 27, 1402 (June 29–July 5): 76.

Matichon Weekly (2007b) Sangkhom Sattha Chatukham-Rammathep Theva Marketing [The society's faith in Chatukham-Rammathep and the marketing of a Deva], 27, 1392 (April 20–6): 9.

Minkler, L. and Cosgel, M. M. (2004) Religious identity and consumption, *Economics Working Papers* Department of Economics, University of Connecticut, http://digitalcommons.uconn.edu/econ_wpapers/200403, accessed January 29, 2009.

Moore, R. L. (1994) *Selling God: American Religion in the Marketplace of Culture*, New York: Oxford University Press.

Muzakki, A. (2008) Islam as a symbolic commodity: transmitting and consuming Islam through public sermons in Indonesia, in P. Kitiarsa (ed.), *Religious Commodifications in Asia:Marketing Gods*, London: Routledge, 205–19.

New, D. S. (2002) *Holy War: The Rise of militant Christian, Jewish, and Islamic Fundamentalism*, Jefferson: McFarland & Co.

Oxford English Dictionary (OED) (1989) Oxford: Oxford University Press (2nd edn.)

Park, J.Z. and Baker, J. (2007) What would Jesus buy: American consumption of religious and spiritual material goods, *Journal of the Scientific Study of Religion* 46 (4): 501–17.

Pattaya Daily News (2007) April 17.

Payangluang, C. (2007) *Phra Thewarat Photthisat Chatukham Rammathep [Chatukham Rammathep. The Bodhisattva King]*, Nonthaburi, Thailand: Samnakphim Utthayan Khwam Ru.

Phra Brahmakhunaphon (P. A. Payutto) (2007) Ruang Phra Brahma, Phra Rahu, Phra Phikhanet ... Khon Thai Ao Thang Nan [Brahma, Rahula, Ganesh ... Thai people worship them all], *Matichon Sudsapda [Matichon Weekly]* 27, 1396 (May 18–24): 25.

Phra Dhammapitaka (P. A. Payutto) (1995a) *Sing Saksit, Thewarit Patihan [Sacred Object, Divine Power, Miracle]* (3rd printing), Bangkok: Munnithi Phutthatham.

Phra Dhammapitaka (P.A. Payutto) (1995b) *Khon Thai Long Thang Reu Rai [Do Thai People Lose Their Way?]* (2nd printing), Bangkok: Munnithi Phutthatham.

Phra Dhammapitaka (P.A. Payutto) (1996) *Sathanakan Phra Phuttha Satsana: Krasae Saiyasat [The Current Situations of Thai Buddhism: The Trends of Supernaturalism]* (2nd printing), Bangkok: Munnithi Phutthatham.

Phra Phaisan Visalo (2003) *Phuttha Satsana Thai Nai Anakhot: Naewnom Lae Thang Ok Chak Wikrit [Thai Buddhism in the Future: Trends and Solutions to the Crisis]* Bangkok: Munnithi Sotsri-Saritwong.

Reader, I. and Tanabe, G. J., Jr (1998) *Practically Religious: Worldly Benefits and the Common Religion of Japan*, Honolulu: University of Hawaii Press.

Roof, W. C. (1999) *Spiritual Marketplace: Baby Boomers and the Remaking of American Religion*. New Jersey: Princeton University Press.

Rotphet, S. (2007) Patihan ... Prakotkan Chatukham [Chatukham ... the Miracle and the Phenomenon], *Manager Online*, www.manager.co.th/asp-bin/PrintNews.aspx?NewsID=9500000062048, accessed June 18, 2008.

Schober, J. (ed.) (1997) *Sacred Biography in the Buddhist Traditions of South and Southeast Asia*, Honolulu: University of Hawaii Press.

Sitthicharphutikun, S. (2007) *Chatukham Rammathep: Thima, Khwam Chue Lae Sattha Haeng Rachan Thale Tai [Chatukham Rammathep: Origin, Belief and Faith in the King of the South Sea]*, Nonthaburi, Thailand: Samnakphim Namo.

Smith, J. A. (2001) Hollywood theology: the commodification in twentieth-century films, *Religion and American Culture* 11 (2): 191–231.

Songsiri, A. (2007) Update Truat Phaeng Chatukham [Checking stocks on Chatukham at the amulet market], *Khao Sod Daily*, April 26.

Strasser, S. (ed.) (2003) *Commodifying Everything: Relations of the Market*, New York: Routledge.

Soontravanich, C. (2004) The regionalization of local Buddhist saints: amulets and crime and violence in post-WW II Thai society, Bangkok: Chulalongkorn University, Faculty of Letters, Department of History (unpublished manuscript).

Swearer, D. K. (1987) Buddhism in southeast Asia, in J. M. Kitagawa (ed.), *The Religious Traditions of Asia*, New York: Macmillan Publishing Company, 119–42.

Tambiah, S. J. (1984) *The Buddhist Saints of the Forest and the Cult of Amulets: A Study in Charisma, Hagiography, Sectarianism and Millennial Buddhism*, Cambridge: Cambridge University Press.

Taussig, M. (1993) Maleficium: state fetishism, in Emily Apter and William Pietz (eds.), *Fetishism as Cultural Discourse*, Ithaca: Cornell University Press, 217–47.

Turner, B. S. (1991) *Religion and Social Theory*, London: Sage.

Twitchell, J. B. (2004) *Branded Nation: The Marketing of Megachurch, College Inc., and Museumworld*, New York: Simon and Schuster.

Twitchell, J. B. (2007) *Shopping for God: How Christianity Went from in Your Heart to in Your Face*, New York: Simon and Schuster.

Vallibhotama, S. (2007) Chatukham Nai Saita Srisak Vallibhotama [Chatukham as seen by Srisak Vallibhotama], in *Cho Chatukham-Khun Phan [Inside Chatukham-Khun Phan]* (3rd printing), Bangkok: Samnakphim Matichon, 277–85.

Ward, G. (2006) The future of religion, *Journal of the American Academy of Religion* 74 (1): 179–86.

Weber, M. (1947) The Protestant sects and the spirit of capitalism, in H. H. Gerth and C. W. Mills (eds.), *From Max Weber: Essays in Sociology*, London: Kegan Paul, Trench, Trubner, 302–22.

Weber, M. (1963; 1965) *The Sociology of Religion*, London: Methuen.

Wiegele, K. L. (2005) *Investing in Miracles: El Shaddai and the Transformation of Popular Catholicism in the Philippines*, Honolulu: University of Hawaii Press.

Wilson, A. (2008) The sacred geography of Bangkok's markets, *International Journal of Urban and Regional Research* 32 (3): 631–42.

26

Women and Piety Movements

RACHEL RINALDO

INTRODUCTION: WHAT IS A PIETY MOVEMENT?

One of the most significant developments of the latter part of the twentieth century was the emergence of religious piety movements around the globe. These movements, which are sometimes referred to as comprising a "religious revival," seek to reinvigorate religious teachings and practices, and have appeared within all the major religious traditions. What distinguishes these movements both from more conventional social movements and from more traditional forms of religious organization is not simply their tendency toward theological conservatism but their emphasis on pious practices. Since Durkheim, many sociologists have understood religion as arising from collective practices that instantiate morals and norms within members of society. More recently, the influence of theorists such as Bourdieu has encouraged social scientists to conceptualize religion less in terms of beliefs and more in terms of practices and habits (Turner 2008; Neitz 2004). This notion of religion as practice undergirds the work of recent scholars such as Mahmood, who maintains that piety movements are distinctive in their purposive cultivation of pious practices such as prayer or veiling (Mahmood 2005).

The term piety generally refers to religious or spiritual devotion. Contemporary usage of the word derives from the Pietist movement of the seventeenth and eighteenth centuries. This movement within German Lutheranism had strong influence on the development of Protestantism. The movement's founder, Philipp Jakob Spener, argued that arcane and divisive theological debates were marginalizing Christian life. He called instead for a return to Christian practices of devotion, greater involvement of the laity in the church, and increased study of the Bible (Stoeffler 1965; Lauchert 1911). Pietist was initially a pejorative term to describe this movement that aimed at the revival of lived Christianity and individual devotion. Pietism's emphasis on personal religious experience and emotion has carried on through the evangelical Protestant tradition. While Pietism peaked in the eighteenth century, scholars have argued that it had an important social impact by preparing the ground for theological rationalism and the individualism of the Enlightenment. Weber's best-known work drew a connection between the asceticism of Puritanism and the accumulation of wealth. Later, sociologist Robert Merton also argued for a correlation between Protestant pietism and the rise of modern science (Cohen 1990).

Some scholars have also drawn connections between the rise of Protestant piety and greater equality for women in the West. Peters (2003) argues that the gradual shift from Roman Catholic piety to Protestant piety in England offered new possibilities of identification for women. While women had a crucial role as household ritual practitioners in Catholicism, Christocentric piety also provided a role for women as religious specialists and perhaps more important, advocated a godly household built on ideas of parity and complementarity (p. 349). Similarly, Parish (1992) maintains that as the Reformation progressed in England female religious figures were active participants in religious debates, and that female piety was seen by ministers as having important political implications at a time of growing sectarianism and struggle.

Turner (2008), building on Weber, considers piety movements to be culturally creative, involving an increased emphasis on religious practices or the invention of practices that are claimed to be truly orthodox. Therefore, piety also requires changes in habits and practices in the material world. Moreover, according to Turner, piety not only creates new standards of behavior, but also creates competition over virtue. Following Turner, this chapter defines piety movements as primarily movements for religious reform. Although many pious movements contest the boundaries between religion and politics, explicitly political religious organizations, such as political parties or pressure groups, will not be discussed here.

Contemporary piety movements may or may not have explicit political aims. For example, while evangelical Christians in the United States are often associated with support for the Republican Party or conservative social mores, many evangelical churches also avoid political discussions or endorsements. Attempts to discern evangelical voting patterns have generated lengthy debates among social scientists (Abramowitz and Saunders 2008; Evans 2006, 2003; Regnerus et al. 1999). As this chapter will show, the relationship between piety movements and politics is complex and often indirect. Nevertheless, insistence on pious acts and morality in the public sphere has consequences for broader politics (Tong and Turner 2008). Some of the most important and visible consequences of piety movements are in the realm of gender.

Even the most cursory examination of contemporary piety movements indicates that women are active participants. As with traditional religion, women provide much of the lay membership, even if they are rarely leaders. This is surprising for many social scientists, given the socially conservative teachings and gender essentialism of many, though not all, of these movements. For many piety movements, in fact, gender is quite a central issue. Evangelical Christianity, for example, is marked by the insistence of many of its key public figures on male authority in the household. Women's participation in piety movements hence gives rise to a whole host of questions about why women participate (and which women), how piety movements affect gender ideologies and gender relations, and how piety movements influence culture and politics in general.

THREE MODES OF ANALYSIS

In this chapter, I outline three principal modes of analysis pursued by scholars studying women and piety movements. The literature on this topic is so vast that this chapter cannot possibly claim to be comprehensive. Therefore, my strategy is to highlight a number of influential and representative studies from a spectrum of religious and social contexts, with the greater focus on evangelical Christianity and revivalist Islam.[1] Because my own area of specialty is Indonesia, I draw special attention to studies of Asia. The literature cited crosses the often fuzzy boundaries between sociology, anthropology, religion, and gender studies, but it also speaks to core issues in sociology, especially the relationship between women, modernity, and religion. Although certainly there are vast differences between, for example, Islam in Egypt and Judaism in the United States, a creative juxtaposition of studies of these phenomena will reveal intriguing patterns that should interest scholars of social change and gender.

The conclusions drawn from surveying the literature in each of these sections lead me to suggest three broad theoretical suppositions that are intended to further scholarly debates. In the first section, I consider explanations of the broad structural factors propelling women's participation in piety movements. In the second section, I examine the growing number of studies which feature micro level explanations of women's involvement. This section analyzes not only the subjective appeal of piety movements for women, but also explores how participation affects women individually and collectively. Finally, I reflect on the consequences of such piety movements for gender relations and gender equality.

This chapter begins from the presupposition that religion and gender are not static elements in the lives of women. Just as gender relations are historically and culturally situated, so too are religious interpretations and practices. Religion is not necessarily the primary determinant of women's daily existences, but women in piety movements have often chosen to make it so. Nevertheless, both religions and gender norms are also increasingly influenced by transnational movements and global structures. To comprehend women's involvement in piety movements, we need to investigate women's often highly localized activities without losing sight of the global context.

PIETY MOVEMENTS IN THE LATE TWENTIETH CENTURY

Contemporary piety movements such as revivalist Islam, Protestant evangelicalism, and Hindu revivalism have their roots in late nineteenth and early twentieth century religious renewal efforts such as Muslim modernism in Egypt and the Arya Samaj organization in India. However, they began to attract greater attention in the 1980s in the wake of events such as the 1979 Iranian revolution, the rise of Islamic terrorism, and the ascendancy of evangelical Christians in American politics. By the 1980s, politicized religious movements such as the Muslim Brotherhood in the Middle East, the Christian Right in the USA, and Hindu Revivalism in India were clearly gaining influence in their respective regions. However, these movements were paralleled by a more generalized religious revival that was propelling many people into formal religious institutions like mosques and schools, but was also generating new informal religious organizations such as prayer groups (Beyer 1994; Kepel 1994; Huntington 1993).

By the early 1990s, it was clear from both scholarly and mass media accounts that women were becoming significant constituents of piety movements in nearly every major religious tradition. In the Middle East, women were rejecting the Westernized clothing of their parents and joining Islamic study groups; women in Southeast Asia were beginning to veil for the first time; women in Latin America and Africa were gravitating toward Pentecostalism and charismatic forms of Christianity; women in the USA were joining evangelical churches and demanding a return to Christian values, or conversely, discarding secular lifestyles in order to take on the strict disciplines of Orthodox Judaism; women in South Asia were joining militant Hindu revivalist organizations; and women in Buddhist countries were increasingly interested in Buddhist practices and beginning to press for ordination as nuns. Though these movements had little in common superficially, many scholars saw them as comparable assertions of cultural identity, reinventions of tradition, and expressions of anxiety about gender amidst rapid globalization and social change (Juergensmeyer 1994; Marty and Appleby 1994; Moghadam 1994).

Women's increasing participation in these movements inspired many novel studies of the gender politics of piety movements, especially those that called for a return to or renewal of traditional values. Scholars noted that gender was not incidental to piety movements of various kinds, but more often, a central preoccupation (Bayes and Tohidi 2001; Marty and Appleby 1994). In particular, authors sought to explore the return of veiling in the Middle East, and to explain the attraction of women in the modern West to the conservative gender ideologies espoused by evangelical churches and orthodox synagogues (Manning 1999; Griffiths 1997; Davidman 1993; Ahmed 1992; Mernissi 1992, 1987; Kaufman 1991; Klatch 1987). This burgeoning literature has produced continuing scholarly debates about religion and feminism, which will be addressed later in this article. But before exploring these ongoing debates, I turn to an exploration of the nature and implications of women's involvement in contemporary piety movements.

MACRO STRUCTURAL EXPLANATIONS

Numerous studies highlight transnational shifts such as modernity and globalization as explanations for women's participation in piety movement. Strikingly, scholars of Islamic revivalism and evangelical Christianity often stress similar aspects of these shifts: especially the unease produced by material affluence and greater inequality. The late twentieth century was marked by the increasing entrance of women into educational institutions and the formal economy, as well as declines in family size and rising age of marriage in many countries. Thus, many analysts also emphasize anxieties over changing gender roles and family structures in driving religious revivalism (Marty and Appleby 1994; Moghadam 1994), as well as the complex ways in which women and gender norms often serve as symbolic community boundaries (Bayes and Tohidi 2001; Ong 1995). Nevertheless, there are also important contrasts between women searching for refuge from dislocating social changes, and those who seek out their own ways of being modern.

An influential and relatively early account of the Islamic revival is Suzanne Brenner's "Reconstructing Self and Society: Javanese Muslim Women and 'the Veil'" (1996). Brenner claims that young, educated women in Indonesia are adopting the veil as part of a rebellion against tradition and against an authoritarian government. Veiling was uncommon in Indonesia until the late 1980s, when some women began adopting a style of veil copied from the Middle East. For these women, a new reformist version of Islam represents an alternative modernity, one that is not Western, yet is still cosmopolitan and forward looking. They reject both the traditions of their parents and the consumerism and hedonism they believe is fostered by the government's embrace of the West. In Islam, they find a vision of a horizontal global community, living by universal rules. While they are indeed motivated by what they see as the negative effects of modernity and especially of Indonesia's 1990s economic boom, they themselves are products of these changes. The women Brenner studies do not reject modernity *per se*, but are instead formulating their own ways of being modern.

A similar sense of longing to be modern, yet wanting to define modernity differently, pervades studies of women and the Islamic revival. In a more recent article on Indonesia, Adamson (2007) argues that mainstream Muslim organizations have adopted ideas of gender equality because they identify them as an essential criterion of modernity. Similarly, Deeb's (2006) study of Shi'a women in Beirut demonstrates that the notion of modernity is crucial to the self-understanding of the community. Like Brenner, Deeb shows how Shi'a women distinguish their new way of practicing Islam as one that depends on education, debate and public participation.

Another early explanation of women and the Islamic revival is Nilufer Göle's *The Forbidden Modern: Civilization and Veiling* (1996). For Göle, the turn to veiling and strict Islamic gender norms are part of a broader reaction against the Turkish state's enforced secularism. Yet much like the women in Brenner's account, the subjects of Göle's study are educated and articulate women who live quite modern lives. They are from families who have recently moved to urban areas, and they seek out opportunities for higher education and careers, while also acceding to male authority. As with the women in the accounts of Brenner and Deeb, the Turkish women in Göle's study reject modernity defined as Western and secular, but not modernity *per se*. Several years later, White's (2002) study of Islamist mobilization in urban Turkey finds that young women are attracted to particular styles of veiling that are seen as being modern and fashionable. Eager to participate in national political life, they define themselves both against the secular elite and against their rural forbears.

In a very different religious context, Jacobson (2006) finds that newly orthodox Jewish women in Buenos Aires are attracted to strict Orthodox Judaism because its emphasis on discipline and order allows them to think of themselves as denizens of the First World, resolving their anxieties about being citizens of a nation that they see as not fully modern. Anxiety plays a similarly critical role in an earlier study of women converts to Orthodox Judaism in the USA, Davidman (1993) contends that women seek out the rigid structures of pious religion as an antidote to the complexities, anomie, and disruptions of modern urban life.

Other scholars also emphasize the tensions of modernity as a critical element in women's involvement in piety movements. Smith-Hefner (2007, 2005) finds that a small but significant number of young women in a university city in Java choose to forgo courtship and romance, instead agreeing to marriages arranged by their Islamic study groups. As the average age of marriage has risen, and increasing numbers of women are entering higher education, more and more young Indonesians are experiencing being unmarried in their late teens and 20s. And increasingly, many live not with their parents, but in dormitory-like accommodation with other students. While some embrace their new freedoms, others seek moral order and structure in their lives. The young women Smith-Hefner studies are drawn to conservative Islamic study groups, and find refuge in arranged marriages from the worrisome freedoms of urban life. Yet, in a very modern way, the women emphasize that they enter these marriages out of choice rather than submission.

Chong (2006) argues that women in Korea are drawn to evangelical Christianity as a response to the crisis of the patriarchal family. South Korea's astounding economic development and rapid modernization have produced great tensions between patriarchal norms and new ideals of modern family relations that are more egalitarian. As elsewhere in Asia, women are increasingly entering higher education, and in many cases, professional careers, yet are still expected to fulfill the ideal of the self-sacrificing wife. In the evangelical church, women find spiritual and institutional resources for managing their dilemmas. Nevertheless, Chong maintains, women's principal coping strategy, an accommodation to religious patriarchy, ends up re-validating and re-legitimizing the conventional gender and family system.

Another macro approach to women and piety movements engages with the intersections of modernity, women, and the nation-state. Kandiyoti (1991) reminds us that the ways religions are practiced and understood are profoundly influenced by their interactions with nation-states. In both Turkey and Iran, discourses of women's rights have in various eras been discredited by their association with secular authoritarian states (Najmabadi 2000; Göle 2002, 1996). This seems to be a more general pattern across the Middle East and Asia, as secular nationalist regimes in the twentieth century identified women's progress with modernity and development (Esposito and Haddad 1998). Nevertheless, despite the lip service to women's equality, the benefits of these secular regimes often were limited to elite women, and even these privileged groups often felt constrained by restrictive state discourses of womanhood (Brenner 1998).

These last analyses touch on one of the remarkable commonalities of studies of women and piety movements from an incredible variety of contexts – that of social class. Although there is not much quantitative data on the topic, anecdotal evidence from these and other studies points to women of the urban lower middle to upper middle classes as constituting a major portion of the membership of piety movements, broadly defined. Yet this makes sense in light of the relationship between modernity and class, as one of the most significant hallmarks of economic development and integration into the global economy is the emergence of an urban middle class. While class cultures are historically and locally constituted, increasing affluence brings access to education, often for both genders. Not only do religious institutions often play an important role in education, but it is also frequently the case that religious participation requires a certain level of literacy and intellectual development. Thus, not only do religious institutions often help women to become middle class, but women of the middle classes are also educated well enough for the demands of religious piety.

Studies of women and piety movements indicate that women are drawn to such movements as a means to resolve issues of modernity and social change. Piety in most cases is seen as being modern, and the pious emphasis on discipline and order is often contrasted to traditional or local practices. While modernity produces great anxiety and tensions, piety movements allow women to both take refuge from dislocating changes and to formulate their own versions of modernity. While modernity is often implicitly conceptualized as secular, for many women modernity and piety go hand in hand.

MICRO EXPLANATIONS: AGENCY AND IDENTITY

Despite the power of structural explanations, there remain many gaps in the understanding of women's involvement in piety movements. Arguments about broader social anxieties related to changing gender and family norms don't necessarily explain how and why women are involved in pious mobilizations. Moreover, these accounts often fail to examine why it is that religious identities become prioritized, rather than ethnic or class identities. An increasing trend in scholarship on women and religion aims for a more thorough comprehension of the subjective appeal of piety, especially for individual women. These scholars ask not only why piety entices women, but how participation in piety movements changes or shapes women's consciousness.

Recent studies of women and piety movements employ ethnographic approaches to consider questions of subjectivity. A broad theme emerging from this body of work is that women derive personal agency from and are also drawn to the self-fashioning aspects of pious practices. While much recent literature focuses on Muslim women, studies of Christian and orthodox Jewish women present noticeably compatible conclusions about pious religion's appeal for women.

The most prominent recent example is Mahmood's (2005) study of women in an Egyptian Islamic piety movement. Mahmood argues that the subjectivity of the women she studies is not one in which the self is autonomous, but one in which the self is constructed within and through social norms. Nevertheless, the women in this movement demonstrate agency through their conscious efforts to cultivate properly pious selves. For Mahmood, the Egyptian women's piety movement shows that agency is not simply an issue of liberation or submission, but can also be about the work of producing a self.

Göle (1996) emphasizes the collective agency women find in pious religious practices. She maintains that Islamist women in Turkey are reconstituting Muslim female identity through their entrance into the public sphere. They define themselves against both tradition and Western versions of modernity, and present a challenge to the older secular elite. Indeed, Göle finds that political Islam in particular presents women with an activist role, emphasizing their participation in creating an Islamic society, while also reinforcing traditional and conservative gender norms.

While Göle concentrates on women's collective agency, Brenner (1996) also makes an important argument about piety and individual agency. While the young, educated Indonesian women in her study are drawn to Islam's universalism, they also find that it offers resources for creating modern selves. Confronted with rapid social change, inequality, and materialism, they embrace the disciplines of Islamic piety, such as prayer and veiling. They see these disciplines as essential parts of Islam's cosmopolitanism and universalism, which they prefer to the older, and more localized religious practices of their parents and grandparents. Like Mahmood, Brenner sees pious disciplines in Foucauldian terms as tools for self-fashioning which allow these women to negotiate an increasingly complicated social world.

Islam is certainly not the only religion that offers tools for producing selves. Chen (2005) finds that both Buddhism and Christianity allow immigrant Taiwanese women in the United States to fashion selves that conform to the values and expectations of their new lives. Another comparative study by Read and Bartkowski (2003, 2000), argues that evangelical Protestant and Muslim women, also in the United States, each draw on the unique cultural repertoires of their religious backgrounds to negotiate changing gender roles and craft their own religious identities.

While there are relatively few studies of women in Buddhist piety movements, the rising intermingling of Buddhism and politics in South Asia and mainland Southeast Asia is drawing the attention of scholars. One of the most interesting developments here has been the increasing interest of women in Theravada Buddhism, particularly in Thailand, Nepal, and Sri Lanka, where women have been demanding ordination into monastic life since the early 1990s (Falk 2008; Findly 2000; Bartholomeusz 1992). Additionally, in some regions of India, Dalit women have converted to Buddhism as part of a search for a voice in the public sphere (Lynch 2000). Many of the women in these studies aim to disseminate more feminist interpretations of Buddhism, and scholars view these movements as part of a broader push for greater female religious authority.

When it comes to Christianity, many authors have emphasized the individual agency women find in religion. Griffiths (1997) maintains that women find freedom from feelings of victimization and an increased sense of personal responsibility in the evangelical subculture. The women Griffiths studies find that developing a relationship with God is a way to come to terms with painful life experiences, family problems, and often unfulfilled desires for intimacy. Brasher (1998) also argues for the importance of evangelical religion in healing the strains of modern life for women. For Griffiths, Brasher, as well as Chong (2008), the communitarian aspects of evangelical Christianity, the spiritual emphasis on a personal relationship to God, and the sense of being able to recover an authentic self, produce feelings of individual agency and empowerment for many women, despite the acceptance of disempowering gender norms.

Pentecostalism, a form of charismatic Christianity that has rapidly gained popularity in Latin America and Africa, seems to have a special appeal to women (Martin 2001). While Pentecostals also espouse an ideology of male domination, scholars note that Pentecostal churches foster female services and prayer groups, allowing women to develop social relationships outside their kin networks (Brusco 1995).

Some scholars have also argued that Pentecostalism's emphasis on asceticism and moral behavior also helps to stigmatize men's behaviors such as drinking and gambling, giving women greater autonomy in household affairs (Smilde 1997; Brusco 1995). Smilde (1997) further maintains that women converts to Pentecostalism in Venezuela see themselves as obedient primarily to God, which greatly limits men's claims to authority and gives women an enhanced sense of their own position in the household.

Scholars of Judaism have also turned to explorations of agency and identity to understand the appeal of Orthodox versions of the religion to women. Avishai (2008) maintains that for pious women, agency must be understood as the conduct and practice of religious ritual. Davidman (1993) shows how Jewish women converts find a "fit" with particular Orthodox communities, which present them with different strategies for accommodating or not accommodating to the secular world. In the process, they fill the voids in their lives and create new identities as Orthodox women. Kaufman (1991) also sees the turn to Orthodoxy as part of a search for female identity and an urge to reconstruct traditional families. Kaufman maintains that Orthodox Judaism's appeal to women is exactly its essentialist gender ideology.

These questions of agency and identity are clearly at the core of contemporary piety movements. But before moving on to the relationship between piety movements and the construction of community, I will delve further into one of the more contentious debates in the literature on women and religious piety: the veil.

THE VEIL

A significant and continuing debate within studies of women and piety movements revolves around the issue of Muslim women's veiling. Beginning with initial questions of the social meanings of veiling, researchers turned their attention to why women veil. As veiling initially gained popularity in the Middle East in the late 1970s and early 1980s, the reaction from feminists was overwhelmingly negative. Early critics such as Mernissi (1987) contended that the push for veiling represented a reassertion of patriarchy on the part of a generation of men for whom the state had failed to provide economic opportunities. Although this argument still has traction in some quarters, scholars of the Middle East soon turned their attention to the women themselves. An important response to Mernissi's claims soon came from Ahmed (1992), who argued that veiling only became an issue because of a colonial discourse in which the veil was considered the primary exemplar of the backwardness of Islam, and that women were now taking up the veil as a symbol of anti-colonial and anti-Western identity.

Veiling has a very different meaning where it is mandatory, as is famously the case in contemporary Iran. During the 1979 revolution, many women eagerly donned the veil as a symbol of their resistance to the secular authoritarian regime of the Shah. An important feature of the revolution was a discourse that placed women at the center of the struggle between Iran and the West. Scholars have described how women were depicted as having lost their dignity during the years of Westernization. Nevertheless, many women were apparently surprised when veiling became mandatory under the new Islamic regime. The rationale was that women's bodies needed to be protected and Islamicized by veiling in public (Moghadam 2003; Najmabadi 2000; Afshar 1998).

Missing from the scholarly debates thus far was much discussion of religious belief or the voices of veiled women. In the late 1980s and early 1990s, however, a new generation of researchers began to ask women why they veiled and how it affected their lives. Macleod (1993, 1992) observed that in urbanizing Egypt, where more women were moving into the formal workforce, veiling is a means for women to assert control over an ambiguous moral situation. She argues that veiling empowers lower middle-class women by blurring class distinctions and affording women enhanced mobility in public spaces.

Nilufer Göle (1996) and Brenner (1996), listening carefully to what Turkish and Indonesian women say about why they adopt the veil, return to the issue of modernity. While veiling has long been practiced in rural areas in Turkey, it was uncommon until the early 1980s in most parts of Indonesia. Yet it has taken hold among the new, urbanizing middle classes in both countries. In both cases, young women are eager to contest definitions of modernity as secular and Western. Both of these accounts emphasize the agency of a new generation of educated women who choose to be pious. In particular, Brenner's account highlights women's attraction to the bodily discipline required by Islam's conventions of female modesty and rigorous prayer schedules. For Brenner, the urge to exert control over one's body and desires is a response to a rapidly changing and increasingly consumerist society.

In a fascinating update on veiling practices in Java, Smith-Hefner (2007) proposes that veiling continues to be a way for young Muslim women to reconcile their new opportunities for individual autonomy and personal choice with their heightened commitment to pious Islam. Noting that veiling has become hegemonic for female medical and technical students, who are positioned to reap the benefits of economic development, Smith-Hefner argues that for middle-class Javanese the veil is a symbol of modern Muslim womanhood. It permits young women to live away from home and have professional careers, helping them resolve their anxieties about moving into what were once predominantly male spaces (p. 415).

The veil is also central to Mahmood's (2005) argument about women and Islamic subjectivity. Mahmood criticizes scholars who conceptualize veiling as an expression of identity. For Mahmood, veiling is one of the most important ways for women to produce themselves as pious subjects. Rather than putting on the veil to express their Islamic identities, she argues that women veil in order to become proper Muslims. Thus, women's selves are not separate from the social world, but produced through interaction with its norms. Mahmood sees this form of personhood as radically different from the normative personhood of the West, or even of the nationalist/secular orientation in Egypt, in which veiling is often a symbol of a religious or cultural identity.

Aihwa Ong (1995) presents a more critical view of the rise of veiling in Malaysia in the late 1980s. For Ong, veiling must be understood within Malaysia's highly charged religious and political context. Ong contends that economic modernization in Malaysia, which has involved large numbers of women working in factories, has intensified anxieties about gender and family, as well as religious and ethnic borders. Both the state and Islamic revivalists seek to control women's bodies as the bearers of Malay ethnic identity, and thereby produce a community in which Malay and Muslim are equated.

More recent accounts by scholars of Malaysia (Mouser 2007; Stivens 2006) also present veiling as the most visible symbol of an ongoing process of Islamization, in which gender relations and notions of the family are critical sites for the production of a purer Islam. Nevertheless, while the veil carries important social meanings, Mouser also emphasizes that Malay women use it in a variety of ways to express their own understandings of their social positions and personal freedoms.

The veil has also become increasingly common in Muslim communities across South Asia. Much like Southeast Asia, South Asian women began to veil in the context of a widespread Islamic revival in the 1990s and early 2000s. Huq and Rashid (2008), studying elite women in a Quranic reading class, find that such women strongly believe that veiling is required for Muslim women, and that it is a social market of religiosity. They argue that the switch to veiling, part of the adoption of other pious Islamic rituals, cuts women off from their pasts, but also gives women a sense of being agents in their own lives, allowing them to assert themselves in their families and social surroundings. Nevertheless, Rosario (2006) warns of the consequences as veiling becomes hegemonic, pointing out that most Bangladeshi women are far from elite, and that there is increasing pressure and harassment of women who do not veil.

While veiling has been framed as a pious religious practice, it has also clearly become a fashion trend. Veiling, of course, rarely means simply wearing the veil. In most countries, to wear the veil also requires a woman to adopt modest clothing, which runs the gamut from Western styles to the notorious *burka* to avant-garde interpretations of traditional garments. Scholars have now begun to examine the veil as a commodity, with designers selling high-priced "Muslim clothing" to wealthy women and luxury hotels featuring Muslim fashion shows. Jones (2007) describes how Islamic clothing in Indonesia now comes in multiple styles and allows women to express their individuality. Amrullah (2008) explores the transnational elements of Indonesian Islamic fashion, and White (2002) demonstrates how particular styles of veiling are closely associated with status distinctions in Turkey.

Recently, scholars have also begun to focus on veiling among Muslim women in North America and Europe. A common observation is that Muslim forms of public self-presentation, especially veiling, clash with liberal public discourses that insist on a secular public sphere (Ismail 2008). Although much attention has centered on state responses to veiling, especially in the case of France (Bowen 2007, Scott 2007), other observers have also parsed themes of identity and piety in relation to veiling. Read and Bartkowski (2003), for example, observe that debates between traditionalists and feminists have emerged among American Muslim women, particularly regarding the issue of veiling. They find that women exhibit remarkable agency in crafting religious identities that draw on their religious faith and the cultural tools that are available to them. In this case, gender traditionalism is manifested through practices like veiling. Yet, influenced by global discourses of Islamic feminism, some women contest the conflation of piety and the veil, arguing that veiling is simply a cultural symbol. These women argue that Muslim women can be true to their religious heritage without veiling.

The debates around veiling reveal that in societies where it is not mandatory, it carries a multiplicity of meanings that are decidedly context dependent. What is clear is that many women make a conscious choice to veil. Though media stereotypes of women being forced to veil persist, nearly all of these empirical studies demonstrate that women see veiling as a form of religious commitment and/or a way of expressing religious identity. This is not to say that veiling does not have broader social outcomes, which I will discuss in the section on "Consequences of Piety Movements." But very much like participation in piety movements more generally, women's veiling can be understood as pious self-fashioning, and as such, a form of agency.

COMMUNITY AND IDENTITY

Women's piety is also linked to the creation of new forms of identity and community. Religious movements, after all, are a form of collective action, and not simply a matter of individual selves. Another striking parallel between studies of women's involvement in piety movements in different parts of the world is the way in which these movements produce new kinds of collective identities.

For example, many scholars (Smith 1998; Manning 1999; Griffiths 1997) view evangelicalism in the United States as a religious subculture. According to some who represent this line of thought, conservative gender ideologies among evangelicals are not as much a reaction to specific social changes as they are a product of a broader conservatism that is a symbolic boundary marker of evangelical cultural identity. Gallagher (2004) probes gender ideologies further to suggest that it is not anti-feminism, but rather, a commitment to male household authority that is vital to constructing the symbolic boundaries of evangelical Protestant identity.

Some scholars also emphasize the ways in which religious piety contributes to the formation of gendered communities. Brasher (1998) maintains that gender segregation in fundamentalist churches allows women to create their own sacred spaces. These communities, according to Brasher, give women stronger social networks and even provide them with the basis for political coalitions. Numerous scholars have also commented on how Islamic study and prayer groups allow women to have autonomy and even certain forms of power within their own gendered spaces (Hegland 2003, 1998; Metcalf 1998; Bernal 1994).

Gender, piety, and community are also linked productively in Deeb's (2006) study of a Shi'a community in Beirut, Lebanon. Deeb shows how women's piety, expressed through veiling and participation in public events and social service work, is essential to the community's conception of itself. She argues that that women's public participation is a marker of morality and modernity by which women are judged within the community, and by which the community also feels that it is judged internationally. Thus, while pious Islam generally buttresses conventional male authority, Deeb maintains that it also provides women with a new and significant public role.

For Chen (2006), evangelical churches foster community by reconstructing family relations. Chen argues that evangelical Christianity democratizes family relationships among Taiwanese immigrants to the USA, a process which also mediates cultural assimilation. While this article does not focus on gender, it is clear that women are leading the turn to Christianity among Asian immigrant groups, partly as a means of managing the complexities of cultural adaptation.

Other writers explore the ways pious religions and gender are intertwined in the construction of new forms of national or transnational communities. This seems to be especially true for Islam, perhaps because gender was often such a central aspect of the colonizing mission in predominantly Muslim countries. Colonial discourses depicted the colonized as backwards because of their treatment of women. From this period onward, gender has been at the heart of the way many former colonies have attempted to differentiate and define their national identities (Esposito and Haddad 1998). In countries which have undergone Islamic revivals, gendered forms of piety are part of defining new identities and collectivities. For example, Brenner (1996) argues that young Indonesian women are attracted to Islam precisely because they perceive it as global. They are eager to identify with an international community of Muslims, and they do so by wearing the veil and practicing Islam in an orthodox manner recognizable to other Muslims around the world. In doing so, they reject both local and state-dominated constructions of womanhood.

Ahmad (2008) finds that women in a piety movement in Pakistan seek to create a stronger Muslim identity through practicing Islam in a stricter manner than has been the country's norm. They adopt Middle Eastern style Muslim clothing and attempt to eliminate all foreign and un-Islamic practices from their lives. While Pakistan has long been majority Muslim, it also has substantial religious minorities, and cultural ties to the rest of South Asia. But the women in Ahmad's study position Pakistan and Muslim as inseparable, emphasizing Pakistan as part of a homogenous and global Muslim culture.

Nevertheless, this urge to construct new forms of community is not limited to Islam. While the Hindu nationalist movement in India is not strictly a piety movement, it is part of a broader pious revival, and for our purposes, it also illustrates the way concerns about community play out on the terrain of religion and gender. Bacchetta (1996) describes how women of the Samiti organization create their feminine Hindu nationalist discourses and their own ideas of what a Hindu nation should mean. In her more recent book, *Gender in the Hindu Nation* (2004), Bacchetta further develops her ideas to demonstrate how women define agency for themselves within the Hindu nationalist ideological structure by positioning Muslims as threatening and often sexualized others.

Stemming from the work of Durkheim, the connection between pious ritual and community has a long tradition in sociology and anthropology. Tong and Turner (2008) explore the gendered aspects of this intersection in Malaysia. They argue that the cultivation of virtuous selves through gender specific religious practices serves to define community membership in the religiously plural Malaysian context. Rituals such as veiling, prayer, and food taboos define a religious *habitus* that is the basis for a group identity, as such norms also work to exclude those who do not follow them.

The relationship between women, piety, agency, and community is certainly not straightforward. Practices of religious piety can facilitate the construction of communities as well as the enforcement of boundaries to exclude others. However, it is clear from even this limited overview of the literature that piety movements often provide women with a sense of agency and personal responsibility, especially in terms of fashioning new selves. Many women therefore feel empowered by participation in such movements. Beyond the cultivation of selves, the collective aspects of piety movements facilitate women in the process of constructing new kinds of communities and social identities.

CONSEQUENCES OF PIETY MOVEMENTS FOR GENDER RELATIONS

Perhaps the most complicated but crucial question for social scientists is what consequences piety movements have for gender relations, as well as their implications for egalitarian or progressive social change. While some scholars take fixed positions on one side or another, most studies emphasize the multiple and sometimes contradictory outcomes of these movements when it comes to gender. Moreover, piety movements have also produced feminist strands, giving rise to both activist and scholarly debates about religion and feminism.

One of the feminist variants which has most intrigued scholars is the movement which has variously been called Muslim or Islamic or Islamist feminism. Though there is disagreement on how to characterize different streams of this movement, scholars have identified a category of pious women who struggle for gender equality from within an Islamic framework (Rinaldo 2008; Mir-Hosseini 2006; Moghadam 2006; Badran 2005; Karam 1998; Afshar 1998). Some of these women embrace the label of feminist, while others reject it for its Western and secular baggage. Another, perhaps larger and overlapping category, does not necessarily see gender equality as Islamic, but argues for greater empowerment and involvement of women in Islamic life (Van Doorn-Harder 2006; Foley 2004). Whatever they are called, Muslim women activists have established transnational networks, and the writings of internationally recognized scholars and theologians such as Fatima Mernissi, Riffat Hassan, Ali Asghar Engineer, and Asma Barlas have significantly influenced their work. Not surprisingly, the organizations that represent these strands tend to be composed of well-educated, urban women. Muslim feminists indeed exert some influence in discourses about Islam and gender. For example, in Indonesia and Malaysia, they speak out against the growing popularity of polygamy by holding public demonstrations, and writing articles and editorials in the mass media (Brenner 2006; Foley 2004). In these countries, Muslim women have indeed challenged the notion that polygamy is intrinsic to Islam. Nevertheless, it is not yet clear whether their activities have much impact on the empowerment of women more generally.

One point on which many scholars agree is that women's involvement in piety movements can lead to greater women's participation in both religious institutions and in the public sphere more broadly. This seems to be especially the case in parts of the world where women have historically not had leadership positions in religion and where women's access to public spaces has been limited. For example, Van Doorn-Harder's (2006) study of Indonesia indicates that women are taking an increasingly active role in Islamic institutions. They are learning to read and interpret Islamic texts, and are passing this knowledge on to other women. Van Doorn-Harder contends that although Muslim women do not agree politically, they share a commitment to women's greater involvement in the religion. She holds that their growing knowledge allows them to debate with extremists who hold much more conservative views about gender, and that they are able to capitalize on opportunities to advocate gender-sensitive and/or egalitarian interpretations of the religion.

Early academic work on women and religious piety tends to depict such movements as either largely empowering or disempowering. Afary (1997), Moghadam (1994), Yuval-Davis and Anthias (1989) and many other feminist scholars initially viewed religious revival movements as attempts to reassert patriarchal control over women. While these scholars certainly raised concerns that are still very much valid, such work was often limited by a strong secular bias or by inattention to the voices of pious women. Responding to these concerns, and drawing on ethnographic fieldwork, authors such as Macleod (1992), Brenner (1996), Brasher (1998), and Griffiths (1997) emphasize the empowering aspects of such movements, highlighting the ways piety movements give women mobility in public space, provide community and healing, and facilitate self-cultivation.

An increasingly significant direction in scholarly approaches to women and religious piety recognizes that pious movements often empower women in certain ways, or empower particular groups of women, but also acknowledges that these movements may also buttress existing conservative gender ideologies, or in some cases, popularize more conservative gender norms (Chong 2006; Deeb 2006; Jacobson 2006; Gole 1996; Davidman 1993). Brenner's (2006, 2005) recent work illuminates the ways in which greater democracy in Indonesia has not brought about women's empowerment, partly because Islamist groups have capitalized on political decentralization to enforce more conservative gender practices, such as requiring women to observe night-time curfews or requiring them to wear Islamic clothing. These authors perhaps provide the most comprehensive and nuanced overviews of how pious women's activities affect gender and politics. Moreover, writers are also beginning to pay greater attention to how gendered pious practices reinforce religious, ethnic, or class boundaries (Tong and Turner 2008; Rinaldo 2008). This more complex understanding of the gender consequences of religious revival is certainly significant for a more sociological understanding of the relationship between religious movements and social change.

Recently, scholars have also attempted to use women's participation in religious movements to rethink the connections between piety and politics. In particular, both Mahmood (2005) and Göle (2002) argue that Muslim women's pious practices contest liberal norms of society and personhood. Such women position Islam firmly in the public sphere, challenging the link between modernity and the secular, and they insist that Islamic norms define who they are as people. They find agency in compliance with Islam rather than in individual liberty or autonomy. Along very similar lines, Avishai (2008) maintains that for Orthodox Jewish Israeli women, agency is in the "doing" or conduct of religious practice. Once again, this is a rather different conception of what it means to be an agent than we often find in the sociological literature, which relies heavily on Westerns traditions of the rational subject. But beyond the issue of contesting liberal norms, these scholars give us little sense of the actual day-to-day social consequences of women's involvement in piety movements.

Nevertheless, the continuing focus on agency with respect to women and piety movements has led scholars to some significant innovations. In their well-known introduction to an edited volume on religious politics and women in South Asia, Basu and Jeffery (1997) conclude that women's agency does not necessarily mean women's empowerment more generally. Pointing to the rising involvement of women in the Hindu right, Basu and Jeffery conclude that the empowerment of some women may result in the disempowerment of others. Moreover, the Hindu right and other religious nationalist movements' incorporation of women helps to legitimize and further propagate conservative ideologies of gender. Similarly, Rosario (2006) concludes from her study of veiling in Bangladesh that individual women's empowerment may be at odds with structural empowerment. Mahmood's (2005) consideration of agency has therefore been especially important in reminding scholars that agency in the feminist literature has too often been conceptualized simply as resistance. Mahmood's contribution is the suggestion that agency needs to be understood far more broadly, not just in terms of resistance or submission, but also as the ability to construct a self from prevailing norms. Nevertheless, too expansive of a conception of women's agency also runs the risk of rendering it meaningless for examining the broader consequences of piety movements for egalitarian social change, if that is indeed our goal.

Despite extensive research on women and piety movements, it is difficult to draw direct correlations between piety and politics, especially regarding gender. While pious forms of religion tend to emphasize conservative gender norms, pious women are politically diverse, with some advocating gender equality. Piety movements seem to have mixed consequences for women participants – producing a sense of individual and/or collective empowerment, while simultaneously underlining or legitimizing conservative gender norms. While piety movements may have important political effects, the outcome of women's involvement in piety movements is not fully understood by social scientists. However, it is clear that women's enhanced agency and public participation do not automatically produce gender equality or egalitarian social change.

CONCLUSIONS

The ever-growing involvement of women in pious religious movements has become a hallmark of the contemporary era. Drawing on diverse studies of women in piety movements around the globe, I have made three wide-ranging suppositions which I hope will further scholarly debates about women, religion, and politics. These suppositions about why women are attracted to piety movements, what piety movements do for women, and how piety movements affect gender relations and politics in general, are intended to serve as a basis for continued research. In addition, I also have outlined several urgent new questions for future empirical and theoretical research.

1   Women are attracted to piety movements as a means to resolve anxieties of modernity and social change. The pious emphasis on discipline and order is viewed as modern, and often contrasted to traditional or local practices.

While modernity produces tensions, especially related to gender and reproduction, piety movements allow women to take refuge from dislocating
changes and to formulate their own versions of modernity. While modernity
is often implicitly understood as secular, for many women modernity and
piety go hand in hand.

2 Pious religious practices, which are often highly gendered, can facilitate the
construction of communities as well as the enforcement of boundaries to
exclude others. Piety movements often provide women with a sense of agency
and personal responsibility, especially in terms of fashioning new selves.
Many women therefore feel empowered by participation in such movements.
Beyond the cultivation of selves, the collective aspects of piety movements
facilitate women in the process of constructing new kinds of communities
and social identities.

3 It is difficult to draw direct correlations between piety and politics, especially
regarding gender. While pious forms of religion tend to emphasize conservative gender norms, pious women are politically diverse. Piety movements
generate a sense of individual and/or collective empowerment for women,
while often simultaneously underlining or legitimizing conservative gender
norms. While piety movements may have significant political effects, the
outcome of women's involvement in piety movements is not fully understood.
However, women's agency and public participation do not automatically
produce gender equality or egalitarian social change.

Despite the vital contributions of the literature surveyed in this chapter, there remain
a great many gaps in our understanding of women and piety movements. Certainly
one fundamental matter is precisely how gender is a part of the rise of piety movements in the modern world. Is it really the case that piety movements are reacting
to tensions over changes in gender relations and family forms? Why is it, for
example, that changes in gender relations and family forms seem to produce such
great anxiety in some places, such as the United States or the Middle East, and not
others, such as Western Europe or China? And is gender really the core issue for
piety movements, as it seems to be for many explicitly political religious movements?
Indeed, how exactly should we distinguish piety movements for political religious
movements, or is this a false distinction to begin with?

Moreover, the links between economic change and women in piety movements
are also not well understood. In particular, the relationship between social class,
gender, and piety movements seems ripe for greater analysis, especially given that
such movements apparently draw heavily from the middle classes.

Another vital set of questions revolves around religion and feminism. Why is it
that feminist varieties of pious religion are so marginal in most places? Will this
change given the increased involvement of women in religious life and the continuing decentralization of religious authority?

Finally, perhaps the most significant question for future investigation is the issue
of whether women's greater involvement in religious life contributes to gender
equality. Despite the conservative gender ideologies espoused by many pious movements, is it possible that the rapidly growing involvement of women in these movements will itself bring about egalitarian social changes? Or are legions of women

more interested in fashioning virtuous selves and building new communities? And is it possible that these seemingly different goals might be commensurable?

Note

1 Catholicism, as the traditional form of Christianity is generally not included in the ranks of piety movements. However, there is a strong charismatic movement within Catholicism which this chapter does not have scope to discuss. For more information on women and piety in the Catholic tradition, see Chesnut 2003 and Manning 1999.

Bibliography

Abramowitz, A. and Saunders, K. (2008) Is polarization a myth?, *Journal of Politics* 542–55.

Adamson, C. (2007) Gendered anxieties: Islam, women's rights and moral hierarchy in Java, *Anthropological Quarterly* 80: 5–37.

Afary, J. (1997) The war against feminism in the name of the almighty: making sense of gender and Islamic fundamentalism, *New Left Review* 89–110.

Afshar, H. (1998) *Islam and Feminisms: An Iranian Case Study*, New York and London: Palgrave Macmillan.

Ahmad, S. (2008) Identity matters, culture wars: an account of al-Huda (re)defining identity and reconfiguring culture in Pakistan, *Culture and Religion* 9: 63–80.

Ahmed, L. (1992) *Women and Gender in Islam: Historical Roots of a Modern Debate*, New Haven: Yale University Press.

Amrullah, E. (2008) Indonesian Muslim fashion styles and designs, *ISIM Review* 22: 22–3.

Avishai, O. (2008) "Doing religion" in a secular world: women in conservative religions and the question of agency, *Gender and Society* 22: 409–433.

Bacchetta, P. (1996) Hindu nationalist women as ideologues: the "Sangh," the "Samiti," and their differential concepts of the Hindu nation, in K. Jayawardena and M. De Alwis (eds.), *Embodied Violence: Communalising Women's Sexuality in South Asia*, London: Zed Books.

Bacchetta, P. (2004) *Gender in the Hindu Nation: RSS Women as Ideologues*, New Delhi: Women Unlimited.

Badran, M. (1999) Feminisms and Islamisms, *Journal of Women's History* 10: 196–204.

Badran, M. (2003) Islamic feminism: what's in a name, *Al-Ahram Weekly Online*.

Badran, M. (2005) Between secular and Islamic feminism(s): reflections on the Middle East and beyond, *Journal of Middle East Women's Studies* 1: 6–28.

Badran, M. (ed.) (1994) *Gender Activism: Feminists and Islamists in Egypt*, Boulder: Westview Press.

Bartholomeusz, T. (1992) The female mendicant in Buddhist Sri Lanka, in J. I. Cabezon (ed.), *Buddhism, Sexuality, and Gender*, New York: SUNY Press.

Basu, Amrita and Jeffery, Patricia (1997) *Appropriating Gender: Women's Activism and Politicized Religion in South Asia*, London: Routledge.

Bayes, J. H. and Tohidi, N. (eds.) (2001) *Globalization, Gender, and Religion: The Politics of Women's Rights in Catholic and Muslim Contexts*, New York: Palgrave Macmillan.

Bernal, Victoria (1994) Gender, culture and capitalism: women and the remaking of Islamic "tradition" in a Sudanese village, *Comparative Studies in Society and History* 36 (1): 36–67.

Beyer, P. (1994) *Religion and Globalization*, London: Sage.

Bowen, J. (2007) *Why the French Don't Like Headscarves: Islam, the State, and Public Space*, Oxford: Princeton University Press.

Brasher, B. (1998) *Godly Women: Fundamentalism and Female Power*, New Brunswick: Rutgers University Press.

Brenner, S. (1996) Reconstructing self and society: Javanese Muslim women and "the veil," *American Ethnologist* 23 (24): 673–97.

Brenner, S. (1998) *The Domestication of Desire: Women, Wealth, and Modernity in Java*, Princeton: Princeton University Press.

Brenner, S. (2005) Islam and gender politics in late new order Indonesia, in A. Willford and K. M. George (eds.), *Spirited Politics: Religion and Public Life in Contemporary Southeast Asia*, Ithaca: Cornell University Press.

Brenner, S. (2006) Democracy, polygamy, and women in post-*Reformasi* Indonesia, *Social Analysis* 50: 164–70.

Brusco, E. E. (1995) *The Reformation of Machismo: Evangelical Conversion and Gender in Colombia*, Austin: University of Texas.

Chen, C. (2005) A self of one's own: Taiwanese immigrant women and religious conversion, *Gender and Society* 19: 336–57.

Chen, C. (2006) From filial piety to religious piety: evangelical Christianity reconstructing Taiwanese immigrant families in the United States, *International Migration Review* 40: 573–602.

Chesnut, R. A. (2003) *Competitive Spirits: Latin America's New Religious Economy*, New York: Oxford University Press.

Chong, K. (2006) Negotiating patriarchy: South Korean evangelical women and the politics of gender, *Gender and Society* 20: 697–724.

Chong, K. (forthcoming) *Deliverance and Submission: Evangelical Women and the Negotiation of Patriarchy in South Korea*, Cambridge, MA: Harvard University Press.

Cohen, B. (ed.) (1990) *Puritanism and the Rise of Modern Science: The Merton Thesis*, New Brunswick: Rutgers University Press.

Davidman, L. (1993) *Tradition in a Rootless World: Women Turn to Orthodox Judaism*, Berkeley: University of California Press.

Deeb, L. (2006) *An Enchanted Modern: Gender and Public Piety in Shi'i Lebanon*, Princeton: Princeton University Press.

Esposito, J. L. and Haddad, Y. (eds.) (1998) *Islam, Gender, and Social Change*, London and New York: Oxford University Press.

Evans, J. H. (2003) Have Americans' attitudes become more polarized? An update, *Social Science Quarterly* 84: 74–90.

Evans, J. H. (2006) Cooperative coalitions on the religious right and left: considering the resiliency of sectarianism, *Journal for the Scientific Study of Religion* 45: 195–215.

Falk, M. L. (2008) *Making Fields of Merit: Buddhist Female Ascetics and Gendered Orders in Thailand*, Seattle: University of Washington Press.

Findly, E. (2000) *Women's Buddhism, Buddhism's Women: Tradition, Revision, Renewal*, Wisdom Publications.

Foley, R. (2004) Muslim women's challenges to Islamic law: the case of Malaysia, *International Feminist Journal of Politics* 6: 53–84.

Gallagher, S. K. (2003) *Evangelical Identity and Gendered Family Life*, New Jersey: Rutgers University Press.

Gallagher, S. K. (2004) The marginalization of evangelical feminism, *Sociology of Religion* 65: 215–37.

Göle, N. (1996) *The Forbidden Modern: Civilization and Veiling*, Ann Arbor: University of Michigan Press.

Göle, N. (2002) Islam in public: new visibilities and new imaginaries, *Public Culture* 14: 173–90.

Griffiths, R. M. (1997) God's daughters: evangelical women and the power of submission, Berkeley: University of California Press.

Hegland, M. E. (2003) Shi'a women's rituals in northwest Pakistan: the shortcomings and significance of resistance, *Anthropological Quarterly* 76: 411–42.

Hood, M. V., III and Smith, M. C. (2002) On the prospect of linking religious-right identification with political behavior: panacea or snipe hunt?, *Journal for the Scientific Study of Religion* 41 (13): 697–710.

Huntington, S. P. (1993) The clash of civilizations?, *Foreign Affairs* 72: 22–49.

Huq, S. and Rashid, S. F. (2008) Refashioning Islam: elite women and piety in Bangladesh, *Contemporary Islam* 2: 7–22.

Ismail, S. (2008) Muslim public self-presentation: interrogating the liberal public sphere, *Political Science and Politics* 41: 25–9.

Jacobson, S. (2006) Modernity, conservative religious movements, and the female subject: newly ultra-orthodox Sephardi women in Buenos Aires, *American Anthropologist* 108: 10.

Jones, C. (2007) Fashion and faith in urban Indonesia, *Theory: The Journal of Dress, Body and Culture* 11 (21): 211–32.

Juergensmeyer, M. (1994) *The New Cold War: Religious Nationalism Confronts the Secular State*, Berkeley: University of California Press.

Kandiyoti, D. (1991) *Women, Islam, and the State: A Comparative Approach*, Philadelphia: Temple University Press.

Karam, A. (1998) *Women, Islams, and the State: Contemporary Feminisms in Egypt*, New York and London: Palgrave Macmillan.

Kaufman, D. R. (1991) *Rachel's Daughters: Newly Orthodox Jewish Women*, New Brunswick: Rutgers University Press.

Kepel, G. (1994) *The Revenge of God: The Resurgence of Islam, Christianity, and Judaism in the Modern World*, Cambridge: Cambridge University Press.

Klatch, R. (1987) *Women of the New Right*, Philadelphia: Temple University Press.

Lauchert, F. (1911) Pietism, *The Catholic Encyclopedia*, New York: Robert Appleton Company.

Lynch, O. M. (2000) Sujata's army: Dalit Buddhist women and self-emancipation, in Findly, E. (ed.), *Women's Buddhism, Buddhism's Women: Tradition, Revision, Renewal*, Wisdom Publications.

Macleod, A. (1992) Hegemonic relations and gender resistance: the new veiling as accommodating protest in Cairo, *Signs: Journal of Women in Culture and Society* 17 (27): 533–57.

Macleod, A. (1993) *Accommodating Protest: Working Women, the New Veiling, and Change in Cairo*, New York: Columbia University Press.

Mahmood, S. (2005) *The Politics of Piety: The Islamic Revival and the Feminist Subject*, Princeton: Princeton University Press.

Manning, C. (1999) *God Gave Us the Right: Conservative Catholic, Evangelical Protestant and Orthodox Jewish Women Grapple with Feminism*, New Jersey: Rutgers University Press.

Martin, B. (2001) From pre- to postmodernity in Latin America: the case of Pentecostalism, in R. K. Fenn (ed.), *The Blackwell Companion to Sociology of Religion*, Oxford: Blackwell.

Marty, M. E. and Appleby, R. S. (eds.) (1994) *Fundamentalisms Observed*, Chicago: University of Chicago Press.

Mernissi, F. (1987) *Beyond the Veil: Male–Female Dynamics in Modern Muslim Society*, Bloomington: Indiana University Press.

Mernissi, F. (1992) *The Veil and the Male Elite: A Feminist Interpretation of Women's Rights in Islam*, New York: Basic Books.

Metcalf, B. (1998) Women and men in a contemporary pietist movement: the case of the Tablighi Jama'at, in A. Basu and P. Jeffery (eds.), *Appropriating Gender: Women's Activism and Politicized Religion in South Asia*, New York: Routledge.

Mir-Hosseini, Z. (2006) Muslim women's quest for equality: between islamic law and feminism, *Critical Inquiry* 32.

Moghadam, V. (1994) *Identity Politics and Women: Cultural Reassertions and Feminisms in International Perspective*, Boulder: Westview Press.

Moghadam, V. (2003) *Modernizing Women: Gender and Social Change in the Middle East*, Boulder: Lynne Rienner.

Moghadam, V. (2006) *Globalizing Women: Transnational Feminist Networks*, Baltimore: Johns Hopkins University Press.

Mouser, A. (2007) Defining "modern" Malay womanhood and the coexistent messages of the veil, *Religion* 37: 164–74.

Najmabadi, A. (2000) Unveiling feminism, *Social Text* 18: 29–45.

Neitz, M. J. (2004) Gender and culture: challenges to the sociology of religion [Genre et culture: défis à la sociologie des religions], *Sociology of Religion* 65 (12): 391–402.

Ong, A. (1995) State versus Islam: Malay families, women's bodies, and the body politic in Malaysia, in A. Ong and M. Peletz (eds.), *Bewitching Women, Pious Men: Gender and Body Politics in Southeast Asia*, Berkeley: University of California Press.

Parish, D. L. (1992) The power of female pietism: women as spiritual authorities and religious role models in seventeenth-century England, *Journal of Religious History* 17: 33–46.

Peters, C. (2003) *Patterns of Piety: Women, Gender and Religion in Late Medieval and Reformation England*, Cambridge: Cambridge University Press.

Read, J. G. and Bartkowski, J. P. (2000) To veil or not to veil? A case study of identity negotiation among Muslim women in Austin, Texas, *Gender and Society* 13 (22): 395–417.

Read, J. G. and Bartkowski, J. P. (2003) Veiled submission: gender, power, and identity among evangelical and Muslim women in the United States, *Qualitative Sociology* 26: 71–92.

Regnerus, Mark, Sikkink, David, and Smith, Christian (1999) Voting with the Christian right: contextual and individual patterns of electoral influence, *Social Forces* 77 (4): 1375–1401.

Rinaldo, R. (2008) "Muslim Women, middle class habitus, and modernity in Indonesia, *Contemporary Islam* 2: 23–39.

Rosario, S. (2006) The new burqa in Bangladesh: empowerment or violation of women's rights?, *Women's Studies International Forum* 29: 368–80.

Scott, J. W. (2007) *The Politics of the Veil*, Princeton: Princeton University Press.

Smilde, D. (1997) The fundamental unity of the conservative and revolutionary tendencies in Venezuelan evangelicalism: the case of conjugal relations, *Religion* 27 (4): 343–59.

Smith, C. (ed.) (1998) *American Evangelicalism: Embattled and Thriving*, Chicago: University of Chicago Press.

Smith-Hefner, N. J. (2005) The new Muslim romance: changing patterns of courtship and marriage among educated Javanese youth, *Journal of Southeast Asian Studies* 36 (18): 441–59.

Smith-Hefner, N. J. (2007) Javanese women and the veil in post-Soeharto Indonesia, *Journal of Asian Studies* 66 (31): 389–420.

Stivens, M. (2006) "Family values" and Islamic revival: gender, rights and state moral projects in Malaysia, *Women's Studies International Forum* 29: 354–67.

Stoeffler, F. E. (1965) *The Rise of Evangelical Pietism*, Leiden: Brill.

Tong, J. K.-C. and Turner, B. S. (2008) Women, piety and practice: a study of women and religious practice in Malaysia, *Contemporary Islam* 2: 41–59.

Turner, B. S. (2008) Acts of piety: the political and the religious, or a tale of two cities, in Engin F. Isin and Greg M. Nielsen (ed.) *Acts of Citizenship*, London: Zed Books.

Van Doorn-Harder, P. (2002) The Indonesian Islamic debate on a woman president, *Sojourn* 17 (26): 164–90.

Van Doorn-Harder, P. (2006) *Women Shaping Islam: Reading the Qur'an in Indonesia*, Chicago: University of Illinois Press.

White, J. (2002) *Islamist Mobilization in Turkey: A Study in Vernacular Politics*, Washington: University of Washington Press.

Yuval-Davis, N. and Anthias, F. (1989) *Woman–Nation–State*, London: Palgrave Macmillan.

27

Religion and Nationalism
A Critical Re-examination

Geneviève Zubrzycki

Introduction

Religious and nationalist conflicts stridently mark the contemporary world, notably in the Middle East, the Indian sub-continent, the Balkans, Northern Ireland, and now in the United States as well. In journalistic accounts and everyday life discourses, it is often assumed to be the result of "age-old hatreds" stemming from irreconcilable worldviews or "civilizational fault lines" – a view that has become conspicuously redundant in the aftermath of September 11. We know how inaccurate this view is from a large body of works that have convincingly revealed how identities, attachments, loyalties, values, and even emotions are socially, culturally and discursively created, changing in time and space (e.g. Anderson 1983; Hobsbawm 1991; Bendelow and Williams 1998). In spite of these corrections, studies of nationalism typically suffer from three interrelated problems that slow further progress in better understanding the relationship between nationalism and religion. Let us briefly consider each, before proposing a different way to think about the relationship and suggesting, through the analysis of the Polish and Québécois cases, a more productive approach to the empirical study of the problem.

Surveying the Field

The evolutionist causal trap

Mainstream scholarship on nations and nationalism often points out that the emergence and rise of nationalism as an ideology is linked to the general trend of the secularization of society (Kedourie 1960; Anderson 1991 [1983]; Gellner 1983; Hobsbawm 1983ab; see A. Smith 2003: 9–18).[1] Historically, in this view, politics replaced religion as the ultimate reference, a process referred to as the "disenchantment of the world" (Weber 2001 [1930]; Gauchet 1985). In view of this historical fact, some scholars have concluded that religion's demise is responsible for the extent of nationalism's success.[2] The argument most paradigmatically goes as follows: Starting with the Reformation, the authority of the Church was seriously diminished in temporal matters. The Enlightenment and later the French Revolution further diminished religion's power as a principle of social organization, as a basis for political legitimacy and sovereignty, and as the source of knowledge. Once the way was cleared, rationalism, politics, and eventually nationalism would become the new sacred principles of the modern era. Historical arguments of the *longue durée* identify these secularizing processes as turning points for the creation of a world system of nation-states, with nationalism – in tandem with, according to some, capitalism – as the new secular orthodoxies.

There is no doubt that these ideological revolutions and the structural changes that accompanied them had a tremendous impact both on the decline of religion as "sacred canopy" (Berger 1969) and on the slow emergence of nationalism and its political project, along with the creation of the nation as a cultural form. In Europe, the Reformation did cause irreparable damage to the Church, and the blows inflicted on religion by the Enlightenment were certainly significant for the emergence of a secular worldview: the Enlightenment not only advocated "Reason" over sentiments, but also claimed moral and political sovereignty from the Church. "*Écraser l'infâme*," in Voltaire's famous words, meant to individually free oneself from religious superstition and to be disenfranchised collectively from the control of the papacy. And a lineage from Locke to Rousseau, and culminating in the French Revolution, was key in forging a new political principle according to which political legitimacy stems from the People, and not from the King's divinely sanctioned rights.

What is problematic in many scholarly narratives, is therefore not those historical observations themselves, but the conclusion that nationalism's emergence and success was (and is) related to religion's demise; that the emergence of nationalism was *caused* by secularization.[3] As Liah Greenfeld points out, "the fact that nationalism replaced religion as the order-creating system (...) implies nothing at all about the historical connection between them and lends no justification to the kind of sociological teleology that is the essence of such reasoning" (1996: 176). The relationship between religious decline and the rise of nationalism is actually much more complex than is often assumed. To wit, historical sociologists have recently argued that nationalism has roots *not* in religious decline, but rather in moments of religious fervor and renewal (Greenfeld 1992, 1996; Gorski 2000b, 2003; Calhoun 1993; Gillis 1994; Marx 2003).[4] One moment of such religious élan was the Reformation, which "replaced the universalistic notion of Christendom with local and regional variants of the common faiths, mobilized popular participation, promulgated vernacular discourse and printed texts, and invoked the theological sovereignty of the people against the Church and monarchs" (Calhoun 1993: 219). Culturally, the Reformation allowed the development of a different kind of memory, one that was neither purely local nor cosmopolitan, as well as a new type of identity among elites, who came to share a bounded self-conception as "God's Englishmen," a proto-national (or national, according to early modernists) identity (Gillis 1994: 7). The Reformation's subsequent launching of national churches throughout Europe is seen as the basis for the development of nation-states, since it emancipated regions from

Rome, fractured the political establishment and furnished new political alliances along confessional lines.

The point, here, is that there is convincing evidence that nationalism's success is not necessarily attributable to religious decline and that we should not take the relationship between nationalism and religion as a zero-sum game, in which one can only win at the expense of the other.

Nationalism as religion: the functionalist trap

The evolutionist view of the rise of nationalism is taken one step further by scholars who suggest, after Émile Durkheim, that nationalism is a substitute for religion in modernity, with immense integrative power in an age of anomie or atomization (Durkheim 1995 [1912]; Hayes 1960; Kohn 1946; Tamir 1995; Llobera 1996; Marvin and Ingle 1999). Nationalism is portrayed as being pervasive in modernity because it fills the void left by religion's retreat. According to this functionalist view, nationalism has not only superseded religion, it has actually replaced it by *itself* becoming a modern religion, fulfilling functions of integration traditional religions once performed.

The words of early scholar of nationalism Carlton Hayes are foundational on this score: "[Nationalism], like *any other* religion, is to a large extent a social function, and its chief rites are public rites performed in the name of and for the salvation of a whole community" (1926: 105. Emphasis mine). Nationalism is not *like* religion; it *is* a religion. It is a religion, moreover, that serves society's survival. At the individual or psychological level, nationalism is seen as a functional substitute for religion in modernity because it fulfils deep human needs (Hayes 1960; Llobera 1996; Hobsbawm 1995: 172–3), whereas at the social level, nationalism fulfils the essential function of consolidating the group and its identity above and beyond individual needs. Indeed, nationalism is so compelling in modernity, according to Yael Tamir (1995), because it offers collective salvation by endowing human action with meaning that endures over time, carrying a promise of eternity. Membership in a nation promises redemption from personal oblivion, offers rescue from alienation, solitude, and anonymity, and it gives individuals the hope of personal renewal through national regeneration (pp. 433–4). Nationalism, then, "is not the pathology of the modern age, but an *answer* to its malaise – to the neurosis, alienation, and meaninglessness characteristic of modern times" (p. 432, emphasis mine). Here, nationalism fulfills the psychological need for individuals to belong and for the group to endure; it is the functional answer to the atomization of modern society.

In a slightly different slant, religion is viewed as having simply "metamorphosed into nationalism" (Llobera 1996: 146): "The success of nationalism in modernity has to be attributed largely to the sacred character the nation inherited from religion. In its essence the nation is the secularized god of our times" (p. 221). What really makes nationalism a religion – what Joseph Llobera calls the "essence" of the nation or of religion – is the functions they both fulfill. Both operate at the level of "deep elementary emotions" (p. 143). Nationalism is a functional equivalent of religion in the modern world, even a religion itself because it has all the trappings and rituals of religion, and also because "it has tapped into the emotional reservoir of human beings" (p. 143).

These arguments are problematic at several levels. First, equating nationalism and religion erases the distinct characteristics of each phenomenon. Second, presupposing psychosocial needs as natural – or eliding the process by which these needs are created and then fulfilled – mystifies as much as it explains. The reification and primordialization of needs imply that national identity is a "natural" phenomenon instead of the product of human agency, and suggests the inevitability of nationalism rather than its historical contingency. Lastly, the functional equivalence of nationalism and religion is dubiously premised upon a historical narrative of the secularization of the West, the vacuum of which was filled by nationalism. The varied and complex history of the relationship between nationalism and religion cannot be narrowed to a simple linear sequence, in which one form of social organization is succeeded by another (from *Gemeinschaft* to *Gesellschaft*), and one type of integrative cement is replaced by another (from religion to nationalism).

In addition to being theoretically and logically flawed, the evolutionist and functionalist perspectives are empirically wrong. Religion is obviously not part of some prior stage, but very much present in the modern world and highly significant in defining the nation and its discourse, as well as in shaping nationalist practices. Those perspectives moreover prevent us from understanding and explaining cases in which religious beliefs, symbols, and practices play a salient role in national identity and nationalism, and lead us to treat these as a residue or "survival" from a pre-modern period, thereby endowing them with primordial, atavistic powers. To escape these problematic generalizations, we need to rethink the relationship in a way that does not a priori preclude the coexistence of religion and nationalism, but instead attends to the historical contingency, the institutional and cultural embeddedness, and the social dynamics of the religion-nation relation. The question is not of the relative primacy of one or the other as carrier of collective identity, but rather to identify the historical conditions under which religion and nationalism are fused, split, or juxtaposed, and to pinpoint how exactly these categories are imbricated in social identities.

The perennialist trap

Unlike the evolutionist and functionalist views, which posit the disappearance of religion as a *sine qua non* for the emergence of nationalism and sees the "age of religion" and the "age of nationalism" as two radically different eras, the "perennialist" position is one that stresses continuity between religion and nationalism: according to its proponents (Smith 1986, 2003; Armstrong 1996; Hastings 1997), ancient religious communities provided the materials from which modern nations could later be built. This view is troubling insofar as it assumes a historical continuity between pre-modern communities, what Anthony D. Smith calls *ethnies*, and modern nations. The problem is that there is no necessary continuity between *ethnies* and modern nations, although – and this is key – such continuity is retrospectively constructed and reinforced in nationalist discourse and narratives. As we will see in the case of Poland, the identity of the nation as primordially and eternally Catholic was created and reinforced in a particular period by interested actors, and is intimately related to structural changes, ideological developments and political interests. This is not to say that Catholicism before the age of nationalism did not play an important role in pre-modern Poland and in the lives of many of its inhabitants. It surely did. But Catholicism has not always been, as nationalists claim, the hallmark of the Polish nation.

The construction of national identity involves the creation of collective memories, rituals and symbols, their institutional maintenance and renewal, and the selective appropriation and annihilation of divisive memories and alternative identities (Renan 1996; Weber 1976; Gellner 1983; Hobsbawm 1983; Anderson 1983; Duara 1995). Claiming a direct continuity with ancient forms of community is therefore far-fetched, although the modern process of nation-creation involves the borrowing from these older communal forms of myths, heroes and symbols that create the illusion of the modern nation's ancient origins and therefore legitimize its modern existence.

Moving ahead

The relationship between religion and nationalism, as these few pages suggest, is extremely complex, and its treatment often problematic in the nationalism literature. Nationalism, Liah Greenfeld pointed out, is a secular form of consciousness that sacralizes the secular, hence the temptation to treat it as a religion (1996:), à la Hayes or Llobera. The temptation to treat nationalism as the religion of modernity must, however, be resisted since it obscures both the nature of religion and of nationalism. To understand the relationship between religion and nation in all its complexity, we must shed modernization theory's *a priori* assumptions, but without reifying the link between pre-modern and modern communal bonds, as perennialists do. The way forward is to highlight how religion can frame identities, shape actions and be used to mobilize masses, as well as show how nationalism impacts on the definition of religious identities and religious movements. Several important works, in the past decade, have undertaken this task under the rubric of "religious nationalism" (eg. Juergensmeyer 1993; Van der Veer 1994; Sells 1996; Tambiah 1996). This literature has been extremely important, taking as its primary focus violent inter-religious and inter-ethnic conflicts and the logics of various forms of group antagonism.[5] Yet for the purposes of this essay they will not be quite sufficient, since they do not take as their specific object of study how religion and national identity become entangled in a given group in the first place – what the fusion or fission between ethnicity (or national identity) and religion is dependent upon, nor when and how that relationship can be renegotiated and reconfigured.

In what follows, I discuss the cases of Poland and Quebec. My objective, in this section, is obviously not to present an exhaustive typology of the relationship between religion and national identity/nationalism, but to provide examples of *how* to study that relationship. The case-studies are illustrative of a way to think about, and a guide for the empirical study of, nationalism and religion. I develop an analytical framework that attends to the social dynamics, the institutional and cultural embeddedness, and the historical contingencies of the religion-nation nexus. Combining historical and ethnographic methods to identify variations in the configuration of nationalism and religion, I reexamine longstanding assumptions about the trajectory of social change and explicate how such categories are articulated in actual social practices "on the ground." I give particular attention to events and symbols that simultaneously point to, and variously link, religious and national references, and their manipulations at key moments of political transition, as it is through those events and symbols that social actors experience, make sense of, and act upon the world.

NATIONALIZING AND DE-NATIONALIZING RELIGION: THE CASE OF POLAND

Post-communist Poland provides a valuable case for research on the relationship between national identity and religion because it is one of the most ethnically and denominationally homogeneous nation-states in the world – its population is 96 percent ethnically Polish and 95 percent Catholic – yet conflicts about national identity and the place of religion in defining that identity have been central public issues in the last two decades. At the root of that phenomenon, I argue, is the reconfiguration of a historically defined relationship between state, nation, and religion in Poland, prompted by the fall of communism and the building of a legitimate national state (Zubrzycki 2006).

For most of the nineteenth and twentieth centuries, in the absence of a state (or of a legitimate state, as under communism) the mobilizing discourse of the nation was articulated in ethno-religious rather than political terms, and the Catholic Church was seen as the "true" guardian and carrier of national values, providing institutional, ideological and symbolic support to civil society. The Catholic narrative of the nation was primarily created in the nineteenth century by Romantic poets who equated the Partitions of Poland – when the Polish state was carved up between Prussia, Austria, and Russia (1795–1918) – with the nation's crucifixion. Poland, in their writings, was the Christ among nations: sacrificed for the sins of the world, it would be brought back to life to save humanity from Despotism. With Poland transformed into a Christ figure, the cross was metamorphosed into a core Polish symbol representing the plight of the nation and its imminent salvation *qua* independence. This representation of the Polish fate became canonical, securely anchored in national self-understanding, and it resurfaced with special intensity under communism. Catholicism and the Catholic Church, during that period, were portrayed by the opposition as the basis of a moral community fighting an evil totalitarian regime imposed from outside and from above, and succeeded in providing a powerful narrative of the nation, one able to mobilize support against the party-state. The narrative was built around Poland's historical suffering, the notion of Poland as a chosen people, as well as the messianic myth of Poland as the bulwark of Christendom. The iconography of national identity and resistance to the oppressive foreign regime emphasized symbols traditionally associated with the nation, such as the miraculous Black Madonna of Częstochowa, as well as motifs taken from the Passion, such as the cross and the crown of thorns.

This narrative and its related "repertoire of action" was especially mobilizing in the context of statelessness; when national identity could not be constructed through official institutions, such as during the Partitions and during communism. But with the fall of communism and an independent state recovered, would Poland be a nation with, or without, the cross?

Indeed, the establishment of a "truly" Polish state in 1989 opened to question both the fusion between nation and religion and the tight bond between civil society and the Church. The construction of a state with the mandate to "genuinely" represent *Polish* interests also entailed specifying what Polishness "is," radically opening the discursive field on the nation. In this context, certain factions advocated maintaining a "Catholic Poland, united under the sign of the cross," while others demanded the confessional neutrality of the state and pressed for a more inclusive, civic-secular definition of national identity. When the state stopped being the "third element" against which civil society and Church could be mobilized, but rather the prism through which identities could be viewed and consciously be constructed, the meaning of Polish religiosity changed, and the provisional nature of what appeared to be a solid fusion of nation and religion began to show its seams.

This became apparent in the debates surrounding the controversial erection of hundreds of crosses just outside Auschwitz in 1998–9. Ultra-nationalist Poles chose the cross as the symbol of choice to mark Auschwitz as the place of *Polish* martyrdom – as opposed to the place of the Jewish Holocaust[6] – and as a strategy to firmly defend a vision of Polishness that was increasingly contested. But in the postcommunist context, the symbol and the gesture signified, for liberal intellectuals from the Left and the Center, the imposition of a set of values and intolerance toward "others." It stood as the rejection of the principles of the *Rechtsstaat*, where particular allegiances are relegated to the private sphere. For liberal Catholics, the crosses at Auschwitz were seen as a vile political instrument, a provocation contrary to the Christian meaning of the symbol, while for many members of the clergy and Episcopate they were the shameful expression of Polish nationalism.

The war of the crosses, as the event came to be known, therefore highlighted deep divisions within Polish society – and within the Church itself – and brought to light the different ways in which various groups actually articulate, "on the ground" and in the public sphere, the relationship between national identity and religion. I show elsewhere (2006) that the event was *not* the confirmation or even the solidification of the nation-religion fusion, but rather a desperate attempt to revitalize a version of national identity in decline. It is precisely at the moment when the fusion of religious and ethno-national categories was being loudly contested in public discourse and civic life, and the categories were divorced in new institutional arrangements – in the 1997 constitution, for example (Zubrzycki 2001) – that strident counter-efforts by minority voices were deployed in an attempt to ossify a vision of the nation that was slowly eroding. That strategy, however, further contributed to the erosion it sought to stop. Though Poles remain overwhelmingly religious[7], the cross they now bear is no longer the symbol of their historical "Passion," nor that of the union of their faith with national identity, but rather – and quite counter-intuitively – a contested symbol expressing deep social tensions regarding Polish Catholicism.

Theories of nationalism and religion revisited

This brief example suggests that contrary to the neat, overly simplified evolutionist-functionalist models, nation and religion are variously interrelated in different historical and political contexts – in communist versus postcommunist Poland, for example – and are evoked and mobilized differently by various social groups. Instead of thinking of the relationship between religion and nation as a dyad, we need to look at it as part of a triad in which the statehood plays a key role. Reading the relationship between nation and religion in Poland requires the analysis of the triadic relationship between state (re)formation, the (re)construction of national identity and the (re)definition of religion's role in society.

Whereas dominant paradigms in the field maintain that nationalism replaced traditional religion and even is a modern religion itself, through the sacralization of politics, this case suggests a much more complex and subtle relationship between nationalism and religion. Historically, the formation of Polish nationalism cannot be related to religious decline, as the evolutionists claim. Religious symbols and stories instead provided a vocabulary and grammar to speak of the nation and its mission after the Partitions. Romantic messianism found a congenial niche for the expression of this emerging form of nationalism in Catholic rituals and everyday practices. Through a slow and complex process in the nineteenth and twentieth centuries, Polish national identity and Catholicism became fused.

This is far from conforming to the functionalist model, however, according to which nationalism, after having superseded religion, replaces it, or even becomes a religion itself. The paradigmatic term for this model is civil religion, sometimes defined as an empirical object, sometimes as an analytical dimension of all social groups. "Civil religion," following the Durkheimian trajectory, attempts to describe or interpret the social sacralization of a given group's symbols.[8] In the modern era, according to this view, civic, or state symbols like the flag are worshiped by citizens as religious icons or totems, and state martyrs are revered as "saints." Nationalism becomes a religion, as "treason" and "heresy" become one and the same. But this will not do either.

Sacred-secular religious nationalism

Liah Greenfeld (1996), we have seen, suggested that the confusion between religion and nationalism stems from the fact that nationalism is a form of consciousness that sacralizes the secular, leading scholars to treat it as a religion, albeit a "civil religion." Although this is useful, it does not go far enough. The Polish case points to a different and overlooked process. Because of Poland's peculiar political history, it was not political institutions and symbols that were sacralized and became the object of religious devotion (following the French revolutionary model), but religious symbols that were first secularized, and then *resacralized as national*. Biblical allegories, religious symbols, hymns, and iconography as well as religious practices like processions, pilgrimages or simple participation in Sunday Mass were, in the nineteenth century, largely politicized as carriers of national identity during the period when the Polish state disappeared from the European map. As such, religion served as an alternative space providing civil society with an area of relative freedom of action in defiance of an oppressive or totalitarian state. A pilgrimage to Częstochowa, in this context, was a way to publicly "vote with one's feet" (Michel 1986: 85). Catholic identity, symbols and acts, were secularized through their politicization and ultimate fusion with national identity. Their significance was heightened or loaded; they became neon hyper-markers, but of Polishness.

The Polish case therefore suggests a peculiar form of the secularization of religion and religious symbols, through their political instrumentalization, and then their *re-sacralization*, now as *national* symbols. The cross in Poland is therefore a *sacred secular* symbol. It is sacred not only because of its Christian semantics (or even in spite of them), but because it traditionally represents, since the nineteenth century, Poland. In the place of religion yielding to nationalism or nationalism becoming a religion, here *religion becomes nationalism.*[9] The national sacralization of religious symbols, however, is meaningful and garners consensual support only in specific politico-structural contexts. The Polish case therefore points to the necessity of looking at the relationship between religion and nationalism as it is embedded within broad systemic processes related to state formation on the one hand, and as it is reflected in specific social dramas and cultural practices on the other.

Beyond secularization

It is in their secular form that Catholicism and its symbols were re-sacralized. They became the sacred symbols of national identity, only to be contested and potentially "secularized" again in the postcommunist period. "Secularization" in the sense I am using the term here would mean, however, returning to a more distinctly (or theologically orthodox) religious interpretation of Catholicism in Poland: to shift the Catholic Church's role in Poland away from identity politics and steer it back toward faith. "The challenge now," in the words of the late priest philosopher Józef Tischner, "is to return to the essence of the Church's mission – to religion," even at the cost of lower church attendance.[10] The goal for many Catholic groups is the de-politicization of religion and a deepening of faith. After Catholicism's long public career, they invite its privatization. According to them, privatization, usually understood as one aspect of secularization, would paradoxically be salutary for Catholicism now that there is no reason for its political role in the public sphere, and now that the "practicing non-believer" lost her reasons to practice. The Polish case thus turns secularization theory on its head: what is commonly seen as religion's revenge – the undeniable strength and pervasiveness of Catholicism in communist Poland's public life (Casanova 1994) – could instead be regarded as its weakening – its instrumentalization as symbolic vehicle of national identity and institutional support to civil society.

What secularization means is thus much more complex than the usual "decline of religion" one-size-fits-all proposition, as Casanova (1994) and Gorski (2000a) argued. For Mark Chaves, for example, secularization is, more specifically, the declining *scope* of religious authority. It is a process, moreover, rooted in concrete social struggles: "Secularization occurs, or not, as the result of social and political conflicts between those social actors who would enhance or maintain religion's social significance and those who would reduce it" (1994: 752). In the Polish case, this struggle is taking place not only between liberal, civic, and secular actors and conservative ethno-nationalist religious elites, but also between two great camps within the Church: that of post-Vatican II "open Catholics" and "purists," who argue for a de-politicization of religion and a deepening of faith, and that of "traditionalists" and "integrists" who maintain that Catholicism is primordially linked with Polishness and that the Church's mission is necessarily political (Zubrzycki

RELIGION AND NATIONALISM 615
2005). The tension is between privatizing and publicizing forces, between opposed
views of the role of religion and of the Church in the public sphere. In the religious
field, the post-1989 period is best described by the polarization, within the Church,
between these two orientations.

But this relative decline in the scope of religious authority and the ensuing privatization of religion do not necessarily imply the decline of religion, merely its decline
as a carrier of sentiments of national affinity and solidarity. The point to be made
here is that secularization turns on multiple axes: one is the level of public engagement in a given national environ, another is the level of authority over the public
sphere in given national context, and still a third reflects the level of privately held
and enacted religious sentiments. Secularization, it turns out, does not mean very
much as a theoretical tool until it is operationalized within a given articulation of
nationness.

Let us now look at another case where national identity, religion, politics and
secularization are peculiarly intertwined.

FROM FRENCH CANADA'S NATIONALIZED RELIGION TO QUEBEC RELIGIO-SECULAR HYBRID[11]

The fusion of Catholicism and national identity in Quebec finds its origins in the
nineteenth century, and, as in Poland, its causes are related to colonial domination
by ethno-religious others. Following the British Conquest of New France in 1759
and the repression of the Patriots' Rebellion, in a series of Republican uprisings
against the British colonial power in 1837, the Catholic Church emerged as the sole
institution able to create, sustain and disseminate a national project. That project,
however, was devoid of political content – the goal was not to change the political
structures and free the nation from the British empire, but to ensure the nation's
very *survival* within the new system by keeping the identity of its members alive.
The survival of the nation therefore rested on maintaining the French language and
the Catholic faith.

To carry that vision, the Church built a retrospective messianic narrative about
the French Canadians' historical destiny in North America that gradually elevated
St John the Baptist as its figurehead. Like the Baptist, whose Providential mission
was to announce the coming of Christ and baptize him, the French had discovered
Canada and brought civilization and Christianity to the pagan natives they evangelized; they also guarded Catholicism, the only "true faith," from the Protestant
heresy surrounding them on the North American continent. The French Canadian
people, in this powerful narrative, were an "apostolic people"; the chosen people,
with a Providential mission supported by "the twin pillars of faith and language,"
according to Jules-Paul Tardivel, a leading clerical nationalist of the time. Religion,
language and ethnicity became increasingly fused, one reinforcing the other, resulting in the creation of a cohesive national identity articulated in a coherent messianic
narrative, and represented in the powerful figure of St Jean-Baptiste.

From the 1840s until the 1960s, the Catholic Church was the center of civic life,
assuming functions usually reserved to the modern state: health, education, and
welfare (Eid 1978). The Church was also active in cultural politics, organizing large

celebrations around Saint-Jean-Baptiste, officially named Patron Saint of French Canadians in North America by Pope Pius IX in 1908. Small bonfires blessed by village priests were succeeded by elaborate processions in the streets of Montreal and Quebec City on the Saint's name Day, June 24th. These religious processions slowly developed into expansive parades combining religious and secular themes and imagery. Hundreds of thousands of spectators gathered along the streets of these cities could admire dozens of floats amidst regiments of Papal Zouaves, religious banners floating with flags, religious hymns sung by children and folkloric airs played by marching bands. While the themes varied and the floats themselves were reinvented every year, the single constant component, year after the year, was the parade's last float, dedicated to the Patron Saint. St Jean-Baptiste was typically represented as a golden child in the company of a lamb[12] emulating popular Italian paintings of the Holy Family where Jesus and John play together. During the 1960s, however, that specific visual depiction of the nation came under harsh attack.

The decade marked the birth of modern *Québécois* nationalism. Despite their frequent conflation in (non-Canadian) English, "French Canadian" and "Québécois" are not synonymous. The two terms rather represent different identities and different visions of the nation, each historically specific. The term "Québécois" is a neologism that came into use only in the early 1960s, when many French Canadians living in Quebec re-imagined the borders of their nation, from the expansive Canada (or even North America as a whole) in which they were a minority, to the circumscribed territory of Quebec, cradle of their civilization, in which they were a majority.[13] The re-imagination of their community, however, also signified the death of the French Canadian nation. Despite the pervasive use of the term outside Canada, "French Canadians" no longer exist, as noted by historian Yves Frenette in the opening sentence of his *Brève histoire des Canadiens-français*.

Besides this territorial fragmentation of French Canadian identity and its subsequent disappearance as a meaningful cultural and political category, much actually distinguishes the French Canadian and the Québécois national visions. While the French language remains a core element of both versions, Catholicism was abandoned as an important or even a desirable marker of the nation in the Québécois project. Likewise, the Church was no longer perceived as a bulwark, but rather as a barrier to the successful development of the nation.[14] While the French Canadian national vision was primarily centered on the notion of ethno-religious survival, the Québécois project explicitly rejected that notion. Its aim was not to survive, but to *develop*. Indeed, the Quiet Revolution's modus operandi was to *catch up* ["rattra-page"] and modernize. The instrument of that modernization was to be the provincial state, whose functions were radically expanded and empowered in order to better represent the interest of the "new" Québécois nation within Canadian federal structures. The influence of the Church in Quebec society – both institutionally and ideologically – was seen as part of the very problem to overcome in order to achieve that goal.

The 1960s were therefore also marked by important structural transformations, chief among them the building of a modern provincial welfare state, which effectively replaced the Church in the spheres of education, health and welfare. This institutional marginalization of the Church was accompanied by the thoroughgoing and extremely rapid secularization of society characterized not only by a stringent critique of the Church and a drastic decline in religious practice,[15] but also by a significant incidence of clergy renouncing their vows to reenter secular society. Within ten years, churches that once thronged with people several days a week now sat empty. Some were bulldozed; others were sold to developers who transformed them into condominiums or hotels; other remained only to be transformed from sites of ritual practices into sites of "cultural heritage."

In the context of the nation's redefinition and the politicization of a new national project during the Quiet Revolution, Saint Jean-Baptiste Day became the battle-ground between two visions of the nation – the French Canadian and the Québécois – and between two primary sets of national actors – the Church and a new wave of secular nationalists. As opposition to the religious narrative of the nation gained ground in the 1960s, it found its preferred target in Saint Jean-Baptiste and his diminutive lamb. The representation of the nation as a pre-pubescent saint was offensive to a new wave of nationalists on two principal grounds: they rejected the *religious* narrative of the nation expressed in, and fomented by the symbol, as ret-rograde; and they found the specific depiction of the nation as a *child* infantilizing because it underlined the nation's dependence.[16] The little St Jean Baptiste and his lamb were symbolic of a vision of the nation that the new Québécois nationalists understood as holding back the nation's potential. They both had to be purged. Under mounting social agitation, the lamb was removed from the traditional float, and at the close of the decade, in 1969, in the face of sufficient protest and even apparent danger to the "actor," the live character was replaced by an *adult statue* of the saint. That same year, the statue was spectacularly beheaded by protesters when they overturned the float during the parade, after which the traditional parades were permanently abolished.

On June 24, 1969, then, French Canada died at the hands of "Young Turks" who pressed for the birth of the Québécois nation, effectively closing a chapter in Quebec history and opening a new one. Gone were the saint and the parade. Yet if the religious icon and its phalanx disappeared, an abstract and secular "St Jean-Baptiste" remained. In 1977, the Parti Québécois' separatist (and secularist) government institutionalized June 24th as Quebec's legal national holiday. Solemn Catholic masses and the traditional parade gave way to secular festivities: "La Fête Natio-nale," the holiday's official designation, has since been celebrated with rock concerts, fireworks and public bonfires where the nation's bards and political figures renew their allegiance to Quebec amidst a sea of blue and white *fleur-de-lis* flags.

Three things here are worth noting: First, the choice of that date as the national holiday of the new Québécois nation; second, the name of the holiday and the use of the adjective "national" in a legal document, which is in itself a political state-ment; and third, the effacement of the association with the saint's day, marking the holiday as stridently secular. The Catholic heritage of the holiday has been thor-oughly occluded in the documentation of the institution responsible for the organi-zation of the Fête (with the exception of a single reference that appeared only very recently; Chartier and Vaudry 2007). In official publications and on the govern-ment's website, ample references were made to the pre-Christian origins of the summer solstice celebrations, and to the traditions inherited from the early days of the colony's festivities, but none to the saint himself, nor to his appropriation by the Catholic Church in the nineteenth century. A century of extraordinary celebrations were simply disregarded, silencing an important chapter in the history of the holiday in Quebec and exorcising the ethno-religious genesis of the French Canadian nation prior to its Québécois redefinition. While the holiday is still commonly referred to as "La Saint-Jean," few under the age of forty could explain why the nation is commemorated on that specific day.[17]

Nationalism and religion: questioning the causal direction

While St Jean Baptiste's career trajectory in Quebec suggests that secular Québécois nationalism has replaced French Canadian ethno-Catholicism, one should be careful not to assume that the former has surfaced *because* of religion's decline – and in order to fill that void – a common assumption, we have seen, in the nationalism literature (Durkheim 1995 [1912]; Hayes 1960; Kohn 1946; Gellner 1983; Hobsbawm 1995). Eric J. Hobsbawm, for example, explains the existence of Québécois nationalism since the 1960s as a *response* to the Quiet Revolution's "social cataclysm," which created a "disorientated generation hungry for new certitudes to replace the collapsing old ones" such that "the rise of militant separatism was a surrogate for the lost traditional Catholicism" (1995: 172).[18] If nationalism in Quebec could be reduced to a simple causal relation – which it cannot – a more plausible argument would be precisely the opposite: the secularization of society was not the cause of the nationalist movement, but its *consequence*. The collapse of the Church as a crypto-state and the rejection of the religious narrative of the nation was the result of the creation of a mobilizing modern, political discourse of the nation and institutional transformations at the level of the provincial state. It was a new wave of nationalists arguing for a novel national project centered on Quebec who were instrumental in initiating the break with the Church and rejecting the religious narrative of the French Canadian nation. The struggles over the figure of Saint Jean-Baptiste and his ultimate "beheading" by left-wing activists could not be more suggestive. The consequence of that action during the parade-turned-protest were to be long-lasting in the way the state organizes its national festivities, how ordinary people celebrate their "national" holiday, and, perhaps most importantly, how Québécois think of and "act out" their nation.

As in the Polish case, the reconfiguration of national identity and religion in the 1960s' Quebec was not only carried out in institutions and through the renegotiation of Church-state relations, but also through the rejection of old narratives and the creation of new ones. That rejection was effected symbolically, in discursive repudiations and in ritual reversals across a decade, when parades became the platforms for protests that chipped away at the figurative castings of ethno-Catholic French Canadianness. Still, the choice of June 24 as the central national celebration monumentalizes in a sense the failure of the separatist national project, and the deep ambivalence toward it among even so-called *Québécois de souche* ("old-stock Québécois"), since the continued use of the saint's day as the National Holiday indexes the conspicuous absence of an Independence Day for Quebec. The Precursor was beheaded and the lamb of God sacrificed, yet the new covenant never arrived.

The fate of St Jean-Baptiste – first beheaded and then buried with the institutionalization of a secular national holiday on the saint's name day – moreover reveals not merely the negation of Catholicism's place in defining the *Québécois* nation (in distinction from its former French Canadian version), but also the continued trace of a religious culture that still informs and infiltrates the "secular" one. Although the saint was beheaded and his float destroyed, St Jean-Baptiste has survived under the guise of a new assumed identity, "la fête nationale." Catholicism, likewise, may have disappeared from the public sphere and from the Québécois' everyday life – few believe and even fewer go to church – but when encountering religious Others, they remain Catholic in their secularism. Recent debates over the "reasonable accommodations" of religious practices of immigrants has demonstrated this quite clearly.[19]

CONCLUSION

The comparative study of nationalism and religion, the analysis of these two cases suggest, would be more productively advanced by devoting less energy to secularization, and more to the specific configurations of religious authority and religious cultures, on one hand, and national institutional contexts and national cultures, on the other. Religion and nationalism each have both institutional and symbolic or discursive forms, such that what began as an apparently straightforward problem of examining religion and nationalism, and their fission or fusion, has now become a more complex one that "secularization" does not usefully address.

For Poland and Quebec, as for other cases where national identity is experienced and expressed through religious channels at some historical point, the estimation of religious decline or ascent in relation to nationalism is a quixotic mission. Where the sacred is secularized and then resacralized in national form, and this transmutation repeated over and over again, the quest after neat models of the substitution of one for the other is a charging of windmills. The relationship between nationalism and religion is far from being fixed, as if on a pre-determined course, but in constant motion.

Events such as the War of the Crosses and the St Jean-Baptiste celebrations, then, become especially important for us to study because it is through such social dramas that the relationship between national identity and religion was actually reconfigured by social actors in post-communist Poland (1990s) and during Quebec's Quiet Revolution (1960s). I showed that by virtue of both the cross and St Jean-Baptiste carrying within them key national narratives, the symbols became objects of contestation through which social actors performed and transformed the relationship between their national identity and Catholicism. By doing so, I argued that the relationship between nation and religion is (re)fashioned at key historical junctures not only in and through political ideologies and institutional re-arrangements, but also in popular rituals such as processions, parades, and protests.

The relationship between national identity and religion is indeed mediated by, expressed in, and reconfigured through the use of symbols and the performance of rituals in concrete sites and during public, and highly publicized, events such as the War of the Crosses in Poland or the St Jean-Baptiste Day parades in Quebec. Dissecting such events and analyzing the debates they generate in the public sphere allows us to grasp the processual dynamics of nationalism and to tease out how broad institutional and structural changes such as state (re)formation and regime transformations are related to micro-sociological phenomena such as identity formation. In the end, I am building a case for why this particular kind of multi-level research approach is not only more complete, but also critical for accurately identifying the mechanisms of social change and explaining the process of identity formation.

These brief empirical case-studies suggest the value of sociological analyses that take symbols and material artifacts seriously. I contend that both the fusion and fission of national and religious identifications, while depending on articulations of statehood, rely on specific events and practices and their manipulations of material artifacts which, despite the differing outcomes in Quebec and Poland, employ an analogous metaphysics of presence – an implicit faith in icons, crosses and banners as being possessed of transforming power. This attribution of power-in-objects is not "totemic," à la Durkheim – the sacralization in a material object of society *as it is* – but rather "polemic" – the graphic pressing of claims through symbols about how society *should be*. Concrete practices and material artifacts are employed by social actors to focus, magnify and exaggerate particular features of the religion-nation configuration, with the objective of changing the relative place of religion in national representations and narratives. And as such, we should pay attention to them.

Notes

1 Secularization theory is highly differentiated. José Casanova, in his remarkable historical-comparative study of public religions in the modern world, argues that secularization, commonly thought to be a single phenomenon (and consequently often developed into a single theory) is actually composed of "three very different, uneven and unintegrated propositions: secularization as differentiation of the secular spheres from religious institutions and norms, secularization as decline of religious beliefs and practices, and secularization as marginalization of religion to a privatized sphere" (1994: 211, see esp. chs. 1 and 8). Philip Gorski (2000a) differentiates between four main types of secularization theories: whereas some posit the disappearance and the decline of religion, others emphasize its privatization and transformation.

2 Benedict Anderson's take on the relationship between secularization and the emergence of nationalism is more nuanced than those of Gellner or Hobsbawm, and he expressly reject a simplistic causal argument: "Needless to say, I am not claiming that the appearance of nationalism towards the end of the eighteenth century was 'produced' by the erosion of religious certainties, or that this erosion does not itself require a complex explanation. Nor am I suggesting that somehow nationalism historically 'supersedes' religion. What I am proposing is that nationalism has to be understood by aligning it, not with self-consciously held political ideologies, but with the large cultural systems that preceded it, *out of which* – as well as *against which* – it came into being" (1991: 12 emphasis mine). For him, there is no *necessary* connection between the dusk of the religious mode of thought and the dawn of nationalism. Rather, the decline of sacred communities, languages and lineages transformed modes of apprehending the world, making the nation "thinkable" (1991: 22).

3 The inverse causal relation is also commonly assumed: the contemporary rise of religious movements and the "re-enchantment of the world" are often attributed to the decline of the nation-state in the face of globalization.

4 The Reformation is either seen as containing the seeds of secularization or as a source of religious revival. According to either interpretation, however, it is a significant event in the formation of nations and nationalism. "Modernists" argue that nationalism is in essence a modern phenomenon, originating in the late eighteenth century, its birth often corresponding to the French Revolution. They look at the Reformation from a greater historical distance, seeing in it its long-term impact on the place of religion in public life. The Reformation, for them, therefore contains the seed of secularization that ultimately allowed the emergence of the nation form. "Early modernists," such as Greenfeld and Gorski, question the modernist position and identify the rise of nationalism in the early modern period. As a result, instead of seeing the Reformation as the beginning of the end of religion that then caused the emergence of nationalism, they understand it as a wave of religious *élan* whose *immediate* effect was to instigate nationalist movements and create national identities. While both positions link the Reformation with the eventual emergence of nationalism, each conceptualizes the relationship between religion and nationalism differently: modernists see nationalism resulting from religious decline, early modernists see its roots in religious enthusiasm.

5 More recently, however, scholars have turned to other concerns, and especially to the role of religious nationalism in state formation, power consolidation, and contemporary (domestic) politics. Roger Friedland (2002) has shown why and in what ways the nation-state is a vehicle of the divine for religious nationalists; Shenhav (2007) has argued that far from transcending religion, nationalism participates in a process of hybridization of the secular and the religious, as exemplified in Zionism and contemporary Israeli politics; and Fukase-Indergaard and Indergaard (2008) have revealed the peculiar role of religious nationalism in the making of the modern Japanese state. Following a different but related literature, Johnson (2005) and Gorski (2008) have resuscitated the concept of civil religion to analyze post 9/11 American politics. Gorski usefully distinguishes between civil religion, which he defines as the "sacralization of the democratic polity and celebration of the sovereign people" and religious nationalism, which is the "sacralization of the national state and a divine deputation of the common people, such that they may serve as the righteous arm of divine judgment."

6 For an analysis of Polish claims to Auschwitz and the ways in which they compete with Jews over the memory of the former death camp, see chs. 3 (" 'Oświęcim'/'Auschwitz': Archeology of a Contested Site and Symbol") and 4 ("The Aesthetics of the War of the Crosses: Mobilizing 'the Nation' ") of my book *The Crosses of Auschwitz: Nationalism and Religion in Post-Communist Poland* (2006).

7 According to recent data, 96% of Polish citizens are Catholic, 95% declare belief in God, and 77% consider religion an integral part of their everyday life. 56% participate in religious services at least once a week and 75% participate once or twice a month (CBOS, *The Meaning of Religion in the Life of Poles*, Statistical Report, Warsaw, 2006).

8 The term "civil religion" was first coined by Jean-Jacques Rousseau in the *Social Contract*. It is mostly associated with Durkheim and Durkheimian perspectives. It was popularized in the United States in the late 1960s with Robert Bellah's article "Civil Religion in America" (1967), on the heels of which a veritable sociological industry grew up before again receding by the 1990s. For an interesting comeback of the concept after the events of September 11, 2001, see Johnson (2005).

9 This is far from the perennialist model of the relationship between nationalism and religion, which claims that the modern nation grew out of already existing religious communities. The association between Catholicism and Polishness was not natural, but historically specific. It is the result of a arduous process of construction that is never

totally completed and that requires extensive maintenance and upkeep in institutions of social reproduction – pedagogy, law, the state, the Church – and by public leaders through speeches, publication, political mobilization, and ritual performance.

10   Father Tischner spoke these words during a public discussion at the Dominican church in Cracow on November 22, 1993 (author's personal recording). This is also the opinion expressed by Jesuit Stanisław Obirek in a personal interview on May 22, 2004. Obirek has since left the Church.

11   This section is based the archival and ethnographic research conducted for a book manuscript in progress on religious narratives, visual symbols and the remaking of the nation in Quebec.

12   The Christian use of the symbol of the lamb originates from the Hebrew tradition. To protect Jews from the 10th plague brought by God to the Egyptians, God told Moses to instruct them to sacrifice lambs and mark their doors with the animals' blood so that the Angel of Death would "pass over" their house and save their firstborn sons from execution. Jesus celebrated his own "Last Supper" with his disciples on Passover, and with his proposal of a new covenant positioned himself as the sacrifice, *agnus Dei*, the saving lamb of God. In the French Canadian narrative, the lamb further signified civilization through the progress of the Christian missions.

13   The territorial narrowing of *Québécois* identity set off a ripple effect throughout Canada, causing other French-speaking Canadian groups to redefine their own identities along provincial lines: Franco-Ontarians, Franco-Manitobans, Saskatchewan's Fransaskois, Franco-Albertans, Franco-Columbians, and so on. Whereas Francophones in Quebec constitute approximately 80 percent of the population, they constitute only 10 to 14 percent of other Canadian provinces' populations, hence their common designation as "Francophones outside Quebec." Quebec has therefore also become, since the 1970s, the reference through which – and sometimes against which – French-speaking Canadians are defined and define themselves. On the transformation and fragmentation of French Canadian identity, see Thériault (1999), and Langlois and Létourneau (2004).

14   The opposition to the ethno-religious vision of the nation and to the clerical power in Quebec did not emerge ex nihilo during the 1960s. It has a long history, with its roots in the Patriots' liberal movement and running through the twentieth century. It however became more meaningful and effective in operating changes during the 1960s because it coincided with, and found its home in that decade's political developments.

15   Stats.

16   The lamb was also viewed as problematic. Recall the theological interpretation of the Saint as the forerunner of the Messiah, and of the lamb as Jesus (as when the Precursor declared, "Behold the Lamb of God, who takes away the sin of the world!" [John 1:29]) and, by extension, French Canadian religion/civilization. Critics emphasized a simpler and more insidious interpretation of the tableau. In their view, John the Baptist was the nation's patron and protector; the lamb was therefore the nation itself, exploited and ultimately sacrificed. In a strategic semantic shift, the new critics began to speak of the *sheep* instead of the lamb to draw attention to the image and push to the foreground a troubling set of associations: one of a docile and dumb nation, a nation that lets wolves "eat the wool off its back," and tamely follows directions when its own interests lay elsewhere. "The sheep" therefore became the symbolic foil against which a new political elite presented their national project, defined around the idea of progress, economic development, and political self-reliance.

17   On selective memory and the invention of tradition in 1970s Quebec, see Richard Handler's *Nationalism and the Politics of Culture in Quebec* (1988).

18 Hobsbawm's functionalist argument is a perfect example of what I call "residual primordialism." He claims that the nation is an invented functional substitute for real, but lost, communities in order to fill an emotional void (1992: 46, 109). From this perspective, nationalism is related to social disorientation and disorganization, as well as to individual uprooting (pp. 172–3).

19 In fall 2006 and winter 2007, several incidents involving religious minorities and Quebec's secular majority prompted vocal opposition to what was perceived as public institutions' *over*-accommodation of minorities' religious needs. In response to public confusion and discontent over the hazy boundaries of "reasonable accommodation," in February 2007 Quebec Premier Jean Charest announced the establishment of the Commission on Practices of Accommodation Related to Cultural Differences (*Commission de consultation sur les pratiques d'accommodement reliées aux différences culturelles*). This public consultation and forum, co-chaired by sociologist Gérard Bouchard and philosopher Charles Taylor, was charged with exploring and explicating the meaning and practice of Quebec's official secularism in the face of increasing religious pluralism created by diverse immigrant populations. Public debate was not solely about the challenges faced by a secular host society and its religious "guests," but one about the very identity and secularity of Quebec, as briefs presented to the commissioners and their own 310-page report attest. Indeed, the year-long investigation of "reasonable accommodation" turned out to be the most significant critical interrogation about Québécois national identity since the 1960s, as political figures, public intellectuals, artists, business people, and ordinary citizens all lent their voices to the commission's work.

Bibliography

Anderson, Benedict (1991) [1983] *Imagined Communities: Reflections on the Origins and Spread of Nationalism*, London and New York: Verso.

Armstrong, John (1996) Nations before nationalism, in J. Hutchison and A. D. Smith (eds.), *Nationalism*, New York: Oxford University Press, 140–7.

Bell, David E. (2003) *The Cult of the Nation in France: Inventing Nationalism, 1680–1800*, Cambridge, MA: Harvard University Press.

Bellah, Robert N. (1967) Civil religion in America, *Daedalus* 96: 1–120.

Bendelow, Gillian and Williams, Simon J. (eds.) (1998). *Emotions in Social Life: Critical Themes and Contemporary issues*, New York: Routledge.

Berger, Peter L. (1969) *The Sacred Canopy: Elements of a Sociological Theory of Religion*, New York: Doubleday.

Berger, Peter L. and Luckman, Thomas (1967) *The Social Construction of Reality: A Treatise in the Sociology of Knowledge*, New York: Doubleday.

Calhoun, Craig (1993) Nationalism and ethnicity, *Annual Review of Sociology* 19: 211–39.

Casanova, José (1994) *Public Religions in the Modern World*, Chicago: University of Chicago Press.

Chartier, Daniel and Vaudry, Catherine (2007) *La fête nationale du Québec. Un peuple, une fierté*, Montreal: Mouvement national des Québécoises et Québécois and Lanctôt Éditeur.

Chaves, Mark (1994) Secularization as declining religious authority, *Social Forces* 72: 749–74.

Duara, Prasenjit (1995) *Rescuing History from the Nation: Questioning Narratives of Modern China*, Chicago: University of Chicago Press.

Durkheim, Émile (1995) [1912] *The Elementary Forms of Religious Life*, tr. K. Fields, New York: Free Press.

Eid, Nadia F. (1978) *Le clergé et le pouvoir politique au Québec: une analyse de l'idéologie ultramontaine au milieu du XIXe siècle*, Montreal: Hurtubise.

Frenette, Yves (1998) *Brève histoire des Canadiens français*, Montreal: Boréal.

Friedland, Roger (2002) Money, sex and god: the erotic logic of religious nationalism, *Sociological Theory* 20 (3): 381–425.

Fukase-Indergaard, Fumiko and Indergaard, Michael (2008) Religious nationalism and the making of the modern Japanese state, *Theory and Society* 37 (4): 343–74.

Gauchet, Marcel (1985) *Le désenchantement du monde. Une histoire politique de la religion*, Paris: Gallimard.

Gellner, Ernest (1983) *Nations and Nationalism*, New York: Cornell University Press.

Gillis, John R. (1994) Memory and identity: the history of a relationship, Pp. 3–24 in J. R. Gillis (ed.), *Commemorations: The Politics of National Identity*, Princeton: Princeton University Press, 3–24.

Gorski, Philip S. (2000a) Historicizing the secularization debate: church, state, and society in late medieval and early modern Europe, ca. 1300 to 1700, *American Sociological Review* 65: 138–67.

Gorski, Philip S. (2000b) The mosaic moment: an early modernist critique of modernist theories of nationalism, *American Journal of Sociology* 105 (5): 1428–68.

Gorski, Philip S. (2003) *The Disciplinary Revolution: Calvinism and the Rise of the State in Early Modern Europe*, Chicago: University of Chicago Press.

Gorski, Philip S. (2008) Class, nation and covenant, SSRC blog posted on the Imanent Frame, http://blogs.ssrc.org/tif/2008/03/21/class-nation-and-covenant, posted on FMarch 21, 2008, accessed on March 22, 2008.

Greenfeld, Liah (1992) *Nationalism: Five Roads to Modernity*, Cambridge, MA: Harvard University Press.

Greenfeld, Liah (1996) Is nationalism the modern religion?, *Critical Review* 10 (2): 169–91.

Handler, Richard (1988) *Nationalism and the Politics of Culture in Quebec*, Madison: University of Wisconsin Press.

Hastings, Adrian (1997) *The Construction of Nationhood: Ethnicity, Religion and Nationalism*, New York: Cambridge University Press.

Hayes, Carlton (1926) *Essays on Nationalism*, New York: Macmillan.

Hayes, Carlton (1960) *Nationalism: A Religion*, New York: Macmillan.

Hobsbawm, Eric J. (1983a) Introduction: inventing traditions, in E. J. Hobsbawm and T. Ranger (eds.), *The Invention of Tradition*, Cambridge: Cambridge University Press, 1–14.

Hobsbawm, Eric J. (1983b) Mass-producing traditions: Europe, 1870–1914, in E. J. Hobsbawm and T. Ranger (eds.), *The Invention of Tradition*, Cambridge: Cambridge University Press, 263–307.

Hobsbawm, Eric J. (1995) [1992] *Nations and Nationalism since 1780* (new revd. edn.), New York and London: Cambridge University Press.

Johnson, Paul C. (2005) Savage civil religion, *Numen* 52: 290–324.

Juergensmeyer, Mark (1993) *The New Cold War? Religious Nationalism Confronts the Secular State*, Berkeley: University of California Press.

Kedourie, Elie (1960) *Nationalism*, New York: Blackwell.

Kohn, Hans (1946) *The Idea of Nationalism: A Study in Its Origins and Background*, New York: Macmillan.

Langlois, Simon and Létourneau, Jocelyn (eds.) (2004). *Aspects de la nouvelle francophonie canadienne*, Ste-Foy: Les Presses de l'Université Laval.

Lincoln, Bruce (2003) *Holy Terrors: Thinking about Religion after September 11*, Chicago: University of Chicago Press.

Llobera, Josep (1996) *The God of Modernity: The Development of Nationalism in Western Europe*, Oxford and Washington: Berg.

Marvin, Carolyn and Ingle, David W. (1999). *Blood Sacrifice and the Nation: Totem Rituals and the American Flag*, Cambridge: Cambridge University Press.

Marx, Anthony W. (2003) *Faith in Nation: Exclusionary Origins of Nationalism*, New York: Oxford University Press.

Michel, Patrick (1986) Y a-t-il un modèle ecclésial polonais?, *Archives des Sciences sociales des Religions* 62 (1): 81–92.

Renan, Ernest (1996) [1882] Qu'est-ce qu'une nation, in G. Eley and R. G. Suny (eds.), *Becoming National: A Reader*, New York: Oxford University Press, 41–55.

Sells, Michael A. (1996) *The Bridge Betrayed: Religion and Genocide in Bosnia*, Berkeley and Los Angeles: University of California Press.

Shenhav, Yehouda (2007) Modernity and the hybridization of nationalism and religion: Zionism and the Jews of the Middle East as a heuristic case, *Theory and Society* 36 (1): 1–30.

Smith, Anthony D. (1986) *The Ethnic Origins of Nations*, New York: Blackwell.

Smith, Anthony D. (2003) *Chosen Peoples: Sacred Sources of National Identity*, New York: Oxford University Press.

Snyder, Louis L. (1990) *Encyclopedia of Nationalism*, New York: Paragon.

Tambiah, Stanley (1996) *Leveling Crowds: Ethnonationalist Conflicts and Collective Violence in South Asia*, Berkeley and Los Angeles: University of California Press.

Tamir, Yael (1995) The enigma of nationalism, *World Politics* 47: 418–40.

Tamir, Yael (1997) Pro Patria Mori!: Death and the State, in R. McKim and J. McMahan (eds.), *The Morality of Nationalism*, New York: Oxford University Press, 227–41.

Thériault, Joseph-Yvon (1999) La nation francophone d'Amérique: Canadiens, Canadiens français, Québécois, in C. Andrew (ed.), *Dislocation et permanence: L'invention du Canada au quotidien*, Ottawa: Ottawa University Press, 111–37.

Van der Veer, Peter (1994) *Religious Nationalism: Hindus and Muslims in India*, Berkeley and Los Angeles: University of California Press.

Van der Veer, Peter and Lehmann, Hartmut (eds.) (1999) *Nation and Religion: Perspectives on Europe and Asia*, Princeton: Princeton University Press.

Weber, Eugen (1976) *Peasants into Frenchmen: The Modernization of Rural France, 1870–1914*, Stanford: Stanford University Press.

Weber, Max (2001) (1930) *The Protestant Ethic and the Spirit of Capitalism*, New York: Routledge.

Zubrzycki, Geneviève (2001) "We, the Polish Nation": Ethnic and Civic Visions of Nationhood in Post-communist Constitutional Debates, *Theory and Society* 30 (5): 629–68.

Zubrzycki, Geneviève (2005) "Poles-Catholics" and "Symbolic Jews": Jewishness as Social Closure in Poland, *Studies in Contemporary Jewry* 21: 65–87.

Zubrzycki, Geneviève (2006) *The Crosses of Auschwitz: Nationalism and Religion in Post-Communist Poland*, Chicago: University of Chicago Press.

Part VII

The Future of Religion

28

The Future of Religion

Andrew Wernick

God is not quite dead. Man is not quite alive. Gardavsky[1]

BACKGROUND TO THE QUESTION

The future of religion is not the same as the future of any particular religion or religious tradition. And yet – from Bacon's *New Atlantis* and Kant's *Religion within the Limits of Reason Alone* to Freud's *Future of an Illusion*, Bataille's musings about Acéphale and on to the crop of books on the topic which seize our attention today – it has been a peculiarly Western question, one marked, indeed, by just this tendency to conflate the regional with the global, and the prospects for Christianity and the civilization it has influenced with those for religion as such.

In the broadest historical terms, and in ways that still reverberate, three factors converged to prompt the question and to set it on its generalizing way.

First was the split of Western Christendom[2] in the Reformation and the question-mark this placed over the future of a religious institution which had held together for almost a millennium. The rift seemed permanent, ratified in the Westphalian principle of *cuius regio illius religio*, as too the spread of sects and movements once the hegemony of a controlling center had been broken. Nevertheless, was unity recoverable through some kind of principled doctrinal harmonization? Long before twentieth-century ecumenism this was already Leibniz's question, who further raised the possibility of a reconciliation between Christianity and Confucianism (Mungello 1977), and thus of an ecumenism that was potentially global.[3] More pragmatically, in states riven by religious conflict, could at least a second-order settlement be forged? Anglicanism, with its fudged doctrine of the Eucharist, and its opening to moderate evangelical and traditionalist tendencies, was a half-step in that direction, but at the cost of politically fraught exclusions. Another way was to project the possibility of a big tent civil religion, prescribing only the minima of Christian belief, for which Locke, in his *Letter on Toleration* provided one model, and Rousseau , in Book IV of the *Social Contract* and "Profession of faith of a Savoyard Vicar" (in *Émile*), another.

In an important respect, however, the schisms of the sixteenth century were quite unlike the credal disputes that had preceded, for example, the Councils of Nicaea (325) and Chalcedon (451). Protestantism, with its emphasis on faith and conscience over dogma and ceremonial, and its elimination of the mediating role of a Church safe-guarded tradition of biblical interpretation, represented a rupture both in belief and in the way that belief was practiced. It was a new form of Christianity, albeit that such resonantly post-medieval features as Luther's "priesthood of all believers," Zwingli's de-magicalizing interpretation of the mass, and Calvinism's levelling congregationalism, were lived as a return to the simplicity of the early church and to the purity of the Biblical Word. How then was Reformed Christianity, and its taking hold in northern Europe, to be regarded? Was the overthrow of priestly authority, iconoclasm and the new *innerlichkeit* a historical step forward, a vital episode of religious evolution, as Hegel (2007: 412–26) saw it, one indeed in which Christianity was itself destined to become something more universal? or was it the herald of a rebellion against all authority, as argued by Catholic conservatives like de Maistre?[4] According to the first, the religious horizon was one of an immanently divine secularization; according to the second, what hovered on the horizon was the spectre of a dissolvent nihilism.

The second factor was the rise of the natural sciences, the detachment of natural philosophy from theology and Scholasticism, and the ambition of an increasingly emancipated rationality to engage the previously off-limit areas of morality, metaphysics and the human. On its critical side, enlightened reason, conjoined with a naturalist ontology, aimed to dissolve all that was mythic, magical or mystical in human (self) understanding. "The premise of all criticism" said the young Marx (1964: 43) is "the criticism of religion." The positive direction of this movement can be traced in the progressive elimination of faith or revelation-based knowledge in the encyclopaedic "tree" that the French Encyclopedists took over from Bacon. It can also be traced in the aim to grasp religion itself, thematized as a generic category, as a natural phenomenon. On the one hand, then religion was historicized and anthropologized, beginning with the proposition that the God of Judaism and Christianity was a socially conditioned projection in a line of such projections that stretched back to an originary animism; and on the other, the search was on for ways to ground, in reason or nature, what could be distilled as universal in Christianity's (and Judaism's) moral truths, a distillate that was in turn projected forwards as the new horizon of religious development.

The third factor, in part driven by the other two, but also corresponding to a differentiating dynamic that came to seem inextricable from capitalist industrialization, was the retreat of religious, especially clerical, authority from the public realm. Correlative with this was the relegation of personal belief to the private sphere ("I have no desire to make windows in men's souls" – Elizabeth I) and, with print and the gradual roll-back of censorship, the opening up of a public space in which ideas about religion could, in relative freedom, be seriously discussed. The question concerning the future of religion, if one fore-grounded this trend, became not only, then, a matter of its future content but of its relative salience, and compartmentalization, within individual and social life.

None of this was a smooth or homogeneous process. As Lucien Goldmann pointed out,[5] the turbulent transition to modernity not only led, in different countries, to different configurations of bourgeois hegemony (and instability), but also to the dominance of different intellectual paradigms (empiricism and utilitarianism in England and Scotland, rationalism in France, idealism in Germany). To which we may add that that these different formations were marked, as well, by different passages through the Reformation and Counter-Reformation and by distinct national problematizations of religion and its future. Particularly striking is the contrast between post-1789 France and Lutheran Germany. In the former, republicanism, in a long drawn out contest with an unreconstructed Catholicism, was associated with practical attempts to complete the new order with a post-theistic cult of society or humanity. In the latter, under conditions of small town backwardness and then top down industrialization, revolution, whether liberal-democratic or more radical, could only be a dream, and speculations by theologians and philosophers about the implications of immanentization (from the god without to the one within) jostled with intimations of a revived or re-invented paganism. Both contrasted with developments across the Channel, where a self-confident progress-through-science empiricism pushed such continental wildness to the side, while the science-religion debate touched off by Darwin's *Origin of Species* largely confined itself to questions of epistemology and the limits of biblical literalism.

Nevertheless, as a cumulative result, by the end of the nineteenth century a rich field of questions, drawing on a multitude of new scholarly specializations, was established within secular thought itself concerning the nature of, and prospects for, the Western religious inheritance. The most dramatic outcome was Nietzsche's assault not just on all metaphysics ("be true to the earth") but on the entire Judaeo-Christian residue of altruistic and communitarian morality. At the same time, the social, political, cultural and even economic dimensions of religion had been thrown dramatically into relief. This paved the way for a historical, comparative and social scientific treatment of the overall relation between modernity, capitalism and religion, a focus that was central to both French and German classical sociology. Besides contrasts with the medieval and antique past, a comparative dimension to such inquiry was also provided by imperialism and the expansion of trade, leading to a more intensified contact with Islam, the religions of India and China, and – which upset all ideas about religion – detailed ethnographic reports about the "primitive" religions of indigenous peoples.

Not surprisingly, the speculations arising from this crucible of issues tended to be ethnocentric. Nor was this only because of what they exoticized or marginalized. In foregrounding the fate of Christianity (and Judaism, though primarily as its antecedent) in the context of modern times, thinking about such matters was saturated in that religion even when taking positions opposing it.[6] The will to truth, as Nietzsche pointed out,[7] was an immanently disruptive element within Christianity itself. Tracing a different genealogy Gillespie (1994) has argued that the absolutization of God in the late middle ages paved the way both for nihilism and for the ego as a replacement foundation for epistemic and moral principles.

Such ethnocentrism could also give itself a good conscience. Christianity, with its gospel of selfless love, was taken, even by most secular thinkers, to be the most universal of religions, and Western societies the most advanced, charting out the future of all humanity. In the grand historicizing of the eighteenth and nineteenth centuries, the ascent of civilization unfolded upwards from "savagery" to "barbarism" and form Sumer to modern Europe. This ascent was also linked to a maturation metaphor. Enlightenment, declared Kant in *What Is Enlightenment?*, is humanity emancipating itself from its self caused tutelage. Freud's *Future of an Illusion* plays with a similar figure of adolescent crisis, though with more doubts about whether it could be successfully overcome. The assertion that the West is the standard bearer, if not the source, of universal human values like freedom and reason is still a common coin of international political discourse. For Max Weber, the West's cultural exceptionalism in being plausibly able to make that claim was indeed a central problem for sociology.[8] Not that Weber's thesis was triumphalist. What had triumphed with Protestantism and capitalism was the disenchantment of the world and instrumental reason, a decidedly limited and two-edged universal.

A generation ago the conventional wisdom, including among sociologists (Wilson 1966; Berger 1973), was broadly in accord with the Enlightenment prognosis. Religion, at least as traditionally understood, was steadily in decline for both individuals and society. Indeed, if current trends in the advanced societies continued, was it not destined ultimately to disappear? Such a view became especially plausible in the two decades following World War II, with secularization of all kinds, from emptying pews to the commercialization of Sundays, proceeding apace. The United States was a notable exception,[9] but even here the trends were in the same direction.

Several things have changed this view. Externally, there has been a resurgence both of Christianity and other world religions, especially Islam, and within that a strong current of neo-traditionalist fundamentalism. In parallel we have seen the collapse of the USSR, leading to the resuscitation of the Russian Orthodox Church, and the decline in the post-colonial world of secular nationalism and socialisms. In part, the resurgence could be regarded as a transitional phenomenon: a mix of reactive anti-modernism and anti-Westernism and of a bridge to capitalist modernization via equivalents of the Protestant ethic (evangelicalism in Central America; the rise of Moslem piety in the small merchant and professional classes in the Middle East). But it is too widespread and variegated a phenomenon to be regarded as ephemeral, and if it represents a displacement of energy from blocked or defeated secular-progressive movements, the relation of ideological forces has also been changed thereby.

In any case, since the 1960s religion has become of increasing salience in the advanced West as well. Among the factors in play have been evangelical and Pentecostal revival; the counter-cultural, but now mainstream, flowering of alternative religions, sects and spiritualities; and changing patterns of religious affiliation and inter-communal relations brought by immigration and policies of multiculturalism, leading to controversies over the spread of "faith schools" and over the place, or non-place, of religion in the symbology of public life. In addition, as Berger had argued in *The Sacred Canopy* (1969), and Harvey Cox in *The Secular City* (1965), secular society itself, even in the flood tide of secularization, could be regarded as more religious than it took itself for.[10] The same point has been made by Mark Taylor (2007: 132): "religion does not return, because it never goes away; to the contrary, religion haunts society, self, and culture even – perhaps especially – when it seems to be absent." The term post-secular (Milbank 1993; Habermas

THE FUTURE OF RELIGION

2008) has come into circulation to describe this new, and newly interpreted, state of affairs.

Against that background my aim in the following remarks is to examine some contemporary approaches to the future of religion which take their bearings from the post-1960s situation. I especially want to focus on the dialogue between Rorty and Vattimo gathered together in a book of that title (Vattimo et al. 2005). I highlight the *Future of Religion* in part because the prominence of its authors – each widely regarded as their country's leading philosopher – has given to the text a certain importance, in part because of the explicitness with which a more broadly postmodern approach to an old question is given voice. The question I want to raise is the extent to which their positions break new ground with respect to the range of positions already established within Western thought over the preceding centuries. The suspicion that I want to test is that in some respects they do not and indeed that something may be missing.

Vattimo and Rorty

The *Future of Religion* (Vattimo et al. 2005) consists of an essay by Rorty, "Anticlericalism and atheism," an essay by Vattimo, "The age of interpretation" and a discussion between them moderated by Zabala, another prominent Italian philosopher, who also edited the book. While the essays by Rorty and Vattimo are occasional pieces, and not the most important of their writings,[11] the text is noteworthy for several reasons. Not the least is the fact of their collaboration itself. Rorty writes as a non-believer (previously a self-described atheist, but here, more consistent with his anti-dogmatism, an agnostic) and as an American liberal-progressive, with John Dewey as his guiding star. Vattimo writes as a practicing Italian Catholic, albeit one who is an "out" campaigner in gay and other causes,[12] and highly critical of the conservative theology that came to predominate under the papacy of John Paul II. Each, one might say, has a faith, but Vattimo's is in the unfolding possibilities of a past, for him transcendent, event, while Rorty's, indistinguishable from hope, is squarely in the human possibilities of the future:

> My sense of the holy is bound up with the hope that someday ... my remote descendants will live in a global civilization in which love is pretty much the only law. In such a society, communication would be domination-free, class and caste would be unknown, hierarchy would be a matter of temporary pragmatic convenience, and power would be entirely at the disposal of the free agreement of a literate and well-educated electorate. (p. 40)

Their philosophical differences are also striking. Vattimo studied hermeneutics with Gadamer and Löwith, and is a post-metaphysical thinker in line with Nietzsche and Heidegger. Rorty (who died in 2007) was a neo-pragmatist engaged with and against the analytic tradition. His early work (Rorty 1979, 1982) concerns the critique of what is metaphysical in the philosophy of science, particularly in its representational view of truth. Where they converge is in their anti-foundationalism, and more especially in their shared recognition (1) that anti-foundationalism applies to itself (i.e. Nietzsche's dictum that "there are no facts only interpretations" is itself only an interpretation) and (2) that such a stance, far from simply throwing us via relativism into anything goes nihilism opens the door to an ethical-political attitude, and practice, that would realize the axial values – love and justice – of the Western religious tradition.

Vattimo, it should be said, is much more interested in bringing out the historical aspect of this point than Rorty. In such works as *The End of Modernism* (Vattimo 1991) and *After Christianity* (Vattimo 2002b) – the titles tell the story – Vattimo explicates his position in detail. Hermeneutics is not to be considered simply as method. It is a reflexive mode of thinking that corresponds to contemporary *dasein*'s being-in-the-world.[13] Hence what he calls "hermeneutical ontology," and hence also his program of "weak thought," focus on dismantling absolutist knowledge claims, while also recognizing that the interpreter cannot escape confinement within his/her own horizon of meaning.

"Weak thought" is seen as fulfilling Nietzsche's and Heidegger's program of depassing Greek and Christian metaphysics. But as an ontological event – interpretation as "what is happening to Being" – it is also seen as completing the *kenosis*, God's self-emptying out, that Vattimo takes to be at the heart of the Christian story (cf. Hegel's "Golgotha of Absolute Spirit"). This is not the only recent instance of Nietzsche's appropriation by Christianity. Another is Altizer's "death of god" theology in the 1960s (Altizer 1966), and Mark Taylor's Derridean development of it in such works as *Erring* and *Altarity*. Inter-related has also been a renewed interest in an older tradition of negative theology that goes back (at least) to Pseudo-Dionysius and Meister Eckhart. But Vattimo's interest in Nietzsche's figure of the death of god is not apophatic, nor for that matter in the nature of divinity. His focus, rather, in line with the historicism of the later Heidegger, is on what the death of God means for the character of the epoch whose signature it is.

In effect, Vattimo's essay identifies awareness of the always-already interpreted character of the world as the fundamental experience of our age, with "the age of interpretation" standing in for Nietzsche's "twilight of the idols." As with Nietzsche, a culture of pan-intepretation undermines the absolutist claims of all authorities, including religious ones. This ultimately spells the end for the hierarchies and dogmas of organized religion, including those of Vattimo's own Church. But whereas, for Nietzsche, European nihilism moves to complete itself through a trans-valuation of good vs evil morality and an ecstatic Dionysianism in which "we ourselves become gods," for Vattimo the visible Church withers while that which is not false in Christianity comes into its own. For him, the future of religion lies in working out (or rather: the working out of) what the saturating prevalence of interpretation implies in the light of Jesus's gospel of love; and also in the light of what, *pace* Girard (1987), demystifying the Crucifixion brings to our understanding of sacrifice, scapegoating, and originary social violence.

But this is not all. The age of interpretation is also identified with the Franciscan visionary Joachim of Fiore's third and culminating "age of spirit," though with two important differences. First, Vattimo's transcription of Joachim's Trinitarian schema disconnects the age of spirit both from monasticism (for Joachim, after the age of the Son, the new age began in the sixth century with St Benedict and the founding of Monte Cassino) and from the apocalyptic communalism of his late medieval heretical followers. Following Hegel, rather, he finds in it a key for understanding modernity. For Vattimo, secondly, the ascendancy of the third person of the Trinity is not to be interpreted as that of an indwelling spirit to be realized in a fusional community, nor indeed as any kind of spiritual substance, but as a metaphor for the rise of a multi-levelled and heterogeneous practice of interpretation which feeds on the generosity it generates.

Rorty had sketched out a comparable position – minus the theological gloss – in *Contingency, Irony and Solidarity* (1989), which offers a critical but sympathetic commentary on the strange goings on in contemporary continental philosophy. What Rorty sees, with approval, as having come to the fore in French post-structuralism, and quintessentially in Derrida's left-inflected deconstruction of Western logocentrism, is a combination of "private irony" (which recognizes the contingency of all language and of all positions including his/her own) and "liberal hope" (for a pluralist community as the outcome of the dismantling of essentialized exclusions). Unlike for Vattimo, and indeed Derrida, however, the espousal of this position – which he had already come to in his critique of positivism – involves no wrestling with the death of God nor with the aporias of escaping metaphysics. There is no god shaped hole to be tremulously left vacant, and no tension, therefore, between the desire for, and impossibility of, belief: a tension that Vattimo et al. (1999) resolves through finding, in his own interpretation of his faith, that he "believes that he believes." Underpinning the agnosticism that Rorty now advances, in fact, is not so much doubt as ironic indifference, including towards the ultimate basis of his own commitments. Hence Rorty's comment, when siding with Lyotard against Habermas's efforts to establish a grand theory of communicative action: "he is not letting the narratives which hold our culture together do their stuff. He is scratching where it does not itch" (Bernstein 1985: 164).

What Rorty foregrounds in his essay, in any case, is the first term in the title: anticlericalism. The future we are bidden to welcome is one in which there is no mandatory public religion, no priestly interference in the public realm, and no restriction placed by clergy of whatever sort on free private interpretation and belief. The clerics inveighed against are not only those of organized religions but secular clerisies too. Like Vattimo, but with an emphasis on the so-to-speak church of the left rather than that of the Catholic Church, his faith, is in the laity, itself understood as a constantly self-reinterpreting community of interpreters. Not that there is any question of a head on campaign against priests or dogmatists. The point, as with the coming of pluralist democracy generally, is to confront hard with weak thought. Weak thought is weak not only because of its (non)grounding in groundlessness, but also because it undermines interpretative authority, as the logos of power. Weak thought, as soft against hard, is the thought of the weak.

In its willingness to straddle, or blur, the line between secular and non-secular modes of thinking *The Future of Religion* exemplifies a more general trend in postmodern thought. Other examples that could be cited are Derrida's engagement with Judaism (Caputo 2002), Baudrillard's play with Manicheism (1990), Eco's early work on Aquinas (1988), and Badiou (2003) and Zizek's (2001) interest in St Paul. This trend is less paradoxical than it might seem. While the anti-foundationalism of Nietzsche and Heidegger continued a critical movement that came to the fore in the Enlightenment, they did so at the expense of Enlightenment certitudes. Their philosophical heirs have simply continued the campaign. Lyotard's characterization of the postmodern condition as "suspicion towards meta-narratives" refers, first and foremost, to those of the Enlightenment itself, including naturalistic objectivism and all stories of progress through demystification.

One casualty has been the exclusive Enlightenment disjunct of reason (= science) and religion (= superstition), and the allergies to boundary crossing that have protected it. It is a stance which now seems like the product of a reaction formation. Its conscious undoing has opened the way for a fresh consideration of archaic themes (e.g. Derrida (1995) on the Abraham and Isaac story, Agamben (1999) on Benjamin's angelology, and Nancy's "Of divine places" 1991: 110–32) and also for a willingness to appropriate traditional religious language while still holding fast to a resolutely this-worldly ontology. Language itself – Bacon's "idol of the market-place" – has come under a destabilizing scrutiny both as the hiding place of metaphysics and for its social and historical arbitrariness as a mediator of thought. If one implication has been the unsettling awareness that language speaks us, another has been what Vattimo (2002a: 16) welcomes "the liberation of metaphor," which is also liberation by metaphor.

Most of the major thinkers associated with the ambiguous turn to religion I am describing are politically to the left – which means, in a post-1960s and post Cold War context, being faced on the one hand with humano-centric commitments to justice that they do not wish to give up and which can no longer easily be expressed in such terms, and on the other hand with the travails of the traditional (Marxist and industrial age) left, both as a political movement and as a mode of thought confidently in tune with the logos of history. It is an uncomfortable place to be, from which religious tropes and locutions have provided, with respect to rethinking the fundaments of a left orientation, a possible line of flight.

The varieties of religiosity put in play by this double exigency, however, and certainly those given expression in *The Future of Religion*, are not to be confounded with mere political retreat. They are neither personal and quietist, nor do they involve a reactive conversion, let alone any recurrence to schemas of individual salvation or life after death. As between a secular humanism that has become conceptually threadbare, and one or another form of retreat into revivalism or otherworldliness, what is envisaged, rather, is a kind of religious third way. This is religion without fixed doctrine, without clerics and cadres, and, with regard to individual religious practice, including ritual and prayer, benignly non-prescriptive. In the sphere of belief, it betokens "neither theism nor atheism" (p. 80), nor indeed the indecisiveness of an older agnosticism, for the question of God's being or non-being has become a non-question.[14] What justifies the term religion in this context is something residual: a transcending yet non-absolutized faith, whose outer expression is in the ethico-political practice (including of interpretation) that it animates. This is (as Caputo puts it) "religion without religion," and above all religion without authority.

NON-RELIGION

Such a view of the religious future, even if regarded only as a beckoning horizon, is no doubt contestable. It leaves popular religion, together with all the indications of its continued vitality and diversification, to one side. It is the religion, Freud would say, of intellectuals. Even, perhaps especially, in its liberal pluralism it never leaves the orbit of the West. But there is a prior question: in what sense is this future, understood as the long-term working out of the consequences of being in "an age of interpretation," the future of *religion*. In what sense are we still talking about religion at all?

The question is sharpened if we compare the positions advanced by Vattimo and Rorty with those advanced by Guyau ([1886] 1897) more than a century earlier. It is not hard to see resemblances. But what the former gesture towards as the future of religion, Guyau, more forthrightly, calls "the *irreligion* (or non-religion) of the future."

Guyau summarized his argument, which entailed a lengthy comparative and historical study and which provides a fascinating link between Durkheim and Nietzsche, as follows:

> The developments of religion and civilization have always proceeded hand in hand, and ... [those of religion] always in the line of a greater independence of spirit, of a less literal and less narrow dogmatism, of a freer speculation. Non-religion [*irreligion*], as we here understand it, may be considered as a higher degree simply of religion and of civilization ... The absence of religion thus conceived is one with a reasoned but hypothetical metaphysics treating of men and the universe. One may designate it as religious independence, or anomy, or individualism. It has, moreover, been preached in some degree by all religious reformers from Sakia-Mouni and Jesus to Luther and Calvin, for they have all of them maintained liberty of conscience and respected so much only of tradition as, in the then state of contemporary religious criticism, they could not help admitting. (Guyau 1897: 11)

Guyau's register is sociological rather than philosophical, and his framework is datedly evolutionist, in the spirit of Comte and, still more, Spencer. Unlike the authors of *The Future of Religion* moreover, Guyau excludes the possibility of such a dispensation coexisting with a plurality of religious survivals. Nor, for him, is there any element of undecidability or metaphor about the defining traits of a religious worldview: it is either myth based or it is reasoned speculation. Nor is Guyau's own position inscribed, as is that, ambiguously, of even Rorty, within a residually Christian faith (in the human, justice, community etc). There are nonetheless striking similarities. Guyau, like Vattimo and Rorty, foresees the emergence of a religio-ideological field in which institutionalized religion has withered away, discourse about ultimate meaning and truth has been freed from myth and doctrinal controls, and in which the deepest ethical, existential and cosmological (and non-mystical) insights of religious founders can be appreciated and debated in clear-eyed terms.

Guyau calls this point of arrival *irreligion*. He does so because attachment and obligation to the otherworldly have gone, there are no gods to worship, and because divinely given truths have been superceded by science on the one side, and by "reasoned speculation" on the other about first principles and deepest truths. Regarding the latter moreover there is no absolute standard of adjudication, and thus no prospect of a non-otherworldly successor to Christianity or other world religions, at least in the form of a unitary and overarching institution. Not that irreligion is a mere absence, any more than "religious anomie or individualism" amounts to chaos or nihilism. Not only does it presuppose a vibrant culture of "moral and metaphysical" inquiry. It also emerges in tandem with a bio-social advance in civilization made possible by enhanced canalization into social bonding of the surplus energy taken to flow through human life (a vitalistic assumption that Guyau shared with Nietzsche, if in a softer and less pagan key).[15] Overall, in fact, if non-religion is taken in conjunction with the wider transformation of which it is taken to be an essential part, it can be taken to play the same orienting and integrating roles as the religions whose series it caps. That is why in the passage cited Guyau can say, confusingly, that "non-religion is a higher form of religion and civilization."

Of course whether, in either case, we have or have not left the terrain of "religion" depends on how the word is defined and understood. But here – and without rehearsing the difficulties caused by the cloud of etymological and historical associations clustering around the word itself – several issues need to be disentangled.

The first concerns the objections that can be raised against any attempt to define religion purely from the subjective side, as a special mode of consciousness, or, more narrowly still, of cognition and belief. This is a standard reproach of sociologists to philosophers, and was indeed Durkheim's main criticism of Guyau (Pickering 1975: 34). If religion is taken to designate such complexes as Buddhism, Christianity etc then what is entailed is much more than a certain form of subjectivity, whether as belief, encounter with something beyond, feeling of absolute dependence, or any other variety of religious experience. It also involves practice, in fact both *a* practice – good works, prayer, rituals, moral regimen – and a body of *collective* practices in which the former are embedded. (In these terms Kant distinguishesd between cult and belief, and Comte between *Culte, dogme* and *regime*.) This we may add is not just a matter of induction. As an Althusserian would say: an apparatus of ritual practice and active symbolism is necessary for reproducing the subjectivity of its adherents, and for reproducing the "ideological social relations" (Colletti 1972) of the social formation as a whole. To peer into the future of religion, then, is not only to wonder about the future of belief and sensibility, it is also to wonder about the future of whatever apparatus of practices clusters around, and sustains, such subjectivity.

There remains the question though of what kind of collective beliefs and practices constitute religion, as opposed to what Althusser himself more broadly calls "ideology." A problem here is that how the line is drawn, and how fuzzily, will depend on the ontology of the drawer. For those who are not religiously musical (as Weber confessed himself to be) it may be hard to draw a line at all. For those who are, but who do not want to posit a realm of the supersensible there remains a dilemma. How, if we stay on the side of subjectivity, can we cogently distinguish between musicality and hallucination, or between what is truly or only apparently religious? How, that is, without recourse to some essential definition (Kant's "true religion") or without finding a satisfactory but propositionless way to speak of what is above and beyond? In line with current theology we may call the elusive ingredient an opening to transcendence, though this only transfers the dilemma onto another term, for such openness is not open if it is not open to what is outside the self as absolutely other – and how are we to understand that? It is in wrestling with this that Derrida (1998: 6) asks, in another instance of collaboration with Vattimo,

"How to 'talk religion'? Of religion? Singularly of religion today? How dare we speak of it in the singular without fear and trembling? who dares speak of it [religion] in the singular?"

On the other hand we can look for an external index, as in Durkheim's "sacred," though upon inspection it carries with it a similar problem. The force of the sacred, as the collective representation of the collective, and of what separates it from the profane, are those of the transcendent collective/we over the individual. It is an understanding that retains a God term – with a universal and sublime aspect that can be experientially encountered – in the shape of a group presumed to be its basis. But then is the sacred precipitated by any and every group, and "nation," comparably sacred? Can we distinguish, perhaps, the (merely) sacred with the(actually) holy? (Lévinas 1977). And in an increasingly complex and individuated society will not that which is held in common as sacred not only diminish, as Durkheim argued, but also disperse? In which case, undermining the Durkheimian ontology completely, the sacred ends up, as Caillois argued in *L'Homme et le sacré* (1988), being whatever each of us projects it to be.

In *The Disenchantment of the World*, Gauchet (1997) has proposed a different definition that would sidestep these issues. For him, what distinguishes religion is its total binding of social life to a sacralized fixed point in the past. It is the tyranny of an Origin. Religion, in this sense, is what there was elementarily, and the historical trajectory, through religion's gradual break-up, is towards an open futurity, for which Christianity, uniquely among the world-religions, has historically paved the way. Ideology (with that of the left as a model, but its forms are pervasive) is a half way house in which what binds is a fixed point in the future. An open future would be free from any binding. From this angle, as pointers to that future, the hybridity of positions of Vattimo and Rorty could be considered less progressive than Guyau's.

A third set of issues, cutting across all the above, concerns the distinction that may be drawn not only between *a* religion, as a wholescale complexes, and religion *as such*, but also between the latter and religion *in general*, understood as the totality of all that can be comprehended in that term. For the nominalist the second distinction may be hard to make, religion without an article being understood in terms of actual religions as the set of their common traits. However, this accords a defining status to past forms which may be a poor guide for capturing the forms of future possibilities. Besides, how in pondering the future of "religion," if conceived as a space occupied by religions understood as unitary complexes, are we to frame an understanding of trends (within modern Christianity for example) towards the separation of subjectivities and practices, of private from public religion, towards, in sum, the break up of the entities abstracted in its concept? The idea of metamorphosis may be just as appropriate as that of entropic decline, in which case a different picture comes into view.

Against Habermas's view that a completed modernity implies the completed, but also communicatively harmonized, separation of social action spheres, the drift we may witnessing is towards a more far-reaching break-up of religious totalities. In a recent book Lough (2006), who like Gauchet emphasizes the seemingly intractable resistance that is met on the way to (past) religion's disappearance, has suggested the latter has been arrested by the very process of religion's disarticulation. In a process he traces ultimately to the rise of the commodity form, what has come to characterize the field of Western religion is that its subjective and existential core has separated from its practical and institutional body. Thence the spirit of religion has migrated into the sublime, where it has tenaciously taken up residence as an untamed, promiscuous and often (for example in the blood-trail of twentieth-century fanaticisms) dangerous element.

Regardless of what concatenation of processes is actually under way, it makes sense to describe the space in which *all* this occurs as religion, thinking it not on the model of a unitary complex, whether in relation to whole societies (Berger's "sacred canopy" or as but as a dimension inhabited by a multiplicity of forms and flavors. Against Guyau, a hypothesis we might entertain is that at a certain point as religions recede, religion-in-general even grows, its vacated spaces filling up again with a swelling cloud of partial, disconnected, and recombinant elements.

THE RELIGION OF HUMANITY

That despite the historical gulf there should be significant overlap between a current and a late nineteenth-century effort to think the (post Christian) future of (Western) religion, is not surprising if we consider the longevity of the question and that, logically speaking, and at the limit, there have always been a finite number of possible answers. The *first* – challenging the premise – is that something recognizably like the old religion (theistic, organized, loyal to its origins and traditions) will, with adaptations and renewals, indefinitely persist. The *second* is that religion of this sort will come to an end and not be replaced. What comes next is non-religion. The *third* is that the old religion will end, but a religion of some new kind will arise in its stead. The *fourth* is that the old religion will die as institution, as ceremonial, as myth, in short as body, but its spirit will be realized immanently in the life, norms and structures of secular society.

In actuality these possibilities are not mutually exclusive. There are gradations and hybrids. The fourth possibility, expressed in the view that secularization is the realization of the spirit of Christianity, is itself a hybrid of the first and second. If we peer into the future of Western religion from the end of the nineteenth century, it is apparent that some combination of all four trends were in store at once. Nevertheless, major positions have clustered around them, and within the matrix they together constitute all possible modern and postmodern futures for religion can be arrayed.

What we might say in these terms is that while Guyau's position exemplifies possibility two (non-religion), Vattimo and Rorty, together with postmodern a/theologians like Mark Taylor and Caputo, blend this with possibility four: no religion as religion fulfilled. A peculiarity of Vattimo's position is that the idea of Christianity fulfilling itself through *kenosis* is, unlike in the paradigm-shaping cases of Kant, Hegel and Feuerbach, linked with a Catholic rather than Protestant understanding of faith and Church. For him, correspondingly, the old church as body does not entirely die. It continues in a porous, self-directing and constantly self-reinterpreting laity. A further peculiarity – though this is typical of the postmodern religious turn, and underpins its hybridity as a religiosity seeking to escape its own metaphysics – is that the thesis of secularization as realized religion is combined with Heidegger's understanding of Nietzsche's death of god, and translated into the terms of completed nihilism. The distinctiveness of Rorty's position , by contrast, is that a horizon of no-religion is combined with a bracketing of the god-question, and that, rather than being ambiguously wedded to Christian tradition, he places his chips in a secular-rationalist liberal-democratism that draws its energy from the American (Rorty 1998), i.e. from the idealist and politically progressive side of what Bellah (1991) has famously called American civil religion.

A tension running through both positions is that the tolerant dispersiveness of weak thought (which eschews being grounded in any Habermas-type rules of communicative engagement) is linked with the aim of fostering community. It is an in-common-ness however that is not constituted around adhesion to any common identity or cognitive foundation. It is a mode of community that arises, rather, in the practice of interpretation itself, that is to say in the ongoing questioning of identities and foundations, and in the charitable spirit with which this is conducted. The parallel between a theology attuned to a divinity, or transcending alterity, without substance and a politics oriented to a decentered and de-essentialized form of community is evident. And if the former is identified with the latter it is more than a parallel. What is missing from Vattimo's and Rorty's reflections is how such a practice, and such a practice as itself a project, might be culturally sustained – and the role played in this, for example, by their own respective faith communities and traditions. For this to come into focus, however, we would have to look at a possible pathway for the future of religion that is absent from their discussion, and indeed from much of contemporary discussion as a whole.

According to that possibility – number three in the grid just sketched out – the destiny of religion is not for the old religion to disappear, nor, in that disappearance, for it to permeate the world and fulfil its promise. It is for a new one to arise in its place. Such a religion would be religious as a binding and gathering that secured the moral and mental ground of the brave new world ushered in by science, industry and capitalism. It would mark a break from the old – whatever the continuities at the level of values – both in giving rise to independently fashioned symbolic and institutional forms, and in being resolutely this-worldly, post-theistic, and human-centered.

The idea, in formal terms, has had two main variants.

In its strongest form, replete with credo, sacred symbols and rituals, and extensions into everyday life, the idea of a new religion makes its appearance in Bacon's allegory of the House of Salomon, a benign order of scientist-priests dedicated "to the knowledge of causes, and secret motions of things; and the enlarging of the bounds of human empire, to the effecting of all things possible." Bacon's vision of technocracy plus philanthropy inspired the formation of royal societies and academies in England and France, and in more oppositional tones was enthusiastically carried forward by the Encyclopedists. But it was not until the cataclysm of the French Revolution that there was impetus to go beyond allegory, and actually try to bring a post-Christian (which in France meant post-Catholic) religious order into being.

The fantastical Jacobin attempt to do so by endowing the revolutionary Republic with a new calendar, roster of festivals (to liberty, reason, nature etc) and, at the climax of the Terror, a deist cult of the Supreme Being, the latter solemnly rolled out on 20th Prairial in a pageant on the Champs de Mars, came to nothing after Thermidor. But in the unstable decades that followed a number of new religion projects surfaced among social reformers, similarly underpinned with humano-philic fervor, coupled with a sense of urgency about the need to complete the insti-tutional transformation begun in the Revolution including at the moral and religious level.

The most notable were Saint-Simon's New Christianity in the 1820s, and Comte's Positive Religion of Humanity announced to the world in 1851, with himself as its *Grand-Pretre*. The Saint-Simonian version was more communitarian ("love one another as brothers"), the Comtean more corporatist and system-obsessed. But common to both was the sacralization of humanity, conceived at once as a lovingly united, and ultimately world-wide, community and as the (true) Great Being, imma-nent and transcendent to the individual. Both also envisaged the growth and suste-nance of humanist faith through a church-like organization with its own rituals and symbols. And both linked the whole construct to a grand totalization of human knowledge with a reflexive science of society at its heart – the equivalent, for the new religion, of what systematic theology had been for the old. Comte's positive polity, we may note, was meant both as a founding doctrinal document, and as a scientific projection of what positive society and positive religion would be like, in the normal state, a lifespan ahead in time (to 1948).

Grandiose attempts by the "prophets of Paris" (Manuel 1962) to found a fully organized religious institution were bound to fail, let alone ones modelled on the integralism, hierarchy and labyrinthine intricacies of the medieval Church. Shorn of excrescences, however, the more general idea of uniting a fractious world by promoting a shared attachment to, and veneration of, the best of what we humans collectively are and aspire to, inspired more limited projects with greater staying power. Their legacies – de Coubertin's modern Olympics, World Fairs, international days of peace and solidarity going back to the Hague Peace Conferences, are still with us. The list of similarly functioning, if no longer so strategically conceived, sites and events has continued to grow. In recent years it has extended to UNESCO World Heritage sites, charity spectaculars like Live Aid, as well as globally media-tized inspirational moments like the moon-landing and the release of Mandela. On its symbolic and ritual side, the entire international left can also be so regarded; and nowhere more so than in the militantly atheist tradition that descends from Marx and Engels. With its Founders, heroes, holy texts, solidarity rituals, festivals, memo-rials and procession of Parties and Internationals, a church-like element in what has consistently put itself forward as the true (and truly demystified) party of humanity has been easy to parody. It can also be regarded, however, as an authentic expres-sion of what was always, superstructurally, part of socialism's vocation. There is a spontaneous dimension to left religiosity too, captured in Lenin's dictum that "revo-lutions are festivals of the oppressed."

This is evidently a heterogeneous field. In each case, moreover, the symbolic and liturgical elements are incidental to some other activity, such as sports, technology promotion, tourism, politics, onto which it has been grafted. What relates them is just that in their disparate modes, all have served, in some symbolically or ritually engaging fashion, to extol humanity's works and benefactors, to mythologize the human story, and to tie the ensemble to a vision of unity, with community or the family of man as a regulative ideal. In short, and strangely, while Comte's Positive Religion did not come to pass, a kind of virtual scattered shadow of it did: a swirl of humanisms – atheist, Christian, neo-hellenic, liberal-universalist, pacifist, socialist – materially anchored in what we can call, in the aggregate, a positive cult of humanity.

If we are to think fully about the future of religion then we must ponder the future of *this* constellation, and not only of those conventionally thought about in such terms. For such an inquiry to proceed, however, we would have to take stock of two other things.

The first concerns changes that have overtaken the humanist complex in the past half century, profoundly unsettling its character. One trend has been long-term and structural: the pressure, in an increasingly consumerized and promotional culture, for its sites, symbols and ceremonies to become absorbed, with loss of aura, into the circuits of profane circulation. The post-Savarin Olympics, a sponsored machine for producing sponsorable star athletes, is a prime example, as also the touristic branding of World Heritage and the showcase function of festivals and charity events. More frontally, the wars, genocides, and totalitarianisms of the twentieth century, and the looming eco-crisis of the twenty first, have dented faith in the all-too-human and cast a pall over any positive collective self sacralization. There has been a theoretical death of Man too: a presumptuous product of the rising up of the subject, according to Heidegger; an evacuated category in *les sciences humaines* as Foucault has shown in *the Order of Things*; a false totality, as feminists, anti-colonialists and critical theorists have all stripes have pointed out, masking difference, domination and multiplicity. On the one hand, then, there has been a discrediting and dismantling of humanity/man as an essential category. On the other hand, the object of worship, humanity, and the cult itself, have lost symbolic power.

However, a paradoxical development has occurred. Out of the same historical traumas that helped to undermine the positive cult of humanity, a so-to-speak negative one has arisen, in its way more powerful, centered on the memorials and museums that sprung up to commemorate victims and safeguard traces of the worst places and events. The most prominent – battlefield graveyards from World War I, Auschwitz–Birkenau, the Hiroshima peace park, and more recently the slave forts in Ghana, and the killing fields of Cambodia – have become places of pilgrimage. They have also become organizing centers for wider networks of remembrance and for missionary efforts like the Hiroshima Peace declaration with its call for "new thinking." To be sure their human universalism can be complicated or dimmed by controversies about responsibility and relative victimhood. But they have not ceased being powerfully sacred sites, radiating with the absolute alterity of the unimaginable suffering, horror and cruelty to which they make us bear witness.[16]

It is a *negative* cult of humanity because these are sites of mourning not celebration, and mourning for the worst that humanity (if we can still retain any notion of a singular collective subject) has inflicted on itself. Negative also because the call that goes out from them is the prohibitive never this again; which is how, at the same time, they belong to a cult of humanity at all. Altogether it as if the replacement deity had itself died, thus in Heidegger's terms, completing nihilism; but that in this very death – a dissolution which mirrors what sociologists like Putnam (2000) fear as declining capital invested in social ties, but which is essentially in the realm of the imaginary, and whose multiple levels Baudrillard (1983) has summarized as "the end of the social" – it has been revived under erasure. What was Humanity, or the collective subject, as an object of worship and veneration, has transmogrified into the face, hospitality, and the multiple, just as the divine we/us which Durkheim ecstatically experienced on Bastille Day in 1880 (Lukes 1972: 48) has transposed into the groundless, negative (Blanchot 1988) or inoperative (Nancy 1991) community.

Whatever the future for the positive and negative cults of humanity, and for the theretico-ideological discourses with which they articulate, a further feature of this complex, common to both, is also worth pondering. This is the distance travelled from what its early visionaries envisaged for it institutionally. With regard to its degree of organization, coherence and depth of social implantation it has not developed at all along the path of a "strong religion," but along that of a "weak" one. Here, in fact, its form begins to converge with that of a second variant of what enlightenment thinkers projected into the space of a new religion for modernity: civil religion.

WORLD CIVIL RELIGION

A defining characteristic of civil religion, whether in Lockian, Rousseauian, or Durkheimian form, is that the principles, symbols, and ceremonials it attaches to citizenship, and places officially in the public realm, overarch the polity. In so doing they complement, and may even in some measure incorporate, but do not replace existing faith communities and their specific practices. To this extent, the embryonic and disparate cult of humanity is a species of civil religion. However, it is on a world scale, whereas civil religion, covering a gap left by the splitting of church and state, was envisaged as a pathway specifically for individual national societies. In actuality, moreover, there has been a bar between the two. Recognizable elements of what might be called civil religion – from founding creeds to flags, monuments, and national days of commemoration or celebration – became ubiquitous features of nineteenth- and twentieth-century nation-states. But the universalism of such complexes, as oriented to something higher than nation, has been restricted by nation-worship, and at the limit by the absolutizing of ethno-cultural particularity.

Nevertheless this is not the only possibility. To the extent of its ethical and political universalism, the civil religion of a modern nation-state can also harbor dreams of going global and providing a sacred canopy for all. Two historic rivals in this respect have been the national civil religions that came into being after the Revolutions of 1776 and 1789. In the French case, the effort to fashion a republican replacement for the Gallican Church merged with the universalisms of the Enlightenment to spin off, in addition to the liberal *civisme* that Durkheim helped to consolidate in the Third Republic, an internationalist version fit for a *civisme* that would be world-wide. In muted form this still continues in the diffusion of rational-humanist rhetoric through such international institutions as UNESCO. In the American case, where Enlightenment motifs crossed with an imperative to bridge across Christian denominations, there resulted a more Deist and biblical variant (one people under God; America as a second Israel). If its missionary side could become indistinguishable from other masks for empire, it could also combine with a prophetic and utopian strain that Lincoln expressed at Gettysburg and that was always part of the mix.

It is in such terms that Robert Bellah, who made the study of American civil religion his own, speculated about the possibility of its giving birth to something larger: a world civil religion.

> The attainment ... of some kind of viable and coherent world order would precipitate a major new set of symbolic forms ... This would ... necessitate the incorporation of vital international symbolism into our civil religion, or, perhaps a better way of putting it, it would result in American civil religion becoming simply one part of a new civil religion of the world ... [This would not] disrupt the American civil religion's continuity. A world civil religion could be accepted as a fulfilment and not as a denial of American civil religion. Indeed such an outcome has been [its] ... eschatological hope ... from the beginning. (Bellah 1991: 185–6).

Bellah's hope is shared by Rorty, and we may want to share it too. One understands why much of the world welcomed Obama after Bush. However, to advance this thought one must take cognizance of the fact that the space of world civil religion is already occupied and that there are other claimants to being the universalizing source from which enveloping forms might spring.

By analogy with the distinction between a religion and religion-in-general, let us call world civil religion without an article that zone of the world social formation in which the positive and negative cults of humanity as well as such putative constructs as Bellah's "new civil religion of the world" all come into play. What Vattimo and Rorty project as the horizon of Western religion they project into that same space. Their very dialogue presupposes it. Yet – in which they are not in the least alone – they do not thematize it, nor the place within it of formations like American liberalism and the Catholic church, both of which vie with one another, *inter alia*, as carriers of the humanist torch. Altogether in fact, world civil religion – understood not as unitary complex, still less as an accomplished fact, but as emergent, multipolar, and overdetermined – is an arena not only of dialogue and link up, but also of ideological and institutional competition involving a host of state and trans-state actors from the United Nations and its agencies to world music festivals and even the traditional world religions on their ecumenical and solidaristic side.

All of which is to say that not only is this aspect of the future of religion global, in its indexation to the wider growth of a global society, but thinking about it from within the self-universalizing worlds of the West will need to become global too.

Notes

1   Cited in McLelland, 1998: 198.
2   The split with the Eastern churches, which had never recognised the primacy of Rome, was ratified in the Great Schism of 1054.
3   In a letter to Bouvet, a Jesuit missionary, Leibniz wrote "I have always been inclined to believe that the ancient Chinese, like the ancient Arabs (witness the Book of Job) and,

perhaps, the ancient Celts (that is to say the ancient Germans and Gauls), were far from idolatry, and were rather worshippers of the sovereign principle." Cited in Walker, 1972: 199.

4 See for example de Maistre's "Reflections on Protestantism in its relations to Sovereignty" and "On the Pope" in Blum (2004) 133–56, 157–96.

5 Goldmann compares the modern German, French and English philosophical traditions in the opening chapters of *Immanuel Kant* (1971). While he reduces these differences to ones between the respective outcomes in these countries of the "bourgeois revolution," the significance of his attempt to delineate the national epistemes that weave together in European thought has been largely overlooked (Wernick, 2000).

6 *Blumenberg vs Lowith*.

7 "We men of knowledge today, we godless men and anti-metaphysicians, we, too, still derive our flame from the fire ignited by a faith millennia old, the Christian faith, which was also Plato's, that God is truth, that truth is divine" (Nietzsche 2001: 201).

8 "A product of modern European civilisation, studying any problem of universal history, is bound to ask himself to what combination of circumstances the fact should be attributed that in Western civilisation, and in Western civilisation only, cultural phenomena have appeared which (as we like to think) line in a line of development having *universal* significance and value" (Weber 2003: 13).

9 For a provocative analysis of the distinctiveness of American religion, as a family of Gnosticisms, focused on what has been growing outside the mainstream denominations, see Bloom 1993.

10 If this is the trend, then, as Berger (Woodhead et al. 2002: 194) has noted, the thesis of American exceptionalism can be turned on its head. "It has often been observed that, in contrast to Europe, the US is a very religious country. But that is not exceptional; [it] conforms to what is the world-wide pattern; Europe is, or seems be, the big exception. And once one accepts the ubiquity of religion in the modern world, one becomes interested in secularisation in a new and very intriguing way – secularisation not as the modern norm, but as a curious case of deviance that requires explanation."

11 A partial list of Rorty's key works would include Rorty 1979, 1982, 1989, and the three volumes of *Philosophical Papers* published by Cambridge University Press in 1991 and 1998. Among Vattimo's are Vattimo 1991, 1997, 1999, 2002a, and 2002b.

12 A human rights and pro-democracy campaigner on many fronts, Vattimo joined the Party of Italian Communists and was a member of the European Partliament from 1999 to 2004.

13 "Hermeneutics is not a philosophy but the enunciation of historical existence itself in the age of the end of metaphysics" (Vattimo, 2005: 45).

14 For a magisterial but controversial statement of this view by a Catholic theologian see Marion (1995).

15 Guyau developed his evolutionary view of instincts and morality in *Esquisse d'une morale sans obligation ni sanction* (1897).

16 What radiates is a kind of negative sublime. For a discussion of the relation between Rudolph Otto's numinously holy and the Holocaust see Cohen 1981.

Bibliography

Agamben, G. (1999) *Potentialities: Collected Essays in Philosophy*, ed. and tr. D. Heller Roazen, Stanford: Stanford University Press.

Altizer, T. J. (1966) *The Gospel of Christian Atheism*, Philadelphia: Westmister Press.

Badiou, A. (2003) *Saint Paul: The Foundation of Universalism*, tr. R. Bressier, Stanford: Stanford University Press.

Baudrillard, J. (1983) *In the Shadow of the Silent Majorities*, New York: Semiotext(e).

Baudrillard, J. (1990) *Fatal Strategies: Crystal Revenge*, New York: Semiotext(e).

Bernstein, J. (ed.) (1985) *Habermas and Modernity*, Cambridge: Polity Press.

Bellah, R. (1991) [1970] *Beyond Belief: Essays on Religion in a Post-traditionalist World*, Berkeley and Los Angeles: University of California Press.

Berger, P. (1969) *The Sacred Canopy: Elements of a Sociological theory of Religion*, New York: Anchor

Berger, P. (1973) *The Social Reality of Religion*, Harmondsworth: Penguin.

Blanchot, M. (1988) *The Unavowable Community*, Barrytown: Station Hill Press.

Bloom, H. (1993) *The American Religion*, New York: Simon and Schuster.

Caputo, J. (2002) *Religion With/out Religion: The Tears and Eros of Jacques Derrida*, London and New York: Routledge.

Cox, H. (1965) *The Secular City*, New York: Macmillan.

Blum, C. (ed. and tr.) (2004) *Critics of the Enlightenment*, Wilmington: ISI Books.

Bottomore, T. (ed. and tr.) (1964) *Karl Marx: Early Writings*, New York: McGraw Hill.

Caillois, R. (1988) *L'Homme et le Sacré*, Paris: Gallmard.

Cohen, A. (1981) *Tremendum: A Theological Interpretation of the Holocaust*, New York: Crossroad.

Colletti, L. (1972) *From Rousseau to Lenin: Studies in Ideology and Society*, London: New Left Books.

Derrida, J. (1995) *The Gift of Death*, Chicago: University of Chicago Press.

Derrida, J. and Vattimo, G. (eds.) (1998) *Religion*, Stanford: Stanford University Press.

Eco, U. (1988). *The Aesthetics of Thomas Aquinas*, tr. H. Bredin, Cambridge, MA: Harvard University Press.

Gardavsky, V. (1973) *God Is Not Yet Dead*, Harmondsworth: Penguin

Gauchet, M. (1997) *The Disenchantment of the World: A Political History of Religion*, Princeton: Princeton University Press.

Gillespie, C. (1994) *Nihilism before Nietzsche*, Chicago: University of Chicago Press.

Girard, R. (1987) *Things Hidden since the Foundation of the World*, Stanford: Stanford University Press.

Goldmann, L. (1971) *Immanuel Kant*, London: New Left Books.

Guyau, J.-M. (1896) *Ésquisse d'une morale sans obligation ni sanction*, Paris: F. Alcan.

Guyau, J.-M. (1897) *The Irreligion of the Future: A Sociological Study*, London: Heinemann.

Habermas, J. (2008) Notes on Post-secular Society, *New Perspectives Quarterly* 25 (4): 17–29.

Hegel, G. (2007) *The Philosophy of History*, New York: Cosimo.

Lévinas, E. (1977) *Du Sacré au Saint*, Paris: Minuit.

Lough, J. (2006) *Weber and the Persistence of Religion: Capitalism, Social Theory and the Sublime*, London: Routledge.

Lukes, S. (1972) *Émile Durkheim: His Life and Work*, New York: Harper and Row.

Manuel, F. (1962) *Prophets of Paris*, Cambridge, MA: Harvard University Press.

Martin, D. (2005) *Secularisation: Towards a Revised General Theory*, Aldershot: Aldgate.

Marion, J.-L. (1995) *God without Being*, Chicago: University of Chicago Press

Marx, Karl (1964) Contribution to the critique of Hegel's philosophy of right, in T. B. Bottomore (ed.), *Karl Marx: Early Writings*, New York: McGraw Hill.

McLelland, J. (1998) *Prometheus Rebound: The Irony of Atheism*, Waterloo, Ontario: Wilfrid Laurier Press.

Mercer, C. (2002) *Leibniz's Metaphysics: Its Origins and Developments*, Cambridge: Cambridge University Press

Milbank, J. (1993) *Theology and Social Theory: Beyond Secular Reason*, Oxford: Blackwell.

Mungello, D. (1977), *Leibnitz and Confucianism: The Struggle for Accord*, Honolulu: University of Hawaii Press.

Nietzsche, F. (2001) *The Gay Science*, ed. B. Williams, Cambridge: Cambridge University Press.

Pickering, W. (ed) (1975) *Durkheim on Religion: A Selection of Readings with Bibliographies*, London: Routledge.

Putnam, R. (2000) *Bowling Alone: The Collapse and Revival of American Community*, New York: Simon and Schuster.

Rorty, R. (1979) *Philosophy and the Mirror of Nature*, Princeton: Princeton University Press.

Rorty, R. (1982) *Consequences of Pragmatism*, Minneapolis: Minnesota University Press.

Rorty, R. (1989) *Contingency, Irony and Solidarity*, Cambridge: Cambridge University Press.

Rorty, R. (1998) *Achieving Our Country: Leftist Thought in Twentieth Century America*, Cambridge: Cambridge University Press

Taylor, M. (2007) *After God*, Chicago: Chicago University Press.

Vattimo, G. (1991) *The End of Modernity: Nihilism and the Hermeneutics in Post-modern Culture*, tr. G. J. Snyder, Cambridge: Polity Press.

Vattimo, G. (1997) *Beyond Interpretation: The meaning of Hermeneutics for Philosophy.*

Vattimo, G. (2002a) *Nietzsche: Philosophy as Cultural Criticism*, Stanford: Stanford University Press.

Vattimo, G. (2002b) *After Christianity*, New York: Columbia University Press.

Vattimo, G. et al. (1999) *Belief*, Cambridge: Polity Press.

Vattimo, G., Rorty, R., and Zabala, S. (eds.) (2005) *The Future of Religion*, New York: Columbia University Press.

Walker, D. P. (1972) *The Ancient Theology: Studies in Christian Platonism from the Fifteenth to the Eighteenth centuries Theology*, Ithaca: Cornell University Press.

Weber, M. (2003) *Protestant Ethic and the Spirit of Capitalism*, New York: Dover.

Wernick, A. (2000) The Rhizomatic genealogy of "The French," *Angelaki: Journal of Theoretical Humanities* 5 (2): 137–49.

Wilson, B. (1966) *Religion in a Secular Society*, London: Watts.

Woodhead, L. et al. (eds) (2002) *Religions in the Modern World: Traditions and Transformations.*

Zizek, S. (2001) *On Belief*, London: Routledge.

29

Religion in a Post-secular Society

Bryan S. Turner

Introduction: The Argument

The concept of "post-secular society" has emerged in sociological discussion from the primarily philosophical debate that has followed the work of Jurgen Habermas (2006) on rationality and religion in contemporary society. The philosophical debate about religion in the modern period has played an important role in how sociologists think about their subject matter. It is of course often difficult to draw a clear distinction between social theory and social philosophy, and therefore there is always some degree of overlap between the sociology and the philosophy of religion. In this interaction between philosophy and sociology, there have been in the past a number of key figures – such as Alasdair MacIntyre, Ernest Gellner, and Peter Winch – who had so to speak a foot in both camps. In the recent discussion about the role of religion in public life, one might argue that it has been the philosophers and theologians- and not the sociologists – who have defined the parameters of discussion about the future of religion. I have in mind, in addition to Habermas, the contributions of Richard Rorty, Charles Taylor, Gianni Vattimo and Jacques Derrida. While it is the philosophers who have raised the major issues concerning the place of religion in apparently secular societies, I shall take a critical stance with respect to their characterization of religion for its lack of engagement with the comparative empirical data that are generated by anthropologists and sociologists. In short, while philosophy has set out the terms of the debate, their work often lacks substance and the quality of discussion now hangs on the injection of anthropological and sociological fieldwork, especially from outside the European and American context, into the public debate. What is at issue here is the very character of secular society, and as a result we are now obliged to give an answer, or at least attend seriously, to the question raised forcefully by Habermas – are we living in a post-secular society?

In this chapter I raise a number of critical reflections on the analysis of religion in contemporary sociology but via an engagement with modern philosophy. In what follows when I refer to "philosophy" I more precisely mean "social philosophy." This critical argument has several components. Philosophers tend, as an inevitable outcome of their professional training, to concentrate on religious beliefs rather than on practice and they almost never look at religious objects. Perhaps even the reference to "beliefs" here is too generous, since much of the actual discussion is about the lack of authority of formal theology in modern public debates. Obviously the major religions make significant truth claims in their official theologies, but the role of religion in everyday life puts practice in the foreground.

Insofar as we think about religious beliefs, we should think more seriously about belief as part of the habitus of individuals and pay more attention to religion and the body, or more specifically to religious habitus and embodiment (Turner 2008). We should try more systematically to incorporate the work of Pierre Bourdieu into the modern study of public religion (Rey 2007). If the body is often missing from the study of religion, the same might be said of the emotions. The sociology of the emotions has in recent years developed as an important field of contemporary research (Barbalet 1998), but it has not played a significant part in recent philosophical debate. Of course William James's *Varieties of Religious Experience* was fundamental to the development of sociology – for example in the work of Émile Durkheim – but there is little attention to the role of emotion in modern religious commitment. Finally, because there is also a marked tendency to look at formal theologies, official statements of belief and formal institutions, there is a tendency to neglect major developments in modern religiosity, namely the growth of "post-institutional spirituality," the development of all forms of popular religion, and the growth of revivalist or fundamentalist religion such as Pentecostalism and charismatic movements. These issues have of course been presented and discussed in various chapters in this volume.

Perhaps the lack of engagement by philosophers with the empirical research of mainstream sociology is the main issue. Philosophical discussions of the crisis of religious belief and authority all too frequently ignore social science empirical investigations and findings. Their abstract speculations rarely refer to any actual findings of social science. Whereas Charles Taylor in *The Secular Age* (2007) happily quotes William James and Émile Durkheim, contemporary research results rarely receive any systematic attention. This lack of attention to the empirical conclusions of modern sociology is compounded by a lack of interest in comparative sociology. Most Western philosophers have had little to say about religion outside Northern Europe and the United States. This is problematic since the point of the post-secular debate has been in part to recognize the peculiarities of the European experience of secularization, on the one hand, and American exceptionalism on the other. In other words, it is very difficult to generalize from the European experience in which the separation of the state and Church with the Westphalian settlement presupposed a history of confessional politics to the modern period and to religions outside the Abrahamic tradition of Judaism, Christianity and Islam. By contrast, contemporary anthropological and sociological research clearly illustrates the vitality of religion in the rest of the world especially as a result of modern pilgrimage, religious revivalism in Asia, and Pentecostal and charismatic movements in South America and Africa. When social philosophers have turned to religious movements outside the West, there is far too much attention given to fundamentalism in general and to radical Islam in particular (Juergensmeyer 2000). There are many forms of revival-ism and growth other than radical or political religion. The majority of Muslims in societies as far removed as Singapore and the United States are well integrated into modern multicultural society (Pew Research Center 2007). More attention to the historical and comparative study of religion would greatly improve, not only our understanding of the recent history of Muslim migration, but also our awareness of the complexity of secularization and post-secularization.

As this volume has shown, there is now general agreement among sociologists that the conventional secularization thesis of the 1960s and 1970s was narrowly focused on northern Europe, providing some insight into post-Christian society in the developed industrial world, but offering little that had relevance outside of that European context. There is an alternative to the simple notion of secularization as membership decline and social irrelevance. In modern societies, religion has been both democratized and commercialized with the growth of megachurches, TV evan-gelism, drive-in confessions, buy-a-prayer, religious tourism and what I have called "low intensity religion" (Turner 2009). Religion survives in Immanuel Kant's terms not so much as a reflective faith but more as health and wealth cults offering a range of services to a variety of this-worldly needs of human beings. Religion is perfectly compatible with secular consumerism as we can observe through the functions of religious markets in providing general spiritual rather than narrowly ecclesiastical services. Some historians might argue that nothing has changed in the sense that the world religions have always satisfied such material interests in the sale of amulets or in providing pilgrimages to the graves of saints. However I argue that in religion there was always an element of sacredness in which the ineffable nature of divinity or holiness was present. I take it that this was the argument of Rudolf Otto (1923) in his account in 1917 of the "numinous" in *The Idea of the Holy*. God could not be known as such and the sacred was manifest through the communication of intermediaries – prophets, angels, mythical creatures, landscapes, or spirits- but the essence of sacredness was ultimately unspeakable. In the modern world with the development of the Internet for example the role of these traditional intermediaries is breaking down and the ineffable hierarchy of beings is being democratized by popular manifestations of religion. The sacred is now effable.

The Political and the Social

I propose that the debate about secularization could be made conceptually more precise and more relevant if we draw a simple distinction between what I shall call "political secularization" and "social secularization." The former refers specifically to public institutions and political arrangements that is to the issues around the historical separation of church and state, while the latter, to questions about values, culture and attitudes. The political dimension is largely institutional and formal, and the social, informal and customary. Political secularization was in fact the cornerstone of the liberal view of tolerance in which we are free to hold our private beliefs provided these do not impinge negatively on public life. In Western terms this liberal solution was associated with the Anglican settlement stemming from Richard Hooker and John Locke. It was initially a local political solution to settle the conflicts between Catholics and Protestants. It is generally agreed that this settlement has broken down or is under considerable social stress, because modern societies tend to be multicultural and multi-faith. The seventeenth-century settlement did not envisage multicultural societies composed of many competing and contradictory religious traditions. Because in modern societies religion often defines identity, it is difficult to sustain a simple division between the public and the private. Furthermore, these identities are typically transnational and hence cannot be confined within the national boundaries of the state. We might argue that public space has been re-sacralized insofar as public religions play a major role in political life. The secular institutions of Western citizenship are straining to cope with these new developments, because the outcome of nineteenth-century citizenship is primarily a legacy of exclusionary national membership.

Political secularization refers to a historical process in which the place of religion in public life was defined and regulated, typically by the state. The separation of religion and state does not been therefore a relationship of equality. One such event occurred when the Virginia Assembly cancelled payment of salaries supported by taxes that had been traditionally paid to Anglican clergy and subsequently, following a number of contentious debates, the bill for Establishing Religious Freedom was passed, serving eventually as the First Amendment. The right to freedom of conscience was closely connected to notions of privacy and hence religious freedom became a major building block of political liberalism and modernity (Casanova 1994). Although this development is often seen to be the outcome of ideals, it is possible to see freedom of religion as a practical outcome of political processes. In the American colonies the irresistible growth in religious pluralism, the need to attract more migrants and the desire of merchants for more trade between the colonies were the material foundations of liberalism and individualism (Abercrombie et al. 1986). In more recent research employing the idea of competition in religious markets, the argument has taken on a more counter-intuitive hue in which it is claimed that "religious liberty is a matter of government regulation" (Gill 2008: 47). This proposition emerges from the argument in Anthony Gill's *The Political Origins of Religious Liberty* in which he asserts that, whereas dominant religious groups seek state regulation of minority religions, religious liberty will be the political objective of marginalized minority religious movements and groups. In terms of political life, this approach leads to the unsurprising but important conclusion that "politicians seek to minimize the cost of ruling" (Gill 2008: 47). Governance is clearly more problematic in pluralistic environments where there is plenty of scope for religious competition and conflicts. Because virtually all modern societies are multicultural and multiracial, the "management of religion" is an inevitable component of political secularization (Turner 2007). In other words, there is a paradox that precisely because religion is important in modern life as the carrier of identity, it has to be controlled by the state to minimize the costs of government. As we will see, Habermas calls this situation post-secular, because, in order to protect public communicative rationality, it is important for there to be some open dialogue with and between religions. The failure of such a dialogue would in all probability lead to political conflict.

By contrast, social secularization refers to issues about social values, practices and customs, namely to everyday life or what we might call the social sphere. This arena is the ensemble of rituals, practices and sites where religion is practiced. We can apprehend this domain through the conventional sociological measures of religious vitality – church membership, belief in God, religious experiences, and acts of devotion such as prayer. This social space encloses a large heterogeneous collection of folk religious, superstitious practices, magical activities and customs as well as elements from more formal world religions. This arena of religion is certainly thriving in both formal and informal dimensions. In this regard, there is little evidence of formal religious decline outside of northern Europe and the conventional secularization thesis has to be either severely modified or abandoned. It is in this religious field that the now famous phrase of Grace Davie also has its maximum currency – believing but not belonging. However, the nature of secularization at the social level is in fact quite complicated. Looking outside Europe, there is obviously very clear evidence of a worldwide revival of religion that is variously described as fundamentalism or pietization. There is evidence of a revival of traditional religions in Asia such as spirit possession in Vietnam, Islam in Southeast Asia, Shinto in Japan and Taoism in China.

This argument provides a conceptually fruitful contrast between the role of religion in the public domain of politics and the social domain of civil society. This distinction is important because, while it is relatively easy for a state to create the conditions for the juridical regulation of religion in the political sphere, it is very difficult in practice for a state to exercise successful control over the social functions of religion. In the post- communist world – Poland, Vietnam, and China for example – it is now clear in retrospect that, while political secularization was relatively successful, religion was never fully eradicated, to use Habermas's terminology, from the life world. One may suppose that attempts in contemporary China to suppress Falungong at the level of ordinary life will in the long run fail (Goldman 2005). Perhaps an even more appropriate example of the differences between the political and the social can be taken from the history of the Russian Orthodox Church in relation to society and state. Although the Church was severely repressed in the early years of the Russian revolution, the close relationship between Orthodoxy and nationalism meant that Christianity could also play a useful role in Russian politics. Since the fall of the Soviet system, the Orthodox Church has made an important come-back under the skilful political leadership of Patriarch Alexy 11 who has forged a powerful alliance with both Vladimir Putin and Dmitry Medvedev (Garrad and Garrad 2009). In 1983 Alexy was successful in securing the return of the Don Monastery in central Moscow to ecclesiastical use. In 1991 he managed to restore the veneration of St Seraphim of Sarov who, dying in 1833, was revered as a patriot by Tsar Nicholas 11. The saint's relics were restored to the Cathedral of Sarov. In 1997 a law on the freedom of religious conscience gave a privileged status to Orthodoxy while Roman Catholicism has been politically marginalized. In Putin's Russia, Orthodoxy has continued to prosper as an official religion offering some degree of spiritual and national legitimacy to the Party and the state. There is also a close relationship between the military and the Church in that religious icons are used to bless warships and the Patriarch offered a thanksgiving service in the anniversary of the creation of the Soviet nuclear arsenal. Although the public role of Orthodoxy has been largely restored, the Church's influence is largely based on cultural nationalism rather than on its spiritual authority. Thus while some 80 percent of Russians describe themselves as "Orthodox," just over 40 percent call themselves "believers." This relationship between the political and the social allows us to say that, while Orthodoxy is a powerful public religion and that public space has been partially re-sacralized, Russian society remains secular. The legacy of atheism and secularism from the past still has a hold over the everyday social world even when religion now plays a considerable part in a nationalist revival. Therefore in any assessment of the notion of "a post-secular society" we need to be careful about whether secularization refers to formal institutions at the political level or whether it refers to lived religion at the social level. It is my contention that the philosophical analysis of the role of religion in public culture is very important, but it may tell us relatively little about how religion is embodied in the social world.

THE RETURN OF RELIGION

Whereas most modern sociologists and political scientists have come to the conclusion that religion has to be taken seriously in debates about the public sphere, such was not the case with major postwar social theorists – Louis Althusser, Pierre Bourdieu, Ralf Dahrendorf, Norbert Elias, Nicos Poulantzas, and others. What has changed? The obvious answer is that there are various transformations of social and political life that have placed religion as an institution at the center of modern society. I shall focus on a number of major macro-social changes that might explain this predominance of religion in the modern world. This account necessarily has to be a mere sketch as the background to understanding post-secularism.

The collapse of organized communism and the decline in Marxist-Leninist ideology allowed religion to flourish once more in European and especially in Poland, the Ukraine and what used to be Yugoslavia. As we have seen, the Orthodox Church has become closely associated with Russian nationalism and, while communist parties have not disappeared in Vietnam, the Renovation Period has allowed the return of religion to public life such as Roman Catholicism in South Vietnam and Protestant sects among the ethnic minorities. Spirit possession cults are also attracting business men from the expanding capitalist sector (Taylor 2007). In various parts of the world from Cuba to Cambodia that were influenced by communism, there was by the 1990s widespread disillusionment with organized communism and the doctrines of Marxist Leninism. Globalization and the Internet have created new opportunities for evangelism even in societies where the Party still attempts to regulate or suppress the flow of information and interaction. In China, Charter 08 calls for, among other things, freedom of religious assembly and practice. While these dissident movements are unlikely to shake the control of the Party or its authoritarian responses to religious revivalism, these developments are likely to see a significant growth in religious activity across both the existing communist and the post-communist world.

Another feature of globalization has been the growth of migration and permanent settlement producing the worldwide emergence of diasporic communities in societies with expanding economies. These diasporic communities are typically held together by their religious beliefs and practices in such a way that in modern societies the distinction between ethnicity and religion begins to become irrelevant. Indeed the

Turks in Germany have become Muslims and around the world Chinese minorities have often become Buddhists. In Malaysia, people of Chinese descent are automatically "Buddhists." The result is that religion has become the major plank of "the politics of identity." Religion becomes a site of ethnic and cultural contestation and hence states become involved in the management of religions, thereby inevitably departing from the traditional division of state and religion in the liberal framework. Paradoxically by intervening to regulate religion in the public domain, the state automatically makes religion more important and prominent. In societies as different as the United States and Singapore, the state intervenes to regulate Islam in the name of incorporating "moderate Muslims" into mainstream society (Kamaludeen et al. 2009). Throughout the modern world, there is a complex interaction between religion and national identity – from Hinduism in India to Catholicism in Poland to Shinto in Japan – whereby religion becomes part of the fabric of public cultures.

Similar arguments might be made about nationalism. In the postwar period, nationalism gained momentum in association with anti-colonial struggles. In the Arab world, this was often combined with pan-Arabism. These secular movements in North Africa and the Middle East enjoyed some political success after the Suez crisis and Nasser was able to mobilize support behind his vision of a post-colonial largely secular Arab world. If political activism increased in the 1940s with the evolution of the Muslim Brotherhood in Egypt, there were further radical developments in the aftermath of the Arab defeat in the 1967 war with Israel. However, the critical event of modern history was the Iranian Revolution in 1978–9. The fall of the secular state in Iran which had promoted a nationalist vision of society over a traditional Islamic framework provided a global example of a spiritual revolution. It provided a singular example of the mobilization of the masses in the name of religious renewal. The message of the Iranian intellectual Ali Shariati against what he called "Westoxification" was embraced by a wide variety of religious movements outside the specific Iranian context (Akbarzadeh and Mansouri 2007).

In the modern debate about post-secularism, the crucial issue, which is often implied rather than stated explicitly, is whether radical forms of Islam can be successfully incorporated through dialogue into a democratic and largely liberal environment. What are the roots of Islamic radicalism? One issue is the intractable problem of the status of Palestine and conflicts with the state of Israel. In a broader historical perspective therefore, Palestine has probably been the single most important issue sustaining political Islam, because it has sustained "a vast collective feeling of injustice [that] continues to hang over our lives with undiminished weight" (Said 2001: 207). In socio-political terms, twentieth-century radical Islam has been interpreted as a product the social frustrations of those social strata (unpaid civil servants, overworked teachers, underemployed engineers, and alienated college teachers) whose interests were not well served and whose aspirations were not well met by either the secular nationalism of post-colonialism with such leaders as Nasser, Suharto or Saddam Hussein, or through the neo-liberal "open-door" policies of Anwar Saddat in Egypt or Chadli Benjedid in Algeria. The social dislocations created by the modern global economy have produced ideal conditions for external Western support of those secular elites in the Arab world who benefit significantly from oil revenues. These conditions of economic growth through the rent extracted from oil production have produced bureaucratic authoritarianism through much of the Middle East. In summary, religious radicalism can be seen as a product of a religious crisis of authority, the failures of authoritarian nationalist governments, and the socio-economic divisions that have been exacerbated by the economic strategies of neo-liberal globalization.

The debate about Islamic radicalism has been heavily dependent upon the work of Gilles Kepel (2002) such as *Jihad*, which was first published in French in 2000; it is influential but also highly controversial. His thesis is relatively simply namely that the last three decades have witnessed both the spectacular rise of "Islamism" and also its political failure. In the 1970s, when sociologists assumed that modernization meant secularization, the sudden irruption of political Islam, especially the importance of Shi'ite theology in popular protests in Iran, appeared to challenge many dominant assumptions about modernity. These religious movements in Iran, especially when they forced women to wear the *chador* and excluded them from public space, were originally defined by leftist intellectuals as a form of religious fascism. Veiling has continued to fuel feminist critiques of the treatment of women in contemporary Iran (Nafisi 2008). Over time, however, Marxists came to realize that Islamism had a popular base and was a powerful force against Western influence, while Western conservatives were attracted by Islamic preaching on moral order, obedience to God and hostility to secular materialists, namely communists and socialists. Western governments were eventually willing to support both Sunni and Shi'a resistance groups against the Russian invasion of Afghanistan after 1979, despite their connections with radical religious groups in Pakistan and Iran.

These religious movements came eventually to fill the political vacuum left by the failures of Arab nationalism that had dominated anti-Western politics since the Suez Crisis. In Kepel's terms, Islamism is the product of both generational pressures and class structure. Religious radicalism has been embraced by young generations in the cities that were created by the postwar demographic explosion in the developing world and the resulting mass exodus of young people from the countryside. This generation was often impoverished, despite its relatively high literacy and access to secondary education. The underclass of the mega-cities became one recruiting ground for religio-political radicalism. However, Islamism also recruited among the middle classes – the descendants of the merchant families from the bazaars and *souks* who had been pushed aside by the processes of decolonization, and from the doctors, engineers and business men, who, while enjoying the salaries made possible by booming oil prices, were nevertheless excluded from political power. The ideological carriers of Islamism at the local level were the "young intellectuals, freshly graduated from technical and science departments, who had themselves been inspired by the ideologues of the 1960s" (Kepel 2002: 6). Traditional Islamic themes of justice and equality were effectively deployed against those regimes that were seen to be corrupt, bankrupt and authoritarian, especially those regimes that had been supported by the West in the Cold War confrontation with the Soviet empire.

The rise of Islamism has to be seen in the context of these international conflicts of the 1980s. The period was dominated by the struggle between the radical Shi'ite regime of Khomeini and the conservative Sunni monarchy of Saudi Arabia. While Tehran attempted to export its revolution abroad, conservative governments in Egypt, Pakistan, the Gulf and Malaysia often encouraged Muslim radicals in their struggles against communism. These governments, such as Malaysia, were often willing to contain Islamism through co-optation and concessions, primarily over the role of religious law (the *Shari'a*). A principal objective of Islamism is to oppose the sequestration of religious law in the private sphere and to bring the *Shari'a* back into prominence in the public arena. According to Kepel's thesis the high point of political success for Islamism came in 1989 when during the Palestinian *intifada* the PLO came under threat from Hamas (the Islamist Resistance Movement) and in Algeria the *Front Islamique du Salut* enjoyed convincing electoral victories in the first free elections since independence. In the same year, a military coup in the Sudan brought the Islamist ideologue Hassan al-Turabi to power, Khomeini symbolically and controversially extended the reach of the *Shari'a* by placing a *fatwa* on Salmon Rushdie's *Satanic Verses* and the Soviet Army finally abandoned its humiliating war in Afghanistan. The collapse of the Berlin Wall was a powerful precursor to the final demise of the Soviet Union in 1992 and Islamism emerged eventually to fill the political and ideological gap in the international system created by the fall of organized communism and the associated failure of Marxist Leninism as its dominant theory.

Kepel's argument is, however, that political Islam has been in decline since 1989, despite the dramatically successful attack by Al Qaeda groups on New York in 2001 and later in London and Madrid. The political opponents of radical Islam have been able to exploit the divided class basis of the movement. For example, the fragile class alliance between the young urban poor, the devout middle classes and alienated intellectuals meant that Islamism was poorly prepared to cope with long-term and systematic opposition from state authorities. Over time governments found ways of dividing these social classes and frustrating the aim of establishing an Islamic state within which the *Shari'a* would have exclusive jurisdiction. Kepel regards the extreme and violent manifestations of Islamism – the Armed Islamist Group in Algeria, the Taliban in Afghanistan and the Al Qaeda network of Osama bin Laden – as evidence of its political disintegration and failure. The re-capture in May 2009 of Mas Selamet bin Kastari, the Indonesian-born Singaporean who had allegedly planned an attack on Changi Airport, brought to an end the immediate threat of terrorist attacks on Singapore under the broad umbrella of Jemaah Islamiyah.

However, opposition to the West is only one aspect, and possibly in the long run the least important aspect of modern Islamic revivalism. The more enduring feature may be connected with personal piety. In particular, modern piety movements appear to have a very strong attraction to women (Tong and Turner 2008). In her *Politics of Piety* (2005), Saba Mahmood has employed the principal concepts of Bourdieu's sociology to explore the growth and implications of the Muslim habitus for pious women in modern Egypt. Her ethnographic study of Cairo provides a fruitful framework for thinking in more global terms about Islamic renewal. In Egypt of course Muslims practice within a predominantly Islamic culture in which other groups such as the Copts are minorities. The need for religious renewal is invoked more sharply when Muslims find themselves in a minority within a larger or more diverse community and hence where the pressures for secularization and assimilation are much greater. Exclusionary group norms come into play more urgently when a religious community is a minority, or where the majority feels it

is under threat by a minority which for example is economically or politically dominant. These everyday norms of pious practice then become especially important for
defining religious differences. Where Muslims are not an overwhelming majority,
there are issues in everyday life as to how social groups should interact without
compromising their piety. One of the prominent examples is diet because piety
involves above all a set of bodily practices for defining social relations that involve
some degree of intimacy. In these situations acts of piety may cause friction and
possibly conflict with other social groups. With the growth of Muslim diasporas,
these movements of renewal may become more frequent and more salient to group
survival and hence the French head-scarf debate becomes in fact a common aspect
of modern multicultural politics.

BELIEF AND PRACTICE IN POST-SECULAR SOCIETY

Returning now to our discussion of the prospects of a post-secular society, much
of the debate about religion in modern society, as I have noted, has been dominated
by philosophers, who largely neglect anthropological and sociological research on
religion. Philosophical commentaries on religion – Habermas, Rorty, Taylor,
Vattimo – have no feel for the ethnographic character of modern social science
accounts of religion. In particular they neglect religious practice in favor of the idea
that the modern problem of religion is a question of belief. As a result in reading
their work, one has no sense of the actual character of everyday religion, only a
sense of their belief systems. Following both Durkheim and Wittgenstein, concentrating on belief to the exclusion of religious practice is a major defect of these
approaches; the vitality of religion is necessarily an aspect of practice. Belief can
only survive if it is embedded in practice. Bourdieu's notion of habitus fits this
critical argument rather well. The significance of religion in everyday life can be
understood by reference to how religious observance is deeply incorporated into the
habitus of a social group.

This argument about the practical nature of religion in the mundane world seems
to me to be the central argument of twentieth-century anthropology especially in
the social anthropology of Mary Douglas. Religion in Western society is weak, not
because it is philosophically incoherent but because it has become de-ritualized, cut
off from a religious calendar and disconnected from both the human life-cycle and
the annual round of agricultural production. In the West one of the few remaining
religious festivals (namely Christmas) is a commercial event in the year that now is
often rolled into New Year as a secular celebration. Kant (1960) in *Religion within
the Limits of Pure Reason* may have been correct in arguing that Christianity (essentially Lutheranism) was its own grave digger because as a reflecting faith it did not
need the practices that Kant associated with "cultic religion." In fact German
Protestantism appeared to be divorced from ritual practices as such.

Much has been written recently about the limitations of the conventional secularization thesis and correspondingly much thought given to the idea of a post-
secular world (Habermas and Mendieta 2002; Habermas and Ratzinger 2006).
Although I have complained about the limitations of much Western thought about
religion, there may be an alternative defense of the secularization thesis, namely the

growth of re gious markets. With the global commodification of modern religions, there is perhaps an alternative view of the secularization thesis after all. If religion is a system of belief and practice based on the ineffable nature of religious communication, modern liberal societies have democratized religion to make it an effable system that is perfectly compatible with the modern world. This "effability" can now be sold as both commodities and services on religious markets.

Much of Habermas's contribution to the idea of a post-secular society has drawn upon work and arguments that are relatively familiar to sociologists of religion. He has for example claimed that the secularization thesis rested on the assumption that the disenchanted world (in a reference I assume to Max Weber) rests on a scientific outlook in which all phenomena can be explained scientifically. Secondly there has been (in reference I assume to Niklas Luhmann) a differentiation of society into specialized functions in which religion becomes increasing a private matter. Finally, the transformation of society from an agrarian basis has improved living standards and reduced risk, removing the dependence of individuals on supernatural forces and reducing their need for help.

Habermas notes correctly that this perspective is based on a narrow European standpoint. America by contrast appears to be vibrantly religious in a society where religion, prosperity and modernization have sat comfortably together. In more global terms, Habermas draws attention to the spread of fundamentalism, the growth of radical Islamic groups, and the presence of religious issues in the public sphere. There appears to be a need to rethink Lockean liberalism because the privatization of religion is no longer a viable political strategy in the separation of state and religion. Habermas's solution to the conflict between radical multiculturalism and radical secularism is to propose a dialogue involving the inclusion of foreign minority cultures into civil society on the one hand and the opening up of subcultures to the state in order to encourage their members to participate actively in political life.

In some respects Habermas,s debate about the pre-political foundations of the liberal state with Joseph Ratzinger (Pope Benedict XVI) at the Catholic Academy of Bavaria on January 19, 2008 was perhaps more interesting, or at least more revealing. Both men were in a reconciliatory or conciliatory mood. Habermas recognized that religion had preserved in tact values and ideas that had been lost elsewhere and that the notion of the fundamental equality of all humans was an important legacy of the Christian faith. Habermas's response to the Pope can be understood against the background of *Kulturprotestantismus* in which there is a general respect for religion and where religion is far more prominent in public life than is the case in the United Kingdom. Habermas's response may have been generous, but it does rest upon the idea that politics (the state) cannot really function without a robust civil society or without a set of shared values. The role of religion – contrary to much critical theory and contrary to the secularization thesis – may be to provide a necessary support of social life as such.

Both Habermas and Ratzinger had one important thing in common – they are both opposed to relativism which they see as a largely destructive force. Habermas in particular is hostile to the postmodern version of relativism. His approach to religion is, at least initially, somewhat different from that of either Rorty or Vattimo. In this discussion I shall refer primarily to their *The Future of Religion* (Zabala

2005). Rorty constructed his relativism out of a mixture of bourgeois postmodernism and pragmatism describing his position as "postmodern bourgeois liberalism"
(Rorty 1991: 199) and as a result we can comfortably align his position with Vattimo's "weak thought." Both philosophers agree that there are "no facts only
interpretations." Their difference lies in relationship to religion since Vattimo is a
practicing Catholic while Rorty belongs to a secular socialist tradition. The role of
philosophy, he argued in *Consequences of Pragmatism* (1982), is not to provide
eternal foundations of Truth, but rather to be a voice alongside literature and art
in the edification of human kind. The measure of philosophical progress is not
demonstrated by philosophy "becoming more rigorous but by becoming more
imaginative" (Rorty 1998: 9). Because Rorty was concerned to establish the proper
limitations of philosophical knowledge in a world which is unstable, changeable
and insecure, his philosophical critique had much in common with postmodernism.
Whereas J.-F. Lyotard defined postmodernism as "incredulity toward metanarra-
tives" (1984: xxiv), Rorty in one of his most influential essays ("Private irony and
liberal hope") defined an ironist as somebody who has "radical and continuing
doubts about the final vocabulary she currently uses" (Rorty 1989: 73). Rorty's
post-professional philosophy attempted to reconcile the pragmatism of Dewey with
the deconstructive intentions of continental philosophy. As Rorty sought to show
in *Achieving our Country* (1998), the Dewey legacy is still highly relevant to progressive attempts to realize the emancipatory spirit of "the American Creed."

In these essays on the future of religion Rorty and Vattimo embrace the idea that
faith, hope and charity – the legacy of New Testament Christianity – provides a
framework for values in modern society. They reject the authority of the Church in
general and papal authority in particular. They also indicate that the Church's
teachings on gender and sexual relations are hopelessly antiquated and involve an
essentialist reduction of women to nature (if not to anatomy). If the Church can
abandon its hierarchical and anti-democratic structures and its commitment to a
sacerdotal priesthood, the Church could serve the needs of modern society – or at
least it would be better equipped to serve those needs. The outcome is implicitly to
endorse Habermas's conciliatory position that the Christian legacy is in many ways
the underpinning of modern Western civilization.

These philosophical discussions are largely directed at political secularization that
is what role religion might play in public life in shaping policies about women,
justice and authority, but they are much less relevant to the analysis of everyday
religion in which embedded practices are less available for philosophical
speculation.

GLOBALIZATION AND RELIGION

One criticism that can be mounted against modern philosophical accounts of religion is that they are simplistic. Habermas thinks that the prominence of religion
today is an effect of missionary work, religious competition and fundamentalism.
But these accounts leave out other developments such as the globalization of piety,
the commodification of religion and the emergence (mainly in the West) of what
sociologists refer to as spirituality. We can summarize these manifestations of reli-

giosity by claiming that the globalization of religion takes three forms. There is a global revivalism that often retains some notion of and commitment to institution-alized religion (whether it is a church, a mosque, a temple or a monastery) with an emphasis on orthodox beliefs that are imposed with some degree of institutional authority. Within revivalism, there are conventional forms of fundamentalism, but also there are the Pentecostal and charismatic churches. Secondly, there is the con-tinuity of various forms of popular and traditional religion which is practiced predominantly by the poorly educated who seek healing, comfort and riches from such traditional religious practices. Religion has less to do with meaning and iden-tity, functioning instead to bring some comfort to those without adequate means of survival. Finally there is also the spread of new spiritualities that are heterodox, urban, commercialized forms of religiosity that typically exist outside the conven-tional churches.

The consequence of these developments is a growing division between "religion" and "spirituality" (Hunt 2005). Globalization thus involves the spread of personal spirituality and these spiritualities typically provide not so much guidance in the everyday world, but subjective, personalized meaning. Such religious phenomena may also be combined with therapeutic or healing services, or the promise of per-sonal enhancement through meditation. While fundamentalist norms of personal discipline appeal to those social groups that are upwardly socially mobile, such as the lower middle-class and newly educated couples, spirituality is an urban phenomenon more closely associated with middle-class singles that have been thoroughly influenced by Western consumer values.

Whereas the traditionally religious find meaning in existing mainstream denomi-national Christianity, spiritual people, according to Courtney Bender (2003: 69) "build and create their own religions in a spiritual market place, intentionally eschewing commitments to traditional religious communities, identities, and theolo-gies." The new religions are closely associated also with themes of therapy, peace and self-help. Of course the idea that religion, especially in the West, has become privatized is hardly a new idea in the sociology of religion (Luckmann 1967). However, these new forms of private subjectivity are no longer confined to Protes-tantism or the American middle classes; they now have global implications.

These popular and informal religious developments are no longer simply local cults, but burgeoning global popular religions carried by the Internet, movies, rock music, popular TV shows and "pulp fiction." These can also be referred to as pick "n" mix or DIY religions because their adherents borrow promiscuously from a great range of religious beliefs and practices. These forms of spirituality are not therefore confined to the West and can also be transmitted by Asian films such as *Hidden Tiger, Crouching Dragon*, and *House of Flying Daggers*. This develop-ment is one aspect of a new technological magic spectacularly presented in the special effects of contemporary blockbuster films. These phenomena have been regarded as aspects of "new religious movements" that are, as we have seen, manifestations of the new spiritual market places. Such forms of religion tend to be highly individualistic, they are unorthodox in the sense that they follow no offi-cial theological creed, they are characterized by their syncretism, and they have little or no connection with public institutions such as churches, mosques or temples. They are post-institutional and in this sense they can be legitimately called postmodern religions. If global fundamentalism involves modernization through personal discipline, the global post-institutional religions are typical of postmodernization.

We live increasingly in a communication environment where images and symbols rather than the written word probably play an important role in interaction. This visual world is therefore iconic rather than one based on a written language. This iconic world requires new skills and expert hierarchies that no longer duplicate the hierarchies of the written word. It is also a new experimental context in which the iconic can also become the iconoclastic as Madonna in her post-Catholic period switched to Rachel and for a while explored the Kabbalah (Hulsether, 2000). This combination of self-help systems, subjectivity, devolved authority structures, iconic discourses and personal theology is an example of low intensity religion. It is a mobile religiosity that can be transported globally by mobile people to new sites where they can mix and match their religious or self-help needs without too much constraint from or concern with hierarchical authorities. It is a low emotional religion because modern conversions tend to be more like a change in consumer brands rather than a deep searching of the soul. If the new religious life styles give rise to emotions at all, these are packaged in ways that can be easily consumed and then discarded. Brand loyalty and commitment on the part of consumers in low intensity religions are also minimal. In a famous article on "religious evolution" in the *American Sociological Review* in 1964, Robert Bellah developed an influential model of religious change from primitive, archaic, historic, early modern to modern religion. The principal characteristics of religion in modern society are its individualism, the decline in the authority of traditional institutions (church and priesthood), a willingness to experiment with diverse idioms of religion and awareness that religious symbols are constructs. Bellah's predictions about modernity have been clearly fulfilled in the growth of popular, de-institutionalized, commercialized and largely post-Christian religions.

In a differentiated global religious market, these segments of the market compete with each other and overlap. The new spirituality is genuinely a consumerist religion and, while fundamentalism appears to challenge consumer (Western) values, it is in fact also selling a life style based on special diets, alternative education, health regimes, practices around prayer and religious meditation, and technologies of the self. All three share a degree of consumerism, but they are also distinctively different, and gender is a crucial feature of the new consumerist religiosity where women increasingly dominate the new spiritualities. Women in both the developed and the developing world who experience new educational opportunities and low fertility rates have the leisure time to invest in religious activity and they will become and to some extent already are the "taste leaders" in the emergent global spiritual market place.

While globalization theory tends to emphasize the triumph of modern fundamentalism (as a critique of traditional and popular religiosity), perhaps the real effect of globalization is the triumph of heterodox, commercial, hybrid popular religion over orthodox, authoritative professional versions of the spiritual life. Their ideological effects cannot be controlled by religious authorities, and they have a greater impact than official messages. In Weber's terms it is the triumph of mass over virtuoso religiosity. The embodied habitus of modern religion is basically compatible with the life styles of a commercial world in which the driving force of the economy is domestic consumption. In the urban environment of global consumer society, megachurches have embraced the sales strategies of late capitalism to get their message out to the public. On these grounds, I would argue that modern religions are compromised because the tension between the world and the religion is lost. We may define this development as social secularization, but paradoxically religion may also retain its influence at the political level because it acts as a transnational carrier of public identities.

To summarize our discussion so far, religion plays a major role in the public domain and in many societies the liberal framework of secularization involving the separation of the church and the state no longer applies. Religion often functions in the public sphere as a profound statement of nationalism or it can be the principal carrier of ethnic identity for minority groups in a diasporic multicultural society. These observations are largely in line with the arguments originally presented by José Casanova in his *Public Religions in the Modern World* (1994). In this respect there has been little significant political secularization. In this political context, the notion of post-secularism functions an aspect of cosmopolitanism and recognition ethics. It provides rational norms of public discourse in which the claims of religion are no longer dismissed as irrational assertions but as legitimate components of public dialogue. Religious developments in the social sphere also show little unambiguous evidence of secularization. The world religions are growing and new religious phenomena are abundant. However, there is also a global commodification of religion which renders much of belief and practice compatible with secular capitalism. The tensions between religion and the secular begin to disappear as a consequence of the incorporation of religion into modern consumerism. Can the sacred survive such a profound secular process of commodification?

WHAT IS AT STAKE? PUBLIC RELIGIONS AND THE SOCIAL

In the introductory chapter to this volume, I argued that the study of religion is important if we want to take the idea of "the social" seriously. In this concluding chapter, I return to Durkheim to argue that the social in the modern world is fragile and fragmented and that the erosion of the social has significant sociological implications for the survival of "the sacred." Let us therefore once more return to Durkheim's formulation of the question of society.

Durkheim (1995) had presented a theory of solidarity in *The Elementary Forms* in terms of a society based on commonalities, collective rituals and shared emotions, but the social world that emerged especially after the Second World War gave rise to very different images and theories of the social. With the growth of worldwide urbanization and the rise of global mega-cities, social life was thought to be increasingly fragmented, producing urban ghettoes and subcultures. The idea of the "lonely crowd" painted a picture of passive and isolated urban dwellers glued to their TVs. In addition it was argued that from 1950 onwards, there were new youth subcultures associated with a growing consumerism. Ethan Watters (2003) in *Urban Tribes* claimed that these new social groups were composed of "never-marrieds" between the ages of 25 and 45 years of age who formed common but ephemeral interest groups. Their new life styles were always shifting forms of identification with these fragmented groups. Dick Hebdige (1979) wrote a classic account of these developments in his *Subculture. The Meaning of Style* to describe the oppositional movements that followed "rock 'n' roll," namely punk, Goths and other rave cultures.

These images of modern tribalism were eventually given a clear and creative sociological statement in Michel Maffesoli's *The Time of the Tribes* in 1996. The subtitle of this work in its English translation of 1988 was *The Decline of Individualism in Mass Society* .Maffesoli argued that various micro-groups were emerging in modern society who share a common, but shallow and transitory culture. While these "tribes" are fleeting, their members share a common emotional bond which is very different from the cold, bureaucratic ties of formal organizations. Punks were probably the classical illustration of such youth interest groups. A year later in 1967 Guy Debord published his *The Society of the Spectacle* in which he developed Marx's theories of economic alienation to argue that modern society was further alienated by the impact of the mass media. Everyday life had been colonized by commodities producing what Marx had originally called the fetish of commodities. We can only experience our world through this mediation and in this alienated world our being had become merely appearing such that the relations between people had become a spectacular world of appearances and commodities. Debord's work on a spectacular society was the ideological foundation of the movement (mainly among students) of the *Situationist International*. Debord encouraged events and demonstrations as a protest against the alienation of a media – dominated world. His ideas had a profound effect on the student protests of 1968. After these social protests of the 1960s, ideas about the media and alienation subsequently became a permanent part of postmodern theory. Jean Baudrillard for example was influenced by Marshall McLuhan and Karl Marx, but criticized Marxism as a theory of production for neglecting consumption (Rojek and Turner 1993). In any case Marx could not have anticipated the growth of media. Baudrillard emphasized the ways in which reality and fiction, substance and appearance had merged in his *The System of Objects* (1968), *The Mirror of Production* (1973) and *Simulation and Simulcra* (1981).

These ideas about social fragmentation, social systems and representation began to influence science fiction and cultural and social theory around the themes of cyberspace and cyberpunk. The works of William Gibson (*Neuromancer* 1984) were said to give expression to a new community of hackers and the technologically literate who were socially disaffected and searching for social forms that could express the connectivity made possible by computerization. The new possibilities might overcome the limitations of the "electronic industrial ghettoes" (Stone 1991: 95) that characterized modern society and some social theorists began to speculate about "cybersociety" as a more attractive alternative to the information city (Jones 1994). These theories also celebrated the merging of fiction and social science writing arguing that traditional social sciences had no chance of capturing even the basic features of the information age.

The point of this excursus into theories of modern tribalism is to suggest that the elementary forms of the social world which Durkheim attempted to describe through the lens of aboriginal tribalism in his sociology of religion are fast disappearing and new but fragmented and ephemeral forms of association are emerging. The new forms of religion that we have broadly referred to as spirituality on the one hand and commodified religion on the other hand are the social expressions of this underlying fragmentation and commericialization of the everyday world. If the division between the sacred and the profane was the cultural expression of the underlying patterns of what we might call "thick solidarity," the new subjective and emotional individualism of modern religion is the cultural expression of the emergence of what we might correspondingly call "thin solidarity." What is at stake therefore in the revival of interest in religion is the possibility of discovering viable forms of social being in a global world of commercial and commodified religiosity. The prospects of sustaining the vitality of the social world appear however to be decidedly unpromising.

Bibliography

Abercrombie, Nicolas, Hill, Stephen, and Turner, Bryan S. (1986) *Sovereign Individuals of Capitalism*, London: Allen & Unwin.

Akbarzadeh, Shahram and Mansouri, Fethi (eds.) (2007) *Islam and Political Violence. Muslim Diaspora and Radicalism in the West*, London: Tauris.

Barbalet, J. M. (1998) *Emotion, Social Theory and Social Structure: A Macrosociological Approach*, Cambridge: Cambridge University Press.

Baudrillard, Jean (1968) *Le Système des objets*. Paris: Gallimard.

Baudrillard, Jean (1973) *Lee Miroir de la production*. Paris: Casterman.

Baudrillard, Jean (1981) *Simulacra and Simulation: The Body in Theory*. Ann Arbor: University of Michigan Press.

Beckford, James (2003) *Social Theory and Religion*, Cambridge: Cambridge University Press.

Bellah, Robert N. (1964) Religious evolution, *American Sociological Review* 29: 358–74.

Bender, Courtney (2003) *Heaven's Kitchen: Living Religion at God's Love We Deliver*, Chicago and London: University of Chicago Press.

Berger, Peter L. (1969) *The Social Reality of Religion*, London: Faber and Faber.

Berger, Peter L. (ed.) (1999) *The Desecularization of the World*, Michigan: William B. Eerdmans.

Bruce, Steve (1990) *Pray TV: Televangelism in America*, London and New York: Routledge.

Casanova, José (1994) *Public Religions in the Modern World*, Chicago: University of Chicago Press.

Davis, M. (1992) *Beyond Blade Runner: Urban Control – the Ecology of Fear*, Westfield: Open Magazine Pamphlet Series.

Debord, Guy (1967) *La société du spectacle*, Paris: Buchet-Chastel.

Douglas, Mary (1966) *Purity and Danger: An analysis of Concepts of Pollution and Taboo*, New York: Praeger.

Durkheim, Émile (1995) *The Elementary Forms of the Religious Life*. New York: Free Press.

Garrad, John and Garrad, Carol (2009) *Russian Orthodoxy Resurgent: Faith and Power in the New Russia*, Princeton: Princeton University Press.

Gibson, William (1984) *Neuromancer*, London: Gollancz.

Gill, Anthony (2008) *The Political Origins of Religious Liberty*, Cambridge: Cambridge University Press.

Goldman, Merle (2005) *From Comrade to Citizen: The Struggle for Political Rights in China*, Cambridge, MA: Harvard University Press.

Habermas, Jürgen (2006) Religion in the public sphere, *European Journal of Philosophy* 14 (1): 1–25.

Habermas, Jürgen and Mendieta, E. (2002) *Religion and Rationality: Essays on Reason, God, and Modernity*, Cambridge, MA: MIT Press.

Habermas, Jurgen and Ratzinger, Joseph (2006) *The Dialectics of Secularization: On Reason and Religion*, San Francisco: Ignatius.

Hebdige, Dick (1979) *Subculture: The Meaning of Style*, London: Routledge.

Hulsether, M. D. (2000) Like a sermon: popular religion in Madonna videos, in B. D. Forbes and J. H. Mahan (eds.), *Religion and Popular Culture*, Berkeley: University of California Press, 77–100.

Hunt, Stephen (2005) *Religion and Everyday Life*, London: Routledge.

Jones, S. (ed.) (1994) *Cybersociety*, London: Sage.

Juergensmeyer, Mark (2000) *Terror on the Mind of God: The Global Rise of Religious Violence*, Berkeley: University of California Press.

Kamaludeen, Mohamed Nasir, Pereira, Alexius A., and Turner, Bryan S. (2009) *Muslims in Singapore: Piety, Politics and Policies*, London: Routledge.

Kant, Immanuel (1960) *Religion within the Limits of Pure Reason*, New York: Harper & Row.

Kepel, Giles (2002) *Jihad: The Trail of Political Islam*, London: I. B. Taurus.

Luckmann, Thomas (1967) *The Invisible Religion: The Problem of Religion in Modern Society*, New York: Macmillan.

Maffesoli, Michael (1996) *The Time of the Tribes: The Decline of Individualism in Mass Society*, tr. Don Smith, London and Thousand Oaks: Sage.

Mahmood, Saba (2005) *Politics of Piety: The Islamic Revival and the Feminist Subject*, Princeton: Princeton University Press.

Mandaville, Peter (2001) *Transnational Muslim Politics: Reimagining the Umma*, London and New York: Routledge.

Martin, David (2002) *Pentecostalism: The World Their Parish*, Oxford: Blackwell.

Mazower, Mark (1998) *Dark Continent: Europe's Twentieth Century*, London: Penguin Books.

Nafisi, Azar (2008) *Reading Lolita in Tehran: A Memoir in Books*, New York: Random House.

Pew Research Center (2007) Muslim Americans: Middle Class and Mostly Mainstream, Washington, DC.

Otto, Rudolf (1923) *The Idea of the Holy*, Oxford: Oxford University Press.

Rey, Terry (2007) *Bourdieu on Religion: Imposing Faith and Legitimacy*, London: Equinox.

Rojek, Chris and Turner, Bryan S. (eds.) (1993) *Forget Baudrillard?*, London: Routledge.

Rorty, Richard (1982) *The Consequences of Pragmatism*, Minneapolis: University of Minnesota Press.

Rorty, Richard (1989) *Contingency, Irony and Solidarity*, Cambridge: Cambridge University Press.

Rorty, Richard (1991) *Essays on Heidegger and Others*, Cambridge: Cambridge University Press.

Rorty, Richard (1998) *Achieving Our Country. Leftist Thought in Twentieth-century America*. Cambridge: Harvard University Press.

Said, Edward W. (2001) Afterword: the consequences of 1948, in E. Rogan and A. Shlaim (eds), *The War for Palestine: Rewriting the History of 1948*, Cambridge: Cambridge University Press, 248–61.

Stone, A. R. (1991) Will the real body please stand up? Boundary stories about virtual cultures, in M. Benedikt (ed.), *Cyberspace: First Steps*, London: MIT Press, 81–118.

Taylor, Charles (2007) *The Secular Age*, Cambridge, MA: Belknap Press.

Taylor, Philip (ed.) (2007) *Modernity and Re-enchantment: Religion in Post-revolutionary Vietnam*, Singapore: ISEAS.

Tong, Joy Kooi-Chin and Turner, Bryan S. (2008) Women, piety and practice: a study of women and religious practice in Malaya, *Contemporary Islam* 2: 41–59.

Turner, Bryan S (2007) Managing religions: state responses to religious diversity, *Contemporary Islam* 1 (2): 123–37.

Turner, Bryan S. (2008) *The Body and Society*, London: Sage.

Turner, Bryan S. (2009) Religious speech: the ineffable nature of religious communication in the information age, *Theory Culture & Society* 25 (7–8): 219–35.

Volpi, Frederic and Turner, Bryan S. (2007) Making Islamic authority matter, *Theory Culture & Society* 24 (2): 1–19.

Ward, Graham (2006) The future of religion, *Journal of the American Academy of Religions* 74 (1): 179–86.

Watters, E. (2003) *Urban Tribes: A Generation Redefines Friendship, Family, and Commitment*, New York: Bloomsbury.

Weber, Max (1966) *Sociology of Religion*, London: Methuen.

Weber, Max (2002) *The Protestant Ethic and the Spirit of Capitalism*, London: Penguin.

Wilson, Bryan (1966) *Religion in Secular Society*, London: Watts.

Wilson, Bryan (1976) *Contemporary Transformations of Religion*, London: Oxford University Press.

Yang, Fenggang and Tamney, Joseph (eds.) (2005) *State, Market and Religions in Chinese Societies*, Leiden: Brill.

Zabala, Santiago (ed.) (2005) *The Future of Religion*, New York: Columbia University Press.

Index